COMPUTER NETWORKS

FIFTH EDITION

COMPUTER NETWORKS

FIFTH EDITION

ANDREW S. TANENBAUM
Vrije Universiteit
Amsterdam, The Netherlands

DAVID J. WETHERALL
University of Washington
Seattle, WA

PEARSON

Credits and acknowledgments borrowed from other sources and reproduced, with permission, in this textbook appear on appropriate page within text.

ISBN 978-81-317-8757-1

First Impression, 2012
Second Impression, 2013
Third Impression

Published by Dorling Kindersley (India) Pvt. Ltd., licensees of Pearson Education in South Asia.

Head Office: 7th Floor, knowledge Boulevard, A-8(A) Sector-62, Noida (U.P) 201309, India
Registered Office: 11 Community Centre, Panchsheel Park, New Delhi 110 017, India.

Printed in India by Manipal Technologies Ltd.

To Suzanne, Barbara, Daniel, Aron, Marvin, Matilde,
and the memory of Bram, and Sweetie π *(AST)*

To Katrin, Lucy, and Pepper (DJW)

CONTENTS

PREFACE

This book is now in its fifth edition. Each edition has corresponded to a different phase in the way computer networks were used. When the first edition appeared in 1980, networks were an academic curiosity. When the second edition appeared in 1988, networks were used by universities and large businesses. When the third edition appeared in 1996, computer networks, especially the Internet, had become a daily reality for millions of people. By the fourth edition, in 2003, wireless networks and mobile computers had become commonplace for accessing the Web and the Internet. Now, in the fifth edition, networks are about content distribution (especially videos using CDNs and peer-to-peer networks) and mobile phones are small computers on the Internet.

New in the Fifth Edition

Among the many changes in this book, the most important one is the addition of Prof. David J. Wetherall as a co-author. David brings a rich background in networking, having cut his teeth designing metropolitan-area networks more than 20 years ago. He has worked with the Internet and wireless networks ever since and is a professor at the University of Washington, where he has been teaching and doing research on computer networks and related topics for the past decade.

Of course, the book also has many changes to keep up with the: ever-changing world of computer networks. Among these are revised and new material on

- Wireless networks (802.12 and 802.16)
- The 3G networks used by smart phones
- RFID and sensor networks
- Content distribution using CDNs
- Peer-to-peer networks
- Real-time media (from stored, streaming, and live sources)
- Internet telephony (voice over IP)
- Delay-tolerant networks

A more detailed chapter-by-chapter list follows.

Chapter 1 has the same introductory function as in the fourth edition, but the contents have been revised and brought up to date. The Internet, mobile phone networks, 802.11, and RFID and sensor networks are discussed as examples of computer networks. Material on the original Ethernet—with its vampire taps—has been removed, along with the material on ATM.

Chapter 2, which covers the physical layer, has expanded coverage of digital modulation (including OFDM as widely used in wireless networks) and 3G networks (based on CDMA). New technologies are discussed, including Fiber to the Home and power-line networking.

Chapter 3, on point-to-point links, has been improved in two ways. The material on codes for error detection and correction has been updated, and also includes a brief description of the modern codes that are important in practice (e.g., convolutional and LDPC codes). The examples of protocols now use Packet over SONET and ADSL. Sadly, the material on protocol verification has been removed as it is little used.

In Chapter 4, on the MAC sublayer, the principles are timeless but the technologies have changed. Sections on the example networks have been redone accordingly, including gigabit Ethernet, 802.11, 802.16, Bluetooth, and RFID. Also updated is the coverage of LAN switching, including VLANs.

Chapter 5, on the network layer, covers the same ground as in the fourth edition. The revisions have been to update material and add depth, particularly for quality of service (relevant for real-time media) and internetworking. The sections on BGP, OSPF and CIDR have been expanded, as has the treatment of multicast routing. Anycast routing is now included.

Chapter 6, on the transport layer, has had material added, revised, and removed. New material describes delay-tolerant networking and congestion control in general. The revised material updates and expands the coverage of TCP congestion control. The material removed described connection-oriented network layers, something rarely seen any more.

Chapter 7, on applications, has also been updated and enlarged. While material on DNS and email is similar to that in the fourth edition, in the past few years there have been many developments in the use of the Web, streaming media and content delivery. Accordingly, sections on the Web and streaming media have been brought up to date. A new section covers content distribution, including CDNs and peer-to-peer networks.

Chapter 8, on security, still covers both symmetric and public-key cryptography for confidentiality and authenticity. Material on the techniques used in practice, including firewalls and VPNs, has been updated, with new material on 802.11 security and Kerberos V5 added.

Chapter 9 contains a renewed list of suggested readings and a comprehensive bibliography of over 300 citations to the current literature. More than half of these are to papers and books written in 2000 or later, and the rest are citations to classic papers.

List of Acronyms

Computer books are full of acronyms. This one is no exception. By the time you are finished reading this one, the following should ring a bell: ADSL, AES, AJAX, AODV, AP, ARP, ARQ, AS, BGP, BOC, CDMA, CDN, CGI, CIDR, CRL, CSMA, CSS, DCT, DES, DHCP, DHT, DIFS, DMCA, DMT, DMZ, DNS, DOCSIS, DOM, DSLAM, DTN, FCFS, FDD, FDDI, FDM, FEC, FIFO, FSK, FTP, GPRS, GSM, HDTV, HFC, HMAC, HTTP, IAB, ICANN, ICMP, IDEA, IETF, IMAP, IMP, IP, IPTV, IRTF, ISO, ISP, ITU, JPEG, JSP, JVM, LAN, LATA, LEC, LEO, LLC, LSR, LTE, MAN, MFJ, MIME, MPEG, MPLS, MSC, MTSO, MTU, NAP, NAT, NRZ, NSAP, OFDM, OSI, OSPF, PAWS, PCM, PGP, PIM, PKI, POP, POTS, PPP, PSTN, QAM, QPSK, RED, RFC, RFID, RPC, RSA, RTSP, SHA, SIP, SMTP, SNR, SOAP, SONET, SPE, SSL, TCP, TDD, TDM, TSAP, UDP, UMTS, URL, VLAN, VSAT, WAN, WDM, and XML. But don't worry. Each will appear in **boldface type** and be carefully defined before it is used. As a fun test, see how many you can identify *before* reading the book, write the number in the margin, then try again *after* reading the book.

How to Use the Book

To help instructors use this book as a text for courses ranging in length from quarters to semesters, we have structured the chapters into core and optional material. The sections marked with a "*" in the table of contents are the optional ones. If a major section (e.g., 2.7) is so marked, all of its subsections are optional. They provide material on network technologies that is useful but can be omitted from a short course without loss of continuity. Of course, students should be encouraged to read those sections as well, to the extent they have time, as all the material is up to date and of value.

Instructors' Resource Materials

The following protected instructors' resource materials are available on the publisher's Web site at *www.pearsonhighered.com/tanenbaum*. For a username and password, please contact your local Pearson representative.

- Solutions manual
- PowerPoint lecture slides

Students' Resource Materials

Resources for students are available through the open-access Companion Web site link on *www.pearsonhighered.com/tanenbaum*, including

- Web resources, links to tutorials, organizations, FAQs, and more
- Figures, tables, and programs from the book
- Steganography demo
- Protocol simulators

Acknowledgements

Many people helped us during the course of the fifth edition. We would especially like to thank Emmanuel Agu (Worcester Polytechnic Institute), Yoris Au (University of Texas at Antonio), Nikhil Bhargava (Aircom International, Inc.), Michael Buettner (University of Washington), John Day (Boston University), Kevin Fall (Intel Labs), Ronald Fulle (Rochester Institute of Technology), Ben Greenstein (Intel Labs), Daniel Halperin (University of Washington), Bob Kinicki (Worcester Polytechnic Institute), Tadayoshi Kohno (University of Washington), Sarvish Kulkarni (Villanova University), Hank Levy (University of Washington), Ratul Mahajan (Microsoft Research), Craig Partridge (BBN), Michael Piatek (University of Washington), Joshua Smith (Intel Labs), Neil Spring (University of Maryland), David Teneyuca (University of Texas at Antonio), Tammy VanDegrift (University of Portland), and Bo Yuan (Rochester Institute of Technology), for providing ideas and feedback. Melody Kadenko and Julie Svendsen provided administrative support to David.

Shivakant Mishra (University of Colorado at Boulder) and Paul Nagin (Chimborazo Publishing, Inc.) thought of many new and challenging end-of-chapter problems. Our editor at Pearson, Tracy Dunkelberger, was her usual helpful self in many ways large and small. Melinda Haggerty and Jeff Holcomb did a good job of keeping things running smoothly. Steve Armstrong (LeTourneau University) prepared the PowerPoint slides. Stephen Turner (University of Michigan at Flint) artfully revised the Web resources and the simulators that accompany the text. Our copyeditor, Rachel Head, is an odd hybrid: she has the eye of an eagle and the memory of an elephant. After reading all her corrections, both of us wondered how we ever made it past third grade.

Finally, we come to the most important people. Suzanne has been through this 19 times now and still has endless patience and love. Barbara and Marvin now know the difference between good textbooks and bad ones and are always an inspiration to produce good ones. Daniel and Matilde are welcome additions to our family. Aron is unlikely to read this book soon, but he likes the nice pictures on page 866 (AST). Katrin and Lucy provided endless support and always managed to keep a smile on my face. Thank you (DJW).

ANDREW S. TANENBAUM

DAVID J. WETHERALL

1

INTRODUCTION

Each of the past three centuries was dominated by a single new technology. The 18th century was the era of the great mechanical systems accompanying the Industrial Revolution. The 19th century was the age of the steam engine. During the 20th century, the key technology was information gathering, processing, and distribution. Among other developments, we saw the installation of worldwide telephone networks, the invention of radio and television, the birth and unprecedented growth of the computer industry, the launching of communication satellites, and, of course, the Internet.

As a result of rapid technological progress, these areas are rapidly converging in the 21st century and the differences between collecting, transporting, storing, and processing information are quickly disappearing. Organizations with hundreds of offices spread over a wide geographical area routinely expect to be able to examine the current status of even their most remote outpost at the push of a button. As our ability to gather, process, and distribute information grows, the demand for ever more sophisticated information processing grows even faster.

Although the computer industry is still young compared to other industries (e.g., automobiles and air transportation), computers have made spectacular progress in a short time. During the first two decades of their existence, computer systems were highly centralized, usually within a single large room. Not infrequently, this room had glass walls, through which visitors could gawk at the great electronic wonder inside. A medium-sized company or university might have had one or two computers, while very large institutions had at most a few dozen. The idea that within forty years vastly more powerful computers smaller than postage stamps would be mass produced by the billions was pure science fiction.

The merging of computers and communications has had a profound influence on the way computer systems are organized. The once-dominant concept of the "computer center" as a room with a large computer to which users bring their work for processing is now totally obsolete (although data centers holding thousands of Internet servers are becoming common). The old model of a single computer serving all of the organization's computational needs has been replaced by one in which a large number of separate but interconnected computers do the job. These systems are called **computer networks**. The design and organization of these networks are the subjects of this book.

Throughout the book we will use the term "computer network" to mean a collection of autonomous computers interconnected by a single technology. Two computers are said to be interconnected if they are able to exchange information. The connection need not be via a copper wire; fiber optics, microwaves, infrared, and communication satellites can also be used. Networks come in many sizes, shapes and forms, as we will see later. They are usually connected together to make larger networks, with the **Internet** being the most well-known example of a network of networks.

There is considerable confusion in the literature between a computer network and a **distributed system**. The key distinction is that in a distributed system, a collection of independent computers appears to its users as a single coherent system. Usually, it has a single model or paradigm that it presents to the users. Often a layer of software on top of the operating system, called **middleware**, is responsible for implementing this model. A well-known example of a distributed system is the **World Wide Web**. It runs on top of the Internet and presents a model in which everything looks like a document (Web page).

In a computer network, this coherence, model, and software are absent. Users are exposed to the actual machines, without any attempt by the system to make the machines look and act in a coherent way. If the machines have different hardware and different operating systems, that is fully visible to the users. If a user wants to run a program on a remote machine, he† has to log onto that machine and run it there.

In effect, a distributed system is a software system built on top of a network. The software gives it a high degree of cohesiveness and transparency. Thus, the distinction between a network and a distributed system lies with the software (especially the operating system), rather than with the hardware.

Nevertheless, there is considerable overlap between the two subjects. For example, both distributed systems and computer networks need to move files around. The difference lies in who invokes the movement, the system or the user.

† "He" should be read as "he or she" throughout this book.

Although this book primarily focuses on networks, many of the topics are also important in distributed systems. For more information about distributed systems, see Tanenbaum and Van Steen (2007).

1.1 USES OF COMPUTER NETWORKS

Before we start to examine the technical issues in detail, it is worth devoting some time to pointing out why people are interested in computer networks and what they can be used for. After all, if nobody were interested in computer networks, few of them would be built. We will start with traditional uses at companies, then move on to home networking and recent developments regarding mobile users, and finish with social issues.

1.1.1 Business Applications

Most companies have a substantial number of computers. For example, a company may have a computer for each worker and use them to design products, write brochures, and do the payroll. Initially, some of these computers may have worked in isolation from the others, but at some point, management may have decided to connect them to be able to distribute information throughout the company.

Put in slightly more general form, the issue here is **resource sharing**. The goal is to make all programs, equipment, and especially data available to anyone on the network without regard to the physical location of the resource or the user. An obvious and widespread example is having a group of office workers share a common printer. None of the individuals really needs a private printer, and a high-volume networked printer is often cheaper, faster, and easier to maintain than a large collection of individual printers.

However, probably even more important than sharing physical resources such as printers, and tape backup systems, is sharing information. Companies small and large are vitally dependent on computerized information. Most companies have customer records, product information, inventories, financial statements, tax information, and much more online. If all of its computers suddenly went down, a bank could not last more than five minutes. A modern manufacturing plant, with a computer-controlled assembly line, would not last even 5 seconds. Even a small travel agency or three-person law firm is now highly dependent on computer networks for allowing employees to access relevant information and documents instantly.

For smaller companies, all the computers are likely to be in a single office or perhaps a single building, but for larger ones, the computers and employees may be scattered over dozens of offices and plants in many countries. Nevertheless, a sales person in New York might sometimes need access to a product inventory database in Singapore. Networks called **VPNs** (**Virtual Private Networks**) may be used to join the individual networks at different sites into one extended network. In other words, the mere fact that a user happens to be 15,000 km away from his data should not prevent him from using the data as though they were local. This goal may be summarized by saying that it is an attempt to end the "tyranny of geography."

In the simplest of terms, one can imagine a company's information system as consisting of one or more databases with company information and some number of employees who need to access them remotely. In this model, the data are stored on powerful computers called **servers**. Often these are centrally housed and maintained by a system administrator. In contrast, the employees have simpler machines, called **clients**, on their desks, with which they access remote data, for example, to include in spreadsheets they are constructing. (Sometimes we will refer to the human user of the client machine as the "client," but it should be clear from the context whether we mean the computer or its user.) The client and server machines are connected by a network, as illustrated in Fig. 1-1. Note that we have shown the network as a simple oval, without any detail. We will use this form when we mean a network in the most abstract sense. When more detail is required, it will be provided.

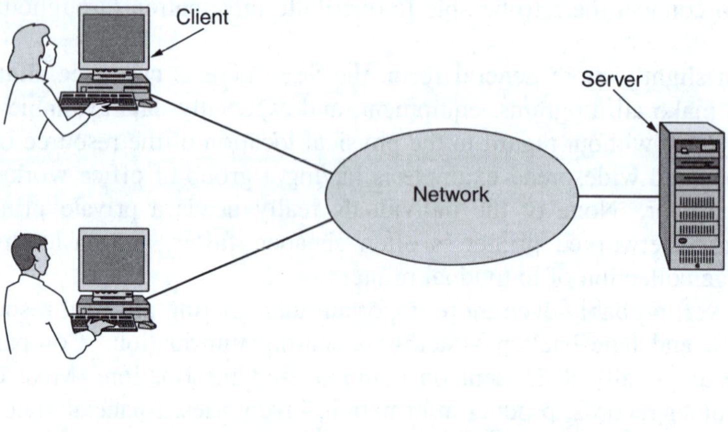

Figure 1-1. A network with two clients and one server.

This whole arrangement is called the **client-server model**. It is widely used and forms the basis of much network usage. The most popular realization is that of a **Web application**, in which the server generates Web pages based on its database in response to client requests that may update the database. The client-server model is applicable when the client and server are both in the same building (and belong to the same company), but also when they are far apart. For example, when a person at home accesses a page on the World Wide Web, the same model is employed, with the remote Web server being the server and the user's personal computer being the client. Under most conditions, one server can handle a large number (hundreds or thousands) of clients simultaneously.

If we look at the client-server model in detail, we see that two processes (i.e., running programs) are involved, one on the client machine and one on the server machine. Communication takes the form of the client process sending a message over the network to the server process. The client process then waits for a reply message. When the server process gets the request, it performs the requested work or looks up the requested data and sends back a reply. These messages are shown in Fig. 1-2.

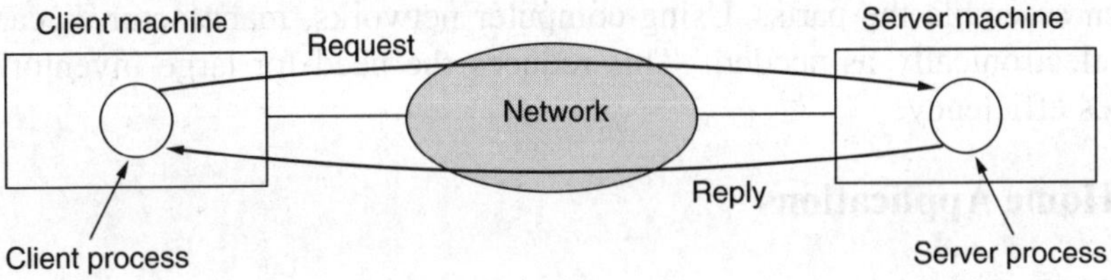

Figure 1-2. The client-server model involves requests and replies.

A second goal of setting up a computer network has to do with people rather than information or even computers. A computer network can provide a powerful **communication medium** among employees. Virtually every company that has two or more computers now has **email** (**electronic mail**), which employees generally use for a great deal of daily communication. In fact, a common gripe around the water cooler is how much email everyone has to deal with, much of it quite meaningless because bosses have discovered that they can send the same (often content-free) message to all their subordinates at the push of a button.

Telephone calls between employees may be carried by the computer network instead of by the phone company. This technology is called **IP telephony** or **Voice over IP (VoIP)** when Internet technology is used. The microphone and speaker at each end may belong to a VoIP-enabled phone or the employee's computer. Companies find this a wonderful way to save on their telephone bills.

Other, richer forms of communication are made possible by computer networks. Video can be added to audio so that employees at distant locations can see and hear each other as they hold a meeting. This technique is a powerful tool for eliminating the cost and time previously devoted to travel. **Desktop sharing** lets remote workers see and interact with a graphical computer screen. This makes it easy for two or more people who work far apart to read and write a shared blackboard or write a report together. When one worker makes a change to an online document, the others can see the change immediately, instead of waiting several days for a letter. Such a speedup makes cooperation among far-flung groups of people easy where it previously had been impossible. More ambitious forms of remote coordination such as telemedicine are only now starting to be used (e.g., remote patient monitoring) but may become much more important. It is sometimes said that communication and transportation are having a race, and whichever wins will make the other obsolete.

A third goal for many companies is doing business electronically, especially with customers and suppliers. This new model is called **e-commerce** (**electronic commerce**) and it has grown rapidly in recent years. Airlines, bookstores, and other retailers have discovered that many customers like the convenience of shopping from home. Consequently, many companies provide catalogs of their goods and services online and take orders online. Manufacturers of automobiles, aircraft, and computers, among others, buy subsystems from a variety of suppliers and then assemble the parts. Using computer networks, manufacturers can place orders electronically as needed. This reduces the need for large inventories and enhances efficiency.

1.1.2 Home Applications

In 1977, Ken Olsen was president of the Digital Equipment Corporation, then the number two computer vendor in the world (after IBM). When asked why Digital was not going after the personal computer market in a big way, he said: "There is no reason for any individual to have a computer in his home." History showed otherwise and Digital no longer exists. People initially bought computers for word processing and games. Recently, the biggest reason to buy a home computer was probably for Internet access. Now, many consumer electronic devices, such as set-top boxes, game consoles, and clock radios, come with embedded computers and computer networks, especially wireless networks, and home networks are broadly used for entertainment, including listening to, looking at, and creating music, photos, and videos.

Internet access provides home users with **connectivity** to remote computers. As with companies, home users can access information, communicate with other people, and buy products and services with e-commerce. The main benefit now comes from connecting outside of the home. Bob Metcalfe, the inventor of Ethernet, hypothesized that the value of a network is proportional to the square of the number of users because this is roughly the number of different connections that may be made (Gilder, 1993). This hypothesis is known as "Metcalfe's law." It helps to explain how the tremendous popularity of the Internet comes from its size.

Access to remote information comes in many forms. It can be surfing the World Wide Web for information or just for fun. Information available includes the arts, business, cooking, government, health, history, hobbies, recreation, science, sports, travel, and many others. Fun comes in too many ways to mention, plus some ways that are better left unmentioned.

Many newspapers have gone online and can be personalized. For example, it is sometimes possible to tell a newspaper that you want everything about corrupt politicians, big fires, scandals involving celebrities, and epidemics, but no football, thank you. Sometimes it is possible to have the selected articles downloaded to your computer while you sleep. As this trend continues, it will cause massive unemployment among 12-year-old paperboys, but newspapers like it because distribution has always been the weakest link in the whole production chain. Of course, to make this model work, they will first have to figure out how to make money in this new world, something not entirely obvious since Internet users expect everything to be free.

The next step beyond newspapers (plus magazines and scientific journals) is the online digital library. Many professional organizations, such as the ACM (*www.acm.org*) and the IEEE Computer Society (*www.computer.org*), already have all their journals and conference proceedings online. Electronic book readers and online libraries may make printed books obsolete. Skeptics should take note of the effect the printing press had on the medieval illuminated manuscript.

Much of this information is accessed using the client-server model, but there is different, popular model for accessing information that goes by the name of **peer-to-peer** communication (Parameswaran et al., 2001). In this form, individuals who form a loose group can communicate with others in the group, as shown in Fig. 1-3. Every person can, in principle, communicate with one or more other people; there is no fixed division into clients and servers.

Figure 1-3. In a peer-to-peer system there are no fixed clients and servers.

Many peer-to-peer systems, such BitTorrent (Cohen, 2003), do not have any central database of content. Instead, each user maintains his own database locally and provides a list of other nearby people who are members of the system. A new user can then go to any existing member to see what he has and get the names of other members to inspect for more content and more names. This lookup process can be repeated indefinitely to build up a large local database of what is out there. It is an activity that would get tedious for people but computers excel at it.

Peer-to-peer communication is often used to share music and videos. It really hit the big time around 2000 with a music sharing service called Napster that was shut down after what was probably the biggest copyright infringement case in all of recorded history (Lam and Tan, 2001; and Macedonia, 2000). Legal applications for peer-to-peer communication also exist. These include fans sharing public domain music, families sharing photos and movies, and users downloading public software packages. In fact, one of the most popular Internet applications of all, email, is inherently peer-to-peer. This form of communication is likely to grow considerably in the future.

All of the above applications involve interactions between a person and a remote database full of information. The second broad category of network use is person-to-person communication, basically the 21st century's answer to the 19th century's telephone. E-mail is already used on a daily basis by millions of people all over the world and its use is growing rapidly. It already routinely contains audio and video as well as text and pictures. Smell may take a while.

Any teenager worth his or her salt is addicted to **instant messaging**. This facility, derived from the UNIX *talk* program in use since around 1970, allows two people to type messages at each other in real time. There are multi-person messaging services too, such as the **Twitter** service that lets people send short text messages called "tweets" to their circle of friends or other willing audiences.

The Internet can be used by applications to carry audio (e.g., Internet radio stations) and video (e.g., YouTube). Besides being a cheap way to call to distant friends, these applications can provide rich experiences such as telelearning, meaning attending 8 A.M. classes without the inconvenience of having to get out of bed first. In the long run, the use of networks to enhance human-to-human communication may prove more important than any of the others. It may become hugely important to people who are geographically challenged, giving them the same access to services as people living in the middle of a big city.

Between person-to-person communications and accessing information are **social network** applications. Here, the flow of information is driven by the relationships that people declare between each other. One of the most popular social networking sites is **Facebook**. It lets people update their personal profiles and shares the updates with other people who they have declared to be their friends. Other social networking applications can make introductions via friends of friends, send news messages to friends such as Twitter above, and much more.

Even more loosely, groups of people can work together to create content. A **wiki**, for example, is a collaborative Web site that the members of a community edit. The most famous wiki is the **Wikipedia**, an encyclopedia anyone can edit, but there are thousands of other wikis.

Our third category is electronic commerce in the broadest sense of the term. Home shopping is already popular and enables users to inspect the online catalogs of thousands of companies. Some of these catalogs are interactive, showing products from different viewpoints and in configurations that can be personalized.

After the customer buys a product electronically but cannot figure out how to use it, online technical support may be consulted.

Another area in which e-commerce is widely used is access to financial institutions. Many people already pay their bills, manage their bank accounts, and handle their investments electronically. This trend will surely continue as networks become more secure.

One area that virtually nobody foresaw is electronic flea markets (e-flea?). Online auctions of second-hand goods have become a massive industry. Unlike traditional e-commerce, which follows the client-server model, online auctions are peer-to-peer in the sense that consumers can act as both buyers and sellers.

Some of these forms of e-commerce have acquired cute little tags based on the fact that "to" and "2" are pronounced the same. The most popular ones are listed in Fig. 1-4.

Tag	Full name	Example
B2C	Business-to-consumer	Ordering books online
B2B	Business-to-business	Car manufacturer ordering tires from supplier
G2C	Government-to-consumer	Government distributing tax forms electronically
C2C	Consumer-to-consumer	Auctioning second-hand products online
P2P	Peer-to-peer	Music sharing

Figure 1-4. Some forms of e-commerce.

Our fourth category is entertainment. This has made huge strides in the home in recent years, with the distribution of music, radio and television programs, and movies over the Internet beginning to rival that of traditional mechanisms. Users can find, buy, and download MP3 songs and DVD-quality movies and add them to their personal collection. TV shows now reach many homes via **IPTV** (**IP TeleVision**) systems that are based on IP technology instead of cable TV or radio transmissions. Media streaming applications let users tune into Internet radio stations or watch recent episodes of their favorite TV shows. Naturally, all of this content can be moved around your house between different devices, displays and speakers, usually with a wireless network.

Soon, it may be possible to search for any movie or television program ever made, in any country, and have it displayed on your screen instantly. New films may become interactive, where the user is occasionally prompted for the story direction (should Macbeth murder Duncan or just bide his time?) with alternative scenarios provided for all cases. Live television may also become interactive, with the audience participating in quiz shows, choosing among contestants, and so on.

Another form of entertainment is game playing. Already we have multiperson real-time simulation games, like hide-and-seek in a virtual dungeon, and flight simulators with the players on one team trying to shoot down the players on the opposing team. Virtual worlds provide a persistent setting in which thousands of users can experience a shared reality with three-dimensional graphics.

Our last category is **ubiquitous computing**, in which computing is embedded into everyday life, as in the vision of Mark Weiser (1991). Many homes are already wired with security systems that include door and window sensors, and there are many more sensors that can be folded in to a smart home monitor, such as energy consumption. Your electricity, gas and water meters could also report usage over the network. This would save money as there would be no need to send out meter readers. And your smoke detectors could call the fire department instead of making a big noise (which has little value if no one is home). As the cost of sensing and communication drops, more and more measurement and reporting will be done with networks.

Increasingly, consumer electronic devices are networked. For example, some high-end cameras already have a wireless network capability and use it to send photos to a nearby display for viewing. Professional sports photographers can also send their photos to their editors in real-time, first wirelessly to an access point then over the Internet. Devices such as televisions that plug into the wall can use **power-line networks** to send information throughout the house over the wires that carry electricity. It may not be very surprising to have these objects on the network, but objects that we do not think of as computers may sense and communicate information too. For example, your shower may record water usage, give you visual feedback while you lather up, and report to a home environmental monitoring application when you are done to help save on your water bill.

A technology called **RFID** (**Radio Frequency IDentification**) will push this idea even further in the future. RFID tags are passive (i.e., have no battery) chips the size of stamps and they can already be affixed to books, passports, pets, credit cards, and other items in the home and out. This lets RFID readers locate and communicate with the items over a distance of up to several meters, depending on the kind of RFID. Originally, RFID was commercialized to replace barcodes. It has not succeeded yet because barcodes are free and RFID tags cost a few cents. Of course, RFID tags offer much more and their price is rapidly declining. They may turn the real world into the Internet of things (ITU, 2005).

1.1.3 Mobile Users

Mobile computers, such as laptop and handheld computers, are one of the fastest-growing segments of the computer industry. Their sales have already overtaken those of desktop computers. Why would anyone want one? People on the go often want to use their mobile devices to read and send email, tweet, watch movies, download music, play games, or simply to surf the Web for information. They want to do all of the things they do at home and in the office. Naturally, they want to do them from anywhere on land, sea or in the air.

Connectivity to the Internet enables many of these mobile uses. Since having a wired connection is impossible in cars, boats, and airplanes, there is a lot of interest in wireless networks. Cellular networks operated by the telephone companies are one familiar kind of wireless network that blankets us with coverage for mobile phones. Wireless **hotspots** based on the 802.11 standard are another kind of wireless network for mobile computers. They have sprung up everywhere that people go, resulting in a patchwork of coverage at cafes, hotels, airports, schools, trains and planes. Anyone with a laptop computer and a wireless modem can just turn on their computer on and be connected to the Internet through the hotspot, as though the computer were plugged into a wired network.

Wireless networks are of great value to fleets of trucks, taxis, delivery vehicles, and repairpersons for keeping in contact with their home base. For example, in many cities, taxi drivers are independent businessmen, rather than being employees of a taxi company. In some of these cities, the taxis have a display the driver can see. When a customer calls up, a central dispatcher types in the pickup and destination points. This information is displayed on the drivers' displays and a beep sounds. The first driver to hit a button on the display gets the call.

Wireless networks are also important to the military. If you have to be able to fight a war anywhere on Earth at short notice, counting on using the local networking infrastructure is probably not a good idea. It is better to bring your own.

Although wireless networking and mobile computing are often related, they are not identical, as Fig. 1-5 shows. Here we see a distinction between **fixed wireless** and **mobile wireless** networks. Even notebook computers are sometimes wired. For example, if a traveler plugs a notebook computer into the wired network jack in a hotel room, he has mobility without a wireless network.

Wireless	Mobile	Typical applications
No	No	Desktop computers in offices
No	Yes	A notebook computer used in a hotel room
Yes	No	Networks in unwired buildings
Yes	Yes	Store inventory with a handheld computer

Figure 1-5. Combinations of wireless networks and mobile computing.

Conversely, some wireless computers are not mobile. In the home, and in offices or hotels that lack suitable cabling, it can be more convenient to connect desktop computers or media players wirelessly than to install wires. Installing a wireless network may require little more than buying a small box with some electronics in it, unpacking it, and plugging it in. This solution may be far cheaper than having workmen put in cable ducts to wire the building.

Finally, there are also true mobile, wireless applications, such as people walking around stores with a handheld computers recording inventory. At many busy airports, car rental return clerks work in the parking lot with wireless mobile computers. They scan the barcodes or RFID chips of returning cars, and their mobile device, which has a built-in printer, calls the main computer, gets the rental information, and prints out the bill on the spot.

Perhaps the key driver of mobile, wireless applications is the mobile phone. **Text messaging** or **texting** is tremendously popular. It lets a mobile phone user type a short message that is then delivered by the cellular network to another mobile subscriber. Few people would have predicted ten years ago that having teenagers tediously typing short text messages on mobile phones would be an immense money maker for telephone companies. But texting (or **Short Message Service** as it is known outside the U.S.) is very profitable since it costs the carrier but a tiny fraction of one cent to relay a text message, a service for which they charge far more.

The long-awaited convergence of telephones and the Internet has finally arrived, and it will accelerate the growth of mobile applications. **Smart phones**, such as the popular iPhone, combine aspects of mobile phones and mobile computers. The (3G and 4G) cellular networks to which they connect can provide fast data services for using the Internet as well as handling phone calls. Many advanced phones connect to wireless hotspots too, and automatically switch between networks to choose the best option for the user.

Other consumer electronics devices can also use cellular and hotspot networks to stay connected to remote computers. Electronic book readers can download a newly purchased book or the next edition of a magazine or today's newspaper wherever they roam. Electronic picture frames can update their displays on cue with fresh images.

Since mobile phones know their locations, often because they are equipped with **GPS (Global Positioning System)** receivers, some services are intentionally location dependent. Mobile maps and directions are an obvious candidate as your GPS-enabled phone and car probably have a better idea of where you are than you do. So, too, are searches for a nearby bookstore or Chinese restaurant, or a local weather forecast. Other services may record location, such as annotating photos and videos with the place at which they were made. This annotation is known as "geo-tagging."

An area in which mobile phones are now starting to be used is **m-commerce (mobile-commerce)** (Senn, 2000). Short text messages from the mobile are used to authorize payments for food in vending machines, movie tickets, and other small items instead of cash and credit cards. The charge then appears on the mobile phone bill. When equipped with **NFC (Near Field Communication)** technology the mobile can act as an RFID smartcard and interact with a nearby reader for payment. The driving forces behind this phenomenon are the mobile device makers and network operators, who are trying hard to figure out how to get a piece of the e-commerce pie. From the store's point of view, this scheme may save them most of the credit card company's fee, which can be several percent.

Of course, this plan may backfire, since customers in a store might use the RFID or barcode readers on their mobile devices to check out competitors' prices before buying and use them to get a detailed report on where else an item can be purchased nearby and at what price.

One huge thing that m-commerce has going for it is that mobile phone users are accustomed to paying for everything (in contrast to Internet users, who expect everything to be free). If an Internet Web site charged a fee to allow its customers to pay by credit card, there would be an immense howling noise from the users. If, however, a mobile phone operator its customers to pay for items in a store by waving the phone at the cash register and then tacked on a fee for this convenience, it would probably be accepted as normal. Time will tell.

No doubt the uses of mobile and wireless computers will grow rapidly in the future as the size of computers shrinks, probably in ways no one can now foresee. Let us take a quick look at some possibilities. **Sensor networks** are made up of nodes that gather and wirelessly relay information they sense about the state of the physical world. The nodes may be part of familiar items such as cars or phones, or they may be small separate devices. For example, your car might gather data on its location, speed, vibration, and fuel efficiency from its on-board diagnostic system and upload this information to a database (Hull et al., 2006). Those data can help find potholes, plan trips around congested roads, and tell you if you are a "gas guzzler" compared to other drivers on the same stretch of road.

Sensor networks are revolutionizing science by providing a wealth of data on behavior that could not previously be observed. One example is tracking the migration of individual zebras by placing a small sensor on each animal (Juang et al., 2002). Researchers have packed a wireless computer into a cube 1 mm on edge (Warneke et al., 2001). With mobile computers this small, even small birds, rodents, and insects can be tracked.

Even mundane uses, such as in parking meters, can be significant because they make use of data that were not previously available. Wireless parking meters can accept credit or debit card payments with instant verification over the wireless link. They can also report when they are in use over the wireless network. This would let drivers download a recent parking map to their car so they can find an available spot more easily. Of course, when a meter expires, it might also check for the presence of a car (by bouncing a signal off it) and report the expiration to parking enforcement. It has been estimated that city governments in the U.S. alone could collect an additional $10 billion this way (Harte et al., 2000).

Wearable computers are another promising application. Smart watches with radios have been part of our mental space since their appearance in the Dick Tracy comic strip in 1946; now you can buy them. Other such devices may be implanted, such as pacemakers and insulin pumps. Some of these can be controlled over a wireless network. This lets doctors test and reconfigure them more easily. It could also lead to some nasty problems if the devices are as insecure as the average PC and can be hacked easily (Halperin et al., 2008).

1.1.4 Social Issues

Computer networks, like the printing press 500 years ago, allow ordinary citizens to distribute and view content in ways that were not previously possible. But along with the good comes the bad, as this new-found freedom brings with it many unsolved social, political, and ethical issues. Let us just briefly mention a few of them; a thorough study would require a full book, at least.

Social networks, message boards, content sharing sites, and a host of other applications allow people to share their views with like-minded individuals. As long as the subjects are restricted to technical topics or hobbies like gardening, not too many problems will arise.

The trouble comes with topics that people actually care about, like politics, religion, or sex. Views that are publicly posted may be deeply offensive to some people. Worse yet, they may not be politically correct. Furthermore, opinions need not be limited to text; high-resolution color photographs and video clips are easily shared over computer networks. Some people take a live-and-let-live view, but others feel that posting certain material (e.g., verbal attacks on particular countries or religions, pornography, etc.) is simply unacceptable and that such content must be censored. Different countries have different and conflicting laws in this area. Thus, the debate rages.

In the past, people have sued network operators, claiming that they are responsible for the contents of what they carry, just as newspapers and magazines are. The inevitable response is that a network is like a telephone company or the post office and cannot be expected to police what its users say.

It should now come only as a slight surprise to learn that some network operators block content for their own reasons. Some users of peer-to-peer applications had their network service cut off because the network operators did not find it profitable to carry the large amounts of traffic sent by those applications. Those same operators would probably like to treat different companies differently. If you are a big company and pay well then you get good service, but if you are a small-time player, you get poor service. Opponents of this practice argue that peer-to-peer and other content should be treated in the same way because they are all just bits to the network. This argument for communications that are not differentiated by their content or source or who is providing the content is known as **network neutrality** (Wu, 2003). It is probably safe to say that this debate will go on for a while.

Many other parties are involved in the tussle over content. For instance, pirated music and movies fueled the massive growth of peer-to-peer networks, which did not please the copyright holders, who have threatened (and sometimes taken) legal action. There are now automated systems that search peer-to-peer networks and fire off warnings to network operators and users who are suspected of infringing copyright. In the United States, these warnings are known as **DMCA takedown notices** after the **Digital Millennium Copyright Act**. This search is an arms' race because it is hard to reliably catch copyright infringement. Even your printer might be mistaken for a culprit (Piatek et al., 2008).

Computer networks make it very easy to communicate. They also make it easy for the people who run the network to snoop on the traffic. This sets up conflicts over issues such as employee rights versus employer rights. Many people read and write email at work. Many employers have claimed the right to read and possibly censor employee messages, including messages sent from a home computer outside working hours. Not all employees agree with this, especially the latter part.

Another conflict is centered around government versus citizen's rights. The FBI has installed systems at many Internet service providers to snoop on all incoming and outgoing email for nuggets of interest. One early system was originally called Carnivore, but bad publicity caused it to be renamed to the more innocent-sounding DCS1000 (Blaze and Bellovin, 2000; Sobel, 2001; and Zacks, 2001). The goal of such systems is to spy on millions of people in the hope of perhaps finding information about illegal activities. Unfortunately for the spies, the Fourth Amendment to the U.S. Constitution prohibits government searches without a search warrant, but the government often ignores it.

Of course, the government does not have a monopoly on threatening people's privacy. The private sector does its bit too by **profiling** users. For example, small files called **cookies** that Web browsers store on users' computers allow companies to track users' activities in cyberspace and may also allow credit card numbers, social security numbers, and other confidential information to leak all over the Internet (Berghel, 2001). Companies that provide Web-based services may maintain large amounts of personal information about their users that allows them to study user activities directly. For example, Google can read your email and show you advertisements based on your interests if you use its email service, **Gmail**.

A new twist with mobile devices is location privacy (Beresford and Stajano, 2003). As part of the process of providing service to your mobile device the network operators learn where you are at different times of day. This allows them to track your movements. They may know which nightclub you frequent and which medical center you visit.

Computer networks also offer the potential to increase privacy by sending anonymous messages. In some situations, this capability may be desirable. Beyond preventing companies from learning your habits, it provides, for example, a way for students, soldiers, employees, and citizens to blow the whistle on illegal behavior on the part of professors, officers, superiors, and politicians without fear of reprisals. On the other hand, in the United States and most other democracies, the law specifically permits an accused person the right to confront and challenge his accuser in court so anonymous accusations cannot be used as evidence.

The Internet makes it possible to find information quickly, but a great deal of it is ill considered, misleading, or downright wrong. That medical advice you plucked from the Internet about the pain in your chest may have come from a Nobel Prize winner or from a high-school dropout.

Other information is frequently unwanted. Electronic junk mail (spam) has become a part of life because spammers have collected millions of email addresses and would-be marketers can cheaply send computer-generated messages to them. The resulting flood of spam rivals the flow messages from real people. Fortunately, filtering software is able to read and discard the spam generated by other computers, with lesser or greater degrees of success.

Still other content is intended for criminal behavior. Web pages and email messages containing active content (basically, programs or macros that execute on the receiver's machine) can contain viruses that take over your computer. They might be used to steal your bank account passwords, or to have your computer send spam as part of a **botnet** or pool of compromised machines.

Phishing messages masquerade as originating from a trustworthy party, for example, your bank, to try to trick you into revealing sensitive information, for example, credit card numbers. Identity theft is becoming a serious problem as thieves collect enough information about a victim to obtain credit cards and other documents in the victim's name.

It can be difficult to prevent computers from impersonating people on the Internet. This problem has led to the development of **CAPTCHAs**, in which a computer asks a person to solve a short recognition task, for example, typing in the letters shown in a distorted image, to show that they are human (von Ahn, 2001). This process is a variation on the famous Turing test in which a person asks questions over a network to judge whether the entity responding is human.

A lot of these problems could be solved if the computer industry took computer security seriously. If all messages were encrypted and authenticated, it would be harder to commit mischief. Such technology is well established and we will study it in detail in Chap. 8. The problem is that hardware and software vendors know that putting in security features costs money and their customers are not demanding such features. In addition, a substantial number of the problems are caused by buggy software, which occurs because vendors keep adding more and more features to their programs, which inevitably means more code and thus more bugs. A tax on new features might help, but that might be a tough sell in some quarters. A refund for defective software might be nice, except it would bankrupt the entire software industry in the first year.

Computer networks raise new legal problems when they interact with old laws. Electronic gambling provides an example. Computers have been simulating things for decades, so why not simulate slot machines, roulette wheels, blackjack dealers, and more gambling equipment? Well, because it is illegal in a lot of places. The trouble is, gambling is legal in a lot of other places (England, for example) and casino owners there have grasped the potential for Internet gambling. What happens if the gambler, the casino, and the server are all in different countries, with conflicting laws? Good question.

1.2 NETWORK HARDWARE

It is now time to turn our attention from the applications and social aspects of networking (the dessert) to the technical issues involved in network design (the spinach). There is no generally accepted taxonomy into which all computer networks fit, but two dimensions stand out as important: transmission technology and scale. We will now examine each of these in turn.

Broadly speaking, there are two types of transmission technology that are in widespread use: **broadcast** links and **point-to-point** links.

Point-to-point links connect individual pairs of machines. To go from the source to the destination on a network made up of point-to-point links, short messages, called **packets** in certain contexts, may have to first visit one or more intermediate machines. Often multiple routes, of different lengths, are possible, so finding good ones is important in point-to-point networks. Point-to-point transmission with exactly one sender and exactly one receiver is sometimes called **unicasting**.

In contrast, on a broadcast network, the communication channel is shared by all the machines on the network; packets sent by any machine are received by all the others. An address field within each packet specifies the intended recipient. Upon receiving a packet, a machine checks the address field. If the packet is intended for the receiving machine, that machine processes the packet; if the packet is intended for some other machine, it is just ignored.

A wireless network is a common example of a broadcast link, with communication shared over a coverage region that depends on the wireless channel and the transmitting machine. As an analogy, consider someone standing in a meeting room and shouting "Watson, come here. I want you." Although the packet may actually be received (heard) by many people, only Watson will respond; the others just ignore it.

Broadcast systems usually also allow the possibility of addressing a packet to *all* destinations by using a special code in the address field. When a packet with this code is transmitted, it is received and processed by every machine on the network. This mode of operation is called **broadcasting**. Some broadcast systems also support transmission to a subset of the machines, which known as **multicasting**.

An alternative criterion for classifying networks is by scale. Distance is important as a classification metric because different technologies are used at different scales.

In Fig. 1-6 we classify multiple processor systems by their rough physical size. At the top are the personal area networks, networks that are meant for one person. Beyond these come longer-range networks. These can be divided into local, metropolitan, and wide area networks, each with increasing scale. Finally, the connection of two or more networks is called an internetwork. The worldwide Internet is certainly the best-known (but not the only) example of an internetwork.

Soon we will have even larger internetworks with the **Interplanetary Internet** that connects networks across space (Burleigh et al., 2003).

Interprocessor distance	Processors located in same	Example
1 m	Square meter	Personal area network
10 m	Room	Local area network
100 m	Building	
1 km	Campus	
10 km	City	Metropolitan area network
100 km	Country	Wide area network
1000 km	Continent	
10,000 km	Planet	The Internet

Figure 1-6. Classification of interconnected processors by scale.

In this book we will be concerned with networks at all these scales. In the following sections, we give a brief introduction to network hardware by scale.

1.2.1 Personal Area Networks

PANs (Personal Area Networks) let devices communicate over the range of a person. A common example is a wireless network that connects a computer with its peripherals. Almost every computer has an attached monitor, keyboard, mouse, and printer. Without using wireless, this connection must be done with cables. So many new users have a hard time finding the right cables and plugging them into the right little holes (even though they are usually color coded) that most computer vendors offer the option of sending a technician to the user's home to do it. To help these users, some companies got together to design a short-range wireless network called **Bluetooth** to connect these components without wires. The idea is that if your devices have Bluetooth, then you need no cables. You just put them down, turn them on, and they work together. For many people, this ease of operation is a big plus.

In the simplest form, Bluetooth networks use the master-slave paradigm of Fig. 1-7. The system unit (the PC) is normally the master, talking to the mouse, keyboard, etc., as slaves. The master tells the slaves what addresses to use, when they can broadcast, how long they can transmit, what frequencies they can use, and so on.

Bluetooth can be used in other settings, too. It is often used to connect a headset to a mobile phone without cords and it can allow your digital music player

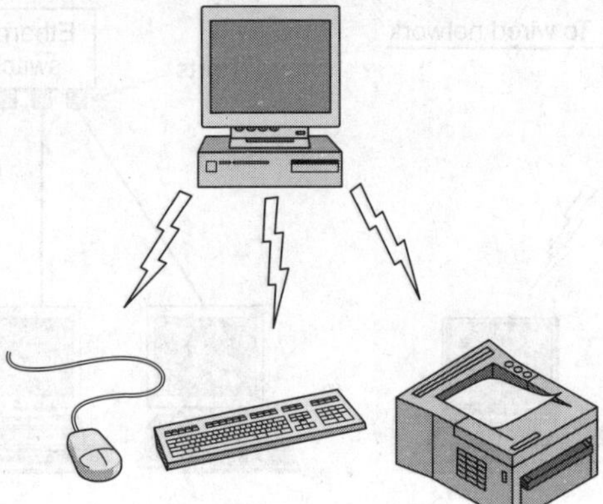

Figure 1-7. Bluetooth PAN configuration.

to connect to your car merely being brought within range. A completely different kind of PAN is formed when an embedded medical device such as a pacemaker, insulin pump, or hearing aid talks to a user-operated remote control. We will discuss Bluetooth in more detail in Chap. 4.

PANs can also be built with other technologies that communicate over short ranges, such as RFID on smartcards and library books. We will study RFID in Chap. 4.

1.2.2 Local Area Networks

The next step up is the **LAN** (**Local Area Network**). A LAN is a privately owned network that operates within and nearby a single building like a home, office or factory. LANs are widely used to connect personal computers and consumer electronics to let them share resources (e.g., printers) and exchange information. When LANs are used by companies, they are called **enterprise networks**.

Wireless LANs are very popular these days, especially in homes, older office buildings, cafeterias, and other places where it is too much trouble to install cables. In these systems, every computer has a radio modem and an antenna that it uses to communicate with other computers. In most cases, each computer talks to a device in the ceiling as shown in Fig. 1-8(a). This device, called an **AP** (**Access Point**), **wireless router**, or **base station**, relays packets between the wireless computers and also between them and the Internet. Being the AP is like being the popular kid as school because everyone wants to talk to you. However, if other computers are close enough, they can communicate directly with one another in a peer-to-peer configuration.

There is a standard for wireless LANs called **IEEE 802.11**, popularly known as **WiFi**, which has become very widespread. It runs at speeds anywhere from 11

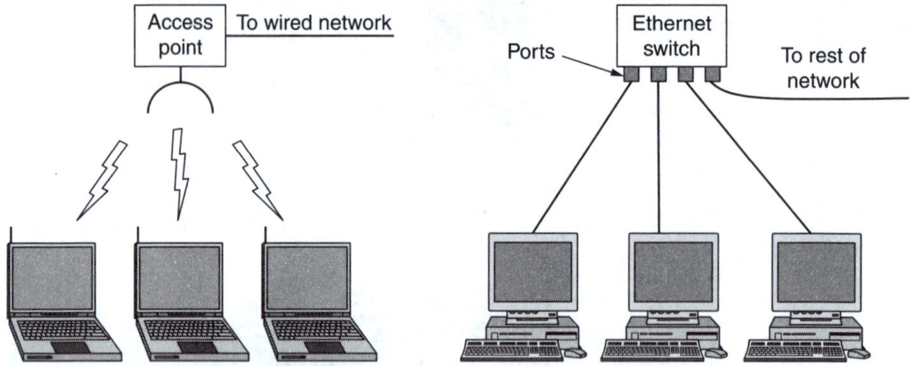

Figure 1-8. Wireless and wired LANs. (a) 802.11. (b) Switched Ethernet.

to hundreds of Mbps. (In this book we will adhere to tradition and measure line speeds in megabits/sec, where 1 Mbps is 1,000,000 bits/sec, and gigabits/sec, where 1 Gbps is 1,000,000,000 bits/sec.) We will discuss 802.11 in Chap. 4.

Wired LANs use a range of different transmission technologies. Most of them use copper wires, but some use optical fiber. LANs are restricted in size, which means that the worst-case transmission time is bounded and known in advance. Knowing these bounds helps with the task of designing network protocols. Typically, wired LANs run at speeds of 100 Mbps to 1 Gbps, have low delay (microseconds or nanoseconds), and make very few errors. Newer LANs can operate at up to 10 Gbps. Compared to wireless networks, wired LANs exceed them in all dimensions of performance. It is just easier to send signals over a wire or through a fiber than through the air.

The topology of many wired LANs is built from point-to-point links. IEEE 802.3, popularly called **Ethernet**, is, by far, the most common type of wired LAN. Fig. 1-8(b) shows a sample topology of **switched Ethernet**. Each computer speaks the Ethernet protocol and connects to a box called a **switch** with a point-to-point link. Hence the name. A switch has multiple **ports**, each of which can connect to one computer. The job of the switch is to relay packets between computers that are attached to it, using the address in each packet to determine which computer to send it to.

To build larger LANs, switches can be plugged into each other using their ports. What happens if you plug them together in a loop? Will the network still work? Luckily, the designers thought of this case. It is the job of the protocol to sort out what paths packets should travel to safely reach the intended computer. We will see how this works in Chap. 4.

It is also possible to divide one large physical LAN into two smaller logical LANs. You might wonder why this would be useful. Sometimes, the layout of the network equipment does not match the organization's structure. For example, the engineering and finance departments of a company might have computers on the same physical LAN because they are in the same wing of the building but it might be easier to manage the system if engineering and finance logically each had its own network **Virtual LAN** or **VLAN**. In this design each port is tagged with a "color," say green for engineering and red for finance. The switch then forwards packets so that computers attached to the green ports are separated from the computers attached to the red ports. Broadcast packets sent on a red port, for example, will not be received on a green port, just as though there were two different LANs. We will cover VLANs at the end of Chap. 4.

There are other wired LAN topologies too. In fact, switched Ethernet is a modern version of the original Ethernet design that broadcast all the packets over a single linear cable. At most one machine could successfully transmit at a time, and a distributed arbitration mechanism was used to resolve conflicts. It used a simple algorithm: computers could transmit whenever the cable was idle. If two or more packets collided, each computer just waited a random time and tried later. We will call that version **classic Ethernet** for clarity, and as you suspected, you will learn about it in Chap. 4.

Both wireless and wired broadcast networks can be divided into static and dynamic designs, depending on how the channel is allocated. A typical static allocation would be to divide time into discrete intervals and use a round-robin algorithm, allowing each machine to broadcast only when its time slot comes up. Static allocation wastes channel capacity when a machine has nothing to say during its allocated slot, so most systems attempt to allocate the channel dynamically (i.e., on demand).

Dynamic allocation methods for a common channel are either centralized or decentralized. In the centralized channel allocation method, there is a single entity, for example, the base station in cellular networks, which determines who goes next. It might do this by accepting multiple packets and prioritizing them according to some internal algorithm. In the decentralized channel allocation method, there is no central entity; each machine must decide for itself whether to transmit. You might think that this approach would lead to chaos, but it does not. Later we will study many algorithms designed to bring order out of the potential chaos.

It is worth spending a little more time discussing LANs in the home. In the future, it is likely that every appliance in the home will be capable of communicating with every other appliance, and all of them will be accessible over the Internet. This development is likely to be one of those visionary concepts that nobody asked for (like TV remote controls or mobile phones), but once they arrived nobody can imagine how they lived without them.

Many devices are already capable of being networked. These include computers, entertainment devices such as TVs and DVDs, phones and other consumer electronics such as cameras, appliances like clock radios, and infrastructure like utility meters and thermostats. This trend will only continue. For instance, the average home probably has a dozen clocks (e.g., in appliances), all of which could adjust to daylight savings time automatically if the clocks were on the Internet. Remote monitoring of the home is a likely winner, as many grown children would be willing to spend some money to help their aging parents live safely in their own homes.

While we could think of the home network as just another LAN, it is more likely to have different properties than other networks. First, the networked devices have to be very easy to install. Wireless routers are the most returned consumer electronic item. People buy one because they want a wireless network at home, find that it does not work "out of the box," and then return it rather than listen to elevator music while on hold on the technical helpline.

Second, the network and devices have to be foolproof in operation. Air conditioners used to have one knob with four settings: OFF, LOW, MEDIUM, and HIGH. Now they have 30-page manuals. Once they are networked, expect the chapter on security alone to be 30 pages. This is a problem because only computer users are accustomed to putting up with products that do not work; the car-, television-, and refrigerator-buying public is far less tolerant. They expect products to work 100% without the need to hire a geek.

Third, low price is essential for success. People will not pay a $50 premium for an Internet thermostat because few people regard monitoring their home temperature from work that important. For $5 extra, though, it might sell.

Fourth, it must be possible to start out with one or two devices and expand the reach of the network gradually. This means no format wars. Telling consumers to buy peripherals with IEEE 1394 (FireWire) interfaces and a few years later retracting that and saying USB 2.0 is the interface-of-the-month and then switching that to 802.11g—oops, no, make that 802.11n—I mean 802.16 (different wireless networks)—is going to make consumers very skittish. The network interface will have to remain stable for decades, like the television broadcasting standards.

Fifth, security and reliability will be very important. Losing a few files to an email virus is one thing; having a burglar disarm your security system from his mobile computer and then plunder your house is something quite different.

An interesting question is whether home networks will be wired or wireless. Convenience and cost favors wireless networking because there are no wires to fit, or worse, retrofit. Security favors wired networking because the radio waves that wireless networks use are quite good at going through walls. Not everyone is overjoyed at the thought of having the neighbors piggybacking on their Internet connection and reading their email. In Chap. 8 we will study how encryption can be used to provide security, but it is easier said than done with inexperienced users.

A third option that may be appealing is to reuse the networks that are already in the home. The obvious candidate is the electric wires that are installed throughout the house. **Power-line networks** let devices that plug into outlets broadcast information throughout the house. You have to plug in the TV anyway, and this way it can get Internet connectivity at the same time. The difficulty is how to carry both power and data signals at the same time. Part of the answer is that they use different frequency bands.

In short, home LANs offer many opportunities and challenges. Most of the latter relate to the need for the networks to be easy to manage, dependable, and secure, especially in the hands of nontechnical users, as well as low cost.

1.2.3 Metropolitan Area Networks

A **MAN** (**Metropolitan Area Network**) covers a city. The best-known examples of MANs are the cable television networks available in many cities. These systems grew from earlier community antenna systems used in areas with poor over-the-air television reception. In those early systems, a large antenna was placed on top of a nearby hill and a signal was then piped to the subscribers' houses.

At first, these were locally designed, ad hoc systems. Then companies began jumping into the business, getting contracts from local governments to wire up entire cities. The next step was television programming and even entire channels designed for cable only. Often these channels were highly specialized, such as all news, all sports, all cooking, all gardening, and so on. But from their inception until the late 1990s, they were intended for television reception only.

When the Internet began attracting a mass audience, the cable TV network operators began to realize that with some changes to the system, they could provide two-way Internet service in unused parts of the spectrum. At that point, the cable TV system began to morph from simply a way to distribute television to a metropolitan area network. To a first approximation, a MAN might look something like the system shown in Fig. 1-9. In this figure we see both television signals and Internet being fed into the centralized **cable headend** for subsequent distribution to people's homes. We will come back to this subject in detail in Chap. 2.

Cable television is not the only MAN, though. Recent developments in high-speed wireless Internet access have resulted in another MAN, which has been standardized as IEEE 802.16 and is popularly known as **WiMAX**. We will look at it in Chap. 4.

1.2.4 Wide Area Networks

A **WAN** (**Wide Area Network**) spans a large geographical area, often a country or continent. We will begin our discussion with wired WANs, using the example of a company with branch offices in different cities.

The WAN in Fig. 1-10 is a network that connects offices in Perth, Melbourne, and Brisbane. Each of these offices contains computers intended for running user (i.e., application) programs. We will follow traditional usage and call these machines **hosts**. The rest of the network that connects these hosts is then called the

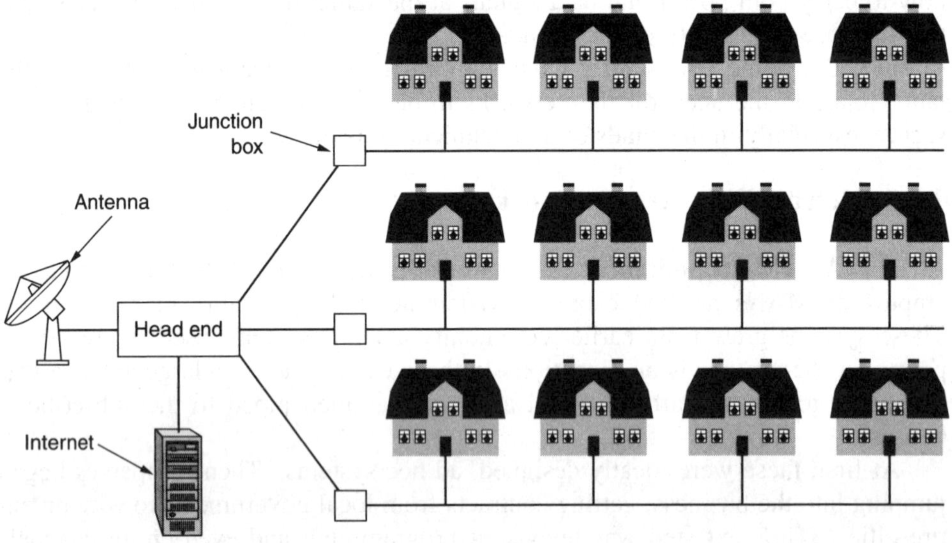

Figure 1-9. A metropolitan area network based on cable TV.

communication subnet, or just **subnet** for short. The job of the subnet is to carry messages from host to host, just as the telephone system carries words (really just sounds) from speaker to listener.

In most WANs, the subnet consists of two distinct components: transmission lines and switching elements. **Transmission lines** move bits between machines. They can be made of copper wire, optical fiber, or even radio links. Most companies do not have transmission lines lying about, so instead they lease the lines from a telecommunications company. **Switching elements**, or just **switches**, are specialized computers that connect two or more transmission lines. When data arrive on an incoming line, the switching element must choose an outgoing line on which to forward them. These switching computers have been called by various names in the past; the name **router** is now most commonly used. Unfortunately, some people pronounce it "rooter" while others have it rhyme with "doubter." Determining the correct pronunciation will be left as an exercise for the reader. (Note: the perceived correct answer may depend on where you live.)

A short comment about the term "subnet" is in order here. Originally, its **only** meaning was the collection of routers and communication lines that moved packets from the source host to the destination host. Readers should be aware that it has acquired a second, more recent meaning in conjunction with network addressing. We will discuss that meaning in Chap. 5 and stick with the original meaning (a collection of lines and routers) until then.

The WAN as we have described it looks similar to a large wired LAN, but there are some important differences that go beyond long wires. Usually in a WAN, the hosts and subnet are owned and operated by different people. In our

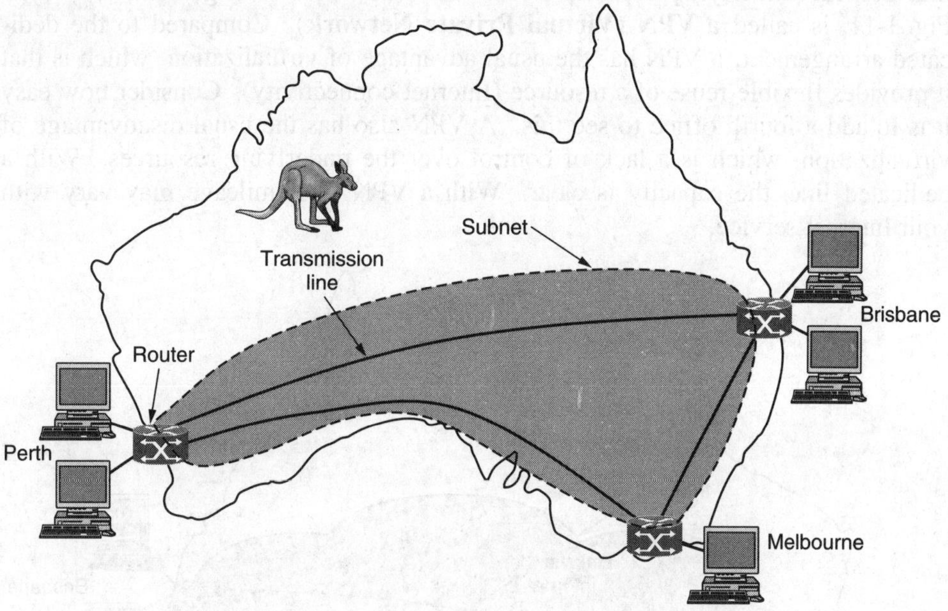

Figure 1-10. WAN that connects three branch offices in Australia.

example, the employees might be responsible for their own computers, while the company's IT department is in charge of the rest of the network. We will see clearer boundaries in the coming examples, in which the network provider or telephone company operates the subnet. Separation of the pure communication aspects of the network (the subnet) from the application aspects (the hosts) greatly simplifies the overall network design.

A second difference is that the routers will usually connect different kinds of networking technology. The networks inside the offices may be switched Ethernet, for example, while the long-distance transmission lines may be SONET links (which we will cover in Chap. 2). Some device needs to join them. The astute reader will notice that this goes beyond our definition of a network. This means that many WANs will in fact be **internetworks**, or composite networks that are made up of more than one network. We will have more to say about internetworks in the next section.

A final difference is in what is connected to the subnet. This could be individual computers, as was the case for connecting to LANs, or it could be entire LANs. This is how larger networks are built from smaller ones. As far as the subnet is concerned, it does the same job.

We are now in a position to look at two other varieties of WANs. First, rather than lease dedicated transmission lines, a company might connect its offices to the Internet This allows connections to be made between the offices as virtual links that use the underlying capacity of the Internet. This arrangement, shown in Fig. 1-11, is called a **VPN (Virtual Private Network)**. Compared to the dedicated arrangement, a VPN has the usual advantage of virtualization, which is that it provides flexible reuse of a resource (Internet connectivity). Consider how easy it is to add a fourth office to see this. A VPN also has the usual disadvantage of virtualization, which is a lack of control over the underlying resources. With a dedicated line, the capacity is clear. With a VPN your mileage may vary with your Internet service.

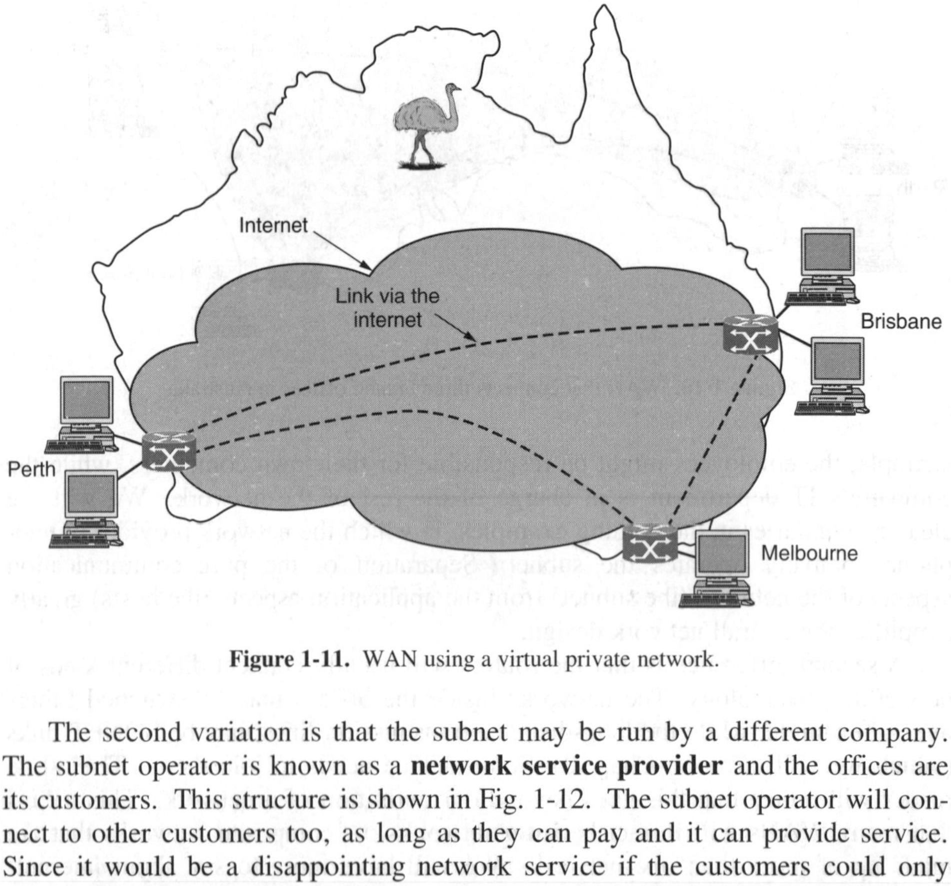

Figure 1-11. WAN using a virtual private network.

The second variation is that the subnet may be run by a different company. The subnet operator is known as a **network service provider** and the offices are its customers. This structure is shown in Fig. 1-12. The subnet operator will connect to other customers too, as long as they can pay and it can provide service. Since it would be a disappointing network service if the customers could only send packets to each other, the subnet operator will also connect to other networks that are part of the Internet. Such a subnet operator is called an **ISP (Internet Service Provider)** and the subnet is an **ISP network**. Its customers who connect to the ISP receive Internet service.

We can use the ISP network to preview some key issues that we will study in later chapters. In most WANs, the network contains many transmission lines, each connecting a pair of routers. If two routers that do not share a transmission line wish to communicate, they must do this indirectly, via other routers. There

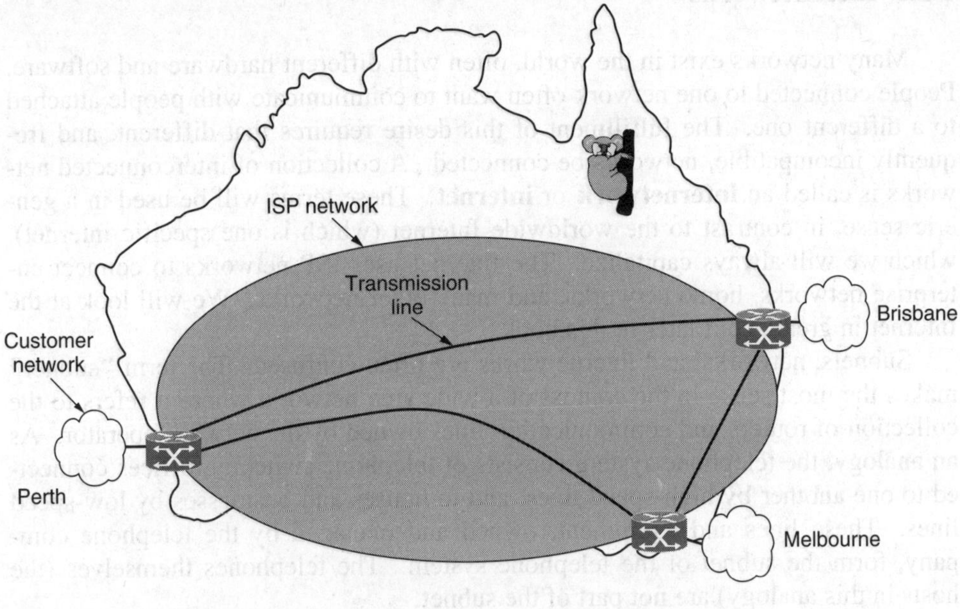

Figure 1-12. WAN using an ISP network.

may be many paths in the network that connect these two routers. How the network makes the decision as to which path to use is called the **routing algorithm**. Many such algorithms exist. How each router makes the decision as to where to send a packet next is called the **forwarding algorithm**. Many of them exist too. We will study some of both types in detail in Chap. 5.

Other kinds of WANs make heavy use of wireless technologies. In satellite systems, each computer on the ground has an antenna through which it can send data to and receive data from to a satellite in orbit. All computers can hear the output *from* the satellite, and in some cases they can also hear the upward transmissions of their fellow computers *to* the satellite as well. Satellite networks are inherently broadcast and are most useful when the broadcast property is important.

The cellular telephone network is another example of a WAN that uses wireless technology. This system has already gone through three generations and a fourth one is on the horizon. The first generation was analog and for voice only. The second generation was digital and for voice only. The third generation is digital and is for both voice and data. Each cellular base station covers a distance much larger than a wireless LAN, with a range measured in kilometers rather than tens of meters. The base stations are connected to each other by a backbone network that is usually wired. The data rates of cellular networks are often on the order of 1 Mbps, much smaller than a wireless LAN that can range up to on the order of 100 Mbps. We will have a lot to say about these networks in Chap. 2.

1.2.5 Internetworks

Many networks exist in the world, often with different hardware and software. People connected to one network often want to communicate with people attached to a different one. The fulfillment of this desire requires that different, and frequently incompatible, networks be connected. A collection of interconnected networks is called an **internetwork** or **internet**. These terms will be used in a generic sense, in contrast to the worldwide Internet (which is one specific internet), which we will always capitalize. The Internet uses ISP networks to connect enterprise networks, home networks, and many other networks. We will look at the Internet in great detail later in this book.

Subnets, networks, and internetworks are often confused. The term "subnet" makes the most sense in the context of a wide area network, where it refers to the collection of routers and communication lines owned by the network operator. As an analogy, the telephone system consists of telephone switching offices connected to one another by high-speed lines, and to houses and businesses by low-speed lines. These lines and equipment, owned and managed by the telephone company, form the subnet of the telephone system. The telephones themselves (the hosts in this analogy) are not part of the subnet.

A network is formed by the combination of a subnet and its hosts. However, the word "network" is often used in a loose sense as well. A subnet might be described as a network, as in the case of the "ISP network" of Fig. 1-12. An internetwork might also be described as a network, as in the case of the WAN in Fig. 1-10. We will follow similar practice, and if we are distinguishing a network from other arrangements, we will stick with our original definition of a collection of computers interconnected by a single technology.

Let us say more about what constitutes an internetwork. We know that an internet is formed when distinct networks are interconnected. In our view, connecting a LAN and a WAN or connecting two LANs is the usual way to form an internetwork, but there is little agreement in the industry over terminology in this area. There are two rules of thumb that are useful. First, if different organizations have paid to construct different parts of the network and each maintains its part, we have an internetwork rather than a single network. Second, if the underlying technology is different in different parts (e.g., broadcast versus point-to-point and wired versus wireless), we probably have an internetwork.

To go deeper, we need to talk about how two different networks can be connected. The general name for a machine that makes a connection between two or more networks and provides the necessary translation, both in terms of hardware and software, is a **gateway**. Gateways are distinguished by the layer at which they operate in the protocol hierarchy. We will have much more to say about layers and protocol hierarchies starting in the next section, but for now imagine that higher layers are more tied to applications, such as the Web, and lower layers are more tied to transmission links, such as Ethernet.

Since the benefit of forming an internet is to connect computers across networks, we do not want to use too low-level a gateway or we will be unable to make connections between different kinds of networks. We do not want to use too high-level a gateway either, or the connection will only work for particular applications. The level in the middle that is "just right" is often called the network layer, and a router is a gateway that switches packets at the network layer. We can now spot an internet by finding a network that has routers.

1.3 NETWORK SOFTWARE

The first computer networks were designed with the hardware as the main concern and the software as an afterthought. This strategy no longer works. Network software is now highly structured. In the following sections we examine the software structuring technique in some detail. The approach described here forms the keystone of the entire book and will occur repeatedly later on.

1.3.1 Protocol Hierarchies

To reduce their design complexity, most networks are organized as a stack of **layers** or **levels**, each one built upon the one below it. The number of layers, the name of each layer, the contents of each layer, and the function of each layer differ from network to network. The purpose of each layer is to offer certain services to the higher layers while shielding those layers from the details of how the offered services are actually implemented. In a sense, each layer is a kind of virtual machine, offering certain services to the layer above it.

This concept is actually a familiar one and is used throughout computer science, where it is variously known as information hiding, abstract data types, data encapsulation, and object-oriented programming. The fundamental idea is that a particular piece of software (or hardware) provides a service to its users but keeps the details of its internal state and algorithms hidden from them.

When layer *n* on one machine carries on a conversation with layer *n* on another machine, the rules and conventions used in this conversation are collectively known as the layer *n* protocol. Basically, a **protocol** is an agreement between the communicating parties on how communication is to proceed. As an analogy, when a woman is introduced to a man, she may choose to stick out her hand. He, in turn, may decide to either shake it or kiss it, depending, for example, on whether she is an American lawyer at a business meeting or a European princess at a formal ball. Violating the protocol will make communication more difficult, if not completely impossible.

A five-layer network is illustrated in Fig. 1-13. The entities comprising the corresponding layers on different machines are called **peers**. The peers may be software processes, hardware devices, or even human beings. In other words, it is the peers that communicate by using the protocol to talk to each other.

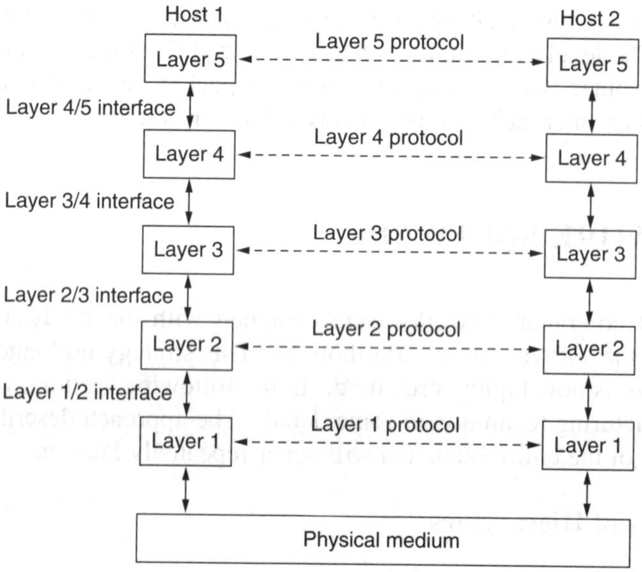

Figure 1-13. Layers, protocols, and interfaces.

In reality, no data are directly transferred from layer n on one machine to layer n on another machine. Instead, each layer passes data and control information to the layer immediately below it, until the lowest layer is reached. Below layer 1 is the **physical medium** through which actual communication occurs. In Fig. 1-13, virtual communication is shown by dotted lines and physical communication by solid lines.

Between each pair of adjacent layers is an **interface**. The interface defines which primitive operations and services the lower layer makes available to the upper one. When network designers decide how many layers to include in a network and what each one should do, one of the most important considerations is defining clean interfaces between the layers. Doing so, in turn, requires that each layer perform a specific collection of well-understood functions. In addition to minimizing the amount of information that must be passed between layers, clear-cut interfaces also make it simpler to replace one layer with a completely different protocol or implementation (e.g., replacing all the telephone lines by satellite channels) because all that is required of the new protocol or implementation is that it offer exactly the same set of services to its upstairs neighbor as the old one did. It is common that different hosts use different implementations of the same protocol (often written by different companies). In fact, the protocol itself can change in some layer without the layers above and below it even noticing.

A set of layers and protocols is called a **network architecture**. The specification of an architecture must contain enough information to allow an implementer to write the program or build the hardware for each layer so that it will correctly obey the appropriate protocol. Neither the details of the implementation nor the specification of the interfaces is part of the architecture because these are hidden away inside the machines and not visible from the outside. It is not even necessary that the interfaces on all machines in a network be the same, provided that each machine can correctly use all the protocols. A list of the protocols used by a certain system, one protocol per layer, is called a **protocol stack**. Network architectures, protocol stacks, and the protocols themselves are the principal subjects of this book.

An analogy may help explain the idea of multilayer communication. Imagine two philosophers (peer processes in layer 3), one of whom speaks Urdu and English and one of whom speaks Chinese and French. Since they have no common language, they each engage a translator (peer processes at layer 2), each of whom in turn contacts a secretary (peer processes in layer 1). Philosopher 1 wishes to convey his affection for *oryctolagus cuniculus* to his peer. To do so, he passes a message (in English) across the 2/3 interface to his translator, saying "I like rabbits," as illustrated in Fig. 1-14. The translators have agreed on a neutral language known to both of them, Dutch, so the message is converted to "Ik vind konijnen leuk." The choice of the language is the layer 2 protocol and is up to the layer 2 peer processes.

The translator then gives the message to a secretary for transmission, for example, by email (the layer 1 protocol). When the message arrives at the other secretary, it is passed to the local translator, who translates it into French and passes it across the 2/3 interface to the second philosopher. Note that each protocol is completely independent of the other ones as long as the interfaces are not changed. The translators can switch from Dutch to, say, Finnish, at will, provided that they both agree and neither changes his interface with either layer 1 or layer 3. Similarly, the secretaries can switch from email to telephone without disturbing (or even informing) the other layers. Each process may add some information intended only for its peer. This information is not passed up to the layer above.

Now consider a more technical example: how to provide communication to the top layer of the five-layer network in Fig. 1-15. A message, *M*, is produced by an application process running in layer 5 and given to layer 4 for transmission. Layer 4 puts a **header** in front of the message to identify the message and passes the result to layer 3. The header includes control information, such as addresses, to allow layer 4 on the destination machine to deliver the message. Other examples of control information used in some layers are sequence numbers (in case the lower layer does not preserve message order), sizes, and times.

In many networks, no limit is placed on the size of messages transmitted in the layer 4 protocol but there is nearly always a limit imposed by the layer 3 protocol. Consequently, layer 3 must break up the incoming messages into smaller

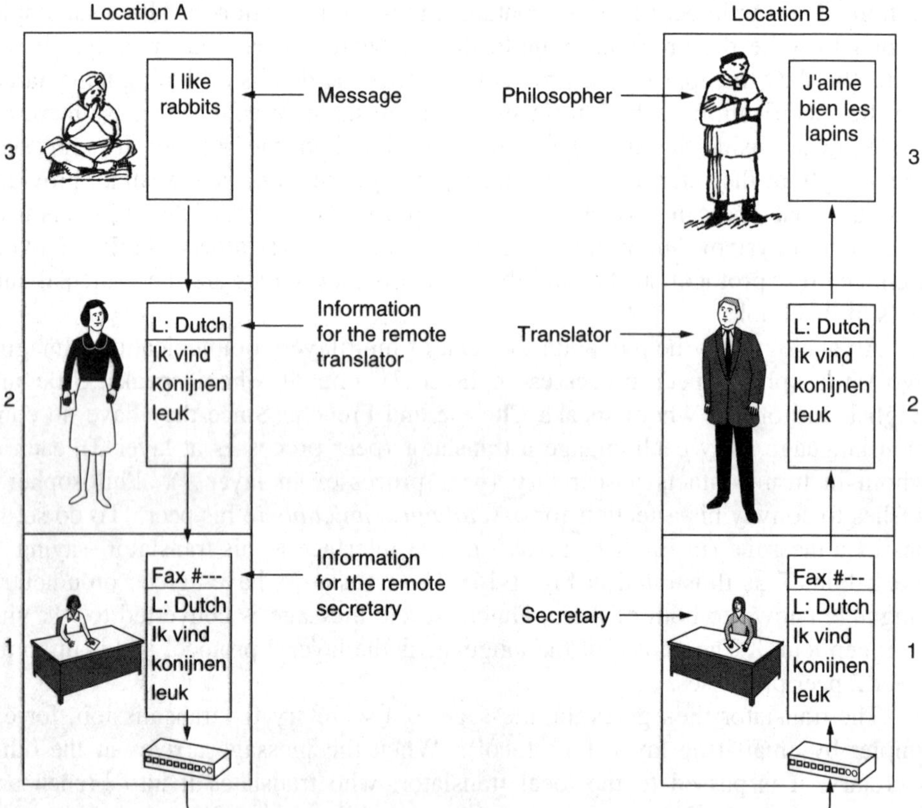

Figure 1-14. The philosopher-translator-secretary architecture.

units, packets, prepending a layer 3 header to each packet. In this example, M is split into two parts, M_1 and M_2, that will be transmitted separately.

Layer 3 decides which of the outgoing lines to use and passes the packets to layer 2. Layer 2 adds to each piece not only a header but also a trailer, and gives the resulting unit to layer 1 for physical transmission. At the receiving machine the message moves upward, from layer to layer, with headers being stripped off as it progresses. None of the headers for layers below n are passed up to layer n.

The important thing to understand about Fig. 1-15 is the relation between the virtual and actual communication and the difference between protocols and interfaces. The peer processes in layer 4, for example, conceptually think of their communication as being "horizontal," using the layer 4 protocol. Each one is likely to have procedures called something like *SendToOtherSide* and *GetFromOtherSide*, even though these procedures actually communicate with lower layers across the 3/4 interface, and not with the other side.

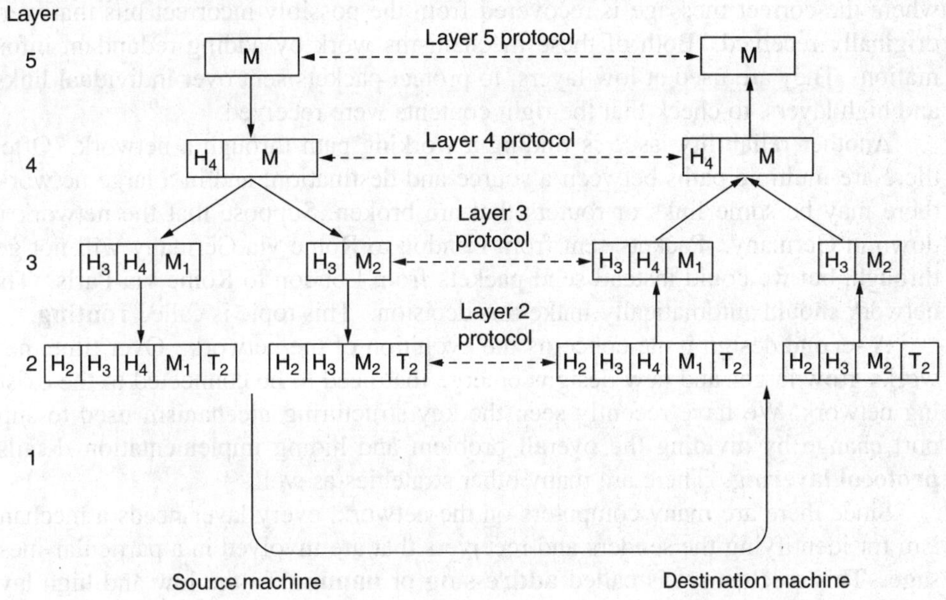

Figure 1-15. Example information flow supporting virtual communication in layer 5.

The peer process abstraction is crucial to all network design. Using it, the unmanageable task of designing the complete network can be broken into several smaller, manageable design problems, namely, the design of the individual layers.

Although Sec. 1.3 is called "Network Software," it is worth pointing out that the lower layers of a protocol hierarchy are frequently implemented in hardware or firmware. Nevertheless, complex protocol algorithms are involved, even if they are embedded (in whole or in part) in hardware.

1.3.2 Design Issues for the Layers

Some of the key design issues that occur in computer networks will come up in layer after layer. Below, we will briefly mention the more important ones.

Reliability is the design issue of making a network that operates correctly even though it is made up of a collection of components that are themselves unreliable. Think about the bits of a packet traveling through the network. There is a chance that some of these bits will be received damaged (inverted) due to fluke electrical noise, random wireless signals, hardware flaws, software bugs and so on. How is it possible that we find and fix these errors?

One mechanism for finding errors in received information uses codes for **error detection**. Information that is incorrectly received can then be retransmitted until it is received correctly. More powerful codes allow for **error correction**, where the correct message is recovered from the possibly incorrect bits that were originally received. Both of these mechanisms work by adding redundant information. They are used at low layers, to protect packets sent over individual links, and high layers, to check that the right contents were received.

Another reliability issue is finding a working path through a network. Often there are multiple paths between a source and destination, and in a large network, there may be some links or routers that are broken. Suppose that the network is down in Germany. Packets sent from London to Rome via Germany will not get through, but we could instead send packets from London to Rome via Paris. The network should automatically make this decision. This topic is called **routing**.

A second design issue concerns the evolution of the network. Over time, networks grow larger and new designs emerge that need to be connected to the existing network. We have recently seen the key structuring mechanism used to support change by dividing the overall problem and hiding implementation details: **protocol layering**. There are many other strategies as well.

Since there are many computers on the network, every layer needs a mechanism for identifying the senders and receivers that are involved in a particular message. This mechanism is called **addressing** or **naming**, in the low and high layers, respectively.

An aspect of growth is that different network technologies often have different limitations. For example, not all communication channels preserve the order of messages sent on them, leading to solutions that number messages. Another example is differences in the maximum size of a message that the networks can transmit. This leads to mechanisms for disassembling, transmitting, and then reassembling messages. This overall topic is called **internetworking**.

When networks get large, new problems arise. Cities can have traffic jams, a shortage of telephone numbers, and it is easy to get lost. Not many people have these problems in their own neighborhood, but citywide they may be a big issue. Designs that continue to work well when the network gets large are said to be **scalable**.

A third design issue is resource allocation. Networks provide a service to hosts from their underlying resources, such as the capacity of transmission lines. To do this well, they need mechanisms that divide their resources so that one host does not interfere with another too much.

Many designs share network bandwidth dynamically, according to the short-term needs of hosts, rather than by giving each host a fixed fraction of the bandwidth that it may or may not use. This design is called **statistical multiplexing**, meaning sharing based on the statistics of demand. It can be applied at low layers for a single link, or at high layers for a network or even applications that use the network.

An allocation problem that occurs at every level is how to keep a fast sender from swamping a slow receiver with data. Feedback from the receiver to the sender is often used. This subject is called **flow control**. Sometimes the problem is that the network is oversubscribed because too many computers want to send too much traffic, and the network cannot deliver it all. This overloading of the network is called **congestion**. One strategy is for each computer to reduce its demand when it experiences congestion. It, too, can be used in all layers.

It is interesting to observe that the network has more resources to offer than simply bandwidth. For uses such as carrying live video, the timeliness of delivery matters a great deal. Most networks must provide service to applications that want this **real-time** delivery at the same time that they provide service to applications that want high throughput. **Quality of service** is the name given to mechanisms that reconcile these competing demands.

The last major design issue is to secure the network by defending it against different kinds of threats. One of the threats we have mentioned previously is that of eavesdropping on communications. Mechanisms that provide **confidentiality** defend against this threat, and they are used in multiple layers. Mechanisms for **authentication** prevent someone from impersonating someone else. They might be used to tell fake banking Web sites from the real one, or to let the cellular network check that a call is really coming from your phone so that you will pay the bill. Other mechanisms for **integrity** prevent surreptitious changes to messages, such as altering "debit my account $10" to "debit my account $1000." All of these designs are based on cryptography, which we shall study in Chap. 8.

1.3.3 Connection-Oriented Versus Connectionless Service

Layers can offer two different types of service to the layers above them: connection-oriented and connectionless. In this section we will look at these two types and examine the differences between them.

Connection-oriented service is modeled after the telephone system. To talk to someone, you pick up the phone, dial the number, talk, and then hang up. Similarly, to use a connection-oriented network service, the service user first establishes a connection, uses the connection, and then releases the connection. The essential aspect of a connection is that it acts like a tube: the sender pushes objects (bits) in at one end, and the receiver takes them out at the other end. In most cases the order is preserved so that the bits arrive in the order they were sent.

In some cases when a connection is established, the sender, receiver, and subnet conduct a **negotiation** about the parameters to be used, such as maximum message size, quality of service required, and other issues. Typically, one side makes a proposal and the other side can accept it, reject it, or make a counterproposal. A **circuit** is another name for a connection with associated resources, such as a fixed bandwidth. This dates from the telephone network in which a circuit was a path over copper wire that carried a phone conversation.

In contrast to connection-oriented service, **connectionless** service is modeled after the postal system. Each message (letter) carries the full destination address, and each one is routed through the intermediate nodes inside the system independent of all the subsequent messages. There are different names for messages in different contexts; a **packet** is a message at the network layer. When the intermediate nodes receive a message in full before sending it on to the next node, this is called **store-and-forward switching**. The alternative, in which the onward transmission of a message at a node starts before it is completely received by the node, is called **cut-through switching**. Normally, when two messages are sent to the same destination, the first one sent will be the first one to arrive. However, it is possible that the first one sent can be delayed so that the second one arrives first.

Each kind of service can further be characterized by its reliability. Some services are reliable in the sense that they never lose data. Usually, a reliable service is implemented by having the receiver acknowledge the receipt of each message so the sender is sure that it arrived. The acknowledgement process introduces overhead and delays, which are often worth it but are sometimes undesirable.

A typical situation in which a reliable connection-oriented service is appropriate is file transfer. The owner of the file wants to be sure that all the bits arrive correctly and in the same order they were sent. Very few file transfer customers would prefer a service that occasionally scrambles or loses a few bits, even if it is much faster.

Reliable connection-oriented service has two minor variations: message sequences and byte streams. In the former variant, the message boundaries are preserved. When two 1024-byte messages are sent, they arrive as two distinct 1024-byte messages, never as one 2048-byte message. In the latter, the connection is simply a stream of bytes, with no message boundaries. When 2048 bytes arrive at the receiver, there is no way to tell if they were sent as one 2048-byte message, two 1024-byte messages, or 2048 1-byte messages. If the pages of a book are sent over a network to a phototypesetter as separate messages, it might be important to preserve the message boundaries. On the other hand, to download a DVD movie, a byte stream from the server to the user's computer is all that is needed. Message boundaries within the movie are not relevant.

For some applications, the transit delays introduced by acknowledgements are unacceptable. One such application is digitized voice traffic for **voice over IP**. It is less disruptive for telephone users to hear a bit of noise on the line from time to time than to experience a delay waiting for acknowledgements. Similarly, when transmitting a video conference, having a few pixels wrong is no problem, but having the image jerk along as the flow stops and starts to correct errors is irritating.

Not all applications require connections. For example, spammers send electronic junk-mail to many recipients. The spammer probably does not want to go to the trouble of setting up and later tearing down a connection to a recipient just to send them one item. Nor is 100 percent reliable delivery essential, especially if it costs more. All that is needed is a way to send a single message that has a high probability of arrival, but no guarantee. Unreliable (meaning not acknowledged) connectionless service is often called **datagram** service, in analogy with telegram service, which also does not return an acknowledgement to the sender. Despite it being unreliable, it is the dominant form in most networks for reasons that will become clear later

In other situations, the convenience of not having to establish a connection to send one message is desired, but reliability is essential. The **acknowledged datagram** service can be provided for these applications. It is like sending a registered letter and requesting a return receipt. When the receipt comes back, the sender is absolutely sure that the letter was delivered to the intended party and not lost along the way. Text messaging on mobile phones is an example.

Still another service is the **request-reply** service. In this service the sender transmits a single datagram containing a request; the reply contains the answer. Request-reply is commonly used to implement communication in the client-server model: the client issues a request and the server responds to it. For example, a mobile phone client might send a query to a map server to retrieve the map data for the current location. Figure 1-16 summarizes the types of services discussed above.

	Service	Example
Connection-oriented	Reliable message stream	Sequence of pages
	Reliable byte stream	Movie download
	Unreliable connection	Voice over IP
Connection-less	Unreliable datagram	Electronic junk mail
	Acknowledged datagram	Text messaging
	Request-reply	Database query

Figure 1-16. Six different types of service.

The concept of using unreliable communication may be confusing at first. After all, why would anyone actually prefer unreliable communication to reliable communication? First of all, reliable communication (in our sense, that is, acknowledged) may not be available in a given layer. For example, Ethernet does not provide reliable communication. Packets can occasionally be damaged in transit. It is up to higher protocol levels to recover from this problem. In particular, many reliable services are built on top of an unreliable datagram service. Second, the delays inherent in providing a reliable service may be unacceptable, especially in real-time applications such as multimedia. For these reasons, both reliable and unreliable communication coexist.

1.3.4 Service Primitives

A service is formally specified by a set of **primitives** (operations) available to user processes to access the service. These primitives tell the service to perform some action or report on an action taken by a peer entity. If the protocol stack is located in the operating system, as it often is, the primitives are normally system calls. These calls cause a trap to kernel mode, which then turns control of the machine over to the operating system to send the necessary packets.

The set of primitives available depends on the nature of the service being provided. The primitives for connection-oriented service are different from those of connectionless service. As a minimal example of the service primitives that might provide a reliable byte stream, consider the primitives listed in Fig. 1-17. They will be familiar to fans of the Berkeley socket interface, as the primitives are a simplified version of that interface.

Primitive	Meaning
LISTEN	Block waiting for an incoming connection
CONNECT	Establish a connection with a waiting peer
ACCEPT	Accept an incoming connection from a peer
RECEIVE	Block waiting for an incoming message
SEND	Send a message to the peer
DISCONNECT	Terminate a connection

Figure 1-17. Six service primitives that provide a simple connection-oriented service.

These primitives might be used for a request-reply interaction in a client-server environment. To illustrate how, We sketch a simple protocol that implements the service using acknowledged datagrams.

First, the server executes LISTEN to indicate that it is prepared to accept incoming connections. A common way to implement LISTEN is to make it a blocking system call. After executing the primitive, the server process is blocked until a request for connection appears.

Next, the client process executes CONNECT to establish a connection with the server. The CONNECT call needs to specify who to connect to, so it might have a parameter giving the server's address. The operating system then typically sends a packet to the peer asking it to connect, as shown by (1) in Fig. 1-18. The client process is suspended until there is a response.

When the packet arrives at the server, the operating system sees that the packet is requesting a connection. It checks to see if there is a listener, and if so it unblocks the listener. The server process can then establish the connection with the ACCEPT call. This sends a response (2) back to the client process to accept the

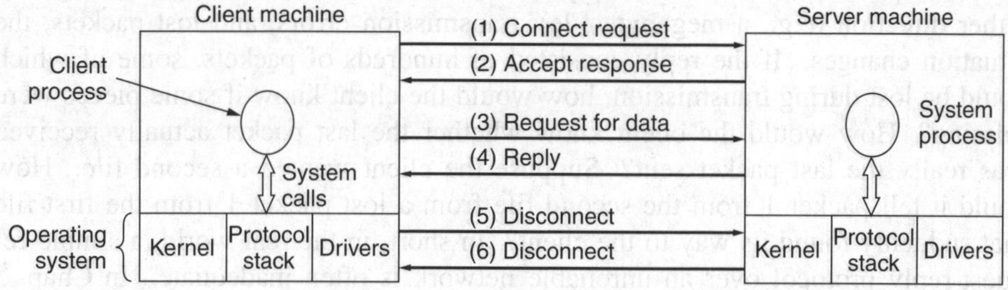

Figure 1-18. A simple client-server interaction using acknowledged datagrams.

connection. The arrival of this response then releases the client. At this point the client and server are both running and they have a connection established.

The obvious analogy between this protocol and real life is a customer (client) calling a company's customer service manager. At the start of the day, the service manager sits next to his telephone in case it rings. Later, a client places a call. When the manager picks up the phone, the connection is established.

The next step is for the server to execute RECEIVE to prepare to accept the first request. Normally, the server does this immediately upon being released from the LISTEN, before the acknowledgement can get back to the client. The RECEIVE call blocks the server.

Then the client executes SEND to transmit its request (3) followed by the execution of RECEIVE to get the reply. The arrival of the request packet at the server machine unblocks the server so it can handle the request. After it has done the work, the server uses SEND to return the answer to the client (4). The arrival of this packet unblocks the client, which can now inspect the answer. If the client has additional requests, it can make them now.

When the client is done, it executes DISCONNECT to terminate the connection (5). Usually, an initial DISCONNECT is a blocking call, suspending the client and sending a packet to the server saying that the connection is no longer needed. When the server gets the packet, it also issues a DISCONNECT of its own, acknowledging the client and releasing the connection (6). When the server's packet gets back to the client machine, the client process is released and the connection is broken. In a nutshell, this is how connection-oriented communication works.

Of course, life is not so simple. Many things can go wrong here. The timing can be wrong (e.g., the CONNECT is done before the LISTEN), packets can get lost, and much more. We will look at these issues in great detail later, but for the moment, Fig. 1-18 briefly summarizes how client-server communication might work with acknowledged datagrams so that we can ignore lost packets.

Given that six packets are required to complete this protocol, one might wonder why a connectionless protocol is not used instead. The answer is that in a perfect world it could be, in which case only two packets would be needed: one for the request and one for the reply. However, in the face of large messages in either direction (e.g., a megabyte file), transmission errors, and lost packets, the situation changes. If the reply consisted of hundreds of packets, some of which could be lost during transmission, how would the client know if some pieces were missing? How would the client know whether the last packet actually received was really the last packet sent? Suppose the client wanted a second file. How could it tell packet 1 from the second file from a lost packet 1 from the first file that suddenly found its way to the client? In short, in the real world, a simple request-reply protocol over an unreliable network is often inadequate. In Chap. 3 we will study a variety of protocols in detail that overcome these and other problems. For the moment, suffice it to say that having a reliable, ordered byte stream between processes is sometimes very convenient.

1.3.5 The Relationship of Services to Protocols

Services and protocols are distinct concepts. This distinction is so important that we emphasize it again here. A *service* is a set of primitives (operations) that a layer provides to the layer above it. The service defines what operations the layer is prepared to perform on behalf of its users, but it says nothing at all about how these operations are implemented. A service relates to an interface between two layers, with the lower layer being the service provider and the upper layer being the service user.

A *protocol*, in contrast, is a set of rules governing the format and meaning of the packets, or messages that are exchanged by the peer entities within a layer. Entities use protocols to implement their service definitions. They are free to change their protocols at will, provided they do not change the service visible to their users. In this way, the service and the protocol are completely decoupled. This is a key concept that any network designer should understand well.

To repeat this crucial point, services relate to the interfaces between layers, as illustrated in Fig. 1-19. In contrast, protocols relate to the packets sent between peer entities on different machines. It is very important not to confuse the two concepts.

An analogy with programming languages is worth making. A service is like an abstract data type or an object in an object-oriented language. It defines operations that can be performed on an object but does not specify how these operations are implemented. In contrast, a protocol relates to the *implementation* of the service and as such is not visible to the user of the service.

Many older protocols did not distinguish the service from the protocol. In effect, a typical layer might have had a service primitive SEND PACKET with the user providing a pointer to a fully assembled packet. This arrangement meant that all changes to the protocol were immediately visible to the users. Most network designers now regard such a design as a serious blunder.

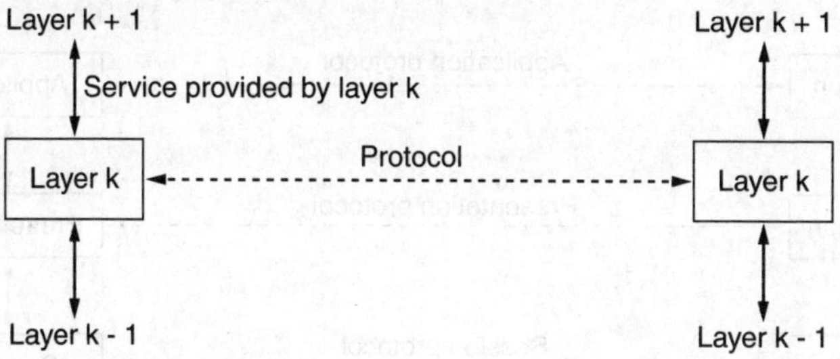

Figure 1-19. The relationship between a service and a protocol.

1.4 REFERENCE MODELS

Now that we have discussed layered networks in the abstract, it is time to look at some examples. We will discuss two important network architectures: the OSI reference model and the TCP/IP reference model. Although the *protocols* associated with the OSI model are not used any more, the *model* itself is actually quite general and still valid, and the features discussed at each layer are still very important. The TCP/IP model has the opposite properties: the model itself is not of much use but the protocols are widely used. For this reason we will look at both of them in detail. Also, sometimes you can learn more from failures than from successes.

1.4.1 The OSI Reference Model

The OSI model (minus the physical medium) is shown in Fig. 1-20. This model is based on a proposal developed by the International Standards Organization (ISO) as a first step toward international standardization of the protocols used in the various layers (Day and Zimmermann, 1983). It was revised in 1995 (Day, 1995). The model is called the ISO **OSI** (**Open Systems Interconnection**) Reference Model because it deals with connecting open systems—that is, systems that are open for communication with other systems. We will just call it the **OSI model** for short.

The OSI model has seven layers. The principles that were applied to arrive at the seven layers can be briefly summarized as follows:

1. A layer should be created where a different abstraction is needed.

2. Each layer should perform a well-defined function.

3. The function of each layer should be chosen with an eye toward defining internationally standardized protocols.

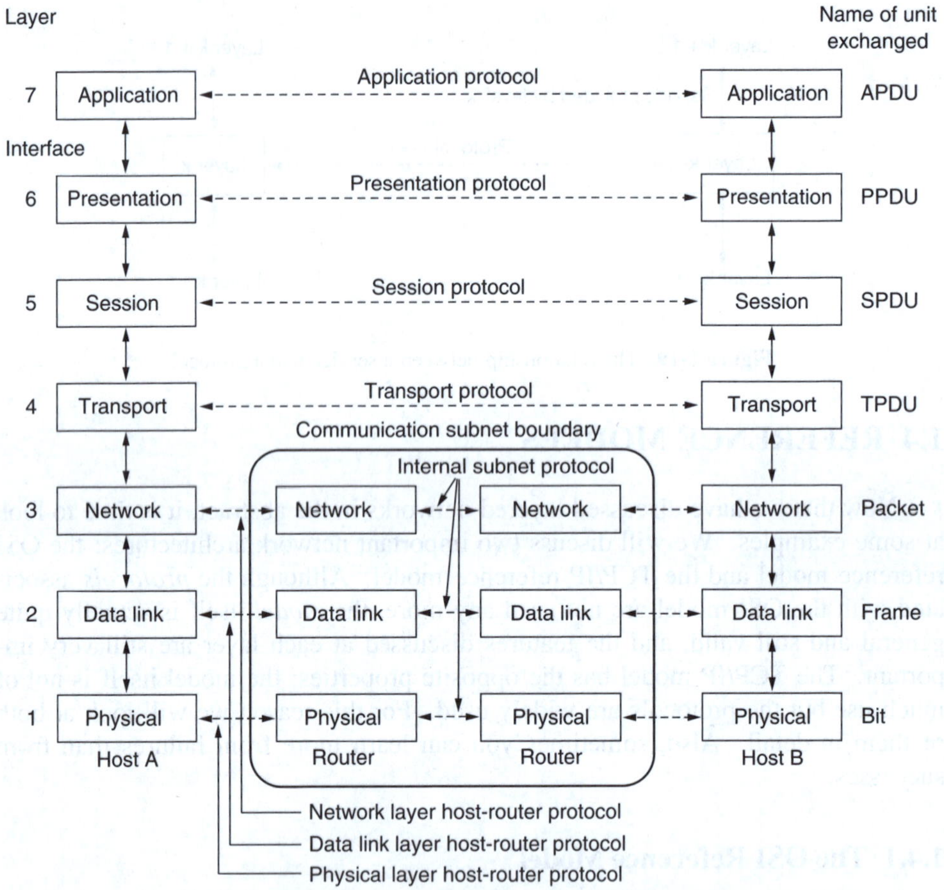

Figure 1-20. The OSI reference model.

4. The layer boundaries should be chosen to minimize the information flow across the interfaces.
5. The number of layers should be large enough that distinct functions need not be thrown together in the same layer out of necessity and small enough that the architecture does not become unwieldy.

Below we will discuss each layer of the model in turn, starting at the bottom layer. Note that the OSI model itself is not a network architecture because it does not specify the exact services and protocols to be used in each layer. It just tells what each layer should do. However, ISO has also produced standards for all the layers, although these are not part of the reference model itself. Each one has been published as a separate international standard. The *model* (in part) is widely used although the associated protocols have been long forgotten.

The Physical Layer

The **physical layer** is concerned with transmitting raw bits over a communication channel. The design issues have to do with making sure that when one side sends a 1 bit it is received by the other side as a 1 bit, not as a 0 bit. Typical questions here are what electrical signals should be used to represent a 1 and a 0, how many nanoseconds a bit lasts, whether transmission may proceed simultaneously in both directions, how the initial connection is established, how it is torn down when both sides are finished, how many pins the network connector has, and what each pin is used for. These design issues largely deal with mechanical, electrical, and timing interfaces, as well as the physical transmission medium, which lies below the physical layer.

The Data Link Layer

The main task of the **data link layer** is to transform a raw transmission facility into a line that appears free of undetected transmission errors. It does so by masking the real errors so the network layer does not see them. It accomplishes this task by having the sender break up the input data into **data frames** (typically a few hundred or a few thousand bytes) and transmit the frames sequentially. If the service is reliable, the receiver confirms correct receipt of each frame by sending back an **acknowledgement frame**.

Another issue that arises in the data link layer (and most of the higher layers as well) is how to keep a fast transmitter from drowning a slow receiver in data. Some traffic regulation mechanism may be needed to let the transmitter know when the receiver can accept more data.

Broadcast networks have an additional issue in the data link layer: how to control access to the shared channel. A special sublayer of the data link layer, the **medium access control** sublayer, deals with this problem.

The Network Layer

The **network layer** controls the operation of the subnet. A key design issue is determining how packets are routed from source to destination. Routes can be based on static tables that are "wired into" the network and rarely changed, or more often they can be updated automatically to avoid failed components. They can also be determined at the start of each conversation, for example, a terminal session, such as a login to a remote machine. Finally, they can be highly dynamic, being determined anew for each packet to reflect the current network load.

If too many packets are present in the subnet at the same time, they will get in one another's way, forming bottlenecks. Handling congestion is also a responsibility of the network layer, in conjunction with higher layers that adapt the load they place on the network. More generally, the quality of service provided (delay, transit time, jitter, etc.) is also a network layer issue.

When a packet has to travel from one network to another to get to its destination, many problems can arise. The addressing used by the second network may be different from that used by the first one. The second one may not accept the packet at all because it is too large. The protocols may differ, and so on. It is up to the network layer to overcome all these problems to allow heterogeneous networks to be interconnected.

In broadcast networks, the routing problem is simple, so the network layer is often thin or even nonexistent.

The Transport Layer

The basic function of the **transport layer** is to accept data from above it, split it up into smaller units if need be, pass these to the network layer, and ensure that the pieces all arrive correctly at the other end. Furthermore, all this must be done efficiently and in a way that isolates the upper layers from the inevitable changes in the hardware technology over the course of time.

The transport layer also determines what type of service to provide to the session layer, and, ultimately, to the users of the network. The most popular type of transport connection is an error-free point-to-point channel that delivers messages or bytes in the order in which they were sent. However, other possible kinds of transport service exist, such as the transporting of isolated messages with no guarantee about the order of delivery, and the broadcasting of messages to multiple destinations. The type of service is determined when the connection is established. (As an aside, an error-free channel is completely impossible to achieve; what people really mean by this term is that the error rate is low enough to ignore in practice.)

The transport layer is a true end-to-end layer; it carries data all the way from the source to the destination. In other words, a program on the source machine carries on a conversation with a similar program on the destination machine, using the message headers and control messages. In the lower layers, each protocols is between a machine and its immediate neighbors, and not between the ultimate source and destination machines, which may be separated by many routers. The difference between layers 1 through 3, which are chained, and layers 4 through 7, which are end-to-end, is illustrated in Fig. 1-20.

The Session Layer

The session layer allows users on different machines to establish **sessions** between them. Sessions offer various services, including **dialog control** (keeping track of whose turn it is to transmit), **token management** (preventing two parties from attempting the same critical operation simultaneously), and **synchronization** (checkpointing long transmissions to allow them to pick up from where they left off in the event of a crash and subsequent recovery).

The Presentation Layer

Unlike the lower layers, which are mostly concerned with moving bits around, the **presentation layer** is concerned with the syntax and semantics of the information transmitted. In order to make it possible for computers with different internal data representations to communicate, the data structures to be exchanged can be defined in an abstract way, along with a standard encoding to be used "on the wire." The presentation layer manages these abstract data structures and allows higher-level data structures (e.g., banking records) to be defined and exchanged.

The Application Layer

The **application layer** contains a variety of protocols that are commonly needed by users. One widely used application protocol is **HTTP** (**HyperText Transfer Protocol**), which is the basis for the World Wide Web. When a browser wants a Web page, it sends the name of the page it wants to the server hosting the page using HTTP. The server then sends the page back. Other application protocols are used for file transfer, electronic mail, and network news.

1.4.2 The TCP/IP Reference Model

Let us now turn from the OSI reference model to the reference model used in the grandparent of all wide area computer networks, the ARPANET, and its successor, the worldwide Internet. Although we will give a brief history of the ARPANET later, it is useful to mention a few key aspects of it now. The ARPANET was a research network sponsored by the DoD (U.S. Department of Defense). It eventually connected hundreds of universities and government installations, using leased telephone lines. When satellite and radio networks were added later, the existing protocols had trouble interworking with them, so a new reference architecture was needed. Thus, from nearly the beginning, the ability to connect multiple networks in a seamless way was one of the major design goals. This architecture later became known as the **TCP/IP Reference Model**, after its two primary protocols. It was first described by Cerf and Kahn (1974), and later refined and defined as a standard in the Internet community (Braden, 1989). The design philosophy behind the model is discussed by Clark (1988).

Given the DoD's worry that some of its precious hosts, routers, and internetwork gateways might get blown to pieces at a moment's notice by an attack from the Soviet Union, another major goal was that the network be able to survive loss of subnet hardware, without existing conversations being broken off. In other words, the DoD wanted connections to remain intact as long as the source and destination machines were functioning, even if some of the machines or transmission lines in between were suddenly put out of operation. Furthermore, since applications with divergent requirements were envisioned, ranging from transferring files to real-time speech transmission, a flexible architecture was needed.

The Link Layer

All these requirements led to the choice of a packet-switching network based on a connectionless layer that runs across different networks. The lowest layer in the model, the **link layer** describes what links such as serial lines and classic Ethernet must do to meet the needs of this connectionless internet layer. It is not really a layer at all, in the normal sense of the term, but rather an interface between hosts and transmission links. Early material on the TCP/IP model has little to say about it.

The Internet Layer

The **internet layer** is the linchpin that holds the whole architecture together. It is shown in Fig. 1-21 as corresponding roughly to the OSI network layer. Its job is to permit hosts to inject packets into any network and have them travel independently to the destination (potentially on a different network). They may even arrive in a completely different order than they were sent, in which case it is the job of higher layers to rearrange them, if in-order delivery is desired. Note that "internet" is used here in a generic sense, even though this layer is present in the Internet.

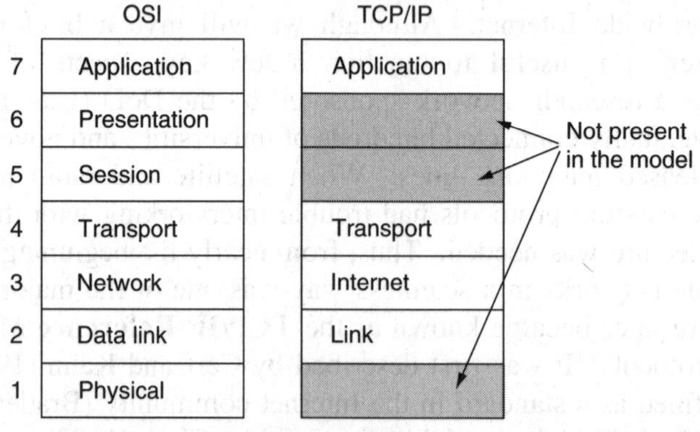

Figure 1-21. The TCP/IP reference model.

The analogy here is with the (snail) mail system. A person can drop a sequence of international letters into a mailbox in one country, and with a little luck, most of them will be delivered to the correct address in the destination country. The letters will probably travel through one or more international mail gateways along the way, but this is transparent to the users. Furthermore, that each country (i.e., each network) has its own stamps, preferred envelope sizes, and delivery rules is hidden from the users.

The internet layer defines an official packet format and protocol called **IP** (**Internet Protocol**), plus a companion protocol called **ICMP** (**Internet Control Message Protocol**) that helps it function. The job of the internet layer is to deliver IP packets where they are supposed to go. Packet routing is clearly a major issue here, as is congestion (though IP has not proven effective at avoiding congestion).

The Transport Layer

The layer above the internet layer in the TCP/IP model is now usually called the **transport layer**. It is designed to allow peer entities on the source and destination hosts to carry on a conversation, just as in the OSI transport layer. Two end-to-end transport protocols have been defined here. The first one, **TCP** (**Transmission Control Protocol**), is a reliable connection-oriented protocol that allows a byte stream originating on one machine to be delivered without error on any other machine in the internet. It segments the incoming byte stream into discrete messages and passes each one on to the internet layer. At the destination, the receiving TCP process reassembles the received messages into the output stream. TCP also handles flow control to make sure a fast sender cannot swamp a slow receiver with more messages than it can handle.

The second protocol in this layer, **UDP** (**User Datagram Protocol**), is an unreliable, connectionless protocol for applications that do not want TCP's sequencing or flow control and wish to provide their own. It is also widely used for one-shot, client-server-type request-reply queries and applications in which prompt delivery is more important than accurate delivery, such as transmitting speech or video. The relation of IP, TCP, and UDP is shown in Fig. 1-22. Since the model was developed, IP has been implemented on many other networks.

The Application Layer

The TCP/IP model does not have session or presentation layers. No need for them was perceived. Instead, applications simply include any session and presentation functions that they require. Experience with the OSI model has proven this view correct: these layers are of little use to most applications.

On top of the transport layer is the **application layer**. It contains all the higher-level protocols. The early ones included virtual terminal (TELNET), file transfer (FTP), and electronic mail (SMTP). Many other protocols have been added to these over the years. Some important ones that we will study, shown in Fig. 1-22,

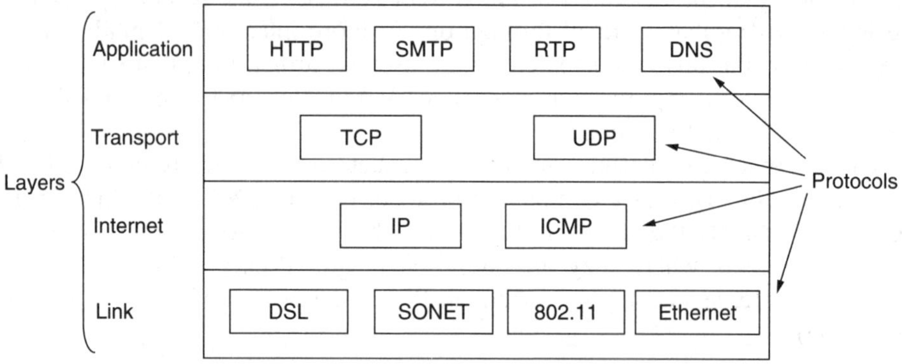

Figure 1-22. The TCP/IP model with some protocols we will study.

include the Domain Name System (DNS), for mapping host names onto their network addresses, HTTP, the protocol for fetching pages on the World Wide Web, and RTP, the protocol for delivering real-time media such as voice or movies.

1.4.3 The Model Used in This Book

As mentioned earlier, the strength of the OSI reference model is the *model* itself (minus the presentation and session layers), which has proven to be exceptionally useful for discussing computer networks. In contrast, the strength of the TCP/IP reference model is the *protocols*, which have been widely used for many years. Since computer scientists like to have their cake and eat it, too, we will use the hybrid model of Fig. 1-23 as the framework for this book.

5	Application
4	Transport
3	Network
2	Link
1	Physical

Figure 1-23. The reference model used in this book.

This model has five layers, running from the physical layer up through the link, network and transport layers to the application layer. The physical layer specifies how to transmit bits across different kinds of media as electrical (or other analog) signals. The link layer is concerned with how to send finite-length messages between directly connected computers with specified levels of reliability. Ethernet and 802.11 are examples of link layer protocols.

The network layer deals with how to combine multiple links into networks, and networks of networks, into internetworks so that we can send packets between distant computers. This includes the task of finding the path along which to send the packets. IP is the main example protocol we will study for this layer. The transport layer strengthens the delivery guarantees of the Network layer, usually with increased reliability, and provide delivery abstractions, such as a reliable byte stream, that match the needs of different applications. TCP is an important example of a transport layer protocol.

Finally, the application layer contains programs that make use of the network. Many, but not all, networked applications have user interfaces, such as a Web browser. Our concern, however, is with the portion of the program that uses the network. This is the HTTP protocol in the case of the Web browser. There are also important support programs in the application layer, such as the DNS, that are used by many applications.

Our chapter sequence is based on this model. In this way, we retain the value of the OSI model for understanding network architectures, but concentrate primarily on protocols that are important in practice, from TCP/IP and related protocols to newer ones such as 802.11, SONET, and Bluetooth.

1.4.4 A Comparison of the OSI and TCP/IP Reference Models

The OSI and TCP/IP reference models have much in common. Both are based on the concept of a stack of independent protocols. Also, the functionality of the layers is roughly similar. For example, in both models the layers up through and including the transport layer are there to provide an end-to-end, network-independent transport service to processes wishing to communicate. These layers form the transport provider. Again in both models, the layers above transport are application-oriented users of the transport service.

Despite these fundamental similarities, the two models also have many differences. In this section we will focus on the key differences between the two reference models. It is important to note that we are comparing the *reference models* here, not the corresponding *protocol stacks*. The protocols themselves will be discussed later. For an entire book comparing and contrasting TCP/IP and OSI, see Piscitello and Chapin (1993).

Three concepts are central to the OSI model:

1. Services.

2. Interfaces.

3. Protocols.

Probably the biggest contribution of the OSI model is that it makes the distinction between these three concepts explicit. Each layer performs some *services* for the layer above it. The service definition tells what the layer does, not how entities above it access it or how the layer works. It defines the layer's semantics.

A layer's *interface* tells the processes above it how to access it. It specifies what the parameters are and what results to expect. It, too, says nothing about how the layer works inside.

Finally, the peer *protocols* used in a layer are the layer's own business. It can use any protocols it wants to, as long as it gets the job done (i.e., provides the offered services). It can also change them at will without affecting software in higher layers.

These ideas fit very nicely with modern ideas about object-oriented programming. An object, like a layer, has a set of methods (operations) that processes outside the object can invoke. The semantics of these methods define the set of services that the object offers. The methods' parameters and results form the object's interface. The code internal to the object is its protocol and is not visible or of any concern outside the object.

The TCP/IP model did not originally clearly distinguish between services, interfaces, and protocols, although people have tried to retrofit it after the fact to make it more OSI-like. For example, the only real services offered by the internet layer are SEND IP PACKET and RECEIVE IP PACKET. As a consequence, the protocols in the OSI model are better hidden than in the TCP/IP model and can be replaced relatively easily as the technology changes. Being able to make such changes transparently is one of the main purposes of having layered protocols in the first place.

The OSI reference model was devised *before* the corresponding protocols were invented. This ordering meant that the model was not biased toward one particular set of protocols, a fact that made it quite general. The downside of this ordering was that the designers did not have much experience with the subject and did not have a good idea of which functionality to put in which layer.

For example, the data link layer originally dealt only with point-to-point networks. When broadcast networks came around, a new sublayer had to be hacked into the model. Furthermore, when people started to build real networks using the OSI model and existing protocols, it was discovered that these networks did not match the required service specifications (wonder of wonders), so convergence sublayers had to be grafted onto the model to provide a place for papering over the differences. Finally, the committee originally expected that each country would have one network, run by the government and using the OSI protocols, so no thought was given to internetworking. To make a long story short, things did not turn out that way.

With TCP/IP the reverse was true: the protocols came first, and the model was really just a description of the existing protocols. There was no problem with the protocols fitting the model. They fit perfectly. The only trouble was that the *model* did not fit any other protocol stacks. Consequently, it was not especially useful for describing other, non-TCP/IP networks.

Turning from philosophical matters to more specific ones, an obvious difference between the two models is the number of layers: the OSI model has seven layers and the TCP/IP model has four. Both have (inter)network, transport, and application layers, but the other layers are different.

Another difference is in the area of connectionless versus connection-oriented communication. The OSI model supports both connectionless and connection-oriented communication in the network layer, but only connection-oriented communication in the transport layer, where it counts (because the transport service is visible to the users). The TCP/IP model supports only one mode in the network layer (connectionless) but both in the transport layer, giving the users a choice. This choice is especially important for simple request-response protocols.

1.4.5 A Critique of the OSI Model and Protocols

Neither the OSI model and its protocols nor the TCP/IP model and its protocols are perfect. Quite a bit of criticism can be, and has been, directed at both of them. In this section and the next one, we will look at some of these criticisms. We will begin with OSI and examine TCP/IP afterward.

At the time the second edition of this book was published (1989), it appeared to many experts in the field that the OSI model and its protocols were going to take over the world and push everything else out of their way. This did not happen. Why? A look back at some of the reasons may be useful. They can be summarized as:

1. Bad timing.
2. Bad technology.
3. Bad implementations.
4. Bad politics.

Bad Timing

First let us look at reason one: bad timing. The time at which a standard is established is absolutely critical to its success. David Clark of M.I.T. has a theory of standards that he calls the *apocalypse of the two elephants*, which is illustrated in Fig. 1-24.

This figure shows the amount of activity surrounding a new subject. When the subject is first discovered, there is a burst of research activity in the form of discussions, papers, and meetings. After a while this activity subsides, corporations discover the subject, and the billion-dollar wave of investment hits.

It is essential that the standards be written in the trough in between the two "elephants." If they are written too early (before the research results are well

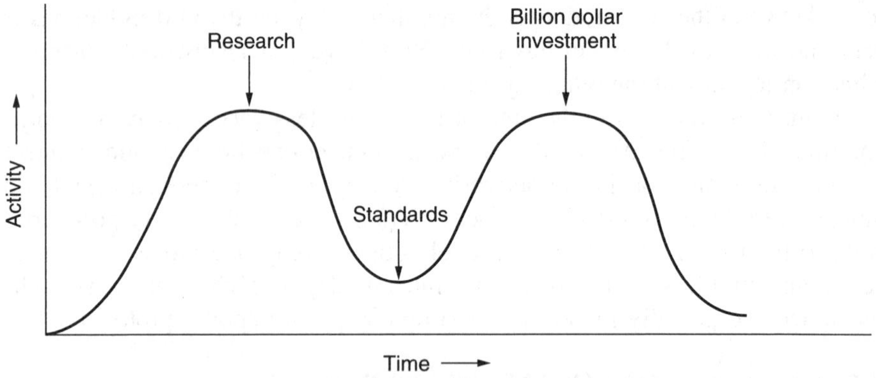

Figure 1-24. The apocalypse of the two elephants.

established), the subject may still be poorly understood; the result is a bad standard. If they are written too late, so many companies may have already made major investments in different ways of doing things that the standards are effectively ignored. If the interval between the two elephants is very short (because everyone is in a hurry to get started), the people developing the standards may get crushed.

It now appears that the standard OSI protocols got crushed. The competing TCP/IP protocols were already in widespread use by research universities by the time the OSI protocols appeared. While the billion-dollar wave of investment had not yet hit, the academic market was large enough that many vendors had begun cautiously offering TCP/IP products. When OSI came around, they did not want to support a second protocol stack until they were forced to, so there were no initial offerings. With every company waiting for every other company to go first, no company went first and OSI never happened.

Bad Technology

The second reason that OSI never caught on is that both the model and the protocols are flawed. The choice of seven layers was more political than technical, and two of the layers (session and presentation) are nearly empty, whereas two other ones (data link and network) are overfull.

The OSI model, along with its associated service definitions and protocols, is extraordinarily complex. When piled up, the printed standards occupy a significant fraction of a meter of paper. They are also difficult to implement and inefficient in operation. In this context, a riddle posed by Paul Mockapetris and cited by Rose (1993) comes to mind:

Q: What do you get when you cross a mobster with an international standard?
A: Someone who makes you an offer you can't understand.

In addition to being incomprehensible, another problem with OSI is that some functions, such as addressing, flow control, and error control, reappear again and again in each layer. Saltzer et al. (1984), for example, have pointed out that to be effective, error control must be done in the highest layer, so that repeating it over and over in each of the lower layers is often unnecessary and inefficient.

Bad Implementations

Given the enormous complexity of the model and the protocols, it will come as no surprise that the initial implementations were huge, unwieldy, and slow. Everyone who tried them got burned. It did not take long for people to associate "OSI" with "poor quality." Although the products improved in the course of time, the image stuck.

In contrast, one of the first implementations of TCP/IP was part of Berkeley UNIX and was quite good (not to mention, free). People began using it quickly, which led to a large user community, which led to improvements, which led to an even larger community. Here the spiral was upward instead of downward.

Bad Politics

On account of the initial implementation, many people, especially in academia, thought of TCP/IP as part of UNIX, and UNIX in the 1980s in academia was not unlike parenthood (then incorrectly called motherhood) and apple pie.

OSI, on the other hand, was widely thought to be the creature of the European telecommunication ministries, the European Community, and later the U.S. Government. This belief was only partly true, but the very idea of a bunch of government bureaucrats trying to shove a technically inferior standard down the throats of the poor researchers and programmers down in the trenches actually developing computer networks did not aid OSI's cause. Some people viewed this development in the same light as IBM announcing in the 1960s that PL/I was the language of the future, or the DoD correcting this later by announcing that it was actually Ada.

1.4.6 A Critique of the TCP/IP Reference Model

The TCP/IP model and protocols have their problems too. First, the model does not clearly distinguish the concepts of services, interfaces, and protocols. Good software engineering practice requires differentiating between the specification and the implementation, something that OSI does very carefully, but TCP/IP does not. Consequently, the TCP/IP model is not much of a guide for designing new networks using new technologies.

Second, the TCP/IP model is not at all general and is poorly suited to describing any protocol stack other than TCP/IP. Trying to use the TCP/IP model to describe Bluetooth, for example, is completely impossible.

Third, the link layer is not really a layer at all in the normal sense of the term as used in the context of layered protocols. It is an interface (between the network and data link layers). The distinction between an interface and a layer is crucial, and one should not be sloppy about it.

Fourth, the TCP/IP model does not distinguish between the physical and data link layers. These are completely different. The physical layer has to do with the transmission characteristics of copper wire, fiber optics, and wireless communication. The data link layer's job is to delimit the start and end of frames and get them from one side to the other with the desired degree of reliability. A proper model should include both as separate layers. The TCP/IP model does not do this.

Finally, although the IP and TCP protocols were carefully thought out and well implemented, many of the other protocols were ad hoc, generally produced by a couple of graduate students hacking away until they got tired. The protocol implementations were then distributed free, which resulted in their becoming widely used, deeply entrenched, and thus hard to replace. Some of them are a bit of an embarrassment now. The virtual terminal protocol, TELNET, for example, was designed for a ten-character-per-second mechanical Teletype terminal. It knows nothing of graphical user interfaces and mice. Nevertheless, it is still in use some 30 years later.

1.5 EXAMPLE NETWORKS

The subject of computer networking covers many different kinds of networks, large and small, well known and less well known. They have different goals, scales, and technologies. In the following sections, we will look at some examples, to get an idea of the variety one finds in the area of computer networking.

We will start with the Internet, probably the best known network, and look at its history, evolution, and technology. Then we will consider the mobile phone network. Technically, it is quite different from the Internet, contrasting nicely with it. Next we will introduce IEEE 802.11, the dominant standard for wireless LANs. Finally, we will look at RFID and sensor networks, technologies that extend the reach of the network to include the physical world and everyday objects.

1.5.1 The Internet

The Internet is not really a network at all, but a vast collection of different networks that use certain common protocols and provide certain common services. It is an unusual system in that it was not planned by anyone and is not controlled by anyone. To better understand it, let us start from the beginning and see how it has developed and why. For a wonderful history of the Internet, John Naughton's (2000) book is highly recommended. It is one of those rare books that is not only fun to read, but also has 20 pages of *ibid.*'s and *op. cit.*'s for the serious historian. Some of the material in this section is based on this book.

Of course, countless technical books have been written about the Internet and its protocols as well. For more information, see, for example, Maufer (1999).

The ARPANET

The story begins in the late 1950s. At the height of the Cold War, the U.S. DoD wanted a command-and-control network that could survive a nuclear war. At that time, all military communications used the public telephone network, which was considered vulnerable. The reason for this belief can be gleaned from Fig. 1-25(a). Here the black dots represent telephone switching offices, each of which was connected to thousands of telephones. These switching offices were, in turn, connected to higher-level switching offices (toll offices), to form a national hierarchy with only a small amount of redundancy. The vulnerability of the system was that the destruction of a few key toll offices could fragment it into many isolated islands.

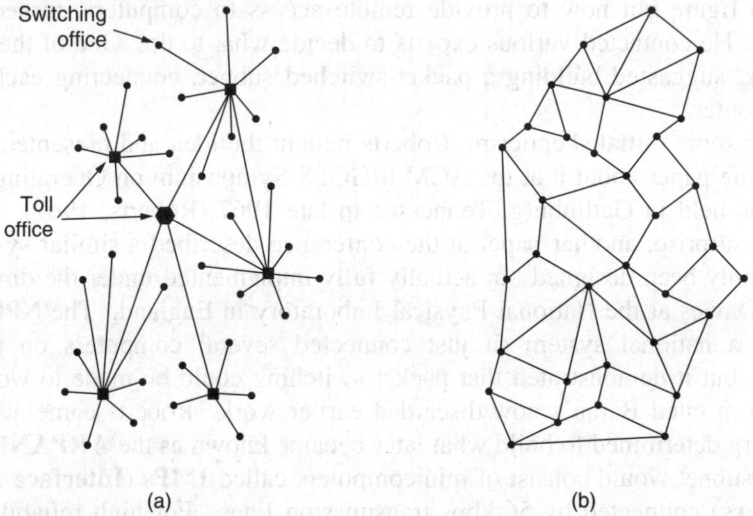

Figure 1-25. (a) Structure of the telephone system. (b) Baran's proposed distributed switching system.

Around 1960, the DoD awarded a contract to the RAND Corporation to find a solution. One of its employees, Paul Baran, came up with the highly distributed and fault-tolerant design of Fig. 1-25(b). Since the paths between any two switching offices were now much longer than analog signals could travel without distortion, Baran proposed using digital packet-switching technology. Baran wrote several reports for the DoD describing his ideas in detail (Baran, 1964). Officials at the Pentagon liked the concept and asked AT&T, then the U.S.' national telephone monopoly, to build a prototype. AT&T dismissed Baran's ideas out of hand. The biggest and richest corporation in the world was not about to allow some young whippersnapper tell it how to build a telephone system. They said Baran's network could not be built and the idea was killed.

Several years went by and still the DoD did not have a better command-and-control system. To understand what happened next, we have to go back all the way to October 1957, when the Soviet Union beat the U.S. into space with the launch of the first artificial satellite, Sputnik. When President Eisenhower tried to find out who was asleep at the switch, he was appalled to find the Army, Navy, and Air Force squabbling over the Pentagon's research budget. His immediate response was to create a single defense research organization, **ARPA**, the **Advanced Research Projects Agency**. ARPA had no scientists or laboratories; in fact, it had nothing more than an office and a small (by Pentagon standards) budget. It did its work by issuing grants and contracts to universities and companies whose ideas looked promising to it.

For the first few years, ARPA tried to figure out what its mission should be. In 1967, the attention of Larry Roberts, a program manager at ARPA who was trying to figure out how to provide remote access to computers, turned to networking. He contacted various experts to decide what to do. One of them, Wesley Clark, suggested building a packet-switched subnet, connecting each host to its own router.

After some initial skepticism, Roberts bought the idea and presented a somewhat vague paper about it at the ACM SIGOPS Symposium on Operating System Principles held in Gatlinburg, Tennessee in late 1967 (Roberts, 1967). Much to Roberts' surprise, another paper at the conference described a similar system that had not only been designed but actually fully implemented under the direction of Donald Davies at the National Physical Laboratory in England. The NPL system was not a national system (it just connected several computers on the NPL campus), but it demonstrated that packet switching could be made to work. Furthermore, it cited Baran's now discarded earlier work. Roberts came away from Gatlinburg determined to build what later became known as the **ARPANET**.

The subnet would consist of minicomputers called **IMPs** (**Interface Message Processors**) connected by 56-kbps transmission lines. For high reliability, each IMP would be connected to at least two other IMPs. The subnet was to be a datagram subnet, so if some lines and IMPs were destroyed, messages could be automatically rerouted along alternative paths.

Each node of the network was to consist of an IMP and a host, in the same room, connected by a short wire. A host could send messages of up to 8063 bits to its IMP, which would then break these up into packets of at most 1008 bits and forward them independently toward the destination. Each packet was received in its entirety before being forwarded, so the subnet was the first electronic store-and-forward packet-switching network.

ARPA then put out a tender for building the subnet. Twelve companies bid for it. After evaluating all the proposals, ARPA selected BBN, a consulting firm based in Cambridge, Massachusetts, and in December 1968 awarded it a contract to build the subnet and write the subnet software. BBN chose to use specially modified Honeywell DDP-316 minicomputers with 12K 16-bit words of core memory as the IMPs. The IMPs did not have disks, since moving parts were considered unreliable. The IMPs were interconnected by 56-kbps lines leased from telephone companies. Although 56 kbps is now the choice of teenagers who cannot afford DSL or cable, it was then the best money could buy.

The software was split into two parts: subnet and host. The subnet software consisted of the IMP end of the host-IMP connection, the IMP-IMP protocol, and a source IMP to destination IMP protocol designed to improve reliability. The original ARPANET design is shown in Fig. 1-26.

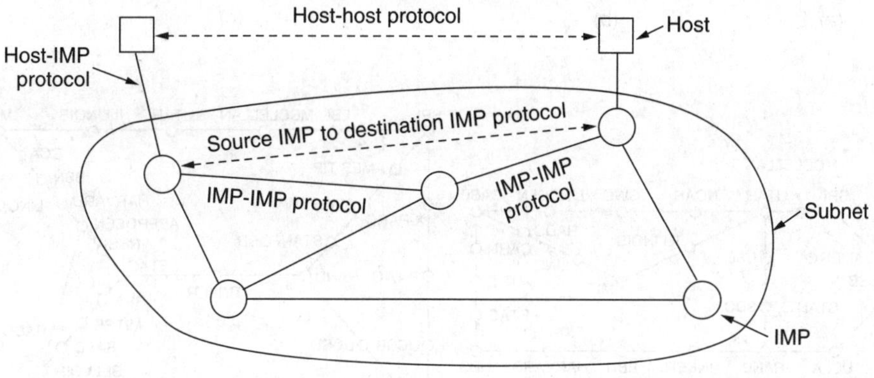

Figure 1-26. The original ARPANET design.

Outside the subnet, software was also needed, namely, the host end of the host-IMP connection, the host-host protocol, and the application software. It soon became clear that BBN was of the opinion that when it had accepted a message on a host-IMP wire and placed it on the host-IMP wire at the destination, its job was done.

Roberts had a problem, though: the hosts needed software too. To deal with it, he convened a meeting of network researchers, mostly graduate students, at Snowbird, Utah, in the summer of 1969. The graduate students expected some network expert to explain the grand design of the network and its software to them and then assign each of them the job of writing part of it. They were astounded when there was no network expert and no grand design. They had to figure out what to do on their own.

Nevertheless, somehow an experimental network went online in December 1969 with four nodes: at UCLA, UCSB, SRI, and the University of Utah. These four were chosen because all had a large number of ARPA contracts, and all had different and completely incompatible host computers (just to make it more fun). The first host-to-host message had been sent two months earlier from the UCLA node by a team led by Len Kleinrock (a pioneer of the theory of packet switching) to the SRI node. The network grew quickly as more IMPs were delivered and installed; it soon spanned the United States. Figure 1-27 shows how rapidly the ARPANET grew in the first 3 years.

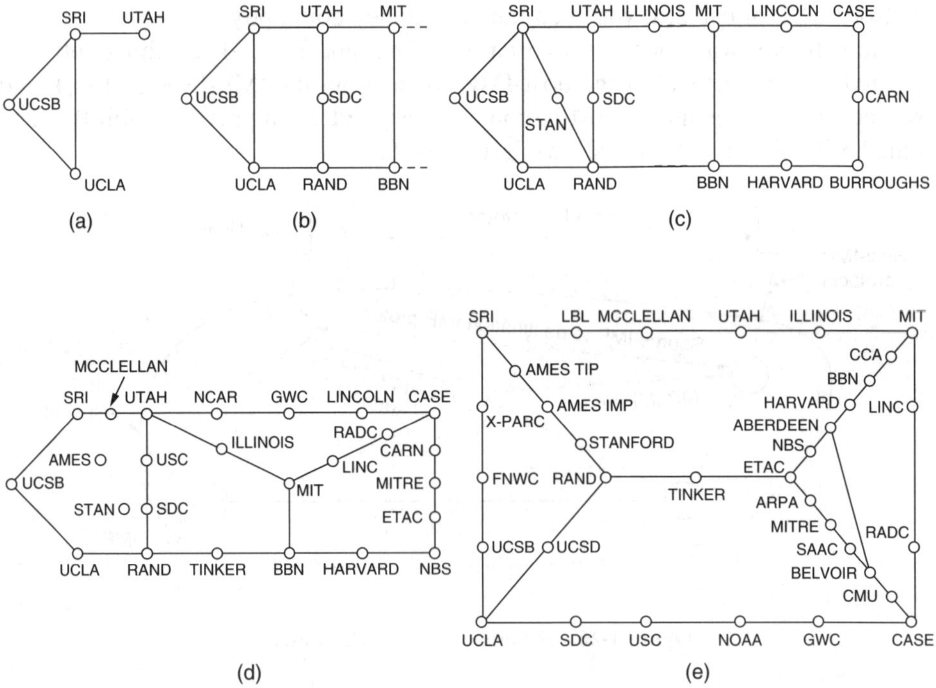

Figure 1-27. Growth of the ARPANET. (a) December 1969. (b) July 1970. (c) March 1971. (d) April 1972. (e) September 1972.

In addition to helping the fledgling ARPANET grow, ARPA also funded research on the use of satellite networks and mobile packet radio networks. In one now famous demonstration, a truck driving around in California used the packet radio network to send messages to SRI, which were then forwarded over the ARPANET to the East Coast, where they were shipped to University College in London over the satellite network. This allowed a researcher in the truck to use a computer in London while driving around in California.

This experiment also demonstrated that the existing ARPANET protocols were not suitable for running over different networks. This observation led to more research on protocols, culminating with the invention of the TCP/IP model and protocols (Cerf and Kahn, 1974). TCP/IP was specifically designed to handle communication over internetworks, something becoming increasingly important as more and more networks were hooked up to the ARPANET.

To encourage adoption of these new protocols, ARPA awarded several contracts to implement TCP/IP on different computer platforms, including IBM, DEC, and HP systems, as well as for Berkeley UNIX. Researchers at the University of California at Berkeley rewrote TCP/IP with a new programming interface called **sockets** for the upcoming 4.2BSD release of Berkeley UNIX. They also wrote many application, utility, and management programs to show how convenient it was to use the network with sockets.

The timing was perfect. Many universities had just acquired a second or third VAX computer and a LAN to connect them, but they had no networking software. When 4.2BSD came along, with TCP/IP, sockets, and many network utilities, the complete package was adopted immediately. Furthermore, with TCP/IP, it was easy for the LANs to connect to the ARPANET, and many did.

During the 1980s, additional networks, especially LANs, were connected to the ARPANET. As the scale increased, finding hosts became increasingly expensive, so **DNS (Domain Name System)** was created to organize machines into domains and map host names onto IP addresses. Since then, DNS has become a generalized, distributed database system for storing a variety of information related to naming. We will study it in detail in Chap. 7.

NSFNET

By the late 1970s, NSF (the U.S. National Science Foundation) saw the enormous impact the ARPANET was having on university research, allowing scientists across the country to share data and collaborate on research projects. However, to get on the ARPANET a university had to have a research contract with the DoD. Many did not have a contract. NSF's initial response was to fund the Computer Science Network (**CSNET**) in 1981. It connected computer science departments and industrial research labs to the ARPANET via dial-up and leased lines. In the late 1980s, the NSF went further and decided to design a successor to the ARPANET that would be open to all university research groups.

To have something concrete to start with, NSF decided to build a backbone network to connect its six supercomputer centers, in San Diego, Boulder, Champaign, Pittsburgh, Ithaca, and Princeton. Each supercomputer was given a little brother, consisting of an LSI-11 microcomputer called a **fuzzball**. The fuzzballs were connected with 56-kbps leased lines and formed the subnet, the same hardware technology the ARPANET used. The software technology was different however: the fuzzballs spoke TCP/IP right from the start, making it the first TCP/IP WAN.

NSF also funded some (eventually about 20) regional networks that connected to the backbone to allow users at thousands of universities, research labs, libraries, and museums to access any of the supercomputers and to communicate with one another. The complete network, including backbone and the regional networks, was called **NSFNET**. It connected to the ARPANET through a link between an

IMP and a fuzzball in the Carnegie-Mellon machine room. The first NSFNET backbone is illustrated in Fig. 1-28 superimposed on a map of the U.S.

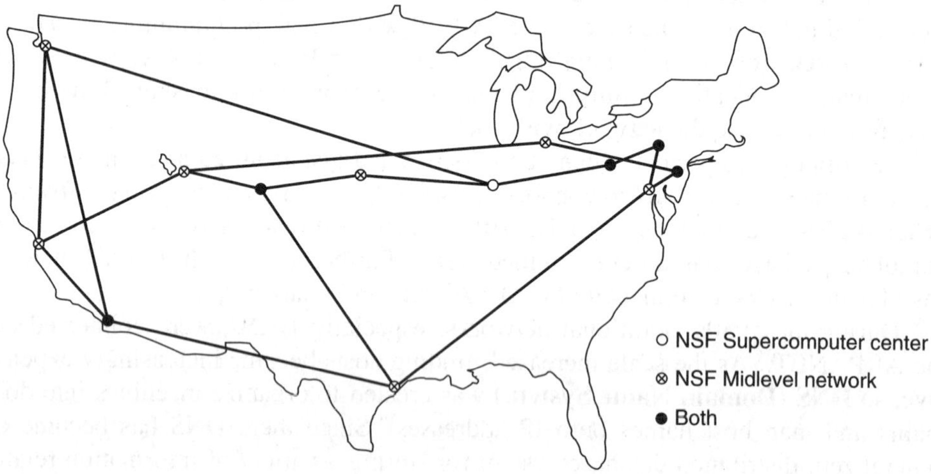

Figure 1-28. The NSFNET backbone in 1988.

NSFNET was an instantaneous success and was overloaded from the word go. NSF immediately began planning its successor and awarded a contract to the Michigan-based MERIT consortium to run it. Fiber optic channels at 448 kbps were leased from MCI (since merged with WorldCom) to provide the version 2 backbone. IBM PC-RTs were used as routers. This, too, was soon overwhelmed, and by 1990, the second backbone was upgraded to 1.5 Mbps.

As growth continued, NSF realized that the government could not continue financing networking forever. Furthermore, commercial organizations wanted to join but were forbidden by NSF's charter from using networks NSF paid for. Consequently, NSF encouraged MERIT, MCI, and IBM to form a nonprofit corporation, **ANS (Advanced Networks and Services)**, as the first step along the road to commercialization. In 1990, ANS took over NSFNET and upgraded the 1.5-Mbps links to 45 Mbps to form **ANSNET**. This network operated for 5 years and was then sold to America Online. But by then, various companies were offering commercial IP service and it was clear the government should now get out of the networking business.

To ease the transition and make sure every regional network could communicate with every other regional network, NSF awarded contracts to four different network operators to establish a **NAP (Network Access Point)**. These operators were PacBell (San Francisco), Ameritech (Chicago), MFS (Washington, D.C.), and Sprint (New York City, where for NAP purposes, Pennsauken, New Jersey counts as New York City). Every network operator that wanted to provide backbone service to the NSF regional networks had to connect to all the NAPs.

This arrangement meant that a packet originating on any regional network had a choice of backbone carriers to get from its NAP to the destination's NAP. Consequently, the backbone carriers were forced to compete for the regional networks' business on the basis of service and price, which was the idea, of course. As a result, the concept of a single default backbone was replaced by a commercially driven competitive infrastructure. Many people like to criticize the Federal Government for not being innovative, but in the area of networking, it was DoD and NSF that created the infrastructure that formed the basis for the Internet and then handed it over to industry to operate.

During the 1990s, many other countries and regions also built national research networks, often patterned on the ARPANET and NSFNET. These included EuropaNET and EBONE in Europe, which started out with 2-Mbps lines and then upgraded to 34-Mbps lines. Eventually, the network infrastructure in Europe was handed over to industry as well.

The Internet has changed a great deal since those early days. It exploded in size with the emergence of the World Wide Web (WWW) in the early 1990s. Recent data from the Internet Systems Consortium puts the number of visible Internet hosts at over 600 million. This guess is only a low-ball estimate, but it far exceeds the few million hosts that were around when the first conference on the WWW was held at CERN in 1994.

The way we use the Internet has also changed radically. Initially, applications such as email-for-academics, newsgroups, remote login, and file transfer dominated. Later it switched to email-for-everyman, then the Web and peer-to-peer content distribution, such as the now-shuttered Napster. Now real-time media distribution, social networks (e.g., Facebook), and microblogging (e.g., Twitter) are taking off. These switches brought richer kinds of media to the Internet and hence much more traffic. In fact, the dominant traffic on the Internet seems to change with some regularity as, for example, new and better ways to work with music or movies can become very popular very quickly.

Architecture of the Internet

The architecture of the Internet has also changed a great deal as it has grown explosively. In this section, we will attempt to give a brief overview of what it looks like today. The picture is complicated by continuous upheavals in the businesses of telephone companies (telcos), cable companies and ISPs that often make it hard to tell who is doing what. One driver of these upheavals is telecommunications convergence, in which one network is used for previously different uses. For example, in a "triple play" one company sells you telephony, TV, and Internet service over the same network connection on the assumption that this will save you money. Consequently, the description given here will be of necessity somewhat simpler than reality. And what is true today may not be true tomorrow.

The big picture is shown in Fig. 1-29. Let us examine this figure piece by piece, starting with a computer at home (at the edges of the figure). To join the Internet, the computer is connected to an **Internet Service Provider**, or simply **ISP**, from who the user purchases **Internet access** or **connectivity**. This lets the computer exchange packets with all of the other accessible hosts on the Internet. The user might send packets to surf the Web or for any of a thousand other uses, it does not matter. There are many kinds of Internet access, and they are usually distinguished by how much bandwidth they provide and how much they cost, but the most important attribute is connectivity.

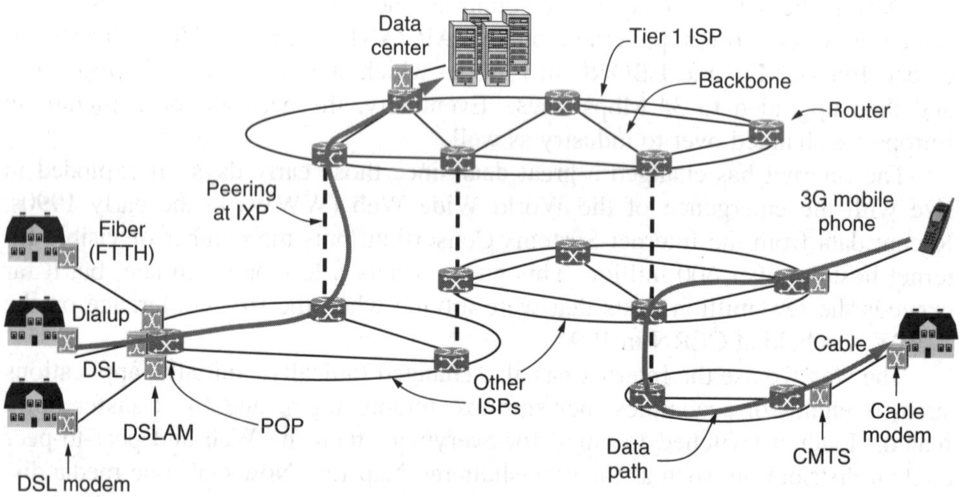

Figure 1-29. Overview of the Internet architecture.

A common way to connect to an ISP is to use the phone line to your house, in which case your phone company is your ISP. **DSL**, short for **Digital Subscriber Line**, reuses the telephone line that connects to your house for digital data transmission. The computer is connected to a device called a **DSL modem** that converts between digital packets and analog signals that can pass unhindered over the telephone line. At the other end, a device called a **DSLAM (Digital Subscriber Line Access Multiplexer)** converts between signals and packets.

Several other popular ways to connect to an ISP are shown in Fig. 1-29. DSL is a higher-bandwidth way to use the local telephone line than to send bits over a traditional telephone call instead of a voice conversation. That is called **dial-up** and done with a different kind of modem at both ends. The word **modem** is short for "*mo*dulator *dem*odulator" and refers to any device that converts between digital bits and analog signals.

Another method is to send signals over the cable TV system. Like DSL, this is a way to reuse existing infrastructure, in this case otherwise unused cable TV channels. The device at the home end is called a **cable modem** and the device at the **cable headend** is called the **CMTS** (**Cable Modem Termination System**).

DSL and cable provide Internet access at rates from a small fraction of a megabit/sec to multiple megabit/sec, depending on the system. These rates are much greater than dial-up rates, which are limited to 56 kbps because of the narrow bandwidth used for voice calls. Internet access at much greater than dial-up speeds is called **broadband**. The name refers to the broader bandwidth that is used for faster networks, rather than any particular speed.

The access methods mentioned so far are limited by the bandwidth of the "last mile" or last leg of transmission. By running optical fiber to residences, faster Internet access can be provided at rates on the order of 10 to 100 Mbps. This design is called **FTTH** (**Fiber to the Home**). For businesses in commercial areas, it may make sense to lease a high-speed transmission line from the offices to the nearest ISP. For example, in North America, a T3 line runs at roughly 45 Mbps.

Wireless is used for Internet access too. An example we will explore shortly is that of 3G mobile phone networks. They can provide data delivery at rates of 1 Mbps or higher to mobile phones and fixed subscribers in the coverage area.

We can now move packets between the home and the ISP. We call the location at which customer packets enter the ISP network for service the ISP's **POP** (**Point of Presence**). We will next explain how packets are moved between the POPs of different ISPs. From this point on, the system is fully digital and packet switched.

ISP networks may be regional, national, or international in scope. We have already seen that their architecture is made up of long-distance transmission lines that interconnect routers at POPs in the different cities that the ISPs serve. This equipment is called the **backbone** of the ISP. If a packet is destined for a host served directly by the ISP, that packet is routed over the backbone and delivered to the host. Otherwise, it must be handed over to another ISP.

ISPs connect their networks to exchange traffic at **IXPs** (**Internet eXchange Points**). The connected ISPs are said to **peer** with each other. There are many IXPs in cities around the world. They are drawn vertically in Fig. 1-29 because ISP networks overlap geographically. Basically, an IXP is a room full of routers, at least one per ISP. A LAN in the room connects all the routers, so packets can be forwarded from any ISP backbone to any other ISP backbone. IXPs can be large and independently owned facilities. One of the largest is the Amsterdam Internet Exchange, to which hundreds of ISPs connect and through which they exchange hundreds of gigabits/sec of traffic.

The peering that happens at IXPs depends on the business relationships between ISPs. There are many possible relationships. For example, a small ISP might pay a larger ISP for Internet connectivity to reach distant hosts, much as a customer purchases service from an Internet provider. In this case, the small ISP is said to pay for **transit**. Alternatively, two large ISPs might decide to exchange traffic so that each ISP can deliver some traffic to the other ISP without having to pay for transit. One of the many paradoxes of the Internet is that ISPs who publicly compete with one another for customers often privately cooperate to do peering (Metz, 2001).

The path a packet takes through the Internet depends on the peering choices of the ISPs. If the ISP delivering a packet peers with the destination ISP, it might deliver the packet directly to its peer. Otherwise, it might route the packet to the nearest place at which it connects to a paid transit provider so that provider can deliver the packet. Two example paths across ISPs are drawn in Fig. 1-29. Often, the path a packet takes will not be the shortest path through the Internet.

At the top of the food chain are a small handful of companies, like AT&T and Sprint, that operate large international backbone networks with thousands of routers connected by high-bandwidth fiber optic links. These ISPs do not pay for transit. They are usually called **tier 1** ISPs and are said to form the backbone of the Internet, since everyone else must connect to them to be able to reach the entire Internet.

Companies that provide lots of content, such as Google and Yahoo!, locate their computers in **data centers** that are well connected to the rest of the Internet. These data centers are designed for computers, not humans, and may be filled with rack upon rack of machines called a **server farm**. **Colocation** or **hosting** data centers let customers put equipment such as servers at ISP POPs so that short, fast connections can be made between the servers and the ISP backbones. The Internet hosting industry has become increasingly virtualized so that it is now common to rent a virtual machine that is run on a server farm instead of installing a physical computer. These data centers are so large (tens or hundreds of thousands of machines) that electricity is a major cost, so data centers are sometimes built in areas where electricity is cheap.

This ends our quick tour of the Internet. We will have a great deal to say about the individual components and their design, algorithms, and protocols in subsequent chapters. One further point worth mentioning here is that what it means to be on the Internet is changing. It used to be that a machine was on the Internet if it: (1) ran the TCP/IP protocol stack; (2) had an IP address; and (3) could send IP packets to all the other machines on the Internet. However, ISPs often reuse IP addresses depending on which computers are in use at the moment, and home networks often share one IP address between multiple computers. This practice undermines the second condition. Security measures such as firewalls can also partly block computers from receiving packets, undermining the third condition. Despite these difficulties, it makes sense to regard such machines as being on the Internet while they are connected to their ISPs.

Also worth mentioning in passing is that some companies have interconnected all their existing internal networks, often using the same technology as the Internet. These **intranets** are typically accessible only on company premises or from company notebooks but otherwise work the same way as the Internet.

1.5.2 Third-Generation Mobile Phone Networks

People love to talk on the phone even more than they like to surf the Internet, and this has made the mobile phone network the most successful network in the world. It has more than four billion subscribers worldwide. To put this number in perspective, it is roughly 60% of the world's population and more than the number of Internet hosts and fixed telephone lines combined (ITU, 2009).

The architecture of the mobile phone network has changed greatly over the past 40 years along with its tremendous growth. First-generation mobile phone systems transmitted voice calls as continuously varying (analog) signals rather than sequences of (digital) bits. **AMPS (Advanced Mobile Phone System)**, which was deployed in the United States in 1982, was a widely used first-generation system. Second-generation mobile phone systems switched to transmitting voice calls in digital form to increase capacity, improve security, and offer text messaging. **GSM (Global System for Mobile communications)**, which was deployed starting in 1991 and has become the most widely used mobile phone system in the world, is a 2G system.

The third generation, or 3G, systems were initially deployed in 2001 and offer both digital voice and broadband digital data services. They also come with a lot of jargon and many different standards to choose from. 3G is loosely defined by the ITU (an international standards body we will discuss in the next section) as providing rates of at least 2 Mbps for stationary or walking users and 384 kbps in a moving vehicle. **UMTS (Universal Mobile Telecommunications System)**, also called **WCDMA (Wideband Code Division Multiple Access)**, is the main 3G system that is being rapidly deployed worldwide. It can provide up to 14 Mbps on the downlink and almost 6 Mbps on the uplink. Future releases will use multiple antennas and radios to provide even greater speeds for users.

The scarce resource in 3G systems, as in 2G and 1G systems before them, is radio spectrum. Governments license the right to use parts of the spectrum to the mobile phone network operators, often using a spectrum auction in which network operators submit bids. Having a piece of licensed spectrum makes it easier to design and operate systems, since no one else is allowed transmit on that spectrum, but it often costs a serious amount of money. In the UK in 2000, for example, five 3G licenses were auctioned for a total of about $40 billion.

It is the scarcity of spectrum that led to the **cellular network** design shown in Fig. 1-30 that is now used for mobile phone networks. To manage the radio interference between users, the coverage area is divided into cells. Within a cell, users are assigned channels that do not interfere with each other and do not cause too much interference for adjacent cells. This allows for good reuse of the spectrum, or **frequency reuse**, in the neighboring cells, which increases the capacity of the network. In 1G systems, which carried each voice call on a specific frequency band, the frequencies were carefully chosen so that they did not conflict with neighboring cells. In this way, a given frequency might only be reused once in several cells. Modern 3G systems allow each cell to use all frequencies, but in a way that results in a tolerable level of interference to the neighboring cells. There are variations on the cellular design, including the use of directional or sectored antennas on cell towers to further reduce interference, but the basic idea is the same.

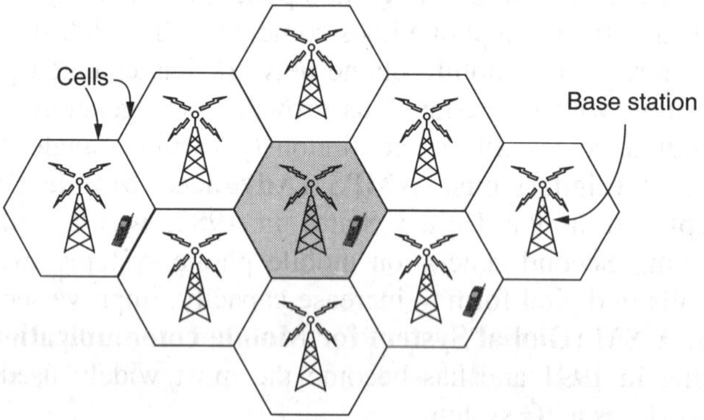

Figure 1-30. Cellular design of mobile phone networks.

The architecture of the mobile phone network is very different than that of the Internet. It has several parts, as shown in the simplified version of the UMTS architecture in Fig. 1-31. First, there is the **air interface**. This term is a fancy name for the radio communication protocol that is used over the air between the mobile device (e.g., the cell phone) and the **cellular base station**. Advances in the air interface over the past decades have greatly increased wireless data rates. The UMTS air interface is based on **Code Division Multiple Access** (**CDMA**), a technique that we will study in Chap. 2.

The cellular base station together with its controller forms the **radio access network**. This part is the wireless side of the mobile phone network. The controller node or **RNC** (**Radio Network Controller**) controls how the spectrum is used. The base station implements the air interface. It is called **Node B**, a temporary label that stuck.

The rest of the mobile phone network carries the traffic for the radio access network. It is called the **core network**. The UMTS core network evolved from the core network used for the 2G GSM system that came before it. However, something surprising is happening in the UMTS core network.

Since the beginning of networking, a war has been going on between the people who support packet networks (i.e., connectionless subnets) and the people who support circuit networks (i.e., connection-oriented subnets). The main proponents of packets come from the Internet community. In a connectionless design, every packet is routed independently of every other packet. As a consequence, if some routers go down during a session, no harm will be done as long as the system can

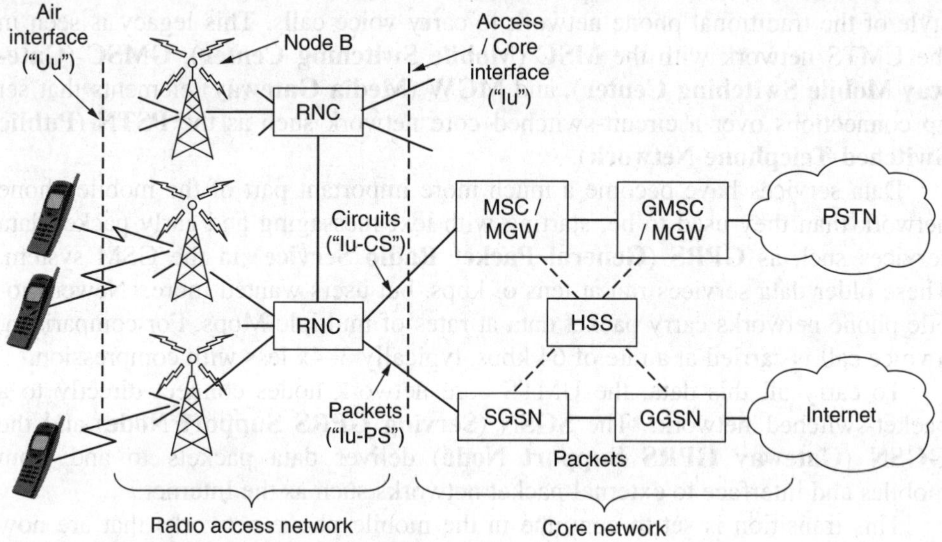

Figure 1-31. Architecture of the UMTS 3G mobile phone network.

dynamically reconfigure itself so that subsequent packets can find some route to the destination, even if it is different from that which previous packets used.

The circuit camp comes from the world of telephone companies. In the telephone system, a caller must dial the called party's number and wait for a connection before talking or sending data. This connection setup establishes a route through the telephone system that is maintained until the call is terminated. All words or packets follow the same route. If a line or switch on the path goes down, the call is aborted, making it less fault tolerant than a connectionless design.

The advantage of circuits is that they can support quality of service more easily. By setting up a connection in advance, the subnet can reserve resources such as link bandwidth, switch buffer space, and CPU. If an attempt is made to set up a call and insufficient resources are available, the call is rejected and the caller gets a kind of busy signal. In this way, once a connection has been set up, the connection will get good service.

With a connectionless network, if too many packets arrive at the same router at the same moment, the router will choke and probably lose packets. The sender will eventually notice this and resend them, but the quality of service will be jerky and unsuitable for audio or video unless the network is lightly loaded. Needless to say, providing adequate audio quality is something telephone companies care about very much, hence their preference for connections.

The surprise in Fig. 1-31 is that there is both packet and circuit switched equipment in the core network. This shows the mobile phone network in transition, with mobile phone companies able to implement one or sometimes both of the alternatives. Older mobile phone networks used a circuit-switched core in the style of the traditional phone network to carry voice calls. This legacy is seen in the UMTS network with the **MSC (Mobile Switching Center)**, **GMSC (Gateway Mobile Switching Center)**, and **MGW (Media Gateway)** elements that set up connections over a circuit-switched core network such as the **PSTN (Public Switched Telephone Network)**.

Data services have become a much more important part of the mobile phone network than they used to be, starting with text messaging and early packet data services such as **GPRS (General Packet Radio Service)** in the GSM system. These older data services ran at tens of kbps, but users wanted more. Newer mobile phone networks carry packet data at rates of multiple Mbps. For comparison, a voice call is carried at a rate of 64 kbps, typically 3–4x less with compression.

To carry all this data, the UMTS core network nodes connect directly to a packet-switched network. The **SGSN (Serving GPRS Support Node)** and the **GGSN (Gateway GPRS Support Node)** deliver data packets to and from mobiles and interface to external packet networks such as the Internet.

This transition is set to continue in the mobile phone networks that are now being planned and deployed. Internet protocols are even used on mobiles to set up connections for voice calls over a packet data network, in the manner of voice-over-IP. IP and packets are used all the way from the radio access through to the core network. Of course, the way that IP networks are designed is also changing to support better quality of service. If it did not, then problems with chopped-up audio and jerky video would not impress paying customers. We will return to this subject in Chap. 5.

Another difference between mobile phone networks and the traditional Internet is mobility. When a user moves out of the range of one cellular base station and into the range of another one, the flow of data must be re-routed from the old to the new cell base station. This technique is known as **handover** or **handoff**, and it is illustrated in Fig. 1-32.

(a) (b)

Figure 1-32. Mobile phone handover (a) before, (b) after.

Either the mobile device or the base station may request a handover when the quality of the signal drops. In some cell networks, usually those based on CDMA technology, it is possible to connect to the new base station before disconnecting from the old base station. This improves the connection quality for the mobile because there is no break in service; the mobile is actually connected to two base stations for a short while. This way of doing a handover is called a **soft handover** to distinguish it from a **hard handover**, in which the mobile disconnects from the old base station before connecting to the new one.

A related issue is how to find a mobile in the first place when there is an incoming call. Each mobile phone network has a **HSS (Home Subscriber Server)** in the core network that knows the location of each subscriber, as well as other profile information that is used for authentication and authorization. In this way, each mobile can be found by contacting the HSS.

A final area to discuss is security. Historically, phone companies have taken security much more seriously than Internet companies for a long time because of the need to bill for service and avoid (payment) fraud. Unfortunately that is not saying much. Nevertheless, in the evolution from 1G through 3G technologies, mobile phone companies have been able to roll out some basic security mechanisms for mobiles.

Starting with the 2G GSM system, the mobile phone was divided into a handset and a removable chip containing the subscriber's identity and account information. The chip is informally called a **SIM card**, short for **Subscriber Identity Module**. SIM cards can be switched to different handsets to activate them, and they provide a basis for security. When GSM customers travel to other countries on vacation or business, they often bring their handsets but buy a new SIM card for few dollars upon arrival in order to make local calls with no roaming charges.

To reduce fraud, information on SIM cards is also used by the mobile phone network to authenticate subscribers and check that they are allowed to use the network. With UMTS, the mobile also uses the information on the SIM card to check that it is talking to a legitimate network.

Another aspect of security is privacy. Wireless signals are broadcast to all nearby receivers, so to make it difficult to eavesdrop on conversations, cryptographic keys on the SIM card are used to encrypt transmissions. This approach provides much better privacy than in 1G systems, which were easily tapped, but is not a panacea due to weaknesses in the encryption schemes.

Mobile phone networks are destined to play a central role in future networks. They are now more about mobile broadband applications than voice calls, and this has major implications for the air interfaces, core network architecture, and security of future networks. 4G technologies that are faster and better are on the drawing board under the name of **LTE (Long Term Evolution)**, even as 3G design and deployment continues. Other wireless technologies also offer broadband Internet access to fixed and mobile clients, notably 802.16 networks under the common name of **WiMAX**. It is entirely possible that LTE and WiMAX are on a collision course with each other and it is hard to predict what will happen to them.

1.5.3 Wireless LANs: 802.11

Almost as soon as laptop computers appeared, many people had a dream of walking into an office and magically having their laptop computer be connected to the Internet. Consequently, various groups began working on ways to accomplish this goal. The most practical approach is to equip both the office and the laptop computers with short-range radio transmitters and receivers to allow them to talk.

Work in this field rapidly led to wireless LANs being marketed by a variety of companies. The trouble was that no two of them were compatible. The proliferation of standards meant that a computer equipped with a brand *X* radio would not work in a room equipped with a brand *Y* base station. In the mid 1990s, the industry decided that a wireless LAN standard might be a good idea, so the IEEE committee that had standardized wired LANs was given the task of drawing up a wireless LAN standard.

The first decision was the easiest: what to call it. All the other LAN standards had numbers like 802.1, 802.2, and 802.3, up to 802.10, so the wireless LAN standard was dubbed 802.11. A common slang name for it is **WiFi** but it is an important standard and deserves respect, so we will call it by its proper name, 802.11.

The rest was harder. The first problem was to find a suitable frequency band that was available, preferably worldwide. The approach taken was the opposite of that used in mobile phone networks. Instead of expensive, licensed spectrum, 802.11 systems operate in unlicensed bands such as the **ISM** (**Industrial, Scientific, and Medical**) bands defined by ITU-R (e.g., 902-928 MHz, 2.4-2.5 GHz, 5.725-5.825 GHz). All devices are allowed to use this spectrum provided that they limit their transmit power to let different devices coexist. Of course, this means that 802.11 radios may find themselves competing with cordless phones, garage door openers, and microwave ovens.

802.11 networks are made up of clients, such as laptops and mobile phones, and infrastructure called **APs** (**access points**) that is installed in buildings. Access points are sometimes called **base stations**. The access points connect to the wired network, and all communication between clients goes through an access point. It is also possible for clients that are in radio range to talk directly, such as two computers in an office without an access point. This arrangement is called an **ad hoc network**. It is used much less often than the access point mode. Both modes are shown in Fig. 1-33.

802.11 transmission is complicated by wireless conditions that vary with even small changes in the environment. At the frequencies used for 802.11, radio signals can be reflected off solid objects so that multiple echoes of a transmission may reach a receiver along different paths. The echoes can cancel or reinforce each other, causing the received signal to fluctuate greatly. This phenomenon is called **multipath fading**, and it is shown in Fig. 1-34.

The key idea for overcoming variable wireless conditions is **path diversity**, or the sending of information along multiple, independent paths. In this way, the

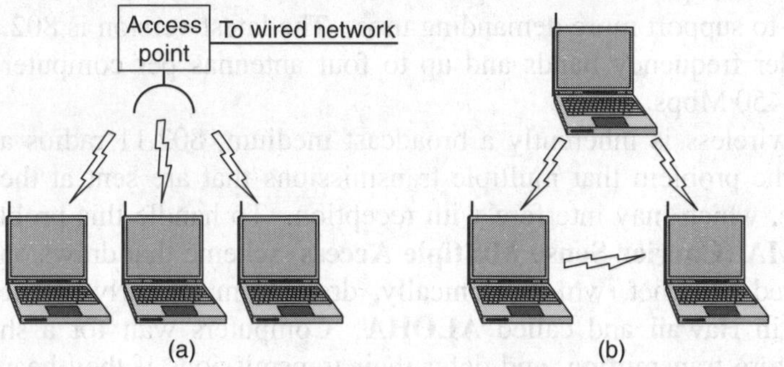

Figure 1-33. (a) Wireless network with an access point. (b) Ad hoc network.

information is likely to be received even if one of the paths happens to be poor due to a fade. These independent paths are typically built into the digital modulation scheme at the physical layer. Options include using different frequencies across the allowed band, following different spatial paths between different pairs of antennas, or repeating bits over different periods of time.

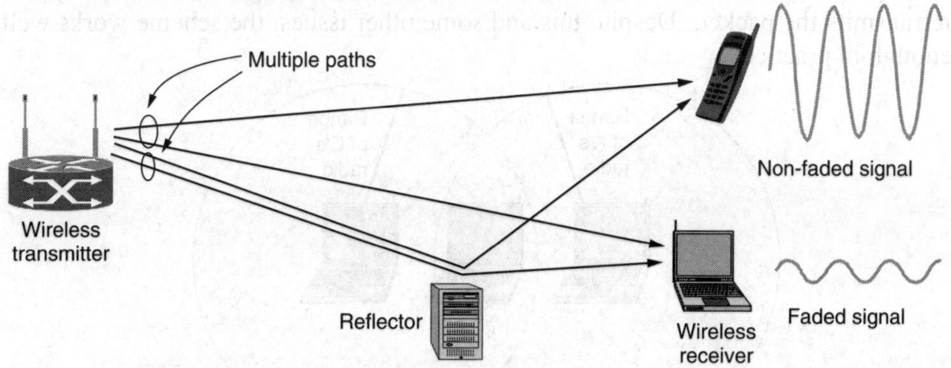

Figure 1-34. Multipath fading.

Different versions of 802.11 have used all of these techniques. The initial (1997) standard defined a wireless LAN that ran at either 1 Mbps or 2 Mbps by hopping between frequencies or spreading the signal across the allowed spectrum. Almost immediately, people complained that it was too slow, so work began on faster standards. The spread spectrum design was extended and became the (1999) 802.11b standard running at rates up to 11 Mbps. The 802.11a (1999) and 802.11g (2003) standards switched to a different modulation scheme called **OFDM** (**Orthogonal Frequency Division Multiplexing**). It divides a wide band of spectrum into many narrow slices over which different bits are sent in parallel. This improved scheme, which we will study in Chap. 2, boosted the 802.11a/g bit rates up to 54 Mbps. That is a significant increase, but people still wanted more throughput to support more demanding uses. The latest version is 802.11n (2009). It uses wider frequency bands and up to four antennas per computer to achieve rates up to 450 Mbps.

Since wireless is inherently a broadcast medium, 802.11 radios also have to deal with the problem that multiple transmissions that are sent at the same time will collide, which may interfere with reception. To handle this problem, 802.11 uses a **CSMA (Carrier Sense Multiple Access)** scheme that draws on ideas from classic wired Ethernet, which, ironically, drew from an early wireless network developed in Hawaii and called **ALOHA**. Computers wait for a short random interval before transmitting, and defer their transmissions if they hear that someone else is already transmitting. This scheme makes it less likely that two computers will send at the same time. It does not work as well as in the case of wired networks, though. To see why, examine Fig. 1-35. Suppose that computer *A* is transmitting to computer *B*, but the radio range of *A*'s transmitter is too short to reach computer *C*. If *C* wants to transmit to *B* it can listen before starting, but the fact that it does not hear anything does not mean that its transmission will succeed. The inability of *C* to hear *A* before starting causes some collisions to occur. After any collision, the sender then waits another, longer, random delay and retransmits the packet. Despite this and some other issues, the scheme works well enough in practice.

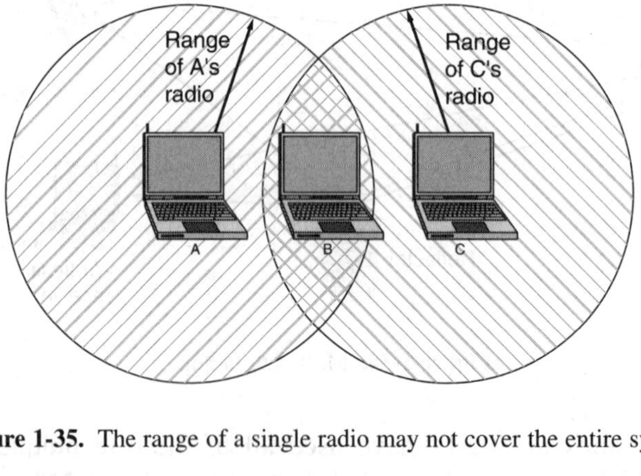

Figure 1-35. The range of a single radio may not cover the entire system.

Another problem is that of mobility. If a mobile client is moved away from the access point it is using and into the range of a different access point, some way of handing it off is needed. The solution is that an 802.11 network can consist of multiple cells, each with its own access point, and a distribution system that connects the cells. The distribution system is often switched Ethernet, but it can use any technology. As the clients move, they may find another access point with a better signal than the one they are currently using and change their association. From the outside, the entire system looks like a single wired LAN.

That said, mobility in 802.11 has been of limited value so far compared to mobility in the mobile phone network. Typically, 802.11 is used by nomadic clients that go from one fixed location to another, rather than being used on-the-go. Mobility is not really needed for nomadic usage. Even when 802.11 mobility is used, it extends over a single 802.11 network, which might cover at most a large building. Future schemes will need to provide mobility across different networks and across different technologies (e.g., 802.21).

Finally, there is the problem of security. Since wireless transmissions are broadcast, it is easy for nearby computers to receive packets of information that were not intended for them. To prevent this, the 802.11 standard included an encryption scheme known as **WEP (Wired Equivalent Privacy)**. The idea was to make wireless security like that of wired security. It is a good idea, but unfortunately the scheme was flawed and soon broken (Borisov et al., 2001). It has since been replaced with newer schemes that have different cryptographic details in the 802.11i standard, also called **WiFi Protected Access**, initially called **WPA** but now replaced by **WPA2**.

802.11 has caused a revolution in wireless networking that is set to continue. Beyond buildings, it is starting to be installed in trains, planes, boats, and automobiles so that people can surf the Internet wherever they go. Mobile phones and all manner of consumer electronics, from game consoles to digital cameras, can communicate with it. We will come back to it in detail in Chap. 4.

1.5.4 RFID and Sensor Networks

The networks we have studied so far are made up of computing devices that are easy to recognize, from computers to mobile phones. With **Radio Frequency IDentification (RFID)**, everyday objects can also be part of a computer network.

An RFID tag looks like a postage stamp-sized sticker that can be affixed to (or embedded in) an object so that it can be tracked. The object might be a cow, a passport, a book or a shipping pallet. The tag consists of a small microchip with a unique identifier and an antenna that receives radio transmissions. RFID readers installed at tracking points find tags when they come into range and interrogate them for their information as shown in Fig. 1-36. Applications include checking identities, managing the supply chain, timing races, and replacing barcodes.

There are many kinds of RFID, each with different properties, but perhaps the most fascinating aspect of RFID technology is that most RFID tags have neither an electric plug nor a battery. Instead, all of the energy needed to operate them is supplied in the form of radio waves by RFID readers. This technology is called **passive RFID** to distinguish it from the (less common) **active RFID** in which there is a power source on the tag.

One common form of RFID is **UHF RFID (Ultra-High Frequency RFID)**. It is used on shipping pallets and some drivers licenses. Readers send signals in

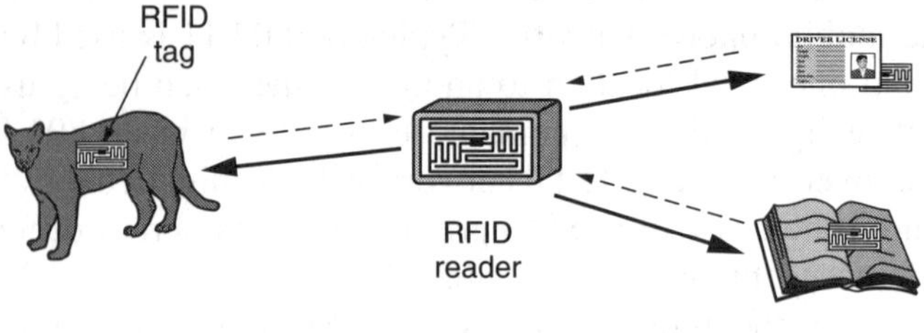

Figure 1-36. RFID used to network everyday objects.

the 902-928 MHz band in the United States. Tags communicate at distances of several meters by changing the way they reflect the reader signals; the reader is able to pick up these reflections. This way of operating is called **backscatter**.

Another popular kind of RFID is **HF RFID (High Frequency RFID)**. It operates at 13.56 MHz and is likely to be in your passport, credit cards, books, and noncontact payment systems. HF RFID has a short range, typically a meter or less, because the physical mechanism is based on induction rather than backscatter. There are also other forms of RFID using other frequencies, such as **LF RFID (Low Frequency RFID)**, which was developed before HF RFID and used for animal tracking. It is the kind of RFID likely to be in your cat.

RFID readers must somehow solve the problem of dealing with multiple tags within reading range. This means that a tag cannot simply respond when it hears a reader, or the signals from multiple tags may collide. The solution is similar to the approach taken in 802.11: tags wait for a short random interval before responding with their identification, which allows the reader to narrow down individual tags and interrogate them further.

Security is another problem. The ability of RFID readers to easily track an object, and hence the person who uses it, can be an invasion of privacy. Unfortunately, it is difficult to secure RFID tags because they lack the computation and communication power to run strong cryptographic algorithms. Instead, weak measures like passwords (which can easily be cracked) are used. If an identity card can be remotely read by an official at a border, what is to stop the same card from being tracked by other people without your knowledge? Not much.

RFID tags started as identification chips, but are rapidly turning into full-fledged computers. For example, many tags have memory that can be updated and later queried, so that information about what has happened to the tagged object can be stored with it. Rieback et al. (2006) demonstrated that this means that all of the usual problems of computer malware apply, only now your cat or your passport might be used to spread an RFID virus.

A step up in capability from RFID is the **sensor network**. Sensor networks are deployed to monitor aspects of the physical world. So far, they have mostly been used for scientific experimentation, such as monitoring bird habitats, volcanic activity, and zebra migration, but business applications including healthcare, monitoring equipment for vibration, and tracking of frozen, refrigerated, or otherwise perishable goods cannot be too far behind.

Sensor nodes are small computers, often the size of a key fob, that have temperature, vibration, and other sensors. Many nodes are placed in the environment that is to be monitored. Typically, they have batteries, though they may scavenge energy from vibrations or the sun. As with RFID, having enough energy is a key challenge, and the nodes must communicate carefully to be able to deliver their sensor information to an external collection point. A common strategy is for the nodes to self-organize to relay messages for each other, as shown in Fig. 1-37. This design is called a **multihop network**.

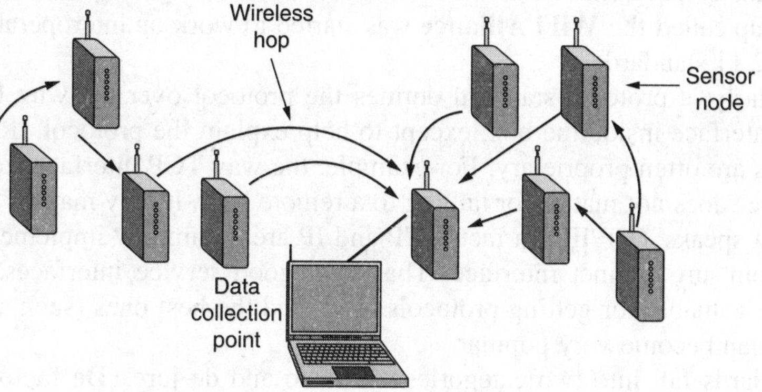

Figure 1-37. Multihop topology of a sensor network.

RFID and sensor networks are likely to become much more capable and pervasive in the future. Researchers have already combined the best of both technologies by prototyping programmable RFID tags with light, movement, and other sensors (Sample et al., 2008).

1.6 NETWORK STANDARDIZATION

Many network vendors and suppliers exist, each with its own ideas of how things should be done. Without coordination, there would be complete chaos, and users would get nothing done. The only way out is to agree on some network standards. Not only do good standards allow different computers to communicate, but they also increase the market for products adhering to the standards. A larger market leads to mass production, economies of scale in manufacturing, better implementations, and other benefits that decrease price and further increase acceptance.

In this section we will take a quick look at the important but little-known, world of international standardization. But let us first discuss what belongs in a standard. A reasonable person might assume that a standard tells you how a protocol should work so that you can do a good job of implementing it. That person would be wrong.

Standards define what is needed for interoperability: no more, no less. That lets the larger market emerge and also lets companies compete on the basis of how good their products are. For example, the 802.11 standard defines many transmission rates but does not say when a sender should use which rate, which is a key factor in good performance. That is up to whoever makes the product. Often getting to interoperability this way is difficult, since there are many implementation choices and standards usually define many options. For 802.11, there were so many problems that, in a strategy that has become common practice, a trade group called the **WiFi Alliance** was started to work on interoperability within the 802.11 standard.

Similarly, a protocol standard defines the protocol over the wire but not the service interface inside the box, except to help explain the protocol. Real service interfaces are often proprietary. For example, the way TCP interfaces to IP within a computer does not matter for talking to a remote host. It only matters that the remote host speaks TCP/IP. In fact, TCP and IP are commonly implemented together without any distinct interface. That said, good service interfaces, like good APIs, are valuable for getting protocols used, and the best ones (such as Berkeley sockets) can become very popular.

Standards fall into two categories: de facto and de jure. **De facto** (Latin for "from the fact") standards are those that have just happened, without any formal plan. HTTP, the protocol on which the Web runs, started life as a de facto standard. It was part of early WWW browsers developed by Tim Berners-Lee at CERN, and its use took off with the growth of the Web. Bluetooth is another example. It was originally developed by Ericsson but now everyone is using it.

De jure (Latin for "by law") standards, in contrast, are adopted through the rules of some formal standardization body. International standardization authorities are generally divided into two classes: those established by treaty among national governments, and those comprising voluntary, nontreaty organizations. In the area of computer network standards, there are several organizations of each type, notably ITU, ISO, IETF and IEEE, all of which we will discuss below.

In practice, the relationships between standards, companies, and standardization bodies are complicated. De facto standards often evolve into de jure standards, especially if they are successful. This happened in the case of HTTP, which was quickly picked up by IETF. Standards bodies often ratify each others' standards, in what looks like patting one another on the back, to increase the market for a technology. These days, many ad hoc business alliances that are formed around particular technologies also play a significant role in developing and refining network standards. For example, **3GPP** (**Third Generation Partnership Project**) is a collaboration between telecommunications associations that drives the UMTS 3G mobile phone standards.

1.6.1 Who's Who in the Telecommunications World

The legal status of the world's telephone companies varies considerably from country to country. At one extreme is the United States, which has over 2000 separate, (mostly very small) privately owned telephone companies. A few more were added with the breakup of AT&T in 1984 (which was then the world's largest corporation, providing telephone service to about 80 percent of America's telephones), and the Telecommunications Act of 1996 that overhauled regulation to foster competition.

At the other extreme are countries in which the national government has a complete monopoly on all communication, including the mail, telegraph, telephone, and often radio and television. Much of the world falls into this category. In some cases the telecommunication authority is a nationalized company, and in others it is simply a branch of the government, usually known as the **PTT** (**Post, Telegraph & Telephone** administration). Worldwide, the trend is toward liberalization and competition and away from government monopoly. Most European countries have now (partially) privatized their PTTs, but elsewhere the process is still only slowly gaining steam.

With all these different suppliers of services, there is clearly a need to provide compatibility on a worldwide scale to ensure that people (and computers) in one country can call their counterparts in another one. Actually, this need has existed for a long time. In 1865, representatives from many European governments met to form the predecessor to today's **ITU** (**International Telecommunication Union**). Its job was to standardize international telecommunications, which in those days meant telegraphy. Even then it was clear that if half the countries used Morse code and the other half used some other code, there was going to be a problem. When the telephone was put into international service, ITU took over the job of standardizing telephony (pronounced te-LEF-ony) as well. In 1947, ITU became an agency of the United Nations.

ITU has about 200 governmental members, including almost every member of the United Nations. Since the United States does not have a PTT, somebody else had to represent it in ITU. This task fell to the State Department, probably on the grounds that ITU had to do with foreign countries, the State Department's specialty. ITU also has more than 700 sector and associate members. They include telephone companies (e.g., AT&T, Vodafone, Sprint), telecom equipment manufacturers (e.g., Cisco, Nokia, Nortel), computer vendors (e.g., Microsoft, Agilent, Toshiba), chip manufacturers (e.g., Intel, Motorola, TI), and other interested companies (e.g., Boeing, CBS, VeriSign).

ITU has three main sectors. We will focus primarily on **ITU-T**, the Telecommunications Standardization Sector, which is concerned with telephone and data communication systems. Before 1993, this sector was called **CCITT**, which is an acronym for its French name, Comité Consultatif International Télégraphique et Téléphonique. **ITU-R**, the Radiocommunications Sector, is concerned with coordinating the use by competing interest groups of radio frequencies worldwide. The other sector is ITU-D, the Development Sector. It promotes the development of information and communication technologies to narrow the "digital divide" between countries with effective access to the information technologies and countries with limited access.

ITU-T's task is to make technical recommendations about telephone, telegraph, and data communication interfaces. These often become internationally recognized standards, though technically the recommendations are only suggestions that governments can adopt or ignore, as they wish (because governments are like 13-year-old boys—they do not take kindly to being given orders). In practice, a country that wishes to adopt a telephone standard different from that used by the rest of the world is free to do so, but at the price of cutting itself off from everyone else. This might work for North Korea, but elsewhere it would be a real problem.

The real work of ITU-T is done in its Study Groups. There are currently 10 Study Groups, often as large as 400 people, that cover topics ranging from telephone billing to multimedia services to security. SG 15, for example, standardizes the DSL technologies popularly used to connect to the Internet. In order to make it possible to get anything at all done, the Study Groups are divided into Working Parties, which are in turn divided into Expert Teams, which are in turn divided into ad hoc groups. Once a bureaucracy, always a bureaucracy.

Despite all this, ITU-T actually does get things done. Since its inception, it has produced more than 3000 recommendations, many of which are widely used in practice. For example, Recommendation H.264 (also an ISO standard known as MPEG-4 AVC) is widely used for video compression, and X.509 public key certificates are used for secure Web browsing and digitally signed email.

As the field of telecommunications completes the transition started in the 1980s from being entirely national to being entirely global, standards will become increasingly important, and more and more organizations will want to become involved in setting them. For more information about ITU, see Irmer (1994).

1.6.2 Who's Who in the International Standards World

International standards are produced and published by **ISO (International Standards Organization**†), a voluntary nontreaty organization founded in 1946. Its members are the national standards organizations of the 157 member countries. These members include ANSI (U.S.), BSI (Great Britain), AFNOR (France), DIN (Germany), and 153 others.

ISO issues standards on a truly vast number of subjects, ranging from nuts and bolts (literally) to telephone pole coatings [not to mention cocoa beans (ISO 2451), fishing nets (ISO 1530), women's underwear (ISO 4416) and quite a few

† For the purist, ISO's true name is the International Organization for Standardization.

other subjects one might not think were subject to standardization]. On issues of telecommunication standards, ISO and ITU-T often cooperate (ISO is a member of ITU-T) to avoid the irony of two official and mutually incompatible international standards.

Over 17,000 standards have been issued, including the OSI standards. ISO has over 200 Technical Committees (TCs), numbered in the order of their creation, each dealing with a specific subject. TC1 deals with the nuts and bolts (standardizing screw thread pitches). JTC1 deals with information technology, including networks, computers, and software. It is the first (and so far only) Joint Technical Committee, created in 1987 by merging TC97 with activities in IEC, yet another standardization body. Each TC has subcommittees (SCs) divided into working groups (WGs).

The real work is done largely in the WGs by over 100,000 volunteers worldwide. Many of these "volunteers" are assigned to work on ISO matters by their employers, whose products are being standardized. Others are government officials keen on having their country's way of doing things become the international standard. Academic experts also are active in many of the WGs.

The procedure used by ISO for adopting standards has been designed to achieve as broad a consensus as possible. The process begins when one of the national standards organizations feels the need for an international standard in some area. A working group is then formed to come up with a **CD** (**Committee Draft**). The CD is then circulated to all the member bodies, which get 6 months to criticize it. If a substantial majority approves, a revised document, called a **DIS** (**Draft International Standard**) is produced and circulated for comments and voting. Based on the results of this round, the final text of the **IS** (**International Standard**) is prepared, approved, and published. In areas of great controversy, a CD or DIS may have to go through several versions before acquiring enough votes, and the whole process can take years.

NIST (**National Institute of Standards and Technology**) is part of the U.S. Department of Commerce. It used to be called the National Bureau of Standards. It issues standards that are mandatory for purchases made by the U.S. Government, except for those of the Department of Defense, which defines its own standards.

Another major player in the standards world is **IEEE** (**Institute of Electrical and Electronics Engineers**), the largest professional organization in the world. In addition to publishing scores of journals and running hundreds of conferences each year, IEEE has a standardization group that develops standards in the area of electrical engineering and computing. IEEE's 802 committee has standardized many kinds of LANs. We will study some of its output later in this book. The actual work is done by a collection of working groups, which are listed in Fig. 1-38. The success rate of the various 802 working groups has been low; having an 802.x number is no guarantee of success. Still, the impact of the success stories (especially 802.3 and 802.11) on the industry and the world has been enormous.

Number	Topic
802.1	Overview and architecture of LANs
802.2 ↓	Logical link control
802.3 *	Ethernet
802.4 ↓	Token bus (was briefly used in manufacturing plants)
802.5	Token ring (IBM's entry into the LAN world)
802.6 ↓	Dual queue dual bus (early metropolitan area network)
802.7 ↓	Technical advisory group on broadband technologies
802.8 †	Technical advisory group on fiber optic technologies
802.9 ↓	Isochronous LANs (for real-time applications)
802.10 ↓	Virtual LANs and security
802.11 *	Wireless LANs (WiFi)
802.12 ↓	Demand priority (Hewlett-Packard's AnyLAN)
802.13	Unlucky number; nobody wanted it
802.14 ↓	Cable modems (defunct: an industry consortium got there first)
802.15 *	Personal area networks (Bluetooth, Zigbee)
802.16 *	Broadband wireless (WiMAX)
802.17	Resilient packet ring
802.18	Technical advisory group on radio regulatory issues
802.19	Technical advisory group on coexistence of all these standards
802.20	Mobile broadband wireless (similar to 802.16e)
802.21	Media independent handoff (for roaming over technologies)
802.22	Wireless regional area network

Figure 1-38. The 802 working groups. The important ones are marked with *. The ones marked with ↓ are hibernating. The one marked with † gave up and disbanded itself.

1.6.3 Who's Who in the Internet Standards World

The worldwide Internet has its own standardization mechanisms, very different from those of ITU-T and ISO. The difference can be crudely summed up by saying that the people who come to ITU or ISO standardization meetings wear suits, while the people who come to Internet standardization meetings wear jeans (except when they meet in San Diego, when they wear shorts and T-shirts).

ITU-T and ISO meetings are populated by corporate officials and government civil servants for whom standardization is their job. They regard standardization as a Good Thing and devote their lives to it. Internet people, on the other hand, prefer anarchy as a matter of principle. However, with hundreds of millions of people all doing their own thing, little communication can occur. Thus, standards, however regrettable, are sometimes needed. In this context, David Clark of M.I.T. once made a now-famous remark about Internet standardization consisting of "rough consensus and running code."

When the ARPANET was set up, DoD created an informal committee to oversee it. In 1983, the committee was renamed the **IAB** (**Internet Activities Board**) and was given a slighter broader mission, namely, to keep the researchers involved with the ARPANET and the Internet pointed more or less in the same direction, an activity not unlike herding cats. The meaning of the acronym "IAB" was later changed to **Internet Architecture Board**.

Each of the approximately ten members of the IAB headed a task force on some issue of importance. The IAB met several times a year to discuss results and to give feedback to the DoD and NSF, which were providing most of the funding at this time. When a standard was needed (e.g., a new routing algorithm), the IAB members would thrash it out and then announce the change so the graduate students who were the heart of the software effort could implement it. Communication was done by a series of technical reports called **RFCs** (**Request For Comments**). RFCs are stored online and can be fetched by anyone interested in them from *www.ietf.org/rfc*. They are numbered in chronological order of creation. Over 5000 now exist. We will refer to many RFCs in this book.

By 1989, the Internet had grown so large that this highly informal style no longer worked. Many vendors by then offered TCP/IP products and did not want to change them just because ten researchers had thought of a better idea. In the summer of 1989, the IAB was reorganized again. The researchers were moved to the **IRTF** (**Internet Research Task Force**), which was made subsidiary to IAB, along with the **IETF** (**Internet Engineering Task Force**). The IAB was repopulated with people representing a broader range of organizations than just the research community. It was initially a self-perpetuating group, with members serving for a 2-year term and new members being appointed by the old ones. Later, the **Internet Society** was created, populated by people interested in the Internet. The Internet Society is thus in a sense comparable to ACM or IEEE. It is governed by elected trustees who appoint the IAB's members.

The idea of this split was to have the IRTF concentrate on long-term research while the IETF dealt with short-term engineering issues. The IETF was divided up into working groups, each with a specific problem to solve. The chairmen of these working groups initially met as a steering committee to direct the engineering effort. The working group topics include new applications, user information, OSI integration, routing and addressing, security, network management, and standards. Eventually, so many working groups were formed (more than 70) that they were grouped into areas and the area chairmen met as the steering committee.

In addition, a more formal standardization process was adopted, patterned after ISOs. To become a **Proposed Standard**, the basic idea must be explained in an RFC and have sufficient interest in the community to warrant consideration.

To advance to the **Draft Standard** stage, a working implementation must have been rigorously tested by at least two independent sites for at least 4 months. If the IAB is convinced that the idea is sound and the software works, it can declare the RFC to be an **Internet Standard**. Some Internet Standards have become DoD standards (MIL-STD), making them mandatory for DoD suppliers.

For Web standards, the **World Wide Web Consortium** (**W3C**) develops protocols and guidelines to facilitate the long-term growth of the Web. It is an industry consortium led by Tim Berners-Lee and set up in 1994 as the Web really begun to take off. W3C now has more than 300 members from around the world and has produced more than 100 W3C Recommendations, as its standards are called, covering topics such as HTML and Web privacy.

1.7 METRIC UNITS

To avoid any confusion, it is worth stating explicitly that in this book, as in computer science in general, metric units are used instead of traditional English units (the furlong-stone-fortnight system). The principal metric prefixes are listed in Fig. 1-39. The prefixes are typically abbreviated by their first letters, with the units greater than 1 capitalized (KB, MB, etc.). One exception (for historical reasons) is kbps for kilobits/sec. Thus, a 1-Mbps communication line transmits 10^6 bits/sec and a 100-psec (or 100-ps) clock ticks every 10^{-10} seconds. Since milli and micro both begin with the letter "m," a choice had to be made. Normally, "m" is used for milli and "μ" (the Greek letter mu) is used for micro.

Exp.	Explicit	Prefix	Exp.	Explicit	Prefix
10^{-3}	0.001	milli	10^{3}	1,000	Kilo
10^{-6}	0.000001	micro	10^{6}	1,000,000	Mega
10^{-9}	0.000000001	nano	10^{9}	1,000,000,000	Giga
10^{-12}	0.000000000001	pico	10^{12}	1,000,000,000,000	Tera
10^{-15}	0.000000000000001	femto	10^{15}	1,000,000,000,000,000	Peta
10^{-18}	0.000000000000000001	atto	10^{18}	1,000,000,000,000,000,000	Exa
10^{-21}	0.000000000000000000001	zepto	10^{21}	1,000,000,000,000,000,000,000	Zetta
10^{-24}	0.000000000000000000000001	yocto	10^{24}	1,000,000,000,000,000,000,000,000	Yotta

Figure 1-39. The principal metric prefixes.

It is also worth pointing out that for measuring memory, disk, file, and database sizes, in common industry practice, the units have slightly different meanings. There, kilo means 2^{10} (1024) rather than 10^3 (1000) because memories are always a power of two. Thus, a 1-KB memory contains 1024 bytes, not 1000 bytes. Note also the capital "B" in that usage to mean "bytes" (units of eight bits), instead of a lowercase "b" that means "bits." Similarly, a 1-MB memory contains 2^{20} (1,048,576) bytes, a 1-GB memory contains 2^{30} (1,073,741,824) bytes, and a 1-TB database contains 2^{40} (1,099,511,627,776) bytes. However, a 1-kbps communication line transmits 1000 bits per second and a 10-Mbps LAN runs at 10,000,000 bits/sec because these speeds are not powers of two. Unfortunately, many people tend to mix up these two systems, especially for disk sizes. To avoid ambiguity, in this book, we will use the symbols KB, MB, GB, and TB for 2^{10}, 2^{20}, 2^{30}, and 2^{40} bytes, respectively, and the symbols kbps, Mbps, Gbps, and Tbps for 10^3, 10^6, 10^9, and 10^{12} bits/sec, respectively.

1.8 OUTLINE OF THE REST OF THE BOOK

This book discusses both the principles and practice of computer networking. Most chapters start with a discussion of the relevant principles, followed by a number of examples that illustrate these principles. These examples are usually taken from the Internet and wireless networks such as the mobile phone network since these are both important and very different. Other examples will be given where relevant.

The book is structured according to the hybrid model of Fig. 1-23. Starting with Chap. 2, we begin working our way up the protocol hierarchy beginning at the bottom. We provide some background in the field of data communication that covers both wired and wireless transmission systems. This material is concerned with how to deliver information over physical channels, although we cover only the architectural rather than the hardware aspects. Several examples of the physical layer, such as the public switched telephone network, the mobile telephone network, and the cable television network are also discussed.

Chapters 3 and 4 discuss the data link layer in two parts. Chap. 3 looks at the problem of how to send packets across a link, including error detection and correction. We look at DSL (used for broadband Internet access over phone lines) as a real-world example of a data link protocol.

In Chap. 4, we examine the medium access sublayer. This is the part of the data link layer that deals with how to share a channel between multiple computers. The examples we look at include wireless, such as 802.11 and RFID, and wired LANs such as classic Ethernet. Link layer switches that connect LANs, such as switched Ethernet, are also discussed here.

Chapter 5 deals with the network layer, especially routing. Many routing algorithms, both static and dynamic, are covered. Even with good routing algorithms, though, if more traffic is offered than the network can handle, some packets will be delayed or discarded. We discuss this issue from how to prevent congestion to how to guarantee a certain quality of service. Connecting heterogeneous networks to form internetworks also leads to numerous problems that are discussed here. The network layer in the Internet is given extensive coverage.

Chapter 6 deals with the transport layer. Much of the emphasis is on connection-oriented protocols and reliability, since many applications need these. Both Internet transport protocols, UDP and TCP, are covered in detail, as are their performance issues.

Chapter 7 deals with the application layer, its protocols, and its applications. The first topic is DNS, which is the Internet's telephone book. Next comes email, including a discussion of its protocols. Then we move on to the Web, with detailed discussions of static and dynamic content, and what happens on the client and server sides. We follow this with a look at networked multimedia, including streaming audio and video. Finally, we discuss content-delivery networks, including peer-to-peer technology.

Chapter 8 is about network security. This topic has aspects that relate to all layers, so it is easiest to treat it after all the layers have been thoroughly explained. The chapter starts with an introduction to cryptography. Later, it shows how cryptography can be used to secure communication, email, and the Web. The chapter ends with a discussion of some areas in which security collides with privacy, freedom of speech, censorship, and other social issues.

Chapter 9 contains an annotated list of suggested readings arranged by chapter. It is intended to help those readers who would like to pursue their study of networking further. The chapter also has an alphabetical bibliography of all the references cited in this book.

The authors' Web site at Pearson:

http://www.pearsonhighered.com/tanenbaum

has a page with links to many tutorials, FAQs, companies, industry consortia, professional organizations, standards organizations, technologies, papers, and more.

1.9 SUMMARY

Computer networks have many uses, both for companies and for individuals, in the home and while on the move. Companies use networks of computers to share corporate information, typically using the client-server model with employee desktops acting as clients accessing powerful servers in the machine room. For individuals, networks offer access to a variety of information and entertainment resources, as well as a way to buy and sell products and services. Individuals often access the Internet via their phone or cable providers at home, though increasingly wireless access is used for laptops and phones. Technology advances are enabling new kinds of mobile applications and networks with computers embedded in appliances and other consumer devices. The same advances raise social issues such as privacy concerns.

Roughly speaking, networks can be divided into LANs, MANs, WANs, and internetworks. LANs typical cover a building and operate at high speeds. MANs usually cover a city. An example is the cable television system, which is now used by many people to access the Internet. WANs may cover a country or a continent. Some of the technologies used to build these networks are point-to-point (e.g., a cable) while others are broadcast (e.g.,wireless). Networks can be interconnected with routers to form internetworks, of which the Internet is the largest and best known example. Wireless networks, for example 802.11 LANs and 3G mobile telephony, are also becoming extremely popular.

Network software is built around protocols, which are rules by which processes communicate. Most networks support protocol hierarchies, with each layer providing services to the layer above it and insulating them from the details of the protocols used in the lower layers. Protocol stacks are typically based either on the OSI model or on the TCP/IP model. Both have link, network, transport, and application layers, but they differ on the other layers. Design issues include reliability, resource allocation, growth, security, and more. Much of this book deals with protocols and their design.

Networks provide various services to their users. These services can range from connectionless best-efforts packet delivery to connection-oriented guaranteed delivery. In some networks, connectionless service is provided in one layer and connection-oriented service is provided in the layer above it.

Well-known networks include the Internet, the 3G mobile telephone network, and 802.11 LANs. The Internet evolved from the ARPANET, to which other networks were added to form an internetwork. The present-day Internet is actually a collection of many thousands of networks that use the TCP/IP protocol stack. The 3G mobile telephone network provides wireless and mobile access to the Internet at speeds of multiple Mbps, and, of course, carries voice calls as well. Wireless LANs based on the IEEE 802.11 standard are deployed in many homes and cafes and can provide connectivity at rates in excess of 100 Mbps. New kinds of networks are emerging too, such as embedded sensor networks and networks based on RFID technology.

Enabling multiple computers to talk to each other requires a large amount of standardization, both in the hardware and software. Organizations such as ITU-T, ISO, IEEE, and IAB manage different parts of the standardization process.

PROBLEMS

1. Imagine that you have trained your St. Bernard, Bernie, to carry a box of three 8-mm tapes instead of a flask of brandy. (When your disk fills up, you consider that an emergency.) These tapes each contain 7 gigabytes. The dog can travel to your side, wherever you may be, at 18 km/hour. For what range of distances does Bernie have a higher data rate than a transmission line whose data rate (excluding overhead) is 150 Mbps? How does your answer change if (i) Bernie's speed is doubled; (ii) each tape capacity is doubled; (iii) the data rate of the transmission line is doubled.

2. An alternative to a LAN is simply a big timesharing system with terminals for all users. Give two advantages of a client-server system using a LAN.

3. The performance of a client-server system is strongly influenced by two major network characteristics: the bandwidth of the network (that is, how many bits/sec it can transport) and the latency (that is, how many seconds it takes for the first bit to get from the client to the server). Give an example of a network that exhibits high bandwidth but also high latency. Then give an example of one that has both low bandwidth and low latency.

4. Besides bandwidth and latency, what other parameter is needed to give a good characterization of the quality of service offered by a network used for (i) digitized voice traffic? (ii) video traffic? (iii) financial transaction traffic?

5. A factor in the delay of a store-and-forward packet-switching system is how long it takes to store and forward a packet through a switch. If switching time is 10 μsec, is this likely to be a major factor in the response of a client-server system where the client is in New York and the server is in California? Assume the propagation speed in copper and fiber to be 2/3 the speed of light in vacuum.

6. A client-server system uses a satellite network, with the satellite at a height of 40,000 km. What is the best-case delay in response to a request?

7. In the future, when everyone has a home terminal connected to a computer network, instant public referendums on important pending legislation will become possible. Ultimately, existing legislatures could be eliminated, to let the will of the people be expressed directly. The positive aspects of such a direct democracy are fairly obvious; discuss some of the negative aspects.

8. Five routers are to be connected in a point-to-point subnet. Between each pair of routers, the designers may put a high-speed line, a medium-speed line, a low-speed line, or no line. If it takes 100 ms of computer time to generate and inspect each topology, how long will it take to inspect all of them?

9. A disadvantage of a broadcast subnet is the capacity wasted when multiple hosts attempt to access the channel at the same time. As a simplistic example, suppose that time is divided into discrete slots, with each of the n hosts attempting to use the channel with probability p during each slot. What fraction of the slots will be wasted due to collisions?

10. What are two reasons for using layered protocols? What is one possible disadvantage of using layered protocols?

11. The president of the Specialty Paint Corp. gets the idea to work with a local beer brewer to produce an invisible beer can (as an anti-litter measure). The president tells her legal department to look into it, and they in turn ask engineering for help. As a result, the chief engineer calls his counterpart at the brewery to discuss the technical aspects of the project. The engineers then report back to their respective legal departments, which then confer by telephone to arrange the legal aspects. Finally, the two corporate presidents discuss the financial side of the deal. What principle of a multilayer protocol in the sense of the OSI model does this communication mechanism violate?

12. Two networks each provide reliable connection-oriented service. One of them offers a reliable byte stream and the other offers a reliable message stream. Are these identical? If so, why is the distinction made? If not, give an example of how they differ.

13. What does "negotiation" mean when discussing network protocols? Give an example.

14. In Fig. 1-19, a service is shown. Are any other services implicit in this figure? If so, where? If not, why not?

15. In some networks, the data link layer handles transmission errors by requesting that damaged frames be retransmitted. If the probability of a frame's being damaged is p, what is the mean number of transmissions required to send a frame? Assume that acknowledgements are never lost.

16. A system has an n-layer protocol hierarchy. Applications generate messages of length M bytes. At each of the layers, an h-byte header is added. What fraction of the network bandwidth is filled with headers?

17. What is the main difference between TCP and UDP?

18. The subnet of Fig. 1-25(b) was designed to withstand a nuclear war. How many bombs would it take to partition the nodes into two disconnected sets? Assume that any bomb wipes out a node and all of the links connected to it.

19. The Internet is roughly doubling in size every 18 months. Although no one really knows for sure, one estimate put the number of hosts on it at 600 million in 2009. Use these data to compute the expected number of Internet hosts in the year 2018. Do you believe this? Explain why or why not.

20. When a file is transferred between two computers, two acknowledgement strategies are possible. In the first one, the file is chopped up into packets, which are individually acknowledged by the receiver, but the file transfer as a whole is not acknowledged. In the second one, the packets are not acknowledged individually, but the entire file is acknowledged when it arrives. Discuss these two approaches.

21. Mobile phone network operators need to know where their subscribers' mobile phones (hence their users) are located. Explain why this is bad for users. Now give reasons why this is good for users.

22. How long was a bit in the original 802.3 standard in meters? Use a transmission speed of 10 Mbps and assume the propagation speed in coax is 2/3 the speed of light in vacuum.

23. An image is 1600×1200 pixels with 3 bytes/pixel. Assume the image is uncompressed. How long does it take to transmit it over a 56-kbps modem channel? Over a 1-Mbps cable modem? Over a 10-Mbps Ethernet? Over 100-Mbps Ethernet? Over gigabit Ethernet?

24. Ethernet and wireless networks have some similarities and some differences. One property of Ethernet is that only one frame at a time can be transmitted on an Ethernet. Does 802.11 share this property with Ethernet? Discuss your answer.

25. List two advantages and two disadvantages of having international standards for network protocols.

26. When a system has a permanent part and a removable part (such as a CD-ROM drive and the CD-ROM), it is important that the system be standardized, so that different companies can make both the permanent and removable parts and everything still works together. Give three examples outside the computer industry where such international standards exist. Now give three areas outside the computer industry where they do not exist.

27. Suppose the algorithms used to implement the operations at layer *k* is changed. How does this impact operations at layers $k - 1$ and $k + 1$?

28. Suppose there is a change in the service (set of operations) provided by layer k. How does this impact services at layers k-1 and k+1?

29. Provide a list of reasons for why the response time of a client may be larger than the best-case delay.

30. What are the disadvantages of using small, fixed-length cells in ATM?

31. Make a list of activities that you do every day in which computer networks are used. How would your life be altered if these networks were suddenly switched off?

32. Find out what networks are used at your school or place of work. Describe the network types, topologies, and switching methods used there.

33. The *ping* program allows you to send a test packet to a given location and see how long it takes to get there and back. Try using *ping* to see how long it takes to get from your location to several known locations. From these data, plot the one-way transit time over the Internet as a function of distance. It is best to use universities since the location of their servers is known very accurately. For example, *berkeley.edu* is in Berkeley, California; *mit.edu* is in Cambridge, Massachusetts; *vu.nl* is in Amsterdam; The Netherlands; *www.usyd.edu.au* is in Sydney, Australia; and *www.uct.ac.za* is in Cape Town, South Africa.

34. Go to IETF's Web site, *www.ietf.org*, to see what they are doing. Pick a project you like and write a half-page report on the problem and the proposed solution.

35. The Internet is made up of a large number of networks. Their arrangement determines the topology of the Internet. A considerable amount of information about the Internet topology is available on line. Use a search engine to find out more about the Internet topology and write a short report summarizing your findings.

36. Search the Internet to find out some of the important peering points used for routing packets in the Internet at present.

37. Write a program that implements message flow from the top layer to the bottom layer of the 7-layer protocol model. Your program should include a separate protocol function for each layer. Protocol headers are sequence up to 64 characters. Each protocol function has two parameters: a message passed from the higher layer protocol (a char buffer) and the size of the message. This function attaches its header in front of the message, prints the new message on the standard output, and then invokes the protocol function of the lower-layer protocol. Program input is an application message (a sequence of 80 characters or less).

2

THE PHYSICAL LAYER

In this chapter we will look at the lowest layer in our protocol model, the physical layer. It defines the electrical, timing and other interfaces by which bits are sent as signals over channels. The physical layer is the foundation on which the network is built. The properties of different kinds of physical channels determine the performance (e.g., throughput, latency, and error rate) so it is a good place to start our journey into networkland.

We will begin with a theoretical analysis of data transmission, only to discover that Mother (Parent?) Nature puts some limits on what can be sent over a channel. Then we will cover three kinds of transmission media: guided (copper wire and fiber optics), wireless (terrestrial radio), and satellite. Each of these technologies has different properties that affect the design and performance of the networks that use them. This material will provide background information on the key transmission technologies used in modern networks.

Next comes digital modulation, which is all about how analog signals are converted into digital bits and back again. After that we will look at multiplexing schemes, exploring how multiple conversations can be put on the same transmission medium at the same time without interfering with one another.

Finally, we will look at three examples of communication systems used in practice for wide area computer networks: the (fixed) telephone system, the mobile phone system, and the cable television system. Each of these is important in practice, so we will devote a fair amount of space to each one.

2.1 THE THEORETICAL BASIS FOR DATA COMMUNICATION

Information can be transmitted on wires by varying some physical property such as voltage or current. By representing the value of this voltage or current as a single-valued function of time, $f(t)$, we can model the behavior of the signal and analyze it mathematically. This analysis is the subject of the following sections.

2.1.1 Fourier Analysis

In the early 19th century, the French mathematician Jean-Baptiste Fourier proved that any reasonably behaved periodic function, $g(t)$ with period T, can be constructed as the sum of a (possibly infinite) number of sines and cosines:

$$g(t) = \frac{1}{2}c + \sum_{n=1}^{\infty} a_n \sin(2\pi nft) + \sum_{n=1}^{\infty} b_n \cos(2\pi nft) \tag{2-1}$$

where $f = 1/T$ is the fundamental frequency, a_n and b_n are the sine and cosine amplitudes of the nth **harmonics** (terms), and c is a constant. Such a decomposition is called a **Fourier series**. From the Fourier series, the function can be reconstructed. That is, if the period, T, is known and the amplitudes are given, the original function of time can be found by performing the sums of Eq. (2-1).

A data signal that has a finite duration, which all of them do, can be handled by just imagining that it repeats the entire pattern over and over forever (i.e., the interval from T to $2T$ is the same as from 0 to T, etc.).

The a_n amplitudes can be computed for any given $g(t)$ by multiplying both sides of Eq. (2-1) by $\sin(2\pi kft)$ and then integrating from 0 to T. Since

$$\int_0^T \sin(2\pi kft)\sin(2\pi nft)\,dt = \begin{cases} 0 \text{ for } k \neq n \\ T/2 \text{ for } k = n \end{cases}$$

only one term of the summation survives: a_n. The b_n summation vanishes completely. Similarly, by multiplying Eq. (2-1) by $\cos(2\pi kft)$ and integrating between 0 and T, we can derive b_n. By just integrating both sides of the equation as it stands, we can find c. The results of performing these operations are as follows:

$$a_n = \frac{2}{T}\int_0^T g(t)\sin(2\pi nft)\,dt \qquad b_n = \frac{2}{T}\int_0^T g(t)\cos(2\pi nft)\,dt \qquad c = \frac{2}{T}\int_0^T g(t)\,dt$$

2.1.2 Bandwidth-Limited Signals

The relevance of all of this to data communication is that real channels affect different frequency signals differently. Let us consider a specific example: the transmission of the ASCII character "b" encoded in an 8-bit byte. The bit pattern that is to be transmitted is 01100010. The left-hand part of Fig. 2-1(a) shows the voltage output by the transmitting computer. The Fourier analysis of this signal yields the coefficients:

$$a_n = \frac{1}{\pi n}[\cos(\pi n/4) - \cos(3\pi n/4) + \cos(6\pi n/4) - \cos(7\pi n/4)]$$

$$b_n = \frac{1}{\pi n}[\sin(3\pi n/4) - \sin(\pi n/4) + \sin(7\pi n/4) - \sin(6\pi n/4)]$$

$$c = 3/4$$

The root-mean-square amplitudes, $\sqrt{a_n^2 + b_n^2}$, for the first few terms are shown on the right-hand side of Fig. 2-1(a). These values are of interest because their squares are proportional to the energy transmitted at the corresponding frequency.

No transmission facility can transmit signals without losing some power in the process. If all the Fourier components were equally diminished, the resulting signal would be reduced in amplitude but not distorted [i.e., it would have the same nice squared-off shape as Fig. 2-1(a)]. Unfortunately, all transmission facilities diminish different Fourier components by different amounts, thus introducing distortion. Usually, for a wire, the amplitudes are transmitted mostly undiminished from 0 up to some frequency f_c [measured in cycles/sec or Hertz (Hz)], with all frequencies above this cutoff frequency attenuated. The width of the frequency range transmitted without being strongly attenuated is called the **bandwidth**. In practice, the cutoff is not really sharp, so often the quoted bandwidth is from 0 to the frequency at which the received power has fallen by half.

The bandwidth is a physical property of the transmission medium that depends on, for example, the construction, thickness, and length of a wire or fiber. Filters are often used to further limit the bandwidth of a signal. 802.11 wireless channels are allowed to use up to roughly 20 MHz, for example, so 802.11 radios filter the signal bandwidth to this size. As another example, traditional (analog) television channels occupy 6 MHz each, on a wire or over the air. This filtering lets more signals share a given region of spectrum, which improves the overall efficiency of the system. It means that the frequency range for some signals will not start at zero, but this does not matter. The bandwidth is still the width of the band of frequencies that are passed, and the information that can be carried depends only on this width and not on the starting and ending frequencies. Signals that run from 0 up to a maximum frequency are called **baseband** signals. Signals that are shifted to occupy a higher range of frequencies, as is the case for all wireless transmissions, are called **passband** signals.

Now let us consider how the signal of Fig. 2-1(a) would look if the bandwidth were so low that only the lowest frequencies were transmitted [i.e., if the function were being approximated by the first few terms of Eq. (2-1)]. Figure 2-1(b) shows the signal that results from a channel that allows only the first harmonic

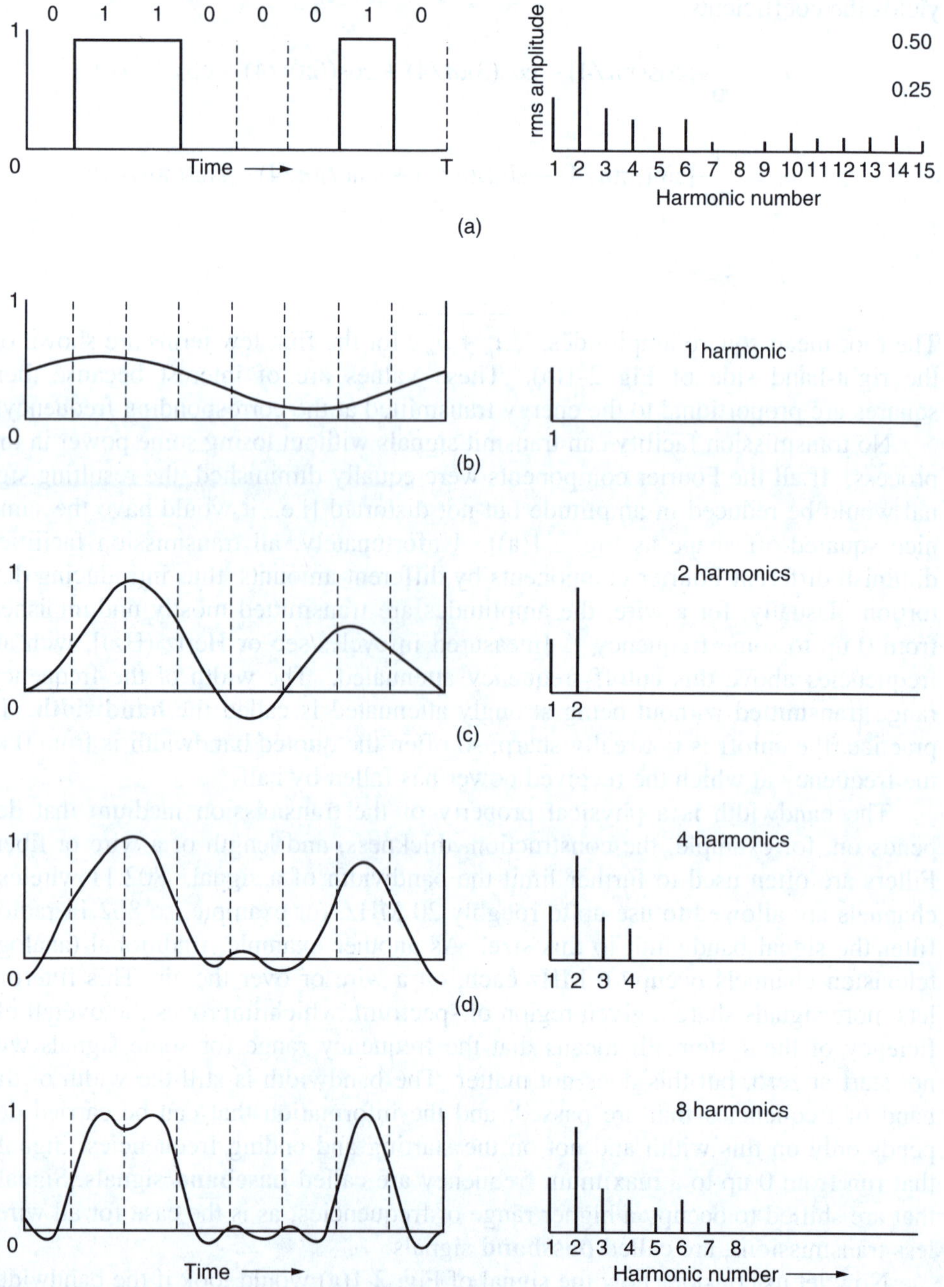

Figure 2-1. (a) A binary signal and its root-mean-square Fourier amplitudes. (b)–(e) Successive approximations to the original signal.

(the fundamental, f) to pass through. Similarly, Fig. 2-1(c)–(e) show the spectra and reconstructed functions for higher-bandwidth channels. For digital transmission, the goal is to receive a signal with just enough fidelity to reconstruct the sequence of bits that was sent. We can already do this easily in Fig. 2-1(e), so it is wasteful to use more harmonics to receive a more accurate replica.

Given a bit rate of b bits/sec, the time required to send the 8 bits in our example 1 bit at a time is $8/b$ sec, so the frequency of the first harmonic of this signal is $b/8$ Hz. An ordinary telephone line, often called a **voice-grade line**, has an artificially introduced cutoff frequency just above 3000 Hz. The presence of this restriction means that the number of the highest harmonic passed through is roughly $3000/(b/8)$, or $24{,}000/b$ (the cutoff is not sharp).

For some data rates, the numbers work out as shown in Fig. 2-2. From these numbers, it is clear that trying to send at 9600 bps over a voice-grade telephone line will transform Fig. 2-1(a) into something looking like Fig. 2-1(c), making accurate reception of the original binary bit stream tricky. It should be obvious that at data rates much higher than 38.4 kbps, there is no hope at all for *binary* signals, even if the transmission facility is completely noiseless. In other words, limiting the bandwidth limits the data rate, even for perfect channels. However, coding schemes that make use of several voltage levels do exist and can achieve higher data rates. We will discuss these later in this chapter.

Bps	T (msec)	First harmonic (Hz)	# Harmonics sent
300	26.67	37.5	80
600	13.33	75	40
1200	6.67	150	20
2400	3.33	300	10
4800	1.67	600	5
9600	0.83	1200	2
19200	0.42	2400	1
38400	0.21	4800	0

Figure 2-2. Relation between data rate and harmonics for our example.

There is much confusion about bandwidth because it means different things to electrical engineers and to computer scientists. To electrical engineers, (analog) bandwidth is (as we have described above) a quantity measured in Hz. To computer scientists, (digital) bandwidth is the maximum data rate of a channel, a quantity measured in bits/sec. That data rate is the end result of using the analog bandwidth of a physical channel for digital transmission, and the two are related, as we discuss next. In this book, it will be clear from the context whether we mean analog bandwidth (Hz) or digital bandwidth (bits/sec).

2.1.3 The Maximum Data Rate of a Channel

As early as 1924, an AT&T engineer, Henry Nyquist, realized that even a perfect channel has a finite transmission capacity. He derived an equation expressing the maximum data rate for a finite-bandwidth noiseless channel. In 1948, Claude Shannon carried Nyquist's work further and extended it to the case of a channel subject to random (that is, thermodynamic) noise (Shannon, 1948). This paper is the most important paper in all of information theory. We will just briefly summarize their now classical results here.

Nyquist proved that if an arbitrary signal has been run through a low-pass filter of bandwidth B, the filtered signal can be completely reconstructed by making only $2B$ (exact) samples per second. Sampling the line faster than $2B$ times per second is pointless because the higher-frequency components that such sampling could recover have already been filtered out. If the signal consists of V discrete levels, Nyquist's theorem states:

$$\text{maximum data rate} = 2B \log_2 V \text{ bits/sec} \qquad (2\text{-}2)$$

For example, a noiseless 3-kHz channel cannot transmit binary (i.e., two-level) signals at a rate exceeding 6000 bps.

So far we have considered only noiseless channels. If random noise is present, the situation deteriorates rapidly. And there is always random (thermal) noise present due to the motion of the molecules in the system. The amount of thermal noise present is measured by the ratio of the signal power to the noise power, called the **SNR** (**Signal-to-Noise Ratio**). If we denote the signal power by S and the noise power by N, the signal-to-noise ratio is S/N. Usually, the ratio is expressed on a log scale as the quantity $10 \log_{10} S/N$ because it can vary over a tremendous range. The units of this log scale are called **decibels** (**dB**), with "deci" meaning 10 and "bel" chosen to honor Alexander Graham Bell, who invented the telephone. An S/N ratio of 10 is 10 dB, a ratio of 100 is 20 dB, a ratio of 1000 is 30 dB, and so on. The manufacturers of stereo amplifiers often characterize the bandwidth (frequency range) over which their products are linear by giving the 3-dB frequency on each end. These are the points at which the amplification factor has been approximately halved (because $10 \log_{10} 0.5 \approx -3$).

Shannon's major result is that the maximum data rate or **capacity** of a noisy channel whose bandwidth is B Hz and whose signal-to-noise ratio is S/N, is given by:

$$\text{maximum number of bits/sec} = B \log_2 (1 + S/N) \qquad (2\text{-}3)$$

This tells us the best capacities that real channels can have. For example, ADSL (Asymmetric Digital Subscriber Line), which provides Internet access over normal telephone lines, uses a bandwidth of around 1 MHz. The SNR depends strongly on the distance of the home from the telephone exchange, and an SNR of around 40 dB for short lines of 1 to 2 km is very good. With these characteristics, the channel can never transmit much more than 13 Mbps, no matter how many or how few signal levels are used and no matter how often or how infrequently samples are taken. In practice, ADSL is specified up to 12 Mbps, though users often see lower rates. This data rate is actually very good, with over 60 years of communications techniques having greatly reduced the gap between the Shannon capacity and the capacity of real systems.

Shannon's result was derived from information-theory arguments and applies to any channel subject to thermal noise. Counterexamples should be treated in the same category as perpetual motion machines. For ADSL to exceed 13 Mbps, it must either improve the SNR (for example by inserting digital repeaters in the lines closer to the customers) or use more bandwidth, as is done with the evolution to ASDL2+.

2.2 GUIDED TRANSMISSION MEDIA

The purpose of the physical layer is to transport bits from one machine to another. Various physical media can be used for the actual transmission. Each one has its own niche in terms of bandwidth, delay, cost, and ease of installation and maintenance. Media are roughly grouped into guided media, such as copper wire and fiber optics, and unguided media, such as terrestrial wireless, satellite, and lasers through the air. We will look at guided media in this section, and unguided media in the next sections.

2.2.1 Magnetic Media

One of the most common ways to transport data from one computer to another is to write them onto magnetic tape or removable media (e.g., recordable DVDs), physically transport the tape or disks to the destination machine, and read them back in again. Although this method is not as sophisticated as using a geosynchronous communication satellite, it is often more cost effective, especially for applications in which high bandwidth or cost per bit transported is the key factor.

A simple calculation will make this point clear. An industry-standard Ultrium tape can hold 800 gigabytes. A box $60 \times 60 \times 60$ cm can hold about 1000 of these tapes, for a total capacity of 800 terabytes, or 6400 terabits (6.4 petabits). A box of tapes can be delivered anywhere in the United States in 24 hours by Federal Express and other companies. The effective bandwidth of this transmission is 6400 terabits/86,400 sec, or a bit over 70 Gbps. If the destination is only an hour away by road, the bandwidth is increased to over 1700 Gbps. No computer network can even approach this. Of course, networks are getting faster, but tape densities are increasing, too.

If we now look at cost, we get a similar picture. The cost of an Ultrium tape is around $40 when bought in bulk. A tape can be reused at least 10 times, so the tape cost is maybe $4000 per box per usage. Add to this another $1000 for shipping (probably much less), and we have a cost of roughly $5000 to ship 800 TB. This amounts to shipping a gigabyte for a little over half a cent. No network can beat that. The moral of the story is:

Never underestimate the bandwidth of a station wagon full of tapes hurtling down the highway.

2.2.2 Twisted Pairs

Although the bandwidth characteristics of magnetic tape are excellent, the delay characteristics are poor. Transmission time is measured in minutes or hours, not milliseconds. For many applications an online connection is needed. One of the oldest and still most common transmission media is **twisted pair**. A twisted pair consists of two insulated copper wires, typically about 1 mm thick. The wires are twisted together in a helical form, just like a DNA molecule. Twisting is done because two parallel wires constitute a fine antenna. When the wires are twisted, the waves from different twists cancel out, so the wire radiates less effectively. A signal is usually carried as the difference in voltage between the two wires in the pair. This provides better immunity to external noise because the noise tends to affect both wires the same, leaving the differential unchanged.

The most common application of the twisted pair is the telephone system. Nearly all telephones are connected to the telephone company (telco) office by a twisted pair. Both telephone calls and ADSL Internet access run over these lines. Twisted pairs can run several kilometers without amplification, but for longer distances the signal becomes too attenuated and repeaters are needed. When many twisted pairs run in parallel for a substantial distance, such as all the wires coming from an apartment building to the telephone company office, they are bundled together and encased in a protective sheath. The pairs in these bundles would interfere with one another if it were not for the twisting. In parts of the world where telephone lines run on poles above ground, it is common to see bundles several centimeters in diameter.

Twisted pairs can be used for transmitting either analog or digital information. The bandwidth depends on the thickness of the wire and the distance traveled, but several megabits/sec can be achieved for a few kilometers in many cases. Due to their adequate performance and low cost, twisted pairs are widely used and are likely to remain so for years to come.

Twisted-pair cabling comes in several varieties. The garden variety deployed in many office buildings is called **Category 5** cabling, or “Cat 5.” A category 5 twisted pair consists of two insulated wires gently twisted together. Four such pairs are typically grouped in a plastic sheath to protect the wires and keep them together. This arrangement is shown in Fig. 2-3.

Different LAN standards may use the twisted pairs differently. For example, 100-Mbps Ethernet uses two (out of the four) pairs, one pair for each direction.

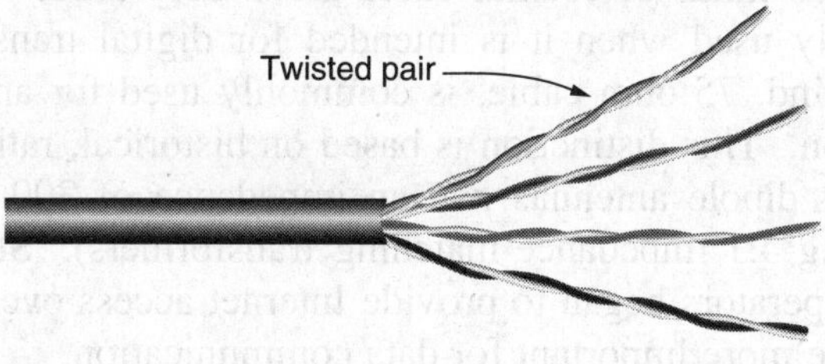

Figure 2-3. Category 5 UTP cable with four twisted pairs.

To reach higher speeds, 1-Gbps Ethernet uses all four pairs in both directions simultaneously; this requires the receiver to factor out the signal that is transmitted locally.

Some general terminology is now in order. Links that can be used in both directions at the same time, like a two-lane road, are called **full-duplex** links. In contrast, links that can be used in either direction, but only one way at a time, like a single-track railroad line. are called **half-duplex** links. A third category consists of links that allow traffic in only one direction, like a one-way street. They are called **simplex** links.

Returning to twisted pair, Cat 5 replaced earlier **Category 3** cables with a similar cable that uses the same connector, but has more twists per meter. More twists result in less crosstalk and a better-quality signal over longer distances, making the cables more suitable for high-speed computer communication, especially 100-Mbps and 1-Gbps Ethernet LANs.

New wiring is more likely to be **Category 6** or even **Category 7**. These categories has more stringent specifications to handle signals with greater bandwidths. Some cables in Category 6 and above are rated for signals of 500 MHz and can support the 10-Gbps links that will soon be deployed.

Through Category 6, these wiring types are referred to as **UTP** (**Unshielded Twisted Pair**) as they consist simply of wires and insulators. In contrast to these, Category 7 cables have shielding on the individual twisted pairs, as well as around the entire cable (but inside the plastic protective sheath). Shielding reduces the susceptibility to external interference and crosstalk with other nearby cables to meet demanding performance specifications. The cables are reminiscent of the high-quality, but bulky and expensive shielded twisted pair cables that IBM introduced in the early 1980s, but which did not prove popular outside of IBM installations. Evidently, it is time to try again.

2.2.3 Coaxial Cable

Another common transmission medium is the **coaxial cable** (known to its many friends as just “coax” and pronounced “co-ax”). It has better shielding and greater bandwidth than unshielded twisted pairs, so it can span longer distances at higher speeds. Two kinds of coaxial cable are widely used. One kind, 50-ohm cable, is commonly used when it is intended for digital transmission from the start. The other kind, 75-ohm cable, is commonly used for analog transmission and cable television. This distinction is based on historical, rather than technical, factors (e.g., early dipole antennas had an impedance of 300 ohms, and it was easy to use existing 4:1 impedance-matching transformers). Starting in the mid-1990s, cable TV operators began to provide Internet access over cable, which has made 75-ohm cable more important for data communication.

A coaxial cable consists of a stiff copper wire as the core, surrounded by an insulating material. The insulator is encased by a cylindrical conductor, often as a closely woven braided mesh. The outer conductor is covered in a protective plastic sheath. A cutaway view of a coaxial cable is shown in Fig. 2-4.

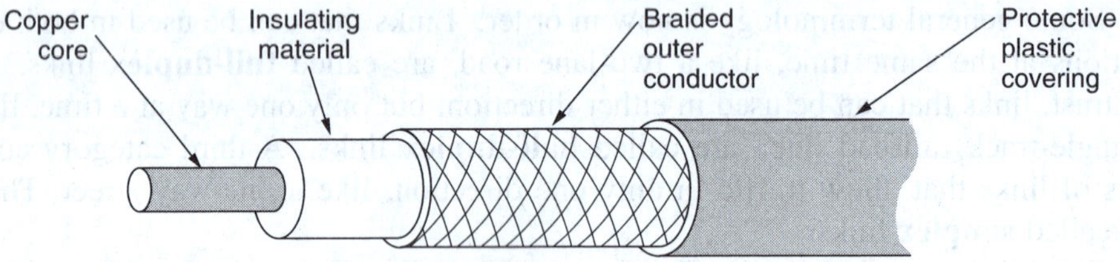

Figure 2-4. A coaxial cable.

The construction and shielding of the coaxial cable give it a good combination of high bandwidth and excellent noise immunity. The bandwidth possible depends on the cable quality and length. Modern cables have a bandwidth of up to a few GHz. Coaxial cables used to be widely used within the telephone system for long-distance lines but have now largely been replaced by fiber optics on long-haul routes. Coax is still widely used for cable television and metropolitan area networks, however.

2.2.4 Power Lines

The telephone and cable television networks are not the only sources of wiring that can be reused for data communication. There is a yet more common kind of wiring: electrical power lines. Power lines deliver electrical power to houses, and electrical wiring within houses distributes the power to electrical outlets.

The use of power lines for data communication is an old idea. Power lines have been used by electricity companies for low-rate communication such as remote metering for many years, as well in the home to control devices (e.g., the X10 standard). In recent years there has been renewed interest in high-rate communication over these lines, both inside the home as a LAN and outside the home for broadband Internet access. We will concentrate on the most common scenario: using electrical wires inside the home.

The convenience of using power lines for networking should be clear. Simply plug a TV and a receiver into the wall, which you must do anyway because they need power, and they can send and receive movies over the electrical wiring. This configuration is shown in Fig. 2-5. There is no other plug or radio. The data signal is superimposed on the low-frequency power signal (on the active or "hot" wire) as both signals use the wiring at the same time.

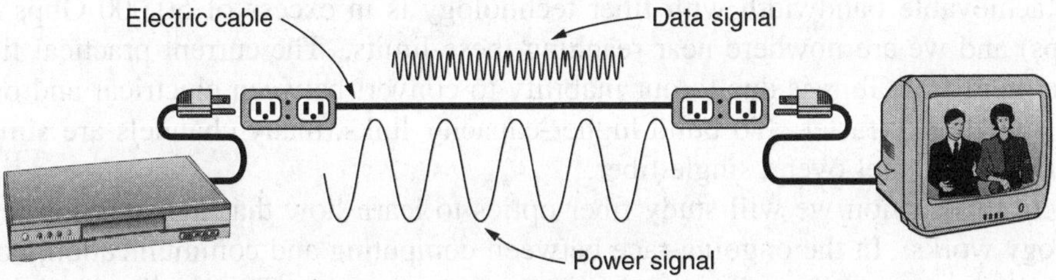

Figure 2-5. A network that uses household electrical wiring.

The difficulty with using household electrical wiring for a network is that it was designed to distribute power signals. This task is quite different than distributing data signals, at which household wiring does a horrible job. Electrical signals are sent at 50–60 Hz and the wiring attenuates the much higher frequency (MHz) signals needed for high-rate data communication. The electrical properties of the wiring vary from one house to the next and change as appliances are turned on and off, which causes data signals to bounce around the wiring. Transient currents when appliances switch on and off create electrical noise over a wide range of frequencies. And without the careful twisting of twisted pairs, electrical wiring acts as a fine antenna, picking up external signals and radiating signals of its own. This behavior means that to meet regulatory requirements, the data signal must exclude licensed frequencies such as the amateur radio bands.

Despite these difficulties, it is practical to send at least 100 Mbps over typical household electrical wiring by using communication schemes that resist impaired frequencies and bursts of errors. Many products use various proprietary standards for power-line networking, so international standards are actively under development.

2.2.5 Fiber Optics

Many people in the computer industry take enormous pride in how fast computer technology is improving as it follows Moore's law, which predicts a doubling of the number of transistors per chip roughly every two years (Schaller,

1997). The original (1981) IBM PC ran at a clock speed of 4.77 MHz. Twenty-eight years later, PCs could run a four-core CPU at 3 GHz. This increase is a gain of a factor of around 2500, or 16 per decade. Impressive.

In the same period, wide area communication links went from 45 Mbps (a T3 line in the telephone system) to 100 Gbps (a modern long distance line). This gain is similarly impressive, more than a factor of 2000 and close to 16 per decade, while at the same time the error rate went from 10^{-5} per bit to almost zero. Furthermore, single CPUs are beginning to approach physical limits, which is why it is now the number of CPUs that is being increased per chip. In contrast, the achievable bandwidth with fiber technology is in excess of 50,000 Gbps (50 Tbps) and we are nowhere near reaching these limits. The current practical limit of around 100 Gbps is due to our inability to convert between electrical and optical signals any faster. To build higher-capacity links, many channels are simply carried in parallel over a single fiber.

In this section we will study fiber optics to learn how that transmission technology works. In the ongoing race between computing and communication, communication may yet win because of fiber optic networks. The implication of this would be essentially infinite bandwidth and a new conventional wisdom that computers are hopelessly slow so that networks should try to avoid computation at all costs, no matter how much bandwidth that wastes. This change will take a while to sink in to a generation of computer scientists and engineers taught to think in terms of the low Shannon limits imposed by copper.

Of course, this scenario does not tell the whole story because it does not include cost. The cost to install fiber over the last mile to reach consumers and bypass the low bandwidth of wires and limited availability of spectrum is tremendous. It also costs more energy to move bits than to compute. We may always have islands of inequities where either computation or communication is essentially free. For example, at the edge of the Internet we throw computation and storage at the problem of compressing and caching content, all to make better use of Internet access links. Within the Internet, we may do the reverse, with companies such as Google moving huge amounts of data across the network to where it is cheaper to store or compute on it.

Fiber optics are used for long-haul transmission in network backbones, high-speed LANs (although so far, copper has always managed catch up eventually), and high-speed Internet access such as **FttH (Fiber to the Home)**. An optical transmission system has three key components: the light source, the transmission medium, and the detector. Conventionally, a pulse of light indicates a 1 bit and the absence of light indicates a 0 bit. The transmission medium is an ultra-thin fiber of glass. The detector generates an electrical pulse when light falls on it. By attaching a light source to one end of an optical fiber and a detector to the other, we have a unidirectional data transmission system that accepts an electrical signal, converts and transmits it by light pulses, and then reconverts the output to an electrical signal at the receiving end.

This transmission system would leak light and be useless in practice were it not for an interesting principle of physics. When a light ray passes from one medium to another—for example, from fused silica to air—the ray is refracted (bent) at the silica/air boundary, as shown in Fig. 2-6(a). Here we see a light ray incident on the boundary at an angle α_1 emerging at an angle β_1. The amount of refraction depends on the properties of the two media (in particular, their indices of refraction). For angles of incidence above a certain critical value, the light is refracted back into the silica; none of it escapes into the air. Thus, a light ray incident at or above the critical angle is trapped inside the fiber, as shown in Fig. 2-6(b), and can propagate for many kilometers with virtually no loss.

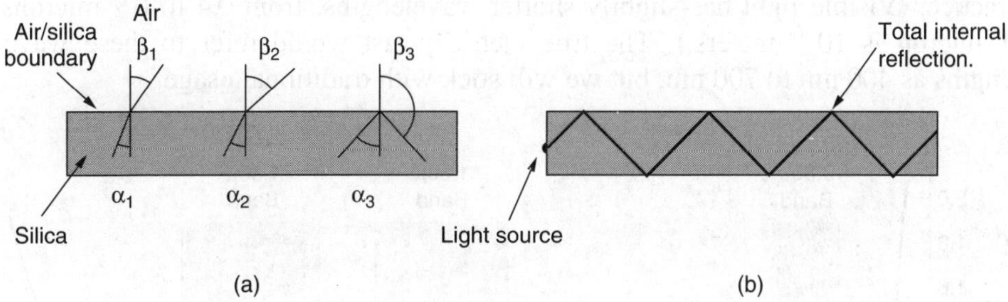

Figure 2-6. (a) Three examples of a light ray from inside a silica fiber impinging on the air/silica boundary at different angles. (b) Light trapped by total internal reflection.

The sketch of Fig. 2-6(b) shows only one trapped ray, but since any light ray incident on the boundary above the critical angle will be reflected internally, many different rays will be bouncing around at different angles. Each ray is said to have a different mode, so a fiber having this property is called a **multimode fiber**.

However, if the fiber's diameter is reduced to a few wavelengths of light the fiber acts like a wave guide and the light can propagate only in a straight line, without bouncing, yielding a **single-mode fiber**. Single-mode fibers are more expensive but are widely used for longer distances. Currently available single-mode fibers can transmit data at 100 Gbps for 100 km without amplification. Even higher data rates have been achieved in the laboratory for shorter distances.

Transmission of Light Through Fiber

Optical fibers are made of glass, which, in turn, is made from sand, an inexpensive raw material available in unlimited amounts. Glassmaking was known to the ancient Egyptians, but their glass had to be no more than 1 mm thick or the light could not shine through. Glass transparent enough to be useful for windows was developed during the Renaissance. The glass used for modern optical fibers is so transparent that if the oceans were full of it instead of water, the seabed would be as visible from the surface as the ground is from an airplane on a clear day.

The attenuation of light through glass depends on the wavelength of the light (as well as on some physical properties of the glass). It is defined as the ratio of input to output signal power. For the kind of glass used in fibers, the attenuation is shown in Fig. 2-7 in units of decibels per linear kilometer of fiber. For example, a factor of two loss of signal power gives an attenuation of $10 \log_{10} 2 = 3$ dB. The figure shows the near-infrared part of the spectrum, which is what is used in practice. Visible light has slightly shorter wavelengths, from 0.4 to 0.7 microns. (1 micron is 10^{-6} meters.) The true metric purist would refer to these wavelengths as 400 nm to 700 nm, but we will stick with traditional usage.

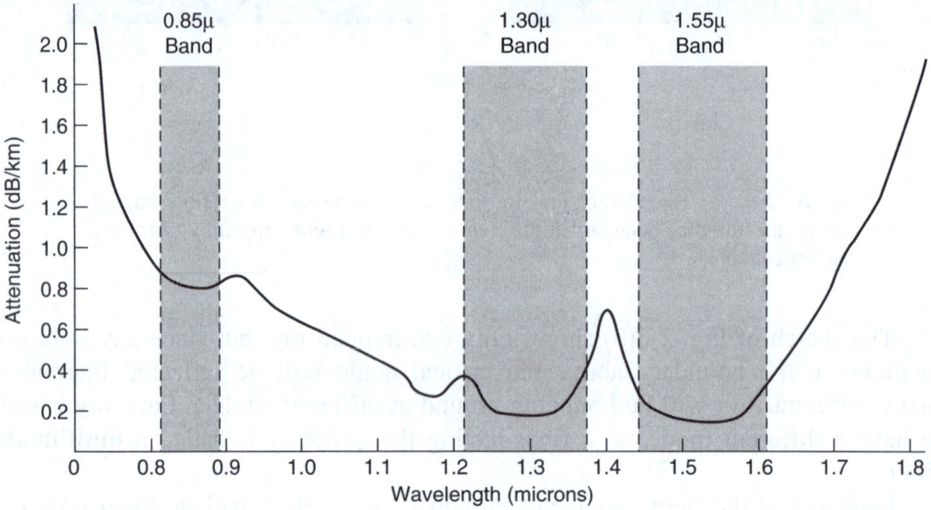

Figure 2-7. Attenuation of light through fiber in the infrared region.

Three wavelength bands are most commonly used at present for optical communication. They are centered at 0.85, 1.30, and 1.55 microns, respectively. All three bands are 25,000 to 30,000 GHz wide. The 0.85-micron band was used first. It has higher attenuation and so is used for shorter distances, but at that wavelength the lasers and electronics could be made from the same material (gallium arsenide). The last two bands have good attenuation properties (less than 5% loss per kilometer). The 1.55-micron band is now widely used with erbium-doped amplifiers that work directly in the optical domain.

Light pulses sent down a fiber spread out in length as they propagate. This spreading is called **chromatic dispersion**. The amount of it is wavelength dependent. One way to keep these spread-out pulses from overlapping is to increase the distance between them, but this can be done only by reducing the signaling rate. Fortunately, it has been discovered that making the pulses in a special shape related to the reciprocal of the hyperbolic cosine causes nearly all the dispersion effects cancel out, so it is possible to send pulses for thousands of kilometers without appreciable shape distortion. These pulses are called **solitons**. A considerable amount of research is going on to take solitons out of the lab and into the field.

Fiber Cables

Fiber optic cables are similar to coax, except without the braid. Figure 2-8(a) shows a single fiber viewed from the side. At the center is the glass core through which the light propagates. In multimode fibers, the core is typically 50 microns in diameter, about the thickness of a human hair. In single-mode fibers, the core is 8 to 10 microns.

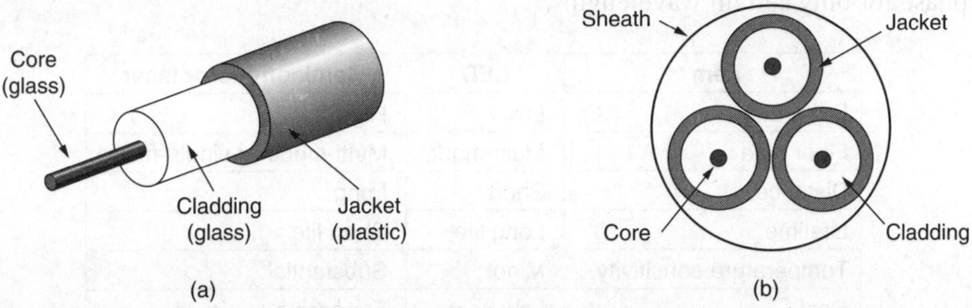

Figure 2-8. (a) Side view of a single fiber. (b) End view of a sheath with three fibers.

The core is surrounded by a glass cladding with a lower index of refraction than the core, to keep all the light in the core. Next comes a thin plastic jacket to protect the cladding. Fibers are typically grouped in bundles, protected by an outer sheath. Figure 2-8(b) shows a sheath with three fibers.

Terrestrial fiber sheaths are normally laid in the ground within a meter of the surface, where they are occasionally subject to attacks by backhoes or gophers. Near the shore, transoceanic fiber sheaths are buried in trenches by a kind of seaplow. In deep water, they just lie on the bottom, where they can be snagged by fishing trawlers or attacked by giant squid.

Fibers can be connected in three different ways. First, they can terminate in connectors and be plugged into fiber sockets. Connectors lose about 10 to 20% of the light, but they make it easy to reconfigure systems.

Second, they can be spliced mechanically. Mechanical splices just lay the two carefully cut ends next to each other in a special sleeve and clamp them in place. Alignment can be improved by passing light through the junction and then making small adjustments to maximize the signal. Mechanical splices take trained personnel about 5 minutes and result in a 10% light loss.

Third, two pieces of fiber can be fused (melted) to form a solid connection. A fusion splice is almost as good as a single drawn fiber, but even here, a small amount of attenuation occurs.

For all three kinds of splices, reflections can occur at the point of the splice, and the reflected energy can interfere with the signal.

Two kinds of light sources are typically used to do the signaling. These are LEDs (Light Emitting Diodes) and semiconductor lasers. They have different properties, as shown in Fig. 2-9. They can be tuned in wavelength by inserting Fabry-Perot or Mach-Zehnder interferometers between the source and the fiber. Fabry-Perot interferometers are simple resonant cavities consisting of two parallel mirrors. The light is incident perpendicular to the mirrors. The length of the cavity selects out those wavelengths that fit inside an integral number of times. Mach-Zehnder interferometers separate the light into two beams. The two beams travel slightly different distances. They are recombined at the end and are in phase for only certain wavelengths.

Item	LED	Semiconductor laser
Data rate	Low	High
Fiber type	Multi-mode	Multi-mode or single-mode
Distance	Short	Long
Lifetime	Long life	Short life
Temperature sensitivity	Minor	Substantial
Cost	Low cost	Expensive

Figure 2-9. A comparison of semiconductor diodes and LEDs as light sources.

The receiving end of an optical fiber consists of a photodiode, which gives off an electrical pulse when struck by light. The response time of photodiodes, which convert the signal from the optical to the electrical domain, limits data rates to about 100 Gbps. Thermal noise is also an issue, so a pulse of light must carry enough energy to be detected. By making the pulses powerful enough, the error rate can be made arbitrarily small.

Comparison of Fiber Optics and Copper Wire

It is instructive to compare fiber to copper. Fiber has many advantages. To start with, it can handle much higher bandwidths than copper. This alone would require its use in high-end networks. Due to the low attenuation, repeaters are needed only about every 50 km on long lines, versus about every 5 km for copper, resulting in a big cost saving. Fiber also has the advantage of not being affected by power surges, electromagnetic interference, or power failures. Nor is it affected by corrosive chemicals in the air, important for harsh factory environments.

Oddly enough, telephone companies like fiber for a different reason: it is thin and lightweight. Many existing cable ducts are completely full, so there is no room to add new capacity. Removing all the copper and replacing it with fiber empties the ducts, and the copper has excellent resale value to copper refiners who see it as very high-grade ore. Also, fiber is much lighter than copper. One thousand twisted pairs 1 km long weigh 8000 kg. Two fibers have more capacity and weigh only 100 kg, which reduces the need for expensive mechanical support systems that must be maintained. For new routes, fiber wins hands down due to its much lower installation cost. Finally, fibers do not leak light and are difficult to tap. These properties give fiber good security against potential wiretappers.

On the downside, fiber is a less familiar technology requiring skills not all engineers have, and fibers can be damaged easily by being bent too much. Since optical transmission is inherently unidirectional, two-way communication requires either two fibers or two frequency bands on one fiber. Finally, fiber interfaces cost more than electrical interfaces. Nevertheless, the future of all fixed data communication over more than short distances is clearly with fiber. For a discussion of all aspects of fiber optics and their networks, see Hecht (2005).

2.3 WIRELESS TRANSMISSION

Our age has given rise to information junkies: people who need to be online all the time. For these mobile users, twisted pair, coax, and fiber optics are of no use. They need to get their "hits" of data for their laptop, notebook, shirt pocket, palmtop, or wristwatch computers without being tethered to the terrestrial communication infrastructure. For these users, wireless communication is the answer.

In the following sections, we will look at wireless communication in general. It has many other important applications besides providing connectivity to users who want to surf the Web from the beach. Wireless has advantages for even fixed devices in some circumstances. For example, if running a fiber to a building is difficult due to the terrain (mountains, jungles, swamps, etc.), wireless may be better. It is noteworthy that modern wireless digital communication began in the Hawaiian Islands, where large chunks of Pacific Ocean separated the users from their computer center and the telephone system was inadequate.

2.3.1 The Electromagnetic Spectrum

When electrons move, they create electromagnetic waves that can propagate through space (even in a vacuum). These waves were predicted by the British physicist James Clerk Maxwell in 1865 and first observed by the German physicist Heinrich Hertz in 1887. The number of oscillations per second of a wave is called its **frequency**, f, and is measured in **Hz** (in honor of Heinrich Hertz). The distance between two consecutive maxima (or minima) is called the **wavelength**, which is universally designated by the Greek letter λ (lambda).

When an antenna of the appropriate size is attached to an electrical circuit, the electromagnetic waves can be broadcast efficiently and received by a receiver some distance away. All wireless communication is based on this principle.

In a vacuum, all electromagnetic waves travel at the same speed, no matter what their frequency. This speed, usually called the **speed of light**, c, is approximately 3×10^8 m/sec, or about 1 foot (30 cm) per nanosecond. (A case could be made for redefining the foot as the distance light travels in a vacuum in 1 nsec rather than basing it on the shoe size of some long-dead king.) In copper or fiber the speed slows to about 2/3 of this value and becomes slightly frequency dependent. The speed of light is the ultimate speed limit. No object or signal can ever move faster than it.

The fundamental relation between f, λ, and c (in a vacuum) is

$$\lambda f = c \tag{2-4}$$

Since c is a constant, if we know f, we can find λ, and vice versa. As a rule of thumb, when λ is in meters and f is in MHz, $\lambda f \approx 300$. For example, 100-MHz waves are about 3 meters long, 1000-MHz waves are 0.3 meters long, and 0.1-meter waves have a frequency of 3000 MHz.

The electromagnetic spectrum is shown in Fig. 2-10. The radio, microwave, infrared, and visible light portions of the spectrum can all be used for transmitting information by modulating the amplitude, frequency, or phase of the waves. Ultraviolet light, X-rays, and gamma rays would be even better, due to their higher frequencies, but they are hard to produce and modulate, do not propagate well through buildings, and are dangerous to living things. The bands listed at the bottom of Fig. 2-10 are the official ITU (International Telecommunication Union) names and are based on the wavelengths, so the LF band goes from 1 km to 10 km (approximately 30 kHz to 300 kHz). The terms LF, MF, and HF refer to Low, Medium, and High Frequency, respectively. Clearly, when the names were assigned nobody expected to go above 10 MHz, so the higher bands were later named the Very, Ultra, Super, Extremely, and Tremendously High Frequency bands. Beyond that there are no names, but Incredibly, Astonishingly, and Prodigiously High Frequency (IHF, AHF, and PHF) would sound nice.

We know from Shannon [Eq. (2-3)] that the amount of information that a signal such as an electromagnetic wave can carry depends on the received power and is proportional to its bandwidth. From Fig. 2-10 it should now be obvious why networking people like fiber optics so much. Many GHz of bandwidth are available to tap for data transmission in the microwave band, and even more in fiber because it is further to the right in our logarithmic scale. As an example, consider the 1.30-micron band of Fig. 2-7, which has a width of 0.17 microns. If we use

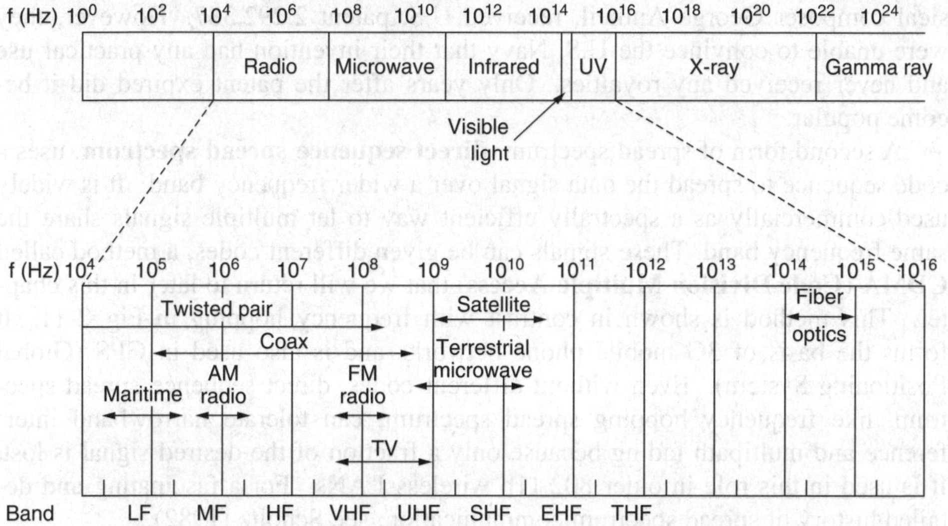

Figure 2-10. The electromagnetic spectrum and its uses for communication.

Eq. (2-4) to find the start and end frequencies from the start and end wavelengths, we find the frequency range to be about 30,000 GHz. With a reasonable signal-to-noise ratio of 10 dB, this is 300 Tbps.

Most transmissions use a relatively narrow frequency band (i.e., $\Delta f / f \ll 1$). They concentrate their signals in this narrow band to use the spectrum efficiently and obtain reasonable data rates by transmitting with enough power. However, in some cases, a wider band is used, with three variations. In **frequency hopping spread spectrum**, the transmitter hops from frequency to frequency hundreds of times per second. It is popular for military communication because it makes transmissions hard to detect and next to impossible to jam. It also offers good resistance to multipath fading and narrowband interference because the receiver will not be stuck on an impaired frequency for long enough to shut down communication. This robustness makes it useful for crowded parts of the spectrum, such as the ISM bands we will describe shortly. This technique is used commercially, for example, in Bluetooth and older versions of 802.11.

As a curious footnote, the technique was coinvented by the Austrian-born sex goddess Hedy Lamarr, the first woman to appear nude in a motion picture (the 1933 Czech film *Extase*). Her first husband was an armaments manufacturer who told her how easy it was to block the radio signals then used to control torpedoes. When she discovered that he was selling weapons to Hitler, she was horrified, disguised herself as a maid to escape him, and fled to Hollywood to continue her career as a movie actress. In her spare time, she invented frequency hopping to help the Allied war effort. Her scheme used 88 frequencies, the number of keys (and frequencies) on the piano. For their invention, she and her friend, the musical composer George Antheil, received U.S. patent 2,292,387. However, they were unable to convince the U.S. Navy that their invention had any practical use and never received any royalties. Only years after the patent expired did it become popular.

A second form of spread spectrum, **direct sequence spread spectrum**, uses a code sequence to spread the data signal over a wider frequency band. It is widely used commercially as a spectrally efficient way to let multiple signals share the same frequency band. These signals can be given different codes, a method called **CDMA (Code Division Multiple Access)** that we will return to later in this chapter. This method is shown in contrast with frequency hopping in Fig. 2-11. It forms the basis of 3G mobile phone networks and is also used in GPS (Global Positioning System). Even without different codes, direct sequence spread spectrum, like frequency hopping spread spectrum, can tolerate narrowband interference and multipath fading because only a fraction of the desired signal is lost. It is used in this role in older 802.11b wireless LANs. For a fascinating and detailed history of spread spectrum communication, see Scholtz (1982).

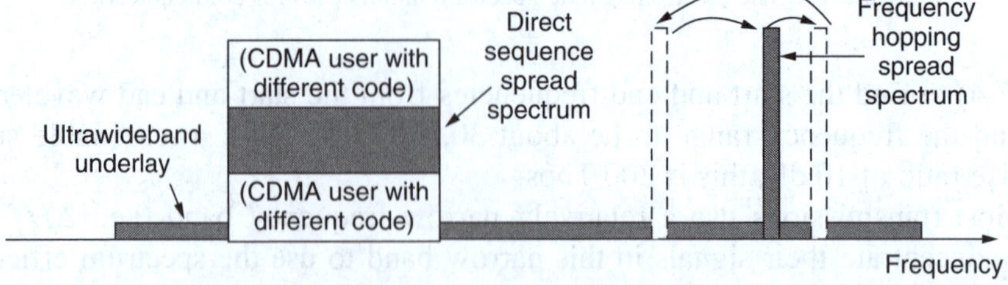

Figure 2-11. Spread spectrum and ultra-wideband (UWB) communication.

A third method of communication with a wider band is **UWB (Ultra-WideBand)** communication. UWB sends a series of rapid pulses, varying their positions to communicate information. The rapid transitions lead to a signal that is spread thinly over a very wide frequency band. UWB is defined as signals that have a bandwidth of at least 500 MHz or at least 20% of the center frequency of their frequency band. UWB is also shown in Fig. 2-11. With this much bandwidth, UWB has the potential to communicate at high rates. Because it is spread across a wide band of frequencies, it can tolerate a substantial amount of relatively strong interference from other narrowband signals. Just as importantly, since UWB has very little energy at any given frequency when used for short-range transmission, it does not cause harmful interference to those other narrowband radio signals. It is said to **underlay** the other signals. This peaceful coexistence has led to its application in wireless PANs that run at up to 1 Gbps, although commercial success has been mixed. It can also be used for imaging through solid objects (ground, walls, and bodies) or as part of precise location systems.

We will now discuss how the various parts of the electromagnetic spectrum of Fig. 2-11 are used, starting with radio. We will assume that all transmissions use a narrow frequency band unless otherwise stated.

2.3.2 Radio Transmission

Radio frequency (RF) waves are easy to generate, can travel long distances, and can penetrate buildings easily, so they are widely used for communication, both indoors and outdoors. Radio waves also are omnidirectional, meaning that they travel in all directions from the source, so the transmitter and receiver do not have to be carefully aligned physically.

Sometimes omnidirectional radio is good, but sometimes it is bad. In the 1970s, General Motors decided to equip all its new Cadillacs with computer-controlled antilock brakes. When the driver stepped on the brake pedal, the computer pulsed the brakes on and off instead of locking them on hard. One fine day an Ohio Highway Patrolman began using his new mobile radio to call headquarters, and suddenly the Cadillac next to him began behaving like a bucking bronco. When the officer pulled the car over, the driver claimed that he had done nothing and that the car had gone crazy.

Eventually, a pattern began to emerge: Cadillacs would sometimes go berserk, but only on major highways in Ohio and then only when the Highway Patrol was watching. For a long, long time General Motors could not understand why Cadillacs worked fine in all the other states and also on minor roads in Ohio. Only after much searching did they discover that the Cadillac's wiring made a fine antenna for the frequency used by the Ohio Highway Patrol's new radio system.

The properties of radio waves are frequency dependent. At low frequencies, radio waves pass through obstacles well, but the power falls off sharply with distance from the source—at least as fast as $1/r^2$ in air—as the signal energy is spread more thinly over a larger surface. This attenuation is called **path loss**. At high frequencies, radio waves tend to travel in straight lines and bounce off obstacles. Path loss still reduces power, though the received signal can depend strongly on reflections as well. High-frequency radio waves are also absorbed by rain and other obstacles to a larger extent than are low-frequency ones. At all frequencies, radio waves are subject to interference from motors and other electrical equipment.

It is interesting to compare the attenuation of radio waves to that of signals in guided media. With fiber, coax and twisted pair, the signal drops by the same fraction per unit distance, for example 20 dB per 100m for twisted pair. With radio, the signal drops by the same fraction as the distance doubles, for example 6 dB per doubling in free space. This behavior means that radio waves can travel long distances, and interference between users is a problem. For this reason, all governments tightly regulate the use of radio transmitters, with few notable exceptions, which are discussed later in this chapter.

In the VLF, LF, and MF bands, radio waves follow the ground, as illustrated in Fig. 2-12(a). These waves can be detected for perhaps 1000 km at the lower frequencies, less at the higher ones. AM radio broadcasting uses the MF band, which is why the ground waves from Boston AM radio stations cannot be heard easily in New York. Radio waves in these bands pass through buildings easily, which is why portable radios work indoors. The main problem with using these bands for data communication is their low bandwidth [see Eq. (2-4)].

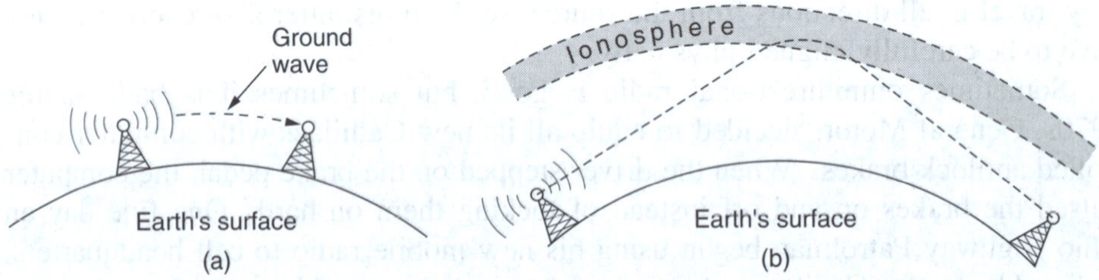

Figure 2-12. (a) In the VLF, LF, and MF bands, radio waves follow the curvature of the earth. (b) In the HF band, they bounce off the ionosphere.

In the HF and VHF bands, the ground waves tend to be absorbed by the earth. However, the waves that reach the ionosphere, a layer of charged particles circling the earth at a height of 100 to 500 km, are refracted by it and sent back to earth, as shown in Fig. 2-12(b). Under certain atmospheric conditions, the signals can bounce several times. Amateur radio operators (hams) use these bands to talk long distance. The military also communicate in the HF and VHF bands.

2.3.3 Microwave Transmission

Above 100 MHz, the waves travel in nearly straight lines and can therefore be narrowly focused. Concentrating all the energy into a small beam by means of a parabolic antenna (like the familiar satellite TV dish) gives a much higher signal-to-noise ratio, but the transmitting and receiving antennas must be accurately aligned with each other. In addition, this directionality allows multiple transmitters lined up in a row to communicate with multiple receivers in a row without interference, provided some minimum spacing rules are observed. Before fiber optics, for decades these microwaves formed the heart of the long-distance telephone transmission system. In fact, MCI, one of AT&T's first competitors after it was deregulated, built its entire system with microwave communications passing between towers tens of kilometers apart. Even the company's name reflected this (MCI stood for Microwave Communications, Inc.). MCI has since gone over to fiber and through a long series of corporate mergers and bankruptcies in the telecommunications shuffle has become part of Verizon.

Microwaves travel in a straight line, so if the towers are too far apart, the earth will get in the way (think about a Seattle-to-Amsterdam link). Thus, repeaters are needed periodically. The higher the towers are, the farther apart they can be. The distance between repeaters goes up very roughly with the square root of the tower height. For 100-meter-high towers, repeaters can be 80 km apart.

Unlike radio waves at lower frequencies, microwaves do not pass through buildings well. In addition, even though the beam may be well focused at the transmitter, there is still some divergence in space. Some waves may be refracted off low-lying atmospheric layers and may take slightly longer to arrive than the direct waves. The delayed waves may arrive out of phase with the direct wave and thus cancel the signal. This effect is called **multipath fading** and is often a serious problem. It is weather and frequency dependent. Some operators keep 10% of their channels idle as spares to switch on when multipath fading temporarily wipes out some frequency band.

The demand for more and more spectrum drives operators to yet higher frequencies. Bands up to 10 GHz are now in routine use, but at about 4 GHz a new problem sets in: absorption by water. These waves are only a few centimeters long and are absorbed by rain. This effect would be fine if one were planning to build a huge outdoor microwave oven for roasting passing birds, but for communication it is a severe problem. As with multipath fading, the only solution is to shut off links that are being rained on and route around them.

In summary, microwave communication is so widely used for long-distance telephone communication, mobile phones, television distribution, and other purposes that a severe shortage of spectrum has developed. It has several key advantages over fiber. The main one is that no right of way is needed to lay down cables. By buying a small plot of ground every 50 km and putting a microwave tower on it, one can bypass the telephone system entirely. This is how MCI managed to get started as a new long-distance telephone company so quickly. (Sprint, another early competitor to the deregulated AT&T, went a completely different route: it was formed by the Southern Pacific Railroad, which already owned a large amount of right of way and just buried fiber next to the tracks.)

Microwave is also relatively inexpensive. Putting up two simple towers (which can be just big poles with four guy wires) and putting antennas on each one may be cheaper than burying 50 km of fiber through a congested urban area or up over a mountain, and it may also be cheaper than leasing the telephone company's fiber, especially if the telephone company has not yet even fully paid for the copper it ripped out when it put in the fiber.

The Politics of the Electromagnetic Spectrum

To prevent total chaos, there are national and international agreements about who gets to use which frequencies. Since everyone wants a higher data rate, everyone wants more spectrum. National governments allocate spectrum for AM and FM radio, television, and mobile phones, as well as for telephone companies, police, maritime, navigation, military, government, and many other competing users. Worldwide, an agency of ITU-R (WRC) tries to coordinate this allocation so devices that work in multiple countries can be manufactured. However, countries are not bound by ITU-R's recommendations, and the FCC (Federal Communication Commission), which does the allocation for the United States, has occasionally rejected ITU-R's recommendations (usually because they required some politically powerful group to give up some piece of the spectrum).

Even when a piece of spectrum has been allocated to some use, such as mobile phones, there is the additional issue of which carrier is allowed to use which frequencies. Three algorithms were widely used in the past. The oldest algorithm, often called the **beauty contest**, requires each carrier to explain why its proposal serves the public interest best. Government officials then decide which of the nice stories they enjoy most. Having some government official award property worth billions of dollars to his favorite company often leads to bribery, corruption, nepotism, and worse. Furthermore, even a scrupulously honest government official who thought that a foreign company could do a better job than any of the national companies would have a lot of explaining to do.

This observation led to algorithm 2, holding a **lottery** among the interested companies. The problem with that idea is that companies with no interest in using the spectrum can enter the lottery. If, say, a fast food restaurant or shoe store chain wins, it can resell the spectrum to a carrier at a huge profit and with no risk.

Bestowing huge windfalls on alert but otherwise random companies has been severely criticized by many, which led to algorithm 3: **auction** off the bandwidth to the highest bidder. When the British government auctioned off the frequencies needed for third-generation mobile systems in 2000, it expected to get about $4 billion. It actually received about $40 billion because the carriers got into a feeding frenzy, scared to death of missing the mobile boat. This event switched on nearby governments' greedy bits and inspired them to hold their own auctions. It worked, but it also left some of the carriers with so much debt that they are close to bankruptcy. Even in the best cases, it will take many years to recoup the licensing fee.

A completely different approach to allocating frequencies is to not allocate them at all. Instead, let everyone transmit at will, but regulate the power used so that stations have such a short range that they do not interfere with each other. Accordingly, most governments have set aside some frequency bands, called the **ISM (Industrial, Scientific, Medical)** bands for unlicensed usage. Garage door openers, cordless phones, radio-controlled toys, wireless mice, and numerous other wireless household devices use the ISM bands. To minimize interference between these uncoordinated devices, the FCC mandates that all devices in the ISM bands limit their transmit power (e.g., to 1 watt) and use other techniques to spread their signals over a range of frequencies. Devices may also need to take care to avoid interference with radar installations.

The location of these bands varies somewhat from country to country. In the United States, for example, the bands that networking devices use in practice without requiring a FCC license are shown in Fig. 2-13. The 900-MHz band was used for early versions of 802.11, but it is crowded. The 2.4-GHz band is available in most countries and widely used for 802.11b/g and Bluetooth, though it is subject to interference from microwave ovens and radar installations. The 5-GHz part of the spectrum includes **U-NII** (**Unlicensed National Information Infrastructure**) bands. The 5-GHz bands are relatively undeveloped but, since they have the most bandwidth and are used by 802.11a, they are quickly gaining in popularity.

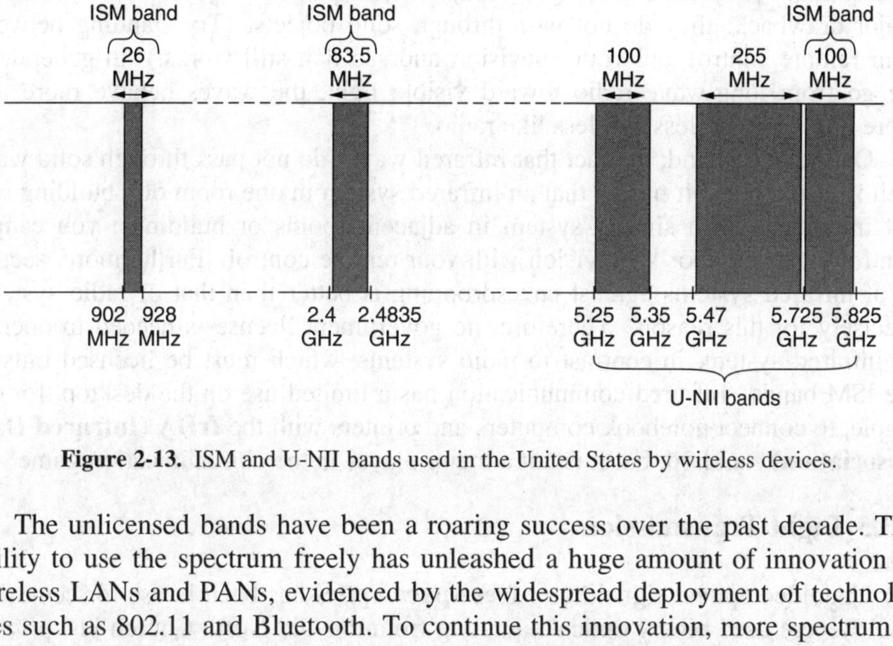

Figure 2-13. ISM and U-NII bands used in the United States by wireless devices.

The unlicensed bands have been a roaring success over the past decade. The ability to use the spectrum freely has unleashed a huge amount of innovation in wireless LANs and PANs, evidenced by the widespread deployment of technologies such as 802.11 and Bluetooth. To continue this innovation, more spectrum is needed. One exciting development in the U.S. is the FCC decision in 2009 to allow unlicensed use of **white spaces** around 700 MHz. White spaces are frequency bands that have been allocated but are not being used locally. The transition from analog to all-digital television broadcasts in the U.S. in 2010 freed up white spaces around 700 MHz. The only difficulty is that, to use the white spaces, unlicensed devices must be able to detect any nearby licensed transmitters, including wireless microphones, that have first rights to use the frequency band.

Another flurry of activity is happening around the 60-GHz band. The FCC opened 57 GHz to 64 GHz for unlicensed operation in 2001. This range is an enormous portion of spectrum, more than all the other ISM bands combined, so it can support the kind of high-speed networks that would be needed to stream high-definition TV through the air across your living room. At 60 GHz, radio waves are absorbed by oxygen. This means that signals do not propagate far, making them well suited to short-range networks. The high frequencies (60 GHz is in the Extremely High Frequency or "millimeter" band, just below infrared radiation) posed an initial challenge for equipment makers, but products are now on the market.

2.3.4 Infrared Transmission

Unguided infrared waves are widely used for short-range communication. The remote controls used for televisions, VCRs, and stereos all use infrared communication. They are relatively directional, cheap, and easy to build but have a major drawback: they do not pass through solid objects. (Try standing between your remote control and your television and see if it still works.) In general, as we go from long-wave radio toward visible light, the waves behave more and more like light and less and less like radio.

On the other hand, the fact that infrared waves do not pass through solid walls well is also a plus. It means that an infrared system in one room of a building will not interfere with a similar system in adjacent rooms or buildings: you cannot control your neighbor's television with your remote control. Furthermore, security of infrared systems against eavesdropping is better than that of radio systems precisely for this reason. Therefore, no government license is needed to operate an infrared system, in contrast to radio systems, which must be licensed outside the ISM bands. Infrared communication has a limited use on the desktop, for example, to connect notebook computers and printers with the **IrDA** (**Infrared Data Association**) standard, but it is not a major player in the communication game.

2.3.5 Light Transmission

Unguided optical signaling or **free-space optics** has been in use for centuries. Paul Revere used binary optical signaling from the Old North Church just prior to his famous ride. A more modern application is to connect the LANs in two buildings via lasers mounted on their rooftops. Optical signaling using lasers is inherently unidirectional, so each end needs its own laser and its own photodetector. This scheme offers very high bandwidth at very low cost and is relatively secure because it is difficult to tap a narrow laser beam. It is also relatively easy to install and, unlike microwave transmission, does not require an FCC license.

The laser's strength, a very narrow beam, is also its weakness here. Aiming a laser beam 1 mm wide at a target the size of a pin head 500 meters away requires the marksmanship of a latter-day Annie Oakley. Usually, lenses are put into the system to defocus the beam slightly. To add to the difficulty, wind and temperature changes can distort the beam and laser beams also cannot penetrate rain or thick fog, although they normally work well on sunny days. However, many of these factors are not an issue when the use is to connect two spacecraft.

One of the authors (AST) once attended a conference at a modern hotel in Europe at which the conference organizers thoughtfully provided a room full of terminals to allow the attendees to read their email during boring presentations. Since the local PTT was unwilling to install a large number of telephone lines for just 3 days, the organizers put a laser on the roof and aimed it at their university's computer science building a few kilometers away. They tested it the night before the conference and it worked perfectly. At 9 A.M. on a bright, sunny day, the link failed completely and stayed down all day. The pattern repeated itself the next two days. It was not until after the conference that the organizers discovered the problem: heat from the sun during the daytime caused convection currents to rise up from the roof of the building, as shown in Fig. 2-14. This turbulent air diverted the beam and made it dance around the detector, much like a shimmering road on a hot day. The lesson here is that to work well in difficult conditions as well as good conditions, unguided optical links need to be engineered with a sufficient margin of error.

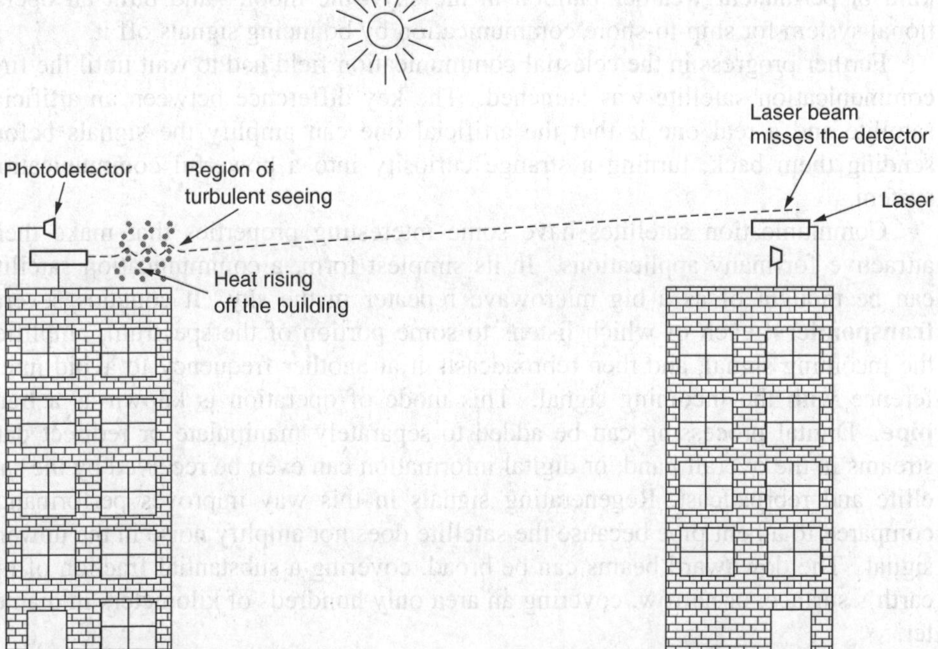

Figure 2-14. Convection currents can interfere with laser communication systems. A bidirectional system with two lasers is pictured here.

Unguided optical communication may seem like an exotic networking technology today, but it might soon become much more prevalent. We are surrounded by cameras (that sense light) and displays (that emit light using LEDs and other technology). Data communication can be layered on top of these displays by encoding information in the pattern at which LEDs turn on and off that is below the threshold of human perception. Communicating with visible light in this way is inherently safe and creates a low-speed network in the immediate vicinity of the display. This could enable all sorts of fanciful ubiquitous computing scenarios. The flashing lights on emergency vehicles might alert nearby traffic lights and vehicles to help clear a path. Informational signs might broadcast maps. Even festive lights might broadcast songs that are synchronized with their display.

2.4 COMMUNICATION SATELLITES

In the 1950s and early 1960s, people tried to set up communication systems by bouncing signals off metallized weather balloons. Unfortunately, the received signals were too weak to be of any practical use. Then the U.S. Navy noticed a kind of permanent weather balloon in the sky—the moon—and built an operational system for ship-to-shore communication by bouncing signals off it.

Further progress in the celestial communication field had to wait until the first communication satellite was launched. The key difference between an artificial satellite and a real one is that the artificial one can amplify the signals before sending them back, turning a strange curiosity into a powerful communication system.

Communication satellites have some interesting properties that make them attractive for many applications. In its simplest form, a communication satellite can be thought of as a big microwave repeater in the sky. It contains several **transponders**, each of which listens to some portion of the spectrum, amplifies the incoming signal, and then rebroadcasts it at another frequency to avoid interference with the incoming signal. This mode of operation is known as a **bent pipe**. Digital processing can be added to separately manipulate or redirect data streams in the overall band, or digital information can even be received by the satellite and rebroadcast. Regenerating signals in this way improves performance compared to a bent pipe because the satellite does not amplify noise in the upward signal. The downward beams can be broad, covering a substantial fraction of the earth's surface, or narrow, covering an area only hundreds of kilometers in diameter.

According to Kepler's law, the orbital period of a satellite varies as the radius of the orbit to the 3/2 power. The higher the satellite, the longer the period. Near the surface of the earth, the period is about 90 minutes. Consequently, low-orbit satellites pass out of view fairly quickly, so many of them are needed to provide continuous coverage and ground antennas must track them. At an altitude of about 35,800 km, the period is 24 hours. At an altitude of 384,000 km, the period is about one month, as anyone who has observed the moon regularly can testify.

A satellite's period is important, but it is not the only issue in determining where to place it. Another issue is the presence of the Van Allen belts, layers of highly charged particles trapped by the earth's magnetic field. Any satellite flying within them would be destroyed fairly quickly by the particles. These factors lead to three regions in which satellites can be placed safely. These regions and some of their properties are illustrated in Fig. 2-15. Below we will briefly describe the satellites that inhabit each of these regions.

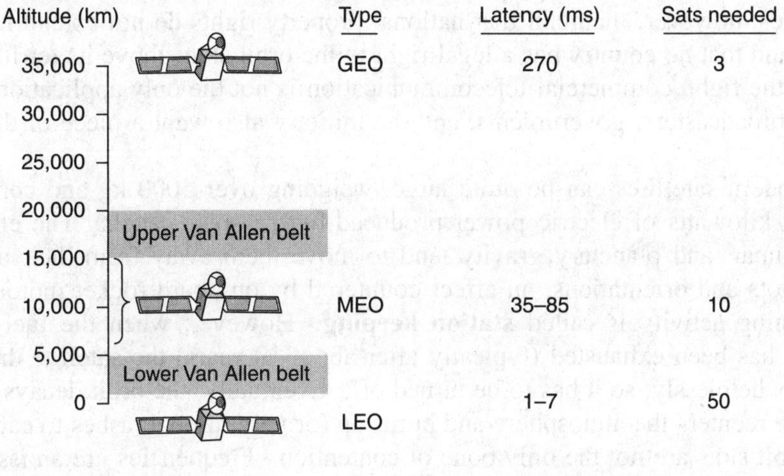

Figure 2-15. Communication satellites and some of their properties, including altitude above the earth, round-trip delay time, and number of satellites needed for global coverage.

2.4.1 Geostationary Satellites

In 1945, the science fiction writer Arthur C. Clarke calculated that a satellite at an altitude of 35,800 km in a circular equatorial orbit would appear to remain motionless in the sky, so it would not need to be tracked (Clarke, 1945). He went on to describe a complete communication system that used these (manned) **geostationary satellites**, including the orbits, solar panels, radio frequencies, and launch procedures. Unfortunately, he concluded that satellites were impractical due to the impossibility of putting power-hungry, fragile vacuum tube amplifiers into orbit, so he never pursued this idea further, although he wrote some science fiction stories about it.

The invention of the transistor changed all that, and the first artificial communication satellite, Telstar, was launched in July 1962. Since then, communication satellites have become a multibillion dollar business and the only aspect of outer space that has become highly profitable. These high-flying satellites are often called **GEO** (**Geostationary Earth Orbit**) satellites.

With current technology, it is unwise to have geostationary satellites spaced much closer than 2 degrees in the 360-degree equatorial plane, to avoid interference. With a spacing of 2 degrees, there can only be 360/2 = 180 of these satellites in the sky at once. However, each transponder can use multiple frequencies and polarizations to increase the available bandwidth.

To prevent total chaos in the sky, orbit slot allocation is done by ITU. This process is highly political, with countries barely out of the stone age demanding "their" orbit slots (for the purpose of leasing them to the highest bidder). Other countries, however, maintain that national property rights do not extend up to the moon and that no country has a legal right to the orbit slots above its territory. To add to the fight, commercial telecommunication is not the only application. Television broadcasters, governments, and the military also want a piece of the orbiting pie.

Modern satellites can be quite large, weighing over 5000 kg and consuming several kilowatts of electric power produced by the solar panels. The effects of solar, lunar, and planetary gravity tend to move them away from their assigned orbit slots and orientations, an effect countered by on-board rocket motors. This fine-tuning activity is called **station keeping**. However, when the fuel for the motors has been exhausted (typically after about 10 years) the satellite drifts and tumbles helplessly, so it has to be turned off. Eventually, the orbit decays and the satellite reenters the atmosphere and burns up (or very rarely crashes to earth).

Orbit slots are not the only bone of contention. Frequencies are an issue, too, because the downlink transmissions interfere with existing microwave users. Consequently, ITU has allocated certain frequency bands to satellite users. The main ones are listed in Fig. 2-16. The C band was the first to be designated for commercial satellite traffic. Two frequency ranges are assigned in it, the lower one for downlink traffic (from the satellite) and the upper one for uplink traffic (to the satellite). To allow traffic to go both ways at the same time, two channels are required. These channels are already overcrowded because they are also used by the common carriers for terrestrial microwave links. The L and S bands were added by international agreement in 2000. However, they are narrow and also crowded.

Band	Downlink	Uplink	Bandwidth	Problems
L	1.5 GHz	1.6 GHz	15 MHz	Low bandwidth; crowded
S	1.9 GHz	2.2 GHz	70 MHz	Low bandwidth; crowded
C	4.0 GHz	6.0 GHz	500 MHz	Terrestrial interference
Ku	11 GHz	14 GHz	500 MHz	Rain
Ka	20 GHz	30 GHz	3500 MHz	Rain, equipment cost

Figure 2-16. The principal satellite bands.

The next-highest band available to commercial telecommunication carriers is the Ku (K under) band. This band is not (yet) congested, and at its higher frequencies, satellites can be spaced as close as 1 degree. However, another problem exists: rain. Water absorbs these short microwaves well. Fortunately, heavy storms are usually localized, so using several widely separated ground stations instead of just one circumvents the problem, but at the price of extra antennas, extra cables, and extra electronics to enable rapid switching between stations. Bandwidth has also been allocated in the Ka (K above) band for commercial satellite traffic, but the equipment needed to use it is expensive. In addition to these commercial bands, many government and military bands also exist.

A modern satellite has around 40 transponders, most often with a 36-MHz bandwidth. Usually, each transponder operates as a bent pipe, but recent satellites have some on-board processing capacity, allowing more sophisticated operation. In the earliest satellites, the division of the transponders into channels was static: the bandwidth was simply split up into fixed frequency bands. Nowadays, each transponder beam is divided into time slots, with various users taking turns. We will study these two techniques (frequency division multiplexing and time division multiplexing) in detail later in this chapter.

The first geostationary satellites had a single spatial beam that illuminated about 1/3 of the earth's surface, called its **footprint**. With the enormous decline in the price, size, and power requirements of microelectronics, a much more sophisticated broadcasting strategy has become possible. Each satellite is equipped with multiple antennas and multiple transponders. Each downward beam can be focused on a small geographical area, so multiple upward and downward transmissions can take place simultaneously. Typically, these so-called **spot beams** are elliptically shaped, and can be as small as a few hundred km in diameter. A communication satellite for the United States typically has one wide beam for the contiguous 48 states, plus spot beams for Alaska and Hawaii.

A recent development in the communication satellite world is the development of low-cost microstations, sometimes called **VSATs (Very Small Aperture Terminals**) (Abramson, 2000). These tiny terminals have 1-meter or smaller antennas (versus 10 m for a standard GEO antenna) and can put out about 1 watt of power. The uplink is generally good for up to 1 Mbps, but the downlink is often up to several megabits/sec. Direct broadcast satellite television uses this technology for one-way transmission.

In many VSAT systems, the microstations do not have enough power to communicate directly with one another (via the satellite, of course). Instead, a special ground station, the **hub**, with a large, high-gain antenna is needed to relay traffic between VSATs, as shown in Fig. 2-17. In this mode of operation, either the sender or the receiver has a large antenna and a powerful amplifier. The trade-off is a longer delay in return for having cheaper end-user stations.

VSATs have great potential in rural areas. It is not widely appreciated, but over half the world's population lives more than hour's walk from the nearest

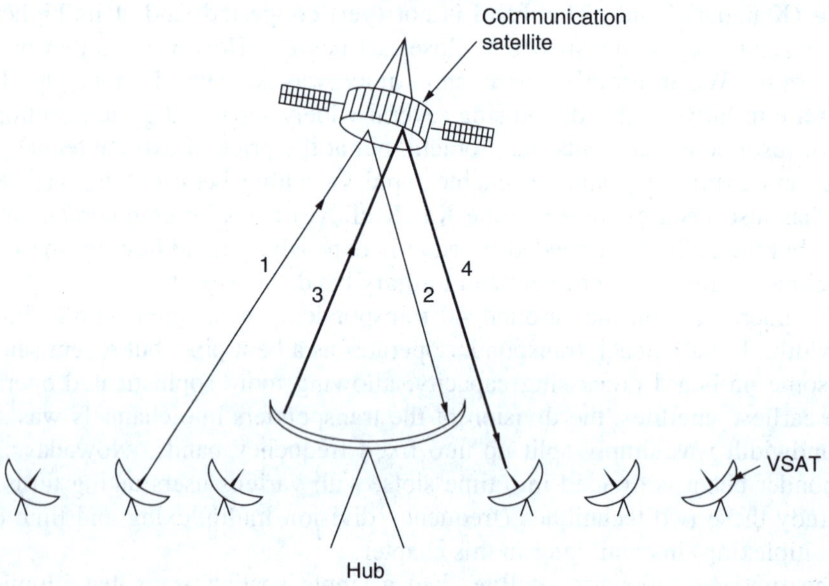

Figure 2-17. VSATs using a hub.

telephone. Stringing telephone wires to thousands of small villages is far beyond the budgets of most Third World governments, but installing 1-meter VSAT dishes powered by solar cells is often feasible. VSATs provide the technology that will wire the world.

Communication satellites have several properties that are radically different from terrestrial point-to-point links. To begin with, even though signals to and from a satellite travel at the speed of light (nearly 300,000 km/sec), the long round-trip distance introduces a substantial delay for GEO satellites. Depending on the distance between the user and the ground station and the elevation of the satellite above the horizon, the end-to-end transit time is between 250 and 300 msec. A typical value is 270 msec (540 msec for a VSAT system with a hub).

For comparison purposes, terrestrial microwave links have a propagation delay of roughly 3 μsec/km, and coaxial cable or fiber optic links have a delay of approximately 5 μsec/km. The latter are slower than the former because electromagnetic signals travel faster in air than in solid materials.

Another important property of satellites is that they are inherently broadcast media. It does not cost more to send a message to thousands of stations within a transponder's footprint than it does to send to one. For some applications, this property is very useful. For example, one could imagine a satellite broadcasting popular Web pages to the caches of a large number of computers spread over a wide area. Even when broadcasting can be simulated with point-to-point lines, satellite broadcasting may be much cheaper. On the other hand, from a privacy point of view, satellites are a complete disaster: everybody can hear everything. Encryption is essential when security is required.

Satellites also have the property that the cost of transmitting a message is independent of the distance traversed. A call across the ocean costs no more to service than a call across the street. Satellites also have excellent error rates and can be deployed almost instantly, a major consideration for disaster response and military communication.

2.4.2 Medium-Earth Orbit Satellites

At much lower altitudes, between the two Van Allen belts, we find the **MEO** (**Medium-Earth Orbit**) satellites. As viewed from the earth, these drift slowly in longitude, taking something like 6 hours to circle the earth. Accordingly, they must be tracked as they move through the sky. Because they are lower than the GEOs, they have a smaller footprint on the ground and require less powerful transmitters to reach them. Currently they are used for navigation systems rather than telecommunications, so we will not examine them further here. The constellation of roughly 30 **GPS** (**Global Positioning System**) satellites orbiting at about 20,200 km are examples of MEO satellites.

2.4.3 Low-Earth Orbit Satellites

Moving down in altitude, we come to the **LEO** (**Low-Earth Orbit**) satellites. Due to their rapid motion, large numbers of them are needed for a complete system. On the other hand, because the satellites are so close to the earth, the ground stations do not need much power, and the round-trip delay is only a few milliseconds. The launch cost is substantially cheaper too. In this section we will examine two examples of satellite constellations for voice service, Iridium and Globalstar.

For the first 30 years of the satellite era, low-orbit satellites were rarely used because they zip into and out of view so quickly. In 1990, Motorola broke new ground by filing an application with the FCC asking for permission to launch 77 low-orbit satellites for the **Iridium** project (element 77 is iridium). The plan was later revised to use only 66 satellites, so the project should have been renamed Dysprosium (element 66), but that probably sounded too much like a disease. The idea was that as soon as one satellite went out of view, another would replace it. This proposal set off a feeding frenzy among other communication companies. All of a sudden, everyone wanted to launch a chain of low-orbit satellites.

After seven years of cobbling together partners and financing, communication service began in November 1998. Unfortunately, the commercial demand for large, heavy satellite telephones was negligible because the mobile phone network had grown in a spectacular way since 1990. As a consequence, Iridium was not profitable and was forced into bankruptcy in August 1999 in one of the most spectacular corporate fiascos in history. The satellites and other assets (worth $5 billion) were later purchased by an investor for $25 million at a kind of extraterrestrial garage sale. Other satellite business ventures promptly followed suit.

The Iridium service restarted in March 2001 and has been growing ever since. It provides voice, data, paging, fax, and navigation service everywhere on land, air, and sea, via hand-held devices that communicate directly with the Iridium satellites. Customers include the maritime, aviation, and oil exploration industries, as well as people traveling in parts of the world lacking a telecom infrastructure (e.g., deserts, mountains, the South Pole, and some Third World countries).

The Iridium satellites are positioned at an altitude of 750 km, in circular polar orbits. They are arranged in north-south necklaces, with one satellite every 32 degrees of latitude, as shown in Fig. 2-18. Each satellite has a maximum of 48 cells (spot beams) and a capacity of 3840 channels, some of which are used for paging and navigation, while others are used for data and voice.

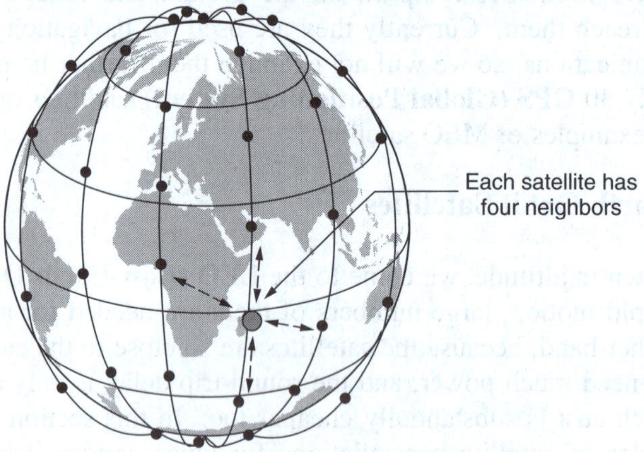

Figure 2-18. The Iridium satellites form six necklaces around the earth.

With six satellite necklaces the entire earth is covered, as suggested by Fig. 2-18. An interesting property of Iridium is that communication between distant customers takes place in space, as shown in Fig. 2-19(a). Here we see a caller at the North Pole contacting a satellite directly overhead. Each satellite has four neighbors with which it can communicate, two in the same necklace (shown) and two in adjacent necklaces (not shown). The satellites relay the call across this grid until it is finally sent down to the callee at the South Pole.

An alternative design to Iridium is **Globalstar**. It is based on 48 LEO satellites but uses a different switching scheme than that of Iridium. Whereas Iridium relays calls from satellite to satellite, which requires sophisticated switching equipment in the satellites, Globalstar uses a traditional bent-pipe design. The call originating at the North Pole in Fig. 2-19(b) is sent back to earth and picked

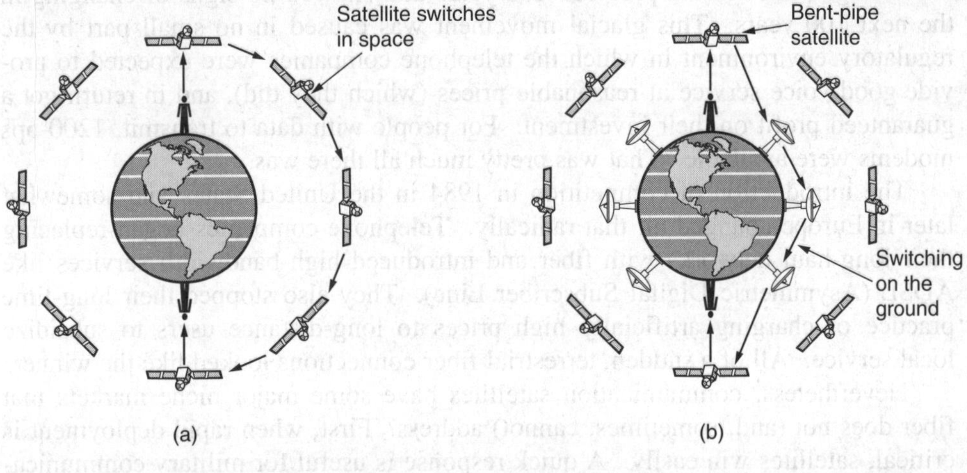

Figure 2-19. (a) Relaying in space. (b) Relaying on the ground.

up by the large ground station at Santa's Workshop. The call is then routed via a terrestrial network to the ground station nearest the callee and delivered by a bent-pipe connection as shown. The advantage of this scheme is that it puts much of the complexity on the ground, where it is easier to manage. Also, the use of large ground station antennas that can put out a powerful signal and receive a weak one means that lower-powered telephones can be used. After all, the telephone puts out only a few milliwatts of power, so the signal that gets back to the ground station is fairly weak, even after having been amplified by the satellite.

Satellites continue to be launched at a rate of around 20 per year, including ever-larger satellites that now weigh over 5000 kilograms. But there are also very small satellites for the more budget-conscious organization. To make space research more accessible, academics from Cal Poly and Stanford got together in 1999 to define a standard for miniature satellites and an associated launcher that would greatly lower launch costs (Nugent et al., 2008). **CubeSats** are satellites in units of 10 cm × 10 cm × 10 cm cubes, each weighing no more than 1 kilogram, that can be launched for as little as $40,000 each. The launcher flies as a secondary payload on commercial space missions. It is basically a tube that takes up to three units of cubesats and uses springs to release them into orbit. Roughly 20 cubesats have launched so far, with many more in the works. Most of them communicate with ground stations on the UHF and VHF bands.

2.4.4 Satellites Versus Fiber

A comparison between satellite communication and terrestrial communication is instructive. As recently as 25 years ago, a case could be made that the future of communication lay with communication satellites. After all, the telephone system had changed little in the previous 100 years and showed no signs of changing in the next 100 years. This glacial movement was caused in no small part by the regulatory environment in which the telephone companies were expected to provide good voice service at reasonable prices (which they did), and in return got a guaranteed profit on their investment. For people with data to transmit, 1200-bps modems were available. That was pretty much all there was.

The introduction of competition in 1984 in the United States and somewhat later in Europe changed all that radically. Telephone companies began replacing their long-haul networks with fiber and introduced high-bandwidth services like ADSL (Asymmetric Digital Subscriber Line). They also stopped their long-time practice of charging artificially high prices to long-distance users to subsidize local service. All of a sudden, terrestrial fiber connections looked like the winner.

Nevertheless, communication satellites have some major niche markets that fiber does not (and, sometimes, cannot) address. First, when rapid deployment is critical, satellites win easily. A quick response is useful for military communication systems in times of war and disaster response in times of peace. Following the massive December 2004 Sumatra earthquake and subsequent tsunami, for example, communications satellites were able to restore communications to first responders within 24 hours. This rapid response was possible because there is a developed satellite service provider market in which large players, such as Intelsat with over 50 satellites, can rent out capacity pretty much anywhere it is needed. For customers served by existing satellite networks, a VSAT can be set up easily and quickly to provide a megabit/sec link to elsewhere in the world.

A second niche is for communication in places where the terrestrial infrastructure is poorly developed. Many people nowadays want to communicate everywhere they go. Mobile phone networks cover those locations with good population density, but do not do an adequate job in other places (e.g., at sea or in the desert). Conversely, Iridium provides voice service everywhere on Earth, even at the South Pole. Terrestrial infrastructure can also be expensive to install, depending on the terrain and necessary rights of way. Indonesia, for example, has its own satellite for domestic telephone traffic. Launching one satellite was cheaper than stringing thousands of undersea cables among the 13,677 islands in the archipelago.

A third niche is when broadcasting is essential. A message sent by satellite can be received by thousands of ground stations at once. Satellites are used to distribute much network TV programming to local stations for this reason. There is now a large market for satellite broadcasts of digital TV and radio directly to end users with satellite receivers in their homes and cars. All sorts of other content can be broadcast too. For example, an organization transmitting a stream of stock, bond, or commodity prices to thousands of dealers might find a satellite system to be much cheaper than simulating broadcasting on the ground.

In short, it looks like the mainstream communication of the future will be terrestrial fiber optics combined with cellular radio, but for some specialized uses, satellites are better. However, there is one caveat that applies to all of this: economics. Although fiber offers more bandwidth, it is conceivable that terrestrial and satellite communication could compete aggressively on price. If advances in technology radically cut the cost of deploying a satellite (e.g., if some future space vehicle can toss out dozens of satellites on one launch) or low-orbit satellites catch on in a big way, it is not certain that fiber will win all markets.

2.5 DIGITAL MODULATION AND MULTIPLEXING

Now that we have studied the properties of wired and wireless channels, we turn our attention to the problem of sending digital information. Wires and wireless channels carry analog signals such as continuously varying voltage, light intensity, or sound intensity. To send digital information, we must devise analog signals to represent bits. The process of converting between bits and signals that represent them is called **digital modulation**.

We will start with schemes that directly convert bits into a signal. These schemes result in **baseband transmission**, in which the signal occupies frequencies from zero up to a maximum that depends on the signaling rate. It is common for wires. Then we will consider schemes that regulate the amplitude, phase, or frequency of a carrier signal to convey bits. These schemes result in **passband transmission**, in which the signal occupies a band of frequencies around the frequency of the carrier signal. It is common for wireless and optical channels for which the signals must reside in a given frequency band.

Channels are often shared by multiple signals. After all, it is much more convenient to use a single wire to carry several signals than to install a wire for every signal. This kind of sharing is called **multiplexing**. It can be accomplished in several different ways. We will present methods for time, frequency, and code division multiplexing.

The modulation and multiplexing techniques we describe in this section are all widely used for wires, fiber, terrestrial wireless, and satellite channels. In the following sections, we will look at examples of networks to see them in action.

2.5.1 Baseband Transmission

The most straightforward form of digital modulation is to use a positive voltage to represent a 1 and a negative voltage to represent a 0. For an optical fiber, the presence of light might represent a 1 and the absence of light might represent a 0. This scheme is called **NRZ** (**Non-Return-to-Zero**). The odd name is for historical reasons, and simply means that the signal follows the data. An example is shown in Fig. 2-20(b).

Once sent, the NRZ signal propagates down the wire. At the other end, the receiver converts it into bits by sampling the signal at regular intervals of time.

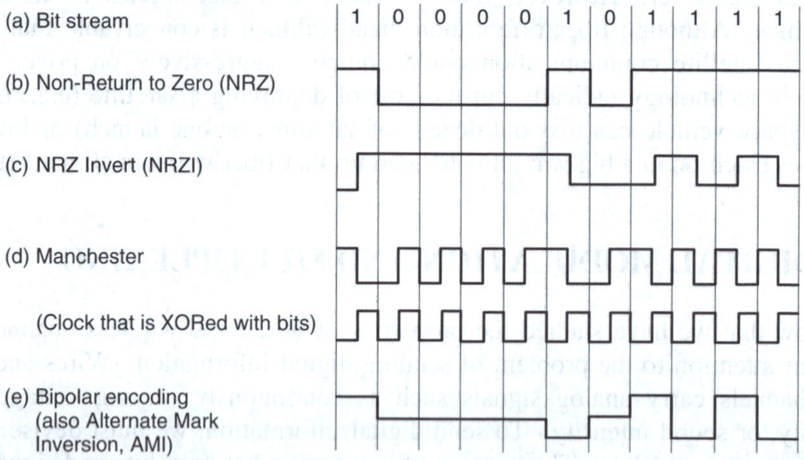

Figure 2-20. Line codes: (a) Bits, (b) NRZ, (c) NRZI, (d) Manchester, (e) Bipolar or AMI.

This signal will not look exactly like the signal that was sent. It will be attenuated and distorted by the channel and noise at the receiver. To decode the bits, the receiver maps the signal samples to the closest symbols. For NRZ, a positive voltage will be taken to indicate that a 1 was sent and a negative voltage will be taken to indicate that a 0 was sent.

NRZ is a good starting point for our studies because it is simple, but it is seldom used by itself in practice. More complex schemes can convert bits to signals that better meet engineering considerations. These schemes are called **line codes**. Below, we describe line codes that help with bandwidth efficiency, clock recovery, and DC balance.

Bandwidth Efficiency

With NRZ, the signal may cycle between the positive and negative levels up to every 2 bits (in the case of alternating 1s and 0s). This means that we need a bandwidth of at least $B/2$ Hz when the bit rate is B bits/sec. This relation comes from the Nyquist rate [Eq. (2-2)]. It is a fundamental limit, so we cannot run NRZ faster without using more bandwidth. Bandwidth is often a limited resource, even for wired channels, Higher-frequency signals are increasingly attenuated, making them less useful, and higher-frequency signals also require faster electronics.

One strategy for using limited bandwidth more efficiently is to use more than two signaling levels. By using four voltages, for instance, we can send 2 bits at once as a single **symbol**. This design will work as long as the signal at the receiver is sufficiently strong to distinguish the four levels. The rate at which the signal changes is then half the bit rate, so the needed bandwidth has been reduced.

We call the rate at which the signal changes the **symbol rate** to distinguish it from the **bit rate**. The bit rate is the symbol rate multiplied by the number of bits per symbol. An older name for the symbol rate, particularly in the context of devices called telephone modems that convey digital data over telephone lines, is the **baud rate**. In the literature, the terms "bit rate" and "baud rate" are often used incorrectly.

Note that the number of signal levels does not need to be a power of two. Often it is not, with some of the levels used for protecting against errors and simplifying the design of the receiver.

Clock Recovery

For all schemes that encode bits into symbols, the receiver must know when one symbol ends and the next symbol begins to correctly decode the bits. With NRZ, in which the symbols are simply voltage levels, a long run of 0s or 1s leaves the signal unchanged. After a while it is hard to tell the bits apart, as 15 zeros look much like 16 zeros unless you have a very accurate clock.

Accurate clocks would help with this problem, but they are an expensive solution for commodity equipment. Remember, we are timing bits on links that run at many megabits/sec, so the clock would have to drift less than a fraction of a microsecond over the longest permitted run. This might be reasonable for slow links or short messages, but it is not a general solution.

One strategy is to send a separate clock signal to the receiver. Another clock line is no big deal for computer buses or short cables in which there are many lines in parallel, but it is wasteful for most network links since if we had another line to send a signal we could use it to send data. A clever trick here is to mix the clock signal with the data signal by XORing them together so that no extra line is needed. The results are shown in Fig. 2-20(d). The clock makes a clock transition in every bit time, so it runs at twice the bit rate. When it is XORed with the 0 level it makes a low-to-high transition that is simply the clock. This transition is a logical 0. When it is XORed with the 1 level it is inverted and makes a high-to-low transition. This transition is a logical 1. This scheme is called **Manchester** encoding and was used for classic Ethernet.

The downside of Manchester encoding is that it requires twice as much bandwidth as NRZ because of the clock, and we have learned that bandwidth often matters. A different strategy is based on the idea that we should code the data to ensure that there are enough transitions in the signal. Consider that NRZ will have clock recovery problems only for long runs of 0s and 1s. If there are frequent transitions, it will be easy for the receiver to stay synchronized with the incoming stream of symbols.

As a step in the right direction, we can simplify the situation by coding a 1 as a transition and a 0 as no transition, or vice versa. This coding is called **NRZI** (**Non-Return-to-Zero Inverted**), a twist on NRZ. An example is shown in

Fig. 2-20(c). The popular **USB (Universal Serial Bus)** standard for connecting computer peripherals uses NRZI. With it, long runs of 1s do not cause a problem.

Of course, long runs of 0s still cause a problem that we must fix. If we were the telephone company, we might simply require that the sender not transmit too many 0s. Older digital telephone lines in the U.S., called **T1 lines**, did in fact require that no more than 15 consecutive 0s be sent for them to work correctly. To really fix the problem we can break up runs of 0s by mapping small groups of bits to be transmitted so that groups with successive 0s are mapped to slightly longer patterns that do not have too many consecutive 0s.

A well-known code to do this is called **4B/5B**. Every 4 bits is mapped into a5-bit pattern with a fixed translation table. The five bit patterns are chosen so that there will never be a run of more than three consecutive 0s. The mapping is shown in Fig. 2-21. This scheme adds 25% overhead, which is better than the 100% overhead of Manchester encoding. Since there are 16 input combinations and 32 output combinations, some of the output combinations are not used. Putting aside the combinations with too many successive 0s, there are still some codes left. As a bonus, we can use these nondata codes to represent physical layer control signals. For example, in some uses "11111" represents an idle line and "11000" represents the start of a frame.

Data (4B)	Codeword (5B)	Data (4B)	Codeword (5B)
0000	11110	1000	10010
0001	01001	1001	10011
0010	10100	1010	10110
0011	10101	1011	10111
0100	01010	1100	11010
0101	01011	1101	11011
0110	01110	1110	11100
0111	01111	1111	11101

Figure 2-21. 4B/5B mapping.

An alternative approach is to make the data look random, known as scrambling. In this case it is very likely that there will be frequent transitions. A **scrambler** works by XORing the data with a pseudorandom sequence before it is transmitted. This mixing will make the data as random as the pseudorandom sequence (assuming it is independent of the pseudorandom sequence). The receiver then XORs the incoming bits with the same pseudorandom sequence to recover the real data. For this to be practical, the pseudorandom sequence must be easy to create. It is commonly given as the seed to a simple random number generator.

Scrambling is attractive because it adds no bandwidth or time overhead. In fact, it often helps to condition the signal so that it does not have its energy in dominant frequency components (caused by repetitive data patterns) that might radiate electromagnetic interference. Scrambling helps because random signals tend to be "white," or have energy spread across the frequency components.

However, scrambling does not guarantee that there will be no long runs. It is possible to get unlucky occasionally. If the data are the same as the pseudorandom sequence, they will XOR to all 0s. This outcome does not generally occur with a long pseudorandom sequence that is difficult to predict. However, with a short or predictable sequence, it might be possible for malicious users to send bit patterns that cause long runs of 0s after scrambling and cause links to fail. Early versions of the standards for sending IP packets over SONET links in the telephone system had this defect (Malis and Simpson, 1999). It was possible for users to send certain "killer packets" that were guaranteed to cause problems.

Balanced Signals

Signals that have as much positive voltage as negative voltage even over short periods of time are called **balanced signals**. They average to zero, which means that they have no DC electrical component. The lack of a DC component is an advantage because some channels, such as coaxial cable or lines with transformers, strongly attenuate a DC component due to their physical properties. Also, one method of connecting the receiver to the channel called **capacitive coupling** passes only the AC portion of a signal. In either case, if we send a signal whose average is not zero, we waste energy as the DC component will be filtered out.

Balancing helps to provide transitions for clock recovery since there is a mix of positive and negative voltages. It also provides a simple way to calibrate receivers because the average of the signal can be measured and used as a decision threshold to decode symbols. With unbalanced signals, the average may be drift away from the true decision level due to a density of 1s, for example, which would cause more symbols to be decoded with errors.

A straightforward way to construct a balanced code is to use two voltage levels to represent a logical 1, (say +1 V or −1 V) with 0 V representing a logical zero. To send a 1, the transmitter alternates between the +1 V and −1 V levels so that they always average out. This scheme is called **bipolar encoding**. In telephone networks it is called **AMI** (**Alternate Mark Inversion**), building on old terminology in which a 1 is called a "mark" and a 0 is called a "space." An example is given in Fig. 2-20(e).

Bipolar encoding adds a voltage level to achieve balance. Alternatively we can use a mapping like 4B/5B to achieve balance (as well as transitions for clock recovery). An example of this kind of balanced code is the **8B/10B** line code. It maps 8 bits of input to 10 bits of output, so it is 80% efficient, just like the 4B/5B line code. The 8 bits are split into a group of 5 bits, which is mapped to 6 bits, and a group of 3 bits, which is mapped to 4 bits. The 6-bit and 4-bit symbols are then concatenated. In each group, some input patterns can be mapped to balanced output patterns that have the same number of 0s and 1s. For example, "001" is mapped to "1001," which is balanced. But there are not enough combinations for all output patterns to be balanced. For these cases, each input pattern is mapped to two output patterns. One will have an extra 1 and the alternate will have an extra 0. For example, "000" is mapped to both "1011" and its complement "0100." As input bits are mapped to output bits, the encoder remembers the **disparity** from the previous symbol. The disparity is the total number of 0s or 1s by which the signal is out of balance. The encoder then selects either an output pattern or its alternate to reduce the disparity. With 8B/10B, the disparity will be at most 2 bits. Thus, the signal will never be far from balanced. There will also never be more than five consecutive 1s or 0s, to help with clock recovery.

2.5.2 Passband Transmission

Often, we want to use a range of frequencies that does not start at zero to send information across a channel. For wireless channels, it is not practical to send very low frequency signals because the size of the antenna needs to be a fraction of the signal wavelength, which becomes large. In any case, regulatory constraints and the need to avoid interference usually dictate the choice of frequencies. Even for wires, placing a signal in a given frequency band is useful to let different kinds of signals coexist on the channel. This kind of transmission is called passband transmission because an arbitrary band of frequencies is used to pass the signal.

Fortunately, our fundamental results from earlier in the chapter are all in terms of bandwidth, or the width of the frequency band. The absolute frequency values do not matter for capacity. This means that we can take a **baseband** signal that occupies 0 to B Hz and shift it up to occupy a **passband** of S to $S+B$ Hz without changing the amount of information that it can carry, even though the signal will look different. To process a signal at the receiver, we can shift it back down to baseband, where it is more convenient to detect symbols.

Digital modulation is accomplished with passband transmission by regulating or modulating a carrier signal that sits in the passband. We can modulate the amplitude, frequency, or phase of the carrier signal. Each of these methods has a corresponding name. In **ASK (Amplitude Shift Keying)**, two different amplitudes are used to represent 0 and 1. An example with a nonzero and a zero level is shown in Fig. 2-22(b). More than two levels can be used to represent more symbols. Similarly, with **FSK (Frequency Shift Keying)**, two or more different tones are used. The example in Fig. 2-21(c) uses just two frequencies. In the simplest form of **PSK (Phase Shift Keying)**, the carrier wave is systematically shifted 0 or 180 degrees at each symbol period. Because there are two phases, it is called **BPSK (Binary Phase Shift Keying)**. "Binary" here refers to the two symbols, not that the symbols represent 2 bits. An example is shown in Fig. 2-22(c). A better scheme that uses the channel bandwidth more efficiently is to use four shifts, e.g., 45, 135, 225, or 315 degrees, to transmit 2 bits of information per symbol. This version is called **QPSK** (**Quadrature Phase Shift Keying**).

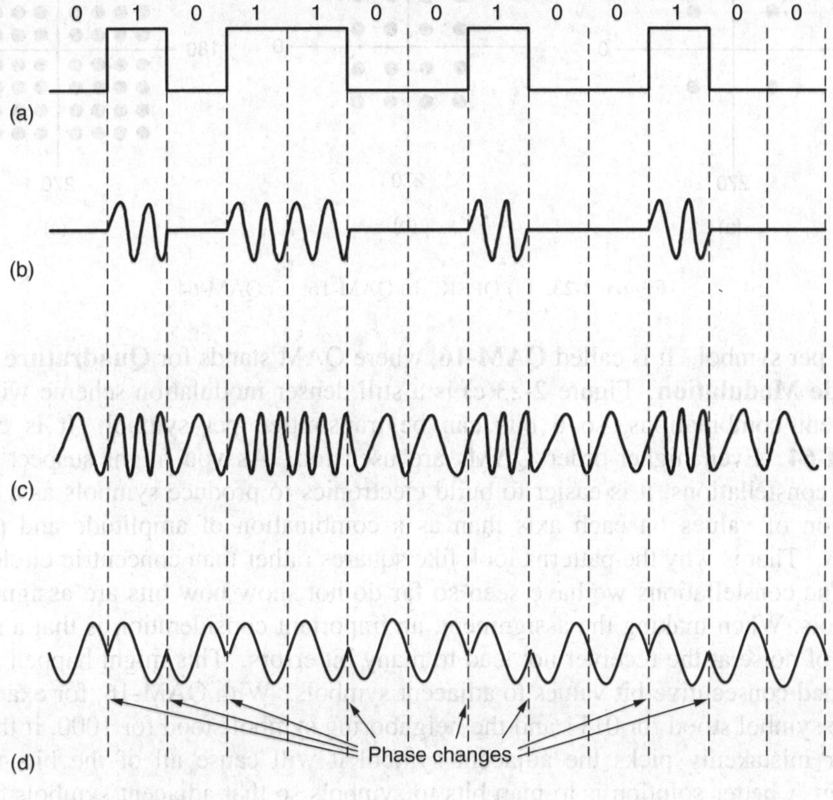

Figure 2-22. (a) A binary signal. (b) Amplitude shift keying. (c) Frequency shift keying. (d) Phase shift keying.

We can combine these schemes and use more levels to transmit more bits per symbol. Only one of frequency and phase can be modulated at a time because they are related, with frequency being the rate of change of phase over time. Usually, amplitude and phase are modulated in combination. Three examples are shown in Fig. 2-23. In each example, the points give the legal amplitude and phase combinations of each symbol. In Fig. 2-23(a), we see equidistant dots at 45, 135, 225, and 315 degrees. The phase of a dot is indicated by the angle a line from it to the origin makes with the positive x-axis. The amplitude of a dot is the distance from the origin. This figure is a representation of QPSK.

This kind of diagram is called a **constellation diagram**. In Fig. 2-23(b) we see a modulation scheme with a denser constellation. Sixteen combinations of amplitudes and phase are used, so the modulation scheme can be used to transmit

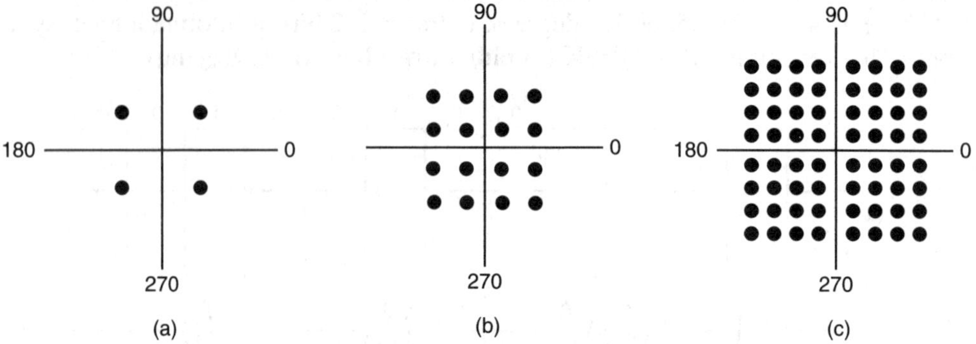

Figure 2-23. (a) QPSK. (b) QAM-16. (c) QAM-64.

4 bits per symbol. It is called **QAM-16**, where QAM stands for **Quadrature Amplitude Modulation**. Figure 2-23(c) is a still denser modulation scheme with 64 different combinations, so 6 bits can be transmitted per symbol. It is called **QAM-64**. Even higher-order QAMs are used too. As you might suspect from these constellations, it is easier to build electronics to produce symbols as a combination of values on each axis than as a combination of amplitude and phase values. That is why the patterns look like squares rather than concentric circles.

The constellations we have seen so far do not show how bits are assigned to symbols. When making the assignment, an important consideration is that a small burst of noise at the receiver not lead to many bit errors. This might happen if we assigned consecutive bit values to adjacent symbols. With QAM-16, for example, if one symbol stood for 0111 and the neighboring symbol stood for 1000, if the receiver mistakenly picks the adjacent symbol it will cause all of the bits to be wrong. A better solution is to map bits to symbols so that adjacent symbols differ in only 1 bit position. This mapping is called a **Gray code**. Fig. 2-24 shows a QAM-16 constellation that has been Gray coded. Now if the receiver decodes the symbol in error, it will make only a single bit error in the expected case that the decoded symbol is close to the transmitted symbol.

2.5.3 Frequency Division Multiplexing

The modulation schemes we have seen let us send one signal to convey bits along a wired or wireless link. However, economies of scale play an important role in how we use networks. It costs essentially the same amount of money to install and maintain a high-bandwidth transmission line as a low-bandwidth line between two different offices (i.e., the costs come from having to dig the trench and not from what kind of cable or fiber goes into it). Consequently, multiplexing schemes have been developed to share lines among many signals.

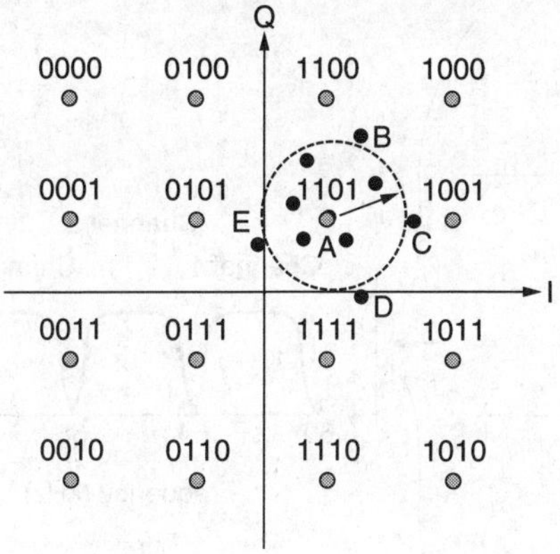

When 1101 is sent:

Point	Decodes as	Bit errors
A	1101	0
B	1100	1
C	1001	1
D	1111	1
E	0101	1

Figure 2-24. Gray-coded QAM-16.

FDM (**Frequency Division Multiplexing**) takes advantage of passband transmission to share a channel. It divides the spectrum into frequency bands, with each user having exclusive possession of some band in which to send their signal. AM radio broadcasting illustrates FDM. The allocated spectrum is about 1 MHz, roughly 500 to 1500 kHz. Different frequencies are allocated to different logical channels (stations), each operating in a portion of the spectrum, with the interchannel separation great enough to prevent interference.

For a more detailed example, in Fig. 2-25 we show three voice-grade telephone channels multiplexed using FDM. Filters limit the usable bandwidth to about 3100 Hz per voice-grade channel. When many channels are multiplexed together, 4000 Hz is allocated per channel. The excess is called a **guard band**. It keeps the channels well separated. First the voice channels are raised in frequency, each by a different amount. Then they can be combined because no two channels now occupy the same portion of the spectrum. Notice that even though there are gaps between the channels thanks to the guard bands, there is some overlap between adjacent channels. The overlap is there because real filters do not have ideal sharp edges. This means that a strong spike at the edge of one channel will be felt in the adjacent one as nonthermal noise.

This scheme has been used to multiplex calls in the telephone system for many years, but multiplexing in time is now preferred instead. However, FDM continues to be used in telephone networks, as well as cellular, terrestrial wireless, and satellite networks at a higher level of granularity.

When sending digital data, it is possible to divide the spectrum efficiently without using guard bands. In **OFDM** (**Orthogonal Frequency Division Multiplexing**), the channel bandwidth is divided into many subcarriers that independently send data (e.g., with QAM). The subcarriers are packed tightly together in the frequency domain. Thus, signals from each subcarrier extend into adjacent ones. However, as seen in Fig. 2-26, the frequency response of each subcarrier is

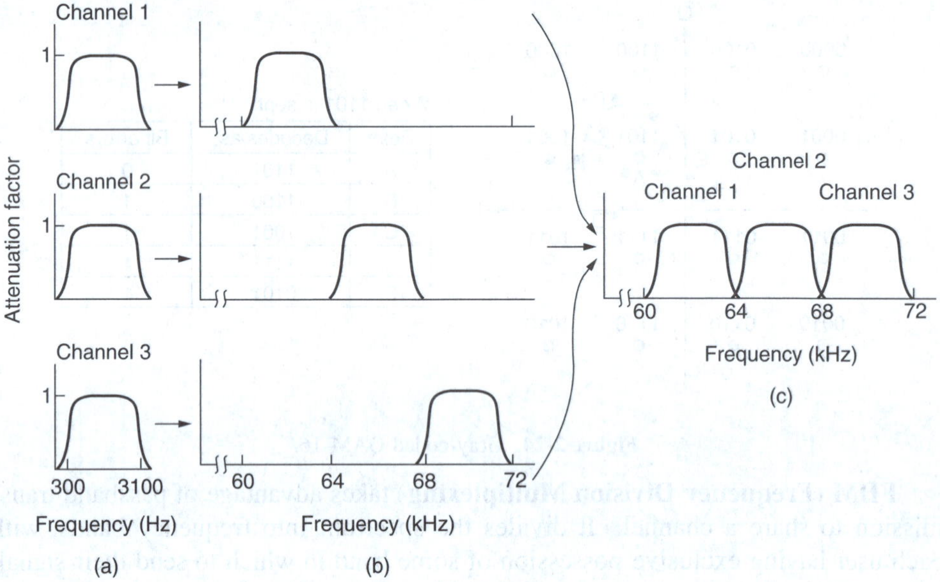

Figure 2-25. Frequency division multiplexing. (a) The original bandwidths. (b) The bandwidths raised in frequency. (c) The multiplexed channel.

designed so that it is zero at the center of the adjacent subcarriers. The subcarriers can therefore be sampled at their center frequencies without interference from their neighbors. To make this work, a guard time is needed to repeat a portion of the symbol signals in time so that they have the desired frequency response. However, this overhead is much less than is needed for many guard bands.

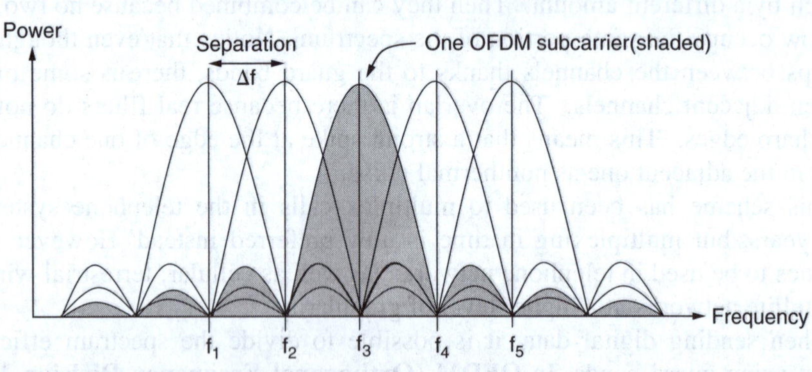

Figure 2-26. Orthogonal frequency division multiplexing (OFDM).

The idea of OFDM has been around for a long time, but it is only in the last decade that it has been widely adopted, following the realization that it is possible to implement OFDM efficiently in terms of a Fourier transform of digital data over all subcarriers (instead of separately modulating each subcarrier). OFDM is used in 802.11, cable networks and power line networking, and is planned for fourth-generation cellular systems. Usually, one high-rate stream of digital information is split into many low-rate streams that are transmitted on the subcarriers in parallel. This division is valuable because degradations of the channel are easier to cope with at the subcarrier level; some subcarriers may be very degraded and excluded in favor of subcarriers that are received well.

2.5.4 Time Division Multiplexing

An alternative to FDM is **TDM** (**Time Division Multiplexing**). Here, the users take turns (in a round-robin fashion), each one periodically getting the entire bandwidth for a little burst of time. An example of three streams being multiplexed with TDM is shown in Fig. 2-27. Bits from each input stream are taken in a fixed **time slot** and output to the aggregate stream. This stream runs at the sum rate of the individual streams. For this to work, the streams must be synchronized in time. Small intervals of **guard time** analogous to a frequency guard band may be added to accommodate small timing variations.

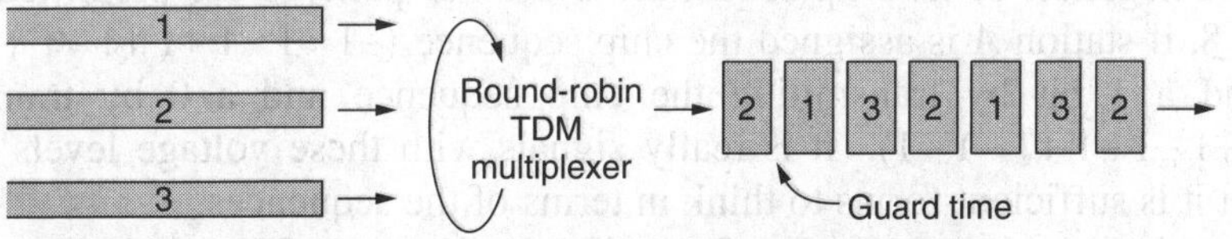

Figure 2-27. Time Division Multiplexing (TDM).

TDM is used widely as part of the telephone and cellular networks. To avoid one point of confusion, let us be clear that it is quite different from the alternative **STDM** (**Statistical Time Division Multiplexing**). The prefix ''statistical'' is added to indicate that the individual streams contribute to the multiplexed stream *not* on a fixed schedule, but according to the statistics of their demand. STDM is packet switching by another name.

2.5.5 Code Division Multiplexing

There is a third kind of multiplexing that works in a completely different way than FDM and TDM. **CDM** (**Code Division Multiplexing**) is a form of **spread spectrum** communication in which a narrowband signal is spread out over a wider frequency band. This can make it more tolerant of interference, as well as allowing multiple signals from different users to share the same frequency band. Because code division multiplexing is mostly used for the latter purpose it is commonly called **CDMA** (**Code Division Multiple Access**).

CDMA allows each station to transmit over the entire frequency spectrum all the time. Multiple simultaneous transmissions are separated using coding theory. Before getting into the algorithm, let us consider an analogy: an airport lounge with many pairs of people conversing. TDM is comparable to pairs of people in the room taking turns speaking. FDM is comparable to the pairs of people speaking at different pitches, some high-pitched and some low-pitched such that each pair can hold its own conversation at the same time as but independently of the others. CDMA is comparable to each pair of people talking at once, but in a different language. The French-speaking couple just hones in on the French, rejecting everything that is not French as noise. Thus, the key to CDMA is to be able to extract the desired signal while rejecting everything else as random noise. A somewhat simplified description of CDMA follows.

In CDMA, each bit time is subdivided into m short intervals called **chips**. Typically, there are 64 or 128 chips per bit, but in the example given here we will use 8 chips/bit for simplicity. Each station is assigned a unique m-bit code called a **chip sequence**. For pedagogical purposes, it is convenient to use a bipolar notation to write these codes as sequences of −1 and +1. We will show chip sequences in parentheses.

To transmit a 1 bit, a station sends its chip sequence. To transmit a 0 bit, it sends the negation of its chip sequence. No other patterns are permitted. Thus, for $m = 8$, if station A is assigned the chip sequence (−1 −1 −1 +1 +1 −1 +1 +1), it can send a 1 bit by transmiting the chip sequence and a 0 by transmitting (+1 +1 +1 −1 −1 +1 −1 −1). It is really signals with these voltage levels that are sent, but it is sufficient for us to think in terms of the sequences.

Increasing the amount of information to be sent from b bits/sec to mb chips/sec for each station means that the bandwidth needed for CDMA is greater by a factor of m than the bandwidth needed for a station not using CDMA (assuming no changes in the modulation or encoding techniques). If we have a 1-MHz band available for 100 stations, with FDM each one would have 10 kHz and could send at 10 kbps (assuming 1 bit per Hz). With CDMA, each station uses the full 1 MHz, so the chip rate is 100 chips per bit to spread the station's bit rate of 10 kbps across the channel.

In Fig. 2-28(a) and (b) we show the chip sequences assigned to four example stations and the signals that they represent. Each station has its own unique chip sequence. Let us use the symbol **S** to indicate the m-chip vector for station S, and $\overline{\mathbf{S}}$ for its negation. All chip sequences are pairwise **orthogonal**, by which we mean that the normalized inner product of any two distinct chip sequences, **S** and **T** (written as **S•T**), is 0. It is known how to generate such orthogonal chip sequences using a method known as **Walsh codes**. In mathematical terms, orthogonality of the chip sequences can be expressed as follows:

$$\mathbf{S} \bullet \mathbf{T} \equiv \frac{1}{m} \sum_{i=1}^{m} S_i T_i = 0 \qquad (2\text{-}5)$$

In plain English, as many pairs are the same as are different. This orthogonality property will prove crucial later. Note that if $\mathbf{S}\bullet\mathbf{T}=0$, then $\mathbf{S}\bullet\overline{\mathbf{T}}$ is also 0. The normalized inner product of any chip sequence with itself is 1:

$$\mathbf{S}\bullet\mathbf{S}=\frac{1}{m}\sum_{i=1}^{m}S_iS_i=\frac{1}{m}\sum_{i=1}^{m}S_i^2=\frac{1}{m}\sum_{i=1}^{m}(\pm 1)^2=1$$

This follows because each of the m terms in the inner product is 1, so the sum is m. Also note that $\mathbf{S}\bullet\overline{\mathbf{S}}=-1$.

A = (−1 −1 −1 +1 +1 −1 +1 +1)
B = (−1 −1 +1 −1 +1 +1 +1 −1)
C = (−1 +1 −1 +1 +1 +1 −1 −1)
D = (−1 +1 −1 −1 −1 −1 +1 −1)

(a)

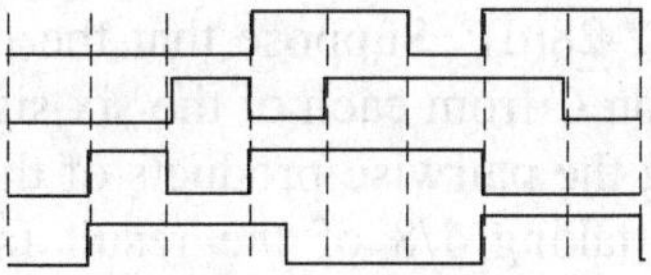

(b)

S_1 = C = (−1 +1 −1 +1 +1 +1 −1 −1)
S_2 = B+C = (−2 0 0 0 +2 +2 0 −2)
S_3 = A+$\overline{\text{B}}$ = (0 0 −2 +2 0 −2 0 +2)
S_4 = A+$\overline{\text{B}}$+C = (−1 +1 −3 +3 +1 −1 −1 +1)
S_5 = A+B+C+D = (−4 0 −2 0 +2 0 +2 −2)
S_6 = A+B+$\overline{\text{C}}$+D = (−2 −2 0 −2 0 −2 +4 0)

(c)

$S_1\bullet$C = [1+1−1+1+1+1−1−1]/8 = 1
$S_2\bullet$C = [2+0+0+0+2+2+0+2]/8 = 1
$S_3\bullet$C = [0+0+2+2+0−2+0−2]/8 = 0
$S_4\bullet$C = [1+1+3+3+1−1+1−1]/8 = 1
$S_5\bullet$C = [4+0+2+0+2+0−2+2]/8 = 1
$S_6\bullet$C = [2−2+0−2+0−2−4+0]/8 = −1

(d)

Figure 2-28. (a) Chip sequences for four stations. (b) Signals the sequences represent (c) Six examples of transmissions. (d) Recovery of station C's signal.

During each bit time, a station can transmit a 1 (by sending its chip sequence), it can transmit a 0 (by sending the negative of its chip sequence), or it can be silent and transmit nothing. We assume for now that all stations are synchronized in time, so all chip sequences begin at the same instant. When two or more stations transmit simultaneously, their bipolar sequences add linearly. For example, if in one chip period three stations output +1 and one station outputs −1, +2 will be received. One can think of this as signals that add as voltages superimposed on the channel: three stations output +1 V and one station outputs −1 V, so that 2 V is received. For instance, in Fig. 2-28(c) we see six examples of one or more stations transmitting 1 bit at the same time. In the first example, C transmits a 1 bit, so we just get C's chip sequence. In the second example, both B and C transmit 1 bits, so we get the sum of their bipolar chip sequences, namely:

$$(-1\ -1\ +1\ -1\ +1\ +1\ +1\ -1)+(-1\ +1\ -1\ +1\ +1\ +1\ -1\ -1)=(-2\ 0\ 0\ 0\ +2\ +2\ 0\ -2)$$

To recover the bit stream of an individual station, the receiver must know that station's chip sequence in advance. It does the recovery by computing the normalized inner product of the received chip sequence and the chip sequence of the station whose bit stream it is trying to recover. If the received chip sequence is **S** and the receiver is trying to listen to a station whose chip sequence is **C**, it just computes the normalized inner product, $\mathbf{S}\bullet\mathbf{C}$.

To see why this works, just imagine that two stations, *A* and *C*, both transmit a 1 bit at the same time that *B* transmits a 0 bit, as is the case in the third example. The receiver sees the sum, $\mathbf{S} = \mathbf{A} + \overline{\mathbf{B}} + \mathbf{C}$, and computes

$$\mathbf{S} \bullet \mathbf{C} = (\mathbf{A} + \overline{\mathbf{B}} + \mathbf{C}) \bullet \mathbf{C} = \mathbf{A} \bullet \mathbf{C} + \overline{\mathbf{B}} \bullet \mathbf{C} + \mathbf{C} \bullet \mathbf{C} = 0 + 0 + 1 = 1$$

The first two terms vanish because all pairs of chip sequences have been carefully chosen to be orthogonal, as shown in Eq. (2-5). Now it should be clear why this property must be imposed on the chip sequences.

To make the decoding process more concrete, we show six examples in Fig. 2-28(d). Suppose that the receiver is interested in extracting the bit sent by station *C* from each of the six signals S_1 through S_6. It calculates the bit by summing the pairwise products of the received **S** and the **C** vector of Fig. 2-28(a) and then taking 1/8 of the result (since $m = 8$ here). The examples include cases where *C* is silent, sends a 1 bit, and sends a 0 bit, individually and in combination with other transmissions. As shown, the correct bit is decoded each time. It is just like speaking French.

In principle, given enough computing capacity, the receiver can listen to all the senders at once by running the decoding algorithm for each of them in parallel. In real life, suffice it to say that this is easier said than done, and it is useful to know which senders might be transmitting.

In the ideal, noiseless CDMA system we have studied here, the number of stations that send concurrently can be made arbitrarily large by using longer chip sequences. For 2^n stations, Walsh codes can provide 2^n orthogonal chip sequences of length 2^n. However, one significant limitation is that we have assumed that all the chips are synchronized in time at the receiver. This synchronization is not even approximately true in some applications, such as cellular networks (in which CDMA has been widely deployed starting in the 1990s). It leads to different designs. We will return to this topic later in the chapter and describe how asynchronous CDMA differs from synchronous CDMA.

As well as cellular networks, CDMA is used by satellites and cable networks. We have glossed over many complicating factors in this brief introduction. Engineers who want to gain a deep understanding of CDMA should read Viterbi (1995) and Lee and Miller (1998). These references require quite a bit of background in communication engineering, however.

2.6 THE PUBLIC SWITCHED TELEPHONE NETWORK

When two computers owned by the same company or organization and located close to each other need to communicate, it is often easiest just to run a cable between them. LANs work this way. However, when the distances are large or there are many computers or the cables have to pass through a public road or other public right of way, the costs of running private cables are usually prohibitive.

Furthermore, in just about every country in the world, stringing private transmission lines across (or underneath) public property is also illegal. Consequently, the network designers must rely on the existing telecommunication facilities.

These facilities, especially the **PSTN** (**Public Switched Telephone Network**), were usually designed many years ago, with a completely different goal in mind: transmitting the human voice in a more-or-less recognizable form. Their suitability for use in computer-computer communication is often marginal at best. To see the size of the problem, consider that a cheap commodity cable running between two computers can transfer data at 1 Gbps or more. In contrast, typical ADSL, the blazingly fast alternative to a telephone modem, runs at around 1 Mbps. The difference between the two is the difference between cruising in an airplane and taking a leisurely stroll.

Nonetheless, the telephone system is tightly intertwined with (wide area) computer networks, so it is worth devoting some time to study it in detail. The limiting factor for networking purposes turns out to be the "last mile" over which customers connect, not the trunks and switches inside the telephone network. This situation is changing with the gradual rollout of fiber and digital technology at the edge of the network, but it will take time and money. During the long wait, computer systems designers used to working with systems that give at least three orders of magnitude better performance have devoted much time and effort to figure out how to use the telephone network efficiently.

In the following sections we will describe the telephone system and show how it works. For additional information about the innards of the telephone system see Bellamy (2000).

2.6.1 Structure of the Telephone System

Soon after Alexander Graham Bell patented the telephone in 1876 (just a few hours ahead of his rival, Elisha Gray), there was an enormous demand for his new invention. The initial market was for the sale of telephones, which came in pairs. It was up to the customer to string a single wire between them. If a telephone owner wanted to talk to n other telephone owners, separate wires had to be strung to all n houses. Within a year, the cities were covered with wires passing over houses and trees in a wild jumble. It became immediately obvious that the model of connecting every telephone to every other telephone, as shown in Fig. 2-29(a), was not going to work.

To his credit, Bell saw this problem early on and formed the Bell Telephone Company, which opened its first switching office (in New Haven, Connecticut) in 1878. The company ran a wire to each customer's house or office. To make a call, the customer would crank the phone to make a ringing sound in the telephone company office to attract the attention of an operator, who would then manually connect the caller to the callee by using a short jumper cable to connect the caller to the callee. The model of a single switching office is illustrated in Fig. 2-29(b).

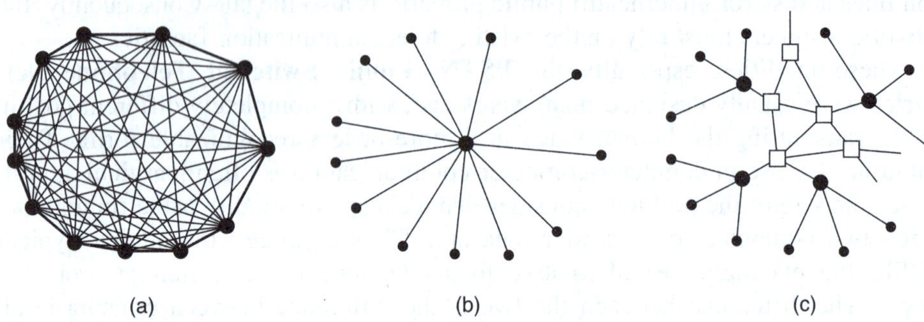

Figure 2-29. (a) Fully interconnected network. (b) Centralized switch. (c) Two-level hierarchy.

Pretty soon, Bell System switching offices were springing up everywhere and people wanted to make long-distance calls between cities, so the Bell System began to connect the switching offices. The original problem soon returned: to connect every switching office to every other switching office by means of a wire between them quickly became unmanageable, so second-level switching offices were invented. After a while, multiple second-level offices were needed, as illustrated in Fig. 2-29(c). Eventually, the hierarchy grew to five levels.

By 1890, the three major parts of the telephone system were in place: the switching offices, the wires between the customers and the switching offices (by now balanced, insulated, twisted pairs instead of open wires with an earth return), and the long-distance connections between the switching offices. For a short technical history of the telephone system, see Hawley (1991).

While there have been improvements in all three areas since then, the basic Bell System model has remained essentially intact for over 100 years. The following description is highly simplified but gives the essential flavor nevertheless. Each telephone has two copper wires coming out of it that go directly to the telephone company's nearest **end office** (also called a **local central office**). The distance is typically 1 to 10 km, being shorter in cities than in rural areas. In the United States alone there are about 22,000 end offices. The two-wire connections between each subscriber's telephone and the end office are known in the trade as the **local loop**. If the world's local loops were stretched out end to end, they would extend to the moon and back 1000 times.

At one time, 80% of AT&T's capital value was the copper in the local loops. AT&T was then, in effect, the world's largest copper mine. Fortunately, this fact was not well known in the investment community. Had it been known, some corporate raider might have bought AT&T, ended all telephone service in the United States, ripped out all the wire, and sold it to a copper refiner for a quick payback.

If a subscriber attached to a given end office calls another subscriber attached to the same end office, the switching mechanism within the office sets up a direct electrical connection between the two local loops. This connection remains intact for the duration of the call.

If the called telephone is attached to another end office, a different procedure has to be used. Each end office has a number of outgoing lines to one or more nearby switching centers, called **toll offices** (or, if they are within the same local area, **tandem offices**). These lines are called **toll connecting trunks**. The number of different kinds of switching centers and their topology varies from country to country depending on the country's telephone density.

If both the caller's and callee's end offices happen to have a toll connecting trunk to the same toll office (a likely occurrence if they are relatively close by), the connection may be established within the toll office. A telephone network consisting only of telephones (the small dots), end offices (the large dots), and toll offices (the squares) is shown in Fig. 2-29(c).

If the caller and callee do not have a toll office in common, a path will have to be established between two toll offices. The toll offices communicate with each other via high-bandwidth **intertoll trunks** (also called **interoffice trunks**). Prior to the 1984 breakup of AT&T, the U.S. telephone system used hierarchical routing to find a path, going to higher levels of the hierarchy until there was a switching office in common. This was then replaced with more flexible, nonhierarchical routing. Figure 2-30 shows how a long-distance connection might be routed.

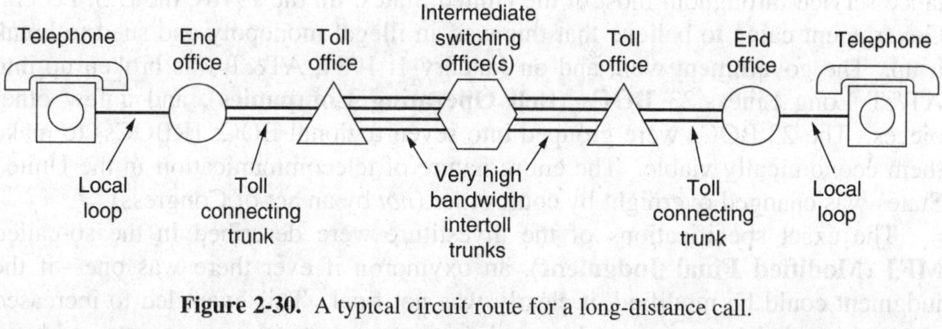

Figure 2-30. A typical circuit route for a long-distance call.

A variety of transmission media are used for telecommunication. Unlike modern office buildings, where the wiring is commonly Category 5, local loops to homes mostly consist of Category 3 twisted pairs, with fiber just starting to appear. Between switching offices, coaxial cables, microwaves, and especially fiber optics are widely used.

In the past, transmission throughout the telephone system was analog, with the actual voice signal being transmitted as an electrical voltage from source to destination. With the advent of fiber optics, digital electronics, and computers, all the trunks and switches are now digital, leaving the local loop as the last piece of analog technology in the system. Digital transmission is preferred because it is not necessary to accurately reproduce an analog waveform after it has passed through many amplifiers on a long call. Being able to correctly distinguish a 0 from a 1 is enough. This property makes digital transmission more reliable than analog. It is also cheaper and easier to maintain.

In summary, the telephone system consists of three major components:

1. Local loops (analog twisted pairs going to houses and businesses).
2. Trunks (digital fiber optic links connecting the switching offices).
3. Switching offices (where calls are moved from one trunk to another).

After a short digression on the politics of telephones, we will come back to each of these three components in some detail. The local loops provide everyone access to the whole system, so they are critical. Unfortunately, they are also the weakest link in the system. For the long-haul trunks, the main issue is how to collect multiple calls together and send them out over the same fiber. This calls for multiplexing, and we apply FDM and TDM to do it. Finally, there are two fundamentally different ways of doing switching; we will look at both.

2.6.2 The Politics of Telephones

For decades prior to 1984, the Bell System provided both local and long-distance service throughout most of the United States. In the 1970s, the U.S. Federal Government came to believe that this was an illegal monopoly and sued to break it up. The government won, and on January 1, 1984, AT&T was broken up into AT&T Long Lines, 23 **BOCs (Bell Operating Companies)**, and a few other pieces. The 23 BOCs were grouped into seven regional BOCs (RBOCs) to make them economically viable. The entire nature of telecommunication in the United States was changed overnight by court order (*not* by an act of Congress).

The exact specifications of the divestiture were described in the so-called **MFJ (Modified Final Judgment)**, an oxymoron if ever there was one—if the judgment could be modified, it clearly was not final. This event led to increased competition, better service, and lower long-distance rates for consumers and businesses. However, prices for local service rose as the cross subsidies from long-distance calling were eliminated and local service had to become self supporting. Many other countries have now introduced competition along similar lines.

Of direct relevance to our studies is that the new competitive framework caused a key technical feature to be added to the architecture of the telephone network. To make it clear who could do what, the United States was divided up into 164 **LATAs (Local Access and Transport Areas)**. Very roughly, a LATA is about as big as the area covered by one area code. Within each LATA, there was one **LEC (Local Exchange Carrier)** with a monopoly on traditional telephone service within its area. The most important LECs were the BOCs, although some LATAs contained one or more of the 1500 independent telephone companies operating as LECs.

The new feature was that all inter-LATA traffic was handled by a different kind of company, an **IXC** (**IntereXchange Carrier**). Originally, AT&T Long Lines was the only serious IXC, but now there are well-established competitors such as Verizon and Sprint in the IXC business. One of the concerns at the breakup was to ensure that all the IXCs would be treated equally in terms of line quality, tariffs, and the number of digits their customers would have to dial to use them. The way this is handled is illustrated in Fig. 2-31. Here we see three example LATAs, each with several end offices. LATAs 2 and 3 also have a small hierarchy with tandem offices (intra-LATA toll offices).

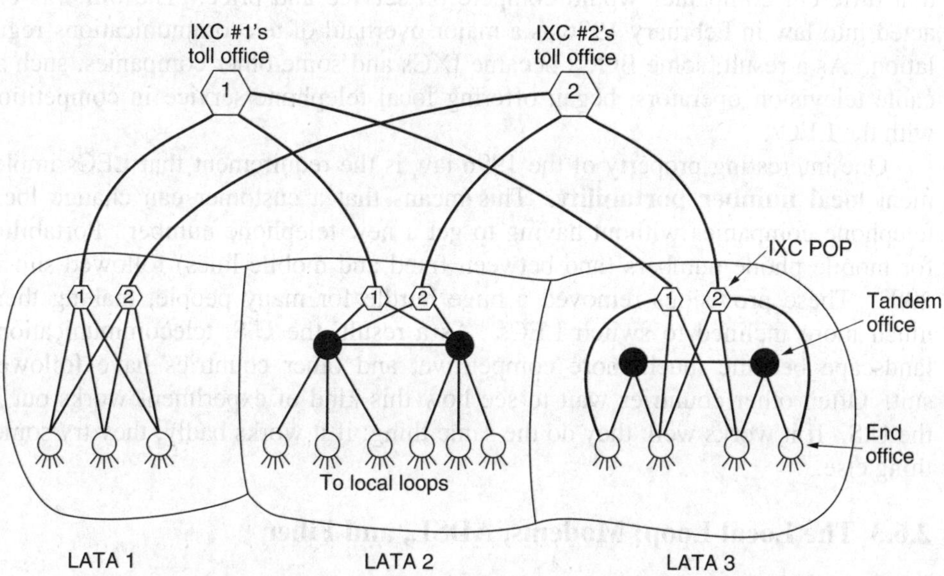

Figure 2-31. The relationship of LATAs, LECs, and IXCs. All the circles are LEC switching offices. Each hexagon belongs to the IXC whose number is in it.

Any IXC that wishes to handle calls originating in a LATA can build a switching office called a **POP** (**Point of Presence**) there. The LEC is required to connect each IXC to every end office, either directly, as in LATAs 1 and 3, or indirectly, as in LATA 2. Furthermore, the terms of the connection, both technical and financial, must be identical for all IXCs. This requirement enables, a subscriber in, say, LATA 1, to choose which IXC to use for calling subscribers in LATA 3.

As part of the MFJ, the IXCs were forbidden to offer local telephone service and the LECs were forbidden to offer inter-LATA telephone service, although both were free to enter any other business, such as operating fried chicken restaurants. In 1984, that was a fairly unambiguous statement. Unfortunately, technology has a funny way of making the law obsolete. Neither cable television nor mobile phones were covered by the agreement. As cable television went from one way to two way and mobile phones exploded in popularity, both LECs and IXCs began buying up or merging with cable and mobile operators.

By 1995, Congress saw that trying to maintain a distinction between the various kinds of companies was no longer tenable and drafted a bill to preserve accessibility for competition but allow cable TV companies, local telephone companies, long-distance carriers, and mobile operators to enter one another's businesses. The idea was that any company could then offer its customers a single integrated package containing cable TV, telephone, and information services and that different companies would compete on service and price. The bill was enacted into law in February 1996 as a major overhaul of telecommunications regulation. As a result, some BOCs became IXCs and some other companies, such as cable television operators, began offering local telephone service in competition with the LECs.

One interesting property of the 1996 law is the requirement that LECs implement **local number portability**. This means that a customer can change local telephone companies without having to get a new telephone number. Portability for mobile phone numbers (and between fixed and mobile lines) followed suit in 2003. These provisions removed a huge hurdle for many people, making them much more inclined to switch LECs. As a result, the U.S. telecommunications landscape became much more competitive, and other countries have followed suit. Often other countries wait to see how this kind of experiment works out in the U.S. If it works well, they do the same thing; if it works badly, they try something else.

2.6.3 The Local Loop: Modems, ADSL, and Fiber

It is now time to start our detailed study of how the telephone system works. Let us begin with the part that most people are familiar with: the two-wire local loop coming from a telephone company end office into houses. The local loop is also frequently referred to as the "last mile," although the length can be up to several miles. It has carried analog information for over 100 years and is likely to continue doing so for some years to come, due to the high cost of converting to digital.

Much effort has been devoted to squeezing data networking out of the copper local loops that are already deployed. Telephone modems send digital data between computers over the narrow channel the telephone network provides for a voice call. They were once widely used, but have been largely displaced by broadband technologies such as ADSL that. reuse the local loop to send digital data from a customer to the end office, where they are siphoned off to the Internet.

Both modems and ADSL must deal with the limitations of old local loops: relatively narrow bandwidth, attenuation and distortion of signals, and susceptibility to electrical noise such as crosstalk.

In some places, the local loop has been modernized by installing optical fiber to (or very close to) the home. Fiber is the way of the future. These installations support computer networks from the ground up, with the local loop having ample bandwidth for data services. The limiting factor is what people will pay, not the physics of the local loop.

In this section we will study the local loop, both old and new. We will cover telephone modems, ADSL, and fiber to the home.

Telephone Modems

To send bits over the local loop, or any other physical channel for that matter, they must be converted to analog signals that can be transmitted over the channel. This conversion is accomplished using the methods for digital modulation that we studied in the previous section. At the other end of the channel, the analog signal is converted back to bits.

A device that converts between a stream of digital bits and an analog signal that represents the bits is called a **modem**, which is short for "*mo*dulator *dem*odulator." Modems come in many varieties: telephone modems, DSL modems, cable modems, wireless modems, etc. The modem may be built into the computer (which is now common for telephone modems) or be a separate box (which is common for DSL and cable modems). Logically, the modem is inserted between the (digital) computer and the (analog) telephone system, as seen in Fig. 2-32.

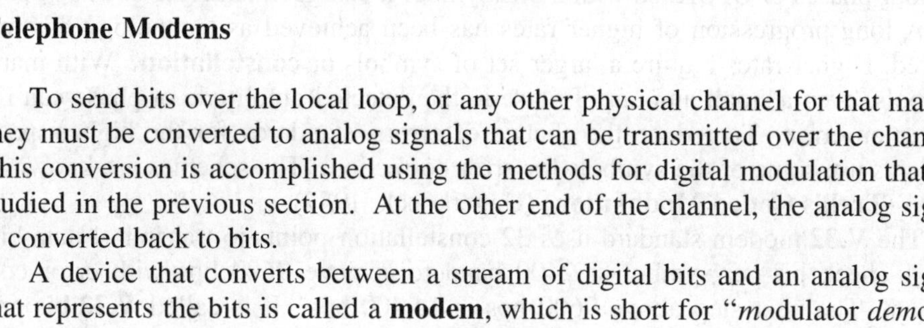

Figure 2-32. The use of both analog and digital transmission for a computer-to-computer call. Conversion is done by the modems and codecs.

Telephone modems are used to send bits between two computers over a voice-grade telephone line, in place of the conversation that usually fills the line. The main difficulty in doing so is that a voice-grade telephone line is limited to 3100 Hz, about what is sufficient to carry a conversation. This bandwidth is more than four orders of magnitude less than the bandwidth that is used for Ethernet or

802.11 (WiFi). Unsurprisingly, the data rates of telephone modems are also four orders of magnitude less than that of Ethernet and 802.11.

Let us run the numbers to see why this is the case. The Nyquist theorem tells us that even with a perfect 3000-Hz line (which a telephone line is decidedly not), there is no point in sending symbols at a rate faster than 6000 baud. In practice, most modems send at a rate of 2400 symbols/sec, or 2400 baud, and focus on getting multiple bits per symbol while allowing traffic in both directions at the same time (by using different frequencies for different directions).

The humble 2400-bps modem uses 0 volts for a logical 0 and 1 volt for a logical 1, with 1 bit per symbol. One step up, it can use four different symbols, as in the four phases of QPSK, so with 2 bits/symbol it can get a data rate of 4800 bps.

A long progression of higher rates has been achieved as technology has improved. Higher rates require a larger set of symbols or **constellation**. With many symbols, even a small amount of noise in the detected amplitude or phase can result in an error. To reduce the chance of errors, standards for the higher-speed modems use some of the symbols for error correction. The schemes are known as **TCM (Trellis Coded Modulation)** (Ungerboeck, 1987).

The **V.32** modem standard uses 32 constellation points to transmit 4 data bits and 1 check bit per symbol at 2400 baud to achieve 9600 bps with error correction. The next step above 9600 bps is 14,400 bps. It is called **V.32 bis** and transmits 6 data bits and 1 check bit per symbol at 2400 baud. Then comes **V.34**, which achieves 28,800 bps by transmitting 12 data bits/symbol at 2400 baud. The constellation now has thousands of points. The final modem in this series is **V.34 bis** which uses 14 data bits/symbol at 2400 baud to achieve 33,600 bps.

Why stop here? The reason that standard modems stop at 33,600 is that the Shannon limit for the telephone system is about 35 kbps based on the average length of local loops and the quality of these lines. Going faster than this would violate the laws of physics (department of thermodynamics).

However, there is one way we can change the situation. At the telephone company end office, the data are converted to digital form for transmission within the telephone network (the core of the telephone network converted from analog to digital long ago). The 35-kbps limit is for the situation in which there are two local loops, one at each end. Each of these adds noise to the signal. If we could get rid of one of these local loops, we would increase the SNR and the maximum rate would be doubled.

This approach is how 56-kbps modems are made to work. One end, typically an ISP, gets a high-quality digital feed from the nearest end office. Thus, when one end of the connection is a high-quality signal, as it is with most ISPs now, the maximum data rate can be as high as 70 kbps. Between two home users with modems and analog lines, the maximum is still 33.6 kbps.

The reason that 56-kbps modems (rather than 70-kbps modems) are in use has to do with the Nyquist theorem. A telephone channel is carried inside the telephone system as digital samples. Each telephone channel is 4000 Hz wide when the guard bands are included. The number of samples per second needed to reconstruct it is thus 8000. The number of bits per sample in the U.S. is 8, one of which may be used for control purposes, allowing 56,000 bits/sec of user data. In Europe, all 8 bits are available to users, so 64,000-bit/sec modems could have been used, but to get international agreement on a standard, 56,000 was chosen.

The end result is the **V.90** and **V.92** modem standards. They provide for a 56-kbps downstream channel (ISP to user) and a 33.6-kbps and 48-kbps upstream channel (user to ISP), respectively. The asymmetry is because there is usually more data transported from the ISP to the user than the other way. It also means that more of the limited bandwidth can be allocated to the downstream channel to increase the chances of it actually working at 56 kbps.

Digital Subscriber Lines

When the telephone industry finally got to 56 kbps, it patted itself on the back for a job well done. Meanwhile, the cable TV industry was offering speeds up to 10 Mbps on shared cables. As Internet access became an increasingly important part of their business, the telephone companies (LECs) began to realize they needed a more competitive product. Their answer was to offer new digital services over the local loop.

Initially, there were many overlapping high-speed offerings, all under the general name of **xDSL** (**Digital Subscriber Line**), for various *x*. Services with more bandwidth than standard telephone service are sometimes called **broadband**, although the term really is more of a marketing concept than a specific technical concept. Later, we will discuss what has become the most popular of these services, **ADSL** (**Asymmetric DSL**). We will also use the term DSL or xDSL as shorthand for all flavors.

The reason that modems are so slow is that telephones were invented for carrying the human voice and the entire system has been carefully optimized for this purpose. Data have always been stepchildren. At the point where each local loop terminates in the end office, the wire runs through a filter that attenuates all frequencies below 300 Hz and above 3400 Hz. The cutoff is not sharp—300 Hz and 3400 Hz are the 3-dB points—so the bandwidth is usually quoted as 4000 Hz even though the distance between the 3 dB points is 3100 Hz. Data on the wire are thus also restricted to this narrow band.

The trick that makes xDSL work is that when a customer subscribes to it, the incoming line is connected to a different kind of switch, one that does not have this filter, thus making the entire capacity of the local loop available. The limiting factor then becomes the physics of the local loop, which supports roughly 1 MHz, not the artificial 3100 Hz bandwidth created by the filter.

Unfortunately, the capacity of the local loop falls rather quickly with distance from the end office as the signal is increasingly degraded along the wire. It also depends on the thickness and general quality of the twisted pair. A plot of the potential bandwidth as a function of distance is given in Fig. 2-33. This figure assumes that all the other factors are optimal (new wires, modest bundles, etc.).

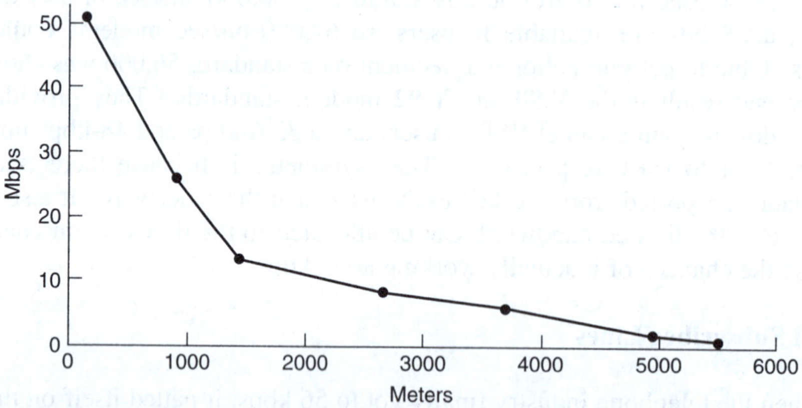

Figure 2-33. Bandwidth versus distance over Category 3 UTP for DSL.

The implication of this figure creates a problem for the telephone company. When it picks a speed to offer, it is simultaneously picking a radius from its end offices beyond which the service cannot be offered. This means that when distant customers try to sign up for the service, they may be told "Thanks a lot for your interest, but you live 100 meters too far from the nearest end office to get this service. Could you please move?" The lower the chosen speed is, the larger the radius and the more customers are covered. But the lower the speed, the less attractive the service is and the fewer the people who will be willing to pay for it. This is where business meets technology.

The xDSL services have all been designed with certain goals in mind. First, the services must work over the existing Category 3 twisted pair local loops. Second, they must not affect customers' existing telephones and fax machines. Third, they must be much faster than 56 kbps. Fourth, they should be always on, with just a monthly charge and no per-minute charge.

To meet the technical goals, the available 1.1 MHz spectrum on the local loop is divided into 256 independent channels of 4312.5 Hz each. This arrangement is shown in Fig. 2-34. The OFDM scheme, which we saw in the previous section, is used to send data over these channels, though it is often called **DMT** (**Discrete MultiTone**) in the context of ADSL. Channel 0 is used for **POTS** (**Plain Old Telephone Service**). Channels 1–5 are not used, to keep the voice and data signals from interfering with each other. Of the remaining 250 channels, one is used for upstream control and one is used for downstream control. The rest are available for user data.

In principle, each of the remaining channels can be used for a full-duplex data stream, but harmonics, crosstalk, and other effects keep practical systems well

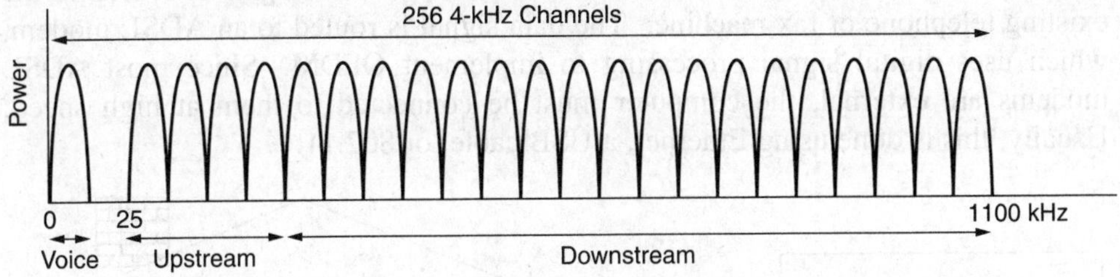

Figure 2-34. Operation of ADSL using discrete multitone modulation.

below the theoretical limit. It is up to the provider to determine how many channels are used for upstream and how many for downstream. A 50/50 mix of upstream and downstream is technically possible, but most providers allocate something like 80–90% of the bandwidth to the downstream channel since most users download more data than they upload. This choice gives rise to the "A" in ADSL. A common split is 32 channels for upstream and the rest downstream. It is also possible to have a few of the highest upstream channels be bidirectional for increased bandwidth, although making this optimization requires adding a special circuit to cancel echoes.

The international ADSL standard, known as **G.dmt**, was approved in 1999. It allows speeds of as much as 8 Mbps downstream and 1 Mbps upstream. It was superseded by a second generation in 2002, called ADSL2, with various improvements to allow speeds of as much as 12 Mbps downstream and 1 Mbps upstream. Now we have ADSL2+, which doubles the downstream speed to 24 Mbps by doubling the bandwidth to use 2.2 MHz over the twisted pair.

However, the numbers quoted here are best-case speeds for good lines close (within 1 to 2 km) to the exchange. Few lines support these rates, and few providers offer these speeds. Typically, providers offer something like 1 Mbps downstream and 256 kbps upstream (standard service), 4 Mbps downstream and 1 Mbps upstream (improved service), and 8 Mbps downstream and 2 Mbps upstream (premium service).

Within each channel, QAM modulation is used at a rate of roughly 4000 symbols/sec. The line quality in each channel is constantly monitored and the data rate is adjusted by using a larger or smaller constellation, like those in Fig. 2-23. Different channels may have different data rates, with up to 15 bits per symbol sent on a channel with a high SNR, and down to 2, 1, or no bits per symbol sent on a channel with a low SNR depending on the standard.

A typical ADSL arrangement is shown in Fig. 2-35. In this scheme, a telephone company technician must install a **NID (Network Interface Device)** on the customer's premises. This small plastic box marks the end of the telephone company's property and the start of the customer's property. Close to the NID (or sometimes combined with it) is a **splitter**, an analog filter that separates the

0–4000-Hz band used by POTS from the data. The POTS signal is routed to the existing telephone or fax machine. The data signal is routed to an ADSL modem, which uses digital signal processing to implement OFDM. Since most ADSL modems are external, the computer must be connected to them at high speed. Usually, this is done using Ethernet, a USB cable, or 802.11.

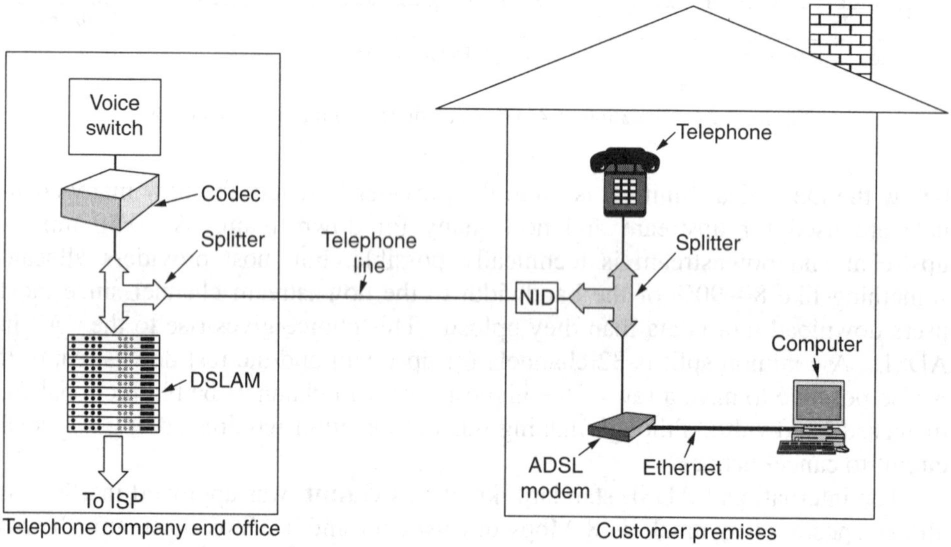

Figure 2-35. A typical ADSL equipment configuration.

At the other end of the wire, on the end office side, a corresponding splitter is installed. Here, the voice portion of the signal is filtered out and sent to the normal voice switch. The signal above 26 kHz is routed to a new kind of device called a **DSLAM** (**Digital Subscriber Line Access Multiplexer**), which contains the same kind of digital signal processor as the ADSL modem. Once the bits have been recovered from the signal, packets are formed and sent off to the ISP.

This complete separation between the voice system and ADSL makes it relatively easy for a telephone company to deploy ADSL. All that is needed is buying a DSLAM and splitter and attaching the ADSL subscribers to the splitter. Other high-bandwidth services (e.g., ISDN) require much greater changes to the existing switching equipment.

One disadvantage of the design of Fig. 2-35 is the need for a NID and splitter on the customer's premises. Installing these can only be done by a telephone company technician, necessitating an expensive "truck roll" (i.e., sending a technician to the customer's premises). Therefore, an alternative, splitterless design, informally called **G.lite**, has also been standardized. It is the same as Fig. 2-35 but without the customer's splitter. The existing telephone line is used as is. The only difference is that a microfilter has to be inserted into each telephone jack between the telephone or ADSL modem and the wire. The microfilter for the telephone is a low-pass filter eliminating frequencies above 3400 Hz; the microfilter for the ADSL modem is a high-pass filter eliminating frequencies below 26 kHz. However, this system is not as reliable as having a splitter, so G.lite can be used only up to 1.5 Mbps (versus 8 Mbps for ADSL with a splitter). For more information about ADSL, see Starr (2003).

Fiber To The Home

Deployed copper local loops limit the performance of ADSL and telephone modems. To let them provide faster and better network services, telephone companies are upgrading local loops at every opportunity by installing optical fiber all the way to houses and offices. The result is called **FttH** (**Fiber To The Home**). While FttH technology has been available for some time, deployments only began to take off in 2005 with growth in the demand for high-speed Internet from customers used to DSL and cable who wanted to download movies. Around 4% of U.S. houses are now connected to FttH with Internet access speeds of up to 100 Mbps.

Several variations of the form "FttX" (where *X* stands for the basement, curb, or neighborhood) exist. They are used to note that the fiber deployment may reach close to the house. In this case, copper (twisted pair or coaxial cable) provides fast enough speeds over the last short distance. The choice of how far to lay the fiber is an economic one, balancing cost with expected revenue. In any case, the point is that optical fiber has crossed the traditional barrier of the "last mile." We will focus on FttH in our discussion.

Like the copper wires before it, the fiber local loop is passive. This means no powered equipment is required to amplify or otherwise process signals. The fiber simply carries signals between the home and the end office. This in turn reduces cost and improves reliability.

Usually, the fibers from the houses are joined together so that only a single fiber reaches the end office per group of up to 100 houses. In the downstream direction, optical splitters divide the signal from the end office so that it reaches all the houses. Encryption is needed for security if only one house should be able to decode the signal. In the upstream direction, optical combiners merge the signals from the houses into a single signal that is received at the end office.

This architecture is called a **PON** (**Passive Optical Network**), and it is shown in Fig. 2-36. It is common to use one wavelength shared between all the houses for downstream transmission, and another wavelength for upstream transmission.

Even with the splitting, the tremendous bandwidth and low attenuation of fiber mean that PONs can provide high rates to users over distances of up to 20 km. The actual data rates and other details depend on the type of PON. Two kinds are common. **GPONs** (**Gigabit-capable PONs**) come from the world of telecommunications, so they are defined by an ITU standard. **EPONs** (**Ethernet PONs**)

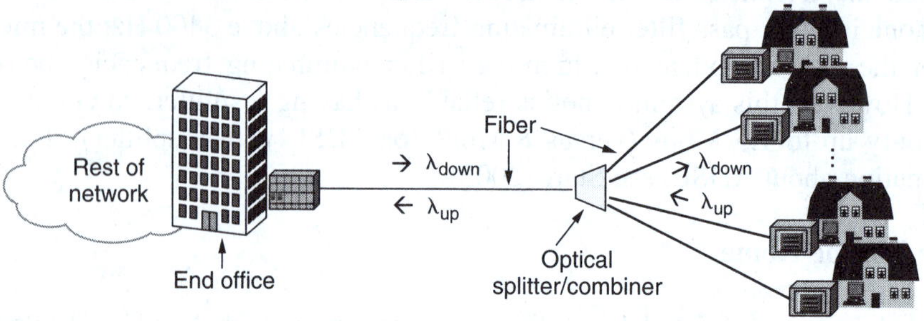

Figure 2-36. Passive optical network for Fiber To The Home.

are more in tune with the world of networking, so they are defined by an IEEE standard. Both run at around a gigabit and can carry traffic for different services, including Internet, video, and voice. For example, GPONs provide 2.4 Gbps downstream and 1.2 or 2.4 Gbps upstream.

Some protocol is needed to share the capacity of the single fiber at the end office between the different houses. The downstream direction is easy. The end office can send messages to each different house in whatever order it likes. In the upstream direction, however, messages from different houses cannot be sent at the same time, or different signals would collide. The houses also cannot hear each other's transmissions so they cannot listen before transmitting. The solution is that equipment at the houses requests and is granted time slots to use by equipment in the end office. For this to work, there is a ranging process to adjust the transmission times from the houses so that all the signals received at the end office are synchronized. The design is similar to cable modems, which we cover later in this chapter. For more information on the future of PONs, see Grobe and Elbers (2008).

2.6.4 Trunks and Multiplexing

Trunks in the telephone network are not only much faster than the local loops, they are different in two other respects. The core of the telephone network carries digital information, not analog information; that is, bits not voice. This necessitates a conversion at the end office to digital form for transmission over the long-haul trunks. The trunks carry thousands, even millions, of calls simultaneously. This sharing is important for achieving economies of scale, since it costs essentially the same amount of money to install and maintain a high-bandwidth trunk as a low-bandwidth trunk between two switching offices. It is accomplished with versions of TDM and FDM multiplexing.

Below we will briefly examine how voice signals are digitized so that they can be transported by the telephone network. After that, we will see how TDM is used to carry bits on trunks, including the TDM system used for fiber optics

(SONET). Then we will turn to FDM as it is applied to fiber optics, which is called wavelength division multiplexing.

Digitizing Voice Signals

Early in the development of the telephone network, the core handled voice calls as analog information. FDM techniques were used for many years to multiplex 4000-Hz voice channels (comprised of 3100 Hz plus guard bands) into larger and larger units. For example, 12 calls in the 60 kHz–to–108 kHz band is known as a **group** and five groups (a total of 60 calls) are known as a **supergroup**, and so on. These FDM methods are still used over some copper wires and microwave channels. However, FDM requires analog circuitry and is not amenable to being done by a computer. In contrast, TDM can be handled entirely by digital electronics, so it has become far more widespread in recent years. Since TDM can only be used for digital data and the local loops produce analog signals, a conversion is needed from analog to digital in the end office, where all the individual local loops come together to be combined onto outgoing trunks.

The analog signals are digitized in the end office by a device called a **codec** (short for "*co*der-*dec*oder"). The codec makes 8000 samples per second (125 μsec/sample) because the Nyquist theorem says that this is sufficient to capture all the information from the 4-kHz telephone channel bandwidth. At a lower sampling rate, information would be lost; at a higher one, no extra information would be gained. Each sample of the amplitude of the signal is quantized to an 8-bit number.

This technique is called **PCM (Pulse Code Modulation)**. It forms the heart of the modern telephone system. As a consequence, virtually all time intervals within the telephone system are multiples of 125 μsec. The standard uncompressed data rate for a voice-grade telephone call is thus 8 bits every 125 μsec, or 64 kbps.

At the other end of the call, an analog signal is recreated from the quantized samples by playing them out (and smoothing them) over time. It will not be exactly the same as the original analog signal, even though we sampled at the Nyquist rate, because the samples were quantized. To reduce the error due to quantization, the quantization levels are unevenly spaced. A logarithmic scale is used that gives relatively more bits to smaller signal amplitudes and relatively fewer bits to large signal amplitudes. In this way the error is proportional to the signal amplitude.

Two versions of quantization are widely used: **μ-law**, used in North America and Japan, and **A-law**, used in Europe and the rest of the world. Both versions are specified in standard ITU G.711. An equivalent way to think about this process is to imagine that the dynamic range of the signal (or the ratio between the largest and smallest possible values) is compressed before it is (evenly) quantized, and then expanded when the analog signal is recreated. For this reason it is called

companding. It is also possible to compress the samples after they are digitized so that they require much less than 64 kbps. However, we will leave this topic for when we explore audio applications such as voice over IP.

Time Division Multiplexing

TDM based on PCM is used to carry multiple voice calls over trunks by sending a sample from each call every 125 μsec. When digital transmission began emerging as a feasible technology, ITU (then called CCITT) was unable to reach agreement on an international standard for PCM. Consequently, a variety of incompatible schemes are now in use in different countries around the world.

The method used in North America and Japan is the **T1** carrier, depicted in Fig. 2-37. (Technically speaking, the format is called DS1 and the carrier is called T1, but following widespread industry tradition, we will not make that subtle distinction here.) The T1 carrier consists of 24 voice channels multiplexed together. Each of the 24 channels, in turn, gets to insert 8 bits into the output stream.

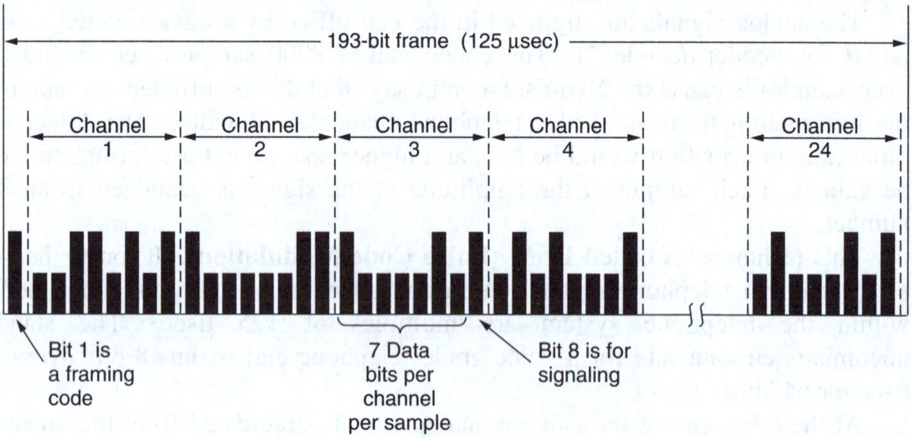

Figure 2-37. The T1 carrier (1.544 Mbps).

A frame consists of $24 \times 8 = 192$ bits plus one extra bit for control purposes, yielding 193 bits every 125 μsec. This gives a gross data rate of 1.544 Mbps, of which 8 kbps is for signaling. The 193rd bit is used for frame synchronization and signaling. In one variation, the 193rd bit is used across a group of 24 frames called an **extended superframe**. Six of the bits, in the 4th, 8th, 12th, 16th, 20th, and 24th positions, take on the alternating pattern 001011 . . . . Normally, the receiver keeps checking for this pattern to make sure that it has not lost synchronization. Six more bits are used to send an error check code to help the receiver confirm that it is synchronized. If it does get out of sync, the receiver can scan for the pattern and validate the error check code to get resynchronized. The remaining 12 bits are used for control information for operating and maintaining the network, such as performance reporting from the remote end.

The T1 format has several variations. The earlier versions sent signaling information **in-band**, meaning in the same channel as the data, by using some of the data bits. This design is one form of **channel-associated signaling**, because each channel has its own private signaling subchannel. In one arrangement, the least significant bit out of an 8-bit sample on each channel is used in every sixth frame. It has the colorful name of **robbed-bit signaling**. The idea is that a few stolen bits will not matter for voice calls. No one will hear the difference.

For data, however, it is another story. Delivering the wrong bits is unhelpful, to say the least. If older versions of T1 are used to carry data, only 7 of 8 bits, or 56 kbps can be used in each of the 24 channels. Instead, newer versions of T1 provide clear channels in which all of the bits may be used to send data. Clear channels are what businesses who lease a T1 line want when they send data across the telephone network in place of voice samples. Signaling for any voice calls is then handled **out-of-band**, meaning in a separate channel from the data. Often, the signaling is done with **common-channel signaling** in which there is a shared signaling channel. One of the 24 channels may be used for this purpose.

Outside North America and Japan, the 2.048-Mbps **E1** carrier is used instead of T1. This carrier has 32 8-bit data samples packed into the basic 125-μsec frame. Thirty of the channels are used for information and up to two are used for signaling. Each group of four frames provides 64 signaling bits, half of which are used for signaling (whether channel-associated or common-channel) and half of which are used for frame synchronization or are reserved for each country to use as it wishes.

Time division multiplexing allows multiple T1 carriers to be multiplexed into higher-order carriers. Figure 2-38 shows how this can be done. At the left we see four T1 channels being multiplexed into one T2 channel. The multiplexing at T2 and above is done bit for bit, rather than byte for byte with the 24 voice channels that make up a T1 frame. Four T1 streams at 1.544 Mbps should generate 6.176 Mbps, but T2 is actually 6.312 Mbps. The extra bits are used for framing and recovery in case the carrier slips. T1 and T3 are widely used by customers, whereas T2 and T4 are only used within the telephone system itself, so they are not well known.

At the next level, seven T2 streams are combined bitwise to form a T3 stream. Then six T3 streams are joined to form a T4 stream. At each step a small amount of overhead is added for framing and recovery in case the synchronization between sender and receiver is lost.

Just as there is little agreement on the basic carrier between the United States and the rest of the world, there is equally little agreement on how it is to be multiplexed into higher-bandwidth carriers. The U.S. scheme of stepping up by 4, 7, and 6 did not strike everyone else as the way to go, so the ITU standard calls for multiplexing four streams into one stream at each level. Also, the framing and

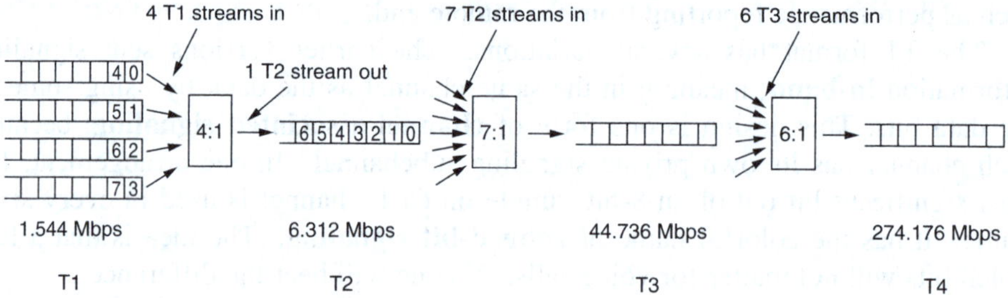

Figure 2-38. Multiplexing T1 streams into higher carriers.

recovery data are different in the U.S. and ITU standards. The ITU hierarchy for 32, 128, 512, 2048, and 8192 channels runs at speeds of 2.048, 8.848, 34.304, 139.264, and 565.148 Mbps.

SONET/SDH

In the early days of fiber optics, every telephone company had its own proprietary optical TDM system. After AT&T was broken up in 1984, local telephone companies had to connect to multiple long-distance carriers, all with different optical TDM systems, so the need for standardization became obvious. In 1985, Bellcore, the RBOC's research arm, began working on a standard, called **SONET (Synchronous Optical NETwork)**.

Later, ITU joined the effort, which resulted in a SONET standard and a set of parallel ITU recommendations (G.707, G.708, and G.709) in 1989. The ITU recommendations are called **SDH (Synchronous Digital Hierarchy)** but differ from SONET only in minor ways. Virtually all the long-distance telephone traffic in the United States, and much of it elsewhere, now uses trunks running SONET in the physical layer. For additional information about SONET, see Bellamy (2000), Goralski (2002), and Shepard (2001).

The SONET design had four major goals. First and foremost, SONET had to make it possible for different carriers to interwork. Achieving this goal required defining a common signaling standard with respect to wavelength, timing, framing structure, and other issues.

Second, some means was needed to unify the U.S., European, and Japanese digital systems, all of which were based on 64-kbps PCM channels but combined them in different (and incompatible) ways.

Third, SONET had to provide a way to multiplex multiple digital channels. At the time SONET was devised, the highest-speed digital carrier actually used widely in the United States was T3, at 44.736 Mbps. T4 was defined, but not used much, and nothing was even defined above T4 speed. Part of SONET's mission was to continue the hierarchy to gigabits/sec and beyond. A standard way to multiplex slower channels into one SONET channel was also needed.

Fourth, SONET had to provide support for operations, administration, and maintenance (OAM), which are needed to manage the network. Previous systems did not do this very well.

An early decision was to make SONET a traditional TDM system, with the entire bandwidth of the fiber devoted to one channel containing time slots for the various subchannels. As such, SONET is a synchronous system. Each sender and receiver is tied to a common clock. The master clock that controls the system has an accuracy of about 1 part in 10^9. Bits on a SONET line are sent out at extremely precise intervals, controlled by the master clock.

The basic SONET frame is a block of 810 bytes put out every 125 μsec. Since SONET is synchronous, frames are emitted whether or not there are any useful data to send. Having 8000 frames/sec exactly matches the sampling rate of the PCM channels used in all digital telephony systems.

The 810-byte SONET frames are best described as a rectangle of bytes, 90 columns wide by 9 rows high. Thus, $8 \times 810 = 6480$ bits are transmitted 8000 times per second, for a gross data rate of 51.84 Mbps. This layout is the basic SONET channel, called **STS-1** (**Synchronous Transport Signal-1**). All SONET trunks are multiples of STS-1.

The first three columns of each frame are reserved for system management information, as illustrated in Fig. 2-39. In this block, the first three rows contain the section overhead; the next six contain the line overhead. The section overhead is generated and checked at the start and end of each section, whereas the line overhead is generated and checked at the start and end of each line.

A SONET transmitter sends back-to-back 810-byte frames, without gaps between them, even when there are no data (in which case it sends dummy data). From the receiver's point of view, all it sees is a continuous bit stream, so how does it know where each frame begins? The answer is that the first 2 bytes of each frame contain a fixed pattern that the receiver searches for. If it finds this pattern in the same place in a large number of consecutive frames, it assumes that it is in sync with the sender. In theory, a user could insert this pattern into the payload in a regular way, but in practice it cannot be done due to the multiplexing of multiple users into the same frame and other reasons.

The remaining 87 columns of each frame hold $87 \times 9 \times 8 \times 8000 = 50.112$ Mbps of user data. This user data could be voice samples, T1 and other carriers swallowed whole, or packets. SONET is simply a convenient container for transporting bits. The **SPE** (**Synchronous Payload Envelope**), which carries the user data does not always begin in row 1, column 4. The SPE can begin anywhere within the frame. A pointer to the first byte is contained in the first row of the line overhead. The first column of the SPE is the path overhead (i.e., the header for the end-to-end path sublayer protocol).

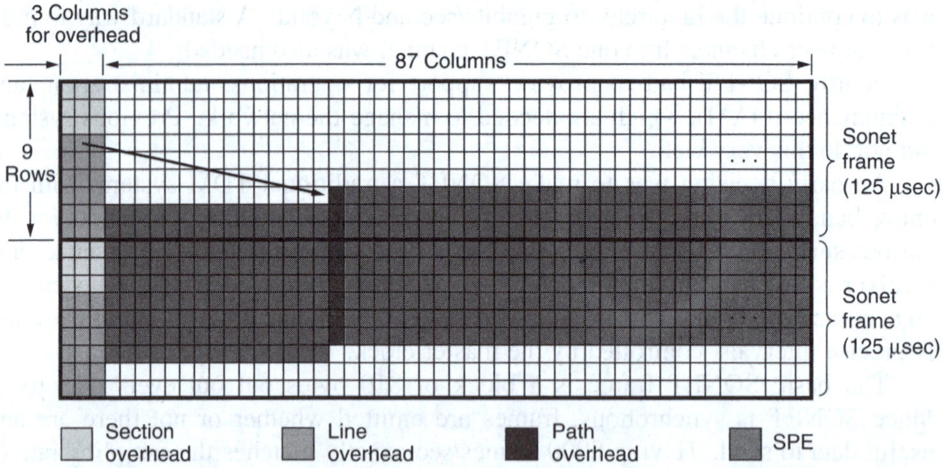

Figure 2-39. Two back-to-back SONET frames.

The ability to allow the SPE to begin anywhere within the SONET frame and even to span two frames, as shown in Fig. 2-39, gives added flexibility to the system. For example, if a payload arrives at the source while a dummy SONET frame is being constructed, it can be inserted into the current frame instead of being held until the start of the next one.

The SONET/SDH multiplexing hierarchy is shown in Fig. 2-40. Rates from STS-1 to STS-768 have been defined, ranging from roughly a T3 line to 40 Gbps. Even higher rates will surely be defined over time, with OC-3072 at 160 Gbps being the next in line if and when it becomes technologically feasible. The optical carrier corresponding to STS-*n* is called OC-*n* but is bit for bit the same except for a certain bit reordering needed for synchronization. The SDH names are different, and they start at OC-3 because ITU-based systems do not have a rate near 51.84 Mbps. We have shown the common rates, which proceed from OC-3 in multiples of four. The gross data rate includes all the overhead. The SPE data rate excludes the line and section overhead. The user data rate excludes all overhead and counts only the 87 payload columns.

As an aside, when a carrier, such as OC-3, is not multiplexed, but carries the data from only a single source, the letter *c* (for concatenated) is appended to the designation, so OC-3 indicates a 155.52-Mbps carrier consisting of three separate OC-1 carriers, but OC-3c indicates a data stream from a single source at 155.52 Mbps. The three OC-1 streams within an OC-3c stream are interleaved by column—first column 1 from stream 1, then column 1 from stream 2, then column 1 from stream 3, followed by column 2 from stream 1, and so on—leading to a frame 270 columns wide and 9 rows deep.

SONET		SDH	Data rate (Mbps)		
Electrical	Optical	Optical	Gross	SPE	User
STS-1	OC-1		51.84	50.112	49.536
STS-3	OC-3	STM-1	155.52	150.336	148.608
STS-12	OC-12	STM-4	622.08	601.344	594.432
STS-48	OC-48	STM-16	2488.32	2405.376	2377.728
STS-192	OC-192	STM-64	9953.28	9621.504	9510.912
STS-768	OC-768	STM-256	39813.12	38486.016	38043.648

Figure 2-40. SONET and SDH multiplex rates.

Wavelength Division Multiplexing

A form of frequency division multiplexing is used as well as TDM to harness the tremendous bandwidth of fiber optic channels. It is called **WDM (Wavelength Division Multiplexing)**. The basic principle of WDM on fibers is depicted in Fig. 2-41. Here four fibers come together at an optical combiner, each with its energy present at a different wavelength. The four beams are combined onto a single shared fiber for transmission to a distant destination. At the far end, the beam is split up over as many fibers as there were on the input side. Each output fiber contains a short, specially constructed core that filters out all but one wavelength. The resulting signals can be routed to their destination or recombined in different ways for additional multiplexed transport.

There is really nothing new here. This way of operating is just frequency division multiplexing at very high frequencies, with the term WDM owing to the description of fiber optic channels by their wavelength or "color" rather than frequency. As long as each channel has its own frequency (i.e., wavelength) range and all the ranges are disjoint, they can be multiplexed together on the long-haul fiber. The only difference with electrical FDM is that an optical system using a diffraction grating is completely passive and thus highly reliable.

The reason WDM is popular is that the energy on a single channel is typically only a few gigahertz wide because that is the current limit of how fast we can convert between electrical and optical signals. By running many channels in parallel on different wavelengths, the aggregate bandwidth is increased linearly with the number of channels. Since the bandwidth of a single fiber band is about 25,000 GHz (see Fig. 2-7), there is theoretically room for 2500 10-Gbps channels even at 1 bit/Hz (and higher rates are also possible).

WDM technology has been progressing at a rate that puts computer technology to shame. WDM was invented around 1990. The first commercial systems had eight channels of 2.5 Gbps per channel. By 1998, systems with 40 channels

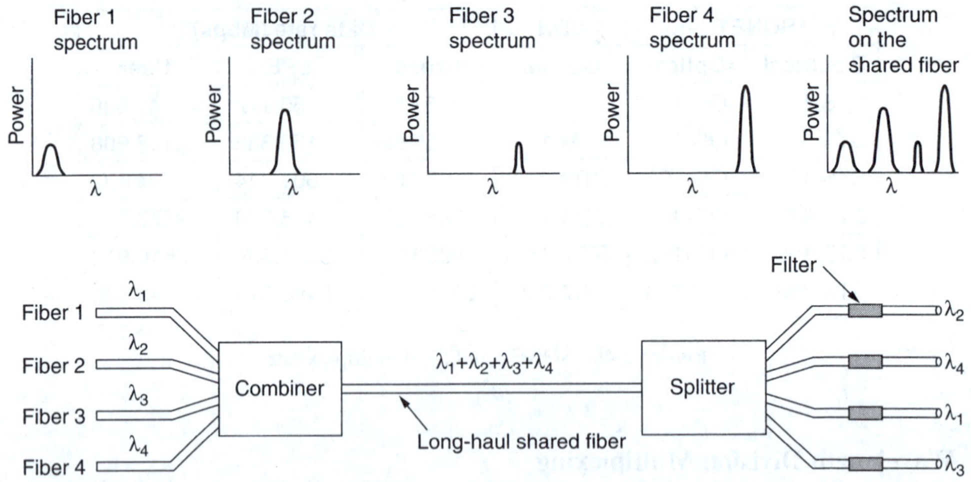

Figure 2-41. Wavelength division multiplexing.

of 2.5 Gbps were on the market. By 2006, there were products with 192 channels of 10 Gbps and 64 channels of 40 Gbps, capable of moving up to 2.56 Tbps. This bandwidth is enough to transmit 80 full-length DVD movies per second. The channels are also packed tightly on the fiber, with 200, 100, or as little as 50 GHz of separation. Technology demonstrations by companies after bragging rights have shown 10 times this capacity in the lab, but going from the lab to the field usually takes at least a few years. When the number of channels is very large and the wavelengths are spaced close together, the system is referred to as **DWDM** (**Dense WDM**).

One of the drivers of WDM technology is the development of all-optical components. Previously, every 100 km it was necessary to split up all the channels and convert each one to an electrical signal for amplification separately before reconverting them to optical signals and combining them. Nowadays, all-optical amplifiers can regenerate the entire signal once every 1000 km without the need for multiple opto-electrical conversions.

In the example of Fig. 2-41, we have a fixed-wavelength system. Bits from input fiber 1 go to output fiber 3, bits from input fiber 2 go to output fiber 1, etc. However, it is also possible to build WDM systems that are switched in the optical domain. In such a device, the output filters are tunable using Fabry-Perot or Mach-Zehnder interferometers. These devices allow the selected frequencies to be changed dynamically by a control computer. This ability provides a large amount of flexibility to provision many different wavelength paths through the telephone network from a fixed set of fibers. For more information about optical networks and WDM, see Ramaswami et al. (2009).

2.6.5 Switching

From the point of view of the average telephone engineer, the phone system is divided into two principal parts: outside plant (the local loops and trunks, since they are physically outside the switching offices) and inside plant (the switches, which are inside the switching offices). We have just looked at the outside plant. Now it is time to examine the inside plant.

Two different switching techniques are used by the network nowadays: circuit switching and packet switching. The traditional telephone system is based on circuit switching, but packet switching is beginning to make inroads with the rise of voice over IP technology. We will go into circuit switching in some detail and contrast it with packet switching. Both kinds of switching are important enough that we will come back to them when we get to the network layer.

Circuit Switching

Conceptually, when you or your computer places a telephone call, the switching equipment within the telephone system seeks out a physical path all the way from your telephone to the receiver's telephone. This technique is called **circuit switching**. It is shown schematically in Fig. 2-42(a). Each of the six rectangles represents a carrier switching office (end office, toll office, etc.). In this example, each office has three incoming lines and three outgoing lines. When a call passes through a switching office, a physical connection is (conceptually) established between the line on which the call came in and one of the output lines, as shown by the dotted lines.

In the early days of the telephone, the connection was made by the operator plugging a jumper cable into the input and output sockets. In fact, a surprising little story is associated with the invention of automatic circuit switching equipment. It was invented by a 19th-century Missouri undertaker named Almon B. Strowger. Shortly after the telephone was invented, when someone died, one of the survivors would call the town operator and say "Please connect me to an undertaker." Unfortunately for Mr. Strowger, there were two undertakers in his town, and the other one's wife was the town telephone operator. He quickly saw that either he was going to have to invent automatic telephone switching equipment or he was going to go out of business. He chose the first option. For nearly 100 years, the circuit-switching equipment used worldwide was known as **Strowger gear**. (History does not record whether the now-unemployed switchboard operator got a job as an information operator, answering questions such as "What is the phone number of an undertaker?")

The model shown in Fig. 2-42(a) is highly simplified, of course, because parts of the physical path between the two telephones may, in fact, be microwave or fiber links onto which thousands of calls are multiplexed. Nevertheless, the basic idea is valid: once a call has been set up, a dedicated path between both ends exists and will continue to exist until the call is finished.

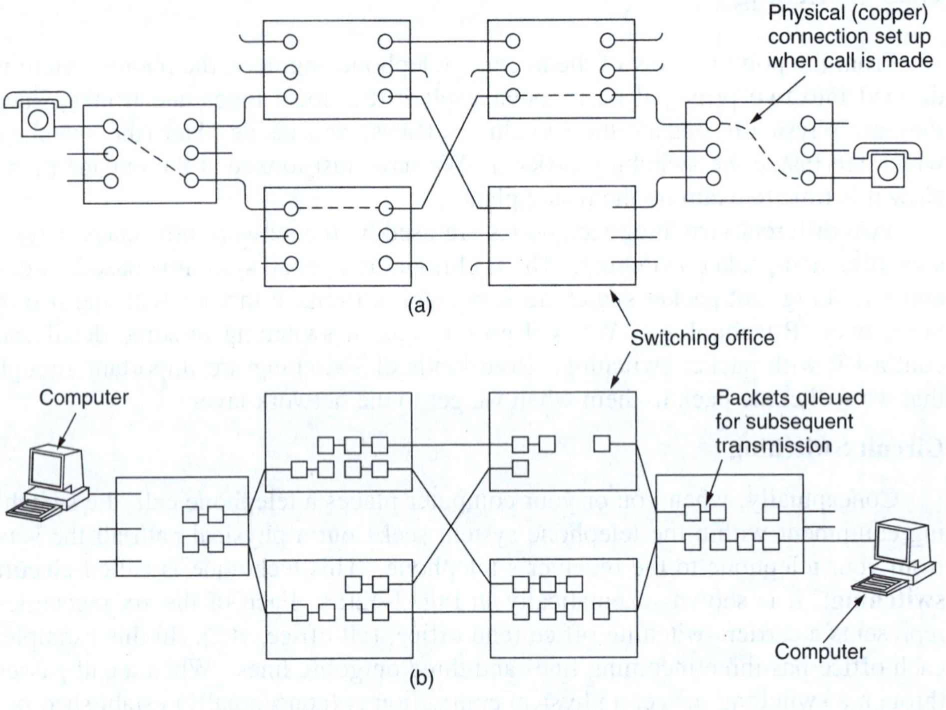

Figure 2-42. (a) Circuit switching. (b) Packet switching.

An important property of circuit switching is the need to set up an end-to-end path *before* any data can be sent. The elapsed time between the end of dialing and the start of ringing can easily be 10 sec, more on long-distance or international calls. During this time interval, the telephone system is hunting for a path, as shown in Fig. 2-43(a). Note that before data transmission can even begin, the call request signal must propagate all the way to the destination and be acknowledged. For many computer applications (e.g., point-of-sale credit verification), long setup times are undesirable.

As a consequence of the reserved path between the calling parties, once the setup has been completed, the only delay for data is the propagation time for the electromagnetic signal, about 5 msec per 1000 km. Also as a consequence of the established path, there is no danger of congestion—that is, once the call has been put through, you never get busy signals. Of course, you might get one before the connection has been established due to lack of switching or trunk capacity.

Packet Switching

The alternative to circuit switching is **packet switching**, shown in Fig. 2-42(b) and described in Chap. 1. With this technology, packets are sent as soon as they are available. There is no need to set up a dedicated path in advance, unlike

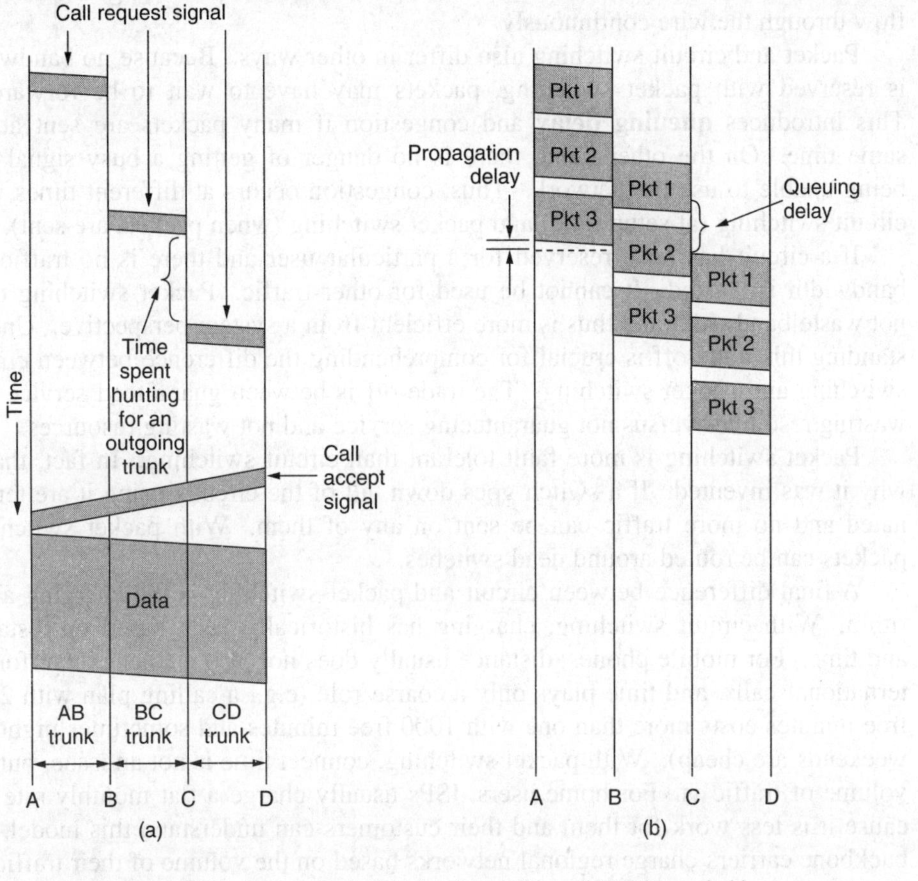

Figure 2-43. Timing of events in (a) circuit switching, (b) packet switching.

with circuit switching. It is up to routers to use store-and-forward transmission to send each packet on its way to the destination on its own. This procedure is unlike circuit switching, in which the result of the connection setup is the reservation of bandwidth all the way from the sender to the receiver. All data on the circuit follows this path. Among other properties, having all the data follow the same path means that it cannot arrive out of order. With packet switching there is no fixed path, so different packets can follow different paths, depending on network conditions at the time they are sent, and they may arrive out of order.

Packet-switching networks place a tight upper limit on the size of packets. This ensures that no user can monopolize any transmission line for very long (e.g., many milliseconds), so that packet-switched networks can handle interactive traffic. It also reduces delay since the first packet of a long message can be forwarded before the second one has fully arrived. However, the store-and-forward delay of accumulating a packet in the router's memory before it is sent on to the next router exceeds that of circuit switching. With circuit switching, the bits just flow through the wire continuously.

Packet and circuit switching also differ in other ways. Because no bandwidth is reserved with packet switching, packets may have to wait to be forwarded. This introduces **queuing delay** and congestion if many packets are sent at the same time. On the other hand, there is no danger of getting a busy signal and being unable to use the network. Thus, congestion occurs at different times with circuit switching (at setup time) and packet switching (when packets are sent).

If a circuit has been reserved for a particular user and there is no traffic, its bandwidth is wasted. It cannot be used for other traffic. Packet switching does not waste bandwidth and thus is more efficient from a system perspective. Understanding this trade-off is crucial for comprehending the difference between circuit switching and packet switching. The trade-off is between guaranteed service and wasting resources versus not guaranteeing service and not wasting resources.

Packet switching is more fault tolerant than circuit switching. In fact, that is why it was invented. If a switch goes down, all of the circuits using it are terminated and no more traffic can be sent on any of them. With packet switching, packets can be routed around dead switches.

A final difference between circuit and packet switching is the charging algorithm. With circuit switching, charging has historically been based on distance and time. For mobile phones, distance usually does not play a role, except for international calls, and time plays only a coarse role (e.g., a calling plan with 2000 free minutes costs more than one with 1000 free minutes and sometimes nights or weekends are cheap). With packet switching, connect time is not an issue, but the volume of traffic is. For home users, ISPs usually charge a flat monthly rate because it is less work for them and their customers can understand this model, but backbone carriers charge regional networks based on the volume of their traffic.

The differences are summarized in Fig. 2-44. Traditionally, telephone networks have used circuit switching to provide high-quality telephone calls, and computer networks have used packet switching for simplicity and efficiency. However, there are notable exceptions. Some older computer networks have been circuit switched under the covers (e.g., X.25) and some newer telephone networks use packet switching with voice over IP technology. This looks just like a standard telephone call on the outside to users, but inside the network packets of voice data are switched. This approach has let upstarts market cheap international calls via calling cards, though perhaps with lower call quality than the incumbents.

2.7 THE MOBILE TELEPHONE SYSTEM

The traditional telephone system, even if it someday gets multigigabit end-to-end fiber, will still not be able to satisfy a growing group of users: people on the go. People now expect to make phone calls and to use their phones to check

Item	Circuit switched	Packet switched
Call setup	Required	Not needed
Dedicated physical path	Yes	No
Each packet follows the same route	Yes	No
Packets arrive in order	Yes	No
Is a switch crash fatal	Yes	No
Bandwidth available	Fixed	Dynamic
Time of possible congestion	At setup time	On every packet
Potentially wasted bandwidth	Yes	No
Store-and-forward transmission	No	Yes
Charging	Per minute	Per packet

Figure 2-44. A comparison of circuit-switched and packet-switched networks.

email and surf the Web from airplanes, cars, swimming pools, and while jogging in the park. Consequently, there is a tremendous amount of interest in wireless telephony. In the following sections we will study this topic in some detail.

The mobile phone system is used for wide area voice and data communication. **Mobile phones** (sometimes called **cell phones**) have gone through three distinct generations, widely called **1G**, **2G**, and **3G**. The generations are:

1. Analog voice.
2. Digital voice.
3. Digital voice and data (Internet, email, etc.).

(Mobile phones should not be confused with **cordless phones** that consist of a base station and a handset sold as a set for use within the home. These are never used for networking, so we will not examine them further.)

Although most of our discussion will be about the technology of these systems, it is interesting to note how political and tiny marketing decisions can have a huge impact. The first mobile system was devised in the U.S. by AT&T and mandated for the whole country by the FCC. As a result, the entire U.S. had a single (analog) system and a mobile phone purchased in California also worked in New York. In contrast, when mobile phones came to Europe, every country devised its own system, which resulted in a fiasco.

Europe learned from its mistake and when digital came around, the government-run PTTs got together and standardized on a single system (GSM), so any European mobile phone will work anywhere in Europe. By then, the U.S. had decided that government should not be in the standardization business, so it left digital to the marketplace. This decision resulted in different equipment manufacturers producing different kinds of mobile phones. As a consequence, in the U.S.

two major—and completely incompatible—digital mobile phone systems were deployed, as well as other minor systems.

Despite an initial lead by the U.S., mobile phone ownership and usage in Europe is now far greater than in the U.S. Having a single system that works anywhere in Europe and with any provider is part of the reason, but there is more. A second area where the U.S. and Europe differed is in the humble matter of phone numbers. In the U.S., mobile phones are mixed in with regular (fixed) telephones. Thus, there is no way for a caller to see if, say, (212) 234-5678 is a fixed telephone (cheap or free call) or a mobile phone (expensive call). To keep people from getting nervous about placing calls, the telephone companies decided to make the mobile phone owner pay for incoming calls. As a consequence, many people hesitated buying a mobile phone for fear of running up a big bill by just receiving calls. In Europe, mobile phone numbers have a special area code (analogous to 800 and 900 numbers) so they are instantly recognizable. Consequently, the usual rule of "caller pays" also applies to mobile phones in Europe (except for international calls, where costs are split).

A third issue that has had a large impact on adoption is the widespread use of prepaid mobile phones in Europe (up to 75% in some areas). These can be purchased in many stores with no more formality than buying a digital camera. You pay and you go. They are preloaded with a balance of, for example, 20 or 50 euros and can be recharged (using a secret PIN code) when the balance drops to zero. As a consequence, practically every teenager and many small children in Europe have (usually prepaid) mobile phones so their parents can locate them, without the danger of the child running up a huge bill. If the mobile phone is used only occasionally, its use is essentially free since there is no monthly charge or charge for incoming calls.

2.7.1 First-Generation (1G) Mobile Phones: Analog Voice

Enough about the politics and marketing aspects of mobile phones. Now let us look at the technology, starting with the earliest system. Mobile radiotelephones were used sporadically for maritime and military communication during the early decades of the 20th century. In 1946, the first system for car-based telephones was set up in St. Louis. This system used a single large transmitter on top of a tall building and had a single channel, used for both sending and receiving. To talk, the user had to push a button that enabled the transmitter and disabled the receiver. Such systems, known as **push-to-talk systems**, were installed in several cities beginning in the late 1950s. CB radio, taxis, and police cars often use this technology.

In the 1960s, **IMTS (Improved Mobile Telephone System)** was installed. It, too, used a high-powered (200-watt) transmitter on top of a hill but it had two frequencies, one for sending and one for receiving, so the push-to-talk button was no longer needed. Since all communication from the mobile telephones went inbound on a different channel than the outbound signals, the mobile users could not hear each other (unlike the push-to-talk system used in taxis).

IMTS supported 23 channels spread out from 150 MHz to 450 MHz. Due to the small number of channels, users often had to wait a long time before getting a dial tone. Also, due to the large power of the hilltop transmitters, adjacent systems had to be several hundred kilometers apart to avoid interference. All in all, the limited capacity made the system impractical.

Advanced Mobile Phone System

All that changed with **AMPS** (**Advanced Mobile Phone System**), invented by Bell Labs and first installed in the United States in 1982. It was also used in England, where it was called TACS, and in Japan, where it was called MCS-L1. AMPS was formally retired in 2008, but we will look at it to understand the context for the 2G and 3G systems that improved on it.

In all mobile phone systems, a geographic region is divided up into **cells**, which is why the devices are sometimes called cell phones. In AMPS, the cells are typically 10 to 20 km across; in digital systems, the cells are smaller. Each cell uses some set of frequencies not used by any of its neighbors. The key idea that gives cellular systems far more capacity than previous systems is the use of relatively small cells and the reuse of transmission frequencies in nearby (but not adjacent) cells. Whereas an IMTS system 100 km across can have only one call on each frequency, an AMPS system might have 100 10-km cells in the same area and be able to have 10 to 15 calls on each frequency, in widely separated cells. Thus, the cellular design increases the system capacity by at least an order of magnitude, more as the cells get smaller. Furthermore, smaller cells mean that less power is needed, which leads to smaller and cheaper transmitters and handsets.

The idea of frequency reuse is illustrated in Fig. 2-45(a). The cells are normally roughly circular, but they are easier to model as hexagons. In Fig. 2-45(a), the cells are all the same size. They are grouped in units of seven cells. Each letter indicates a group of frequencies. Notice that for each frequency set, there is a buffer about two cells wide where that frequency is not reused, providing for good separation and low interference.

Finding locations high in the air to place base station antennas is a major issue. This problem has led some telecommunication carriers to forge alliances with the Roman Catholic Church, since the latter owns a substantial number of exalted potential antenna sites worldwide, all conveniently under a single management.

In an area where the number of users has grown to the point that the system is overloaded, the power can be reduced and the overloaded cells split into smaller

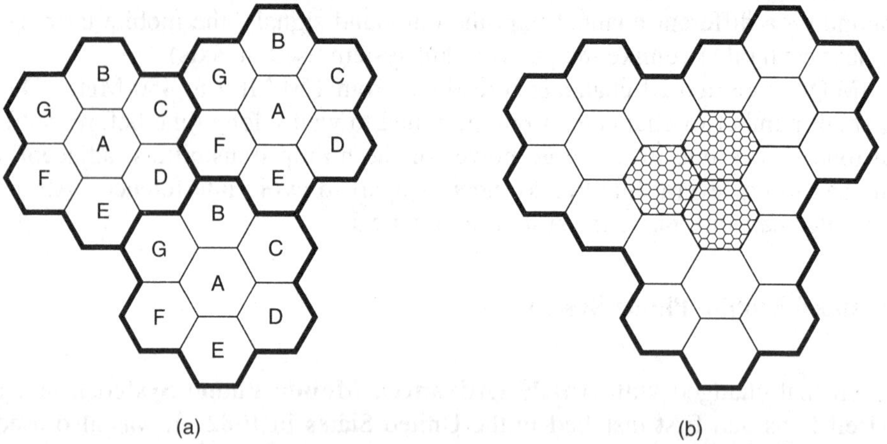

Figure 2-45. (a) Frequencies are not reused in adjacent cells. (b) To add more users, smaller cells can be used.

microcells to permit more frequency reuse, as shown in Fig. 2-45(b). Telephone companies sometimes create temporary microcells, using portable towers with satellite links at sporting events, rock concerts, and other places where large numbers of mobile users congregate for a few hours.

At the center of each cell is a base station to which all the telephones in the cell transmit. The base station consists of a computer and transmitter/receiver connected to an antenna. In a small system, all the base stations are connected to a single device called an **MSC** (**Mobile Switching Center**) or **MTSO** (**Mobile Telephone Switching Office**). In a larger one, several MSCs may be needed, all of which are connected to a second-level MSC, and so on. The MSCs are essentially end offices as in the telephone system, and are in fact connected to at least one telephone system end office. The MSCs communicate with the base stations, each other, and the PSTN using a packet-switching network.

At any instant, each mobile telephone is logically in one specific cell and under the control of that cell's base station. When a mobile telephone physically leaves a cell, its base station notices the telephone's signal fading away and asks all the surrounding base stations how much power they are getting from it. When the answers come back, the base station then transfers ownership to the cell getting the strongest signal; under most conditions that is the cell where the telephone is now located. The telephone is then informed of its new boss, and if a call is in progress, it is asked to switch to a new channel (because the old one is not reused in any of the adjacent cells). This process, called **handoff**, takes about 300 msec. Channel assignment is done by the MSC, the nerve center of the system. The base stations are really just dumb radio relays.

Channels

AMPS uses FDM to separate the channels. The system uses 832 full-duplex channels, each consisting of a pair of simplex channels. This arrangement is known as **FDD (Frequency Division Duplex)**. The 832 simplex channels from 824 to 849 MHz are used for mobile to base station transmission, and 832 simplex channels from 869 to 894 MHz are used for base station to mobile transmission. Each of these simplex channels is 30 kHz wide.

The 832 channels are divided into four categories. Control channels (base to mobile) are used to manage the system. Paging channels (base to mobile) alert mobile users to calls for them. Access channels (bidirectional) are used for call setup and channel assignment. Finally, data channels (bidirectional) carry voice, fax, or data. Since the same frequencies cannot be reused in nearby cells and 21 channels are reserved in each cell for control, the actual number of voice channels available per cell is much smaller than 832, typically about 45.

Call Management

Each mobile telephone in AMPS has a 32-bit serial number and a 10-digit telephone number in its programmable read-only memory. The telephone number is represented as a 3-digit area code in 10 bits and a 7-digit subscriber number in 24 bits. When a phone is switched on, it scans a preprogrammed list of 21 control channels to find the most powerful signal. The phone then broadcasts its 32-bit serial number and 34-bit telephone number. Like all the control information in AMPS, this packet is sent in digital form, multiple times, and with an error-correcting code, even though the voice channels themselves are analog.

When the base station hears the announcement, it tells the MSC, which records the existence of its new customer and also informs the customer's home MSC of his current location. During normal operation, the mobile telephone reregisters about once every 15 minutes.

To make a call, a mobile user switches on the phone, enters the number to be called on the keypad, and hits the SEND button. The phone then transmits the number to be called and its own identity on the access channel. If a collision occurs there, it tries again later. When the base station gets the request, it informs the MSC. If the caller is a customer of the MSC's company (or one of its partners), the MSC looks for an idle channel for the call. If one is found, the channel number is sent back on the control channel. The mobile phone then automatically switches to the selected voice channel and waits until the called party picks up the phone.

Incoming calls work differently. To start with, all idle phones continuously listen to the paging channel to detect messages directed at them. When a call is placed to a mobile phone (either from a fixed phone or another mobile phone), a packet is sent to the callee's home MSC to find out where it is. A packet is then sent to the base station in its current cell, which sends a broadcast on the paging channel of the form "Unit 14, are you there?" The called phone responds with a "Yes" on the access channel. The base then says something like: "Unit 14, call for you on channel 3." At this point, the called phone switches to channel 3 and starts making ringing sounds (or playing some melody the owner was given as a birthday present).

2.7.2 Second-Generation (2G) Mobile Phones: Digital Voice

The first generation of mobile phones was analog; the second generation is digital. Switching to digital has several advantages. It provides capacity gains by allowing voice signals to be digitized and compressed. It improves security by allowing voice and control signals to be encrypted. This in turn deters fraud and eavesdropping, whether from intentional scanning or echoes of other calls due to RF propagation. Finally, it enables new services such as text messaging.

Just as there was no worldwide standardization during the first generation, there was also no worldwide standardization during the second, either. Several different systems were developed, and three have been widely deployed. **D-AMPS (Digital Advanced Mobile Phone System)** is a digital version of AMPS that coexists with AMPS and uses TDM to place multiple calls on the same frequency channel. It is described in International Standard IS-54 and its successor IS-136. **GSM (Global System for Mobile communications)** has emerged as the dominant system, and while it was slow to catch on in the U.S. it is now used virtually everywhere in the world. Like D-AMPS, GSM is based on a mix of FDM and TDM. **CDMA (Code Division Multiple Access)**, described in **International Standard IS-95**, is a completely different kind of system and is based on neither FDM mor TDM. While CDMA has not become the dominant 2G system, its technology has become the basis for 3G systems.

Also, the name **PCS (Personal Communications Services)** is sometimes used in the marketing literature to indicate a second-generation (i.e., digital) system. Originally it meant a mobile phone using the 1900 MHz band, but that distinction is rarely made now.

We will now describe GSM, since it is the dominant 2G system. In the next section we will have more to say about CDMA when we describe 3G systems.

GSM—The Global System for Mobile Communications

GSM started life in the 1980s as an effort to produce a single European 2G standard. The task was assigned to a telecommunications group called (in French) Groupe Specialé Mobile. The first GSM systems were deployed starting in 1991 and were a quick success. It soon became clear that GSM was going to be more than a European success, with uptake stretching to countries as far away as Australia, so GSM was renamed to have a more worldwide appeal.

GSM and the other mobile phone systems we will study retain from 1G systems a design based on cells, frequency reuse across cells, and mobility with handoffs as subscribers move. It is the details that differ. Here, we will briefly discuss some of the main properties of GSM. However, the printed GSM standard is over 5000 [sic] pages long. A large fraction of this material relates to engineering aspects of the system, especially the design of receivers to handle multipath signal propagation, and synchronizing transmitters and receivers. None of this will be even mentioned here.

Fig. 2-46 shows that the GSM architecture is similar to the AMPS architecture, though the components have different names. The mobile itself is now divided into the handset and a removable chip with subscriber and account information called a **SIM card**, short for **Subscriber Identity Module**. It is the SIM card that activates the handset and contains secrets that let the mobile and the network identify each other and encrypt conversations. A SIM card can be removed and plugged into a different handset to turn that handset into your mobile as far as the network is concerned.

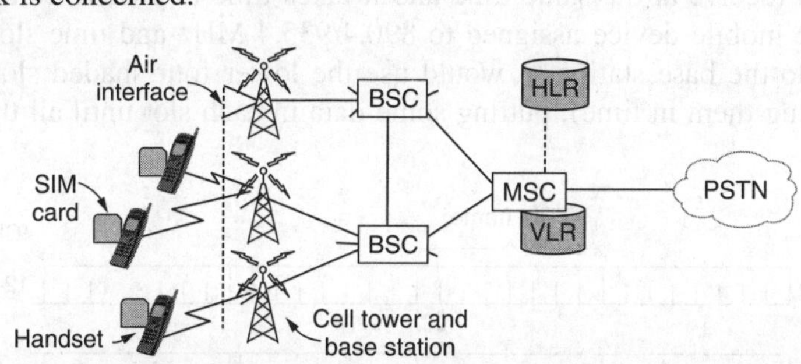

Figure 2-46. GSM mobile network architecture.

The mobile talks to cell base stations over an **air interface** that we will describe in a moment. The cell base stations are each connected to a **BSC** (**Base Station Controller**) that controls the radio resources of cells and handles handoff. The BSC in turn is connected to an MSC (as in AMPS) that routes calls and connects to the PSTN (Public Switched Telephone Network).

To be able to route calls, the MSC needs to know where mobiles can currently be found. It maintains a database of nearby mobiles that are associated with the cells it manages. This database is called the **VLR** (**Visitor Location Register**). There is also a database in the mobile network that gives the last known location of each mobile. It is called the **HLR** (**Home Location Register**). This database is used to route incoming calls to the right locations. Both databases must be kept up to date as mobiles move from cell to cell.

We will now describe the air interface in some detail. GSM runs on a range of frequencies worldwide, including 900, 1800, and 1900 MHz. More spectrum is allocated than for AMPS in order to support a much larger number of users. GSM is a frequency division duplex cellular system, like AMPS. That is, each mobile transmits on one frequency and receives on another, higher frequency (55 MHz higher for GSM versus 80 MHz higher for AMPS). However, unlike with AMPS, with GSM a single frequency pair is split by time-division multiplexing into time slots. In this way it is shared by multiple mobiles.

To handle multiple mobiles, GSM channels are much wider than the AMPS channels (200-kHz versus 30 kHz). One 200-kHz channel is shown in Fig. 2-47. A GSM system operating in the 900-MHz region has 124 pairs of simplex channels. Each simplex channel is 200 kHz wide and supports eight separate connections on it, using time division multiplexing. Each currently active station is assigned one time slot on one channel pair. Theoretically, 992 channels can be supported in each cell, but many of them are not available, to avoid frequency conflicts with neighboring cells. In Fig. 2-47, the eight shaded time slots all belong to the same connection, four of them in each direction. Transmitting and receiving does not happen in the same time slot because the GSM radios cannot transmit and receive at the same time and it takes time to switch from one to the other. If the mobile device assigned to 890.4/935.4 MHz and time slot 2 wanted to transmit to the base station, it would use the lower four shaded slots (and the ones following them in time), putting some data in each slot until all the data had been sent.

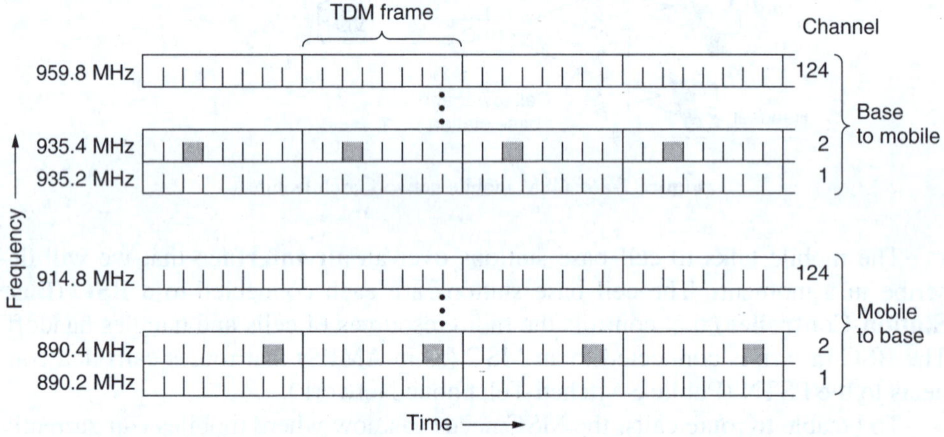

Figure 2-47. GSM uses 124 frequency channels, each of which uses an eight-slot TDM system.

The TDM slots shown in Fig. 2-47 are part of a complex framing hierarchy. Each TDM slot has a specific structure, and groups of TDM slots form multiframes, also with a specific structure. A simplified version of this hierarchy is shown in Fig. 2-48. Here we can see that each TDM slot consists of a 148-bit data frame that occupies the channel for 577 μsec (including a 30-μsec guard time after each slot). Each data frame starts and ends with three 0 bits, for frame delineation purposes. It also contains two 57-bit *Information* fields, each one having a control bit that indicates whether the following *Information* field is for voice or data. Between the *Information* fields is a 26-bit *Sync* (training) field that is used by the receiver to synchronize to the sender's frame boundaries.

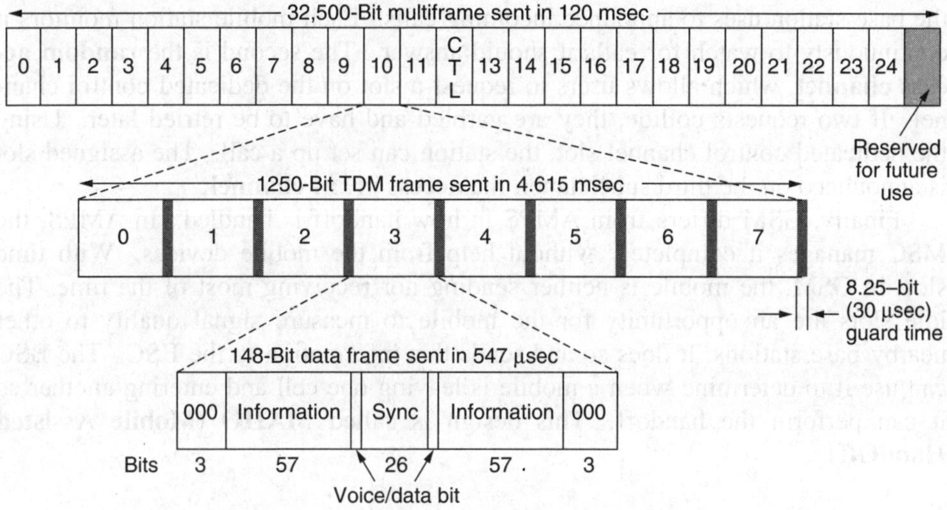

Figure 2-48. A portion of the GSM framing structure.

A data frame is transmitted in 547 μsec, but a transmitter is only allowed to send one data frame every 4.615 msec, since it is sharing the channel with seven other stations. The gross rate of each channel is 270,833 bps, divided among eight users. However, as with AMPS, the overhead eats up a large fraction of the bandwidth, ultimately leaving 24.7 kbps worth of payload per user before error correction. After error correction, 13 kbps is left for speech. While this is substantially less than 64 kbps PCM for uncompressed voice signals in the fixed telephone network, compression on the mobile device can reach these levels with little loss of quality.

As can be seen from Fig. 2-48, eight data frames make up a TDM frame and 26 TDM frames make up a 120-msec multiframe. Of the 26 TDM frames in a multiframe, slot 12 is used for control and slot 25 is reserved for future use, so only 24 are available for user traffic.

However, in addition to the 26-slot multiframe shown in Fig. 2-48, a 51-slot multiframe (not shown) is also used. Some of these slots are used to hold several control channels used to manage the system. The **broadcast control channel** is a continuous stream of output from the base station containing the base station's identity and the channel status. All mobile stations monitor their signal strength to see when they have moved into a new cell.

The **dedicated control channel** is used for location updating, registration, and call setup. In particular, each BSC maintains a database of mobile stations currently under its jurisdiction, the VLR. Information needed to maintain the VLR is sent on the dedicated control channel.

Finally, there is the **common control channel**, which is split up into three logical subchannels. The first of these subchannels is the **paging channel**, which the base station uses to announce incoming calls. Each mobile station monitors it continuously to watch for calls it should answer. The second is the **random access channel**, which allows users to request a slot on the dedicated control channel. If two requests collide, they are garbled and have to be retried later. Using the dedicated control channel slot, the station can set up a call. The assigned slot is announced on the third subchannel, the **access grant channel**.

Finally, GSM differs from AMPS in how handoff is handled. In AMPS, the MSC manages it completely without help from the mobile devices. With time slots in GSM, the mobile is neither sending nor receiving most of the time. The idle slots are an opportunity for the mobile to measure signal quality to other nearby base stations. It does so and sends this information to the BSC. The BSC can use it to determine when a mobile is leaving one cell and entering another so it can perform the handoff. This design is called **MAHO (Mobile Assisted HandOff)**.

2.7.3 Third-Generation (3G) Mobile Phones: Digital Voice and Data

The first generation of mobile phones was analog voice, and the second generation was digital voice. The third generation of mobile phones, or **3G** as it is called, is all about digital voice *and* data.

A number of factors are driving the industry. First, data traffic already exceeds voice traffic on the fixed network and is growing exponentially, whereas voice traffic is essentially flat. Many industry experts expect data traffic to dominate voice on mobile devices as well soon. Second, the telephone, entertainment, and computer industries have all gone digital and are rapidly converging. Many people are drooling over lightweight, portable devices that act as a telephone, music and video player, email terminal, Web interface, gaming machine, and more, all with worldwide wireless connectivity to the Internet at high bandwidth.

Apple's iPhone is a good example of this kind of 3G device. With it, people get hooked on wireless data services, and AT&T wireless data volumes are rising steeply with the popularity of iPhones. The trouble is, the iPhone uses a 2.5G network (an enhanced 2G network, but not a true 3G network) and there is not enough data capacity to keep users happy. 3G mobile telephony is all about providing enough wireless bandwidth to keep these future users happy.

ITU tried to get a bit more specific about this vision starting back around 1992. It issued a blueprint for getting there called **IMT-2000**, where IMT stood for **International Mobile Telecommunications**. The basic services that the IMT-2000 network was supposed to provide to its users are:

1. High-quality voice transmission.
2. Messaging (replacing email, fax, SMS, chat, etc.).
3. Multimedia (playing music, viewing videos, films, television, etc.).
4. Internet access (Web surfing, including pages with audio and video).

Additional services might be video conferencing, telepresence, group game playing, and m-commerce (waving your telephone at the cashier to pay in a store). Furthermore, all these services are supposed to be available worldwide (with automatic connection via a satellite when no terrestrial network can be located), instantly (always on), and with quality of service guarantees.

ITU envisioned a single worldwide technology for IMT-2000, so manufacturers could build a single device that could be sold and used anywhere in the world (like CD players and computers and unlike mobile phones and televisions). Having a single technology would also make life much simpler for network operators and would encourage more people to use the services. Format wars, such as the Betamax versus VHS battle with videorecorders, are not good for business.

As it turned out, this was a bit optimistic. The number 2000 stood for three things: (1) the year it was supposed to go into service, (2) the frequency it was supposed to operate at (in MHz), and (3) the bandwidth the service should have (in kbps). It did not make it on any of the three counts. Nothing was implemented by 2000. ITU recommended that all governments reserve spectrum at 2 GHz so devices could roam seamlessly from country to country. China reserved the required bandwidth but nobody else did. Finally, it was recognized that 2 Mbps is not currently feasible for users who are *too* mobile (due to the difficulty of performing handoffs quickly enough). More realistic is 2 Mbps for stationary indoor users (which will compete head-on with ADSL), 384 kbps for people walking, and 144 kbps for connections in cars.

Despite these initial setbacks, much has been accomplished since then. Several IMT proposals were made and, after some winnowing, it came down to two main ones. The first one, **WCDMA (Wideband CDMA)**, was proposed by Ericsson and was pushed by the European Union, which called it **UMTS (Universal Mobile Telecommunications System)**. The other contender was **CDMA2000**, proposed by Qualcomm.

Both of these systems are more similar than different in that they are based on broadband CDMA; WCDMA uses 5-MHz channels and CDMA2000 uses 1.25-MHz channels. If the Ericsson and Qualcomm engineers were put in a room and told to come to a common design, they probably could find one fairly quickly. The trouble is that the real problem is not engineering, but politics (as usual). Europe wanted a system that interworked with GSM, whereas the U.S. wanted a system that was compatible with one already widely deployed in the U.S. (IS-95). Each side also supported its local company (Ericsson is based in Sweden; Qualcomm is in California). Finally, Ericsson and Qualcomm were involved in numerous lawsuits over their respective CDMA patents.

Worldwide, 10–15% of mobile subscribers already use 3G technologies. In North America and Europe, around a third of mobile subscribers are 3G. Japan was an early adopter and now nearly all mobile phones in Japan are 3G. These figures include the deployment of both UMTS and CDMA2000, and 3G continues to be one great cauldron of activity as the market shakes out. To add to the confusion, UMTS became a single 3G standard with multiple incompatible options, including CDMA2000. This change was an effort to unify the various camps, but it just papers over the technical differences and obscures the focus of ongoing efforts. We will use UMTS to mean WCDMA, as distinct from CDMA2000.

We will focus our discussion on the use of CDMA in cellular networks, as it is the distinguishing feature of both systems. CDMA is neither FDM nor TDM but a kind of mix in which each user sends on the same frequency band at the same time. When it was first proposed for cellular systems, the industry gave it approximately the same reaction that Columbus first got from Queen Isabella when he proposed reaching India by sailing in the wrong direction. However, through the persistence of a single company, Qualcomm, CDMA succeeded as a 2G system (IS-95) and matured to the point that it became the technical basis for 3G.

To make CDMA work in the mobile phone setting requires more than the basic CDMA technique that we described in the previous section. Specifically, we described synchronous CDMA, in which the chip sequences are exactly orthogonal. This design works when all users are synchronized on the start time of their chip sequences, as in the case of the base station transmitting to mobiles. The base station can transmit the chip sequences starting at the same time so that the signals will be orthogonal and able to be separated. However, it is difficult to synchronize the transmissions of independent mobile phones. Without care, their transmissions would arrive at the base station at different times, with no guarantee of orthogonality. To let mobiles send to the base station without synchronization, we want code sequences that are orthogonal to each other at all possible offsets, not simply when they are aligned at the start.

While it is not possible to find sequences that are exactly orthogonal for this general case, long pseudorandom sequences come close enough. They have the property that, with high probability, they have a low **cross-correlation** with each other at all offsets. This means that when one sequence is multiplied by another sequence and summed up to compute the inner product, the result will be small; it would be zero if they were orthogonal. (Intuitively, random sequences should always look different from each other. Multiplying them together should then produce a random signal, which will sum to a small result.) This lets a receiver filter unwanted transmissions out of the received signal. Also, the **auto-correlation** of pseudorandom sequences is also small, with high probability, except at a zero offset. This means that when one sequence is multiplied by a delayed copy of itself and summed, the result will be small, except when the delay is zero. (Intuitively, a delayed random sequence looks like a different random sequence, and we are back to the cross-correlation case.) This lets a receiver lock onto the beginning of the wanted transmission in the received signal.

The use of pseudorandom sequences lets the base station receive CDMA messages from unsynchronized mobiles. However, an implicit assumption in our discussion of CDMA is that the power levels of all mobiles are the same at the receiver. If they are not, a small cross-correlation with a powerful signal might overwhelm a large auto-correlation with a weak signal. Thus, the transmit power on mobiles must be controlled to minimize interference between competing signals. It is this interference that limits the capacity of CDMA systems.

The power levels received at a base station depend on how far away the transmitters are as well as how much power they transmit. There may be many mobile stations at varying distances from the base station. A good heuristic to equalize the received power is for each mobile station to transmit to the base station at the inverse of the power level it receives from the base station. In other words, a mobile station receiving a weak signal from the base station will use more power than one getting a strong signal. For more accuracy, the base station also gives each mobile feedback to increase, decrease, or hold steady its transmit power. The feedback is frequent (1500 times per second) because good power control is important to minimize interference.

Another improvement over the basic CDMA scheme we described earlier is to allow different users to send data at different rates. This trick is accomplished naturally in CDMA by fixing the rate at which chips are transmitted and assigning users chip sequences of different lengths. For example, in WCDMA, the chip rate is 3.84 Mchips/sec and the spreading codes vary from 4 to 256 chips. With a 256-chip code, around 12 kbps is left after error correction, and this capacity is sufficient for a voice call. With a 4-chip code, the user data rate is close to 1 Mbps. Intermediate-length codes give intermediate rates; to get to multiple Mbps, the mobile must use more than one 5-MHz channel at once.

Now let us describe the advantages of CDMA, given that we have dealt with the problems of getting it to work. It has three main advantages. First, CDMA can improve capacity by taking advantage of small periods when some transmitters are silent. In polite voice calls, one party is silent while the other talks. On average, the line is busy only 40% of the time. However, the pauses may be small and are difficult to predict. With TDM or FDM systems, it is not possible to reassign time slots or frequency channels quickly enough to benefit from these small silences. However, in CDMA, by simply not transmitting one user lowers the interference for other users, and it is likely that some fraction of users will not be transmitting in a busy cell at any given time. Thus CDMA takes advantage of expected silences to allow a larger number of simultaneous calls.

Second, with CDMA each cell uses the same frequencies. Unlike GSM and AMPS, FDM is not needed to separate the transmissions of different users. This eliminates complicated frequency planning tasks and improves capacity. It also makes it easy for a base station to use multiple directional antennas, or **sectored antennas**, instead of an omnidirectional antenna. Directional antennas concentrate a signal in the intended direction and reduce the signal, and hence interference, in other directions. This in turn increases capacity. Three sector designs are common. The base station must track the mobile as it moves from sector to sector. This tracking is easy with CDMA because all frequencies are used in all sectors.

Third, CDMA facilitates **soft handoff**, in which the mobile is acquired by the new base station before the previous one signs off. In this way there is no loss of continuity. Soft handoff is shown in Fig. 2-49. It is easy with CDMA because all frequencies are used in each cell. The alternative is a **hard handoff**, in which the old base station drops the call before the new one acquires it. If the new one is unable to acquire it (e.g., because there is no available frequency), the call is disconnected abruptly. Users tend to notice this, but it is inevitable occasionally with the current design. Hard handoff is the norm with FDM designs to avoid the cost of having the mobile transmit or receive on two frequencies simultaneously.

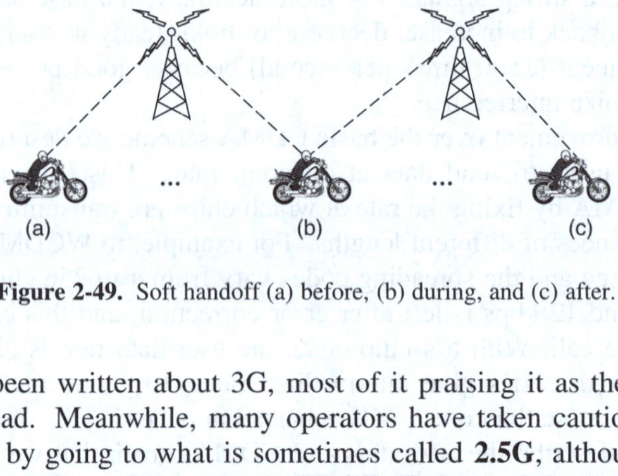

Figure 2-49. Soft handoff (a) before, (b) during, and (c) after.

Much has been written about 3G, most of it praising it as the greatest thing since sliced bread. Meanwhile, many operators have taken cautious steps in the direction of 3G by going to what is sometimes called **2.5G**, although 2.1G might be more accurate. One such system is **EDGE (Enhanced Data rates for GSM Evolution)**, which is just GSM with more bits per symbol. The trouble is, more bits per symbol also means more errors per symbol, so EDGE has nine different schemes for modulation and error correction, differing in terms of how much of the bandwidth is devoted to fixing the errors introduced by the higher speed. EDGE is one step along an evolutionary path that is defined from GSM to WCDMA. Similarly, there is an evolutionary path defined for operators to upgrade from IS-95 to CDMA2000 networks.

Even though 3G networks are not fully deployed yet, some researchers regard 3G as a done deal. These people are already working on 4G systems under the name of **LTE** (**Long Term Evolution**). Some of the proposed features of 4G include: high bandwidth; ubiquity (connectivity everywhere); seamless integration with other wired and wireless IP networks, including 802.11 access points; adaptive resource and spectrum management; and high quality of service for multimedia. For more information see Astely et al. (2009) and Larmo et al. (2009).

Meanwhile, wireless networks with 4G levels of performance are already available. The main example is **802.16**, also known as **WiMAX**. For an overview of mobile WiMAX see Ahmadi (2009). To say the industry is in a state of flux is a huge understatement. Check back in a few years to see what has happened.

2.8 CABLE TELEVISION

We have now studied both the fixed and wireless telephone systems in a fair amount of detail. Both will clearly play a major role in future networks. But there is another major player that has emerged over the past decade for Internet access: cable television networks. Many people nowadays get their telephone and Internet service over cable. In the following sections we will look at cable television as a network in more detail and contrast it with the telephone systems we have just studied. Some relevant references for more information are Donaldson and Jones (2001), Dutta-Roy (2001), and Fellows and Jones (2001).

2.8.1 Community Antenna Television

Cable television was conceived in the late 1940s as a way to provide better reception to people living in rural or mountainous areas. The system initially consisted of a big antenna on top of a hill to pluck the television signal out of the air, an amplifier, called the **headend**, to strengthen it, and a coaxial cable to deliver it to people's houses, as illustrated in Fig. 2-50.

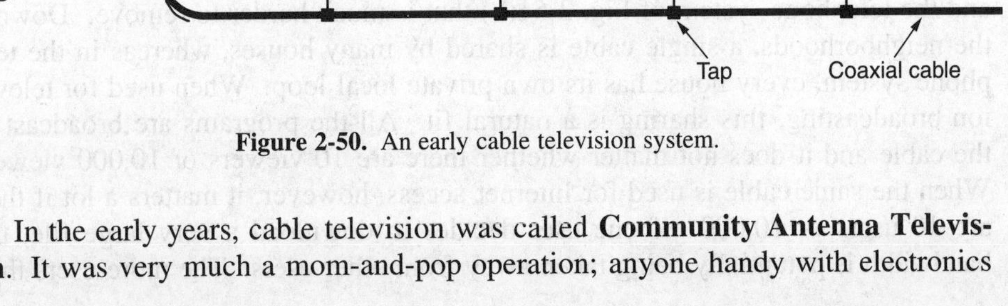

Figure 2-50. An early cable television system.

In the early years, cable television was called **Community Antenna Television**. It was very much a mom-and-pop operation; anyone handy with electronics could set up a service for his town, and the users would chip in to pay the costs. As the number of subscribers grew, additional cables were spliced onto the original cable and amplifiers were added as needed. Transmission was one way, from the headend to the users. By 1970, thousands of independent systems existed.

In 1974, Time Inc. started a new channel, Home Box Office, with new content (movies) distributed only on cable. Other cable-only channels followed, focusing on news, sports, cooking, and many other topics. This development gave rise to two changes in the industry. First, large corporations began buying up existing cable systems and laying new cable to acquire new subscribers. Second, there was now a need to connect multiple systems, often in distant cities, in order to distribute the new cable channels. The cable companies began to lay cable between the cities to connect them all into a single system. This pattern was analogous to what happened in the telephone industry 80 years earlier with the connection of previously isolated end offices to make long-distance calling possible.

2.8.2 Internet over Cable

Over the course of the years the cable system grew and the cables between the various cities were replaced by high-bandwidth fiber, similar to what happened in the telephone system. A system with fiber for the long-haul runs and coaxial cable to the houses is called an **HFC (Hybrid Fiber Coax)** system. The electro-optical converters that interface between the optical and electrical parts of the system are called **fiber nodes**. Because the bandwidth of fiber is so much greater than that of coax, a fiber node can feed multiple coaxial cables. Part of a modern HFC system is shown in Fig. 2-51(a).

Over the past decade, many cable operators decided to get into the Internet access business, and often the telephony business as well. Technical differences between the cable plant and telephone plant had an effect on what had to be done to achieve these goals. For one thing, all the one-way amplifiers in the system had to be replaced by two-way amplifiers to support upstream as well as downstream transmissions. While this was happening, early Internet over cable systems used the cable television network for downstream transmissions and a dial-up connection via the telephone network for upstream transmissions. It was a clever workaround, but not much of a network compared to what it could be.

However, there is another difference between the HFC system of Fig. 2-51(a) and the telephone system of Fig. 2-51(b) that is much harder to remove. Down in the neighborhoods, a single cable is shared by many houses, whereas in the telephone system, every house has its own private local loop. When used for television broadcasting, this sharing is a natural fit. All the programs are broadcast on the cable and it does not matter whether there are 10 viewers or 10,000 viewers. When the same cable is used for Internet access, however, it matters a lot if there are 10 users or 10,000. If one user decides to download a very large file, that bandwidth is potentially being taken away from other users. The more users there

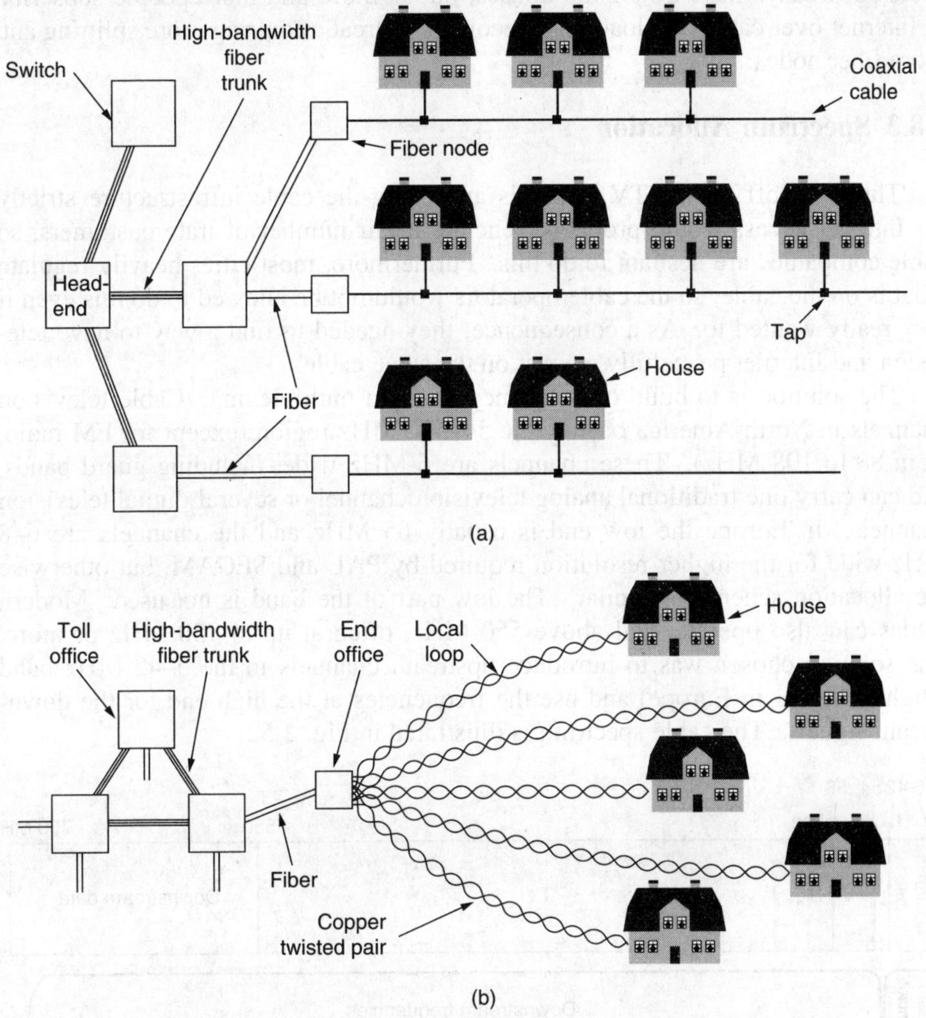

Figure 2-51. (a) Cable television. (b) The fixed telephone system.

are, the more competition there is for bandwidth. The telephone system does not have this particular property: downloading a large file over an ADSL line does not reduce your neighbor's bandwidth. On the other hand, the bandwidth of coax is much higher than that of twisted pairs, so you can get lucky if your neighbors do not use the Internet much.

The way the cable industry has tackled this problem is to split up long cables and connect each one directly to a fiber node. The bandwidth from the headend to each fiber node is effectively infinite, so as long as there are not too many subscribers on each cable segment, the amount of traffic is manageable. Typical cables nowadays have 500–2000 houses, but as more and more people subscribe to Internet over cable, the load may become too great, requiring more splitting and more fiber nodes.

2.8.3 Spectrum Allocation

Throwing off all the TV channels and using the cable infrastructure strictly for Internet access would probably generate a fair number of irate customers, so cable companies are hesitant to do this. Furthermore, most cities heavily regulate what is on the cable, so the cable operators would not be allowed to do this even if they really wanted to. As a consequence, they needed to find a way to have television and Internet peacefully coexist on the same cable.

The solution is to build on frequency division multiplexing. Cable television channels in North America occupy the 54–550 MHz region (except for FM radio, from 88 to 108 MHz). These channels are 6-MHz wide, including guard bands, and can carry one traditional analog television channel or several digital television channels. In Europe the low end is usually 65 MHz and the channels are 6–8 MHz wide for the higher resolution required by PAL and SECAM, but otherwise the allocation scheme is similar. The low part of the band is not used. Modern cables can also operate well above 550 MHz, often at up to 750 MHz or more. The solution chosen was to introduce upstream channels in the 5–42 MHz band (slightly higher in Europe) and use the frequencies at the high end for the downstream signals. The cable spectrum is illustrated in Fig. 2-52.

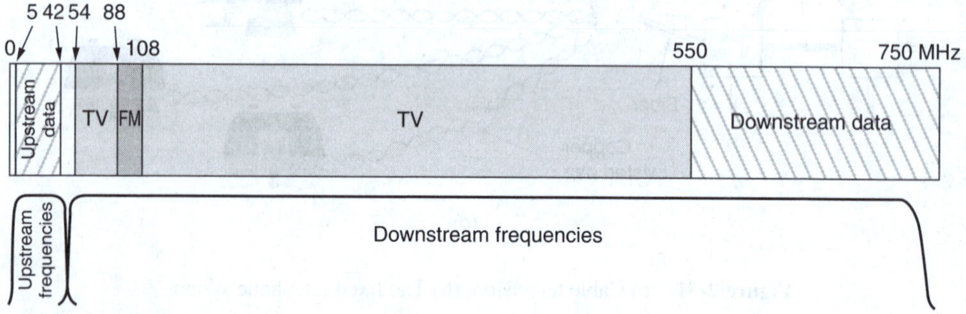

Figure 2-52. Frequency allocation in a typical cable TV system used for Internet access.

Note that since the television signals are all downstream, it is possible to use upstream amplifiers that work only in the 5–42 MHz region and downstream amplifiers that work only at 54 MHz and up, as shown in the figure. Thus, we get an asymmetry in the upstream and downstream bandwidths because more spectrum is available above television than below it. On the other hand, most users want more downstream traffic, so cable operators are not unhappy with this fact of life. As we saw earlier, telephone companies usually offer an asymmetric DSL service, even though they have no technical reason for doing so.

In addition to upgrading the amplifiers, the operator has to upgrade the headend, too, from a dumb amplifier to an intelligent digital computer system with a high-bandwidth fiber interface to an ISP. Often the name gets upgraded as well, from "headend" to **CMTS** (**Cable Modem Termination System**). In the following text, we will refrain from doing a name upgrade and stick with the traditional "headend."

2.8.4 Cable Modems

Internet access requires a cable modem, a device that has two interfaces on it: one to the computer and one to the cable network. In the early years of cable Internet, each operator had a proprietary cable modem, which was installed by a cable company technician. However, it soon became apparent that an open standard would create a competitive cable modem market and drive down prices, thus encouraging use of the service. Furthermore, having the customers buy cable modems in stores and install them themselves (as they do with wireless access points) would eliminate the dreaded truck rolls.

Consequently, the larger cable operators teamed up with a company called CableLabs to produce a cable modem standard and to test products for compliance. This standard, called **DOCSIS** (**Data Over Cable Service Interface Specification**), has mostly replaced proprietary modems. DOCSIS version 1.0 came out in 1997, and was soon followed by DOCSIS 2.0 in 2001. It increased upstream rates to better support symmetric services such as IP telephony. The most recent version of the standard is DOCSIS 3.0, which came out in 2006. It uses more bandwidth to increase rates in both directions. The European version of these standards is called **EuroDOCSIS**. Not all cable operators like the idea of a standard, however, since many of them were making good money leasing their modems to their captive customers. An open standard with dozens of manufacturers selling cable modems in stores ends this lucrative practice.

The modem-to-computer interface is straightforward. It is normally Ethernet, or occasionally USB. The other end is more complicated as it uses all of FDM, TDM, and CDMA to share the bandwidth of the cable between subscribers.

When a cable modem is plugged in and powered up, it scans the downstream channels looking for a special packet periodically put out by the headend to provide system parameters to modems that have just come online. Upon finding this packet, the new modem announces its presence on one of the upstream channels. The headend responds by assigning the modem to its upstream and downstream channels. These assignments can be changed later if the headend deems it necessary to balance the load.

The use of 6-MHz or 8-MHz channels is the FDM part. Each cable modem sends data on one upstream and one downstream channel, or multiple channels under DOCSIS 3.0. The usual scheme is to take each 6 (or 8) MHz downstream channel and modulate it with QAM-64 or, if the cable quality is exceptionally good, QAM-256. With a 6-MHz channel and QAM-64, we get about 36 Mbps. When the overhead is subtracted, the net payload is about 27 Mbps. With QAM-256, the net payload is about 39 Mbps. The European values are 1/3 larger.

For upstream, there is more RF noise because the system was not originally designed for data, and noise from multiple subscribers is funneled to the headend, so a more conservative scheme is used. This ranges from QPSK to QAM-128, where some of the symbols are used for error protection with Trellis Coded Modulation. With fewer bits per symbol on the upstream, the asymmetry between upstream and downstream rates is much more than suggested by Fig. 2-52.

TDM is then used to share bandwidth on the upstream across multiple subscribers. Otherwise their transmissions would collide at the headend. Time is divided into **minislots** and different subscribers send in different minislots. To make this work, the modem determines its distance from the headend by sending it a special packet and seeing how long it takes to get the response. This process is called **ranging**. It is important for the modem to know its distance to get the timing right. Each upstream packet must fit in one or more consecutive minislots at the headend when it is received. The headend announces the start of a new round of minislots periodically, but the starting gun is not heard at all modems simultaneously due to the propagation time down the cable. By knowing how far it is from the headend, each modem can compute how long ago the first minislot really started. Minislot length is network dependent. A typical payload is 8 bytes.

During initialization, the headend assigns each modem to a minislot to use for requesting upstream bandwidth. When a computer wants to send a packet, it transfers the packet to the modem, which then requests the necessary number of minislots for it. If the request is accepted, the headend puts an acknowledgement on the downstream channel telling the modem which minislots have been reserved for its packet. The packet is then sent, starting in the minislot allocated to it. Additional packets can be requested using a field in the header.

As a rule, multiple modems will be assigned the same minislot, which leads to contention. Two different possibilities exist for dealing with it. The first is that CDMA is used to share the minislot between subscribers. This solves the contention problem because all subscribers with a CDMA code sequence can send at the same time, albeit at a reduced rate. The second option is that CDMA is not used, in which case there may be no acknowledgement to the request because of a collision. In this case, the modem just waits a random time and tries again. After each successive failure, the randomization time is doubled. (For readers already somewhat familiar with networking, this algorithm is just slotted ALOHA with binary exponential backoff. Ethernet cannot be used on cable because stations cannot sense the medium. We will come back to these issues in Chap. 4.)

The downstream channels are managed differently from the upstream channels. For starters, there is only one sender (the headend), so there is no contention and no need for minislots, which is actually just statistical time division multiplexing. For another, the amount of traffic downstream is usually much larger than upstream, so a fixed packet size of 204 bytes is used. Part of that is a Reed-Solomon error-correcting code and some other overhead, leaving a user payload of 184 bytes. These numbers were chosen for compatibility with digital television using MPEG-2, so the TV and downstream data channels are formatted the same way. Logically, the connections are as depicted in Fig. 2-53.

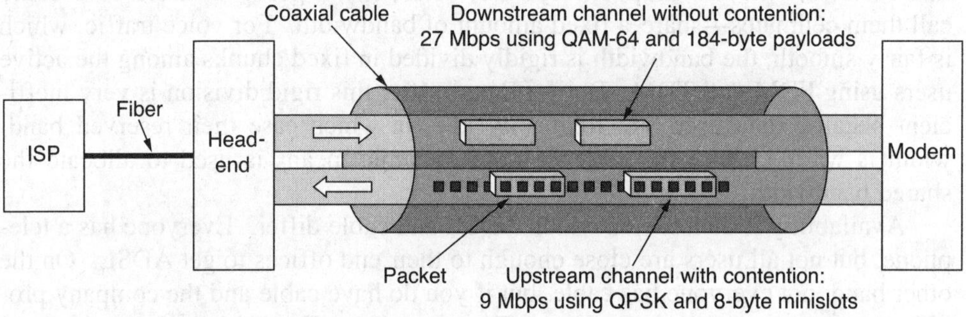

Figure 2-53. Typical details of the upstream and downstream channels in North America.

2.8.5 ADSL Versus Cable

Which is better, ADSL or cable? That is like asking which operating system is better. Or which language is better. Or which religion. Which answer you get depends on whom you ask. Let us compare ADSL and cable on a few points. Both use fiber in the backbone, but they differ on the edge. Cable uses coax; ADSL uses twisted pair. The theoretical carrying capacity of coax is hundreds of times more than twisted pair. However, the full capacity of the cable is not available for data users because much of the cable's bandwidth is wasted on useless stuff such as television programs.

In practice, it is hard to generalize about effective capacity. ADSL providers give specific statements about the bandwidth (e.g., 1 Mbps downstream, 256 kbps upstream) and generally achieve about 80% of it consistently. Cable providers may artificially cap the bandwidth to each user to help them make performance predictions, but they cannot really give guarantees because the effective capacity depends on how many people are currently active on the user's cable segment. Sometimes it may be better than ADSL and sometimes it may be worse. What can be annoying, though, is the unpredictability. Having great service one minute does not guarantee great service the next minute since the biggest bandwidth hog in town may have just turned on his computer.

As an ADSL system acquires more users, their increasing numbers have little effect on existing users, since each user has a dedicated connection. With cable, as more subscribers sign up for Internet service, performance for existing users will drop. The only cure is for the cable operator to split busy cables and connect each one to a fiber node directly. Doing so costs time and money, so there are business pressures to avoid it.

As an aside, we have already studied another system with a shared channel like cable: the mobile telephone system. Here, too, a group of users—we could call them cellmates—share a fixed amount of bandwidth. For voice traffic, which is fairly smooth, the bandwidth is rigidly divided in fixed chunks among the active users using FDM and TDM. But for data traffic, this rigid division is very inefficient because data users are frequently idle, in which case their reserved bandwidth is wasted. As with cable, a more dynamic means is used to allocate the shared bandwidth.

Availability is an issue on which ADSL and cable differ. Everyone has a telephone, but not all users are close enough to their end offices to get ADSL. On the other hand, not everyone has cable, but if you do have cable and the company provides Internet access, you can get it. Distance to the fiber node or headend is not an issue. It is also worth noting that since cable started out as a television distribution medium, few businesses have it.

Being a point-to-point medium, ADSL is inherently more secure than cable. Any cable user can easily read all the packets going down the cable. For this reason, any decent cable provider will encrypt all traffic in both directions. Nevertheless, having your neighbor get your encrypted messages is still less secure than having him not get anything at all.

The telephone system is generally more reliable than cable. For example, it has backup power and continues to work normally even during a power outage. With cable, if the power to any amplifier along the chain fails, all downstream users are cut off instantly.

Finally, most ADSL providers offer a choice of ISPs. Sometimes they are even required to do so by law. Such is not always the case with cable operators.

The conclusion is that ADSL and cable are much more alike than they are different. They offer comparable service and, as competition between them heats up, probably comparable prices.

2.9 SUMMARY

The physical layer is the basis of all networks. Nature imposes two fundamental limits on all channels, and these determine their bandwidth. These limits are the Nyquist limit, which deals with noiseless channels, and the Shannon limit, which deals with noisy channels.

Transmission media can be guided or unguided. The principal guided media are twisted pair, coaxial cable, and fiber optics. Unguided media include terrestrial radio, microwaves, infrared, lasers through the air, and satellites.

Digital modulation methods send bits over guided and unguided media as analog signals. Line codes operate at baseband, and signals can be placed in a passband by modulating the amplitude, frequency, and phase of a carrier. Channels can be shared between users with time, frequency and code division multiplexing.

A key element in most wide area networks is the telephone system. Its main components are the local loops, trunks, and switches. ADSL offers speeds up to 40 Mbps over the local loop by dividing it into many subcarriers that run in parallel. This far exceeds the rates of telephone modems. PONs bring fiber to the home for even greater access rates than ADSL.

Trunks carry digital information. They are multiplexed with WDM to provision many high capacity links over individual fibers, as well as with TDM to share each high rate link between users. Both circuit switching and packet switching are important.

For mobile applications, the fixed telephone system is not suitable. Mobile phones are currently in widespread use for voice, and increasingly for data. They have gone through three generations. The first generation, 1G, was analog and dominated by AMPS. 2G was digital, with GSM presently the most widely deployed mobile phone system in the world. 3G is digital and based on broadband CDMA, with WCDMA and also CDMA2000 now being deployed.

An alternative system for network access is the cable television system. It has gradually evolved from coaxial cable to hybrid fiber coax, and from television to television and Internet. Potentially, it offers very high bandwidth, but the bandwidth in practice depends heavily on the other users because it is shared.

PROBLEMS

1. Compute the Fourier coefficients for the function $f(t) = t \quad (0 \le t \le 1)$.
2. A noiseless 4-kHz channel is sampled every 1 msec. What is the maximum data rate? How does the maximum data rate change if the channel is noisy, with a signal-to-noise ratio of 30 dB?
3. Television channels are 6 MHz wide. How many bits/sec can be sent if four-level digital signals are used? Assume a noiseless channel.
4. If a binary signal is sent over a 3-kHz channel whose signal-to-noise ratio is 20 dB, what is the maximum achievable data rate?
5. What signal-to-noise ratio is needed to put a T1 carrier on a 50-kHz line?
6. What are the advantages of fiber optics over copper as a transmission medium? Is there any downside of using fiber optics over copper?

7. How much bandwidth is there in 0.1 microns of spectrum at a wavelength of 1 micron?

8. It is desired to send a sequence of computer screen images over an optical fiber. The screen is 2560×1600 pixels, each pixel being 24 bits. There are 60 screen images per second. How much bandwidth is needed, and how many microns of wavelength are needed for this band at 1.30 microns?

9. Is the Nyquist theorem true for high-quality single-mode optical fiber or only for copper wire?

10. Radio antennas often work best when the diameter of the antenna is equal to the wavelength of the radio wave. Reasonable antennas range from 1 cm to 5 meters in diameter. What frequency range does this cover?

11. A laser beam 1 mm wide is aimed at a detector 1 mm wide 100 m away on the roof of a building. How much of an angular diversion (in degrees) does the laser have to have before it misses the detector?

12. The 66 low-orbit satellites in the Iridium project are divided into six necklaces around the earth. At the altitude they are using, the period is 90 minutes. What is the average interval for handoffs for a stationary transmitter?

13. Calculate the end-to-end transit time for a packet for both GEO (altitude: 35,800 km), MEO (altitude: 18,000 km) and LEO (altitude: 750 km) satellites.

14. What is the latency of a call originating at the North Pole to reach the South Pole if the call is routed via Iridium satellites? Assume that the switching time at the satellites is 10 microseconds and earth's radius is 6371 km.

15. What is the minimum bandwidth needed to achieve a data rate of B bits/sec if the signal is transmitted using NRZ, MLT-3, and Manchester encoding? Explain your answer.

16. Prove that in 4B/5B encoding, a signal transition will occur at least every four bit times.

17. How many end office codes were there pre-1984, when each end office was named by its three-digit area code and the first three digits of the local number? Area codes started with a digit in the range 2–9, had a 0 or 1 as the second digit, and ended with any digit. The first two digits of a local number were always in the range 2–9. The third digit could be any digit.

18. A simple telephone system consists of two end offices and a single toll office to which each end office is connected by a 1-MHz full-duplex trunk. The average telephone is used to make four calls per 8-hour workday. The mean call duration is 6 min. Ten percent of the calls are long distance (i.e., pass through the toll office). What is the maximum number of telephones an end office can support? (Assume 4 kHz per circuit.) Explain why a telephone company may decide to support a lesser number of telephones than this maximum number at the end office.

19. A regional telephone company has 10 million subscribers. Each of their telephones is connected to a central office by a copper twisted pair. The average length of these twisted pairs is 10 km. How much is the copper in the local loops worth? Assume that the cross section of each strand is a circle 1 mm in diameter, the density of copper is 9.0 grams/cm^3, and that copper sells for $6 per kilogram.

20. Is an oil pipeline a simplex system, a half-duplex system, a full-duplex system, or none of the above? What about a river or a walkie-talkie-style communication?

21. The cost of a fast microprocessor has dropped to the point where it is now possible to put one in each modem. How does that affect the handling of telephone line errors? Does it negate the need for error checking/correction in layer 2?

22. A modem constellation diagram similar to Fig. 2-23 has data points at the following coordinates: (1, 1), (1, −1), (−1, 1), and (−1, −1). How many bps can a modem with these parameters achieve at 1200 symbols/second?

23. What is the maximum bit rate achievable in a V.32 standard modem if the baud rate is 1200 and no error correction is used?

24. How many frequencies does a full-duplex QAM-64 modem use?

25. Ten signals, each requiring 4000 Hz, are multiplexed onto a single channel using FDM. What is the minimum bandwidth required for the multiplexed channel? Assume that the guard bands are 400 Hz wide.

26. Why has the PCM sampling time been set at 125 μsec?

27. What is the percent overhead on a T1 carrier? That is, what percent of the 1.544 Mbps are not delivered to the end user? How does it relate to the percent overhead in OC-1 or OC-768 lines?

28. Compare the maximum data rate of a noiseless 4-kHz channel using
(a) Analog encoding (e.g., QPSK) with 2 bits per sample.
(b) The T1 PCM system.

29. If a T1 carrier system slips and loses track of where it is, it tries to resynchronize using the first bit in each frame. How many frames will have to be inspected on average to resynchronize with a probability of 0.001 of being wrong?

30. What is the difference, if any, between the demodulator part of a modem and the coder part of a codec? (After all, both convert analog signals to digital ones.)

31. SONET clocks have a drift rate of about 1 part in 10^9. How long does it take for the drift to equal the width of 1 bit? Do you see any practical implications of this calculation? If so, what?

32. How long will it take to transmit a 1-GB file from one VSAT to another using a hub as shown in Figure 2-17? Assume that the uplink is 1 Mbps, the downlink is 7 Mbps, and circuit switching is used with 1.2 sec circuit setup time.

33. Calculate the transmit time in the previous problem if packet switching is used instead. Assume that the packet size is 64 KB, the switching delay in the satellite and hub is 10 microseconds, and the packet header size is 32 bytes.

34. In Fig. 2-40, the user data rate for OC-3 is stated to be 148.608 Mbps. Show how this number can be derived from the SONET OC-3 parameters. What will be the gross, SPE, and user data rates of an OC-3072 line?

35. To accommodate lower data rates than STS-1, SONET has a system of virtual tributaries (VTs). A VT is a partial payload that can be inserted into an STS-1 frame and combined with other partial payloads to fill the data frame. VT1.5 uses 3 columns, VT2 uses 4 columns, VT3 uses 6 columns, and VT6 uses 12 columns of an STS-1 frame. Which VT can accommodate

(a) A DS-1 service (1.544 Mbps)?
(b) European CEPT-1 service (2.048 Mbps)?
(c) A DS-2 service (6.312 Mbps)?

36. What is the available user bandwidth in an OC-12c connection?

37. Three packet-switching networks each contain *n* nodes. The first network has a star topology with a central switch, the second is a (bidirectional) ring, and the third is fully interconnected, with a wire from every node to every other node. What are the best-, average-, and worst-case transmission paths in hops?

38. Compare the delay in sending an *x*-bit message over a *k*-hop path in a circuit-switched network and in a (lightly loaded) packet-switched network. The circuit setup time is *s* sec, the propagation delay is *d* sec per hop, the packet size is *p* bits, and the data rate is *b* bps. Under what conditions does the packet network have a lower delay? Also, explain the conditions under which a packet-switched network is preferable to a circuit-switched network.

39. Suppose that *x* bits of user data are to be transmitted over a *k*-hop path in a packet-switched network as a series of packets, each containing *p* data bits and *h* header bits, with $x \gg p + h$. The bit rate of the lines is *b* bps and the propagation delay is negligible. What value of *p* minimizes the total delay?

40. In a typical mobile phone system with hexagonal cells, it is forbidden to reuse a frequency band in an adjacent cell. If 840 frequencies are available, how many can be used in a given cell?

41. The actual layout of cells is seldom as regular that as shown in Fig. 2-45. Even the shapes of individual cells are typically irregular. Give a possible reason why this might be. How do these irregular shapes affect frequency assignment to each cell?

42. Make a rough estimate of the number of PCS microcells 100 m in diameter it would take to cover San Francisco (120 square km).

43. Sometimes when a mobile user crosses the boundary from one cell to another, the current call is abruptly terminated, even though all transmitters and receivers are functioning perfectly. Why?

44. Suppose that *A*, *B*, and *C* are simultaneously transmitting 0 bits, using a CDMA system with the chip sequences of Fig. 2-28(a). What is the resulting chip sequence?

45. Consider a different way of looking at the orthogonality property of CDMA chip sequences. Each bit in a pair of sequences can match or not match. Express the orthogonality property in terms of matches and mismatches.

46. A CDMA receiver gets the following chips: (−1 +1 −3 +1 −1 −3 +1 +1). Assuming the chip sequences defined in Fig. 2-28(a), which stations transmitted, and which bits did each one send?

47. In Figure 2-28, there are four stations that can transmit. Suppose four more stations are added. Provide the chip sequences of these stations.

48. At the low end, the telephone system is star shaped, with all the local loops in a neighborhood converging on an end office. In contrast, cable television consists of a single long cable snaking its way past all the houses in the same neighborhood. Suppose that a future TV cable were 10-Gbps fiber instead of copper. Could it be used to simulate the telephone model of everybody having their own private line to the end office? If so, how many one-telephone houses could be hooked up to a single fiber?

49. A cable company decides to provide Internet access over cable in a neighborhood consisting of 5000 houses. The company uses a coaxial cable and spectrum allocation allowing 100 Mbps downstream bandwidth per cable. To attract customers, the company decides to guarantee at least 2 Mbps downstream bandwidth to each house at any time. Describe what the cable company needs to do to provide this guarantee.

50. Using the spectral allocation shown in Fig. 2-52 and the information given in the text, how many Mbps does a cable system allocate to upstream and how many to downstream?

51. How fast can a cable user receive data if the network is otherwise idle? Assume that the user interface is
(a) 10-Mbps Ethernet
(b) 100-Mbps Ethernet
(c) 54-Mbps Wireless.

52. Multiplexing STS-1 multiple data streams, called tributaries, plays an important role in SONET. A 3:1 multiplexer multiplexes three input STS-1 tributaries onto one output STS-3 stream. This multiplexing is done byte for byte. That is, the first three output bytes are the first bytes of tributaries 1, 2, and 3, respectively. the next three output bytes are the second bytes of tributaries 1, 2, and 3, respectively, and so on. Write a program that simulates this 3:1 multiplexer. Your program should consist of five processes. The main process creates four processes, one each for the three STS-1 tributaries and one for the multiplexer. Each tributary process reads in an STS-1 frame from an input file as a sequence of 810 bytes. They send their frames (byte by byte) to the multiplexer process. The multiplexer process receives these bytes and outputs an STS-3 frame (byte by byte) by writing it to standard output. Use pipes for communication among processes.

53. Write a program to implement CDMA. Assume that the length of a chip sequence is eight and the number of stations transmitting is four. Your program consists of three sets of processes: four transmitter processes (t0, t1, t2, and t3), one joiner process, and four receiver processes (r0, r1, r2, and r3). The main program, which also acts as the joiner process first reads four chip sequences (bipolar notation) from the standard input and a sequence of 4 bits (1 bit per transmitter process to be transmitted), and forks off four pairs of transmitter and receiver processes. Each pair of transmitter/receiver processes (t0,r0; t1,r1; t2,r2; t3,r3) is assigned one chip sequence and each transmitter process is assigned 1 bit (first bit to t0, second bit to t1, and so on). Next, each transmitter process computes the signal to be transmitted (a sequence of 8 bits) and sends it to the joiner process. After receiving signals from all four transmitter processes, the joiner process combines the signals and sends the combined signal to the four receiver processes. Each receiver process then computes the bit it has received and prints it to standard output. Use pipes for communication between processes.

3

THE DATA LINK LAYER

In this chapter we will study the design principles for the second layer in our model, the data link layer. This study deals with algorithms for achieving reliable, efficient communication of whole units of information called frames (rather than individual bits, as in the physical layer) between two adjacent machines. By adjacent, we mean that the two machines are connected by a communication channel that acts conceptually like a wire (e.g., a coaxial cable, telephone line, or wireless channel). The essential property of a channel that makes it "wire-like" is that the bits are delivered in exactly the same order in which they are sent.

At first you might think this problem is so trivial that there is nothing to study—machine *A* just puts the bits on the wire, and machine *B* just takes them off. Unfortunately, communication channels make errors occasionally. Furthermore, they have only a finite data rate, and there is a nonzero propagation delay between the time a bit is sent and the time it is received. These limitations have important implications for the efficiency of the data transfer. The protocols used for communications must take all these factors into consideration. These protocols are the subject of this chapter.

After an introduction to the key design issues present in the data link layer, we will start our study of its protocols by looking at the nature of errors and how they can be detected and corrected. Then we will study a series of increasingly complex protocols, each one solving more and more of the problems present in this layer. Finally, we will conclude with some examples of data link protocols.

3.1 DATA LINK LAYER DESIGN ISSUES

The data link layer uses the services of the physical layer to send and receive bits over communication channels. It has a number of functions, including:

1. Providing a well-defined service interface to the network layer.
2. Dealing with transmission errors.
3. Regulating the flow of data so that slow receivers are not swamped by fast senders.

To accomplish these goals, the data link layer takes the packets it gets from the network layer and encapsulates them into **frames** for transmission. Each frame contains a frame header, a payload field for holding the packet, and a frame trailer, as illustrated in Fig. 3-1. Frame management forms the heart of what the data link layer does. In the following sections we will examine all the above-mentioned issues in detail.

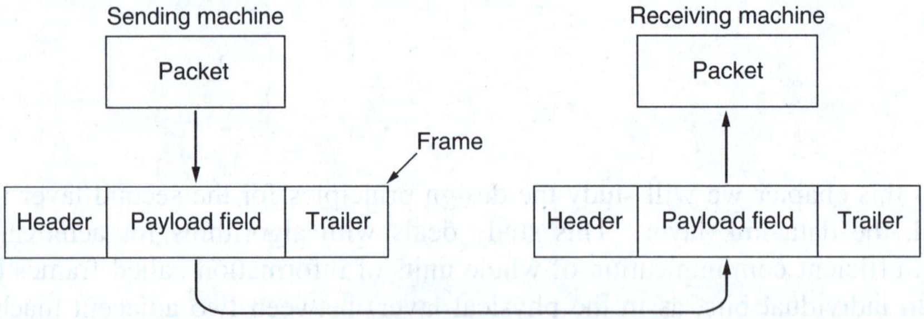

Figure 3-1. Relationship between packets and frames.

Although this chapter is explicitly about the data link layer and its protocols, many of the principles we will study here, such as error control and flow control, are found in transport and other protocols as well. That is because reliability is an overall goal, and it is achieved when all the layers work together. In fact, in many networks, these functions are found mostly in the upper layers, with the data link layer doing the minimal job that is "good enough." However, no matter where they are found, the principles are pretty much the same. They often show up in their simplest and purest forms in the data link layer, making this a good place to examine them in detail.

3.1.1 Services Provided to the Network Layer

The function of the data link layer is to provide services to the network layer. The principal service is transferring data from the network layer on the source machine to the network layer on the destination machine. On the source machine is an entity, call it a process, in the network layer that hands some bits to the data link layer for transmission to the destination. The job of the data link layer is to transmit the bits to the destination machine so they can be handed over to the network layer there, as shown in Fig. 3-2(a). The actual transmission follows the path of Fig. 3-2(b), but it is easier to think in terms of two data link layer processes communicating using a data link protocol. For this reason, we will implicitly use the model of Fig. 3-2(a) throughout this chapter.

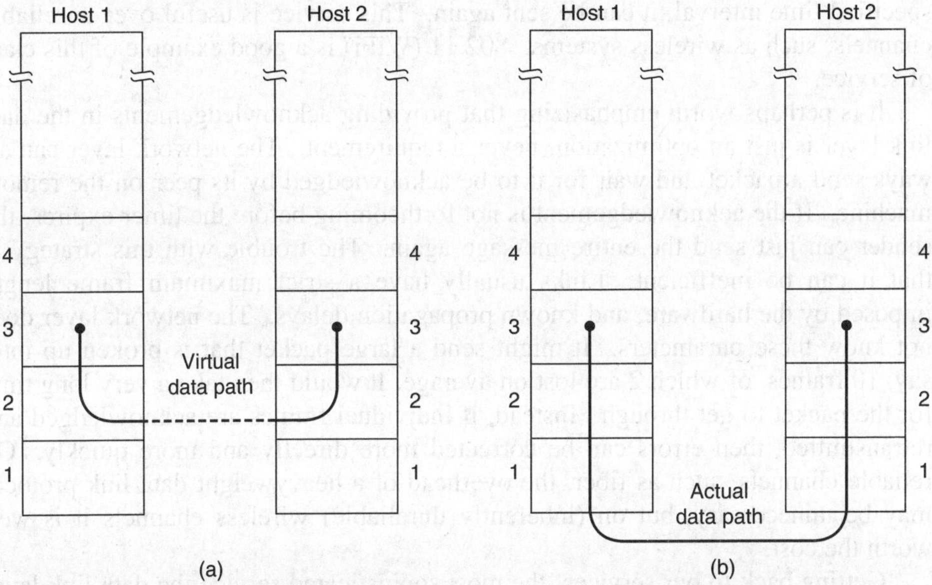

Figure 3-2. (a) Virtual communication. (b) Actual communication.

The data link layer can be designed to offer various services. The actual services that are offered vary from protocol to protocol. Three reasonable possibilities that we will consider in turn are:

1. Unacknowledged connectionless service.
2. Acknowledged connectionless service.
3. Acknowledged connection-oriented service.

Unacknowledged connectionless service consists of having the source machine send independent frames to the destination machine without having the destination machine acknowledge them. Ethernet is a good example of a data link layer that provides this class of service. No logical connection is established beforehand or released afterward. If a frame is lost due to noise on the line, no attempt is made to detect the loss or recover from it in the data link layer. This class of service is appropriate when the error rate is very low, so recovery is left to higher layers. It is also appropriate for real-time traffic, such as voice, in which late data are worse than bad data.

The next step up in terms of reliability is acknowledged connectionless service. When this service is offered, there are still no logical connections used, but each frame sent is individually acknowledged. In this way, the sender knows whether a frame has arrived correctly or been lost. If it has not arrived within a specified time interval, it can be sent again. This service is useful over unreliable channels, such as wireless systems. 802.11 (WiFi) is a good example of this class of service.

It is perhaps worth emphasizing that providing acknowledgements in the data link layer is just an optimization, never a requirement. The network layer can always send a packet and wait for it to be acknowledged by its peer on the remote machine. If the acknowledgement is not forthcoming before the timer expires, the sender can just send the entire message again. The trouble with this strategy is that it can be inefficient. Links usually have a strict maximum frame length imposed by the hardware, and known propagation delays. The network layer does not know these parameters. It might send a large packet that is broken up into, say, 10 frames, of which 2 are lost on average. It would then take a very long time for the packet to get through. Instead, if individual frames are acknowledged and retransmitted, then errors can be corrected more directly and more quickly. On reliable channels, such as fiber, the overhead of a heavyweight data link protocol may be unnecessary, but on (inherently unreliable) wireless channels it is well worth the cost.

Getting back to our services, the most sophisticated service the data link layer can provide to the network layer is connection-oriented service. With this service, the source and destination machines establish a connection before any data are transferred. Each frame sent over the connection is numbered, and the data link layer guarantees that each frame sent is indeed received. Furthermore, it guarantees that each frame is received exactly once and that all frames are received in the right order. Connection-oriented service thus provides the network layer processes with the equivalent of a reliable bit stream. It is appropriate over long, unreliable links such as a satellite channel or a long-distance telephone circuit. If acknowledged connectionless service were used, it is conceivable that lost acknowledgements could cause a frame to be sent and received several times, wasting bandwidth.

When connection-oriented service is used, transfers go through three distinct phases. In the first phase, the connection is established by having both sides initialize variables and counters needed to keep track of which frames have been received and which ones have not. In the second phase, one or more frames are actually transmitted. In the third and final phase, the connection is released, freeing up the variables, buffers, and other resources used to maintain the connection.

3.1.2 Framing

To provide service to the network layer, the data link layer must use the service provided to it by the physical layer. What the physical layer does is accept a raw bit stream and attempt to deliver it to the destination. If the channel is noisy, as it is for most wireless and some wired links, the physical layer will add some redundancy to its signals to reduce the bit error rate to a tolerable level. However, the bit stream received by the data link layer is not guaranteed to be error free. Some bits may have different values and the number of bits received may be less than, equal to, or more than the number of bits transmitted. It is up to the data link layer to detect and, if necessary, correct errors.

The usual approach is for the data link layer to break up the bit stream into discrete frames, compute a short token called a checksum for each frame, and include the checksum in the frame when it is transmitted. (Checksum algorithms will be discussed later in this chapter.) When a frame arrives at the destination, the checksum is recomputed. If the newly computed checksum is different from the one contained in the frame, the data link layer knows that an error has occurred and takes steps to deal with it (e.g., discarding the bad frame and possibly also sending back an error report).

Breaking up the bit stream into frames is more difficult than it at first appears. A good design must make it easy for a receiver to find the start of new frames while using little of the channel bandwidth. We will look at four methods:

1. Byte count.
2. Flag bytes with byte stuffing.
3. Flag bits with bit stuffing.
4. Physical layer coding violations.

The first framing method uses a field in the header to specify the number of bytes in the frame. When the data link layer at the destination sees the byte count, it knows how many bytes follow and hence where the end of the frame is. This technique is shown in Fig. 3-3(a) for four small example frames of sizes 5, 5, 8, and 8 bytes, respectively.

The trouble with this algorithm is that the count can be garbled by a transmission error. For example, if the byte count of 5 in the second frame of Fig. 3-3(b) becomes a 7 due to a single bit flip, the destination will get out of synchronization. It will then be unable to locate the correct start of the next frame. Even if the checksum is incorrect so the destination knows that the frame is bad, it still has no way of telling where the next frame starts. Sending a frame back to the source asking for a retransmission does not help either, since the destination does not know how many bytes to skip over to get to the start of the retransmission. For this reason, the byte count method is rarely used by itself.

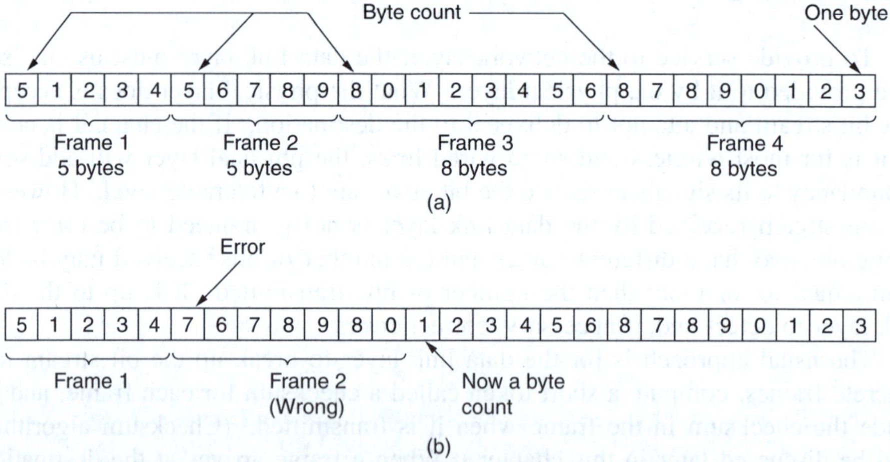

Figure 3-3. A byte stream. (a) Without errors. (b) With one error.

The second framing method gets around the problem of resynchronization after an error by having each frame start and end with special bytes. Often the same byte, called a **flag byte**, is used as both the starting and ending delimiter. This byte is shown in Fig. 3-4(a) as FLAG. Two consecutive flag bytes indicate the end of one frame and the start of the next. Thus, if the receiver ever loses synchronization it can just search for two flag bytes to find the end of the current frame and the start of the next frame.

However, there is a still a problem we have to solve. It may happen that the flag byte occurs in the data, especially when binary data such as photographs or songs are being transmitted. This situation would interfere with the framing. One way to solve this problem is to have the sender's data link layer insert a special escape byte (ESC) just before each "accidental" flag byte in the data. Thus, a framing flag byte can be distinguished from one in the data by the absence or presence of an escape byte before it. The data link layer on the receiving end removes the escape bytes before giving the data to the network layer. This technique is called **byte stuffing**.

Of course, the next question is: what happens if an escape byte occurs in the middle of the data? The answer is that it, too, is stuffed with an escape byte. At the receiver, the first escape byte is removed, leaving the data byte that follows it (which might be another escape byte or the flag byte). Some examples are shown in Fig. 3-4(b). In all cases, the byte sequence delivered after destuffing is exactly the same as the original byte sequence. We can still search for a frame boundary by looking for two flag bytes in a row, without bothering to undo escapes.

The byte-stuffing scheme depicted in Fig. 3-4 is a slight simplification of the one used in **PPP** (**Point-to-Point Protocol**), which is used to carry packets over communications links. We will discuss PPP near the end of this chapter.

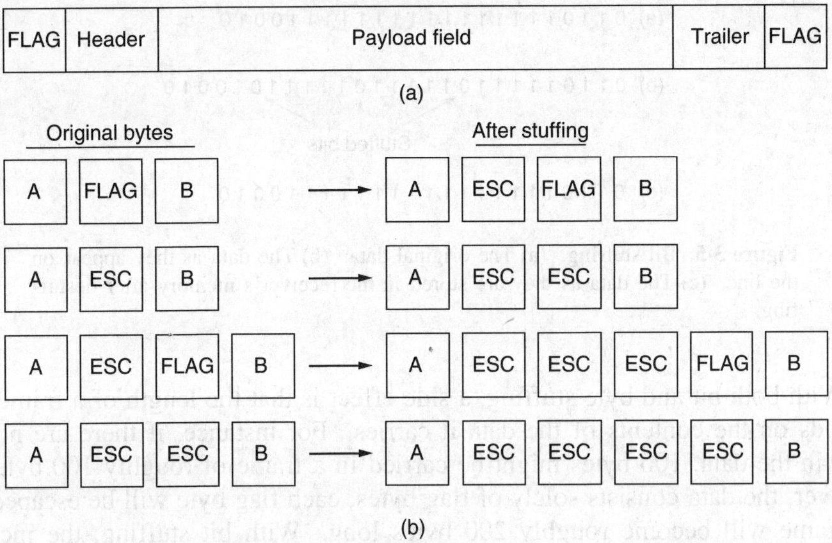

Figure 3-4. (a) A frame delimited by flag bytes. (b) Four examples of byte sequences before and after byte stuffing.

The third method of delimiting the bit stream gets around a disadvantage of byte stuffing, which is that it is tied to the use of 8-bit bytes. Framing can be also be done at the bit level, so frames can contain an arbitrary number of bits made up of units of any size. It was developed for the once very popular **HDLC (High-level Data Link Control)** protocol. Each frame begins and ends with a special bit pattern, 01111110 or 0x7E in hexadecimal. This pattern is a flag byte. Whenever the sender's data link layer encounters five consecutive 1s in the data, it automatically stuffs a 0 bit into the outgoing bit stream. This **bit stuffing** is analogous to byte stuffing, in which an escape byte is stuffed into the outgoing character stream before a flag byte in the data. It also ensures a minimum density of transitions that help the physical layer maintain synchronization. USB (Universal Serial Bus) uses bit stuffing for this reason.

When the receiver sees five consecutive incoming 1 bits, followed by a 0 bit, it automatically destuffs (i.e., deletes) the 0 bit. Just as byte stuffing is completely transparent to the network layer in both computers, so is bit stuffing. If the user data contain the flag pattern, 01111110, this flag is transmitted as 011111010 but stored in the receiver's memory as 01111110. Figure 3-5 gives an example of bit stuffing.

With bit stuffing, the boundary between two frames can be unambiguously recognized by the flag pattern. Thus, if the receiver loses track of where it is, all it has to do is scan the input for flag sequences, since they can only occur at frame boundaries and never within the data.

(a) 0 1 1 0 1 1 1 1 1 1 1 1 1 1 1 1 1 1 1 1 0 0 1 0

(b) 0 1 1 0 1 1 1 1 1 0 1 1 1 1 1 0 1 1 1 1 1 0 1 0 0 1 0

Stuffed bits

(c) 0 1 1 0 1 1 1 1 1 1 1 1 1 1 1 1 1 1 1 1 0 0 1 0

Figure 3-5. Bit stuffing. (a) The original data. (b) The data as they appear on the line. (c) The data as they are stored in the receiver's memory after destuffing.

With both bit and byte stuffing, a side effect is that the length of a frame now depends on the contents of the data it carries. For instance, if there are no flag bytes in the data, 100 bytes might be carried in a frame of roughly 100 bytes. If, however, the data consists solely of flag bytes, each flag byte will be escaped and the frame will become roughly 200 bytes long. With bit stuffing, the increase would be roughly 12.5% as 1 bit is added to every byte.

The last method of framing is to use a shortcut from the physical layer. We saw in Chap. 2 that the encoding of bits as signals often includes redundancy to help the receiver. This redundancy means that some signals will not occur in regular data. For example, in the 4B/5B line code 4 data bits are mapped to 5 signal bits to ensure sufficient bit transitions. This means that 16 out of the 32 signal possibilities are not used. We can use some reserved signals to indicate the start and end of frames. In effect, we are using "coding violations" to delimit frames. The beauty of this scheme is that, because they are reserved signals, it is easy to find the start and end of frames and there is no need to stuff the data.

Many data link protocols use a combination of these methods for safety. A common pattern used for Ethernet and 802.11 is to have a frame begin with a well-defined pattern called a **preamble**. This pattern might be quite long (72 bits is typical for 802.11) to allow the receiver to prepare for an incoming packet. The preamble is then followed by a length (i.e., count) field in the header that is used to locate the end of the frame.

3.1.3 Error Control

Having solved the problem of marking the start and end of each frame, we come to the next problem: how to make sure all frames are eventually delivered to the network layer at the destination and in the proper order. Assume for the moment that the receiver can tell whether a frame that it receives contains correct or faulty information (we will look at the codes that are used to detect and correct transmission errors in Sec. 3.2). For unacknowledged connectionless service it might be fine if the sender just kept outputting frames without regard to whether they were arriving properly. But for reliable, connection-oriented service it would not be fine at all.

The usual way to ensure reliable delivery is to provide the sender with some feedback about what is happening at the other end of the line. Typically, the protocol calls for the receiver to send back special control frames bearing positive or negative acknowledgements about the incoming frames. If the sender receives a positive acknowledgement about a frame, it knows the frame has arrived safely. On the other hand, a negative acknowledgement means that something has gone wrong and the frame must be transmitted again.

An additional complication comes from the possibility that hardware troubles may cause a frame to vanish completely (e.g., in a noise burst). In this case, the receiver will not react at all, since it has no reason to react. Similarly, if the acknowledgement frame is lost, the sender will not know how to proceed. It should be clear that a protocol in which the sender transmits a frame and then waits for an acknowledgement, positive or negative, will hang forever if a frame is ever lost due to, for example, malfunctioning hardware or a faulty communication channel.

This possibility is dealt with by introducing timers into the data link layer. When the sender transmits a frame, it generally also starts a timer. The timer is set to expire after an interval long enough for the frame to reach the destination, be processed there, and have the acknowledgement propagate back to the sender. Normally, the frame will be correctly received and the acknowledgement will get back before the timer runs out, in which case the timer will be canceled.

However, if either the frame or the acknowledgement is lost, the timer will go off, alerting the sender to a potential problem. The obvious solution is to just transmit the frame again. However, when frames may be transmitted multiple times there is a danger that the receiver will accept the same frame two or more times and pass it to the network layer more than once. To prevent this from happening, it is generally necessary to assign sequence numbers to outgoing frames, so that the receiver can distinguish retransmissions from originals.

The whole issue of managing the timers and sequence numbers so as to ensure that each frame is ultimately passed to the network layer at the destination exactly once, no more and no less, is an important part of the duties of the data link layer (and higher layers). Later in this chapter, we will look at a series of increasingly sophisticated examples to see how this management is done.

3.1.4 Flow Control

Another important design issue that occurs in the data link layer (and higher layers as well) is what to do with a sender that systematically wants to transmit frames faster than the receiver can accept them. This situation can occur when the sender is running on a fast, powerful computer and the receiver is running on a slow, low-end machine. A common situation is when a smart phone requests a Web page from a far more powerful server, which then turns on the fire hose and blasts the data at the poor helpless phone until it is completely swamped. Even if the transmission is error free, the receiver may be unable to handle the frames as fast as they arrive and will lose some.

Clearly, something has to be done to prevent this situation. Two approaches are commonly used. In the first one, **feedback-based flow control**, the receiver sends back information to the sender giving it permission to send more data, or at least telling the sender how the receiver is doing. In the second one, **rate-based flow control**, the protocol has a built-in mechanism that limits the rate at which senders may transmit data, without using feedback from the receiver.

In this chapter we will study feedback-based flow control schemes, primarily because rate-based schemes are only seen as part of the transport layer (Chap. 5). Feedback-based schemes are seen at both the link layer and higher layers. The latter is more common these days, in which case the link layer hardware is designed to run fast enough that it does not cause loss. For example, hardware implementations of the link layer as **NICs (Network Interface Cards)** are sometimes said to run at "wire speed," meaning that they can handle frames as fast as they can arrive on the link. Any overruns are then not a link problem, so they are handled by higher layers.

Various feedback-based flow control schemes are known, but most of them use the same basic principle. The protocol contains well-defined rules about when a sender may transmit the next frame. These rules often prohibit frames from being sent until the receiver has granted permission, either implicitly or explicitly. For example, when a connection is set up the receiver might say: "You may send me *n* frames now, but after they have been sent, do not send any more until I have told you to continue." We will examine the details shortly.

3.2 ERROR DETECTION AND CORRECTION

We saw in Chap. 2 that communication channels have a range of characteristics. Some channels, like optical fiber in telecommunications networks, have tiny error rates so that transmission errors are a rare occurrence. But other channels, especially wireless links and aging local loops, have error rates that are orders of magnitude larger. For these links, transmission errors are the norm. They cannot be avoided at a reasonable expense or cost in terms of performance. The conclusion is that transmission errors are here to stay. We have to learn how to deal with them.

Network designers have developed two basic strategies for dealing with errors. Both add redundant information to the data that is sent. One strategy is to include enough redundant information to enable the receiver to deduce what the transmitted data must have been. The other is to include only enough redundancy to allow the receiver to deduce that an error has occurred (but not which error) and have it request a retransmission. The former strategy uses **error-correcting codes** and the latter uses **error-detecting codes**. The use of error-correcting codes is often referred to as **FEC (Forward Error Correction)**.

Each of these techniques occupies a different ecological niche. On channels that are highly reliable, such as fiber, it is cheaper to use an error-detecting code and just retransmit the occasional block found to be faulty. However, on channels such as wireless links that make many errors, it is better to add redundancy to each block so that the receiver is able to figure out what the originally transmitted block was. FEC is used on noisy channels because retransmissions are just as likely to be in error as the first transmission.

A key consideration for these codes is the type of errors that are likely to occur. Neither error-correcting codes nor error-detecting codes can handle all possible errors since the redundant bits that offer protection are as likely to be received in error as the data bits (which can compromise their protection). It would be nice if the channel treated redundant bits differently than data bits, but it does not. They are all just bits to the channel. This means that to avoid undetected errors the code must be strong enough to handle the expected errors.

One model is that errors are caused by extreme values of thermal noise that overwhelm the signal briefly and occasionally, giving rise to isolated single-bit errors. Another model is that errors tend to come in bursts rather than singly. This model follows from the physical processes that generate them—such as a deep fade on a wireless channel or transient electrical interference on a wired channel/

Both models matter in practice, and they have different trade-offs. Having the errors come in bursts has both advantages and disadvantages over isolated single-bit errors. On the advantage side, computer data are always sent in blocks of bits. Suppose that the block size was 1000 bits and the error rate was 0.001 per bit. If errors were independent, most blocks would contain an error. If the errors came in bursts of 100, however, only one block in 100 would be affected, on average. The disadvantage of burst errors is that when they do occur they are much harder to correct than isolated errors.

Other types of errors also exist. Sometimes, the location of an error will be known, perhaps because the physical layer received an analog signal that was far from the expected value for a 0 or 1 and declared the bit to be lost. This situation is called an **erasure channel**. It is easier to correct errors in erasure channels than in channels that flip bits because even if the value of the bit has been lost, at least we know which bit is in error. However, we often do not have the benefit of erasures.

We will examine both error-correcting codes and error-detecting codes next. Please keep two points in mind, though. First, we cover these codes in the link layer because this is the first place that we have run up against the problem of reliably transmitting groups of bits. However, the codes are widely used because reliability is an overall concern. Error-correcting codes are also seen in the physical layer, particularly for noisy channels, and in higher layers, particularly for real-time media and content distribution. Error-detecting codes are commonly used in link, network, and transport layers.

The second point to bear in mind is that error codes are applied mathematics. Unless you are particularly adept at Galois fields or the properties of sparse matrices, you should get codes with good properties from a reliable source rather than making up your own. In fact, this is what many protocol standards do, with the same codes coming up again and again. In the material below, we will study a simple code in detail and then briefly describe advanced codes. In this way, we can understand the trade-offs from the simple code and talk about the codes that are used in practice via the advanced codes.

3.2.1 Error-Correcting Codes

We will examine four different error-correcting codes:

1. Hamming codes.
2. Binary convolutional codes.
3. Reed-Solomon codes.
4. Low-Density Parity Check codes.

All of these codes add redundancy to the information that is sent. A frame consists of m data (i.e., message) bits and r redundant (i.e. check) bits. In a **block code**, the r check bits are computed solely as a function of the m data bits with which they are associated, as though the m bits were looked up in a large table to find their corresponding r check bits. In a **systematic code**, the m data bits are sent directly, along with the check bits, rather than being encoded themselves before they are sent. In a **linear code**, the r check bits are computed as a linear function of the m data bits. Exclusive OR (XOR) or modulo 2 addition is a popular choice. This means that encoding can be done with operations such as matrix multiplications or simple logic circuits. The codes we will look at in this section are linear, systematic block codes unless otherwise noted.

Let the total length of a block be n (i.e., $n = m + r$). We will describe this as an (n,m) code. An n-bit unit containing data and check bits is referred to as an n-bit **codeword**. The **code rate**, or simply rate, is the fraction of the codeword that carries information that is not redundant, or m/n. The rates used in practice vary widely. They might be 1/2 for a noisy channel, in which case half of the received information is redundant, or close to 1 for a high-quality channel, with only a small number of check bits added to a large message.

To understand how errors can be handled, it is necessary to first look closely at what an error really is. Given any two codewords that may be transmitted or received—say, 10001001 and 10110001—it is possible to determine how many corresponding bits differ. In this case, 3 bits differ. To determine how many bits differ, just XOR the two codewords and count the number of 1 bits in the result. For example:

```
10001001
10110001
--------
00111000
```

The number of bit positions in which two codewords differ is called the **Hamming distance** (Hamming, 1950). Its significance is that if two codewords are a Hamming distance d apart, it will require d single-bit errors to convert one into the other.

Given the algorithm for computing the check bits, it is possible to construct a complete list of the legal codewords, and from this list to find the two codewords with the smallest Hamming distance. This distance is the Hamming distance of the complete code.

In most data transmission applications, all 2^m possible data messages are legal, but due to the way the check bits are computed, not all of the 2^n possible codewords are used. In fact, when there are r check bits, only the small fraction of $2^m/2^n$ or $1/2^r$ of the possible messages will be legal codewords. It is the sparseness with which the message is embedded in the space of codewords that allows the receiver to detect and correct errors.

The error-detecting and error-correcting properties of a block code depend on its Hamming distance. To reliably detect d errors, you need a distance $d + 1$ code because with such a code there is no way that d single-bit errors can change a valid codeword into another valid codeword. When the receiver sees an illegal codeword, it can tell that a transmission error has occurred. Similarly, to correct d errors, you need a distance $2d + 1$ code because that way the legal codewords are so far apart that even with d changes the original codeword is still closer than any other codeword. This means the original codeword can be uniquely determined based on the assumption that a larger number of errors are less likely.

As a simple example of an error-correcting code, consider a code with only four valid codewords:

0000000000, 0000011111, 1111100000, and 1111111111

This code has a distance of 5, which means that it can correct double errors or detect quadruple errors. If the codeword 0000000111 arrives and we expect only single- or double-bit errors, the receiver will know that the original must have been 0000011111. If, however, a triple error changes 0000000000 into 0000000111, the error will not be corrected properly. Alternatively, if we expect all of these errors, we can detect them. None of the received codewords are legal codewords so an error must have occurred. It should be apparent that in this example we cannot both correct double errors and detect quadruple errors because this would require us to interpret a received codeword in two different ways.

In our example, the task of decoding by finding the legal codeword that is closest to the received codeword can be done by inspection. Unfortunately, in the most general case where all codewords need to be evaluated as candidates, this task can be a time-consuming search. Instead, practical codes are designed so that they admit shortcuts to find what was likely the original codeword.

Imagine that we want to design a code with m message bits and r check bits that will allow all single errors to be corrected. Each of the 2^m legal messages has n illegal codewords at a distance of 1 from it. These are formed by systematically inverting each of the n bits in the n-bit codeword formed from it. Thus, each of the 2^m legal messages requires $n+1$ bit patterns dedicated to it. Since the total number of bit patterns is 2^n, we must have $(n+1)2^m \le 2^n$. Using $n = m + r$, this requirement becomes

$$(m + r + 1) \le 2^r \qquad (3\text{-}1)$$

Given m, this puts a lower limit on the number of check bits needed to correct single errors.

This theoretical lower limit can, in fact, be achieved using a method due to Hamming (1950). In **Hamming codes** the bits of the codeword are numbered consecutively, starting with bit 1 at the left end, bit 2 to its immediate right, and so on. The bits that are powers of 2 (1, 2, 4, 8, 16, etc.) are check bits. The rest (3, 5, 6, 7, 9, etc.) are filled up with the m data bits. This pattern is shown for an (11,7) Hamming code with 7 data bits and 4 check bits in Fig. 3-6. Each check bit forces the modulo 2 sum, or parity, of some collection of bits, including itself, to be even (or odd). A bit may be included in several check bit computations. To see which check bits the data bit in position k contributes to, rewrite k as a sum of powers of 2. For example, $11 = 1 + 2 + 8$ and $29 = 1 + 4 + 8 + 16$. A bit is checked by just those check bits occurring in its expansion (e.g., bit 11 is checked by bits 1, 2, and 8). In the example, the check bits are computed for even parity sums for a message that is the ASCII letter "A."

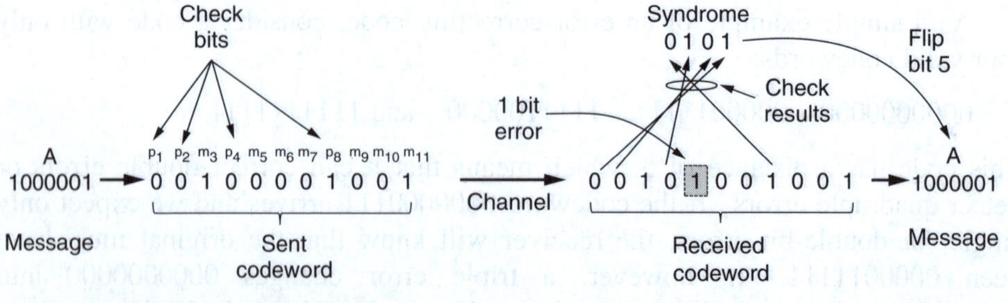

Figure 3-6. Example of an (11, 7) Hamming code correcting a single-bit error.

This construction gives a code with a Hamming distance of 3, which means that it can correct single errors (or detect double errors). The reason for the very careful numbering of message and check bits becomes apparent in the decoding process. When a codeword arrives, the receiver redoes the check bit computations including the values of the received check bits. We call these the check results. If the check bits are correct then, for even parity sums, each check result should be zero. In this case the codeword is accepted as valid.

If the check results are not all zero, however, an error has been detected. The set of check results forms the **error syndrome** that is used to pinpoint and correct the error. In Fig. 3-6, a single-bit error occurred on the channel so the check results are 0, 1, 0, and 1 for $k = 8, 4, 2,$ and 1, respectively. This gives a syndrome of 0101 or $4 + 1 = 5$. By the design of the scheme, this means that the fifth bit is in error. Flipping the incorrect bit (which might be a check bit or a data bit) and discarding the check bits gives the correct message of an ASCII "A."

Hamming distances are valuable for understanding block codes, and Hamming codes are used in error-correcting memory. However, most networks use stronger codes. The second code we will look at is a **convolutional code**. This code is the only one we will cover that is not a block code. In a convolutional code, an encoder processes a sequence of input bits and generates a sequence of output bits. There is no natural message size or encoding boundary as in a block code. The output depends on the current and previous input bits. That is, the encoder has memory. The number of previous bits on which the output depends is called the **constraint length** of the code. Convolutional codes are specified in terms of their rate and constraint length.

Convolutional codes are widely used in deployed networks, for example, as part of the GSM mobile phone system, in satellite communications, and in 802.11. As an example, a popular convolutional code is shown in Fig. 3-7. This code is known as the NASA convolutional code of $r = 1/2$ and $k = 7$, since it was first used for the Voyager space missions starting in 1977. Since then it has been liberally reused, for example, as part of 802.11.

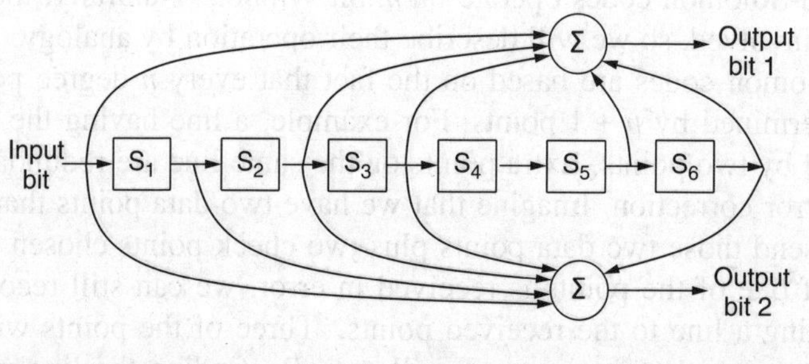

Figure 3-7. The NASA binary convolutional code used in 802.11.

In Fig. 3-7, each input bit on the left-hand side produces two output bits on the right-hand side that are XOR sums of the input and internal state. Since it deals with bits and performs linear operations, this is a binary, linear convolutional code. Since 1 input bit produces 2 output bits, the code rate is 1/2. It is not systematic since none of the output bits is simply the input bit.

The internal state is kept in six memory registers. Each time another bit is input the values in the registers are shifted to the right. For example, if 111 is input and the initial state is all zeros, the internal state, written left to right, will become 100000, 110000, and 111000 after the first, second, and third bits have been input. The output bits will be 11, followed by 10, and then 01. It takes seven shifts to flush an input completely so that it does not affect the output. The constraint length of this code is thus $k = 7$.

A convolutional code is decoded by finding the sequence of input bits that is most likely to have produced the observed sequence of output bits (which includes any errors). For small values of k, this is done with a widely used algorithm developed by Viterbi (Forney, 1973). The algorithm walks the observed sequence, keeping for each step and for each possible internal state the input sequence that would have produced the observed sequence with the fewest errors. The input sequence requiring the fewest errors at the end is the most likely message.

Convolutional codes have been popular in practice because it is easy to factor the uncertainty of a bit being a 0 or a 1 into the decoding. For example, suppose −1V is the logical 0 level and +1V is the logical 1 level, we might receive 0.9V and −0.1V for 2 bits. Instead of mapping these signals to 1 and 0 right away, we would like to treat 0.9V as "very likely a 1" and −0.1V as "maybe a 0" and correct the sequence as a whole. Extensions of the Viterbi algorithm can work with these uncertainties to provide stronger error correction. This approach of working with the uncertainty of a bit is called **soft-decision decoding**. Conversely, deciding whether each bit is a 0 or a 1 before subsequent error correction is called **hard-decision decoding**.

The third kind of error-correcting code we will describe is the **Reed-Solomon code**. Like Hamming codes, Reed-Solomon codes are linear block codes, and they are often systematic too. Unlike Hamming codes, which operate on individual bits, Reed-Solomon codes operate on m bit symbols. Naturally, the mathematics are more involved, so we will describe their operation by analogy.

Reed-Solomon codes are based on the fact that every n degree polynomial is uniquely determined by $n + 1$ points. For example, a line having the form $ax + b$ is determined by two points. Extra points on the same line are redundant, which is helpful for error correction. Imagine that we have two data points that represent a line and we send those two data points plus two check points chosen to lie on the same line. If one of the points is received in error, we can still recover the data points by fitting a line to the received points. Three of the points will lie on the line, and one point, the one in error, will not. By finding the line we have corrected the error.

Reed-Solomon codes are actually defined as polynomials that operate over finite fields, but they work in a similar manner. For m bit symbols, the codewords are $2^m - 1$ symbols long. A popular choice is to make $m = 8$ so that symbols are bytes. A codeword is then 255 bytes long. The (255, 233) code is widely used; it adds 32 redundant symbols to 233 data symbols. Decoding with error correction is done with an algorithm developed by Berlekamp and Massey that can efficiently perform the fitting task for moderate-length codes (Massey, 1969).

Reed-Solomon codes are widely used in practice because of their strong error-correction properties, particularly for burst errors. They are used for DSL, data over cable, satellite communications, and perhaps most ubiquitously on CDs, DVDs, and Blu-ray discs. Because they are based on *m* bit symbols, a single-bit error and an *m*-bit burst error are both treated simply as one symbol error. When *2t* redundant symbols are added, a Reed-Solomon code is able to correct up to *t* errors in any of the transmitted symbols. This means, for example, that the (255, 233) code, which has 32 redundant symbols, can correct up to 16 symbol errors. Since the symbols may be consecutive and they are each 8 bits, an error burst of up to 128 bits can be corrected. The situation is even better if the error model is one of erasures (e.g., a scratch on a CD that obliterates some symbols). In this case, up to *2t* errors can be corrected.

Reed-Solomon codes are often used in combination with other codes such as a convolutional code. The thinking is as follows. Convolutional codes are effective at handling isolated bit errors, but they will fail, likely with a burst of errors, if there are too many errors in the received bit stream. By adding a Reed-Solomon code within the convolutional code, the Reed-Solomon decoding can mop up the error bursts, a task at which it is very good. The overall code then provides good protection against both single and burst errors.

The final error-correcting code we will cover is the **LDPC (Low-Density Parity Check)** code. LDPC codes are linear block codes that were invented by Robert Gallagher in his doctoral thesis (Gallagher, 1962). Like most theses, they were promptly forgotten, only to be reinvented in 1995 when advances in computing power had made them practical.

In an LDPC code, each output bit is formed from only a fraction of the input bits. This leads to a matrix representation of the code that has a low density of 1s, hence the name for the code. The received codewords are decoded with an approximation algorithm that iteratively improves on a best fit of the received data to a legal codeword. This corrects errors.

LDPC codes are practical for large block sizes and have excellent error-correction abilities that outperform many other codes (including the ones we have looked at) in practice. For this reason they are rapidly being included in new protocols. They are part of the standard for digital video broadcasting, 10 Gbps Ethernet, power-line networks, and the latest version of 802.11. Expect to see more of them in future networks.

3.2.2 Error-Detecting Codes

Error-correcting codes are widely used on wireless links, which are notoriously noisy and error prone when compared to optical fibers. Without error-correcting codes, it would be hard to get anything through. However, over fiber or high-quality copper, the error rate is much lower, so error detection and retransmission is usually more efficient there for dealing with the occasional error.

We will examine three different error-detecting codes. They are all linear, systematic block codes:

1. Parity.
2. Checksums.
3. Cyclic Redundancy Checks (CRCs).

To see how they can be more efficient than error-correcting codes, consider the first error-detecting code, in which a single **parity bit** is appended to the data. The parity bit is chosen so that the number of 1 bits in the codeword is even (or odd). Doing this is equivalent to computing the (even) parity bit as the modulo 2 sum or XOR of the data bits. For example, when 1011010 is sent in even parity, a bit is added to the end to make it 10110100. With odd parity 1011010 becomes 10110101. A code with a single parity bit has a distance of 2, since any single-bit error produces a codeword with the wrong parity. This means that it can detect single-bit errors.

Consider a channel on which errors are isolated and the error rate is 10^{-6} per bit. This may seem a tiny error rate, but it is at best a fair rate for a long wired cable that is challenging for error detection. Typical LAN links provide bit error rates of 10^{-10}. Let the block size be 1000 bits. To provide error correction for 1000-bit blocks, we know from Eq. (3-1) that 10 check bits are needed. Thus, a megabit of data would require 10,000 check bits. To merely detect a block with a single 1-bit error, one parity bit per block will suffice. Once every 1000 blocks, a block will be found to be in error and an extra block (1001 bits) will have to be transmitted to repair the error. The total overhead for the error detection and retransmission method is only 2001 bits per megabit of data, versus 10,000 bits for a Hamming code.

One difficulty with this scheme is that a single parity bit can only reliably detect a single-bit error in the block. If the block is badly garbled by a long burst error, the probability that the error will be detected is only 0.5, which is hardly acceptable. The odds can be improved considerably if each block to be sent is regarded as a rectangular matrix n bits wide and k bits high. Now, if we compute and send one parity bit for each row, up to k bit errors will be reliably detected as long as there is at most one error per row.

However, there is something else we can do that provides better protection against burst errors: we can compute the parity bits over the data in a different order than the order in which the data bits are transmitted. Doing so is called **interleaving**. In this case, we will compute a parity bit for each of the n columns and send all the data bits as k rows, sending the rows from top to bottom and the bits in each row from left to right in the usual manner. At the last row, we send the n parity bits. This transmission order is shown in Fig. 3-8 for $n = 7$ and $k = 7$.

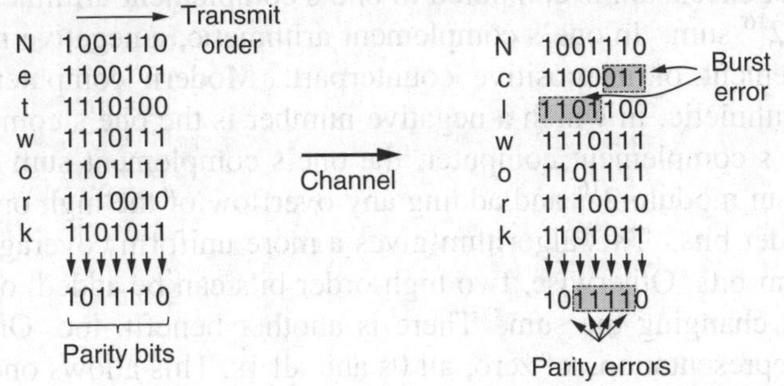

Figure 3-8. Interleaving of parity bits to detect a burst error.

Interleaving is a general technique to convert a code that detects (or corrects) isolated errors into a code that detects (or corrects) burst errors. In Fig. 3-8, when a burst error of length $n = 7$ occurs, the bits that are in error are spread across different columns. (A burst error does not imply that all the bits are wrong; it just implies that at least the first and last are wrong. In Fig. 3-8, 4 bits were flipped over a range of 7 bits.) At most 1 bit in each of the n columns will be affected, so the parity bits on those columns will detect the error. This method uses n parity bits on blocks of kn data bits to detect a single burst error of length n or less.

A burst of length $n + 1$ will pass undetected, however, if the first bit is inverted, the last bit is inverted, and all the other bits are correct. If the block is badly garbled by a long burst or by multiple shorter bursts, the probability that any of the n columns will have the correct parity by accident is 0.5, so the probability of a bad block being accepted when it should not be is 2^{-n}.

The second kind of error-detecting code, the **checksum**, is closely related to groups of parity bits. The word "checksum" is often used to mean a group of check bits associated with a message, regardless of how are calculated. A group of parity bits is one example of a checksum. However, there are other, stronger checksums based on a running sum of the data bits of the message. The checksum is usually placed at the end of the message, as the complement of the sum function. This way, errors may be detected by summing the entire received codeword, both data bits and checksum. If the result comes out to be zero, no error has been detected.

One example of a checksum is the 16-bit Internet checksum used on all Internet packets as part of the IP protocol (Braden et al., 1988). This checksum is a sum of the message bits divided into 16-bit words. Because this method operates on words rather than on bits, as in parity, errors that leave the parity unchanged can still alter the sum and be detected. For example, if the lowest order bit in two different words is flipped from a 0 to a 1, a parity check across these bits would fail to detect an error. However, two 1s will be added to the 16-bit checksum to produce a different result. The error can then be detected.

The Internet checksum is computed in one's complement arithmetic instead of as the modulo 2^{16} sum. In one's complement arithmetic, a negative number is the bitwise complement of its positive counterpart. Modern computers run two's complement arithmetic, in which a negative number is the one's complement plus one. On a two's complement computer, the one's complement sum is equivalent to taking the sum modulo 2^{16} and adding any overflow of the high order bits back into the low-order bits. This algorithm gives a more uniform coverage of the data by the checksum bits. Otherwise, two high-order bits can be added, overflow, and be lost without changing the sum. There is another benefit, too. One's complement has two representations of zero, all 0s and all 1s. This allows one value (e.g., all 0s) to indicate that there is no checksum, without the need for another field.

For decades, it has always been assumed that frames to be checksummed contain random bits. All analyses of checksum algorithms have been made under this assumption. Inspection of real data by Partridge et al. (1995) has shown this assumption to be quite wrong. As a consequence, undetected errors are in some cases much more common than had been previously thought.

The Internet checksum in particular is efficient and simple but provides weak protection in some cases precisely because it is a simple sum. It does not detect the deletion or addition of zero data, nor swapping parts of the message, and it provides weak protection against message splices in which parts of two packets are put together. These errors may seem very unlikely to occur by random processes, but they are just the sort of errors that can occur with buggy hardware.

A better choice is **Fletcher's checksum** (Fletcher, 1982). It includes a positional component, adding the product of the data and its position to the running sum. This provides stronger detection of changes in the position of data.

Although the two preceding schemes may sometimes be adequate at higher layers, in practice, a third and stronger kind of error-detecting code is in widespread use at the link layer: the **CRC (Cyclic Redundancy Check)**, also known as a **polynomial code**. Polynomial codes are based upon treating bit strings as representations of polynomials with coefficients of 0 and 1 only. A k-bit frame is regarded as the coefficient list for a polynomial with k terms, ranging from x^{k-1} to x^0. Such a polynomial is said to be of degree $k-1$. The high-order (leftmost) bit is the coefficient of x^{k-1}, the next bit is the coefficient of x^{k-2}, and so on. For example, 110001 has 6 bits and thus represents a six-term polynomial with coefficients 1, 1, 0, 0, 0, and 1: $1x^5 + 1x^4 + 0x^3 + 0x^2 + 0x^1 + 1x^0$.

Polynomial arithmetic is done modulo 2, according to the rules of algebraic field theory. It does not have carries for addition or borrows for subtraction. Both addition and subtraction are identical to exclusive OR. For example:

$$\begin{array}{r} 10011011 \\ +\,11001010 \\ \hline 01010001 \end{array} \qquad \begin{array}{r} 00110011 \\ +\,11001101 \\ \hline 11111110 \end{array} \qquad \begin{array}{r} 11110000 \\ -\,10100110 \\ \hline 01010110 \end{array} \qquad \begin{array}{r} 01010101 \\ -\,10101111 \\ \hline 11111010 \end{array}$$

Long division is carried out in exactly the same way as it is in binary except that the subtraction is again done modulo 2. A divisor is said "to go into" a dividend if the dividend has as many bits as the divisor.

When the polynomial code method is employed, the sender and receiver must agree upon a **generator polynomial**, $G(x)$, in advance. Both the high- and low-order bits of the generator must be 1. To compute the CRC for some frame with m bits corresponding to the polynomial $M(x)$, the frame must be longer than the generator polynomial. The idea is to append a CRC to the end of the frame in such a way that the polynomial represented by the checksummed frame is divisible by $G(x)$. When the receiver gets the checksummed frame, it tries dividing it by $G(x)$. If there is a remainder, there has been a transmission error.

The algorithm for computing the CRC is as follows:

1. Let r be the degree of $G(x)$. Append r zero bits to the low-order end of the frame so it now contains $m + r$ bits and corresponds to the polynomial $x^r M(x)$.
2. Divide the bit string corresponding to $G(x)$ into the bit string corresponding to $x^r M(x)$, using modulo 2 division.
3. Subtract the remainder (which is always r or fewer bits) from the bit string corresponding to $x^r M(x)$ using modulo 2 subtraction. The result is the checksummed frame to be transmitted. Call its polynomial $T(x)$.

Figure 3-9 illustrates the calculation for a frame 1101011111 using the generator $G(x) = x^4 + x + 1$.

It should be clear that $T(x)$ is divisible (modulo 2) by $G(x)$. In any division problem, if you diminish the dividend by the remainder, what is left over is divisible by the divisor. For example, in base 10, if you divide 210,278 by 10,941, the remainder is 2399. If you then subtract 2399 from 210,278, what is left over (207,879) is divisible by 10,941.

Now let us analyze the power of this method. What kinds of errors will be detected? Imagine that a transmission error occurs, so that instead of the bit string for $T(x)$ arriving, $T(x) + E(x)$ arrives. Each 1 bit in $E(x)$ corresponds to a bit that has been inverted. If there are k 1 bits in $E(x)$, k single-bit errors have occurred. A single burst error is characterized by an initial 1, a mixture of 0s and 1s, and a final 1, with all other bits being 0.

Upon receiving the checksummed frame, the receiver divides it by $G(x)$; that is, it computes $[T(x) + E(x)]/G(x)$. $T(x)/G(x)$ is 0, so the result of the computation is simply $E(x)/G(x)$. Those errors that happen to correspond to polynomials containing $G(x)$ as a factor will slip by; all other errors will be caught.

If there has been a single-bit error, $E(x) = x^i$, where i determines which bit is in error. If $G(x)$ contains two or more terms, it will never divide into $E(x)$, so all single-bit errors will be detected.

```
Frame:       1 1 0 1 0 1 1 1 1 1
Generator:   1 0 0 1 1

                    1 1 0 0 0 0 1 1 1 0  ← Quotient (thrown away)
1 0 0 1 1 / 1 1 0 1 0 1 1 1 1 1 0 0 0 0  ← Frame with four zeros appended
            1 0 0 1 1
            ---------
              1 0 0 1 1
              1 0 0 1 1
              ---------
                0 0 0 0 1
                0 0 0 0 0
                ---------
                  0 0 0 1 1
                  0 0 0 0 0
                  ---------
                    0 0 1 1 1
                    0 0 0 0 0
                    ---------
                      0 1 1 1 1
                      0 0 0 0 0
                      ---------
                        1 1 1 1 0
                        1 0 0 1 1
                        ---------
                          1 1 0 1 0
                          1 0 0 1 1
                          ---------
                            1 0 0 1 0
                            1 0 0 1 1
                            ---------
                              0 0 0 1 0
                              0 0 0 0 0
                              ---------
                                    1 0  ← Remainder

Transmitted frame: 1 1 0 1 0 1 1 1 1 1 0 0 1 0  ← Frame with four zeros appended
                                                   minus remainder
```

Figure 3-9. Example calculation of the CRC.

If there have been two isolated single-bit errors, $E(x) = x^i + x^j$, where $i > j$. Alternatively, this can be written as $E(x) = x^j(x^{i-j} + 1)$. If we assume that $G(x)$ is not divisible by x, a sufficient condition for all double errors to be detected is that $G(x)$ does not divide $x^k + 1$ for any k up to the maximum value of $i - j$ (i.e., up to the maximum frame length). Simple, low-degree polynomials that give protection to long frames are known. For example, $x^{15} + x^{14} + 1$ will not divide $x^k + 1$ for any value of k below 32,768.

If there are an odd number of bits in error, $E(X)$ contains an odd number of terms (e.g., $x^5 + x^2 + 1$, but not $x^2 + 1$). Interestingly, no polynomial with an odd number of terms has $x + 1$ as a factor in the modulo 2 system. By making $x + 1$ a factor of $G(x)$, we can catch all errors with an odd number of inverted bits.

Finally, and importantly, a polynomial code with r check bits will detect all burst errors of length $\le r$. A burst error of length k can be represented by $x^i(x^{k-1} + \ldots + 1)$, where i determines how far from the right-hand end of the received frame the burst is located. If $G(x)$ contains an x^0 term, it will not have x^i as a factor, so if the degree of the parenthesized expression is less than the degree of $G(x)$, the remainder can never be zero.

If the burst length is $r+1$, the remainder of the division by $G(x)$ will be zero if and only if the burst is identical to $G(x)$. By definition of a burst, the first and last bits must be 1, so whether it matches depends on the $r-1$ intermediate bits. If all combinations are regarded as equally likely, the probability of such an incorrect frame being accepted as valid is $\frac{1}{2}^{r-1}$.

It can also be shown that when an error burst longer than $r+1$ bits occurs or when several shorter bursts occur, the probability of a bad frame getting through unnoticed is $\frac{1}{2}^{r}$, assuming that all bit patterns are equally likely.

Certain polynomials have become international standards. The one used in IEEE 802 followed the example of Ethernet and is

$$x^{32}+x^{26}+x^{23}+x^{22}+x^{16}+x^{12}+x^{11}+x^{10}+x^{8}+x^{7}+x^{5}+x^{4}+x^{2}+x^{1}+1$$

Among other desirable properties, it has the property that it detects all bursts of length 32 or less and all bursts affecting an odd number of bits. It has been used widely since the 1980s. However, this does not mean it is the best choice. Using an exhaustive computational search, Castagnoli et al. (1993) and Koopman (2002) found the best CRCs. These CRCs have a Hamming distance of 6 for typical message sizes, while the IEEE standard CRC-32 has a Hamming distance of only 4.

Although the calculation required to compute the CRC may seem complicated, it is easy to compute and verify CRCs in hardware with simple shift register circuits (Peterson and Brown, 1961). In practice, this hardware is nearly always used. Dozens of networking standards include various CRCs, including virtually all LANs (e.g., Ethernet, 802.11) and point-to-point links (e.g., packets over SONET).

3.3 ELEMENTARY DATA LINK PROTOCOLS

To introduce the subject of protocols, we will begin by looking at three protocols of increasing complexity. For interested readers, a simulator for these and subsequent protocols is available via the Web (see the preface). Before we look at the protocols, it is useful to make explicit some of the assumptions underlying the model of communication.

To start with, we assume that the physical layer, data link layer, and network layer are independent processes that communicate by passing messages back and forth. A common implementation is shown in Fig. 3-10. The physical layer process and some of the data link layer process run on dedicate hardware called a **NIC** (**Network Interface Card**). The rest of the link layer process and the network layer process run on the main CPU as part of the operating system, with the software for the link layer process often taking the form of a **device driver**. However, other implementations are also possible (e.g., three processes offloaded to dedicated hardware called a **network accelerator**, or three processes running on the main CPU on a software-defined ratio). Actually, the preferred implementation changes from decade to decade with technology trade-offs. In any event, treating the three layers as separate processes makes the discussion conceptually cleaner and also serves to emphasize the independence of the layers.

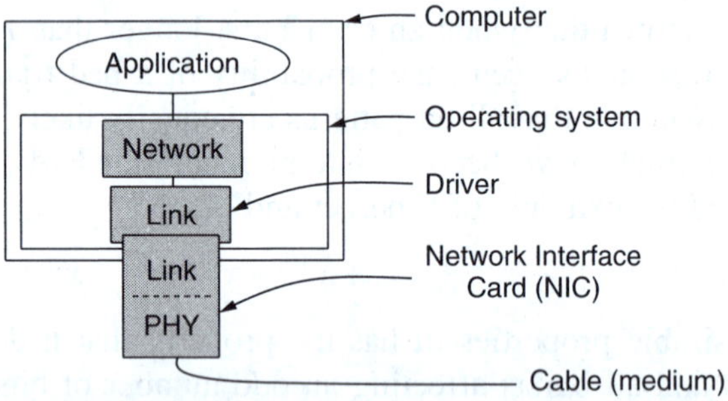

Figure 3-10. Implementation of the physical, data link, and network layers.

Another key assumption is that machine *A* wants to send a long stream of data to machine *B*, using a reliable, connection-oriented service. Later, we will consider the case where *B* also wants to send data to *A* simultaneously. *A* is assumed to have an infinite supply of data ready to send and never has to wait for data to be produced. Instead, when *A*'s data link layer asks for data, the network layer is always able to comply immediately. (This restriction, too, will be dropped later.)

We also assume that machines do not crash. That is, these protocols deal with communication errors, but not the problems caused by computers crashing and rebooting.

As far as the data link layer is concerned, the packet passed across the interface to it from the network layer is pure data, whose every bit is to be delivered to the destination's network layer. The fact that the destination's network layer may interpret part of the packet as a header is of no concern to the data link layer.

When the data link layer accepts a packet, it encapsulates the packet in a frame by adding a data link header and trailer to it (see Fig. 3-1). Thus, a frame consists of an embedded packet, some control information (in the header), and a checksum (in the trailer). The frame is then transmitted to the data link layer on the other machine. We will assume that there exist suitable library procedures *to_physical_layer* to send a frame and *from_physical_layer* to receive a frame. These procedures compute and append or check the checksum (which is usually done in hardware) so that we do not need to worry about it as part of the protocols we develop in this section. They might use the CRC algorithm discussed in the previous section, for example.

Initially, the receiver has nothing to do. It just sits around waiting for something to happen. In the example protocols throughout this chapter we will indicate that the data link layer is waiting for something to happen by the procedure call

```
#define MAX_PKT 1024                          /* determines packet size in bytes */

typedef enum {false, true} boolean;           /* boolean type */
typedef unsigned int seq_nr;                  /* sequence or ack numbers */
typedef struct {unsigned char data[MAX_PKT];} packet; /* packet definition */
typedef enum {data, ack, nak} frame_kind;     /* frame_kind definition */

typedef struct {                              /* frames are transported in this layer */
  frame_kind kind;                            /* what kind of frame is it? */
  seq_nr seq;                                 /* sequence number */
  seq_nr ack;                                 /* acknowledgement number */
  packet info;                                /* the network layer packet */
} frame;

/* Wait for an event to happen; return its type in event. */
void wait_for_event(event_type *event);

/* Fetch a packet from the network layer for transmission on the channel. */
void from_network_layer(packet *p);

/* Deliver information from an inbound frame to the network layer. */
void to_network_layer(packet *p);

/* Go get an inbound frame from the physical layer and copy it to r. */
void from_physical_layer(frame *r);

/* Pass the frame to the physical layer for transmission. */
void to_physical_layer(frame *s);

/* Start the clock running and enable the timeout event. */
void start_timer(seq_nr k);

/* Stop the clock and disable the timeout event. */
void stop_timer(seq_nr k);

/* Start an auxiliary timer and enable the ack_timeout event. */
void start_ack_timer(void);

/* Stop the auxiliary timer and disable the ack_timeout event. */
void stop_ack_timer(void);

/* Allow the network layer to cause a network_layer_ready event. */
void enable_network_layer(void);

/* Forbid the network layer from causing a network_layer_ready event. */
void disable_network_layer(void);

/* Macro inc is expanded in-line: increment k circularly. */
#define inc(k) if (k < MAX_SEQ) k = k + 1; else k = 0
```

Figure 3-11. Some definitions needed in the protocols to follow. These definitions are located in the file *protocol.h*.

wait_for_event(&*event*). This procedure only returns when something has happened (e.g., a frame has arrived). Upon return, the variable *event* tells what happened. The set of possible events differs for the various protocols to be described and will be defined separately for each protocol. Note that in a more realistic situation, the data link layer will not sit in a tight loop waiting for an event, as we have suggested, but will receive an interrupt, which will cause it to stop whatever it was doing and go handle the incoming frame. Nevertheless, for simplicity we will ignore all the details of parallel activity within the data link layer and assume that it is dedicated full time to handling just our one channel.

When a frame arrives at the receiver, the checksum is recomputed. If the checksum in the frame is incorrect (i.e., there was a transmission error), the data link layer is so informed (*event* = *cksum_err*). If the inbound frame arrived undamaged, the data link layer is also informed (*event* = *frame_arrival*) so that it can acquire the frame for inspection using *from_physical_layer*. As soon as the receiving data link layer has acquired an undamaged frame, it checks the control information in the header, and, if everything is all right, passes the packet portion to the network layer. Under no circumstances is a frame header ever given to a network layer.

There is a good reason why the network layer must never be given any part of the frame header: to keep the network and data link protocols completely separate. As long as the network layer knows nothing at all about the data link protocol or the frame format, these things can be changed without requiring changes to the network layer's software. This happens whenever a new NIC is installed in a computer. Providing a rigid interface between the network and data link layers greatly simplifies the design task because communication protocols in different layers can evolve independently.

Figure 3-11 shows some declarations (in C) common to many of the protocols to be discussed later. Five data structures are defined there: *boolean*, *seq_nr*, *packet*, *frame_kind*, and *frame*. A *boolean* is an enumerated type and can take on the values *true* and *false*. A *seq_nr* is a small integer used to number the frames so that we can tell them apart. These sequence numbers run from 0 up to and including *MAX_SEQ*, which is defined in each protocol needing it. A *packet* is the unit of information exchanged between the network layer and the data link layer on the same machine, or between network layer peers. In our model it always contains *MAX_PKT* bytes, but more realistically it would be of variable length.

A *frame* is composed of four fields: *kind*, *seq*, *ack*, and *info*, the first three of which contain control information and the last of which may contain actual data to be transferred. These control fields are collectively called the **frame header**.

The *kind* field tells whether there are any data in the frame, because some of the protocols distinguish frames containing only control information from those containing data as well. The *seq* and *ack* fields are used for sequence numbers and acknowledgements, respectively; their use will be described in more detail later. The *info* field of a data frame contains a single packet; the *info* field of a control frame is not used. A more realistic implementation would use a variable-length *info* field, omitting it altogether for control frames.

Again, it is important to understand the relationship between a packet and a frame. The network layer builds a packet by taking a message from the transport layer and adding the network layer header to it. This packet is passed to the data link layer for inclusion in the *info* field of an outgoing frame. When the frame arrives at the destination, the data link layer extracts the packet from the frame and passes the packet to the network layer. In this manner, the network layer can act as though machines can exchange packets directly.

A number of procedures are also listed in Fig. 3-11. These are library routines whose details are implementation dependent and whose inner workings will not concern us further in the following discussions. The procedure *wait_for_event* sits in a tight loop waiting for something to happen, as mentioned earlier. The procedures *to_network_layer* and *from_network_layer* are used by the data link layer to pass packets to the network layer and accept packets from the network layer, respectively. Note that *from_physical_layer* and *to_physical_layer* pass frames between the data link layer and the physical layer. In other words, *to_network_layer* and *from_network_layer* deal with the interface between layers 2 and 3, whereas *from_physical_layer* and *to_physical_layer* deal with the interface between layers 1 and 2.

In most of the protocols, we assume that the channel is unreliable and loses entire frames upon occasion. To be able to recover from such calamities, the sending data link layer must start an internal timer or clock whenever it sends a frame. If no reply has been received within a certain predetermined time interval, the clock times out and the data link layer receives an interrupt signal.

In our protocols this is handled by allowing the procedure *wait_for_event* to return *event = timeout*. The procedures *start_timer* and *stop_timer* turn the timer on and off, respectively. Timeout events are possible only when the timer is running and before *stop_timer* is called. It is explicitly permitted to call *start_timer* while the timer is running; such a call simply resets the clock to cause the next timeout after a full timer interval has elapsed (unless it is reset or turned off).

The procedures *start_ack_timer* and *stop_ack_timer* control an auxiliary timer used to generate acknowledgements under certain conditions.

The procedures *enable_network_layer* and *disable_network_layer* are used in the more sophisticated protocols, where we no longer assume that the network layer always has packets to send. When the data link layer enables the network layer, the network layer is then permitted to interrupt when it has a packet to be sent. We indicate this with *event = network_layer_ready*. When the network layer is disabled, it may not cause such events. By being careful about when it enables and disables its network layer, the data link layer can prevent the network layer from swamping it with packets for which it has no buffer space.

Frame sequence numbers are always in the range 0 to *MAX_SEQ* (inclusive), where *MAX_SEQ* is different for the different protocols. It is frequently necessary to advance a sequence number by 1 circularly (i.e., *MAX_SEQ* is followed by 0). The macro *inc* performs this incrementing. It has been defined as a macro because it is used in-line within the critical path. As we will see later, the factor limiting network performance is often protocol processing, so defining simple operations like this as macros does not affect the readability of the code but does improve performance.

The declarations of Fig. 3-11 are part of each of the protocols we will discuss shortly. To save space and to provide a convenient reference, they have been extracted and listed together, but conceptually they should be merged with the protocols themselves. In C, this merging is done by putting the definitions in a special header file, in this case *protocol.h*, and using the #include facility of the C preprocessor to include them in the protocol files.

3.3.1 A Utopian Simplex Protocol

As an initial example we will consider a protocol that is as simple as it can be because it does not worry about the possibility of anything going wrong. Data are transmitted in one direction only. Both the transmitting and receiving network layers are always ready. Processing time can be ignored. Infinite buffer space is available. And best of all, the communication channel between the data link layers never damages or loses frames. This thoroughly unrealistic protocol, which we will nickname "Utopia," is simply to show the basic structure on which we will build. It's implementation is shown in Fig. 3-12.

The protocol consists of two distinct procedures, a sender and a receiver. The sender runs in the data link layer of the source machine, and the receiver runs in the data link layer of the destination machine. No sequence numbers or acknowledgements are used here, so *MAX_SEQ* is not needed. The only event type possible is *frame_arrival* (i.e., the arrival of an undamaged frame).

The sender is in an infinite while loop just pumping data out onto the line as fast as it can. The body of the loop consists of three actions: go fetch a packet from the (always obliging) network layer, construct an outbound frame using the variable *s*, and send the frame on its way. Only the *info* field of the frame is used by this protocol, because the other fields have to do with error and flow control and there are no errors or flow control restrictions here.

The receiver is equally simple. Initially, it waits for something to happen, the only possibility being the arrival of an undamaged frame. Eventually, the frame arrives and the procedure *wait_for_event* returns, with *event* set to *frame_arrival* (which is ignored anyway). The call to *from_physical_layer* removes the newly arrived frame from the hardware buffer and puts it in the variable *r*, where the receiver code can get at it. Finally, the data portion is passed on to the network layer, and the data link layer settles back to wait for the next frame, effectively suspending itself until the frame arrives.

```
/* Protocol 1 (Utopia) provides for data transmission in one direction only, from
   sender to receiver. The communication channel is assumed to be error free
   and the receiver is assumed to be able to process all the input infinitely quickly.
   Consequently, the sender just sits in a loop pumping data out onto the line as
   fast as it can. */

typedef enum {frame_arrival} event_type;
#include "protocol.h"

void sender1(void)
{
  frame s;                              /* buffer for an outbound frame */
  packet buffer;                        /* buffer for an outbound packet */

  while (true) {
      from_network_layer(&buffer);      /* go get something to send */
      s.info = buffer;                  /* copy it into s for transmission */
      to_physical_layer(&s);            /* send it on its way */
  }                                     /* Tomorrow, and tomorrow, and tomorrow,
                                           Creeps in this petty pace from day to day
                                           To the last syllable of recorded time.
                                                – Macbeth, V, v */
}

void receiver1(void)
{
  frame r;
  event_type event;                     /* filled in by wait, but not used here */

  while (true) {
      wait_for_event(&event);           /* only possibility is frame_arrival */
      from_physical_layer(&r);          /* go get the inbound frame */
      to_network_layer(&r.info);        /* pass the data to the network layer */
  }
}
```

Figure 3-12. A utopian simplex protocol.

The utopia protocol is unrealistic because it does not handle either flow control or error correction. Its processing is close to that of an unacknowledged connectionless service that relies on higher layers to solve these problems, though even an unacknowledged connectionless service would do some error detection.

3.3.2 A Simplex Stop-and-Wait Protocol for an Error-Free Channel

Now we will tackle the problem of preventing the sender from flooding the receiver with frames faster than the latter is able to process them. This situation can easily happen in practice so being able to prevent it is of great importance.

The communication channel is still assumed to be error free, however, and the data traffic is still simplex.

One solution is to build the receiver to be powerful enough to process a continuous stream of back-to-back frames (or, equivalently, define the link layer to be slow enough that the receiver can keep up). It must have sufficient buffering and processing abilities to run at the line rate and must be able to pass the frames that are received to the network layer quickly enough. However, this is a worst-case solution. It requires dedicated hardware and can be wasteful of resources if the utilization of the link is mostly low. Moreover, it just shifts the problem of dealing with a sender that is too fast elsewhere; in this case to the network layer.

A more general solution to this problem is to have the receiver provide feedback to the sender. After having passed a packet to its network layer, the receiver sends a little dummy frame back to the sender which, in effect, gives the sender permission to transmit the next frame. After having sent a frame, the sender is required by the protocol to bide its time until the little dummy (i.e., acknowledgement) frame arrives. This delay is a simple example of a flow control protocol.

Protocols in which the sender sends one frame and then waits for an acknowledgement before proceeding are called **stop-and-wait**. Figure 3-13 gives an example of a simplex stop-and-wait protocol.

Although data traffic in this example is simplex, going only from the sender to the receiver, frames do travel in both directions. Consequently, the communication channel between the two data link layers needs to be capable of bidirectional information transfer. However, this protocol entails a strict alternation of flow: first the sender sends a frame, then the receiver sends a frame, then the sender sends another frame, then the receiver sends another one, and so on. A half-duplex physical channel would suffice here.

As in protocol 1, the sender starts out by fetching a packet from the network layer, using it to construct a frame, and sending it on its way. But now, unlike in protocol 1, the sender must wait until an acknowledgement frame arrives before looping back and fetching the next packet from the network layer. The sending data link layer need not even inspect the incoming frame as there is only one possibility. The incoming frame is always an acknowledgement.

The only difference between *receiver1* and *receiver2* is that after delivering a packet to the network layer, *receiver2* sends an acknowledgement frame back to the sender before entering the wait loop again. Because only the arrival of the frame back at the sender is important, not its contents, the receiver need not put any particular information in it.

3.3.3 A Simplex Stop-and-Wait Protocol for a Noisy Channel

Now let us consider the normal situation of a communication channel that makes errors. Frames may be either damaged or lost completely. However, we assume that if a frame is damaged in transit, the receiver hardware will detect this

```
/* Protocol 2 (Stop-and-wait) also provides for a one-directional flow of data from
   sender to receiver. The communication channel is once again assumed to be error
   free, as in protocol 1. However, this time the receiver has only a finite buffer
   capacity and a finite processing speed, so the protocol must explicitly prevent
   the sender from flooding the receiver with data faster than it can be handled. */

typedef enum {frame_arrival} event_type;
#include "protocol.h"

void sender2(void)
{
  frame s;                           /* buffer for an outbound frame */
  packet buffer;                     /* buffer for an outbound packet */
  event_type event;                  /* frame_arrival is the only possibility */

  while (true) {
      from_network_layer(&buffer);   /* go get something to send */
      s.info = buffer;               /* copy it into s for transmission */
      to_physical_layer(&s);         /* bye-bye little frame */
      wait_for_event(&event);        /* do not proceed until given the go ahead */
  }
}

void receiver2(void)
{
  frame r, s;                        /* buffers for frames */
  event_type event;                  /* frame_arrival is the only possibility */
  while (true) {
      wait_for_event(&event);        /* only possibility is frame_arrival */
      from_physical_layer(&r);       /* go get the inbound frame */
      to_network_layer(&r.info);     /* pass the data to the network layer */
      to_physical_layer(&s);         /* send a dummy frame to awaken sender */
  }
}
```

Figure 3-13. A simplex stop-and-wait protocol.

when it computes the checksum. If the frame is damaged in such a way that the checksum is nevertheless correct—an unlikely occurrence—this protocol (and all other protocols) can fail (i.e., deliver an incorrect packet to the network layer).

At first glance it might seem that a variation of protocol 2 would work: adding a timer. The sender could send a frame, but the receiver would only send an acknowledgement frame if the data were correctly received. If a damaged frame arrived at the receiver, it would be discarded. After a while the sender would time out and send the frame again. This process would be repeated until the frame finally arrived intact.

This scheme has a fatal flaw in it though. Think about the problem and try to discover what might go wrong before reading further.

To see what might go wrong, remember that the goal of the data link layer is to provide error-free, transparent communication between network layer processes. The network layer on machine *A* gives a series of packets to its data link layer, which must ensure that an identical series of packets is delivered to the network layer on machine *B* by its data link layer. In particular, the network layer on *B* has no way of knowing that a packet has been lost or duplicated, so the data link layer must guarantee that no combination of transmission errors, however unlikely, can cause a duplicate packet to be delivered to a network layer.

Consider the following scenario:

1. The network layer on *A* gives packet 1 to its data link layer. The packet is correctly received at *B* and passed to the network layer on *B*. *B* sends an acknowledgement frame back to *A*.
2. The acknowledgement frame gets lost completely. It just never arrives at all. Life would be a great deal simpler if the channel mangled and lost only data frames and not control frames, but sad to say, the channel is not very discriminating.
3. The data link layer on *A* eventually times out. Not having received an acknowledgement, it (incorrectly) assumes that its data frame was lost or damaged and sends the frame containing packet 1 again.
4. The duplicate frame also arrives intact at the data link layer on *B* and is unwittingly passed to the network layer there. If *A* is sending a file to *B*, part of the file will be duplicated (i.e., the copy of the file made by *B* will be incorrect and the error will not have been detected). In other words, the protocol will fail.

Clearly, what is needed is some way for the receiver to be able to distinguish a frame that it is seeing for the first time from a retransmission. The obvious way to achieve this is to have the sender put a sequence number in the header of each frame it sends. Then the receiver can check the sequence number of each arriving frame to see if it is a new frame or a duplicate to be discarded.

Since the protocol must be correct and the sequence number field in the header is likely to be small to use the link efficiently, the question arises: what is the minimum number of bits needed for the sequence number? The header might provide 1 bit, a few bits, 1 byte, or multiple bytes for a sequence number depending on the protocol. The important point is that it must carry sequence numbers that are large enough for the protocol to work correctly, or it is not much of a protocol.

The only ambiguity in this protocol is between a frame, m, and its direct successor, $m + 1$. If frame m is lost or damaged, the receiver will not acknowledge it, so the sender will keep trying to send it. Once it has been correctly received, the receiver will send an acknowledgement to the sender. It is here that the potential trouble crops up. Depending upon whether the acknowledgement frame gets back to the sender correctly or not, the sender may try to send m or $m + 1$.

At the sender, the event that triggers the transmission of frame $m + 1$ is the arrival of an acknowledgement for frame m. But this situation implies that $m - 1$ has been correctly received, and furthermore that its acknowledgement has also been correctly received by the sender. Otherwise, the sender would not have begun with m, let alone have been considering $m + 1$. As a consequence, the only ambiguity is between a frame and its immediate predecessor or successor, not between the predecessor and successor themselves.

A 1-bit sequence number (0 or 1) is therefore sufficient. At each instant of time, the receiver expects a particular sequence number next. When a frame containing the correct sequence number arrives, it is accepted and passed to the network layer, then acknowledged. Then the expected sequence number is incremented modulo 2 (i.e., 0 becomes 1 and 1 becomes 0). Any arriving frame containing the wrong sequence number is rejected as a duplicate. However, the last valid acknowledgement is repeated so that the sender can eventually discover that the frame has been received.

An example of this kind of protocol is shown in Fig. 3-14. Protocols in which the sender waits for a positive acknowledgement before advancing to the next data item are often called **ARQ** (**Automatic Repeat reQuest**) or **PAR** (**Positive Acknowledgement with Retransmission**). Like protocol 2, this one also transmits data only in one direction.

Protocol 3 differs from its predecessors in that both sender and receiver have a variable whose value is remembered while the data link layer is in the wait state. The sender remembers the sequence number of the next frame to send in *next_frame_to_send*; the receiver remembers the sequence number of the next frame expected in *frame_expected*. Each protocol has a short initialization phase before entering the infinite loop.

After transmitting a frame, the sender starts the timer running. If it was already running, it will be reset to allow another full timer interval. The interval should be chosen to allow enough time for the frame to get to the receiver, for the receiver to process it in the worst case, and for the acknowledgement frame to propagate back to the sender. Only when that interval has elapsed is it safe to assume that either the transmitted frame or its acknowledgement has been lost, and to send a duplicate. If the timeout interval is set too short, the sender will transmit unnecessary frames. While these extra frames will not affect the correctness of the protocol, they will hurt performance.

After transmitting a frame and starting the timer, the sender waits for something exciting to happen. Only three possibilities exist: an acknowledgement frame arrives undamaged, a damaged acknowledgement frame staggers in, or the timer expires. If a valid acknowledgement comes in, the sender fetches the next packet from its network layer and puts it in the buffer, overwriting the previous packet. It also advances the sequence number. If a damaged frame arrives or the timer expires, neither the buffer nor the sequence number is changed so that a duplicate can be sent. In all cases, the contents of the buffer (either the next packet or a duplicate) are then sent.

When a valid frame arrives at the receiver, its sequence number is checked to see if it is a duplicate. If not, it is accepted, passed to the network layer, and an acknowledgement is generated. Duplicates and damaged frames are not passed to the network layer, but they do cause the last correctly received frame to be acknowledged to signal the sender to advance to the next frame or retransmit a damaged frame.

3.4 SLIDING WINDOW PROTOCOLS

In the previous protocols, data frames were transmitted in one direction only. In most practical situations, there is a need to transmit data in both directions. One way of achieving full-duplex data transmission is to run two instances of one of the previous protocols, each using a separate link for simplex data traffic (in different directions). Each link is then comprised of a "forward" channel (for data) and a "reverse" channel (for acknowledgements). In both cases the capacity of the reverse channel is almost entirely wasted.

A better idea is to use the same link for data in both directions. After all, in protocols 2 and 3 it was already being used to transmit frames both ways, and the reverse channel normally has the same capacity as the forward channel. In this model the data frames from *A* to *B* are intermixed with the acknowledgement frames from *A* to *B*. By looking at the *kind* field in the header of an incoming frame, the receiver can tell whether the frame is data or an acknowledgement.

Although interleaving data and control frames on the same link is a big improvement over having two separate physical links, yet another improvement is possible. When a data frame arrives, instead of immediately sending a separate control frame, the receiver restrains itself and waits until the network layer passes it the next packet. The acknowledgement is attached to the outgoing data frame (using the *ack* field in the frame header). In effect, the acknowledgement gets a free ride on the next outgoing data frame. The technique of temporarily delaying outgoing acknowledgements so that they can be hooked onto the next outgoing data frame is known as **piggybacking**.

The principal advantage of using piggybacking over having distinct acknowledgement frames is a better use of the available channel bandwidth. The *ack* field in the frame header costs only a few bits, whereas a separate frame would need a header, the acknowledgement, and a checksum. In addition, fewer frames sent generally means a lighter processing load at the receiver. In the next protocol to be examined, the piggyback field costs only 1 bit in the frame header. It rarely costs more than a few bits.

However, piggybacking introduces a complication not present with separate acknowledgements. How long should the data link layer wait for a packet onto

```
/* Protocol 3 (PAR) allows unidirectional data flow over an unreliable channel. */

#define MAX_SEQ 1                          /* must be 1 for protocol 3 */
typedef enum {frame_arrival, cksum_err, timeout} event_type;
#include "protocol.h"

void sender3(void)
{
 seq_nr next_frame_to_send;               /* seq number of next outgoing frame */
 frame s;                                 /* scratch variable */
 packet buffer;                           /* buffer for an outbound packet */
 event_type event;

 next_frame_to_send = 0;                  /* initialize outbound sequence numbers */
 from_network_layer(&buffer);             /* fetch first packet */
 while (true) {
   s.info = buffer;                       /* construct a frame for transmission */
   s.seq = next_frame_to_send;            /* insert sequence number in frame */
   to_physical_layer(&s);                 /* send it on its way */
   start_timer(s.seq);                    /* if answer takes too long, time out */
   wait_for_event(&event);                /* frame_arrival, cksum_err, timeout */
   if (event == frame_arrival) {
        from_physical_layer(&s);          /* get the acknowledgement */
        if (s.ack == next_frame_to_send) {
             stop_timer(s.ack);           /* turn the timer off */
             from_network_layer(&buffer); /* get the next one to send */
             inc(next_frame_to_send);     /* invert next_frame_to_send */
        }
   }
 }
}

void receiver3(void)
{
 seq_nr frame_expected;
 frame r, s;
 event_type event;

 frame_expected = 0;
 while (true) {
   wait_for_event(&event);                /* possibilities: frame_arrival, cksum_err */
   if (event == frame_arrival) {          /* a valid frame has arrived */
        from_physical_layer(&r);          /* go get the newly arrived frame */
        if (r.seq == frame_expected) {    /* this is what we have been waiting for */
             to_network_layer(&r.info);   /* pass the data to the network layer */
             inc(frame_expected);         /* next time expect the other sequence nr */
        }
        s.ack = 1 – frame_expected;       /* tell which frame is being acked */
        to_physical_layer(&s);            /* send acknowledgement */
   }
 }
}
```

Figure 3-14. A positive acknowledgement with retransmission protocol.

which to piggyback the acknowledgement? If the data link layer waits longer than the sender's timeout period, the frame will be retransmitted, defeating the whole purpose of having acknowledgements. If the data link layer were an oracle and could foretell the future, it would know when the next network layer packet was going to come in and could decide either to wait for it or send a separate acknowledgement immediately, depending on how long the projected wait was going to be. Of course, the data link layer cannot foretell the future, so it must resort to some ad hoc scheme, such as waiting a fixed number of milliseconds. If a new packet arrives quickly, the acknowledgement is piggybacked onto it. Otherwise, if no new packet has arrived by the end of this time period, the data link layer just sends a separate acknowledgement frame.

The next three protocols are bidirectional protocols that belong to a class called **sliding window** protocols. The three differ among themselves in terms of efficiency, complexity, and buffer requirements, as discussed later. In these, as in all sliding window protocols, each outbound frame contains a sequence number, ranging from 0 up to some maximum. The maximum is usually $2^n - 1$ so the sequence number fits exactly in an n-bit field. The stop-and-wait sliding window protocol uses $n = 1$, restricting the sequence numbers to 0 and 1, but more sophisticated versions can use an arbitrary n.

The essence of all sliding window protocols is that at any instant of time, the sender maintains a set of sequence numbers corresponding to frames it is permitted to send. These frames are said to fall within the **sending window**. Similarly, the receiver also maintains a **receiving window** corresponding to the set of frames it is permitted to accept. The sender's window and the receiver's window need not have the same lower and upper limits or even have the same size. In some protocols they are fixed in size, but in others they can grow or shrink over the course of time as frames are sent and received.

Although these protocols give the data link layer more freedom about the order in which it may send and receive frames, we have definitely not dropped the requirement that the protocol must deliver packets to the destination network layer in the same order they were passed to the data link layer on the sending machine. Nor have we changed the requirement that the physical communication channel is "wire-like," that is, it must deliver all frames in the order sent.

The sequence numbers within the sender's window represent frames that have been sent or can be sent but are as yet not acknowledged. Whenever a new packet arrives from the network layer, it is given the next highest sequence number, and the upper edge of the window is advanced by one. When an acknowledgement comes in, the lower edge is advanced by one. In this way the window continuously maintains a list of unacknowledged frames. Figure 3-15 shows an example.

Since frames currently within the sender's window may ultimately be lost or damaged in transit, the sender must keep all of these frames in its memory for possible retransmission. Thus, if the maximum window size is n, the sender needs n buffers to hold the unacknowledged frames. If the window ever grows to its

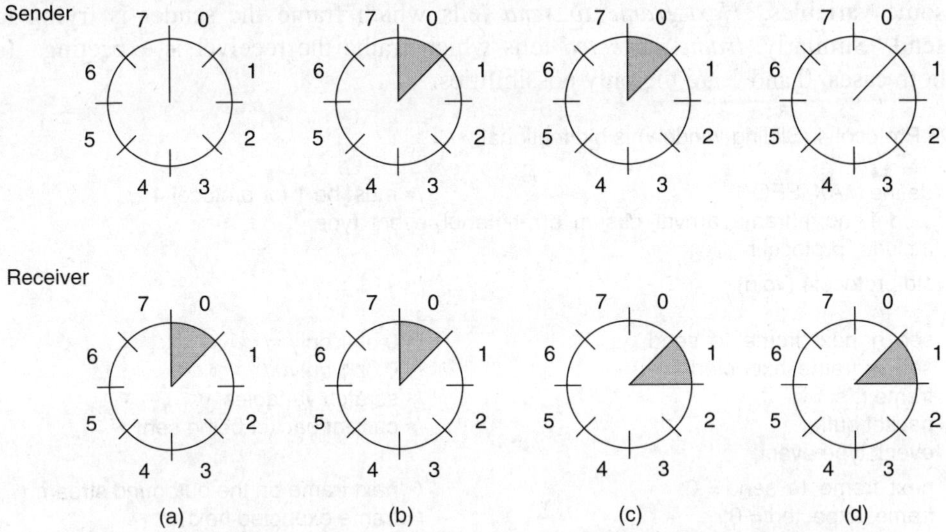

Figure 3-15. A sliding window of size 1, with a 3-bit sequence number. (a) Initially. (b) After the first frame has been sent. (c) After the first frame has been received. (d) After the first acknowledgement has been received.

maximum size, the sending data link layer must forcibly shut off the network layer until another buffer becomes free.

The receiving data link layer's window corresponds to the frames it may accept. Any frame falling within the window is put in the receiver's buffer. When a frame whose sequence number is equal to the lower edge of the window is received, it is passed to the network layer and the window is rotated by one. Any frame falling outside the window is discarded. In all of these cases, a subsequent acknowledgement is generated so that the sender may work out how to proceed. Note that a window size of 1 means that the data link layer only accepts frames in order, but for larger windows this is not so. The network layer, in contrast, is always fed data in the proper order, regardless of the data link layer's window size.

Figure 3-15 shows an example with a maximum window size of 1. Initially, no frames are outstanding, so the lower and upper edges of the sender's window are equal, but as time goes on, the situation progresses as shown. Unlike the sender's window, the receiver's window always remains at its initial size, rotating as the next frame is accepted and delivered to the network layer.

3.4.1 A One-Bit Sliding Window Protocol

Before tackling the general case, let us examine a sliding window protocol with a window size of 1. Such a protocol uses stop-and-wait since the sender transmits a frame and waits for its acknowledgement before sending the next one.

Figure 3-16 depicts such a protocol. Like the others, it starts out by defining some variables. *Next_frame_to_send* tells which frame the sender is trying to send. Similarly, *frame_expected* tells which frame the receiver is expecting. In both cases, 0 and 1 are the only possibilities.

```
/* Protocol 4 (Sliding window) is bidirectional. */

#define MAX_SEQ 1                                    /* must be 1 for protocol 4 */
typedef enum {frame_arrival, cksum_err, timeout} event_type;
#include "protocol.h"
void protocol4 (void)
{
 seq_nr next_frame_to_send;                          /* 0 or 1 only */
 seq_nr frame_expected;                              /* 0 or 1 only */
 frame r, s;                                         /* scratch variables */
 packet buffer;                                      /* current packet being sent */
 event_type event;

 next_frame_to_send = 0;                             /* next frame on the outbound stream */
 frame_expected = 0;                                 /* frame expected next */
 from_network_layer(&buffer);                        /* fetch a packet from the network layer */
 s.info = buffer;                                    /* prepare to send the initial frame */
 s.seq = next_frame_to_send;                         /* insert sequence number into frame */
 s.ack = 1 – frame_expected;                         /* piggybacked ack */
 to_physical_layer(&s);                              /* transmit the frame */
 start_timer(s.seq);                                 /* start the timer running */
 while (true) {
    wait_for_event(&event);                          /* frame_arrival, cksum_err, or timeout */
    if (event == frame_arrival) {                    /* a frame has arrived undamaged */
         from_physical_layer(&r);                    /* go get it */
         if (r.seq == frame_expected) {              /* handle inbound frame stream */
               to_network_layer(&r.info);            /* pass packet to network layer */
               inc(frame_expected);                  /* invert seq number expected next */
         }
         if (r.ack == next_frame_to_send) {          /* handle outbound frame stream */
               stop_timer(r.ack);                    /* turn the timer off */
               from_network_layer(&buffer);          /* fetch new pkt from network layer */
               inc(next_frame_to_send);              /* invert sender's sequence number */
         }
    }
    s.info = buffer;                                 /* construct outbound frame */
    s.seq = next_frame_to_send;                      /* insert sequence number into it */
    s.ack = 1 – frame_expected;                      /* seq number of last received frame */
    to_physical_layer(&s);                           /* transmit a frame */
    start_timer(s.seq);                              /* start the timer running */
 }
}
```

Figure 3-16. A 1-bit sliding window protocol.

Under normal circumstances, one of the two data link layers goes first and transmits the first frame. In other words, only one of the data link layer programs should contain the *to_physical_layer* and *start_timer* procedure calls outside the main loop. The starting machine fetches the first packet from its network layer, builds a frame from it, and sends it. When this (or any) frame arrives, the receiving data link layer checks to see if it is a duplicate, just as in protocol 3. If the frame is the one expected, it is passed to the network layer and the receiver's window is slid up.

The acknowledgement field contains the number of the last frame received without error. If this number agrees with the sequence number of the frame the sender is trying to send, the sender knows it is done with the frame stored in *buffer* and can fetch the next packet from its network layer. If the sequence number disagrees, it must continue trying to send the same frame. Whenever a frame is received, a frame is also sent back.

Now let us examine protocol 4 to see how resilient it is to pathological scenarios. Assume that computer *A* is trying to send its frame 0 to computer *B* and that *B* is trying to send its frame 0 to *A*. Suppose that *A* sends a frame to *B*, but *A*'s timeout interval is a little too short. Consequently, *A* may time out repeatedly, sending a series of identical frames, all with $seq = 0$ and $ack = 1$.

When the first valid frame arrives at computer *B*, it will be accepted and *frame_expected* will be set to a value of 1. All the subsequent frames received will be rejected because *B* is now expecting frames with sequence number 1, not 0. Furthermore, since all the duplicates will have $ack = 1$ and *B* is still waiting for an acknowledgement of 0, *B* will not go and fetch a new packet from its network layer.

After every rejected duplicate comes in, *B* will send *A* a frame containing $seq = 0$ and $ack = 0$. Eventually, one of these will arrive correctly at *A*, causing *A* to begin sending the next packet. No combination of lost frames or premature timeouts can cause the protocol to deliver duplicate packets to either network layer, to skip a packet, or to deadlock. The protocol is correct.

However, to show how subtle protocol interactions can be, we note that a peculiar situation arises if both sides simultaneously send an initial packet. This synchronization difficulty is illustrated by Fig. 3-17. In part (a), the normal operation of the protocol is shown. In (b) the peculiarity is illustrated. If *B* waits for *A*'s first frame before sending one of its own, the sequence is as shown in (a), and every frame is accepted.

However, if *A* and *B* simultaneously initiate communication, their first frames cross, and the data link layers then get into situation (b). In (a) each frame arrival brings a new packet for the network layer; there are no duplicates. In (b) half of the frames contain duplicates, even though there are no transmission errors. Similar situations can occur as a result of premature timeouts, even when one side clearly starts first. In fact, if multiple premature timeouts occur, frames may be sent three or more times, wasting valuable bandwidth.

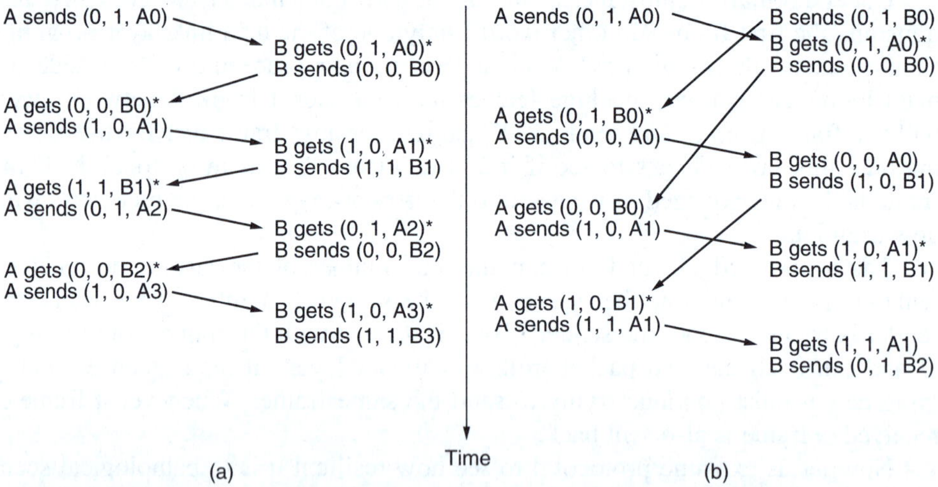

Figure 3-17. Two scenarios for protocol 4. (a) Normal case. (b) Abnormal case. The notation is (seq, ack, packet number). An asterisk indicates where a network layer accepts a packet.

3.4.2 A Protocol Using Go-Back-N

Until now we have made the tacit assumption that the transmission time required for a frame to arrive at the receiver plus the transmission time for the acknowledgement to come back is negligible. Sometimes this assumption is clearly false. In these situations the long round-trip time can have important implications for the efficiency of the bandwidth utilization. As an example, consider a 50-kbps satellite channel with a 500-msec round-trip propagation delay. Let us imagine trying to use protocol 4 to send 1000-bit frames via the satellite. At $t = 0$ the sender starts sending the first frame. At $t = 20$ msec the frame has been completely sent. Not until $t = 270$ msec has the frame fully arrived at the receiver, and not until $t = 520$ msec has the acknowledgement arrived back at the sender, under the best of circumstances (of no waiting in the receiver and a short acknowledgement frame). This means that the sender was blocked 500/520 or 96% of the time. In other words, only 4% of the available bandwidth was used. Clearly, the combination of a long transit time, high bandwidth, and short frame length is disastrous in terms of efficiency.

The problem described here can be viewed as a consequence of the rule requiring a sender to wait for an acknowledgement before sending another frame. If we relax that restriction, much better efficiency can be achieved. Basically, the solution lies in allowing the sender to transmit up to *w* frames before blocking, instead of just 1. With a large enough choice of *w* the sender will be able to continuously transmit frames since the acknowledgements will arrive for previous frames before the window becomes full, preventing the sender from blocking.

To find an appropriate value for w we need to know how many frames can fit inside the channel as they propagate from sender to receiver. This capacity is determined by the bandwidth in bits/sec multiplied by the one-way transit time, or the **bandwidth-delay product** of the link. We can divide this quantity by the number of bits in a frame to express it as a number of frames. Call this quantity BD. Then w should be set to $2BD + 1$. Twice the bandwidth-delay is the number of frames that can be outstanding if the sender continuously sends frames when the round-trip time to receive an acknowledgement is considered. The "+1" is because an acknowledgement frame will not be sent until after a complete frame is received.

For the example link with a bandwidth of 50 kbps and a one-way transit time of 250 msec, the bandwidth-delay product is 12.5 kbit or 12.5 frames of 1000 bits each. $2BD + 1$ is then 26 frames. Assume the sender begins sending frame 0 as before and sends a new frame every 20 msec. By the time it has finished sending 26 frames, at $t = 520$ msec, the acknowledgement for frame 0 will have just arrived. Thereafter, acknowledgements will arrive every 20 msec, so the sender will always get permission to continue just when it needs it. From then onwards, 25 or 26 unacknowledged frames will always be outstanding. Put in other terms, the sender's maximum window size is 26.

For smaller window sizes, the utilization of the link will be less than 100% since the sender will be blocked sometimes. We can write the utilization as the fraction of time that the sender is not blocked:

$$\text{link utilization} \le \frac{w}{1 + 2BD}$$

This value is an upper bound because it does not allow for any frame processing time and treats the acknowledgement frame as having zero length, since it is usually short. The equation shows the need for having a large window w whenever the bandwidth-delay product is large. If the delay is high, the sender will rapidly exhaust its window even for a moderate bandwidth, as in the satellite example. If the bandwidth is high, even for a moderate delay the sender will exhaust its window quickly unless it has a large window (e.g., a 1-Gbps link with 1-msec delay holds 1 megabit). With stop-and-wait for which $w = 1$, if there is even one frame's worth of propagation delay the efficiency will be less than 50%.

This technique of keeping multiple frames in flight is an example of **pipelining**. Pipelining frames over an unreliable communication channel raises some serious issues. First, what happens if a frame in the middle of a long stream is damaged or lost? Large numbers of succeeding frames will arrive at the receiver before the sender even finds out that anything is wrong. When a damaged frame arrives at the receiver, it obviously should be discarded, but what should the receiver do with all the correct frames following it? Remember that the receiving data link layer is obligated to hand packets to the network layer in sequence.

Two basic approaches are available for dealing with errors in the presence of pipelining, both of which are shown in Fig. 3-18.

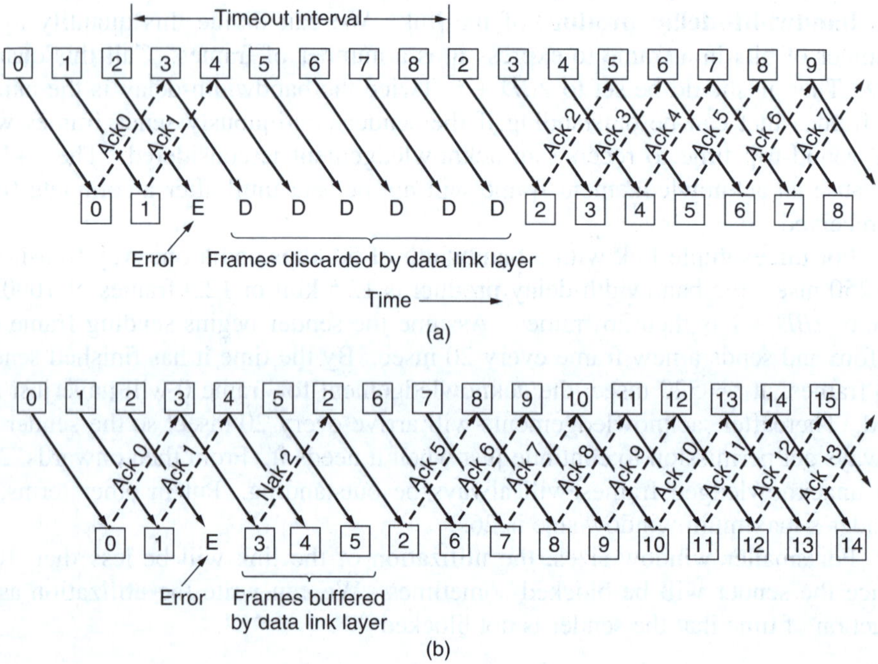

Figure 3-18. Pipelining and error recovery. Effect of an error when (a) receiver's window size is 1 and (b) receiver's window size is large.

One option, called **go-back-n**, is for the receiver simply to discard all subsequent frames, sending no acknowledgements for the discarded frames. This strategy corresponds to a receive window of size 1. In other words, the data link layer refuses to accept any frame except the next one it must give to the network layer. If the sender's window fills up before the timer runs out, the pipeline will begin to empty. Eventually, the sender will time out and retransmit all unacknowledged frames in order, starting with the damaged or lost one. This approach can waste a lot of bandwidth if the error rate is high.

In Fig. 3-18(b) we see go-back-n for the case in which the receiver's window is large. Frames 0 and 1 are correctly received and acknowledged. Frame 2, however, is damaged or lost. The sender, unaware of this problem, continues to send frames until the timer for frame 2 expires. Then it backs up to frame 2 and starts over with it, sending 2, 3, 4, etc. all over again.

The other general strategy for handling errors when frames are pipelined is called **selective repeat**. When it is used, a bad frame that is received is discarded, but any good frames received after it are accepted and buffered. When the sender times out, only the oldest unacknowledged frame is retransmitted. If that frame arrives correctly, the receiver can deliver to the network layer, in sequence, all the frames it has buffered. Selective repeat corresponds to a receiver window larger than 1. This approach can require large amounts of data link layer memory if the window is large.

Selective repeat is often combined with having the receiver send a negative acknowledgement (NAK) when it detects an error, for example, when it receives a checksum error or a frame out of sequence. NAKs stimulate retransmission before the corresponding timer expires and thus improve performance.

In Fig. 3-18(b), frames 0 and 1 are again correctly received and acknowledged and frame 2 is lost. When frame 3 arrives at the receiver, the data link layer there notices that it has missed a frame, so it sends back a NAK for 2 but buffers 3. When frames 4 and 5 arrive, they, too, are buffered by the data link layer instead of being passed to the network layer. Eventually, the NAK 2 gets back to the sender, which immediately resends frame 2. When that arrives, the data link layer now has 2, 3, 4, and 5 and can pass all of them to the network layer in the correct order. It can also acknowledge all frames up to and including 5, as shown in the figure. If the NAK should get lost, eventually the sender will time out for frame 2 and send it (and only it) of its own accord, but that may be a quite a while later.

These two alternative approaches are trade-offs between efficient use of bandwidth and data link layer buffer space. Depending on which resource is scarcer, one or the other can be used. Figure 3-19 shows a go-back-n protocol in which the receiving data link layer only accepts frames in order; frames following an error are discarded. In this protocol, for the first time we have dropped the assumption that the network layer always has an infinite supply of packets to send. When the network layer has a packet it wants to send, it can cause a *network_layer_ready* event to happen. However, to enforce the flow control limit on the sender window or the number of unacknowledged frames that may be outstanding at any time, the data link layer must be able to keep the network layer from bothering it with more work. The library procedures *enable_network_layer* and *disable_network_layer* do this job.

The maximum number of frames that may be outstanding at any instant is not the same as the size of the sequence number space. For go-back-n, *MAX_SEQ* frames may be outstanding at any instant, even though there are *MAX_SEQ* + 1 distinct sequence numbers (which are 0, 1, . . . , *MAX_SEQ*). We will see an even tighter restriction for the next protocol, selective repeat. To see why this restriction is required, consider the following scenario with *MAX_SEQ* = 7:

1. The sender sends frames 0 through 7.
2. A piggybacked acknowledgement for 7 comes back to the sender.
3. The sender sends another eight frames, again with sequence numbers 0 through 7.
4. Now another piggybacked acknowledgement for frame 7 comes in.

```
/* Protocol 5 (Go-back-n) allows multiple outstanding frames. The sender may transmit up
   to MAX_SEQ frames without waiting for an ack. In addition, unlike in the previous
   protocols, the network layer is not assumed to have a new packet all the time. Instead,
   the network layer causes a network_layer_ready event when there is a packet to send. */

#define MAX_SEQ 7
typedef enum {frame_arrival, cksum_err, timeout, network_layer_ready} event_type;
#include "protocol.h"

static boolean between(seq_nr a, seq_nr b, seq_nr c)
{
/* Return true if a <= b < c circularly; false otherwise. */
 if (((a <= b) && (b < c)) || ((c < a) && (a <= b)) || ((b < c) && (c < a)))
     return(true);
  else
     return(false);
}

static void send_data(seq_nr frame_nr, seq_nr frame_expected, packet buffer[ ])
{
/* Construct and send a data frame. */
 frame s;                                   /* scratch variable */

 s.info = buffer[frame_nr];                 /* insert packet into frame */
 s.seq = frame_nr;                          /* insert sequence number into frame */
 s.ack = (frame_expected + MAX_SEQ) % (MAX_SEQ + 1);/* piggyback ack */
 to_physical_layer(&s);                     /* transmit the frame */
 start_timer(frame_nr);                     /* start the timer running */
}

void protocol5(void)
{
 seq_nr next_frame_to_send;                 /* MAX_SEQ > 1; used for outbound stream */
 seq_nr ack_expected;                       /* oldest frame as yet unacknowledged */
 seq_nr frame_expected;                     /* next frame expected on inbound stream */
 frame r;                                   /* scratch variable */
 packet buffer[MAX_SEQ + 1];                /* buffers for the outbound stream */
 seq_nr nbuffered;                          /* number of output buffers currently in use */
 seq_nr i;                                  /* used to index into the buffer array */
 event_type event;

 enable_network_layer();                    /* allow network_layer_ready events */
 ack_expected = 0;                          /* next ack expected inbound */
 next_frame_to_send = 0;                    /* next frame going out */
 frame_expected = 0;                        /* number of frame expected inbound */
 nbuffered = 0;                             /* initially no packets are buffered */

 while (true) {
   wait_for_event(&event);                  /* four possibilities: see event_type above */
```

```
  switch(event) {
    case network_layer_ready:               /* the network layer has a packet to send */
          /* Accept, save, and transmit a new frame. */
          from_network_layer(&buffer[next_frame_to_send]); /* fetch new packet */
          nbuffered = nbuffered + 1;        /* expand the sender's window */
          send_data(next_frame_to_send, frame_expected, buffer);/* transmit the frame */
          inc(next_frame_to_send);          /* advance sender's upper window edge */
          break;

    case frame_arrival:                     /* a data or control frame has arrived */
          from_physical_layer(&r);          /* get incoming frame from physical layer */

          if (r.seq == frame_expected) {
                /* Frames are accepted only in order. */
                to_network_layer(&r.info);  /* pass packet to network layer */
                inc(frame_expected);        /* advance lower edge of receiver's window */
          }

          /* Ack n implies n − 1, n − 2, etc. Check for this. */
          while (between(ack_expected, r.ack, next_frame_to_send)) {
                /* Handle piggybacked ack. */
                nbuffered = nbuffered − 1;  /* one frame fewer buffered */
                stop_timer(ack_expected);   /* frame arrived intact; stop timer */
                inc(ack_expected);          /* contract sender's window */
          }
          break;

    case cksum_err: break;                  /* just ignore bad frames */

    case timeout:                           /* trouble; retransmit all outstanding frames */
          next_frame_to_send = ack_expected;    /* start retransmitting here */
          for (i = 1; i <= nbuffered; i++) {
                send_data(next_frame_to_send, frame_expected, buffer);/* resend frame */
                inc(next_frame_to_send);    /* prepare to send the next one */
          }

  }

  if (nbuffered < MAX_SEQ)
          enable_network_layer();
  else
          disable_network_layer();
 }
}
```

Figure 3-19. A sliding window protocol using go-back-n.

The question is this: did all eight frames belonging to the second batch arrive successfully, or did all eight get lost (counting discards following an error as lost)? In both cases the receiver would be sending frame 7 as the acknowledgement.

The sender has no way of telling. For this reason the maximum number of outstanding frames must be restricted to *MAX_SEQ*.

Although protocol 5 does not buffer the frames arriving after an error, it does not escape the problem of buffering altogether. Since a sender may have to retransmit all the unacknowledged frames at a future time, it must hang on to all transmitted frames until it knows for sure that they have been accepted by the receiver. When an acknowledgement comes in for frame n, frames $n - 1$, $n - 2$, and so on are also automatically acknowledged. This type of acknowledgement is called a **cumulative acknowledgement**. This property is especially important when some of the previous acknowledgement-bearing frames were lost or garbled. Whenever any acknowledgement comes in, the data link layer checks to see if any buffers can now be released. If buffers can be released (i.e., there is some room available in the window), a previously blocked network layer can now be allowed to cause more *network_layer_ready* events.

For this protocol, we assume that there is always reverse traffic on which to piggyback acknowledgements. Protocol 4 does not need this assumption since it sends back one frame every time it receives a frame, even if it has already sent that frame. In the next protocol we will solve the problem of one-way traffic in an elegant way.

Because protocol 5 has multiple outstanding frames, it logically needs multiple timers, one per outstanding frame. Each frame times out independently of all the other ones. However, all of these timers can easily be simulated in software using a single hardware clock that causes interrupts periodically. The pending timeouts form a linked list, with each node of the list containing the number of clock ticks until the timer expires, the frame being timed, and a pointer to the next node.

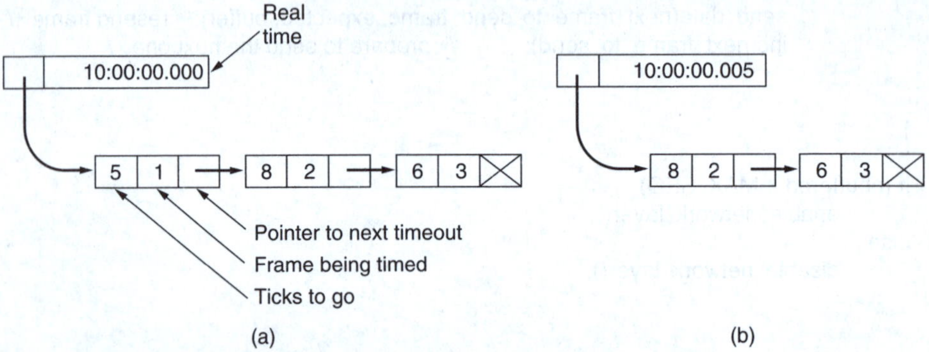

Figure 3-20. Simulation of multiple timers in software. (a) The queued timeouts. (b) The situation after the first timeout has expired.

As an illustration of how the timers could be implemented, consider the example of Fig. 3-20(a). Assume that the clock ticks once every 1 msec. Initially, the real time is 10:00:00.000; three timeouts are pending, at 10:00:00.005, 10:00:00.013, and 10:00:00.019. Every time the hardware clock ticks, the real time is updated and the tick counter at the head of the list is decremented. When the tick counter becomes zero, a timeout is caused and the node is removed from the list, as shown in Fig. 3-20(b). Although this organization requires the list to be scanned when *start_timer* or *stop_timer* is called, it does not require much work per tick. In protocol 5, both of these routines have been given a parameter indicating which frame is to be timed.

3.4.3 A Protocol Using Selective Repeat

The go-back-n protocol works well if errors are rare, but if the line is poor it wastes a lot of bandwidth on retransmitted frames. An alternative strategy, the selective repeat protocol, is to allow the receiver to accept and buffer the frames following a damaged or lost one.

In this protocol, both sender and receiver maintain a window of outstanding and acceptable sequence numbers, respectively. The sender's window size starts out at 0 and grows to some predefined maximum. The receiver's window, in contrast, is always fixed in size and equal to the predetermined maximum. The receiver has a buffer reserved for each sequence number within its fixed window. Associated with each buffer is a bit (*arrived*) telling whether the buffer is full or empty. Whenever a frame arrives, its sequence number is checked by the function *between* to see if it falls within the window. If so and if it has not already been received, it is accepted and stored. This action is taken without regard to whether or not the frame contains the next packet expected by the network layer. Of course, it must be kept within the data link layer and not passed to the network layer until all the lower-numbered frames have already been delivered to the network layer in the correct order. A protocol using this algorithm is given in Fig. 3-21.

Nonsequential receive introduces further constraints on frame sequence numbers compared to protocols in which frames are only accepted in order. We can illustrate the trouble most easily with an example. Suppose that we have a 3-bit sequence number, so that the sender is permitted to transmit up to seven frames before being required to wait for an acknowledgement. Initially, the sender's and receiver's windows are as shown in Fig. 3-22(a). The sender now transmits frames 0 through 6. The receiver's window allows it to accept any frame with a sequence number between 0 and 6 inclusive. All seven frames arrive correctly, so the receiver acknowledges them and advances its window to allow receipt of 7, 0, 1, 2, 3, 4, or 5, as shown in Fig. 3-22(b). All seven buffers are marked empty.

It is at this point that disaster strikes in the form of a lightning bolt hitting the telephone pole and wiping out all the acknowledgements. The protocol should operate correctly despite this disaster. The sender eventually times out and retransmits frame 0. When this frame arrives at the receiver, a check is made to see if it falls within the receiver's window. Unfortunately, in Fig. 3-22(b) frame 0 is

```
/* Protocol 6 (Selective repeat) accepts frames out of order but passes packets to the
   network layer in order. Associated with each outstanding frame is a timer. When the timer
   expires, only that frame is retransmitted, not all the outstanding frames, as in protocol 5. */

#define MAX_SEQ 7                                    /* should be 2^n - 1 */
#define NR_BUFS ((MAX_SEQ + 1)/2)
typedef enum {frame_arrival, cksum_err, timeout, network_layer_ready, ack_timeout} event_type;
#include "protocol.h"
boolean no_nak = true;                               /* no nak has been sent yet */
seq_nr oldest_frame = MAX_SEQ + 1;                   /* initial value is only for the simulator */

static boolean between(seq_nr a, seq_nr b, seq_nr c)
{
/* Same as between in protocol 5, but shorter and more obscure. */
  return ((a <= b) && (b < c)) || ((c < a) && (a <= b)) || ((b < c) && (c < a));
}

static void send_frame(frame_kind fk, seq_nr frame_nr, seq_nr frame_expected, packet buffer[ ])
{
/* Construct and send a data, ack, or nak frame. */
  frame s;                                           /* scratch variable */

  s.kind = fk;                                       /* kind == data, ack, or nak */
  if (fk == data) s.info = buffer[frame_nr % NR_BUFS];
  s.seq = frame_nr;                                  /* only meaningful for data frames */
  s.ack = (frame_expected + MAX_SEQ) % (MAX_SEQ + 1);
  if (fk == nak) no_nak = false;                     /* one nak per frame, please */
  to_physical_layer(&s);                             /* transmit the frame */
  if (fk == data) start_timer(frame_nr % NR_BUFS);
  stop_ack_timer();                                  /* no need for separate ack frame */
}

void protocol6(void)
{
  seq_nr ack_expected;                               /* lower edge of sender's window */
  seq_nr next_frame_to_send;                         /* upper edge of sender's window + 1 */
  seq_nr frame_expected;                             /* lower edge of receiver's window */
  seq_nr too_far;                                    /* upper edge of receiver's window + 1 */
  int i;                                             /* index into buffer pool */
  frame r;                                           /* scratch variable */
  packet out_buf[NR_BUFS];                           /* buffers for the outbound stream */
  packet in_buf[NR_BUFS];                            /* buffers for the inbound stream */
  boolean arrived[NR_BUFS];                          /* inbound bit map */
  seq_nr nbuffered;                                  /* how many output buffers currently used */
  event_type event;

  enable_network_layer();                            /* initialize */
  ack_expected = 0;                                  /* next ack expected on the inbound stream */
  next_frame_to_send = 0;                            /* number of next outgoing frame */
  frame_expected = 0;
  too_far = NR_BUFS;
  nbuffered = 0;                                     /* initially no packets are buffered */
  for (i = 0; i < NR_BUFS; i++) arrived[i] = false;
```

```
while (true) {
  wait_for_event(&event);                    /* five possibilities: see event_type above */
  switch(event) {
   case network_layer_ready:                 /* accept, save, and transmit a new frame */
        nbuffered = nbuffered + 1;           /* expand the window */
        from_network_layer(&out_buf[next_frame_to_send % NR_BUFS]); /* fetch new packet */
        send_frame(data, next_frame_to_send, frame_expected, out_buf);/* transmit the frame */
        inc(next_frame_to_send);             /* advance upper window edge */
        break;

   case frame_arrival:                       /* a data or control frame has arrived */
        from_physical_layer(&r);             /* fetch incoming frame from physical layer */
        if (r.kind == data) {
             /* An undamaged frame has arrived. */
             if ((r.seq != frame_expected) && no_nak)
                send_frame(nak, 0, frame_expected, out_buf); else start_ack_timer();
             if (between(frame_expected,r.seq,too_far) && (arrived[r.seq%NR_BUFS]==false)) {
                  /* Frames may be accepted in any order. */
                  arrived[r.seq % NR_BUFS] = true;    /* mark buffer as full */
                  in_buf[r.seq % NR_BUFS] = r.info;   /* insert data into buffer */
                  while (arrived[frame_expected % NR_BUFS]) {
                       /* Pass frames and advance window. */
                       to_network_layer(&in_buf[frame_expected % NR_BUFS]);
                       no_nak = true;
                       arrived[frame_expected % NR_BUFS] = false;
                       inc(frame_expected);      /* advance lower edge of receiver's window */
                       inc(too_far);             /* advance upper edge of receiver's window */
                       start_ack_timer();        /* to see if a separate ack is needed */
                  }
             }
        }
        if((r.kind==nak) && between(ack_expected,(r.ack+1)%(MAX_SEQ+1),next_frame_to_send))
             send_frame(data, (r.ack+1) % (MAX_SEQ + 1), frame_expected, out_buf);

        while (between(ack_expected, r.ack, next_frame_to_send)) {
             nbuffered = nbuffered - 1;          /* handle piggybacked ack */
             stop_timer(ack_expected % NR_BUFS);   /* frame arrived intact */
             inc(ack_expected);                  /* advance lower edge of sender's window */
        }
        break;

   case cksum_err:
        if (no_nak) send_frame(nak, 0, frame_expected, out_buf); /* damaged frame */
        break;

   case timeout:
        send_frame(data, oldest_frame, frame_expected, out_buf); /* we timed out */
        break;

   case ack_timeout:
        send_frame(ack,0,frame_expected, out_buf);    /* ack timer expired; send ack */
  }
  if (nbuffered < NR_BUFS) enable_network_layer(); else disable_network_layer();
 }
}
```

Figure 3-21. A sliding window protocol using selective repeat.

within the new window, so it is accepted as a new frame. The receiver also sends a (piggybacked) acknowledgement for frame 6, since 0 through 6 have been received.

The sender is happy to learn that all its transmitted frames did actually arrive correctly, so it advances its window and immediately sends frames 7, 0, 1, 2, 3, 4, and 5. Frame 7 will be accepted by the receiver and its packet will be passed directly to the network layer. Immediately thereafter, the receiving data link layer checks to see if it has a valid frame 0 already, discovers that it does, and passes the old buffered packet to the network layer as if it were a new packet. Consequently, the network layer gets an incorrect packet, and the protocol fails.

The essence of the problem is that after the receiver advanced its window, the new range of valid sequence numbers overlapped the old one. Consequently, the following batch of frames might be either duplicates (if all the acknowledgements were lost) or new ones (if all the acknowledgements were received). The poor receiver has no way of distinguishing these two cases.

The way out of this dilemma lies in making sure that after the receiver has advanced its window there is no overlap with the original window. To ensure that there is no overlap, the maximum window size should be at most half the range of the sequence numbers. This situation is shown in Fig. 3-22(c) and Fig. 3-22(d). With 3 bits, the sequence numbers range from 0 to 7. Only four unacknowledged frames should be outstanding at any instant. That way, if the receiver has just accepted frames 0 through 3 and advanced its window to permit acceptance of frames 4 through 7, it can unambiguously tell if subsequent frames are retransmissions (0 through 3) or new ones (4 through 7). In general, the window size for protocol 6 will be $(MAX\_SEQ + 1)/2$.

An interesting question is: how many buffers must the receiver have? Under no conditions will it ever accept frames whose sequence numbers are below the lower edge of the window or frames whose sequence numbers are above the upper edge of the window. Consequently, the number of buffers needed is equal to the window size, not to the range of sequence numbers. In the preceding example of a 3-bit sequence number, four buffers, numbered 0 through 3, are needed. When frame i arrives, it is put in buffer i mod 4. Notice that although i and $(i + 4)$ mod 4 are "competing" for the same buffer, they are never within the window at the same time, because that would imply a window size of at least 5.

For the same reason, the number of timers needed is equal to the number of buffers, not to the size of the sequence space. Effectively, a timer is associated with each buffer. When the timer runs out, the contents of the buffer are retransmitted.

Protocol 6 also relaxes the implicit assumption that the channel is heavily loaded. We made this assumption in protocol 5 when we relied on frames being sent in the reverse direction on which to piggyback acknowledgements. If the reverse traffic is light, the acknowledgements may be held up for a long period of time, which can cause problems. In the extreme, if there is a lot of traffic in one

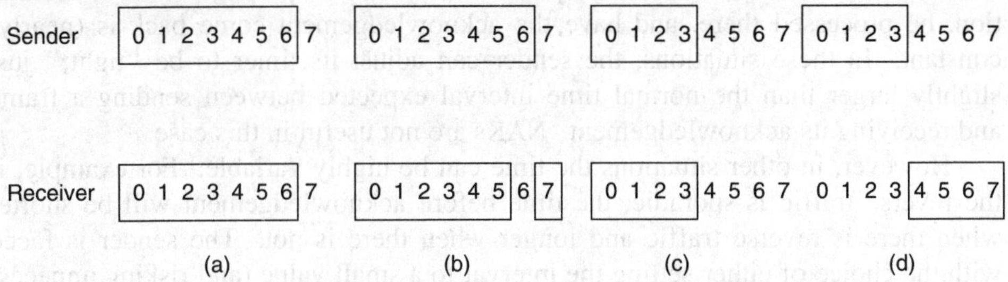

Figure 3-22. (a) Initial situation with a window of size7. (b) After 7 frames have been sent and received but not acknowledged. (c) Initial situation with a window size of 4. (d) After 4 frames have been sent and received but not acknowledged.

direction and no traffic in the other direction, the protocol will block when the sender window reaches its maximum.

To relax this assumption, an auxiliary timer is started by *start_ack_timer* after an in-sequence data frame arrives. If no reverse traffic has presented itself before this timer expires, a separate acknowledgement frame is sent. An interrupt due to the auxiliary timer is called an *ack_timeout* event. With this arrangement, traffic flow in only one direction is possible because the lack of reverse data frames onto which acknowledgements can be piggybacked is no longer an obstacle. Only one auxiliary timer exists, and if *start_ack_timer* is called while the timer is running, it has no effect. The timer is not reset or extended since its purpose is to provide some minimum rate of acknowledgements.

It is essential that the timeout associated with the auxiliary timer be appreciably shorter than the timeout used for timing out data frames. This condition is required to ensure that a correctly received frame is acknowledged early enough that the frame's retransmission timer does not expire and retransmit the frame.

Protocol 6 uses a more efficient strategy than protocol 5 for dealing with errors. Whenever the receiver has reason to suspect that an error has occurred, it sends a negative acknowledgement (NAK) frame back to the sender. Such a frame is a request for retransmission of the frame specified in the NAK. In two cases, the receiver should be suspicious: when a damaged frame arrives or a frame other than the expected one arrives (potential lost frame). To avoid making multiple requests for retransmission of the same lost frame, the receiver should keep track of whether a NAK has already been sent for a given frame. The variable *no_nak* in protocol 6 is *true* if no NAK has been sent yet for *frame_expected*. If the NAK gets mangled or lost, no real harm is done, since the sender will eventually time out and retransmit the missing frame anyway. If the wrong frame arrives after a NAK has been sent and lost, *no_nak* will be *true* and the auxiliary timer will be started. When it expires, an ACK will be sent to resynchronize the sender to the receiver's current status.

In some situations, the time required for a frame to propagate to the destination, be processed there, and have the acknowledgement come back is (nearly) constant. In these situations, the sender can adjust its timer to be "tight," just slightly larger than the normal time interval expected between sending a frame and receiving its acknowledgement. NAKs are not useful in this case.

However, in other situations the time can be highly variable. For example, if the reverse traffic is sporadic, the time before acknowledgement will be shorter when there is reverse traffic and longer when there is not. The sender is faced with the choice of either setting the interval to a small value (and risking unnecessary retransmissions), or setting it to a large value (and going idle for a long period after an error). Both choices waste bandwidth. In general, if the standard deviation of the acknowledgement interval is large compared to the interval itself, the timer is set "loose" to be conservative. NAKs can then appreciably speed up retransmission of lost or damaged frames.

Closely related to the matter of timeouts and NAKs is the question of determining which frame caused a timeout. In protocol 5, it is always *ack_expected*, because it is always the oldest. In protocol 6, there is no trivial way to determine who timed out. Suppose that frames 0 through 4 have been transmitted, meaning that the list of outstanding frames is 01234, in order from oldest to youngest. Now imagine that 0 times out, 5 (a new frame) is transmitted, 1 times out, 2 times out, and 6 (another new frame) is transmitted. At this point the list of outstanding frames is 3405126, from oldest to youngest. If all inbound traffic (i.e., acknowledgement-bearing frames) is lost for a while, the seven outstanding frames will time out in that order.

To keep the example from getting even more complicated than it already is, we have not shown the timer administration. Instead, we just assume that the variable *oldest_frame* is set upon timeout to indicate which frame timed out.

3.5 EXAMPLE DATA LINK PROTOCOLS

Within a single building, LANs are widely used for interconnection, but most wide-area network infrastructure is built up from point-to-point lines. In Chap. 4, we will look at LANs. Here we will examine the data link protocols found on point-to-point lines in the Internet in two common situations. The first situation is when packets are sent over SONET optical fiber links in wide-area networks. These links are widely used, for example, to connect routers in the different locations of an ISP's network.

The second situation is for ADSL links running on the local loop of the telephone network at the edge of the Internet. These links connect millions of individuals and businesses to the Internet.

The Internet needs point-to-point links for these uses, as well as dial-up modems, leased lines, and cable modems, and so on. A standard protocol called **PPP**

(**Point-to-Point Protocol**) is used to send packets over these links. PPP is defined in RFC 1661 and further elaborated in RFC 1662 and other RFCs (Simpson, 1994a, 1994b). SONET and ADSL links both apply PPP, but in different ways.

3.5.1 Packet over SONET

SONET, which we covered in Sec. 2.6.4, is the physical layer protocol that is most commonly used over the wide-area optical fiber links that make up the backbone of communications networks, including the telephone system. It provides a bitstream that runs at a well-defined rate, for example 2.4 Gbps for an OC-48 link. This bitstream is organized as fixed-size byte payloads that recur every 125 μsec, whether or not there is user data to send.

To carry packets across these links, some framing mechanism is needed to distinguish occasional packets from the continuous bitstream in which they are transported. PPP runs on IP routers to provide this mechanism, as shown in Fig. 3-23.

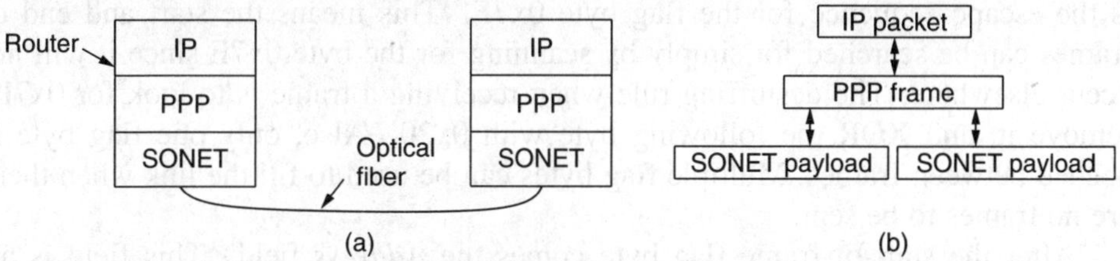

Figure 3-23. Packet over SONET. (a) A protocol stack. (b) Frame relationships.

PPP improves on an earlier, simpler protocol called **SLIP** (**Serial Line Internet Protocol**) and is used to handle error detection link configuration, support multiple protocols, permit authentication, and more. With a wide set of options, PPP provides three main features:

1. A framing method that unambiguously delineates the end of one frame and the start of the next one. The frame format also handles error detection.

2. A link control protocol for bringing lines up, testing them, negotiating options, and bringing them down again gracefully when they are no longer needed. This protocol is called **LCP** (**Link Control Protocol**).

3. A way to negotiate network-layer options in a way that is independent of the network layer protocol to be used. The method chosen is to have a different **NCP** (**Network Control Protocol**) for each network layer supported.

The PPP frame format was chosen to closely resemble the frame format of **HDLC (High-level Data Link Control)**, a widely used instance of an earlier family of protocols, since there was no need to reinvent the wheel.

The primary difference between PPP and HDLC is that PPP is byte oriented rather than bit oriented. In particular, PPP uses byte stuffing and all frames are an integral number of bytes. HDLC uses bit stuffing and allows frames of, say, 30.25 bytes.

There is a second major difference in practice, however. HDLC provides reliable transmission with a sliding window, acknowledgements, and timeouts in the manner we have studied. PPP can also provide reliable transmission in noisy environments, such as wireless networks; the exact details are defined in RFC 1663. However, this is rarely done in practice. Instead, an "unnumbered mode" is nearly always used in the Internet to provide connectionless unacknowledged service.

The PPP frame format is shown in Fig. 3-24. All PPP frames begin with the standard HDLC flag byte of 0x7E (01111110). The flag byte is stuffed if it occurs within the *Payload* field using the escape byte 0x7D. The following byte is the escaped byte XORed with 0x20, which flips the 5th bit. For example, 0x7D 0x5E is the escape sequence for the flag byte 0x7E. This means the start and end of frames can be searched for simply by scanning for the byte 0x7E since it will not occur elsewhere. The destuffing rule when receiving a frame is to look for 0x7D, remove it, and XOR the following byte with 0x20. Also, only one flag byte is needed between frames. Multiple flag bytes can be used to fill the link when there are no frames to be sent.

After the start-of-frame flag byte comes the *Address* field. This field is always set to the binary value 11111111 to indicate that all stations are to accept the frame. Using this value avoids the issue of having to assign data link addresses.

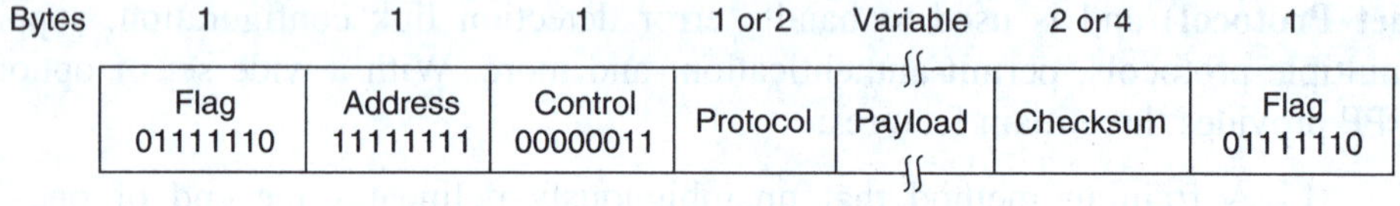

Figure 3-24. The PPP full frame format for unnumbered mode operation.

The *Address* field is followed by the *Control* field, the default value of which is 00000011. This value indicates an unnumbered frame.

Since the *Address* and *Control* fields are always constant in the default configuration, LCP provides the necessary mechanism for the two parties to negotiate an option to omit them altogether and save 2 bytes per frame.

The fourth PPP field is the *Protocol* field. Its job is to tell what kind of packet is in the *Payload* field. Codes starting with a 0 bit are defined for IP version 4, IP version 6, and other network layer protocols that might be used, such as IPX and

AppleTalk. Codes starting with a 1 bit are used for PPP configuration protocols, including LCP and a different NCP for each network layer protocol supported. The default size of the *Protocol* field is 2 bytes, but it can be negotiated down to 1 byte using LCP. The designers were perhaps overly cautious in thinking that someday there might be more than 256 protocols in use.

The *Payload* field is variable length, up to some negotiated maximum. If the length is not negotiated using LCP during line setup, a default length of 1500 bytes is used. Padding may follow the payload if it is needed.

After the *Payload* field comes the *Checksum* field, which is normally 2 bytes, but a 4-byte checksum can be negotiated. The 4-byte checksum is in fact the same 32-bit CRC whose generator polynomial is given at the end of Sec. 3.2.2. The 2-byte checksum is also an industry-standard CRC.

PPP is a framing mechanism that can carry the packets of multiple protocols over many types of physical layers. To use PPP over SONET, the choices to make are spelled out in RFC 2615 (Malis and Simpson, 1999). A 4-byte checksum is used, since this is the primary means of detecting transmission errors over the physical, link, and network layers. It is recommended that the *Address*, *Control*, and *Protocol* fields not be compressed, since SONET links already run at relatively high rates.

There is also one unusual feature. The PPP payload is scrambled (as described in Sec. 2.5.1) before it is inserted into the SONET payload. Scrambling XORs the payload with a long pseudorandom sequence before it is transmitted. The issue is that the SONET bitstream needs frequent bit transitions for synchronization. These transitions come naturally with the variation in voice signals, but in data communication the user chooses the information that is sent and might send a packet with a long run of 0s. With scrambling, the likelihood of a user being able to cause problems by sending a long run of 0s is made extremely low.

Before PPP frames can be carried over SONET lines, the PPP link must be established and configured. The phases that the link goes through when it is brought up, used, and taken down again are shown in Fig. 3-25.

The link starts in the *DEAD* state, which means that there is no connection at the physical layer. When a physical layer connection is established, the link moves to *ESTABLISH*. At this point, the PPP peers exchange a series of LCP packets, each carried in the *Payload* field of a PPP frame, to select the PPP options for the link from the possibilities mentioned above. The initiating peer proposes options, and the responding peer either accepts or rejects them, in whole or part. The responder can also make alternative proposals.

If LCP option negotiation is successful, the link reaches the *AUTHENTICATE* state. Now the two parties can check each other's identities, if desired. If authentication is successful, the *NETWORK* state is entered and a series of NCP packets are sent to configure the network layer. It is difficult to generalize about the NCP protocols because each one is specific to some network layer protocol and allows configuration requests to be made that are specific to that protocol.

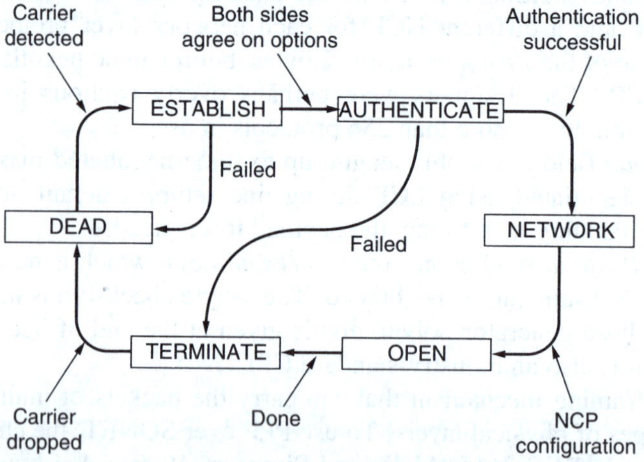

Figure 3-25. State diagram for bringing a PPP link up and down.

For IP, for example, the assignment of IP addresses to both ends of the link is the most important possibility.

Once *OPEN* is reached, data transport can take place. It is in this state that IP packets are carried in PPP frames across the SONET line. When data transport is finished, the link moves into the *TERMINATE* state, and from there it moves back to the *DEAD* state when the physical layer connection is dropped.

3.5.2 ADSL (Asymmetric Digital Subscriber Loop)

ADSL connects millions of home subscribers to the Internet at megabit/sec rates over the same telephone local loop that is used for plain old telephone service. In Sec. 2.5.3, we described how a device called a DSL modem is added on the home side. It sends bits over the local loop to a device called a DSLAM (DSL Access Multiplexer), pronounced "dee-slam," in the telephone company's local office. Now we will explore in more detail how packets are carried over ADSL links.

The overall picture for the protocols and devices used with ADSL is shown in Fig. 3-26. Different protocols are deployed in different networks, so we have chosen to show the most popular scenario. Inside the home, a computer such as a PC sends IP packets to the DSL modem using a link layer like Ethernet. The DSL modem then sends the IP packets over the local loop to the DSLAM using the protocols that we are about to study. At the DSLAM (or a router connected to it depending on the implementation) the IP packets are extracted and enter an ISP network so that they may reach any destination on the Internet.

The protocols shown over the ADSL link in Fig. 3-26 start at the bottom with the ADSL physical layer. They are based on a digital modulation scheme called

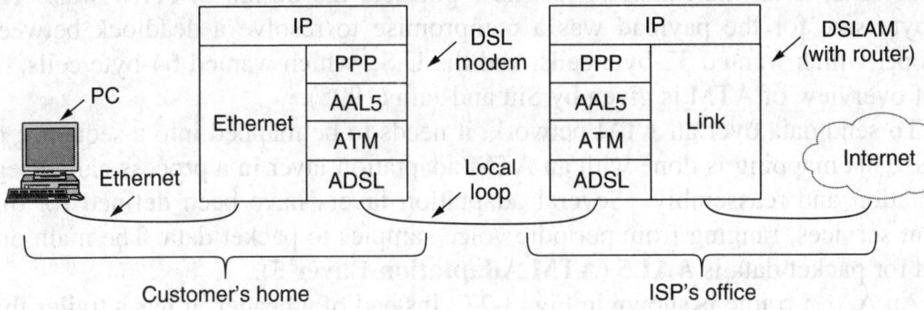

Figure 3-26. ADSL protocol stacks.

orthogonal frequency division multiplexing (also known as discrete multitone), as we saw in Sec 2.5.3. Near the top of the stack, just below the IP network layer, is PPP. This protocol is the same PPP that we have just studied for packet over SONET transports. It works in the same way to establish and configure the link and carry IP packets.

In between ADSL and PPP are ATM and AAL5. These are new protocols that we have not seen before. **ATM** (**Asynchronous Transfer Mode**) was designed in the early 1990s and launched with incredible hype. It promised a network technology that would solve the world's telecommunications problems by merging voice, data, cable television, telegraph, carrier pigeon, tin cans connected by strings, tom toms, and everything else into an integrated system that could do everything for everyone. This did not happen. In large part, the problems of ATM were similar to those we described concerning the OSI protocols, that is, bad timing, technology, implementation, and politics. Nevertheless, ATM was much more successful than OSI. While it has not taken over the world, it remains widely used in niches including broadband access lines such as DSL, and WAN links inside telephone networks.

ATM is a link layer that is based on the transmission of fixed-length **cells** of information. The "Asynchronous" in its name means that the cells do not always need to be sent in the way that bits are continuously sent over synchronous lines, as in SONET. Cells only need to be sent when there is information to carry. ATM is a connection-oriented technology. Each cell carries a **virtual circuit** identifier in its header and devices use this identifier to forward cells along the paths of established connections.

The cells are each 53 bytes long, consisting of a 48-byte payload plus a 5-byte header. By using small cells, ATM can flexibly divide the bandwidth of a physical layer link among different users in fine slices. This ability is useful when, for example, sending both voice and data over one link without having long data packets that would cause large variations in the delay of the voice samples. The unusual choice for the cell length (e.g., compared to the more natural choice of a power of 2) is an indication of just how political the design of ATM was. The 48-byte size for the payload was a compromise to resolve a deadlock between Europe, which wanted 32-byte cells, and the U.S., which wanted 64-byte cells. A brief overview of ATM is given by Siu and Jain (1995).

To send data over an ATM network, it needs to be mapped into a sequence of cells. This mapping is done with an ATM adaptation layer in a process called segmentation and reassembly. Several adaptation layers have been defined for different services, ranging from periodic voice samples to packet data. The main one used for packet data is **AAL5 (ATM Adaptation Layer 5)**.

An AAL5 frame is shown in Fig. 3-27. Instead of a header, it has a trailer that gives the length and has a 4-byte CRC for error detection. Naturally, the CRC is the same one used for PPP and IEEE 802 LANs like Ethernet. Wang and Crowcroft (1992) have shown that it is strong enough to detect nontraditional errors such as cell reordering. As well as a payload, the AAL5 frame has padding. This rounds out the overall length to be a multiple of 48 bytes so that the frame can be evenly divided into cells. No addresses are needed on the frame as the virtual circuit identifier carried in each cell will get it to the right destination.

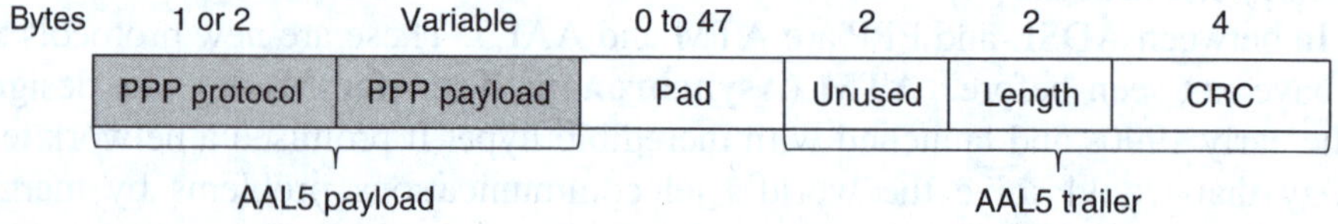

Figure 3-27. AAL5 frame carrying PPP data.

Now that we have described ATM, we have only to describe how PPP makes use of ATM in the case of ADSL. It is done with yet another standard called **PPPoA (PPP over ATM)**. This standard is not really a protocol (so it does not appear in Fig. 3-26) but more a specification of how to work with both PPP and AAL5 frames. It is described in RFC 2364 (Gross et al., 1998).

Only the PPP protocol and payload fields are placed in the AAL5 payload, as shown in Fig. 3-27. The protocol field indicates to the DSLAM at the far end whether the payload is an IP packet or a packet from another protocol such as LCP. The far end knows that the cells contain PPP information because an ATM virtual circuit is set up for this purpose.

Within the AAL5 frame, PPP framing is not needed as it would serve no purpose; ATM and AAL5 already provide the framing. More framing would be worthless. The PPP CRC is also not needed because AAL5 already includes the very same CRC. This error detection mechanism supplements the ADSL physical layer coding of a Reed-Solomon code for error correction and a 1-byte CRC for the detection of any remaining errors not otherwise caught. This scheme has a much more sophisticated error-recovery mechanism than when packets are sent over a SONET line because ADSL is a much noisier channel.

3.6 SUMMARY

The task of the data link layer is to convert the raw bit stream offered by the physical layer into a stream of frames for use by the network layer. The link layer can present this stream with varying levels of reliability, ranging from connectionless, unacknowledged service to reliable, connection-oriented service.

Various framing methods are used, including byte count, byte stuffing, and bit stuffing. Data link protocols can provide error control to detect or correct damaged frames and to retransmit lost frames. To prevent a fast sender from overrunning a slow receiver, the data link protocol can also provide flow control. The sliding window mechanism is widely used to integrate error control and flow control in a simple way. When the window size is 1 packet, the protocol is stop-and-wait.

Codes for error correction and detection add redundant information to messages by using a variety of mathematical techniques. Convolutional codes and Reed-Solomon codes are widely deployed for error correction, with low-density parity check codes increasing in popularity. The codes for error detection that are used in practice include cyclic redundancy checks and checksums. All these codes can be applied at the link layer, as well as at the physical layer and higher layers.

We examined a series of protocols that provide a reliable link layer using acknowledgements and retransmissions, or ARQ (Automatic Repeat reQuest), under more realistic assumptions. Starting from an error-free environment in which the receiver can handle any frame sent to it, we introduced flow control, followed by error control with sequence numbers and the stop-and-wait algorithm. Then we used the sliding window algorithm to allow bidirectional communication and introduce the concept of piggybacking. The last two protocols pipeline the transmission of multiple frames to prevent the sender from blocking on a link with a long propagation delay. The receiver can either discard all frames other than the next one in sequence, or buffer out-of-order frames and send negative acknowledgements for greater bandwidth efficiency. The former strategy is a go-back-n protocol, and the latter strategy is a selective repeat protocol.

The Internet uses PPP as the main data link protocol over point-to-point lines. It provides a connectionless unacknowledged service, using flag bytes to delimit frames and a CRC for error detection. It is used to carry packets across a range of links, including SONET links in wide-area networks and ADSL links for the home.

PROBLEMS

1. An upper-layer packet is split into 10 frames, each of which has an 80% chance of arriving undamaged. If no error control is done by the data link protocol, how many times must the message be sent on average to get the entire thing through?

2. The following character encoding is used in a data link protocol:
A: 01000111 B: 11100011 FLAG: 01111110 ESC: 11100000
Show the bit sequence transmitted (in binary) for the four-character frame A B ESC FLAG when each of the following framing methods is used:
(a) Byte count.
(b) Flag bytes with byte stuffing.
(c) Starting and ending flag bytes with bit stuffing.
3. The following data fragment occurs in the middle of a data stream for which the byte-stuffing algorithm described in the text is used: A B ESC C ESC FLAG FLAG D. What is the output after stuffing?
4. What is the maximum overhead in byte-stuffing algorithm?
5. One of your classmates, Scrooge, has pointed out that it is wasteful to end each frame with a flag byte and then begin the next one with a second flag byte. One flag byte could do the job as well, and a byte saved is a byte earned. Do you agree?
6. A bit string, 0111101111101111110, needs to be transmitted at the data link layer. What is the string actually transmitted after bit stuffing?
7. Can you think of any circumstances under which an open-loop protocol (e.g., a Hamming code) might be preferable to the feedback-type protocols discussed throughout this chapter?
8. To provide more reliability than a single parity bit can give, an error-detecting coding scheme uses one parity bit for checking all the odd-numbered bits and a second parity bit for all the even-numbered bits. What is the Hamming distance of this code?
9. Sixteen-bit messages are transmitted using a Hamming code. How many check bits are needed to ensure that the receiver can detect and correct single-bit errors? Show the bit pattern transmitted for the message 1101001100110101. Assume that even parity is used in the Hamming code.
10. A 12-bit Hamming code whose hexadecimal value is 0xE4F arrives at a receiver. What was the original value in hexadecimal? Assume that not more than 1 bit is in error.
11. One way of detecting errors is to transmit data as a block of n rows of k bits per row and add parity bits to each row and each column. The bitin the lower-right corner is a parity bit that checks its row and its column. Will this scheme detect all single errors? Double errors? Triple errors? Show that this scheme cannot detect some four-bit errors.
12. Suppose that data are transmitted in blocks of sizes 1000 bits. What is the maximum error rate under which error detection and retransmission mechanism (1 parity bit per block) is better than using Hamming code? Assume that bit errors are independent of one another and no bit error occurs during retransmission.
13. A block of bits with n rows and k columns uses horizontal and vertical parity bits for error detection. Suppose that exactly 4 bits are inverted due to transmission errors. Derive an expression for the probability that the error will be undetected.

14. Using the convolutional coder of Fig. 3-7, what is the output sequence when the input sequence is 10101010 (left to right) and the internal state is initially all zero?

15. Suppose that a message 1001 1100 1010 0011 is transmitted using Internet Checksum (4-bit word). What is the value of the checksum?

16. What is the remainder obtained by dividing $x^7 + x^5 + 1$ by the generator polynomial $x^3 + 1$?

17. A bit stream 10011101 is transmitted using the standard CRC method described in the text. The generator polynomial is $x^3 + 1$. Show the actual bit string transmitted. Suppose that the third bit from the left is inverted during transmission. Show that this error is detected at the receiver's end. Give an example of bit errors in the bit string transmitted that will not be detected by the receiver.

18. A 1024-bit message is sent that contains 992 data bits and 32 CRC bits. CRC is computed using the IEEE 802 standardized, 32-degree CRC polynomial. For each of the following, explain whether the errors during message transmission will be detected by the receiver:
(a) There was a single-bit error.
(b) There were two isolated bit errors.
(c) There were 18 isolated bit errors.
(d) There were 47 isolated bit errors.
(e) There was a 24-bit long burst error.
(f) There was a 35-bit long burst error.

19. In the discussion of ARQ protocol in Section 3.3.3, a scenario was outlined that resulted in the receiver accepting two copies of the same frame due to a loss of acknowledgement frame. Is it possible that a receiver may accept multiple copies of the same frame when none of the frames (message or acknowledgement) are lost?

20. A channel has a bit rate of 4 kbps and a propagation delay of 20 msec. For what range of frame sizes does stop-and-wait give an efficiency of at least 50%?

21. In protocol 3, is it possible for the sender to start the timer when it is already running? If so, how might this occur? If not, why is it impossible?

22. A 3000-km-long T1 trunk is used to transmit 64-byte frames using protocol 5. If the propagation speed is 6 μsec/km, how many bits should the sequence numbers be?

23. Imagine a sliding window protocol using so many bits for sequence numbers that wraparound never occurs. What relations must hold among the four window edges and the window size, which is constant and the same for both the sender and the receiver?

24. If the procedure *between* in protocol 5 checked for the condition $a \le b \le c$ instead of the condition $a \le b < c$, would that have any effect on the protocol's correctness or efficiency? Explain your answer.

25. In protocol 6, when a data frame arrives, a check is made to see if the sequence number differs from the one expected and *no_nak* is true. If both conditions hold, a NAK is sent. Otherwise, the auxiliary timer is started. Suppose that the else clause were omitted. Would this change affect the protocol's correctness?

26. Suppose that the three-statement while loop near the end of protocol 6 was removed from the code. Would this affect the correctness of the protocol or just the performance? Explain your answer.

27. The distance from earth to a distant planet is approximately 9×10^{10} m. What is the channel utilization if a stop-and-wait protocol is used for frame transmission on a 64 Mbps point-to-point link? Assume that the frame size is 32 KB and the speed of light is 3×10^8 m/s.

28. In the previous problem, suppose a sliding window protocol is used instead. For what send window size will the link utilization be 100%? You may ignore the protocol processing times at the sender and the receiver.

29. In protocol 6, the code for *frame_arrival* has a section used for NAKs. This section is invoked if the incoming frame is a NAK and another condition is met. Give a scenario where the presence of this other condition is essential.

30. Consider the operation of protocol 6 over a 1-Mbps perfect (i.e., error-free) line. The maximum frame size is 1000 bits. New packets are generated 1 second apart. The timeout interval is 10 msec. If the special acknowledgement timer were eliminated, unnecessary timeouts would occur. How many times would the average message be transmitted?

31. In protocol 6, $MAX\_SEQ = 2^n - 1$. While this condition is obviously desirable to make efficient use of header bits, we have not demonstrated that it is essential. Does the protocol work correctly for $MAX\_SEQ = 4$, for example?

32. Frames of 1000 bits are sent over a 1-Mbps channel using a geostationary satellite whose propagation time from the earth is 270 msec. Acknowledgements are always piggybacked onto data frames. The headers are very short. Three-bit sequence numbers are used. What is the maximum achievable channel utilization for

(a) Stop-and-wait?
(b) Protocol 5?
(c) Protocol 6?

33. Compute the fraction of the bandwidth that is wasted on overhead (headers and retransmissions) for protocol 6 on a heavily loaded 50-kbps satellite channel with data frames consisting of 40 header and 3960 data bits. Assume that the signal propagation time from the earth to the satellite is 270 msec. ACK frames never occur. NAK frames are 40 bits. The error rate for data frames is 1%, and the error rate for NAK frames is negligible. The sequence numbers are 8 bits.

34. Consider an error-free 64-kbps satellite channel used to send 512-byte data frames in one direction, with very short acknowledgements coming back the other way. What is the maximum throughput for window sizes of 1, 7, 15, and 127? The earth-satellite propagation time is 270 msec.

35. A 100-km-long cable runs at the T1 data rate. The propagation speed in the cable is 2/3 the speed of light in vacuum. How many bits fit in the cable?

36. Give at least one reason why PPP uses byte stuffing instead of bit stuffing to prevent accidental flag bytes within the payload from causing confusion.

37. What is the minimum overhead to send an IP packet using PPP? Count only the overhead introduced by PPP itself, not the IP header overhead. What is the maximum overhead?

38. A 100-byte IP packet is transmitted over a local loop using ADSL protocol stack. How many ATM cells will be transmitted? Briefly describe their contents.

39. The goal of this lab exercise is to implement an error-detection mechanism using the standard CRC algorithm described in the text. Write two programs, *generator* and *verifier*. The *generator* program reads from standard input a line of ASCII text containing an n-bit message consisting of a string of 0s and 1s. The second line is the k-bit polynomial, also in ASCII. It outputs to standard output a line of ASCII text with $n + k$ 0s and 1s representing the message to be transmitted. Then it outputs the polynomial, just as it read it in. The verifier program reads in the output of the generator program and outputs a message indicating whether it is correct or not. Finally, write a program, *alter*, that inverts 1 bit on the first line depending on its argument (the bit number counting the leftmost bit as 1) but copies the rest of the two lines correctly. By typing

```
generator <file | verifier
```

you should see that the message is correct, but by typing

```
generator <file | alter arg | verifier
```

you should get the error message.

4

THE MEDIUM ACCESS CONTROL SUBLAYER

Network links can be divided into two categories: those using point-to-point connections and those using broadcast channels. We studied point-to-point links in Chap. 2; this chapter deals with broadcast links and their protocols.

In any broadcast network, the key issue is how to determine who gets to use the channel when there is competition for it. To make this point, consider a conference call in which six people, on six different telephones, are all connected so that each one can hear and talk to all the others. It is very likely that when one of them stops speaking, two or more will start talking at once, leading to chaos. In a face-to-face meeting, chaos is avoided by external means. For example, at a meeting, people raise their hands to request permission to speak. When only a single channel is available, it is much harder to determine who should go next. Many protocols for solving the problem are known. They form the contents of this chapter. In the literature, broadcast channels are sometimes referred to as **multiaccess channels** or **random access channels**.

The protocols used to determine who goes next on a multiaccess channel belong to a sublayer of the data link layer called the **MAC** (**Medium Access Control**) sublayer. The MAC sublayer is especially important in LANs, particularly wireless ones because wireless is naturally a broadcast channel. WANs, in contrast, use point-to-point links, except for satellite networks. Because multiaccess channels and LANs are so closely related, in this chapter we will discuss LANs in general, including a few issues that are not strictly part of the MAC sublayer, but the main subject here will be control of the channel.

Technically, the MAC sublayer is the bottom part of the data link layer, so logically we should have studied it before examining all the point-to-point protocols in Chap. 3. Nevertheless, for most people, it is easier to understand protocols involving multiple parties after two-party protocols are well understood. For that reason we have deviated slightly from a strict bottom-up order of presentation.

4.1 THE CHANNEL ALLOCATION PROBLEM

The central theme of this chapter is how to allocate a single broadcast channel among competing users. The channel might be a portion of the wireless spectrum in a geographic region, or a single wire or optical fiber to which multiple nodes are connected. It does not matter. In both cases, the channel connects each user to all other users and any user who makes full use of the channel interferes with other users who also wish to use the channel.

We will first look at the shortcomings of static allocation schemes for bursty traffic. Then, we will lay out the key assumptions used to model the dynamic schemes that we examine in the following sections.

4.1.1 Static Channel Allocation

The traditional way of allocating a single channel, such as a telephone trunk, among multiple competing users is to chop up its capacity by using one of the multiplexing schemes we described in Sec. 2.5, such as FDM (Frequency Division Multiplexing). If there are N users, the bandwidth is divided into N equal-sized portions, with each user being assigned one portion. Since each user has a private frequency band, there is now no interference among users. When there is only a small and constant number of users, each of which has a steady stream or a heavy load of traffic, this division is a simple and efficient allocation mechanism. A wireless example is FM radio stations. Each station gets a portion of the FM band and uses it most of the time to broadcast its signal.

However, when the number of senders is large and varying or the traffic is bursty, FDM presents some problems. If the spectrum is cut up into N regions and fewer than N users are currently interested in communicating, a large piece of valuable spectrum will be wasted. And if more than N users want to communicate, some of them will be denied permission for lack of bandwidth, even if some of the users who have been assigned a frequency band hardly ever transmit or receive anything.

Even assuming that the number of users could somehow be held constant at N, dividing the single available channel into some number of static subchannels is inherently inefficient. The basic problem is that when some users are quiescent, their bandwidth is simply lost. They are not using it, and no one else is allowed to use it either. A static allocation is a poor fit to most computer systems, in which data traffic is extremely bursty, often with peak traffic to mean traffic ratios of 1000:1. Consequently, most of the channels will be idle most of the time.

The poor performance of static FDM can easily be seen with a simple queueing theory calculation. Let us start by finding the mean time delay, T, to send a frame onto a channel of capacity C bps. We assume that the frames arrive randomly with an average arrival rate of λ frames/sec, and that the frames vary in length with an average length of $1/\mu$ bits. With these parameters, the service rate of the channel is μC frames/sec. A standard queueing theory result is

$$T = \frac{1}{\mu C - \lambda}$$

(For the curious, this result is for an "M/M/1" queue. It requires that the randomness of the times between frame arrivals and the frame lengths follow an exponential distribution, or equivalently be the result of a Poisson process.)

In our example, if C is 100 Mbps, the mean frame length, $1/\mu$, is 10,000 bits, and the frame arrival rate, λ, is 5000 frames/sec, then $T = 200$ μsec. Note that if we ignored the queueing delay and just asked how long it takes to send a 10,000-bit frame on a 100-Mbps network, we would get the (incorrect) answer of 100 μsec. That result only holds when there is no contention for the channel.

Now let us divide the single channel into N independent subchannels, each with capacity C/N bps. The mean input rate on each of the subchannels will now be λ/N. Recomputing T, we get

$$T_N = \frac{1}{\mu(C/N) - (\lambda/N)} = \frac{N}{\mu C - \lambda} = NT \tag{4-1}$$

The mean delay for the divided channel is N times worse than if all the frames were somehow magically arranged orderly in a big central queue. This same result says that a bank lobby full of ATM machines is better off having a single queue feeding all the machines than a separate queue in front of each machine.

Precisely the same arguments that apply to FDM also apply to other ways of statically dividing the channel. If we were to use time division multiplexing (TDM) and allocate each user every Nth time slot, if a user does not use the allocated slot, it would just lie fallow. The same would hold if we split up the networks physically. Using our previous example again, if we were to replace the 100-Mbps network with 10 networks of 10 Mbps each and statically allocate each user to one of them, the mean delay would jump from 200 μsec to 2 msec.

Since none of the traditional static channel allocation methods work well at all with bursty traffic, we will now explore dynamic methods.

4.1.2 Assumptions for Dynamic Channel Allocation

Before we get to the first of the many channel allocation methods in this chapter, it is worthwhile to carefully formulate the allocation problem. Underlying all the work done in this area are the following five key assumptions:

1. **Independent Traffic**. The model consists of *N* independent **stations** (e.g., computers, telephones), each with a program or user that generates frames for transmission. The expected number of frames generated in an interval of length Δt is $\lambda \Delta t$, where λ is a constant (the arrival rate of new frames). Once a frame has been generated, the station is blocked and does nothing until the frame has been successfully transmitted.

2. **Single Channel**. A single channel is available for all communication. All stations can transmit on it and all can receive from it. The stations are assumed to be equally capable, though protocols may assign them different roles (e.g., priorities).

3. **Observable Collisions**. If two frames are transmitted simultaneously, they overlap in time and the resulting signal is garbled. This event is called a **collision**. All stations can detect that a collision has occurred. A collided frame must be transmitted again later. No errors other than those generated by collisions occur.

4. **Continuous or Slotted Time**. Time may be assumed continuous, in which case frame transmission can begin at any instant. Alternatively, time may be slotted or divided into discrete intervals (called slots). Frame transmissions must then begin at the start of a slot. A slot may contain 0, 1, or more frames, corresponding to an idle slot, a successful transmission, or a collision, respectively.

5. **Carrier Sense or No Carrier Sense**. With the carrier sense assumption, stations can tell if the channel is in use before trying to use it. No station will attempt to use the channel while it is sensed as busy. If there is no carrier sense, stations cannot sense the channel before trying to use it. They just go ahead and transmit. Only later can they determine whether the transmission was successful.

Some discussion of these assumptions is in order. The first one says that frame arrivals are independent, both across stations and at a particular station, and that frames are generated unpredictably but at a constant rate. Actually, this assumption is not a particularly good model of network traffic, as it is well known that packets come in bursts over a range of time scales (Paxson and Floyd, 1995; and Leland et al., 1994). Nonetheless, **Poisson models**, as they are frequently called, are useful because they are mathematically tractable. They help us analyze protocols to understand roughly how performance changes over an operating range and how it compares with other designs.

The single-channel assumption is the heart of the model. No external ways to communicate exist. Stations cannot raise their hands to request that the teacher call on them, so we will have to come up with better solutions.

The remaining three assumptions depend on the engineering of the system, and we will say which assumptions hold when we examine a particular protocol.

The collision assumption is basic. Stations need some way to detect collisions if they are to retransmit frames rather than let them be lost. For wired channels, node hardware can be designed to detect collisions when they occur. The stations can then terminate their transmissions prematurely to avoid wasting capacity. This detection is much harder for wireless channels, so collisions are usually inferred after the fact by the lack of an expected acknowledgement frame. It is also possible for some frames involved in a collision to be successfully received, depending on the details of the signals and the receiving hardware. However, this situation is not the common case, so we will assume that all frames involved in a collision are lost. We will also see protocols that are designed to prevent collisions from occurring in the first place.

The reason for the two alternative assumptions about time is that slotted time can be used to improve performance. However, it requires the stations to follow a master clock or synchronize their actions with each other to divide time into discrete intervals. Hence, it is not always available. We will discuss and analyze systems with both kinds of time. For a given system, only one of them holds.

Similarly, a network may have carrier sensing or not have it. Wired networks will generally have carrier sense. Wireless networks cannot always use it effectively because not every station may be within radio range of every other station. Similarly, carrier sense will not be available in other settings in which a station cannot communicate directly with other stations, for example a cable modem in which stations must communicate via the cable headend. Note that the word "carrier" in this sense refers to a signal on the channel and has nothing to do with the common carriers (e.g., telephone companies) that date back to the days of the Pony Express.

To avoid any misunderstanding, it is worth noting that no multiaccess protocol guarantees reliable delivery. Even in the absence of collisions, the receiver may have copied some of the frame incorrectly for various reasons. Other parts of the link layer or higher layers provide reliability.

4.2 MULTIPLE ACCESS PROTOCOLS

Many algorithms for allocating a multiple access channel are known. In the following sections, we will study a small sample of the more interesting ones and give some examples of how they are commonly used in practice.

4.2.1 ALOHA

The story of our first MAC starts out in pristine Hawaii in the early 1970s. In this case, "pristine" can be interpreted as "not having a working telephone system." This did not make life more pleasant for researcher Norman Abramson and his colleagues at the University of Hawaii who were trying to connect users on remote islands to the main computer in Honolulu. Stringing their own cables under the Pacific Ocean was not in the cards, so they looked for a different solution.

The one they found used short-range radios, with each user terminal sharing the same upstream frequency to send frames to the central computer. It included a simple and elegant method to solve the channel allocation problem. Their work has been extended by many researchers since then (Schwartz and Abramson, 2009). Although Abramson's work, called the ALOHA system, used ground-based radio broadcasting, the basic idea is applicable to any system in which uncoordinated users are competing for the use of a single shared channel.

We will discuss two versions of ALOHA here: pure and slotted. They differ with respect to whether time is continuous, as in the pure version, or divided into discrete slots into which all frames must fit.

Pure ALOHA

The basic idea of an ALOHA system is simple: let users transmit whenever they have data to be sent. There will be collisions, of course, and the colliding frames will be damaged. Senders need some way to find out if this is the case. In the ALOHA system, after each station has sent its frame to the central computer, this computer rebroadcasts the frame to all of the stations. A sending station can thus listen for the broadcast from the hub to see if its frame has gotten through. In other systems, such as wired LANs, the sender might be able to listen for collisions while transmitting.

If the frame was destroyed, the sender just waits a random amount of time and sends it again. The waiting time must be random or the same frames will collide over and over, in lockstep. Systems in which multiple users share a common channel in a way that can lead to conflicts are known as **contention** systems.

A sketch of frame generation in an ALOHA system is given in Fig. 4-1. We have made the frames all the same length because the throughput of ALOHA systems is maximized by having a uniform frame size rather than by allowing variable-length frames.

Whenever two frames try to occupy the channel at the same time, there will be a collision (as seen in Fig. 4-1) and both will be garbled. If the first bit of a new frame overlaps with just the last bit of a frame that has almost finished, both frames will be totally destroyed (i.e., have incorrect checksums) and both will have to be retransmitted later. The checksum does not (and should not) distinguish between a total loss and a near miss. Bad is bad.

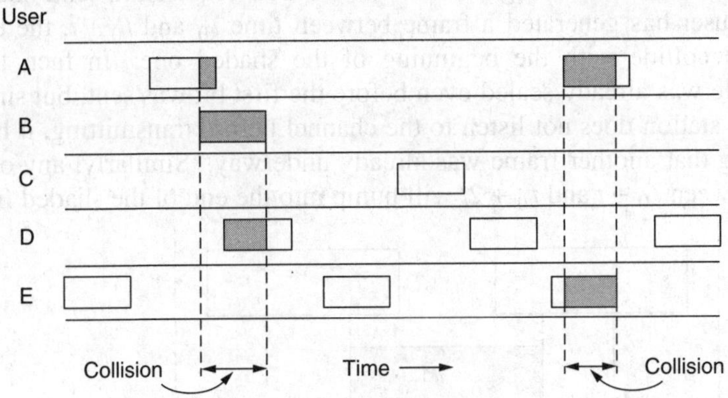

Figure 4-1. In pure ALOHA, frames are transmitted at completely arbitrary times.

An interesting question is: what is the efficiency of an ALOHA channel? In other words, what fraction of all transmitted frames escape collisions under these chaotic circumstances? Let us first consider an infinite collection of users typing at their terminals (stations). A user is always in one of two states: typing or waiting. Initially, all users are in the typing state. When a line is finished, the user stops typing, waiting for a response. The station then transmits a frame containing the line over the shared channel to the central computer and checks the channel to see if it was successful. If so, the user sees the reply and goes back to typing. If not, the user continues to wait while the station retransmits the frame over and over until it has been successfully sent.

Let the "frame time" denote the amount of time needed to transmit the standard, fixed-length frame (i.e., the frame length divided by the bit rate). At this point, we assume that the new frames generated by the stations are well modeled by a Poisson distribution with a mean of N frames per frame time. (The infinite-population assumption is needed to ensure that N does not decrease as users become blocked.) If $N > 1$, the user community is generating frames at a higher rate than the channel can handle, and nearly every frame will suffer a collision. For reasonable throughput, we would expect $0 < N < 1$.

In addition to the new frames, the stations also generate retransmissions of frames that previously suffered collisions. Let us further assume that the old and new frames combined are well modeled by a Poisson distribution, with mean of G frames per frame time. Clearly, $G \geq N$. At low load (i.e., $N \approx 0$), there will be few collisions, hence few retransmissions, so $G \approx N$. At high load, there will be many collisions, so $G > N$. Under all loads, the throughput, S, is just the offered load, G, times the probability, P_0, of a transmission succeeding—that is, $S = GP_0$, where P_0 is the probability that a frame does not suffer a collision.

A frame will not suffer a collision if no other frames are sent within one frame time of its start, as shown in Fig. 4-2. Under what conditions will the shaded frame arrive undamaged? Let t be the time required to send one frame. If any other user has generated a frame between time t_0 and $t_0 + t$, the end of that frame will collide with the beginning of the shaded one. In fact, the shaded frame's fate was already sealed even before the first bit was sent, but since in pure ALOHA a station does not listen to the channel before transmitting, it has no way of knowing that another frame was already underway. Similarly, any other frame started between $t_0 + t$ and $t_0 + 2t$ will bump into the end of the shaded frame.

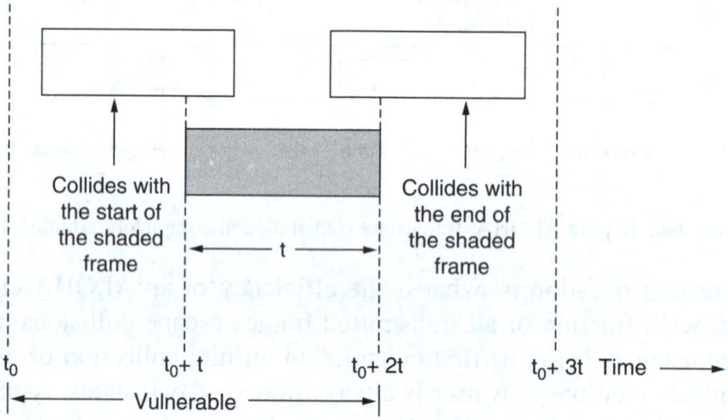

Figure 4-2. Vulnerable period for the shaded frame.

The probability that k frames are generated during a given frame time, in which G frames are expected, is given by the Poisson distribution

$$\Pr[k] = \frac{G^k e^{-G}}{k!} \tag{4-2}$$

so the probability of zero frames is just e^{-G}. In an interval two frame times long, the mean number of frames generated is $2G$. The probability of no frames being initiated during the entire vulnerable period is thus given by $P_0 = e^{-2G}$. Using $S = GP_0$, we get

$$S = Ge^{-2G}$$

The relation between the offered traffic and the throughput is shown in Fig. 4-3. The maximum throughput occurs at $G = 0.5$, with $S = 1/2e$, which is about 0.184. In other words, the best we can hope for is a channel utilization of 18%. This result is not very encouraging, but with everyone transmitting at will, we could hardly have expected a 100% success rate.

Slotted ALOHA

Soon after ALOHA came onto the scene, Roberts (1972) published a method for doubling the capacity of an ALOHA system. His proposal was to divide time into discrete intervals called **slots**, each interval corresponding to one frame. This

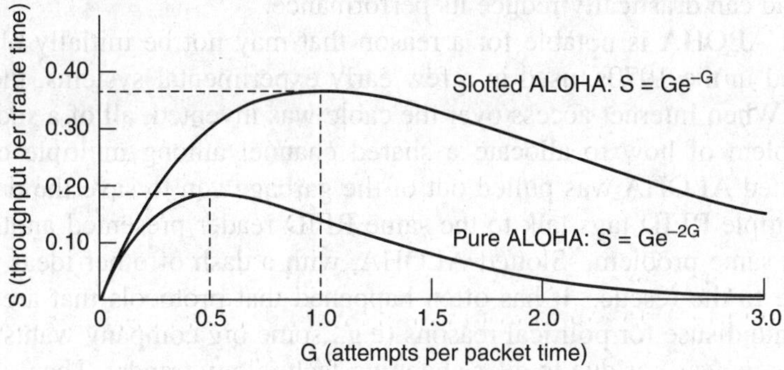

Figure 4-3. Throughput versus offered traffic for ALOHA systems.

approach requires the users to agree on slot boundaries. One way to achieve synchronization would be to have one special station emit a pip at the start of each interval, like a clock.

In Roberts' method, which has come to be known as **slotted ALOHA**—in contrast to Abramson's **pure ALOHA**—a station is not permitted to send whenever the user types a line. Instead, it is required to wait for the beginning of the next slot. Thus, the continuous time ALOHA is turned into a discrete time one. This halves the vulnerable period. To see this, look at Fig. 4-3 and imagine the collisions that are now possible. The probability of no other traffic during the same slot as our test frame is then e^{-G}, which leads to

$$S = Ge^{-G} \tag{4-3}$$

As you can see from Fig. 4-3, slotted ALOHA peaks at $G = 1$, with a throughput of $S = 1/e$ or about 0.368, twice that of pure ALOHA. If the system is operating at $G = 1$, the probability of an empty slot is 0.368 (from Eq. 4-2). The best we can hope for using slotted ALOHA is 37% of the slots empty, 37% successes, and 26% collisions. Operating at higher values of G reduces the number of empties but increases the number of collisions exponentially. To see how this rapid growth of collisions with G comes about, consider the transmission of a test frame. The probability that it will avoid a collision is e^{-G}, which is the probability that all the other stations are silent in that slot. The probability of a collision is then just $1 - e^{-G}$. The probability of a transmission requiring exactly k attempts (i.e., $k - 1$ collisions followed by one success) is

$$P_k = e^{-G}(1 - e^{-G})^{k-1}$$

The expected number of transmissions, E, per line typed at a terminal is then

$$E = \sum_{k=1}^{\infty} kP_k = \sum_{k=1}^{\infty} ke^{-G}(1 - e^{-G})^{k-1} = e^G$$

As a result of the exponential dependence of E upon G, small increases in the channel load can drastically reduce its performance.

Slotted ALOHA is notable for a reason that may not be initially obvious. It was devised in the 1970s, used in a few early experimental systems, then almost forgotten. When Internet access over the cable was invented, all of a sudden there was a problem of how to allocate a shared channel among multiple competing users. Slotted ALOHA was pulled out of the garbage can to save the day. Later, having multiple RFID tags talk to the same RFID reader presented another variation on the same problem. Slotted ALOHA, with a dash of other ideas mixed in, again came to the rescue. It has often happened that protocols that are perfectly valid fall into disuse for political reasons (e.g., some big company wants everyone to do things its way) or due to ever-changing technology trends. Then, years later some clever person realizes that a long-discarded protocol solves his current problem. For this reason, in this chapter we will study a number of elegant protocols that are not currently in widespread use but might easily be used in future applications, provided that enough network designers are aware of them. Of course, we will also study many protocols that are in current use as well.

4.2.2 Carrier Sense Multiple Access Protocols

With slotted ALOHA, the best channel utilization that can be achieved is $1/e$. This low result is hardly surprising, since with stations transmitting at will, without knowing what the other stations are doing there are bound to be many collisions. In LANs, however, it is often possible for stations to detect what other stations are doing, and thus adapt their behavior accordingly. These networks can achieve a much better utilization than $1/e$. In this section, we will discuss some protocols for improving performance.

Protocols in which stations listen for a carrier (i.e., a transmission) and act accordingly are called **carrier sense protocols**. A number of them have been proposed, and they were long ago analyzed in detail. For example, see Kleinrock and Tobagi (1975). Below we will look at several versions of carrier sense protocols.

Persistent and Nonpersistent CSMA

The first carrier sense protocol that we will study here is called **1-persistent CSMA (Carrier Sense Multiple Access)**. That is a bit of a mouthful for the simplest CSMA scheme. When a station has data to send, it first listens to the channel to see if anyone else is transmitting at that moment. If the channel is idle, the stations sends its data. Otherwise, if the channel is busy, the station just waits until it becomes idle. Then the station transmits a frame. If a collision occurs, the station waits a random amount of time and starts all over again. The protocol is called 1-persistent because the station transmits with a probability of 1 when it finds the channel idle.

You might expect that this scheme avoids collisions except for the rare case of simultaneous sends, but it in fact it does not. If two stations become ready in the middle of a third station's transmission, both will wait politely until the transmission ends, and then both will begin transmitting exactly simultaneously, resulting in a collision. If they were not so impatient, there would be fewer collisions.

More subtly, the propagation delay has an important effect on collisions. There is a chance that just after a station begins sending, another station will become ready to send and sense the channel. If the first station's signal has not yet reached the second one, the latter will sense an idle channel and will also begin sending, resulting in a collision. This chance depends on the number of frames that fit on the channel, or the **bandwidth-delay product** of the channel. If only a tiny fraction of a frame fits on the channel, which is the case in most LANs since the propagation delay is small, the chance of a collision happening is small. The larger the bandwidth-delay product, the more important this effect becomes, and the worse the performance of the protocol.

Even so, this protocol has better performance than pure ALOHA because both stations have the decency to desist from interfering with the third station's frame. Exactly the same holds for slotted ALOHA.

A second carrier sense protocol is **nonpersistent CSMA**. In this protocol, a conscious attempt is made to be less greedy than in the previous one. As before, a station senses the channel when it wants to send a frame, and if no one else is sending, the station begins doing so itself. However, if the channel is already in use, the station does not continually sense it for the purpose of seizing it immediately upon detecting the end of the previous transmission. Instead, it waits a random period of time and then repeats the algorithm. Consequently, this algorithm leads to better channel utilization but longer delays than 1-persistent CSMA.

The last protocol is **p-persistent CSMA**. It applies to slotted channels and works as follows. When a station becomes ready to send, it senses the channel. If it is idle, it transmits with a probability p. With a probability $q = 1 - p$, it defers until the next slot. If that slot is also idle, it either transmits or defers again, with probabilities p and q. This process is repeated until either the frame has been transmitted or another station has begun transmitting. In the latter case, the unlucky station acts as if there had been a collision (i.e., it waits a random time and starts again). If the station initially senses that the channel is busy, it waits until the next slot and applies the above algorithm. IEEE 802.11 uses a refinement of p-persistent CSMA that we will discuss in Sec. 4.4.

Figure 4-4 shows the computed throughput versus offered traffic for all three protocols, as well as for pure and slotted ALOHA.

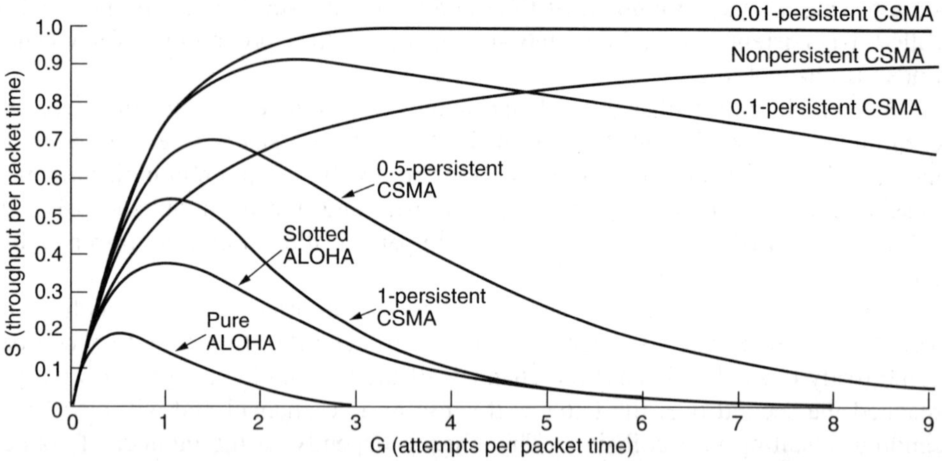

Figure 4-4. Comparison of the channel utilization versus load for various random access protocols.

CSMA with Collision Detection

Persistent and nonpersistent CSMA protocols are definitely an improvement over ALOHA because they ensure that no station begins to transmit while the channel is busy. However, if two stations sense the channel to be idle and begin transmitting simultaneously, their signals will still collide. Another improvement is for the stations to quickly detect the collision and abruptly stop transmitting, (rather than finishing them) since they are irretrievably garbled anyway. This strategy saves time and bandwidth.

This protocol, known as **CSMA/CD (CSMA with Collision Detection)**, is the basis of the classic Ethernet LAN, so it is worth devoting some time to looking at it in detail. It is important to realize that collision detection is an analog process. The station's hardware must listen to the channel while it is transmitting. If the signal it reads back is different from the signal it is putting out, it knows that a collision is occurring. The implications are that a received signal must not be tiny compared to the transmitted signal (which is difficult for wireless, as received signals may be 1,000,000 times weaker than transmitted signals) and that the modulation must be chosen to allow collisions to be detected (e.g., a collision of two 0-volt signals may well be impossible to detect).

CSMA/CD, as well as many other LAN protocols, uses the conceptual model of Fig. 4-5. At the point marked t_0, a station has finished transmitting its frame. Any other station having a frame to send may now attempt to do so. If two or more stations decide to transmit simultaneously, there will be a collision. If a station detects a collision, it aborts its transmission, waits a random period of time, and then tries again (assuming that no other station has started transmitting in the meantime). Therefore, our model for CSMA/CD will consist of alternating contention and transmission periods, with idle periods occurring when all stations are quiet (e.g., for lack of work).

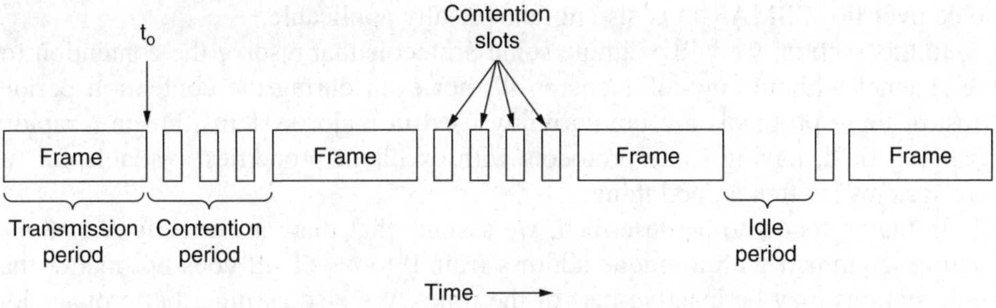

Figure 4-5. CSMA/CD can be in contention, transmission, or idle state.

Now let us look at the details of the contention algorithm. Suppose that two stations both begin transmitting at exactly time t_0. How long will it take them to realize that they have collided? The answer is vital to determining the length of the contention period and hence what the delay and throughput will be.

The minimum time to detect the collision is just the time it takes the signal to propagate from one station to the other. Based on this information, you might think that a station that has not heard a collision for a time equal to the full cable propagation time after starting its transmission can be sure it has seized the cable. By "seized," we mean that all other stations know it is transmitting and will not interfere. This conclusion is wrong.

Consider the following worst-case scenario. Let the time for a signal to propagate between the two farthest stations be τ. At t_0, one station begins transmitting. At $t_0 + \tau - \varepsilon$, an instant before the signal arrives at the most distant station, that station also begins transmitting. Of course, it detects the collision almost instantly and stops, but the little noise burst caused by the collision does not get back to the original station until time $2\tau - \varepsilon$. In other words, in the worst case a station cannot be sure that it has seized the channel until it has transmitted for 2τ without hearing a collision.

With this understanding, we can think of CSMA/CD contention as a slotted ALOHA system with a slot width of 2τ. On a 1-km long coaxial cable, $\tau \approx 5$ μsec. The difference for CSMA/CD compared to slotted ALOHA is that slots in which only one station transmits (i.e., in which the channel is seized) are followed by the rest of a frame. This difference will greatly improve performance if the frame time is much longer than the propagation time.

4.2.3 Collision-Free Protocols

Although collisions do not occur with CSMA/CD once a station has unambiguously captured the channel, they can still occur during the contention period. These collisions adversely affect the system performance, especially when the bandwidth-delay product is large, such as when the cable is long (i.e., large τ) and the frames are short. Not only do collisions reduce bandwidth, but they make the time to send a frame variable, which is not a good fit for real-time traffic such as voice over IP. CSMA/CD is also not universally applicable.

In this section, we will examine some protocols that resolve the contention for the channel without any collisions at all, not even during the contention period. Most of these protocols are not currently used in major systems, but in a rapidly changing field, having some protocols with excellent properties available for future systems is often a good thing.

In the protocols to be described, we assume that there are exactly N stations, each programmed with a unique address from 0 to $N - 1$. It does not matter that some stations may be inactive part of the time. We also assume that propagation delay is negligible. The basic question remains: which station gets the channel after a successful transmission? We continue using the model of Fig. 4-5 with its discrete contention slots.

A Bit-Map Protocol

In our first collision-free protocol, the **basic bit-map method**, each contention period consists of exactly N slots. If station 0 has a frame to send, it transmits a 1 bit during the slot 0. No other station is allowed to transmit during this slot. Regardless of what station 0 does, station 1 gets the opportunity to transmit a 1 bit during slot 1, but only if it has a frame queued. In general, station j may announce that it has a frame to send by inserting a 1 bit into slot j. After all N slots have passed by, each station has complete knowledge of which stations wish to transmit. At that point, they begin transmitting frames in numerical order (see Fig. 4-6).

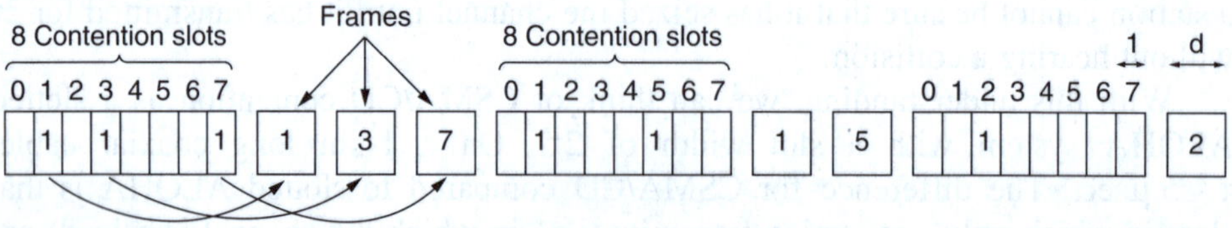

Figure 4-6. The basic bit-map protocol.

Since everyone agrees on who goes next, there will never be any collisions. After the last ready station has transmitted its frame, an event all stations can easily monitor, another N-bit contention period is begun. If a station becomes ready just after its bit slot has passed by, it is out of luck and must remain silent until every station has had a chance and the bit map has come around again.

Protocols like this in which the desire to transmit is broadcast before the actual transmission are called **reservation protocols** because they reserve channel ownership in advance and prevent collisions. Let us briefly analyze the performance of this protocol. For convenience, we will measure time in units of the contention bit slot, with data frames consisting of d time units.

Under conditions of low load, the bit map will simply be repeated over and over, for lack of data frames. Consider the situation from the point of view of a low-numbered station, such as 0 or 1. Typically, when it becomes ready to send, the "current" slot will be somewhere in the middle of the bit map. On average, the station will have to wait $N/2$ slots for the current scan to finish and another full N slots for the following scan to run to completion before it may begin transmitting.

The prospects for high-numbered stations are brighter. Generally, these will only have to wait half a scan ($N/2$ bit slots) before starting to transmit. High-numbered stations rarely have to wait for the next scan. Since low-numbered stations must wait on average $1.5N$ slots and high-numbered stations must wait on average $0.5N$ slots, the mean for all stations is N slots.

The channel efficiency at low load is easy to compute. The overhead per frame is N bits and the amount of data is d bits, for an efficiency of $d/(d+N)$.

At high load, when all the stations have something to send all the time, the N-bit contention period is prorated over N frames, yielding an overhead of only 1 bit per frame, or an efficiency of $d/(d+1)$. The mean delay for a frame is equal to the sum of the time it queues inside its station, plus an additional $(N-1)d+N$ once it gets to the head of its internal queue. This interval is how long it takes to wait for all other stations to have their turn sending a frame and another bitmap.

Token Passing

The essence of the bit-map protocol is that it lets every station transmit a frame in turn in a predefined order. Another way to accomplish the same thing is to pass a small message called a **token** from one station to the next in the same predefined order. The token represents permission to send. If a station has a frame queued for transmission when it receives the token, it can send that frame before it passes the token to the next station. If it has no queued frame, it simply passes the token.

In a **token ring** protocol, the topology of the network is used to define the order in which stations send. The stations are connected one to the next in a single ring. Passing the token to the next station then simply consists of receiving the token in from one direction and transmitting it out in the other direction, as seen in Fig. 4-7. Frames are also transmitted in the direction of the token. This way they will circulate around the ring and reach whichever station is the destination. However, to stop the frame circulating indefinitely (like the token), some station needs to remove it from the ring. This station may be either the one that originally sent the frame, after it has gone through a complete cycle, or the station that was the intended recipient of the frame.

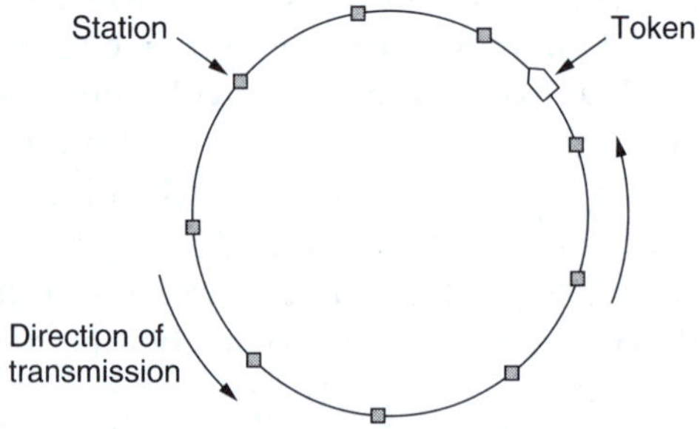

Figure 4-7. Token ring.

Note that we do not need a physical ring to implement token passing. The channel connecting the stations might instead be a single long bus. Each station then uses the bus to send the token to the next station in the predefined sequence. Possession of the token allows a station to use the bus to send one frame, as before. This protocol is called **token bus**.

The performance of token passing is similar to that of the bit-map protocol, though the contention slots and frames of one cycle are now intermingled. After sending a frame, each station must wait for all N stations (including itself) to send the token to their neighbors and the other $N - 1$ stations to send a frame, if they have one. A subtle difference is that, since all positions in the cycle are equivalent, there is no bias for low- or high-numbered stations. For token ring, each station is also sending the token only as far as its neighboring station before the protocol takes the next step. Each token does not need to propagate to all stations before the protocol advances to the next step.

Token rings have cropped up as MAC protocols with some consistency. An early token ring protocol (called "Token Ring" and standardized as IEEE 802.5) was popular in the 1980s as an alternative to classic Ethernet. In the 1990s, a much faster token ring called **FDDI** (**Fiber Distributed Data Interface**) was beaten out by switched Ethernet. In the 2000s, a token ring called **RPR** (**Resilient Packet Ring**) was defined as IEEE 802.17 to standardize the mix of metropolitan area rings in use by ISPs. We wonder what the 2010s will have to offer.

Binary Countdown

A problem with the basic bit-map protocol, and by extension token passing, is that the overhead is 1 bit per station, so it does not scale well to networks with thousands of stations. We can do better than that by using binary station addresses with a channel that combines transmissions. A station wanting to use the channel now broadcasts its address as a binary bit string, starting with the high-order bit. All addresses are assumed to be the same length. The bits in each address position from different stations are BOOLEAN ORed together by the channel when they are sent at the same time. We will call this protocol **binary countdown**. It was used in Datakit (Fraser, 1987). It implicitly assumes that the transmission delays are negligible so that all stations see asserted bits essentially instantaneously.

To avoid conflicts, an arbitration rule must be applied: as soon as a station sees that a high-order bit position that is 0 in its address has been overwritten with a 1, it gives up. For example, if stations 0010, 0100, 1001, and 1010 are all trying to get the channel, in the first bit time the stations transmit 0, 0, 1, and 1, respectively. These are ORed together to form a 1. Stations 0010 and 0100 see the 1 and know that a higher-numbered station is competing for the channel, so they give up for the current round. Stations 1001 and 1010 continue.

The next bit is 0, and both stations continue. The next bit is 1, so station 1001 gives up. The winner is station 1010 because it has the highest address. After winning the bidding, it may now transmit a frame, after which another bidding cycle starts. The protocol is illustrated in Fig. 4-8. It has the property that higher-numbered stations have a higher priority than lower-numbered stations, which may be either good or bad, depending on the context.

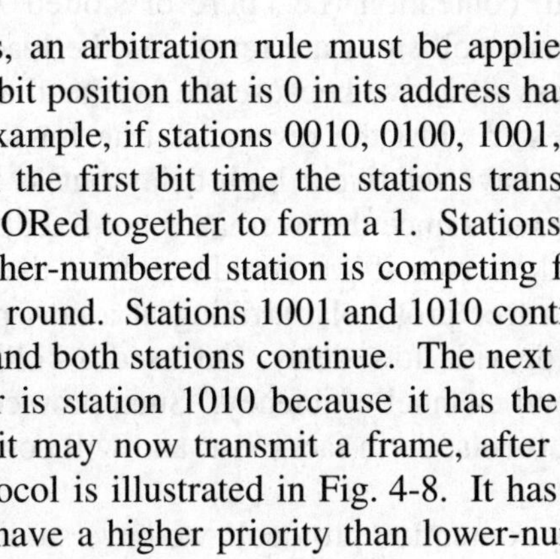

Figure 4-8. The binary countdown protocol. A dash indicates silence.

The channel efficiency of this method is $d/(d + \log_2 N)$. If, however, the frame format has been cleverly chosen so that the sender's address is the first field in the frame, even these $\log_2 N$ bits are not wasted, and the efficiency is 100%.

Binary countdown is an example of a simple, elegant, and efficient protocol that is waiting to be rediscovered. Hopefully, it will find a new home some day.

4.2.4 Limited-Contention Protocols

We have now considered two basic strategies for channel acquisition in a broadcast network: contention, as in CSMA, and collision-free protocols. Each strategy can be rated as to how well it does with respect to the two important performance measures, delay at low load and channel efficiency at high load. Under conditions of light load, contention (i.e., pure or slotted ALOHA) is preferable due to its low delay (since collisions are rare). As the load increases, contention becomes increasingly less attractive because the overhead associated with channel arbitration becomes greater. Just the reverse is true for the collision-free protocols. At low load, they have relatively high delay but as the load increases, the channel efficiency improves (since the overheads are fixed).

Obviously, it would be nice if we could combine the best properties of the contention and collision-free protocols, arriving at a new protocol that used contention at low load to provide low delay, but used a collision-free technique at high load to provide good channel efficiency. Such protocols, which we will call **limited-contention protocols**, do in fact exist, and will conclude our study of carrier sense networks.

Up to now, the only contention protocols we have studied have been symmetric. That is, each station attempts to acquire the channel with some probability, p, with all stations using the same p. Interestingly enough, the overall system performance can sometimes be improved by using a protocol that assigns different probabilities to different stations.

Before looking at the asymmetric protocols, let us quickly review the performance of the symmetric case. Suppose that k stations are contending for channel access. Each has a probability p of transmitting during each slot. The probability that some station successfully acquires the channel during a given slot is the probability that any one station transmits, with probability p, and all other $k-1$ stations defer, each with probability $1-p$. This value is $kp(1-p)^{k-1}$. To find the optimal value of p, we differentiate with respect to p, set the result to zero, and solve for p. Doing so, we find that the best value of p is $1/k$. Substituting $p = 1/k$, we get

$$\Pr[\text{success with optimal } p] = \left[\frac{k-1}{k}\right]^{k-1} \qquad (4\text{-}4)$$

This probability is plotted in Fig. 4-9. For small numbers of stations, the chances of success are good, but as soon as the number of stations reaches even five, the probability has dropped close to its asymptotic value of $1/e$.

From Fig. 4-9, it is fairly obvious that the probability of some station acquiring the channel can be increased only by decreasing the amount of competition. The limited-contention protocols do precisely that. They first divide the stations into (not necessarily disjoint) groups. Only the members of group 0 are permitted

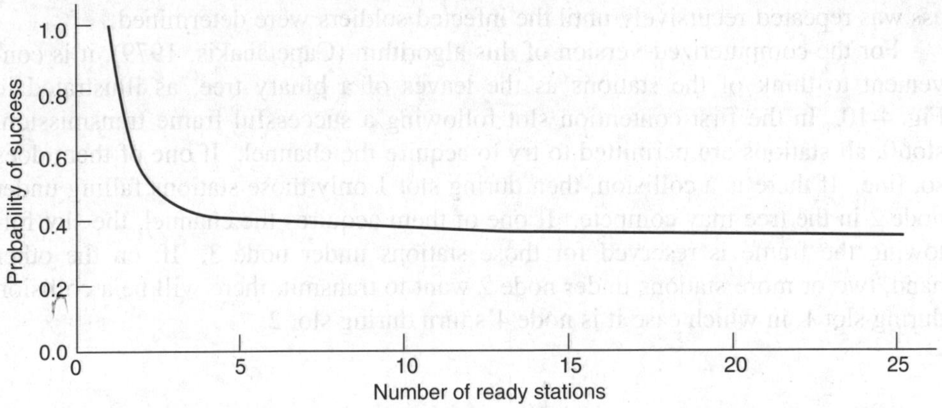

Figure 4-9. Acquisition probability for a symmetric contention channel.

to compete for slot 0. If one of them succeeds, it acquires the channel and transmits its frame. If the slot lies fallow or if there is a collision, the members of group 1 contend for slot 1, etc. By making an appropriate division of stations into groups, the amount of contention for each slot can be reduced, thus operating each slot near the left end of Fig. 4-9.

The trick is how to assign stations to slots. Before looking at the general case, let us consider some special cases. At one extreme, each group has but one member. Such an assignment guarantees that there will never be collisions because at most one station is contending for any given slot. We have seen such protocols before (e.g., binary countdown). The next special case is to assign two stations per group. The probability that both will try to transmit during a slot is p^2, which for a small p is negligible. As more and more stations are assigned to the same slot, the probability of a collision grows, but the length of the bit-map scan needed to give everyone a chance shrinks. The limiting case is a single group containing all stations (i.e., slotted ALOHA). What we need is a way to assign stations to slots dynamically, with many stations per slot when the load is low and few (or even just one) station per slot when the load is high.

The Adaptive Tree Walk Protocol

One particularly simple way of performing the necessary assignment is to use the algorithm devised by the U.S. Army for testing soldiers for syphilis during World War II (Dorfman, 1943). In short, the Army took a blood sample from N soldiers. A portion of each sample was poured into a single test tube. This mixed sample was then tested for antibodies. If none were found, all the soldiers in the group were declared healthy. If antibodies were present, two new mixed samples were prepared, one from soldiers 1 through $N/2$ and one from the rest. The process was repeated recursively until the infected soldiers were determined.

For the computerized version of this algorithm (Capetanakis, 1979), it is convenient to think of the stations as the leaves of a binary tree, as illustrated in Fig. 4-10. In the first contention slot following a successful frame transmission, slot 0, all stations are permitted to try to acquire the channel. If one of them does so, fine. If there is a collision, then during slot 1 only those stations falling under node 2 in the tree may compete. If one of them acquires the channel, the slot following the frame is reserved for those stations under node 3. If, on the other hand, two or more stations under node 2 want to transmit, there will be a collision during slot 1, in which case it is node 4's turn during slot 2.

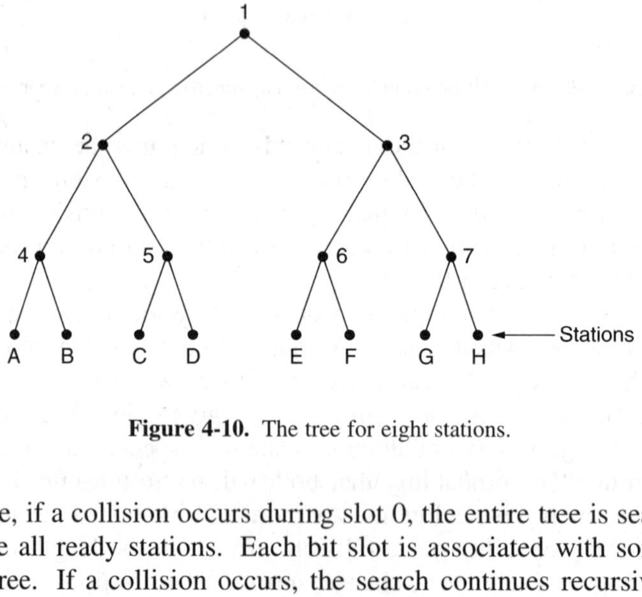

Figure 4-10. The tree for eight stations.

In essence, if a collision occurs during slot 0, the entire tree is searched, depth first, to locate all ready stations. Each bit slot is associated with some particular node in the tree. If a collision occurs, the search continues recursively with the node's left and right children. If a bit slot is idle or if only one station transmits in it, the searching of its node can stop because all ready stations have been located. (Were there more than one, there would have been a collision.)

When the load on the system is heavy, it is hardly worth the effort to dedicate slot 0 to node 1 because that makes sense only in the unlikely event that precisely one station has a frame to send. Similarly, one could argue that nodes 2 and 3 should be skipped as well for the same reason. Put in more general terms, at what level in the tree should the search begin? Clearly, the heavier the load, the farther down the tree the search should begin. We will assume that each station has a good estimate of the number of ready stations, q, for example, from monitoring recent traffic.

To proceed, let us number the levels of the tree from the top, with node 1 in Fig. 4-10 at level 0, nodes 2 and 3 at level 1, etc. Notice that each node at level i

has a fraction 2^{-i} of the stations below it. If the q ready stations are uniformly distributed, the expected number of them below a specific node at level i is just $2^{-i}q$. Intuitively, we would expect the optimal level to begin searching the tree to be the one at which the mean number of contending stations per slot is 1, that is, the level at which $2^{-i}q = 1$. Solving this equation, we find that $i = \log_2 q$.

Numerous improvements to the basic algorithm have been discovered and are discussed in some detail by Bertsekas and Gallager (1992). For example, consider the case of stations *G* and *H* being the only ones wanting to transmit. At node 1 a collision will occur, so 2 will be tried and discovered idle. It is pointless to probe node 3 since it is guaranteed to have a collision (we know that two or more stations under 1 are ready and none of them are under 2, so they must all be under 3). The probe of 3 can be skipped and 6 tried next. When this probe also turns up nothing, 7 can be skipped and node *G* tried next.

4.2.5 Wireless LAN Protocols

A system of laptop computers that communicate by radio can be regarded as a wireless LAN, as we discussed in Sec. 1.5.3. Such a LAN is an example of a broadcast channel. It also has somewhat different properties than a wired LAN, which leads to different MAC protocols. In this section, we will examine some of these protocols. In Sec. 4.4, we will look at 802.11 (WiFi) in detail.

A common configuration for a wireless LAN is an office building with access points (APs) strategically placed around the building. The APs are wired together using copper or fiber and provide connectivity to the stations that talk to them. If the transmission power of the APs and laptops is adjusted to have a range of tens of meters, nearby rooms become like a single cell and the entire building becomes like the cellular telephony systems we studied in Chap. 2, except that each cell only has one channel. This channel is shared by all the stations in the cell, including the AP. It typically provides megabit/sec bandwidths, up to 600 Mbps.

We have already remarked that wireless systems cannot normally detect a collision while it is occurring. The received signal at a station may be tiny, perhaps a million times fainter than the signal that is being transmitted. Finding it is like looking for a ripple on the ocean. Instead, acknowledgements are used to discover collisions and other errors after the fact.

There is an even more important difference between wireless LANs and wired LANs. A station on a wireless LAN may not be able to transmit frames to or receive frames from all other stations because of the limited radio range of the stations. In wired LANs, when one station sends a frame, all other stations receive it. The absence of this property in wireless LANs causes a variety of complications.

We will make the simplifying assumption that each radio transmitter has some fixed range, represented by a circular coverage region within which another station can sense and receive the station's transmission. It is important to realize that in practice coverage regions are not nearly so regular because the propagation of radio signals depends on the environment. Walls and other obstacles that attenuate and reflect signals may cause the range to differ markedly in different directions. But a simple circular model will do for our purposes.

A naive approach to using a wireless LAN might be to try CSMA: just listen for other transmissions and only transmit if no one else is doing so. The trouble is, this protocol is not really a good way to think about wireless because what matters for reception is interference at the receiver, not at the sender. To see the nature of the problem, consider Fig. 4-11, where four wireless stations are illustrated. For our purposes, it does not matter which are APs and which are laptops. The radio range is such that *A* and *B* are within each other's range and can potentially interfere with one another. *C* can also potentially interfere with both *B* and *D*, but not with *A*.

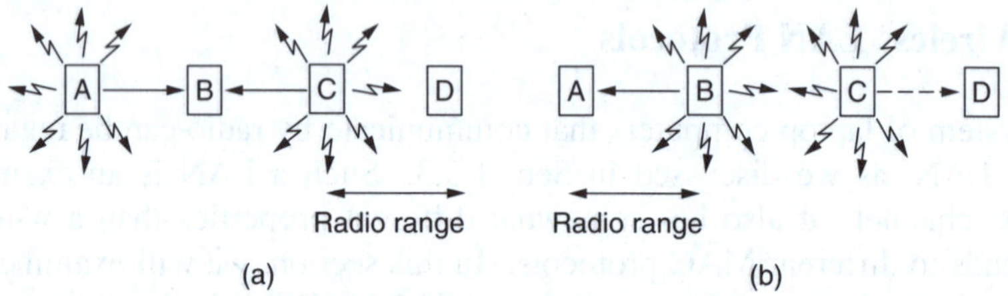

Figure 4-11. A wireless LAN. (a) *A* and *C* are hidden terminals when transmitting to *B*. (b) *B* and *C* are exposed terminals when transmitting to *A* and *D*.

First consider what happens when *A* and *C* transmit to *B*, as depicted in Fig. 4-11(a). If *A* sends and then *C* immediately senses the medium, it will not hear *A* because *A* is out of range. Thus *C* will falsely conclude that it can transmit to *B*. If *C* does start transmitting, it will interfere at *B*, wiping out the frame from *A*. (We assume here that no CDMA-type scheme is used to provide multiple channels, so collisions garble the signal and destroy both frames.) We want a MAC protocol that will prevent this kind of collision from happening because it wastes bandwidth. The problem of a station not being able to detect a potential competitor for the medium because the competitor is too far away is called the **hidden terminal problem**.

Now let us look at a different situation: *B* transmitting to *A* at the same time that *C* wants to transmit to *D*, as shown in Fig. 4-11(b). If *C* senses the medium, it will hear a transmission and falsely conclude that it may not send to *D* (shown as a dashed line). In fact, such a transmission would cause bad reception only in the zone between *B* and *C*, where neither of the intended receivers is located. We want a MAC protocol that prevents this kind of deferral from happening because it wastes bandwidth. The problem is called the **exposed terminal problem**.

The difficulty is that, before starting a transmission, a station really wants to know whether there is radio activity around the receiver. CSMA merely tells it whether there is activity near the transmitter by sensing the carrier. With a wire, all signals propagate to all stations, so this distinction does not exist. However, only one transmission can then take place at once anywhere in the system. In a system based on short-range radio waves, multiple transmissions can occur simultaneously if they all have different destinations and these destinations are out of range of one another. We want this concurrency to happen as the cell gets larger and larger, in the same way that people at a party should not wait for everyone in the room to go silent before they talk; multiple conversations can take place at once in a large room as long as they are not directed to the same location.

An early and influential protocol that tackles these problems for wireless LANs is **MACA** (**Multiple Access with Collision Avoidance**) (Karn, 1990). The basic idea behind it is for the sender to stimulate the receiver into outputting a short frame, so stations nearby can detect this transmission and avoid transmitting for the duration of the upcoming (large) data frame. This technique is used instead of carrier sense.

MACA is illustrated in Fig. 4-12. Let us see how *A* sends a frame to *B*. *A* starts by sending an **RTS** (**Request To Send**) frame to *B*, as shown in Fig. 4-12(a). This short frame (30 bytes) contains the length of the data frame that will eventually follow. Then *B* replies with a **CTS** (**Clear To Send**) frame, as shown in Fig. 4-12(b). The CTS frame contains the data length (copied from the RTS frame). Upon receipt of the CTS frame, *A* begins transmission.

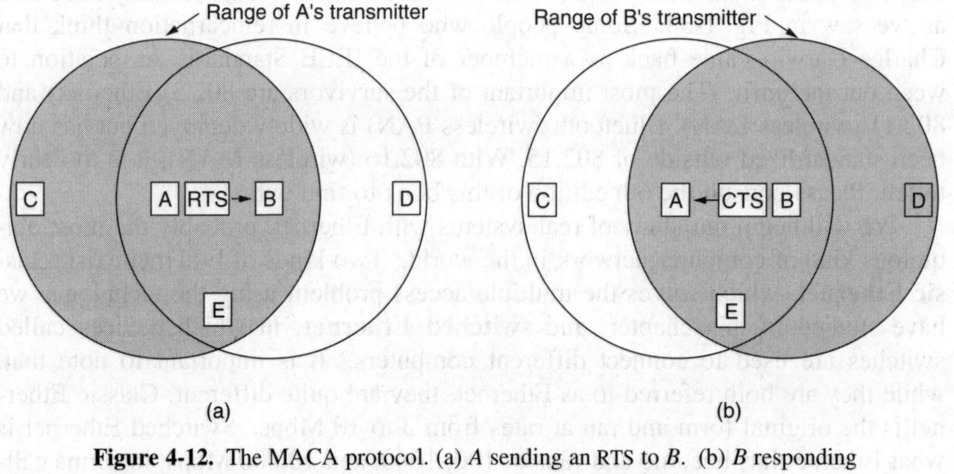

Figure 4-12. The MACA protocol. (a) *A* sending an RTS to *B*. (b) *B* responding with a CTS to *A*.

Now let us see how stations overhearing either of these frames react. Any station hearing the RTS is clearly close to *A* and must remain silent long enough for the CTS to be transmitted back to *A* without conflict. Any station hearing the CTS is clearly close to *B* and must remain silent during the upcoming data transmission, whose length it can tell by examining the CTS frame.

In Fig. 4-12, *C* is within range of *A* but not within range of *B*. Therefore, it hears the RTS from *A* but not the CTS from *B*. As long as it does not interfere with the CTS, it is free to transmit while the data frame is being sent. In contrast, *D* is within range of *B* but not *A*. It does not hear the RTS but does hear the CTS. Hearing the CTS tips it off that it is close to a station that is about to receive a frame, so it defers sending anything until that frame is expected to be finished. Station *E* hears both control messages and, like *D*, must be silent until the data frame is complete.

Despite these precautions, collisions can still occur. For example, *B* and *C* could both send RTS frames to *A* at the same time. These will collide and be lost. In the event of a collision, an unsuccessful transmitter (i.e., one that does not hear a CTS within the expected time interval) waits a random amount of time and tries again later.

4.3 ETHERNET

We have now finished our discussion of channel allocation protocols in the abstract, so it is time to see how these principles apply to real systems. Many of the designs for personal, local, and metropolitan area networks have been standardized under the name of IEEE 802. A few have survived but many have not, as we saw in Fig. 1-38. Some people who believe in reincarnation think that Charles Darwin came back as a member of the IEEE Standards Association to weed out the unfit. The most important of the survivors are 802.3 (Ethernet) and 802.11 (wireless LAN). Bluetooth (wireless PAN) is widely deployed but has now been standardized outside of 802.15. With 802.16 (wireless MAN), it is too early to tell. Please consult the 6th edition of this book to find out.

We will begin our study of real systems with Ethernet, probably the most ubiquitous kind of computer network in the world. Two kinds of Ethernet exist: **classic Ethernet**, which solves the multiple access problem using the techniques we have studied in this chapter; and **switched Ethernet**, in which devices called switches are used to connect different computers. It is important to note that, while they are both referred to as Ethernet, they are quite different. Classic Ethernet is the original form and ran at rates from 3 to 10 Mbps. Switched Ethernet is what Ethernet has become and runs at 100, 1000, and 10,000 Mbps, in forms called fast Ethernet, gigabit Ethernet, and 10 gigabit Ethernet. In practice, only switched Ethernet is used nowadays.

We will discuss these historical forms of Ethernet in chronological order showing how they developed. Since Ethernet and IEEE 802.3 are identical except for a minor difference (which we will discuss shortly), many people use the terms "Ethernet" and "IEEE 802.3" interchangeably. We will do so, too. For more information about Ethernet, see Spurgeon (2000).

4.3.1 Classic Ethernet Physical Layer

The story of Ethernet starts about the same time as that of ALOHA, when a student named Bob Metcalfe got his bachelor's degree at M.I.T. and then moved up the river to get his Ph.D. at Harvard. During his studies, he was exposed to Abramson's work. He became so interested in it that after graduating from Harvard, he decided to spend the summer in Hawaii working with Abramson before starting work at Xerox PARC (Palo Alto Research Center). When he got to PARC, he saw that the researchers there had designed and built what would later be called personal computers. But the machines were isolated. Using his knowledge of Abramson's work, he, together with his colleague David Boggs, designed and implemented the first local area network (Metcalfe and Boggs, 1976). It used a single long, thick coaxial cable and ran at 3 Mbps.

They called the system **Ethernet** after the *luminiferous ether*, through which electromagnetic radiation was once thought to propagate. (When the 19th-century British physicist James Clerk Maxwell discovered that electromagnetic radiation could be described by a wave equation, scientists assumed that space must be filled with some ethereal medium in which the radiation was propagating. Only after the famous Michelson-Morley experiment in 1887 did physicists discover that electromagnetic radiation could propagate in a vacuum.)

The Xerox Ethernet was so successful that DEC, Intel, and Xerox drew up a standard in 1978 for a 10-Mbps Ethernet, called the **DIX standard**. With a minor change, the DIX standard became the IEEE 802.3 standard in 1983. Unfortunately for Xerox, it already had a history of making seminal inventions (such as the personal computer) and then failing to commercialize on them, a story told in *Fumbling the Future* (Smith and Alexander, 1988). When Xerox showed little interest in doing anything with Ethernet other than helping standardize it, Metcalfe formed his own company, 3Com, to sell Ethernet adapters for PCs. It sold many millions of them.

Classic Ethernet snaked around the building as a single long cable to which all the computers were attached. This architecture is shown in Fig. 4-13. The first variety, popularly called **thick Ethernet,** resembled a yellow garden hose, with markings every 2.5 meters to show where to attach computers. (The 802.3 standard did not actually *require* the cable to be yellow, but it did *suggest* it.) It was succeeded by **thin Ethernet,** which bent more easily and made connections using industry-standard BNC connectors. Thin Ethernet was much cheaper and easier to install, but it could run for only 185 meters per segment (instead of 500 m with thick Ethernet), each of which could handle only 30 machines (instead of 100).

Each version of Ethernet has a maximum cable length per segment (i.e., unamplified length) over which the signal will propagate. To allow larger networks, multiple cables can be connected by **repeaters**. A repeater is a physical layer device that receives, amplifies (i.e., regenerates), and retransmits signals in both directions. As far as the software is concerned, a series of cable segments

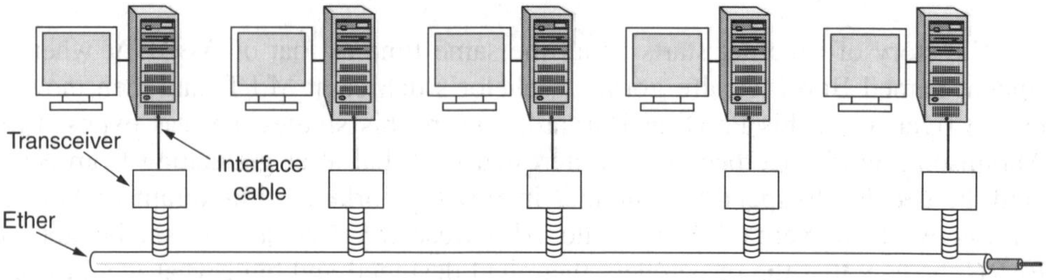

Figure 4-13. Architecture of classic Ethernet.

connected by repeaters is no different from a single cable (except for a small amount of delay introduced by the repeaters).

Over each of these cables, information was sent using the Manchester encoding we studied in Sec. 2.5. An Ethernet could contain multiple cable segments and multiple repeaters, but no two transceivers could be more than 2.5 km apart and no path between any two transceivers could traverse more than four repeaters. The reason for this restriction was so that the MAC protocol, which we will look at next, would work correctly.

4.3.2 Classic Ethernet MAC Sublayer Protocol

The format used to send frames is shown in Fig. 4-14. First comes a *Preamble* of 8 bytes, each containing the bit pattern 10101010 (with the exception of the last byte, in which the last 2 bits are set to 11). This last byte is called the *Start of Frame* delimiter for 802.3. The Manchester encoding of this pattern produces a 10-MHz square wave for 6.4 μsec to allow the receiver's clock to synchronize with the sender's. The last two 1 bits tell the receiver that the rest of the frame is about to start.

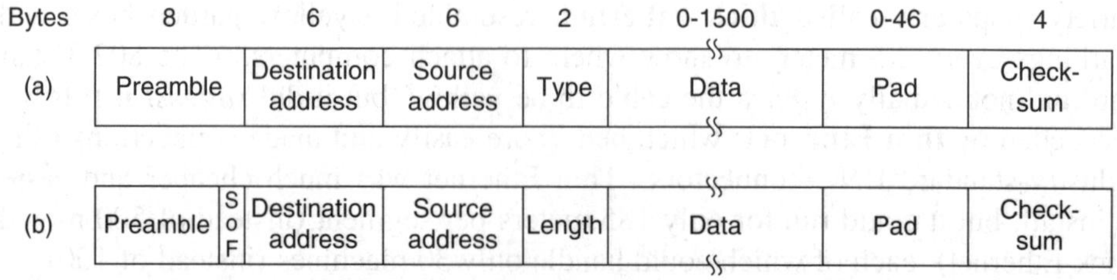

Figure 4-14. Frame formats. (a) Ethernet (DIX). (b) IEEE 802.3.

Next come two addresses, one for the destination and one for the source. They are each 6 bytes long. The first transmitted bit of the destination address is a 0 for ordinary addresses and a 1 for group addresses. Group addresses allow multiple stations to listen to a single address. When a frame is sent to a group address, all the stations in the group receive it. Sending to a group of stations is called **multicasting**. The special address consisting of all 1 bits is reserved for **broadcasting**. A frame containing all 1s in the destination field is accepted by all stations on the network. Multicasting is more selective, but it involves group management to define which stations are in the group. Conversely, broadcasting does not differentiate between stations at all, so it does not require any group management.

An interesting feature of station source addresses is that they are globally unique, assigned centrally by IEEE to ensure that no two stations anywhere in the world have the same address. The idea is that any station can uniquely address any other station by just giving the right 48-bit number. To do this, the first 3 bytes of the address field are used for an **OUI (Organizationally Unique Identifier)**. Values for this field are assigned by IEEE and indicate a manufacturer. Manufacturers are assigned blocks of 2^{24} addresses. The manufacturer assigns the last 3 bytes of the address and programs the complete address into the NIC before it is sold.

Next comes the *Type* or *Length* field, depending on whether the frame is Ethernet or IEEE 802.3. Ethernet uses a *Type* field to tell the receiver what to do with the frame. Multiple network-layer protocols may be in use at the same time on the same machine, so when an Ethernet frame arrives, the operating system has to know which one to hand the frame to. The *Type* field specifies which process to give the frame to. For example, a type code of 0x0800 means that the data contains an IPv4 packet.

IEEE 802.3, in its wisdom, decided that this field would carry the length of the frame, since the Ethernet length was determined by looking inside the data—a layering violation if ever there was one. Of course, this meant there was no way for the receiver to figure out what to do with an incoming frame. That problem was handled by the addition of another header for the **LLC (Logical Link Control)** protocol within the data. It uses 8 bytes to convey the 2 bytes of protocol type information.

Unfortunately, by the time 802.3 was published, so much hardware and software for DIX Ethernet was already in use that few manufacturers and users were enthusiastic about repackaging the *Type* and *Length* fields. In 1997, IEEE threw in the towel and said that both ways were fine with it. Fortunately, all the *Type* fields in use before 1997 had values greater than 1500, then well established as the maximum data size. Now the rule is that any number there less than or equal to 0x600 (1536) can be interpreted as *Length*, and any number greater than 0x600 can be interpreted as *Type*. Now IEEE can maintain that everyone is using its standard and everybody else can keep on doing what they were already doing (not bothering with LLC) without feeling guilty about it.

Next come the data, up to 1500 bytes. This limit was chosen somewhat arbitrarily at the time the Ethernet standard was cast in stone, mostly based on the fact that a transceiver needs enough RAM to hold an entire frame and RAM was expensive in 1978. A larger upper limit would have meant more RAM, and hence a more expensive transceiver.

In addition to there being a maximum frame length, there is also a minimum frame length. While a data field of 0 bytes is sometimes useful, it causes a problem. When a transceiver detects a collision, it truncates the current frame, which means that stray bits and pieces of frames appear on the cable all the time. To make it easier to distinguish valid frames from garbage, Ethernet requires that valid frames must be at least 64 bytes long, from destination address to checksum, including both. If the data portion of a frame is less than 46 bytes, the *Pad* field is used to fill out the frame to the minimum size.

Another (and more important) reason for having a minimum length frame is to prevent a station from completing the transmission of a short frame before the first bit has even reached the far end of the cable, where it may collide with another frame. This problem is illustrated in Fig. 4-15. At time 0, station *A*, at one end of the network, sends off a frame. Let us call the propagation time for this frame to reach the other end τ. Just before the frame gets to the other end (i.e., at time $\tau - \varepsilon$), the most distant station, *B*, starts transmitting. When *B* detects that it is receiving more power than it is putting out, it knows that a collision has occurred, so it aborts its transmission and generates a 48-bit noise burst to warn all other stations. In other words, it jams the ether to make sure the sender does not miss the collision. At about time 2τ, the sender sees the noise burst and aborts its transmission, too. It then waits a random time before trying again.

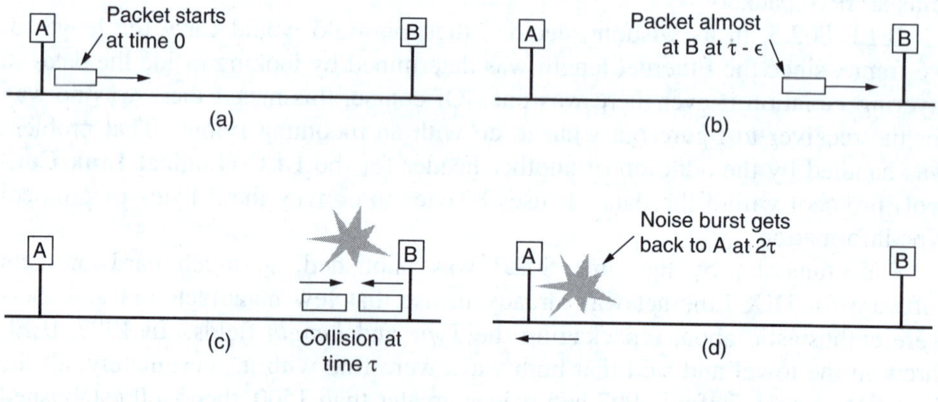

Figure 4-15. Collision detection can take as long as 2τ.

If a station tries to transmit a very short frame, it is conceivable that a collision will occur, but the transmission will have completed before the noise burst gets back to the station at 2τ. The sender will then incorrectly conclude that the frame was successfully sent. To prevent this situation from occurring, all frames must take more than 2τ to send so that the transmission is still taking place when the noise burst gets back to the sender. For a 10-Mbps LAN with a maximum length of 2500 meters and four repeaters (from the 802.3 specification), the round-trip time (including time to propagate through the four repeaters) has been determined to be nearly 50 μsec in the worst case. Therefore, the shortest allowed frame must take at least this long to transmit. At 10 Mbps, a bit takes 100 nsec, so 500 bits is the smallest frame that is guaranteed to work. To add some margin of safety, this number was rounded up to 512 bits or 64 bytes.

The final field is the *Checksum*. It is a 32-bit CRC of the kind we studied in Sec. 3.2. In fact, it is defined exactly by the generator polynomial we gave there, which popped up for PPP, ADSL, and other links too. This CRC is an error-detecting code that is used to determine if the bits of the frame have been received correctly. It just does error detection, with the frame dropped if an error is detected.

CSMA/CD with Binary Exponential Backoff

Classic Ethernet uses the 1-persistent CSMA/CD algorithm that we studied in Sec. 4.2. This descriptor just means that stations sense the medium when they have a frame to send and send the frame as soon as the medium becomes idle. They monitor the channel for collisions as they send. If there is a collision, they abort the transmission with a short jam signal and retransmit after a random interval.

Let us now see how the random interval is determined when a collision occurs, as it is a new method. The model is still that of Fig. 4-5. After a collision, time is divided into discrete slots whose length is equal to the worst-case round-trip propagation time on the ether (2τ). To accommodate the longest path allowed by Ethernet, the slot time has been set to 512 bit times, or 51.2 μsec.

After the first collision, each station waits either 0 or 1 slot times at random before trying again. If two stations collide and each one picks the same random number, they will collide again. After the second collision, each one picks either 0, 1, 2, or 3 at random and waits that number of slot times. If a third collision occurs (the probability of this happening is 0.25), the next time the number of slots to wait is chosen at random from the interval 0 to $2^3 - 1$.

In general, after i collisions, a random number between 0 and $2^i - 1$ is chosen, and that number of slots is skipped. However, after 10 collisions have been reached, the randomization interval is frozen at a maximum of 1023 slots. After 16 collisions, the controller throws in the towel and reports failure back to the computer. Further recovery is up to higher layers.

This algorithm, called **binary exponential backoff**, was chosen to dynamically adapt to the number of stations trying to send. If the randomization interval for all collisions were 1023, the chance of two stations colliding for a second time would be negligible, but the average wait after a collision would be hundreds of slot times, introducing significant delay. On the other hand, if each station always delayed for either 0 or 1 slots, then if 100 stations ever tried to send at once they would collide over and over until 99 of them picked 1 and the remaining station picked 0. This might take years. By having the randomization interval grow exponentially as more and more consecutive collisions occur, the algorithm ensures a low delay when only a few stations collide but also ensures that the collisions are resolved in a reasonable interval when many stations collide. Truncating the backoff at 1023 keeps the bound from growing too large.

If there is no collision, the sender assumes that the frame was probably successfully delivered. That is, neither CSMA/CD nor Ethernet provides acknowledgements. This choice is appropriate for wired and optical fiber channels that have low error rates. Any errors that do occur must then be detected by the CRC and recovered by higher layers. For wireless channels that have more errors, we will see that acknowledgements are used.

4.3.3 Ethernet Performance

Now let us briefly examine the performance of classic Ethernet under conditions of heavy and constant load, that is, with k stations always ready to transmit. A rigorous analysis of the binary exponential backoff algorithm is complicated. Instead, we will follow Metcalfe and Boggs (1976) and assume a constant retransmission probability in each slot. If each station transmits during a contention slot with probability p, the probability A that some station acquires the channel in that slot is

$$A = kp(1-p)^{k-1} \tag{4-5}$$

A is maximized when $p = 1/k$, with $A \rightarrow 1/e$ as $k \rightarrow \infty$. The probability that the contention interval has exactly j slots in it is $A(1-A)^{j-1}$, so the mean number of slots per contention is given by

$$\sum_{j=0}^{\infty} jA(1-A)^{j-1} = \frac{1}{A}$$

Since each slot has a duration 2τ, the mean contention interval, w, is $2\tau/A$. Assuming optimal p, the mean number of contention slots is never more than e, so w is at most $2\tau e \approx 5.4\tau$.

If the mean frame takes P sec to transmit, when many stations have frames to send,

$$\text{Channel efficiency} = \frac{P}{P + 2\tau/A} \tag{4-6}$$

Here we see where the maximum cable distance between any two stations enters into the performance figures. The longer the cable, the longer the contention interval, which is why the Ethernet standard specifies a maximum cable length.

It is instructive to formulate Eq. (4-6) in terms of the frame length, F, the network bandwidth, B, the cable length, L, and the speed of signal propagation, c, for the optimal case of e contention slots per frame. With $P = F/B$, Eq. (4-6) becomes

$$\text{Channel efficiency} = \frac{1}{1 + 2BLe/cF} \tag{4-7}$$

When the second term in the denominator is large, network efficiency will be low. More specifically, increasing network bandwidth or distance (the BL product) reduces efficiency for a given frame size. Unfortunately, much research on network hardware is aimed precisely at increasing this product. People want high bandwidth over long distances (fiber optic MANs, for example), yet classic Ethernet implemented in this manner is not the best system for these applications. We will see other ways of implementing Ethernet in the next section.

In Fig. 4-16, the channel efficiency is plotted versus the number of ready stations for $2\tau = 51.2$ μsec and a data rate of 10 Mbps, using Eq. (4-7). With a 64-byte slot time, it is not surprising that 64-byte frames are not efficient. On the other hand, with 1024-byte frames and an asymptotic value of e 64-byte slots per contention interval, the contention period is 174 bytes long and the efficiency is 85%. This result is much better than the 37% efficiency of slotted ALOHA.

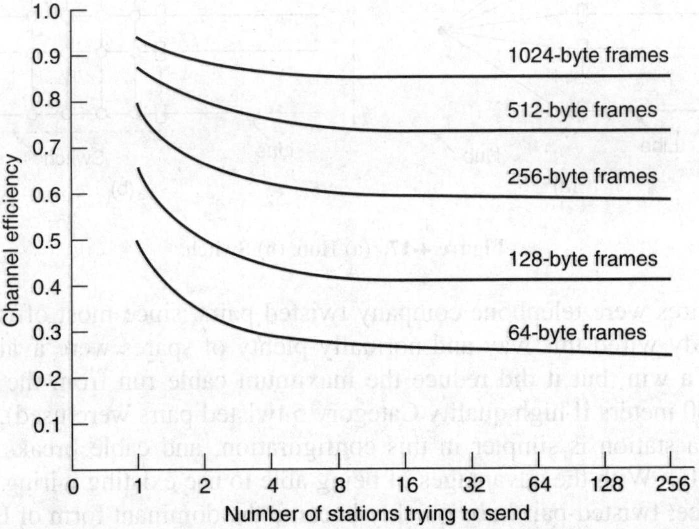

Figure 4-16. Efficiency of Ethernet at 10 Mbps with 512-bit slot times.

It is probably worth mentioning that there has been a large amount of theoretical performance analysis of Ethernet (and other networks). Most of the results should be taken with a grain (or better yet, a metric ton) of salt, for two reasons.

First, virtually all of the theoretical work assumes Poisson traffic. As researchers have begun looking at real data, it now appears that network traffic is rarely Poisson. Instead, it is self-similar or bursty over a range of time scales (Paxson and Floyd, 1995; and Leland et al., 1994). What this means is that averaging over long periods of time does not smooth out the traffic. As well as using questionable models, many of the analyses focus on the "interesting" performance cases of abnormally high load. Boggs et al. (1988) showed by experimentation that Ethernet works well in reality, even at moderately high load.

4.3.4 Switched Ethernet

Ethernet soon began to evolve away from the single long cable architecture of classic Ethernet. The problems associated with finding breaks or loose connections drove it toward a different kind of wiring pattern, in which each station has a dedicated cable running to a central **hub**. A hub simply connects all the attached wires electrically, as if they were soldered together. This configuration is shown in Fig. 4-17(a).

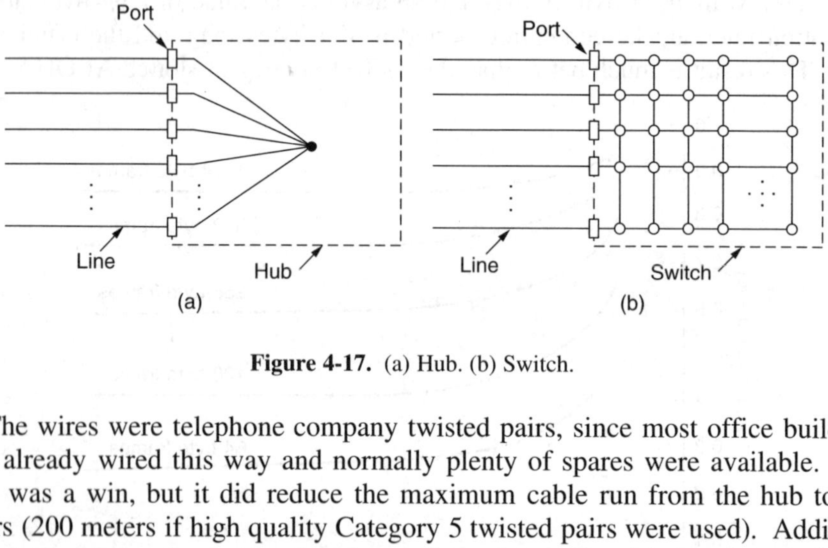

Figure 4-17. (a) Hub. (b) Switch.

The wires were telephone company twisted pairs, since most office buildings were already wired this way and normally plenty of spares were available. This reuse was a win, but it did reduce the maximum cable run from the hub to 100 meters (200 meters if high quality Category 5 twisted pairs were used). Adding or removing a station is simpler in this configuration, and cable breaks can be detected easily. With the advantages of being able to use existing wiring and ease of maintenance, twisted-pair hubs quickly became the dominant form of Ethernet.

However, hubs do not increase capacity because they are logically equivalent to the single long cable of classic Ethernet. As more and more stations are added, each station gets a decreasing share of the fixed capacity. Eventually, the LAN will saturate. One way out is to go to a higher speed, say, from 10 Mbps to 100 Mbps, 1 Gbps, or even higher speeds. But with the growth of multimedia and powerful servers, even a 1-Gbps Ethernet can become saturated.

Fortunately, there is an another way to deal with increased load: switched Ethernet. The heart of this system is a **switch** containing a high-speed backplane that connects all of the ports, as shown in Fig. 4-17(b). From the outside, a switch looks just like a hub. They are both boxes, typically with 4 to 48 ports, each with a standard RJ-45 connector for a twisted-pair cable. Each cable connects the switch or hub to a single computer, as shown in Fig. 4-18. A switch has the same advantages as a hub, too. It is easy to add or remove a new station by plugging or unplugging a wire, and it is easy to find most faults since a flaky cable or port will usually affect just one station. There is still a shared component that can fail—the switch itself—but if all stations lose connectivity the IT folks know what to do to fix the problem: replace the whole switch.

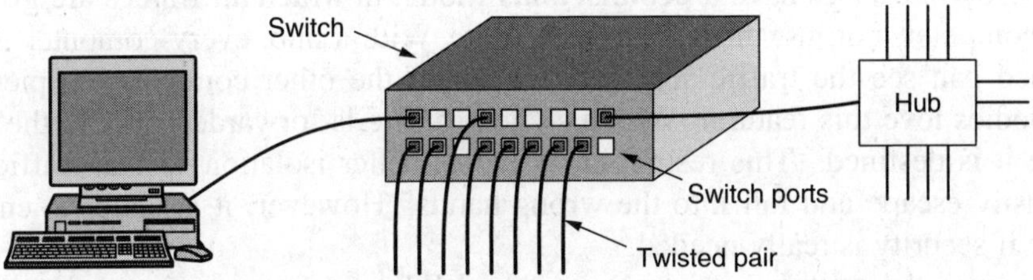

Figure 4-18. An Ethernet switch.

Inside the switch, however, something very different is happening. Switches only output frames to the ports for which those frames are destined. When a switch port receives an Ethernet frame from a station, the switch checks the Ethernet addresses to see which port the frame is destined for. This step requires the switch to be able to work out which ports correspond to which addresses, a process that we will describe in Sec. 4.8 when we get to the general case of switches connected to other switches. For now, just assume that the switch knows the frame's destination port. The switch then forwards the frame over its high-speed backplane to the destination port. The backplane typically runs at many Gbps, using a proprietary protocol that does not need to be standardized because it is entirely hidden inside the switch. The destination port then transmits the frame on the wire so that it reaches the intended station. None of the other ports even knows the frame exists.

What happens if more than one of the stations or ports wants to send a frame at the same time? Again, switches differ from hubs. In a hub, all stations are in the same **collision domain**. They must use the CSMA/CD algorithm to schedule their transmissions. In a switch, each port is its own independent collision domain. In the common case that the cable is full duplex, both the station and the port can send a frame on the cable at the same time, without worrying about other ports and stations. Collisions are now impossible and CSMA/CD is not needed. However, if the cable is half duplex, the station and the port must contend for transmission with CSMA/CD in the usual way.

A switch improves performance over a hub in two ways. First, since there are no collisions, the capacity is used more efficiently. Second, and more importantly, with a switch multiple frames can be sent simultaneously (by different stations). These frames will reach the switch ports and travel over the switch's backplane to be output on the proper ports. However, since two frames might be sent to the same output port at the same time, the switch must have buffering so that it can temporarily queue an input frame until it can be transmitted to the output port. Overall, these improvements give a large performance win that is not possible with a hub. The total system throughput can often be increased by an order of magnitude, depending on the number of ports and traffic patterns.

The change in the ports on which frames are output also has security benefits. Most LAN interfaces have a **promiscuous mode**, in which *all* frames are given to each computer, not just those addressed to it. With a hub, every computer that is attached can see the traffic sent between all of the other computers. Spies and busybodies love this feature. With a switch, traffic is forwarded only to the ports where it is destined. This restriction provides better isolation so that traffic will not easily escape and fall into the wrong hands. However, it is better to encrypt traffic if security is really needed.

Because the switch just expects standard Ethernet frames on each input port, it is possible to use some of the ports as concentrators. In Fig. 4-18, the port in the upper-right corner is connected not to a single station, but to a 12-port hub instead. As frames arrive at the hub, they contend for the ether in the usual way, including collisions and binary backoff. Successful frames make it through the hub to the switch and are treated there like any other incoming frames. The switch does not know they had to fight their way in. Once in the switch, they are sent to the correct output line over the high-speed backplane. It is also possible that the correct destination was one on the lines attached to the hub, in which case the frame has already been delivered so the switch just drops it. Hubs are simpler and cheaper than switches, but due to falling switch prices they have become an endangered species. Modern networks largely use switched Ethernet. Nevertheless, legacy hubs still exist.

4.3.5 Fast Ethernet

At the same time that switches were becoming popular, the speed of 10-Mbps Ethernet was coming under pressure. At first, 10 Mbps seemed like heaven, just as cable modems seemed like heaven to the users of telephone modems. But the novelty wore off quickly. As a kind of corollary to Parkinson's Law ("Work expands to fill the time available for its completion"), it seemed that data expanded to fill the bandwidth available for their transmission.

Many installations needed more bandwidth and thus had numerous 10-Mbps LANs connected by a maze of repeaters, hubs, and switches, although to the network managers it sometimes felt that they were being held together by bubble gum and chicken wire. But even with Ethernet switches, the maximum bandwidth of a single computer was limited by the cable that connected it to the switch port.

It was in this environment that IEEE reconvened the 802.3 committee in 1992 with instructions to come up with a faster LAN. One proposal was to keep 802.3 exactly as it was, but just make it go faster. Another proposal was to redo it totally and give it lots of new features, such as real-time traffic and digitized voice, but just keep the old name (for marketing reasons). After some wrangling, the committee decided to keep 802.3 the way it was, and just make it go faster. This strategy would get the job done before the technology changed and avoid unforeseen problems with a brand new design. The new design would also be backward-compatible with existing Ethernet LANs. The people behind the losing proposal did what any self-respecting computer-industry people would have done under these circumstances: they stomped off and formed their own committee and standardized their LAN anyway (eventually as 802.12). It flopped miserably.

The work was done quickly (by standards committees' norms), and the result, 802.3u, was approved by IEEE in June 1995. Technically, 802.3u is not a new standard, but an addendum to the existing 802.3 standard (to emphasize its backward compatibility). This strategy is used a lot. Since practically everyone calls it **fast Ethernet**, rather than 802.3u, we will do that, too.

The basic idea behind fast Ethernet was simple: keep all the old frame formats, interfaces, and procedural rules, but reduce the bit time from 100 nsec to 10 nsec. Technically, it would have been possible to copy 10-Mbps classic Ethernet and still detect collisions on time by just reducing the maximum cable length by a factor of 10. However, the advantages of twisted-pair wiring were so overwhelming that fast Ethernet is based entirely on this design. Thus, all fast Ethernet systems use hubs and switches; multidrop cables with vampire taps or BNC connectors are not permitted.

Nevertheless, some choices still had to be made, the most important being which wire types to support. One contender was Category 3 twisted pair. The argument for it was that practically every office in the Western world had at least four Category 3 (or better) twisted pairs running from it to a telephone wiring closet within 100 meters. Sometimes two such cables existed. Thus, using Category 3 twisted pair would make it possible to wire up desktop computers using fast Ethernet without having to rewire the building, an enormous advantage for many organizations.

The main disadvantage of a Category 3 twisted pair is its inability to carry 100 Mbps over 100 meters, the maximum computer-to-hub distance specified for 10-Mbps hubs. In contrast, Category 5 twisted pair wiring can handle 100 m easily, and fiber can go much farther. The compromise chosen was to allow all three possibilities, as shown in Fig. 4-19, but to pep up the Category 3 solution to give it the additional carrying capacity needed.

The Category 3 UTP scheme, called **100Base-T4**, used a signaling speed of 25 MHz, only 25% faster than standard Ethernet's 20 MHz. (Remember that

Name	Cable	Max. segment	Advantages
100Base-T4	Twisted pair	100 m	Uses category 3 UTP
100Base-TX	Twisted pair	100 m	Full duplex at 100 Mbps (Cat 5 UTP)
100Base-FX	Fiber optics	2000 m	Full duplex at 100 Mbps; long runs

Figure 4-19. The original fast Ethernet cabling.

Manchester encoding, discussed in Sec. 2.5, requires two clock periods for each of the 10 million bits sent each second.) However, to achieve the necessary bit rate, 100Base-T4 requires four twisted pairs. Of the four pairs, one is always to the hub, one is always from the hub, and the other two are switchable to the current transmission direction. To get 100 Mbps out of the three twisted pairs in the transmission direction, a fairly involved scheme is used on each twisted pair. It involves sending ternary digits with three different voltage levels. This scheme is not likely to win any prizes for elegance, and we will skip the details. However, since standard telephone wiring for decades has had four twisted pairs per cable, most offices are able to use the existing wiring plant. Of course, it means giving up your office telephone, but that is surely a small price to pay for faster email.

100Base-T4 fell by the wayside as many office buildings were rewired with Category 5 UTP for **100Base-TX** Ethernet, which came to dominate the market. This design is simpler because the wires can handle clock rates of 125 MHz. Only two twisted pairs per station are used, one to the hub and one from it. Neither straight binary coding (i.e., NRZ) nor Manchester coding is used. Instead, the **4B/5B** encoding we described in Sec 2.5 is used. 4 data bits are encoded as 5 signal bits and sent at 125 MHz to provide 100 Mbps. This scheme is simple but has sufficient transitions for synchronization and uses the bandwidth of the wire relatively well. The 100Base-TX system is full duplex; stations can transmit at 100 Mbps on one twisted pair and receive at 100 Mbps on another twisted pair at the same time.

The last option, **100Base-FX**, uses two strands of multimode fiber, one for each direction, so it, too, can run full duplex with 100 Mbps in each direction. In this setup, the distance between a station and the switch can be up to 2 km.

Fast Ethernet allows interconnection by either hubs or switches. To ensure that the CSMA/CD algorithm continues to work, the relationship between the minimum frame size and maximum cable length must be maintained as the network speed goes up from 10 Mbps to 100 Mbps. So, either the minimum frame size of 64 bytes must go up or the maximum cable length of 2500 m must come down, proportionally. The easy choice was for the maximum distance between any two stations to come down by a factor of 10, since a hub with 100-m cables falls within this new maximum already. However, 2-km 100Base-FX cables are too long to permit a 100-Mbps hub with the normal Ethernet collision algorithm. These cables must instead be connected to a switch and operate in a full-duplex mode so that there are no collisions.

Users quickly started to deploy fast Ethernet, but they were not about to throw away 10-Mbps Ethernet cards on older computers. As a consequence, virtually all fast Ethernet switches can handle a mix of 10-Mbps and 100-Mbps stations. To make upgrading easy, the standard itself provides a mechanism called **autonegotiation** that lets two stations automatically negotiate the optimum speed (10 or 100 Mbps) and duplexity (half or full). It works well most of the time but is known to lead to duplex mismatch problems when one end of the link autonegotiates but the other end does not and is set to full-duplex mode (Shalunov and Carlson, 2005). Most Ethernet products use this feature to configure themselves.

4.3.6 Gigabit Ethernet

The ink was barely dry on the fast Ethernet standard when the 802 committee began working on a yet faster Ethernet, quickly dubbed **gigabit Ethernet**. IEEE ratified the most popular form as 802.3ab in 1999. Below we will discuss some of the key features of gigabit Ethernet. More information is given by Spurgeon (2000).

The committee's goals for gigabit Ethernet were essentially the same as the committee's goals for fast Ethernet: increase performance tenfold while maintaining compatibility with all existing Ethernet standards. In particular, gigabit Ethernet had to offer unacknowledged datagram service with both unicast and broadcast, use the same 48-bit addressing scheme already in use, and maintain the same frame format, including the minimum and maximum frame sizes. The final standard met all these goals.

Like fast Ethernet, all configurations of gigabit Ethernet use point-to-point links. In the simplest configuration, illustrated in Fig. 4-20(a), two computers are directly connected to each other. The more common case, however, uses a switch or a hub connected to multiple computers and possibly additional switches or hubs, as shown in Fig. 4-20(b). In both configurations, each individual Ethernet cable has exactly two devices on it, no more and no fewer.

Also like fast Ethernet, gigabit Ethernet supports two different modes of operation: full-duplex mode and half-duplex mode. The "normal" mode is full-duplex mode, which allows traffic in both directions at the same time. This mode is used when there is a central switch connected to computers (or other switches) on the periphery. In this configuration, all lines are buffered so each computer and switch is free to send frames whenever it wants to. The sender does not have to sense the channel to see if anybody else is using it because contention is impossible. On the line between a computer and a switch, the computer is the only possible sender to the switch, and the transmission will succeed even if the switch is currently sending a frame to the computer (because the line is full duplex). Since

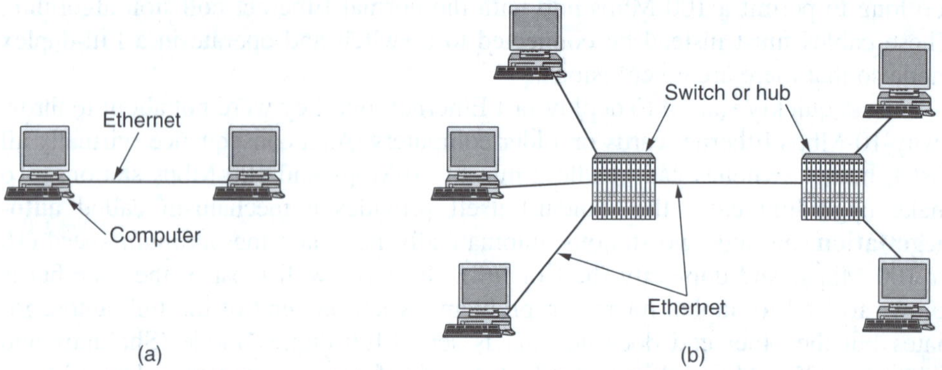

Figure 4-20. (a) A two-station Ethernet. (b) A multistation Ethernet.

no contention is possible, the CSMA/CD protocol is not used, so the maximum length of the cable is determined by signal strength issues rather than by how long it takes for a noise burst to propagate back to the sender in the worst case. Switch\%es are free to mix and match speeds. Autonegotiation is supported just as in fast Ethernet, only now the choice is among 10, 100, and 1000 Mbps.

The other mode of operation, half-duplex, is used when the computers are connected to a hub rather than a switch. A hub does not buffer incoming frames. Instead, it electrically connects all the lines internally, simulating the multidrop cable used in classic Ethernet. In this mode, collisions are possible, so the standard CSMA/CD protocol is required. Because a 64-byte frame (the shortest allowed) can now be transmitted 100 times faster than in classic Ethernet, the maximum cable length must be 100 times less, or 25 meters, to maintain the essential property that the sender is still transmitting when the noise burst gets back to it, even in the worst case. With a 2500-meter-long cable, the sender of a 64-byte frame at 1 Gbps would be long finished before the frame got even a tenth of the way to the other end, let alone to the end and back.

This length restriction was painful enough that two features were added to the standard to increase the maximum cable length to 200 meters, which is probably enough for most offices. The first feature, called **carrier extension**, essentially tells the hardware to add its own padding after the normal frame to extend the frame to 512 bytes. Since this padding is added by the sending hardware and removed by the receiving hardware, the software is unaware of it, meaning that no changes are needed to existing software. The downside is that using 512 bytes worth of bandwidth to transmit 46 bytes of user data (the payload of a 64-byte frame) has a line efficiency of only 9%.

The second feature, called **frame bursting**, allows a sender to transmit a concatenated sequence of multiple frames in a single transmission. If the total burst is less than 512 bytes, the hardware pads it again. If enough frames are waiting for transmission, this scheme is very efficient and preferred over carrier extension.

In all fairness, it is hard to imagine an organization buying modern computers with gigabit Ethernet cards and then connecting them with an old-fashioned hub to simulate classic Ethernet with all its collisions. Gigabit Ethernet interfaces and switches used to be expensive, but their prices fell rapidly as sales volumes picked up. Still, backward compatibility is sacred in the computer industry, so the committee was required to put it in. Today, most computers ship with an Ethernet interface that is capable of 10-, 100-, and 1000-Mbps operation and compatible with all of them.

Gigabit Ethernet supports both copper and fiber cabling, as listed in Fig. 4-21. Signaling at or near 1 Gbps requires encoding and sending a bit every nanosecond. This trick was initially accomplished with short, shielded copper cables (the 1000Base-CX version) and optical fibers. For the optical fibers, two wavelengths are permitted and result in two different versions: 0.85 microns (short, for 1000Base-SX) and 1.3 microns (long, for 1000Base-LX).

Name	Cable	Max. segment	Advantages
1000Base-SX	Fiber optics	550 m	Multimode fiber (50, 62.5 microns)
1000Base-LX	Fiber optics	5000 m	Single (10 μ) or multimode (50, 62.5 μ)
1000Base-CX	2 Pairs of STP	25 m	Shielded twisted pair
1000Base-T	4 Pairs of UTP	100 m	Standard category 5 UTP

Figure 4-21. Gigabit Ethernet cabling.

Signaling at the short wavelength can be achieved with cheaper LEDs. It is used with multimode fiber and is useful for connections within a building, as it can run up to 500 m for 50-micron fiber. Signaling at the long wavelength requires more expensive lasers. On the other hand, when combined with single-mode (10-micron) fiber, the cable length can be up to 5 km. This limit allows long distance connections between buildings, such as for a campus backbone, as a dedicated point-to-point link. Later variations of the standard allowed even longer links over single-mode fiber.

To send bits over these versions of gigabit Ethernet, the **8B/10B** encoding we described in Sec. 2.5 was borrowed from another networking technology called Fibre Channel. That scheme encodes 8 bits of data into 10-bit codewords that are sent over the wire or fiber, hence the name 8B/10B. The codewords were chosen so that they could be balanced (i.e., have the same number of 0s and 1s) with sufficient transitions for clock recovery. Sending the coded bits with NRZ requires a signaling bandwidth of 25% more than that required for the uncoded bits, a big improvement over the 100% expansion of Manchester coding.

However, all of these options required new copper or fiber cables to support the faster signaling. None of them made use of the large amount of Category 5 UTP that had been installed along with fast Ethernet. Within a year, 1000Base-T came along to fill this gap, and it has been the most popular form of gigabit Ethernet ever since. People apparently dislike rewiring their buildings.

More complicated signaling is needed to make Ethernet run at 1000 Mbps over Category 5 wires. To start, all four twisted pairs in the cable are used, and each pair is used in both directions at the same time by using digital signal processing to separate signals. Over each wire, five voltage levels that carry 2 bits are used for signaling at 125 Msymbols/sec. The mapping to produce the symbols from the bits is not straightforward. It involves scrambling, for transitions, followed by an error correcting code in which four values are embedded into five signal levels.

A speed of 1 Gbps is quite fast. For example, if a receiver is busy with some other task for even 1 msec and does not empty the input buffer on some line, up to 1953 frames may have accumulated in that gap. Also, when a computer on a gigabit Ethernet is shipping data down the line to a computer on a classic Ethernet, buffer overruns are very likely. As a consequence of these two observations, gigabit Ethernet supports flow control. The mechanism consists of one end sending a special control frame to the other end telling it to pause for some period of time. These PAUSE control frames are normal Ethernet frames containing a type of 0x8808. Pauses are given in units of the minimum frame time. For gigabit Ethernet, the time unit is 512 nsec, allowing for pauses as long as 33.6 msec.

There is one more extension that was introduced along with gigabit Ethernet. **Jumbo frames** allow for frames to be longer than 1500 bytes, usually up to 9 KB. This extension is proprietary. It is not recognized by the standard because if it is used then Ethernet is no longer compatible with earlier versions, but most vendors support it anyway. The rationale is that 1500 bytes is a short unit at gigabit speeds. By manipulating larger blocks of information, the frame rate can be decreased, along with the processing associated with it, such as interrupting the processor to say that a frame has arrived, or splitting up and recombining messages that were too long to fit in one Ethernet frame.

4.3.7 10-Gigabit Ethernet

As soon as gigabit Ethernet was standardized, the 802 committee got bored and wanted to get back to work. IEEE told them to start on 10-gigabit Ethernet. This work followed much the same pattern as the previous Ethernet standards, with standards for fiber and shielded copper cable appearing first in 2002 and 2004, followed by the standard for copper twisted pair in 2006.

10 Gbps is a truly prodigious speed, 1000x faster than the original Ethernet. Where could it be needed? The answer is inside data centers and exchanges to connect high-end routers, switches, and servers, as well as in long-distance, high bandwidth trunks between offices that are enabling entire metropolitan area networks based on Ethernet and fiber. The long distance connections use optical fiber, while the short connections may use copper or fiber.

All versions of 10-gigabit Ethernet support only full-duplex operation. CSMA/CD is no longer part of the design, and the standards concentrate on the details of physical layers that can run at very high speed. Compatibility still matters, though, so 10-gigabit Ethernet interfaces autonegotiate and fall back to the highest speed supported by both ends of the line.

The main kinds of 10-gigabit Ethernet are listed in Fig. 4-22. Multimode fiber with the 0.85μ (short) wavelength is used for medium distances, and single-mode fiber at 1.3μ (long) and 1.5μ (extended) is used for long distances. 10GBase-ER can run for distances of 40 km, making it suitable for wide area applications. All of these versions send a serial stream of information that is produced by scrambling the data bits, then encoding them with a **64B/66B** code. This encoding has less overhead than an 8B/10B code.

Name	Cable	Max. segment	Advantages
10GBase-SR	Fiber optics	Up to 300 m	Multimode fiber (0.85μ)
10GBase-LR	Fiber optics	10 km	Single-mode fiber (1.3μ)
10GBase-ER	Fiber optics	40 km	Single-mode fiber (1.5μ)
10GBase-CX4	4 Pairs of twinax	15 m	Twinaxial copper
10GBase-T	4 Pairs of UTP	100 m	Category 6a UTP

Figure 4-22. 10-Gigabit Ethernet cabling.

The first copper version defined, 10GBase-CX4, uses a cable with four pairs of twinaxial copper wiring. Each pair uses 8B/10B coding and runs at 3.125 Gsymbols/second to reach 10 Gbps. This version is cheaper than fiber and was early to market, but it remains to be seen whether it will be beat out in the long run by 10-gigabit Ethernet over more garden variety twisted pair wiring.

10GBase-T is the version that uses UTP cables. While it calls for Category 6a wiring, for shorter runs, it can use lower categories (including Category 5) to allow some reuse of installed cabling. Not surprisingly, the physical layer is quite involved to reach 10 Gbps over twisted pair. We will only sketch some of the high-level details. Each of the four twisted pairs is used to send 2500 Mbps in both directions. This speed is reached using a signaling rate of 800 Msymbols/sec with symbols that use 16 voltage levels. The symbols are produced by scrambling the data, protecting it with a LDPC (Low Density Parity Check) code, and further coding for error correction.

10-gigabit Ethernet is still shaking out in the market, but the 802.3 committee has already moved on. At the end of 2007, IEEE created a group to standardize Ethernet operating at 40 Gbps and 100 Gbps. This upgrade will let Ethernet compete in very high-performance settings, including long-distance connections in backbone networks and short connections over the equipment backplanes. The standard is not yet complete, but proprietary products are already available.

4.3.8 Retrospective on Ethernet

Ethernet has been around for over 30 years and has no serious competitors in sight, so it is likely to be around for many years to come. Few CPU architectures, operating systems, or programming languages have been king of the mountain for three decades going on strong. Clearly, Ethernet did something right. What?

Probably the main reason for its longevity is that Ethernet is simple and flexible. In practice, simple translates into reliable, cheap, and easy to maintain. Once the hub and switch architecture was adopted, failures became extremely rare. People hesitate to replace something that works perfectly all the time, especially when they know that an awful lot of things in the computer industry work very poorly, so that many so-called "upgrades" are worse than what they replaced.

Simple also translates into cheap. Twisted-pair wiring is relatively inexpensive as are the hardware components. They may start out expensive when there is a transition, for example, new gigabit Ethernet NICs or switches, but they are merely additions to a well established network (not a replacement of it) and the prices fall quickly as the sales volume picks up.

Ethernet is easy to maintain. There is no software to install (other than the drivers) and not much in the way of configuration tables to manage (and get wrong). Also, adding new hosts is as simple as just plugging them in.

Another point is that Ethernet interworks easily with TCP/IP, which has become dominant. IP is a connectionless protocol, so it fits perfectly with Ethernet, which is also connectionless. IP fits much less well with connection-oriented alternatives such as ATM. This mismatch definitely hurt ATM's chances.

Lastly, and perhaps most importantly, Ethernet has been able to evolve in certain crucial ways. Speeds have gone up by several orders of magnitude and hubs and switches have been introduced, but these changes have not required changing the software and have often allowed the existing cabling to be reused for a time. When a network salesman shows up at a large installation and says "I have this fantastic new network for you. All you have to do is throw out all your hardware and rewrite all your software," he has a problem.

Many alternative technologies that you have probably not even heard of were faster than Ethernet when they were introduced. As well as ATM, this list includes FDDI (Fiber Distributed Data Interface) and Fibre Channel,† two ring-based optical LANs. Both were incompatible with Ethernet. Neither one made it. They were too complicated, which led to complex chips and high prices. The lesson that should have been learned here was KISS (Keep It Simple, Stupid). Eventually, Ethernet caught up with them in terms of speed, often by borrowing some of their technology, for example, the 4B/5B coding from FDDI and the 8B/10B coding from Fibre Channel. Then they had no advantages left and quietly died off or fell into specialized roles.

† It is called "Fibre Channel" and not "Fiber Channel" because the document editor was British.

It looks like Ethernet will continue to expand in its applications for some time. 10-gigabit Ethernet has freed it from the distance constraints of CSMA/CD. Much effort is being put into **carrier-grade Ethernet** to let network providers offer Ethernet-based services to their customers for metropolitan and wide area networks (Fouli and Maler, 2009). This application carries Ethernet frames long distances over fiber and calls for better management features to help operators offer reliable, high-quality services. Very high speed networks are also finding uses in backplanes connecting components in large routers or servers. Both of these uses are in addition to that of sending frames between computers in offices.

4.4 WIRELESS LANS

Wireless LANs are increasingly popular, and homes, offices, cafes, libraries, airports, zoos, and other public places are being outfitted with them to connect computers, PDAs, and smart phones to the Internet. Wireless LANs can also be used to let two or more nearby computers communicate without using the Internet.

The main wireless LAN standard is 802.11. We gave some background information on it in Sec. 1.5.3. Now it is time to take a closer look at the technology. In the following sections, we will look at the protocol stack, physical-layer radio transmission techniques, the MAC sublayer protocol, the frame structure, and the services provided. For more information about 802.11, see Gast (2005). To get the truth from the mouth of the horse, consult the published standard, IEEE 802.11-2007 itself.

4.4.1 The 802.11 Architecture and Protocol Stack

802.11 networks can be used in two modes. The most popular mode is to connect clients, such as laptops and smart phones, to another network, such as a company intranet or the Internet. This mode is shown in Fig. 4-23(a). In infrastructure mode, each client is associated with an **AP** (**Access Point**) that is in turn connected to the other network. The client sends and receives its packets via the AP. Several access points may be connected together, typically by a wired network called a **distribution system**, to form an extended 802.11 network. In this case, clients can send frames to other clients via their APs.

The other mode, shown in Fig. 4-23(b), is an **ad hoc network**. This mode is a collection of computers that are associated so that they can directly send frames to each other. There is no access point. Since Internet access is the killer application for wireless, ad hoc networks are not very popular.

Now we will look at the protocols. All the 802 protocols, including 802.11 and Ethernet, have a certain commonality of structure. A partial view of the 802.11 protocol stack is given in Fig. 4-24. The stack is the same for clients and

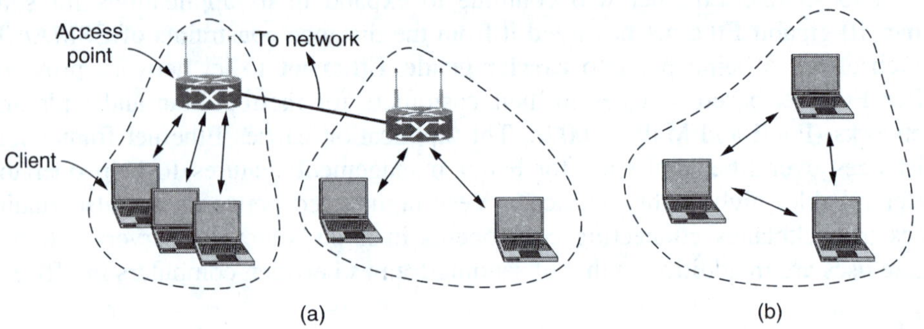

Figure 4-23. 802.11 architecture. (a) Infrastructure mode. (b) Ad-hoc mode.

APs. The physical layer corresponds fairly well to the OSI physical layer, but the data link layer in all the 802 protocols is split into two or more sublayers. In 802.11, the MAC (Medium Access Control) sublayer determines how the channel is allocated, that is, who gets to transmit next. Above it is the LLC (Logical Link Control) sublayer, whose job it is to hide the differences between the different 802 variants and make them indistinguishable as far as the network layer is concerned. This could have been a significant responsibility, but these days the LLC is a glue layer that identifies the protocol (e.g., IP) that is carried within an 802.11 frame.

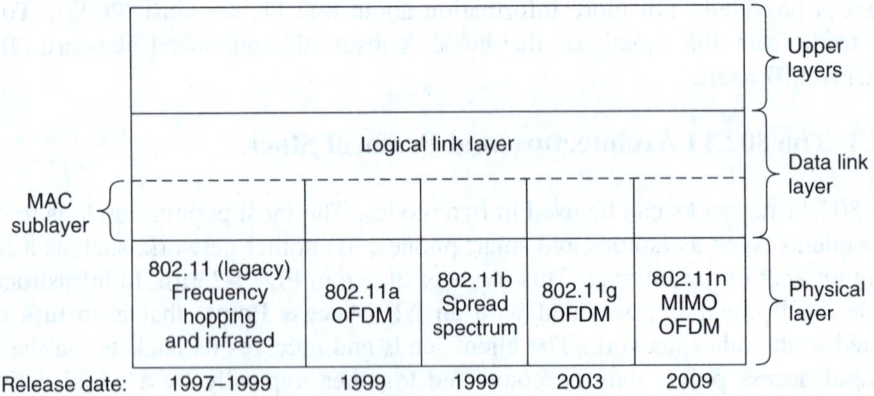

Figure 4-24. Part of the 802.11 protocol stack.

Several transmission techniques have been added to the physical layer as 802.11 has evolved since it first appeared in 1997. Two of the initial techniques, infrared in the manner of television remote controls and frequency hopping in the 2.4-GHz band, are now defunct. The third initial technique, direct sequence spread spectrum at 1 or 2 Mbps in the 2.4-GHz band, was extended to run at rates up to 11 Mbps and quickly became a hit. It is now known as 802.11b.

To give wireless junkies a much-wanted speed boost, new transmission techniques based on the OFDM (Orthogonal Frequency Division Multiplexing) scheme we described in Sec. 2.5.3 were introduced in 1999 and 2003. The first is called 802.11a and uses a different frequency band, 5 GHz. The second stuck with 2.4 GHz and compatibility. It is called 802.11g. Both give rates up to 54 Mbps.

Most recently, transmission techniques that simultaneously use multiple antennas at the transmitter and receiver for a speed boost were finalized as 802.11n in Oct. 2009. With four antennas and wider channels, the 802.11 standard now defines rates up to a startling 600 Mbps.

We will now examine each of these transmission techniques briefly. We will only cover those that are in use, however, skipping the legacy 802.11 transmission methods. Technically, these belong to the physical layer and should have been examined in Chap. 2, but since they are so closely tied to LANs in general and the 802.11 LAN in particular, we treat them here instead.

4.4.2 The 802.11 Physical Layer

Each of the transmission techniques makes it possible to send a MAC frame over the air from one station to another. They differ, however, in the technology used and speeds achievable. A detailed discussion of these technologies is far beyond the scope of this book, but a few words on each one will relate the techniques to the material we covered in Sec. 2.5 and will provide interested readers with the key terms to search for elsewhere for more information.

All of the 802.11 techniques use short-range radios to transmit signals in either the 2.4-GHz or the 5-GHz ISM frequency bands, both described in Sec. 2.3.3. These bands have the advantage of being unlicensed and hence freely available to any transmitter willing to meet some restrictions, such as radiated power of at most 1 W (though 50 mW is more typical for wireless LAN radios). Unfortunately, this fact is also known to the manufacturers of garage door openers, cordless phones, microwave ovens, and countless other devices, all of which compete with laptops for the same spectrum. The 2.4-GHz band tends to be more crowded than the 5-GHz band, so 5 GHz can be better for some applications even though it has shorter range due to the higher frequency.

All of the transmission methods also define multiple rates. The idea is that different rates can be used depending on the current conditions. If the wireless signal is weak, a low rate can be used. If the signal is clear, the highest rate can be used. This adjustment is called **rate adaptation**. Since the rates vary by a factor of 10 or more, good rate adaptation is important for good performance. Of course, since it is not needed for interoperability, the standards do not say how rate adaptation should be done.

The first transmission method we shall look at is **802.11b**. It is a spread-spectrum method that supports rates of 1, 2, 5.5, and 11 Mbps, though in practice the operating rate is nearly always 11 Mbps. It is similar to the CDMA system we examined in Sec. 2.5, except that there is only one spreading code that is shared by all users. Spreading is used to satisfy the FCC requirement that power be spread over the ISM band. The spreading sequence used by 201.11b is a **Barker sequence**. It has the property that its autocorrelation is low except when the sequences are aligned. This property allows a receiver to lock onto the start of a transmission. To send at a rate of 1 Mbps, the Barker sequence is used with BPSK modulation to send 1 bit per 11 chips. The chips are transmitted at a rate of 11 Mchips/sec. To send at 2 Mbps, it is used with QPSK modulation to send 2 bits per 11 chips. The higher rates are different. These rates use a technique called **CCK** (**Complementary Code Keying**) to construct codes instead of the Barker sequence. The 5.5-Mbps rate sends 4 bits in every 8-chip code, and the 11-Mbps rate sends 8 bits in every 8-chip code.

Next we come to **802.11a**, which supports rates up to 54 Mbps in the 5-GHz ISM band. You might have expected that 802.11a to come before 802.11b, but that was not the case. Although the 802.11a group was set up first, the 802.11b standard was approved first and its product got to market well ahead of the 802.11a products, partly because of the difficulty of operating in the higher 5-GHz band.

The 802.11a method is based on **OFDM** (**Orthogonal Frequency Division Multiplexing**) because OFDM uses the spectrum efficiently and resists wireless signal degradations such as multipath. Bits are sent over 52 subcarriers in parallel, 48 carrying data and 4 used for synchronization. Each symbol lasts 4μs and sends 1, 2, 4, or 6 bits. The bits are coded for error correction with a binary convolutional code first, so only 1/2, 2/3, or 3/4 of the bits are not redundant. With different combinations, 802.11a can run at eight different rates, ranging from 6 to 54 Mbps. These rates are significantly faster than 802.11b rates, and there is less interference in the 5-GHz band. However, 802.11b has a range that is about seven times greater than that of 802.11a, which is more important in many situations.

Even with the greater range, the 802.11b people had no intention of letting this upstart win the speed championship. Fortunately, in May 2002, the FCC dropped its long-standing rule requiring all wireless communications equipment operating in the ISM bands in the U.S. to use spread spectrum, so it got to work on **802.11g**, which was approved by IEEE in 2003. It copies the OFDM modulation methods of 802.11a but operates in the narrow 2.4-GHz ISM band along with 802.11b. It offers the same rates as 802.11a (6 to 54 Mbps) plus of course compatibility with any 802.11b devices that happen to be nearby. All of these different choices can be confusing for customers, so it is common for products to support 802.11a/b/g in a single NIC.

Not content to stop there, the IEEE committee began work on a high-throughput physical layer called **802.11n**. It was ratified in 2009. The goal for 802.11n was throughput of at least 100 Mbps after all the wireless overheads were removed. This goal called for a raw speed increase of at least a factor of four. To make it happen, the committee doubled the channels from 20 MHz to 40 MHz and reduced framing overheads by allowing a group of frames to be sent together. More significantly, however, 802.11n uses up to four antennas to transmit up to four streams of information at the same time. The signals of the streams interfere at the receiver, but they can be separated using **MIMO** (**Multiple Input Multiple Output**) communications techniques. The use of multiple antennas gives a large speed boost, or better range and reliability instead. MIMO, like OFDM, is one of those clever communications ideas that is changing wireless designs and which we are all likely to hear a lot about in the future. For a brief introduction to multiple antennas in 802.11 see Halperin et al. (2010).

4.4.3 The 802.11 MAC Sublayer Protocol

Let us now return from the land of electrical engineering to the land of computer science. The 802.11 MAC sublayer protocol is quite different from that of Ethernet, due to two factors that are fundamental to wireless communication.

First, radios are nearly always half duplex, meaning that they cannot transmit and listen for noise bursts at the same time on a single frequency. The received signal can easily be a million times weaker than the transmitted signal, so it cannot be heard at the same time. With Ethernet, a station just waits until the ether goes silent and then starts transmitting. If it does not receive a noise burst back while transmitting the first 64 bytes, the frame has almost assuredly been delivered correctly. With wireless, this collision detection mechanism does not work.

Instead, 802.11 tries to avoid collisions with a protocol called **CSMA/CA** (**CSMA with Collision Avoidance**). This protocol is conceptually similar to Ethernet's CSMA/CD, with channel sensing before sending and exponential back off after collisions. However, a station that has a frame to send starts with a random backoff (except in the case that it has not used the channel recently and the channel is idle). It does not wait for a collision. The number of slots to backoff is chosen in the range 0 to, say, 15 in the case of the OFDM physical layer. The station waits until the channel is idle, by sensing that there is no signal for a short period of time (called the DIFS, as we explain below), and counts down idle slots, pausing when frames are sent. It sends its frame when the counter reaches 0. If the frame gets through, the destination immediately sends a short acknowledgement. Lack of an acknowledgement is inferred to indicate an error, whether a collision or otherwise. In this case, the sender doubles the backoff period and tries again, continuing with exponential backoff as in Ethernet until the frame has been successfully transmitted or the maximum number of retransmissions has been reached.

An example timeline is shown in Fig. 4-25. Station *A* is the first to send a frame. While *A* is sending, stations *B* and *C* become ready to send. They see that the channel is busy and wait for it to become idle. Shortly after *A* receives an acknowledgement, the channel goes idle. However, rather than sending a frame right away and colliding, *B* and *C* both perform a backoff. *C* picks a short backoff, and thus sends first. *B* pauses its countdown while it senses that *C* is using the channel, and resumes after *C* has received an acknowledgement. *B* soon completes its backoff and sends its frame.

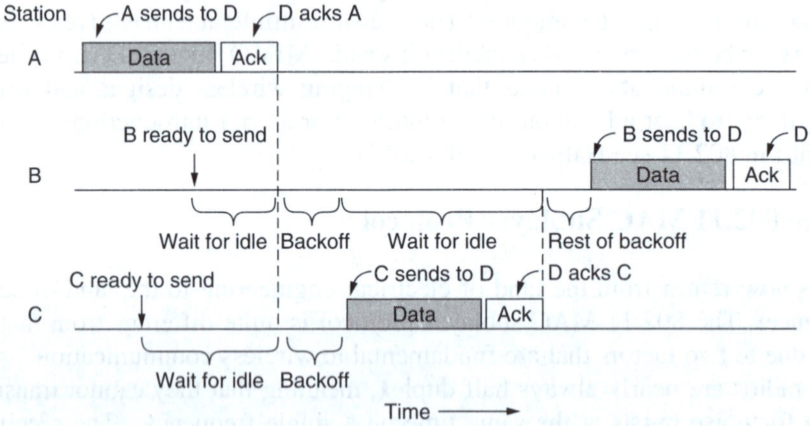

Figure 4-25. Sending a frame with CSMA/CA.

Compared to Ethernet, there are two main differences. First, starting backoffs early helps to avoid collisions. This avoidance is worthwhile because collisions are expensive, as the entire frame is transmitted even if one occurs. Second, acknowledgements are used to infer collisions because collisions cannot be detected.

This mode of operation is called **DCF** (**Distributed Coordination Function**) because each station acts independently, without any kind of central control. The standard also includes an optional mode of operation called **PCF** (**Point Coordination Function**) in which the access point controls all activity in its cell, just like a cellular base station. However, PCF is not used in practice because there is normally no way to prevent stations in another nearby network from transmitting competing traffic.

The second problem is that the transmission ranges of different stations may be different. With a wire, the system is engineered so that all stations can hear each other. With the complexities of RF propagation this situation does not hold for wireless stations. Consequently, situations such as the hidden terminal problem mentioned earlier and illustrated again in Fig. 4-26(a) can arise. Since not all stations are within radio range of each other, transmissions going on in one part of a cell may not be received elsewhere in the same cell. In this example, station *C* is transmitting to station *B*. If *A* senses the channel, it will not hear anything and will falsely conclude that it may now start transmitting to *B*. This decision leads to a collision.

The inverse situation is the exposed terminal problem, illustrated in Fig. 4-26(b). Here, *B* wants to send to *C*, so it listens to the channel. When it hears a

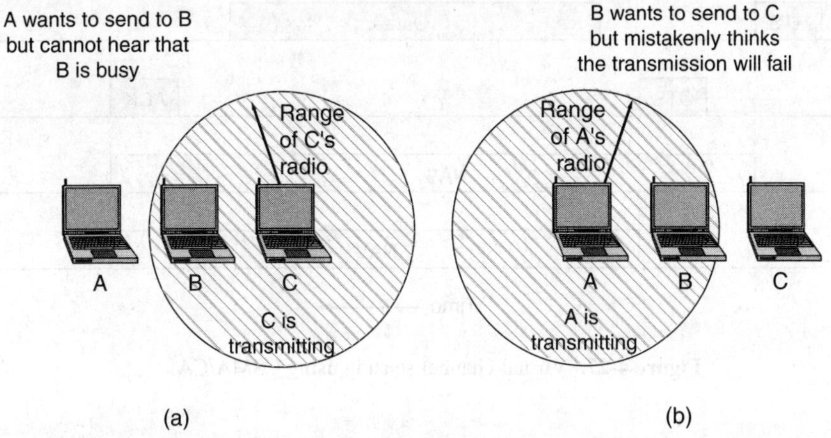

Figure 4-26. (a) The hidden terminal problem. (b) The exposed terminal problem.

transmission, it falsely concludes that it may not send to *C*, even though *A* may in fact be transmitting to *D* (not shown). This decision wastes a transmission opportunity.

To reduce ambiguities about which station is sending, 802.11 defines channel sensing to consist of both physical sensing and virtual sensing. Physical sensing simply checks the medium to see if there is a valid signal. With virtual sensing, each station keeps a logical record of when the channel is in use by tracking the **NAV (Network Allocation Vector)**. Each frame carries a NAV field that says how long the sequence of which this frame is part will take to complete. Stations that overhear this frame know that the channel will be busy for the period indicated by the NAV, regardless of whether they can sense a physical signal. For example, the NAV of a data frame includes the time needed to send an acknowledgement. All stations that hear the data frame will defer during the acknowledgement period, whether or not they can hear the acknowledgement.

An optional RTS/CTS mechanism uses the NAV to prevent terminals from sending frames at the same time as hidden terminals. It is shown in Fig. 4-27. In this example, *A* wants to send to *B*. *C* is a station within range of *A* (and possibly within range of *B*, but that does not matter). *D* is a station within range of *B* but not within range of *A*.

The protocol starts when *A* decides it wants to send data to *B*. *A* begins by sending an RTS frame to *B* to request permission to send it a frame. If *B* receives this request, it answers with a CTS frame to indicate that the channel is clear to send. Upon receipt of the CTS, *A* sends its frame and starts an ACK timer. Upon correct receipt of the data frame, *B* responds with an ACK frame, completing the exchange. If *A*'s ACK timer expires before the ACK gets back to it, it is treated as a collision and the whole protocol is run again after a backoff.

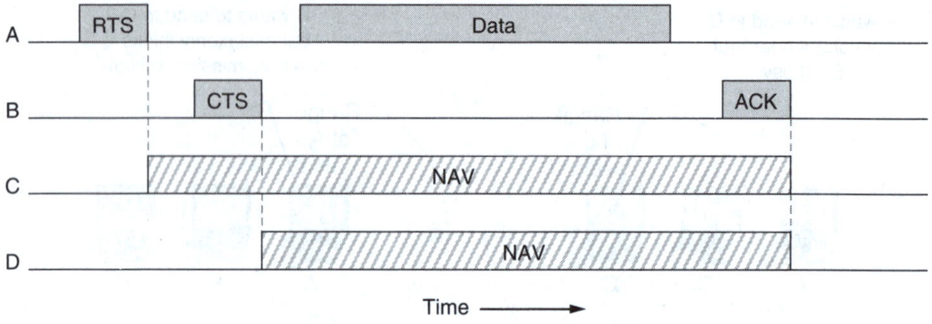

Figure 4-27. Virtual channel sensing using CSMA/CA.

Now let us consider this exchange from the viewpoints of *C* and *D*. *C* is within range of *A*, so it may receive the RTS frame. If it does, it realizes that someone is going to send data soon. From the information provided in the RTS request, it can estimate how long the sequence will take, including the final ACK. So, for the good of all, it desists from transmitting anything until the exchange is completed. It does so by updating its record of the NAV to indicate that the channel is busy, as shown in Fig. 4-27. *D* does not hear the RTS, but it does hear the CTS, so it also updates its NAV. Note that the NAV signals are not transmitted; they are just internal reminders to keep quiet for a certain period of time.

However, while RTS/CTS sounds good in theory, it is one of those designs that has proved to be of little value in practice. Several reasons why it is seldom used are known. It does not help for short frames (which are sent in place of the RTS) or for the AP (which everyone can hear, by definition). For other situations, it only slows down operation. RTS/CTS in 802.11 is a little different than in the MACA protocol we saw in Sec 4.2 because everyone hearing the RTS or CTS remains quiet for the duration to allow the ACK to get through without collision. Because of this, it does not help with exposed terminals as MACA did, only with hidden terminals. Most often there are few hidden terminals, and CSMA/CA already helps them by slowing down stations that transmit unsuccessfully, whatever the cause, to make it more likely that transmissions will succeed.

CSMA/CA with physical and virtual sensing is the core of the 802.11 protocol. However, there are several other mechanisms that have been developed to go with it. Each of these mechanisms was driven by the needs of real operation, so we will look at them briefly.

The first need we will look at is reliability. In contrast to wired networks, wireless networks are noisy and unreliable, in no small part due to interference from other kinds of devices, such as microwave ovens, which also use the unlicensed ISM bands. The use of acknowledgements and retransmissions is of little help if the probability of getting a frame through is small in the first place.

The main strategy that is used to increase successful transmissions is to lower the transmission rate. Slower rates use more robust modulations that are more likely to be received correctly for a given signal-to-noise ratio. If too many frames are lost, a station can lower the rate. If frames are delivered with little loss, a station can occasionally test a higher rate to see if it should be used.

Another strategy to improve the chance of the frame getting through undamaged is to send shorter frames. If the probability of any bit being in error is p, the probability of an n-bit frame being received entirely correctly is $(1-p)^n$. For example, for $p = 10^{-4}$, the probability of receiving a full Ethernet frame (12,144 bits) correctly is less than 30%. Most frames will be lost. But if the frames are only a third as long (4048 bits) two thirds of them will be received correctly. Now most frames will get through and fewer retransmissions will be needed.

Shorter frames can be implemented by reducing the maximum size of the message that is accepted from the network layer. Alternatively, 802.11 allows frames to be split into smaller pieces, called **fragments**, each with its own checksum. The fragment size is not fixed by the standard, but is a parameter that can be adjusted by the AP. The fragments are individually numbered and acknowledged using a stop-and-wait protocol (i.e., the sender may not transmit fragment $k + 1$ until it has received the acknowledgement for fragment k). Once the channel has been acquired, multiple fragments are sent as a burst. They go one after the other with an acknowledgement (and possibly retransmissions) in between, until either the whole frame has been successfully sent or the transmission time reaches the maximum allowed. The NAV mechanism keeps other stations quiet only until the next acknowledgement, but another mechanism (see below) is used to allow a burst of fragments to be sent without other stations sending a frame in the middle.

The second need we will discuss is saving power. Battery life is always an issue with mobile wireless devices. The 802.11 standard pays attention to the issue of power management so that clients need not waste power when they have neither information to send nor to receive.

The basic mechanism for saving power builds on **beacon frames**. Beacons are periodic broadcasts by the AP (e.g., every 100 msec). The frames advertise the presence of the AP to clients and carry system parameters, such as the identifier of the AP, the time, how long until the next beacon, and security settings.

Clients can set a power-management bit in frames that they send to the AP to tell it that they are entering **power-save mode**. In this mode, the client can doze and the AP will buffer traffic intended for it. To check for incoming traffic, the client wakes up for every beacon, and checks a traffic map that is sent as part of the beacon. This map tells the client if there is buffered traffic. If so, the client sends a poll message to the AP, which then sends the buffered traffic. The client can then go back to sleep until the next beacon is sent.

Another power-saving mechanism, called **APSD (Automatic Power Save Delivery)**, was also added to 802.11 in 2005. With this new mechanism, the AP buffers frames and sends them to a client just after the client sends frames to the

AP. The client can then go to sleep until it has more traffic to send (and receive). This mechanism works well for applications such as VoIP that have frequent traffic in both directions. For example, a VoIP wireless phone might use it to send and receive frames every 20 msec, much more frequently than the beacon interval of 100 msec, while dozing in between.

The third and last need we will examine is quality of service. When the VoIP traffic in the preceding example competes with peer-to-peer traffic, the VoIP traffic will suffer. It will be delayed due to contention with the high-bandwidth peer-to-peer traffic, even though the VoIP bandwidth is low. These delays are likely to degrade the voice calls. To prevent this degradation, we would like to let the VoIP traffic go ahead of the peer-to-peer traffic, as it is of higher priority.

IEEE 802.11 has a clever mechanism to provide this kind of quality of service that was introduced as set of extensions under the name 802.11e in 2005. It works by extending CSMA/CA with carefully defined intervals between frames. After a frame has been sent, a certain amount of idle time is required before any station may send a frame to check that the channel is no longer in use. The trick is to define different time intervals for different kinds of frames.

Five intervals are depicted in Fig. 4-28. The interval between regular data frames is called the **DIFS (DCF InterFrame Spacing)**. Any station may attempt to acquire the channel to send a new frame after the medium has been idle for DIFS. The usual contention rules apply, and binary exponential backoff may be needed if a collision occurs. The shortest interval is **SIFS (Short InterFrame Spacing)**. It is used to allow the parties in a single dialog the chance to go first. Examples include letting the receiver send an ACK, other control frame sequences like RTS and CTS, or letting a sender transmit a burst of fragments. Sending the next fragment after waiting only SIFS is what prevents another station from jumping in with a frame in the middle of the exchange.

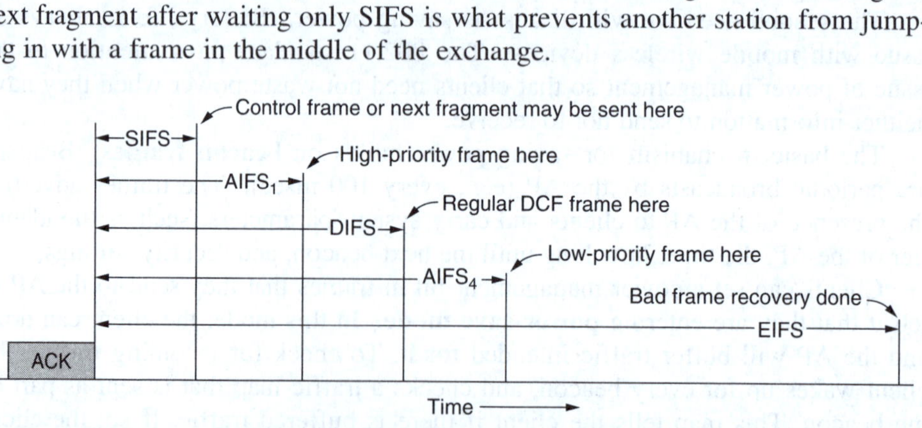

Figure 4-28. Interframe spacing in 802.11.

The two **AIFS (Arbitration InterFrame Space)** intervals show examples of two different priority levels. The short interval, $AIFS_1$, is smaller than DIFS but longer than SIFS. It can be used by the AP to move voice or other high-priority traffic to the head of the line. The AP will wait for a shorter interval before it sends the voice traffic, and thus send it before regular traffic. The long interval, $AIFS_4$, is larger than DIFS. It is used for background traffic that can be deferred until after regular traffic. The AP will wait for a longer interval before it sends this traffic, giving regular traffic the opportunity to transmit first. The complete quality of service mechanism defines four different priority levels that have different backoff parameters as well as different idle parameters.

The last time interval, **EIFS** (**Extended InterFrame Spacing**), is used only by a station that has just received a bad or unknown frame, to report the problem. The idea is that since the receiver may have no idea of what is going on, it should wait a while to avoid interfering with an ongoing dialog between two stations.

A further part of the quality of service extensions is the notion of a **TXOP** or **transmission opportunity**. The original CSMA/CA mechanism let stations send one frame at a time. This design was fine until the range of rates increased. With 802.11a/g, one station might be sending at 6 Mbps and another station be sending at 54 Mbps. They each get to send one frame, but the 6-Mbps station takes nine times as long (ignoring fixed overheads) as the 54-Mbps station to send its frame. This disparity has the unfortunate side effect of slowing down a fast sender who is competing with a slow sender to roughly the rate of the slow sender. For example, again ignoring fixed overheads, when sending alone the 6-Mbps and 54-Mbps senders will get their own rates, but when sending together they will both get 5.4 Mbps on average. It is a stiff penalty for the fast sender. This issue is known as the **rate anomaly** (Heusse et al., 2003).

With transmission opportunities, each station gets an equal amount of airtime, not an equal number of frames. Stations that send at a higher rate for their airtime will get higher throughput. In our example, when sending together the 6-Mbps and 54-Mbps senders will now get 3 Mbps and 27 Mbps, respectively.

4.4.4 The 802.11 Frame Structure

The 802.11 standard defines three different classes of frames in the air: data, control, and management. Each of these has a header with a variety of fields used within the MAC sublayer. In addition, there are some headers used by the physical layer, but these mostly deal with the modulation techniques used, so we will not discuss them here.

We will look at the format of the data frame as an example. It is shown in Fig. 4-29. First comes the *Frame control* field, which is made up of 11 subfields. The first of these is the *Protocol version*, set to 00. It is there to allow future versions of 802.11 to operate at the same time in the same cell. Then come the *Type* (data, control, or management) and *Subtype* fields (e.g., RTS or CTS). For a regular data frame (without quality of service), they are set to 10 and 0000 in binary. The *To DS* and *From DS* bits are set to indicate whether the frame is going to or coming from the network connected to the APs, which is called the distribution system. The *More fragments* bit means that more fragments will follow. The *Retry* bit marks a retransmission of a frame sent earlier. The *Power management* bit indicates that the sender is going into power-save mode. The *More data* bit indicates that the sender has additional frames for the receiver. The *Protected Frame* bit indicates that the frame body has been encrypted for security. We will discuss security briefly in the next section. Finally, the *Order* bit tells the receiver that the higher layer expects the sequence of frames to arrive strictly in order.

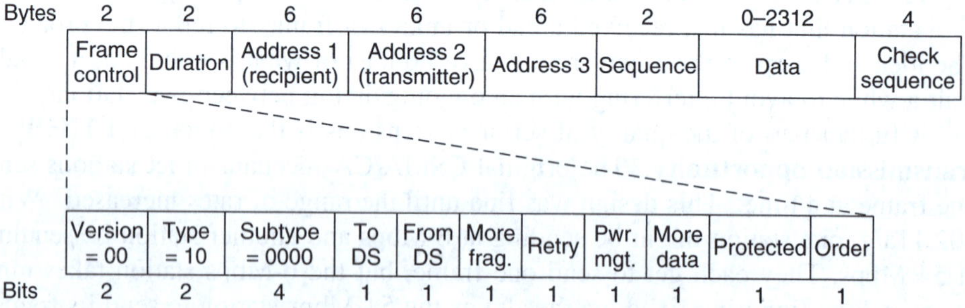

Figure 4-29. Format of the 802.11 data frame.

The second field of the data frame, the *Duration* field, tells how long the frame and its acknowledgement will occupy the channel, measured in microseconds. It is present in all types of frames, including control frames, and is what stations use to manage the NAV mechanism.

Next come addresses. Data frames sent to or from an AP have three addresses, all in standard IEEE 802 format. The first address is the receiver, and the second address is the transmitter. They are obviously needed, but what is the third address for? Remember that the AP is simply a relay point for frames as they travel between a client and another point on the network, perhaps a distant client or a portal to the Internet. The third address gives this distant endpoint.

The *Sequence* field numbers frames so that duplicates can be detected. Of the 16 bits available, 4 identify the fragment and 12 carry a number that is advanced with each new transmission. The *Data* field contains the payload, up to 2312 bytes. The first bytes of this payload are in a format known as **LLC** (**Logical Link Control**). This layer is the glue that identifies the higher-layer protocol (e.g., IP) to which the payloads should be passed. Last comes the *Frame check sequence*, which is the same 32-bit CRC we saw in Sec. 3.2.2 and elsewhere.

Management frames have the same format as data frames, plus a format for the data portion that varies with the subtype (e.g., parameters in beacon frames). Control frames are short. Like all frames, they have the *Frame control*, *Duration*, and *Frame check sequence* fields. However, they may have only one address and no data portion. Most of the key information is conveyed with the *Subtype* field (e.g., ACK, RTS and CTS).

4.4.5 Services

The 802.11 standard defines the services that the clients, the access points, and the network connecting them must be a conformant wireless LAN. These services cluster into several groups.

The **association** service is used by mobile stations to connect themselves to APs. Typically, it is used just after a station moves within radio range of the AP. Upon arrival, the station learns the identity and capabilities of the AP, either from beacon frames or by directly asking the AP. The capabilities include the data rates supported, security arrangements, power-saving capabilities, quality of service support, and more. The station sends a request to associate with the AP. The AP may accept or reject the request.

Reassociation lets a station change its preferred AP. This facility is useful for mobile stations moving from one AP to another AP in the same extended 802.11 LAN, like a handover in the cellular network. If it is used correctly, no data will be lost as a consequence of the handover. (But 802.11, like Ethernet, is just a best-effort service.) Either the station or the AP may also **disassociate**, breaking their relationship. A station should use this service before shutting down or leaving the network. The AP may use it before going down for maintenance.

Stations must also **authenticate** before they can send frames via the AP, but authentication is handled in different ways depending on the choice of security scheme. If the 802.11 network is "open," anyone is allowed to use it. Otherwise, credentials are needed to authenticate. The recommended scheme, called **WPA2** (**WiFi Protected Access 2**), implements security as defined in the 802.11i standard. (Plain WPA is an interim scheme that implements a subset of 802.11i. We will skip it and go straight to the complete scheme.) With WPA2, the AP can talk to an authentication server that has a username and password database to determine if the station is allowed to access the network. Alternatively a pre-shared key, which is a fancy name for a network password, may be configured. Several frames are exchanged between the station and the AP with a challenge and response that lets the station prove it has the right credentials. This exchange happens after association.

The scheme that was used before WPA is called **WEP** (**Wired Equivalent Privacy**). For this scheme, authentication with a preshared key happens before association. However, its use is discouraged because of design flaws that make WEP easy to compromise. The first practical demonstration that WEP was broken came when Adam Stubblefield was a summer intern at AT&T (Stubblefield et al., 2002). He was able to code up and test an attack in one week, much of which was spent getting permission from management to buy the WiFi cards needed for experiments. Software to crack WEP passwords is now freely available.

Once frames reach the AP, the **distribution** service determines how to route them. If the destination is local to the AP, the frames can be sent out directly over the air. Otherwise, they will have to be forwarded over the wired network. The

integration service handles any translation that is needed for a frame to be sent outside the 802.11 LAN, or to arrive from outside the 802.11 LAN. The common case here is connecting the wireless LAN to the Internet.

Data transmission is what it is all about, so 802.11 naturally provides a **data delivery** service. This service lets stations transmit and receive data using the protocols we described earlier in this chapter. Since 802.11 is modeled on Ethernet and transmission over Ethernet is not guaranteed to be 100% reliable, transmission over 802.11 is not guaranteed to be reliable either. Higher layers must deal with detecting and correcting errors.

Wireless is a broadcast signal. For information sent over a wireless LAN to be kept confidential, it must be encrypted. This goal is accomplished with a **privacy** service that manages the details of encryption and decryption. The encryption algorithm for WPA2 is based on **AES (Advanced Encryption Standard)**, a U.S. government standard approved in 2002. The keys that are used for encryption are determined during the authentication procedure.

To handle traffic with different priorities, there is a **QOS traffic scheduling** service. It uses the protocols we described to give voice and video traffic preferential treatment compared to best-effort and background traffic. A companion service also provides higher-layer timer synchronization. This lets stations coordinate their actions, which may be useful for media processing.

Finally, there are two services that help stations manage their use of the spectrum. The **transmit power control** service gives stations the information they need to meet regulatory limits on transmit power that vary from region to region. The **dynamic frequency selection** service give stations the information they need to avoid transmitting on frequencies in the 5-GHz band that are being used for radar in the proximity.

With these services, 802.11 provides a rich set of functionality for connecting nearby mobile clients to the Internet. It has been a huge success, and the standard has repeatedly been amended to add more functionality. For a perspective on where the standard has been and where it is heading, see Hiertz et al. (2010).

4.5 BROADBAND WIRELESS

We have been indoors too long. Let us go outdoors, where there is quite a bit of interesting networking over the so-called "last mile." With the deregulation of the telephone systems in many countries, competitors to the entrenched telephone companies are now often allowed to offer local voice and high-speed Internet service. There is certainly plenty of demand. The problem is that running fiber or coax to millions of homes and businesses is prohibitively expensive. What is a competitor to do?

The answer is broadband wireless. Erecting a big antenna on a hill just outside of town is much easier and cheaper than digging many trenches and stringing cables. Thus, companies have begun to experiment with providing multimegabit wireless communication services for voice, Internet, movies on demand, etc.

To stimulate the market, IEEE formed a group to standardize a broadband wireless metropolitan area network. The next number available in the 802 numbering space was **802.16**, so the standard got this number. Informally the technology is called **WiMAX (Worldwide Interoperability for Microwave Access)**. We will use the terms 802.16 and WiMAX interchangeably.

The first 802.16 standard was approved in December 2001. Early versions provided a wireless local loop between fixed points with a line of sight to each other. This design soon changed to make WiMAX a more competitive alternative to cable and DSL for Internet access. By January 2003, 802.16 had been revised to support non-line-of-sight links by using OFDM technology at frequencies between 2 GHz and 10 GHz. This change made deployment much easier, though stations were still fixed locations. The rise of 3G cellular networks posed a threat by promising high data rates *and* mobility. In response, 802.16 was enhanced again to allow mobility at vehicular speeds by December 2005. Mobile broadband Internet access is the target of the current standard, IEEE 802.16-2009.

Like the other 802 standards, 802.16 was heavily influenced by the OSI model, including the (sub)layers, terminology, service primitives, and more. Unfortunately, also like OSI, it is fairly complicated. In fact, the **WiMAX Forum** was created to define interoperable subsets of the standard for commercial offerings. In the following sections, we will give a brief description of some of the highlights of the common forms of 802.16 air interface, but this treatment is far from complete and leaves out many details. For additional information about WiMAX and broadband wireless in general, see Andrews et al. (2007).

4.5.1 Comparison of 802.16 with 802.11 and 3G

At this point you may be thinking: why devise a new standard? Why not just use 802.11 or 3G? In fact, WiMAX combines aspects of both 802.11 and 3G, making it more like a 4G technology.

Like 802.11, WiMAX is all about wirelessly connecting devices to the Internet at megabit/sec speeds, instead of using cable or DSL. The devices may be mobile, or at least portable. WiMAX did not start by adding low-rate data on the side of voice-like cellular networks; 802.16 was designed to carry IP packets over the air and to connect to an IP-based wired network with a minimum of fuss. The packets may carry peer-to-peer traffic, VoIP calls, or streaming media to support a range of applications. Also like 802.11, it is based on OFDM technology to ensure good performance in spite of wireless signal degradations such as multipath fading, and on MIMO technology to achieve high levels of throughput.

However, WiMAX is more like 3G (and thus unlike 802.11) in several key respects. The key technical problem is to achieve high capacity by the efficient use of spectrum, so that a large number of subscribers in a coverage area can all get high throughput. The typical distances are at least 10 times larger than for an 802.11 network. Consequently, WiMAX base stations are more powerful than 802.11 Access Points (APs). To handle weaker signals over larger distances, the base station uses more power and better antennas, and it performs more processing to handle errors. To maximize throughput, transmissions are carefully scheduled by the base station for each particular subscriber; spectrum use is not left to chance with CSMA/CA, which may waste capacity with collisions.

Licensed spectrum is the expected case for WiMAX, typically around 2.5 GHz in the U.S. The whole system is substantially more optimized than 802.11. This complexity is worth it, considering the large amount of money involved for licensed spectrum. Unlike 802.11, the result is a managed and reliable service with good support for quality of service.

With all of these features, 802.16 most closely resembles the 4G cellular networks that are now being standardized under the name **LTE (Long Term Evolution)**. While 3G cellular networks are based on CDMA and support voice and data, 4G cellular networks will be based on OFDM with MIMO, and they will target data, with voice as just one application. It looks like WiMAX and 4G are on a collision course in terms of technology and applications. Perhaps this convergence is unsurprising, given that the Internet is the killer application and OFDM and MIMO are the best-known technologies for efficiently using the spectrum.

4.5.2 The 802.16 Architecture and Protocol Stack

The 802.16 architecture is shown in Fig. 4-30. Base stations connect directly to the provider's backbone network, which is in turn connected to the Internet. The base stations communicate with stations over the wireless air interface. Two kinds of stations exist. Subscriber stations remain in a fixed location, for example, broadband Internet access for homes. Mobile stations can receive service while they are moving, for example, a car equipped with WiMAX.

The 802.16 protocol stack that is used across the air interface is shown in Fig. 4-31. The general structure is similar to that of the other 802 networks, but with more sublayers. The bottom layer deals with transmission, and here we have shown only the popular offerings of 802.16, fixed and mobile WiMAX. There is a different physical layer for each offering. Both layers operate in licensed spectrum below 11 GHz and use OFDM, but in different ways.

Above the physical layer, the data link layer consists of three sublayers. The bottom one deals with privacy and security, which is far more crucial for public outdoor networks than for private indoor networks. It manages encryption, decryption, and key management.

Next comes the MAC common sublayer part. This part is where the main protocols, such as channel management, are located. The model here is that the base station completely controls the system. It can schedule the downlink (i.e., base to subscriber) channels very efficiently and plays a major role in managing

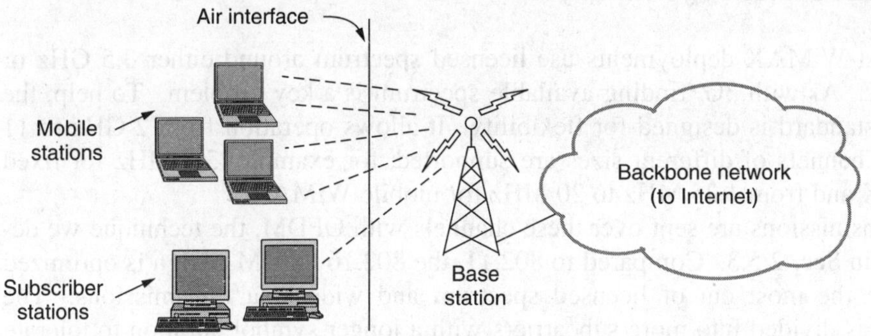

Figure 4-30. The 802.16 architecture.

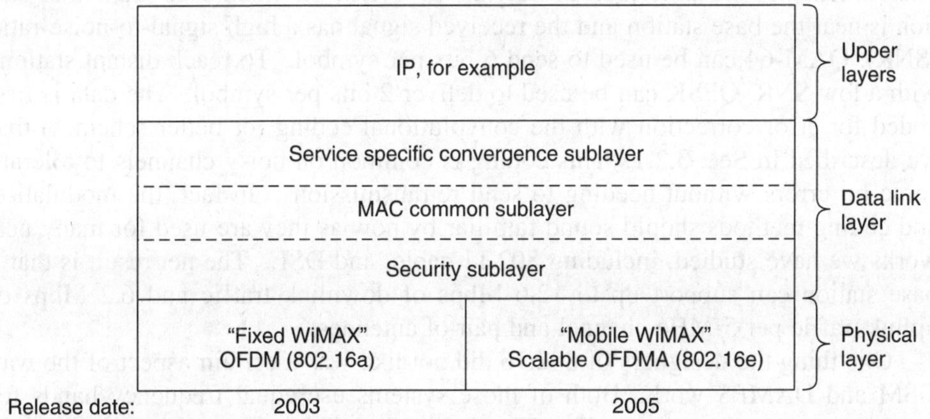

Figure 4-31. The 802.16 protocol stack.

the uplink (i.e., subscriber to base) channels as well. An unusual feature of this MAC sublayer is that, unlike those of the other 802 protocols, it is completely connection oriented, in order to provide quality of service guarantees for telephony and multimedia communication.

The service-specific convergence sublayer takes the place of the logical link sublayer in the other 802 protocols. Its function is to provide an interface to the network layer. Different convergence layers are defined to integrate seamlessly with different upper layers. The important choice is IP, though the standard defines mappings for protocols such as Ethernet and ATM too. Since IP is connectionless and the 802.16 MAC sublayer is connection-oriented, this layer must map between addresses and connections.

4.5.3 The 802.16 Physical Layer

Most WiMAX deployments use licensed spectrum around either 3.5 GHz or 2.5 GHz. As with 3G, finding available spectrum is a key problem. To help, the 802.16 standard is designed for flexibility. It allows operation from 2 GHz to 11 GHz. Channels of different sizes are supported, for example, 3.5 MHz for fixed WiMAX and from 1.25 MHz to 20 MHz for mobile WiMAX.

Transmissions are sent over these channels with OFDM, the technique we described in Sec. 2.5.3. Compared to 802.11, the 802.16 OFDM design is optimized to make the most out of licensed spectrum and wide area transmissions. The channel is divided into more subcarriers with a longer symbol duration to tolerate larger wireless signal degradations; WiMAX parameters are around 20 times larger than comparable 802.11 parameters. For example, in mobile WiMAX there are 512 subcarriers for a 5-MHz channel and the time to send a symbol on each subcarrier is roughly 100 μsec.

Symbols on each subcarrier are sent with QPSK, QAM-16, or QAM-64, modulation schemes we described in Sec. 2.5.3. When the mobile or subscriber station is near the base station and the received signal has a high signal-to-noise ratio (SNR), QAM-64 can be used to send 6 bits per symbol. To reach distant stations with a low SNR, QPSK can be used to deliver 2 bits per symbol. The data is first coded for error correction with the convolutional coding (or better schemes) that we described in Sec. 3.2.1. This coding is common on noisy channels to tolerate some bit errors without needing to send retransmissions. In fact, the modulation and coding methods should sound familiar by now as they are used for many networks we have studied, including 802.11 cable, and DSL. The net result is that a base station can support up to 12.6 Mbps of downlink traffic and 6.2 Mbps of uplink traffic per 5-MHz channel and pair of antennas.

One thing the designers of 802.16 did not like was a certain aspect of the way GSM and DAMPS work. Both of those systems use equal frequency bands for upstream and downstream traffic. That is, they implicitly assume there is as much upstream traffic as downstream traffic. For voice, traffic is symmetric for the most part, but for Internet access (and certainly Web surfing) there is often more downstream traffic than upstream traffic. The ratio is often 2:1, 3:1, or more:1.

So, the designers chose a flexible scheme for dividing the channel between stations, called **OFDMA** (**Orthogonal Frequency Division Multiple Access**). With OFDMA, different sets of subcarriers can be assigned to different stations, so that more than one station can send or receive at once. If this were 802.11, all subcarriers would be used by one station to send at any given moment. The added flexibility in how bandwidth is assigned can increase performance because a given subcarrier might be faded at one receiver due to multipath effects but clear at another. Subcarriers can be assigned to the stations that can use them best.

As well as having asymmetric traffic, stations usually alternate between sending and receiving. This method is called **TDD** (**Time Division Duplex**). The alternative method, in which a station sends and receives at the same time (on different subcarrier frequencies), is called **FDD (Frequency Division Duplex)**. WiMAX allows both methods, but TDD is preferred because it is easier to implement and more flexible.

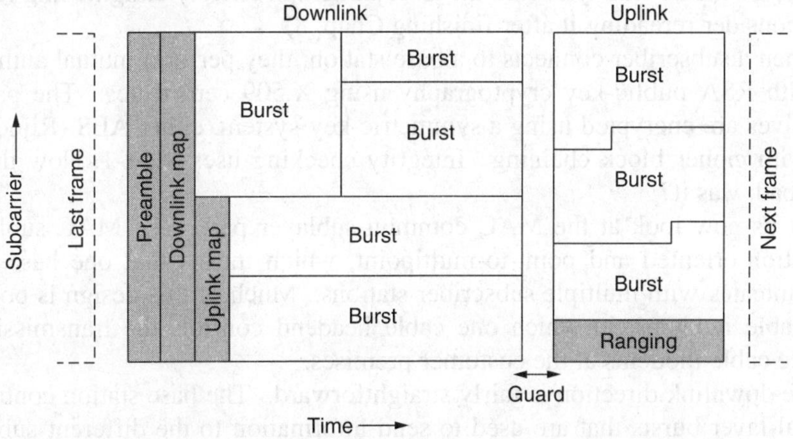

Figure 4-32. Frame structure for OFDMA with time division duplexing.

Fig. 4-32 shows an example of the frame structure that is repeated over time. It starts with a preamble to synchronize all stations, followed by downlink transmissions from the base station. First, the base station sends maps that tell all stations how the downlink and uplink subcarriers are assigned over the frame. The base station controls the maps, so it can allocate different amounts of bandwidth to stations from frame to frame depending on the needs of each station.

Next, the base station sends bursts of traffic to different subscriber and mobile stations on the subcarriers at the times given in the map. The downlink transmissions end with a guard time for stations to switch from receiving to transmitting. Finally, the subscriber and mobile stations send their bursts of traffic to the base station in the uplink positions that were reserved for them in the map. One of these uplink bursts is reserved for **ranging**, which is the process by which new stations adjust their timing and request initial bandwidth to connect to the base station. Since no connection is set up at this stage, new stations just transmit and hope there is no collision.

4.5.4 The 802.16 MAC Sublayer Protocol

The data link layer is divided into three sublayers, as we saw in Fig. 4-31. Since we will not study cryptography until Chap. 8, it is difficult to explain now how the security sublayer works. Suffice it to say that encryption is used to keep secret all data transmitted. Only the frame payloads are encrypted; the headers are not. This property means that a snooper can see who is talking to whom but cannot tell what they are saying to each other.

If you already know something about cryptography, what follows is a one-paragraph explanation of the security sublayer. If you know nothing about cryptography, you are not likely to find the next paragraph terribly enlightening (but you might consider rereading it after finishing Chap. 8).

When a subscriber connects to a base station, they perform mutual authentication with RSA public-key cryptography using X.509 certificates. The payloads themselves are encrypted using a symmetric-key system, either AES (Rijndael) or DES with cipher block chaining. Integrity checking uses SHA-1. Now that was not so bad, was it?

Let us now look at the MAC common sublayer part. The MAC sublayer is connection-oriented and point-to-multipoint, which means that one base station communicates with multiple subscriber stations. Much of this design is borrowed from cable modems, in which one cable headend controls the transmissions of multiple cable modems at the customer premises.

The downlink direction is fairly straightforward. The base station controls the physical-layer bursts that are used to send information to the different subscriber stations. The MAC sublayer simply packs its frames into this structure. To reduce overhead, there are several different options. For example, MAC frames may be sent individually, or packed back-to-back into a group.

The uplink channel is more complicated since there are competing subscribers that need access to it. Its allocation is tied closely to the quality of service issue. Four classes of service are defined, as follows:

1. Constant bit rate service.
2. Real-time variable bit rate service.
3. Non-real-time variable bit rate service.
4. Best-effort service.

All service in 802.16 is connection-oriented. Each connection gets one of these service classes, determined when the connection is set up. This design is different from that of 802.11 or Ethernet, which are connectionless in the MAC sublayer.

Constant bit rate service is intended for transmitting uncompressed voice. This service needs to send a predetermined amount of data at predetermined time intervals. It is accommodated by dedicating certain bursts to each connection of this type. Once the bandwidth has been allocated, the bursts are available automatically, without the need to ask for each one.

Real-time variable bit rate service is for compressed multimedia and other soft real-time applications in which the amount of bandwidth needed at each instant may vary. It is accommodated by the base station polling the subscriber at a fixed interval to ask how much bandwidth is needed this time.

Non-real-time variable bit rate service is for heavy transmissions that are not real time, such as large file transfers. For this service, the base station polls the subscriber often, but not at rigidly prescribed time intervals. Connections with this service can also use best-effort service, described next, to request bandwidth.

Best-effort service is for everything else. No polling is done and the subscriber must contend for bandwidth with other best-effort subscribers. Requests for bandwidth are sent in bursts marked in the uplink map as available for contention. If a request is successful, its success will be noted in the next downlink map. If it is not successful, the unsuccessful subscriber have to try again later. To minimize collisions, the Ethernet binary exponential backoff algorithm is used.

4.5.5 The 802.16 Frame Structure

All MAC frames begin with a generic header. The header is followed by an optional payload and an optional checksum (CRC), as illustrated in Fig. 4-33. The payload is not needed in control frames, for example, those requesting channel slots. The checksum is (surprisingly) also optional, due to the error correction in the physical layer and the fact that no attempt is ever made to retransmit real-time frames. If no retransmissions will be attempted, why even bother with a checksum? But if there is a checksum, it is the standard IEEE 802 CRC, and acknowledgements and retransmissions are used for reliability.

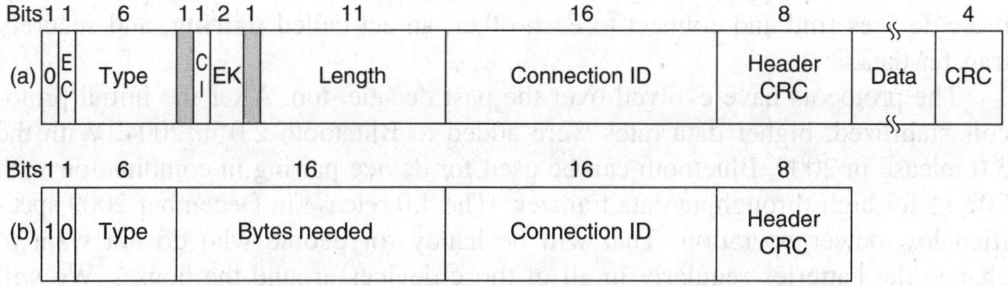

Figure 4-33. (a) A generic frame. (b) A bandwidth request frame.

A quick rundown of the header fields of Fig. 4-33(a) follows. The *EC* bit tells whether the payload is encrypted. The *Type* field identifies the frame type, mostly telling whether packing and fragmentation are present. The *CI* field indicates the presence or absence of the final checksum. The *EK* field tells which of the encryption keys is being used (if any). The *Length* field gives the complete length of the frame, including the header. The *Connection identifier* tells which connection this frame belongs to. Finally, the *Header CRC* field is a checksum over the header only, using the polynomial $x^8 + x^2 + x + 1$.

The 802.16 protocol has many kinds of frames. An example of a different type of frame, one that is used to request bandwidth, is shown in Fig. 4-33(b). It starts with a 1 bit instead of a 0 bit and is otherwise similar to the generic header except that the second and third bytes form a 16-bit number telling how much bandwidth is needed to carry the specified number of bytes. Bandwidth request frames do not carry a payload or full-frame CRC.

A great deal more could be said about 802.16, but this is not the place to say it. For more information, please consult the IEEE 802.16-2009 standard itself.

4.6 BLUETOOTH

In 1994, the L. M. Ericsson company became interested in connecting its mobile phones to other devices (e.g., laptops) without cables. Together with four other companies (IBM, Intel, Nokia, and Toshiba), it formed a SIG (Special Interest Group, i.e., consortium) in 1998 to develop a wireless standard for interconnecting computing and communication devices and accessories using short-range, low-power, inexpensive wireless radios. The project was named **Bluetooth**, after Harald Blaatand (Bluetooth) II (940–981), a Viking king who unified (i.e., conquered) Denmark and Norway, also without cables.

Bluetooth 1.0 was released in July 1999, and since then the SIG has never looked back. All manner of consumer electronic devices now use Bluetooth, from mobile phones and laptops to headsets, printers, keyboards, mice, gameboxes, watches, music players, navigation units, and more. The Bluetooth protocols let these devices find and connect to each other, an act called **pairing**, and securely transfer data.

The protocols have evolved over the past decade, too. After the initial protocols stabilized, higher data rates were added to Bluetooth 2.0 in 2004. With the 3.0 release in 2009, Bluetooth can be used for device pairing in combination with 802.11 for high-throughput data transfer. The 4.0 release in December 2009 specified low-power operation. That will be handy for people who do not want to change the batteries regularly in all of those devices around the house. We will cover the main aspects of Bluetooth below.

4.6.1 Bluetooth Architecture

Let us start our study of the Bluetooth system with a quick overview of what it contains and what it is intended to do. The basic unit of a Bluetooth system is a **piconet**, which consists of a master node and up to seven active slave nodes within a distance of 10 meters. Multiple piconets can exist in the same (large) room and can even be connected via a bridge node that takes part in multiple piconets, as in Fig. 4-34. An interconnected collection of piconets is called a **scatternet**.

In addition to the seven active slave nodes in a piconet, there can be up to 255 parked nodes in the net. These are devices that the master has switched to a low-power state to reduce the drain on their batteries. In parked state, a device cannot

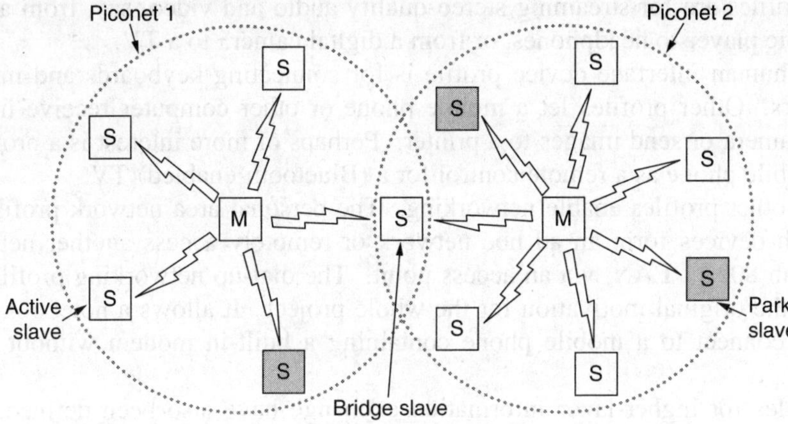

Figure 4-34. Two piconets can be connected to form a scatternet.

do anything except respond to an activation or beacon signal from the master. Two intermediate power states, hold and sniff, also exist, but these will not concern us here.

The reason for the master/slave design is that the designers intended to facilitate the implementation of complete Bluetooth chips for under \$5. The consequence of this decision is that the slaves are fairly dumb, basically just doing whatever the master tells them to do. At its heart, a piconet is a centralized TDM system, with the master controlling the clock and determining which device gets to communicate in which time slot. All communication is between the master and a slave; direct slave-slave communication is not possible.

4.6.2 Bluetooth Applications

Most network protocols just provide channels between communicating entities and let application designers figure out what they want to use them for. For example, 802.11 does not specify whether users should use their notebook computers for reading email, surfing the Web, or something else. In contrast, the Bluetooth SIG specifies particular applications to be supported and provides different protocol stacks for each one. At the time of writing, there are 25 applications, which are called **profiles**. Unfortunately, this approach leads to a very large amount of complexity. We will omit the complexity here but will briefly look at the profiles to see more clearly what the Bluetooth SIG is trying to accomplish.

Six of the profiles are for different uses of audio and video. For example, the intercom profile allows two telephones to connect as walkie-talkies. The headset and hands-free profiles both provide voice communication between a headset and its base station, as might be used for hands-free telephony while driving a car.

Other profiles are for streaming stereo-quality audio and video, say, from a portable music player to headphones, or from a digital camera to a TV.

The human interface device profile is for connecting keyboards and mice to computers. Other profiles let a mobile phone or other computer receive images from a camera or send images to a printer. Perhaps of more interest is a profile to use a mobile phone as a remote control for a (Bluetooth-enabled) TV.

Still other profiles enable networking. The personal area network profile lets Bluetooth devices form an ad hoc network or remotely access another network, such as an 802.11 LAN, via an access point. The dial-up networking profile was actually the original motivation for the whole project. It allows a notebook computer to connect to a mobile phone containing a built-in modem without using wires.

Profiles for higher-layer information exchange have also been defined. The synchronization profile is intended for loading data into a mobile phone when it leaves home and collecting data from it when it returns.

We will skip the rest of the profiles, except to mention that some profiles serve as building blocks on which the above profiles are built. The generic access profile, on which all of the other profiles are built, provides a way to establish and maintain secure links (channels) between the master and the slaves. The other generic profiles define the basics of object exchange and audio and video transport. Utility profiles are used widely for functions such as emulating a serial line, which is especially useful for many legacy applications.

Was it really necessary to spell out all these applications in detail and provide different protocol stacks for each one? Probably not, but there were a number of different working groups that devised different parts of the standard, and each one just focused on its specific problem and generated its own profile. Think of this as Conway's Law in action. (In the April 1968 issue of *Datamation* magazine, Melvin Conway observed that if you assign *n* people to write a compiler, you will get an *n*-pass compiler, or more generally, the software structure mirrors the structure of the group that produced it.) It would probably have been possible to get away with two protocol stacks instead of 25, one for file transfer and one for streaming real-time communication.

4.6.3 The Bluetooth Protocol Stack

The Bluetooth standard has many protocols grouped loosely into the layers shown in Fig. 4-35. The first observation to make is that the structure does not follow the OSI model, the TCP/IP model, the 802 model, or any other model.

The bottom layer is the physical radio layer, which corresponds fairly well to the physical layer in the OSI and 802 models. It deals with radio transmission and modulation. Many of the concerns here have to do with the goal of making the system inexpensive so that it can become a mass-market item.

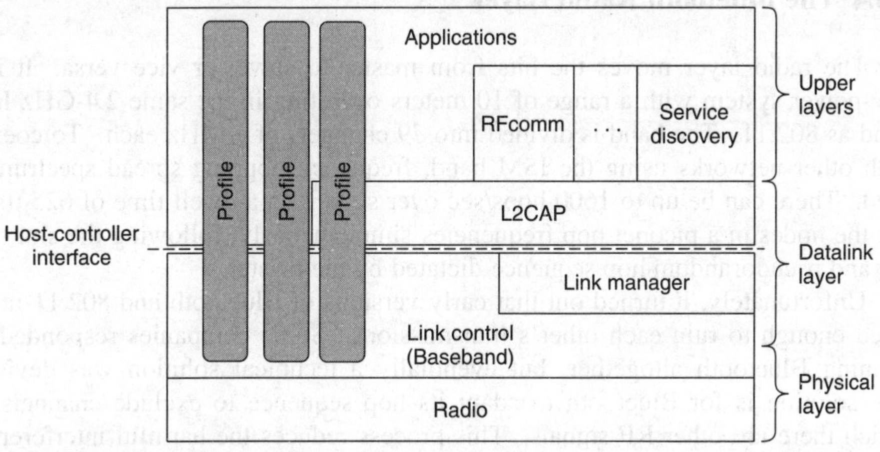

Figure 4-35. The Bluetooth protocol architecture.

The link control (or baseband) layer is somewhat analogous to the MAC sublayer but also includes elements of the physical layer. It deals with how the master controls time slots and how these slots are grouped into frames.

Next come two protocols that use the link control protocol. The link manager handles the establishment of logical channels between devices, including power management, pairing and encryption, and quality of service. It lies below the host controller interface line. This interface is a convenience for implementation: typically, the protocols below the line will be implemented on a Bluetooth chip, and the protocols above the line will be implemented on the Bluetooth device that hosts the chip.

The link protocol above the line is **L2CAP** (**Logical Link Control Adaptation Protocol**). It frames variable-length messages and provides reliability if needed. Many protocols use L2CAP, such as the two utility protocols that are shown. The service discovery protocol is used to locate services within the network. The RFcomm (Radio Frequency communication) protocol emulates the standard serial port found on PCs for connecting the keyboard, mouse, and modem, among other devices.

The top layer is where the applications are located. The profiles are represented by vertical boxes because they each define a slice of the protocol stack for a particular purpose. Specific profiles, such as the headset profile, usually contain only those protocols needed by that application and no others. For example, profiles may include L2CAP if they have packets to send but skip L2CAP if they have only a steady flow of audio samples.

In the following sections, we will examine the Bluetooth radio layer and various link protocols, since these roughly correspond to the physical and MAC sublayers in the other procotol stacks we have studied.

4.6.4 The Bluetooth Radio Layer

The radio layer moves the bits from master to slave, or vice versa. It is a low-power system with a range of 10 meters operating in the same 2.4-GHz ISM band as 802.11. The band is divided into 79 channels of 1 MHz each. To coexist with other networks using the ISM band, frequency hopping spread spectrum is used. There can be up to 1600 hops/sec over slots with a dwell time of 625 μsec. All the nodes in a piconet hop frequencies simultaneously, following the slot timing and pseudorandom hop sequence dictated by the master.

Unfortunately, it turned out that early versions of Bluetooth and 802.11 interfered enough to ruin each other's transmissions. Some companies responded by banning Bluetooth altogether, but eventually a technical solution was devised. The solution is for Bluetooth to adapt its hop sequence to exclude channels on which there are other RF signals. This process reduces the harmful interference. It is called **adaptive frequency hopping**.

Three forms of modulation are used to send bits on a channel. The basic scheme is to use frequency shift keying to send a 1-bit symbol every microsecond, giving a gross data rate of 1 Mbps. Enhanced rates were introduced with the 2.0 version of Bluetooth. These rates use phase shift keying to send either 2 or 3 bits per symbol, for gross data rates of 2 or 3 Mbps. The enhanced rates are only used in the data portion of frames.

4.6.5 The Bluetooth Link Layers

The link control (or baseband) layer is the closest thing Bluetooth has to a MAC sublayer. It turns the raw bit stream into frames and defines some key formats. In the simplest form, the master in each piconet defines a series of 625-μsec time slots, with the master's transmissions starting in the even slots and the slaves' transmissions starting in the odd ones. This scheme is traditional time division multiplexing, with the master getting half the slots and the slaves sharing the other half. Frames can be 1, 3, or 5 slots long. Each frame has an overhead of 126 bits for an access code and header, plus a settling time of 250–260 μsec per hop to allow the inexpensive radio circuits to become stable. The payload of the frame can be encrypted for confidentiality with a key that is chosen when the master and slave connect. Hops only happen between frames, not during a frame. The result is that a 5-slot frame is much more efficient than a 1-slot frame because the overhead is constant but more data is sent.

The link manager protocol sets up logical channels, called **links**, to carry frames between the master and a slave device that have discovered each other. A pairing procedure is followed to make sure that the two devices are allowed to communicate before the link is used. The old pairing method is that both devices must be configured with the same four-digit PIN (Personal Identification Number). The matching PIN is how each device would know that it was connecting to the right remote device. However, unimaginative users and devices default to PINs such as "0000" and "1234" meant that this method provided very little security in practice.

The new **secure simple pairing** method enables users to confirm that both devices are displaying the same passkey, or to observe the passkey on one device and enter it into the second device. This method is more secure because users do not have to choose or set a PIN. They merely confirm a longer, device-generated passkey. Of course, it cannot be used on some devices with limited input/output, such as a hands-free headset.

Once pairing is complete, the link manager protocol sets up the links. Two main kinds of links exist to carry user data. The first is the **SCO (Synchronous Connection Oriented)** link. It is used for real-time data, such as telephone connections. This type of link is allocated a fixed slot in each direction. A slave may have up to three SCO links with its master. Each SCO link can transmit one 64,000-bps PCM audio channel. Due to the time-critical nature of SCO links, frames sent over them are never retransmitted. Instead, forward error correction can be used to increase reliability.

The other kind is the **ACL (Asynchronous ConnectionLess)** link. This type of link is used for packet-switched data that is available at irregular intervals. ACL traffic is delivered on a best-effort basis. No guarantees are given. Frames can be lost and may have to be retransmitted. A slave may have only one ACL link to its master.

The data sent over ACL links come from the L2CAP layer. This layer has four major functions. First, it accepts packets of up to 64 KB from the upper layers and breaks them into frames for transmission. At the far end, the frames are reassembled into packets. Second, it handles the multiplexing and demultiplexing of multiple packet sources. When a packet has been reassembled, the L2CAP layer determines which upper-layer protocol to hand it to, for example, RFcomm or service discovery. Third, L2CAP handles error control and retransmission. It detects errors and resends packets that were not acknowledged. Finally, L2CAP enforces quality of service requirements between multiple links.

4.6.6 The Bluetooth Frame Structure

Bluetooth defines several frame formats, the most important of which is shown in two forms in Fig. 4-36. It begins with an access code that usually identifies the master so that slaves within radio range of two masters can tell which traffic is for them. Next comes a 54-bit header containing typical MAC sublayer fields. If the frame is sent at the basic rate, the data field comes next. It has up to 2744 bits for a five-slot transmission. For a single time slot, the format is the same except that the data field is 240 bits.

If the frame is sent at the enhanced rate, the data portion may have up to two or three times as many bits because each symbol carries 2 or 3 bits instead of 1

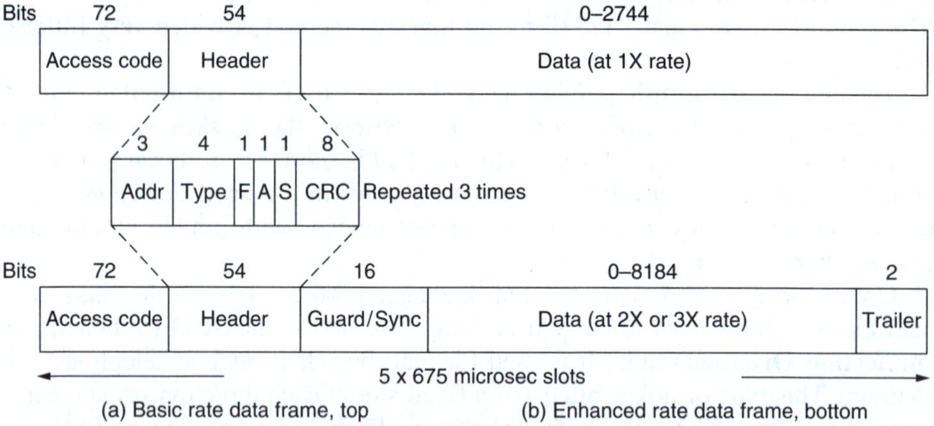

Figure 4-36. Typical Bluetooth data frame at (a) basic and (b) enhanced, data rates.

bit. These data are preceded by a guard field and a synchronization pattern that is used to switch to the faster data rate. That is, the access code and header are carried at the basic rate and only the data portion is carried at the faster rate. Enhanced-rate frames end with a short trailer.

Let us take a quick look at the common header. The *Address* field identifies which of the eight active devices the frame is intended for. The *Type* field identifies the frame type (ACL, SCO, poll, or null), the type of error correction used in the data field, and how many slots long the frame is. The *Flow* bit is asserted by a slave when its buffer is full and cannot receive any more data. This bit enables a primitive form of flow control. The *Acknowledgement* bit is used to piggyback an ACK onto a frame. The *Sequence* bit is used to number the frames to detect retransmissions. The protocol is stop-and-wait, so 1 bit is enough. Then comes the 8-bit header *Checksum*. The entire 18-bit header is repeated three times to form the 54-bit header shown in Fig. 4-36. On the receiving side, a simple circuit examines all three copies of each bit. If all three are the same, the bit is accepted. If not, the majority opinion wins. Thus, 54 bits of transmission capacity are used to send 10 bits of header. The reason is that to reliably send data in a noisy environment using cheap, low-powered (2.5 mW) devices with little computing capacity, a great deal of redundancy is needed.

Various formats are used for the data field for ACL and SCO frames. The basic-rate SCO frames are a simple example to study: the data field is always 240 bits. Three variants are defined, permitting 80, 160, or 240 bits of actual payload, with the rest being used for error correction. In the most reliable version (80-bit payload), the contents are just repeated three times, the same as the header.

We can work out the capacity with this frame as follows. Since the slave may use only the odd slots, it gets 800 slots/sec, just as the master does. With an 80-bit payload, the channel capacity from the slave is 64,000 bps as is the channel capacity from the master. This capacity is exactly enough for a single full-duplex PCM voice channel (which is why a hop rate of 1600 hops/sec was chosen). That is, despite a raw bandwidth of 1 Mbps, a single full-duplex uncompressed voice channel can completely saturate the piconet. The efficiency of 13% is the result of spending 41% of the capacity on settling time, 20% on headers, and 26% on repetition coding. This shortcoming highlights the value of the enhanced rates and frames of more than a single slot.

There is much more to be said about Bluetooth, but no more space to say it here. For the curious, the Bluetooth 4.0 specification contains all the details.

4.7 RFID

We have looked at MAC designs from LANs up to MANs and down to PANs. As a last example, we will study a category of low-end wireless devices that people may not recognize as forming a computer network: the **RFID** (**Radio Frequency IDentification**) tags and readers that we described in Sec. 1.5.4.

RFID technology takes many forms, used in smartcards, implants for pets, passports, library books, and more. The form that we will look at was developed in the quest for an **EPC** (**Electronic Product Code**) that started with the Auto-ID Center at the Massachusetts Institute of Technology in 1999. An EPC is a replacement for a barcode that can carry a larger amount of information and is electronically readable over distances up to 10 m, even when it is not visible. It is different technology than, for example, the RFID used in passports,which must be placed quite close to a reader to perform a transaction. The ability to communicate over a distance makes EPCs more relevant to our studies.

EPCglobal was formed in 2003 to commercialize the RFID technology developed by the Auto-ID Center. The effort got a boost in 2005 when Walmart required its top 100 suppliers to label all shipments with RFID tags. Widespread deployment has been hampered by the difficulty of competing with cheap printed barcodes, but new uses, such as in drivers licenses, are now growing. We will describe the second generation of this technology, which is informally called **EPC Gen 2** (EPCglobal, 2008).

4.7.1 EPC Gen 2 Architecture

The architecture of an EPC Gen 2 RFID network is shown in Fig. 4-37. It has two key components: tags and readers. RFID tags are small, inexpensive devices that have a unique 96-bit EPC identifier and a small amount of memory that can be read and written by the RFID reader. The memory might be used to record the location history of an item, for example, as it moves through the supply chain.

Often, the tags look like stickers that can be placed on, for example, pairs of jeans on the shelves in a store. Most of the sticker is taken up by an antenna that is printed onto it. A tiny dot in the middle is the RFID integrated circuit. Alternatively, the RFID tags can be integrated into an object, such as a driver's license. In both cases, the tags have no battery and they must gather power from the radio transmissions of a nearby RFID reader to run. This kind of tag is called a "Class 1" tag to distinguish it from more capable tags that have batteries.

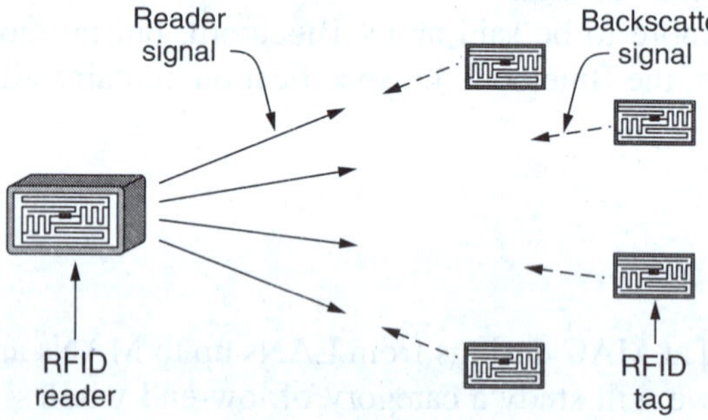

Figure 4-37. RFID architecture.

The readers are the intelligence in the system, analogous to base stations and access points in cellular and WiFi networks. Readers are much more powerful than tags. They have their own power sources, often have multiple antennas, and are in charge of when tags send and receive messages. As there will commonly be multiple tags within the reading range, the readers must solve the multiple access problem. There may be multiple readers that can contend with each other in the same area, too.

The main job of the reader is to inventory the tags in the neighborhood, that is, to discover the identifiers of the nearby tags. The inventory is accomplished with the physical layer protocol and the tag-identification protocol that are outlined in the following sections.

4.7.2 EPC Gen 2 Physical Layer

The physical layer defines how bits are sent between the RFID reader and tags. Much of it uses methods for sending wireless signals that we have seen previously. In the U.S., transmissions are sent in the unlicensed 902–928 MHz ISM band. This band falls in the UHF (Ultra High Frequency) range, so the tags are referred to as UHF RFID tags. The reader performs frequency hopping at least every 400 msec to spread its signal across the channel, to limit interference and satisfy regulatory requirements. The reader and tags use forms of ASK (Amplitude Shift Keying) modulation that we described in Sec. 2.5.2 to encode bits. They take turns to send bits, so the link is half duplex.

There are two main differences from other physical layers that we have studied. The first is that the reader is always transmitting a signal, regardless of whether it is the reader or tag that is communicating. Naturally, the reader transmits a signal to send bits to tags. For the tags to send bits to the reader, the reader transmits a fixed carrier signal that carries no bits. The tags harvest this signal to get the power they need to run; otherwise, a tag would not be able to transmit in the first place. To send data, a tag changes whether it is reflecting the signal from the reader, like a radar signal bouncing off a target, or absorbing it.

This method is called **backscatter**. It differs from all the other wireless situations we have seen so far, in which the sender and receiver never both transmit at the same time. Backscatter is a low-energy way for the tag to create a weak signal of its own that shows up at the reader. For the reader to decode the incoming signal, it must filter out the outgoing signal that it is transmitting. Because the tag signal is weak, tags can only send bits to the reader at a low rate, and tags cannot receive or even sense transmissions from other tags.

The second difference is that very simple forms of modulation are used so that they can be implemented on a tag that runs on very little power and costs only a few cents to make. To send data to the tags, the reader uses two amplitude levels. Bits are determined to be either a 0 or a 1, depending on how long the reader waits before a low-power period. The tag measures the time between low-power periods and compares this time to a reference measured during a preamble. As shown in Fig. 4-38, 1s are longer than 0s.

Tag responses consist of the tag alternating its backscatter state at fixed intervals to create a series of pulses in the signal. Anywhere from one to eight pulse periods can be used to encode each 0 or 1, depending on the need for reliability. 1s have fewer transitions than 0s, as is shown with an example of two-pulse period coding in Fig. 4-38.

Figure 4-38. Reader and tag backscatter signals.

4.7.3 EPC Gen 2 Tag Identification Layer

To inventory the nearby tags, the reader needs to receive a message from each tag that gives the identifier for the tag. This situation is a multiple access problem for which the number of tags is unknown in the general case. The reader might broadcast a query to ask all tags to send their identifiers. However, tags that replied right away would then collide in much the same way as stations on a classic Ethernet.

We have seen many ways of tackling the multiple access problem in this chapter. The closest protocol for the current situation, in which the tags cannot hear each others' transmissions, is slotted ALOHA, one of the earliest protocols we studied. This protocol is adapted for use in Gen 2 RFID.

The sequence of messages used to identify a tag is shown in Fig. 4-39. In the first slot (slot 0), the reader sends a *Query* message to start the process. Each *QRepeat* message advances to the next slot. The reader also tells the tags the range of slots over which to randomize transmissions. Using a range is necessary because the reader synchronizes tags when it starts the process; unlike stations on an Ethernet, tags do not wake up with a message at a time of their choosing.

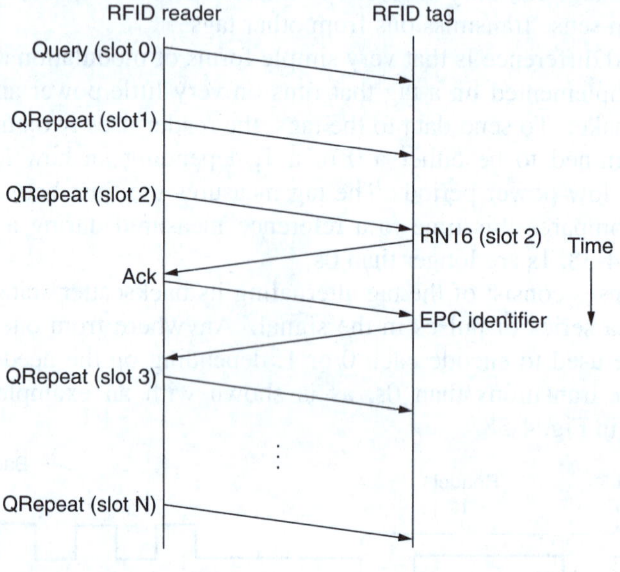

Figure 4-39. Example message exchange to identify a tag.

Tags pick a random slot in which to reply. In Fig. 4-39, the tag replies in slot 2. However, tags do not send their identifiers when they first reply. Instead, a tag sends a short 16-bit random number in an *RN16* message. If there is no collision, the reader receives this message and sends an *ACK* message of its own. At this stage, the tag has acquired the slot and sends its EPC identifier.

The reason for this exchange is that EPC identifiers are long, so collisions on these messages would be expensive. Instead, a short exchange is used to test whether the tag can safely use the slot to send its identifier. Once its identifier has been successfully transmitted, the tag temporarily stops responding to new *Query* messages so that all the remaining tags can be identified.

A key problem is for the reader to adjust the number of slots to avoid collisions, but without using so many slots that performance suffers. This adjustment is analogous to binary exponential backoff in Ethernet. If the reader sees too many slots with no responses or too many slots with collisions, it can send a *QAdjust* message to decrease or increase the range of slots over which the tags are responding.

The RFID reader can perform other operations on the tags. For example, it can select a subset of tags before running an inventory, allowing it to collect responses from, say, tagged jeans but not tagged shirts. The reader can also write data to tags as they are identified. This feature could be used to record the point of sale or other relevant information.

4.7.4 Tag Identification Message Formats

The format of the *Query* message is shown in Fig. 4-40 as an example of a reader-to-tag message. The message is compact because the downlink rates are limited, from 27 kbps up to 128 kbps. The *Command* field carries the code 1000 to identify the message as a *Query*.

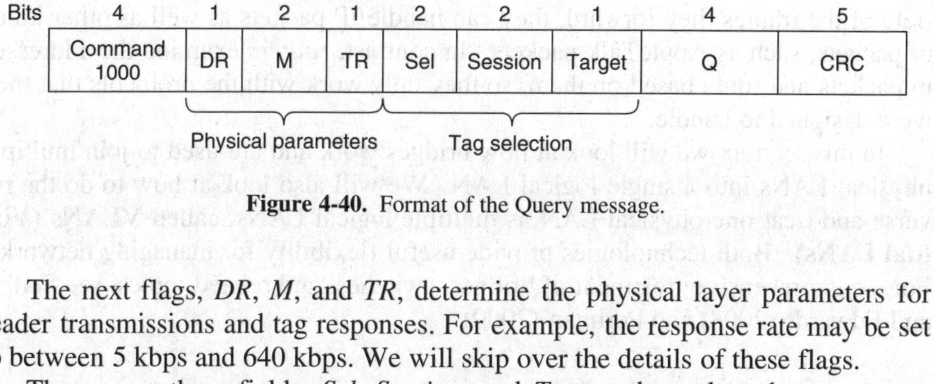

Figure 4-40. Format of the Query message.

The next flags, *DR*, *M*, and *TR*, determine the physical layer parameters for reader transmissions and tag responses. For example, the response rate may be set to between 5 kbps and 640 kbps. We will skip over the details of these flags.

Then come three fields, *Sel*, *Session*, and *Target*, that select the tags to respond. As well as the readers being able to select a subset of identifiers, the tags keep track of up to four concurrent sessions and whether they have been identified in those sessions. In this way, multiple readers can operate in overlapping coverage areas by using different sessions.

Next is the most important parameter for this command, *Q*. This field defines the range of slots over which tags will respond, from 0 to 2^Q-1. Finally, there is a CRC to protect the message fields. At 5 bits, it is shorter than most CRCs we have seen, but the *Query* message is much shorter than most packets too.

Tag-to-reader messages are simpler. Since the reader is in control, it knows what message to expect in response to each of its transmissions. The tag responses simply carry data, such as the EPC identifier.

Originally the tags were just for identification purposes. However, they have grown over time to resemble very small computers. Some research tags have sensors and are able to run small programs to gather and process data (Sample et al., 2008). One vision for this technology is the "Internet of things" that connects objects in the physical world to the Internet (Welbourne et al., 2009; and Gershenfeld et al., 2004).

4.8 DATA LINK LAYER SWITCHING

Many organizations have multiple LANs and wish to connect them. Would it not be convenient if we could just join the LANs together to make a larger LAN? In fact, we can do this when the connections are made with devices called **bridges**. The Ethernet switches we described in Sec. 4.3.4 are a modern name for bridges; they provide functionality that goes beyond classic Ethernet and Ethernet hubs to make it easy to join multiple LANs into a larger and faster network. We shall use the terms "bridge" and "switch" interchangeably.

Bridges operate in the data link layer, so they examine the data link layer addresses to forward frames. Since they are not supposed to examine the payload field of the frames they forward, they can handle IP packets as well as other kinds of packets, such as AppleTalk packets. In contrast, *routers* examine the addresses in packets and route based on them, so they only work with the protocols that they were designed to handle.

In this section, we will look at how bridges work and are used to join multiple physical LANs into a single logical LAN. We will also look at how to do the reverse and treat one physical LAN as multiple logical LANs, called **VLANs (Virtual LANs)**. Both technologies provide useful flexibility for managing networks. For a comprehensive treatment of bridges, switches, and related topics, see Seifert and Edwards (2008) and Perlman (2000).

4.8.1 Uses of Bridges

Before getting into the technology of bridges, let us take a look at some common situations in which bridges are used. We will mention three reasons why a single organization may end up with multiple LANs.

First, many university and corporate departments have their own LANs to connect their own personal computers, servers, and devices such as printers. Since the goals of the various departments differ, different departments may set up different LANs, without regard to what other departments are doing. Sooner or later, though, there is a need for interaction, so bridges are needed. In this example, multiple LANs come into existence due to the autonomy of their owners.

Second, the organization may be geographically spread over several buildings separated by considerable distances. It may be cheaper to have separate LANs in each building and connect them with bridges and a few long-distance fiber optic links than to run all the cables to a single central switch. Even if laying the cables is easy to do, there are limits on their lengths (e.g., 200 m for twisted-pair gigabit Ethernet). The network would not work for longer cables due to the excessive signal attenuation or round-trip delay. The only solution is to partition the LAN and install bridges to join the pieces to increase the total physical distance that can be covered.

Third, it may be necessary to split what is logically a single LAN into separate LANs (connected by bridges) to accommodate the load. At many large universities, for example, thousands of workstations are available for student and faculty computing. Companies may also have thousands of employees. The scale of this system precludes putting all the workstations on a single LAN—there are more computers than ports on any Ethernet hub and more stations than allowed on a single classic Ethernet.

Even if it were possible to wire all the workstations together, putting more stations on an Ethernet hub or classic Ethernet would not add capacity. All of the stations share the same, fixed amount of bandwidth. The more stations there are, the less average bandwidth per station.

However, two separate LANs have twice the capacity of a single LAN. Bridges let the LANs be joined together while keeping this capacity. The key is not to send traffic onto ports where it is not needed, so that each LAN can run at full speed. This behavior also increases reliability, since on a single LAN a defective node that keeps outputting a continuous stream of garbage can clog up the entire LAN. By deciding what to forward and what not to forward, bridges act like fire doors in a building, preventing a single node that has gone berserk from bringing down the entire system.

To make these benefits easily available, ideally bridges should be completely transparent. It should be possible to go out and buy bridges, plug the LAN cables into the bridges, and have everything work perfectly, instantly. There should be no hardware changes required, no software changes required, no setting of address switches, no downloading of routing tables or parameters, nothing at all. Just plug in the cables and walk away. Furthermore, the operation of the existing LANs should not be affected by the bridges at all. As far as the stations are concerned, there should be no observable difference whether or not they are part of a bridged LAN. It should be as easy to move stations around the bridged LAN as it is to move them around a single LAN.

Surprisingly enough, it is actually possible to create bridges that are transparent. Two algorithms are used: a backward learning algorithm to stop traffic being sent where it is not needed; and a spanning tree algorithm to break loops that may be formed when switches are cabled together willy-nilly. Let us now take a look at these algorithms in turn to learn how this magic is accomplished.

4.8.2 Learning Bridges

The topology of two LANs bridged together is shown in Fig. 4-41 for two cases. On the left-hand side, two multidrop LANs, such as classic Ethernets, are joined by a special station—the bridge—that sits on both LANs. On the right-hand side, LANs with point-to-point cables, including one hub, are joined together. The bridges are the devices to which the stations and hub are attached. If the LAN technology is Ethernet, the bridges are better known as Ethernet switches.

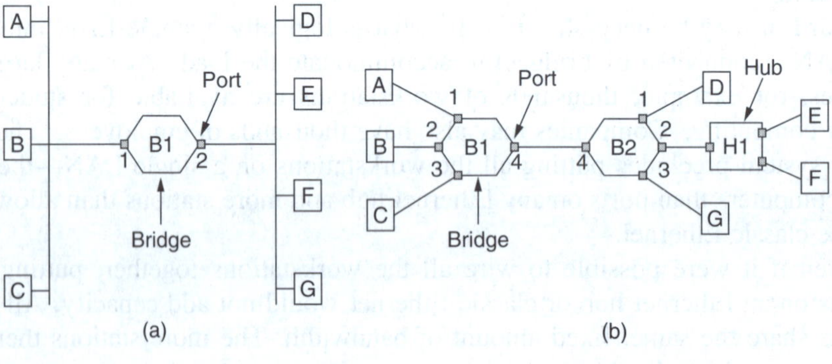

Figure 4-41. (a) Bridge connecting two multidrop LANs. (b) Bridges (and a hub) connecting seven point-to-point stations.

Bridges were developed when classic Ethernets were in use, so they are often shown in topologies with multidrop cables, as in Fig. 4-41(a). However, all the topologies that are encountered today are comprised of point-to-point cables and switches. The bridges work the same way in both settings. All of the stations attached to the same port on a bridge belong to the same collision domain, and this is different than the collision domain for other ports. If there is more than one station, as in a classic Ethernet, a hub, or a half-duplex link, the CSMA/CD protocol is used to send frames.

There is a difference, however, in how the bridged LANs are built. To bridge multidrop LANs, a bridge is added as a new station on each of the multidrop LANs, as in Fig. 4-41(a). To bridge point-to-point LANs, the hubs are either connected to a bridge or, preferably, replaced with a bridge to increase performance. In Fig. 4-41(b), bridges have replaced all but one hub.

Different kinds of cables can also be attached to one bridge. For example, the cable connecting bridge *B1* to bridge *B2* in Fig. 4-41(b) might be a long-distance fiber optic link, while the cable connecting the bridges to stations might be a short-haul twisted-pair line. This arrangement is useful for bridging LANs in different buildings.

Now let us consider what happens inside the bridges. Each bridge operates in promiscuous mode, that is, it accepts every frame transmitted by the stations attached to each of its ports. The bridge must decide whether to forward or discard each frame, and, if the former, on which port to output the frame. This decision is made by using the destination address. As an example, consider the topology of Fig. 4-41(a). If station *A* sends a frame to station *B*, bridge *B1* will receive the frame on port 1. This frame can be immediately discarded without further ado because it is already on the correct port. However, in the topology of Fig. 4-41(b) suppose that *A* sends a frame to *D*. Bridge *B1* will receive the frame on port 1 and output it on port 4. Bridge *B2* will then receive the frame on its port 4 and output it on its port 1.

A simple way to implement this scheme is to have a big (hash) table inside the bridge. The table can list each possible destination and which output port it belongs on. For example, in Fig. 4-41(b), the table at *B1* would list *D* as belonging to port 4, since all *B1* has to know is which port to put frames on to reach *D*. That, in fact, more forwarding will happen later when the frame hits *B2* is not of interest to *B1*.

When the bridges are first plugged in, all the hash tables are empty. None of the bridges know where any of the destinations are, so they use a flooding algorithm: every incoming frame for an unknown destination is output on all the ports to which the bridge is connected except the one it arrived on. As time goes on, the bridges learn where destinations are. Once a destination is known, frames destined for it are put only on the proper port; they are not flooded.

The algorithm used by the bridges is **backward learning**. As mentioned above, the bridges operate in promiscuous mode, so they see every frame sent on any of their ports. By looking at the source addresses, they can tell which machines are accessible on which ports. For example, if bridge *B1* in Fig. 4-41(b) sees a frame on port 3 coming from *C*, it knows that *C* must be reachable via port 3, so it makes an entry in its hash table. Any subsequent frame addressed to *C* coming in to *B1* on any other port will be forwarded to port 3.

The topology can change as machines and bridges are powered up and down and moved around. To handle dynamic topologies, whenever a hash table entry is made, the arrival time of the frame is noted in the entry. Whenever a frame whose source is already in the table arrives, its entry is updated with the current time. Thus, the time associated with every entry tells the last time a frame from that machine was seen.

Periodically, a process in the bridge scans the hash table and purges all entries more than a few minutes old. In this way, if a computer is unplugged from its LAN, moved around the building, and plugged in again somewhere else, within a few minutes it will be back in normal operation, without any manual intervention. This algorithm also means that if a machine is quiet for a few minutes, any traffic sent to it will have to be flooded until it next sends a frame itself.

The routing procedure for an incoming frame depends on the port it arrives on (the source port) and the address to which it is destined (the destination address). The procedure is as follows.

1. If the port for the destination address is the same as the source port, discard the frame.

2. If the port for the destination address and the source port are different, forward the frame on to the destination port.

3. If the destination port is unknown, use flooding and send the frame on all ports except the source port.

You might wonder whether the first case can occur with point-to-point links. The answer is that it can occur if hubs are used to connect a group of computers to a bridge. An example is shown in Fig. 4-41(b) where stations *E* and *F* are connected to hub *H*1, which is in turn connected to bridge *B2*. If *E* sends a frame to *F*, the hub will relay it to *B2* as well as to *F*. That is what hubs do—they wire all ports together so that a frame input on one port is simply output on all other ports. The frame will arrive at *B2* on port 4, which is already the right output port to reach the destination. Bridge *B2* need only discard the frame.

As each frame arrives, this algorithm must be applied, so it is usually implemented with special-purpose VLSI chips. The chips do the lookup and update the table entry, all in a few microseconds. Because bridges only look at the MAC addresses to decide how to forward frames, it is possible to start forwarding as soon as the destination header field has come in, before the rest of the frame has arrived (provided the output line is available, of course). This design reduces the latency of passing through the bridge, as well as the number of frames that the bridge must be able to buffer. It is referred to as **cut-through switching** or **wormhole routing** and is usually handled in hardware.

We can look at the operation of a bridge in terms of protocol stacks to understand what it means to be a link layer device. Consider a frame sent from station *A* to station *D* in the configuration of Fig. 4-41(a), in which the LANs are Ethernet. The frame will pass through one bridge. The protocol stack view of processing is shown in Fig. 4-42.

The packet comes from a higher layer and descends into the Ethernet MAC layer. It acquires an Ethernet header (and also a trailer, not shown in the figure). This unit is passed to the physical layer, goes out over the cable, and is picked up by the bridge.

In the bridge, the frame is passed up from the physical layer to the Ethernet MAC layer. This layer has extended processing compared to the Ethernet MAC layer at a station. It passes the frame to a relay, still within the MAC layer. The bridge relay function uses only the Ethernet MAC header to determine how to handle the frame. In this case, it passes the frame to the Ethernet MAC layer of the port used to reach station *D*, and the frame continues on its way.

In the general case, relays at a given layer can rewrite the headers for that layer. VLANs will provide an example shortly. In no case should the bridge look inside the frame and learn that it is carrying an IP packet; that is irrelevant to the

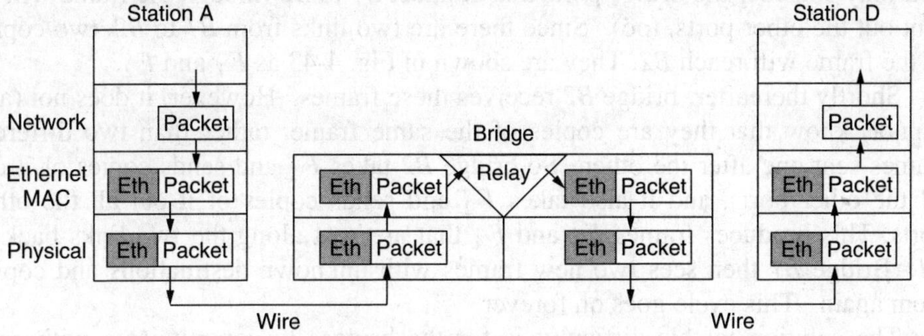

Figure 4-42. Protocol processing at a bridge.

bridge processing and would violate protocol layering. Also note that a bridge with *k* ports will have *k* instances of MAC and physical layers. The value of *k* is 2 for our simple example.

4.8.3 Spanning Tree Bridges

To increase reliability, redundant links can be used between bridges. In the example of Fig. 4-43, there are two links in parallel between a pair of bridges. This design ensures that if one link is cut, the network will not be partitioned into two sets of computers that cannot talk to each other.

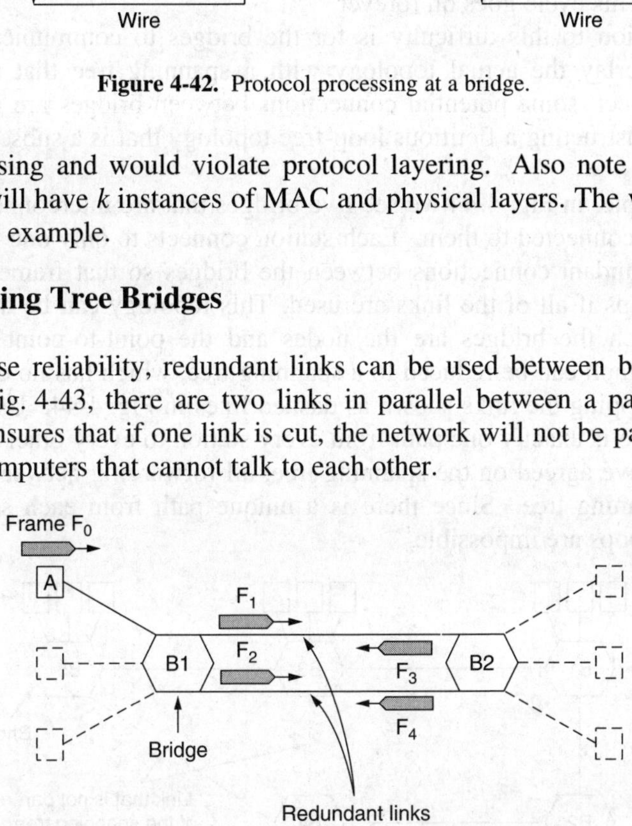

Figure 4-43. Bridges with two parallel links.

However, this redundancy introduces some additional problems because it creates loops in the topology. An example of these problems can be seen by looking at how a frame sent by *A* to a previously unobserved destination is handled in Fig. 4-43. Each bridge follows the normal rule for handling unknown destinations, which is to flood the frame. Call the frame from *A* that reaches bridge *B1* frame F_0. The bridge sends copies of this frame out all of its other ports. We will only consider the bridge ports that connect *B1* to *B2* (though the frame will be sent out the other ports, too). Since there are two links from *B1* to *B2*, two copies of the frame will reach *B2*. They are shown in Fig. 4-43 as F_1 and F_2.

Shortly thereafter, bridge *B2* receives these frames. However, it does not (and cannot) know that they are copies of the same frame, rather than two different frames sent one after the other. So bridge *B2* takes F_1 and sends copies of it out all the other ports, and it also takes F_2 and sends copies of it out all the other ports. This produces frames F_3 and F_4 that are sent along the two links back to *B1*. Bridge *B1* then sees two new frames with unknown destinations and copies them again. This cycle goes on forever.

The solution to this difficulty is for the bridges to communicate with each other and overlay the actual topology with a spanning tree that reaches every bridge. In effect, some potential connections between bridges are ignored in the interest of constructing a fictitious loop-free topology that is a subset of the actual topology.

For example, in Fig. 4-44 we see five bridges that are interconnected and also have stations connected to them. Each station connects to only one bridge. There are some redundant connections between the bridges so that frames will be forwarded in loops if all of the links are used. This topology can be thought of as a graph in which the bridges are the nodes and the point-to-point links are the edges. The graph can be reduced to a spanning tree, which has no cycles by definition, by dropping the links shown as dashed lines in Fig. 4-44. Using this spanning tree, there is exactly one path from every station to every other station. Once the bridges have agreed on the spanning tree, all forwarding between stations follows the spanning tree. Since there is a unique path from each source to each destination, loops are impossible.

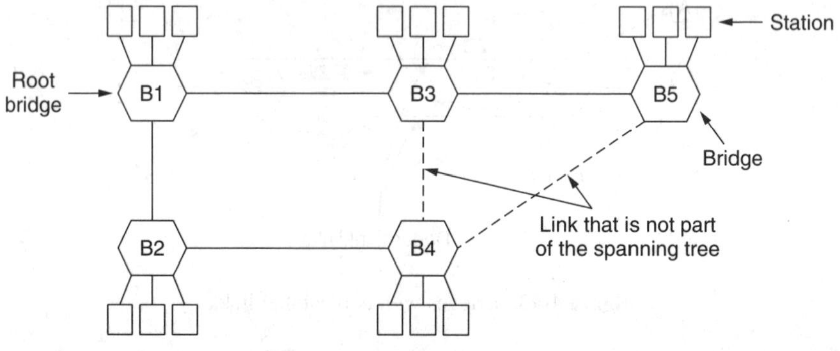

Figure 4-44. A spanning tree connecting five bridges. The dashed lines are links that are not part of the spanning tree.

To build the spanning tree, the bridges run a distributed algorithm. Each bridge periodically broadcasts a configuration message out all of its ports to its neighbors and processes the messages it receives from other bridges, as described next. These messages are not forwarded, since their purpose is to build the tree, which can then be used for forwarding.

The bridges must first choose one bridge to be the root of the spanning tree. To make this choice, they each include an identifier based on their MAC address in the configuration message, as well as the identifier of the bridge they believe to be the root. MAC addresses are installed by the manufacturer and guaranteed to be unique worldwide, which makes these identifiers convenient and unique. The bridges choose the bridge with the lowest identifier to be the root. After enough messages have been exchanged to spread the news, all bridges will agree on which bridge is the root. In Fig. 4-44, bridge *B1* has the lowest identifier and becomes the root.

Next, a tree of shortest paths from the root to every bridge is constructed. In Fig. 4-44, bridges *B2* and *B3* can each be reached from bridge *B1* directly, in one hop that is a shortest path. Bridge *B4* can be reached in two hops, via either *B2* or *B3*. To break this tie, the path via the bridge with the lowest identifier is chosen, so *B4* is reached via *B2*. Bridge *B5* can be reached in two hops via *B3*.

To find these shortest paths, bridges include the distance from the root in their configuration messages. Each bridge remembers the shortest path it finds to the root. The bridges then turn off ports that are not part of the shortest path.

Although the tree spans all the bridges, not all the links (or even bridges) are necessarily present in the tree. This happens because turning off the ports prunes some links from the network to prevent loops. Even after the spanning tree has been established, the algorithm continues to run during normal operation to automatically detect topology changes and update the tree.

The algorithm for constructing the spanning tree was invented by Radia Perlman. Her job was to solve the problem of joining LANs without loops. She was given a week to do it, but she came up with the idea for the spanning tree algorithm in a day. Fortunately, this left her enough time to write it as a poem (Perlman, 1985):

I think that I shall never see
A graph more lovely than a tree.
A tree whose crucial property
Is loop-free connectivity.
A tree which must be sure to span.
So packets can reach every LAN.
First the Root must be selected
By ID it is elected.
Least cost paths from Root are traced
In the tree these paths are placed.
A mesh is made by folks like me
Then bridges find a spanning tree.

The spanning tree algorithm was then standardized as IEEE 802.1D and used for many years. In 2001, it was revised to more rapidly find a new spanning tree after a topology change. For a detailed treatment of bridges, see Perlman (2000).

4.8.4 Repeaters, Hubs, Bridges, Switches, Routers, and Gateways

So far in this book, we have looked at a variety of ways to get frames and packets from one computer to another. We have mentioned repeaters, hubs, bridges, switches, routers, and gateways. All of these devices are in common use, but they all differ in subtle and not-so-subtle ways. Since there are so many of them, it is probably worth taking a look at them together to see what the similarities and differences are.

The key to understanding these devices is to realize that they operate in different layers, as illustrated in Fig. 4-45(a). The layer matters because different devices use different pieces of information to decide how to switch. In a typical scenario, the user generates some data to be sent to a remote machine. Those data are passed to the transport layer, which then adds a header (for example, a TCP header) and passes the resulting unit down to the network layer. The network layer adds its own header to form a network layer packet (e.g., an IP packet). In Fig. 4-45(b), we see the IP packet shaded in gray. Then the packet goes to the data link layer, which adds its own header and checksum (CRC) and gives the resulting frame to the physical layer for transmission, for example, over a LAN.

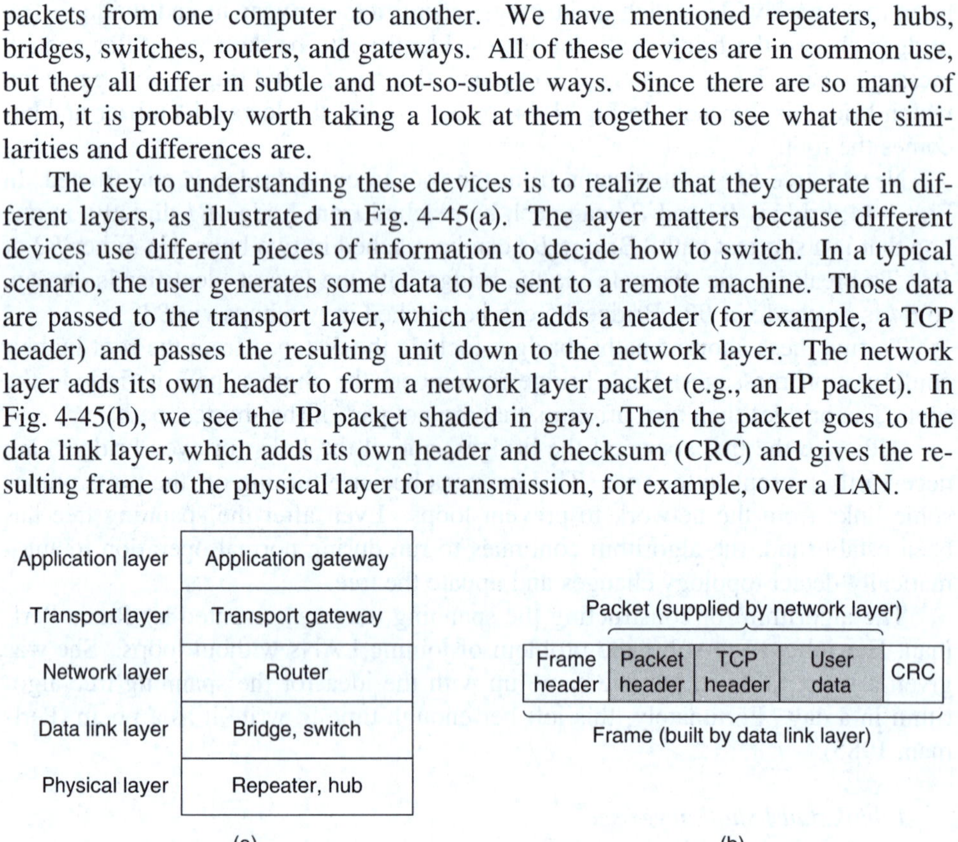

Figure 4-45. (a) Which device is in which layer. (b) Frames, packets, and headers.

Now let us look at the switching devices and see how they relate to the packets and frames. At the bottom, in the physical layer, we find the repeaters. These are analog devices that work with signals on the cables to which they are connected. A signal appearing on one cable is cleaned up, amplified, and put out on another cable. Repeaters do not understand frames, packets, or headers. They understand the symbols that encode bits as volts. Classic Ethernet, for example, was designed to allow four repeaters that would boost the signal to extend the maximum cable length from 500 meters to 2500 meters.

Next we come to the hubs. A hub has a number of input lines that it joins electrically. Frames arriving on any of the lines are sent out on all the others. If two frames arrive at the same time, they will collide, just as on a coaxial cable. All the lines coming into a hub must operate at the same speed. Hubs differ from repeaters in that they do not (usually) amplify the incoming signals and are designed for multiple input lines, but the differences are slight. Like repeaters, hubs are physical layer devices that do not examine the link layer addresses or use them in any way.

Now let us move up to the data link layer, where we find bridges and switches. We just studied bridges at some length. A bridge connects two or more LANs. Like a hub, a modern bridge has multiple ports, usually enough for 4 to 48 input lines of a certain type. Unlike in a hub, each port is isolated to be its own collision domain; if the port has a full-duplex point-to-point line, the CSMA/CD algorithm is not needed. When a frame arrives, the bridge extracts the destination address from the frame header and looks it up in a table to see where to send the frame. For Ethernet, this address is the 48-bit destination address shown in Fig. 4-14. The bridge only outputs the frame on the port where it is needed and can forward multiple frames at the same time.

Bridges offer much better performance than hubs, and the isolation between bridge ports also means that the input lines may run at different speeds, possibly even with different network types. A common example is a bridge with ports that connect to 10-, 100-, and 1000-Mbps Ethernet. Buffering within the bridge is needed to accept a frame on one port and transmit the frame out on a different port. If frames come in faster than they can be retransmitted, the bridge may run out of buffer space and have to start discarding frames. For example, if a gigabit Ethernet is pouring bits into a 10-Mbps Ethernet at top speed, the bridge will have to buffer them, hoping not to run out of memory. This problem still exists even if all the ports run at the same speed because more than one port may be sending frames to a given destination port.

Bridges were originally intended to be able to join different kinds of LANs, for example, an Ethernet and a Token Ring LAN. However, this never worked well because of differences between the LANs. Different frame formats require copying and reformatting, which takes CPU time, requires a new checksum calculation, and introduces the possibility of undetected errors due to bad bits in the bridge's memory. Different maximum frame lengths are also a serious problem with no good solution. Basically, frames that are too large to be forwarded must be discarded. So much for transparency.

Two other areas where LANs can differ are security and quality of service. Some LANs have link-layer encryption, for example 802.11, and some do not, for example Ethernet. Some LANs have quality of service features such as priorities, for example 802.11, and some do not, for example Ethernet. Consequently, when a frame must travel between these LANs, the security or quality of service expected by the sender may not be able to be provided. For all of these reasons, modern bridges usually work for one network type, and routers, which we will come to soon, are used instead to join networks of different types.

Switches are modern bridges by another name. The differences are more to do with marketing than technical issues, but there are a few points worth knowing. Bridges were developed when classic Ethernet was in use, so they tend to join relatively few LANs and thus have relatively few ports. The term "switch" is more popular nowadays. Also, modern installations all use point-to-point links, such as twisted-pair cables, so individual computers plug directly into a switch and thus the switch will tend to have many ports. Finally, "switch" is also used as a general term. With a bridge, the functionality is clear. On the other hand, a switch may refer to an Ethernet switch or a completely different kind of device that makes forwarding decisions, such as a telephone switch.

So far, we have seen repeaters and hubs, which are actually quite similar, as well as bridges and switches, which are even more similar to each other. Now we move up to routers, which are different from all of the above. When a packet comes into a router, the frame header and trailer are stripped off and the packet located in the frame's payload field (shaded in Fig. 4-45) is passed to the routing software. This software uses the packet header to choose an output line. For an IP packet, the packet header will contain a 32-bit (IPv4) or 128-bit (IPv6) address, but not a 48-bit IEEE 802 address. The routing software does not see the frame addresses and does not even know whether the packet came in on a LAN or a point-to-point line. We will study routers and routing in Chap. 5.

Up another layer, we find transport gateways. These connect two computers that use different connection-oriented transport protocols. For example, suppose a computer using the connection-oriented TCP/IP protocol needs to talk to a computer using a different connection-oriented transport protocol called SCTP. The transport gateway can copy the packets from one connection to the other, reformatting them as need be.

Finally, application gateways understand the format and contents of the data and can translate messages from one format to another. An email gateway could translate Internet messages into SMS messages for mobile phones, for example. Like "switch," "gateway" is somewhat of a general term. It refers to a forwarding process that runs at a high layer.

4.8.5 Virtual LANs

In the early days of local area networking, thick yellow cables snaked through the cable ducts of many office buildings. Every computer they passed was plugged in. No thought was given to which computer belonged on which LAN. All the people in adjacent offices were put on the same LAN, whether they belonged together or not. Geography trumped corporate organization charts.

With the advent of twisted pair and hubs in the 1990s, all that changed. Buildings were rewired (at considerable expense) to rip out all the yellow garden hoses and install twisted pairs from every office to central wiring closets at the end of each corridor or in a central machine room, as illustrated in Fig. 4-46. If the Vice President in Charge of Wiring was a visionary, Category 5 twisted pairs were installed; if he was a bean counter, the existing (Category 3) telephone wiring was used (only to be replaced a few years later, when fast Ethernet emerged).

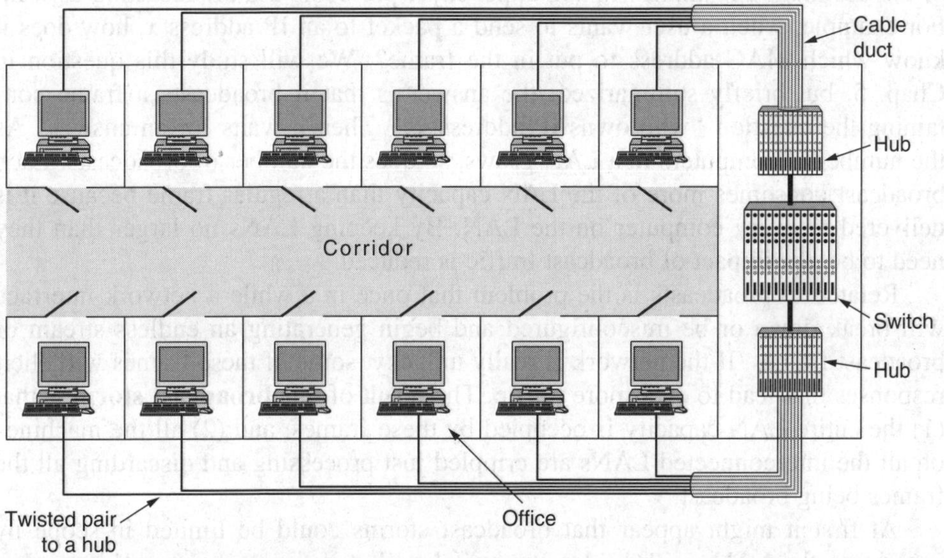

Figure 4-46. A building with centralized wiring using hubs and a switch.

Today, the cables have changed and hubs have become switches, but the wiring pattern is still the same. This pattern makes it possible to configure LANs logically rather than physically. For example, if a company wants *k* LANs, it could buy *k* switches. By carefully choosing which connectors to plug into which switches, the occupants of a LAN can be chosen in a way that makes organizational sense, without too much regard to geography.

Does it matter who is on which LAN? After all, in nearly all organizations, all the LANs are interconnected. In short, yes, it often matters. Network administrators like to group users on LANs to reflect the organizational structure rather than the physical layout of the building, for a variety of reasons. One issue is security. One LAN might host Web servers and other computers intended for public use. Another LAN might host computers containing the records of the Human Resources department that are not to be passed outside of the department. In such a situation, putting all the computers on a single LAN and not letting any of the servers be accessed from off the LAN makes sense. Management tends to frown when hearing that such an arrangement is impossible.

A second issue is load. Some LANs are more heavily used than others and it may be desirable to separate them. For example, if the folks in research are running all kinds of nifty experiments that sometimes get out of hand and saturate their LAN, the folks in management may not be enthusiastic about donating some of the capacity they were using for videoconferencing to help out. Then again, this might impress on management the need to install a faster network.

A third issue is broadcast traffic. Bridges broadcast traffic when the location of the destination is unknown, and upper-layer protocols use broadcasting as well. For example, when a user wants to send a packet to an IP address *x*, how does it know which MAC address to put in the frame? We will study this question in Chap. 5, but briefly summarized, the answer is that it broadcasts a frame containing the question "who owns IP address *x*?" Then it waits for an answer. As the number of computers in a LAN grows, so does the number of broadcasts. Each broadcast consumes more of the LAN capacity than a regular frame because it is delivered to every computer on the LAN. By keeping LANs no larger than they need to be, the impact of broadcast traffic is reduced.

Related to broadcasts is the problem that once in a while a network interface will break down or be misconfigured and begin generating an endless stream of broadcast frames. If the network is really unlucky, some of these frames will elicit responses that lead to ever more traffic. The result of this **broadcast storm** is that (1) the entire LAN capacity is occupied by these frames, and (2) all the machines on all the interconnected LANs are crippled just processing and discarding all the frames being broadcast.

At first it might appear that broadcast storms could be limited in scope by separating the LANs with bridges or switches, but if the goal is to achieve transparency (i.e., a machine can be moved to a different LAN across the bridge without anyone noticing it), then bridges have to forward broadcast frames.

Having seen why companies might want multiple LANs with restricted scopes, let us get back to the problem of decoupling the logical topology from the physical topology. Building a physical topology to reflect the organizational structure can add work and cost, even with centralized wiring and switches. For example, if two people in the same department work in different buildings, it may be easier to wire them to different switches that are part of different LANs. Even if this is not the case, a user might be shifted within the company from one department to another without changing offices, or might change offices without changing departments. This might result in the user being on the wrong LAN until an administrator changes the user's connector from one switch to another. Furthermore, the number of computers that belong to different departments may not be a good match for the number of ports on switches; some departments may be too small and others so big that they require multiple switches. This results in wasted switch ports that are not used.

In many companies, organizational changes occur all the time, meaning that system administrators spend a lot of time pulling out plugs and pushing them back in somewhere else. Also, in some cases, the change cannot be made at all because the twisted pair from the user's machine is too far from the correct switch (e.g., in the wrong building), or the available switch ports are on the wrong LAN.

In response to customer requests for more flexibility, network vendors began working on a way to rewire buildings entirely in software. The resulting concept is called a **VLAN (Virtual LAN)**. It has been standardized by the IEEE 802 committee and is now widely deployed in many organizations. Let us now take a look at it. For additional information about VLANs, see Seifert and Edwards (2008).

VLANs are based on VLAN-aware switches. To set up a VLAN-based network, the network administrator decides how many VLANs there will be, which computers will be on which VLAN, and what the VLANs will be called. Often the VLANs are (informally) named by colors, since it is then possible to print color diagrams showing the physical layout of the machines, with the members of the red LAN in red, members of the green LAN in green, and so on. In this way, both the physical and logical layouts are visible in a single view.

As an example, consider the bridged LAN of Fig. 4-47, in which nine of the machines belong to the G (gray) VLAN and five belong to the W (white) VLAN. Machines from the gray VLAN are spread across two switches, including two machines that connect to a switch via a hub.

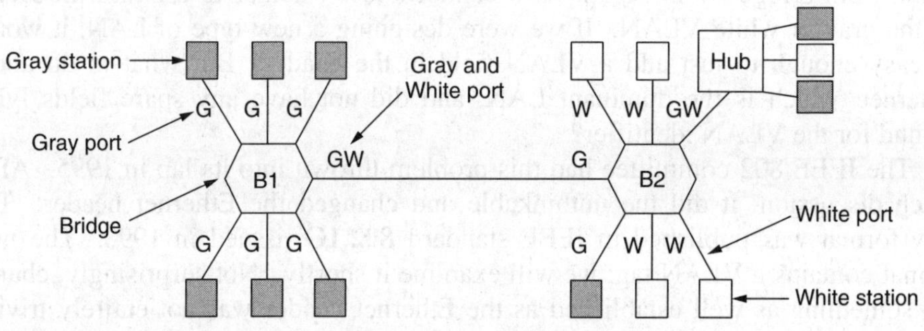

Figure 4-47. Two VLANs, gray and white, on a bridged LAN.

To make the VLANs function correctly, configuration tables have to be set up in the bridges. These tables tell which VLANs are accessible via which ports. When a frame comes in from, say, the gray VLAN, it must be forwarded on all the ports marked with a G. This holds for ordinary (i.e., unicast) traffic for which the bridges have not learned the location of the destination, as well as for multicast and broadcast traffic. Note that a port may be labeled with multiple VLAN colors.

As an example, suppose that one of the gray stations plugged into bridge *B1* in Fig. 4-47 sends a frame to a destination that has not been observed beforehand. Bridge *B1* will receive the frame and see that it came from a machine on the gray

VLAN, so it will flood the frame on all ports labeled G (except the incoming port). The frame will be sent to the five other gray stations attached to *B1* as well as over the link from *B1* to bridge *B2*. At bridge *B2*, the frame is similarly forwarded on all ports labeled G. This sends the frame to one further station and the hub (which will transmit the frame to all of its stations). The hub has both labels because it connects to machines from both VLANs. The frame is not sent on other ports without G in the label because the bridge knows that there are no machines on the gray VLAN that can be reached via these ports.

In our example, the frame is only sent from bridge *B1* to bridge *B2* because there are machines on the gray VLAN that are connected to *B2*. Looking at the white VLAN, we can see that the bridge *B2* port that connects to bridge *B1* is *not* labeled W. This means that a frame on the white VLAN will not be forwarded from bridge *B2* to bridge *B1*. This behavior is correct because no stations on the white VLAN are connected to *B1*.

The IEEE 802.1Q Standard

To implement this scheme, bridges need to know to which VLAN an incoming frame belongs. Without this information, for example, when bridge *B2* gets a frame from bridge *B1* in Fig. 4-47, it cannot know whether to forward the frame on the gray or white VLAN. If we were designing a new type of LAN, it would be easy enough to just add a VLAN field in the header. But what to do about Ethernet, which is the dominant LAN, and did not have any spare fields lying around for the VLAN identifier?

The IEEE 802 committee had this problem thrown into its lap in 1995. After much discussion, it did the unthinkable and changed the Ethernet header. The new format was published in IEEE standard **802.1Q**, issued in 1998. The new format contains a VLAN tag; we will examine it shortly. Not surprisingly, changing something as well established as the Ethernet header was not entirely trivial. A few questions that come to mind are:

1. Need we throw out several hundred million existing Ethernet cards?
2. If not, who generates the new fields?
3. What happens to frames that are already the maximum size?

Of course, the 802 committee was (only too painfully) aware of these problems and had to come up with solutions, which it did.

The key to the solution is to realize that the VLAN fields are only actually used by the bridges and switches and *not* by the user machines. Thus, in Fig. 4-47, it is not really essential that they are present on the lines going out to the end stations as long as they are on the line between the bridges. Also, to use VLANs, the bridges have to be VLAN aware. This fact makes the design feasible.

As to throwing out all existing Ethernet cards, the answer is no. Remember that the 802.3 committee could not even get people to change the *Type* field into a *Length* field. You can imagine the reaction to an announcement that all existing Ethernet cards had to be thrown out. However, new Ethernet cards are 802.1Q compliant and can correctly fill in the VLAN fields.

Because there can be computers (and switches) that are not VLAN aware, the first VLAN-aware bridge to touch a frame adds VLAN fields and the last one down the road removes them. An example of a mixed topology is shown in Fig. 4-48. In this figure, VLAN-aware computers generate tagged (i.e., 802.1Q) frames directly, and further switching uses these tags. The shaded symbols are VLAN-aware and the empty ones are not.

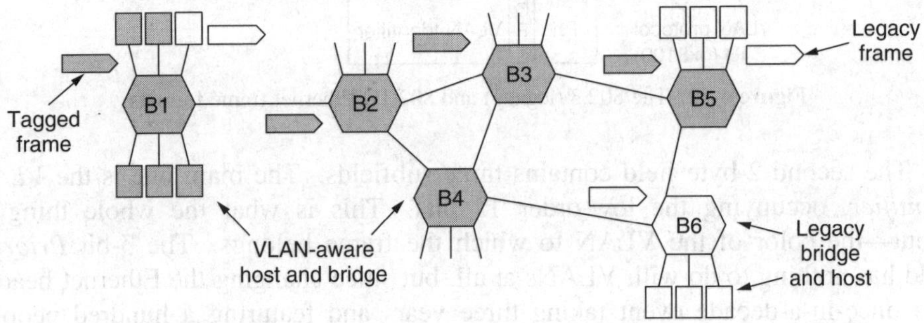

Figure 4-48. Bridged LAN that is only partly VLAN aware. The shaded symbols are VLAN aware. The empty ones are not.

With 802.1Q, frames are colored depending on the port on which they are received. For this method to work, all machines on a port must belong to the same VLAN, which reduces flexibility. For example, in Fig. 4-48, this property holds for all ports where an individual computer connects to a bridge, but not for the port where the hub connects to bridge *B2*.

Additionally, the bridge can use the higher-layer protocol to select the color. In this way, frames arriving on a port might be placed in different VLANs depending on whether they carry IP packets or PPP frames.

Other methods are possible, but they are not supported by 802.1Q. As one example, the MAC address can be used to select the VLAN color. This might be useful for frames coming in from a nearby 802.11 LAN in which laptops send frames via different ports as they move. One MAC address would then be mapped to a fixed VLAN regardless of which port it entered the LAN on.

As to the problem of frames longer than 1518 bytes, 802.1Q just raised the limit to 1522 bytes. Luckily, only VLAN-aware computers and switches must support these longer frames.

Now let us take a look at the 802.1Q frame format. It is shown in Fig. 4-49. The only change is the addition of a pair of 2-byte fields. The first one is the

VLAN protocol ID. It always has the value 0x8100. Since this number is greater than 1500, all Ethernet cards interpret it as a type rather than a length. What a legacy card does with such a frame is moot since such frames are not supposed to be sent to legacy cards.

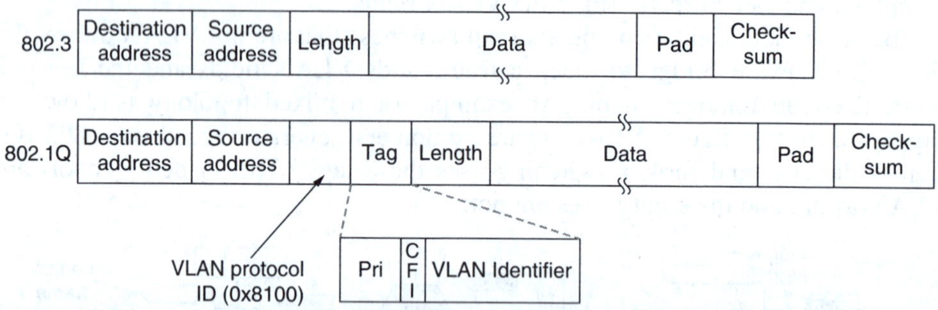

Figure 4-49. The 802.3 (legacy) and 802.1Q Ethernet frame formats.

The second 2-byte field contains three subfields. The main one is the *VLAN identifier*, occupying the low-order 12 bits. This is what the whole thing is about—the color of the VLAN to which the frame belongs. The 3-bit *Priority* field has nothing to do with VLANs at all, but since changing the Ethernet header is a once-in-a-decade event taking three years and featuring a hundred people, why not put in some other good things while you are at it? This field makes it possible to distinguish hard real-time traffic from soft real-time traffic from time-insensitive traffic in order to provide better quality of service over Ethernet. It is needed for voice over Ethernet (although in all fairness, IP has had a similar field for a quarter of a century and nobody ever used it).

The last field, *CFI* (*Canonical format indicator*), should have been called the *CEI* (*Corporate ego indicator*). It was originally intended to indicate the order of the bits in the MAC addresses (little-endian versus big-endian), but that use got lost in other controversies. Its presence now indicates that the payload contains a freeze-dried 802.5 frame that is hoping to find another 802.5 LAN at the destination while being carried by Ethernet in between. This whole arrangement, of course, has nothing whatsoever to do with VLANs. But standards' committee politics are not unlike regular politics: if you vote for my bit, I will vote for your bit.

As we mentioned above, when a tagged frame arrives at a VLAN-aware switch, the switch uses the VLAN identifier as an index into a table to find out which ports to send it on. But where does the table come from? If it is manually constructed, we are back to square zero: manual configuration of bridges. The beauty of the transparent bridge is that it is plug-and-play and does not require any manual configuration. It would be a terrible shame to lose that property. Fortunately, VLAN-aware bridges can also autoconfigure themselves based on observing the tags that come by. If a frame tagged as VLAN 4 comes in on port

3, apparently some machine on port 3 is on VLAN 4. The 802.1Q standard explains how to build the tables dynamically, mostly by referencing appropriate portions of the 802.1D standard.

Before leaving the subject of VLAN routing, it is worth making one last observation. Many people in the Internet and Ethernet worlds are fanatically in favor of connectionless networking and violently opposed to anything smacking of connections in the data link or network layers. Yet VLANs introduce something that is surprisingly similar to a connection. To use VLANs properly, each frame carries a new special identifier that is used as an index into a table inside the switch to look up where the frame is supposed to be sent. That is precisely what happens in connection-oriented networks. In connectionless networks, it is the destination address that is used for routing, not some kind of connection identifier. We will see more of this creeping connectionism in Chap. 5.

4.9 SUMMARY

Some networks have a single channel that is used for all communication. In these networks, the key design issue is the allocation of this channel among the competing stations wishing to use it. FDM and TDM are simple, efficient allocation schemes when the number of stations is small and fixed and the traffic is continuous. Both are widely used under these circumstances, for example, for dividing up the bandwidth on telephone trunks. However, when the number of stations is large and variable or the traffic is fairly bursty—the common case in computer networks—FDM and TDM are poor choices.

Numerous dynamic channel allocation algorithms have been devised. The ALOHA protocol, with and without slotting, is used in many derivatives in real systems, for example, cable modems and RFID. As an improvement when the state of the channel can be sensed, stations can avoid starting a transmission while another station is transmitting. This technique, carrier sensing, has led to a variety of CSMA protocols for LANs and MANs. It is the basis for classic Ethernet and 802.11 networks.

A class of protocols that eliminates contention altogether, or at least reduces it considerably, is well known. The bitmap protocol, topologies such as rings, and the binary countdown protocol completely eliminate contention. The tree walk protocol reduces it by dynamically dividing the stations into two disjoint groups of different sizes and allowing contention only within one group; ideally that group is chosen so that only one station is ready to send when it is permitted to do so.

Wireless LANs have the added problems that it is difficult to sense colliding transmissions, and that the coverage regions of stations may differ. In the dominant wireless LAN, IEEE 802.11, stations use CSMA/CA to mitigate the first problem by leaving small gaps to avoid collisions. The stations can also use the RTS/CTS protocol to combat hidden terminals that arise because of the second problem. IEEE 802.11 is commonly used to connect laptops and other devices to wireless access points, but it can also be used between devices. Any of several physical layers can be used, including multichannel FDM with and without multiple antennas, and spread spectrum.

Like 802.11, RFID readers and tags use a random access protocol to communicate identifiers. Other wireless PANs and MANs have different designs. The Bluetooth system connects headsets and many kinds of peripherals to computers without wires. IEEE 802.16 provides a wide area wireless Internet data service for stationary and mobile computers. Both of these networks use a centralized, connection-oriented design in which the Bluetooth master and the WiMAX base station decide when each station may send or receive data. For 802.16, this design supports different quality of service for real-time traffic like telephone calls and interactive traffic like Web browsing. For Bluetooth, placing the complexity in the master leads to inexpensive slave devices.

Ethernet is the dominant form of wired LAN. Classic Ethernet used CSMA/CD for channel allocation on a yellow cable the size of a garden hose that snaked from machine to machine. The architecture has changed as speeds have risen from 10 Mbps to 10 Gbps and continue to climb. Now, point-to-point links such as twisted pair are attached to hubs and switches. With modern switches and full-duplex links, there is no contention on the links and the switch can forward frames between different ports in parallel.

With buildings full of LANs, a way is needed to interconnect them all. Plug-and-play bridges are used for this purpose. The bridges are built with a backward learning algorithm and a spanning tree algorithm. Since this functionality is built into modern switches, the terms "bridge" and "switch" are used interchangeably. To help with the management of bridged LANs, VLANs let the physical topology be divided into different logical topologies. The VLAN standard, IEEE 802.1Q, introduces a new format for Ethernet frames.

PROBLEMS

1. For this problem, use a formula from this chapter, but first state the formula. Frames arrive randomly at a 100-Mbps channel for transmission. If the channel is busy when a frame arrives, it waits its turn in a queue. Frame length is exponentially distributed with a mean of 10,000 bits/frame. For each of the following frame arrival rates, give the delay experienced by the average frame, including both queueing time and transmission time.

(a) 90 frames/sec.
(b) 900 frames/sec.
(c) 9000 frames/sec.

2. A group of N stations share a 56-kbps pure ALOHA channel. Each station outputs a 1000-bit frame on average once every 100 sec, even if the previous one has not yet been sent (e.g., the stations can buffer outgoing frames). What is the maximum value of N?

3. Consider the delay of pure ALOHA versus slotted ALOHA at low load. Which one is less? Explain your answer.

4. A large population of ALOHA users manages to generate 50 requests/sec, including both originals and retransmissions. Time is slotted in units of 40 msec.
(a) What is the chance of success on the first attempt?
(b) What is the probability of exactly k collisions and then a success?
(c) What is the expected number of transmission attempts needed?

5. In an infinite-population slotted ALOHA system, the mean number of slots a station waits between a collision and a retransmission is 4. Plot the delay versus throughput curve for this system.

6. What is the length of a contention slot in CSMA/CD for (a) a 2-km twin-lead cable (signal propagation speed is 82% of the signal propagation speed in vacuum)?, and (b) a 40-km multimode fiber optic cable (signal propagation speed is 65% of the signal propagation speed in vacuum)?

7. How long does a station, s, have to wait in the worst case before it can start transmitting its frame over a LAN that uses the basic bit-map protocol?

8. In the binary countdown protocol, explain how a lower-numbered station may be starved from sending a packet.

9. Sixteen stations, numbered 1 through 16, are contending for the use of a shared channel by using the adaptive tree walk protocol. If all the stations whose addresses are prime numbers suddenly become ready at once, how many bit slots are needed to resolve the contention?

10. Consider five wireless stations, A, B, C, D, and E. Station A can communicate with all other stations. B can communicate with A, C and E. C can communicate with A, B and D. D can communicate with A, C and E. E can communicate A, D and B.

(a) When A is sending to B, what other communications are possible?
(b) When B is sending to A, what other communications are possible?
(c) When B is sending to C, what other communications are possible?

11. Six stations, A through F, communicate using the MACA protocol. Is it possible for two transmissions to take place simultaneously? Explain your answer.

12. A seven-story office building has 15 adjacent offices per floor. Each office contains a wall socket for a terminal in the front wall, so the sockets form a rectangular grid in the vertical plane, with a separation of 4 m between sockets, both horizontally and vertically. Assuming that it is feasible to run a straight cable between any pair of sockets, horizontally, vertically, or diagonally, how many meters of cable are needed to connect all sockets using

(a) A star configuration with a single router in the middle?
(b) A classic 802.3 LAN?

13. What is the baud rate of classic 10-Mbps Ethernet?

14. Sketch the Manchester encoding on a classic Ethernet for the bit stream 0001110101.

15. A 1-km-long, 10-Mbps CSMA/CD LAN (not 802.3) has a propagation speed of 200 m/μsec. Repeaters are not allowed in this system. Data frames are 256 bits long, including 32 bits of header, checksum, and other overhead. The first bit slot after a successful transmission is reserved for the receiver to capture the channel in order to send a 32-bit acknowledgement frame. What is the effective data rate, excluding overhead, assuming that there are no collisions?

16. Two CSMA/CD stations are each trying to transmit long (multiframe) files. After each frame is sent, they contend for the channel, using the binary exponential backoff algorithm. What is the probability that the contention ends on round k, and what is the mean number of rounds per contention period?

17. An IP packet to be transmitted by Ethernet is 60 bytes long, including all its headers. If LLC is not in use, is padding needed in the Ethernet frame, and if so, how many bytes?

18. Ethernet frames must be at least 64 bytes long to ensure that the transmitter is still going in the event of a collision at the far end of the cable. Fast Ethernet has the same 64-byte minimum frame size but can get the bits out ten times faster. How is it possible to maintain the same minimum frame size?

19. Some books quote the maximum size of an Ethernet frame as 1522 bytes instead of 1500 bytes. Are they wrong? Explain your answer.

20. How many frames per second can gigabit Ethernet handle? Think carefully and take into account all the relevant cases. *Hint*: the fact that it is *gigabit* Ethernet matters.

21. Name two networks that allow frames to be packed back-to-back. Why is this feature worth having?

22. In Fig. 4-27, four stations, *A*, *B*, *C*, and *D*, are shown. Which of the last two stations do you think is closest to *A* and why?

23. Give an example to show that the RTS/CTS in the 802.11 protocol is a little different than in the MACA protocol.

24. A wireless LAN with one AP has 10 client stations. Four stations have data rates of 6 Mbps, four stations have data rates of 18 Mbps, and the last two stations have data rates of 54 Mbps. What is the data rate experienced by each station when all ten stations are sending data together, and

(a) TXOP is not used?
(b) TXOP is used?

25. Suppose that an 11-Mbps 802.11b LAN is transmitting 64-byte frames back-to-back over a radio channel with a bit error rate of 10^{-7}. How many frames per second will be damaged on average?

26. An 802.16 network has a channel width of 20 MHz. How many bits/sec can be sent to a subscriber station?

27. Give two reasons why networks might use an error-correcting code instead of error detection and retransmission.

28. List two ways in which WiMAX is similar to 802.11, and two ways in which it is different from 802.11.

29. From Fig. 4-34, we see that a Bluetooth device can be in two piconets at the same time. Is there any reason why one device cannot be the master in both of them at the same time?

30. What is the maximum size of the data field for a 3-slot Bluetooth frame at basic rate? Explain your answer.

31. Figure 4-24 shows several physical layer protocols. Which of these is closest to the Bluetooth physical layer protocol? What is the biggest difference between the two?

32. It is mentioned in Section 4.6.6 that the efficiency of a 1-slot frame with repetition encoding is about 13% at basic data rate. What will the efficiency be if a 5-slot frame with repetition encoding is used at basic data rate instead?

33. Beacon frames in the frequency hopping spread spectrum variant of 802.11 contain the dwell time. Do you think the analogous beacon frames in Bluetooth also contain the dwell time? Discuss your answer.

34. Suppose that there are 10 RFID tags around an RFID reader. What is the best value of Q? How likely is it that one tag responds with no collision in a given slot?

35. List some of the security concerns of an RFID system.

36. A switch designed for use with fast Ethernet has a backplane that can move 10 Gbps. How many frames/sec can it handle in the worst case?

37. Briefly describe the difference between store-and-forward and cut-through switches.

38. Consider the extended LAN connected using bridges *B1* and *B2* in Fig. 4-41(b). Suppose the hash tables in the two bridges are empty. List all ports on which a packet will be forwarded for the following sequence of data transmissions:

(a) *A* sends a packet to *C*.
(b) *E* sends a packet to *F*.
(c) *F* sends a packet to *E*.
(d) *G* sends a packet to *E*.
(e) *D* sends a packet to *A*.
(f) *B* sends a packet to *F*.

39. Store-and-forward switches have an advantage over cut-through switches with respect to damaged frames. Explain what it is.

40. It is mentioned in Section 4.8.3 that some bridges may not even be present in the spanning tree. Outline a scenario where a bridge may not be present in the spanning tree.

41. To make VLANs work, configuration tables are needed in the bridges. What if the VLANs of Fig. 4-47 used hubs rather than switches? Do the hubs need configuration tables, too? Why or why not?

42. In Fig. 4-48, the switch in the legacy end domain on the right is a VLAN-aware switch. Would it be possible to use a legacy switch there? If so, how would that work? If not, why not?

43. Write a program to simulate the behavior of the CSMA/CD protocol over Ethernet when there are *N* stations ready to transmit while a frame is being transmitted. Your program should report the times when each station successfully starts sending its frame. Assume that a clock tick occurs once every slot time (51.2 μsec) and a collision detection and sending of a jamming sequence takes one slot time. All frames are the maximum length allowed.

5

THE NETWORK LAYER

The network layer is concerned with getting packets from the source all the way to the destination. Getting to the destination may require making many hops at intermediate routers along the way. This function clearly contrasts with that of the data link layer, which has the more modest goal of just moving frames from one end of a wire to the other. Thus, the network layer is the lowest layer that deals with end-to-end transmission.

To achieve its goals, the network layer must know about the topology of the network (i.e., the set of all routers and links) and choose appropriate paths through it, even for large networks. It must also take care when choosing routes to avoid overloading some of the communication lines and routers while leaving others idle. Finally, when the source and destination are in different networks, new problems occur. It is up to the network layer to deal with them. In this chapter we will study all these issues and illustrate them, primarily using the Internet and its network layer protocol, IP.

5.1 NETWORK LAYER DESIGN ISSUES

In the following sections, we will give an introduction to some of the issues that the designers of the network layer must grapple with. These issues include the service provided to the transport layer and the internal design of the network.

5.1.1 Store-and-Forward Packet Switching

Before starting to explain the details of the network layer, it is worth restating the context in which the network layer protocols operate. This context can be seen in Fig. 5-1. The major components of the network are the ISP's equipment (routers connected by transmission lines), shown inside the shaded oval, and the customers' equipment, shown outside the oval. Host *H1* is directly connected to one of the ISP's routers, *A*, perhaps as a home computer that is plugged into a DSL modem. In contrast, *H2* is on a LAN, which might be an office Ethernet, with a router, *F*, owned and operated by the customer. This router has a leased line to the ISP's equipment. We have shown *F* as being outside the oval because it does not belong to the ISP. For the purposes of this chapter, however, routers on customer premises are considered part of the ISP network because they run the same algorithms as the ISP's routers (and our main concern here is algorithms).

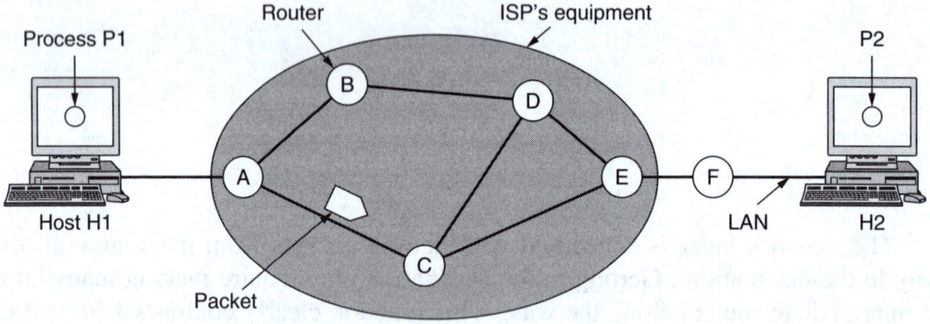

Figure 5-1. The environment of the network layer protocols.

This equipment is used as follows. A host with a packet to send transmits it to the nearest router, either on its own LAN or over a point-to-point link to the ISP. The packet is stored there until it has fully arrived and the link has finished its processing by verifying the checksum. Then it is forwarded to the next router along the path until it reaches the destination host, where it is delivered. This mechanism is store-and-forward packet switching, as we have seen in previous chapters.

5.1.2 Services Provided to the Transport Layer

The network layer provides services to the transport layer at the network layer/transport layer interface. An important question is precisely what kind of services the network layer provides to the transport layer. The services need to be carefully designed with the following goals in mind:

1. The services should be independent of the router technology.
2. The transport layer should be shielded from the number, type, and topology of the routers present.
3. The network addresses made available to the transport layer should use a uniform numbering plan, even across LANs and WANs.

Given these goals, the designers of the network layer have a lot of freedom in writing detailed specifications of the services to be offered to the transport layer. This freedom often degenerates into a raging battle between two warring factions. The discussion centers on whether the network layer should provide connection-oriented service or connectionless service.

One camp (represented by the Internet community) argues that the routers' job is moving packets around and nothing else. In this view (based on 40 years of experience with a real computer network), the network is inherently unreliable, no matter how it is designed. Therefore, the hosts should accept this fact and do error control (i.e., error detection and correction) and flow control themselves.

This viewpoint leads to the conclusion that the network service should be connectionless, with primitives SEND PACKET and RECEIVE PACKET and little else. In particular, no packet ordering and flow control should be done, because the hosts are going to do that anyway and there is usually little to be gained by doing it twice. This reasoning is an example of the **end-to-end argument**, a design principle that has been very influential in shaping the Internet (Saltzer et al., 1984). Furthermore, each packet must carry the full destination address, because each packet sent is carried independently of its predecessors, if any.

The other camp (represented by the telephone companies) argues that the network should provide a reliable, connection-oriented service. They claim that 100 years of successful experience with the worldwide telephone system is an excellent guide. In this view, quality of service is the dominant factor, and without connections in the network, quality of service is very difficult to achieve, especially for real-time traffic such as voice and video.

Even after several decades, this controversy is still very much alive. Early, widely used data networks, such as X.25 in the 1970s and its successor Frame Relay in the 1980s, were connection-oriented. However, since the days of the ARPANET and the early Internet, connectionless network layers have grown tremendously in popularity. The IP protocol is now an ever-present symbol of success. It was undeterred by a connection-oriented technology called ATM that was developed to overthrow it in the 1980s; instead, it is ATM that is now found in niche uses and IP that is taking over telephone networks. Under the covers, however, the Internet is evolving connection-oriented features as quality of service becomes more important. Two examples of connection-oriented technologies are MPLS (MultiProtocol Label Switching), which we will describe in this chapter, and VLANs, which we saw in Chap. 4. Both technologies are widely used.

5.1.3 Implementation of Connectionless Service

Having looked at the two classes of service the network layer can provide to its users, it is time to see how this layer works inside. Two different organizations are possible, depending on the type of service offered. If connectionless service is offered, packets are injected into the network individually and routed independently of each other. No advance setup is needed. In this context, the packets are frequently called **datagrams** (in analogy with telegrams) and the network is called a **datagram network**. If connection-oriented service is used, a path from the source router all the way to the destination router must be established before any data packets can be sent. This connection is called a **VC** (**virtual circuit**), in analogy with the physical circuits set up by the telephone system, and the network is called a **virtual-circuit network**. In this section, we will examine datagram networks; in the next one, we will examine virtual-circuit networks.

Let us now see how a datagram network works. Suppose that the process *P1* in Fig. 5-2 has a long message for *P2*. It hands the message to the transport layer, with instructions to deliver it to process *P2* on host *H2*. The transport layer code runs on *H1*, typically within the operating system. It prepends a transport header to the front of the message and hands the result to the network layer, probably just another procedure within the operating system.

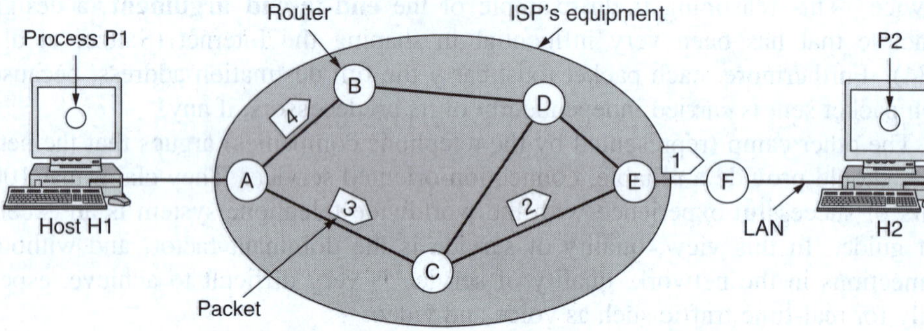

A's table (initially) Dest.	Line	A's table (later) Dest.	Line	C's table Dest.	Line	E's table Dest.	Line
A	–	A	–	A	A	A	C
B	B	B	B	B	A	B	D
C	C	C	C	C	–	C	C
D	B	D	B	D	E	D	D
E	C	E	B	E	E	E	–
F	C	F	B	F	E	F	F

Figure 5-2. Routing within a datagram network.

Let us assume for this example that the message is four times longer than the maximum packet size, so the network layer has to break it into four packets, 1, 2,

3, and 4, and send each of them in turn to router *A* using some point-to-point protocol, for example, PPP. At this point the ISP takes over. Every router has an internal table telling it where to send packets for each of the possible destinations. Each table entry is a pair consisting of a destination and the outgoing line to use for that destination. Only directly connected lines can be used. For example, in Fig. 5-2, *A* has only two outgoing lines—to *B* and to *C*—so every incoming packet must be sent to one of these routers, even if the ultimate destination is to some other router. *A*'s initial routing table is shown in the figure under the label "initially."

At *A*, packets 1, 2, and 3 are stored briefly, having arrived on the incoming link and had their checksums verified. Then each packet is forwarded according to *A*'s table, onto the outgoing link to *C* within a new frame. Packet 1 is then forwarded to *E* and then to *F*. When it gets to *F*, it is sent within a frame over the LAN to *H2*. Packets 2 and 3 follow the same route.

However, something different happens to packet 4. When it gets to *A* it is sent to router *B*, even though it is also destined for *F*. For some reason, *A* decided to send packet 4 via a different route than that of the first three packets. Perhaps it has learned of a traffic jam somewhere along the *ACE* path and updated its routing table, as shown under the label "later." The algorithm that manages the tables and makes the routing decisions is called the **routing algorithm**. Routing algorithms are one of the main topics we will study in this chapter. There are several different kinds of them, as we will see.

IP (Internet Protocol), which is the basis for the entire Internet, is the dominant example of a connectionless network service. Each packet carries a destination IP address that routers use to individually forward each packet. The addresses are 32 bits in IPv4 packets and 128 bits in IPv6 packets. We will describe IP in much detail later in this chapter.

5.1.4 Implementation of Connection-Oriented Service

For connection-oriented service, we need a virtual-circuit network. Let us see how that works. The idea behind virtual circuits is to avoid having to choose a new route for every packet sent, as in Fig. 5-2. Instead, when a connection is established, a route from the source machine to the destination machine is chosen as part of the connection setup and stored in tables inside the routers. That route is used for all traffic flowing over the connection, exactly the same way that the telephone system works. When the connection is released, the virtual circuit is also terminated. With connection-oriented service, each packet carries an identifier telling which virtual circuit it belongs to.

As an example, consider the situation shown in Fig. 5-3. Here, host *H1* has established connection 1 with host *H2*. This connection is remembered as the first entry in each of the routing tables. The first line of *A*'s table says that if a packet bearing connection identifier 1 comes in from *H1*, it is to be sent to router *C* and given connection identifier 1. Similarly, the first entry at *C* routes the packet to *E*, also with connection identifier 1.

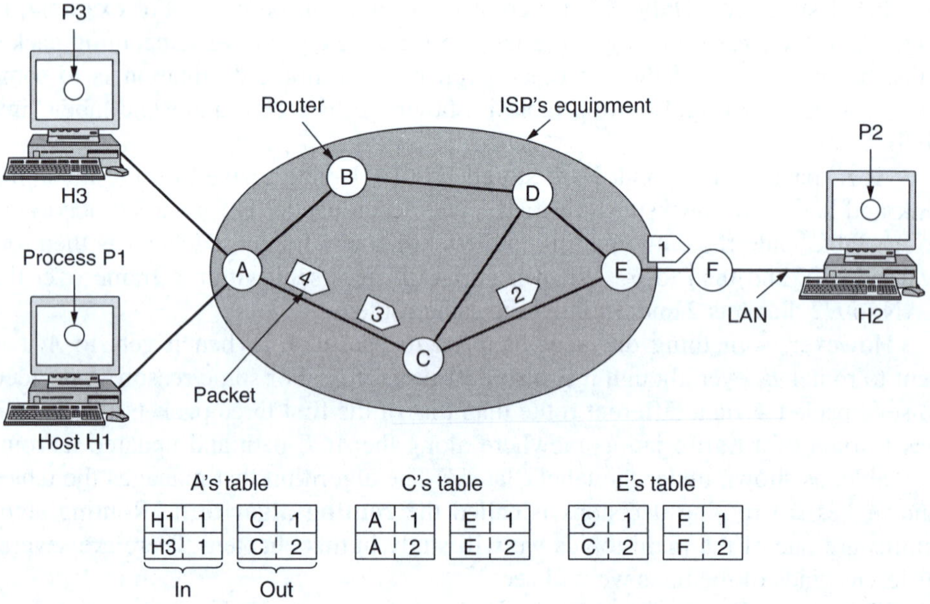

Figure 5-3. Routing within a virtual-circuit network.

Now let us consider what happens if *H3* also wants to establish a connection to *H2*. It chooses connection identifier 1 (because it is initiating the connection and this is its only connection) and tells the network to establish the virtual circuit. This leads to the second row in the tables. Note that we have a conflict here because although *A* can easily distinguish connection 1 packets from *H1* from connection 1 packets from *H3*, *C* cannot do this. For this reason, *A* assigns a different connection identifier to the outgoing traffic for the second connection. Avoiding conflicts of this kind is why routers need the ability to replace connection identifiers in outgoing packets.

In some contexts, this process is called **label switching**. An example of a connection-oriented network service is **MPLS** (**MultiProtocol Label Switching**). It is used within ISP networks in the Internet, with IP packets wrapped in an MPLS header having a 20-bit connection identifier or label. MPLS is often hidden from customers, with the ISP establishing long-term connections for large amounts of traffic, but it is increasingly being used to help when quality of service is important but also with other ISP traffic management tasks. We will have more to say about MPLS later in this chapter.

5.1.5 Comparison of Virtual-Circuit and Datagram Networks

Both virtual circuits and datagrams have their supporters and their detractors. We will now attempt to summarize both sets of arguments. The major issues are listed in Fig. 5-4, although purists could probably find a counterexample for everything in the figure.

Issue	Datagram network	Virtual-circuit network
Circuit setup	Not needed	Required
Addressing	Each packet contains the full source and destination address	Each packet contains a short VC number
State information	Routers do not hold state information about connections	Each VC requires router table space per connection
Routing	Each packet is routed independently	Route chosen when VC is set up; all packets follow it
Effect of router failures	None, except for packets lost during the crash	All VCs that passed through the failed router are terminated
Quality of service	Difficult	Easy if enough resources can be allocated in advance for each VC
Congestion control	Difficult	Easy if enough resources can be allocated in advance for each VC

Figure 5-4. Comparison of datagram and virtual-circuit networks.

Inside the network, several trade-offs exist between virtual circuits and datagrams. One trade-off is setup time versus address parsing time. Using virtual circuits requires a setup phase, which takes time and consumes resources. However, once this price is paid, figuring out what to do with a data packet in a virtual-circuit network is easy: the router just uses the circuit number to index into a table to find out where the packet goes. In a datagram network, no setup is needed but a more complicated lookup procedure is required to locate the entry for the destination.

A related issue is that the destination addresses used in datagram networks are longer than circuit numbers used in virtual-circuit networks because they have a global meaning. If the packets tend to be fairly short, including a full destination address in every packet may represent a significant amount of overhead, and hence a waste of bandwidth.

Yet another issue is the amount of table space required in router memory. A datagram network needs to have an entry for every possible destination, whereas a virtual-circuit network just needs an entry for each virtual circuit. However, this advantage is somewhat illusory since connection setup packets have to be routed too, and they use destination addresses, the same as datagrams do.

Virtual circuits have some advantages in guaranteeing quality of service and avoiding congestion within the network because resources (e.g., buffers, bandwidth, and CPU cycles) can be reserved in advance, when the connection is established. Once the packets start arriving, the necessary bandwidth and router capacity will be there. With a datagram network, congestion avoidance is more difficult.

For transaction processing systems (e.g., stores calling up to verify credit card purchases), the overhead required to set up and clear a virtual circuit may easily dwarf the use of the circuit. If the majority of the traffic is expected to be of this kind, the use of virtual circuits inside the network makes little sense. On the other hand, for long-running uses such as VPN traffic between two corporate offices, permanent virtual circuits (that are set up manually and last for months or years) may be useful.

Virtual circuits also have a vulnerability problem. If a router crashes and loses its memory, even if it comes back up a second later, all the virtual circuits passing through it will have to be aborted. In contrast, if a datagram router goes down, only those users whose packets were queued in the router at the time need suffer (and probably not even then since the sender is likely to retransmit them shortly). The loss of a communication line is fatal to virtual circuits using it, but can easily be compensated for if datagrams are used. Datagrams also allow the routers to balance the traffic throughout the network, since routes can be changed partway through a long sequence of packet transmissions.

5.2 ROUTING ALGORITHMS

The main function of the network layer is routing packets from the source machine to the destination machine. In most networks, packets will require multiple hops to make the journey. The only notable exception is for broadcast networks, but even here routing is an issue if the source and destination are not on the same network segment. The algorithms that choose the routes and the data structures that they use are a major area of network layer design.

The **routing algorithm** is that part of the network layer software responsible for deciding which output line an incoming packet should be transmitted on. If the network uses datagrams internally, this decision must be made anew for every arriving data packet since the best route may have changed since last time. If the network uses virtual circuits internally, routing decisions are made only when a new virtual circuit is being set up. Thereafter, data packets just follow the already established route. The latter case is sometimes called **session routing** because a route remains in force for an entire session (e.g., while logged in over a VPN).

It is sometimes useful to make a distinction between routing, which is making the decision which routes to use, and forwarding, which is what happens when a packet arrives. One can think of a router as having two processes inside it. One of them handles each packet as it arrives, looking up the outgoing line to use for it in the routing tables. This process is **forwarding**. The other process is responsible for filling in and updating the routing tables. That is where the routing algorithm comes into play.

Regardless of whether routes are chosen independently for each packet sent or only when new connections are established, certain properties are desirable in a routing algorithm: correctness, simplicity, robustness, stability, fairness, and efficiency. Correctness and simplicity hardly require comment, but the need for robustness may be less obvious at first. Once a major network comes on the air, it may be expected to run continuously for years without system-wide failures. During that period there will be hardware and software failures of all kinds. Hosts, routers, and lines will fail repeatedly, and the topology will change many times. The routing algorithm should be able to cope with changes in the topology and traffic without requiring all jobs in all hosts to be aborted. Imagine the havoc if the network needed to be rebooted every time some router crashed!

Stability is also an important goal for the routing algorithm. There exist routing algorithms that never converge to a fixed set of paths, no matter how long they run. A stable algorithm reaches equilibrium and stays there. It should converge quickly too, since communication may be disrupted until the routing algorithm has reached equilibrium.

Fairness and efficiency may sound obvious—surely no reasonable person would oppose them—but as it turns out, they are often contradictory goals. As a simple example of this conflict, look at Fig. 5-5. Suppose that there is enough traffic between A and A', between B and B', and between C and C' to saturate the horizontal links. To maximize the total flow, the X to X' traffic should be shut off altogether. Unfortunately, X and X' may not see it that way. Evidently, some compromise between global efficiency and fairness to individual connections is needed.

Before we can even attempt to find trade-offs between fairness and efficiency, we must decide what it is we seek to optimize. Minimizing the mean packet delay is an obvious candidate to send traffic through the network effectively, but so is maximizing total network throughput. Furthermore, these two goals are also in conflict, since operating any queueing system near capacity implies a long queueing delay. As a compromise, many networks attempt to minimize the distance a packet must travel, or simply reduce the number of hops a packet must make. Either choice tends to improve the delay and also reduce the amount of bandwidth consumed per packet, which tends to improve the overall network throughput as well.

Routing algorithms can be grouped into two major classes: nonadaptive and adaptive. **Nonadaptive algorithms** do not base their routing decisions on any

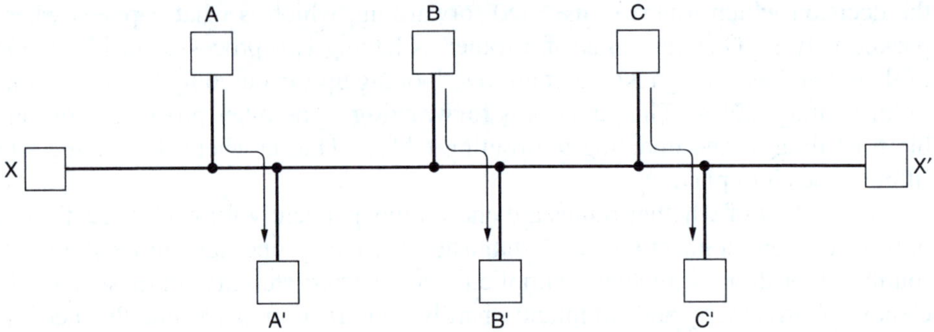

Figure 5-5. Network with a conflict between fairness and efficiency.

measurements or estimates of the current topology and traffic. Instead, the choice of the route to use to get from *I* to *J* (for all *I* and *J*) is computed in advance, offline, and downloaded to the routers when the network is booted. This procedure is sometimes called **static routing**. Because it does not respond to failures, static routing is mostly useful for situations in which the routing choice is clear. For example, router *F* in Fig. 5-3 should send packets headed into the network to router *E* regardless of the ultimate destination.

Adaptive algorithms, in contrast, change their routing decisions to reflect changes in the topology, and sometimes changes in the traffic as well. These **dynamic routing** algorithms differ in where they get their information (e.g., locally, from adjacent routers, or from all routers), when they change the routes (e.g., when the topology changes, or every ΔT seconds as the load changes), and what metric is used for optimization (e.g., distance, number of hops, or estimated transit time).

In the following sections, we will discuss a variety of routing algorithms. The algorithms cover delivery models besides sending a packet from a source to a destination. Sometimes the goal is to send the packet to multiple, all, or one of a set of destinations. All of the routing algorithms we describe here make decisions based on the topology; we defer the possibility of decisions based on the traffic levels to Sec 5.3.

5.2.1 The Optimality Principle

Before we get into specific algorithms, it may be helpful to note that one can make a general statement about optimal routes without regard to network topology or traffic. This statement is known as the **optimality principle** (Bellman, 1957). It states that if router *J* is on the optimal path from router *I* to router *K*, then the optimal path from *J* to *K* also falls along the same route. To see this, call the part of the route from *I* to *J* r_1 and the rest of the route r_2. If a route better than r_2 existed from *J* to *K*, it could be concatenated with r_1 to improve the route from *I* to *K*, contradicting our statement that $r_1 r_2$ is optimal.

As a direct consequence of the optimality principle, we can see that the set of optimal routes from all sources to a given destination form a tree rooted at the destination. Such a tree is called a **sink tree** and is illustrated in Fig. 5-6(b), where the distance metric is the number of hops. The goal of all routing algorithms is to discover and use the sink trees for all routers.

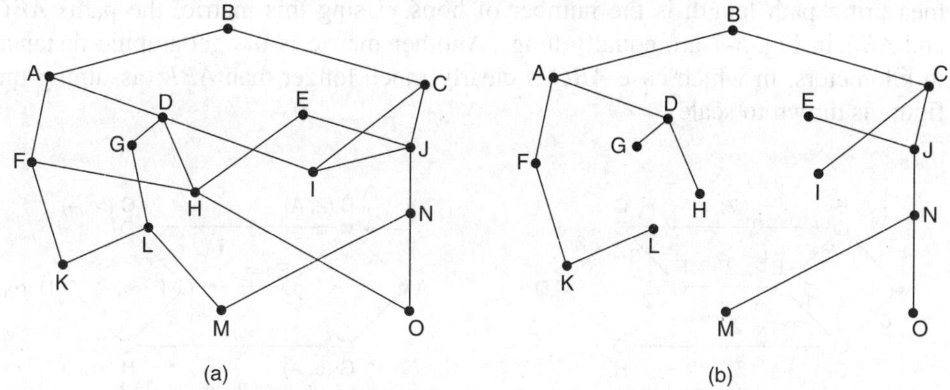

Figure 5-6. (a) A network. (b) A sink tree for router *B*.

Note that a sink tree is not necessarily unique; other trees with the same path lengths may exist. If we allow all of the possible paths to be chosen, the tree becomes a more general structure called a **DAG** (**Directed Acyclic Graph**). DAGs have no loops. We will use sink trees as a convenient shorthand for both cases. Both cases also depend on the technical assumption that the paths do not interfere with each other so, for example, a traffic jam on one path will not cause another path to divert.

Since a sink tree is indeed a tree, it does not contain any loops, so each packet will be delivered within a finite and bounded number of hops. In practice, life is not quite this easy. Links and routers can go down and come back up during operation, so different routers may have different ideas about the current topology. Also, we have quietly finessed the issue of whether each router has to individually acquire the information on which to base its sink tree computation or whether this information is collected by some other means. We will come back to these issues shortly. Nevertheless, the optimality principle and the sink tree provide a benchmark against which other routing algorithms can be measured.

5.2.2 Shortest Path Algorithm

Let us begin our study of routing algorithms with a simple technique for computing optimal paths given a complete picture of the network. These paths are the ones that we want a distributed routing algorithm to find, even though not all routers may know all of the details of the network.

The idea is to build a graph of the network, with each node of the graph representing a router and each edge of the graph representing a communication line, or link. To choose a route between a given pair of routers, the algorithm just finds the shortest path between them on the graph.

The concept of a **shortest path** deserves some explanation. One way of measuring path length is the number of hops. Using this metric, the paths *ABC* and *ABE* in Fig. 5-7 are equally long. Another metric is the geographic distance in kilometers, in which case *ABC* is clearly much longer than *ABE* (assuming the figure is drawn to scale).

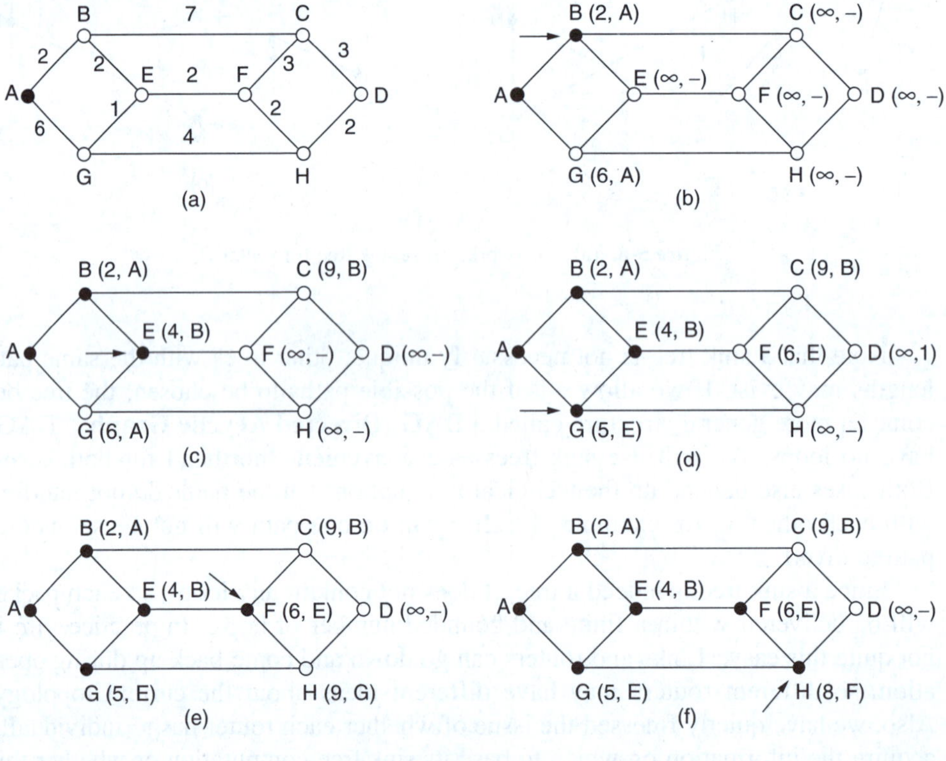

Figure 5-7. The first six steps used in computing the shortest path from *A* to *D*. The arrows indicate the working node.

However, many other metrics besides hops and physical distance are also possible. For example, each edge could be labeled with the mean delay of a standard test packet, as measured by hourly runs. With this graph labeling, the shortest path is the fastest path rather than the path with the fewest edges or kilometers.

In the general case, the labels on the edges could be computed as a function of the distance, bandwidth, average traffic, communication cost, measured delay, and other factors. By changing the weighting function, the algorithm would then compute the "shortest" path measured according to any one of a number of criteria or to a combination of criteria.

Several algorithms for computing the shortest path between two nodes of a graph are known. This one is due to Dijkstra (1959) and finds the shortest paths between a source and all destinations in the network. Each node is labeled (in parentheses) with its distance from the source node along the best known path. The distances must be non-negative, as they will be if they are based on real quantities like bandwidth and delay. Initially, no paths are known, so all nodes are labeled with infinity. As the algorithm proceeds and paths are found, the labels may change, reflecting better paths. A label may be either tentative or permanent. Initially, all labels are tentative. When it is discovered that a label represents the shortest possible path from the source to that node, it is made permanent and never changed thereafter.

To illustrate how the labeling algorithm works, look at the weighted, undirected graph of Fig. 5-7(a), where the weights represent, for example, distance. We want to find the shortest path from *A* to *D*. We start out by marking node *A* as permanent, indicated by a filled-in circle. Then we examine, in turn, each of the nodes adjacent to *A* (the working node), relabeling each one with the distance to *A*. Whenever a node is relabeled, we also label it with the node from which the probe was made so that we can reconstruct the final path later. If the network had more than one shortest path from *A* to *D* and we wanted to find all of them, we would need to remember all of the probe nodes that could reach a node with the same distance.

Having examined each of the nodes adjacent to *A*, we examine all the tentatively labeled nodes in the whole graph and make the one with the smallest label permanent, as shown in Fig. 5-7(b). This one becomes the new working node.

We now start at *B* and examine all nodes adjacent to it. If the sum of the label on *B* and the distance from *B* to the node being considered is less than the label on that node, we have a shorter path, so the node is relabeled.

After all the nodes adjacent to the working node have been inspected and the tentative labels changed if possible, the entire graph is searched for the tentatively labeled node with the smallest value. This node is made permanent and becomes the working node for the next round. Figure 5-7 shows the first six steps of the algorithm.

To see why the algorithm works, look at Fig. 5-7(c). At this point we have just made *E* permanent. Suppose that there were a shorter path than *ABE*, say

AXYZE (for some *X* and *Y*). There are two possibilities: either node *Z* has already been made permanent, or it has not been. If it has, then *E* has already been probed (on the round following the one when *Z* was made permanent), so the *AXYZE* path has not escaped our attention and thus cannot be a shorter path.

Now consider the case where *Z* is still tentatively labeled. If the label at *Z* is greater than or equal to that at *E*, then *AXYZE* cannot be a shorter path than *ABE*. If the label is less than that of *E*, then *Z* and not *E* will become permanent first, allowing *E* to be probed from *Z*.

This algorithm is given in Fig. 5-8. The global variables *n* and *dist* describe the graph and are initialized before *shortest_path* is called. The only difference between the program and the algorithm described above is that in Fig. 5-8, we compute the shortest path starting at the terminal node, *t*, rather than at the source node, *s*.

Since the shortest paths from *t* to *s* in an undirected graph are the same as the shortest paths from *s* to *t*, it does not matter at which end we begin. The reason for searching backward is that each node is labeled with its predecessor rather than its successor. When the final path is copied into the output variable, *path*, the path is thus reversed. The two reversal effects cancel, and the answer is produced in the correct order.

5.2.3 Flooding

When a routing algorithm is implemented, each router must make decisions based on local knowledge, not the complete picture of the network. A simple local technique is **flooding**, in which every incoming packet is sent out on every outgoing line except the one it arrived on.

Flooding obviously generates vast numbers of duplicate packets, in fact, an infinite number unless some measures are taken to damp the process. One such measure is to have a hop counter contained in the header of each packet that is decremented at each hop, with the packet being discarded when the counter reaches zero. Ideally, the hop counter should be initialized to the length of the path from source to destination. If the sender does not know how long the path is, it can initialize the counter to the worst case, namely, the full diameter of the network.

Flooding with a hop count can produce an exponential number of duplicate packets as the hop count grows and routers duplicate packets they have seen before. A better technique for damming the flood is to have routers keep track of which packets have been flooded, to avoid sending them out a second time. One way to achieve this goal is to have the source router put a sequence number in each packet it receives from its hosts. Each router then needs a list per source router telling which sequence numbers originating at that source have already been seen. If an incoming packet is on the list, it is not flooded.

```
#define MAX_NODES 1024                    /* maximum number of nodes */
#define INFINITY 1000000000               /* a number larger than every maximum path */
int n, dist[MAX_NODES][MAX_NODES];        /* dist[i][j] is the distance from i to j */

void shortest_path(int s, int t, int path[])
{ struct state {                          /* the path being worked on */
      int predecessor;                    /* previous node */
      int length;                         /* length from source to this node */
      enum {permanent, tentative} label;  /* label state */
  } state[MAX_NODES];

  int i, k, min;
  struct state *p;

  for (p = &state[0]; p < &state[n]; p++) {   /* initialize state */
      p->predecessor = -1;
      p->length = INFINITY;
      p->label = tentative;
  }
  state[t].length = 0; state[t].label = permanent;
  k = t;                                  /* k is the initial working node */
  do {                                    /* Is there a better path from k? */
      for (i = 0; i < n; i++)             /* this graph has n nodes */
           if (dist[k][i] != 0 && state[i].label == tentative) {
                 if (state[k].length + dist[k][i] < state[i].length) {
                      state[i].predecessor = k;
                      state[i].length = state[k].length + dist[k][i];
                 }
           }

      /* Find the tentatively labeled node with the smallest label. */
      k = 0; min = INFINITY;
      for (i = 0; i < n; i++)
           if (state[i].label == tentative && state[i].length < min) {
                 min = state[i].length;
                 k = i;
           }
      state[k].label = permanent;
  } while (k != s);

  /* Copy the path into the output array. */
  i = 0; k = s;
  do {path[i++] = k; k = state[k].predecessor; } while (k >= 0);
}
```

Figure 5-8. Dijkstra's algorithm to compute the shortest path through a graph.

To prevent the list from growing without bound, each list should be augmented by a counter, *k*, meaning that all sequence numbers through *k* have been seen. When a packet comes in, it is easy to check if the packet has already been flooded (by comparing its sequence number to *k*; if so, it is discarded. Furthermore, the full list below *k* is not needed, since *k* effectively summarizes it.

Flooding is not practical for sending most packets, but it does have some important uses. First, it ensures that a packet is delivered to every node in the network. This may be wasteful if there is a single destination that needs the packet, but it is effective for broadcasting information. In wireless networks, all messages transmitted by a station can be received by all other stations within its radio range, which is, in fact, flooding, and some algorithms utilize this property.

Second, flooding is tremendously robust. Even if large numbers of routers are blown to bits (e.g., in a military network located in a war zone), flooding will find a path if one exists, to get a packet to its destination. Flooding also requires little in the way of setup. The routers only need to know their neighbors. This means that flooding can be used as a building block for other routing algorithms that are more efficient but need more in the way of setup. Flooding can also be used as a metric against which other routing algorithms can be compared. Flooding always chooses the shortest path because it chooses every possible path in parallel. Consequently, no other algorithm can produce a shorter delay (if we ignore the overhead generated by the flooding process itself).

5.2.4 Distance Vector Routing

Computer networks generally use dynamic routing algorithms that are more complex than flooding, but more efficient because they find shortest paths for the current topology. Two dynamic algorithms in particular, distance vector routing and link state routing, are the most popular. In this section, we will look at the former algorithm. In the following section, we will study the latter algorithm.

A **distance vector routing** algorithm operates by having each router maintain a table (i.e., a vector) giving the best known distance to each destination and which link to use to get there. These tables are updated by exchanging information with the neighbors. Eventually, every router knows the best link to reach each destination.

The distance vector routing algorithm is sometimes called by other names, most commonly the distributed **Bellman-Ford** routing algorithm, after the researchers who developed it (Bellman, 1957; and Ford and Fulkerson, 1962). It was the original ARPANET routing algorithm and was also used in the Internet under the name RIP.

In distance vector routing, each router maintains a routing table indexed by, and containing one entry for each router in the network. This entry has two parts: the preferred outgoing line to use for that destination and an estimate of the distance to that destination. The distance might be measured as the number of hops or using another metric, as we discussed for computing shortest paths.

The router is assumed to know the "distance" to each of its neighbors. If the metric is hops, the distance is just one hop. If the metric is propagation delay, the router can measure it directly with special ECHO packets that the receiver just timestamps and sends back as fast as it can.

As an example, assume that delay is used as a metric and that the router knows the delay to each of its neighbors. Once every *T* msec, each router sends to each neighbor a list of its estimated delays to each destination. It also receives a similar list from each neighbor. Imagine that one of these tables has just come in from neighbor *X*, with X_i being *X*'s estimate of how long it takes to get to router *i*. If the router knows that the delay to *X* is *m* msec, it also knows that it can reach router *i* via *X* in $X_i + m$ msec. By performing this calculation for each neighbor, a router can find out which estimate seems the best and use that estimate and the corresponding link in its new routing table. Note that the old routing table is not used in the calculation.

This updating process is illustrated in Fig. 5-9. Part (a) shows a network. The first four columns of part (b) show the delay vectors received from the neighbors of router *J*. *A* claims to have a 12-msec delay to *B*, a 25-msec delay to *C*, a 40-msec delay to *D*, etc. Suppose that *J* has measured or estimated its delay to its neighbors, *A*, *I*, *H*, and *K*, as 8, 10, 12, and 6 msec, respectively.

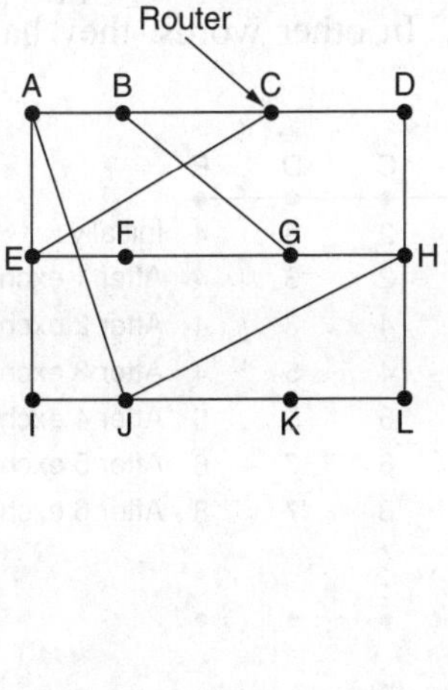

(a)

To	A	I	H	K	New estimated delay from J	Line
A	0	24	20	21	8	A
B	12	36	31	28	20	A
C	25	18	19	36	28	I
D	40	27	8	24	20	H
E	14	7	30	22	17	I
F	23	20	19	40	30	I
G	18	31	6	31	18	H
H	17	20	0	19	12	H
I	21	0	14	22	10	I
J	9	11	7	10	0	–
K	24	22	22	0	6	K
L	29	33	9	9	15	K
	JA delay is 8	JI delay is 10	JH delay is 12	JK delay is 6	New routing table for J	

Vectors received from J's four neighbors

(b)

Figure 5-9. (a) A network. (b) Input from *A*, *I*, *H*, *K*, and the new routing table for *J*.

Consider how *J* computes its new route to router *G*. It knows that it can get to *A* in 8 msec, and furthermore *A* claims to be able to get to *G* in 18 msec, so *J* knows it can count on a delay of 26 msec to *G* if it forwards packets bound for *G* to *A*. Similarly, it computes the delay to *G* via *I*, *H*, and *K* as 41 (31 + 10), 18 (6 + 12), and 37 (31 + 6) msec, respectively. The best of these values is 18, so it makes an entry in its routing table that the delay to *G* is 18 msec and that the route to use is via *H*. The same calculation is performed for all the other destinations, with the new routing table shown in the last column of the figure.

The Count-to-Infinity Problem

The settling of routes to best paths across the network is called **convergence**. Distance vector routing is useful as a simple technique by which routers can collectively compute shortest paths, but it has a serious drawback in practice: although it converges to the correct answer, it may do so slowly. In particular, it reacts rapidly to good news, but leisurely to bad news. Consider a router whose best route to destination *X* is long. If, on the next exchange, neighbor *A* suddenly reports a short delay to *X*, the router just switches over to using the line to *A* to send traffic to *X*. In one vector exchange, the good news is processed.

To see how fast good news propagates, consider the five-node (linear) network of Fig. 5-10, where the delay metric is the number of hops. Suppose *A* is down initially and all the other routers know this. In other words, they have all recorded the delay to *A* as infinity.

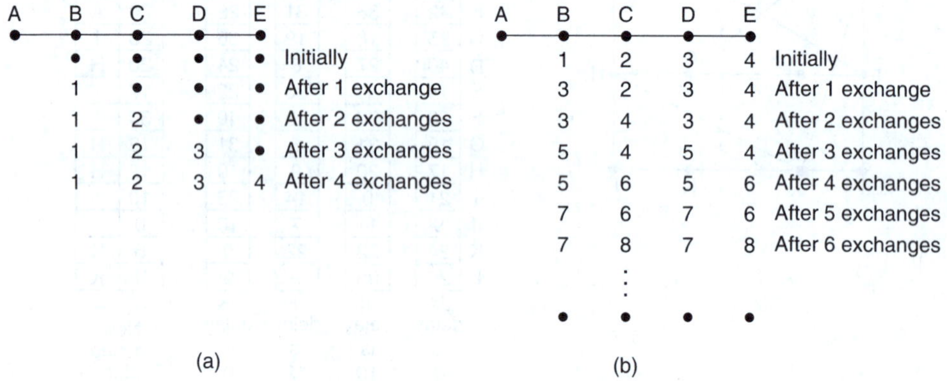

Figure 5-10. The count-to-infinity problem.

When *A* comes up, the other routers learn about it via the vector exchanges. For simplicity, we will assume that there is a gigantic gong somewhere that is struck periodically to initiate a vector exchange at all routers simultaneously. At the time of the first exchange, *B* learns that its left-hand neighbor has zero delay to *A*. *B* now makes an entry in its routing table indicating that *A* is one hop away to the left. All the other routers still think that *A* is down. At this point, the routing table entries for *A* are as shown in the second row of Fig. 5-10(a). On the next exchange, *C* learns that *B* has a path of length 1 to *A*, so it updates its routing table to indicate a path of length 2, but *D* and *E* do not hear the good news until later. Clearly, the good news is spreading at the rate of one hop per exchange. In a network whose longest path is of length *N* hops, within *N* exchanges everyone will know about newly revived links and routers.

Now let us consider the situation of Fig. 5-10(b), in which all the links and routers are initially up. Routers *B*, *C*, *D*, and *E* have distances to *A* of 1, 2, 3, and 4 hops, respectively. Suddenly, either *A* goes down or the link between *A* and *B* is cut (which is effectively the same thing from *B*'s point of view).

At the first packet exchange, *B* does not hear anything from *A*. Fortunately, *C* says "Do not worry; I have a path to *A* of length 2." Little does *B* suspect that *C*'s path runs through *B* itself. For all *B* knows, *C* might have ten links all with separate paths to *A* of length 2. As a result, *B* thinks it can reach *A* via *C*, with a path length of 3. *D* and *E* do not update their entries for *A* on the first exchange.

On the second exchange, *C* notices that each of its neighbors claims to have a path to *A* of length 3. It picks one of them at random and makes its new distance to *A* 4, as shown in the third row of Fig. 5-10(b). Subsequent exchanges produce the history shown in the rest of Fig. 5-10(b).

From this figure, it should be clear why bad news travels slowly: no router ever has a value more than one higher than the minimum of all its neighbors. Gradually, all routers work their way up to infinity, but the number of exchanges required depends on the numerical value used for infinity. For this reason, it is wise to set infinity to the longest path plus 1.

Not entirely surprisingly, this problem is known as the **count-to-infinity** problem. There have been many attempts to solve it, for example, preventing routers from advertising their best paths back to the neighbors from which they heard them with the split horizon with poisoned reverse rule discussed in RFC 1058. However, none of these heuristics work well in practice despite the colorful names. The core of the problem is that when *X* tells *Y* that it has a path somewhere, *Y* has no way of knowing whether it itself is on the path.

5.2.5 Link State Routing

Distance vector routing was used in the ARPANET until 1979, when it was replaced by link state routing. The primary problem that caused its demise was that the algorithm often took too long to converge after the network topology changed (due to the count-to-infinity problem). Consequently, it was replaced by an entirely new algorithm, now called **link state routing**. Variants of link state routing called IS-IS and OSPF are the routing algorithms that are most widely used inside large networks and the Internet today.

The idea behind link state routing is fairly simple and can be stated as five parts. Each router must do the following things to make it work:

1. Discover its neighbors and learn their network addresses.
2. Set the distance or cost metric to each of its neighbors.
3. Construct a packet telling all it has just learned.
4. Send this packet to and receive packets from all other routers.
5. Compute the shortest path to every other router.

In effect, the complete topology is distributed to every router. Then Dijkstra's algorithm can be run at each router to find the shortest path to every other router. Below we will consider each of these five steps in more detail.

Learning about the Neighbors

When a router is booted, its first task is to learn who its neighbors are. It accomplishes this goal by sending a special HELLO packet on each point-to-point line. The router on the other end is expected to send back a reply giving its name. These names must be globally unique because when a distant router later hears that three routers are all connected to *F*, it is essential that it can determine whether all three mean the same *F*.

When two or more routers are connected by a broadcast link (e.g., a switch, ring, or classic Ethernet), the situation is slightly more complicated. Fig. 5-11(a) illustrates a broadcast LAN to which three routers, *A*, *C*, and *F*, are directly connected. Each of these routers is connected to one or more additional routers, as shown.

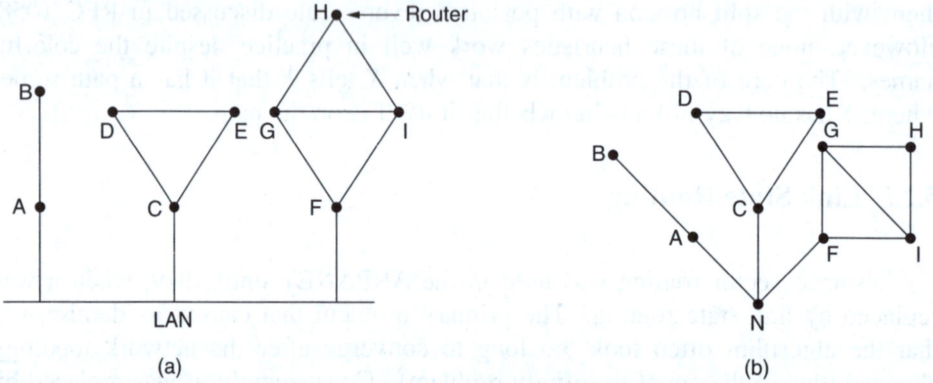

Figure 5-11. (a) Nine routers and a broadcast LAN. (b) A graph model of (a).

The broadcast LAN provides connectivity between each pair of attached routers. However, modeling the LAN as many point-to-point links increases the size of the topology and leads to wasteful messages. A better way to model the LAN is to consider it as a node itself, as shown in Fig. 5-11(b). Here, we have introduced a new, artificial node, *N*, to which *A*, *C*, and *F* are connected. One **designated router** on the LAN is selected to play the role of *N* in the routing protocol. The fact that it is possible to go from *A* to *C* on the LAN is represented by the path *ANC* here.

Setting Link Costs

The link state routing algorithm requires each link to have a distance or cost metric for finding shortest paths. The cost to reach neighbors can be set automatically, or configured by the network operator. A common choice is to make the cost inversely proportional to the bandwidth of the link. For example, 1-Gbps Ethernet may have a cost of 1 and 100-Mbps Ethernet a cost of 10. This makes higher-capacity paths better choices.

If the network is geographically spread out, the delay of the links may be factored into the cost so that paths over shorter links are better choices. The most direct way to determine this delay is to send over the line a special ECHO packet that the other side is required to send back immediately. By measuring the round-trip time and dividing it by two, the sending router can get a reasonable estimate of the delay.

Building Link State Packets

Once the information needed for the exchange has been collected, the next step is for each router to build a packet containing all the data. The packet starts with the identity of the sender, followed by a sequence number and age (to be described later) and a list of neighbors. The cost to each neighbor is also given. An example network is presented in Fig. 5-12(a) with costs shown as labels on the lines. The corresponding link state packets for all six routers are shown in Fig. 5-12(b).

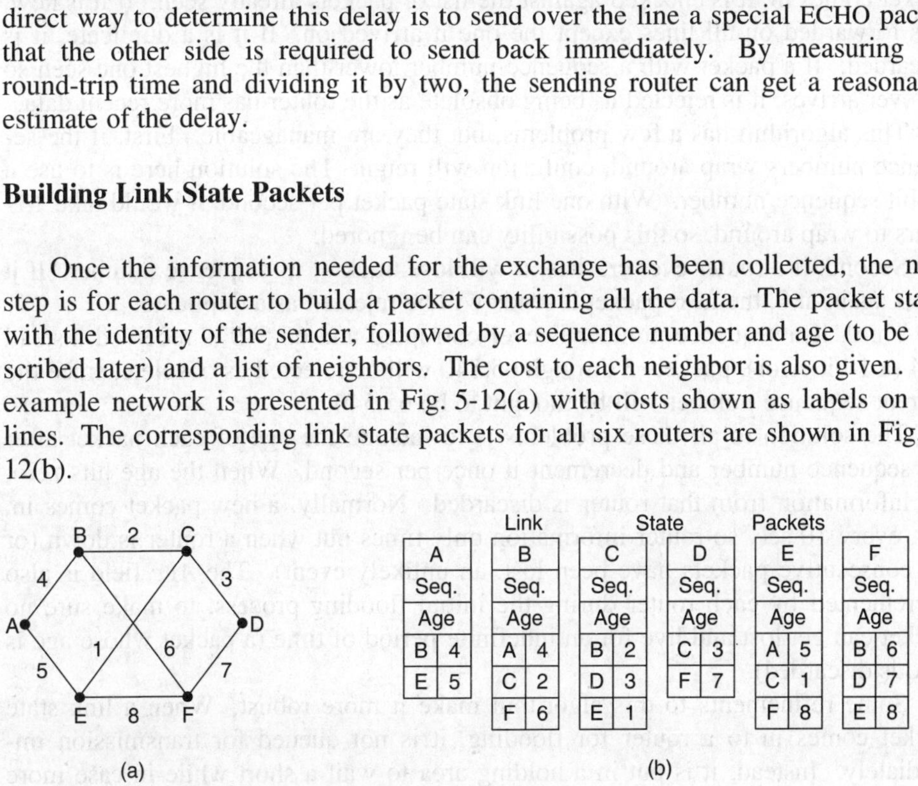

Figure 5-12. (a) A network. (b) The link state packets for this network.

Building the link state packets is easy. The hard part is determining when to build them. One possibility is to build them periodically, that is, at regular intervals. Another possibility is to build them when some significant event occurs, such as a line or neighbor going down or coming back up again or changing its properties appreciably.

Distributing the Link State Packets

The trickiest part of the algorithm is distributing the link state packets. All of the routers must get all of the link state packets quickly and reliably. If different routers are using different versions of the topology, the routes they compute can have inconsistencies such as loops, unreachable machines, and other problems.

First, we will describe the basic distribution algorithm. After that we will give some refinements. The fundamental idea is to use flooding to distribute the link state packets to all routers. To keep the flood in check, each packet contains a sequence number that is incremented for each new packet sent. Routers keep track of all the (source router, sequence) pairs they see. When a new link state packet comes in, it is checked against the list of packets already seen. If it is new, it is forwarded on all lines except the one it arrived on. If it is a duplicate, it is discarded. If a packet with a sequence number lower than the highest one seen so far ever arrives, it is rejected as being obsolete as the router has more recent data.

This algorithm has a few problems, but they are manageable. First, if the sequence numbers wrap around, confusion will reign. The solution here is to use a 32-bit sequence number. With one link state packet per second, it would take 137 years to wrap around, so this possibility can be ignored.

Second, if a router ever crashes, it will lose track of its sequence number. If it starts again at 0, the next packet it sends will be rejected as a duplicate.

Third, if a sequence number is ever corrupted and 65,540 is received instead of 4 (a 1-bit error), packets 5 through 65,540 will be rejected as obsolete, since the current sequence number will be thought to be 65,540.

The solution to all these problems is to include the age of each packet after the sequence number and decrement it once per second. When the age hits zero, the information from that router is discarded. Normally, a new packet comes in, say, every 10 sec, so router information only times out when a router is down (or six consecutive packets have been lost, an unlikely event). The *Age* field is also decremented by each router during the initial flooding process, to make sure no packet can get lost and live for an indefinite period of time (a packet whose age is zero is discarded).

Some refinements to this algorithm make it more robust. When a link state packet comes in to a router for flooding, it is not queued for transmission immediately. Instead, it is put in a holding area to wait a short while in case more links are coming up or going down. If another link state packet from the same source comes in before the first packet is transmitted, their sequence numbers are compared. If they are equal, the duplicate is discarded. If they are different, the older one is thrown out. To guard against errors on the links, all link state packets are acknowledged.

The data structure used by router *B* for the network shown in Fig. 5-12(a) is depicted in Fig. 5-13. Each row here corresponds to a recently arrived, but as yet not fully processed, link state packet. The table records where the packet originated, its sequence number and age, and the data. In addition, there are send and acknowledgement flags for each of *B*'s three links (to *A*, *C*, and *F*, respectively). The send flags mean that the packet must be sent on the indicated link. The acknowledgement flags mean that it must be acknowledged there.

			Send flags			ACK flags			
Source	Seq.	Age	A	C	F	A	C	F	Data
A	21	60	0	1	1	1	0	0	
F	21	60	1	1	0	0	0	1	
E	21	59	0	1	0	1	0	1	
C	20	60	1	0	1	0	1	0	
D	21	59	1	0	0	0	1	1	

Figure 5-13. The packet buffer for router *B* in Fig. 5-12(a).

In Fig. 5-13, the link state packet from *A* arrives directly, so it must be sent to *C* and *F* and acknowledged to *A*, as indicated by the flag bits. Similarly, the packet from *F* has to be forwarded to *A* and *C* and acknowledged to *F*.

However, the situation with the third packet, from *E*, is different. It arrives twice, once via *EAB* and once via *EFB*. Consequently, it has to be sent only to *C* but must be acknowledged to both *A* and *F*, as indicated by the bits.

If a duplicate arrives while the original is still in the buffer, bits have to be changed. For example, if a copy of *C*'s state arrives from *F* before the fourth entry in the table has been forwarded, the six bits will be changed to 100011 to indicate that the packet must be acknowledged to *F* but not sent there.

Computing the New Routes

Once a router has accumulated a full set of link state packets, it can construct the entire network graph because every link is represented. Every link is, in fact, represented twice, once for each direction. The different directions may even have different costs. The shortest-path computations may then find different paths from router *A* to *B* than from router *B* to *A*.

Now Dijkstra's algorithm can be run locally to construct the shortest paths to all possible destinations. The results of this algorithm tell the router which link to use to reach each destination. This information is installed in the routing tables, and normal operation is resumed.

Compared to distance vector routing, link state routing requires more memory and computation. For a network with *n* routers, each of which has *k* neighbors, the memory required to store the input data is proportional to *kn*, which is at least as large as a routing table listing all the destinations. Also, the computation time grows faster than *kn*, even with the most efficient data structures, an issue in large networks. Nevertheless, in many practical situations, link state routing works well because it does not suffer from slow convergence problems.

Link state routing is widely used in actual networks, so a few words about some example protocols are in order. Many ISPs use the **IS-IS (Intermediate System-Intermediate System)** link state protocol (Oran, 1990). It was designed for an early network called DECnet, later adopted by ISO for use with the OSI protocols and then modified to handle other protocols as well, most notably, IP. **OSPF (Open Shortest Path First)** is the other main link state protocol. It was designed by IETF several years after IS-IS and adopted many of the innovations designed for IS-IS. These innovations include a self-stabilizing method of flooding link state updates, the concept of a designated router on a LAN, and the method of computing and supporting path splitting and multiple metrics. As a consequence, there is very little difference between IS-IS and OSPF. The most important difference is that IS-IS can carry information about multiple network layer protocols at the same time (e.g., IP, IPX, and AppleTalk). OSPF does not have this feature, and it is an advantage in large multiprotocol environments. We will go over OSPF in Sec. 5.6.6.

A general comment on routing algorithms is also in order. Link state, distance vector, and other algorithms rely on processing at all the routers to compute routes. Problems with the hardware or software at even a small number of routers can wreak havoc across the network. For example, if a router claims to have a link it does not have or forgets a link it does have, the network graph will be incorrect. If a router fails to forward packets or corrupts them while forwarding them, the route will not work as expected. Finally, if it runs out of memory or does the routing calculation wrong, bad things will happen. As the network grows into the range of tens or hundreds of thousands of nodes, the probability of some router failing occasionally becomes nonnegligible. The trick is to try to arrange to limit the damage when the inevitable happens. Perlman (1988) discusses these problems and their possible solutions in detail.

5.2.6 Hierarchical Routing

As networks grow in size, the router routing tables grow proportionally. Not only is router memory consumed by ever-increasing tables, but more CPU time is needed to scan them and more bandwidth is needed to send status reports about them. At a certain point, the network may grow to the point where it is no longer feasible for every router to have an entry for every other router, so the routing will have to be done hierarchically, as it is in the telephone network.

When hierarchical routing is used, the routers are divided into what we will call **regions**. Each router knows all the details about how to route packets to destinations within its own region but knows nothing about the internal structure of other regions. When different networks are interconnected, it is natural to regard each one as a separate region to free the routers in one network from having to know the topological structure of the other ones.

For huge networks, a two-level hierarchy may be insufficient; it may be necessary to group the regions into clusters, the clusters into zones, the zones into groups, and so on, until we run out of names for aggregations. As an example of a multilevel hierarchy, consider how a packet might be routed from Berkeley, California, to Malindi, Kenya. The Berkeley router would know the detailed topology within California but would send all out-of-state traffic to the Los Angeles router. The Los Angeles router would be able to route traffic directly to other domestic routers but would send all foreign traffic to New York. The New York router would be programmed to direct all traffic to the router in the destination country responsible for handling foreign traffic, say, in Nairobi. Finally, the packet would work its way down the tree in Kenya until it got to Malindi.

Figure 5-14 gives a quantitative example of routing in a two-level hierarchy with five regions. The full routing table for router *1A* has 17 entries, as shown in Fig. 5-14(b). When routing is done hierarchically, as in Fig. 5-14(c), there are entries for all the local routers, as before, but all other regions are condensed into a single router, so all traffic for region 2 goes via the *1B-2A* line, but the rest of the remote traffic goes via the *1C-3B* line. Hierarchical routing has reduced the table from 17 to 7 entries. As the ratio of the number of regions to the number of routers per region grows, the savings in table space increase.

Unfortunately, these gains in space are not free. There is a penalty to be paid: increased path length. For example, the best route from *1A* to *5C* is via region 2, but with hierarchical routing all traffic to region 5 goes via region 3, because that is better for most destinations in region 5.

When a single network becomes very large, an interesting question is "how many levels should the hierarchy have?" For example, consider a network with 720 routers. If there is no hierarchy, each router needs 720 routing table entries. If the network is partitioned into 24 regions of 30 routers each, each router needs 30 local entries plus 23 remote entries for a total of 53 entries. If a three-level hierarchy is chosen, with 8 clusters each containing 9 regions of 10 routers, each router needs 10 entries for local routers, 8 entries for routing to other regions within its own cluster, and 7 entries for distant clusters, for a total of 25 entries. Kamoun and Kleinrock (1979) discovered that the optimal number of levels for an N router network is $\ln N$, requiring a total of $e \ln N$ entries per router. They have also shown that the increase in effective mean path length caused by hierarchical routing is sufficiently small that it is usually acceptable.

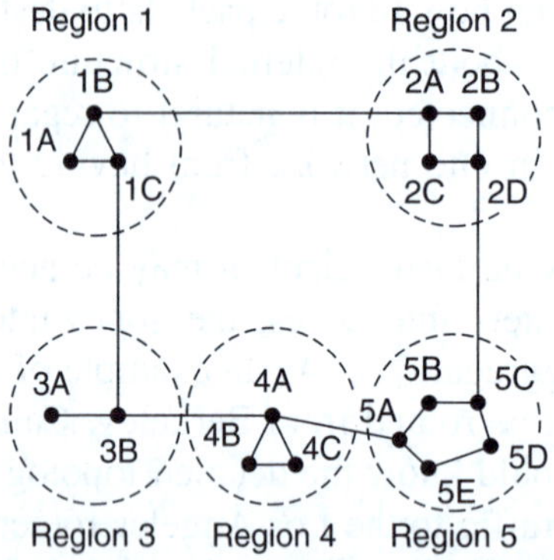

(a)

Full table for 1A

Dest.	Line	Hops
1A	–	–
1B	1B	1
1C	1C	1
2A	1B	2
2B	1B	3
2C	1B	3
2D	1B	4
3A	1C	3
3B	1C	2
4A	1C	3
4B	1C	4
4C	1C	4
5A	1C	4
5B	1C	5
5C	1B	5
5D	1C	6
5E	1C	5

(b)

Hierarchical table for 1A

Dest.	Line	Hops
1A	–	–
1B	1B	1
1C	1C	1
2	1B	2
3	1C	2
4	1C	3
5	1C	4

(c)

Figure 5-14. Hierarchical routing.

5.2.7 Broadcast Routing

In some applications, hosts need to send messages to many or all other hosts. For example, a service distributing weather reports, stock market updates, or live radio programs might work best by sending to all machines and letting those that are interested read the data. Sending a packet to all destinations simultaneously is called **broadcasting**. Various methods have been proposed for doing it.

One broadcasting method that requires no special features from the network is for the source to simply send a distinct packet to each destination. Not only is the method wasteful of bandwidth and slow, but it also requires the source to have a complete list of all destinations. This method is not desirable in practice, even though it is widely applicable.

An improvement is **multidestination routing**, in which each packet contains either a list of destinations or a bit map indicating the desired destinations. When a packet arrives at a router, the router checks all the destinations to determine the set of output lines that will be needed. (An output line is needed if it is the best route to at least one of the destinations.) The router generates a new copy of the packet for each output line to be used and includes in each packet only those destinations that are to use the line. In effect, the destination set is partitioned among the output lines. After a sufficient number of hops, each packet will carry only one destination like a normal packet. Multidestination routing is like using separately addressed packets, except that when several packets must follow the same route, one of them pays full fare and the rest ride free. The network bandwidth is therefore used more efficiently. However, this scheme still requires the source to know all the destinations, plus it is as much work for a router to determine where to send one multidestination packet as it is for multiple distinct packets.

We have already seen a better broadcast routing technique: flooding. When implemented with a sequence number per source, flooding uses links efficiently with a decision rule at routers that is relatively simple. Although flooding is ill-suited for ordinary point-to-point communication, it rates serious consideration for broadcasting. However, it turns out that we can do better still once the shortest path routes for regular packets have been computed.

The idea for **reverse path forwarding** is elegant and remarkably simple once it has been pointed out (Dalal and Metcalfe, 1978). When a broadcast packet arrives at a router, the router checks to see if the packet arrived on the link that is normally used for sending packets *toward* the source of the broadcast. If so, there is an excellent chance that the broadcast packet itself followed the best route from the router and is therefore the first copy to arrive at the router. This being the case, the router forwards copies of it onto all links except the one it arrived on. If, however, the broadcast packet arrived on a link other than the preferred one for reaching the source, the packet is discarded as a likely duplicate.

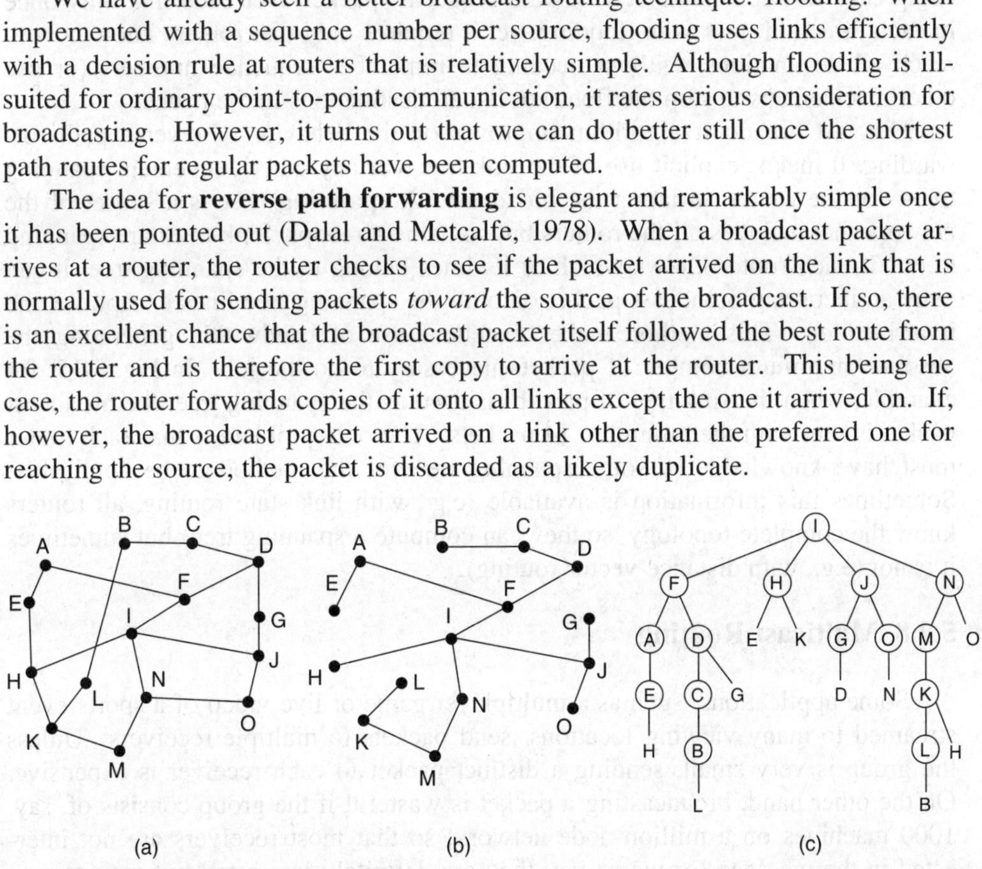

Figure 5-15. Reverse path forwarding. (a) A network. (b) A sink tree. (c) The tree built by reverse path forwarding.

An example of reverse path forwarding is shown in Fig. 5-15. Part (a) shows a network, part (b) shows a sink tree for router *I* of that network, and part (c) shows how the reverse path algorithm works. On the first hop, *I* sends packets to *F*, *H*, *J*, and *N*, as indicated by the second row of the tree. Each of these packets arrives on the preferred path to *I* (assuming that the preferred path falls along the sink tree) and is so indicated by a circle around the letter. On the second hop, eight packets are generated, two by each of the routers that received a packet on the first hop. As it turns out, all eight of these arrive at previously unvisited routers, and five of these arrive along the preferred line. Of the six packets generated on the third hop, only three arrive on the preferred path (at *C*, *E*, and *K*); the others are duplicates. After five hops and 24 packets, the broadcasting terminates, compared with four hops and 14 packets had the sink tree been followed exactly.

The principal advantage of reverse path forwarding is that it is efficient while being easy to implement. It sends the broadcast packet over each link only once in each direction, just as in flooding, yet it requires only that routers know how to reach all destinations, without needing to remember sequence numbers (or use other mechanisms to stop the flood) or list all destinations in the packet.

Our last broadcast algorithm improves on the behavior of reverse path forwarding. It makes explicit use of the sink tree—or any other convenient spanning tree—for the router initiating the broadcast. A **spanning tree** is a subset of the network that includes all the routers but contains no loops. Sink trees are spanning trees. If each router knows which of its lines belong to the spanning tree, it can copy an incoming broadcast packet onto all the spanning tree lines except the one it arrived on. This method makes excellent use of bandwidth, generating the absolute minimum number of packets necessary to do the job. In Fig. 5-15, for example, when the sink tree of part (b) is used as the spanning tree, the broadcast packet is sent with the minimum 14 packets. The only problem is that each router must have knowledge of some spanning tree for the method to be applicable. Sometimes this information is available (e.g., with link state routing, all routers know the complete topology, so they can compute a spanning tree) but sometimes it is not (e.g., with distance vector routing).

5.2.8 Multicast Routing

Some applications, such as a multiplayer game or live video of a sports event streamed to many viewing locations, send packets to multiple receivers. Unless the group is very small, sending a distinct packet to each receiver is expensive. On the other hand, broadcasting a packet is wasteful if the group consists of, say, 1000 machines on a million-node network, so that most receivers are not interested in the message (or worse yet, they are definitely interested but are not supposed to see it). Thus, we need a way to send messages to well-defined groups that are numerically large in size but small compared to the network as a whole.

Sending a message to such a group is called **multicasting**, and the routing algorithm used is called **multicast routing**. All multicasting schemes require some way to create and destroy groups and to identify which routers are members of a group. How these tasks are accomplished is not of concern to the routing algorithm. For now, we will assume that each group is identified by a multicast address and that routers know the groups to which they belong. We will revisit group membership when we describe the network layer of the Internet in Sec. 5.6.

Multicast routing schemes build on the broadcast routing schemes we have already studied, sending packets along spanning trees to deliver the packets to the members of the group while making efficient use of bandwidth. However, the best spanning tree to use depends on whether the group is dense, with receivers scattered over most of the network, or sparse, with much of the network not belonging to the group. In this section we will consider both cases.

If the group is dense, broadcast is a good start because it efficiently gets the packet to all parts of the network. But broadcast will reach some routers that are not members of the group, which is wasteful. The solution explored by Deering and Cheriton (1990) is to prune the broadcast spanning tree by removing links that do not lead to members. The result is an efficient multicast spanning tree.

As an example, consider the two groups, 1 and 2, in the network shown in Fig. 5-16(a). Some routers are attached to hosts that belong to one or both of these groups, as indicated in the figure. A spanning tree for the leftmost router is shown in Fig. 5-16(b). This tree can be used for broadcast but is overkill for multicast, as can be seen from the two pruned versions that are shown next. In Fig. 5-16(c), all the links that do not lead to hosts that are members of group 1 have been removed. The result is the multicast spanning tree for the leftmost router to send to group 1. Packets are forwarded only along this spanning tree, which is more efficient than the broadcast tree because there are 7 links instead of 10. Fig. 5-16(d) shows the multicast spanning tree after pruning for group 2. It is efficient too, with only five links this time. It also shows that different multicast groups have different spanning trees.

Various ways of pruning the spanning tree are possible. The simplest one can be used if link state routing is used and each router is aware of the complete topology, including which hosts belong to which groups. Each router can then construct its own pruned spanning tree for each sender to the group in question by constructing a sink tree for the sender as usual and then removing all links that do not connect group members to the sink node. **MOSPF** (**Multicast OSPF**) is an example of a link state protocol that works in this way (Moy, 1994).

With distance vector routing, a different pruning strategy can be followed. The basic algorithm is reverse path forwarding. However, whenever a router with no hosts interested in a particular group and no connections to other routers receives a multicast message for that group, it responds with a PRUNE message, telling the neighbor that sent the message not to send it any more multicasts from the sender for that group. When a router with no group members among its own hosts has received such messages on all the lines to which it sends the multicast, it, too, can respond with a PRUNE message. In this way, the spanning tree is recursively pruned. **DVMRP** (**Distance Vector Multicast Routing Protocol**) is an example of a multicast routing protocol that works this way (Waitzman et al., 1988).

Pruning results in efficient spanning trees that use only the links that are actually needed to reach members of the group. One potential disadvantage is that it is lots of work for routers, especially for large networks. Suppose that a network

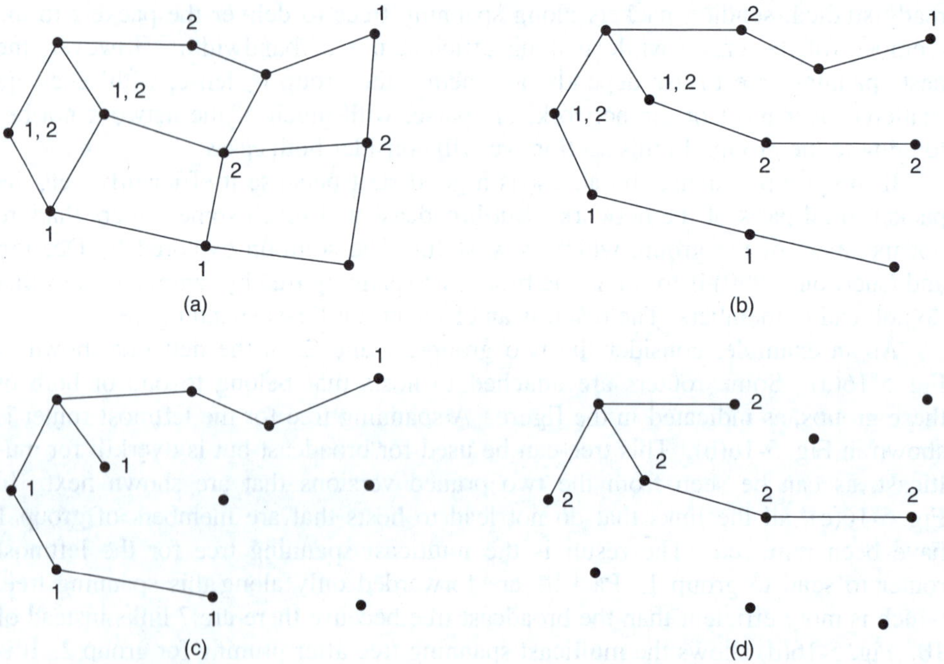

Figure 5-16. (a) A network. (b) A spanning tree for the leftmost router. (c) A multicast tree for group 1. (d) A multicast tree for group 2.

has *n* groups, each with an average of *m* nodes. At each router and for each group, *m* pruned spanning trees must be stored, for a total of *mn* trees. For example, Fig. 5-16(c) gives the spanning tree for the leftmost router to send to group 1. The spanning tree for the rightmost router to send to group 1 (not shown) will look quite different, as packets will head directly for group members rather than via the left side of the graph. This in turn means that routers must forward packets destined to group 1 in different directions depending on which node is sending to the group. When many large groups with many senders exist, considerable storage is needed to store all the trees.

An alternative design uses **core-based trees** to compute a single spanning tree for the group (Ballardie et al., 1993). All of the routers agree on a root (called the **core** or **rendezvous point**) and build the tree by sending a packet from each member to the root. The tree is the union of the paths traced by these packets. Fig. 5-17(a) shows a core-based tree for group 1. To send to this group, a sender sends a packet to the core. When the packet reaches the core, it is forwarded down the tree. This is shown in Fig. 5-17(b) for the sender on the righthand side of the network. As a performance optimization, packets destined for the group do not need to reach the core before they are multicast. As soon as a packet reaches the tree, it can be forwarded up toward the root, as well as down all the other branches. This is the case for the sender at the top of Fig. 5-17(b).

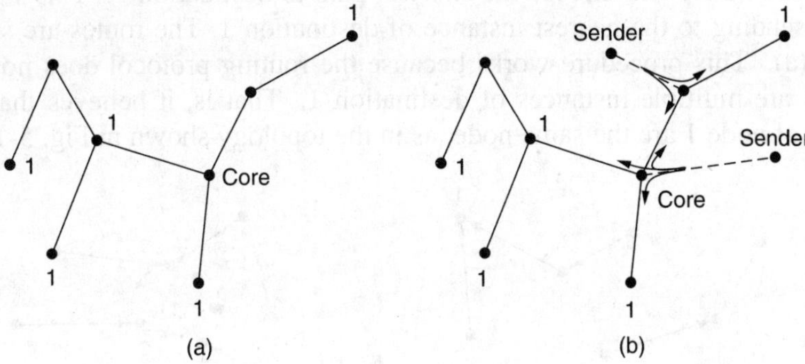

Figure 5-17. (a) Core-based tree for group 1. (b) Sending to group 1.

Having a shared tree is not optimal for all sources. For example, in Fig. 5-17(b), the packet from the sender on the righthand side reaches the top-right group member via the core in three hops, instead of directly. The inefficiency depends on where the core and senders are located, but often it is reasonable when the core is in the middle of the senders. When there is only a single sender, as in a video that is streamed to a group, using the sender as the core is optimal.

Also of note is that shared trees can be a major savings in storage costs, messages sent, and computation. Each router has to keep only one tree per group, instead of *m* trees. Further, routers that are not part of the tree do no work at all to support the group. For this reason, shared tree approaches like core-based trees are used for multicasting to sparse groups in the Internet as part of popular protocols such as **PIM** (**Protocol Independent Multicast**) (Fenner et al., 2006).

5.2.9 Anycast Routing

So far, we have covered delivery models in which a source sends to a single destination (called **unicast**), to all destinations (called broadcast), and to a group of destinations (called multicast). Another delivery model, called **anycast** is sometimes also useful. In anycast, a packet is delivered to the nearest member of a group (Partridge et al., 1993). Schemes that find these paths are called **anycast routing**.

Why would we want anycast? Sometimes nodes provide a service, such as time of day or content distribution for which it is getting the right information all that matters, not the node that is contacted; any node will do. For example, anycast is used in the Internet as part of DNS, as we will see in Chap. 7.

Luckily, we will not have to devise new routing schemes for anycast because regular distance vector and link state routing can produce anycast routes. Suppose we want to anycast to the members of group 1. They will all be given the address "1," instead of different addresses. Distance vector routing will distribute vectors as usual, and nodes will choose the shortest path to destination 1. This will result in nodes sending to the nearest instance of destination 1. The routes are shown in Fig. 5-18(a). This procedure works because the routing protocol does not realize that there are multiple instances of destination 1. That is, it believes that all the instances of node 1 are the same node, as in the topology shown in Fig. 5-18(b).

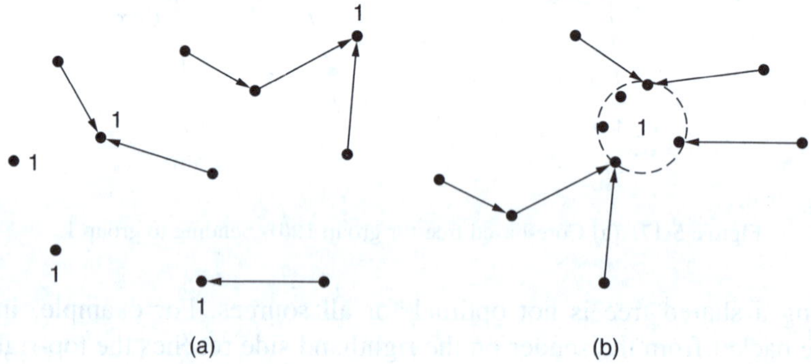

Figure 5-18. (a) Anycast routes to group 1. (b) Topology seen by the routing protocol.

This procedure works for link state routing as well, although there is the added consideration that the routing protocol must not find seemingly short paths that pass through node 1. This would result in jumps through hyperspace, since the instances of node 1 are really nodes located in different parts of the network. However, link state protocols already make this distinction between routers and hosts. We glossed over this fact earlier because it was not needed for our discussion.

5.2.10 Routing for Mobile Hosts

Millions of people use computers while on the go, from truly mobile situations with wireless devices in moving cars, to nomadic situations in which laptop computers are used in a series of different locations. We will use the term **mobile hosts** to mean either category, as distinct from stationary hosts that never move. Increasingly, people want to stay connected wherever in the world they may be, as easily as if they were at home. These mobile hosts introduce a new complication: to route a packet to a mobile host, the network first has to find it.

The model of the world that we will consider is one in which all hosts are assumed to have a permanent **home location** that never changes. Each hosts also has a permanent home address that can be used to determine its home location, analogous to the way the telephone number 1-212-5551212 indicates the United States (country code 1) and Manhattan (212). The routing goal in systems with mobile hosts is to make it possible to send packets to mobile hosts using their fixed home addresses and have the packets efficiently reach them wherever they may be. The trick, of course, is to find them.

Some discussion of this model is in order. A different model would be to recompute routes as the mobile host moves and the topology changes. We could then simply use the routing schemes described earlier in this section. However, with a growing number of mobile hosts, this model would soon lead to the entire network endlessly computing new routes. Using the home addresses greatly reduces this burden.

Another alternative would be to provide mobility above the network layer, which is what typically happens with laptops today. When they are moved to new Internet locations, laptops acquire new network addresses. There is no association between the old and new addresses; the network does not know that they belonged to the same laptop. In this model, a laptop can be used to browse the Web, but other hosts cannot send packets to it (for example, for an incoming call), without building a higher layer location service, for example, signing into Skype *again* after moving. Moreover, connections cannot be maintained while the host is moving; new connections must be started up instead. Network-layer mobility is useful to fix these problems.

The basic idea used for mobile routing in the Internet and cellular networks is for the mobile host to tell a host at the home location where it is now. This host, which acts on behalf of the mobile host, is called the **home agent**. Once it knows where the mobile host is currently located, it can forward packets so that they are delivered.

Fig. 5-19 shows mobile routing in action. A sender in the northwest city of Seattle wants to send a packet to a host normally located across the United States in New York. The case of interest to us is when the mobile host is not at home. Instead, it is temporarily in San Diego.

The mobile host in San Diego must acquire a local network address before it can use the network. This happens in the normal way that hosts obtain network addresses; we will cover how this works for the Internet later in this chapter. The local address is called a **care of address**. Once the mobile host has this address, it can tell its home agent where it is now. It does this by sending a registration message to the home agent (step 1) with the care of address. The message is shown with a dashed line in Fig. 5-19 to indicate that it is a control message, not a data message.

Next, the sender sends a data packet to the mobile host using its permanent address (step 2). This packet is routed by the network to the host's home location because that is where the home address belongs. In New York, the home agent intercepts this packet because the mobile host is away from home. It then wraps or **encapsulates** the packet with a new header and sends this bundle to the care of address (step 3). This mechanism is called **tunneling**. It is very important in the Internet so we will look at it in more detail later.

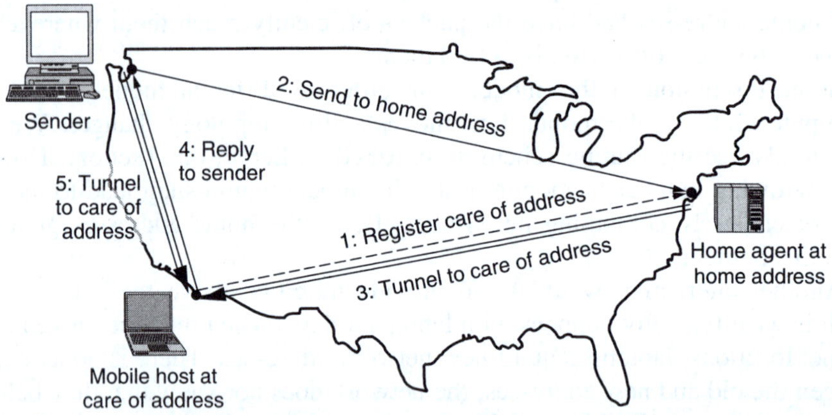

Figure 5-19. Packet routing for mobile hosts.

When the encapsulated packet arrives at the care of address, the mobile host unwraps it and retrieves the packet from the sender. The mobile host then sends its reply packet directly to the sender (step 4). The overall route is called **triangle routing** because it may be circuitous if the remote location is far from the home location. As part of step 4, the sender may learn the current care of address. Subsequent packets can be routed directly to the mobile host by tunneling them to the care of address (step 5), bypassing the home location entirely. If connectivity is lost for any reason as the mobile moves, the home address can always be used to reach the mobile.

An important aspect that we have omitted from this description is security. In general, when a host or router gets a message of the form "Starting right now, please send all of Stephany's mail to me," it might have a couple of questions about whom it is talking to and whether this is a good idea. Security information is included in the messages so that their validity can be checked with cryptographic protocols that we will study in Chap. 8.

There are many variations on mobile routing. The scheme above is modeled on IPv6 mobility, the form of mobility used in the Internet (Johnson et al., 2004) and as part of IP-based cellular networks such as UMTS. We showed the sender to be a stationary node for simplicity, but the designs let both nodes be mobile hosts. Alternatively, the host may be part of a mobile network, for example a computer in a plane. Extensions of the basic scheme support mobile networks with no work on the part of the hosts (Devarapalli et al., 2005).

Some schemes make use of a foreign (i.e., remote) agent, similar to the home agent but at the foreign location, or analogous to the VLR (Visitor Location Register) in cellular networks. However, in more recent schemes, the foreign agent is not needed; mobile hosts act as their own foreign agents. In either case, knowledge of the temporary location of the mobile host is limited to a small number of hosts (e.g., the mobile, home agent, and senders) so that the many routers in a large network do not need to recompute routes.

For more information about mobile routing, see also Perkins (1998, 2002) and Snoeren and Balakrishnan (2000).

5.2.11 Routing in Ad Hoc Networks

We have now seen how to do routing when the hosts are mobile but the routers are fixed. An even more extreme case is one in which the routers themselves are mobile. Among the possibilities are emergency workers at an earthquake site, military vehicles on a battlefield, a fleet of ships at sea, or a gathering of people with laptop computers in an area lacking 802.11.

In all these cases, and others, each node communicates wirelessly and acts as both a host and a router. Networks of nodes that just happen to be near each other are called **ad hoc networks** or **MANETs** (**Mobile Ad hoc NETworks**). Let us now examine them briefly. More information can be found in Perkins (2001).

What makes ad hoc networks different from wired networks is that the topology is suddenly tossed out the window. Nodes can come and go or appear in new places at the drop of a bit. With a wired network, if a router has a valid path to some destination, that path continues to be valid barring failures, which are hopefully rare. With an ad hoc network, the topology may be changing all the time, so the desirability and even the validity of paths can change spontaneously without warning. Needless to say, these circumstances make routing in ad hoc networks more challenging than routing in their fixed counterparts.

Many, many routing algorithms for ad hoc networks have been proposed. However, since ad hoc networks have been little used in practice compared to mobile networks, it is unclear which of these protocols are most useful. As an example, we will look at one of the most popular routing algorithms, **AODV** (**Ad hoc On-demand Distance Vector**) (Perkins and Royer, 1999). It is a relative of the distance vector algorithm that has been adapted to work in a mobile environment, in which nodes often have limited bandwidth and battery lifetimes. Let us now see how it discovers and maintains routes.

Route Discovery

In AODV, routes to a destination are discovered on demand, that is, only when a somebody wants to send a packet to that destination. This saves much work that would otherwise be wasted when the topology changes before the route is used. At any instant, the topology of an ad hoc network can be described by a graph of connected nodes. Two nodes are connected (i.e., have an arc between them in the graph) if they can communicate directly using their radios. A basic but adequate model that is sufficient for our purposes is that each node can communicate with all other nodes that lie within its coverage circle. Real networks are more complicated, with buildings, hills, and other obstacles that block communication, and nodes for which *A* is connected to *B* but *B* is not connected to *A* because *A* has a more powerful transmitter than *B*. However, for simplicity, we will assume all connections are symmetric.

To describe the algorithm, consider the newly formed ad hoc network of Fig. 5-20. Suppose that a process at node *A* wants to send a packet to node *I*. The AODV algorithm maintains a distance vector table at each node, keyed by destination, giving information about that destination, including the neighbor to which to send packets to reach the destination. First, *A* looks in its table and does not find an entry for *I*. It now has to discover a route to *I*. This property of discovering routes only when they are needed is what makes this algorithm "on demand."

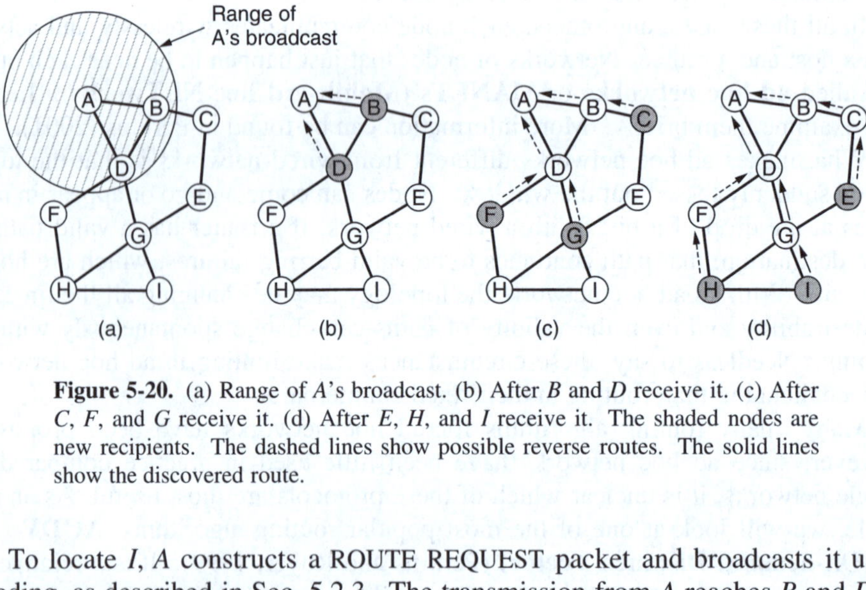

Figure 5-20. (a) Range of *A*'s broadcast. (b) After *B* and *D* receive it. (c) After *C*, *F*, and *G* receive it. (d) After *E*, *H*, and *I* receive it. The shaded nodes are new recipients. The dashed lines show possible reverse routes. The solid lines show the discovered route.

To locate *I*, *A* constructs a ROUTE REQUEST packet and broadcasts it using flooding, as described in Sec. 5.2.3. The transmission from *A* reaches *B* and *D*, as illustrated in Fig. 5-20(a). Each node rebroadcasts the request, which continues to reach nodes *F*, *G*, and *C* in Fig. 5-20(c) and nodes *H*, *E*, and *I* in Fig. 5-20(d). A sequence number set at the source is used to weed out duplicates during the flood. For example, *D* discards the transmission from *B* in Fig. 5-20(c) because it has already forwarded the request.

Eventually, the request reaches node *I*, which constructs a ROUTE REPLY packet. This packet is unicast to the sender along the reverse of the path followed by the request. For this to work, each intermediate node must remember the node that sent it the request. The arrows in Fig. 5-20(b)–(d) show the reverse route information that is stored. Each intermediate node also increments a hop count as it forwards the reply. This tells the nodes how far they are from the destination. The replies tell each intermediate node which neighbor to use to reach the destination: it is the node that sent them the reply. Intermediate nodes *G* and *D* put the best route they hear into their routing tables as they process the reply. When the reply reaches *A*, a new route, *ADGI*, has been created.

In a large network, the algorithm generates many broadcasts, even for destinations that are close by. To reduce overhead, the scope of the broadcasts is limited using the IP packet's *Time to live* field. This field is initialized by the sender and decremented on each hop. If it hits 0, the packet is discarded instead of being broadcast. The route discovery process is then modified as follows. To locate a destination, the sender broadcasts a ROUTE REQUEST packet with *Time to live* set to 1. If no response comes back within a reasonable time, another one is sent, this time with *Time to live* set to 2. Subsequent attempts use 3, 4, 5, etc. In this way, the search is first attempted locally, then in increasingly wider rings.

Route Maintenance

Because nodes can move or be switched off, the topology can change spontaneously. For example, in Fig. 5-20, if *G* is switched off, *A* will not realize that the route it was using to *I* (*ADGI*) is no longer valid. The algorithm needs to be able to deal with this. Periodically, each node broadcasts a *Hello* message. Each of its neighbors is expected to respond to it. If no response is forthcoming, the broadcaster knows that that neighbor has moved out of range or failed and is no longer connected to it. Similarly, if it tries to send a packet to a neighbor that does not respond, it learns that the neighbor is no longer available.

This information is used to purge routes that no longer work. For each possible destination, each node, *N*, keeps track of its active neighbors that have fed it a packet for that destination during the last ΔT seconds. When any of *N*'s neighbors becomes unreachable, it checks its routing table to see which destinations have routes using the now-gone neighbor. For each of these routes, the active neighbors are informed that their route via *N* is now invalid and must be purged from their routing tables. In our example, *D* purges its entries for *G* and *I* from its routing table and notifies *A*, which purges its entry for *I*. In the general case, the active neighbors tell their active neighbors, and so on, recursively, until all routes depending on the now-gone node are purged from all routing tables.

At this stage, the invalid routes have been purged from the network, and senders can find new, valid routes by using the discovery mechanism that we described. However, there is a complication. Recall that distance vector protocols can suffer from slow convergence or count-to-infinity problems after a topology change in which they confuse old, invalid routes with new, valid routes.

To ensure rapid convergence, routes include a sequence number that is controlled by the destination. The destination sequence number is like a logical clock. The destination increments it every time that it sends a fresh ROUTE REPLY. Senders ask for a fresh route by including in the ROUTE REQUEST the destination sequence number of the last route they used, which will either be the sequence number of the route that was just purged, or 0 as an initial value. The request will be broadcast until a route with a higher sequence number is found. Intermediate nodes store the routes that have a higher sequence number, or the fewest hops for the current sequence number.

In the spirit of an on demand protocol, intermediate nodes only store the routes that are in use. Other route information learned during broadcasts is timed out after a short delay. Discovering and storing only the routes that are used helps to save bandwidth and battery life compared to a standard distance vector protocol that periodically broadcasts updates.

So far, we have considered only a single route, from *A* to *I*. To further save resources, route discovery and maintenance are shared when routes overlap. For instance, if *B* also wants to send packets to *I*, it will perform route discovery. However, in this case the request will first reach *D*, which already has a route to *I*. Node *D* can then generate a reply to tell *B* the route without any additional work being required.

There are many other ad hoc routing schemes. Another well-known on demand scheme is DSR (Dynamic Source Routing) (Johnson et al., 2001). A different strategy based on geography is explored by GPSR (Greedy Perimeter Stateless Routing) (Karp and Kung, 2000). If all nodes know their geographic positions, forwarding to a destination can proceed without route computation by simply heading in the right direction and circling back to escape any dead ends. Which protocols win out will depend on the kinds of ad hoc networks that prove useful in practice.

5.3 CONGESTION CONTROL ALGORITHMS

Too many packets present in (a part of) the network causes packet delay and loss that degrades performance. This situation is called **congestion**. The network and transport layers share the responsibility for handling congestion. Since congestion occurs within the network, it is the network layer that directly experiences it and must ultimately determine what to do with the excess packets. However, the most effective way to control congestion is to reduce the load that the transport layer is placing on the network. This requires the network and transport layers to work together. In this chapter we will look at the network aspects of congestion. In Chap. 6, we will complete the topic by covering the transport aspects of congestion.

Figure 5-21 depicts the onset of congestion. When the number of packets hosts send into the network is well within its carrying capacity, the number delivered is proportional to the number sent. If twice as many are sent, twice as many are delivered. However, as the offered load approaches the carrying capacity, bursts of traffic occasionally fill up the buffers inside routers and some packets are lost. These lost packets consume some of the capacity, so the number of delivered packets falls below the ideal curve. The network is now congested.

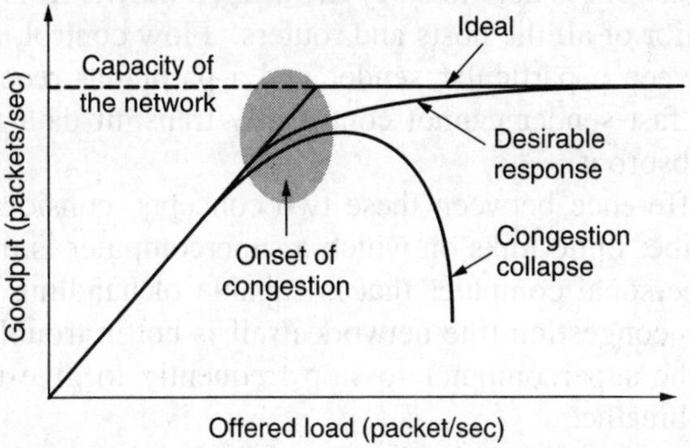

Figure 5-21. With too much traffic, performance drops sharply.

Unless the network is well designed, it may experience a **congestion collapse**, in which performance plummets as the offered load increases beyond the capacity. This can happen because packets can be sufficiently delayed inside the network that they are no longer useful when they leave the network. For example, in the early Internet, the time a packet spent waiting for a backlog of packets ahead of it to be sent over a slow 56-kbps link could reach the maximum time it was allowed to remain in the network. It then had to be thrown away. A different failure mode occurs when senders retransmit packets that are greatly delayed, thinking that they have been lost. In this case, copies of the same packet will be delivered by the network, again wasting its capacity. To capture these factors, the y-axis of Fig. 5-21 is given as **goodput**, which is the rate at which *useful* packets are delivered by the network.

We would like to design networks that avoid congestion where possible and do not suffer from congestion collapse if they do become congested. Unfortunately, congestion cannot wholly be avoided. If all of a sudden, streams of packets begin arriving on three or four input lines and all need the same output line, a queue will build up. If there is insufficient memory to hold all of them, packets will be lost. Adding more memory may help up to a point, but Nagle (1987) realized that if routers have an infinite amount of memory, congestion gets worse, not better. This is because by the time packets get to the front of the queue, they have already timed out (repeatedly) and duplicates have been sent. This makes matters worse, not better—it leads to congestion collapse.

Low-bandwidth links or routers that process packets more slowly than the line rate can also become congested. In this case, the situation can be improved by directing some of the traffic away from the bottleneck to other parts of the network. Eventually, however, all regions of the network will be congested. In this situation, there is no alternative but to shed load or build a faster network.

It is worth pointing out the difference between congestion control and flow control, as the relationship is a very subtle one. Congestion control has to do with making sure the network is able to carry the offered traffic. It is a global issue, involving the behavior of all the hosts and routers. Flow control, in contrast, relates to the traffic between a particular sender and a particular receiver. Its job is to make sure that a fast sender cannot continually transmit data faster than the receiver is able to absorb it.

To see the difference between these two concepts, consider a network made up of 100-Gbps fiber optic links on which a supercomputer is trying to force feed a large file to a personal computer that is capable of handling only 1 Gbps. Although there is no congestion (the network itself is not in trouble), flow control is needed to force the supercomputer to stop frequently to give the personal computer a chance to breathe.

At the other extreme, consider a network with 1-Mbps lines and 1000 large computers, half of which are trying to transfer files at 100 kbps to the other half. Here, the problem is not that of fast senders overpowering slow receivers, but that the total offered traffic exceeds what the network can handle.

The reason congestion control and flow control are often confused is that the best way to handle both problems is to get the host to slow down. Thus, a host can get a "slow down" message either because the receiver cannot handle the load or because the network cannot handle it. We will come back to this point in Chap. 6.

We will start our study of congestion control by looking at the approaches that can be used at different time scales. Then we will look at approaches to preventing congestion from occurring in the first place, followed by approaches for coping with it once it has set in.

5.3.1 Approaches to Congestion Control

The presence of congestion means that the load is (temporarily) greater than the resources (in a part of the network) can handle. Two solutions come to mind: increase the resources or decrease the load. As shown in Fig. 5-22, these solutions are usually applied on different time scales to either prevent congestion or react to it once it has occurred.

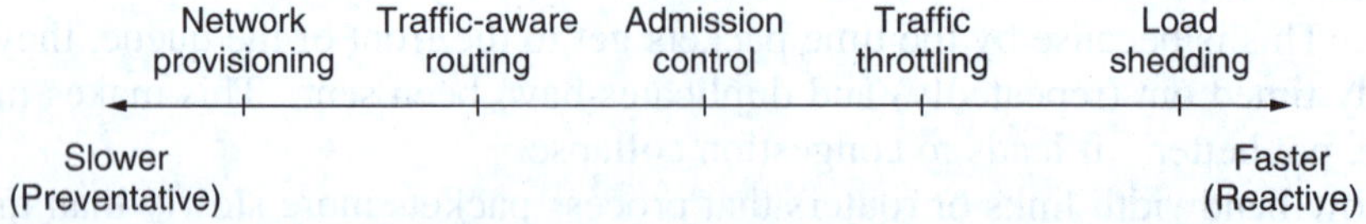

Figure 5-22. Timescales of approaches to congestion control.

The most basic way to avoid congestion is to build a network that is well matched to the traffic that it carries. If there is a low-bandwidth link on the path along which most traffic is directed, congestion is likely. Sometimes resources can be added dynamically when there is serious congestion, for example, turning on spare routers or enabling lines that are normally used only as backups (to make the system fault tolerant) or purchasing bandwidth on the open market. More often, links and routers that are regularly heavily utilized are upgraded at the earliest opportunity. This is called **provisioning** and happens on a time scale of months, driven by long-term traffic trends.

To make the most of the existing network capacity, routes can be tailored to traffic patterns that change during the day as network users wake and sleep in different time zones. For example, routes may be changed to shift traffic away from heavily used paths by changing the shortest path weights. Some local radio stations have helicopters flying around their cities to report on road congestion to make it possible for their mobile listeners to route their packets (cars) around hotspots. This is called **traffic-aware routing**. Splitting traffic across multiple paths is also helpful.

However, sometimes it is not possible to increase capacity. The only way then to beat back the congestion is to decrease the load. In a virtual-circuit network, new connections can be refused if they would cause the network to become congested. This is called **admission control**.

At a finer granularity, when congestion is imminent the network can deliver feedback to the sources whose traffic flows are responsible for the problem. The network can request these sources to throttle their traffic, or it can slow down the traffic itself.

Two difficulties with this approach are how to identify the onset of congestion, and how to inform the source that needs to slow down. To tackle the first issue, routers can monitor the average load, queueing delay, or packet loss. In all cases, rising numbers indicate growing congestion.

To tackle the second issue, routers must participate in a feedback loop with the sources. For a scheme to work correctly, the time scale must be adjusted carefully. If every time two packets arrive in a row, a router yells STOP and every time a router is idle for 20 μsec, it yells GO, the system will oscillate wildly and never converge. On the other hand, if it waits 30 minutes to make sure before saying anything, the congestion-control mechanism will react too sluggishly to be of any use. Delivering timely feedback is a nontrivial matter. An added concern is having routers send more messages when the network is already congested.

Finally, when all else fails, the network is forced to discard packets that it cannot deliver. The general name for this is **load shedding**. A good policy for choosing which packets to discard can help to prevent congestion collapse.

5.3.2 Traffic-Aware Routing

The first approach we will examine is traffic-aware routing. The routing schemes we looked at in Sec 5.2 used fixed link weights. These schemes adapted to changes in topology, but not to changes in load. The goal in taking load into account when computing routes is to shift traffic away from hotspots that will be the first places in the network to experience congestion.

The most direct way to do this is to set the link weight to be a function of the (fixed) link bandwidth and propagation delay plus the (variable) measured load or average queuing delay. Least-weight paths will then favor paths that are more lightly loaded, all else being equal.

Traffic-aware routing was used in the early Internet according to this model (Khanna and Zinky, 1989). However, there is a peril. Consider the network of Fig. 5-23, which is divided into two parts, East and West, connected by two links, *CF* and *EI*. Suppose that most of the traffic between East and West is using link *CF*, and, as a result, this link is heavily loaded with long delays. Including queueing delay in the weight used for the shortest path calculation will make *EI* more attractive. After the new routing tables have been installed, most of the East-West traffic will now go over *EI*, loading this link. Consequently, in the next update, *CF* will appear to be the shortest path. As a result, the routing tables may oscillate wildly, leading to erratic routing and many potential problems.

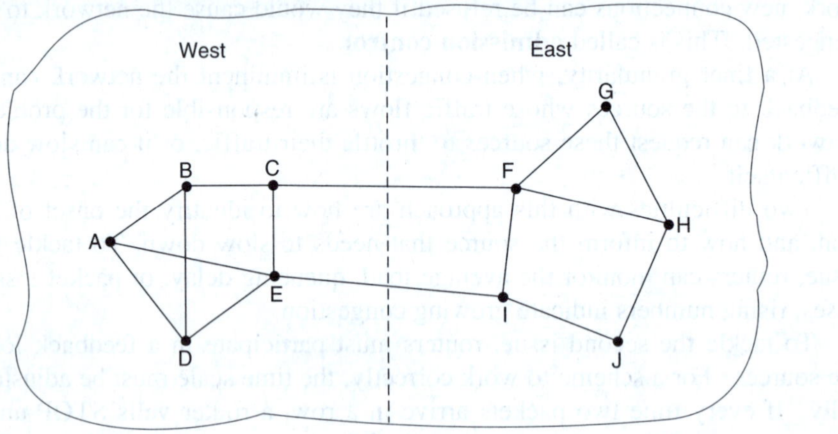

Figure 5-23. A network in which the East and West parts are connected by two links.

If load is ignored and only bandwidth and propagation delay are considered, this problem does not occur. Attempts to include load but change weights within a narrow range only slow down routing oscillations. Two techniques can contribute to a successful solution. The first is multipath routing, in which there can be multiple paths from a source to a destination. In our example this means that the traffic can be spread across both of the East to West links. The second one is for the routing scheme to shift traffic across routes slowly enough that it is able to converge, as in the scheme of Gallagher (1977).

Given these difficulties, in the Internet routing protocols do not generally adjust their routes depending on the load. Instead, adjustments are made outside the routing protocol by slowly changing its inputs. This is called **traffic engineering**.

5.3.3 Admission Control

One technique that is widely used in virtual-circuit networks to keep congestion at bay is **admission control**. The idea is simple: do not set up a new virtual circuit unless the network can carry the added traffic without becoming congested. Thus, attempts to set up a virtual circuit may fail. This is better than the alternative, as letting more people in when the network is busy just makes matters worse. By analogy, in the telephone system, when a switch gets overloaded it practices admission control by not giving dial tones.

The trick with this approach is working out when a new virtual circuit will lead to congestion. The task is straightforward in the telephone network because of the fixed bandwidth of calls (64 kbps for uncompressed audio). However, virtual circuits in computer networks come in all shapes and sizes. Thus, the circuit must come with some characterization of its traffic if we are to apply admission control.

Traffic is often described in terms of its rate and shape. The problem of how to describe it in a simple yet meaningful way is difficult because traffic is typically bursty—the average rate is only half the story. For example, traffic that varies while browsing the Web is more difficult to handle than a streaming movie with the same long-term throughput because the bursts of Web traffic are more likely to congest routers in the network. A commonly used descriptor that captures this effect is the **leaky bucket** or **token bucket**. A leaky bucket has two parameters that bound the average rate and the instantaneous burst size of traffic. Since leaky buckets are widely used for quality of service, we will go over them in detail in Sec. 5.4.

Armed with traffic descriptions, the network can decide whether to admit the new virtual circuit. One possibility is for the network to reserve enough capacity along the paths of each of its virtual circuits that congestion will not occur. In this case, the traffic description is a service agreement for what the network will guarantee its users. We have prevented congestion but veered into the related topic of quality of service a little too early; we will return to it in the next section.

Even without making guarantees, the network can use traffic descriptions for admission control. The task is then to estimate how many circuits will fit within the carrying capacity of the network without congestion. Suppose that virtual circuits that may blast traffic at rates up to 10 Mbps all pass through the same 100-Mbps physical link. How many circuits should be admitted? Clearly, 10 circuits can be admitted without risking congestion, but this is wasteful in the normal case since it may rarely happen that all 10 are transmitting full blast at the same time. In real networks, measurements of past behavior that capture the statistics of transmissions can be used to estimate the number of circuits to admit, to trade better performance for acceptable risk.

Admission control can also be combined with traffic-aware routing by considering routes around traffic hotspots as part of the setup procedure. For example, consider the network illustrated in Fig. 5-24(a), in which two routers are congested, as indicated.

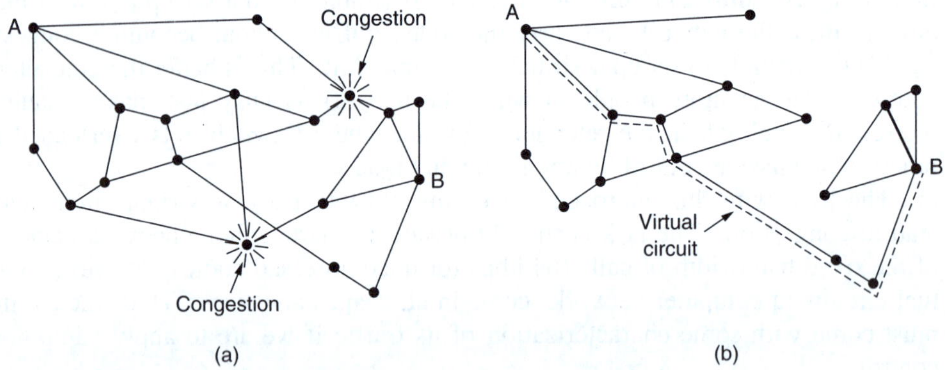

Figure 5-24. (a) A congested network. (b) The portion of the network that is not congested. A virtual circuit from *A* to *B* is also shown.

Suppose that a host attached to router *A* wants to set up a connection to a host attached to router *B*. Normally, this connection would pass through one of the congested routers. To avoid this situation, we can redraw the network as shown in Fig. 5-24(b), omitting the congested routers and all of their lines. The dashed line shows a possible route for the virtual circuit that avoids the congested routers. Shaikh et al. (1999) give a design for this kind of load-sensitive routing.

5.3.4 Traffic Throttling

In the Internet and many other computer networks, senders adjust their transmissions to send as much traffic as the network can readily deliver. In this setting, the network aims to operate just before the onset of congestion. When congestion is imminent, it must tell the senders to throttle back their transmissions and slow down. This feedback is business as usual rather than an exceptional situation. The term **congestion avoidance** is sometimes used to contrast this operating point with the one in which the network has become (overly) congested.

Let us now look at some approaches to throttling traffic that can be used in both datagram networks and virtual-circuit networks. Each approach must solve two problems. First, routers must determine when congestion is approaching, ideally before it has arrived. To do so, each router can continuously monitor the resources it is using. Three possibilities are the utilization of the output links, the buffering of queued packets inside the router, and the number of packets that are lost due to insufficient buffering. Of these possibilities, the second one is the most useful. Averages of utilization do not directly account for the burstiness of most traffic—a utilization of 50% may be low for smooth traffic and too high for highly variable traffic. Counts of packet losses come too late. Congestion has already set in by the time that packets are lost.

The queueing delay inside routers directly captures any congestion experienced by packets. It should be low most of time, but will jump when there is a burst of traffic that generates a backlog. To maintain a good estimate of the queueing delay, d, a sample of the instantaneous queue length, s, can be made periodically and d updated according to

$$d_{new} = \alpha d_{old} + (1 - \alpha)s$$

where the constant α determines how fast the router forgets recent history. This is called an **EWMA** (**Exponentially Weighted Moving Average**). It smoothes out fluctuations and is equivalent to a low-pass filter. Whenever d moves above the threshold, the router notes the onset of congestion.

The second problem is that routers must deliver timely feedback to the senders that are causing the congestion. Congestion is experienced in the network, but relieving congestion requires action on behalf of the senders that are using the network. To deliver feedback, the router must identify the appropriate senders. It must then warn them carefully, without sending many more packets into the already congested network. Different schemes use different feedback mechanisms, as we will now describe.

Choke Packets

The most direct way to notify a sender of congestion is to tell it directly. In this approach, the router selects a congested packet and sends a **choke packet** back to the source host, giving it the destination found in the packet. The original packet may be tagged (a header bit is turned on) so that it will not generate any more choke packets farther along the path and then forwarded in the usual way. To avoid increasing load on the network during a time of congestion, the router may only send choke packets at a low rate.

When the source host gets the choke packet, it is required to reduce the traffic sent to the specified destination, for example, by 50%. In a datagram network, simply picking packets at random when there is congestion is likely to cause choke packets to be sent to fast senders, because they will have the most packets in the queue. The feedback implicit in this protocol can help prevent congestion yet not throttle any sender unless it causes trouble. For the same reason, it is likely that multiple choke packets will be sent to a given host and destination. The host should ignore these additional chokes for the fixed time interval until its reduction in traffic takes effect. After that period, further choke packets indicate that the network is still congested.

An example of a choke packet used in the early Internet is the SOURCE-QUENCH message (Postel, 1981). It never caught on, though, partly because the circumstances in which it was generated and the effect it had were not clearly specified. The modern Internet uses an alternative notification design that we will describe next.

Explicit Congestion Notification

Instead of generating additional packets to warn of congestion, a router can tag any packet it forwards (by setting a bit in the packet's header) to signal that it is experiencing congestion. When the network delivers the packet, the destination can note that there is congestion and inform the sender when it sends a reply packet. The sender can then throttle its transmissions as before.

This design is called **ECN** (**Explicit Congestion Notification**) and is used in the Internet (Ramakrishnan et al., 2001). It is a refinement of early congestion signaling protocols, notably the binary feedback scheme of Ramakrishnan and Jain (1988) that was used in the DECNET architecture. Two bits in the IP packet header are used to record whether the packet has experienced congestion. Packets are unmarked when they are sent, as illustrated in Fig. 5-25. If any of the routers they pass through is congested, that router will then mark the packet as having experienced congestion as it is forwarded. The destination will then echo any marks back to the sender as an explicit congestion signal in its next reply packet. This is shown with a dashed line in the figure to indicate that it happens above the IP level (e.g., in TCP). The sender must then throttle its transmissions, as in the case of choke packets.

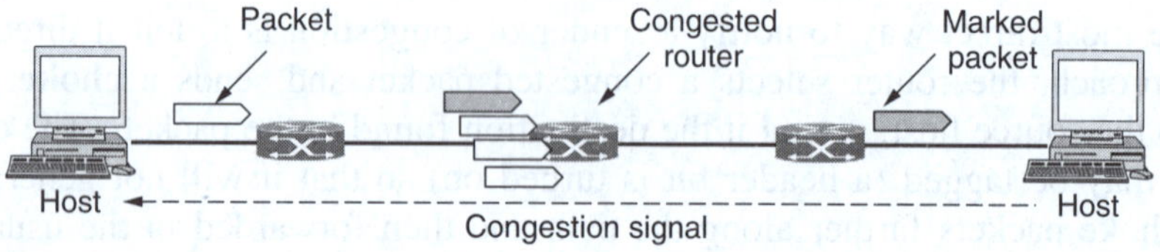

Figure 5-25. Explicit congestion notification

Hop-by-Hop Backpressure

At high speeds or over long distances, many new packets may be transmitted after congestion has been signaled because of the delay before the signal takes effect. Consider, for example, a host in San Francisco (router *A* in Fig. 5-26) that is sending traffic to a host in New York (router *D* in Fig. 5-26) at the OC-3 speed of 155 Mbps. If the New York host begins to run out of buffers, it will take about 40 msec for a choke packet to get back to San Francisco to tell it to slow down. An ECN indication will take even longer because it is delivered via the destination. Choke packet propagation is illustrated as the second, third, and fourth steps in

Fig. 5-26(a). In those 40 msec, another 6.2 megabits will have been sent. Even if the host in San Francisco completely shuts down immediately, the 6.2 megabits in the pipe will continue to pour in and have to be dealt with. Only in the seventh diagram in Fig. 5-26(a) will the New York router notice a slower flow.

An alternative approach is to have the choke packet take effect at every hop it passes through, as shown in the sequence of Fig. 5-26(b). Here, as soon as the choke packet reaches *F*, *F* is required to reduce the flow to *D*. Doing so will require *F* to devote more buffers to the connection, since the source is still sending away at full blast, but it gives *D* immediate relief, like a headache remedy in a television commercial. In the next step, the choke packet reaches *E*, which tells *E* to reduce the flow to *F*. This action puts a greater demand on *E*'s buffers but gives *F* immediate relief. Finally, the choke packet reaches *A* and the flow genuinely slows down.

The net effect of this hop-by-hop scheme is to provide quick relief at the point of congestion, at the price of using up more buffers upstream. In this way, congestion can be nipped in the bud without losing any packets. The idea is discussed in detail by Mishra et al. (1996).

5.3.5 Load Shedding

When none of the above methods make the congestion disappear, routers can bring out the heavy artillery: load shedding. **Load shedding** is a fancy way of saying that when routers are being inundated by packets that they cannot handle, they just throw them away. The term comes from the world of electrical power generation, where it refers to the practice of utilities intentionally blacking out certain areas to save the entire grid from collapsing on hot summer days when the demand for electricity greatly exceeds the supply.

The key question for a router drowning in packets is which packets to drop. The preferred choice may depend on the type of applications that use the network. For a file transfer, an old packet is worth more than a new one. This is because dropping packet 6 and keeping packets 7 through 10, for example, will only force the receiver to do more work to buffer data that it cannot yet use. In contrast, for real-time media, a new packet is worth more than an old one. This is because packets become useless if they are delayed and miss the time at which they must be played out to the user.

The former policy (old is better than new) is often called **wine** and the latter (new is better than old) is often called **milk** because most people would rather drink new milk and old wine than the alternative.

More intelligent load shedding requires cooperation from the senders. An example is packets that carry routing information. These packets are more important than regular data packets because they establish routes; if they are lost, the network may lose connectivity. Another example is that algorithms for compressing video, like MPEG, periodically transmit an entire frame and then send subsequent

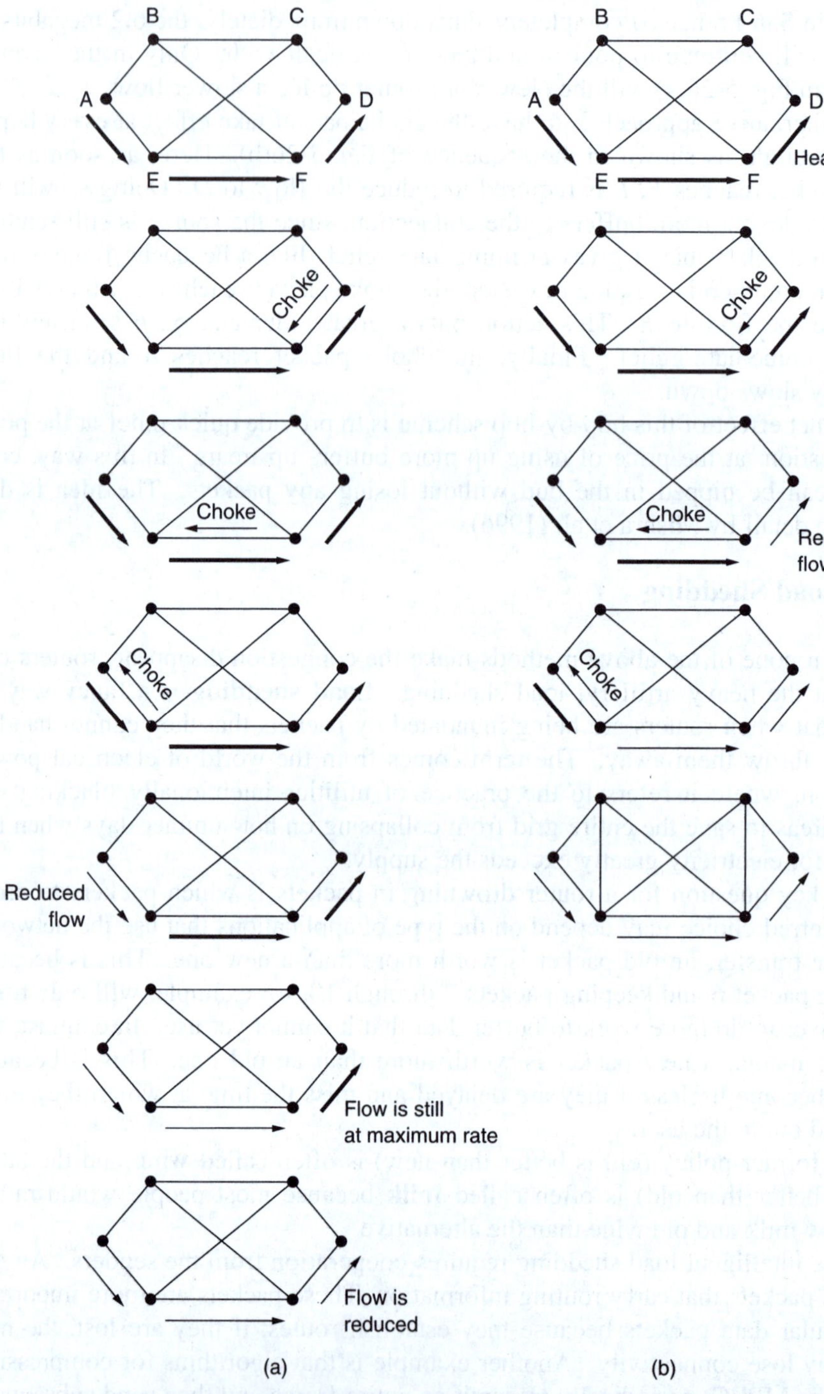

Figure 5-26. (a) A choke packet that affects only the source. (b) A choke packet that affects each hop it passes through.

frames as differences from the last full frame. In this case, dropping a packet that is part of a difference is preferable to dropping one that is part of a full frame because future packets depend on the full frame.

To implement an intelligent discard policy, applications must mark their packets to indicate to the network how important they are. Then, when packets have to be discarded, routers can first drop packets from the least important class, then the next most important class, and so on.

Of course, unless there is some significant incentive to avoid marking every packet as VERY IMPORTANT—NEVER, EVER DISCARD, nobody will do it. Often accounting and money are used to discourage frivolous marking. For example, the network might let senders send faster than the service they purchased allows if they mark excess packets as low priority. Such a strategy is actually not a bad idea because it makes more efficient use of idle resources, allowing hosts to use them as long as nobody else is interested, but without establishing a right to them when times get tough.

Random Early Detection

Dealing with congestion when it first starts is more effective than letting it gum up the works and then trying to deal with it. This observation leads to an interesting twist on load shedding, which is to discard packets before all the buffer space is really exhausted.

The motivation for this idea is that most Internet hosts do not yet get congestion signals from routers in the form of ECN. Instead, the only reliable indication of congestion that hosts get from the network is packet loss. After all, it is difficult to build a router that does not drop packets when it is overloaded. Transport protocols such as TCP are thus hardwired to react to loss as congestion, slowing down the source in response. The reasoning behind this logic is that TCP was designed for wired networks and wired networks are very reliable, so lost packets are mostly due to buffer overruns rather than transmission errors. Wireless links must recover transmission errors at the link layer (so they are not seen at the network layer) to work well with TCP.

This situation can be exploited to help reduce congestion. By having routers drop packets early, before the situation has become hopeless, there is time for the source to take action before it is too late. A popular algorithm for doing this is called **RED (Random Early Detection)** (Floyd and Jacobson, 1993). To determine when to start discarding, routers maintain a running average of their queue lengths. When the average queue length on some link exceeds a threshold, the link is said to be congested and a small fraction of the packets are dropped at random. Picking packets at random makes it more likely that the fastest senders will see a packet drop; this is the best option since the router cannot tell which source is causing the most trouble in a datagram network. The affected sender will notice the loss when there is no acknowledgement, and then the transport protocol will slow down. The lost packet is thus delivering the same message as a choke packet, but implicitly, without the router sending any explicit signal.

RED routers improve performance compared to routers that drop packets only when their buffers are full, though they may require tuning to work well. For example, the ideal number of packets to drop depends on how many senders need to be notified of congestion. However, ECN is the preferred option if it is available. It works in exactly the same manner, but delivers a congestion signal explicitly rather than as a loss; RED is used when hosts cannot receive explicit signals.

5.4 QUALITY OF SERVICE

The techniques we looked at in the previous sections are designed to reduce congestion and improve network performance. However, there are applications (and customers) that demand stronger performance guarantees from the network than "the best that could be done under the circumstances.'' Multimedia applications in particular, often need a minimum throughput and maximum latency to work. In this section, we will continue our study of network performance, but now with a sharper focus on ways to provide quality of service that is matched to application needs. This is an area in which the Internet is undergoing a long-term upgrade.

An easy solution to provide good quality of service is to build a network with enough capacity for whatever traffic will be thrown at it. The name for this solution is **overprovisioning**. The resulting network will carry application traffic without significant loss and, assuming a decent routing scheme, will deliver packets with low latency. Performance doesn't get any better than this. To some extent, the telephone system is overprovisioned because it is rare to pick up a telephone and not get a dial tone instantly. There is simply so much capacity available that demand can almost always be met.

The trouble with this solution is that it is expensive. It is basically solving a problem by throwing money at it. Quality of service mechanisms let a network with less capacity meet application requirements just as well at a lower cost. Moreover, overprovisioning is based on expected traffic. All bets are off if the traffic pattern changes too much. With quality of service mechanisms, the network can honor the performance guarantees that it makes even when traffic spikes, at the cost of turning down some requests.

Four issues must be addressed to ensure quality of service:

1. What applications need from the network.
2. How to regulate the traffic that enters the network.
3. How to reserve resources at routers to guarantee performance.
4. Whether the network can safely accept more traffic.

No single technique deals efficiently with all these issues. Instead, a variety of techniques have been developed for use at the network (and transport) layer. Practical quality-of-service solutions combine multiple techniques. To this end, we will describe two versions of quality of service for the Internet called Integrated Services and Differentiated Services.

5.4.1 Application Requirements

A stream of packets from a source to a destination is called a **flow** (Clark, 1988). A flow might be all the packets of a connection in a connection-oriented network, or all the packets sent from one process to another process in a connectionless network. The needs of each flow can be characterized by four primary parameters: bandwidth, delay, jitter, and loss. Together, these determine the **QoS (Quality of Service)** the flow requires.

Several common applications and the stringency of their network requirements are listed in Fig. 5-27. Note that network requirements are less demanding than application requirements in those cases that the application can improve on the service provided by the network. In particular, networks do not need to be lossless for reliable file transfer, and they do not need to deliver packets with identical delays for audio and video playout. Some amount of loss can be repaired with retransmissions, and some amount of jitter can be smoothed by buffering packets at the receiver. However, there is nothing applications can do to remedy the situation if the network provides too little bandwidth or too much delay.

Application	Bandwidth	Delay	Jitter	Loss
Email	Low	Low	Low	Medium
File sharing	High	Low	Low	Medium
Web access	Medium	Medium	Low	Medium
Remote login	Low	Medium	Medium	Medium
Audio on demand	Low	Low	High	Low
Video on demand	High	Low	High	Low
Telephony	Low	High	High	Low
Videoconferencing	High	High	High	Low

Figure 5-27. Stringency of applications' quality-of-service requirements.

The applications differ in their bandwidth needs, with email, audio in all forms, and remote login not needing much, but file sharing and video in all forms needing a great deal.

More interesting are the delay requirements. File transfer applications, including email and video, are not delay sensitive. If all packets are delayed uniformly by a few seconds, no harm is done. Interactive applications, such as Web surfing and remote login, are more delay sensitive. Real-time applications, such as telephony and videoconferencing, have strict delay requirements. If all the words in a telephone call are each delayed by too long, the users will find the connection unacceptable. On the other hand, playing audio or video files from a server does not require low delay.

The variation (i.e., standard deviation) in the delay or packet arrival times is called **jitter**. The first three applications in Fig. 5-27 are not sensitive to the packets arriving with irregular time intervals between them. Remote login is somewhat sensitive to that, since updates on the screen will appear in little bursts if the connection suffers much jitter. Video and especially audio are extremely sensitive to jitter. If a user is watching a video over the network and the frames are all delayed by exactly 2.000 seconds, no harm is done. But if the transmission time varies randomly between 1 and 2 seconds, the result will be terrible unless the application hides the jitter. For audio, a jitter of even a few milliseconds is clearly audible.

The first four applications have more stringent requirements on loss than audio and video because all bits must be delivered correctly. This goal is usually achieved with retransmissions of packets that are lost in the network by the transport layer. This is wasted work; it would be better if the network refused packets it was likely to lose in the first place. Audio and video applications can tolerate some lost packets without retransmission because people do not notice short pauses or occasional skipped frames.

To accommodate a variety of applications, networks may support different categories of QoS. An influential example comes from ATM networks, which were once part of a grand vision for networking but have since become a niche technology. They support:

1. Constant bit rate (e.g., telephony).
2. Real-time variable bit rate (e.g., compressed videoconferencing).
3. Non-real-time variable bit rate (e.g., watching a movie on demand).
4. Available bit rate (e.g., file transfer).

These categories are also useful for other purposes and other networks. Constant bit rate is an attempt to simulate a wire by providing a uniform bandwidth and a uniform delay. Variable bit rate occurs when video is compressed, with some frames compressing more than others. Sending a frame with a lot of detail in it may require sending many bits, whereas a shot of a white wall may compress extremely well. Movies on demand are not actually real time because a few seconds of video can easily be buffered at the receiver before playback starts, so jitter on the network merely causes the amount of stored-but-not-played video to vary. Available bit rate is for applications such as email that are not sensitive to delay or jitter and will take what bandwidth they can get.

5.4.2 Traffic Shaping

Before the network can make QoS guarantees, it must know what traffic is being guaranteed. In the telephone network, this characterization is simple. For example, a voice call (in uncompressed format) needs 64 kbps and consists of one 8-bit sample every 125 μsec. However, traffic in data networks is **bursty**. It typically arrives at nonuniform rates as the traffic rate varies (e.g., videoconferencing with compression), users interact with applications (e.g., browsing a new Web page), and computers switch between tasks. Bursts of traffic are more difficult to handle than constant-rate traffic because they can fill buffers and cause packets to be lost.

Traffic shaping is a technique for regulating the average rate and burstiness of a flow of data that enters the network. The goal is to allow applications to transmit a wide variety of traffic that suits their needs, including some bursts, yet have a simple and useful way to describe the possible traffic patterns to the network. When a flow is set up, the user and the network (i.e., the customer and the provider) agree on a certain traffic pattern (i.e., shape) for that flow. In effect, the customer says to the provider "My transmission pattern will look like this; can you handle it?"

Sometimes this agreement is called an **SLA** (**Service Level Agreement**), especially when it is made over aggregate flows and long periods of time, such as all of the traffic for a given customer. As long as the customer fulfills her part of the bargain and only sends packets according to the agreed-on contract, the provider promises to deliver them all in a timely fashion.

Traffic shaping reduces congestion and thus helps the network live up to its promise. However, to make it work, there is also the issue of how the provider can tell if the customer is following the agreement and what to do if the customer is not. Packets in excess of the agreed pattern might be dropped by the network, or they might be marked as having lower priority. Monitoring a traffic flow is called **traffic policing**.

Shaping and policing are not so important for peer-to-peer and other transfers that will consume any and all available bandwidth, but they are of great importance for real-time data, such as audio and video connections, which have stringent quality-of-service requirements.

Leaky and Token Buckets

We have already seen one way to limit the amount of data an application sends: the sliding window, which uses one parameter to limit how much data is in transit at any given time, which indirectly limits the rate. Now we will look at a more general way to characterize traffic, with the leaky bucket and token bucket algorithms. The formulations are slightly different but give an equivalent result.

Try to imagine a bucket with a small hole in the bottom, as illustrated in Fig. 5-28(b). No matter the rate at which water enters the bucket, the outflow is at a constant rate, *R*, when there is any water in the bucket and zero when the bucket is empty. Also, once the bucket is full to capacity *B*, any additional water entering it spills over the sides and is lost.

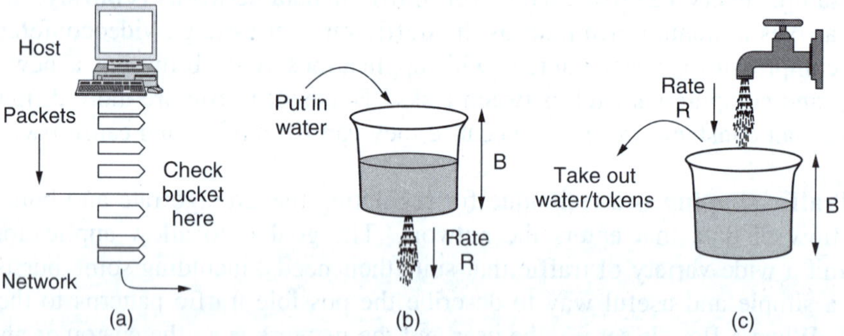

Figure 5-28. (a) Shaping packets. (b) A leaky bucket. (c) A token bucket.

This bucket can be used to shape or police packets entering the network, as shown in Fig. 5-28(a). Conceptually, each host is connected to the network by an interface containing a leaky bucket. To send a packet into the network, it must be possible to put more water into the bucket. If a packet arrives when the bucket is full, the packet must either be queued until enough water leaks out to hold it or be discarded. The former might happen at a host shaping its traffic for the network as part of the operating system. The latter might happen in hardware at a provider network interface that is policing traffic entering the network. This technique was proposed by Turner (1986) and is called the **leaky bucket algorithm**.

A different but equivalent formulation is to imagine the network interface as a bucket that is being filled, as shown in Fig. 5-28(c). The tap is running at rate *R* and the bucket has a capacity of *B*, as before. Now, to send a packet we must be able to take water, or tokens, as the contents are commonly called, out of the bucket (rather than putting water into the bucket). No more than a fixed number of tokens, *B*, can accumulate in the bucket, and if the bucket is empty, we must wait until more tokens arrive before we can send another packet. This algorithm is called the **token bucket algorithm**.

Leaky and token buckets limit the long-term rate of a flow but allow short-term bursts up to a maximum regulated length to pass through unaltered and without suffering any artificial delays. Large bursts will be smoothed by a leaky bucket traffic shaper to reduce congestion in the network. As an example, imagine that a computer can produce data at up to 1000 Mbps (125 million bytes/sec) and that the first link of the network also runs at this speed. The pattern of traffic the host generates is shown in Fig. 5-29(a). This pattern is bursty. The average rate over one second is 200 Mbps, even though the host sends a burst of 16,000 KB at the top speed of 1000 Mbps (for 1/8 of the second).

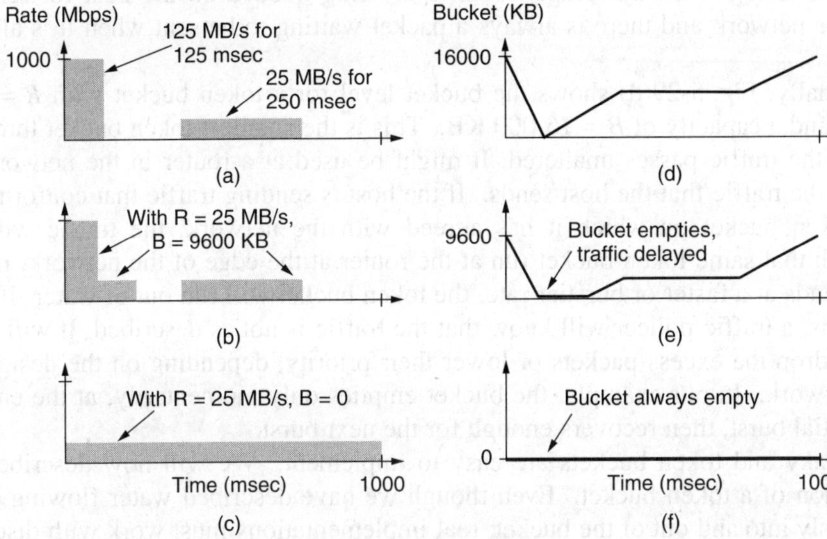

Figure 5-29. (a) Traffic from a host. Output shaped by a token bucket of rate 200 Mbps and capacity (b) 9600 KB and (c) 0 KB. Token bucket level for shaping with rate 200 Mbps and capacity (d) 16,000 KB, (e) 9600 KB, and (f) 0 KB.

Now suppose that the routers can accept data at the top speed only for short intervals, until their buffers fill up. The buffer size is 9600 KB, smaller than the traffic burst. For long intervals, the routers work best at rates not exceeding 200 Mbps (say, because this is all the bandwidth given to the customer). The implication is that if traffic is sent in this pattern, some of it will be dropped in the network because it does not fit into the buffers at routers.

To avoid this packet loss, we can shape the traffic at the host with a token bucket. If we use a rate, R, of 200 Mbps and a capacity, B, of 9600 KB, the traffic will fall within what the network can handle. The output of this token bucket is shown in Fig. 5-29(b). The host can send full throttle at 1000 Mbps for a short while until it has drained the bucket. Then it has to cut back to 200 Mbps until the burst has been sent. The effect is to spread out the burst over time because it was too large to handle all at once. The level of the token bucket is shown in Fig. 5-29(e). It starts off full and is depleted by the initial burst. When it reaches zero, new packets can be sent only at the rate at which the buffer is filling; there can be no more bursts until the bucket has recovered. The bucket fills when no traffic is being sent and stays flat when traffic is being sent at the fill rate.

We can also shape the traffic to be less bursty. Fig. 5-29(c) shows the output of a token bucket with $R = 200$ Mbps and a capacity of 0. This is the extreme case in which the traffic has been completely smoothed. No bursts are allowed, and the traffic enters the network at a steady rate. The corresponding bucket level, shown in Fig. 5-29(f), is always empty. Traffic is being queued on the host for release into the network and there is always a packet waiting to be sent when it is allowed.

Finally, Fig. 5-29(d) shows the bucket level for a token bucket with $R = 200$ Mbps and a capacity of $B = 16{,}000$ KB. This is the smallest token bucket through which the traffic passes unaltered. It might be used at a router in the network to police the traffic that the host sends. If the host is sending traffic that conforms to the token bucket on which it has agreed with the network, the traffic will fit through that same token bucket run at the router at the edge of the network. If the host sends at a faster or burstier rate, the token bucket will run out of water. If this happens, a traffic policer will know that the traffic is not as described. It will then either drop the excess packets or lower their priority, depending on the design of the network. In our example, the bucket empties only momentarily, at the end of the initial burst, then recovers enough for the next burst.

Leaky and token buckets are easy to implement. We will now describe the operation of a token bucket. Even though we have described water flowing continuously into and out of the bucket, real implementations must work with discrete quantities. A token bucket is implemented with a counter for the level of the bucket. The counter is advanced by $R/\Delta T$ units at every clock tick of ΔT seconds. This would be 200 Kbit every 1 msec in our example above. Every time a unit of traffic is sent into the network, the counter is decremented, and traffic may be sent until the counter reaches zero.

When the packets are all the same size, the bucket level can just be counted in packets (e.g., 200 Mbit is 20 packets of 1250 bytes). However, often variable-sized packets are being used. In this case, the bucket level is counted in bytes. If the residual byte count is too low to send a large packet, the packet must wait until the next tick (or even longer, if the fill rate is small).

Calculating the length of the maximum burst (until the bucket empties) is slightly tricky. It is longer than just 9600 KB divided by 125 MB/sec because while the burst is being output, more tokens arrive. If we call the burst length S sec., the maximum output rate M bytes/sec, the token bucket capacity B bytes, and the token arrival rate R bytes/sec, we can see that an output burst contains a maximum of $B + RS$ bytes. We also know that the number of bytes in a maximum-speed burst of length S seconds is MS. Hence, we have

$$B + RS = MS$$

We can solve this equation to get $S = B/(M - R)$. For our parameters of $B = 9600$ KB, $M = 125$ MB/sec, and $R = 25$ MB/sec, we get a burst time of about 94 msec.

A potential problem with the token bucket algorithm is that it reduces large bursts down to the long-term rate R. It is frequently desirable to reduce the peak rate, but without going down to the long-term rate (and also without raising the long-term rate to allow more traffic into the network). One way to get smoother traffic is to insert a second token bucket after the first one. The rate of the second bucket should be much higher than the first one. Basically, the first bucket characterizes the traffic, fixing its average rate but allowing some bursts. The second bucket reduces the peak rate at which the bursts are sent into the network. For example, if the rate of the second token bucket is set to be 500 Mbps and the capacity is set to 0, the initial burst will enter the network at a peak rate of 500 Mbps, which is lower than the 1000 Mbps rate we had previously.

Using all of these buckets can be a bit tricky. When token buckets are used for traffic shaping at hosts, packets are queued and delayed until the buckets permit them to be sent. When token buckets are used for traffic policing at routers in the network, the algorithm is simulated to make sure that no more packets are sent than permitted. Nevertheless, these tools provide ways to shape the network traffic into more manageable forms to assist in meeting quality-of-service requirements.

5.4.3 Packet Scheduling

Being able to regulate the shape of the offered traffic is a good start. However, to provide a performance guarantee, we must reserve sufficient resources along the route that the packets take through the network. To do this, we are assuming that the packets of a flow follow the same route. Spraying them over routers at random makes it hard to guarantee anything. As a consequence, something similar to a virtual circuit has to be set up from the source to the destination, and all the packets that belong to the flow must follow this route.

Algorithms that allocate router resources among the packets of a flow and between competing flows are called **packet scheduling algorithms**. Three different kinds of resources can potentially be reserved for different flows:

1. Bandwidth.
2. Buffer space.
3. CPU cycles.

The first one, bandwidth, is the most obvious. If a flow requires 1 Mbps and the outgoing line has a capacity of 2 Mbps, trying to direct three flows through that line is not going to work. Thus, reserving bandwidth means not oversubscribing any output line.

A second resource that is often in short supply is buffer space. When a packet arrives, it is buffered inside the router until it can be transmitted on the chosen outgoing line. The purpose of the buffer is to absorb small bursts of traffic as the flows contend with each other. If no buffer is available, the packet has to be discarded since there is no place to put it. For good quality of service, some buffers might be reserved for a specific flow so that flow does not have to compete for buffers with other flows. Up to some maximum value, there will always be a buffer available when the flow needs one.

Finally, CPU cycles may also be a scarce resource. It takes router CPU time to process a packet, so a router can process only a certain number of packets per second. While modern routers are able to process most packets quickly, some kinds of packets require greater CPU processing, such as the ICMP packets we will describe in Sec. 5.6. Making sure that the CPU is not overloaded is needed to ensure timely processing of these packets.

Packet scheduling algorithms allocate bandwidth and other router resources by determining which of the buffered packets to send on the output line next. We already described the most straightforward scheduler when explaining how routers work. Each router buffers packets in a queue for each output line until they can be sent, and they are sent in the same order that they arrived. This algorithm is known as **FIFO** (**First-In First-Out**), or equivalently **FCFS** (**First-Come First-Serve**).

FIFO routers usually drop newly arriving packets when the queue is full. Since the newly arrived packet would have been placed at the end of the queue, this behavior is called **tail drop**. It is intuitive, and you may be wondering what alternatives exist. In fact, the RED algorithm we described in Sec. 5.3.5 chose a newly arriving packet to drop at random when the average queue length grew large. The other scheduling algorithms that we will describe also create other opportunities for deciding which packet to drop when the buffers are full.

FIFO scheduling is simple to implement, but it is not suited to providing good quality of service because when there are multiple flows, one flow can easily affect the performance of the other flows. If the first flow is aggressive and sends large bursts of packets, they will lodge in the queue. Processing packets in the order of their arrival means that the aggressive sender can hog most of the capacity of the routers its packets traverse, starving the other flows and reducing their quality of service. To add insult to injury, the packets of the other flows that do get through are likely to be delayed because they had to sit in the queue behind many packets from the aggressive sender.

Many packet scheduling algorithms have been devised that provide stronger isolation between flows and thwart attempts at interference (Bhatti and Crowcroft, 2000). One of the first ones was the **fair queueing** algorithm devised by Nagle (1987). The essence of this algorithm is that routers have separate queues, one for each flow for a given output line. When the line becomes idle, the router scans the queues round-robin, as shown in Fig. 5-30. It then takes the first packet on the next queue. In this way, with *n* hosts competing for the output line, each host gets to send one out of every *n* packets. It is fair in the sense that all flows get to send packets at the same rate. Sending more packets will not improve this rate.

Although a start, the algorithm has a flaw: it gives more bandwidth to hosts that use large packets than to hosts that use small packets. Demers et al. (1990) suggested an improvement in which the round-robin is done in such a way as to

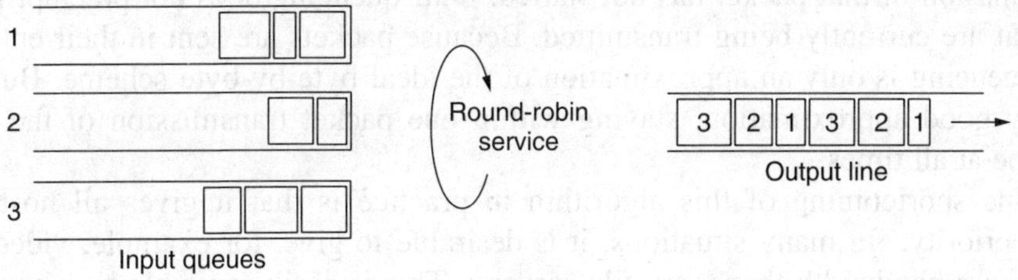

Figure 5-30. Round-robin fair queueing.

simulate a byte-by-byte round-robin, instead of a packet-by-packet round-robin. The trick is to compute a virtual time that is the number of the round at which each packet would finish being sent. Each round drains a byte from all of the queues that have data to send. The packets are then sorted in order of their finishing times and sent in that order.

This algorithm and an example of finish times for packets arriving in three flows are illustrated in Fig. 5-31. If a packet has length *L*, the round at which it will finish is simply *L* rounds after the start time. The start time is either the finish time of the previous packet, or the arrival time of the packet, if the queue is empty when it arrives.

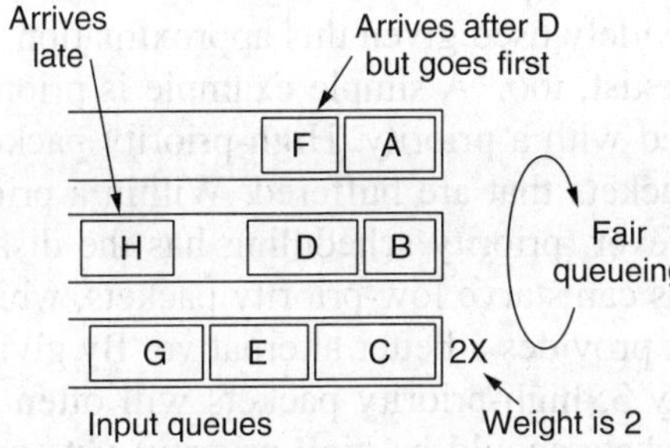

(a)

Packet	Arrival time	Length	Finish time	Output order
A	0	8	8	1
B	5	6	11	3
C	5	10	10	2
D	8	9	20	7
E	8	8	14	4
F	10	6	16	5
G	11	10	19	6
H	20	8	28	8

(b)

Figure 5-31. (a) Weighted Fair Queueing. (b) Finishing times for the packets.

From the table in Fig. 5-32(b), and looking only at the first two packets in the top two queues, packets arrive in the order *A*, *B*, *D*, and *F*. Packet *A* arrives at round 0 and is 8 bytes long, so its finish time is round 8. Similarly the finish time for packet *B* is 11. Packet *D* arrives while *B* is being sent. Its finish time is 9 byte-rounds after it starts when *B* finishes, or 20. Similarly, the finish time for *F* is 16. In the absence of new arrivals, the relative sending order is *A*, *B*, *F*, *D*, even though *F* arrived after *D*. It is possible that another small packet will arrive on the top flow and obtain a finish time before *D*. It will only jump ahead of *D* if the transmission of that packet has not started. Fair queueing does not preempt packets that are currently being transmitted. Because packets are sent in their entirety, fair queueing is only an approximation of the ideal byte-by-byte scheme. But it is a very good approximation, staying within one packet transmission of the ideal scheme at all times.

One shortcoming of this algorithm in practice is that it gives all hosts the same priority. In many situations, it is desirable to give, for example, video servers more bandwidth than, say, file servers. This is easily possible by giving the video server two or more bytes per round. This modified algorithm is called **WFQ (Weighted Fair Queueing)**. Letting the number of bytes per round be the weight of a flow, W, we can now give the formula for computing the finish time:

$$F_i = \max(A_i, F_{i-1}) + L_i / W$$

where A_i is the arrival time, F_i is the finish time, and L_i is the length of packet i. The bottom queue of Fig. 5-31(a) has a weight of 2, so its packets are sent more quickly as you can see in the finish times given in Fig. 5-31(b).

Another practical consideration is implementation complexity. WFQ requires that packets be inserted by their finish time into a sorted queue. With N flows, this is at best an $O(\log N)$ operation per packet, which is difficult to achieve for many flows in high-speed routers. Shreedhar and Varghese (1995) describe an approximation called **deficit round robin** that can be implemented very efficiently, with only $O(1)$ operations per packet. WFQ is widely used given this approximation.

Other kinds of scheduling algorithms exist, too. A simple example is priority scheduling, in which each packet is marked with a priority. High-priority packets are always sent before any low-priority packets that are buffered. Within a priority, packets are sent in FIFO order. However, priority scheduling has the disadvantage that a burst of high-priority packets can starve low-priority packets, which may have to wait indefinitely. WFQ often provides a better alternative. By giving the high-priority queue a large weight, say 3, high-priority packets will often go through a short line (as relatively few packets should be high priority) yet some fraction of low priority packets will continue to be sent even when there is high priority traffic. A high and low priority system is essentially a two-queue WFQ system in which the high priority has infinite weight.

As a final example of a scheduler, packets might carry timestamps and be sent in timestamp order. Clark et al. (1992) describe a design in which the timestamp records how far the packet is behind or ahead of schedule as it is sent through a sequence of routers on the path. Packets that have been queued behind other packets at a router will tend to be behind schedule, and the packets that have been serviced first will tend to be ahead of schedule. Sending packets in order of their timestamps has the beneficial effect of speeding up slow packets while at the same time slowing down fast packets. The result is that all packets are delivered by the network with a more consistent delay.

5.4.4 Admission Control

We have now seen all the necessary elements for QoS and it is time to put them together to actually provide it. QoS guarantees are established through the process of admission control. We first saw admission control used to control congestion, which is a performance guarantee, albeit a weak one. The guarantees we are considering now are stronger, but the model is the same. The user offers a flow with an accompanying QoS requirement to the network. The network then decides whether to accept or reject the flow based on its capacity and the commitments it has made to other flows. If it accepts, the network reserves capacity in advance at routers to guarantee QoS when traffic is sent on the new flow.

The reservations must be made at all of the routers along the route that the packets take through the network. Any routers on the path without reservations might become congested, and a single congested router can break the QoS guarantee. Many routing algorithms find the single best path between each source and each destination and send all traffic over the best path. This may cause some flows to be rejected if there is not enough spare capacity along the best path. QoS guarantees for new flows may still be accommodated by choosing a different route for the flow that has excess capacity. This is called **QoS routing**. Chen and Nahrstedt (1998) give an overview of these techniques. It is also possible to split the traffic for each destination over multiple paths to more easily find excess capacity. A simple method is for routers to choose equal-cost paths and to divide the traffic equally or in proportion to the capacity of the outgoing links. However, more sophisticated algorithms are also available (Nelakuditi and Zhang, 2002).

Given a path, the decision to accept or reject a flow is not a simple matter of comparing the resources (bandwidth, buffers, cycles) requested by the flow with the router's excess capacity in those three dimensions. It is a little more complicated than that. To start with, although some applications may know about their bandwidth requirements, few know about buffers or CPU cycles, so at the minimum, a different way is needed to describe flows and translate this description to router resources. We will get to this shortly.

Next, some applications are far more tolerant of an occasional missed deadline than others. The applications must choose from the type of guarantees that the network can make, whether hard guarantees or behavior that will hold most of the time. All else being equal, everyone would like hard guarantees, but the difficulty is that they are expensive because they constrain worst case behavior. Guarantees for most of the packets are often sufficient for applications, and more flows with this guarantee can be supported for a fixed capacity.

Finally, some applications may be willing to haggle about the flow parameters and others may not. For example, a movie viewer that normally runs at 30 frames/sec may be willing to drop back to 25 frames/sec if there is not enough free bandwidth to support 30 frames/sec. Similarly, the number of pixels per frame, audio bandwidth, and other properties may be adjustable.

Because many parties may be involved in the flow negotiation (the sender, the receiver, and all the routers along the path between them), flows must be described accurately in terms of specific parameters that can be negotiated. A set of such parameters is called a **flow specification**. Typically, the sender (e.g., the video server) produces a flow specification proposing the parameters it would like to use. As the specification propagates along the route, each router examines it and modifies the parameters as need be. The modifications can only reduce the flow, not increase it (e.g., a lower data rate, not a higher one). When it gets to the other end, the parameters can be established.

As an example of what can be in a flow specification, consider the example of Fig. 5-32. This is based on RFCs 2210 and 2211 for Integrated Services, a QoS design we will cover in the next section. It has five parameters. The first two parameters, the *token bucket rate* and *token bucket size*, use a token bucket to give the maximum sustained rate the sender may transmit, averaged over a long time interval, and the largest burst it can send over a short time interval.

Parameter	Unit
Token bucket rate	Bytes/sec
Token bucket size	Bytes
Peak data rate	Bytes/sec
Minimum packet size	Bytes
Maximum packet size	Bytes

Figure 5-32. An example flow specification.

The third parameter, the *peak data rate*, is the maximum transmission rate tolerated, even for brief time intervals. The sender must never exceed this rate even for short bursts.

The last two parameters specify the minimum and maximum packet sizes, including the transport and network layer headers (e.g., TCP and IP). The minimum size is useful because processing each packet takes some fixed time, no matter how short. A router may be prepared to handle 10,000 packets/sec of 1 KB each, but not be prepared to handle 100,000 packets/sec of 50 bytes each, even though this represents a lower data rate. The maximum packet size is important due to internal network limitations that may not be exceeded. For example, if part of the path goes over an Ethernet, the maximum packet size will be restricted to no more than 1500 bytes no matter what the rest of the network can handle.

An interesting question is how a router turns a flow specification into a set of specific resource reservations. At first glance, it might appear that if a router has a link that runs at, say, 1 Gbps and the average packet is 1000 bits, it can process 1 million packets/sec. This observation is not the case, though, because there will always be idle periods on the link due to statistical fluctuations in the load. If the link needs every bit of capacity to get its work done, idling for even a few bits creates a backlog it can never get rid of.

Even with a load slightly below the theoretical capacity, queues can build up and delays can occur. Consider a situation in which packets arrive at random with a mean arrival rate of λ packets/sec. The packets have random lengths and can be sent on the link with a mean service rate of μ packets/sec. Under the assumption that both the arrival and service distributions are Poisson distributions (what is called an M/M/1 queueing system, where "M" stands for Markov, i.e., Poisson), it can be proven using queueing theory that the mean delay experienced by a packet, T, is

$$T = \frac{1}{\mu} \times \frac{1}{1 - \lambda/\mu} = \frac{1}{\mu} \times \frac{1}{1 - \rho}$$

where $\rho = \lambda/\mu$ is the CPU utilization. The first factor, $1/\mu$, is what the service time would be in the absence of competition. The second factor is the slowdown due to competition with other flows. For example, if $\lambda = 950{,}000$ packets/sec and $\mu = 1{,}000{,}000$ packets/sec, then $\rho = 0.95$ and the mean delay experienced by each packet will be 20 μsec instead of 1 μsec. This time accounts for both the queueing time and the service time, as can be seen when the load is very low ($\lambda/\mu \approx 0$). If there are, say, 30 routers along the flow's route, queueing delay alone will account for 600 μsec of delay.

One method of relating flow specifications to router resources that correspond to bandwidth and delay performance guarantees is given by Parekh and Gallagher (1993, 1994). It is based on traffic sources shaped by (R, B) token buckets and WFQ at routers. Each flow is given a WFQ weight W large enough to drain its token bucket rate R as shown in Fig. 5-33. For example, if the flow has a rate of 1 Mbps and the router and output link have a capacity of 1 Gbps, the weight for the flow must be greater than 1/1000th of the total of the weights for all of the flows at that router for the output link. This guarantees the flow a minimum bandwidth. If it cannot be given a large enough rate, the flow cannot be admitted.

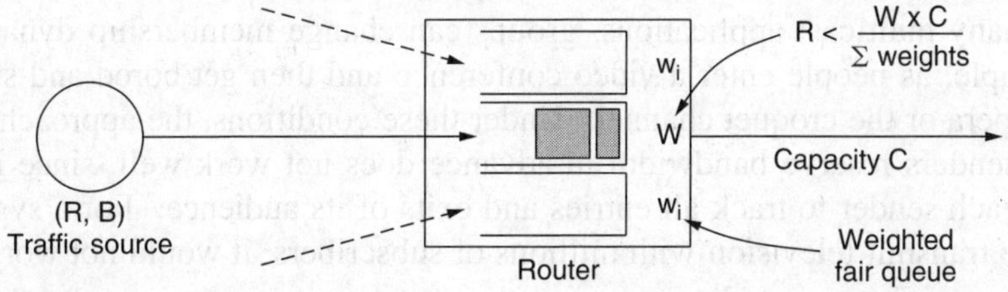

Figure 5-33. Bandwidth and delay guarantees with token buckets and WFQ.

The largest queueing delay the flow will see is a function of the burst size of the token bucket. Consider the two extreme cases. If the traffic is smooth, without any bursts, packets will be drained from the router just as quickly as they arrive. There will be no queueing delay (ignoring packetization effects). On the other hand, if the traffic is saved up in bursts, then a maximum-size burst, B, may arrive at the router all at once. In this case the maximum queueing delay, D, will be the time taken to drain this burst at the guaranteed bandwidth, or B/R (again, ignoring packetization effects). If this delay is too large, the flow must request more bandwidth from the network.

These guarantees are hard. The token buckets bound the burstiness of the source, and fair queueing isolates the bandwidth given to different flows. This means that the flow will meet its bandwidth and delay guarantees regardless of how the other competing flows behave at the router. Those other flows cannot break the guarantee even by saving up traffic and all sending at once.

Moreover, the result holds for a path through multiple routers in any network topology. Each flow gets a minimum bandwidth because that bandwidth is guaranteed at each router. The reason each flow gets a maximum delay is more subtle. In the worst case that a burst of traffic hits the first router and competes with the traffic of other flows, it will be delayed up to the maximum delay of D. However, this delay will also smooth the burst. In turn, this means that the burst will incur no further queueing delays at later routers. The overall queueing delay will be at most D.

5.4.5 Integrated Services

Between 1995 and 1997, IETF put a lot of effort into devising an architecture for streaming multimedia. This work resulted in over two dozen RFCs, starting with RFCs 2205–2212. The generic name for this work is **integrated services**. It was aimed at both unicast and multicast applications. An example of the former is a single user streaming a video clip from a news site. An example of the latter is a collection of digital television stations broadcasting their programs as streams of IP packets to many receivers at various locations. Below we will concentrate on multicast, since unicast is a special case of multicast.

In many multicast applications, groups can change membership dynamically, for example, as people enter a video conference and then get bored and switch to a soap opera or the croquet channel. Under these conditions, the approach of having the senders reserve bandwidth in advance does not work well, since it would require each sender to track all entries and exits of its audience. For a system designed to transmit television with millions of subscribers, it would not work at all.

RSVP—The Resource reSerVation Protocol

The main part of the integrated services architecture that is visible to the users of the network is **RSVP**. It is described in RFCs 2205–2210. This protocol is used for making the reservations; other protocols are used for sending the data.

RSVP allows multiple senders to transmit to multiple groups of receivers, permits individual receivers to switch channels freely, and optimizes bandwidth use while at the same time eliminating congestion.

In its simplest form, the protocol uses multicast routing using spanning trees, as discussed earlier. Each group is assigned a group address. To send to a group, a sender puts the group's address in its packets. The standard multicast routing algorithm then builds a spanning tree covering all group members. The routing algorithm is not part of RSVP. The only difference from normal multicasting is a little extra information that is multicast to the group periodically to tell the routers along the tree to maintain certain data structures in their memories.

As an example, consider the network of Fig. 5-34(a). Hosts 1 and 2 are multicast senders, and hosts 3, 4, and 5 are multicast receivers. In this example, the senders and receivers are disjoint, but in general, the two sets may overlap. The multicast trees for hosts 1 and 2 are shown in Fig. 5-34(b) and Fig. 5-34(c), respectively.

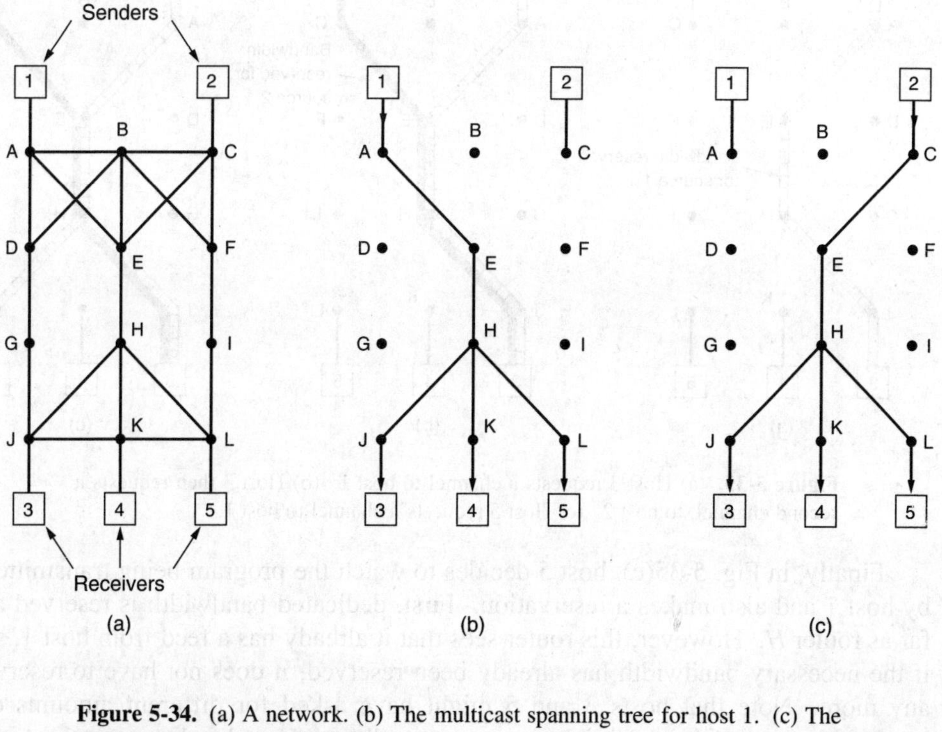

Figure 5-34. (a) A network. (b) The multicast spanning tree for host 1. (c) The multicast spanning tree for host 2.

To get better reception and eliminate congestion, any of the receivers in a group can send a reservation message up the tree to the sender. The message is propagated using the reverse path forwarding algorithm discussed earlier. At each hop, the router notes the reservation and reserves the necessary bandwidth. We saw in the previous section how a weighted fair queueing scheduler can be used to make this reservation. If insufficient bandwidth is available, it reports back failure. By the time the message gets back to the source, bandwidth has been reserved all the way from the sender to the receiver making the reservation request along the spanning tree.

An example of such a reservation is shown in Fig. 5-35(a). Here host 3 has requested a channel to host 1. Once it has been established, packets can flow from 1 to 3 without congestion. Now consider what happens if host 3 next reserves a channel to the other sender, host 2, so the user can watch two television programs at once. A second path is reserved, as illustrated in Fig. 5-35(b). Note that two separate channels are needed from host 3 to router *E* because two independent streams are being transmitted.

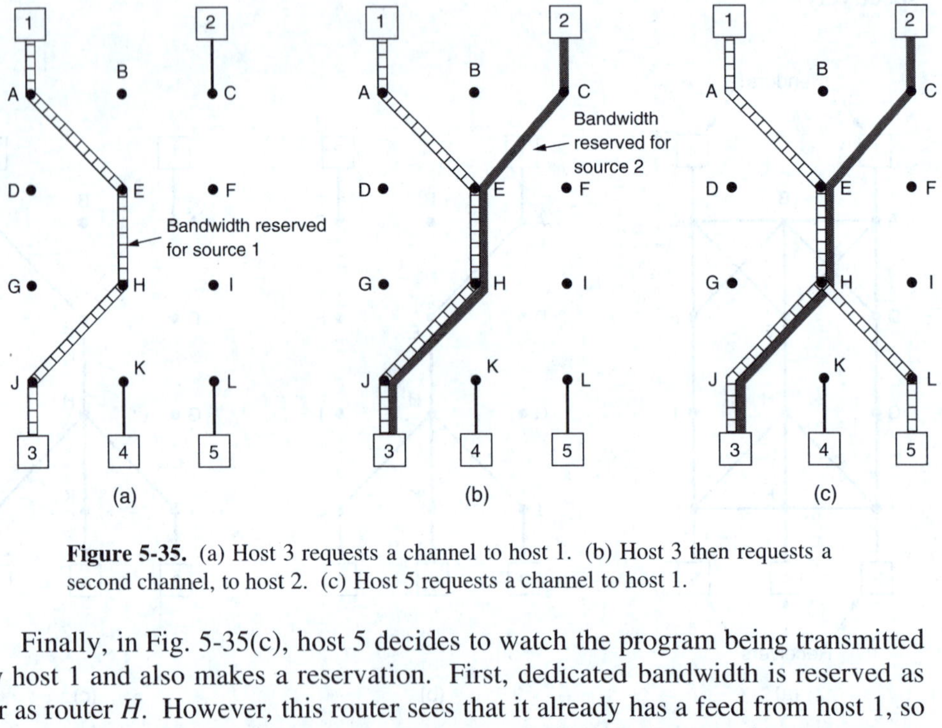

Figure 5-35. (a) Host 3 requests a channel to host 1. (b) Host 3 then requests a second channel, to host 2. (c) Host 5 requests a channel to host 1.

Finally, in Fig. 5-35(c), host 5 decides to watch the program being transmitted by host 1 and also makes a reservation. First, dedicated bandwidth is reserved as far as router *H*. However, this router sees that it already has a feed from host 1, so if the necessary bandwidth has already been reserved, it does not have to reserve any more. Note that hosts 3 and 5 might have asked for different amounts of bandwidth (e.g., if host 3 is playing on a small screen and only wants the low-resolution information), so the capacity reserved must be large enough to satisfy the greediest receiver.

When making a reservation, a receiver can (optionally) specify one or more sources that it wants to receive from. It can also specify whether these choices are fixed for the duration of the reservation or whether the receiver wants to keep open the option of changing sources later. The routers use this information to optimize bandwidth planning. In particular, two receivers are only set up to share a path if they both agree not to change sources later on.

The reason for this strategy in the fully dynamic case is that reserved bandwidth is decoupled from the choice of source. Once a receiver has reserved bandwidth, it can switch to another source and keep that portion of the existing path that is valid for the new source. If host 2 is transmitting several video streams in real time, for example a TV broadcaster with multiple channels, host 3 may switch between them at will without changing its reservation: the routers do not care what program the receiver is watching.

5.4.6 Differentiated Services

Flow-based algorithms have the potential to offer good quality of service to one or more flows because they reserve whatever resources are needed along the route. However, they also have a downside. They require an advance setup to establish each flow, something that does not scale well when there are thousands or millions of flows. Also, they maintain internal per-flow state in the routers, making them vulnerable to router crashes. Finally, the changes required to the router code are substantial and involve complex router-to-router exchanges for setting up the flows. As a consequence, while work continues to advance integrated services, few deployments of it or anything like it exist yet.

For these reasons, IETF has also devised a simpler approach to quality of service, one that can be largely implemented locally in each router without advance setup and without having the whole path involved. This approach is known as **class-based** (as opposed to flow-based) quality of service. IETF has standardized an architecture for it, called **differentiated services**, which is described in RFCs 2474, 2475, and numerous others. We will now describe it.

Differentiated services can be offered by a set of routers forming an administrative domain (e.g., an ISP or a telco). The administration defines a set of service classes with corresponding forwarding rules. If a customer subscribes to differentiated services, customer packets entering the domain are marked with the class to which they belong. This information is carried in the *Differentiated services* field of IPv4 and IPv6 packets (described in Sec. 5.6). The classes are defined as **per hop behaviors** because they correspond to the treatment the packet will receive at each router, not a guarantee across the network. Better service is provided to packets with some per-hop behaviors (e.g., premium service) than to others (e.g., regular service). Traffic within a class may be required to conform to some specific shape, such as a leaky bucket with some specified drain rate. An operator with a nose for business might charge extra for each premium packet transported or might allow up to N premium packets per month for a fixed additional monthly fee. Note that this scheme requires no advance setup, no resource reservation, and no time-consuming end-to-end negotiation for each flow, as with integrated services. This makes differentiated services relatively easy to implement.

Class-based service also occurs in other industries. For example, package delivery companies often offer overnight, two-day, and three-day service. Airlines offer first class, business class, and cattle-class service. Long-distance trains often have multiple service classes. Even the Paris subway has two different service classes. For packets, the classes may differ in terms of delay, jitter, and probability of being discarded in the event of congestion, among other possibilities (but probably not roomier Ethernet frames).

To make the difference between flow-based quality of service and class-based quality of service clearer, consider an example: Internet telephony. With a flow-based scheme, each telephone call gets its own resources and guarantees. With a class-based scheme, all the telephone calls together get the resources reserved for the class telephony. These resources cannot be taken away by packets from the Web browsing class or other classes, but no telephone call gets any private resources reserved for it alone.

Expedited Forwarding

The choice of service classes is up to each operator, but since packets are often forwarded between networks run by different operators, IETF has defined some network-independent service classes. The simplest class is **expedited forwarding**, so let us start with that one. It is described in RFC 3246.

The idea behind expedited forwarding is very simple. Two classes of service are available: regular and expedited. The vast majority of the traffic is expected to be regular, but a limited fraction of the packets are expedited. The expedited packets should be able to transit the network as though no other packets were present. In this way they will get low loss, low delay and low jitter service—just what is needed for VoIP. A symbolic representation of this "two-tube" system is given in Fig. 5-36. Note that there is still just one physical line. The two logical pipes shown in the figure represent a way to reserve bandwidth for different classes of service, not a second physical line.

One way to implement this strategy is as follows. Packets are classified as expedited or regular and marked accordingly. This step might be done on the sending host or in the ingress (first) router. The advantage of doing classification on the sending host is that more information is available about which packets belong to which flows. This task may be performed by networking software or even the operating system, to avoid having to change existing applications. For example, it is becoming common for VoIP packets to be marked for expedited service by hosts. If the packets pass through a corporate network or ISP that supports expedited service, they will receive preferential treatment. If the network does not support expedited service, no harm is done.

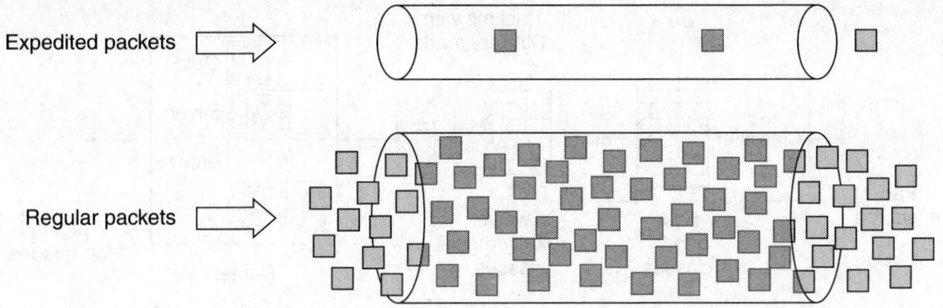

Figure 5-36. Expedited packets experience a traffic-free network.

Of course, if the marking is done by the host, the ingress router is likely to police the traffic to make sure that customers are not sending more expedited traffic than they have paid for. Within the network, the routers may have two output queues for each outgoing line, one for expedited packets and one for regular packets. When a packet arrives, it is queued accordingly. The expedited queue is given priority over the regular one, for example, by using a priority scheduler. In this way, expedited packets see an unloaded network, even when there is, in fact, a heavy load of regular traffic.

Assured Forwarding

A somewhat more elaborate scheme for managing the service classes is called **assured forwarding**. It is described in RFC 2597. Assured forwarding specifies that there shall be four priority classes, each class having its own resources. The top three classes might be called gold, silver, and bronze. In addition, it defines three discard classes for packets that are experiencing congestion: low, medium, and high. Taken together, these two factors define 12 service classes.

Figure 5-37 shows one way packets might be processed under assured forwarding. The first step is to classify the packets into one of the four priority classes. As before, this step might be done on the sending host (as shown in the figure) or in the ingress router, and the rate of higher-priority packets may be limited by the operator as part of the service offering.

The next step is to determine the discard class for each packet. This is done by passing the packets of each priority class through a traffic policer such as a token bucket. The policer lets all of the traffic through, but it identifies packets that fit within small bursts as low discard, packets that exceed small bursts as medium discard, and packets that exceed large bursts as high discard. The combination of priority and discard class is then encoded in each packet.

Finally, the packets are processed by routers in the network with a packet scheduler that distinguishes the different classes. A common choice is to use

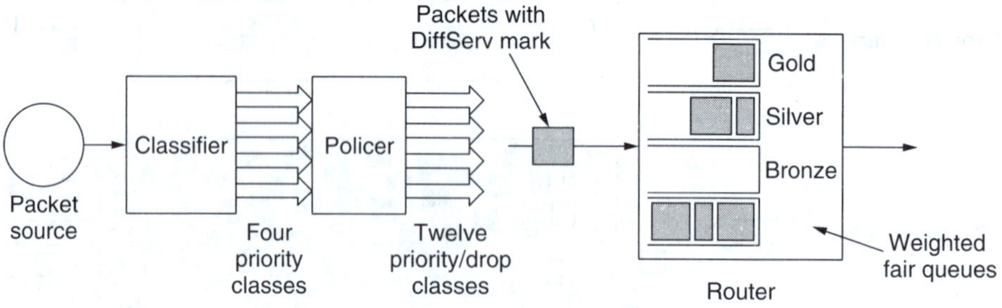

Figure 5-37. A possible implementation of assured forwarding.

weighted fair queueing for the four priority classes, with higher classes given higher weights. In this way, the higher classes will get most of the bandwidth, but the lower classes will not be starved of bandwidth entirely. For example, if the weights double from one class to the next higher class, the higher class will get twice the bandwidth. Within a priority class, packets with a higher discard class can be preferentially dropped by running an algorithm such as RED (Random Early Detection), which we saw in Sec. 5.3.5. RED will start to drop packets as congestion builds but before the router has run out of buffer space. At this stage, there is still buffer space with which to accept low discard packets while dropping high discard packets.

5.5 INTERNETWORKING

Until now, we have implicitly assumed that there is a single homogeneous network, with each machine using the same protocol in each layer. Unfortunately, this assumption is wildly optimistic. Many different networks exist, including PANs, LANs, MANs, and WANs. We have described Ethernet, Internet over cable, the fixed and mobile telephone networks, 802.11, 802.16, and more. Numerous protocols are in widespread use across these networks in every layer. In the following sections, we will take a careful look at the issues that arise when two or more networks are connected to form an **internetwork**, or more simply an **internet**.

It would be much simpler to join networks together if everyone used a single networking technology, and it is often the case that there is a dominant kind of network, such as Ethernet. Some pundits speculate that the multiplicity of technologies will go away as soon as everyone realizes how wonderful [fill in your favorite network] is. Do not count on it. History shows this to be wishful thinking. Different kinds of networks grapple with different problems, so, for example, Ethernet and satellite networks are always likely to differ. Reusing existing systems, such as running data networks on top of cable, the telephone network, and power lines, adds constraints that cause the features of the networks to diverge. Heterogeneity is here to stay.

If there will always be different networks, it would be simpler if we did not need to interconnect them. This also is unlikely. Bob Metcalfe postulated that the value of a network with N nodes is the number of connections that may be made between the nodes, or N^2 (Gilder, 1993). This means that large networks are much more valuable than small networks because they allow many more connections, so there always will be an incentive to combine smaller networks.

The Internet is the prime example of this interconnection. (We will write Internet with a capital "I" to distinguish it from other internets, or connected networks.) The purpose of joining all these networks is to allow users on any of them to communicate with users on all the other ones. When you pay an ISP for Internet service, you may be charged depending on the bandwidth of your line, but what you are really paying for is the ability to exchange packets with any other host that is also connected to the Internet. After all, the Internet would not be very popular if you could only send packets to other hosts in the same city.

Since networks often differ in important ways, getting packets from one network to another is not always so easy. We must address problems of heterogeneity, and also problems of scale as the resulting internet grows very large. We will begin by looking at how networks can differ to see what we are up against. Then we shall see the approach used so successfully by IP (Internet Protocol), the network layer protocol of the Internet, including techniques for tunneling through networks, routing in internetworks, and packet fragmentation.

5.5.1 How Networks Differ

Networks can differ in many ways. Some of the differences, such as different modulation techniques or frame formats, are internal to the physical and data link layers. These differences will not concern us here. Instead, in Fig. 5-38 we list some of the differences that can be exposed to the network layer. It is papering over these differences that makes internetworking more difficult than operating within a single network.

When packets sent by a source on one network must transit one or more foreign networks before reaching the destination network, many problems can occur at the interfaces between networks. To start with, the source needs to be able to address the destination. What do we do if the source is on an Ethernet network and the destination is on a WiMAX network? Assuming we can even specify a WiMAX destination from an Ethernet network, packets would cross from a connectionless network to a connection-oriented one. This may require that a new connection be set up on short notice, which injects a delay, and much overhead if the connection is not used for many more packets.

Many specific differences may have to be accommodated as well. How do we multicast a packet to a group with some members on a network that does not

Item	Some Possibilities
Service offered	Connectionless versus connection oriented
Addressing	Different sizes, flat or hierarchical
Broadcasting	Present or absent (also multicast)
Packet size	Every network has its own maximum
Ordering	Ordered and unordered delivery
Quality of service	Present or absent; many different kinds
Reliability	Different levels of loss
Security	Privacy rules, encryption, etc.
Parameters	Different timeouts, flow specifications, etc.
Accounting	By connect time, packet, byte, or not at all

Figure 5-38. Some of the many ways networks can differ.

support multicast? The differing max packet sizes used by different networks can be a major nuisance, too. How do you pass an 8000-byte packet through a network whose maximum size is 1500 bytes? If packets on a connection-oriented network transit a connectionless network, they may arrive in a different order than they were sent. That is something the sender likely did not expect, and it might come as an (unpleasant) surprise to the receiver as well.

These kinds of differences can be papered over, with some effort. For example, a gateway joining two networks might generate separate packets for each destination in lieu of better network support for multicasting. A large packet might be broken up, sent in pieces, and then joined back together. Receivers might buffer packets and deliver them in order.

Networks also can differ in large respects that are more difficult to reconcile. The clearest example is quality of service. If one network has strong QoS and the other offers best effort service, it will be impossible to make bandwidth and delay guarantees for real-time traffic end to end. In fact, they can likely only be made while the best-effort network is operated at a low utilization, or hardly used, which is unlikely to be the goal of most ISPs. Security mechanisms are problematic, but at least encryption for confidentiality and data integrity can be layered on top of networks that do not already include it. Finally, differences in accounting can lead to unwelcome bills when normal usage suddenly becomes expensive, as roaming mobile phone users with data plans have discovered.

5.5.2 How Networks Can Be Connected

There are two basic choices for connecting different networks: we can build devices that translate or convert packets from each kind of network into packets for each other network, or, like good computer scientists, we can try to solve the problem by adding a layer of indirection and building a common layer on top of the different networks. In either case, the devices are placed at the boundaries between networks.

Early on, Cerf and Kahn (1974) argued for a common layer to hide the differences of existing networks. This approach has been tremendously successful, and the layer they proposed was eventually separated into the TCP and IP protocols. Almost four decades later, IP is the foundation of the modern Internet. For this accomplishment, Cerf and Kahn were awarded the 2004 Turing Award, informally known as the Nobel Prize of computer science. IP provides a universal packet format that all routers recognize and that can be passed through almost every network. IP has extended its reach from computer networks to take over the telephone network. It also runs on sensor networks and other tiny devices that were once presumed too resource-constrained to support it.

We have discussed several different devices that connect networks, including repeaters, hubs, switches, bridges, routers, and gateways. Repeaters and hubs just move bits from one wire to another. They are mostly analog devices and do not understand anything about higher layer protocols. Bridges and switches operate at the link layer. They can be used to build networks, but only with minor protocol translation in the process, for example, between 10, 100 and 1000 Mbps Ethernet switches. Our focus in this section is interconnection devices that operate at the network layer, namely the routers. We will leave gateways, which are higher-layer interconnection devices, until later.

Let us first explore at a high level how interconnection with a common network layer can be used to interconnect dissimilar networks. An internet comprised of 802.11, MPLS, and Ethernet networks is shown in Fig. 5-39(a). Suppose that the source machine on the 802.11 network wants to send a packet to the destination machine on the Ethernet network. Since these technologies are different, and they are further separated by another kind of network (MPLS), some added processing is needed at the boundaries between the networks.

Because different networks may, in general, have different forms of addressing, the packet carries a network layer address that can identify any host across the three networks. The first boundary the packet reaches is when it transitions from an 802.11 network to an MPLS network. 802.11 provides a connectionless service, but MPLS provides a connection-oriented service. This means that a virtual circuit must be set up to cross that network. Once the packet has traveled along the virtual circuit, it will reach the Ethernet network. At this boundary, the packet may be too large to be carried, since 802.11 can work with larger frames than Ethernet. To handle this problem, the packet is divided into fragments, and each fragment is sent separately. When the fragments reach the destination, they are reassembled. Then the packet has completed its journey.

The protocol processing for this journey is shown in Fig. 5-39(b). The source accepts data from the transport layer and generates a packet with the common network layer header, which is IP in this example. The network header contains the

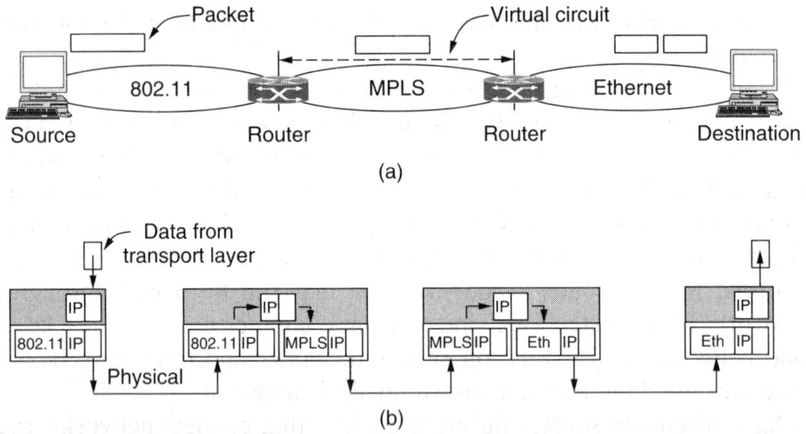

Figure 5-39. (a) A packet crossing different networks. (b) Network and link layer protocol processing.

ultimate destination address, which is used to determine that the packet should be sent via the first router. So the packet is encapsulated in an 802.11 frame whose destination is the first router and transmitted. At the router, the packet is removed from the frame's data field and the 802.11 frame header is discarded. The router now examines the IP address in the packet and looks up this address in its routing table. Based on this address, it decides to send the packet to the second router next. For this part of the path, an MPLS virtual circuit must be established to the second router and the packet must be encapsulated with MPLS headers that travel this circuit. At the far end, the MPLS header is discarded and the network address is again consulted to find the next network layer hop. It is the destination itself. Since the packet is too long to be sent over Ethernet, it is split into two portions. Each of these portions is put into the data field of an Ethernet frame and sent to the Ethernet address of the destination. At the destination, the Ethernet header is stripped from each of the frames, and the contents are reassembled. The packet has finally reached its destination.

Observe that there is an essential difference between the routed case and the switched (or bridged) case. With a router, the packet is extracted from the frame and the network address in the packet is used for deciding where to send it. With a switch (or bridge), the entire frame is transported on the basis of its MAC address. Switches do not have to understand the network layer protocol being used to switch packets. Routers do.

Unfortunately, internetworking is not as easy as we have made it sound. In fact, when bridges were introduced, it was intended that they would join different types of networks, or at least different types of LANs. They were to do this by translating frames from one LAN into frames from another LAN. However, this did not work well, for the same reason that internetworking is difficult: the differences in the features of LANs, such as different maximum packet sizes and LANs with and without priority classes, are hard to mask. Today, bridges are predominantly used to connect the same kind of network at the link layer, and routers connect different networks at the network layer.

Internetworking has been very successful at building large networks, but it only works when there is a common network layer. There have, in fact, been many network protocols over time. Getting everybody to agree on a single format is difficult when companies perceive it to their commercial advantage to have a proprietary format that they control. Examples besides IP, which is now the near-universal network protocol, were IPX, SNA, and AppleTalk. None of these protocols are still in widespread use, but there will always be other protocols. The most relevant example now is probably IPv4 and IPv6. While these are both versions of IP, they are not compatible (or it would not have been necessary to create IPv6).

A router that can handle multiple network protocols is called a **multiprotocol router**. It must either translate the protocols, or leave connection for a higher protocol layer. Neither approach is entirely satisfactory. Connection at a higher layer, say, by using TCP, requires that all the networks implement TCP (which may not be the case). Then, it limits usage across the networks to applications that use TCP (which does not include many real-time applications).

The alternative is to translate packets between the networks. However, unless the packet formats are close relatives with the same information fields, such conversions will always be incomplete and often doomed to failure. For example, IPv6 addresses are 128 bits long. They will not fit in a 32-bit IPv4 address field, no matter how hard the router tries. Getting IPv4 and IPv6 to run in the same network has proven to be a major obstacle to the deployment of IPv6. (To be fair, so has getting customers to understand why they should want IPv6 in the first place.) Greater problems can be expected when translating between fundamentally different protocols, such as connectionless and connection-oriented network protocols. Given these difficulties, conversion is only rarely attempted. Arguably, even IP has only worked so well by serving as a kind of lowest common denominator. It requires little of the networks on which it runs, but offers only best-effort service as a result.

5.5.3 Tunneling

Handling the general case of making two different networks interwork is exceedingly difficult. However, there is a common special case that is manageable even for different network protocols. This case is where the source and destination hosts are on the same type of network, but there is a different network in between. As an example, think of an international bank with an IPv6 network in Paris, an IPv6 network in London and connectivity between the offices via the IPv4 Internet. This situation is shown in Fig. 5-40.

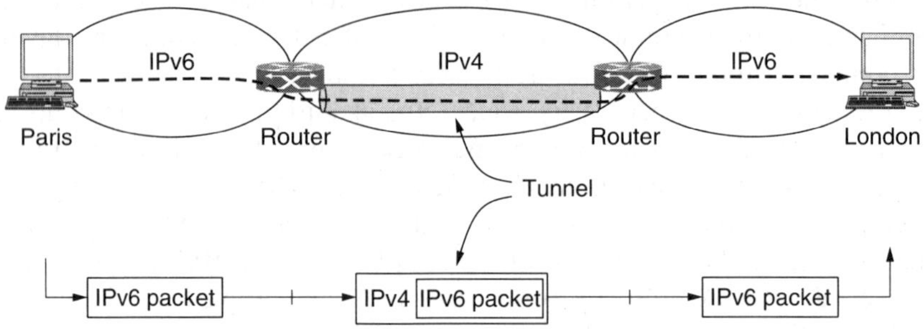

Figure 5-40. Tunneling a packet from Paris to London.

The solution to this problem is a technique called **tunneling**. To send an IP packet to a host in the London office, a host in the Paris office constructs the packet containing an IPv6 address in London, and sends it to the multiprotocol router that connects the Paris IPv6 network to the IPv4 Internet. When this router gets the IPv6 packet, it encapsulates the packet with an IPv4 header addressed to the IPv4 side of the multiprotocol router that connects to the London IPv6 network. That is, the router puts a (IPv6) packet inside a (IPv4) packet. When this wrapped packet arrives, the London router removes the original IPv6 packet and sends it onward to the destination host.

The path through the IPv4 Internet can be seen as a big tunnel extending from one multiprotocol router to the other. The IPv6 packet just travels from one end of the tunnel to the other, snug in its nice box. It does not have to worry about dealing with IPv4 at all. Neither do the hosts in Paris or London. Only the multiprotocol routers have to understand both IPv4 and IPv6 packets. In effect, the entire trip from one multiprotocol router to the other is like a hop over a single link.

An analogy may make tunneling clearer. Consider a person driving her car from Paris to London. Within France, the car moves under its own power, but when it hits the English Channel, it is loaded onto a high-speed train and transported to England through the Chunnel (cars are not permitted to drive through the Chunnel). Effectively, the car is being carried as freight, as depicted in Fig. 5-41. At the far end, the car is let loose on the English roads and once again continues to move under its own power. Tunneling of packets through a foreign network works the same way.

Tunneling is widely used to connect isolated hosts and networks using other networks. The network that results is called an **overlay** since it has effectively been overlaid on the base network. Deployment of a network protocol with a new feature is a common reason, as our "IPv6 over IPv4" example shows. The disadvantage of tunneling is that none of the hosts on the network that is tunneled over can be reached because the packets cannot escape in the middle of the tunnel.

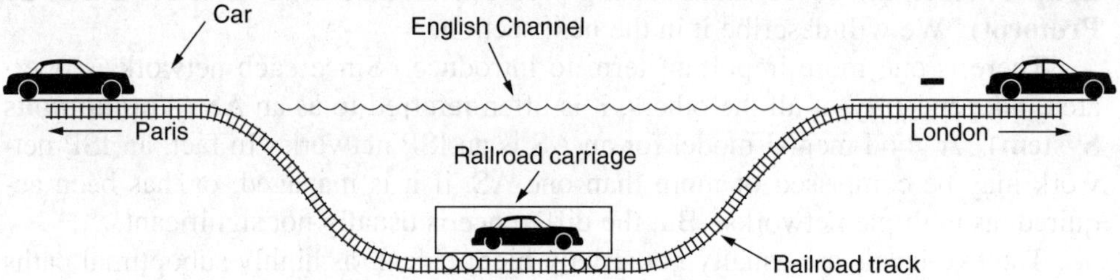

Figure 5-41. Tunneling a car from France to England.

However, this limitation of tunnels is turned into an advantage with **VPNs** (**Virtual Private Networks**). A VPN is simply an overlay that is used to provide a measure of security. We will explore VPNs when we get to Chap. 8.

5.5.4 Internetwork Routing

Routing through an internet poses the same basic problem as routing within a single network, but with some added complications. To start, the networks may internally use different routing algorithms. For example, one network may use link state routing and another distance vector routing. Since link state algorithms need to know the topology but distance vector algorithms do not, this difference alone would make it unclear how to find the shortest paths across the internet.

Networks run by different operators lead to bigger problems. First, the operators may have different ideas about what is a good path through the network. One operator may want the route with the least delay, while another may want the most inexpensive route. This will lead the operators to use different quantities to set the shortest-path costs (e.g., milliseconds of delay vs. monetary cost). The weights will not be comparable across networks, so shortest paths on the internet will not be well defined.

Worse yet, one operator may not want another operator to even know the details of the paths in its network, perhaps because the weights and paths may reflect sensitive information (such as the monetary cost) that represents a competitive business advantage.

Finally, the internet may be much larger than any of the networks that comprise it. It may therefore require routing algorithms that scale well by using a hierarchy, even if none of the individual networks need to use a hierarchy.

All of these considerations lead to a two-level routing algorithm. Within each network, an **intradomain** or **interior gateway protocol** is used for routing. ("Gateway" is an older term for "router.") It might be a link state protocol of the kind we have already described. Across the networks that make up the internet, an **interdomain** or **exterior gateway protocol** is used. The networks may all use different intradomain protocols, but they must use the same interdomain protocol.

In the Internet, the interdomain routing protocol is called **BGP** (**Border Gateway Protocol**). We will describe it in the next section.

There is one more important term to introduce. Since each network is operated independently of all the others, it is often referred to as an **AS** (**Autonomous System**). A good mental model for an AS is an ISP network. In fact, an ISP network may be comprised of more than one AS, if it is managed, or, has been acquired, as multiple networks. But the difference is usually not significant.

The two levels are usually not strictly hierarchical, as highly suboptimal paths might result if a large international network and a small regional network were both abstracted to be a single network. However, relatively little information about routes within the networks is exposed to find routes across the internetwork. This helps to address all of the complications. It improves scaling and lets operators freely select routes within their own networks using a protocol of their choosing. It also does not require weights to be compared across networks or expose sensitive information outside of networks.

However, we have said little so far about how the routes across the networks of the internet are determined. In the Internet, a large determining factor is the business arrangements between ISPs. Each ISP may charge or receive money from the other ISPs for carrying traffic. Another factor is that if internetwork routing requires crossing international boundaries, various laws may suddenly come into play, such as Sweden's strict privacy laws about exporting personal data about Swedish citizens from Sweden. All of these nontechnical factors are wrapped up in the concept of a **routing policy** that governs the way autonomous networks select the routes that they use. We will return to routing policies when we describe BGP.

5.5.5 Packet Fragmentation

Each network or link imposes some maximum size on its packets. These limits have various causes, among them

1. Hardware (e.g., the size of an Ethernet frame).
2. Operating system (e.g., all buffers are 512 bytes).
3. Protocols (e.g., the number of bits in the packet length field).
4. Compliance with some (inter)national standard.
5. Desire to reduce error-induced retransmissions to some level.
6. Desire to prevent one packet from occupying the channel too long.

The result of all these factors is that the network designers are not free to choose any old maximum packet size they wish. Maximum payloads for some common technologies are 1500 bytes for Ethernet and 2272 bytes for 802.11. IP is more generous, allows for packets as big as 65,515 bytes.

Hosts usually prefer to transmit large packets because this reduces packet overheads such as bandwidth wasted on header bytes. An obvious internetworking problem appears when a large packet wants to travel through a network whose maximum packet size is too small. This nuisance has been a persistent issue, and solutions to it have evolved along with much experience gained on the Internet.

One solution is to make sure the problem does not occur in the first place. However, this is easier said than done. A source does not usually know the path a packet will take through the network to a destination, so it certainly does not know how small packets must be to get there. This packet size is called the **Path MTU** (**Path Maximum Transmission Unit**). Even if the source did know the path MTU, packets are routed independently in a connectionless network such as the Internet. This routing means that paths may suddenly change, which can unexpectedly change the path MTU.

The alternative solution to the problem is to allow routers to break up packets into **fragments**, sending each fragment as a separate network layer packet. However, as every parent of a small child knows, converting a large object into small fragments is considerably easier than the reverse process. (Physicists have even given this effect a name: the second law of thermodynamics.) Packet-switching networks, too, have trouble putting the fragments back together again.

Two opposing strategies exist for recombining the fragments back into the original packet. The first strategy is to make fragmentation caused by a "small-packet" network transparent to any subsequent networks through which the packet must pass on its way to the ultimate destination. This option is shown in Fig. 5-42(a). In this approach, when an oversized packet arrives at *G1*, the router breaks it up into fragments. Each fragment is addressed to the same exit router, *G2*, where the pieces are recombined. In this way, passage through the small-packet network is made transparent. Subsequent networks are not even aware that fragmentation has occurred.

Transparent fragmentation is straightforward but has some problems. For one thing, the exit router must know when it has received all the pieces, so either a count field or an "end of packet" bit must be provided. Also, because all packets must exit via the same router so that they can be reassembled, the routes are constrained. By not allowing some fragments to follow one route to the ultimate destination and other fragments a disjoint route, some performance may be lost. More significant is the amount of work that the router may have to do. It may need to buffer the fragments as they arrive, and decide when to throw them away if not all of the fragments arrive. Some of this work may be wasteful, too, as the packet may pass through a series of small packet networks and need to be repeatedly fragmented and reassembled.

The other fragmentation strategy is to refrain from recombining fragments at any intermediate routers. Once a packet has been fragmented, each fragment is

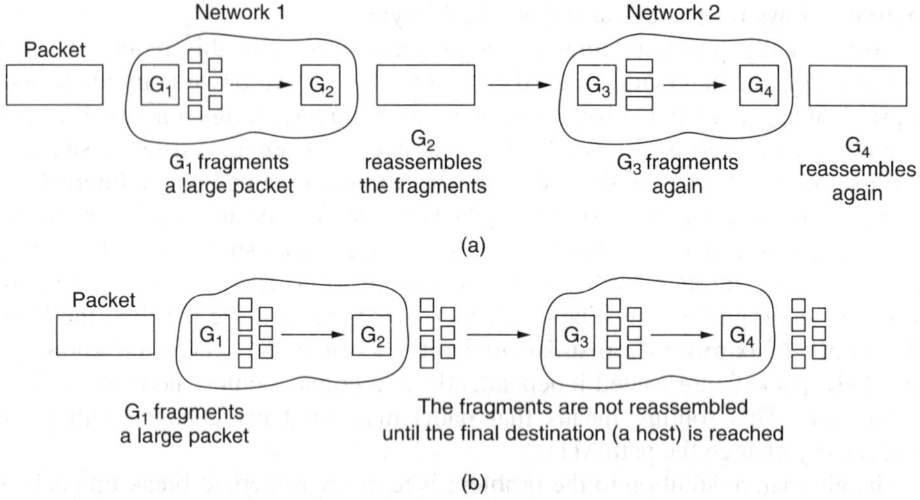

Figure 5-42. (a) Transparent fragmentation. (b) Nontransparent fragmentation.

treated as though it were an original packet. The routers pass the fragments, as shown in Fig. 5-42(b), and reassembly is performed only at the destination host.

The main advantage of nontransparent fragmentation is that it requires routers to do less work. IP works this way. A complete design requires that the fragments be numbered in such a way that the original data stream can be reconstructed. The design used by IP is to give every fragment a packet number (carried on all packets), an absolute byte offset within the packet, and a flag indicating whether it is the end of the packet. An example is shown in Fig. 5-43. While simple, this design has some attractive properties. Fragments can be placed in a buffer at the destination in the right place for reassembly, even if they arrive out of order. Fragments can also be fragmented if they pass over a network with a yet smaller MTU. This is shown in Fig. 5-43(c). Retransmissions of the packet (if all fragments were not received) can be fragmented into different pieces. Finally, fragments can be of arbitrary size, down to a single byte plus the packet header. In all cases, the destination simply uses the packet number and fragment offset to place the data in the right position, and the end-of-packet flag to determine when it has the complete packet.

Unfortunately, this design still has problems. The overhead can be higher than with transparent fragmentation because fragment headers are now carried over some links where they may not be needed. But the real problem is the existence of fragments in the first place. Kent and Mogul (1987) argued that fragmentation is detrimental to performance because, as well as the header overheads, a whole packet is lost if any of its fragments are lost, and because fragmentation is more of a burden for hosts than was originally realized.

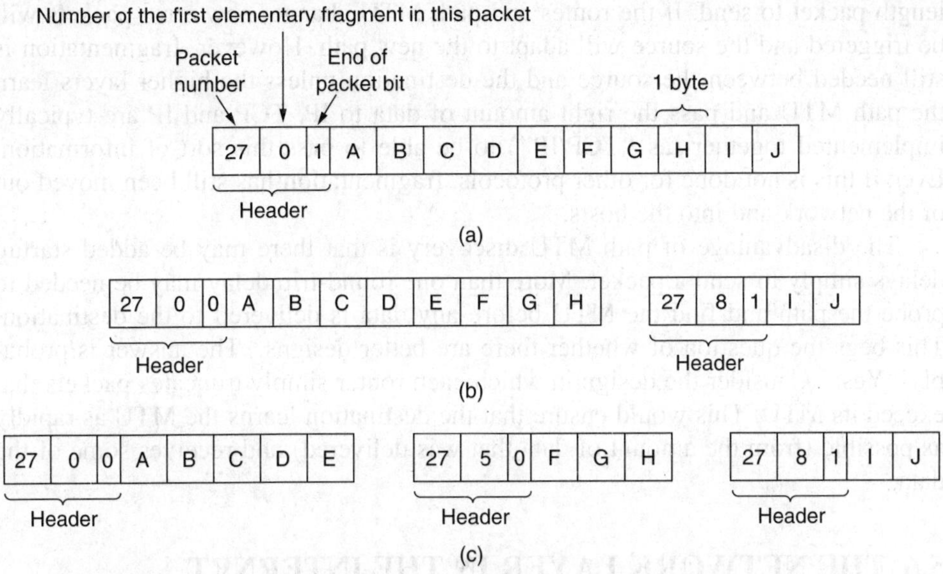

Figure 5-43. Fragmentation when the elementary data size is 1 byte. (a) Original packet, containing 10 data bytes. (b) Fragments after passing through a network with maximum packet size of 8 payload bytes plus header. (c) Fragments after passing through a size 5 gateway.

This leads us back to the original solution of getting rid of fragmentation in the network, the strategy used in the modern Internet. The process is called **path MTU discovery** (Mogul and Deering, 1990). It works as follows. Each IP packet is sent with its header bits set to indicate that no fragmentation is allowed to be performed. If a router receives a packet that is too large, it generates an error packet, returns it to the source, and drops the packet. This is shown in Fig. 5-44. When the source receives the error packet, it uses the information inside to refragment the packet into pieces that are small enough for the router to handle. If a router further down the path has an even smaller MTU, the process is repeated.

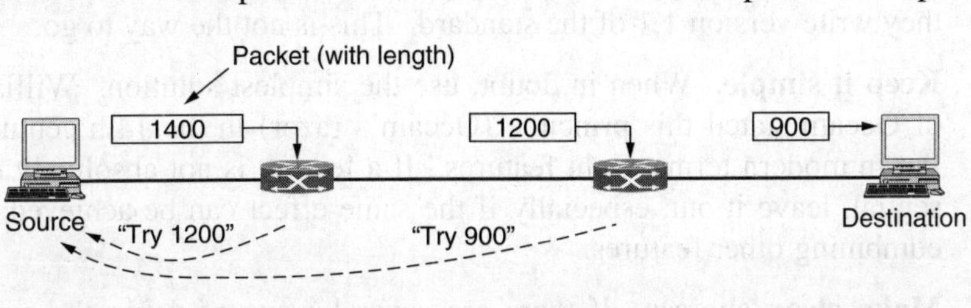

Figure 5-44. Path MTU discovery.

The advantage of path MTU discovery is that the source now knows what length packet to send. If the routes and path MTU change, new error packets will be triggered and the source will adapt to the new path. However, fragmentation is still needed between the source and the destination unless the higher layers learn the path MTU and pass the right amount of data to IP. TCP and IP are typically implemented together (as "TCP/IP") to be able to pass this sort of information. Even if this is not done for other protocols, fragmentation has still been moved out of the network and into the hosts.

The disadvantage of path MTU discovery is that there may be added startup delays simply to send a packet. More than one round-trip delay may be needed to probe the path and find the MTU before any data is delivered to the destination. This begs the question of whether there are better designs. The answer is probably "Yes." Consider the design in which each router simply truncates packets that exceed its MTU. This would ensure that the destination learns the MTU as rapidly as possible (from the amount of data that was delivered) and receives some of the data.

5.6 THE NETWORK LAYER IN THE INTERNET

It is now time to discuss the network layer of the Internet in detail. But before getting into specifics, it is worth taking a look at the principles that drove its design in the past and made it the success that it is today. All too often, nowadays, people seem to have forgotten them. These principles are enumerated and discussed in RFC 1958, which is well worth reading (and should be mandatory for all protocol designers—with a final exam at the end). This RFC draws heavily on ideas put forth by Clark (1988) and Saltzer et al. (1984). We will now summarize what we consider to be the top 10 principles (from most important to least important).

1. **Make sure it works.** Do not finalize the design or standard until multiple prototypes have successfully communicated with each other. All too often, designers first write a 1000-page standard, get it approved, then discover it is deeply flawed and does not work. Then they write version 1.1 of the standard. This is not the way to go.

2. **Keep it simple.** When in doubt, use the simplest solution. William of Occam stated this principle (Occam's razor) in the 14th century. Put in modern terms: fight features. If a feature is not absolutely essential, leave it out, especially if the same effect can be achieved by combining other features.

3. **Make clear choices.** If there are several ways of doing the same thing, choose one. Having two or more ways to do the same thing is looking for trouble. Standards often have multiple options or modes

or parameters because several powerful parties insist that their way is best. Designers should strongly resist this tendency. Just say no.

4. **Exploit modularity.** This principle leads directly to the idea of having protocol stacks, each of whose layers is independent of all the other ones. In this way, if circumstances require one module or layer to be changed, the other ones will not be affected.

5. **Expect heterogeneity.** Different types of hardware, transmission facilities, and applications will occur on any large network. To handle them, the network design must be simple, general, and flexible.

6. **Avoid static options and parameters.** If parameters are unavoidable (e.g., maximum packet size), it is best to have the sender and receiver negotiate a value rather than defining fixed choices.

7. **Look for a good design; it need not be perfect.** Often, the designers have a good design but it cannot handle some weird special case. Rather than messing up the design, the designers should go with the good design and put the burden of working around it on the people with the strange requirements.

8. **Be strict when sending and tolerant when receiving.** In other words, send only packets that rigorously comply with the standards, but expect incoming packets that may not be fully conformant and try to deal with them.

9. **Think about scalability.** If the system is to handle millions of hosts and billions of users effectively, no centralized databases of any kind are tolerable and load must be spread as evenly as possible over the available resources.

10. **Consider performance and cost.** If a network has poor performance or outrageous costs, nobody will use it.

Let us now leave the general principles and start looking at the details of the Internet's network layer. In the network layer, the Internet can be viewed as a collection of networks or **ASes** (**Autonomous Systems**) that are interconnected. There is no real structure, but several major backbones exist. These are constructed from high-bandwidth lines and fast routers. The biggest of these backbones, to which everyone else connects to reach the rest of the Internet, are called **Tier 1 networks**. Attached to the backbones are ISPs (Internet Service Providers) that provide Internet access to homes and businesses, data centers and colocation facilities full of server machines, and regional (mid-level) networks. The data centers serve much of the content that is sent over the Internet. Attached to the regional networks are more ISPs, LANs at many universities and companies, and other edge networks. A sketch of this quasihierarchical organization is given in Fig. 5-45.

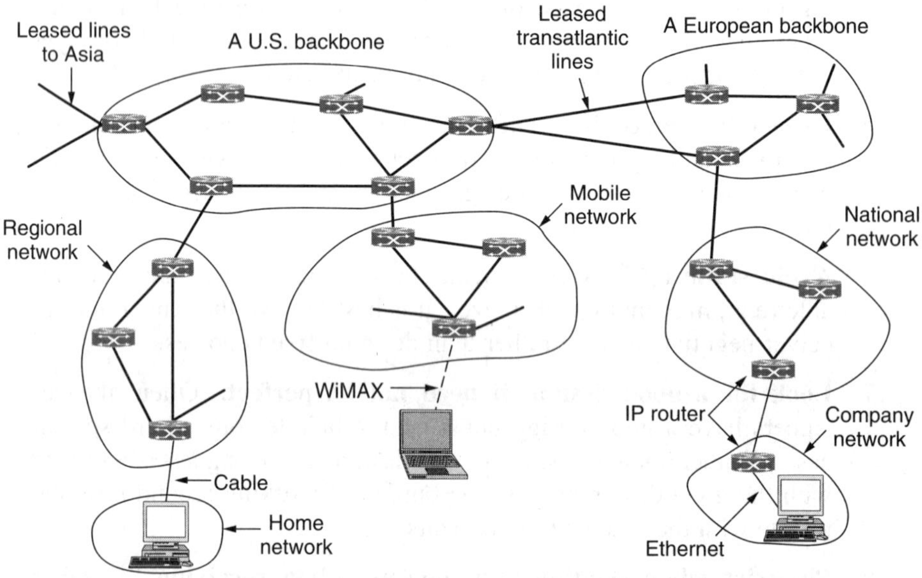

Figure 5-45. The Internet is an interconnected collection of many networks.

The glue that holds the whole Internet together is the network layer protocol, **IP (Internet Protocol)**. Unlike most older network layer protocols, IP was designed from the beginning with internetworking in mind. A good way to think of the network layer is this: its job is to provide a best-effort (i.e., not guaranteed) way to transport packets from source to destination, without regard to whether these machines are on the same network or whether there are other networks in between them.

Communication in the Internet works as follows. The transport layer takes data streams and breaks them up so that they may be sent as IP packets. In theory, packets can be up to 64 KB each, but in practice they are usually not more than 1500 bytes (so they fit in one Ethernet frame). IP routers forward each packet through the Internet, along a path from one router to the next, until the destination is reached. At the destination, the network layer hands the data to the transport layer, which gives it to the receiving process. When all the pieces finally get to the destination machine, they are reassembled by the network layer into the original datagram. This datagram is then handed to the transport layer.

In the example of Fig. 5-45, a packet originating at a host on the home network has to traverse four networks and a large number of IP routers before even getting to the company network on which the destination host is located. This is not unusual in practice, and there are many longer paths. There is also much redundant connectivity in the Internet, with backbones and ISPs connecting to each other in multiple locations. This means that there are many possible paths between two hosts. It is the job of the IP routing protocols to decide which paths to use.

5.6.1 The IP Version 4 Protocol

An appropriate place to start our study of the network layer in the Internet is with the format of the IP datagrams themselves. An IPv4 datagram consists of a header part and a body or payload part. The header has a 20-byte fixed part and a variable-length optional part. The header format is shown in Fig. 5-46. The bits are transmitted from left to right and top to bottom, with the high-order bit of the *Version* field going first. (This is a "big-endian" network byte order. On little-endian machines, such as Intel x86 computers, a software conversion is required on both transmission and reception.) In retrospect, little endian would have been a better choice, but at the time IP was designed, no one knew it would come to dominate computing.

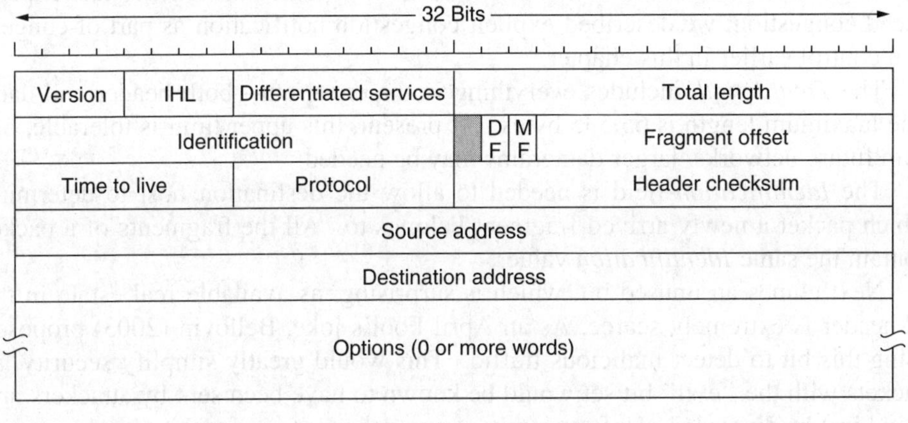

Figure 5-46. The IPv4 (Internet Protocol) header.

The *Version* field keeps track of which version of the protocol the datagram belongs to. Version 4 dominates the Internet today, and that is where we have started our discussion. By including the version at the start of each datagram, it becomes possible to have a transition between versions over a long period of time. In fact, IPv6, the next version of IP, was defined more than a decade ago, yet is only just beginning to be deployed. We will describe it later in this section. Its use will eventually be forced when each of China's almost 2^{31} people has a desktop PC, a laptop, and an IP phone. As an aside on numbering, IPv5 was an experimental real-time stream protocol that was never widely used.

Since the header length is not constant, a field in the header, *IHL*, is provided to tell how long the header is, in 32-bit words. The minimum value is 5, which applies when no options are present. The maximum value of this 4-bit field is 15, which limits the header to 60 bytes, and thus the *Options* field to 40 bytes. For some options, such as one that records the route a packet has taken, 40 bytes is far too small, making those options useless.

The *Differentiated services* field is one of the few fields that has changed its meaning (slightly) over the years. Originally, it was called the *Type of service* field. It was and still is intended to distinguish between different classes of service. Various combinations of reliability and speed are possible. For digitized voice, fast delivery beats accurate delivery. For file transfer, error-free transmission is more important than fast transmission. The *Type of service* field provided 3 bits to signal priority and 3 bits to signal whether a host cared more about delay, throughput, or reliability. However, no one really knew what to do with these bits at routers, so they were left unused for many years. When differentiated services were designed, IETF threw in the towel and reused this field. Now, the top 6 bits are used to mark the packet with its service class; we described the expedited and assured services earlier in this chapter. The bottom 2 bits are used to carry explicit congestion notification information, such as whether the packet has experienced congestion; we described explicit congestion notification as part of congestion control earlier in this chapter.

The *Total length* includes everything in the datagram—both header and data. The maximum length is 65,535 bytes. At present, this upper limit is tolerable, but with future networks, larger datagrams may be needed.

The *Identification* field is needed to allow the destination host to determine which packet a newly arrived fragment belongs to. All the fragments of a packet contain the same *Identification* value.

Next comes an unused bit, which is surprising, as available real estate in the IP header is extremely scarce. As an April Fool's joke, Bellovin (2003) proposed using this bit to detect malicious traffic. This would greatly simplify security, as packets with the "evil" bit set would be known to have been sent by attackers and could just be discarded. Unfortunately, network security is not this simple.

Then come two 1-bit fields related to fragmentation. *DF* stands for Don't Fragment. It is an order to the routers not to fragment the packet. Originally, it was intended to support hosts incapable of putting the pieces back together again. Now it is used as part of the process to discover the path MTU, which is the largest packet that can travel along a path without being fragmented. By marking the datagram with the *DF* bit, the sender knows it will either arrive in one piece, or an error message will be returned to the sender.

MF stands for More Fragments. All fragments except the last one have this bit set. It is needed to know when all fragments of a datagram have arrived.

The *Fragment offset* tells where in the current packet this fragment belongs. All fragments except the last one in a datagram must be a multiple of 8 bytes, the elementary fragment unit. Since 13 bits are provided, there is a maximum of 8192 fragments per datagram, supporting a maximum packet length up to the limit of the *Total length* field. Working together, the *Identification*, *MF*, and *Fragment offset* fields are used to implement fragmentation as described in Sec. 5.5.5.

The *TtL (Time to live)* field is a counter used to limit packet lifetimes. It was originally supposed to count time in seconds, allowing a maximum lifetime of 255 sec. It must be decremented on each hop and is supposed to be decremented multiple times when a packet is queued for a long time in a router. In practice, it just counts hops. When it hits zero, the packet is discarded and a warning packet is sent back to the source host. This feature prevents packets from wandering around forever, something that otherwise might happen if the routing tables ever become corrupted.

When the network layer has assembled a complete packet, it needs to know what to do with it. The *Protocol* field tells it which transport process to give the packet to. TCP is one possibility, but so are UDP and some others. The numbering of protocols is global across the entire Internet. Protocols and other assigned numbers were formerly listed in RFC 1700, but nowadays they are contained in an online database located at *www.iana.org*.

Since the header carries vital information such as addresses, it rates its own checksum for protection, the *Header checksum*. The algorithm is to add up all the 16-bit halfwords of the header as they arrive, using one's complement arithmetic, and then take the one's complement of the result. For purposes of this algorithm, the *Header checksum* is assumed to be zero upon arrival. Such a checksum is useful for detecting errors while the packet travels through the network. Note that it must be recomputed at each hop because at least one field always changes (the *Time to live* field), but tricks can be used to speed up the computation.

The *Source address* and *Destination address* indicate the IP address of the source and destination network interfaces. We will discuss Internet addresses in the next section.

The *Options* field was designed to provide an escape to allow subsequent versions of the protocol to include information not present in the original design, to permit experimenters to try out new ideas, and to avoid allocating header bits to information that is rarely needed. The options are of variable length. Each begins with a 1-byte code identifying the option. Some options are followed by a 1-byte option length field, and then one or more data bytes. The *Options* field is padded out to a multiple of 4 bytes. Originally, the five options listed in Fig. 5-47 were defined.

The *Security* option tells how secret the information is. In theory, a military router might use this field to specify not to route packets through certain countries the military considers to be "bad guys." In practice, all routers ignore it, so its only practical function is to help spies find the good stuff more easily.

The *Strict source routing* option gives the complete path from source to destination as a sequence of IP addresses. The datagram is required to follow that

Option	Description
Security	Specifies how secret the datagram is
Strict source routing	Gives the complete path to be followed
Loose source routing	Gives a list of routers not to be missed
Record route	Makes each router append its IP address
Timestamp	Makes each router append its address and timestamp

Figure 5-47. Some of the IP options.

exact route. It is most useful for system managers who need to send emergency packets when the routing tables have been corrupted, or for making timing measurements.

The *Loose source routing* option requires the packet to traverse the list of routers specified, in the order specified, but it is allowed to pass through other routers on the way. Normally, this option will provide only a few routers, to force a particular path. For example, to force a packet from London to Sydney to go west instead of east, this option might specify routers in New York, Los Angeles, and Honolulu. This option is most useful when political or economic considerations dictate passing through or avoiding certain countries.

The *Record route* option tells each router along the path to append its IP address to the *Options* field. This allows system managers to track down bugs in the routing algorithms ("Why are packets from Houston to Dallas visiting Tokyo first?"). When the ARPANET was first set up, no packet ever passed through more than nine routers, so 40 bytes of options was plenty. As mentioned above, now it is too small.

Finally, the *Timestamp* option is like the *Record route* option, except that in addition to recording its 32-bit IP address, each router also records a 32-bit timestamp. This option, too, is mostly useful for network measurement.

Today, IP options have fallen out of favor. Many routers ignore them or do not process them efficiently, shunting them to the side as an uncommon case. That is, they are only partly supported and they are rarely used.

5.6.2 IP Addresses

A defining feature of IPv4 is its 32-bit addresses. Every host and router on the Internet has an IP address that can be used in the *Source address* and *Destination address* fields of IP packets. It is important to note that an IP address does not actually refer to a host. It really refers to a network interface, so if a host is on two networks, it must have two IP addresses. However, in practice, most hosts are on one network and thus have one IP address. In contrast, routers have multiple interfaces and thus multiple IP addresses.

Prefixes

IP addresses are hierarchical, unlike Ethernet addresses. Each 32-bit address is comprised of a variable-length network portion in the top bits and a host portion in the bottom bits. The network portion has the same value for all hosts on a single network, such as an Ethernet LAN. This means that a network corresponds to a contiguous block of IP address space. This block is called a **prefix**.

IP addresses are written in **dotted decimal notation**. In this format, each of the 4 bytes is written in decimal, from 0 to 255. For example, the 32-bit hexadecimal address 80D00297 is written as 128.208.2.151. Prefixes are written by giving the lowest IP address in the block and the size of the block. The size is determined by the number of bits in the network portion; the remaining bits in the host portion can vary. This means that the size must be a power of two. By convention, it is written after the prefix IP address as a slash followed by the length in bits of the network portion. In our example, if the prefix contains 2^8 addresses and so leaves 24 bits for the network portion, it is written as 128.208.0.0/24.

Since the prefix length cannot be inferred from the IP address alone, routing protocols must carry the prefixes to routers. Sometimes prefixes are simply described by their length, as in a "/16" which is pronounced "slash 16." The length of the prefix corresponds to a binary mask of 1s in the network portion. When written out this way, it is called a **subnet mask**. It can be ANDed with the IP address to extract only the network portion. For our example, the subnet mask is 255.255.255.0. Fig. 5-48 shows a prefix and a subnet mask.

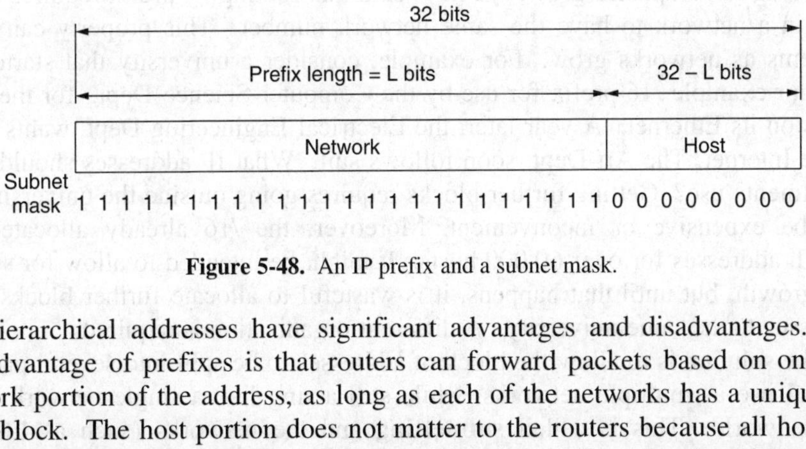

Figure 5-48. An IP prefix and a subnet mask.

Hierarchical addresses have significant advantages and disadvantages. The key advantage of prefixes is that routers can forward packets based on only the network portion of the address, as long as each of the networks has a unique address block. The host portion does not matter to the routers because all hosts on the same network will be sent in the same direction. It is only when the packets reach the network for which they are destined that they are forwarded to the correct host. This makes the routing tables much smaller than they would otherwise be. Consider that the number of hosts on the Internet is approaching one billion. That would be a very large table for every router to keep. However, by using a hierarchy, routers need to keep routes for only around 300,000 prefixes.

While using a hierarchy lets Internet routing scale, it has two disadvantages. First, the IP address of a host depends on where it is located in the network. An Ethernet address can be used anywhere in the world, but every IP address belongs to a specific network, and routers will only be able to deliver packets destined to that address to the network. Designs such as mobile IP are needed to support hosts that move between networks but want to keep the same IP addresses.

The second disadvantage is that the hierarchy is wasteful of addresses unless it is carefully managed. If addresses are assigned to networks in (too) large blocks, there will be (many) addresses that are allocated but not in use. This allocation would not matter much if there were plenty of addresses to go around. However, it was realized more than two decades ago that the tremendous growth of the Internet was rapidly depleting the free address space. IPv6 is the solution to this shortage, but until it is widely deployed there will be great pressure to allocate IP addresses so that they are used very efficiently.

Subnets

Network numbers are managed by a nonprofit corporation called **ICANN** (**Internet Corporation for Assigned Names and Numbers**), to avoid conflicts. In turn, ICANN has delegated parts of the address space to various regional authorities, which dole out IP addresses to ISPs and other companies. This is the process by which a company is allocated a block of IP addresses.

However, this process is only the start of the story, as IP address assignment is ongoing as companies grow. We have said that routing by prefix requires all the hosts in a network to have the same network number. This property can cause problems as networks grow. For example, consider a university that started out with our example /16 prefix for use by the Computer Science Dept. for the computers on its Ethernet. A year later, the Electrical Engineering Dept. wants to get on the Internet. The Art Dept. soon follows suit. What IP addresses should these departments use? Getting further blocks requires going outside the university and may be expensive or inconvenient. Moreover, the /16 already allocated has enough addresses for over 60,000 hosts. It might be intended to allow for significant growth, but until that happens, it is wasteful to allocate further blocks of IP addresses to the same university. A different organization is required.

The solution is to allow the block of addresses to be split into several parts for internal use as multiple networks, while still acting like a single network to the outside world. This is called **subnetting** and the networks (such as Ethernet LANs) that result from dividing up a larger network are called **subnets**. As we mentioned in Chap. 1, you should be aware that this new usage of the term conflicts with older usage of "subnet" to mean the set of all routers and communication lines in a network.

Fig. 5-49 shows how subnets can help with our example. The single /16 has been split into pieces. This split does not need to be even, but each piece must be aligned so that any bits can be used in the lower host portion. In this case, half of the block (a /17) is allocated to the Computer Science Dept, a quarter is allocated to the Electrical Engineering Dept. (a /18), and one eighth (a /19) to the Art Dept. The remaining eighth is unallocated. A different way to see how the block was divided is to look at the resulting prefixes when written in binary notation:

```
Computer Science:   10000000  11010000  1|xxxxxxx  xxxxxxxx
Electrical Eng.:    10000000  11010000  00|xxxxxx  xxxxxxxx
Art:                10000000  11010000  011|xxxxx  xxxxxxxx
```

Here, the vertical bar (|) shows the boundary between the subnet number and the host portion.

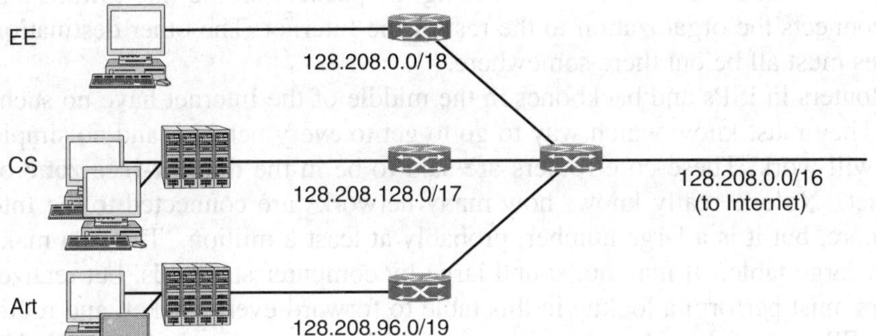

Figure 5-49. Splitting an IP prefix into separate networks with subnetting.

When a packet comes into the main router, how does the router know which subnet to give it to? This is where the details of our prefixes come in. One way would be for each router to have a table with 65,536 entries telling it which outgoing line to use for each host on campus. But this would undermine the main scaling benefit we get from using a hierarchy. Instead, the routers simply need to know the subnet masks for the networks on campus.

When a packet arrives, the router looks at the destination address of the packet and checks which subnet it belongs to. The router can do this by ANDing the destination address with the mask for each subnet and checking to see if the result is the corresponding prefix. For example, consider a packet destined for IP address 128.208.2.151. To see if it is for the Computer Science Dept., we AND with 255.255.128.0 to take the first 17 bits (which is 128.208.0.0) and see if they match the prefix address (which is 128.208.128.0). They do not match. Checking the first 18 bits for the Electrical Engineering Dept., we get 128.208.0.0 when ANDing with the subnet mask. This does match the prefix address, so the packet is forwarded onto the interface which leads to the Electrical Engineering network.

The subnet divisions can be changed later if necessary, by updating all subnet masks at routers inside the university. Outside the network, the subnetting is not visible, so allocating a new subnet does not require contacting ICANN or changing any external databases.

CIDR—Classless InterDomain Routing

Even if blocks of IP addresses are allocated so that the addresses are used efficiently, there is still a problem that remains: routing table explosion.

Routers in organizations at the edge of a network, such as a university, need to have an entry for each of their subnets, telling the router which line to use to get to that network. For routes to destinations outside of the organization, they can use the simple default rule of sending the packets on the line toward the ISP that connects the organization to the rest of the Internet. The other destination addresses must all be out there somewhere.

Routers in ISPs and backbones in the middle of the Internet have no such luxury. They must know which way to go to get to every network and no simple default will work. These core routers are said to be in the **default-free zone** of the Internet. No one really knows how many networks are connected to the Internet any more, but it is a large number, probably at least a million. This can make for a very large table. It may not sound large by computer standards, but realize that routers must perform a lookup in this table to forward every packet, and routers at large ISPs may forward up to millions of packets per second. Specialized hardware and fast memory are needed to process packets at these rates, not a general-purpose computer.

In addition, routing algorithms require each router to exchange information about the addresses it can reach with other routers. The larger the tables, the more information needs to be communicated and processed. The processing grows at least linearly with the table size. Greater communication increases the likelihood that some parts will get lost, at least temporarily, possibly leading to routing instabilities.

The routing table problem could have been solved by going to a deeper hierarchy, like the telephone network. For example, having each IP address contain a country, state/province, city, network, and host field might work. Then, each router would only need to know how to get to each country, the states or provinces in its own country, the cities in its state or province, and the networks in its city. Unfortunately, this solution would require considerably more than 32 bits for IP addresses and would use addresses inefficiently (and Liechtenstein would have as many bits in its addresses as the United States).

Fortunately, there is something we can do to reduce routing table sizes. We can apply the same insight as subnetting: routers at different locations can know about a given IP address as belonging to prefixes of different sizes. However, instead of splitting an address block into subnets, here we combine multiple small prefixes into a single larger prefix. This process is called **route aggregation**. The resulting larger prefix is sometimes called a **supernet**, to contrast with subnets as the division of blocks of addresses.

With aggregation, IP addresses are contained in prefixes of varying sizes. The same IP address that one router treats as part of a /22 (a block containing 2^{10} addresses) may be treated by another router as part of a larger /20 (which contains 2^{12} addresses). It is up to each router to have the corresponding prefix information. This design works with subnetting and is called **CIDR** (**Classless Inter-Domain Routing**), which is pronounced "cider," as in the drink. The most recent version of it is specified in RFC 4632 (Fuller and Li, 2006). The name highlights the contrast with addresses that encode hierarchy with classes, which we will describe shortly.

To make CIDR easier to understand, let us consider an example in which a block of 8192 IP addresses is available starting at 194.24.0.0. Suppose that Cambridge University needs 2048 addresses and is assigned the addresses 194.24.0.0 through 194.24.7.255, along with mask 255.255.248.0. This is a /21 prefix. Next, Oxford University asks for 4096 addresses. Since a block of 4096 addresses must lie on a 4096-byte boundary, Oxford cannot be given addresses starting at 194.24.8.0. Instead, it gets 194.24.16.0 through 194.24.31.255, along with subnet mask 255.255.240.0. Finally, the University of Edinburgh asks for 1024 addresses and is assigned addresses 194.24.8.0 through 194.24.11.255 and mask 255.255.252.0. These assignments are summarized in Fig. 5-50.

University	First address	Last address	How many	Prefix
Cambridge	194.24.0.0	194.24.7.255	2048	194.24.0.0/21
Edinburgh	194.24.8.0	194.24.11.255	1024	194.24.8.0/22
(Available)	194.24.12.0	194.24.15.255	1024	194.24.12.0/22
Oxford	194.24.16.0	194.24.31.255	4096	194.24.16.0/20

Figure 5-50. A set of IP address assignments.

All of the routers in the default-free zone are now told about the IP addresses in the three networks. Routers close to the universities may need to send on a different outgoing line for each of the prefixes, so they need an entry for each of the prefixes in their routing tables. An example is the router in London in Fig. 5-51.

Now let us look at these three universities from the point of view of a distant router in New York. All of the IP addresses in the three prefixes should be sent from New York (or the U.S. in general) to London. The routing process in London notices this and combines the three prefixes into a single aggregate entry for the prefix 194.24.0.0/19 that it passes to the New York router. This prefix contains 8K addresses and covers the three universities and the otherwise unallocated 1024 addresses. By using aggregation, three prefixes have been reduced to one, reducing

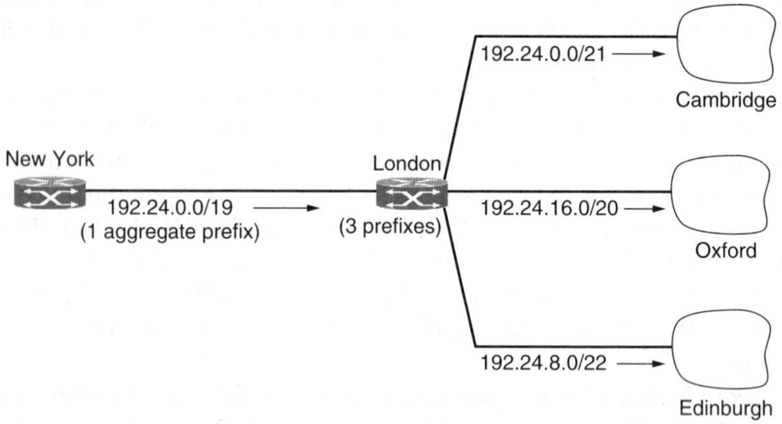

Figure 5-51. Aggregation of IP prefixes.

the prefixes that the New York router must be told about and the routing table entries in the New York router.

When aggregation is turned on, it is an automatic process. It depends on which prefixes are located where in the Internet not on the actions of an administrator assigning addresses to networks. Aggregation is heavily used throughout the Internet and can reduce the size of router tables to around 200,000 prefixes.

As a further twist, prefixes are allowed to overlap. The rule is that packets are sent in the direction of the most specific route, or the **longest matching prefix** that has the fewest IP addresses. Longest matching prefix routing provides a useful degree of flexibility, as seen in the behavior of the router at New York in Fig. 5-52. This router still uses a single aggregate prefix to send traffic for the three universities to London. However, the previously available block of addresses within this prefix has now been allocated to a network in San Francisco. One possibility is for the New York router to keep four prefixes, sending packets for three of them to London and packets for the fourth to San Francisco. Instead, longest matching prefix routing can handle this forwarding with the two prefixes that are shown. One overall prefix is used to direct traffic for the entire block to London. One more specific prefix is also used to direct a portion of the larger prefix to San Francisco. With the longest matching prefix rule, IP addresses within the San Francisco network will be sent on the outgoing line to San Francisco, and all other IP addresses in the larger prefix will be sent to London.

Conceptually, CIDR works as follows. When a packet comes in, the routing table is scanned to determine if the destination lies within the prefix. It is possible that multiple entries with different prefix lengths will match, in which case the entry with the longest prefix is used. Thus, if there is a match for a /20 mask and a /24 mask, the /24 entry is used to look up the outgoing line for the packet. However, this process would be tedious if the table were really scanned entry by entry.

Figure 5-52. Longest matching prefix routing at the New York router.

Instead, complex algorithms have been devised to speed up the address matching process (Ruiz-Sanchez et al., 2001). Commercial routers use custom VLSI chips with these algorithms embedded in hardware.

Classful and Special Addressing

To help you better appreciate why CIDR is so useful, we will briefly relate the design that predated it. Before 1993, IP addresses were divided into the five categories listed in Fig. 5-53. This allocation has come to be called **classful addressing**.

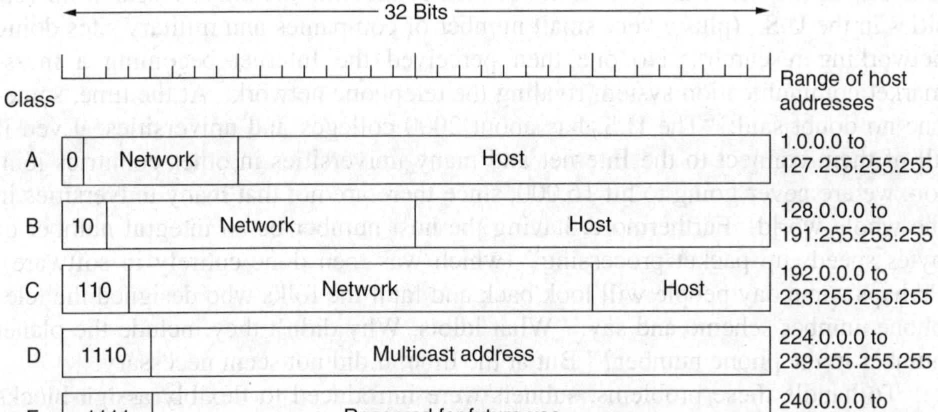

Figure 5-53. IP address formats.

The class A, B, and C formats allow for up to 128 networks with 16 million hosts each, 16,384 networks with up to 65,536 hosts each, and 2 million networks (e.g., LANs) with up to 256 hosts each (although a few of these are special). Also supported is multicast (the class D format), in which a datagram is directed to multiple hosts. Addresses beginning with 1111 are reserved for use in the future. They would be valuable to use now given the depletion of the IPv4 address space.

Unfortunately, many hosts will not accept these addresses as valid because they have been off-limits for so long and it is hard to teach old hosts new tricks.

This is a hierarchical design, but unlike CIDR the sizes of the address blocks are fixed. Over 2 billion addresses exist, but organizing the address space by classes wastes millions of them. In particular, the real villain is the class B network. For most organizations, a class A network, with 16 million addresses, is too big, and a class C network, with 256 addresses is too small. A class B network, with 65,536, is just right. In Internet folklore, this situation is known as the **three bears problem** [as in *Goldilocks and the Three Bears* (Southey, 1848)].

In reality, though, a class B address is far too large for most organizations. Studies have shown that more than half of all class B networks have fewer than 50 hosts. A class C network would have done the job, but no doubt every organization that asked for a class B address thought that one day it would outgrow the 8-bit host field. In retrospect, it might have been better to have had class C networks use 10 bits instead of 8 for the host number, allowing 1022 hosts per network. Had this been the case, most organizations would probably have settled for a class C network, and there would have been half a million of them (versus only 16,384 class B networks).

It is hard to fault the Internet's designers for not having provided more (and smaller) class B addresses. At the time the decision was made to create the three classes, the Internet was a research network connecting the major research universities in the U.S. (plus a very small number of companies and military sites doing networking research). No one then perceived the Internet becoming a mass-market communication system rivaling the telephone network. At the time, someone no doubt said: "The U.S. has about 2000 colleges and universities. Even if all of them connect to the Internet and many universities in other countries join, too, we are never going to hit 16,000, since there are not that many universities in the whole world. Furthermore, having the host number be an integral number of bytes speeds up packet processing" (which was then done entirely in software). Perhaps some day people will look back and fault the folks who designed the telephone number scheme and say: "What idiots. Why didn't they include the planet number in the phone number?" But at the time, it did not seem necessary.

To handle these problems, subnets were introduced to flexibly assign blocks of addresses within an organization. Later, CIDR was added to reduce the size of the global routing table. Today, the bits that indicate whether an IP address belongs to class A, B, or C network are no longer used, though references to these classes in the literature are still common.

To see how dropping the classes made forwarding more complicated, consider how simple it was in the old classful system. When a packet arrived at a router, a copy of the IP address was shifted right 28 bits to yield a 4-bit class number. A 16-way branch then sorted packets into A, B, C (and D and E) classes, with eight of the cases for class A, four of the cases for class B, and two of the cases for class C. The code for each class then masked off the 8-, 16-, or 24-bit network number and right aligned it in a 32-bit word. The network number was then looked up in the A, B, or C table, usually by indexing for A and B networks and hashing for C networks. Once the entry was found, the outgoing line could be looked up and the packet forwarded. This is much simpler than the longest matching prefix operation, which can no longer use a simple table lookup because an IP address may have any length prefix.

Class D addresses continue to be used in the Internet for multicast. Actually, it might be more accurate to say that they are starting to be used for multicast, since Internet multicast has not been widely deployed in the past.

There are also several other addresses that have special meanings, as shown in Fig. 5-54. The IP address 0.0.0.0, the lowest address, is used by hosts when they are being booted. It means "this network" or "this host." IP addresses with 0 as the network number refer to the current network. These addresses allow machines to refer to their own network without knowing its number (but they have to know the network mask to know how many 0s to include). The address consisting of all 1s, or 255.255.255.255—the highest address—is used to mean all hosts on the indicated network. It allows broadcasting on the local network, typically a LAN. The addresses with a proper network number and all 1s in the host field allow machines to send broadcast packets to distant LANs anywhere in the Internet. However, many network administrators disable this feature as it is mostly a security hazard. Finally, all addresses of the form 127.*xx.yy.zz* are reserved for loopback testing. Packets sent to that address are not put out onto the wire; they are processed locally and treated as incoming packets. This allows packets to be sent to the host without the sender knowing its number, which is useful for testing.

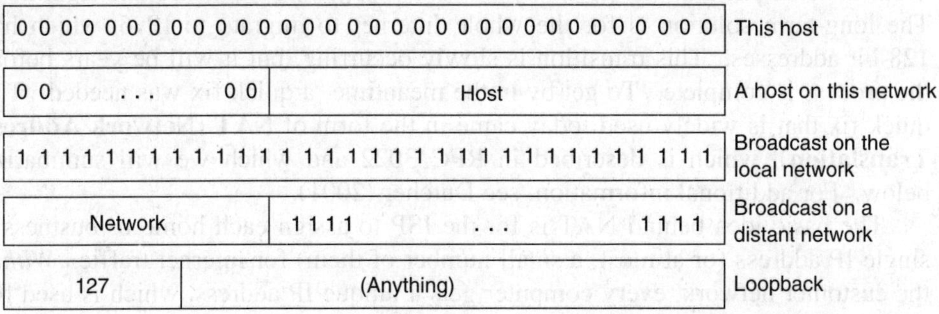

Figure 5-54. Special IP addresses.

NAT—Network Address Translation

IP addresses are scarce. An ISP might have a /16 address, giving it 65,534 usable host numbers. If it has more customers than that, it has a problem.

This scarcity has led to techniques to use IP addresses sparingly. One approach is to dynamically assign an IP address to a computer when it is on and using the network, and to take the IP address back when the host becomes inactive. The IP address can then be assigned to another computer that becomes active. In this way, a single /16 address can handle up to 65,534 active users.

This strategy works well in some cases, for example, for dialup networking and mobile and other computers that may be temporarily absent or powered off. However, it does not work very well for business customers. Many PCs in businesses are expected to be on continuously. Some are employee machines, backed up at night, and some are servers that may have to serve a remote request at a moment's notice. These businesses have an access line that always provides connectivity to the rest of the Internet.

Increasingly, this situation also applies to home users subscribing to ADSL or Internet over cable, since there is no connection charge (just a monthly flat rate charge). Many of these users have two or more computers at home, often one for each family member, and they all want to be online all the time. The solution is to connect all the computers into a home network via a LAN and put a (wireless) router on it. The router then connects to the ISP. From the ISP's point of view, the family is now the same as a small business with a handful of computers. Welcome to Jones, Inc. With the techniques we have seen so far, each computer must have its own IP address all day long. For an ISP with many thousands of customers, particularly business customers and families that are just like small businesses, the demand for IP addresses can quickly exceed the block that is available.

The problem of running out of IP addresses is not a theoretical one that might occur at some point in the distant future. It is happening right here and right now. The long-term solution is for the whole Internet to migrate to IPv6, which has 128-bit addresses. This transition is slowly occurring, but it will be years before the process is complete. To get by in the meantime, a quick fix was needed. The quick fix that is widely used today came in the form of **NAT** (**Network Address Translation**), which is described in RFC 3022 and which we will summarize below. For additional information, see Dutcher (2001).

The basic idea behind NAT is for the ISP to assign each home or business a single IP address (or at most, a small number of them) for Internet traffic. *Within* the customer network, every computer gets a unique IP address, which is used for routing intramural traffic. However, just before a packet exits the customer network and goes to the ISP, an address translation from the unique internal IP address to the shared public IP address takes place. This translation makes use of three ranges of IP addresses that have been declared as private. Networks may use them internally as they wish. The only rule is that no packets containing these addresses may appear on the Internet itself. The three reserved ranges are:

```
10.0.0.0    – 10.255.255.255/8     (16,777,216 hosts)
172.16.0.0  – 172.31.255.255/12    (1,048,576 hosts)
192.168.0.0 – 192.168.255.255/16   (65,536 hosts)
```

The first range provides for 16,777,216 addresses (except for all 0s and all 1s, as usual) and is the usual choice, even if the network is not large.

The operation of NAT is shown in Fig. 5-55. Within the customer premises, every machine has a unique address of the form 10.*x*.*y*.*z*. However, before a packet leaves the customer premises, it passes through a **NAT box** that converts the internal IP source address, 10.0.0.1 in the figure, to the customer's true IP address, 198.60.42.12 in this example. The NAT box is often combined in a single device with a firewall, which provides security by carefully controlling what goes into the customer network and what comes out of it. We will study firewalls in Chap. 8. It is also possible to integrate the NAT box into a router or ADSL modem.

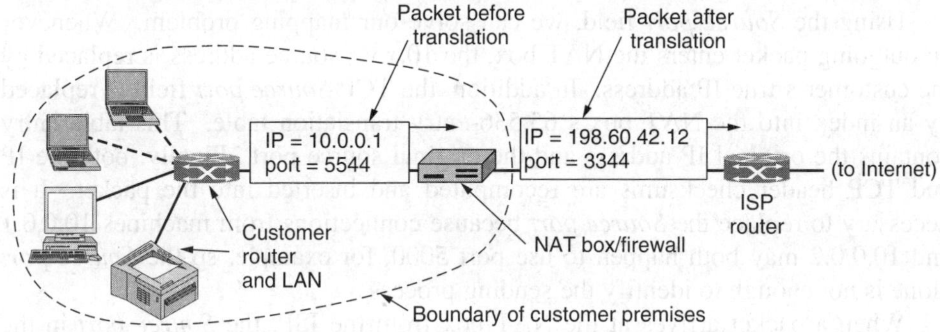

Figure 5-55. Placement and operation of a NAT box.

So far, we have glossed over one tiny but crucial detail: when the reply comes back (e.g., from a Web server), it is naturally addressed to 198.60.42.12, so how does the NAT box know which internal address to replace it with? Herein lies the problem with NAT. If there were a spare field in the IP header, that field could be used to keep track of who the real sender was, but only 1 bit is still unused. In principle, a new option could be created to hold the true source address, but doing so would require changing the IP code on all the machines on the entire Internet to handle the new option. This is not a promising alternative for a quick fix.

What actually happens is as follows. The NAT designers observed that most IP packets carry either TCP or UDP payloads. When we study TCP and UDP in Chap. 6, we will see that both of these have headers containing a source port and a destination port. Below we will just discuss TCP ports, but exactly the same story holds for UDP ports. The ports are 16-bit integers that indicate where the TCP connection begins and ends. These ports provide the field needed to make NAT work.

When a process wants to establish a TCP connection with a remote process, it attaches itself to an unused TCP port on its own machine. This is called the **source port** and tells the TCP code where to send incoming packets belonging to this connection. The process also supplies a **destination port** to tell who to give the packets to on the remote side. Ports 0–1023 are reserved for well-known services. For example, port 80 is the port used by Web servers, so remote clients can locate them. Each outgoing TCP message contains both a source port and a destination port. Together, these ports serve to identify the processes using the connection on both ends.

An analogy may make the use of ports clearer. Imagine a company with a single main telephone number. When people call the main number, they reach an operator who asks which extension they want and then puts them through to that extension. The main number is analogous to the customer's IP address and the extensions on both ends are analogous to the ports. Ports are effectively an extra 16 bits of addressing that identify which process gets which incoming packet.

Using the *Source port* field, we can solve our mapping problem. Whenever an outgoing packet enters the NAT box, the 10.*x*.*y*.*z* source address is replaced by the customer's true IP address. In addition, the TCP *Source port* field is replaced by an index into the NAT box's 65,536-entry translation table. This table entry contains the original IP address and the original source port. Finally, both the IP and TCP header checksums are recomputed and inserted into the packet. It is necessary to replace the *Source port* because connections from machines 10.0.0.1 and 10.0.0.2 may both happen to use port 5000, for example, so the *Source port* alone is not enough to identify the sending process.

When a packet arrives at the NAT box from the ISP, the *Source port* in the TCP header is extracted and used as an index into the NAT box's mapping table. From the entry located, the internal IP address and original TCP *Source port* are extracted and inserted into the packet. Then, both the IP and TCP checksums are recomputed and inserted into the packet. The packet is then passed to the customer router for normal delivery using the 10.*x*.*y*.*z* address.

Although this scheme sort of solves the problem, networking purists in the IP community have a tendency to regard it as an abomination-on-the-face-of-the-earth. Briefly summarized, here are some of the objections. First, NAT violates the architectural model of IP, which states that every IP address uniquely identifies a single machine worldwide. The whole software structure of the Internet is built on this fact. With NAT, thousands of machines may (and do) use address 10.0.0.1.

Second, NAT breaks the end-to-end connectivity model of the Internet, which says that any host can send a packet to any other host at any time. Since the mapping in the NAT box is set up by outgoing packets, incoming packets cannot be accepted until after outgoing ones. In practice, this means that a home user with NAT can make TCP/IP connections to a remote Web server, but a remote user cannot make connections to a game server on the home network. Special configuration or **NAT traversal** techniques are needed to support this kind of situation.

Third, NAT changes the Internet from a connectionless network to a peculiar kind of connection-oriented network. The problem is that the NAT box must maintain information (i.e., the mapping) for each connection passing through it.

Having the network maintain connection state is a property of connection-oriented networks, not connectionless ones. If the NAT box crashes and its mapping table is lost, all its TCP connections are destroyed. In the absence of NAT, a router can crash and restart with no long-term effect on TCP connections. The sending process just times out within a few seconds and retransmits all unacknowledged packets. With NAT, the Internet becomes as vulnerable as a circuit-switched network.

Fourth, NAT violates the most fundamental rule of protocol layering: layer k may not make any assumptions about what layer $k + 1$ has put into the payload field. This basic principle is there to keep the layers independent. If TCP is later upgraded to TCP-2, with a different header layout (e.g., 32-bit ports), NAT will fail. The whole idea of layered protocols is to ensure that changes in one layer do not require changes in other layers. NAT destroys this independence.

Fifth, processes on the Internet are not required to use TCP or UDP. If a user on machine *A* decides to use some new transport protocol to talk to a user on machine *B* (for example, for a multimedia application), introduction of a NAT box will cause the application to fail because the NAT box will not be able to locate the TCP *Source port* correctly.

A sixth and related problem is that some applications use multiple TCP/IP connections or UDP ports in prescribed ways. For example, **FTP**, the standard **File Transfer Protocol**, inserts IP addresses in the body of packet for the receiver to extract and use. Since NAT knows nothing about these arrangements, it cannot rewrite the IP addresses or otherwise account for them. This lack of understanding means that FTP and other applications such as the H.323 Internet telephony protocol (which we will study in Chap. 7) will fail in the presence of NAT unless special precautions are taken. It is often possible to patch NAT for these cases, but having to patch the code in the NAT box every time a new application comes along is not a good idea.

Finally, since the TCP *Source port* field is 16 bits, at most 65,536 machines can be mapped onto an IP address. Actually, the number is slightly less because the first 4096 ports are reserved for special uses. However, if multiple IP addresses are available, each one can handle up to 61,440 machines.

A view of these and other problems with NAT is given in RFC 2993. Despite the issues, NAT is widely used in practice, especially for home and small business networks, as the only expedient technique to deal with the IP address shortage. It has become wrapped up with firewalls and privacy because it blocks unsolicited incoming packets by default. For this reason, it is unlikely to go away even when IPv6 is widely deployed.

5.6.3 IP Version 6

IP has been in heavy use for decades. It has worked extremely well, as demonstrated by the exponential growth of the Internet. Unfortunately, IP has become a victim of its own popularity: it is close to running out of addresses. Even with CIDR and NAT using addresses more sparingly, the last IPv4 addresses are expected to be assigned by ICANN before the end of 2012. This looming disaster was recognized almost two decades ago, and it sparked a great deal of discussion and controversy within the Internet community about what to do about it.

In this section, we will describe both the problem and several proposed solutions. The only long-term solution is to move to larger addresses. **IPv6 (IP version 6)** is a replacement design that does just that. It uses 128-bit addresses; a shortage of these addresses is not likely any time in the foreseeable future. However, IPv6 has proved very difficult to deploy. It is a different network layer protocol that does not really interwork with IPv4, despite many similarities. Also, companies and users are not really sure why they should want IPv6 in any case. The result is that IPv6 is deployed and used on only a tiny fraction of the Internet (estimates are 1%) despite having been an Internet Standard since 1998. The next several years will be an interesting time, as the few remaining IPv4 addresses are allocated. Will people start to auction off their IPv4 addresses on eBay? Will a black market in them spring up? Who knows.

In addition to the address problems, other issues loom in the background. In its early years, the Internet was largely used by universities, high-tech industries, and the U.S. Government (especially the Dept. of Defense). With the explosion of interest in the Internet starting in the mid-1990s, it began to be used by a different group of people, often with different requirements. For one thing, numerous people with smart phones use it to keep in contact with their home bases. For another, with the impending convergence of the computer, communication, and entertainment industries, it may not be that long before every telephone and television set in the world is an Internet node, resulting in a billion machines being used for audio and video on demand. Under these circumstances, it became apparent that IP had to evolve and become more flexible.

Seeing these problems on the horizon, in 1990 IETF started work on a new version of IP, one that would never run out of addresses, would solve a variety of other problems, and be more flexible and efficient as well. Its major goals were:

1. Support billions of hosts, even with inefficient address allocation.
2. Reduce the size of the routing tables.
3. Simplify the protocol, to allow routers to process packets faster.
4. Provide better security (authentication and privacy).
5. Pay more attention to the type of service, particularly for real-time data.
6. Aid multicasting by allowing scopes to be specified.
7. Make it possible for a host to roam without changing its address.
8. Allow the protocol to evolve in the future.
9. Permit the old and new protocols to coexist for years.

The design of IPv6 presented a major opportunity to improve all of the features in IPv4 that fall short of what is now wanted. To develop a protocol that met all these requirements, IETF issued a call for proposals and discussion in RFC 1550. Twenty-one responses were initially received. By December 1992, seven serious proposals were on the table. They ranged from making minor patches to IP, to throwing it out altogether and replacing it with a completely different protocol.

One proposal was to run TCP over CLNP, the network layer protocol designed for OSI. With its 160-bit addresses, CLNP would have provided enough address space forever as it could give every molecule of water in the oceans enough addresses (roughly 2^5) to set up a small network. This choice would also have unified two major network layer protocols. However, many people felt that this would have been an admission that something in the OSI world was actually done right, a statement considered Politically Incorrect in Internet circles. CLNP was patterned closely on IP, so the two are not really that different. In fact, the protocol ultimately chosen differs from IP far more than CLNP does. Another strike against CLNP was its poor support for service types, something required to transmit multimedia efficiently.

Three of the better proposals were published in *IEEE Network* (Deering, 1993; Francis, 1993; and Katz and Ford, 1993). After much discussion, revision, and jockeying for position, a modified combined version of the Deering and Francis proposals, by now called **SIPP** (**Simple Internet Protocol Plus**) was selected and given the designation **IPv6.**

IPv6 meets IETF's goals fairly well. It maintains the good features of IP, discards or deemphasizes the bad ones, and adds new ones where needed. In general, IPv6 is not compatible with IPv4, but it is compatible with the other auxiliary Internet protocols, including TCP, UDP, ICMP, IGMP, OSPF, BGP, and DNS, with small modifications being required to deal with longer addresses. The main features of IPv6 are discussed below. More information about it can be found in RFCs 2460 through 2466.

First and foremost, IPv6 has longer addresses than IPv4. They are 128 bits long, which solves the problem that IPv6 set out to solve: providing an effectively unlimited supply of Internet addresses. We will have more to say about addresses shortly.

The second major improvement of IPv6 is the simplification of the header. It contains only seven fields (versus 13 in IPv4). This change allows routers to process packets faster and thus improves throughput and delay. We will discuss the header shortly, too.

The third major improvement is better support for options. This change was essential with the new header because fields that previously were required are now optional (because they are not used so often). In addition, the way options are represented is different, making it simple for routers to skip over options not intended for them. This feature speeds up packet processing time.

A fourth area in which IPv6 represents a big advance is in security. IETF had its fill of newspaper stories about precocious 12-year-olds using their personal computers to break into banks and military bases all over the Internet. There was a strong feeling that something had to be done to improve security. Authentication and privacy are key features of the new IP. These were later retrofitted to IPv4, however, so in the area of security the differences are not so great any more.

Finally, more attention has been paid to quality of service. Various half-hearted efforts to improve QoS have been made in the past, but now, with the growth of multimedia on the Internet, the sense of urgency is greater.

The Main IPv6 Header

The IPv6 header is shown in Fig. 5-56. The *Version* field is always 6 for IPv6 (and 4 for IPv4). During the transition period from IPv4, which has already taken more than a decade, routers will be able to examine this field to tell what kind of packet they have. As an aside, making this test wastes a few instructions in the critical path, given that the data link header usually indicates the network protocol for demultiplexing, so some routers may skip the check. For example, the Ethernet *Type* field has different values to indicate an IPv4 or an IPv6 payload. The discussions between the "Do it right" and "Make it fast" camps will no doubt be lengthy and vigorous.

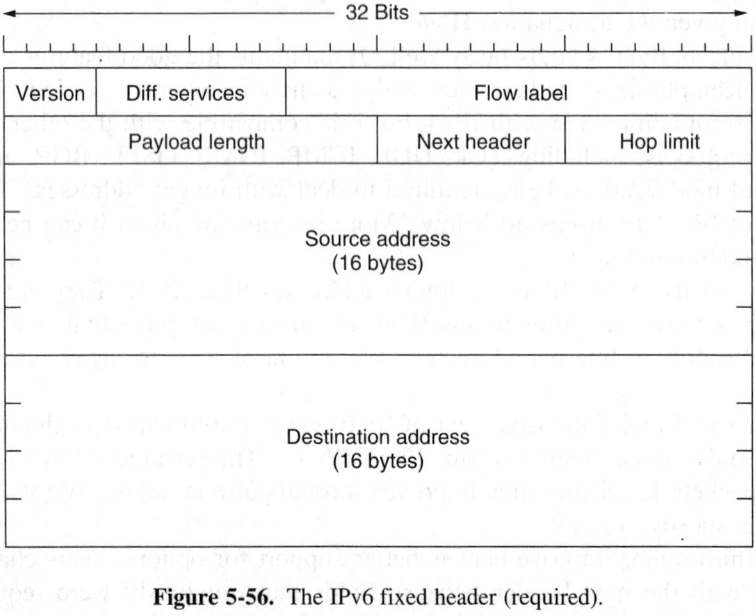

Figure 5-56. The IPv6 fixed header (required).

The *Differentiated services* field (originally called *Traffic class*) is used to distinguish the class of service for packets with different real-time delivery requirements. It is used with the differentiated service architecture for quality of service in the same manner as the field of the same name in the IPv4 packet. Also, the low-order 2 bits are used to signal explicit congestion indications, again in the same way as with IPv4.

The *Flow label* field provides a way for a source and destination to mark groups of packets that have the same requirements and should be treated in the same way by the network, forming a pseudoconnection. For example, a stream of packets from one process on a certain source host to a process on a specific destination host might have stringent delay requirements and thus need reserved bandwidth. The flow can be set up in advance and given an identifier. When a packet with a nonzero *Flow label* shows up, all the routers can look it up in internal tables to see what kind of special treatment it requires. In effect, flows are an attempt to have it both ways: the flexibility of a datagram network and the guarantees of a virtual-circuit network.

Each flow for quality of service purposes is designated by the source address, destination address, and flow number. This design means that up to 2^{20} flows may be active at the same time between a given pair of IP addresses. It also means that even if two flows coming from different hosts but with the same flow label pass through the same router, the router will be able to tell them apart using the source and destination addresses. It is expected that flow labels will be chosen randomly, rather than assigned sequentially starting at 1, so routers are expected to hash them.

The *Payload length* field tells how many bytes follow the 40-byte header of Fig. 5-56. The name was changed from the IPv4 *Total length* field because the meaning was changed slightly: the 40 header bytes are no longer counted as part of the length (as they used to be). This change means the payload can now be 65,535 bytes instead of a mere 65,515 bytes.

The *Next header* field lets the cat out of the bag. The reason the header could be simplified is that there can be additional (optional) extension headers. This field tells which of the (currently) six extension headers, if any, follow this one. If this header is the last IP header, the *Next header* field tells which transport protocol handler (e.g., TCP, UDP) to pass the packet to.

The *Hop limit* field is used to keep packets from living forever. It is, in practice, the same as the *Time to live* field in IPv4, namely, a field that is decremented on each hop. In theory, in IPv4 it was a time in seconds, but no router used it that way, so the name was changed to reflect the way it is actually used.

Next come the *Source address* and *Destination address* fields. Deering's original proposal, SIP, used 8-byte addresses, but during the review process many people felt that with 8-byte addresses IPv6 would run out of addresses within a few decades, whereas with 16-byte addresses it would never run out. Other people argued that 16 bytes was overkill, whereas still others favored using 20-byte addresses to be compatible with the OSI datagram protocol. Still another faction wanted variable-sized addresses. After much debate and more than a few words unprintable in an academic textbook, it was decided that fixed-length 16-byte addresses were the best compromise.

A new notation has been devised for writing 16-byte addresses. They are written as eight groups of four hexadecimal digits with colons between the groups, like this:

8000:0000:0000:0000:0123:4567:89AB:CDEF

Since many addresses will have many zeros inside them, three optimizations have been authorized. First, leading zeros within a group can be omitted, so 0123 can be written as 123. Second, one or more groups of 16 zero bits can be replaced by a pair of colons. Thus, the above address now becomes

8000::123:4567:89AB:CDEF

Finally, IPv4 addresses can be written as a pair of colons and an old dotted decimal number, for example:

::192.31.20.46

Perhaps it is unnecessary to be so explicit about it, but there are a lot of 16-byte addresses. Specifically, there are 2^{128} of them, which is approximately 3×10^{38}. If the entire earth, land and water, were covered with computers, IPv6 would allow 7×10^{23} IP addresses per square meter. Students of chemistry will notice that this number is larger than Avogadro's number. While it was not the intention to give every molecule on the surface of the earth its own IP address, we are not that far off.

In practice, the address space will not be used efficiently, just as the telephone number address space is not (the area code for Manhattan, 212, is nearly full, but that for Wyoming, 307, is nearly empty). In RFC 3194, Durand and Huitema calculated that, using the allocation of telephone numbers as a guide, even in the most pessimistic scenario there will still be well over 1000 IP addresses per square meter of the entire earth's surface (land and water). In any likely scenario, there will be trillions of them per square meter. In short, it seems unlikely that we will run out in the foreseeable future.

It is instructive to compare the IPv4 header (Fig. 5-46) with the IPv6 header (Fig. 5-56) to see what has been left out in IPv6. The *IHL* field is gone because the IPv6 header has a fixed length. The *Protocol* field was taken out because the *Next header* field tells what follows the last IP header (e.g., a UDP or TCP segment).

All the fields relating to fragmentation were removed because IPv6 takes a different approach to fragmentation. To start with, all IPv6-conformant hosts are expected to dynamically determine the packet size to use. They do this using the path MTU discovery procedure we described in Sec. 5.5.5. In brief, when a host sends an IPv6 packet that is too large, instead of fragmenting it, the router that is unable to forward it drops the packet and sends an error message back to the sending host. This message tells the host to break up all future packets to that destination. Having the host send packets that are the right size in the first place is ultimately much more efficient than having the routers fragment them on the fly. Also, the minimum-size packet that routers must be able to forward has been raised from 576 to 1280 bytes to allow 1024 bytes of data and many headers.

Finally, the *Checksum* field is gone because calculating it greatly reduces performance. With the reliable networks now used, combined with the fact that the data link layer and transport layers normally have their own checksums, the value of yet another checksum was deemed not worth the performance price it extracted. Removing all these features has resulted in a lean and mean network layer protocol. Thus, the goal of IPv6—a fast, yet flexible, protocol with plenty of address space—is met by this design.

Extension Headers

Some of the missing IPv4 fields are occasionally still needed, so IPv6 introduces the concept of (optional) **extension headers**. These headers can be supplied to provide extra information, but encoded in an efficient way. Six kinds of extension headers are defined at present, as listed in Fig. 5-57. Each one is optional, but if more than one is present they must appear directly after the fixed header, and preferably in the order listed.

Extension header	Description
Hop-by-hop options	Miscellaneous information for routers
Destination options	Additional information for the destination
Routing	Loose list of routers to visit
Fragmentation	Management of datagram fragments
Authentication	Verification of the sender's identity
Encrypted security payload	Information about the encrypted contents

Figure 5-57. IPv6 extension headers.

Some of the headers have a fixed format; others contain a variable number of variable-length options. For these, each item is encoded as a (*Type, Length, Value*) tuple. The *Type* is a 1-byte field telling which option this is. The *Type* values have been chosen so that the first 2 bits tell routers that do not know how to process the option what to do. The choices are: skip the option; discard the packet; discard the packet and send back an ICMP packet; and discard the packet but do not send ICMP packets for multicast addresses (to prevent one bad multicast packet from generating millions of ICMP reports).

The *Length* is also a 1-byte field. It tells how long the value is (0 to 255 bytes). The *Value* is any information required, up to 255 bytes.

The hop-by-hop header is used for information that all routers along the path must examine. So far, one option has been defined: support of datagrams exceeding 64 KB. The format of this header is shown in Fig. 5-58. When it is used, the *Payload length* field in the fixed header is set to 0.

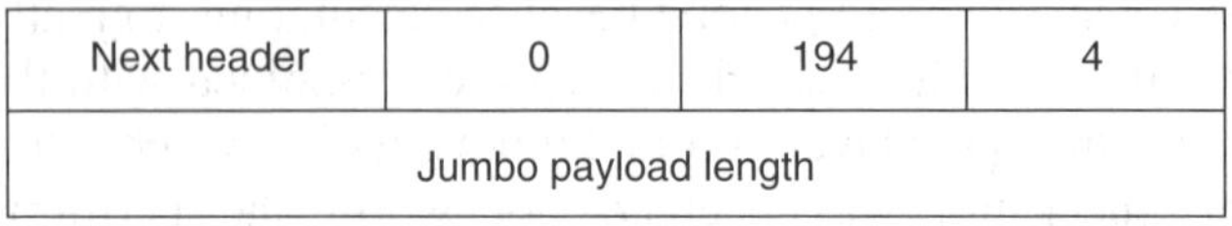

Figure 5-58. The hop-by-hop extension header for large datagrams (jumbograms).

As with all extension headers, this one starts with a byte telling what kind of header comes next. This byte is followed by one telling how long the hop-by-hop header is in bytes, excluding the first 8 bytes, which are mandatory. All extensions begin this way.

The next 2 bytes indicate that this option defines the datagram size (code 194) and that the size is a 4-byte number. The last 4 bytes give the size of the datagram. Sizes less than 65,536 bytes are not permitted and will result in the first router discarding the packet and sending back an ICMP error message. Datagrams using this header extension are called **jumbograms**. The use of jumbograms is important for supercomputer applications that must transfer gigabytes of data efficiently across the Internet.

The destination options header is intended for fields that need only be interpreted at the destination host. In the initial version of IPv6, the only options defined are null options for padding this header out to a multiple of 8 bytes, so initially it will not be used. It was included to make sure that new routing and host software can handle it, in case someone thinks of a destination option some day.

The routing header lists one or more routers that must be visited on the way to the destination. It is very similar to the IPv4 loose source routing in that all addresses listed must be visited in order, but other routers not listed may be visited in between. The format of the routing header is shown in Fig. 5-59.

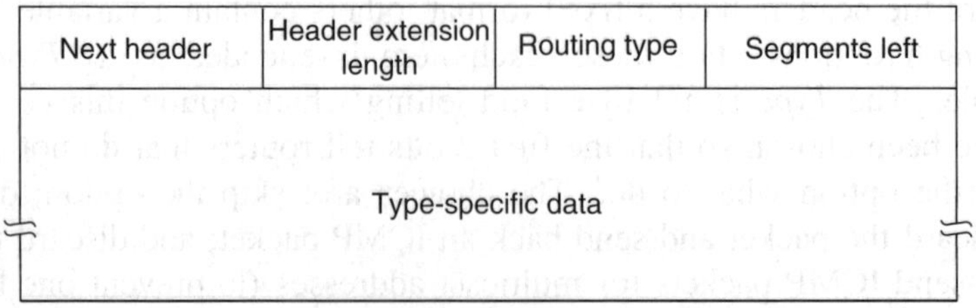

Figure 5-59. The extension header for routing.

The first 4 bytes of the routing extension header contain four 1-byte integers. The *Next header* and *Header extension length* fields were described above. The *Routing type* field gives the format of the rest of the header. Type 0 says that a reserved 32-bit word follows the first word, followed by some number of IPv6 addresses. Other types may be invented in the future, as needed. Finally, the *Segments left* field keeps track of how many of the addresses in the list have not yet been visited. It is decremented every time one is visited. When it hits 0, the packet is on its own with no more guidance about what route to follow. Usually, at this point it is so close to the destination that the best route is obvious.

The fragment header deals with fragmentation similarly to the way IPv4 does. The header holds the datagram identifier, fragment number, and a bit telling whether more fragments will follow. In IPv6, unlike in IPv4, only the source host can fragment a packet. Routers along the way may not do this. This change is a major philosophical break with the original IP, but in keeping with current practice for IPv4. Plus, it simplifies the routers' work and makes routing go faster. As mentioned above, if a router is confronted with a packet that is too big, it discards the packet and sends an ICMP error packet back to the source. This information allows the source host to fragment the packet into smaller pieces using this header and try again.

The authentication header provides a mechanism by which the receiver of a packet can be sure of who sent it. The encrypted security payload makes it possible to encrypt the contents of a packet so that only the intended recipient can read it. These headers use the cryptographic techniques that we will describe in Chap. 8 to accomplish their missions.

Controversies

Given the open design process and the strongly held opinions of many of the people involved, it should come as no surprise that many choices made for IPv6 were highly controversial, to say the least. We will summarize a few of these briefly below. For all the gory details, see the RFCs.

We have already mentioned the argument about the address length. The result was a compromise: 16-byte fixed-length addresses.

Another fight developed over the length of the *Hop limit* field. One camp felt strongly that limiting the maximum number of hops to 255 (implicit in using an 8-bit field) was a gross mistake. After all, paths of 32 hops are common now, and 10 years from now much longer paths may be common. These people argued that using a huge address size was farsighted but using a tiny hop count was shortsighted. In their view, the greatest sin a computer scientist can commit is to provide too few bits somewhere.

The response was that arguments could be made to increase every field, leading to a bloated header. Also, the function of the *Hop limit* field is to keep packets from wandering around for too long a time and 65,535 hops is far, far too long.

Finally, as the Internet grows, more and more long-distance links will be built, making it possible to get from any country to any other country in half a dozen hops at most. If it takes more than 125 hops to get from the source and the destination to their respective international gateways, something is wrong with the national backbones. The 8-bitters won this one.

Another hot potato was the maximum packet size. The supercomputer community wanted packets in excess of 64 KB. When a supercomputer gets started transferring, it really means business and does not want to be interrupted every 64 KB. The argument against large packets is that if a 1-MB packet hits a 1.5-Mbps T1 line, that packet will tie the line up for over 5 seconds, producing a very noticeable delay for interactive users sharing the line. A compromise was reached here: normal packets are limited to 64 KB, but the hop-by-hop extension header can be used to permit jumbograms.

A third hot topic was removing the IPv4 checksum. Some people likened this move to removing the brakes from a car. Doing so makes the car lighter so it can go faster, but if an unexpected event happens, you have a problem.

The argument against checksums was that any application that really cares about data integrity has to have a transport layer checksum anyway, so having another one in IP (in addition to the data link layer checksum) is overkill. Furthermore, experience showed that computing the IP checksum was a major expense in IPv4. The antichecksum camp won this one, and IPv6 does not have a checksum.

Mobile hosts were also a point of contention. If a portable computer flies halfway around the world, can it continue operating there with the same IPv6 address, or does it have to use a scheme with home agents? Some people wanted to build explicit support for mobile hosts into IPv6. That effort failed when no consensus could be found for any specific proposal.

Probably the biggest battle was about security. Everyone agreed it was essential. The war was about where to put it and how. First where. The argument for putting it in the network layer is that it then becomes a standard service that all applications can use without any advance planning. The argument against it is that really secure applications generally want nothing less than end-to-end encryption, where the source application does the encryption and the destination application undoes it. With anything less, the user is at the mercy of potentially buggy network layer implementations over which he has no control. The response to this argument is that these applications can just refrain from using the IP security features and do the job themselves. The rejoinder to that is that the people who do not trust the network to do it right do not want to pay the price of slow, bulky IP implementations that have this capability, even if it is disabled.

Another aspect of where to put security relates to the fact that many (but not all) countries have very stringent export laws concerning cryptography. Some, notably France and Iraq, also restrict its use domestically, so that people cannot have secrets from the government. As a result, any IP implementation that used a cryptographic system strong enough to be of much value could not be exported from the United States (and many other countries) to customers worldwide. Having to maintain two sets of software, one for domestic use and one for export, is something most computer vendors vigorously oppose.

One point on which there was no controversy is that no one expects the IPv4 Internet to be turned off on a Sunday evening and come back up as an IPv6 Internet Monday morning. Instead, isolated "islands" of IPv6 will be converted, initially communicating via tunnels, as we showed in Sec. 5.5.3. As the IPv6 islands grow, they will merge into bigger islands. Eventually, all the islands will merge, and the Internet will be fully converted.

At least, that was the plan. Deployment has proved the Achilles heel of IPv6. It remains little used, even though all major operating systems fully support it. Most deployments are new situations in which a network operator—for example, a mobile phone operator— needs a large number of IP addresses. Many strategies have been defined to help ease the transition. Among them are ways to automatically configure the tunnels that carry IPv6 over the IPv4 Internet, and ways for hosts to automatically find the tunnel endpoints. Dual-stack hosts have an IPv4 and an IPv6 implementation so that they can select which protocol to use depending on the destination of the packet. These strategies will streamline the substantial deployment that seems inevitable when IPv4 addresses are exhausted. For more information about IPv6, see Davies (2008).

5.6.4 Internet Control Protocols

In addition to IP, which is used for data transfer, the Internet has several companion control protocols that are used in the network layer. They include ICMP, ARP, and DHCP. In this section, we will look at each of these in turn, describing the versions that correspond to IPv4 because they are the protocols that are in common use. ICMP and DHCP have similar versions for IPv6; the equivalent of ARP is called NDP (Neighbor Discovery Protocol) for IPv6.

IMCP—The Internet Control Message Protocol

The operation of the Internet is monitored closely by the routers. When something unexpected occurs during packet processing at a router, the event is reported to the sender by the **ICMP** (**Internet Control Message Protocol**). ICMP is also used to test the Internet. About a dozen types of ICMP messages are defined. Each ICMP message type is carried encapsulated in an IP packet. The most important ones are listed in Fig. 5-60.

The DESTINATION UNREACHABLE message is used when the router cannot locate the destination or when a packet with the *DF* bit cannot be delivered because a "small-packet" network stands in the way.

Message type	Description
Destination unreachable	Packet could not be delivered
Time exceeded	Time to live field hit 0
Parameter problem	Invalid header field
Source quench	Choke packet
Redirect	Teach a router about geography
Echo and echo reply	Check if a machine is alive
Timestamp request/reply	Same as Echo, but with timestamp
Router advertisement/solicitation	Find a nearby router

Figure 5-60. The principal ICMP message types.

The TIME EXCEEDED message is sent when a packet is dropped because its *TtL (Time to live)* counter has reached zero. This event is a symptom that packets are looping, or that the counter values are being set too low.

One clever use of this error message is the **traceroute** utility that was developed by Van Jacobson in 1987. Traceroute finds the routers along the path from the host to a destination IP address. It finds this information without any kind of privileged network support. The method is simply to send a sequence of packets to the destination, first with a TtL of 1, then a TtL of 2, 3, and so on. The counters on these packets will reach zero at successive routers along the path. These routers will each obediently send a TIME EXCEEDED message back to the host. From those messages, the host can determine the IP addresses of the routers along the path, as well as keep statistics and timings on parts of the path. It is not what the TIME EXCEEDED message was intended for, but it is perhaps the most useful network debugging tool of all time.

The PARAMETER PROBLEM message indicates that an illegal value has been detected in a header field. This problem indicates a bug in the sending host's IP software or possibly in the software of a router transited.

The SOURCE QUENCH message was long ago used to throttle hosts that were sending too many packets. When a host received this message, it was expected to slow down. It is rarely used anymore because when congestion occurs, these packets tend to add more fuel to the fire and it is unclear how to respond to them. Congestion control in the Internet is now done largely by taking action in the transport layer, using packet losses as a congestion signal; we will study it in detail in Chap. 6.

The REDIRECT message is used when a router notices that a packet seems to be routed incorrectly. It is used by the router to tell the sending host to update to a better route.

The ECHO and ECHO REPLY messages are sent by hosts to see if a given destination is reachable and currently alive. Upon receiving the ECHO message, the destination is expected to send back an ECHO REPLY message. These messages are used in the **ping** utility that checks if a host is up and on the Internet.

The TIMESTAMP REQUEST and TIMESTAMP REPLY messages are similar, except that the arrival time of the message and the departure time of the reply are recorded in the reply. This facility can be used to measure network performance.

The ROUTER ADVERTISEMENT and ROUTER SOLICITATION messages are used to let hosts find nearby routers. A host needs to learn the IP address of at least one router to be able to send packets off the local network.

In addition to these messages, others have been defined. The online list is now kept at *www.iana.org/assignments/icmp-parameters*.

ARP—The Address Resolution Protocol

Although every machine on the Internet has one or more IP addresses, these addresses are not sufficient for sending packets. Data link layer NICs (Network Interface Cards) such as Ethernet cards do not understand Internet addresses. In the case of Ethernet, every NIC ever manufactured comes equipped with a unique 48-bit Ethernet address. Manufacturers of Ethernet NICs request a block of Ethernet addresses from IEEE to ensure that no two NICs have the same address (to avoid conflicts should the two NICs ever appear on the same LAN). The NICs send and receive frames based on 48-bit Ethernet addresses. They know nothing at all about 32-bit IP addresses.

The question now arises, how do IP addresses get mapped onto data link layer addresses, such as Ethernet? To explain how this works, let us use the example of Fig. 5-61, in which a small university with two /24 networks is illustrated. One network (CS) is a switched Ethernet in the Computer Science Dept. It has the prefix 192.32.65.0/24. The other LAN (EE), also switched Ethernet, is in Electrical Engineering and has the prefix 192.32.63.0/24. The two LANs are connected by an IP router. Each machine on an Ethernet and each interface on the router has a unique Ethernet address, labeled *E1* through *E6*, and a unique IP address on the CS or EE network.

Let us start out by seeing how a user on host 1 sends a packet to a user on host 2 on the CS network. Let us assume the sender knows the name of the intended receiver, possibly something like *eagle.cs.uni.edu*. The first step is to find the IP address for host 2. This lookup is performed by DNS, which we will study in Chap. 7. For the moment, we will just assume that DNS returns the IP address for host 2 (192.32.65.5).

The upper layer software on host 1 now builds a packet with 192.32.65.5 in the *Destination address* field and gives it to the IP software to transmit. The IP software can look at the address and see that the destination is on the CS network, (i.e., its own network). However, it still needs some way to find the destination's Ethernet address to send the frame. One solution is to have a configuration file somewhere in the system that maps IP addresses onto Ethernet addresses. While

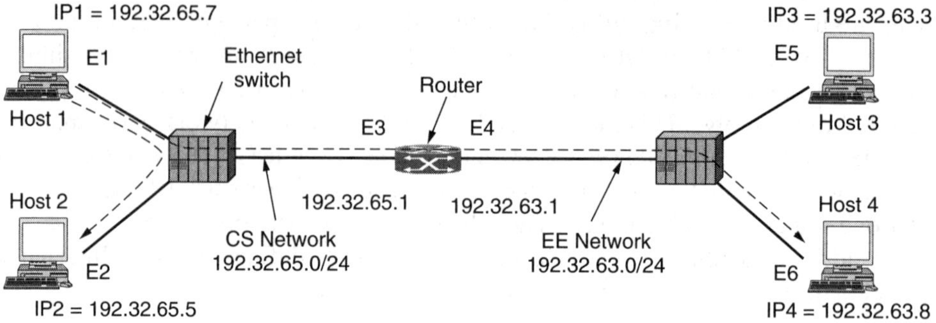

Frame	Source IP	Source Eth.	Destination IP	Destination Eth.
Host 1 to 2, on CS net	IP1	E1	IP2	E2
Host 1 to 4, on CS net	IP1	E1	IP4	E3
Host 1 to 4, on EE net	IP1	E4	IP4	E6

Figure 5-61. Two switched Ethernet LANs joined by a router.

this solution is certainly possible, for organizations with thousands of machines keeping all these files up to date is an error-prone, time-consuming job.

A better solution is for host 1 to output a broadcast packet onto the Ethernet asking who owns IP address 192.32.65.5. The broadcast will arrive at every machine on the CS Ethernet, and each one will check its IP address. Host 2 alone will respond with its Ethernet address (*E2*). In this way host 1 learns that IP address 192.32.65.5 is on the host with Ethernet address *E2*. The protocol used for asking this question and getting the reply is called **ARP (Address Resolution Protocol)**. Almost every machine on the Internet runs it. ARP is defined in RFC 826.

The advantage of using ARP over configuration files is the simplicity. The system manager does not have to do much except assign each machine an IP address and decide about subnet masks. ARP does the rest.

At this point, the IP software on host 1 builds an Ethernet frame addressed to *E2*, puts the IP packet (addressed to 192.32.65.5) in the payload field, and dumps it onto the Ethernet. The IP and Ethernet addresses of this packet are given in Fig. 5-61. The Ethernet NIC of host 2 detects this frame, recognizes it as a frame for itself, scoops it up, and causes an interrupt. The Ethernet driver extracts the IP packet from the payload and passes it to the IP software, which sees that it is correctly addressed and processes it.

Various optimizations are possible to make ARP work more efficiently. To start with, once a machine has run ARP, it caches the result in case it needs to contact the same machine shortly. Next time it will find the mapping in its own cache, thus eliminating the need for a second broadcast. In many cases, host 2 will need to send back a reply, forcing it, too, to run ARP to determine the sender's Ethernet address. This ARP broadcast can be avoided by having host 1 include its IP-to-Ethernet mapping in the ARP packet. When the ARP broadcast arrives at host 2, the pair (192.32.65.7, *E1*) is entered into host 2's ARP cache. In fact, all machines on the Ethernet can enter this mapping into their ARP caches.

To allow mappings to change, for example, when a host is configured to use a new IP address (but keeps its old Ethernet address), entries in the ARP cache should time out after a few minutes. A clever way to help keep the cached information current and to optimize performance is to have every machine broadcast its mapping when it is configured. This broadcast is generally done in the form of an ARP looking for its own IP address. There should not be a response, but a side effect of the broadcast is to make or update an entry in everyone's ARP cache. This is known as a **gratuitous ARP**. If a response does (unexpectedly) arrive, two machines have been assigned the same IP address. The error must be resolved by the network manager before both machines can use the network.

Now let us look at Fig. 5-61 again, only this time assume that host 1 wants to send a packet to host 4 (192.32.63.8) on the EE network. Host 1 will see that the destination IP address is not on the CS network. It knows to send all such off-network traffic to the router, which is also known as the **default gateway**. By convention, the default gateway is the lowest address on the network (198.31.65.1). To send a frame to the router, host 1 must still know the Ethernet address of the router interface on the CS network. It discovers this by sending an ARP broadcast for 198.31.65.1, from which it learns *E3*. It then sends the frame. The same lookup mechanisms are used to send a packet from one router to the next over a sequence of routers in an Internet path.

When the Ethernet NIC of the router gets this frame, it gives the packet to the IP software. It knows from the network masks that the packet should be sent onto the EE network where it will reach host 4. If the router does not know the Ethernet address for host 4, then it will use ARP again. The table in Fig. 5-61 lists the source and destination Ethernet and IP addresses that are present in the frames as observed on the CS and EE networks. Observe that the Ethernet addresses change with the frame on each network while the IP addresses remain constant (because they indicate the endpoints across all of the interconnected networks).

It is also possible to send a packet from host 1 to host 4 without host 1 knowing that host 4 is on a different network. The solution is to have the router answer ARPs on the CS network for host 4 and give its Ethernet address, *E3*, as the response. It is not possible to have host 4 reply directly because it will not see the ARP request (as routers do not forward Ethernet-level broadcasts). The router will then receive frames sent to 192.32.63.8 and forward them onto the EE network. This solution is called **proxy ARP**. It is used in special cases in which a host wants to appear on a network even though it actually resides on another network. A common situation, for example, is a mobile computer that wants some other node to pick up packets for it when it is not on its home network.

DHCP—The Dynamic Host Configuration Protocol

ARP (as well as other Internet protocols) makes the assumption that hosts are configured with some basic information, such as their own IP addresses. How do hosts get this information? It is possible to manually configure each computer, but that is tedious and error-prone. There is a better way, and it is called **DHCP (Dynamic Host Configuration Protocol)**.

With DHCP, every network must have a DHCP server that is responsible for configuration. When a computer is started, it has a built-in Ethernet or other link layer address embedded in the NIC, but no IP address. Much like ARP, the computer broadcasts a request for an IP address on its network. It does this by using a DHCP DISCOVER packet. This packet must reach the DHCP server. If that server is not directly attached to the network, the router will be configured to receive DHCP broadcasts and relay them to the DHCP server, wherever it is located.

When the server receives the request, it allocates a free IP address and sends it to the host in a DHCP OFFER packet (which again may be relayed via the router). To be able to do this work even when hosts do not have IP addresses, the server identifies a host using its Ethernet address (which is carried in the DHCP DISCOVER packet)

An issue that arises with automatic assignment of IP addresses from a pool is for how long an IP address should be allocated. If a host leaves the network and does not return its IP address to the DHCP server, that address will be permanently lost. After a period of time, many addresses may be lost. To prevent that from happening, IP address assignment may be for a fixed period of time, a technique called **leasing**. Just before the lease expires, the host must ask for a DHCP renewal. If it fails to make a request or the request is denied, the host may no longer use the IP address it was given earlier.

DHCP is described in RFCs 2131 and 2132. It is widely used in the Internet to configure all sorts of parameters in addition to providing hosts with IP addresses. As well as in business and home networks, DHCP is used by ISPs to set the parameters of devices over the Internet access link, so that customers do not need to phone their ISPs to get this information. Common examples of the information that is configured include the network mask, the IP address of the default gateway, and the IP addresses of DNS and time servers. DHCP has largely replaced earlier protocols (called RARP and BOOTP) with more limited functionality.

5.6.5 Label Switching and MPLS

So far, on our tour of the network layer of the Internet, we have focused exclusively on packets as datagrams that are forwarded by IP routers. There is also another kind of technology that is starting to be widely used, especially by ISPs, in order to move Internet traffic across their networks. This technology is called **MPLS** (**MultiProtocol Label Switching**) and it is perilously close to circuit switching. Despite the fact that many people in the Internet community have an intense dislike for connection-oriented networking, the idea seems to keep coming back. As Yogi Berra once put it, it is like deja vu all over again. However, there are essential differences between the way the Internet handles route construction and the way connection-oriented networks do it, so the technique is certainly not traditional circuit switching.

MPLS adds a label in front of each packet, and forwarding is based on the label rather than on the destination address. Making the label an index into an internal table makes finding the correct output line just a matter of table lookup. Using this technique, forwarding can be done very quickly. This advantage was the original motivation behind MPLS, which began as proprietary technology known by various names including **tag switching**. Eventually, IETF began to standardize the idea. It is described in RFC 3031 and many other RFCs. The main benefits over time have come to be routing that is flexible and forwarding that is suited to quality of service as well as fast.

The first question to ask is where does the label go? Since IP packets were not designed for virtual circuits, there is no field available for virtual-circuit numbers within the IP header. For this reason, a new MPLS header had to be added in front of the IP header. On a router-to-router line using PPP as the framing protocol, the frame format, including the PPP, MPLS, IP, and TCP headers, is as shown in Fig. 5-62.

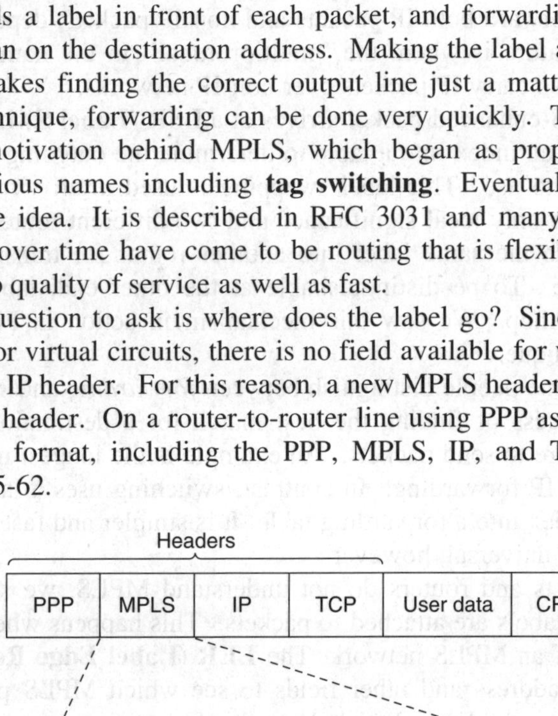

Figure 5-62. Transmitting a TCP segment using IP, MPLS, and PPP.

The generic MPLS header is 4 bytes long and has four fields. Most important is the *Label* field, which holds the index. The *QoS* field indicates the class of service. The *S* field relates to stacking multiple labels (which is discussed below). The *TtL* field indicates how many more times the packet may be forwarded. It is decremented at each router, and if it hits 0, the packet is discarded. This feature prevents infinite looping in the case of routing instability.

MPLS falls between the IP network layer protocol and the PPP link layer protocol. It is not really a layer 3 protocol because it depends on IP or other network layer addresses to set up label paths. It is not really a layer 2 protocol either because it forwards packets across multiple hops, not a single link. For this reason, MPLS is sometimes described as a layer 2.5 protocol. It is an illustration that real protocols do not always fit neatly into our ideal layered protocol model.

On the brighter side, because the MPLS headers are not part of the network layer packet or the data link layer frame, MPLS is to a large extent independent of both layers. Among other things, this property means it is possible to build MPLS switches that can forward both IP packets and non-IP packets, depending on what shows up. This feature is where the "multiprotocol" in the name MPLS came from. MPLS can also carry IP packets over non-IP networks.

When an MPLS-enhanced packet arrives at a **LSR** (**Label Switched Router**), the label is used as an index into a table to determine the outgoing line to use and also the new label to use. This label swapping is used in all virtual-circuit networks. Labels have only local significance and two different routers can feed unrelated packets with the same label into another router for transmission on the same outgoing line. To be distinguishable at the other end, labels have to be remapped at every hop. We saw this mechanism in action in Fig. 5-3. MPLS uses the same technique.

As an aside, some people distinguish between *forwarding* and *switching*. Forwarding is the process of finding the best match for a destination address in a table to decide where to send packets. An example is the longest matching prefix algorithm used for IP forwarding. In contrast, switching uses a label taken from the packet as an index into a forwarding table. It is simpler and faster. These definitions are far from universal, however.

Since most hosts and routers do not understand MPLS, we should also ask when and how the labels are attached to packets. This happens when an IP packet reaches the edge of an MPLS network. The **LER** (**Label Edge Router**) inspects the destination IP address and other fields to see which MPLS path the packet should follow, and puts the right label on the front of the packet. Within the MPLS network, this label is used to forward the packet. At the other edge of the MPLS network, the label has served its purpose and is removed, revealing the IP packet again for the next network. This process is shown in Fig. 5-63. One difference from traditional virtual circuits is the level of aggregation. It is certainly possible for each flow to have its own set of labels through the MPLS network. However, it is more common for routers to group multiple flows that end at a particular router or LAN and use a single label for them. The flows that are grouped together under a single label are said to belong to the same **FEC** (**Forwarding Equivalence Class**). This class covers not only where the packets are going, but also their service class (in the differentiated services sense) because all the packets are treated the same way for forwarding purposes.

With traditional virtual-circuit routing, it is not possible to group several distinct paths with different endpoints onto the same virtual-circuit identifier because there would be no way to distinguish them at the final destination. With MPLS,

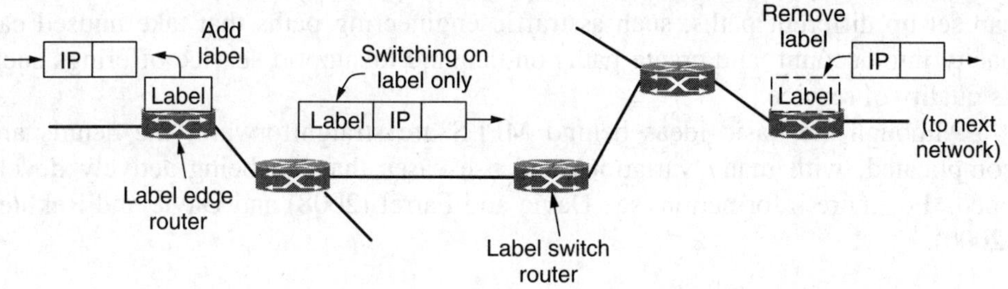

Figure 5-63. Forwarding an IP packet through an MPLS network.

the packets still contain their final destination address, in addition to the label. At the end of the labeled route, the label header can be removed and forwarding can continue the usual way, using the network layer destination address.

Actually, MPLS goes even further. It can operate at multiple levels at once by adding more than one label to the front of a packet. For example, suppose that there are many packets that already have different labels (because we want to treat the packets differently somewhere in the network) that should follow a common path to some destination. Instead of setting up many label switching paths, one for each of the different labels, we can set up a single path. When the already-labeled packets reach the start of this path, another label is added to the front. This is called a stack of labels. The outermost label guides the packets along the path. It is removed at the end of the path, and the labels revealed, if any, are used to forward the packet further. The *S* bit in Fig. 5-62 allows a router removing a label to know if there are any additional labels left. It is set to 1 for the bottom label and 0 for all the other labels.

The final question we will ask is how the label forwarding tables are set up so that packets follow them. This is one area of major difference between MPLS and conventional virtual-circuit designs. In traditional virtual-circuit networks, when a user wants to establish a connection, a setup packet is launched into the network to create the path and make the forwarding table entries. MPLS does not involve users in the setup phase. Requiring users to do anything other than send a datagram would break too much existing Internet software.

Instead, the forwarding information is set up by protocols that are a combination of routing protocols and connection setup protocols. These control protocols are cleanly separated from label forwarding, which allows multiple, different control protocols to be used. One of the variants works like this. When a router is booted, it checks to see which routes it is the final destination for (e.g., which prefixes belong to its interfaces). It then creates one or more FECs for them, allocates a label for each one, and passes the labels to its neighbors. They, in turn, enter the labels in their forwarding tables and send new labels to their neighbors, until all the routers have acquired the path. Resources can also be reserved as the path is constructed to guarantee an appropriate quality of service. Other variants can set up different paths, such as traffic engineering paths that take unused capacity into account, and create paths on-demand to support service offerings such as quality of service.

Although the basic ideas behind MPLS are straightforward, the details are complicated, with many variations and use cases that are being actively developed. For more information, see Davie and Farrel (2008) and Davie and Rekhter (2000).

5.6.6 OSPF—An Interior Gateway Routing Protocol

We have now finished our study of how packets are forwarded in the Internet. It is time to move on to the next topic: routing in the Internet. As we mentioned earlier, the Internet is made up of a large number of independent networks or **ASes** (**Autonomous Systems**) that are operated by different organizations, usually a company, university, or ISP. Inside of its own network, an organization can use its own algorithm for internal routing, or **intradomain routing**, as it is more commonly known. Nevertheless, there are only a handful of standard protocols that are popular. In this section, we will study the problem of intradomain routing and look at the OSPF protocol that is widely used in practice. An intradomain routing protocol is also called an **interior gateway protocol**. In the next section, we will study the problem of routing between independently operated networks, or **interdomain routing**. For that case, all networks must use the same interdomain routing protocol or **exterior gateway protocol**. The protocol that is used in the Internet is BGP (Border Gateway Protocol).

Early intradomain routing protocols used a distance vector design, based on the distributed Bellman-Ford algorithm inherited from the ARPANET. RIP (Routing Information Protocol) is the main example that is used to this day. It works well in small systems, but less well as networks get larger. It also suffers from the count-to-infinity problem and generally slow convergence. The ARPANET switched over to a link state protocol in May 1979 because of these problems, and in 1988 IETF began work on a link state protocol for intradomain routing. That protocol, called **OSPF** (**Open Shortest Path First**), became a standard in 1990. It drew on a protocol called **IS-IS** (**Intermediate-System to Intermediate-System**), which became an ISO standard. Because of their shared heritage, the two protocols are much more alike than different. For the complete story, see RFC 2328. They are the dominant intradomain routing protocols, and most router vendors now support both of them. OSPF is more widely used in company networks, and IS-IS is more widely used in ISP networks. Of the two, we will give a sketch of how OSPF works.

Given the long experience with other routing protocols, the group designing OSPF had a long list of requirements that had to be met. First, the algorithm had to be published in the open literature, hence the “O” in OSPF. A proprietary solution owned by one company would not do. Second, the new protocol had to support a variety of distance metrics, including physical distance, delay, and so on. Third, it had to be a dynamic algorithm, one that adapted to changes in the topology automatically and quickly.

Fourth, and new for OSPF, it had to support routing based on type of service. The new protocol had to be able to route real-time traffic one way and other traffic a different way. At the time, IP had a *Type of service* field, but no existing routing protocol used it. This field was included in OSPF but still nobody used it, and it was eventually removed. Perhaps this requirement was ahead of its time, as it preceded IETF's work on differentiated services, which has rejuvenated classes of service.

Fifth, and related to the above, OSPF had to do load balancing, splitting the load over multiple lines. Most previous protocols sent all packets over a single best route, even if there were two routes that were equally good. The other route was not used at all. In many cases, splitting the load over multiple routes gives better performance.

Sixth, support for hierarchical systems was needed. By 1988, some networks had grown so large that no router could be expected to know the entire topology. OSPF had to be designed so that no router would have to.

Seventh, some modicum of security was required to prevent fun-loving students from spoofing routers by sending them false routing information. Finally, provision was needed for dealing with routers that were connected to the Internet via a tunnel. Previous protocols did not handle this well.

OSPF supports both point-to-point links (e.g., SONET) and broadcast networks (e.g., most LANs). Actually, it is able to support networks with multiple routers, each of which can communicate directly with the others (called **multiaccess networks**) even if they do not have broadcast capability. Earlier protocols did not handle this case well.

An example of an autonomous system network is given in Fig. 5-64(a). Hosts are omitted because they do not generally play a role in OSPF, while routers and networks (which may contain hosts) do. Most of the routers in Fig. 5-64(a) are connected to other routers by point-to-point links, and to networks to reach the hosts on those networks. However, routers *R3*, *R4*, and *R5* are connected by a broadcast LAN such as switched Ethernet.

OSPF operates by abstracting the collection of actual networks, routers, and links into a directed graph in which each arc is assigned a weight (distance, delay, etc.). A point-to-point connection between two routers is represented by a pair of arcs, one in each direction. Their weights may be different. A broadcast network is represented by a node for the network itself, plus a node for each router. The arcs from that network node to the routers have weight 0. They are important nonetheless, as without them there is no path through the network. Other networks, which have only hosts, have only an arc reaching them and not one returning. This structure gives routes to hosts, but not through them.

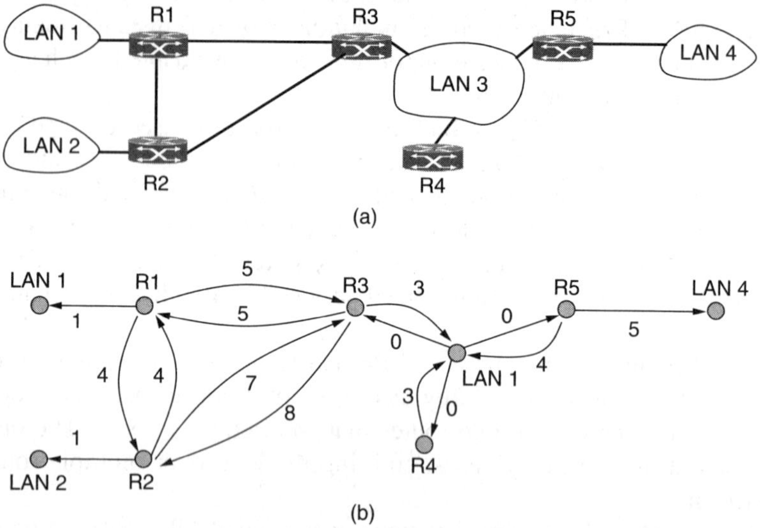

Figure 5-64. (a) An autonomous system. (b) A graph representation of (a).

Figure 5-64(b) shows the graph representation of the network of Fig. 5-64(a). What OSPF fundamentally does is represent the actual network as a graph like this and then use the link state method to have every router compute the shortest path from itself to all other nodes. Multiple paths may be found that are equally short. In this case, OSPF remembers the set of shortest paths and during packet forwarding, traffic is split across them. This helps to balance load. It is called **ECMP (Equal Cost MultiPath)**.

Many of the ASes in the Internet are themselves large and nontrivial to manage. To work at this scale, OSPF allows an AS to be divided into numbered **areas**, where an area is a network or a set of contiguous networks. Areas do not overlap but need not be exhaustive, that is, some routers may belong to no area. Routers that lie wholly within an area are called **internal routers**. An area is a generalization of an individual network. Outside an area, its destinations are visible but not its topology. This characteristic helps routing to scale.

Every AS has a **backbone area**, called area 0. The routers in this area are called **backbone routers**. All areas are connected to the backbone, possibly by tunnels, so it is possible to go from any area in the AS to any other area in the AS via the backbone. A tunnel is represented in the graph as just another arc with a cost. As with other areas, the topology of the backbone is not visible outside the backbone.

Each router that is connected to two or more areas is called an **area border router**. It must also be part of the backbone. The job of an area border router is to summarize the destinations in one area and to inject this summary into the other areas to which it is connected. This summary includes cost information but not all the details of the topology within an area. Passing cost information allows hosts in other areas to find the best area border router to use to enter an area. Not passing topology information reduces traffic and simplifies the shortest-path computations of routers in other areas. However, if there is only one border router out of an area, even the summary does not need to be passed. Routes to destinations out of the area always start with the instruction "Go to the border router." This kind of area is called a **stub area**.

The last kind of router is the **AS boundary router**. It injects routes to external destinations on other ASes into the area. The external routes then appear as destinations that can be reached via the AS boundary router with some cost. An external route can be injected at one or more AS boundary routers. The relationship between ASes, areas, and the various kinds of routers is shown in Fig. 5-65. One router may play multiple roles, for example, a border router is also a backbone router.

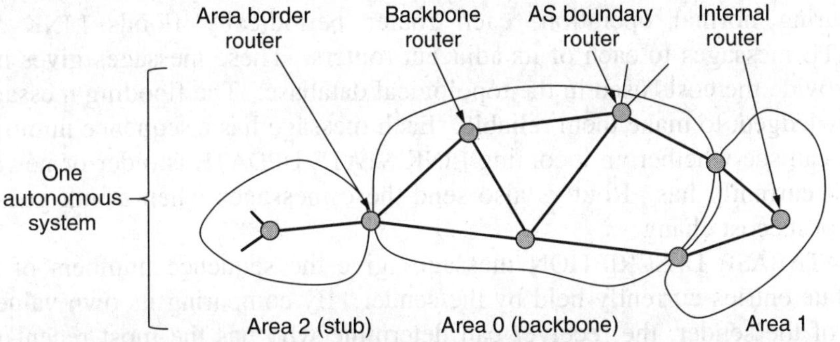

Figure 5-65. The relation between ASes, backbones, and areas in OSPF.

During normal operation, each router within an area has the same link state database and runs the same shortest path algorithm. Its main job is to calculate the shortest path from itself to every other router and network in the entire AS. An area border router needs the databases for all the areas to which it is connected and must run the shortest path algorithm for each area separately.

For a source and destination in the same area, the best intra-area route (that lies wholly within the area) is chosen. For a source and destination in different areas, the inter-area route must go from the source to the backbone, across the backbone to the destination area, and then to the destination. This algorithm forces a star configuration on OSPF, with the backbone being the hub and the other areas being spokes. Because the route with the lowest cost is chosen, routers in different parts of the network may use different area border routers to enter the backbone and destination area. Packets are routed from source to destination "as is." They are not encapsulated or tunneled (unless going to an area whose only connection to the backbone is a tunnel). Also, routes to external destinations may include the external cost from the AS boundary router over the external path, if desired, or just the cost internal to the AS.

When a router boots, it sends HELLO messages on all of its point-to-point lines and multicasts them on LANs to the group consisting of all the other routers. From the responses, each router learns who its neighbors are. Routers on the same LAN are all neighbors.

OSPF works by exchanging information between adjacent routers, which is not the same as between neighboring routers. In particular, it is inefficient to have every router on a LAN talk to every other router on the LAN. To avoid this situation, one router is elected as the **designated router**. It is said to be **adjacent** to all the other routers on its LAN, and exchanges information with them. In effect, it is acting as the single node that represents the LAN. Neighboring routers that are not adjacent do not exchange information with each other. A backup designated router is always kept up to date to ease the transition should the primary designated router crash and need to be replaced immediately.

During normal operation, each router periodically floods LINK STATE UPDATE messages to each of its adjacent routers. These messages gives its state and provide the costs used in the topological database. The flooding messages are acknowledged, to make them reliable. Each message has a sequence number, so a router can see whether an incoming LINK STATE UPDATE is older or newer than what it currently has. Routers also send these messages when a link goes up or down or its cost changes.

DATABASE DESCRIPTION messages give the sequence numbers of all the link state entries currently held by the sender. By comparing its own values with those of the sender, the receiver can determine who has the most recent values. These messages are used when a link is brought up.

Either partner can request link state information from the other one by using LINK STATE REQUEST messages. The result of this algorithm is that each pair of adjacent routers checks to see who has the most recent data, and new information is spread throughout the area this way. All these messages are sent directly in IP packets. The five kinds of messages are summarized in Fig. 5-66.

Message type	Description
Hello	Used to discover who the neighbors are
Link state update	Provides the sender's costs to its neighbors
Link state ack	Acknowledges link state update
Database description	Announces which updates the sender has
Link state request	Requests information from the partner

Figure 5-66. The five types of OSPF messages.

Finally, we can put all the pieces together. Using flooding, each router informs all the other routers in its area of its links to other routers and networks and the cost of these links. This information allows each router to construct the graph for its area(s) and compute the shortest paths. The backbone area does this work, too. In addition, the backbone routers accept information from the area border routers in order to compute the best route from each backbone router to every other router. This information is propagated back to the area border routers, which advertise it within their areas. Using this information, internal routers can select the best route to a destination outside their area, including the best exit router to the backbone.

5.6.7 BGP—The Exterior Gateway Routing Protocol

Within a single AS, OSPF and IS-IS are the protocols that are commonly used. Between ASes, a different protocol, called **BGP** (**Border Gateway Protocol**), is used. A different protocol is needed because the goals of an intradomain protocol and an interdomain protocol are not the same. All an intradomain protocol has to do is move packets as efficiently as possible from the source to the destination. It does not have to worry about politics.

In contrast, interdomain routing protocols have to worry about politics a great deal (Metz, 2001). For example, a corporate AS might want the ability to send packets to any Internet site and receive packets from any Internet site. However, it might be unwilling to carry transit packets originating in a foreign AS and ending in a different foreign AS, even if its own AS is on the shortest path between the two foreign ASes ("That's their problem, not ours"). On the other hand, it might be willing to carry transit traffic for its neighbors, or even for specific other ASes that paid it for this service. Telephone companies, for example, might be happy to act as carriers for their customers, but not for others. Exterior gateway protocols in general, and BGP in particular, have been designed to allow many kinds of routing policies to be enforced in the interAS traffic.

Typical policies involve political, security, or economic considerations. A few examples of possible routing constraints are:

1. Do not carry commercial traffic on the educational network.
2. Never send traffic from the Pentagon on a route through Iraq.
3. Use TeliaSonera instead of Verizon because it is cheaper.
4. Don't use AT&T in Australia because performance is poor.
5. Traffic starting or ending at Apple should not transit Google.

As you might imagine from this list, routing policies can be highly individual. They are often proprietary because they contain sensitive business information.

However, we can describe some patterns that capture the reasoning of the company above and that are often used as a starting point.

A routing policy is implemented by deciding what traffic can flow over which of the links between ASes. One common policy is that a customer ISP pays another provider ISP to deliver packets to any other destination on the Internet and receive packets sent from any other destination. The customer ISP is said to buy **transit service** from the provider ISP. This is just like a customer at home buying Internet access service from an ISP. To make it work, the provider should advertise routes to all destinations on the Internet to the customer over the link that connects them. In this way, the customer will have a route to use to send packets anywhere. Conversely, the customer should advertise routes only to the destinations on its network to the provider. This will let the provider send traffic to the customer only for those addresses; the customer does not want to handle traffic intended for other destinations.

We can see an example of transit service in Fig. 5-67. There are four ASes that are connected. The connection is often made with a link at **IXPs** (**Internet eXchange Points**), facilities to which many ISPs have a link for the purpose of connecting with other ISPs. *AS2*, *AS3*, and *AS4* are customers of *AS1*. They buy transit service from it. Thus, when source *A* sends to destination *C*, the packets travel from *AS2* to *AS1* and finally to *AS4*. The routing advertisements travel in the opposite direction to the packets. *AS4* advertises *C* as a destination to its transit provider, *AS1*, to let sources reach *C* via *AS1*. Later, *AS1* advertises a route to *C* to its other customers, including *AS2*, to let the customers know that they can send traffic to *C* via *AS1*.

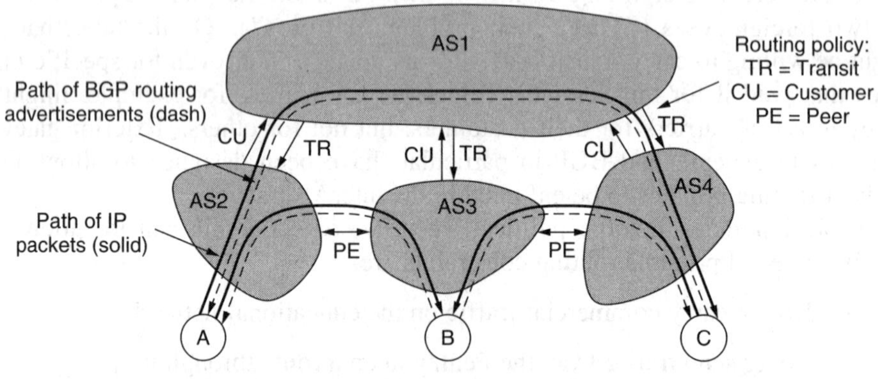

Figure 5-67. Routing policies between four autonomous systems.

In Fig. 5-67, all of the other ASes buy transit service from *AS1*. This provides them with connectivity so they can interact with any host on the Internet. However, they have to pay for this privilege. Suppose that *AS2* and *AS3* exchange a lot of traffic. Given that their networks are connected already, if they want to, they can use a different policy—they can send traffic directly to each other for free. This will reduce the amount of traffic they must have *AS1* deliver on their behalf, and hopefully it will reduce their bills. This policy is called **peering**.

To implement peering, two ASes send routing advertisements to each other for the addresses that reside in their networks. Doing so makes it possible for *AS2* to send *AS3* packets from *A* destined to *B* and vice versa. However, note that peering is not transitive. In Fig. 5-67, *AS3* and *AS4* also peer with each other. This peering allows traffic from *C* destined for *B* to be sent directly to *AS4*. What happens if *C* sends a packet to *A*? *AS3* is only advertising a route to *B* to *AS4*. It is not advertising a route to *A*. The consequence is that traffic will not pass from *AS4* to *AS3* to *AS2*, even though a physical path exists. This restriction is exactly what *AS3* wants. It peers with *AS4* to exchange traffic, but does not want to carry traffic from *AS4* to other parts of the Internet since it is not being paid to so do. Instead, *AS4* gets transit service from *AS1*. Thus, it is *AS1* who will carry the packet from *C* to *A*.

Now that we know about transit and peering, we can also see that *A*, *B*, and *C* have transit arrangements. For example, *A* must buy Internet access from *AS2*. *A* might be a single home computer or a company network with many LANs. However, it does not need to run BGP because it is a **stub network** that is connected to the rest of the Internet by only one link. So the only place for it to send packets destined outside of the network is over the link to *AS2*. There is nowhere else to go. This path can be arranged simply by setting up a default route. For this reason, we have not shown *A*, *B*, and *C* as ASes that participate in interdomain routing.

On the other hand, some company networks are connected to multiple ISPs. This technique is used to improve reliability, since if the path through one ISP fails, the company can use the path via the other ISP. This technique is called **multihoming**. In this case, the company network is likely to run an interdomain routing protocol (e.g., BGP) to tell other ASes which addresses should be reached via which ISP links.

Many variations on these transit and peering policies are possible, but they already illustrate how business relationships and control over where route advertisements go can implement different kinds of policies. Now we will consider in more detail how routers running BGP advertise routes to each other and select paths over which to forward packets.

BGP is a form of distance vector protocol, but it is quite unlike intradomain distance vector protocols such as RIP. We have already seen that policy, instead of minimum distance, is used to pick which routes to use. Another large difference is that instead of maintaining just the cost of the route to each destination, each BGP router keeps track of the path used. This approach is called a **path vector protocol**. The path consists of the next hop router (which may be on the other side of the ISP, not adjacent) and the sequence of ASes, or **AS path**, that the route has followed (given in reverse order). Finally, pairs of BGP routers communicate with each other by establishing TCP connections. Operating this way provides reliable communication and also hides all the details of the network being passed through.

An example of how BGP routes are advertised is shown in Fig. 5-68. There are three ASes and the middle one is providing transit to the left and right ISPs. A route advertisement to prefix *C* starts in *AS3*. When it is propagated across the link to *R2c* at the top of the figure, it has the AS path of simply *AS3* and the next hop router of *R3a*. At the bottom, it has the same AS path but a different next hop because it came across a different link. This advertisement continues to propagate and crosses the boundary into *AS1*. At router *R1a*, at the top of the figure, the AS path is *AS2*, *AS3* and the next hop is *R2a*.

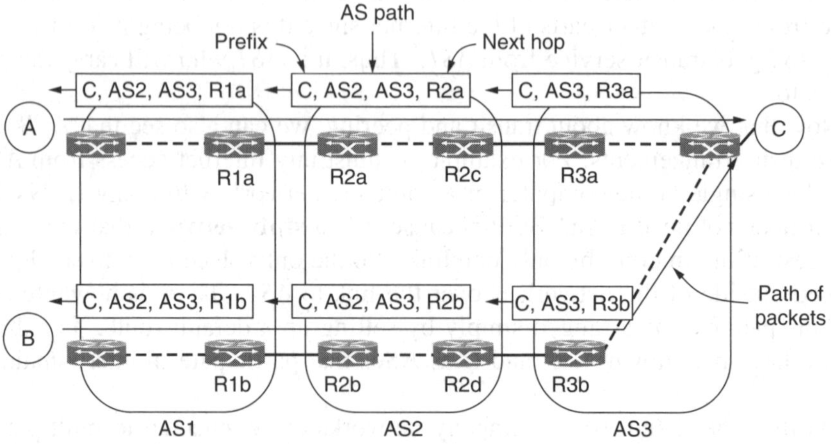

Figure 5-68. Propagation of BGP route advertisements.

Carrying the complete path with the route makes it easy for the receiving router to detect and break routing loops. The rule is that each router that sends a route outside of the AS prepends its own AS number to the route. (This is why the list is in reverse order.) When a router receives a route, it checks to see if its own AS number is already in the AS path. If it is, a loop has been detected and the advertisement is discarded. However, and somewhat ironically, it was realized in the late 1990s that despite this precaution BGP suffers from a version of the count-to-infinity problem (Labovitz et al., 2001). There are no long-lived loops, but routes can sometimes be slow to converge and have transient loops.

Giving a list of ASes is a very coarse way to specify a path. An AS might be a small company, or an international backbone network. There is no way of telling from the route. BGP does not even try because different ASes may use different intradomain protocols whose costs cannot be compared. Even if they could be compared, an AS may not want to reveal its internal metrics. This is one of the ways that interdomain routing protocols differ from intradomain protocols.

So far we have seen how a route advertisement is sent across the link between two ISPs. We still need some way to propagate BGP routes from one side of the ISP to the other, so they can be sent on to the next ISP. This task could be handled by the intradomain protocol, but because BGP is very good at scaling to large networks, a variant of BGP is often used. It is called **iBGP (internal BGP)** to distinguish it from the regular use of BGP as **eBGP (external BGP)**.

The rule for propagating routes inside an ISP is that every router at the boundary of the ISP learns of all the routes seen by all the other boundary routers, for consistency. If one boundary router on the ISP learns of a prefix to IP 128.208.0.0/16, all the other routers will learn of this prefix. The prefix will then be reachable from all parts of the ISP, no matter how packets enter the ISP from other ASes.

We have not shown this propagation in Fig. 5-68 to avoid clutter, but, for example, router *R2b* will know that it can reach *C* via either router *R2c* at top or router *R2d* at bottom. The next hop is updated as the route crosses within the ISP so that routers on the far side of the ISP know which router to use to exit the ISP on the other side. This can be seen in the leftmost routes in which the next hop points to a router in the same ISP and not a router in the next ISP.

We can now describe the key missing piece, which is how BGP routers choose which route to use for each destination. Each BGP router may learn a route for a given destination from the router it is connected to in the next ISP and from all of the other boundary routers (which have heard different routes from the routers they are connected to in other ISPs). Each router must decide which route in this set of routes is the best one to use. Ultimately the answer is that it is up to the ISP to write some policy to pick the preferred route. However, this explanation is very general and not at all satisfying, so we can at least describe some common strategies.

The first strategy is that routes via peered networks are chosen in preference to routes via transit providers. The former are free; the latter cost money. A similar strategy is that customer routes are given the highest preference. It is only good business to send traffic directly to the paying customers.

A different kind of strategy is the default rule that shorter AS paths are better. This is debatable given that an AS could be a network of any size, so a path through three small ASes could actually be shorter than a path through one big AS. However, shorter tends to be better on average, and this rule is a common tiebreaker.

The final strategy is to prefer the route that has the lowest cost within the ISP. This is the strategy implemented in Fig. 5-68. Packets sent from *A* to *C* exit *AS1* at the top router, *R1a*. Packets sent from *B* exit via the bottom router, *R1b*. The reason is that both *A* and *B* are taking the lowest-cost path or quickest route out of *AS1*. Because they are located in different parts of the ISP, the quickest exit for each one is different. The same thing happens as the packets pass through *AS2*. On the last leg, *AS3* has to carry the packet from *B* through its own network.

This strategy is known as **early exit** or **hot-potato routing**. It has the curious side effect of tending to make routes asymmetric. For example, consider the path taken when *C* sends a packet back to *B*. The packet will exit *AS3* quickly, at the top router, to avoid wasting its resources. Similarly, it will stay at the top when *AS2* passes it to *AS1* as quickly as possible. Then the packet will have a longer journey in *AS1*. This is a mirror image of the path taken from *B* to *C*.

The above discussion should make clear that each BGP router chooses its own best route from the known possibilities. It is not the case, as might naively be expected, that BGP chooses a path to follow at the AS level and OSPF chooses paths within each of the ASes. BGP and the interior gateway protocol are integrated much more deeply. This means that, for example, BGP can find the best exit point from one ISP to the next and this point will vary across the ISP, as in the case of the hot-potato policy. It also means that BGP routers in different parts of one AS may choose different AS paths to reach the same destination. Care must be exercised by the ISP to configure all of the BGP routers to make compatible choices given all of this freedom, but this can be done in practice.

Amazingly, we have only scratched the surface of BGP. For more information, see the BGP version 4 specification in RFC 4271 and related RFCs. However, realize that much of its complexity lies with policies, which are not described in the specification of the BGP protocol.

5.6.8 Internet Multicasting

Normal IP communication is between one sender and one receiver. However, for some applications, it is useful for a process to be able to send to a large number of receivers simultaneously. Examples are streaming a live sports event to many viewers, delivering program updates to a pool of replicated servers, and handling digital conference (i.e., multiparty) telephone calls.

IP supports one-to-many communication, or multicasting, using class D IP addresses. Each class D address identifies a group of hosts. Twenty-eight bits are available for identifying groups, so over 250 million groups can exist at the same time. When a process sends a packet to a class D address, a best-effort attempt is made to deliver it to all the members of the group addressed, but no guarantees are given. Some members may not get the packet.

The range of IP addresses 224.0.0.0/24 is reserved for multicast on the local network. In this case, no routing protocol is needed. The packets are multicast by simply broadcasting them on the LAN with a multicast address. All hosts on the LAN receive the broadcasts, and hosts that are members of the group process the packet. Routers do not forward the packet off the LAN. Some examples of local multicast addresses are:

224.0.0.1 All systems on a LAN
224.0.0.2 All routers on a LAN
224.0.0.5 All OSPF routers on a LAN
224.0.0.251 All DNS servers on a LAN

Other multicast addresses may have members on different networks. In this case, a routing protocol is needed. But first the multicast routers need to know which hosts are members of a group. A process asks its host to join in a specific group. It can also ask its host to leave the group. Each host keeps track of which groups its processes currently belong to. When the last process on a host leaves a group, the host is no longer a member of that group. About once a minute, each multicast router sends a query packet to all the hosts on its LAN (using the local multicast address of 224.0.0.1, of course) asking them to report back on the groups to which they currently belong. The multicast routers may or may not be colocated with the standard routers. Each host sends back responses for all the class D addresses it is interested in. These query and response packets use a protocol called **IGMP** (**Internet Group Management Protocol**). It is described in RFC 3376.

Any of several multicast routing protocols may be used to build multicast spanning trees that give paths from senders to all of the members of the group. The algorithms that are used are the ones we described in Sec. 5.2.8. Within an AS, the main protocol used is **PIM** (**Protocol Independent Multicast**). PIM comes in several flavors. In Dense Mode PIM, a pruned reverse path forwarding tree is created. This is suited to situations in which members are everywhere in the network, such as distributing files to many servers within a data center network. In Sparse Mode PIM, spanning trees that are built are similar to core-based trees. This is suited to situations such as a content provider multicasting TV to subscribers on its IP network. A variant of this design, called Source-Specific Multicast PIM, is optimized for the case that there is only one sender to the group. Finally, multicast extensions to BGP or tunnels need to be used to create multicast routes when the group members are in more than one AS.

5.6.9 Mobile IP

Many users of the Internet have mobile computers and want to stay connected when they are away from home and even on the road in between. Unfortunately, the IP addressing system makes working far from home easier said than done, as we will describe shortly. When people began demanding the ability anyway, IETF set up a Working Group to find a solution. The Working Group quickly formulated a number of goals considered desirable in any solution. The major ones were:

1. Each mobile host must be able to use its home IP address anywhere.
2. Software changes to the fixed hosts were not permitted.
3. Changes to the router software and tables were not permitted.
4. Most packets for mobile hosts should not make detours on the way.
5. No overhead should be incurred when a mobile host is at home.

The solution chosen was the one described in Sec. 5.2.10. In brief, every site that wants to allow its users to roam has to create a helper at the site called a **home agent**. When a mobile host shows up at a foreign site, it obtains a new IP address (called a care-of address) at the foreign site. The mobile then tells the home agent where it is now by giving it the care-of address. When a packet for the mobile arrives at the home site and the mobile is elsewhere, the home agent grabs the packet and tunnels it to the mobile at the current care-of address. The mobile can send reply packets directly to whoever it is communicating with, but still using its home address as the source address. This solution meets all the requirements stated above except that packets for mobile hosts do make detours.

Now that we have covered the network layer of the Internet, we can go into the solution in more detail. The need for mobility support in the first place comes from the IP addressing scheme itself. Every IP address contains a network number and a host number. For example, consider the machine with IP address 160.80.40.20/16. The 160.80 gives the network number; the 40.20 is the host number. Routers all over the world have routing tables telling which link to use to get to network 160.80. Whenever a packet comes in with a destination IP address of the form 160.80.xxx.yyy, it goes out on that line. If all of a sudden, the machine with that address is carted off to some distant site, the packets for it will continue to be routed to its home LAN (or router).

At this stage, there are two options—both unattractive. The first is that we could create a route to a more specific prefix. That is, if the distant site advertises a route to 160.80.40.20/32, packets sent to the destination will start arriving in the right place again. This option depends on the longest matching prefix algorithm that is used at routers. However, we have added a route to an IP prefix with a single IP address in it. All ISPs in the world will learn about this prefix. If everyone changes global IP routes in this way when they move their computer, each router would have millions of table entries, at astronomical cost to the Internet. This option is not workable.

The second option is to change the IP address of the mobile. True, packets sent to the home IP address will no longer be delivered until all the relevant people, programs, and databases are informed of the change. But the mobile can still use the Internet at the new location to browse the Web and run other applications. This option handles mobility at a higher layer. It is what typically happens when a user takes a laptop to a coffee store and uses the Internet via the local wireless network. The disadvantage is that it breaks some applications, and it does not keep connectivity as the mobile moves around.

As an aside, mobility can also be handled at a lower layer, the link layer. This is what happens when using a laptop on a single 802.11 wireless network. The IP address of the mobile does not change and the network path remains the same. It is the wireless link that is providing mobility. However, the degree of mobility is limited. If the laptop moves too far, it will have to connect to the Internet via another network with a different IP address.

The mobile IP solution for IPv4 is given in RFC 3344. It works with the existing Internet routing and allows hosts to stay connected with their own IP addresses as they move about. For it to work, the mobile must be able to discover when it has moved. This is accomplished with ICMP router advertisement and solicitation messages. Mobiles listen for periodic router advertisements or send a solicitation to discover the nearest router. If this router is not the usual address of the router when the mobile is at home, it must be on a foreign network. If this router has changed since last time, the mobile has moved to another foreign network. This same mechanism lets mobile hosts find their home agents.

To get a care-of IP address on the foreign network, a mobile can simply use DHCP. Alternatively, if IPv4 addresses are in short supply, the mobile can send and receive packets via a foreign agent that already has an IP address on the network. The mobile host finds a foreign agent using the same ICMP mechanism used to find the home agent. After the mobile obtains an IP address or finds a foreign agent, it is able to use the network to send a message to its home agent, informing the home agent of its current location.

The home agent needs a way to intercept packets sent to the mobile only when the mobile is not at home. ARP provides a convenient mechanism. To send a packet over an Ethernet to an IP host, the router needs to know the Ethernet address of the host. The usual mechanism is for the router to send an ARP query to ask, for example, what is the Ethernet address of 160.80.40.20. When the mobile is at home, it answers ARP queries for its IP address with its own Ethernet address. When the mobile is away, the home agent responds to this query by giving its Ethernet address. The router then sends packets for 160.80.40.20 to the home agent. Recall that this is called a proxy ARP.

To quickly update ARP mappings back and forth when the mobile leaves home or arrives back home, another ARP technique called a **gratuitous ARP** can be used. Basically, the mobile or home agent send themselves an ARP query for the mobile IP address that supplies the right answer so that the router notices and updates its mapping.

Tunneling to send a packet between the home agent and the mobile host at the care-of address is done by encapsulating the packet with another IP header destined for the care-of address. When the encapsulated packet arrives at the care-of address, the outer IP header is removed to reveal the packet.

As with many Internet protocols, the devil is in the details, and most often the details of compatibility with other protocols that are deployed. There are two complications. First, NAT boxes depend on peeking past the IP header to look at the TCP or UDP header. The original form of tunneling for mobile IP did not use these headers, so it did not work with NAT boxes. The solution was to change the encapsulation to include a UDP header.

The second complication is that some ISPs check the source IP addresses of packets to see that they match where the routing protocol believes the source should be located. This technique is called **ingress filtering**, and it is a security measure intended to discard traffic with seemingly incorrect addresses that may be malicious. However, packets sent from the mobile to other Internet hosts when it is on a foreign network will have a source IP address that is out of place, so they will be discarded. To get around this problem, the mobile can use the care-of address as a source to tunnel the packets back to the home agent. From here, they are sent into the Internet from what appears to be the right location. The cost is that the route is more roundabout.

Another issue we have not discussed is security. When a home agent gets a message asking it to please forward all of Roberta's packets to some IP address, it had better not comply unless it is convinced that Roberta is the source of this request, and not somebody trying to impersonate her. Cryptographic authentication protocols are used for this purpose. We will study such protocols in Chap. 8.

Mobility protocols for IPv6 build on the IPv4 foundation. The scheme above suffers from the triangle routing problem in which packets sent to the mobile take a dogleg through a distant home agent. In IPv6, route optimization is used to follow a direct path between the mobile and other IP addresses after the initial packets have followed the long route. Mobile IPv6 is defined in RFC 3775.

There is another kind of mobility that is also being defined for the Internet. Some airplanes have built-in wireless networking that passengers can use to connect their laptops to the Internet. The plane has a router that connects to the rest of the Internet via a wireless link. (Did you expect a wired link?) So now we have a flying router, which means that the whole network is mobile. Network mobility designs support this situation without the laptops realizing that the plane is mobile. As far as they are concerned, it is just another network. Of course, some of the laptops may be using mobile IP to keep their home addresses while they are on the plane, so we have two levels of mobility. Network mobility is defined for IPv6 in RFC 3963.

5.7 SUMMARY

The network layer provides services to the transport layer. It can be based on either datagrams or virtual circuits. In both cases, its main job is routing packets from the source to the destination. In datagram networks, a routing decision is made on every packet. In virtual-circuit networks, it is made when the virtual circuit is set up.

Many routing algorithms are used in computer networks. Flooding is a simple algorithm to send a packet along all paths. Most algorithms find the shortest path and adapt to changes in the network topology. The main algorithms are distance vector routing and link state routing. Most actual networks use one of these. Other important routing topics are the use of hierarchy in large networks, routing for mobile hosts, and broadcast, multicast, and anycast routing.

Networks can easily become congested, leading to increased delay and lost packets. Network designers attempt to avoid congestion by designing the network to have enough capacity, choosing uncongested routes, refusing to accept more traffic, signaling sources to slow down, and shedding load.

The next step beyond just dealing with congestion is to actually try to achieve a promised quality of service. Some applications care more about throughput whereas others care more about delay and jitter. The methods that can be used to provide different qualities of service include a combination of traffic shaping, reserving resources at routers, and admission control. Approaches that have been designed for good quality of service include IETF integrated services (including RSVP) and differentiated services.

Networks differ in various ways, so when multiple networks are interconnected, problems can occur. When different networks have different maximum packet sizes, fragmentation may be needed. Different networks may run different routing protocols internally but need to run a common protocol externally. Sometimes the problems can be finessed by tunneling a packet through a hostile network, but if the source and destination networks are different, this approach fails.

The Internet has a rich variety of protocols related to the network layer. These include the datagram protocol, IP, and associated control protocols such as ICMP, ARP, and DHCP. A connection-oriented protocol called MPLS carries IP packets across some networks. One of the main routing protocols used within networks is OSPF, and the routing protocol used across networks is BGP. The Internet is rapidly running out of IP addresses, so a new version of IP, IPv6, has been developed and is ever-so-slowly being deployed.

PROBLEMS

1. Give two example computer applications for which connection-oriented service is appropriate. Now give two examples for which connectionless service is best.
2. Datagram networks route each packet as a separate unit, independent of all others. Virtual-circuit networks do not have to do this, since each data packet follows a predetermined route. Does this observation mean that virtual-circuit networks do not need the capability to route isolated packets from an arbitrary source to an arbitrary destination? Explain your answer.
3. Give three examples of protocol parameters that might be negotiated when a connection is set up.
4. Assuming that all routers and hosts are working properly and that all software in both is free of all errors, is there any chance, however small, that a packet will be delivered to the wrong destination?

5. Give a simple heuristic for finding two paths through a network from a given source to a given destination that can survive the loss of any communication line (assuming two such paths exist). The routers are considered reliable enough, so it is not necessary to worry about the possibility of router crashes.

6. Consider the network of Fig. 5-12(a). Distance vector routing is used, and the following vectors have just come in to router *C*: from *B*: (5, 0, 8, 12, 6, 2); from *D*: (16, 12, 6, 0, 9, 10); and from *E*: (7, 6, 3, 9, 0, 4). The cost of the links from *C* to *B*, *D*, and *E*, are 6, 3, and 5, respectively. What is *C*'s new routing table? Give both the outgoing line to use and the cost.

7. If costs are recorded as 8-bit numbers in a 50-router network, and distance vectors are exchanged twice a second, how much bandwidth per (full-duplex) line is chewed up by the distributed routing algorithm? Assume that each router has three lines to other routers.

8. In Fig. 5-13 the Boolean OR of the two sets of ACF bits are 111 in every row. Is this just an accident here, or does it hold for all networks under all circumstances?

9. For hierarchical routing with 4800 routers, what region and cluster sizes should be chosen to minimize the size of the routing table for a three-layer hierarchy? A good starting place is the hypothesis that a solution with *k* clusters of *k* regions of *k* routers is close to optimal, which means that *k* is about the cube root of 4800 (around 16). Use trial and error to check out combinations where all three parameters are in the general vicinity of 16.

10. In the text it was stated that when a mobile host is not at home, packets sent to its home LAN are intercepted by its home agent on that LAN. For an IP network on an 802.3 LAN, how does the home agent accomplish this interception?

11. Looking at the network of Fig. 5-6, how many packets are generated by a broadcast from *B*, using

(a) reverse path forwarding?
(b) the sink tree?

12. Consider the network of Fig. 5-15(a). Imagine that one new line is added, between *F* and *G*, but the sink tree of Fig. 5-15(b) remains unchanged. What changes occur to Fig. 5-15(c)?

13. Compute a multicast spanning tree for router *C* in the following network for a group with members at routers *A*, *B*, *C*, *D*, *E*, *F*, *I*, and *K*.

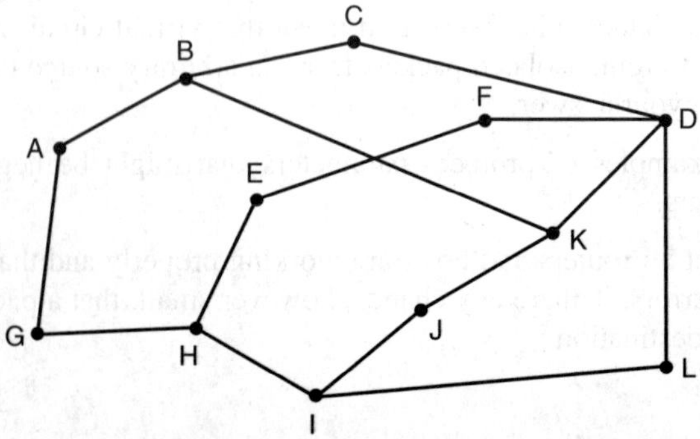

14. Suppose that node B in Fig. 5-20 has just rebooted and has no routing information in its tables. It suddenly needs a route to H. It sends out broadcasts with TtL set to 1, 2, 3, and so on. How many rounds does it take to find a route?

15. As a possible congestion control mechanism in a network using virtual circuits internally, a router could refrain from acknowledging a received packet until (1) it knows its last transmission along the virtual circuit was received successfully and (2) it has a free buffer. For simplicity, assume that the routers use a stop-and-wait protocol and that each virtual circuit has one buffer dedicated to it for each direction of traffic. If it takes T sec to transmit a packet (data or acknowledgement) and there are n routers on the path, what is the rate at which packets are delivered to the destination host? Assume that transmission errors are rare and that the host-router connection is infinitely fast.

16. A datagram network allows routers to drop packets whenever they need to. The probability of a router discarding a packet is p. Consider the case of a source host connected to the source router, which is connected to the destination router, and then to the destination host. If either of the routers discards a packet, the source host eventually times out and tries again. If both host-router and router-router lines are counted as hops, what is the mean number of

(a) hops a packet makes per transmission?
(b) transmissions a packet makes?
(c) hops required per received packet?

17. Describe two major differences between the ECN method and the RED method of congestion avoidance.

18. A token bucket scheme is used for traffic shaping. A new token is put into the bucket every 5 μsec. Each token is good for one short packet, which contains 48 bytes of data. What is the maximum sustainable data rate?

19. A computer on a 6-Mbps network is regulated by a token bucket. The token bucket is filled at a rate of 1 Mbps. It is initially filled to capacity with 8 megabits. How long can the computer transmit at the full 6 Mbps?

20. The network of Fig. 5-34 uses RSVP with multicast trees for hosts 1 and 2 as shown. Suppose that host 3 requests a channel of bandwidth 2 MB/sec for a flow from host 1 and another channel of bandwidth 1 MB/sec for a flow from host 2. At the same time, host 4 requests a channel of bandwidth 2 MB/sec for a flow from host 1 and host 5 requests a channel of bandwidth 1 MB/sec for a flow from host 2. How much total bandwidth will be reserved for these requests at routers A, B, C, E, H, J, K, and L?

21. A router can process 2 million packets/sec. The load offered to it is 1.5 million packets/sec on average. If a route from source to destination contains 10 routers, how much time is spent being queued and serviced by the router?

22. Consider the user of differentiated services with expedited forwarding. Is there a guarantee that expedited packets experience a shorter delay than regular packets? Why or why not?

23. Suppose that host *A* is connected to a router *R* 1, *R* 1 is connected to another router, *R* 2, and *R* 2 is connected to host *B*. Suppose that a TCP message that contains 900 bytes of data and 20 bytes of TCP header is passed to the IP code at host *A* for delivery to *B*. Show the *Total length, Identification*, *DF*, *MF*, and *Fragment offset* fields of the IP header in each packet transmitted over the three links. Assume that link *A-R1* can support a maximum frame size of 1024 bytes including a 14-byte frame header, link *R1-R2* can support a maximum frame size of 512 bytes, including an 8-byte frame header, and link *R2-B* can support a maximum frame size of 512 bytes including a 12-byte frame header.

24. A router is blasting out IP packets whose total length (data plus header) is 1024 bytes. Assuming that packets live for 10 sec, what is the maximum line speed the router can operate at without danger of cycling through the IP datagram ID number space?

25. An IP datagram using the *Strict source routing* option has to be fragmented. Do you think the option is copied into each fragment, or is it sufficient to just put it in the first fragment? Explain your answer.

26. Suppose that instead of using 16 bits for the network part of a class B address originally, 20 bits had been used. How many class B networks would there have been?

27. Convert the IP address whose hexadecimal representation is C22F1582 to dotted decimal notation.

28. A network on the Internet has a subnet mask of 255.255.240.0. What is the maximum number of hosts it can handle?

29. While IP addresses are tried to specific networks, Ethernet addresses are not. Can you think of a good reason why they are not?

30. A large number of consecutive IP addresses are available starting at 198.16.0.0. Suppose that four organizations, *A*, *B*, *C*, and *D*, request 4000, 2000, 4000, and 8000 addresses, respectively, and in that order. For each of these, give the first IP address assigned, the last IP address assigned, and the mask in the *w.x.y.z/s* notation.

31. A router has just received the following new IP addresses: 57.6.96.0/21, 57.6.104.0/21, 57.6.112.0/21, and 57.6.120.0/21. If all of them use the same outgoing line, can they be aggregated? If so, to what? If not, why not?

32. The set of IP addresses from 29.18.0.0 to 19.18.128.255 has been aggregated to 29.18.0.0/17. However, there is a gap of 1024 unassigned addresses from 29.18.60.0 to 29.18.63.255 that are now suddenly assigned to a host using a different outgoing line. Is it now necessary to split up the aggregate address into its constituent blocks, add the new block to the table, and then see if any reaggregation is possible? If not, what can be done instead?

33. A router has the following (CIDR) entries in its routing table:

Address/mask	**Next hop**
135.46.56.0/22	Interface 0
135.46.60.0/22	Interface 1
192.53.40.0/23	Router 1
default	Router 2

For each of the following IP addresses, what does the router do if a packet with that address arrives?

(a) 135.46.63.10
(b) 135.46.57.14
(c) 135.46.52.2
(d) 192.53.40.7
(e) 192.53.56.7

34. Many companies have a policy of having two (or more) routers connecting the company to the Internet to provide some redundancy in case one of them goes down. Is this policy still possible with NAT? Explain your answer.

35. You have just explained the ARP protocol to a friend. When you are all done, he says: "I've got it. ARP provides a service to the network layer, so it is part of the data link layer." What do you say to him?

36. Describe a way to reassemble IP fragments at the destination.

37. Most IP datagram reassembly algorithms have a timer to avoid having a lost fragment tie up reassembly buffers forever. Suppose that a datagram is fragmented into four fragments. The first three fragments arrive, but the last one is delayed. Eventually, the timer goes off and the three fragments in the receiver's memory are discarded. A little later, the last fragment stumbles in. What should be done with it?

38. In IP, the checksum covers only the header and not the data. Why do you suppose this design was chosen?

39. A person who lives in Boston travels to Minneapolis, taking her portable computer with her. To her surprise, the LAN at her destination in Minneapolis is a wireless IP LAN, so she does not have to plug in. Is it still necessary to go through the entire business with home agents and foreign agents to make email and other traffic arrive correctly?

40. IPv6 uses 16-byte addresses. If a block of 1 million addresses is allocated every picosecond, how long will the addresses last?

41. The *Protocol* field used in the IPv4 header is not present in the fixed IPv6 header. Why not?

42. When the IPv6 protocol is introduced, does the ARP protocol have to be changed? If so, are the changes conceptual or technical?

43. Write a program to simulate routing using flooding. Each packet should contain a counter that is decremented on each hop. When the counter gets to zero, the packet is discarded. Time is discrete, with each line handling one packet per time interval. Make three versions of the program: all lines are flooded, all lines except the input line are flooded, and only the (statically chosen) best k lines are flooded. Compare flooding with deterministic routing ($k = 1$) in terms of both delay and the bandwidth used.

44. Write a program that simulates a computer network using discrete time. The first packet on each router queue makes one hop per time interval. Each router has only a finite number of buffers. If a packet arrives and there is no room for it, it is discarded and not retransmitted. Instead, there is an end-to-end protocol, complete with timeouts and acknowledgement packets, that eventually regenerates the packet from the source router. Plot the throughput of the network as a function of the end-to-end timeout interval, parameterized by error rate.

45. Write a function to do forwarding in an IP router. The procedure has one parameter, an IP address. It also has access to a global table consisting of an array of triples. Each triple contains three integers: an IP address, a subnet mask, and the outline line to use. The function looks up the IP address in the table using CIDR and returns the line to use as its value.

46. Use the *traceroute* (UNIX) or *tracert* (Windows) programs to trace the route from your computer to various universities on other continents. Make a list of transoceanic links you have discovered. Some sites to try are

www.berkeley.edu (California)
www.mit.edu (Massachusetts)
www.vu.nl (Amsterdam)
www.ucl.ac.uk (London)
www.usyd.edu.au (Sydney)
www.u-tokyo.ac.jp (Tokyo)
www.uct.ac.za (Cape Town)

6

THE TRANSPORT LAYER

Together with the network layer, the transport layer is the heart of the protocol hierarchy. The network layer provides end-to-end packet delivery using datagrams or virtual circuits. The transport layer builds on the network layer to provide data transport from a process on a source machine to a process on a destination machine with a desired level of reliability that is independent of the physical networks currently in use. It provides the abstractions that applications need to use the network. Without the transport layer, the whole concept of layered protocols would make little sense. In this chapter, we will study the transport layer in detail, including its services and choice of API design to tackle issues of reliability, connections and congestion control, protocols such as TCP and UDP, and performance.

6.1 THE TRANSPORT SERVICE

In the following sections, we will provide an introduction to the transport service. We look at what kind of service is provided to the application layer. To make the issue of transport service more concrete, we will examine two sets of transport layer primitives. First comes a simple (but hypothetical) one to show the basic ideas. Then comes the interface commonly used in the Internet.

6.1.1 Services Provided to the Upper Layers

The ultimate goal of the transport layer is to provide efficient, reliable, and cost-effective data transmission service to its users, normally processes in the application layer. To achieve this, the transport layer makes use of the services provided by the network layer. The software and/or hardware within the transport layer that does the work is called the **transport entity**. The transport entity can be located in the operating system kernel, in a library package bound into network applications, in a separate user process, or even on the network interface card. The first two options are most common on the Internet. The (logical) relationship of the network, transport, and application layers is illustrated in Fig. 6-1.

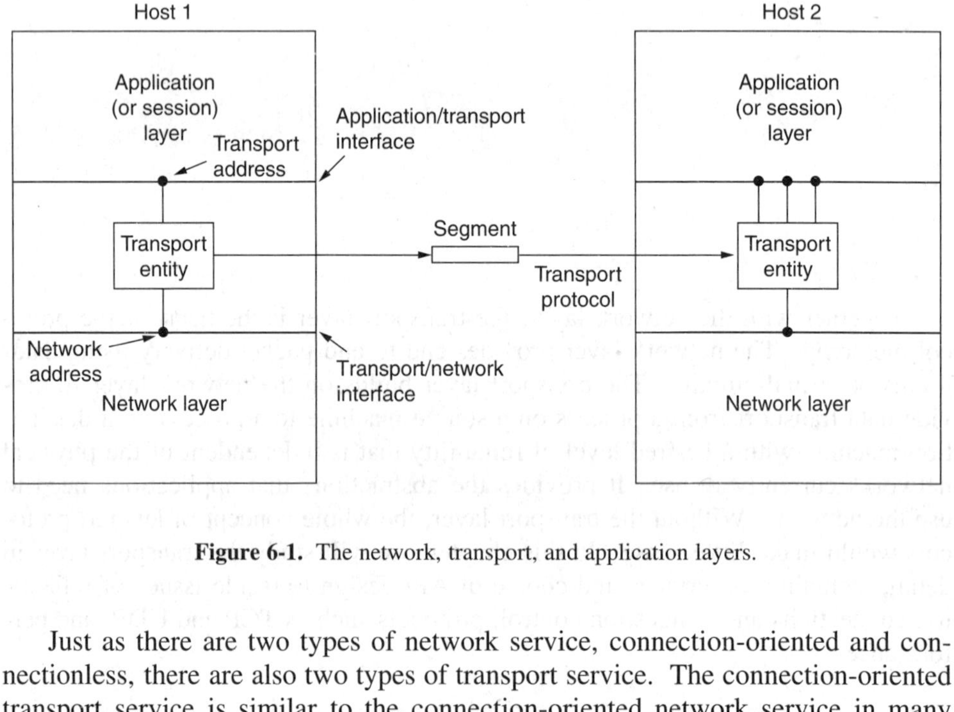

Figure 6-1. The network, transport, and application layers.

Just as there are two types of network service, connection-oriented and connectionless, there are also two types of transport service. The connection-oriented transport service is similar to the connection-oriented network service in many ways. In both cases, connections have three phases: establishment, data transfer, and release. Addressing and flow control are also similar in both layers. Furthermore, the connectionless transport service is also very similar to the connectionless network service. However, note that it can be difficult to provide a connectionless transport service on top of a connection-oriented network service, since it is inefficient to set up a connection to send a single packet and then tear it down immediately afterwards.

The obvious question is this: if the transport layer service is so similar to the network layer service, why are there two distinct layers? Why is one layer not adequate? The answer is subtle, but crucial. The transport code runs entirely on the users' machines, but the network layer mostly runs on the routers, which are operated by the carrier (at least for a wide area network). What happens if the network layer offers inadequate service? What if it frequently loses packets? What happens if routers crash from time to time?

Problems occur, that's what. The users have no real control over the network layer, so they cannot solve the problem of poor service by using better routers or putting more error handling in the data link layer because they don't own the routers. The only possibility is to put on top of the network layer another layer that improves the quality of the service. If, in a connectionless network, packets are lost or mangled, the transport entity can detect the problem and compensate for it by using retransmissions. If, in a connection-oriented network, a transport entity is informed halfway through a long transmission that its network connection has been abruptly terminated, with no indication of what has happened to the data currently in transit, it can set up a new network connection to the remote transport entity. Using this new network connection, it can send a query to its peer asking which data arrived and which did not, and knowing where it was, pick up from where it left off.

In essence, the existence of the transport layer makes it possible for the transport service to be more reliable than the underlying network. Furthermore, the transport primitives can be implemented as calls to library procedures to make them independent of the network primitives. The network service calls may vary considerably from one network to another (e.g., calls based on a connectionless Ethernet may be quite different from calls on a connection-oriented WiMAX network). Hiding the network service behind a set of transport service primitives ensures that changing the network merely requires replacing one set of library procedures with another one that does the same thing with a different underlying service.

Thanks to the transport layer, application programmers can write code according to a standard set of primitives and have these programs work on a wide variety of networks, without having to worry about dealing with different network interfaces and levels of reliability. If all real networks were flawless and all had the same service primitives and were guaranteed never, ever to change, the transport layer might not be needed. However, in the real world it fulfills the key function of isolating the upper layers from the technology, design, and imperfections of the network.

For this reason, many people have made a qualitative distinction between layers 1 through 4 on the one hand and layer(s) above 4 on the other. The bottom four layers can be seen as the **transport service provider**, whereas the upper layer(s) are the **transport service user**. This distinction of provider versus user has a considerable impact on the design of the layers and puts the transport layer in a key position, since it forms the major boundary between the provider and user of the reliable data transmission service. It is the level that applications see.

6.1.2 Transport Service Primitives

To allow users to access the transport service, the transport layer must provide some operations to application programs, that is, a transport service interface. Each transport service has its own interface. In this section, we will first examine a simple (hypothetical) transport service and its interface to see the bare essentials. In the following section, we will look at a real example.

The transport service is similar to the network service, but there are also some important differences. The main difference is that the network service is intended to model the service offered by real networks, warts and all. Real networks can lose packets, so the network service is generally unreliable.

The connection-oriented transport service, in contrast, is reliable. Of course, real networks are not error-free, but that is precisely the purpose of the transport layer—to provide a reliable service on top of an unreliable network.

As an example, consider two processes on a single machine connected by a pipe in UNIX (or any other interprocess communication facility). They assume the connection between them is 100% perfect. They do not want to know about acknowledgements, lost packets, congestion, or anything at all like that. What they want is a 100% reliable connection. Process *A* puts data into one end of the pipe, and process *B* takes it out of the other. This is what the connection-oriented transport service is all about—hiding the imperfections of the network service so that user processes can just assume the existence of an error-free bit stream even when they are on different machines.

As an aside, the transport layer can also provide unreliable (datagram) service. However, there is relatively little to say about that besides "it's datagrams," so we will mainly concentrate on the connection-oriented transport service in this chapter. Nevertheless, there are some applications, such as client-server computing and streaming multimedia, that build on a connectionless transport service, and we will say a little bit about that later on.

A second difference between the network service and transport service is whom the services are intended for. The network service is used only by the transport entities. Few users write their own transport entities, and thus few users or programs ever see the bare network service. In contrast, many programs (and thus programmers) see the transport primitives. Consequently, the transport service must be convenient and easy to use.

To get an idea of what a transport service might be like, consider the five primitives listed in Fig. 6-2. This transport interface is truly bare bones, but it gives the essential flavor of what a connection-oriented transport interface has to do. It allows application programs to establish, use, and then release connections, which is sufficient for many applications.

To see how these primitives might be used, consider an application with a server and a number of remote clients. To start with, the server executes a LISTEN primitive, typically by calling a library procedure that makes a system call that

Primitive	Packet sent	Meaning
LISTEN	(none)	Block until some process tries to connect
CONNECT	CONNECTION REQ.	Actively attempt to establish a connection
SEND	DATA	Send information
RECEIVE	(none)	Block until a DATA packet arrives
DISCONNECT	DISCONNECTION REQ.	Request a release of the connection

Figure 6-2. The primitives for a simple transport service.

blocks the server until a client turns up. When a client wants to talk to the server, it executes a CONNECT primitive. The transport entity carries out this primitive by blocking the caller and sending a packet to the server. Encapsulated in the payload of this packet is a transport layer message for the server's transport entity.

A quick note on terminology is now in order. For lack of a better term, we will use the term **segment** for messages sent from transport entity to transport entity. TCP, UDP and other Internet protocols use this term. Some older protocols used the ungainly name **TPDU (Transport Protocol Data Unit)**. That term is not used much any more now but you may see it in older papers and books.

Thus, segments (exchanged by the transport layer) are contained in packets (exchanged by the network layer). In turn, these packets are contained in frames (exchanged by the data link layer). When a frame arrives, the data link layer processes the frame header and, if the destination address matches for local delivery, passes the contents of the frame payload field up to the network entity. The network entity similarly processes the packet header and then passes the contents of the packet payload up to the transport entity. This nesting is illustrated in Fig. 6-3.

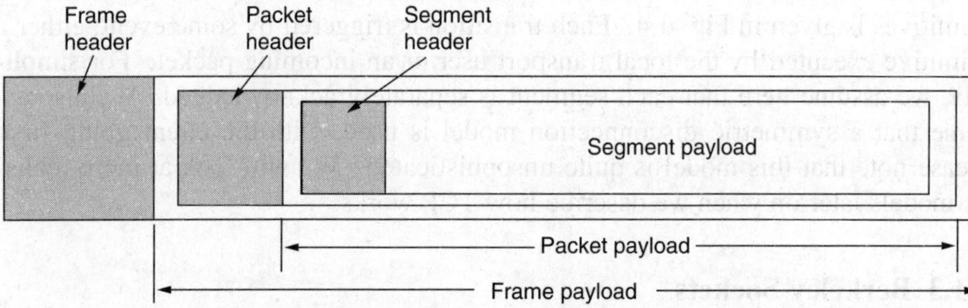

Figure 6-3. Nesting of segments, packets, and frames.

Getting back to our client-server example, the client's CONNECT call causes a CONNECTION REQUEST segment to be sent to the server. When it arrives, the transport entity checks to see that the server is blocked on a LISTEN (i.e., is interested in handling requests). If so, it then unblocks the server and sends a CONNECTION ACCEPTED segment back to the client. When this segment arrives, the client is unblocked and the connection is established.

Data can now be exchanged using the SEND and RECEIVE primitives. In the simplest form, either party can do a (blocking) RECEIVE to wait for the other party to do a SEND. When the segment arrives, the receiver is unblocked. It can then process the segment and send a reply. As long as both sides can keep track of whose turn it is to send, this scheme works fine.

Note that in the transport layer, even a simple unidirectional data exchange is more complicated than at the network layer. Every data packet sent will also be acknowledged (eventually). The packets bearing control segments are also acknowledged, implicitly or explicitly. These acknowledgements are managed by the transport entities, using the network layer protocol, and are not visible to the transport users. Similarly, the transport entities need to worry about timers and retransmissions. None of this machinery is visible to the transport users. To the transport users, a connection is a reliable bit pipe: one user stuffs bits in and they magically appear in the same order at the other end. This ability to hide complexity is the reason that layered protocols are such a powerful tool.

When a connection is no longer needed, it must be released to free up table space within the two transport entities. Disconnection has two variants: asymmetric and symmetric. In the asymmetric variant, either transport user can issue a DISCONNECT primitive, which results in a DISCONNECT segment being sent to the remote transport entity. Upon its arrival, the connection is released.

In the symmetric variant, each direction is closed separately, independently of the other one. When one side does a DISCONNECT, that means it has no more data to send but it is still willing to accept data from its partner. In this model, a connection is released when both sides have done a DISCONNECT.

A state diagram for connection establishment and release for these simple primitives is given in Fig. 6-4. Each transition is triggered by some event, either a primitive executed by the local transport user or an incoming packet. For simplicity, we assume here that each segment is separately acknowledged. We also assume that a symmetric disconnection model is used, with the client going first. Please note that this model is quite unsophisticated. We will look at more realistic models later on when we describe how TCP works.

6.1.3 Berkeley Sockets

Let us now briefly inspect another set of transport primitives, the socket primitives as they are used for TCP. Sockets were first released as part of the Berkeley UNIX 4.2BSD software distribution in 1983. They quickly became popular. The primitives are now widely used for Internet programming on many operating

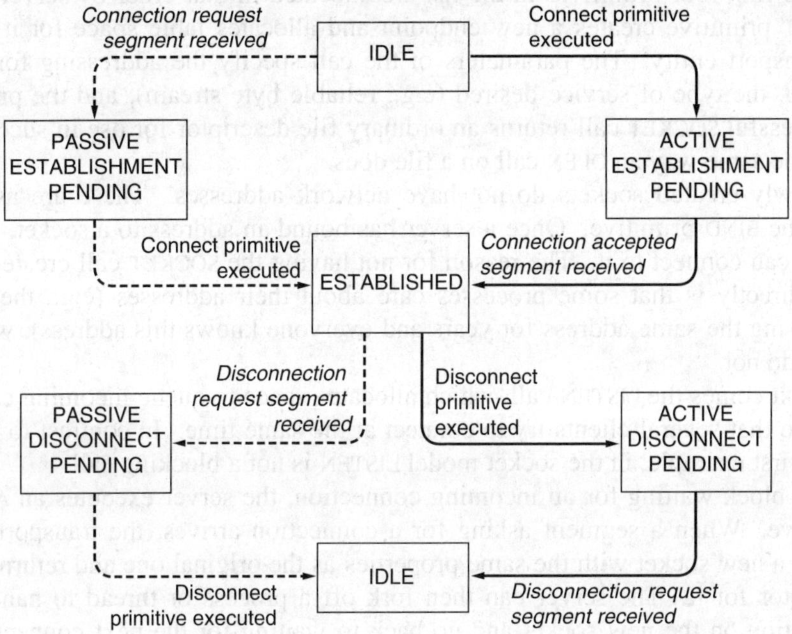

Figure 6-4. A state diagram for a simple connection management scheme. Transitions labeled in italics are caused by packet arrivals. The solid lines show the client's state sequence. The dashed lines show the server's state sequence.

systems, especially UNIX-based systems, and there is a socket-style API for Windows called "winsock."

The primitives are listed in Fig. 6-5. Roughly speaking, they follow the model of our first example but offer more features and flexibility. We will not look at the corresponding segments here. That discussion will come later.

Primitive	Meaning
SOCKET	Create a new communication endpoint
BIND	Associate a local address with a socket
LISTEN	Announce willingness to accept connections; give queue size
ACCEPT	Passively establish an incoming connection
CONNECT	Actively attempt to establish a connection
SEND	Send some data over the connection
RECEIVE	Receive some data from the connection
CLOSE	Release the connection

Figure 6-5. The socket primitives for TCP.

The first four primitives in the list are executed in that order by servers. The SOCKET primitive creates a new endpoint and allocates table space for it within the transport entity. The parameters of the call specify the addressing format to be used, the type of service desired (e.g., reliable byte stream), and the protocol. A successful SOCKET call returns an ordinary file descriptor for use in succeeding calls, the same way an OPEN call on a file does.

Newly created sockets do not have network addresses. These are assigned using the BIND primitive. Once a server has bound an address to a socket, remote clients can connect to it. The reason for not having the SOCKET call create an address directly is that some processes care about their addresses (e.g., they have been using the same address for years and everyone knows this address), whereas others do not.

Next comes the LISTEN call, which allocates space to queue incoming calls for the case that several clients try to connect at the same time. In contrast to LISTEN in our first example, in the socket model LISTEN is not a blocking call.

To block waiting for an incoming connection, the server executes an ACCEPT primitive. When a segment asking for a connection arrives, the transport entity creates a new socket with the same properties as the original one and returns a file descriptor for it. The server can then fork off a process or thread to handle the connection on the new socket and go back to waiting for the next connection on the original socket. ACCEPT returns a file descriptor, which can be used for reading and writing in the standard way, the same as for files.

Now let us look at the client side. Here, too, a socket must first be created using the SOCKET primitive, but BIND is not required since the address used does not matter to the server. The CONNECT primitive blocks the caller and actively starts the connection process. When it completes (i.e., when the appropriate segment is received from the server), the client process is unblocked and the connection is established. Both sides can now use SEND and RECEIVE to transmit and receive data over the full-duplex connection. The standard UNIX READ and WRITE system calls can also be used if none of the special options of SEND and RECEIVE are required.

Connection release with sockets is symmetric. When both sides have executed a CLOSE primitive, the connection is released.

Sockets have proved tremendously popular and are the de facto standard for abstracting transport services to applications. The socket API is often used with the TCP protocol to provide a connection-oriented service called a **reliable byte stream**, which is simply the reliable bit pipe that we described. However, other protocols could be used to implement this service using the same API. It should all be the same to the transport service users.

A strength of the socket API is that is can be used by an application for other transport services. For instance, sockets can be used with a connectionless transport service. In this case, CONNECT sets the address of the remote transport peer and SEND and RECEIVE send and receive datagrams to and from the remote peer.

(It is also common to use an expanded set of calls, for example, SENDTO and RECEIVEFROM, that emphasize messages and do not limit an application to a single transport peer.) Sockets can also be used with transport protocols that provide a message stream rather than a byte stream and that do or do not have congestion control. For example, **DCCP** (**Datagram Congestion Controlled Protocol**) is a version of UDP with congestion control (Kohler et al., 2006). It is up to the transport users to understand what service they are getting.

However, sockets are not likely to be the final word on transport interfaces. For example, applications often work with a group of related streams, such as a Web browser that requests several objects from the same server. With sockets, the most natural fit is for application programs to use one stream per object. This structure means that congestion control is applied separately for each stream, not across the group, which is suboptimal. It punts to the application the burden of managing the set. Newer protocols and interfaces have been devised that support groups of related streams more effectively and simply for the application. Two examples are **SCTP** (**Stream Control Transmission Protocol**) defined in RFC 4960 and **SST** (**Structured Stream Transport**) (Ford, 2007). These protocols must change the socket API slightly to get the benefits of groups of related streams, and they also support features such as a mix of connection-oriented and connectionless traffic and even multiple network paths. Time will tell if they are successful.

6.1.4 An Example of Socket Programming: An Internet File Server

As an example of the nitty-gritty of how real socket calls are made, consider the client and server code of Fig. 6-6. Here we have a very primitive Internet file server along with an example client that uses it. The code has many limitations (discussed below), but in principle the server code can be compiled and run on any UNIX system connected to the Internet. The client code can be compiled and run on any other UNIX machine on the Internet, anywhere in the world. The client code can be executed with appropriate parameters to fetch any file to which the server has access on its machine. The file is written to standard output, which, of course, can be redirected to a file or pipe.

Let us look at the server code first. It starts out by including some standard headers, the last three of which contain the main Internet-related definitions and data structures. Next comes a definition of *SERVER_PORT* as 12345. This number was chosen arbitrarily. Any number between 1024 and 65535 will work just as well, as long as it is not in use by some other process; ports below 1023 are reserved for privileged users.

The next two lines in the server define two constants needed. The first one determines the chunk size in bytes used for the file transfer. The second one determines how many pending connections can be held before additional ones are discarded upon arrival.

```
/* This page contains a client program that can request a file from the server program
 * on the next page. The server responds by sending the whole file.
 */

#include <sys/types.h>
#include <sys/socket.h>
#include <netinet/in.h>
#include <netdb.h>

#define SERVER_PORT 12345                /* arbitrary, but client & server must agree */
#define BUF_SIZE 4096                    /* block transfer size */

int main(int argc, char **argv)
{
  int c, s, bytes;
  char buf[BUF_SIZE];                    /* buffer for incoming file */
  struct hostent *h;                     /* info about server */
  struct sockaddr_in channel;            /* holds IP address */

  if (argc != 3) fatal("Usage: client server-name file-name");
  h = gethostbyname(argv[1]);            /* look up host's IP address */
  if (!h) fatal("gethostbyname failed");

  s = socket(PF_INET, SOCK_STREAM, IPPROTO_TCP);
  if (s <0) fatal("socket");
  memset(&channel, 0, sizeof(channel));
  channel.sin_family= AF_INET;
  memcpy(&channel.sin_addr.s_addr, h->h_addr, h->h_length);
  channel.sin_port= htons(SERVER_PORT);

  c = connect(s, (struct sockaddr *) &channel, sizeof(channel));
  if (c < 0) fatal("connect failed");

  /* Connection is now established. Send file name including 0 byte at end. */
  write(s, argv[2], strlen(argv[2])+1);

  /* Go get the file and write it to standard output. */
  while (1) {
      bytes = read(s, buf, BUF_SIZE);    /* read from socket */
      if (bytes <= 0) exit(0);           /* check for end of file */
      write(1, buf, bytes);              /* write to standard output */
  }
}

fatal(char *string)
{
  printf("%s\n", string);
  exit(1);
}
```

Figure 6-6. Client code using sockets. The server code is on the next page.

```
#include <sys/types.h>                     /* This is the server code */
#include <sys/fcntl.h>
#include <sys/socket.h>
#include <netinet/in.h>
#include <netdb.h>

#define SERVER_PORT 12345                  /* arbitrary, but client & server must agree */
#define BUF_SIZE 4096                      /* block transfer size */
#define QUEUE_SIZE 10

int main(int argc, char *argv[])
{
 int s, b, l, fd, sa, bytes, on = 1;
 char buf[BUF_SIZE];                       /* buffer for outgoing file */
 struct sockaddr_in channel;               /* holds IP address */

 /* Build address structure to bind to socket. */
 memset(&channel, 0, sizeof(channel));     /* zero channel */
 channel.sin_family = AF_INET;
 channel.sin_addr.s_addr = htonl(INADDR_ANY);
 channel.sin_port = htons(SERVER_PORT);

 /* Passive open. Wait for connection. */
 s = socket(AF_INET, SOCK_STREAM, IPPROTO_TCP);   /* create socket */
 if (s < 0) fatal("socket failed");
 setsockopt(s, SOL_SOCKET, SO_REUSEADDR, (char *) &on, sizeof(on));

 b = bind(s, (struct sockaddr *) &channel, sizeof(channel));
 if (b < 0) fatal("bind failed");

 l = listen(s, QUEUE_SIZE);                /* specify queue size */
 if (l < 0) fatal("listen failed");

 /* Socket is now set up and bound. Wait for connection and process it. */
 while (1) {
     sa = accept(s, 0, 0);                 /* block for connection request */
     if (sa < 0) fatal("accept failed");

     read(sa, buf, BUF_SIZE);              /* read file name from socket */

     /* Get and return the file. */
     fd = open(buf, O_RDONLY);             /* open the file to be sent back */
     if (fd < 0) fatal("open failed");

     while (1) {
          bytes = read(fd, buf, BUF_SIZE); /* read from file */
          if (bytes <= 0) break;           /* check for end of file */
          write(sa, buf, bytes);           /* write bytes to socket */
     }
     close(fd);                            /* close file */
     close(sa);                            /* close connection */
 }
}
```

After the declarations of local variables, the server code begins. It starts out by initializing a data structure that will hold the server's IP address. This data structure will soon be bound to the server's socket. The call to *memset* sets the data structure to all 0s. The three assignments following it fill in three of its fields. The last of these contains the server's port. The functions *htonl* and *htons* have to do with converting values to a standard format so the code runs correctly on both little-endian machines (e.g., Intel x86) and big-endian machines (e.g., the SPARC). Their exact semantics are not relevant here.

Next, the server creates a socket and checks for errors (indicated by $s < 0$). In a production version of the code, the error message could be a trifle more explanatory. The call to *setsockopt* is needed to allow the port to be reused so the server can run indefinitely, fielding request after request. Now the IP address is bound to the socket and a check is made to see if the call to *bind* succeeded. The final step in the initialization is the call to *listen* to announce the server's willingness to accept incoming calls and tell the system to hold up to *QUEUE_SIZE* of them in case new requests arrive while the server is still processing the current one. If the queue is full and additional requests arrive, they are quietly discarded.

At this point, the server enters its main loop, which it never leaves. The only way to stop it is to kill it from outside. The call to *accept* blocks the server until some client tries to establish a connection with it. If the *accept* call succeeds, it returns a socket descriptor that can be used for reading and writing, analogous to how file descriptors can be used to read from and write to pipes. However, unlike pipes, which are unidirectional, sockets are bidirectional, so *sa* (the accepted socket) can be used for reading from the connection and also for writing to it. A pipe file descriptor is for reading or writing but not both.

After the connection is established, the server reads the file name from it. If the name is not yet available, the server blocks waiting for it. After getting the file name, the server opens the file and enters a loop that alternately reads blocks from the file and writes them to the socket until the entire file has been copied. Then the server closes the file and the connection and waits for the next connection to show up. It repeats this loop forever.

Now let us look at the client code. To understand how it works, it is necessary to understand how it is invoked. Assuming it is called *client*, a typical call is

```
client flits.cs.vu.nl /usr/tom/filename >f
```

This call only works if the server is already running on *flits.cs.vu.nl* and the file */usr/tom/filename* exists and the server has read access to it. If the call is successful, the file is transferred over the Internet and written to *f*, after which the client program exits. Since the server continues after a transfer, the client can be started again and again to get other files.

The client code starts with some includes and declarations. Execution begins by checking to see if it has been called with the right number of arguments (*argc* = 3 means the program name plus two arguments). Note that *argv* [1] contains the name of the server (e.g., *flits.cs.vu.nl*) and is converted to an IP address by *gethostbyname*. This function uses DNS to look up the name. We will study DNS in Chap. 7.

Next, a socket is created and initialized. After that, the client attempts to establish a TCP connection to the server, using *connect*. If the server is up and running on the named machine and attached to *SERVER_PORT* and is either idle or has room in its *listen* queue, the connection will (eventually) be established. Using the connection, the client sends the name of the file by writing on the socket. The number of bytes sent is one larger than the name proper, since the 0 byte terminating the name must also be sent to tell the server where the name ends.

Now the client enters a loop, reading the file block by block from the socket and copying it to standard output. When it is done, it just exits.

The procedure *fatal* prints an error message and exits. The server needs the same procedure, but it was omitted due to lack of space on the page. Since the client and server are compiled separately and normally run on different computers, they cannot share the code of *fatal*.

These two programs (as well as other material related to this book) can be fetched from the book's Web site

http://www.pearsonhighered.com/tanenbaum

Just for the record, this server is not the last word in serverdom. Its error checking is meager and its error reporting is mediocre. Since it handles all requests strictly sequentially (because it has only a single thread), its performance is poor. It has clearly never heard about security, and using bare UNIX system calls is not the way to gain platform independence. It also makes some assumptions that are technically illegal, such as assuming that the file name fits in the buffer and is transmitted atomically. These shortcomings notwithstanding, it is a working Internet file server. In the exercises, the reader is invited to improve it. For more information about programming with sockets, see Donahoo and Calvert (2008, 2009).

6.2 ELEMENTS OF TRANSPORT PROTOCOLS

The transport service is implemented by a **transport protocol** used between the two transport entities. In some ways, transport protocols resemble the data link protocols we studied in detail in Chap. 3. Both have to deal with error control, sequencing, and flow control, among other issues.

However, significant differences between the two also exist. These differences are due to major dissimilarities between the environments in which the two protocols operate, as shown in Fig. 6-7. At the data link layer, two routers communicate directly via a physical channel, whether wired or wireless, whereas at the transport layer, this physical channel is replaced by the entire network. This difference has many important implications for the protocols.

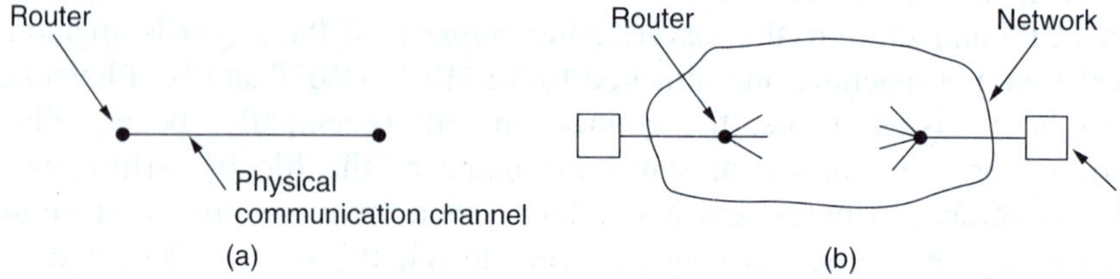

Figure 6-7. (a) Environment of the data link layer. (b) Environment of the transport layer.

For one thing, over point-to-point links such as wires or optical fiber, it is usually not necessary for a router to specify which router it wants to talk to—each outgoing line leads directly to a particular router. In the transport layer, explicit addressing of destinations is required.

For another thing, the process of establishing a connection over the wire of Fig. 6-7(a) is simple: the other end is always there (unless it has crashed, in which case it is not there). Either way, there is not much to do. Even on wireless links, the process is not much different. Just sending a message is sufficient to have it reach all other destinations. If the message is not acknowledged due to an error, it can be resent. In the transport layer, initial connection establishment is complicated, as we will see.

Another (exceedingly annoying) difference between the data link layer and the transport layer is the potential existence of storage capacity in the network. When a router sends a packet over a link, it may arrive or be lost, but it cannot bounce around for a while, go into hiding in a far corner of the world, and suddenly emerge after other packets that were sent much later. If the network uses datagrams, which are independently routed inside, there is a nonnegligible probability that a packet may take the scenic route and arrive late and out of the expected order, or even that duplicates of the packet will arrive. The consequences of the network's ability to delay and duplicate packets can sometimes be disastrous and can require the use of special protocols to correctly transport information.

A final difference between the data link and transport layers is one of degree rather than of kind. Buffering and flow control are needed in both layers, but the presence in the transport layer of a large and varying number of connections with bandwidth that fluctuates as the connections compete with each other may require a different approach than we used in the data link layer. Some of the protocols discussed in Chap. 3 allocate a fixed number of buffers to each line, so that when a frame arrives a buffer is always available. In the transport layer, the larger number of connections that must be managed and variations in the bandwidth each connection may receive make the idea of dedicating many buffers to each one less attractive. In the following sections, we will examine all of these important issues, and others.

6.2.1 Addressing

When an application (e.g., a user) process wishes to set up a connection to a remote application process, it must specify which one to connect to. (Connectionless transport has the same problem: to whom should each message be sent?) The method normally used is to define transport addresses to which processes can listen for connection requests. In the Internet, these endpoints are called **ports**. We will use the generic term **TSAP** (**Transport Service Access Point**) to mean a specific endpoint in the transport layer. The analogous endpoints in the network layer (i.e., network layer addresses) are not-surprisingly called **NSAPs** (**Network Service Access Points**). IP addresses are examples of NSAPs.

Figure 6-8 illustrates the relationship between the NSAPs, the TSAPs, and a transport connection. Application processes, both clients and servers, can attach themselves to a local TSAP to establish a connection to a remote TSAP. These connections run through NSAPs on each host, as shown. The purpose of having TSAPs is that in some networks, each computer has a single NSAP, so some way is needed to distinguish multiple transport endpoints that share that NSAP.

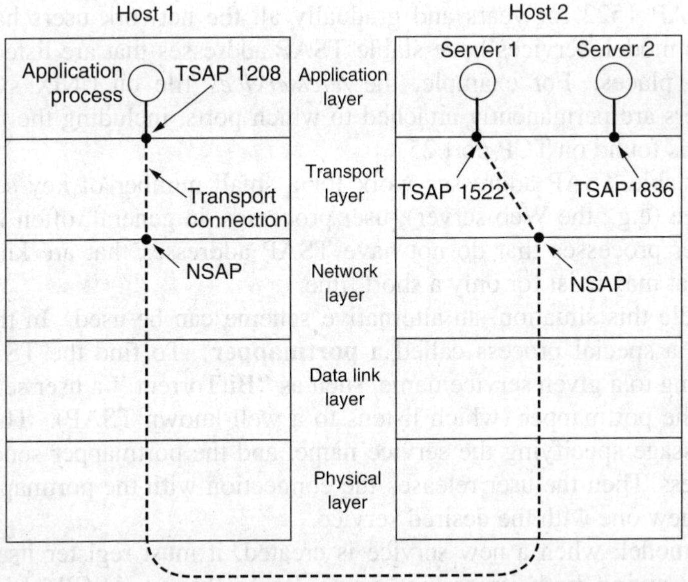

Figure 6-8. TSAPs, NSAPs, and transport connections.

A possible scenario for a transport connection is as follows:

1. A mail server process attaches itself to TSAP 1522 on host 2 to wait for an incoming call. How a process attaches itself to a TSAP is outside the networking model and depends entirely on the local operating system. A call such as our LISTEN might be used, for example.
2. An application process on host 1 wants to send an email message, so it attaches itself to TSAP 1208 and issues a CONNECT request. The request specifies TSAP 1208 on host 1 as the source and TSAP 1522 on host 2 as the destination. This action ultimately results in a transport connection being established between the application process and the server.
3. The application process sends over the mail message.
4. The mail server responds to say that it will deliver the message.
5. The transport connection is released.

Note that there may well be other servers on host 2 that are attached to other TSAPs and are waiting for incoming connections that arrive over the same NSAP.

The picture painted above is fine, except we have swept one little problem under the rug: how does the user process on host 1 know that the mail server is attached to TSAP 1522? One possibility is that the mail server has been attaching itself to TSAP 1522 for years and gradually all the network users have learned this. In this model, services have stable TSAP addresses that are listed in files in well-known places. For example, the */etc/services* file on UNIX systems lists which servers are permanently attached to which ports, including the fact that the mail server is found on TCP port 25.

While stable TSAP addresses work for a small number of key services that never change (e.g., the Web server), user processes, in general, often want to talk to other user processes that do not have TSAP addresses that are known in advance, or that may exist for only a short time.

To handle this situation, an alternative scheme can be used. In this scheme, there exists a special process called a **portmapper**. To find the TSAP address corresponding to a given service name, such as "BitTorrent," a user sets up a connection to the portmapper (which listens to a well-known TSAP). The user then sends a message specifying the service name, and the portmapper sends back the TSAP address. Then the user releases the connection with the portmapper and establishes a new one with the desired service.

In this model, when a new service is created, it must register itself with the portmapper, giving both its service name (typically, an ASCII string) and its TSAP. The portmapper records this information in its internal database so that when queries come in later, it will know the answers.

The function of the portmapper is analogous to that of a directory assistance operator in the telephone system—it provides a mapping of names onto numbers. Just as in the telephone system, it is essential that the address of the well-known TSAP used by the portmapper is indeed well known. If you do not know the number of the information operator, you cannot call the information operator to find it out. If you think the number you dial for information is obvious, try it in a foreign country sometime.

Many of the server processes that can exist on a machine will be used only rarely. It is wasteful to have each of them active and listening to a stable TSAP address all day long. An alternative scheme is shown in Fig. 6-9 in a simplified form. It is known as the **initial connection protocol**. Instead of every conceivable server listening at a well-known TSAP, each machine that wishes to offer services to remote users has a special **process server** that acts as a proxy for less heavily used servers. This server is called *inetd* on UNIX systems. It listens to a set of ports at the same time, waiting for a connection request. Potential users of a service begin by doing a CONNECT request, specifying the TSAP address of the service they want. If no server is waiting for them, they get a connection to the process server, as shown in Fig. 6-9(a).

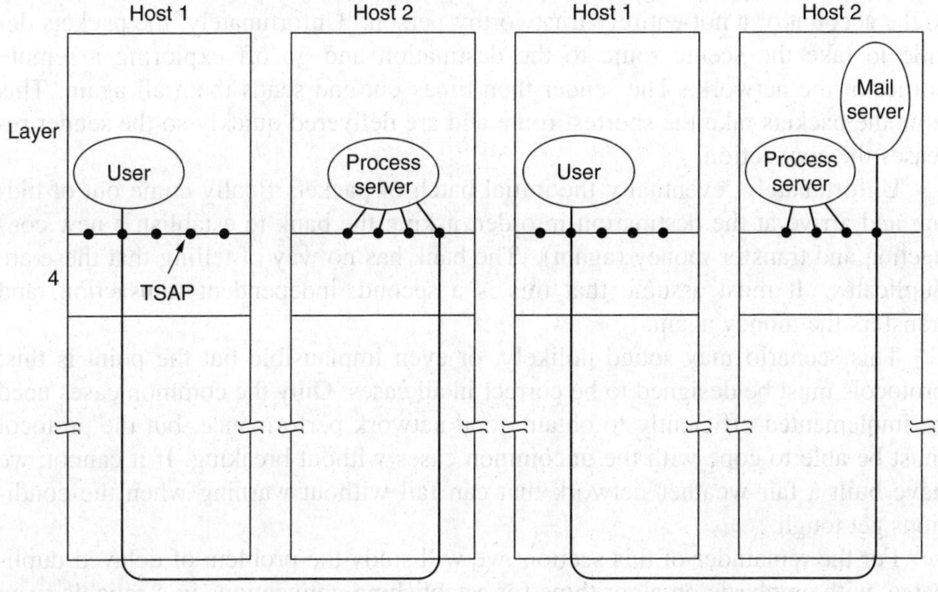

Figure 6-9. How a user process in host 1 establishes a connection with a mail server in host 2 via a process server.

After it gets the incoming request, the process server spawns the requested server, allowing it to inherit the existing connection with the user. The new server does the requested work, while the process server goes back to listening for new requests, as shown in Fig. 6-9(b). This method is only applicable when servers can be created on demand.

6.2.2 Connection Establishment

Establishing a connection sounds easy, but it is actually surprisingly tricky. At first glance, it would seem sufficient for one transport entity to just send a CONNECTION REQUEST segment to the destination and wait for a CONNECTION ACCEPTED reply. The problem occurs when the network can lose, delay, corrupt, and duplicate packets. This behavior causes serious complications.

Imagine a network that is so congested that acknowledgements hardly ever get back in time and each packet times out and is retransmitted two or three times. Suppose that the network uses datagrams inside and that every packet follows a different route. Some of the packets might get stuck in a traffic jam inside the network and take a long time to arrive. That is, they may be delayed in the network and pop out much later, when the sender thought that they had been lost.

The worst possible nightmare is as follows. A user establishes a connection with a bank, sends messages telling the bank to transfer a large amount of money to the account of a not-entirely-trustworthy person. Unfortunately, the packets decide to take the scenic route to the destination and go off exploring a remote corner of the network. The sender then times out and sends them all again. This time the packets take the shortest route and are delivered quickly so the sender releases the connection.

Unfortunately, eventually the initial batch of packets finally come out of hiding and arrive at the destination in order, asking the bank to establish a new connection and transfer money (again). The bank has no way of telling that these are duplicates. It must assume that this is a second, independent transaction, and transfers the money again.

This scenario may sound unlikely, or even implausible but the point is this: protocols must be designed to be correct in all cases. Only the common cases need be implemented efficiently to obtain good network performance, but the protocol must be able to cope with the uncommon cases without breaking. If it cannot, we have built a fair-weather network that can fail without warning when the conditions get tough.

For the remainder of this section, we will study the problem of delayed duplicates, with emphasis on algorithms for establishing connections in a reliable way, so that nightmares like the one above cannot happen. The crux of the problem is that the delayed duplicates are thought to be new packets. We cannot prevent packets from being duplicated and delayed. But if and when this happens, the packets must be rejected as duplicates and not processed as fresh packets.

The problem can be attacked in various ways, none of them very satisfactory. One way is to use throwaway transport addresses. In this approach, each time a transport address is needed, a new one is generated. When a connection is released, the address is discarded and never used again. Delayed duplicate packets then never find their way to a transport process and can do no damage. However, this approach makes it more difficult to connect with a process in the first place.

Another possibility is to give each connection a unique identifier (i.e., a sequence number incremented for each connection established) chosen by the initiating party and put in each segment, including the one requesting the connection. After each connection is released, each transport entity can update a table listing obsolete connections as (peer transport entity, connection identifier) pairs. Whenever a connection request comes in, it can be checked against the table to see if it belongs to a previously released connection.

Unfortunately, this scheme has a basic flaw: it requires each transport entity to maintain a certain amount of history information indefinitely. This history must persist at both the source and destination machines. Otherwise, if a machine crashes and loses its memory, it will no longer know which connection identifiers have already been used by its peers.

Instead, we need to take a different tack to simplify the problem. Rather than allowing packets to live forever within the network, we devise a mechanism to kill off aged packets that are still hobbling about. With this restriction, the problem becomes somewhat more manageable.

Packet lifetime can be restricted to a known maximum using one (or more) of the following techniques:

1. Restricted network design.
2. Putting a hop counter in each packet.
3. Timestamping each packet.

The first technique includes any method that prevents packets from looping, combined with some way of bounding delay including congestion over the (now known) longest possible path. It is difficult, given that internets may range from a single city to international in scope. The second method consists of having the hop count initialized to some appropriate value and decremented each time the packet is forwarded. The network protocol simply discards any packet whose hop counter becomes zero. The third method requires each packet to bear the time it was created, with the routers agreeing to discard any packet older than some agreed-upon time. This latter method requires the router clocks to be synchronized, which itself is a nontrivial task, and in practice a hop counter is a close enough approximation to age.

In practice, we will need to guarantee not only that a packet is dead, but also that all acknowledgements to it are dead, too, so we will now introduce a period *T*, which is some small multiple of the true maximum packet lifetime. The maximum packet lifetime is a conservative constant for a network; for the Internet, it is somewhat arbitrarily taken to be 120 seconds. The multiple is protocol dependent and simply has the effect of making T longer. If we wait a time T secs after a packet has been sent, we can be sure that all traces of it are now gone and that neither it nor its acknowledgements will suddenly appear out of the blue to complicate matters.

With packet lifetimes bounded, it is possible to devise a practical and foolproof way to reject delayed duplicate segments. The method described below is due to Tomlinson (1975), as refined by Sunshine and Dalal (1978). Variants of it are widely used in practice, including in TCP.

The heart of the method is for the source to label segments with sequence numbers that will not be reused within T secs. The period, T, and the rate of packets per second determine the size of the sequence numbers. In this way, only one packet with a given sequence number may be outstanding at any given time. Duplicates of this packet may still occur, and they must be discarded by the destination. However, it is no longer the case that a delayed duplicate of an old packet may beat a new packet with the same sequence number and be accepted by the destination in its stead.

To get around the problem of a machine losing all memory of where it was after a crash, one possibility is to require transport entities to be idle for T secs after a recovery. The idle period will let all old segments die off, so the sender can start again with any sequence number. However, in a complex internetwork, T may be large, so this strategy is unattractive.

Instead, Tomlinson proposed equipping each host with a time-of-day clock. The clocks at different hosts need not be synchronized. Each clock is assumed to take the form of a binary counter that increments itself at uniform intervals. Furthermore, the number of bits in the counter must equal or exceed the number of bits in the sequence numbers. Last, and most important, the clock is assumed to continue running even if the host goes down.

When a connection is set up, the low-order k bits of the clock are used as the k-bit initial sequence number. Thus, unlike our protocols of Chap. 3, each connection starts numbering its segments with a different initial sequence number. The sequence space should be so large that by the time sequence numbers wrap around, old segments with the same sequence number are long gone. This linear relation between time and initial sequence numbers is shown in Fig. 6-10(a). The forbidden region shows the times for which segment sequence numbers are illegal leading up to their use. If any segment is sent with a sequence number in this region, it could be delayed and impersonate a different packet with the same sequence number that will be issued slightly later. For example, if the host crashes and restarts at time 70 seconds, it will use initial sequence numbers based on the clock to pick up after it left off; the host does not start with a lower sequence number in the forbidden region.

Once both transport entities have agreed on the initial sequence number, any sliding window protocol can be used for data flow control. This window protocol will correctly find and discard duplicates of packets after they have already been

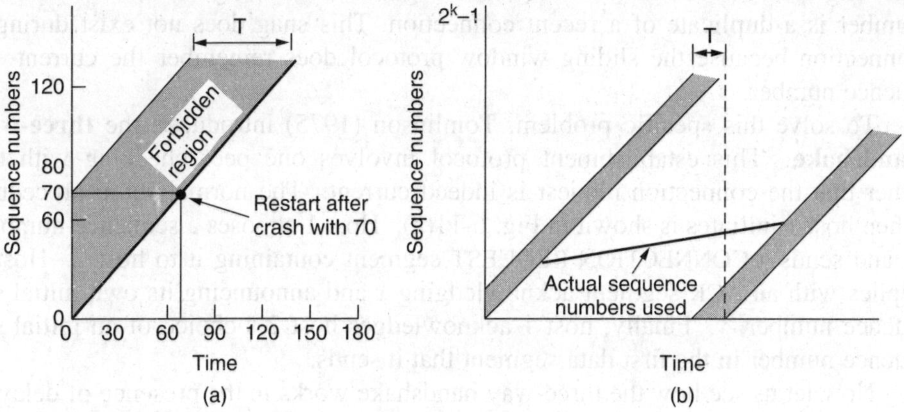

Figure 6-10. (a) Segments may not enter the forbidden region. (b) The resynchronization problem.

accepted. In reality, the initial sequence number curve (shown by the heavy line) is not linear, but a staircase, since the clock advances in discrete steps. For simplicity, we will ignore this detail.

To keep packet sequence numbers out of the forbidden region, we need to take care in two respects. We can get into trouble in two distinct ways. If a host sends too much data too fast on a newly opened connection, the actual sequence number versus time curve may rise more steeply than the initial sequence number versus time curve, causing the sequence number to enter the forbidden region. To prevent this from happening, the maximum data rate on any connection is one segment per clock tick. This also means that the transport entity must wait until the clock ticks before opening a new connection after a crash restart, lest the same number be used twice. Both of these points argue in favor of a short clock tick (1 μsec or less). But the clock cannot tick too fast relative to the sequence number. For a clock rate of C and a sequence number space of size S, we must have $S/C > T$ so that the sequence numbers cannot wrap around too quickly.

Entering the forbidden region from underneath by sending too fast is not the only way to get into trouble. From Fig. 6-10(b), we see that at any data rate less than the clock rate, the curve of actual sequence numbers used versus time will eventually run into the forbidden region from the left as the sequence numbers wrap around. The greater the slope of the actual sequence numbers, the longer this event will be delayed. Avoiding this situation limits how slowly sequence numbers can advance on a connection (or how long the connections may last).

The clock-based method solves the problem of not being able to distinguish delayed duplicate segments from new segments. However, there is a practical snag for using it for establishing connections. Since we do not normally remember sequence numbers across connections at the destination, we still have no way of knowing if a CONNECTION REQUEST segment containing an initial sequence number is a duplicate of a recent connection. This snag does not exist during a connection because the sliding window protocol does remember the current sequence number.

To solve this specific problem, Tomlinson (1975) introduced the **three-way handshake**. This establishment protocol involves one peer checking with the other that the connection request is indeed current. The normal setup procedure when host 1 initiates is shown in Fig. 6-11(a). Host 1 chooses a sequence number, x, and sends a CONNECTION REQUEST segment containing it to host 2. Host 2 replies with an ACK segment acknowledging x and announcing its own initial sequence number, y. Finally, host 1 acknowledges host 2's choice of an initial sequence number in the first data segment that it sends.

Now let us see how the three-way handshake works in the presence of delayed duplicate control segments. In Fig. 6-11(b), the first segment is a delayed duplicate CONNECTION REQUEST from an old connection. This segment arrives at host 2 without host 1's knowledge. Host 2 reacts to this segment by sending host 1 an ACK segment, in effect asking for verification that host 1 was indeed trying to set up a new connection. When host 1 rejects host 2's attempt to establish a connection, host 2 realizes that it was tricked by a delayed duplicate and abandons the connection. In this way, a delayed duplicate does no damage.

The worst case is when both a delayed CONNECTION REQUEST and an ACK are floating around in the subnet. This case is shown in Fig. 6-11(c). As in the previous example, host 2 gets a delayed CONNECTION REQUEST and replies to it. At this point, it is crucial to realize that host 2 has proposed using y as the initial sequence number for host 2 to host 1 traffic, knowing full well that no segments containing sequence number y or acknowledgements to y are still in existence. When the second delayed segment arrives at host 2, the fact that z has been acknowledged rather than y tells host 2 that this, too, is an old duplicate. The important thing to realize here is that there is no combination of old segments that can cause the protocol to fail and have a connection set up by accident when no one wants it.

TCP uses this three-way handshake to establish connections. Within a connection, a timestamp is used to extend the 32-bit sequence number so that it will not wrap within the maximum packet lifetime, even for gigabit-per-second connections. This mechanism is a fix to TCP that was needed as it was used on faster and faster links. It is described in RFC 1323 and called **PAWS (Protection Against Wrapped Sequence numbers)**. Across connections, for the initial sequence numbers and before PAWS can come into play, TCP originally used the clock-based scheme just described. However, this turned out to have a security vulnerability. The clock made it easy for an attacker to predict the next initial sequence number and send packets that tricked the three-way handshake and established a forged connection. To close this hole, pseudorandom initial sequence numbers are used for connections in practice. However, it remains important that

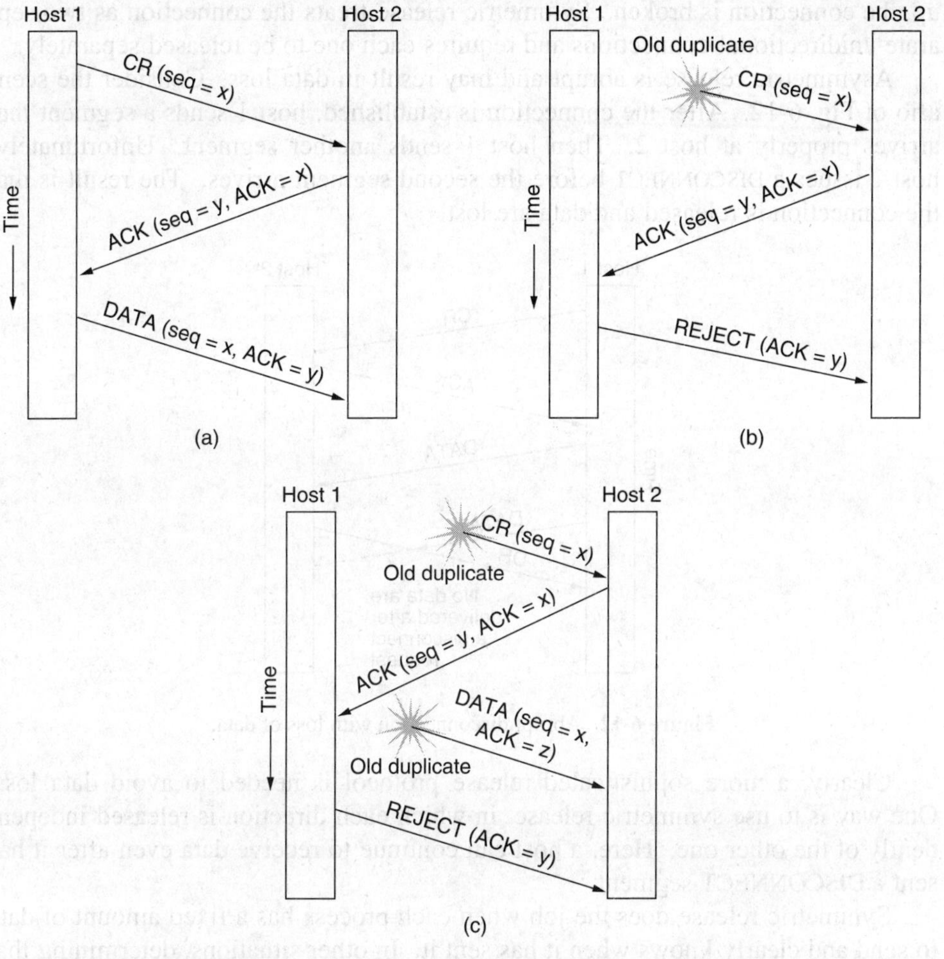

Figure 6-11. Three protocol scenarios for establishing a connection using a three-way handshake. CR denotes CONNECTION REQUEST. (a) Normal operation. (b) Old duplicate CONNECTION REQUEST appearing out of nowhere. (c) Duplicate CONNECTION REQUEST and duplicate ACK.

the initial sequence numbers not repeat for an interval even though they appear random to an observer. Otherwise, delayed duplicates can wreak havoc.

6.2.3 Connection Release

Releasing a connection is easier than establishing one. Nevertheless, there are more pitfalls than one might expect here. As we mentioned earlier, there are two styles of terminating a connection: asymmetric release and symmetric release.

Asymmetric release is the way the telephone system works: when one party hangs up, the connection is broken. Symmetric release treats the connection as two separate unidirectional connections and requires each one to be released separately.

Asymmetric release is abrupt and may result in data loss. Consider the scenario of Fig. 6-12. After the connection is established, host 1 sends a segment that arrives properly at host 2. Then host 1 sends another segment. Unfortunately, host 2 issues a DISCONNECT before the second segment arrives. The result is that the connection is released and data are lost.

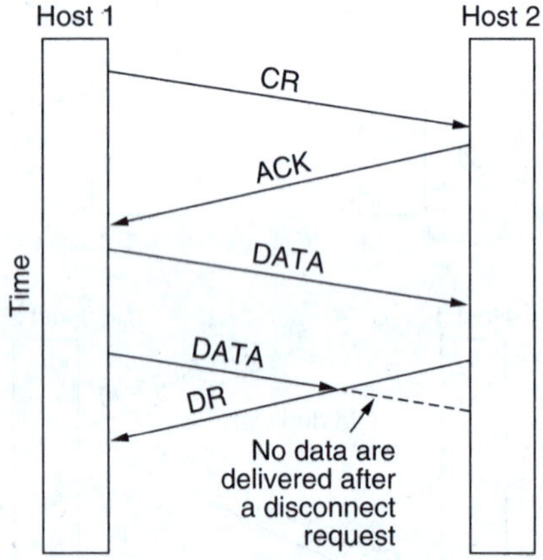

Figure 6-12. Abrupt disconnection with loss of data.

Clearly, a more sophisticated release protocol is needed to avoid data loss. One way is to use symmetric release, in which each direction is released independently of the other one. Here, a host can continue to receive data even after it has sent a DISCONNECT segment.

Symmetric release does the job when each process has a fixed amount of data to send and clearly knows when it has sent it. In other situations, determining that all the work has been done and the connection should be terminated is not so obvious. One can envision a protocol in which host 1 says "I am done. Are you done too?" If host 2 responds: "I am done too. Goodbye, the connection can be safely released."

Unfortunately, this protocol does not always work. There is a famous problem that illustrates this issue. It is called the **two-army problem**. Imagine that a white army is encamped in a valley, as shown in Fig. 6-13. On both of the surrounding hillsides are blue armies. The white army is larger than either of the blue armies alone, but together the blue armies are larger than the white army. If either blue army attacks by itself, it will be defeated, but if the two blue armies attack simultaneously, they will be victorious.

The blue armies want to synchronize their attacks. However, their only communication medium is to send messengers on foot down into the valley, where

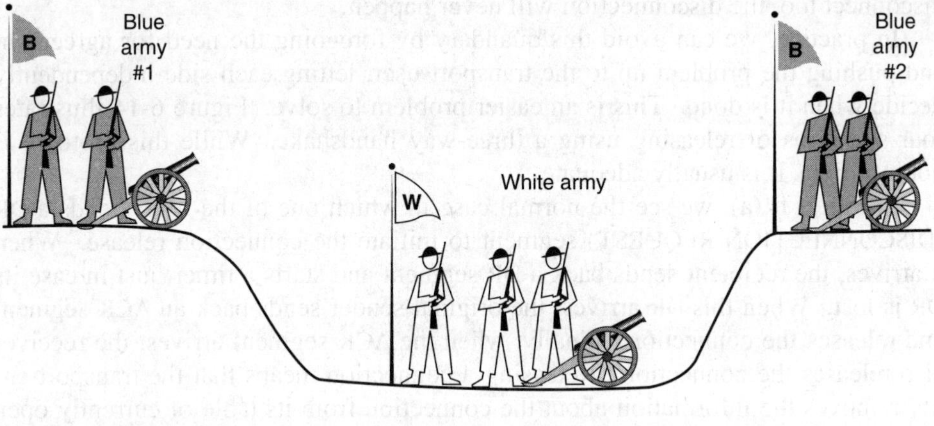

Figure 6-13. The two-army problem.

they might be captured and the message lost (i.e., they have to use an unreliable communication channel). The question is: does a protocol exist that allows the blue armies to win?

Suppose that the commander of blue army #1 sends a message reading: "I propose we attack at dawn on March 29. How about it?" Now suppose that the message arrives, the commander of blue army #2 agrees, and his reply gets safely back to blue army #1. Will the attack happen? Probably not, because commander #2 does not know if his reply got through. If it did not, blue army #1 will not attack, so it would be foolish for him to charge into battle.

Now let us improve the protocol by making it a three-way handshake. The initiator of the original proposal must acknowledge the response. Assuming no messages are lost, blue army #2 will get the acknowledgement, but the commander of blue army #1 will now hesitate. After all, he does not know if his acknowledgement got through, and if it did not, he knows that blue army #2 will not attack. We could now make a four-way handshake protocol, but that does not help either.

In fact, it can be proven that no protocol exists that works. Suppose that some protocol did exist. Either the last message of the protocol is essential, or it is not. If it is not, we can remove it (and any other unessential messages) until we are left with a protocol in which every message is essential. What happens if the final message does not get through? We just said that it was essential, so if it is lost, the attack does not take place. Since the sender of the final message can never be sure of its arrival, he will not risk attacking. Worse yet, the other blue army knows this, so it will not attack either.

To see the relevance of the two-army problem to releasing connections, rather than to military affairs, just substitute "disconnect" for "attack." If neither side is prepared to disconnect until it is convinced that the other side is prepared to disconnect too, the disconnection will never happen.

In practice, we can avoid this quandary by foregoing the need for agreement and pushing the problem up to the transport user, letting each side independently decide when it is done. This is an easier problem to solve. Figure 6-14 illustrates four scenarios of releasing using a three-way handshake. While this protocol is not infallible, it is usually adequate.

In Fig. 6-14(a), we see the normal case in which one of the users sends a DR (DISCONNECTION REQUEST) segment to initiate the connection release. When it arrives, the recipient sends back a DR segment and starts a timer, just in case its DR is lost. When this DR arrives, the original sender sends back an ACK segment and releases the connection. Finally, when the ACK segment arrives, the receiver also releases the connection. Releasing a connection means that the transport entity removes the information about the connection from its table of currently open connections and signals the connection's owner (the transport user) somehow. This action is different from a transport user issuing a DISCONNECT primitive.

If the final ACK segment is lost, as shown in Fig. 6-14(b), the situation is saved by the timer. When the timer expires, the connection is released anyway.

Now consider the case of the second DR being lost. The user initiating the disconnection will not receive the expected response, will time out, and will start all over again. In Fig. 6-14(c), we see how this works, assuming that the second time no segments are lost and all segments are delivered correctly and on time.

Our last scenario, Fig. 6-14(d), is the same as Fig. 6-14(c) except that now we assume all the repeated attempts to retransmit the DR also fail due to lost segments. After *N* retries, the sender just gives up and releases the connection. Meanwhile, the receiver times out and also exits.

While this protocol usually suffices, in theory it can fail if the initial DR and *N* retransmissions are all lost. The sender will give up and release the connection, while the other side knows nothing at all about the attempts to disconnect and is still fully active. This situation results in a half-open connection.

We could have avoided this problem by not allowing the sender to give up after *N* retries and forcing it to go on forever until it gets a response. However, if the other side is allowed to time out, the sender will indeed go on forever, because no response will ever be forthcoming. If we do not allow the receiving side to time out, the protocol hangs in Fig. 6-14(d).

One way to kill off half-open connections is to have a rule saying that if no segments have arrived for a certain number of seconds, the connection is automatically disconnected. That way, if one side ever disconnects, the other side will detect the lack of activity and also disconnect. This rule also takes care of the case where the connection is broken (because the network can no longer deliver packets between the hosts) without either end disconnecting first. Of course, if this rule is introduced, it is necessary for each transport entity to have a timer that is stopped and then restarted whenever a segment is sent. If this timer expires, a

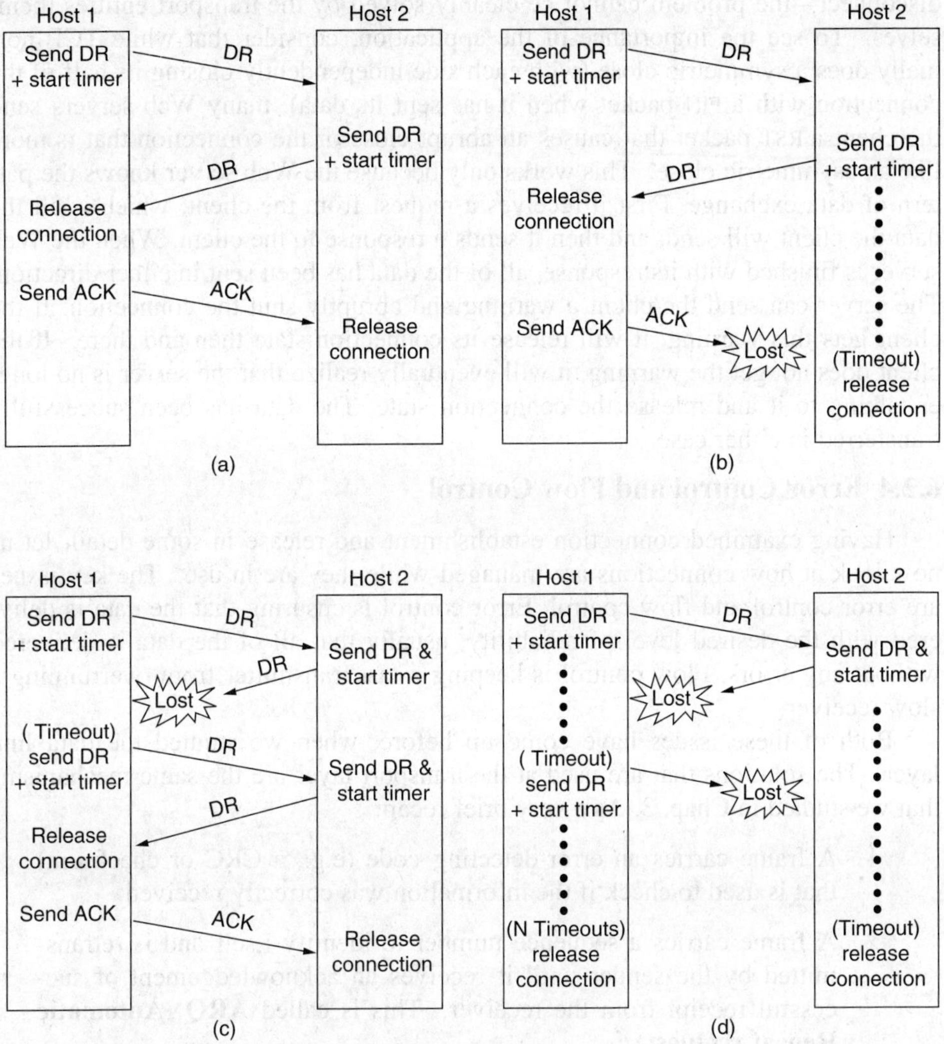

Figure 6-14. Four protocol scenarios for releasing a connection. (a) Normal case of three-way handshake. (b) Final ACK lost. (c) Response lost. (d) Response lost and subsequent DRs lost.

dummy segment is transmitted, just to keep the other side from disconnecting. On the other hand, if the automatic disconnect rule is used and too many dummy segments in a row are lost on an otherwise idle connection, first one side, then the other will automatically disconnect.

We will not belabor this point any more, but by now it should be clear that releasing a connection without data loss is not nearly as simple as it first appears. The lesson here is that the transport user must be involved in deciding when to disconnect—the problem cannot be cleanly solved by the transport entities themselves. To see the importance of the application, consider that while TCP normally does a symmetric close (with each side independently closing its half of the connection with a FIN packet when it has sent its data), many Web servers send the client a RST packet that causes an abrupt close of the connection that is more like an asymmetric close. This works only because the Web server knows the pattern of data exchange. First it receives a request from the client, which is all the data the client will send, and then it sends a response to the client. When the Web server is finished with its response, all of the data has been sent in either direction. The server can send the client a warning and abruptly shut the connection. If the client gets this warning, it will release its connection state then and there. If the client does not get the warning, it will eventually realize that the server is no longer talking to it and release the connection state. The data has been successfully transferred in either case.

6.2.4 Error Control and Flow Control

Having examined connection establishment and release in some detail, let us now look at how connections are managed while they are in use. The key issues are error control and flow control. Error control is ensuring that the data is delivered with the desired level of reliability, usually that all of the data is delivered without any errors. Flow control is keeping a fast transmitter from overrunning a slow receiver.

Both of these issues have come up before, when we studied the data link layer. The solutions that are used at the transport layer are the same mechanisms that we studied in Chap. 3. As a very brief recap:

1. A frame carries an error-detecting code (e.g., a CRC or checksum) that is used to check if the information was correctly received.
2. A frame carries a sequence number to identify itself and is retransmitted by the sender until it receives an acknowledgement of successful receipt from the receiver. This is called **ARQ** (**Automatic Repeat reQuest**).
3. There is a maximum number of frames that the sender will allow to be outstanding at any time, pausing if the receiver is not acknowledging frames quickly enough. If this maximum is one packet the protocol is called **stop-and-wait**. Larger windows enable pipelining and improve performance on long, fast links.
4. The **sliding window** protocol combines these features and is also used to support bidirectional data transfer.

Given that these mechanisms are used on frames at the link layer, it is natural to wonder why they would be used on segments at the transport layer as well.

However, there is little duplication between the link and transport layers in practice. Even though the same mechanisms are used, there are differences in function and degree.

For a difference in function, consider error detection. The link layer checksum protects a frame while it crosses a single link. The transport layer checksum protects a segment while it crosses an entire network path. It is an end-to-end check, which is not the same as having a check on every link. Saltzer et al. (1984) describe a situation in which packets were corrupted inside a router. The link layer checksums protected the packets only while they traveled across a link, not while they were inside the router. Thus, packets were delivered incorrectly even though they were correct according to the checks on every link.

This and other examples led Saltzer et al. to articulate the **end-to-end argument**. According to this argument, the transport layer check that runs end-to-end is essential for correctness, and the link layer checks are not essential but nonetheless valuable for improving performance (since without them a corrupted packet can be sent along the entire path unnecessarily).

As a difference in degree, consider retransmissions and the sliding window protocol. Most wireless links, other than satellite links, can have only a single frame outstanding from the sender at a time. That is, the bandwidth-delay product for the link is small enough that not even a whole frame can be stored inside the link. In this case, a small window size is sufficient for good performance. For example, 802.11 uses a stop-and-wait protocol, transmitting or retransmitting each frame and waiting for it to be acknowledged before moving on to the next frame. Having a window size larger than one frame would add complexity without improving performance. For wired and optical fiber links, such as (switched) Ethernet or ISP backbones, the error-rate is low enough that link-layer retransmissions can be omitted because the end-to-end retransmissions will repair the residual frame loss.

On the other hand, many TCP connections have a bandwidth-delay product that is much larger than a single segment. Consider a connection sending data across the U.S. at 1 Mbps with a round-trip time of 100 msec. Even for this slow connection, 200 Kbit of data will be stored at the receiver in the time it takes to send a segment and receive an acknowledgement. For these situations, a large sliding window must be used. Stop-and-wait will cripple performance. In our example it would limit performance to one segment every 200 msec, or 5 segments/sec no matter how fast the network really is.

Given that transport protocols generally use larger sliding windows, we will look at the issue of buffering data more carefully. Since a host may have many connections, each of which is treated separately, it may need a substantial amount of buffering for the sliding windows. The buffers are needed at both the sender and the receiver. Certainly they are needed at the sender to hold all transmitted but as yet unacknowledged segments. They are needed there because these segments may be lost and need to be retransmitted.

However, since the sender is buffering, the receiver may or may not dedicate specific buffers to specific connections, as it sees fit. The receiver may, for example, maintain a single buffer pool shared by all connections. When a segment comes in, an attempt is made to dynamically acquire a new buffer. If one is available, the segment is accepted; otherwise, it is discarded. Since the sender is prepared to retransmit segments lost by the network, no permanent harm is done by having the receiver drop segments, although some resources are wasted. The sender just keeps trying until it gets an acknowledgement.

The best trade-off between source buffering and destination buffering depends on the type of traffic carried by the connection. For low-bandwidth bursty traffic, such as that produced by an interactive terminal, it is reasonable not to dedicate any buffers, but rather to acquire them dynamically at both ends, relying on buffering at the sender if segments must occasionally be discarded. On the other hand, for file transfer and other high-bandwidth traffic, it is better if the receiver does dedicate a full window of buffers, to allow the data to flow at maximum speed. This is the strategy that TCP uses.

There still remains the question of how to organize the buffer pool. If most segments are nearly the same size, it is natural to organize the buffers as a pool of identically sized buffers, with one segment per buffer, as in Fig. 6-15(a). However, if there is wide variation in segment size, from short requests for Web pages to large packets in peer-to-peer file transfers, a pool of fixed-sized buffers presents problems. If the buffer size is chosen to be equal to the largest possible segment, space will be wasted whenever a short segment arrives. If the buffer size is chosen to be less than the maximum segment size, multiple buffers will be needed for long segments, with the attendant complexity.

Another approach to the buffer size problem is to use variable-sized buffers, as in Fig. 6-15(b). The advantage here is better memory utilization, at the price of more complicated buffer management. A third possibility is to dedicate a single large circular buffer per connection, as in Fig. 6-15(c). This system is simple and elegant and does not depend on segment sizes, but makes good use of memory only when the connections are heavily loaded.

As connections are opened and closed and as the traffic pattern changes, the sender and receiver need to dynamically adjust their buffer allocations. Consequently, the transport protocol should allow a sending host to request buffer space at the other end. Buffers could be allocated per connection, or collectively, for all the connections running between the two hosts. Alternatively, the receiver, knowing its buffer situation (but not knowing the offered traffic) could tell the sender "I have reserved *X* buffers for you." If the number of open connections should increase, it may be necessary for an allocation to be reduced, so the protocol should provide for this possibility.

A reasonably general way to manage dynamic buffer allocation is to decouple the buffering from the acknowledgements, in contrast to the sliding window protocols of Chap. 3. Dynamic buffer management means, in effect, a variable-sized

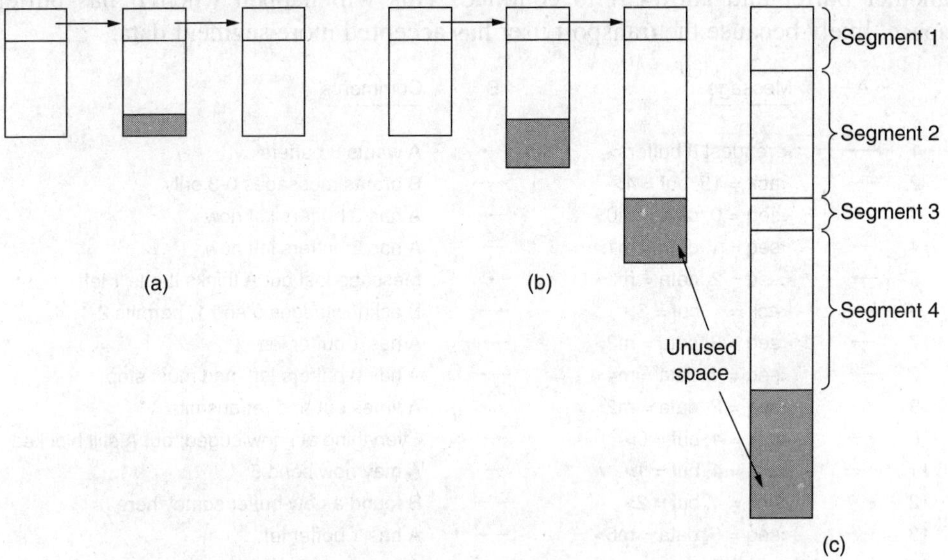

Figure 6-15. (a) Chained fixed-size buffers. (b) Chained variable-sized buffers. (c) One large circular buffer per connection.

window. Initially, the sender requests a certain number of buffers, based on its expected needs. The receiver then grants as many of these as it can afford. Every time the sender transmits a segment, it must decrement its allocation, stopping altogether when the allocation reaches zero. The receiver separately piggybacks both acknowledgements and buffer allocations onto the reverse traffic. TCP uses this scheme, carrying buffer allocations in a header field called *Window size*.

Figure 6-16 shows an example of how dynamic window management might work in a datagram network with 4-bit sequence numbers. In this example, data flows in segments from host *A* to host *B* and acknowledgements and buffer allocations flow in segments in the reverse direction. Initially, *A* wants eight buffers, but it is granted only four of these. It then sends three segments, of which the third is lost. Segment 6 acknowledges receipt of all segments up to and including sequence number 1, thus allowing *A* to release those buffers, and furthermore informs *A* that it has permission to send three more segments starting beyond 1 (i.e., segments 2, 3, and 4). *A* knows that it has already sent number 2, so it thinks that it may send segments 3 and 4, which it proceeds to do. At this point it is blocked and must wait for more buffer allocation. Timeout-induced retransmissions (line 9), however, may occur while blocked, since they use buffers that have already been allocated. In line 10, *B* acknowledges receipt of all segments up to and including 4 but refuses to let *A* continue. Such a situation is impossible with the fixed-window protocols of Chap. 3. The next segment from *B* to *A* allocates another buffer and allows *A* to continue. This will happen when *B* has buffer space, likely because the transport user has accepted more segment data.

	A	Message	B	Comments
1	→	< request 8 buffers>	→	A wants 8 buffers
2	←	<ack = 15, buf = 4>	←	B grants messages 0-3 only
3	→	<seq = 0, data = m0>	→	A has 3 buffers left now
4	→	<seq = 1, data = m1>	→	A has 2 buffers left now
5	→	<seq = 2, data = m2>	• • •	Message lost but A thinks it has 1 left
6	←	<ack = 1, buf = 3>	←	B acknowledges 0 and 1, permits 2-4
7	→	<seq = 3, data = m3>	→	A has 1 buffer left
8	→	<seq = 4, data = m4>	→	A has 0 buffers left, and must stop
9	→	<seq = 2, data = m2>	→	A times out and retransmits
10	←	<ack = 4, buf = 0>	←	Everything acknowledged, but A still blocked
11	←	<ack = 4, buf = 1>	←	A may now send 5
12	←	<ack = 4, buf = 2>	←	B found a new buffer somewhere
13	→	<seq = 5, data = m5>	→	A has 1 buffer left
14	→	<seq = 6, data = m6>	→	A is now blocked again
15	←	<ack = 6, buf = 0>	←	A is still blocked
16	• • •	<ack = 6, buf = 4>	←	Potential deadlock

Figure 6-16. Dynamic buffer allocation. The arrows show the direction of transmission. An ellipsis (...) indicates a lost segment.

Problems with buffer allocation schemes of this kind can arise in datagram networks if control segments can get lost—which they most certainly can. Look at line 16. *B* has now allocated more buffers to *A*, but the allocation segment was lost. Oops. Since control segments are not sequenced or timed out, *A* is now deadlocked. To prevent this situation, each host should periodically send control segments giving the acknowledgement and buffer status on each connection. That way, the deadlock will be broken, sooner or later.

Until now we have tacitly assumed that the only limit imposed on the sender's data rate is the amount of buffer space available in the receiver. This is often not the case. Memory was once expensive but prices have fallen dramatically. Hosts may be equipped with sufficient memory that the lack of buffers is rarely, if ever, a problem, even for wide area connections. Of course, this depends on the buffer size being set to be large enough, which has not always been the case for TCP (Zhang et al., 2002).

When buffer space no longer limits the maximum flow, another bottleneck will appear: the carrying capacity of the network. If adjacent routers can exchange at most x packets/sec and there are k disjoint paths between a pair of hosts, there is no way that those hosts can exchange more than kx segments/sec, no matter how much buffer space is available at each end. If the sender pushes too hard (i.e., sends more than *kx* segments/sec), the network will become congested because it will be unable to deliver segments as fast as they are coming in.

What is needed is a mechanism that limits transmissions from the sender based on the network's carrying capacity rather than on the receiver's buffering capacity. Belsnes (1975) proposed using a sliding window flow-control scheme in which the sender dynamically adjusts the window size to match the network's carrying capacity. This means that a dynamic sliding window can implement both flow control and congestion control. If the network can handle *c* segments/sec and the round-trip time (including transmission, propagation, queueing, processing at the receiver, and return of the acknowledgement) is *r*, the sender's window should be *cr*. With a window of this size, the sender normally operates with the pipeline full. Any small decrease in network performance will cause it to block. Since the network capacity available to any given flow varies over time, the window size should be adjusted frequently, to track changes in the carrying capacity. As we will see later, TCP uses a similar scheme.

6.2.5 Multiplexing

Multiplexing, or sharing several conversations over connections, virtual circuits, and physical links plays a role in several layers of the network architecture. In the transport layer, the need for multiplexing can arise in a number of ways. For example, if only one network address is available on a host, all transport connections on that machine have to use it. When a segment comes in, some way is needed to tell which process to give it to. This situation, called **multiplexing**, is shown in Fig. 6-17(a). In this figure, four distinct transport connections all use the same network connection (e.g., IP address) to the remote host.

Multiplexing can also be useful in the transport layer for another reason. Suppose, for example, that a host has multiple network paths that it can use. If a user needs more bandwidth or more reliability than one of the network paths can provide, a way out is to have a connection that distributes the traffic among multiple network paths on a round-robin basis, as indicated in Fig. 6-17(b). This modus operandi is called **inverse multiplexing**. With *k* network connections open, the effective bandwidth might be increased by a factor of *k*. An example of inverse multiplexing is **SCTP** (**Stream Control Transmission Protocol**), which can run a connection using multiple network interfaces. In contrast, TCP uses a single network endpoint. Inverse multiplexing is also found at the link layer, when several low-rate links are used in parallel as one high-rate link.

6.2.6 Crash Recovery

If hosts and routers are subject to crashes or connections are long-lived (e.g., large software or media downloads), recovery from these crashes becomes an issue. If the transport entity is entirely within the hosts, recovery from network

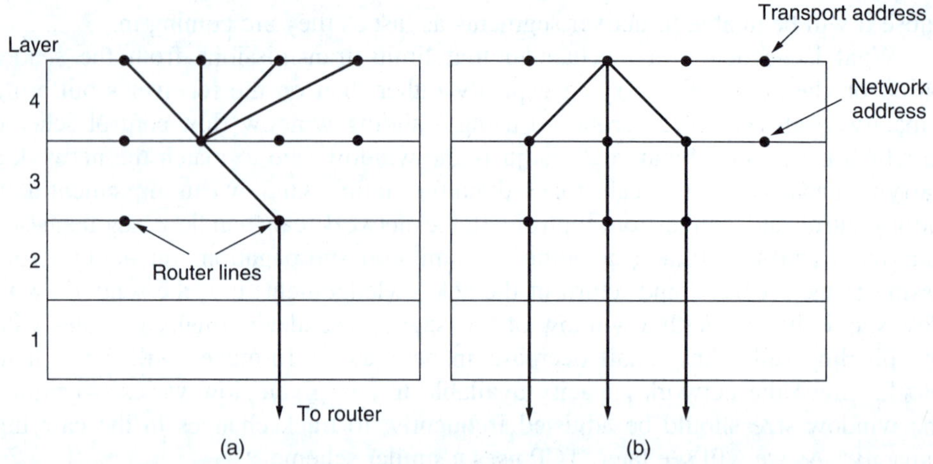

Figure 6-17. (a) Multiplexing. (b) Inverse multiplexing.

and router crashes is straightforward. The transport entities expect lost segments all the time and know how to cope with them by using retransmissions.

A more troublesome problem is how to recover from host crashes. In particular, it may be desirable for clients to be able to continue working when servers crash and quickly reboot. To illustrate the difficulty, let us assume that one host, the client, is sending a long file to another host, the file server, using a simple stop-and-wait protocol. The transport layer on the server just passes the incoming segments to the transport user, one by one. Partway through the transmission, the server crashes. When it comes back up, its tables are reinitialized, so it no longer knows precisely where it was.

In an attempt to recover its previous status, the server might send a broadcast segment to all other hosts, announcing that it has just crashed and requesting that its clients inform it of the status of all open connections. Each client can be in one of two states: one segment outstanding, *S1*, or no segments outstanding, *S0*. Based on only this state information, the client must decide whether to retransmit the most recent segment.

At first glance, it would seem obvious: the client should retransmit if and only if it has an unacknowledged segment outstanding (i.e., is in state *S1*) when it learns of the crash. However, a closer inspection reveals difficulties with this naive approach. Consider, for example, the situation in which the server's transport entity first sends an acknowledgement and then, when the acknowledgement has been sent, writes to the application process. Writing a segment onto the output stream and sending an acknowledgement are two distinct events that cannot be done simultaneously. If a crash occurs after the acknowledgement has been sent but before the write has been fully completed, the client will receive the acknowledgement and thus be in state *S0* when the crash recovery announcement arrives. The client will therefore not retransmit, (incorrectly) thinking that the segment has arrived. This decision by the client leads to a missing segment.

At this point you may be thinking: "That problem can be solved easily. All you have to do is reprogram the transport entity to first do the write and then send the acknowledgement." Try again. Imagine that the write has been done but the crash occurs before the acknowledgement can be sent. The client will be in state *S1* and thus retransmit, leading to an undetected duplicate segment in the output stream to the server application process.

No matter how the client and server are programmed, there are always situations where the protocol fails to recover properly. The server can be programmed in one of two ways: acknowledge first or write first. The client can be programmed in one of four ways: always retransmit the last segment, never retransmit the last segment, retransmit only in state *S0*, or retransmit only in state *S1*. This gives eight combinations, but as we shall see, for each combination there is some set of events that makes the protocol fail.

Three events are possible at the server: sending an acknowledgement (*A*), writing to the output process (*W*), and crashing (*C*). The three events can occur in six different orderings: *AC*(*W*), *AWC*, *C*(*AW*), *C*(*WA*), *WAC*, and *WC*(*A*), where the parentheses are used to indicate that neither *A* nor *W* can follow *C* (i.e., once it has crashed, it has crashed). Figure 6-18 shows all eight combinations of client and server strategies and the valid event sequences for each one. Notice that for each strategy there is some sequence of events that causes the protocol to fail. For example, if the client always retransmits, the *AWC* event will generate an undetected duplicate, even though the other two events work properly.

	Strategy used by receiving host					
	First ACK, then write			First write, then ACK		
Strategy used by sending host	AC(W)	AWC	C(AW)	C(WA)	W AC	WC(A)
Always retransmit	OK	DUP	OK	OK	DUP	DUP
Never retransmit	LOST	OK	LOST	LOST	OK	OK
Retransmit in S0	OK	DUP	LOST	LOST	DUP	OK
Retransmit in S1	LOST	OK	OK	OK	OK	DUP

OK = Protocol functions correctly
DUP = Protocol generates a duplicate message
LOST = Protocol loses a message

Figure 6-18. Different combinations of client and server strategies.

Making the protocol more elaborate does not help. Even if the client and server exchange several segments before the server attempts to write, so that the client knows exactly what is about to happen, the client has no way of knowing whether a crash occurred just before or just after the write. The conclusion is inescapable: under our ground rules of no simultaneous events—that is, separate events happen one after another not at the same time—host crash and recovery cannot be made transparent to higher layers.

Put in more general terms, this result can be restated as "recovery from a layer N crash can only be done by layer $N + 1$," and then only if the higher layer retains enough status information to reconstruct where it was before the problem occurred. This is consistent with the case mentioned above that the transport layer can recover from failures in the network layer, provided that each end of a connection keeps track of where it is.

This problem gets us into the issue of what a so-called end-to-end acknowledgement really means. In principle, the transport protocol is end-to-end and not chained like the lower layers. Now consider the case of a user entering requests for transactions against a remote database. Suppose that the remote transport entity is programmed to first pass segments to the next layer up and then acknowledge. Even in this case, the receipt of an acknowledgement back at the user's machine does not necessarily mean that the remote host stayed up long enough to actually update the database. A truly end-to-end acknowledgement, whose receipt means that the work has actually been done and lack thereof means that it has not, is probably impossible to achieve. This point is discussed in more detail by Saltzer et al. (1984).

6.3 CONGESTION CONTROL

If the transport entities on many machines send too many packets into the network too quickly, the network will become congested, with performance degraded as packets are delayed and lost. Controlling congestion to avoid this problem is the combined responsibility of the network and transport layers. Congestion occurs at routers, so it is detected at the network layer. However, congestion is ultimately caused by traffic sent into the network by the transport layer. The only effective way to control congestion is for the transport protocols to send packets into the network more slowly.

In Chap. 5, we studied congestion control mechanisms in the network layer. In this section, we will study the other half of the problem, congestion control mechanisms in the transport layer. After describing the goals of congestion control, we will describe how hosts can regulate the rate at which they send packets into the network. The Internet relies heavily on the transport layer for congestion control, and specific algorithms are built into TCP and other protocols.

6.3.1 Desirable Bandwidth Allocation

Before we describe how to regulate traffic, we must understand what we are trying to achieve by running a congestion control algorithm. That is, we must specify the state in which a good congestion control algorithm will operate the network. The goal is more than to simply avoid congestion. It is to find a good allocation of bandwidth to the transport entities that are using the network. A good allocation will deliver good performance because it uses all the available bandwidth but avoids congestion, it will be fair across competing transport entities, and it will quickly track changes in traffic demands. We will make each of these criteria more precise in turn.

Efficiency and Power

An efficient allocation of bandwidth across transport entities will use all of the network capacity that is available. However, it is not quite right to think that if there is a 100-Mbps link, five transport entities should get 20 Mbps each. They should usually get less than 20 Mbps for good performance. The reason is that the traffic is often bursty. Recall that in Sec. 5.3 we described the **goodput** (or rate of useful packets arriving at the receiver) as a function of the offered load. This curve and a matching curve for the delay as a function of the offered load are given in Fig. 6-19.

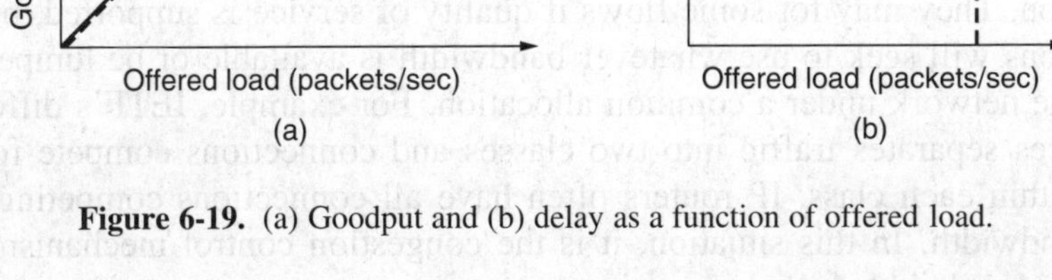

Figure 6-19. (a) Goodput and (b) delay as a function of offered load.

As the load increases in Fig. 6-19(a) goodput initially increases at the same rate, but as the load approaches the capacity, goodput rises more gradually. This falloff is because bursts of traffic can occasionally mount up and cause some losses at buffers inside the network. If the transport protocol is poorly designed and retransmits packets that have been delayed but not lost, the network can enter congestion collapse. In this state, senders are furiously sending packets, but increasingly little useful work is being accomplished.

The corresponding delay is given in Fig. 6-19(b) Initially the delay is fixed, representing the propagation delay across the network. As the load approaches the capacity, the delay rises, slowly at first and then much more rapidly. This is again because of bursts of traffic that tend to mound up at high load. The delay cannot really go to infinity, except in a model in which the routers have infinite buffers. Instead, packets will be lost after experiencing the maximum buffering delay.

For both goodput and delay, performance begins to degrade at the onset of congestion. Intuitively, we will obtain the best performance from the network if we allocate bandwidth up until the delay starts to climb rapidly. This point is below the capacity. To identify it, Kleinrock (1979) proposed the metric of **power**, where

$$power = \frac{load}{delay}$$

Power will initially rise with offered load, as delay remains small and roughly constant, but will reach a maximum and fall as delay grows rapidly. The load with the highest power represents an efficient load for the transport entity to place on the network.

Max-Min Fairness

In the preceding discussion, we did not talk about how to divide bandwidth between different transport senders. This sounds like a simple question to answer—give all the senders an equal fraction of the bandwidth—but it involves several considerations.

Perhaps the first consideration is to ask what this problem has to do with congestion control. After all, if the network gives a sender some amount of bandwidth to use, the sender should just use that much bandwidth. However, it is often the case that networks do not have a strict bandwidth reservation for each flow or connection. They may for some flows if quality of service is supported, but many connections will seek to use whatever bandwidth is available or be lumped together by the network under a common allocation. For example, IETF's differentiated services separates traffic into two classes and connections compete for bandwidth within each class. IP routers often have all connections competing for the same bandwidth. In this situation, it is the congestion control mechanism that is allocating bandwidth to the competing connections.

A second consideration is what a fair portion means for flows in a network. It is simple enough if N flows use a single link, in which case they can all have $1/N$ of the bandwidth (although efficiency will dictate that they use slightly less if the traffic is bursty). But what happens if the flows have different, but overlapping, network paths? For example, one flow may cross three links, and the other flows may cross one link. The three-link flow consumes more network resources. It might be fairer in some sense to give it less bandwidth than the one-link flows. It should certainly be possible to support more one-link flows by reducing the bandwidth of the three-link flow. This point demonstrates an inherent tension between fairness and efficiency.

However, we will adopt a notion of fairness that does not depend on the length of the network path. Even with this simple model, giving connections an equal fraction of bandwidth is a bit complicated because different connections will take different paths through the network and these paths will themselves have different capacities. In this case, it is possible for a flow to be bottlenecked on a downstream link and take a smaller portion of an upstream link than other flows; reducing the bandwidth of the other flows would slow them down but would not help the bottlenecked flow at all.

The form of fairness that is often desired for network usage is **max-min fairness**. An allocation is max-min fair if the bandwidth given to one flow cannot be increased without decreasing the bandwidth given to another flow with an allocation that is no larger. That is, increasing the bandwidth of a flow will only make the situation worse for flows that are less well off.

Let us see an example. A max-min fair allocation is shown for a network with four flows, *A*, *B*, *C*, and *D*, in Fig. 6-20. Each of the links between routers has the same capacity, taken to be 1 unit, though in the general case the links will have different capacities. Three flows compete for the bottom-left link between routers *R4* and *R5*. Each of these flows therefore gets 1/3 of the link. The remaining flow, *A*, competes with *B* on the link from *R2* to *R3*. Since *B* has an allocation of 1/3, *A* gets the remaining 2/3 of the link. Notice that all of the other links have spare capacity. However, this capacity cannot be given to any of the flows without decreasing the capacity of another, lower flow. For example, if more of the bandwidth on the link between *R2* and *R3* is given to flow *B*, there will be less for flow *A*. This is reasonable as flow *A* already has more bandwidth. However, the capacity of flow *C* or *D* (or both) must be decreased to give more bandwidth to *B*, and these flows will have less bandwidth than *B*. Thus, the allocation is max-min fair.

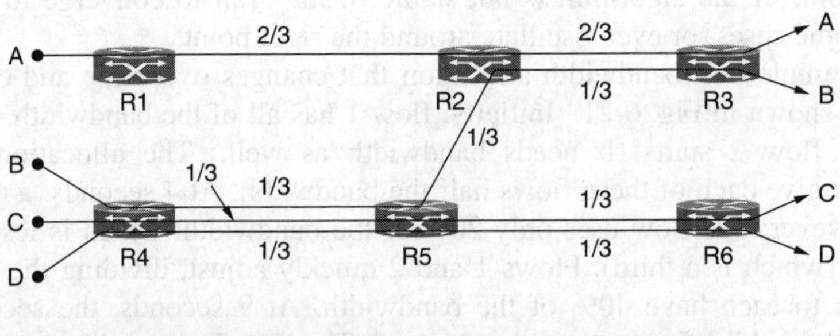

Figure 6-20. Max-min bandwidth allocation for four flows.

Max-min allocations can be computed given a global knowledge of the network. An intuitive way to think about them is to imagine that the rate for all of the flows starts at zero and is slowly increased. When the rate reaches a bottleneck for any flow, then that flow stops increasing. The other flows all continue to increase, sharing equally in the available capacity, until they too reach their respective bottlenecks.

A third consideration is the level over which to consider fairness. A network could be fair at the level of connections, connections between a pair of hosts, or all connections per host. We examined this issue when we were discussing WFQ (Weighted Fair Queueing) in Sec. 5.4 and concluded that each of these definitions has its problems. For example, defining fairness per host means that a busy server will fare no better than a mobile phone, while defining fairness per connection encourages hosts to open more connections. Given that there is no clear answer, fairness is often considered per connection, but precise fairness is usually not a concern. It is more important in practice that no connection be starved of bandwidth than that all connections get precisely the same amount of bandwidth. In fact, with TCP it is possible to open multiple connections and compete for bandwidth more aggressively. This tactic is used by bandwidth-hungry applications such as BitTorrent for peer-to-peer file sharing.

Convergence

A final criterion is that the congestion control algorithm converge quickly to a fair and efficient allocation of bandwidth. The discussion of the desirable operating point above assumes a static network environment. However, connections are always coming and going in a network, and the bandwidth needed by a given connection will vary over time too, for example, as a user browses Web pages and occasionally downloads large videos.

Because of the variation in demand, the ideal operating point for the network varies over time. A good congestion control algorithm should rapidly converge to the ideal operating point, and it should track that point as it changes over time. If the convergence is too slow, the algorithm will never be close to the changing operating point. If the algorithm is not stable, it may fail to converge to the right point in some cases, or even oscillate around the right point.

An example of a bandwidth allocation that changes over time and converges quickly is shown in Fig. 6-21. Initially, flow 1 has all of the bandwidth. One second later, flow 2 starts. It needs bandwidth as well. The allocation quickly changes to give each of these flows half the bandwidth. At 4 seconds, a third flow joins. However, this flow uses only 20% of the bandwidth, which is less than its fair share (which is a third). Flows 1 and 2 quickly adjust, dividing the available bandwidth to each have 40% of the bandwidth. At 9 seconds, the second flow leaves, and the third flow remains unchanged. The first flow quickly captures 80% of the bandwidth. At all times, the total allocated bandwidth is approximately 100%, so that the network is fully used, and competing flows get equal treatment (but do not have to use more bandwidth than they need).

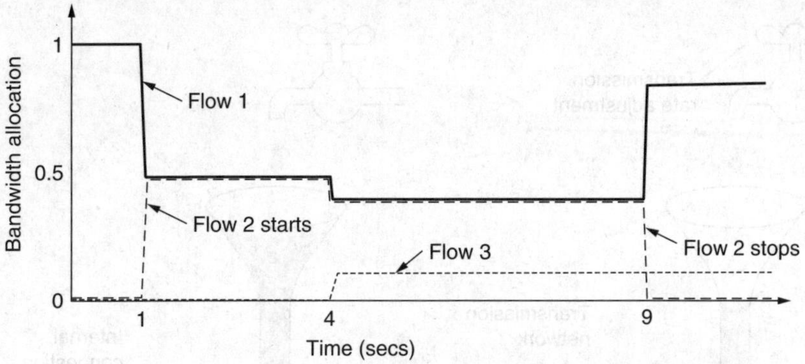

Figure 6-21. Changing bandwidth allocation over time.

6.3.2 Regulating the Sending Rate

Now it is time for the main course. How do we regulate the sending rates to obtain a desirable bandwidth allocation? The sending rate may be limited by two factors. The first is flow control, in the case that there is insufficient buffering at the receiver. The second is congestion, in the case that there is insufficient capacity in the network. In Fig. 6-22, we see this problem illustrated hydraulically. In Fig. 6-22(a), we see a thick pipe leading to a small-capacity receiver. This is a flow-control limited situation. As long as the sender does not send more water than the bucket can contain, no water will be lost. In Fig. 6-22(b), the limiting factor is not the bucket capacity, but the internal carrying capacity of the network. If too much water comes in too fast, it will back up and some will be lost (in this case, by overflowing the funnel).

These cases may appear similar to the sender, as transmitting too fast causes packets to be lost. However, they have different causes and call for different solutions. We have already talked about a flow-control solution with a variable-sized window. Now we will consider a congestion control solution. Since either of these problems can occur, the transport protocol will in general need to run both solutions and slow down if either problem occurs.

The way that a transport protocol should regulate the sending rate depends on the form of the feedback returned by the network. Different network layers may return different kinds of feedback. The feedback may be explicit or implicit, and it may be precise or imprecise.

An example of an explicit, precise design is when routers tell the sources the rate at which they may send. Designs in the literature such as XCP (eXplicit Congestion Protocol) operate in this manner (Katabi et al., 2002). An explicit, imprecise design is the use of ECN (Explicit Congestion Notification) with TCP. In this design, routers set bits on packets that experience congestion to warn the senders to slow down, but they do not tell them how much to slow down.

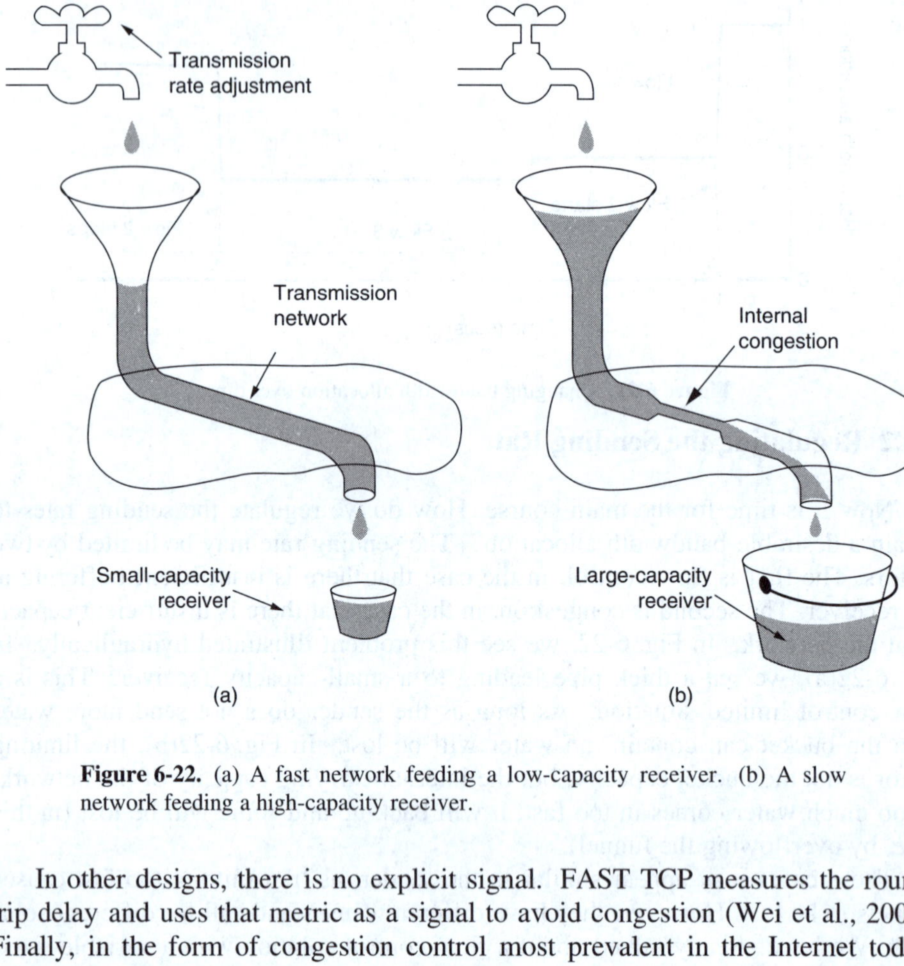

Figure 6-22. (a) A fast network feeding a low-capacity receiver. (b) A slow network feeding a high-capacity receiver.

In other designs, there is no explicit signal. FAST TCP measures the round-trip delay and uses that metric as a signal to avoid congestion (Wei et al., 2006). Finally, in the form of congestion control most prevalent in the Internet today, TCP with drop-tail or RED routers, packet loss is inferred and used to signal that the network has become congested. There are many variants of this form of TCP, including CUBIC TCP, which is used in Linux (Ha et al., 2008). Combinations are also possible. For example, Windows includes Compound TCP that uses both packet loss and delay as feedback signals (Tan et al., 2006). These designs are summarized in Fig. 6-23.

If an explicit and precise signal is given, the transport entity can use that signal to adjust its rate to the new operating point. For example, if XCP tells senders the rate to use, the senders may simply use that rate. In the other cases, however, some guesswork is involved. In the absence of a congestion signal, the senders should decrease their rates. When a congestion signal is given, the senders should decrease their rates. The way in which the rates are increased or decreased is given by a **control law**. These laws have a major effect on performance.

Protocol	Signal	Explicit?	Precise?
XCP	Rate to use	Yes	Yes
TCP with ECN	Congestion warning	Yes	No
FAST TCP	End-to-end delay	No	Yes
Compound TCP	Packet loss & end-to-end delay	No	Yes
CUBIC TCP	Packet loss	No	No
TCP	Packet loss	No	No

Figure 6-23. Signals of some congestion control protocols.

Chiu and Jain (1989) studied the case of binary congestion feedback and concluded that **AIMD (Additive Increase Multiplicative Decrease)** is the appropriate control law to arrive at the efficient and fair operating point. To argue this case, they constructed a graphical argument for the simple case of two connections competing for the bandwidth of a single link. The graph in Fig. 6-24 shows the bandwidth allocated to user 1 on the x-axis and to user 2 on the y-axis. When the allocation is fair, both users will receive the same amount of bandwidth. This is shown by the dotted fairness line. When the allocations sum to 100%, the capacity of the link, the allocation is efficient. This is shown by the dotted efficiency line. A congestion signal is given by the network to both users when the sum of their allocations crosses this line. The intersection of these lines is the desired operating point, when both users have the same bandwidth and all of the network bandwidth is used.

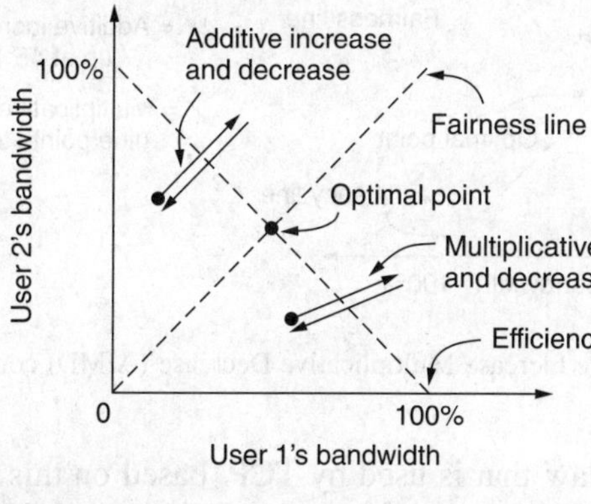

Figure 6-24. Additive and multiplicative bandwidth adjustments.

Consider what happens from some starting allocation if both user 1 and user 2 additively increase their respective bandwidths over time. For example, the users may each increase their sending rate by 1 Mbps every second. Eventually, the operating point crosses the efficiency line and both users receive a congestion signal from the network. At this stage, they must reduce their allocations. However, an additive decrease would simply cause them to oscillate along an additive line. This situation is shown in Fig. 6-24. The behavior will keep the operating point close to efficient, but it will not necessarily be fair.

Similarly, consider the case when both users multiplicatively increase their bandwidth over time until they receive a congestion signal. For example, the users may increase their sending rate by 10% every second. If they then multiplicatively decrease their sending rates, the operating point of the users will simply oscillate along a multiplicative line. This behavior is also shown in Fig. 6-24. The multiplicative line has a different slope than the additive line. (It points to the origin, while the additive line has an angle of 45 degrees.) But it is otherwise no better. In neither case will the users converge to the optimal sending rates that are both fair and efficient.

Now consider the case that the users additively increase their bandwidth allocations and then multiplicatively decrease them when congestion is signaled. This behavior is the AIMD control law, and it is shown in Fig. 6-25. It can be seen that the path traced by this behavior does converge to the optimal point that is both fair and efficient. This convergence happens no matter what the starting point, making AIMD broadly useful. By the same argument, the only other combination, multiplicative increase and additive decrease, would diverge from the optimal point.

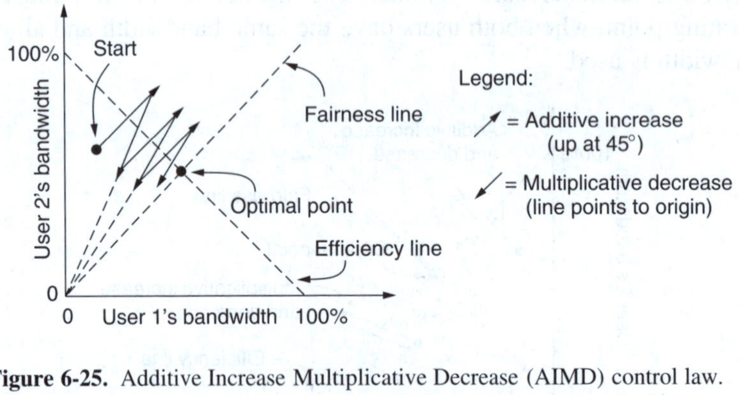

Figure 6-25. Additive Increase Multiplicative Decrease (AIMD) control law.

AIMD is the control law that is used by TCP, based on this argument and another stability argument (that it is easy to drive the network into congestion and difficult to recover, so the increase policy should be gentle and the decrease policy aggressive). It is not quite fair, since TCP connections adjust their window size by a given amount every round-trip time. Different connections will have different round-trip times. This leads to a bias in which connections to closer hosts receive more bandwidth than connections to distant hosts, all else being equal.

In Sec. 6.5, we will describe in detail how TCP implements an AIMD control law to adjust the sending rate and provide congestion control. This task is more difficult than it sounds because rates are measured over some interval and traffic is bursty. Instead of adjusting the rate directly, a strategy that is often used in practice is to adjust the size of a sliding window. TCP uses this strategy. If the window size is *W* and the round-trip time is *RTT*, the equivalent rate is *W/RTT*. This strategy is easy to combine with flow control, which already uses a window, and has the advantage that the sender paces packets using acknowledgements and hence slows down in one *RTT* if it stops receiving reports that packets are leaving the network.

As a final issue, there may be many different transport protocols that send traffic into the network. What will happen if the different protocols compete with different control laws to avoid congestion? Unequal bandwidth allocations, that is what. Since TCP is the dominant form of congestion control in the Internet, there is significant community pressure for new transport protocols to be designed so that they compete fairly with it. The early streaming media protocols caused problems by excessively reducing TCP throughput because they did not compete fairly. This led to the notion of **TCP-friendly** congestion control in which TCP and non-TCP transport protocols can be freely mixed with no ill effects (Floyd et al., 2000).

6.3.3 Wireless Issues

Transport protocols such as TCP that implement congestion control should be independent of the underlying network and link layer technologies. That is a good theory, but in practice there are issues with wireless networks. The main issue is that packet loss is often used as a congestion signal, including by TCP as we have just discussed. Wireless networks lose packets all the time due to transmission errors.

With the AIMD control law, high throughput requires very small levels of packet loss. Analyses by Padhye et al. (1998) show that the throughput goes up as the inverse square-root of the packet loss rate. What this means in practice is that the loss rate for fast TCP connections is very small; 1% is a moderate loss rate, and by the time the loss rate reaches 10% the connection has effectively stopped working. However, for wireless networks such as 802.11 LANs, frame loss rates of at least 10% are common. This difference means that, absent protective measures, congestion control schemes that use packet loss as a signal will unnecessarily throttle connections that run over wireless links to very low rates.

To function well, the only packet losses that the congestion control algorithm should observe are losses due to insufficient bandwidth, not losses due to transmission errors. One solution to this problem is to mask the wireless losses by using retransmissions over the wireless link. For example, 802.11 uses a stop-and-wait protocol to deliver each frame, retrying transmissions multiple times if need be before reporting a packet loss to the higher layer. In the normal case, each packet is delivered despite transient transmission errors that are not visible to the higher layers.

Fig. 6-26 shows a path with a wired and wireless link for which the masking strategy is used. There are two aspects to note. First, the sender does not necessarily know that the path includes a wireless link, since all it sees is the wired link to which it is attached. Internet paths are heterogeneous and there is no general method for the sender to tell what kind of links comprise the path. This complicates the congestion control problem, as there is no easy way to use one protocol for wireless links and another protocol for wired links.

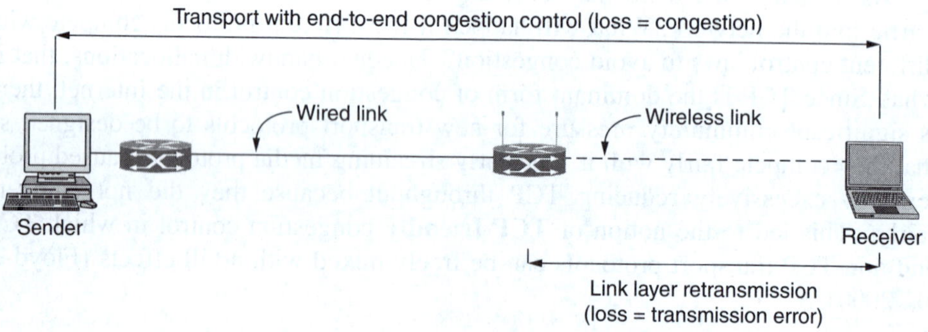

Figure 6-26. Congestion control over a path with a wireless link.

The second aspect is a puzzle. The figure shows two mechanisms that are driven by loss: link layer frame retransmissions, and transport layer congestion control. The puzzle is how these two mechanisms can co-exist without getting confused. After all, a loss should cause only one mechanism to take action because it is either a transmission error or a congestion signal. It cannot be both. If both mechanisms take action (by retransmitting the frame and slowing down the sending rate) then we are back to the original problem of transports that run far too slowly over wireless links. Consider this puzzle for a moment and see if you can solve it.

The solution is that the two mechanisms act at different timescales. Link layer retransmissions happen on the order of microseconds to milliseconds for wireless links such as 802.11. Loss timers in transport protocols fire on the order of milliseconds to seconds. The difference is three orders of magnitude. This allows wireless links to detect frame losses and retransmit frames to repair transmission errors long before packet loss is inferred by the transport entity.

The masking strategy is sufficient to let most transport protocols run well across most wireless links. However, it is not always a fitting solution. Some wireless links have long round-trip times, such as satellites. For these links other techniques must be used to mask loss, such as FEC (Forward Error Correction), or the transport protocol must use a non-loss signal for congestion control.

A second issue with congestion control over wireless links is variable capacity. That is, the capacity of a wireless link changes over time, sometimes abruptly, as nodes move and the signal-to-noise ratio varies with the changing channel conditions. This is unlike wired links whose capacity is fixed. The transport protocol must adapt to the changing capacity of wireless links, otherwise it will either congest the network or fail to use the available capacity.

One possible solution to this problem is simply not to worry about it. This strategy is feasible because congestion control algorithms must already handle the case of new users entering the network or existing users changing their sending rates. Even though the capacity of wired links is fixed, the changing behavior of other users presents itself as variability in the bandwidth that is available to a given user. Thus it is possible to simply run TCP over a path with an 802.11 wireless link and obtain reasonable performance.

However, when there is much wireless variability, transport protocols designed for wired links may have trouble keeping up and deliver poor performance. The solution in this case is a transport protocol that is designed for wireless links. A particularly challenging setting is a wireless mesh network in which multiple, interfering wireless links must be crossed, routes change due to mobility, and there is lots of loss. Research in this area is ongoing. See Li et al. (2009) for an example of wireless transport protocol design.

6.4 THE INTERNET TRANSPORT PROTOCOLS: UDP

The Internet has two main protocols in the transport layer, a connectionless protocol and a connection-oriented one. The protocols complement each other. The connectionless protocol is UDP. It does almost nothing beyond sending packets between applications, letting applications build their own protocols on top as needed. The connection-oriented protocol is TCP. It does almost everything. It makes connections and adds reliability with retransmissions, along with flow control and congestion control, all on behalf of the applications that use it.

In the following sections, we will study UDP and TCP. We will start with UDP because it is simplest. We will also look at two uses of UDP. Since UDP is a transport layer protocol that typically runs in the operating system and protocols that use UDP typically run in user space, these uses might be considered applications. However, the techniques they use are useful for many applications and are better considered to belong to a transport service, so we will cover them here.

6.4.1 Introduction to UDP

The Internet protocol suite supports a connectionless transport protocol called **UDP (User Datagram Protocol)**. UDP provides a way for applications to send encapsulated IP datagrams without having to establish a connection. UDP is described in RFC 768.

UDP transmits **segments** consisting of an 8-byte header followed by the payload. The header is shown in Fig. 6-27. The two **ports** serve to identify the endpoints within the source and destination machines. When a UDP packet arrives, its payload is handed to the process attached to the destination port. This attachment occurs when the BIND primitive or something similar is used, as we saw in Fig. 6-6 for TCP (the binding process is the same for UDP). Think of ports as mailboxes that applications can rent to receive packets. We will have more to say about them when we describe TCP, which also uses ports. In fact, the main value of UDP over just using raw IP is the addition of the source and destination ports. Without the port fields, the transport layer would not know what to do with each incoming packet. With them, it delivers the embedded segment to the correct application.

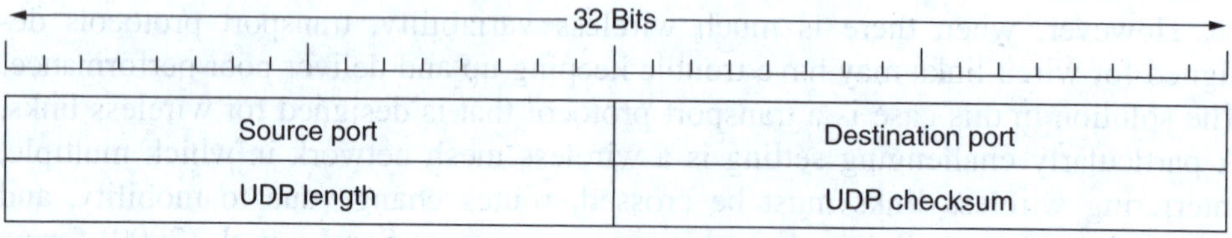

Figure 6-27. The UDP header.

The source port is primarily needed when a reply must be sent back to the source. By copying the *Source port* field from the incoming segment into the *Destination port* field of the outgoing segment, the process sending the reply can specify which process on the sending machine is to get it.

The *UDP length* field includes the 8-byte header and the data. The minimum length is 8 bytes, to cover the header. The maximum length is 65,515 bytes, which is lower than the largest number that will fit in 16 bits because of the size limit on IP packets.

An optional *Checksum* is also provided for extra reliability. It checksums the header, the data, and a conceptual IP pseudoheader. When performing this computation, the *Checksum* field is set to zero and the data field is padded out with an additional zero byte if its length is an odd number. The checksum algorithm is simply to add up all the 16-bit words in one's complement and to take the one's complement of the sum. As a consequence, when the receiver performs the calculation on the entire segment, including the *Checksum* field, the result should be 0. If the checksum is not computed, it is stored as a 0, since by a happy coincidence of one's complement arithmetic a true computed 0 is stored as all 1s. However, turning it off is foolish unless the quality of the data does not matter (e.g., for digitized speech).

The pseudoheader for the case of IPv4 is shown in Fig. 6-28. It contains the 32-bit IPv4 addresses of the source and destination machines, the protocol number for UDP (17), and the byte count for the UDP segment (including the header). It is different but analogous for IPv6. Including the pseudoheader in the UDP checksum computation helps detect misdelivered packets, but including it also violates the protocol hierarchy since the IP addresses in it belong to the IP layer, not to the UDP layer. TCP uses the same pseudoheader for its checksum.

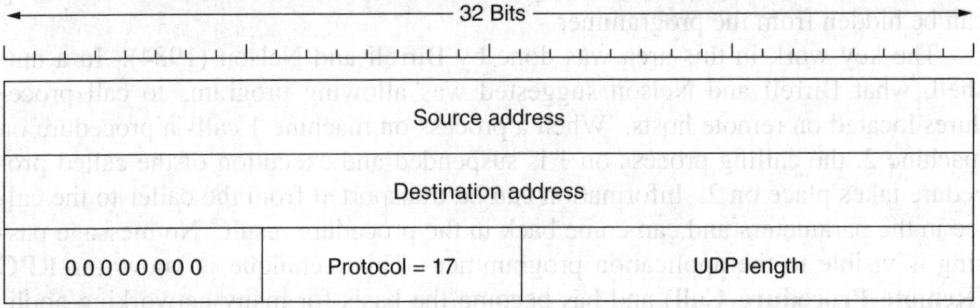

Figure 6-28. The IPv4 pseudoheader included in the UDP checksum.

It is probably worth mentioning explicitly some of the things that UDP does *not* do. It does not do flow control, congestion control, or retransmission upon receipt of a bad segment. All of that is up to the user processes. What it does do is provide an interface to the IP protocol with the added feature of demultiplexing multiple processes using the ports and optional end-to-end error detection. That is all it does.

For applications that need to have precise control over the packet flow, error control, or timing, UDP provides just what the doctor ordered. One area where it is especially useful is in client-server situations. Often, the client sends a short request to the server and expects a short reply back. If either the request or the reply is lost, the client can just time out and try again. Not only is the code simple, but fewer messages are required (one in each direction) than with a protocol requiring an initial setup like TCP.

An application that uses UDP this way is DNS (Domain Name System), which we will study in Chap. 7. In brief, a program that needs to look up the IP address of some host name, for example, *www.cs.berkeley.edu*, can send a UDP packet containing the host name to a DNS server. The server replies with a UDP packet containing the host's IP address. No setup is needed in advance and no release is needed afterward. Just two messages go over the network.

6.4.2 Remote Procedure Call

In a certain sense, sending a message to a remote host and getting a reply back is a lot like making a function call in a programming language. In both cases, you start with one or more parameters and you get back a result. This observation has led people to try to arrange request-reply interactions on networks to be cast in the form of procedure calls. Such an arrangement makes network applications much easier to program and more familiar to deal with. For example, just imagine a procedure named *get_IP_address*(*host_name*) that works by sending a UDP packet to a DNS server and waiting for the reply, timing out and trying again if one is not forthcoming quickly enough. In this way, all the details of networking can be hidden from the programmer.

The key work in this area was done by Birrell and Nelson (1984). In a nutshell, what Birrell and Nelson suggested was allowing programs to call procedures located on remote hosts. When a process on machine 1 calls a procedure on machine 2, the calling process on 1 is suspended and execution of the called procedure takes place on 2. Information can be transported from the caller to the callee in the parameters and can come back in the procedure result. No message passing is visible to the application programmer. This technique is known as **RPC** (**Remote Procedure Call**) and has become the basis for many networking applications. Traditionally, the calling procedure is known as the client and the called procedure is known as the server, and we will use those names here too.

The idea behind RPC is to make a remote procedure call look as much as possible like a local one. In the simplest form, to call a remote procedure, the client program must be bound with a small library procedure, called the **client stub**, that represents the server procedure in the client's address space. Similarly, the server is bound with a procedure called the **server stub**. These procedures hide the fact that the procedure call from the client to the server is not local.

The actual steps in making an RPC are shown in Fig. 6-29. Step 1 is the client calling the client stub. This call is a local procedure call, with the parameters pushed onto the stack in the normal way. Step 2 is the client stub packing the parameters into a message and making a system call to send the message. Packing the parameters is called **marshaling**. Step 3 is the operating system sending the message from the client machine to the server machine. Step 4 is the operating system passing the incoming packet to the server stub. Finally, step 5 is the server stub calling the server procedure with the unmarshaled parameters. The reply traces the same path in the other direction.

The key item to note here is that the client procedure, written by the user, just makes a normal (i.e., local) procedure call to the client stub, which has the same name as the server procedure. Since the client procedure and client stub are in the same address space, the parameters are passed in the usual way. Similarly, the server procedure is called by a procedure in its address space with the parameters it expects. To the server procedure, nothing is unusual. In this way, instead of I/O being done on sockets, network communication is done by faking a normal procedure call.

Despite the conceptual elegance of RPC, there are a few snakes hiding under the grass. A big one is the use of pointer parameters. Normally, passing a pointer to a procedure is not a problem. The called procedure can use the pointer in the same way the caller can because both procedures live in the same virtual address

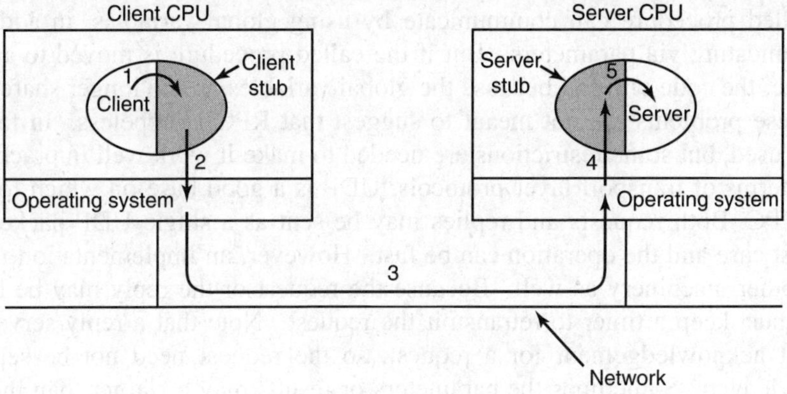

Figure 6-29. Steps in making a remote procedure call. The stubs are shaded.

space. With RPC, passing pointers is impossible because the client and server are in different address spaces.

In some cases, tricks can be used to make it possible to pass pointers. Suppose that the first parameter is a pointer to an integer, *k*. The client stub can marshal *k* and send it along to the server. The server stub then creates a pointer to *k* and passes it to the server procedure, just as it expects. When the server procedure returns control to the server stub, the latter sends *k* back to the client, where the new *k* is copied over the old one, just in case the server changed it. In effect, the standard calling sequence of call-by-reference has been replaced by call-by-copy-restore. Unfortunately, this trick does not always work, for example, if the pointer points to a graph or other complex data structure. For this reason, some restrictions must be placed on parameters to procedures called remotely, as we shall see.

A second problem is that in weakly typed languages, like C, it is perfectly legal to write a procedure that computes the inner product of two vectors (arrays), without specifying how large either one is. Each could be terminated by a special value known only to the calling and called procedures. Under these circumstances, it is essentially impossible for the client stub to marshal the parameters: it has no way of determining how large they are.

A third problem is that it is not always possible to deduce the types of the parameters, not even from a formal specification or the code itself. An example is *printf*, which may have any number of parameters (at least one), and the parameters can be an arbitrary mixture of integers, shorts, longs, characters, strings, floating-point numbers of various lengths, and other types. Trying to call *printf* as a remote procedure would be practically impossible because C is so permissive. However, a rule saying that RPC can be used provided that you do not program in C (or C++) would not be popular with a lot of programmers.

A fourth problem relates to the use of global variables. Normally, the calling and called procedure can communicate by using global variables, in addition to communicating via parameters. But if the called procedure is moved to a remote machine, the code will fail because the global variables are no longer shared.

These problems are not meant to suggest that RPC is hopeless. In fact, it is widely used, but some restrictions are needed to make it work well in practice.

In terms of transport layer protocols, UDP is a good base on which to implement RPC. Both requests and replies may be sent as a single UDP packet in the simplest case and the operation can be fast. However, an implementation must include other machinery as well. Because the request or the reply may be lost, the client must keep a timer to retransmit the request. Note that a reply serves as an implicit acknowledgement for a request, so the request need not be separately acknowledged. Sometimes the parameters or results may be larger than the maximum UDP packet size, in which case some protocol is needed to deliver large messages. If multiple requests and replies can overlap (as in the case of concurrent programming), an identifier is needed to match the request with the reply.

A higher-level concern is that the operation may not be idempotent (i.e., safe to repeat). The simple case is idempotent operations such as DNS requests and replies. The client can safely retransmit these requests again and again if no replies are forthcoming. It does not matter whether the server never received the request, or it was the reply that was lost. The answer, when it finally arrives, will be the same (assuming the DNS database is not updated in the meantime). However, not all operations are idempotent, for example, because they have important side-effects such as incrementing a counter. RPC for these operations requires stronger semantics so that when the programmer calls a procedure it is not executed multiple times. In this case, it may be necessary to set up a TCP connection and send the request over it rather than using UDP.

6.4.3 Real-Time Transport Protocols

Client-server RPC is one area in which UDP is widely used. Another one is for real-time multimedia applications. In particular, as Internet radio, Internet telephony, music-on-demand, videoconferencing, video-on-demand, and other multimedia applications became more commonplace, people have discovered that each application was reinventing more or less the same real-time transport protocol. It gradually became clear that having a generic real-time transport protocol for multiple applications would be a good idea.

Thus was **RTP (Real-time Transport Protocol)** born. It is described in RFC 3550 and is now in widespread use for multimedia applications. We will describe two aspects of real-time transport. The first is the RTP protocol for transporting audio and video data in packets. The second is the processing that takes place, mostly at the receiver, to play out the audio and video at the right time. These functions fit into the protocol stack as shown in Fig. 6-30.

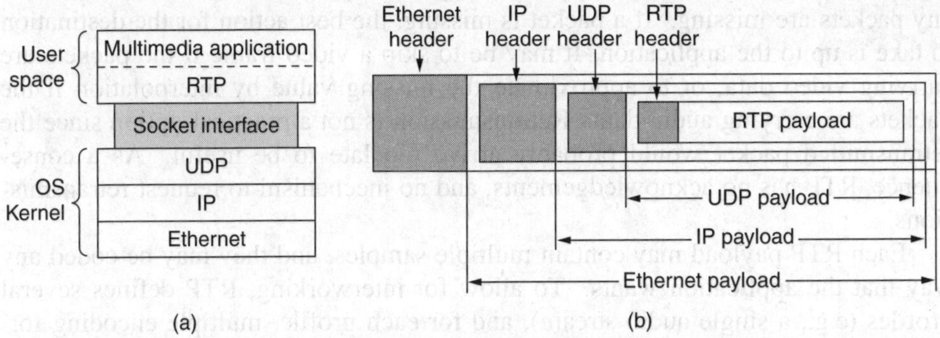

Figure 6-30. (a) The position of RTP in the protocol stack. (b) Packet nesting.

RTP normally runs in user space over UDP (in the operating system). It operates as follows. The multimedia application consists of multiple audio, video, text, and possibly other streams. These are fed into the RTP library, which is in user space along with the application. This library multiplexes the streams and encodes them in RTP packets, which it stuffs into a socket. On the operating system side of the socket, UDP packets are generated to wrap the RTP packets and handed to IP for transmission over a link such as Ethernet. The reverse process happens at the receiver. The multimedia application eventually receives multimedia data from the RTP library. It is responsible for playing out the media. The protocol stack for this situation is shown in Fig. 6-30(a). The packet nesting is shown in Fig. 6-30(b).

As a consequence of this design, it is a little hard to say which layer RTP is in. Since it runs in user space and is linked to the application program, it certainly looks like an application protocol. On the other hand, it is a generic, application-independent protocol that just provides transport facilities, so it also looks like a transport protocol. Probably the best description is that it is a transport protocol that just happens to be implemented in the application layer, which is why we are covering it in this chapter.

RTP—The Real-time Transport Protocol

The basic function of RTP is to multiplex several real-time data streams onto a single stream of UDP packets. The UDP stream can be sent to a single destination (unicasting) or to multiple destinations (multicasting). Because RTP just uses normal UDP, its packets are not treated specially by the routers unless some normal IP quality-of-service features are enabled. In particular, there are no special guarantees about delivery, and packets may be lost, delayed, corrupted, etc.

The RTP format contains several features to help receivers work with multimedia information. Each packet sent in an RTP stream is given a number one higher than its predecessor. This numbering allows the destination to determine if any packets are missing. If a packet is missing, the best action for the destination to take is up to the application. It may be to skip a video frame if the packets are carrying video data, or to approximate the missing value by interpolation if the packets are carrying audio data. Retransmission is not a practical option since the retransmitted packet would probably arrive too late to be useful. As a consequence, RTP has no acknowledgements, and no mechanism to request retransmissions.

Each RTP payload may contain multiple samples, and they may be coded any way that the application wants. To allow for interworking, RTP defines several profiles (e.g., a single audio stream), and for each profile, multiple encoding formats may be allowed. For example, a single audio stream may be encoded as 8-bit PCM samples at 8 kHz using delta encoding, predictive encoding, GSM encoding, MP3 encoding, and so on. RTP provides a header field in which the source can specify the encoding but is otherwise not involved in how encoding is done.

Another facility many real-time applications need is timestamping. The idea here is to allow the source to associate a timestamp with the first sample in each packet. The timestamps are relative to the start of the stream, so only the differences between timestamps are significant. The absolute values have no meaning. As we will describe shortly, this mechanism allows the destination to do a small amount of buffering and play each sample the right number of milliseconds after the start of the stream, independently of when the packet containing the sample arrived.

Not only does timestamping reduce the effects of variation in network delay, but it also allows multiple streams to be synchronized with each other. For example, a digital television program might have a video stream and two audio streams. The two audio streams could be for stereo broadcasts or for handling films with an original language soundtrack and a soundtrack dubbed into the local language, giving the viewer a choice. Each stream comes from a different physical device, but if they are timestamped from a single counter, they can be played back synchronously, even if the streams are transmitted and/or received somewhat erratically.

The RTP header is illustrated in Fig. 6-31. It consists of three 32-bit words and potentially some extensions. The first word contains the *Version* field, which is already at 2. Let us hope this version is very close to the ultimate version since there is only one code point left (although 3 could be defined as meaning that the real version was in an extension word).

The *P* bit indicates that the packet has been padded to a multiple of 4 bytes. The last padding byte tells how many bytes were added. The *X* bit indicates that an extension header is present. The format and meaning of the extension header are not defined. The only thing that is defined is that the first word of the extension gives the length. This is an escape hatch for any unforeseen requirements.

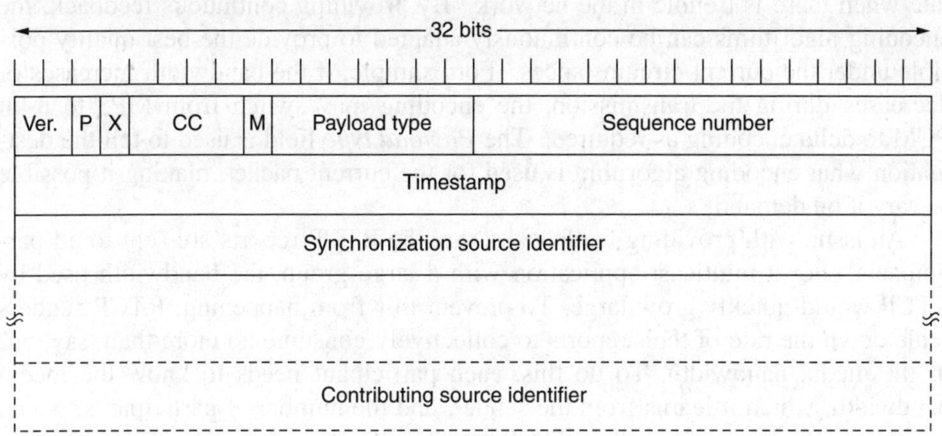

Figure 6-31. The RTP header.

The *CC* field tells how many contributing sources are present, from 0 to 15 (see below). The *M* bit is an application-specific marker bit. It can be used to mark the start of a video frame, the start of a word in an audio channel, or something else that the application understands. The *Payload type* field tells which encoding algorithm has been used (e.g., uncompressed 8-bit audio, MP3, etc.). Since every packet carries this field, the encoding can change during transmission. The *Sequence number* is just a counter that is incremented on each RTP packet sent. It is used to detect lost packets.

The *Timestamp* is produced by the stream's source to note when the first sample in the packet was made. This value can help reduce timing variability called jitter at the receiver by decoupling the playback from the packet arrival time. The *Synchronization source identifier* tells which stream the packet belongs to. It is the method used to multiplex and demultiplex multiple data streams onto a single stream of UDP packets. Finally, the *Contributing source identifiers*, if any, are used when mixers are present in the studio. In that case, the mixer is the synchronizing source, and the streams being mixed are listed here.

RTCP—The Real-time Transport Control Protocol

RTP has a little sister protocol (little sibling protocol?) called **RTCP (Realtime Transport Control Protocol)**. It is defined along with RTP in RFC 3550 and handles feedback, synchronization, and the user interface. It does not transport any media samples.

The first function can be used to provide feedback on delay, variation in delay or jitter, bandwidth, congestion, and other network properties to the sources. This information can be used by the encoding process to increase the data rate (and give better quality) when the network is functioning well and to cut back the data rate when there is trouble in the network. By providing continuous feedback, the encoding algorithms can be continuously adapted to provide the best quality possible under the current circumstances. For example, if the bandwidth increases or decreases during the transmission, the encoding may switch from MP3 to 8-bit PCM to delta encoding as required. The *Payload type* field is used to tell the destination what encoding algorithm is used for the current packet, making it possible to vary it on demand.

An issue with providing feedback is that the RTCP reports are sent to all participants. For a multicast application with a large group, the bandwidth used by RTCP would quickly grow large. To prevent this from happening, RTCP senders scale down the rate of their reports to collectively consume no more than, say, 5% of the media bandwidth. To do this, each participant needs to know the media bandwidth, which it learns from the sender, and the number of participants, which it estimates by listening to other RTCP reports.

RTCP also handles interstream synchronization. The problem is that different streams may use different clocks, with different granularities and different drift rates. RTCP can be used to keep them in sync.

Finally, RTCP provides a way for naming the various sources (e.g., in ASCII text). This information can be displayed on the receiver's screen to indicate who is talking at the moment.

More information about RTP can be found in Perkins (2003).

Playout with Buffering and Jitter Control

Once the media information reaches the receiver, it must be played out at the right time. In general, this will not be the time at which the RTP packet arrived at the receiver because packets will take slightly different amounts of time to transit the network. Even if the packets are injected with exactly the right intervals between them at the sender, they will reach the receiver with different relative times. This variation in delay is called **jitter**. Even a small amount of packet jitter can cause distracting media artifacts, such as jerky video frames and unintelligible audio, if the media is simply played out as it arrives.

The solution to this problem is to **buffer** packets at the receiver before they are played out to reduce the jitter. As an example, in Fig. 6-32 we see a stream of packets being delivered with a substantial amount of jitter. Packet 1 is sent from the server at $t = 0$ sec and arrives at the client at $t = 1$ sec. Packet 2 undergoes more delay and takes 2 sec to arrive. As the packets arrive, they are buffered on the client machine.

At $t = 10$ sec, playback begins. At this time, packets 1 through 6 have been buffered so that they can be removed from the buffer at uniform intervals for smooth play. In the general case, it is not necessary to use uniform intervals because the RTP timestamps tell when the media should be played.

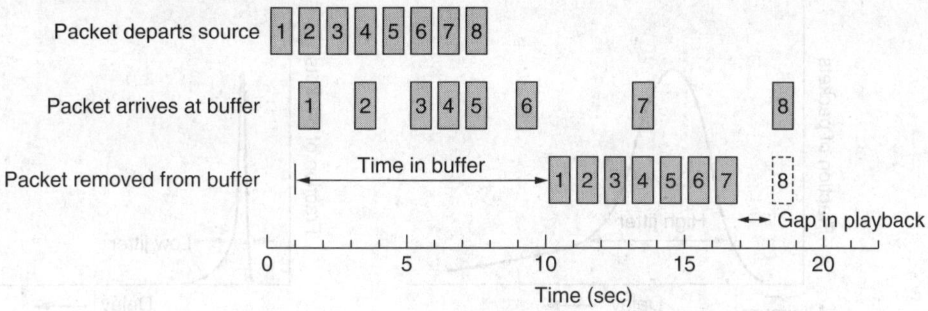

Figure 6-32. Smoothing the output stream by buffering packets.

Unfortunately, we can see that packet 8 has been delayed so much that it is not available when its play slot comes up. There are two options. Packet 8 can be skipped and the player can move on to subsequent packets. Alternatively, playback can stop until packet 8 arrives, creating an annoying gap in the music or movie. In a live media application like a voice-over-IP call, the packet will typically be skipped. Live applications do not work well on hold. In a streaming media application, the player might pause. This problem can be alleviated by delaying the starting time even more, by using a larger buffer. For a streaming audio or video player, buffers of about 10 seconds are often used to ensure that the player receives all of the packets (that are not dropped in the network) in time. For live applications like videoconferencing, short buffers are needed for responsiveness.

A key consideration for smooth playout is the **playback point**, or how long to wait at the receiver for media before playing it out. Deciding how long to wait depends on the jitter. The difference between a low-jitter and high-jitter connection is shown in Fig. 6-33. The average delay may not differ greatly between the two, but if there is high jitter the playback point may need to be much further out to capture 99% of the packets than if there is low jitter.

To pick a good playback point, the application can measure the jitter by looking at the difference between the RTP timestamps and the arrival time. Each difference gives a sample of the delay (plus an arbitrary, fixed offset). However, the delay can change over time due to other, competing traffic and changing routes. To accommodate this change, applications can adapt their playback point while they are running. However, if not done well, changing the playback point can produce an observable glitch to the user. One way to avoid this problem for audio is to adapt the playback point between **talkspurts**, in the gaps in a conversation. No one will notice the difference between a short and slightly longer silence. RTP lets applications set the *M* marker bit to indicate the start of a new talkspurt for this purpose.

If the absolute delay until media is played out is too long, live applications will suffer. Nothing can be done to reduce the propagation delay if a direct path is

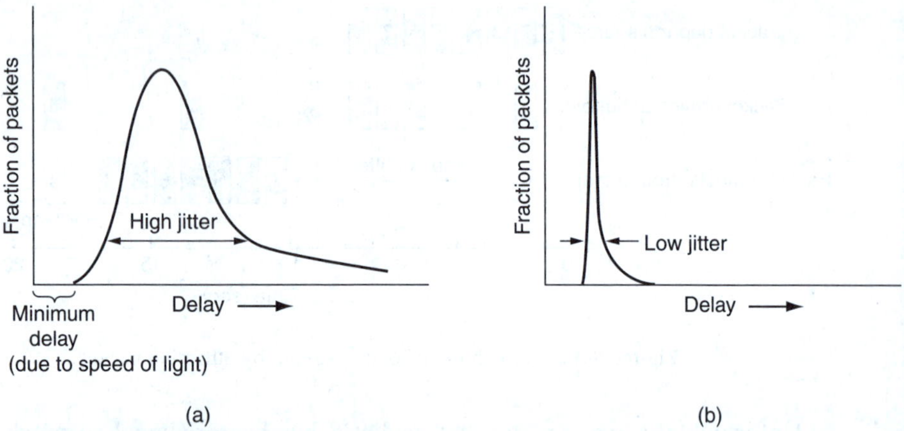

Figure 6-33. (a) High jitter. (b) Low jitter.

already being used. The playback point can be pulled in by simply accepting that a larger fraction of packets will arrive too late to be played. If this is not acceptable, the only way to pull in the playback point is to reduce the jitter by using a better quality of service, for example, the expedited forwarding differentiated service. That is, a better network is needed.

6.5 THE INTERNET TRANSPORT PROTOCOLS: TCP

UDP is a simple protocol and it has some very important uses, such as client-server interactions and multimedia, but for most Internet applications, reliable, sequenced delivery is needed. UDP cannot provide this, so another protocol is required. It is called TCP and is the main workhorse of the Internet. Let us now study it in detail.

6.5.1 Introduction to TCP

TCP (Transmission Control Protocol) was specifically designed to provide a reliable end-to-end byte stream over an unreliable internetwork. An internetwork differs from a single network because different parts may have wildly different topologies, bandwidths, delays, packet sizes, and other parameters. TCP was designed to dynamically adapt to properties of the internetwork and to be robust in the face of many kinds of failures.

TCP was formally defined in RFC 793 in September 1981. As time went on, many improvements have been made, and various errors and inconsistencies have been fixed. To give you a sense of the extent of TCP, the important RFCs are now RFC 793 plus: clarifications and bug fixes in RFC 1122; extensions for high-performance in RFC 1323; selective acknowledgements in RFC 2018; congestion control in RFC 2581; repurposing of header fields for quality of service in RFC 2873; improved retransmission timers in RFC 2988; and explicit congestion notification in RFC 3168. The full collection is even larger, which led to a guide to the many RFCs, published of course as another RFC document, RFC 4614.

Each machine supporting TCP has a TCP transport entity, either a library procedure, a user process, or most commonly part of the kernel. In all cases, it manages TCP streams and interfaces to the IP layer. A TCP entity accepts user data streams from local processes, breaks them up into pieces not exceeding 64 KB (in practice, often 1460 data bytes in order to fit in a single Ethernet frame with the IP and TCP headers), and sends each piece as a separate IP datagram. When datagrams containing TCP data arrive at a machine, they are given to the TCP entity, which reconstructs the original byte streams. For simplicity, we will sometimes use just "TCP" to mean the TCP transport entity (a piece of software) or the TCP protocol (a set of rules). From the context it will be clear which is meant. For example, in "The user gives TCP the data," the TCP transport entity is clearly intended.

The IP layer gives no guarantee that datagrams will be delivered properly, nor any indication of how fast datagrams may be sent. It is up to TCP to send datagrams fast enough to make use of the capacity but not cause congestion, and to time out and retransmit any datagrams that are not delivered. Datagrams that do arrive may well do so in the wrong order; it is also up to TCP to reassemble them into messages in the proper sequence. In short, TCP must furnish good performance with the reliability that most applications want and that IP does not provide.

6.5.2 The TCP Service Model

TCP service is obtained by both the sender and the receiver creating end points, called **sockets**, as discussed in Sec. 6.1.3. Each socket has a socket number (address) consisting of the IP address of the host and a 16-bit number local to that host, called a **port**. A port is the TCP name for a TSAP. For TCP service to be obtained, a connection must be explicitly established between a socket on one machine and a socket on another machine. The socket calls are listed in Fig. 6-5.

A socket may be used for multiple connections at the same time. In other words, two or more connections may terminate at the same socket. Connections are identified by the socket identifiers at both ends, that is, (*socket1*, *socket2*). No virtual circuit numbers or other identifiers are used.

Port numbers below 1024 are reserved for standard services that can usually only be started by privileged users (e.g., root in UNIX systems). They are called **well-known ports**. For example, any process wishing to remotely retrieve mail from a host can connect to the destination host's port 143 to contact its IMAP daemon. The list of well-known ports is given at *www.iana.org*. Over 700 have been assigned. A few of the better-known ones are listed in Fig. 6-34.

Port	Protocol	Use
20, 21	FTP	File transfer
22	SSH	Remote login, replacement for Telnet
25	SMTP	Email
80	HTTP	World Wide Web
110	POP-3	Remote email access
143	IMAP	Remote email access
443	HTTPS	Secure Web (HTTP over SSL/TLS)
543	RTSP	Media player control
631	IPP	Printer sharing

Figure 6-34. Some assigned ports.

Other ports from 1024 through 49151 can be registered with IANA for use by unprivileged users, but applications can and do choose their own ports. For example, the BitTorrent peer-to-peer file-sharing application (unofficially) uses ports 6881–6887, but may run on other ports as well.

It would certainly be possible to have the FTP daemon attach itself to port 21 at boot time, the SSH daemon attach itself to port 22 at boot time, and so on. However, doing so would clutter up memory with daemons that were idle most of the time. Instead, what is commonly done is to have a single daemon, called **inetd** (**Internet daemon**) in UNIX, attach itself to multiple ports and wait for the first incoming connection. When that occurs, *inetd* forks off a new process and executes the appropriate daemon in it, letting that daemon handle the request. In this way, the daemons other than *inetd* are only active when there is work for them to do. Inetd learns which ports it is to use from a configuration file. Consequently, the system administrator can set up the system to have permanent daemons on the busiest ports (e.g., port 80) and *inetd* on the rest.

All TCP connections are full duplex and point-to-point. Full duplex means that traffic can go in both directions at the same time. Point-to-point means that each connection has exactly two end points. TCP does not support multicasting or broadcasting.

A TCP connection is a byte stream, not a message stream. Message boundaries are not preserved end to end. For example, if the sending process does four 512-byte writes to a TCP stream, these data may be delivered to the receiving process as four 512-byte chunks, two 1024-byte chunks, one 2048-byte chunk (see Fig. 6-35), or some other way. There is no way for the receiver to detect the unit(s) in which the data were written, no matter how hard it tries.

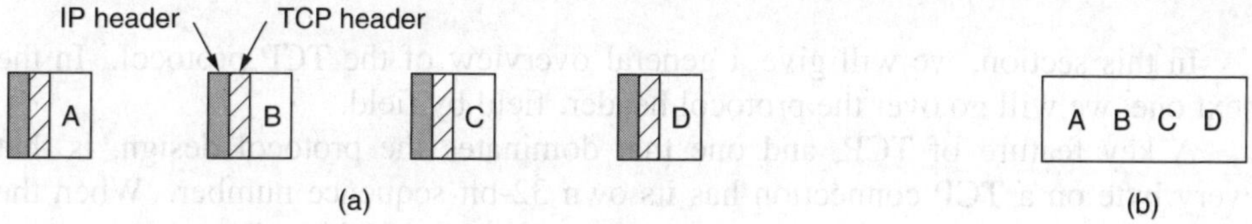

Figure 6-35. (a) Four 512-byte segments sent as separate IP datagrams. (b) The 2048 bytes of data delivered to the application in a single READ call.

Files in UNIX have this property too. The reader of a file cannot tell whether the file was written a block at a time, a byte at a time, or all in one blow. As with a UNIX file, the TCP software has no idea of what the bytes mean and no interest in finding out. A byte is just a byte.

When an application passes data to TCP, TCP may send it immediately or buffer it (in order to collect a larger amount to send at once), at its discretion. However, sometimes the application really wants the data to be sent immediately. For example, suppose a user of an interactive game wants to send a stream of updates. It is essential that the updates be sent immediately, not buffered until there is a collection of them. To force data out, TCP has the notion of a PUSH flag that is carried on packets. The original intent was to let applications tell TCP implementations via the PUSH flag not to delay the transmission. However, applications cannot literally set the PUSH flag when they send data. Instead, different operating systems have evolved different options to expedite transmission (e.g., TCP_NODELAY in Windows and Linux).

For Internet archaeologists, we will also mention one interesting feature of TCP service that remains in the protocol but is rarely used: **urgent data**. When an application has high priority data that should be processed immediately, for example, if an interactive user hits the CTRL-C key to break off a remote computation that has already begun, the sending application can put some control information in the data stream and give it to TCP along with the URGENT flag. This event causes TCP to stop accumulating data and transmit everything it has for that connection immediately.

When the urgent data are received at the destination, the receiving application is interrupted (e.g., given a signal in UNIX terms) so it can stop whatever it was doing and read the data stream to find the urgent data. The end of the urgent data is marked so the application knows when it is over. The start of the urgent data is not marked. It is up to the application to figure that out.

This scheme provides a crude signaling mechanism and leaves everything else up to the application. However, while urgent data is potentially useful, it found no compelling application early on and fell into disuse. Its use is now discouraged because of implementation differences, leaving applications to handle their own signaling. Perhaps future transport protocols will provide better signaling.

6.5.3 The TCP Protocol

In this section, we will give a general overview of the TCP protocol. In the next one, we will go over the protocol header, field by field.

A key feature of TCP, and one that dominates the protocol design, is that every byte on a TCP connection has its own 32-bit sequence number. When the Internet began, the lines between routers were mostly 56-kbps leased lines, so a host blasting away at full speed took over 1 week to cycle through the sequence numbers. At modern network speeds, the sequence numbers can be consumed at an alarming rate, as we will see later. Separate 32-bit sequence numbers are carried on packets for the sliding window position in one direction and for acknowledgements in the reverse direction, as discussed below.

The sending and receiving TCP entities exchange data in the form of segments. A **TCP segment** consists of a fixed 20-byte header (plus an optional part) followed by zero or more data bytes. The TCP software decides how big segments should be. It can accumulate data from several writes into one segment or can split data from one write over multiple segments. Two limits restrict the segment size. First, each segment, including the TCP header, must fit in the 65,515-byte IP payload. Second, each link has an **MTU** (**Maximum Transfer Unit**). Each segment must fit in the MTU at the sender and receiver so that it can be sent and received in a single, unfragmented packet. In practice, the MTU is generally 1500 bytes (the Ethernet payload size) and thus defines the upper bound on segment size.

However, it is still possible for IP packets carrying TCP segments to be fragmented when passing over a network path for which some link has a small MTU. If this happens, it degrades performance and causes other problems (Kent and Mogul, 1987). Instead, modern TCP implementations perform **path MTU discovery** by using the technique outlined in RFC 1191 that we described in Sec. 5.5.5. This technique uses ICMP error messages to find the smallest MTU for any link on the path. TCP then adjusts the segment size downwards to avoid fragmentation.

The basic protocol used by TCP entities is the sliding window protocol with a dynamic window size. When a sender transmits a segment, it also starts a timer. When the segment arrives at the destination, the receiving TCP entity sends back a segment (with data if any exist, and otherwise without) bearing an acknowledgement number equal to the next sequence number it expects to receive and the remaining window size. If the sender's timer goes off before the acknowledgement is received, the sender transmits the segment again.

Although this protocol sounds simple, there are many sometimes subtle ins and outs, which we will cover below. Segments can arrive out of order, so bytes 3072–4095 can arrive but cannot be acknowledged because bytes 2048–3071 have not turned up yet. Segments can also be delayed so long in transit that the sender times out and retransmits them. The retransmissions may include different byte ranges than the original transmission, requiring careful administration to keep track of which bytes have been correctly received so far. However, since each byte in the stream has its own unique offset, it can be done.

TCP must be prepared to deal with these problems and solve them in an efficient way. A considerable amount of effort has gone into optimizing the performance of TCP streams, even in the face of network problems. A number of the algorithms used by many TCP implementations will be discussed below.

6.5.4 The TCP Segment Header

Figure 6-36 shows the layout of a TCP segment. Every segment begins with a fixed-format, 20-byte header. The fixed header may be followed by header options. After the options, if any, up to $65,535 - 20 - 20 = 65,495$ data bytes may follow, where the first 20 refer to the IP header and the second to the TCP header. Segments without any data are legal and are commonly used for acknowledgements and control messages.

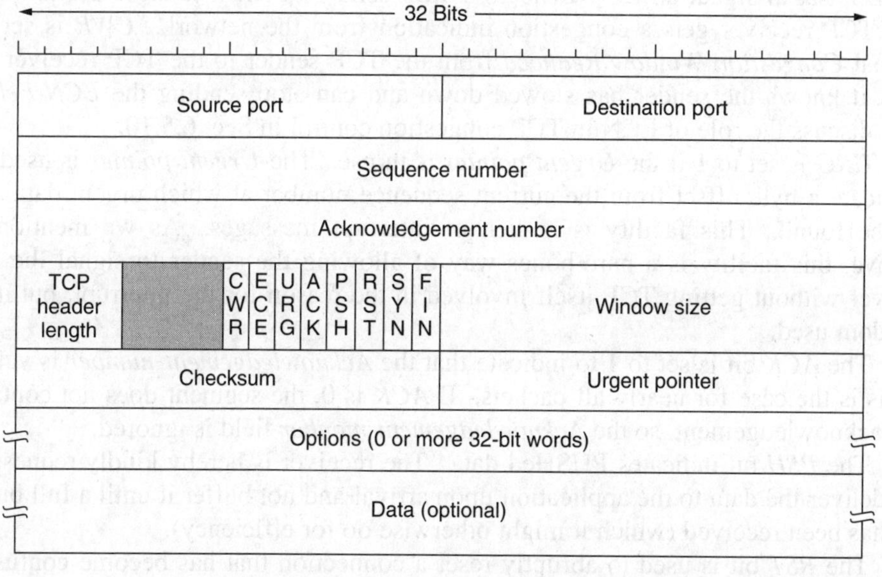

Figure 6-36. The TCP header.

Let us dissect the TCP header field by field. The *Source port* and *Destination port* fields identify the local end points of the connection. A TCP port plus its host's IP address forms a 48-bit unique end point. The source and destination end points together identify the connection. This connection identifier is called a **5 tuple** because it consists of five pieces of information: the protocol (TCP), source IP and source port, and destination IP and destination port.

The *Sequence number* and *Acknowledgement number* fields perform their usual functions. Note that the latter specifies the next in-order byte expected, not the last byte correctly received. It is a **cumulative acknowledgement** because it summarizes the received data with a single number. It does not go beyond lost data. Both are 32 bits because every byte of data is numbered in a TCP stream.

The *TCP header length* tells how many 32-bit words are contained in the TCP header. This information is needed because the *Options* field is of variable length, so the header is, too. Technically, this field really indicates the start of the data within the segment, measured in 32-bit words, but that number is just the header length in words, so the effect is the same.

Next comes a 4-bit field that is not used. The fact that these bits have remained unused for 30 years (as only 2 of the original reserved 6 bits have been reclaimed) is testimony to how well thought out TCP is. Lesser protocols would have needed these bits to fix bugs in the original design.

Now come eight 1-bit flags. *CWR* and *ECE* are used to signal congestion when ECN (Explicit Congestion Notification) is used, as specified in RFC 3168. *ECE* is set to signal an *ECN-Echo* to a TCP sender to tell it to slow down when the TCP receiver gets a congestion indication from the network. *CWR* is set to signal *Congestion Window Reduced* from the TCP sender to the TCP receiver so that it knows the sender has slowed down and can stop sending the *ECN-Echo*. We discuss the role of ECN in TCP congestion control in Sec. 6.5.10.

URG is set to 1 if the *Urgent pointer* is in use. The *Urgent pointer* is used to indicate a byte offset from the current sequence number at which urgent data are to be found. This facility is in lieu of interrupt messages. As we mentioned above, this facility is a bare-bones way of allowing the sender to signal the receiver without getting TCP itself involved in the reason for the interrupt, but it is seldom used.

The *ACK* bit is set to 1 to indicate that the *Acknowledgement number* is valid. This is the case for nearly all packets. If *ACK* is 0, the segment does not contain an acknowledgement, so the *Acknowledgement number* field is ignored.

The *PSH* bit indicates PUSHed data. The receiver is hereby kindly requested to deliver the data to the application upon arrival and not buffer it until a full buffer has been received (which it might otherwise do for efficiency).

The *RST* bit is used to abruptly reset a connection that has become confused due to a host crash or some other reason. It is also used to reject an invalid segment or refuse an attempt to open a connection. In general, if you get a segment with the *RST* bit on, you have a problem on your hands.

The *SYN* bit is used to establish connections. The connection request has *SYN* = 1 and *ACK* = 0 to indicate that the piggyback acknowledgement field is not in use. The connection reply does bear an acknowledgement, however, so it has *SYN* = 1 and *ACK* = 1. In essence, the *SYN* bit is used to denote both CONNECTION REQUEST and CONNECTION ACCEPTED, with the *ACK* bit used to distinguish between those two possibilities.

The *FIN* bit is used to release a connection. It specifies that the sender has no more data to *transmit*. However, after closing a connection, the closing process may continue to *receive* data indefinitely. Both *SYN* and *FIN* segments have sequence numbers and are thus guaranteed to be processed in the correct order.

Flow control in TCP is handled using a variable-sized sliding window. The *Window size* field tells how many bytes may be sent starting at the byte acknowledged. A *Window size* field of 0 is legal and says that the bytes up to and including *Acknowledgement number* – 1 have been received, but that the receiver has not had a chance to consume the data and would like no more data for the moment, thank you. The receiver can later grant permission to send by transmitting a segment with the same *Acknowledgement number* and a nonzero *Window size* field.

In the protocols of Chap. 3, acknowledgements of frames received and permission to send new frames were tied together. This was a consequence of a fixed window size for each protocol. In TCP, acknowledgements and permission to send additional data are completely decoupled. In effect, a receiver can say: "I have received bytes up through *k* but I do not want any more just now, thank you." This decoupling (in fact, a variable-sized window) gives additional flexibility. We will study it in detail below.

A *Checksum* is also provided for extra reliability. It checksums the header, the data, and a conceptual pseudoheader in exactly the same way as UDP, except that the pseudoheader has the protocol number for TCP (6) and the checksum is mandatory. Please see Sec. 6.4.1 for details.

The *Options* field provides a way to add extra facilities not covered by the regular header. Many options have been defined and several are commonly used. The options are of variable length, fill a multiple of 32 bits by using padding with zeros, and may extend to 40 bytes to accommodate the longest TCP header that can be specified. Some options are carried when a connection is established to negotiate or inform the other side of capabilities. Other options are carried on packets during the lifetime of the connection. Each option has a Type-Length-Value encoding.

A widely used option is the one that allows each host to specify the **MSS** (**Maximum Segment Size**) it is willing to accept. Using large segments is more efficient than using small ones because the 20-byte header can be amortized over more data, but small hosts may not be able to handle big segments. During connection setup, each side can announce its maximum and see its partner's. If a host does not use this option, it defaults to a 536-byte payload. All Internet hosts are required to accept TCP segments of 536 + 20 = 556 bytes. The maximum segment size in the two directions need not be the same.

For lines with high bandwidth, high delay, or both, the 64-KB window corresponding to a 16-bit field is a problem. For example, on an OC-12 line (of roughly 600 Mbps), it takes less than 1 msec to output a full 64-KB window. If the round-trip propagation delay is 50 msec (which is typical for a transcontinental fiber), the sender will be idle more than 98% of the time waiting for acknowledgements. A larger window size would allow the sender to keep pumping data out. The **window scale** option allows the sender and receiver to negotiate a window scale factor at the start of a connection. Both sides use the scale factor to shift the *Window size* field up to 14 bits to the left, thus allowing windows of up to 2^{30} bytes. Most TCP implementations support this option.

The **timestamp** option carries a timestamp sent by the sender and echoed by the receiver. It is included in every packet, once its use is established during connection setup, and used to compute round-trip time samples that are used to estimate when a packet has been lost. It is also used as a logical extension of the 32-bit sequence number. On a fast connection, the sequence number may wrap around quickly, leading to possible confusion between old and new data. The **PAWS** (**Protection Against Wrapped Sequence numbers**) scheme discards arriving segments with old timestamps to prevent this problem.

Finally, the **SACK** (**Selective ACKnowledgement**) option lets a receiver tell a sender the ranges of sequence numbers that it has received. It supplements the *Acknowledgement number* and is used after a packet has been lost but subsequent (or duplicate) data has arrived. The new data is not reflected by the *Acknowledgement number* field in the header because that field gives only the next in-order byte that is expected. With SACK, the sender is explicitly aware of what data the receiver has and hence can determine what data should be retransmitted. SACK is defined in RFC 2108 and RFC 2883 and is increasingly used. We describe the use of SACK along with congestion control in Sec. 6.5.10.

6.5.5 TCP Connection Establishment

Connections are established in TCP by means of the three-way handshake discussed in Sec. 6.2.2. To establish a connection, one side, say, the server, passively waits for an incoming connection by executing the LISTEN and ACCEPT primitives in that order, either specifying a specific source or nobody in particular.

The other side, say, the client, executes a CONNECT primitive, specifying the IP address and port to which it wants to connect, the maximum TCP segment size it is willing to accept, and optionally some user data (e.g., a password). The CONNECT primitive sends a TCP segment with the *SYN* bit on and *ACK* bit off and waits for a response.

When this segment arrives at the destination, the TCP entity there checks to see if there is a process that has done a LISTEN on the port given in the *Destination port* field. If not, it sends a reply with the *RST* bit on to reject the connection.

If some process is listening to the port, that process is given the incoming TCP segment. It can either accept or reject the connection. If it accepts, an acknowledgement segment is sent back. The sequence of TCP segments sent in the normal case is shown in Fig. 6-37(a). Note that a *SYN* segment consumes 1 byte of sequence space so that it can be acknowledged unambiguously.

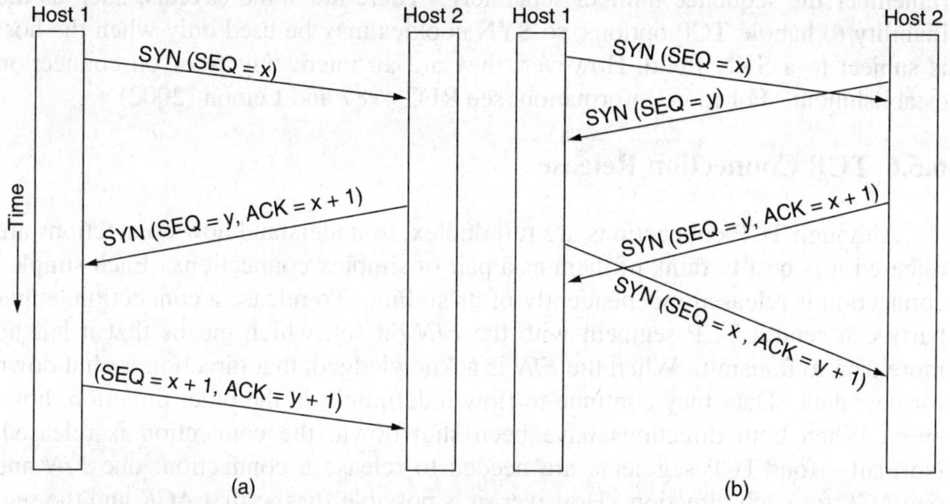

Figure 6-37. (a) TCP connection establishment in the normal case. (b) Simultaneous connection establishment on both sides.

In the event that two hosts simultaneously attempt to establish a connection between the same two sockets, the sequence of events is as illustrated in Fig. 6-37(b). The result of these events is that just one connection is established, not two, because connections are identified by their end points. If the first setup results in a connection identified by (x, y) and the second one does too, only one table entry is made, namely, for (x, y).

Recall that the initial sequence number chosen by each host should cycle slowly, rather than be a constant such as 0. This rule is to protect against delayed duplicate packets, as we discussed in Sec 6.2.2. Originally this was accomplished with a clock-based scheme in which the clock ticked every 4 μsec.

However, a vulnerability with implementing the three-way handshake is that the listening process must remember its sequence number as soon it responds with its own *SYN* segment. This means that a malicious sender can tie up resources on a host by sending a stream of *SYN* segments and never following through to complete the connection. This attack is called a **SYN flood**, and it crippled many Web servers in the 1990s.

One way to defend against this attack is to use **SYN cookies**. Instead of remembering the sequence number, a host chooses a cryptographically generated sequence number, puts it on the outgoing segment, and forgets it. If the three-way handshake completes, this sequence number (plus 1) will be returned to the host. It can then regenerate the correct sequence number by running the same cryptographic function, as long as the inputs to that function are known, for example, the other host's IP address and port, and a local secret. This procedure allows the host to check that an acknowledged sequence number is correct without having to remember the sequence number separately. There are some caveats, such as the inability to handle TCP options, so SYN cookies may be used only when the host is subject to a SYN flood. However, they are an interesting twist on connection establishment. For more information, see RFC 4987 and Lemon (2002).

6.5.6 TCP Connection Release

Although TCP connections are full duplex, to understand how connections are released it is best to think of them as a pair of simplex connections. Each simplex connection is released independently of its sibling. To release a connection, either party can send a TCP segment with the *FIN* bit set, which means that it has no more data to transmit. When the *FIN* is acknowledged, that direction is shut down for new data. Data may continue to flow indefinitely in the other direction, however. When both directions have been shut down, the connection is released. Normally, four TCP segments are needed to release a connection: one *FIN* and one *ACK* for each direction. However, it is possible for the first *ACK* and the second *FIN* to be contained in the same segment, reducing the total count to three.

Just as with telephone calls in which both people say goodbye and hang up the phone simultaneously, both ends of a TCP connection may send *FIN* segments at the same time. These are each acknowledged in the usual way, and the connection is shut down. There is, in fact, no essential difference between the two hosts releasing sequentially or simultaneously.

To avoid the two-army problem (discussed in Sec. 6.2.3), timers are used. If a response to a *FIN* is not forthcoming within two maximum packet lifetimes, the sender of the *FIN* releases the connection. The other side will eventually notice that nobody seems to be listening to it anymore and will time out as well. While this solution is not perfect, given the fact that a perfect solution is theoretically impossible, it will have to do. In practice, problems rarely arise.

6.5.7 TCP Connection Management Modeling

The steps required to establish and release connections can be represented in a finite state machine with the 11 states listed in Fig. 6-38. In each state, certain events are legal. When a legal event happens, some action may be taken. If some other event happens, an error is reported.

Each connection starts in the *CLOSED* state. It leaves that state when it does either a passive open (LISTEN) or an active open (CONNECT). If the other side does the opposite one, a connection is established and the state becomes *ESTABLISHED*. Connection release can be initiated by either side. When it is complete, the state returns to *CLOSED*.

The finite state machine itself is shown in Fig. 6-39. The common case of a client actively connecting to a passive server is shown with heavy lines—solid for the client, dotted for the server. The lightface lines are unusual event sequences.

State	Description
CLOSED	No connection is active or pending
LISTEN	The server is waiting for an incoming call
SYN RCVD	A connection request has arrived; wait for ACK
SYN SENT	The application has started to open a connection
ESTABLISHED	The normal data transfer state
FIN WAIT 1	The application has said it is finished
FIN WAIT 2	The other side has agreed to release
TIME WAIT	Wait for all packets to die off
CLOSING	Both sides have tried to close simultaneously
CLOSE WAIT	The other side has initiated a release
LAST ACK	Wait for all packets to die off

Figure 6-38. The states used in the TCP connection management finite state machine.

Each line in Fig. 6-39 is marked by an *event/action* pair. The event can either be a user-initiated system call (CONNECT, LISTEN, SEND, or CLOSE), a segment arrival (*SYN*, *FIN*, *ACK*, or *RST*), or, in one case, a timeout of twice the maximum packet lifetime. The action is the sending of a control segment (*SYN*, *FIN*, or *RST*) or nothing, indicated by —. Comments are shown in parentheses.

One can best understand the diagram by first following the path of a client (the heavy solid line), then later following the path of a server (the heavy dashed line). When an application program on the client machine issues a CONNECT request, the local TCP entity creates a connection record, marks it as being in the *SYN SENT* state, and shoots off a *SYN* segment. Note that many connections may be open (or being opened) at the same time on behalf of multiple applications, so the state is per connection and recorded in the connection record. When the *SYN+ACK* arrives, TCP sends the final *ACK* of the three-way handshake and switches into the *ESTABLISHED* state. Data can now be sent and received.

When an application is finished, it executes a CLOSE primitive, which causes the local TCP entity to send a *FIN* segment and wait for the corresponding *ACK* (dashed box marked "active close"). When the *ACK* arrives, a transition is made to the state *FIN WAIT 2* and one direction of the connection is closed. When the other side closes, too, a *FIN* comes in, which is acknowledged. Now both sides are closed, but TCP waits a time equal to twice the maximum packet lifetime to guarantee that all packets from the connection have died off, just in case the acknowledgement was lost. When the timer goes off, TCP deletes the connection record.

Now let us examine connection management from the server's viewpoint. The server does a LISTEN and settles down to see who turns up. When a *SYN*

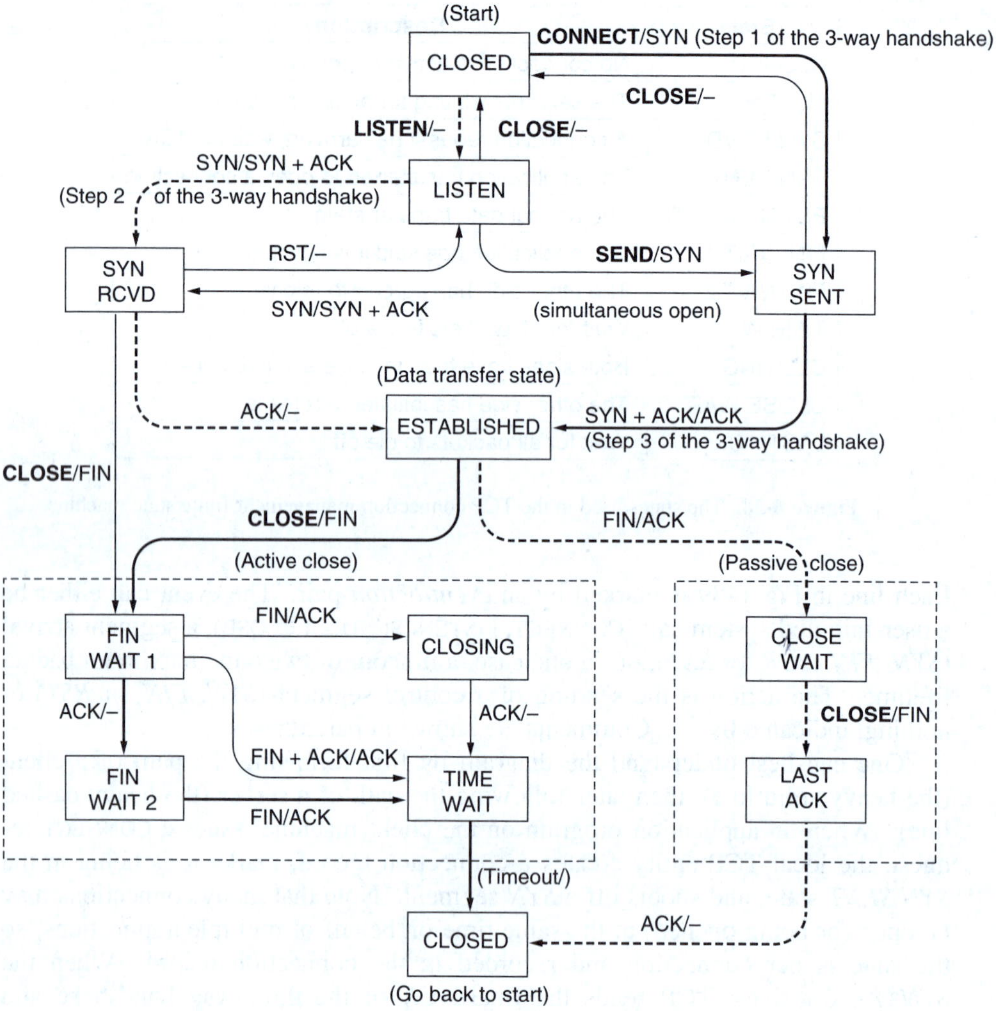

Figure 6-39. TCP connection management finite state machine. The heavy solid line is the normal path for a client. The heavy dashed line is the normal path for a server. The light lines are unusual events. Each transition is labeled with the event causing it and the action resulting from it, separated by a slash.

comes in, it is acknowledged and the server goes to the *SYN RCVD* state. When the server's *SYN* is itself acknowledged, the three-way handshake is complete and the server goes to the *ESTABLISHED* state. Data transfer can now occur.

When the client is done transmitting its data, it does a CLOSE, which causes a *FIN* to arrive at the server (dashed box marked "passive close"). The server is then signaled. When it, too, does a CLOSE, a *FIN* is sent to the client. When the client's acknowledgement shows up, the server releases the connection and deletes the connection record.

6.5.8 TCP Sliding Window

As mentioned earlier, window management in TCP decouples the issues of acknowledgement of the correct receipt of segments and receiver buffer allocation. For example, suppose the receiver has a 4096-byte buffer, as shown in Fig. 6-40. If the sender transmits a 2048-byte segment that is correctly received, the receiver will acknowledge the segment. However, since it now has only 2048 bytes of buffer space (until the application removes some data from the buffer), it will advertise a window of 2048 starting at the next byte expected.

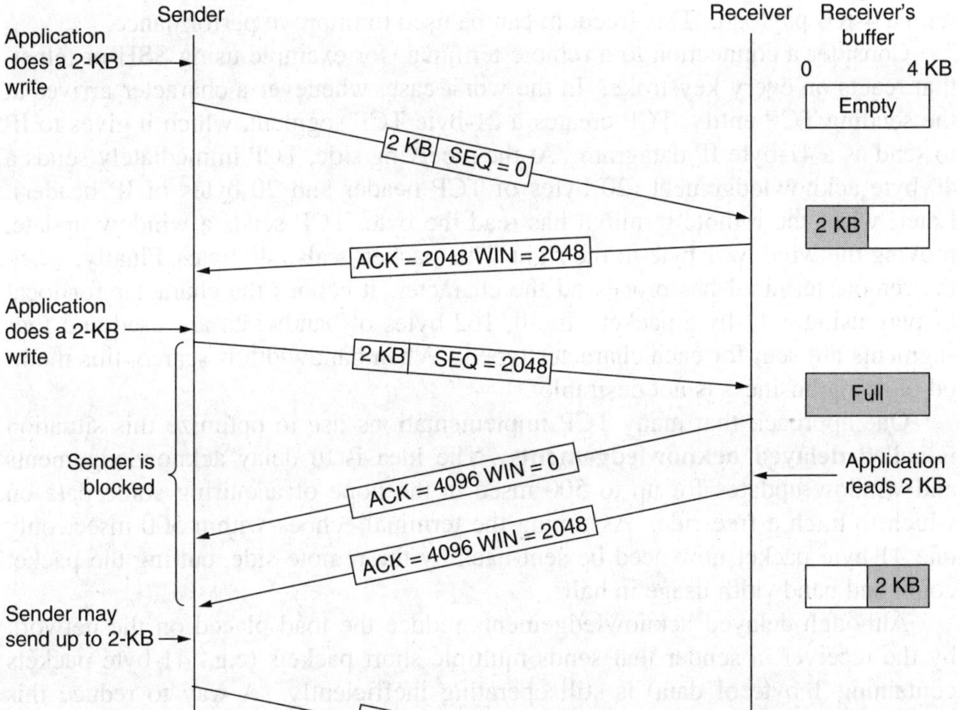

Figure 6-40. Window management in TCP.

Now the sender transmits another 2048 bytes, which are acknowledged, but the advertised window is of size 0. The sender must stop until the application process on the receiving host has removed some data from the buffer, at which time TCP can advertise a larger window and more data can be sent.

When the window is 0, the sender may not normally send segments, with two exceptions. First, urgent data may be sent, for example, to allow the user to kill the process running on the remote machine. Second, the sender may send a 1-byte segment to force the receiver to reannounce the next byte expected and the window size. This packet is called a **window probe**. The TCP standard explicitly provides this option to prevent deadlock if a window update ever gets lost.

Senders are not required to transmit data as soon as they come in from the application. Neither are receivers required to send acknowledgements as soon as possible. For example, in Fig. 6-40, when the first 2 KB of data came in, TCP, knowing that it had a 4-KB window, would have been completely correct in just buffering the data until another 2 KB came in, to be able to transmit a segment with a 4-KB payload. This freedom can be used to improve performance.

Consider a connection to a remote terminal, for example using SSH or telnet, that reacts on every keystroke. In the worst case, whenever a character arrives at the sending TCP entity, TCP creates a 21-byte TCP segment, which it gives to IP to send as a 41-byte IP datagram. At the receiving side, TCP immediately sends a 40-byte acknowledgement (20 bytes of TCP header and 20 bytes of IP header). Later, when the remote terminal has read the byte, TCP sends a window update, moving the window 1 byte to the right. This packet is also 40 bytes. Finally, when the remote terminal has processed the character, it echoes the character for local display using a 41-byte packet. In all, 162 bytes of bandwidth are used and four segments are sent for each character typed. When bandwidth is scarce, this method of doing business is not desirable.

One approach that many TCP implementations use to optimize this situation is called **delayed acknowledgements**. The idea is to delay acknowledgements and window updates for up to 500 msec in the hope of acquiring some data on which to hitch a free ride. Assuming the terminal echoes within 500 msec, only one 41-byte packet now need be sent back by the remote side, cutting the packet count and bandwidth usage in half.

Although delayed acknowledgements reduce the load placed on the network by the receiver, a sender that sends multiple short packets (e.g., 41-byte packets containing 1 byte of data) is still operating inefficiently. A way to reduce this usage is known as **Nagle's algorithm** (Nagle, 1984). What Nagle suggested is simple: when data come into the sender in small pieces, just send the first piece and buffer all the rest until the first piece is acknowledged. Then send all the buffered data in one TCP segment and start buffering again until the next segment is acknowledged. That is, only one short packet can be outstanding at any time. If many pieces of data are sent by the application in one round-trip time, Nagle's algorithm will put the many pieces in one segment, greatly reducing the bandwidth used. The algorithm additionally says that a new segment should be sent if enough data have trickled in to fill a maximum segment.

Nagle's algorithm is widely used by TCP implementations, but there are times when it is better to disable it. In particular, in interactive games that are run over the Internet, the players typically want a rapid stream of short update packets. Gathering the updates to send them in bursts makes the game respond erratically, which makes for unhappy users. A more subtle problem is that Nagle's algorithm can sometimes interact with delayed acknowledgements to cause a temporary deadlock: the receiver waits for data on which to piggyback an acknowledgement, and the sender waits on the acknowledgement to send more data. This interaction can delay the downloads of Web pages. Because of these problems, Nagle's algorithm can be disabled (which is called the *TCP_NODELAY* option). Mogul and Minshall (2001) discuss this and other solutions.

Another problem that can degrade TCP performance is the **silly window syndrome** (Clark, 1982). This problem occurs when data are passed to the sending TCP entity in large blocks, but an interactive application on the receiving side reads data only 1 byte at a time. To see the problem, look at Fig. 6-41. Initially, the TCP buffer on the receiving side is full (i.e., it has a window of size 0) and the sender knows this. Then the interactive application reads one character from the TCP stream. This action makes the receiving TCP happy, so it sends a window update to the sender saying that it is all right to send 1 byte. The sender obliges and sends 1 byte. The buffer is now full, so the receiver acknowledges the 1-byte segment and sets the window to 0. This behavior can go on forever.

Clark's solution is to prevent the receiver from sending a window update for 1 byte. Instead, it is forced to wait until it has a decent amount of space available and advertise that instead. Specifically, the receiver should not send a window update until it can handle the maximum segment size it advertised when the connection was established or until its buffer is half empty, whichever is smaller. Furthermore, the sender can also help by not sending tiny segments. Instead, it should wait until it can send a full segment, or at least one containing half of the receiver's buffer size.

Nagle's algorithm and Clark's solution to the silly window syndrome are complementary. Nagle was trying to solve the problem caused by the sending application delivering data to TCP a byte at a time. Clark was trying to solve the problem of the receiving application sucking the data up from TCP a byte at a time. Both solutions are valid and can work together. The goal is for the sender not to send small segments and the receiver not to ask for them.

The receiving TCP can go further in improving performance than just doing window updates in large units. Like the sending TCP, it can also buffer data, so it can block a READ request from the application until it has a large chunk of data for it. Doing so reduces the number of calls to TCP (and the overhead). It also increases the response time, but for noninteractive applications like file transfer, efficiency may be more important than response time to individual requests.

Another issue that the receiver must handle is that segments may arrive out of order. The receiver will buffer the data until it can be passed up to the application

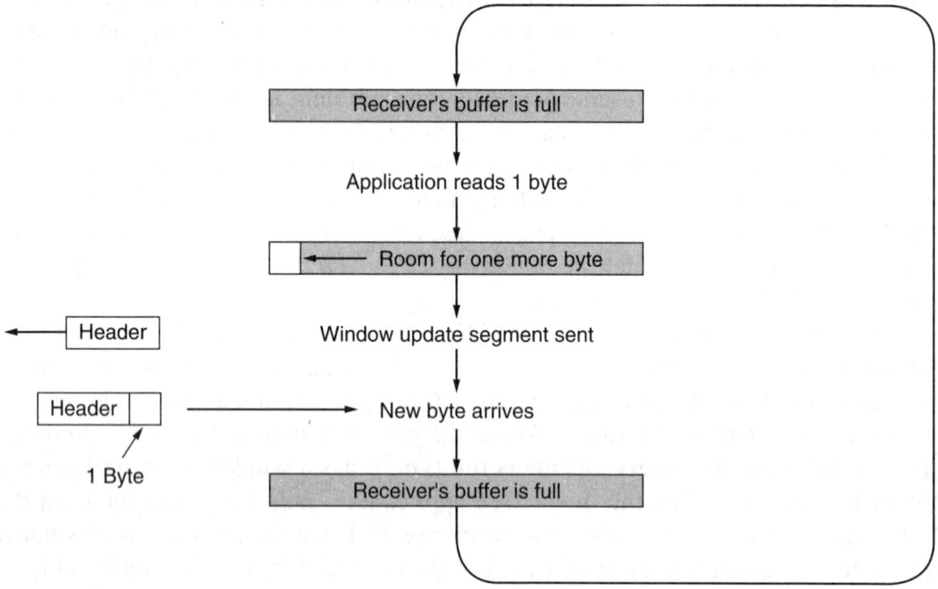

Figure 6-41. Silly window syndrome.

in order. Actually, nothing bad would happen if out-of-order segments were discarded, since they would eventually be retransmitted by the sender, but it would be wasteful.

Acknowledgements can be sent only when all the data up to the byte acknowledged have been received. This is called a **cumulative acknowledgement**. If the receiver gets segments 0, 1, 2, 4, 5, 6, and 7, it can acknowledge everything up to and including the last byte in segment 2. When the sender times out, it then retransmits segment 3. As the receiver has buffered segments 4 through 7, upon receipt of segment 3 it can acknowledge all bytes up to the end of segment 7.

6.5.9 TCP Timer Management

TCP uses multiple timers (at least conceptually) to do its work. The most important of these is the **RTO (Retransmission TimeOut)**. When a segment is sent, a retransmission timer is started. If the segment is acknowledged before the timer expires, the timer is stopped. If, on the other hand, the timer goes off before the acknowledgement comes in, the segment is retransmitted (and the timer os started again). The question that arises is: how long should the timeout be?

This problem is much more difficult in the transport layer than in data link protocols such as 802.11. In the latter case, the expected delay is measured in microseconds and is highly predictable (i.e., has a low variance), so the timer can be set to go off just slightly after the acknowledgement is expected, as shown in Fig. 6-42(a). Since acknowledgements are rarely delayed in the data link layer (due to lack of congestion), the absence of an acknowledgement at the expected time generally means either the frame or the acknowledgement has been lost.

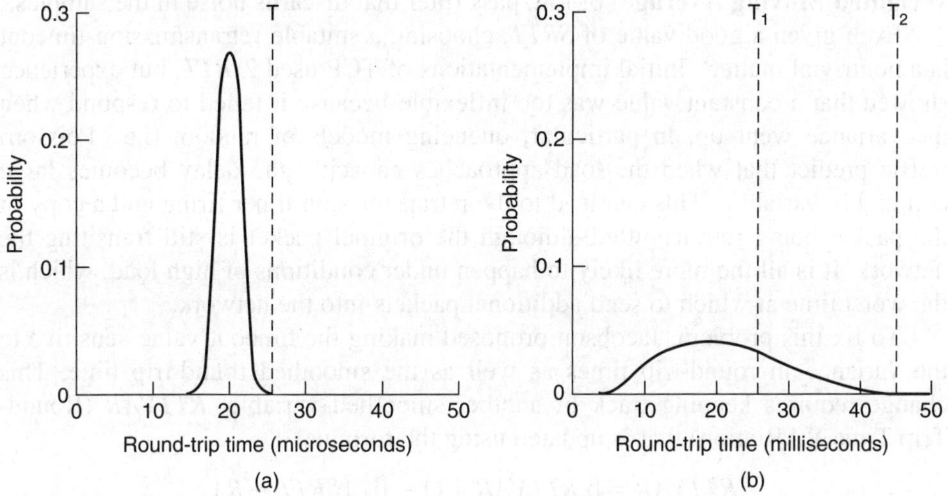

Figure 6-42. (a) Probability density of acknowledgement arrival times in the data link layer. (b) Probability density of acknowledgement arrival times for TCP.

TCP is faced with a radically different environment. The probability density function for the time it takes for a TCP acknowledgement to come back looks more like Fig. 6-42(b) than Fig. 6-42(a). It is larger and more variable. Determining the round-trip time to the destination is tricky. Even when it is known, deciding on the timeout interval is also difficult. If the timeout is set too short, say, T_1 in Fig. 6-42(b), unnecessary retransmissions will occur, clogging the Internet with useless packets. If it is set too long (e.g., T_2), performance will suffer due to the long retransmission delay whenever a packet is lost. Furthermore, the mean and variance of the acknowledgement arrival distribution can change rapidly within a few seconds as congestion builds up or is resolved.

The solution is to use a dynamic algorithm that constantly adapts the timeout interval, based on continuous measurements of network performance. The algorithm generally used by TCP is due to Jacobson (1988) and works as follows. For each connection, TCP maintains a variable, *SRTT* (Smoothed Round-Trip Time), that is the best current estimate of the round-trip time to the destination in question. When a segment is sent, a timer is started, both to see how long the acknowledgement takes and also to trigger a retransmission if it takes too long. If the acknowledgement gets back before the timer expires, TCP measures how long the acknowledgement took, say, R. It then updates $SRTT$ according to the formula

$$SRTT = \alpha \, SRTT + (1 - \alpha) \, R$$

where α is a smoothing factor that determines how quickly the old values are forgotten. Typically, $\alpha = 7/8$. This kind of formula is an **EWMA** (**Exponentially Weighted Moving Average**) or low-pass filter that discards noise in the samples.

Even given a good value of $SRTT$, choosing a suitable retransmission timeout is a nontrivial matter. Initial implementations of TCP used $2xRTT$, but experience showed that a constant value was too inflexible because it failed to respond when the variance went up. In particular, queueing models of random (i.e., Poisson) traffic predict that when the load approaches capacity, the delay becomes large and highly variable. This can lead to the retransmission timer firing and a copy of the packet being retransmitted although the original packet is still transiting the network. It is all the more likely to happen under conditions of high load, which is the worst time at which to send additional packets into the network.

To fix this problem, Jacobson proposed making the timeout value sensitive to the variance in round-trip times as well as the smoothed round-trip time. This change requires keeping track of another smoothed variable, $RTTVAR$ (Round-Trip Time VARiation) that is updated using the formula

$$RTTVAR = \beta \, RTTVAR + (1 - \beta) \, | SRTT - R |$$

This is an EWMA as before, and typically $\beta = 3/4$. The retransmission timeout, RTO, is set to be

$$RTO = SRTT + 4 \times RTTVAR$$

The choice of the factor 4 is somewhat arbitrary, but multiplication by 4 can be done with a single shift, and less than 1% of all packets come in more than four standard deviations late. Note that $RTTVAR$ is not exactly the same as the standard deviation (it is really the mean deviation), but it is close enough in practice. Jacobson's paper is full of clever tricks to compute timeouts using only integer adds, subtracts, and shifts. This economy is not needed for modern hosts, but it has become part of the culture that allows TCP to run on all manner of devices, from supercomputers down to tiny devices. So far nobody has put it on an RFID chip, but someday? Who knows.

More details of how to compute this timeout, including initial settings of the variables, are given in RFC 2988. The retransmission timer is also held to a minimum of 1 second, regardless of the estimates. This is a conservative value chosen to prevent spurious retransmissions based on measurements (Allman and Paxson, 1999).

One problem that occurs with gathering the samples, R, of the round-trip time is what to do when a segment times out and is sent again. When the acknowledgement comes in, it is unclear whether the acknowledgement refers to the first transmission or a later one. Guessing wrong can seriously contaminate the retransmission timeout. Phil Karn discovered this problem the hard way. Karn is an amateur radio enthusiast interested in transmitting TCP/IP packets by ham radio, a notoriously unreliable medium. He made a simple proposal: do not update estimates on any segments that have been retransmitted. Additionally, the timeout is doubled on each successive retransmission until the segments get through the first time. This fix is called **Karn's algorithm** (Karn and Partridge, 1987). Most TCP implementations use it.

The retransmission timer is not the only timer TCP uses. A second timer is the **persistence timer**. It is designed to prevent the following deadlock. The receiver sends an acknowledgement with a window size of 0, telling the sender to wait. Later, the receiver updates the window, but the packet with the update is lost. Now the sender and the receiver are each waiting for the other to do something. When the persistence timer goes off, the sender transmits a probe to the receiver. The response to the probe gives the window size. If it is still 0, the persistence timer is set again and the cycle repeats. If it is nonzero, data can now be sent.

A third timer that some implementations use is the **keepalive timer**. When a connection has been idle for a long time, the keepalive timer may go off to cause one side to check whether the other side is still there. If it fails to respond, the connection is terminated. This feature is controversial because it adds overhead and may terminate an otherwise healthy connection due to a transient network partition.

The last timer used on each TCP connection is the one used in the *TIME WAIT* state while closing. It runs for twice the maximum packet lifetime to make sure that when a connection is closed, all packets created by it have died off.

6.5.10 TCP Congestion Control

We have saved one of the key functions of TCP for last: congestion control. When the load offered to any network is more than it can handle, congestion builds up. The Internet is no exception. The network layer detects congestion when queues grow large at routers and tries to manage it, if only by dropping packets. It is up to the transport layer to receive congestion feedback from the network layer and slow down the rate of traffic that it is sending into the network. In the Internet, TCP plays the main role in controlling congestion, as well as the main role in reliable transport. That is why it is such a special protocol.

We covered the general situation of congestion control in Sec. 6.3. One key takeaway was that a transport protocol using an AIMD (Additive Increase Multiplicative Decrease) control law in response to binary congestion signals from the network would converge to a fair and efficient bandwidth allocation. TCP congestion control is based on implementing this approach using a window and with packet loss as the binary signal. To do so, TCP maintains a **congestion window** whose size is the number of bytes the sender may have in the network at any time. The corresponding rate is the window size divided by the round-trip time of the connection. TCP adjusts the size of the window according to the AIMD rule.

Recall that the congestion window is maintained *in addition* to the flow control window, which specifies the number of bytes that the receiver can buffer. Both windows are tracked in parallel, and the number of bytes that may be sent is the smaller of the two windows. Thus, the effective window is the smaller of what the sender thinks is all right and what the receiver thinks is all right. It takes two to tango. TCP will stop sending data if either the congestion or the flow control window is temporarily full. If the receiver says "send 64 KB" but the sender knows that bursts of more than 32 KB clog the network, it will send 32 KB. On the other hand, if the receiver says "send 64 KB" and the sender knows that bursts of up to 128 KB get through effortlessly, it will send the full 64 KB requested. The flow control window was described earlier, and in what follows we will only describe the congestion window.

Modern congestion control was added to TCP largely through the efforts of Van Jacobson (1988). It is a fascinating story. Starting in 1986, the growing popularity of the early Internet led to the first occurrence of what became known as a **congestion collapse**, a prolonged period during which goodput dropped precipitously (i.e., by more than a factor of 100) due to congestion in the network. Jacobson (and many others) set out to understand what was happening and remedy the situation.

The high-level fix that Jacobson implemented was to approximate an AIMD congestion window. The interesting part, and much of the complexity of TCP congestion control, is how he added this to an existing implementation without changing any of the message formats, which made it instantly deployable. To start, he observed that packet loss is a suitable signal of congestion. This signal comes a little late (as the network is already congested) but it is quite dependable. After all, it is difficult to build a router that does not drop packets when it is overloaded. This fact is unlikely to change. Even when terabyte memories appear to buffer vast numbers of packets, we will probably have terabit/sec networks to fill up those memories.

However, using packet loss as a congestion signal depends on transmission errors being relatively rare. This is not normally the case for wireless links such as 802.11, which is why they include their own retransmission mechanism at the link layer. Because of wireless retransmissions, network layer packet loss due to transmission errors is normally masked on wireless networks. It is also rare on other links because wires and optical fibers typically have low bit-error rates.

All the Internet TCP algorithms assume that lost packets are caused by congestion and monitor timeouts and look for signs of trouble the way miners watch their canaries. A good retransmission timer is needed to detect packet loss signals accurately and in a timely manner. We have already discussed how the TCP retransmission timer includes estimates of the mean and variation in round-trip times. Fixing this timer, by including the variation factor, was an important step in Jacobson's work. Given a good retransmission timeout, the TCP sender can track the outstanding number of bytes, which are loading the network. It simply looks at the difference between the sequence numbers that are transmitted and acknowledged.

Now it seems that our task is easy. All we need to do is to track the congestion window, using sequence and acknowledgement numbers, and adjust the congestion window using an AIMD rule. As you might have expected, it is more complicated than that. A first consideration is that the way packets are sent into the network, even over short periods of time, must be matched to the network path. Otherwise the traffic will cause congestion. For example, consider a host with a congestion window of 64 KB attached to a 1-Gbps switched Ethernet. If the host sends the entire window at once, this burst of traffic may travel over a slow 1-Mbps ADSL line further along the path. The burst that took only half a millisecond on the 1-Gbps line will clog the 1-Mbps line for half a second, completely disrupting protocols such as voice over IP. This behavior might be a good idea for a protocol designed to cause congestion, but not for a protocol to control it.

However, it turns out that we can use small bursts of packets to our advantage. Fig. 6-43 shows what happens when a sender on a fast network (the 1-Gbps link) sends a small burst of four packets to a receiver on a slow network (the 1-Mbps link) that is the bottleneck or slowest part of the path. Initially the four packets travel over the link as quickly as they can be sent by the sender. At the router, they are queued while being sent because it takes longer to send a packet over the slow link than to receive the next packet over the fast link. But the queue is not large because only a small number of packets were sent at once. Note the increased length of the packets on the slow link. The same packet, of 1 KB say, is now longer because it takes more time to send it on a slow link than on a fast one.

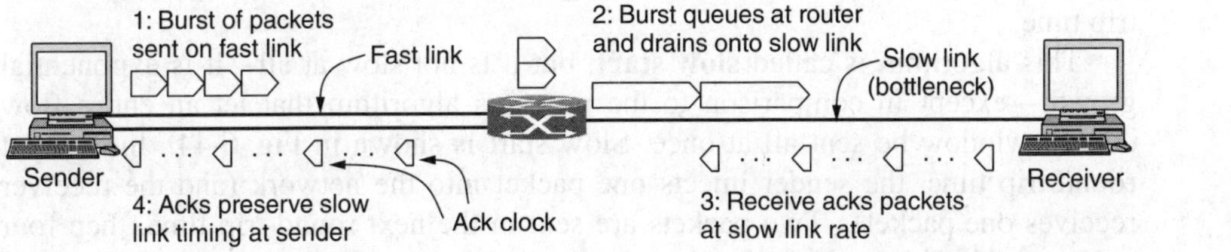

Figure 6-43. A burst of packets from a sender and the returning ack clock.

Eventually the packets get to the receiver, where they are acknowledged. The times for the acknowledgements reflect the times at which the packets arrived at the receiver after crossing the slow link. They are spread out compared to the original packets on the fast link. As these acknowledgements travel over the network and back to the sender they preserve this timing.

The key observation is this: the acknowledgements return to the sender at about the rate that packets can be sent over the slowest link in the path. This is precisely the rate that the sender wants to use. If it injects new packets into the network at this rate, they will be sent as fast as the slow link permits, but they will not queue up and congest any router along the path. This timing is known as an **ack clock**. It is an essential part of TCP. By using an ack clock, TCP smoothes out traffic and avoids unnecessary queues at routers.

A second consideration is that the AIMD rule will take a very long time to reach a good operating point on fast networks if the congestion window is started from a small size. Consider a modest network path that can support 10 Mbps with an RTT of 100 msec. The appropriate congestion window is the bandwidth-delay product, which is 1 Mbit or 100 packets of 1250 bytes each. If the congestion window starts at 1 packet and increases by 1 packet every RTT, it will be 100 RTTs or 10 seconds before the connection is running at about the right rate. That is a long time to wait just to get to the right speed for a transfer. We could reduce this startup time by starting with a larger initial window, say of 50 packets. But this window would be far too large for slow or short links. It would cause congestion if used all at once, as we have just described.

Instead, the solution Jacobson chose to handle both of these considerations is a mix of linear and multiplicative increase. When a connection is established, the sender initializes the congestion window to a small initial value of at most four segments; the details are described in RFC 3390, and the use of four segments is an increase from an earlier initial value of one segment based on experience. The sender then sends the initial window. The packets will take a round-trip time to be acknowledged. For each segment that is acknowledged before the retransmission timer goes off, the sender adds one segment's worth of bytes to the congestion window. Plus, as that segment has been acknowledged, there is now one less segment in the network. The upshot is that every acknowledged segment allows two more segments to be sent. The congestion window is doubling every round-trip time.

This algorithm is called **slow start**, but it is not slow at all—it is exponential growth—except in comparison to the previous algorithm that let an entire flow control window be sent all at once. Slow start is shown in Fig. 6-44. In the first round-trip time, the sender injects one packet into the network (and the receiver receives one packet). Two packets are sent in the next round-trip time, then four packets in the third round-trip time.

Slow-start works well over a range of link speeds and round-trip times, and uses an ack clock to match the rate of sender transmissions to the network path. Take a look at the way acknowledgements return from the sender to the receiver in Fig. 6-44. When the sender gets an acknowledgement, it increases the congestion window by one and immediately sends two packets into the network. (One packet is the increase by one; the other packet is a replacement for the packet that has been acknowledged and left the network. At all times, the number of

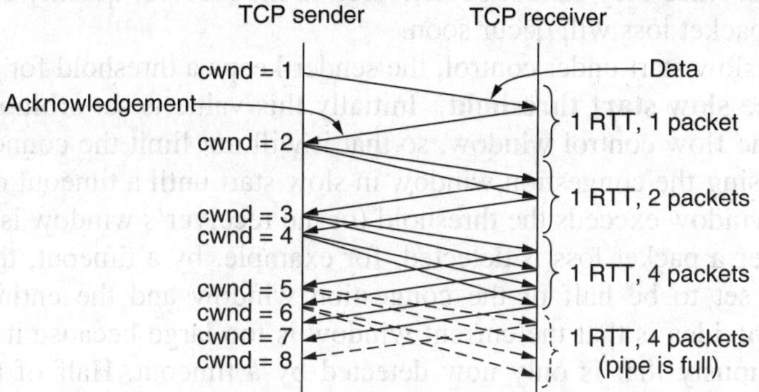

Figure 6-44. Slow start from an initial congestion window of one segment.

unacknowledged packets is given by the congestion window.) However, these two packets will not necessarily arrive at the receiver as closely spaced as when they were sent. For example, suppose the sender is on a 100-Mbps Ethernet. Each packet of 1250 bytes takes 100 μsec to send. So the delay between the packets can be as small as 100 μsec. The situation changes if these packets go across a 1-Mbps ADSL link anywhere along the path. It now takes 10 msec to send the same packet. This means that the minimum spacing between the two packets has grown by a factor of 100. Unless the packets have to wait together in a queue on a later link, the spacing will remain large.

In Fig. 6-44, this effect is shown by enforcing a minimum spacing between data packets arriving at the receiver. The same spacing is kept when the receiver sends acknowledgements, and thus when the sender receives the acknowledgements. If the network path is slow, acknowledgements will come in slowly (after a delay of an RTT). If the network path is fast, acknowledgements will come in quickly (again, after the RTT). All the sender has to do is follow the timing of the ack clock as it injects new packets, which is what slow start does.

Because slow start causes exponential growth, eventually (and sooner rather than later) it will send too many packets into the network too quickly. When this happens, queues will build up in the network. When the queues are full, one or more packets will be lost. After this happens, the TCP sender will time out when an acknowledgement fails to arrive in time. There is evidence of slow start growing too fast in Fig. 6-44. After three RTTs, four packets are in the network. These four packets take an entire RTT to arrive at the receiver. That is, a congestion window of four packets is the right size for this connection. However, as these packets are acknowledged, slow start continues to grow the congestion window, reaching eight packets in another RTT. Only four of these packets can reach the receiver in one RTT, no matter how many are sent. That is, the network pipe is full. Additional packets placed into the network by the sender will build up in router queues, since they cannot be delivered to the receiver quickly enough. Congestion and packet loss will occur soon.

To keep slow start under control, the sender keeps a threshold for the connection called the **slow start threshold**. Initially this value is set arbitrarily high, to the size of the flow control window, so that it will not limit the connection. TCP keeps increasing the congestion window in slow start until a timeout occurs or the congestion window exceeds the threshold (or the receiver's window is filled).

Whenever a packet loss is detected, for example, by a timeout, the slow start threshold is set to be half of the congestion window and the entire process is restarted. The idea is that the current window is too large because it caused congestion previously that is only now detected by a timeout. Half of the window, which was used successfully at an earlier time, is probably a better estimate for a congestion window that is close to the path capacity but will not cause loss. In our example in Fig. 6-44, growing the congestion window to eight packets may cause loss, while the congestion window of four packets in the previous RTT was the right value. The congestion window is then reset to its small initial value and slow start resumes.

Whenever the slow start threshold is crossed, TCP switches from slow start to additive increase. In this mode, the congestion window is increased by one segment every round-trip time. Like slow start, this is usually implemented with an increase for every segment that is acknowledged, rather than an increase once per RTT. Call the congestion window *cwnd* and the maximum segment size *MSS*. A common approximation is to increase *cwnd* by $(MSS \times MSS)/cwnd$ for each of the $cwnd/MSS$ packets that may be acknowledged. This increase does not need to be fast. The whole idea is for a TCP connection to spend a lot of time with its congestion window close to the optimum value—not so small that throughput will be low, and not so large that congestion will occur.

Additive increase is shown in Fig. 6-45 for the same situation as slow start. At the end of every RTT, the sender's congestion window has grown enough that it can inject an additional packet into the network. Compared to slow start, the linear rate of growth is much slower. It makes little difference for small congestion windows, as is the case here, but a large difference in the time taken to grow the congestion window to 100 segments, for example.

There is something else that we can do to improve performance too. The defect in the scheme so far is waiting for a timeout. Timeouts are relatively long because they must be conservative. After a packet is lost, the receiver cannot acknowledge past it, so the acknowledgement number will stay fixed, and the sender will not be able to send any new packets into the network because its congestion window remains full. This condition can continue for a relatively long period until the timer fires and the lost packet is retransmitted. At that stage, TCP slow starts again.

There is a quick way for the sender to recognize that one of its packets has been lost. As packets beyond the lost packet arrive at the receiver, they trigger

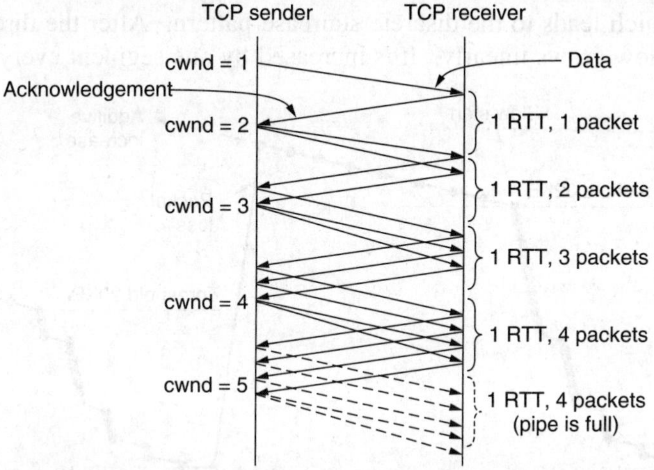

Figure 6-45. Additive increase from an initial congestion window of one segment.

acknowledgements that return to the sender. These acknowledgements bear the same acknowledgement number. They are called **duplicate acknowledgements**. Each time the sender receives a duplicate acknowledgement, it is likely that another packet has arrived at the receiver and the lost packet still has not shown up.

Because packets can take different paths through the network, they can arrive out of order. This will trigger duplicate acknowledgements even though no packets have been lost. However, this is uncommon in the Internet much of the time. When there is reordering across multiple paths, the received packets are usually not reordered too much. Thus, TCP somewhat arbitrarily assumes that three duplicate acknowledgements imply that a packet has been lost. The identity of the lost packet can be inferred from the acknowledgement number as well. It is the very next packet in sequence. This packet can then be retransmitted right away, before the retransmission timeout fires.

This heuristic is called **fast retransmission**. After it fires, the slow start threshold is still set to half the current congestion window, just as with a timeout. Slow start can be restarted by setting the congestion window to one packet. With this window size, a new packet will be sent after the one round-trip time that it takes to acknowledge the retransmitted packet along with all data that had been sent before the loss was detected.

An illustration of the congestion algorithm we have built up so far is shown in Fig. 6-46. This version of TCP is called TCP Tahoe after the 4.2BSD Tahoe release in 1988 in which it was included. The maximum segment size here is 1 KB. Initially, the congestion window was 64 KB, but a timeout occurred, so the threshold is set to 32 KB and the congestion window to 1 KB for transmission 0. The congestion window grows exponentially until it hits the threshold (32 KB). The window is increased every time a new acknowledgement arrives rather than continuously, which leads to the discrete staircase pattern. After the threshold is passed, the window grows linearly. It is increased by one segment every RTT.

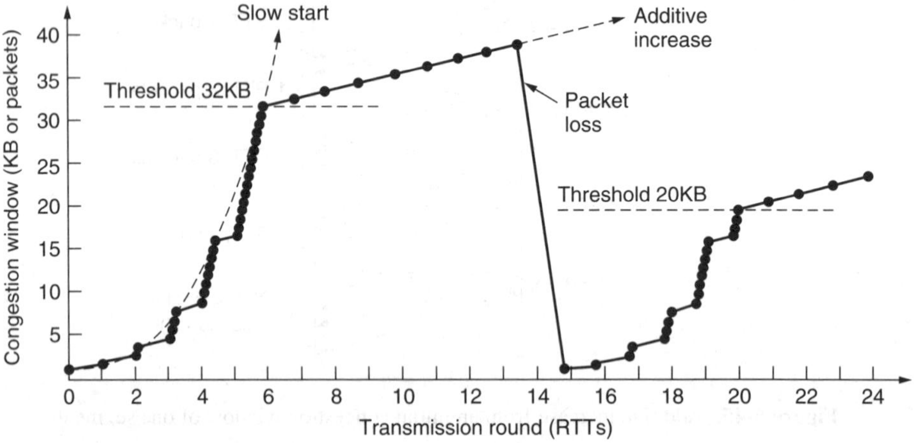

Figure 6-46. Slow start followed by additive increase in TCP Tahoe.

The transmissions in round 13 are unlucky (they should have known), and one of them is lost in the network. This is detected when three duplicate acknowledgements arrive. At that time, the lost packet is retransmitted, the threshold is set to half the current window (by now 40 KB, so half is 20 KB), and slow start is initiated all over again. Restarting with a congestion window of one packet takes one round-trip time for all of the previously transmitted data to leave the network and be acknowledged, including the retransmitted packet. The congestion window grows with slow start as it did previously, until it reaches the new threshold of 20 KB. At that time, the growth becomes linear again. It will continue in this fashion until another packet loss is detected via duplicate acknowledgements or a timeout (or the receiver's window becomes the limit).

TCP Tahoe (which included good retransmission timers) provided a working congestion control algorithm that solved the problem of congestion collapse. Jacobson realized that it is possible to do even better. At the time of the fast retransmission, the connection is running with a congestion window that is too large, but it is still running with a working ack clock. Every time another duplicate acknowledgement arrives, it is likely that another packet has left the network. Using duplicate acknowledgements to count the packets in the network, makes it possible to let some packets exit the network and continue to send a new packet for each additional duplicate acknowledgement.

Fast recovery is the heuristic that implements this behavior. It is a temporary mode that aims to maintain the ack clock running with a congestion window that is the new threshold, or half the value of the congestion window at the time of the fast retransmission. To do this, duplicate acknowledgements are counted (including the three that triggered fast retransmission) until the number of packets in the network has fallen to the new threshold. This takes about half a round-trip time. From then on, a new packet can be sent for each duplicate acknowledgement that is received. One round-trip time after the fast retransmission, the lost packet will have been acknowledged. At that time, the stream of duplicate acknowledgements will cease and fast recovery mode will be exited. The congestion window will be set to the new slow start threshold and grows by linear increase.

The upshot of this heuristic is that TCP avoids slow start, except when the connection is first started and when a timeout occurs. The latter can still happen when more than one packet is lost and fast retransmission does not recover adequately. Instead of repeated slow starts, the congestion window of a running connection follows a **sawtooth** pattern of additive increase (by one segment every RTT) and multiplicative decrease (by half in one RTT). This is exactly the AIMD rule that we sought to implement.

This sawtooth behavior is shown in Fig. 6-47. It is produced by TCP Reno, named after the 4.3BSD Reno release in 1990 in which it was included. TCP Reno is essentially TCP Tahoe plus fast recovery. After an initial slow start, the congestion window climbs linearly until a packet loss is detected by duplicate acknowledgements. The lost packet is retransmitted and fast recovery is used to keep the ack clock running until the retransmission is acknowledged. At that time, the congestion window is resumed from the new slow start threshold, rather than from 1. This behavior continues indefinitely, and the connection spends most of the time with its congestion window close to the optimum value of the bandwidth-delay product.

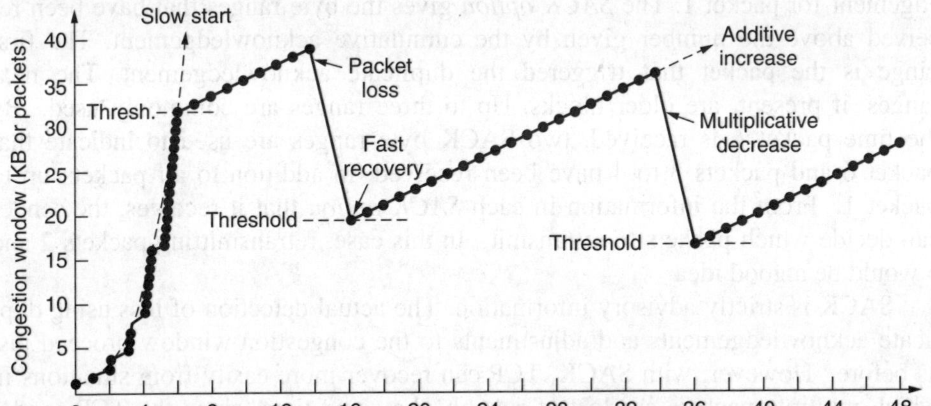

Figure 6-47. Fast recovery and the sawtooth pattern of TCP Reno.

TCP Reno with its mechanisms for adjusting the congestion window has formed the basis for TCP congestion control for more than two decades. Most of the changes in the intervening years have adjusted these mechanisms in minor ways, for example, by changing the choices of the initial window and removing various ambiguities. Some improvements have been made for recovering from two or more losses in a window of packets. For example, the TCP NewReno version uses a partial advance of the acknowledgement number after a retransmission to find and repair another loss (Hoe, 1996), as described in RFC 3782. Since the mid-1990s, several variations have emerged that follow the principles we have described but use slightly different control laws. For example, Linux uses a variant called CUBIC TCP (Ha et al., 2008) and Windows includes a variant called Compound TCP (Tan et al., 2006).

Two larger changes have also affected TCP implementations. First, much of the complexity of TCP comes from inferring from a stream of duplicate acknowledgements which packets have arrived and which packets have been lost. The cumulative acknowledgement number does not provide this information. A simple fix is the use of **SACK (Selective ACKnowledgements)**, which lists up to three ranges of bytes that have been received. With this information, the sender can more directly decide what packets to retransmit and track the packets in flight to implement the congestion window.

When the sender and receiver set up a connection, they each send the *SACK permitted* TCP option to signal that they understand selective acknowledgements. Once SACK is enabled for a connection, it works as shown in Fig. 6-48. A receiver uses the TCP *Acknowledgement number* field in the normal manner, as a cumulative acknowledgement of the highest in-order byte that has been received. When it receives packet 3 out of order (because packet 2 was lost), it sends a *SACK option* for the received data along with the (duplicate) cumulative acknowledgement for packet 1. The *SACK option* gives the byte ranges that have been received above the number given by the cumulative acknowledgement. The first range is the packet that triggered the duplicate acknowledgement. The next ranges, if present, are older blocks. Up to three ranges are commonly used. By the time packet 6 is received, two SACK byte ranges are used to indicate that packet 6 and packets 3 to 4 have been received, in addition to all packets up to packet 1. From the information in each *SACK option* that it receives, the sender can decide which packets to retransmit. In this case, retransmitting packets 2 and 5 would be a good idea.

SACK is strictly advisory information. The actual detection of loss using duplicate acknowledgements and adjustments to the congestion window proceed just as before. However, with SACK, TCP can recover more easily from situations in which multiple packets are lost at roughly the same time, since the TCP sender knows which packets have not been received. SACK is now widely deployed. It is described in RFC 2883, and TCP congestion control using SACK is described in RFC 3517.

The second change is the use of ECN (Explicit Congestion Notification) in addition to packet loss as a congestion signal. ECN is an IP layer mechanism to

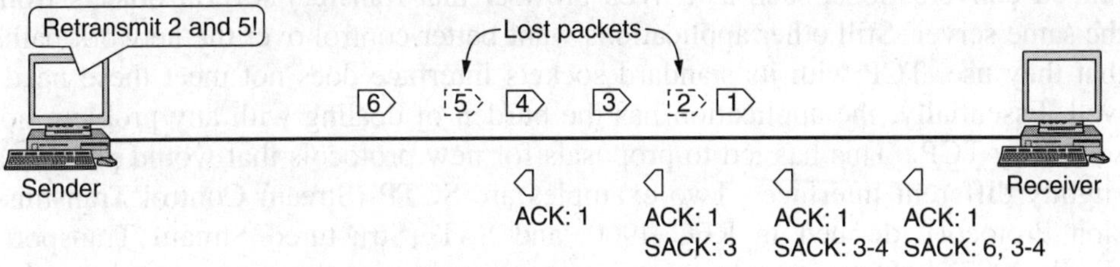

Figure 6-48. Selective acknowledgements.

notify hosts of congestion that we described in Sec. 5.3.4. With it, the TCP receiver can receive congestion signals from IP.

The use of ECN is enabled for a TCP connection when both the sender and receiver indicate that they are capable of using ECN by setting the *ECE* and *CWR* bits during connection establishment. If ECN is used, each packet that carries a TCP segment is flagged in the IP header to show that it can carry an ECN signal. Routers that support ECN will set a congestion signal on packets that can carry ECN flags when congestion is approaching, instead of dropping those packets after congestion has occurred.

The TCP receiver is informed if any packet that arrives carries an ECN congestion signal. The receiver then uses the *ECE* (ECN Echo) flag to signal the TCP sender that its packets have experienced congestion. The sender tells the receiver that it has heard the signal by using the *CWR* (Congestion Window Reduced) flag.

The TCP sender reacts to these congestion notifications in exactly the same way as it does to packet loss that is detected via duplicate acknowledgements. However, the situation is strictly better. Congestion has been detected and no packet was harmed in any way. ECN is described in RFC 3168. It requires both host and router support, and is not yet widely used on the Internet.

For more information on the complete set of congestion control behaviors that are implemented in TCP, see RFC 5681.

6.5.11 The Future of TCP

As the workhorse of the Internet, TCP has been used for many applications and extended over time to give good performance over a wide range of networks. Many versions are deployed with slightly different implementations than the classic algorithms we have described, especially for congestion control and robustness against attacks. It is likely that TCP will continue to evolve with the Internet. We will mention two particular issues.

The first one is that TCP does not provide the transport semantics that all applications want. For example, some applications want to send messages or records whose boundaries need to be preserved. Other applications work with a group of related conversations, such as a Web browser that transfers several objects from the same server. Still other applications want better control over the network paths that they use. TCP with its standard sockets interface does not meet these needs well. Essentially, the application has the burden of dealing with any problem not solved by TCP. This has led to proposals for new protocols that would provide a slightly different interface. Two examples are SCTP (Stream Control Transmission Protocol), defined in RFC 4960, and SST (Structured Stream Transport) (Ford, 2007). However, whenever someone proposes changing something that has worked so well for so long, there is always a huge battle between the "Users are demanding more features" and "If it ain't broke, don't fix it" camps.

The second issue is congestion control. You may have expected that this is a solved problem after our deliberations and the mechanisms that have been developed over time. Not so. The form of TCP congestion control that we described, and which is widely used, is based on packet losses as a signal of congestion. When Padhye et al. (1998) modeled TCP throughput based on the sawtooth pattern, they found that the packet loss rate must drop off rapidly with increasing speed. To reach a throughput of 1 Gbps with a round-trip time of 100 ms and 1500 byte packets, one packet can be lost approximately every 10 minutes. That is a packet loss rate of 2×10^{-8}, which is incredibly small. It is too infrequent to serve as a good congestion signal, and any other source of loss (e.g., packet transmission error rates of 10^{-7}) can easily dominate it, limiting the throughput.

This relationship has not been a problem in the past, but networks are getting faster and faster, leading many people to revisit congestion control. One possibility is to use an alternate congestion control in which the signal is not packet loss at all. We gave several examples in Sec. 6.2. The signal might be round-trip time, which grows when the network becomes congested, as is used by FAST TCP (Wei et al., 2006). Other approaches are possible too, and time will tell which is the best.

6.6 PERFORMANCE ISSUES

Performance issues are very important in computer networks. When hundreds or thousands of computers are interconnected, complex interactions, with unforeseen consequences, are common. Frequently, this complexity leads to poor performance and no one knows why. In the following sections, we will examine many issues related to network performance to see what kinds of problems exist and what can be done about them.

Unfortunately, understanding network performance is more an art than a science. There is little underlying theory that is actually of any use in practice. The best we can do is give some rules of thumb gained from hard experience and present examples taken from the real world. We have delayed this discussion until we studied the transport layer because the performance that applications receive depends on the combined performance of the transport, network and link layers, and to be able to use TCP as an example in various places.

In the next sections, we will look at six aspects of network performance:

1. Performance problems.
2. Measuring network performance.
3. Host design for fast networks.
4. Fast segment processing.
5. Header compression.
6. Protocols for "long fat" networks.

These aspects consider network performance both at the host and across the network, and as networks are increased in speed and size.

6.6.1 Performance Problems in Computer Networks

Some performance problems, such as congestion, are caused by temporary resource overloads. If more traffic suddenly arrives at a router than the router can handle, congestion will build up and performance will suffer. We studied congestion in detail in this and the previous chapter.

Performance also degrades when there is a structural resource imbalance. For example, if a gigabit communication line is attached to a low-end PC, the poor host will not be able to process the incoming packets fast enough and some will be lost. These packets will eventually be retransmitted, adding delay, wasting bandwidth, and generally reducing performance.

Overloads can also be synchronously triggered. As an example, if a segment contains a bad parameter (e.g., the port for which it is destined), in many cases the receiver will thoughtfully send back an error notification. Now consider what could happen if a bad segment is broadcast to 1000 machines: each one might send back an error message. The resulting **broadcast storm** could cripple the network. UDP suffered from this problem until the ICMP protocol was changed to cause hosts to refrain from responding to errors in UDP segments sent to broadcast addresses. Wireless networks must be particularly careful to avoid unchecked broadcast responses because broadcast occurs naturally and the wireless bandwidth is limited.

A second example of synchronous overload is what happens after an electrical power failure. When the power comes back on, all the machines simultaneously start rebooting. A typical reboot sequence might require first going to some (DHCP) server to learn one's true identity, and then to some file server to get a copy of the operating system. If hundreds of machines in a data center all do this at once, the server will probably collapse under the load.

Even in the absence of synchronous overloads and the presence of sufficient resources, poor performance can occur due to lack of system tuning. For example, if a machine has plenty of CPU power and memory but not enough of the memory has been allocated for buffer space, flow control will slow down segment reception and limit performance. This was a problem for many TCP connections as the Internet became faster but the default size of the flow control window stayed fixed at 64 KB.

Another tuning issue is setting timeouts. When a segment is sent, a timer is set to guard against loss of the segment. If the timeout is set too short, unnecessary retransmissions will occur, clogging the wires. If the timeout is set too long, unnecessary delays will occur after a segment is lost. Other tunable parameters include how long to wait for data on which to piggyback before sending a separate acknowledgement, and how many retransmissions to make before giving up.

Another performance problem that occurs with real-time applications like audio and video is jitter. Having enough bandwidth on average is not sufficient for good performance. Short transmission delays are also required. Consistently achieving short delays demands careful engineering of the load on the network, quality-of-service support at the link and network layers, or both.

6.6.2 Network Performance Measurement

When a network performs poorly, its users often complain to the folks running it, demanding improvements. To improve the performance, the operators must first determine exactly what is going on. To find out what is really happening, the operators must make measurements. In this section, we will look at network performance measurements. Much of the discussion below is based on the seminal work of Mogul (1993).

Measurements can be made in different ways and at many locations (both in the protocol stack and physically). The most basic kind of measurement is to start a timer when beginning some activity and see how long that activity takes. For example, knowing how long it takes for a segment to be acknowledged is a key measurement. Other measurements are made with counters that record how often some event has happened (e.g., number of lost segments). Finally, one is often interested in knowing the amount of something, such as the number of bytes processed in a certain time interval.

Measuring network performance and parameters has many potential pitfalls. We list a few of them here. Any systematic attempt to measure network performance should be careful to avoid these.

Make Sure That the Sample Size Is Large Enough

Do not measure the time to send one segment, but repeat the measurement, say, one million times and take the average. Startup effects, such as the 802.16 NIC or cable modem getting a bandwidth reservation after an idle period, can slow the first segment, and queueing introduces variability. Having a large sample will reduce the uncertainty in the measured mean and standard deviation. This uncertainty can be computed using standard statistical formulas.

Make Sure That the Samples Are Representative

Ideally, the whole sequence of one million measurements should be repeated at different times of the day and the week to see the effect of different network conditions on the measured quantity. Measurements of congestion, for example, are of little use if they are made at a moment when there is no congestion. Sometimes the results may be counterintuitive at first, such as heavy congestion at 11 A.M., and 1 P.M., but no congestion at noon (when all the users are at lunch).

With wireless networks, location is an important variable because of signal propagation. Even a measurement node placed close to a wireless client may not observe the same packets as the client due to differences in the antennas. It is best to take measurements from the wireless client under study to see what it sees. Failing that, it is possible to use techniques to combine the wireless measurements taken at different vantage points to gain a more complete picture of what is going on (Mahajan et al., 2006).

Caching Can Wreak Havoc with Measurements

Repeating a measurement many times will return an unexpectedly fast answer if the protocols use caching mechanisms. For instance, fetching a Web page or looking up a DNS name (to find the IP address) may involve a network exchange the first time, and then return the answer from a local cache without sending any packets over the network. The results from such a measurement are essentially worthless (unless you want to measure cache performance).

Buffering can have a similar effect. TCP/IP performance tests have been known to report that UDP can achieve a performance substantially higher than the network allows. How does this occur? A call to UDP normally returns control as soon as the message has been accepted by the kernel and added to the transmission queue. If there is sufficient buffer space, timing 1000 UDP calls does not mean that all the data have been sent. Most of them may still be in the kernel, but the performance test program thinks they have all been transmitted.

Caution is advised to be absolutely sure that you understand how data can be cached and buffered as part of a network operation.

Be Sure That Nothing Unexpected Is Going On during Your Tests

Making measurements at the same time that some user has decided to run a video conference over your network will often give different results than if there is no video conference. It is best to run tests on an idle network and create the entire workload yourself. Even this approach has pitfalls, though. While you might think nobody will be using the network at 3 A.M., that might be when the automatic backup program begins copying all the disks to tape. Or, there might be heavy traffic for your wonderful Web pages from distant time zones.

Wireless networks are challenging in this respect because it is often not possible to separate them from all sources of interference. Even if there are no other wireless networks sending traffic nearby, someone may microwave popcorn and inadvertently cause interference that degrades 802.11 performance. For these reasons, it is a good practice to monitor the overall network activity so that you can at least realize when something unexpected does happen.

Be Careful When Using a Coarse-Grained Clock

Computer clocks function by incrementing some counter at regular intervals. For example, a millisecond timer adds 1 to a counter every 1 msec. Using such a timer to measure an event that takes less than 1 msec is possible but requires some care. Some computers have more accurate clocks, of course, but there are always shorter events to measure too. Note that clocks are not always as accurate as the precision with which the time is returned when they are read.

To measure the time to make a TCP connection, for example, the clock (say, in milliseconds) should be read out when the transport layer code is entered and again when it is exited. If the true connection setup time is 300 μsec, the difference between the two readings will be either 0 or 1, both wrong. However, if the measurement is repeated one million times and the total of all measurements is added up and divided by one million, the mean time will be accurate to better than 1 μsec.

Be Careful about Extrapolating the Results

Suppose that you make measurements with simulated network loads running from 0 (idle) to 0.4 (40% of capacity). For example, the response time to send a voice-over-IP packet over an 802.11 network might be as shown by the data points and solid line through them in Fig. 6-49. It may be tempting to extrapolate linearly, as shown by the dotted line. However, many queueing results involve a factor of $1/(1 - \rho)$, where ρ is the load, so the true values may look more like the dashed line, which rises much faster than linearly when the load gets high. That is, beware contention effects that become much more pronounced at high load.

6.6.3 Host Design for Fast Networks

Measuring and tinkering can improve performance considerably, but they cannot substitute for good design in the first place. A poorly designed network can be improved only so much. Beyond that, it has to be redesigned from scratch.

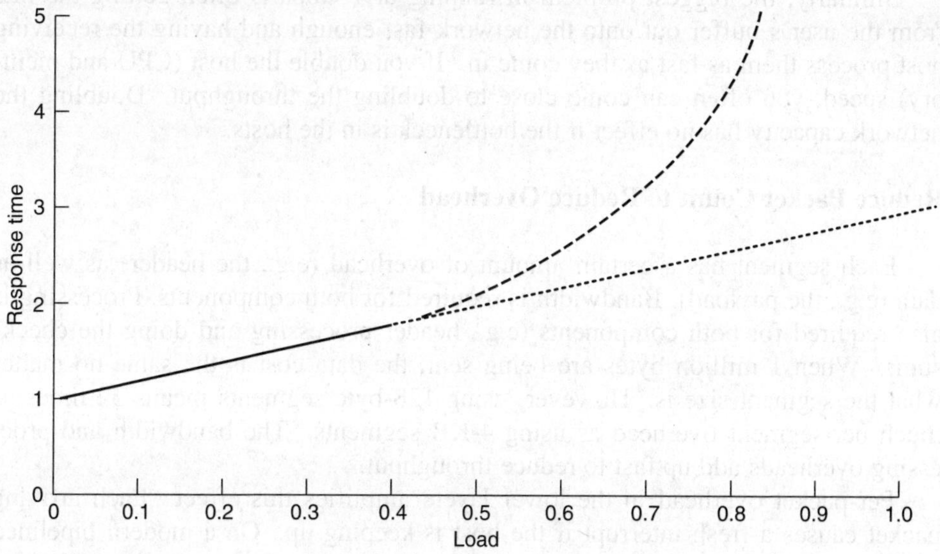

Figure 6-49. Response as a function of load.

In this section, we will present some rules of thumb for software implementation of network protocols on hosts. Surprisingly, experience shows that this is often a performance bottleneck on otherwise fast networks, for two reasons. First, NICs (Network Interface Cards) and routers have already been engineered (with hardware support) to run at "wire speed." This means that they can process packets as quickly as the packets can possibly arrive on the link. Second, the relevant performance is that which applications obtain. It is not the link capacity, but the throughput and delay after network and transport processing.

Reducing software overheads improves performance by increasing throughput and decreasing delay. It can also reduce the energy that is spent on networking, which is an important consideration for mobile computers. Most of these ideas have been common knowledge to network designers for years. They were first stated explicitly by Mogul (1993); our treatment largely follows his. Another relevant source is Metcalfe (1993).

Host Speed Is More Important Than Network Speed

Long experience has shown that in nearly all fast networks, operating system and protocol overhead dominate actual time on the wire. For example, in theory, the minimum RPC time on a 1-Gbps Ethernet is 1 μsec, corresponding to a minimum (512-byte) request followed by a minimum (512-byte) reply. In practice, overcoming the software overhead and getting the RPC time anywhere near there is a substantial achievement. It rarely happens in practice.

Similarly, the biggest problem in running at 1 Gbps is often getting the bits from the user's buffer out onto the network fast enough and having the receiving host process them as fast as they come in. If you double the host (CPU and memory) speed, you often can come close to doubling the throughput. Doubling the network capacity has no effect if the bottleneck is in the hosts.

Reduce Packet Count to Reduce Overhead

Each segment has a certain amount of overhead (e.g., the header) as well as data (e.g., the payload). Bandwidth is required for both components. Processing is also required for both components (e.g., header processing and doing the checksum). When 1 million bytes are being sent, the data cost is the same no matter what the segment size is. However, using 128-byte segments means 32 times as much per-segment overhead as using 4-KB segments. The bandwidth and processing overheads add up fast to reduce throughput.

Per-packet overhead in the lower layers amplifies this effect. Each arriving packet causes a fresh interrupt if the host is keeping up. On a modern pipelined processor, each interrupt breaks the CPU pipeline, interferes with the cache, requires a change to the memory management context, voids the branch prediction table, and forces a substantial number of CPU registers to be saved. An n-fold reduction in segments sent thus reduces the interrupt and packet overhead by a factor of n.

You might say that both people and computers are poor at multitasking. This observation underlies the desire to send MTU packets that are as large as will pass along the network path without fragmentation. Mechanisms such as Nagle's algorithm and Clark's solution are also attempts to avoid sending small packets.

Minimize Data Touching

The most straightforward way to implement a layered protocol stack is with one module for each layer. Unfortunately, this leads to copying (or at least accessing the data on multiple passes) as each layer does its own work. For example, after a packet is received by the NIC, it is typically copied to a kernel buffer. From there, it is copied to a network layer buffer for network layer processing, then to a transport layer buffer for transport layer processing, and finally to the receiving application process. It is not unusual for an incoming packet to be copied three or four times before the segment enclosed in it is delivered.

All this copying can greatly degrade performance because memory operations are an order of magnitude slower than register–register instructions. For example, if 20% of the instructions actually go to memory (i.e., are cache misses), which is likely when touching incoming packets, the average instruction execution time is slowed down by a factor of 2.8 ($0.8 \times 1 + 0.2 \times 10$). Hardware assistance will not help here. The problem is too much copying by the operating system.

A clever operating system will minimize copying by combining the processing of multiple layers. For example, TCP and IP are usually implemented together (as "TCP/IP") so that it is not necessary to copy the payload of the packet as processing switches from network to transport layer. Another common trick is to perform multiple operations within a layer in a single pass over the data. For example, checksums are often computed while copying the data (when it has to be copied) and the newly computed checksum is appended to the end.

Minimize Context Switches

A related rule is that context switches (e.g., from kernel mode to user mode) are deadly. They have the bad properties of interrupts and copying combined. This cost is why transport protocols are often implemented in the kernel. Like reducing packet count, context switches can be reduced by having the library procedure that sends data do internal buffering until it has a substantial amount of them. Similarly, on the receiving side, small incoming segments should be collected together and passed to the user in one fell swoop instead of individually, to minimize context switches.

In the best case, an incoming packet causes a context switch from the current user to the kernel, and then a switch to the receiving process to give it the newly arrived data. Unfortunately, with some operating systems, additional context switches happen. For example, if the network manager runs as a special process in user space, a packet arrival is likely to cause a context switch from the current user to the kernel, then another one from the kernel to the network manager, followed by another one back to the kernel, and finally one from the kernel to the receiving process. This sequence is shown in Fig. 6-50. All these context switches on each packet are wasteful of CPU time and can have a devastating effect on network performance.

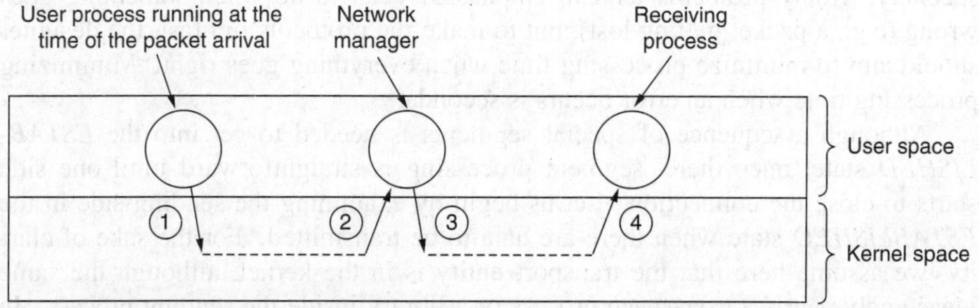

Figure 6-50. Four context switches to handle one packet with a user-space network manager.

Avoiding Congestion Is Better Than Recovering from It

The old maxim that an ounce of prevention is worth a pound of cure certainly holds for network congestion. When a network is congested, packets are lost, bandwidth is wasted, useless delays are introduced, and more. All of these costs are unnecessary, and recovering from congestion takes time and patience. Not having it occur in the first place is better. Congestion avoidance is like getting your DTP vaccination: it hurts a little at the time you get it, but it prevents something that would hurt a lot more in the future.

Avoid Timeouts

Timers are necessary in networks, but they should be used sparingly and timeouts should be minimized. When a timer goes off, some action is generally repeated. If it is truly necessary to repeat the action, so be it, but repeating it unnecessarily is wasteful.

The way to avoid extra work is to be careful that timers are set a little bit on the conservative side. A timer that takes too long to expire adds a small amount of extra delay to one connection in the (unlikely) event of a segment being lost. A timer that goes off when it should not have uses up host resources, wastes bandwidth, and puts extra load on perhaps dozens of routers for no good reason.

6.6.4 Fast Segment Processing

Now that we have covered general rules, we will look at some specific methods for speeding up segment processing. For more information, see Clark et al. (1989), and Chase et al. (2001).

Segment processing overhead has two components: overhead per segment and overhead per byte. Both must be attacked. The key to fast segment processing is to separate out the normal, successful case (one-way data transfer) and handle it specially. Many protocols tend to emphasize what to do when something goes wrong (e.g., a packet getting lost), but to make the protocols run fast, the designer should aim to minimize processing time when everything goes right. Minimizing processing time when an error occurs is secondary.

Although a sequence of special segments is needed to get into the *ESTABLISHED* state, once there, segment processing is straightforward until one side starts to close the connection. Let us begin by examining the sending side in the *ESTABLISHED* state when there are data to be transmitted. For the sake of clarity, we assume here that the transport entity is in the kernel, although the same ideas apply if it is a user-space process or a library inside the sending process. In Fig. 6-51, the sending process traps into the kernel to do the SEND. The first thing the transport entity does is test to see if this is the normal case: the state is *ESTABLISHED*, neither side is trying to close the connection, a regular (i.e., not an out-of-band) full segment is being sent, and enough window space is available at the receiver. If all conditions are met, no further tests are needed and the fast path through the sending transport entity can be taken. Typically, this path is taken most of the time.

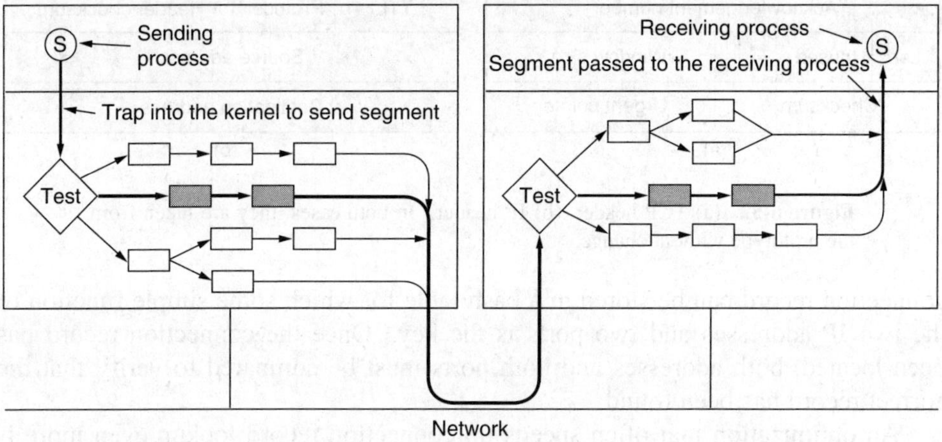

Figure 6-51. The fast path from sender to receiver is shown with a heavy line. The processing steps on this path are shaded.

In the usual case, the headers of consecutive data segments are almost the same. To take advantage of this fact, a prototype header is stored within the transport entity. At the start of the fast path, it is copied as fast as possible to a scratch buffer, word by word. Those fields that change from segment to segment are overwritten in the buffer. Frequently, these fields are easily derived from state variables, such as the next sequence number. A pointer to the full segment header plus a pointer to the user data are then passed to the network layer. Here, the same strategy can be followed (not shown in Fig. 6-51). Finally, the network layer gives the resulting packet to the data link layer for transmission.

As an example of how this principle works in practice, let us consider TCP/IP. Fig. 6-52(a) shows the TCP header. The fields that are the same between consecutive segments on a one-way flow are shaded. All the sending transport entity has to do is copy the five words from the prototype header into the output buffer, fill in the next sequence number (by copying it from a word in memory), compute the checksum, and increment the sequence number in memory. It can then hand the header and data to a special IP procedure for sending a regular, maximum segment. IP then copies its five-word prototype header [see Fig. 6-52(b)] into the buffer, fills in the *Identification* field, and computes its checksum. The packet is now ready for transmission.

Now let us look at fast path processing on the receiving side of Fig. 6-51. Step 1 is locating the connection record for the incoming segment. For TCP, the

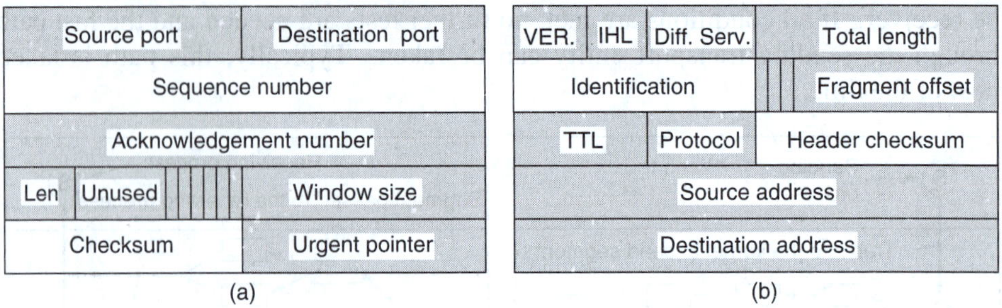

Figure 6-52. (a) TCP header. (b) IP header. In both cases, they are taken from the prototype without change.

connection record can be stored in a hash table for which some simple function of the two IP addresses and two ports is the key. Once the connection record has been located, both addresses and both ports must be compared to verify that the correct record has been found.

An optimization that often speeds up connection record lookup even more is to maintain a pointer to the last one used and try that one first. Clark et al. (1989) tried this and observed a hit rate exceeding 90%.

The segment is checked to see if it is a normal one: the state is *ESTABLISHED*, neither side is trying to close the connection, the segment is a full one, no special flags are set, and the sequence number is the one expected. These tests take just a handful of instructions. If all conditions are met, a special fast path TCP procedure is called.

The fast path updates the connection record and copies the data to the user. While it is copying, it also computes the checksum, eliminating an extra pass over the data. If the checksum is correct, the connection record is updated and an acknowledgement is sent back. The general scheme of first making a quick check to see if the header is what is expected and then having a special procedure handle that case is called **header prediction**. Many TCP implementations use it. When this optimization and all the other ones discussed in this chapter are used together, it is possible to get TCP to run at 90% of the speed of a local memory-to-memory copy, assuming the network itself is fast enough.

Two other areas where major performance gains are possible are buffer management and timer management. The issue in buffer management is avoiding unnecessary copying, as mentioned above. Timer management is important because nearly all timers set do not expire. They are set to guard against segment loss, but most segments and their acknowledgements arrive correctly. Hence, it is important to optimize timer management for the case of timers rarely expiring.

A common scheme is to use a linked list of timer events sorted by expiration time. The head entry contains a counter telling how many ticks away from expiry it is. Each successive entry contains a counter telling how many ticks after the previous entry it is. Thus, if timers expire in 3, 10, and 12 ticks, respectively, the three counters are 3, 7, and 2, respectively.

At every clock tick, the counter in the head entry is decremented. When it hits zero, its event is processed and the next item on the list becomes the head. Its counter does not have to be changed. This way, inserting and deleting timers are expensive operations, with execution times proportional to the length of the list.

A much more efficient approach can be used if the maximum timer interval is bounded and known in advance. Here, an array called a **timing wheel** can be used, as shown in Fig. 6-53. Each slot corresponds to one clock tick. The current time shown is $T = 4$. Timers are scheduled to expire at 3, 10, and 12 ticks from now. If a new timer suddenly is set to expire in seven ticks, an entry is just made in slot 11. Similarly, if the timer set for $T + 10$ has to be canceled, the list starting in slot 14 has to be searched and the required entry removed. Note that the array of Fig. 6-53 cannot accommodate timers beyond $T + 15$.

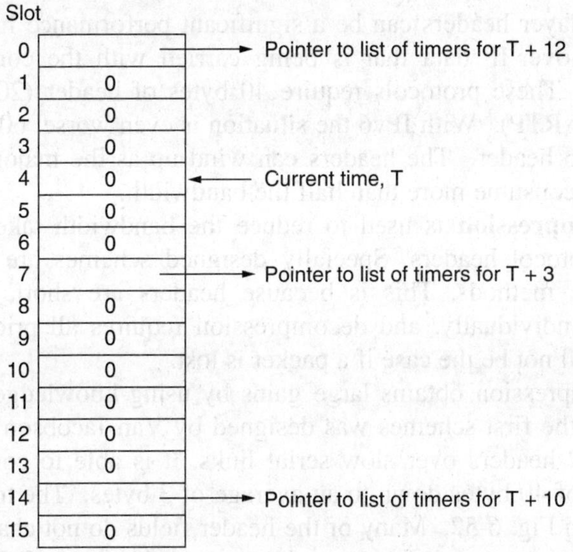

Figure 6-53. A timing wheel.

When the clock ticks, the current time pointer is advanced by one slot (circularly). If the entry now pointed to is nonzero, all of its timers are processed. Many variations on the basic idea are discussed by Varghese and Lauck (1987).

6.6.5 Header Compression

We have been looking at fast networks for too long. There is more out there. Let us now consider performance on wireless and other networks in which bandwidth is limited. Reducing software overhead can help mobile computers run more efficiently, but it does nothing to improve performance when the network links are the bottleneck.

To use bandwidth well, protocol headers and payloads should be carried with the minimum of bits. For payloads, this means using compact encodings of information, such as images that are in JPEG format rather than a bitmap, or document formats such as PDF that include compression. It also means application-level caching mechanisms, such as Web caches that reduce transfers in the first place.

What about for protocol headers? At the link layer, headers for wireless networks are typically compact because they were designed with scarce bandwidth in mind. For example, 802.16 headers have short connection identifiers instead of longer addresses. However, higher layer protocols such as IP, TCP and UDP come in one version for all link layers, and they are not designed with compact headers. In fact, streamlined processing to reduce software overhead often leads to headers that are not as compact as they could otherwise be (e.g., IPv6 has a more loosely packed headers than IPv4).

The higher-layer headers can be a significant performance hit. Consider, for example, voice-over-IP data that is being carried with the combination of IP, UDP, and RTP. These protocols require 40 bytes of header (20 for IPv4, 8 for UDP, and 12 for RTP). With IPv6 the situation is even worse: 60 bytes, including the 40-byte IPv6 header. The headers can wind up as the majority of the transmitted data and consume more than half the bandwidth.

Header compression is used to reduce the bandwidth taken over links by higher-layer protocol headers. Specially designed schemes are used instead of general purpose methods. This is because headers are short, so they do not compress well individually, and decompression requires all prior data to be received. This will not be the case if a packet is lost.

Header compression obtains large gains by using knowledge of the protocol format. One of the first schemes was designed by Van Jacobson (1990) for compressing TCP/IP headers over slow serial links. It is able to compress a typical TCP/IP header of 40 bytes down to an average of 3 bytes. The trick to this method is hinted at in Fig. 6-52. Many of the header fields do not change from packet to packet. There is no need, for example, to send the same IP TTL or the same TCP port numbers in each and every packet. They can be omitted on the sending side of the link and filled in on the receiving side.

Similarly, other fields change in a predictable manner. For example, barring loss, the TCP sequence number advances with the data. In these cases, the receiver can predict the likely value. The actual number only needs to be carried when it differs from what is expected. Even then, it may be carried as a small change from the previous value, as when the acknowledgement number increases when new data is received in the reverse direction.

With header compression, it is possible to have simple headers in higher-layer protocols and compact encodings over low bandwidth links. **ROHC** (**RObust Header Compression**) is a modern version of header compression that is defined as a framework in RFC 5795. It is designed to tolerate the loss that can occur on wireless links. There is a profile for each set of protocols to be compressed, such as IP/UDP/RTP. Compressed headers are carried by referring to a context, which is essentially a connection; header fields may easily be predicted for packets of the same connection, but not for packets of different connections. In typical operation, ROHC reduces IP/UDP/RTP headers from 40 bytes to 1 to 3 bytes.

While header compression is mainly targeted at reducing bandwidth needs, it can also be useful for reducing delay. Delay is comprised of propagation delay, which is fixed given a network path, and transmission delay, which depends on the bandwidth and amount of data to be sent. For example, a 1-Mbps link sends 1 bit in 1 μsec. In the case of media over wireless networks, the network is relatively slow so transmission delay may be an important factor in overall delay and consistently low delay is important for quality of service.

Header compression can help by reducing the amount of data that is sent, and hence reducing transmission delay. The same effect can be achieved by sending smaller packets. This will trade increased software overhead for decreased transmission delay. Note that another potential source of delay is queueing delay to access the wireless link. This can also be significant because wireless links are often heavily used as the limited resource in a network. In this case, the wireless link must have quality-of-service mechanisms that give low delay to real-time packets. Header compression alone is not sufficient.

6.6.6 Protocols for Long Fat Networks

Since the 1990s, there have been gigabit networks that transmit data over large distances. Because of the combination of a fast network, or "fat pipe," and long delay, these networks are called **long fat networks**. When these networks arose, people's first reaction was to use the existing protocols on them, but various problems quickly arose. In this section, we will discuss some of the problems with scaling up the speed and delay of network protocols.

The first problem is that many protocols use 32-bit sequence numbers. When the Internet began, the lines between routers were mostly 56-kbps leased lines, so a host blasting away at full speed took over 1 week to cycle through the sequence numbers. To the TCP designers, 2^{32} was a pretty decent approximation of infinity because there was little danger of old packets still being around a week after they were transmitted. With 10-Mbps Ethernet, the wrap time became 57 minutes, much shorter, but still manageable. With a 1-Gbps Ethernet pouring data out onto the Internet, the wrap time is about 34 seconds, well under the 120-sec maximum packet lifetime on the Internet. All of a sudden, 2^{32} is not nearly as good an approximation to infinity since a fast sender can cycle through the sequence space while old packets still exist.

The problem is that many protocol designers simply assumed, without stating it, that the time required to use up the entire sequence space would greatly exceed the maximum packet lifetime. Consequently, there was no need to even worry about the problem of old duplicates still existing when the sequence numbers wrapped around. At gigabit speeds, that unstated assumption fails. Fortunately, it proved possible to extend the effective sequence number by treating the timestamp that can be carried as an option in the TCP header of each packet as the high-order bits. This mechanism is called PAWS (Protection Against Wrapped Sequence numbers) and is described in RFC 1323.

A second problem is that the size of the flow control window must be greatly increased. Consider, for example, sending a 64-KB burst of data from San Diego to Boston in order to fill the receiver's 64-KB buffer. Suppose that the link is 1 Gbps and the one-way speed-of-light-in-fiber delay is 20 msec. Initially, at $t = 0$, the pipe is empty, as illustrated in Fig. 6-54(a). Only 500 μsec later, in Fig. 6-54(b), all the segments are out on the fiber. The lead segment will now be somewhere in the vicinity of Brawley, still deep in Southern California. However, the transmitter must stop until it gets a window update.

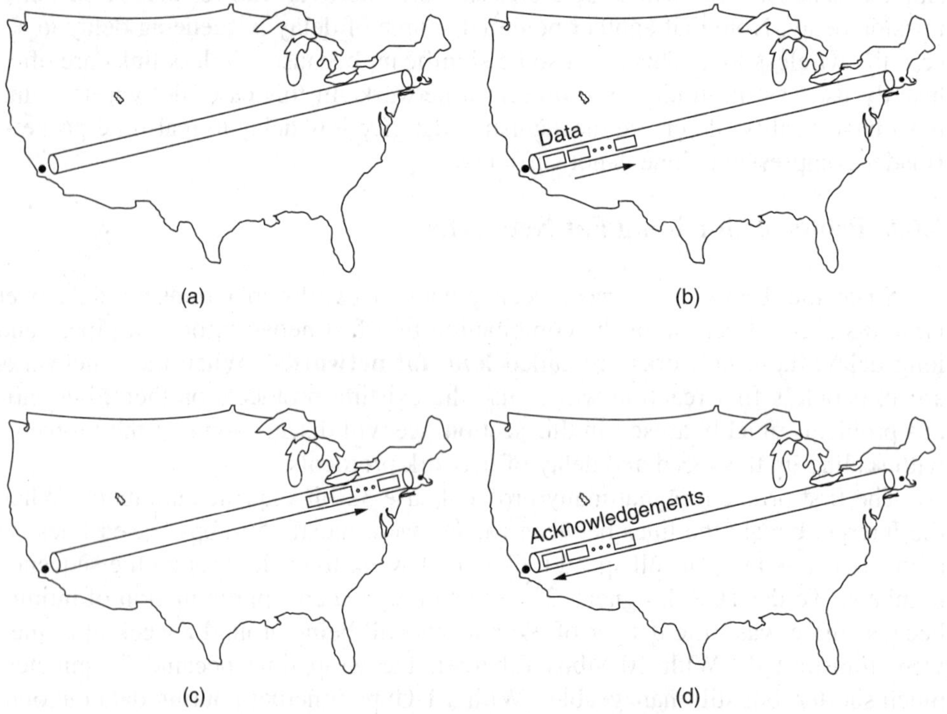

Figure 6-54. The state of transmitting 1 Mbit from San Diego to Boston. (a) At $t = 0$. (b) After 500 μsec. (c) After 20 msec. (d) After 40 msec.

After 20 msec, the lead segment hits Boston, as shown in Fig. 6-54(c), and is acknowledged. Finally, 40 msec after starting, the first acknowledgement gets back to the sender and the second burst can be transmitted. Since the transmission line was used for 1.25 msec out of 100, the efficiency is about 1.25%. This situation is typical of an older protocols running over gigabit lines.

A useful quantity to keep in mind when analyzing network performance is the **bandwidth-delay product**. It is obtained by multiplying the bandwidth (in bits/sec) by the round-trip delay time (in sec). The product is the capacity of the pipe from the sender to the receiver and back (in bits).

For the example of Fig. 6-54, the bandwidth-delay product is 40 million bits. In other words, the sender would have to transmit a burst of 40 million bits to be able to keep going full speed until the first acknowledgement came back. It takes this many bits to fill the pipe (in both directions). This is why a burst of half a million bits only achieves a 1.25% efficiency: it is only 1.25% of the pipe's capacity.

The conclusion that can be drawn here is that for good performance, the receiver's window must be at least as large as the bandwidth-delay product, and preferably somewhat larger since the receiver may not respond instantly. For a transcontinental gigabit line, at least 5 MB are required.

A third and related problem is that simple retransmission schemes, such as the go-back-n protocol, perform poorly on lines with a large bandwidth-delay product. Consider, the 1-Gbps transcontinental link with a round-trip transmission time of 40 msec. A sender can transmit 5 MB in one round trip. If an error is detected, it will be 40 msec before the sender is told about it. If go-back-n is used, the sender will have to retransmit not just the bad packet, but also the 5 MB worth of packets that came afterward. Clearly, this is a massive waste of resources. More complex protocols such as selective-repeat are needed.

A fourth problem is that gigabit lines are fundamentally different from megabit lines in that long gigabit lines are delay limited rather than bandwidth limited. In Fig. 6-55 we show the time it takes to transfer a 1-Mbit file 4000 km at various transmission speeds. At speeds up to 1 Mbps, the transmission time is dominated by the rate at which the bits can be sent. By 1 Gbps, the 40-msec round-trip delay dominates the 1 msec it takes to put the bits on the fiber. Further increases in bandwidth have hardly any effect at all.

Figure 6-55 has unfortunate implications for network protocols. It says that stop-and-wait protocols, such as RPC, have an inherent upper bound on their performance. This limit is dictated by the speed of light. No amount of technological progress in optics will ever improve matters (new laws of physics would help, though). Unless some other use can be found for a gigabit line while a host is waiting for a reply, the gigabit line is no better than a megabit line, just more expensive.

A fifth problem is that communication speeds have improved faster than computing speeds. (Note to computer engineers: go out and beat those communication engineers! We are counting on you.) In the 1970s, the ARPANET ran at 56 kbps and had computers that ran at about 1 MIPS. Compare these numbers to

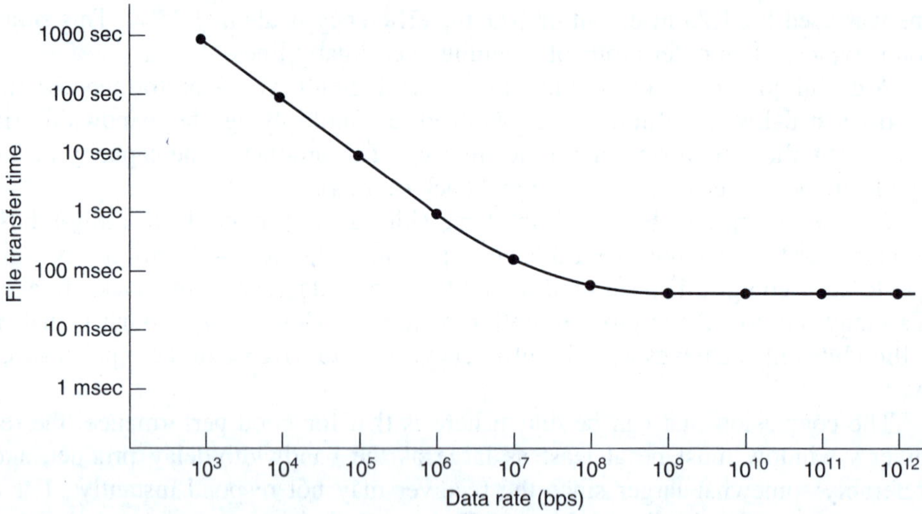

Figure 6-55. Time to transfer and acknowledge a 1-Mbit file over a 4000-km line.

1000-MIPS computers exchanging packets over a 1-Gbps line. The number of instructions per byte has decreased by more than a factor of 10. The exact numbers are debatable depending on dates and scenarios, but the conclusion is this: there is less time available for protocol processing than there used to be, so protocols must become simpler.

Let us now turn from the problems to ways of dealing with them. The basic principle that all high-speed network designers should learn by heart is:

Design for speed, not for bandwidth optimization.

Old protocols were often designed to minimize the number of bits on the wire, frequently by using small fields and packing them together into bytes and words. This concern is still valid for wireless networks, but not for gigabit networks. Protocol processing is the problem, so protocols should be designed to minimize it. The IPv6 designers clearly understood this principle.

A tempting way to go fast is to build fast network interfaces in hardware. The difficulty with this strategy is that unless the protocol is exceedingly simple, hardware just means a plug-in board with a second CPU and its own program. To make sure the network coprocessor is cheaper than the main CPU, it is often a slower chip. The consequence of this design is that much of the time the main (fast) CPU is idle waiting for the second (slow) CPU to do the critical work. It is a myth to think that the main CPU has other work to do while waiting. Furthermore, when two general-purpose CPUs communicate, race conditions can occur, so elaborate protocols are needed between the two processors to synchronize them correctly and avoid races. Usually, the best approach is to make the protocols simple and have the main CPU do the work.

Packet layout is an important consideration in gigabit networks. The header should contain as few fields as possible, to reduce processing time, and these fields should be big enough to do the job and be word-aligned for fast processing. In this context, "big enough" means that problems such as sequence numbers wrapping around while old packets still exist, receivers being unable to advertise enough window space because the window field is too small, etc. do not occur.

The maximum data size should be large, to reduce software overhead and permit efficient operation. 1500 bytes is too small for high-speed networks, which is why gigabit Ethernet supports jumbo frames of up to 9 KB and IPv6 supports jumbogram packets in excess of 64 KB.

Let us now look at the issue of feedback in high-speed protocols. Due to the (relatively) long delay loop, feedback should be avoided: it takes too long for the receiver to signal the sender. One example of feedback is governing the transmission rate by using a sliding window protocol. Future protocols may switch to rate-based protocols to avoid the (long) delays inherent in the receiver sending window updates to the sender. In such a protocol, the sender can send all it wants to, provided it does not send faster than some rate the sender and receiver have agreed upon in advance.

A second example of feedback is Jacobson's slow start algorithm. This algorithm makes multiple probes to see how much the network can handle. With high-speed networks, making half a dozen or so small probes to see how the network responds wastes a huge amount of bandwidth. A more efficient scheme is to have the sender, receiver, and network all reserve the necessary resources at connection setup time. Reserving resources in advance also has the advantage of making it easier to reduce jitter. In short, going to high speeds inexorably pushes the design toward connection-oriented operation, or something fairly close to it.

Another valuable feature is the ability to send a normal amount of data along with the connection request. In this way, one round-trip time can be saved.

6.7 DELAY-TOLERANT NETWORKING

We will finish this chapter by describing a new kind of transport that may one day be an important component of the Internet. TCP and most other transport protocols are based on the assumption that the sender and the receiver are continuously connected by some working path, or else the protocol fails and data cannot be delivered. In some networks there is often no end-to-end path. An example is a space network as LEO (Low-Earth Orbit) satellites pass in and out of range of ground stations. A given satellite may be able to communicate to a ground station only at particular times, and two satellites may never be able to communicate with each other at any time, even via a ground station, because one of the satellites may always be out of range. Other example networks involve submarines, buses, mobile phones, and other devices with computers for which there is intermittent connectivity due to mobility or extreme conditions.

In these occasionally connected networks, data can still be communicated by storing them at nodes and forwarding them later when there is a working link. This technique is called **message switching**. Eventually the data will be relayed to the destination. A network whose architecture is based on this approach is called a **DTN** (**Delay-Tolerant Network**, or a **Disruption-Tolerant Network**).

Work on DTNs started in 2002 when IETF set up a research group on the topic. The inspiration for DTNs came from an unlikely source: efforts to send packets in space. Space networks must deal with intermittent communication and very long delays. Kevin Fall observed that the ideas for these Interplanetary Internets could be applied to networks on Earth in which intermittent connectivity was the norm (Fall, 2003). This model gives a useful generalization of the Internet in which storage and delays can occur during communication. Data delivery is akin to delivery in the postal system, or electronic mail, rather than packet switching at routers.

Since 2002, the DTN architecture has been refined, and the applications of the DTN model have grown. As a mainstream application, consider large datasets of many terabytes that are produced by scientific experiments, media events, or Web-based services and need to be copied to datacenters at different locations around the world. Operators would like to send this bulk traffic at off-peak times to make use of bandwidth that has already been paid for but is not being used, and are willing to tolerate some delay. It is like doing the backups at night when other applications are not making heavy use of the network. The problem is that, for global services, the off-peak times are different at locations around the world. There may be little overlap in the times when datacenters in Boston and Perth have off-peak network bandwidth because night for one city is day for the other.

However, DTN models allow for storage and delays during transfer. With this model, it becomes possible to send the dataset from Boston to Amsterdam using off-peak bandwidth, as the cities have time zones that are only 6 hours apart. The dataset is then stored in Amsterdam until there is off-peak bandwidth between Amsterdam and Perth. It is then sent to Perth to complete the transfer. Laoutaris et al. (2009) have studied this model and find that it can provide substantial capacity at little cost, and that the use of a DTN model often doubles that capacity compared with a traditional end-to-end model.

In what follows, we will describe the IETF DTN architecture and protocols.

6.7.1 DTN Architecture

The main assumption in the Internet that DTNs seek to relax is that an end-to-end path between a source and a destination exists for the entire duration of a communication session. When this is not the case, the normal Internet protocols fail. DTNs get around the lack of end-to-end connectivity with an architecture that is based on message switching, as shown in Fig. 6-56. It is also intended to tolerate links with low reliability and large delays. The architecture is specified in RFC 4838.

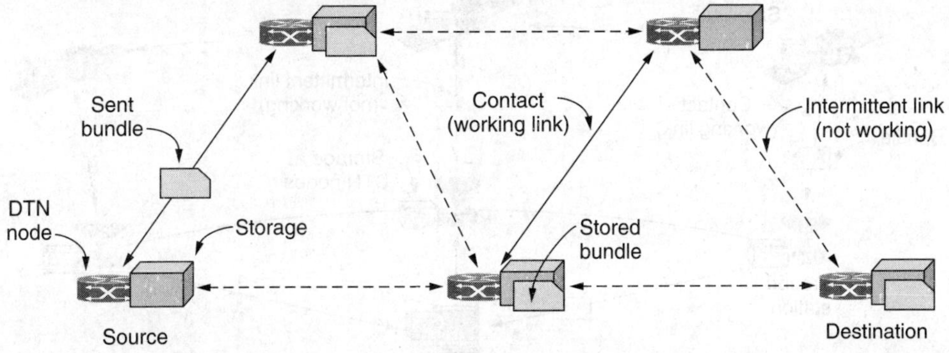

Figure 6-56. Delay-tolerant networking architecture.

In DTN terminology, a message is called a **bundle**. DTN nodes are equipped with storage, typically persistent storage such as a disk or flash memory. They store bundles until links become available and then forward the bundles. The links work intermittently. Fig. 6-56 shows five intermittent links that are not currently working, and two links that are working. A working link is called a **contact**. Fig. 6-56 also shows bundles stored at two DTN nodes awaiting contacts to send the bundles onward. In this way, the bundles are relayed via contacts from the source to their destination.

The storing and forwarding of bundles at DTN nodes sounds similar to the queueing and forwarding of packets at routers, but there are qualitative differences. In routers in the Internet, queueing occurs for milliseconds or at most seconds. At DTN nodes, bundles may be stored for hours, until a bus arrives in town, while an airplane completes a flight, until a sensor node harvests enough solar energy to run, until a sleeping computer wakes up, and so forth. These examples also point to a second difference, which is that nodes may move (with a bus or plane) while they hold stored data, and this movement may even be a key part of data delivery. Routers in the Internet are not allowed to move. The whole process of moving bundles might be better known as "store-carry-forward."

As an example, consider the scenario shown in Fig. 6-57 that was the first use of DTN protocols in space (Wood et al., 2008). The source of bundles is an LEO satellite that is recording Earth images as part of the Disaster Monitoring Constellation of satellites. The images must be returned to the collection point. However, the satellite has only intermittent contact with three ground stations as it orbits the Earth. It comes into contact with each ground station in turn. Each of the satellite, ground stations, and collection point act as a DTN node. At each contact, a bundle (or a portion of a bundle) is sent to a ground station. The bundles are then sent over a backhaul terrestrial network to the collection point to complete the transfer.

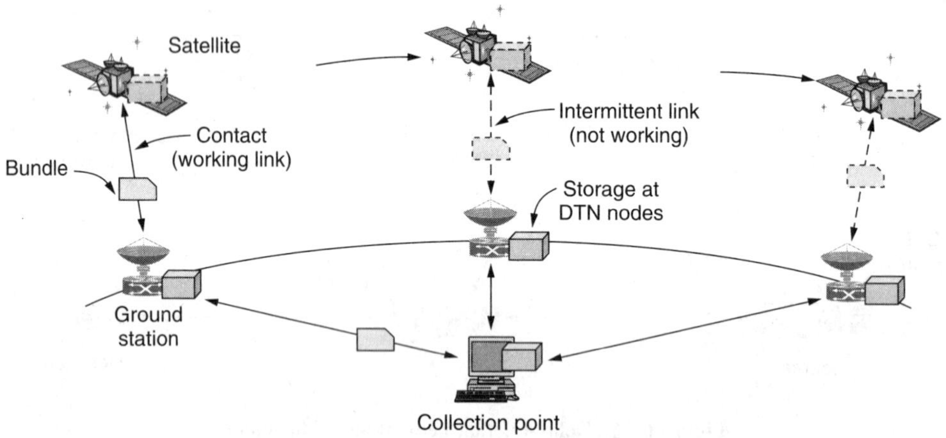

Figure 6-57. Use of a DTN in space.

The primary advantage of the DTN architecture in this example is that it naturally fits the situation of the satellite needing to store images because there is no connectivity at the time the image is taken. There are two further advantages. First, there may be no single contact long enough to send the images. However, they can be spread across the contacts with three ground stations. Second, the use of the link between the satellite and ground station is decoupled from the link over the backhaul network. This means that the satellite download is not limited by a slow terrestrial link. It can proceed at full speed, with the bundle stored at the ground station until it can be relayed to the collection point.

An important issue that is not specified by the architecture is how to find good routes via DTN nodes. A route in this path to use. Good routes depend on the nature of the architecture describes when to send data, and also which contacts. Some contacts are known ahead of time. A good example is the motion of heavenly bodies in the space example. For the space experiment, it was known ahead of time when contacts would occur, that the contact intervals ranged from 5 to 14 minutes per pass with each ground station, and that the downlink capacity was 8.134 Mbps. Given this knowledge, the transport of a bundle of images can be planned ahead of time.

In other cases, the contacts can be predicted, but with less certainty. Examples include buses that make contact with each other in mostly regular ways, due to a timetable, yet with some variation, and the times and amount of off-peak bandwidth in ISP networks, which are predicted from past data. At the other extreme, the contacts are occasional and random. One example is carrying data from user to user on mobile phones depending on which users make contact with each other during the day. When there is unpredictability in contacts, one routing strategy is to send copies of the bundle along different paths in the hope that one of the copies is delivered to the destination before the lifetime is reached.

6.7.2 The Bundle Protocol

To take a closer look at the operation of DTNs, we will now look at the IETF protocols. DTNs are an emerging kind of network, and experimental DTNs have used different protocols, as there is no requirement that the IETF protocols be used. However, they are at least a good place to start and highlight many of the key issues.

The DTN protocol stack is shown in Fig. 6-58. The key protocol is the **Bundle protocol**, which is specified in RFC 5050. It is responsible for accepting messages from the application and sending them as one or more bundles via store-carry-forward operations to the destination DTN node. It is also apparent from Fig. 6-58 that the Bundle protocol runs above the level of TCP/IP. In other words, TCP/IP may be used over each contact to move bundles between DTN nodes. This positioning raises the issue of whether the Bundle protocol is a transport layer protocol or an application layer protocol. Just as with RTP, we take the position that, despite running over a transport protocol, the Bundle protocol is providing a transport service to many different applications, and so we cover DTNs in this chapter.

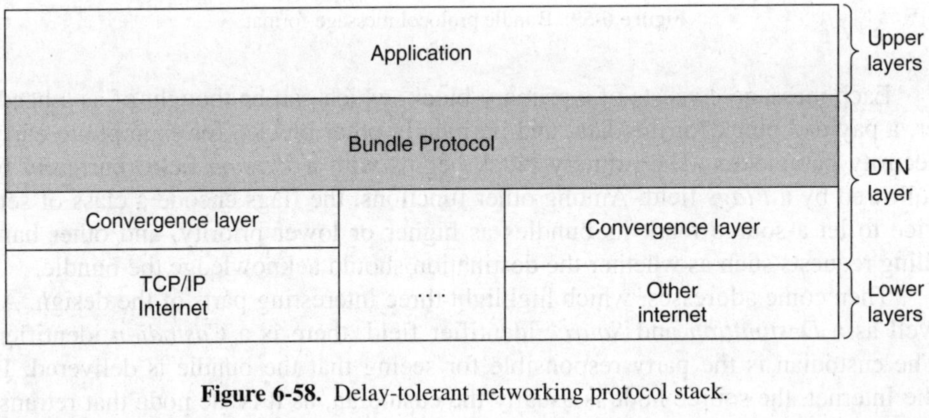

Figure 6-58. Delay-tolerant networking protocol stack.

In Fig. 6-58, we see that the Bundle protocol may be run over other kinds of protocols such as UDP, or even other kinds of internets. For example, in a space network the links may have very long delays. The round-trip time between Earth and Mars can easily be 20 minutes depending on the relative position of the planets. Imagine how well TCP acknowledgements and retransmissions will work over that link, especially for relatively short messages. Not well at all. Instead, another protocol that uses error-correcting codes might be used. Or in sensor networks that are very resource constrained, a more lightweight protocol than TCP may be used.

Since the Bundle protocol is fixed, yet it is intended to run over a variety of transports, there is must be a gap in functionality between the protocols. That gap is the reason for the inclusion of a convergence layer in Fig. 6-58. The convergence layer is just a glue layer that matches the interfaces of the protocols that it joins. By definition there is a different convergence layer for each different lower layer transport. Convergence layers are commonly found in standards to join new and existing protocols.

The format of Bundle protocol messages is shown in Fig. 6-59. The different fields in these messages tell us some of the key issues that are handled by the Bundle protocol.

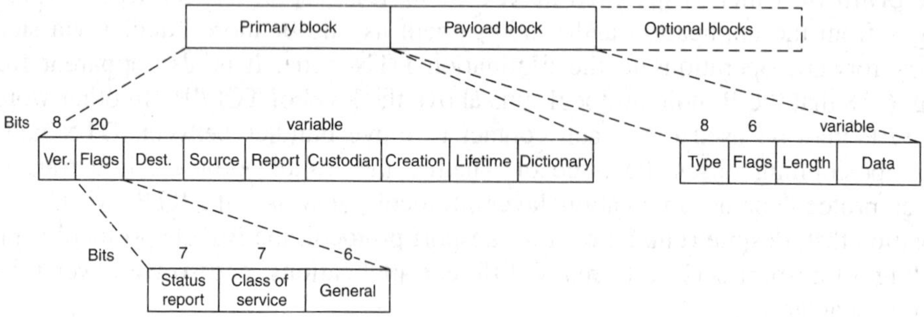

Figure 6-59. Bundle protocol message format.

Each message consists of a primary block, which can be thought of as a header, a payload block for the data, and optionally other blocks, for example to carry security parameters. The primary block begins with a *Version* field (currently 6) followed by a *Flags* field. Among other functions, the flags encode a class of service to let a source mark its bundles as higher or lower priority, and other handling requests such as whether the destination should acknowledge the bundle.

Then come addresses, which highlight three interesting parts of the design. As well as a *Destination* and *Source* identifier field, there is a *Custodian* identifier. The custodian is the party responsible for seeing that the bundle is delivered. In the Internet, the source node is usually the custodian, as it is the node that retransmits if the data is not ultimately delivered to the destination. However, in a DTN, the source node may not always be connected and may have no way of knowing whether the data has been delivered. DTNs deal with this problem using the notion of **custody transfer**, in which another node, closer to the destination, can assume responsibility for seeing the data safely delivered. For example, if a bundle is stored on an airplane for forwarding at a later time and location, the airplane may become the custodian of the bundle.

The second interesting aspect is that these identifiers are *not* IP addresses. Because the Bundle protocol is intended to work across a variety of transports and internets, it defines its own identifiers. These identifiers are really more like high-level names, such as Web page URLs, than low-level addresses, such as IP addresses. They give DTNs an aspect of application-level routing, such as email delivery or the distribution of software updates.

The third interesting aspect is the way the identifiers are encoded. There is also a *Report* identifier for diagnostic messages. All of the identifiers are encoded as references to a variable length *Dictionary* field. This provides compression when the custodian or report nodes are the same as the source or the destination. In fact, much of the message format has been designed with both extensibility and efficiency in mind by using a compact representation of variable length fields. The compact representation is important for wireless links and resource-constrained nodes such as in a sensor network.

Next comes a *Creation* field carrying the time at which the bundle was created, along with a sequence number from the source for ordering, plus a *Lifetime* field that tells the time at which the bundle data is no longer useful. These fields exist because data may be stored for a long period at DTN nodes and there must be some way to remove stale data from the network. Unlike the Internet, they require that DTN nodes have loosely synchronized clocks.

The primary block is completed with the *Dictionary* field. Then comes the payload block. This block starts with a short *Type* field that identifies it as a payload, followed by a small set of *Flags* that describe processing options. Then comes the *Data* field, preceded by a *Length* field. Finally, there may be other, optional blocks, such as a block that carries security parameters.

Many aspects of DTNs are being explored in the research community. Good strategies for routing depend on the nature of the contacts, as was mentioned above. Storing data inside the network raises other issues. Now congestion control must consider storage at nodes as another kind of resource that can be depleted. The lack of end-to-end communication also exacerbates security problems. Before a DTN node takes custody of a bundle, it may want to know that the sender is authorized to use the network and that the bundle is probably wanted by the destination. Solutions to these problems will depend on the kind of DTN, as space networks are different from sensor networks.

6.8 SUMMARY

The transport layer is the key to understanding layered protocols. It provides various services, the most important of which is an end-to-end, reliable, connection-oriented byte stream from sender to receiver. It is accessed through service primitives that permit the establishment, use, and release of connections. A common transport layer interface is the one provided by Berkeley sockets.

Transport protocols must be able to do connection management over unreliable networks. Connection establishment is complicated by the existence of delayed duplicate packets that can reappear at inopportune moments. To deal with them, three-way handshakes are needed to establish connections. Releasing a connection is easier than establishing one but is still far from trivial due to the two-army problem.

Even when the network layer is completely reliable, the transport layer has plenty of work to do. It must handle all the service primitives, manage connections and timers, allocate bandwidth with congestion control, and run a variable-sized sliding window for flow control.

Congestion control should allocate all of the available bandwidth between competing flows fairly, and it should track changes in the usage of the network. The AIMD control law converges to a fair and efficient allocation.

The Internet has two main transport protocols: UDP and TCP. UDP is a connectionless protocol that is mainly a wrapper for IP packets with the additional feature of multiplexing and demultiplexing multiple processes using a single IP address. UDP can be used for client-server interactions, for example, using RPC. It can also be used for building real-time protocols such as RTP.

The main Internet transport protocol is TCP. It provides a reliable, bidirectional, congestion-controlled byte stream with a 20-byte header on all segments. A great deal of work has gone into optimizing TCP performance, using algorithms from Nagle, Clark, Jacobson, Karn, and others.

Network performance is typically dominated by protocol and segment processing overhead, and this situation gets worse at higher speeds. Protocols should be designed to minimize the number of segments and work for large bandwidth-delay paths. For gigabit networks, simple protocols and streamlined processing are called for.

Delay-tolerant networking provides a delivery service across networks that have occasional connectivity or long delays across links. Intermediate nodes store, carry, and forward bundles of information so that it is eventually delivered, even if there is no working path from sender to receiver at any time.

PROBLEMS

1. In our example transport primitives of Fig. 6-2, LISTEN is a blocking call. Is this strictly necessary? If not, explain how a nonblocking primitive could be used. What advantage would this have over the scheme described in the text?
2. Primitives of transport service assume asymmetry between the two end points during connection establishment, one end (server) executes LISTEN while the other end (client) executes CONNECT. However, in peer to peer applications such file sharing

systems, e.g. BitTorrent, all end points are peers. There is no server or client functionality. How can transport service primitives may be used to build such peer to peer applications?

3. In the underlying model of Fig. 6-4, it is assumed that packets may be lost by the network layer and thus must be individually acknowledged. Suppose that the network layer is 100 percent reliable and never loses packets. What changes, if any, are needed to Fig. 6-4?

4. In both parts of Fig. 6-6, there is a comment that the value of *SERVER_PORT* must be the same in both client and server. Why is this so important?

5. In the Internet File Server example (Figure 6-6), can the connect( ) system call on the client fail for any reason other than listen queue being full on the server? Assume that the network is perfect.

6. One criteria for deciding whether to have a server active all the time or have it start on demand using a process server is how frequently the service provided is used. Can you think of any other criteria for making this decision?

7. Suppose that the clock-driven scheme for generating initial sequence numbers is used with a 15-bit wide clock counter. The clock ticks once every 100 msec, and the maximum packet lifetime is 60 sec. How often need resynchronization take place

   (a) in the worst case?

   (b) when the data consumes 240 sequence numbers/min?

8. Why does the maximum packet lifetime, *T*, have to be large enough to ensure that not only the packet but also its acknowledgements have vanished?

9. Imagine that a two-way handshake rather than a three-way handshake were used to set up connections. In other words, the third message was not required. Are deadlocks now possible? Give an example or show that none exist.

10. Imagine a generalized *n*-army problem, in which the agreement of any two of the blue armies is sufficient for victory. Does a protocol exist that allows blue to win?

11. Consider the problem of recovering from host crashes (i.e., Fig. 6-18). If the interval between writing and sending an acknowledgement, or vice versa, can be made relatively small, what are the two best sender-receiver strategies for minimizing the chance of a protocol failure?

12. In Figure 6-20, suppose a new flow *E* is added that takes a path from *R1* to *R2* to *R6*. How does the max-min bandwidth allocation change for the five flows?

13. Discuss the advantages and disadvantages of credits versus sliding window protocols.

14. Some other policies for fairness in congestion control are Additive Increase Additive Decrease (AIAD), Multiplicative Increase Additive Decrease (MIAD), and Multiplicative Increase Multiplicative Decrease (MIMD). Discuss these three policies in terms of convergence and stability.

15. Why does UDP exist? Would it not have been enough to just let user processes send raw IP packets?

16. Consider a simple application-level protocol built on top of UDP that allows a client to retrieve a file from a remote server residing at a well-known address. The client first sends a request with a file name, and the server responds with a sequence of data packets containing different parts of the requested file. To ensure reliability and sequenced delivery, client and server use a stop-and-wait protocol. Ignoring the obvious performance issue, do you see a problem with this protocol? Think carefully about the possibility of processes crashing.

17. A client sends a 128-byte request to a server located 100 km away over a 1-gigabit optical fiber. What is the efficiency of the line during the remote procedure call?

18. Consider the situation of the previous problem again. Compute the minimum possible response time both for the given 1-Gbps line and for a 1-Mbps line. What conclusion can you draw?

19. Both UDP and TCP use port numbers to identify the destination entity when delivering a message. Give two reasons why these protocols invented a new abstract ID (port numbers), instead of using process IDs, which already existed when these protocols were designed.

20. Several RPC implementations provide an option to the client to use RPC implemented over UDP or RPC implemented over TCP. Under what conditions will a client prefer to use RPC over UDP and under what conditions will he prefer to use RPC over TCP?

21. Consider two networks, $N1$ and $N2$, that have the same average delay between a source A and a destination D. In $N1$, the delay experienced by different packets is unformly distributed with maximum delay being 10 seconds, while in $N2$, 99% of the packets experience less than one second delay with no limit on maximum delay. Discuss how RTP may be used in these two cases to transmit live audio/video stream.

22. What is the total size of the minimum TCP MTU, including TCP and IP overhead but not including data link layer overhead?

23. Datagram fragmentation and reassembly are handled by IP and are invisible to TCP. Does this mean that TCP does not have to worry about data arriving in the wrong order?

24. RTP is used to transmit CD-quality audio, which makes a pair of 16-bit samples 44,100 times/sec, one sample for each of the stereo channels. How many packets per second must RTP transmit?

25. Would it be possible to place the RTP code in the operating system kernel, along with the UDP code? Explain your answer.

26. A process on host 1 has been assigned port p, and a process on host 2 has been assigned port q. Is it possible for there to be two or more TCP connections between these two ports at the same time?

27. In Fig. 6-36 we saw that in addition to the 32-bit *acknowledgement* field, there is an *ACK* bit in the fourth word. Does this really add anything? Why or why not?

28. The maximum payload of a TCP segment is 65,495 bytes. Why was such a strange number chosen?

29. Describe two ways to get into the *SYN RCVD* state of Fig. 6-39.

30. Consider the effect of using slow start on a line with a 10-msec round-trip time and no congestion. The receive window is 24 KB and the maximum segment size is 2 KB. How long does it take before the first full window can be sent?

31. Suppose that the TCP congestion window is set to 18 KB and a timeout occurs. How big will the window be if the next four transmission bursts are all successful? Assume that the maximum segment size is 1 KB.

32. If the TCP round-trip time, *RTT*, is currently 30 msec and the following acknowledgements come in after 26, 32, and 24 msec, respectively, what is the new *RTT* estimate using the Jacobson algorithm? Use $\alpha = 0.9$.

33. A TCP machine is sending full windows of 65,535 bytes over a 1-Gbps channel that has a 10-msec one-way delay. What is the maximum throughput achievable? What is the line efficiency?

34. What is the fastest line speed at which a host can blast out 1500-byte TCP payloads with a 120-sec maximum packet lifetime without having the sequence numbers wrap around? Take TCP, IP, and Ethernet overhead into consideration. Assume that Ethernet frames may be sent continuously.

35. To address the limitations of IP version 4, a major effort had to be undertaken via IETF that resulted in the design of IP version 6 and there are still is significant reluctance in the adoption of this new version. However, no such major effort is needed to address the limitations of TCP. Explain why this is the case.

36. In a network whose max segment is 128 bytes, max segment lifetime is 30 sec, and has 8-bit sequence numbers, what is the maximum data rate per connection?

37. Suppose that you are measuring the time to receive a segment. When an interrupt occurs, you read out the system clock in milliseconds. When the segment is fully processed, you read out the clock again. You measure 0 msec 270,000 times and msec 730,000 times. How long does it take to receive a segment?

38. A CPU executes instructions at the rate of 1000 MIPS. Data can be copied 64 bits at a time, with each word copied costing 10 instructions. If an coming packet has to be copied four times, can this system handle a 1-Gbps line? For simplicity, assume that all instructions, even those instructions that read or write memory, run at the full 1000-MIPS rate.

39. To get around the problem of sequence numbers wrapping around while old packets still exist, one could use 64-bit sequence numbers. However, theoretically, an optical fiber can run at 75 Tbps. What maximum packet lifetime is required to make sure that future 75-Tbps networks do not have wraparound problems even with 64-bit sequence numbers? Assume that each byte has its own sequence number, as TCP does.

40. In Sec. 6.6.5, we calculated that a gigabit line dumps 80,000 packets/sec on the host, giving it only 6250 instructions to process it and leaving half the CPU time for applications. This calculation assumed a 1500-byte packet. Redo the calculation for an ARPANET-sized packet (128 bytes). In both cases, assume that the packet sizes given include all overhead.

41. For a 1-Gbps network operating over 4000 km, the delay is the limiting factor, not the bandwidth. Consider a MAN with the average source and destination 20 km apart. At what data rate does the round-trip delay due to the speed of light equal the transmission delay for a 1-KB packet?

42. Calculate the bandwidth-delay product for the following networks: (1) T1 (1.5 Mbps), (2) Ethernet (10 Mbps), (3) T3 (45 Mbps), and (4) STS-3 (155 Mbps). Assume an RTT of 100 msec. Recall that a TCP header has 16 bits reserved for Window Size. What are its implications in light of your calculations?

43. What is the bandwidth-delay product for a 50-Mbps channel on a geostationary satellite? If the packets are all 1500 bytes (including overhead), how big should the window be in packets?

44. The file server of Fig. 6-6 is far from perfect and could use a few improvements. Make the following modifications.

(a) Give the client a third argument that specifies a byte range.
(b) Add a client flag –w that allows the file to be written to the server.

45. One common function that all network protocols need is to manipulate messages. Recall that protocols manipulate messages by adding/striping headers. Some protocols may break a single message into multiple fragments, and later join these multiple fragments back into a single message. To this end, design and implement a message management library that provides support for creating a new message, attaching a header to a message, stripping a header from a message, breaking a message into two messages, combining two messages into a single message, and saving a copy of a message. Your implementation must minimize data copying from one buffer to another as much as possible. It is critical that the operations that manipulate messages do not touch the data in a message, but rather, only manipulate pointers.

46. Design and implement a chat system that allows multiple groups of users to chat. A chat coordinator resides at a well-known network address, uses UDP for communication with chat clients, sets up chat servers for each chat session, and maintains a chat session directory. There is one chat server per chat session. A chat server uses TCP for communication with clients. A chat client allows users to start, join, and leave a chat session. Design and implement the coordinator, server, and client code.

7

THE APPLICATION LAYER

Having finished all the preliminaries, we now come to the layer where all the applications are found. The layers below the application layer are there to provide transport services, but they do not do real work for users. In this chapter, we will study some real network applications.

However, even in the application layer there is a need for support protocols, to allow the applications to function. Accordingly, we will look at an important one of these before starting with the applications themselves. The item in question is DNS, which handles naming within the Internet. After that, we will examine three real applications: electronic mail, the World Wide Web, and multimedia. We will finish the chapter by saying more about content distribution, including by peer-to-peer networks.

7.1 DNS—THE DOMAIN NAME SYSTEM

Although programs theoretically could refer to Web pages, mailboxes, and other resources by using the network (e.g., IP) addresses of the computers on which they are stored, these addresses are hard for people to remember. Also, browsing a company's Web pages from *128.111.24.41* means that if the company moves the Web server to a different machine with a different IP address, everyone needs to be told the new IP address. Consequently, high-level, readable names were introduced in order to decouple machine names from machine addresses. In this way, the company's Web server might be known as *www.cs.washington.edu* regardless of its IP address. Nevertheless, since the network itself understands only numerical addresses, some mechanism is required to convert the names to network addresses. In the following sections, we will study how this mapping is accomplished in the Internet.

Way back in the ARPANET days, there was simply a file, *hosts.txt*, that listed all the computer names and their IP addresses. Every night, all the hosts would fetch it from the site at which it was maintained. For a network of a few hundred large timesharing machines, this approach worked reasonably well.

However, well before many millions of PCs were connected to the Internet, everyone involved with it realized that this approach could not continue to work forever. For one thing, the size of the file would become too large. However, even more importantly, host name conflicts would occur constantly unless names were centrally managed, something unthinkable in a huge international network due to the load and latency. To solve these problems, **DNS (Domain Name System)** was invented in 1983. It has been a key part of the Internet ever since.

The essence of DNS is the invention of a hierarchical, domain-based naming scheme and a distributed database system for implementing this naming scheme. It is primarily used for mapping host names to IP addresses but can also be used for other purposes. DNS is defined in RFCs 1034, 1035, 2181, and further elaborated in many others.

Very briefly, the way DNS is used is as follows. To map a name onto an IP address, an application program calls a library procedure called the **resolver**, passing it the name as a parameter. We saw an example of a resolver, *gethostbyname*, in Fig. 6-6. The resolver sends a query containing the name to a local DNS server, which looks up the name and returns a response containing the IP address to the resolver, which then returns it to the caller. The query and response messages are sent as UDP packets. Armed with the IP address, the program can then establish a TCP connection with the host or send it UDP packets.

7.1.1 The DNS Name Space

Managing a large and constantly changing set of names is a nontrivial problem. In the postal system, name management is done by requiring letters to specify (implicitly or explicitly) the country, state or province, city, street address, and name of the addressee. Using this kind of hierarchical addressing ensures that there is no confusion between the Marvin Anderson on Main St. in White Plains, N.Y. and the Marvin Anderson on Main St. in Austin, Texas. DNS works the same way.

For the Internet, the top of the naming hierarchy is managed by an organization called **ICANN (Internet Corporation for Assigned Names and Numbers)**. ICANN was created for this purpose in 1998, as part of the maturing of the Internet to a worldwide, economic concern. Conceptually, the Internet is divided into over 250 **top-level domains**, where each domain covers many hosts. Each domain is partitioned into subdomains, and these are further partitioned, and so on. All these domains can be represented by a tree, as shown in Fig. 7-1. The leaves of the tree represent domains that have no subdomains (but do contain machines, of course). A leaf domain may contain a single host, or it may represent a company and contain thousands of hosts.

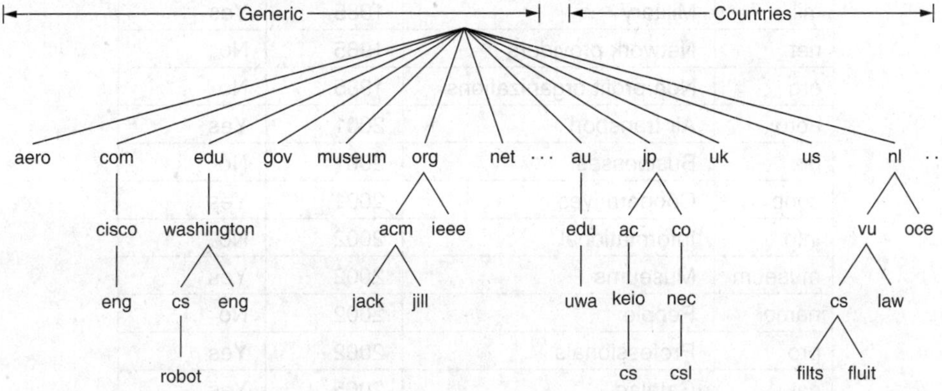

Figure 7-1. A portion of the Internet domain name space.

The top-level domains come in two flavors: generic and countries. The generic domains, listed in Fig. 7-2, include original domains from the 1980s and domains introduced via applications to ICANN. Other generic top-level domains will be added in the future.

The country domains include one entry for every country, as defined in ISO 3166. Internationalized country domain names that use non-Latin alphabets were introduced in 2010. These domains let people name hosts in Arabic, Cyrillic, Chinese, or other languages.

Getting a second-level domain, such as *name-of-company.com*, is easy. The top-level domains are run by **registrars** appointed by ICANN. Getting a name merely requires going to a corresponding registrar (for *com* in this case) to check if the desired name is available and not somebody else's trademark. If there are no problems, the requester pays the registrar a small annual fee and gets the name.

However, as the Internet has become more commercial and more international, it has also become more contentious, especially in matters related to naming. This controversy includes ICANN itself. For example, the creation of the *xxx* domain took several years and court cases to resolve. Is voluntarily placing adult content in its own domain a good or a bad thing? (Some people did not want adult content available at all on the Internet while others wanted to put it all in one domain so nanny filters could easily find and block it from children). Some of the domains self-organize, while others have restrictions on who can obtain a name, as noted in Fig. 7-2. But what restrictions are appropriate? Take the *pro* domain,

Domain	Intended use	Start date	Restricted?
com	Commercial	1985	No
edu	Educational institutions	1985	Yes
gov	Government	1985	Yes
int	International organizations	1988	Yes
mil	Military	1985	Yes
net	Network providers	1985	No
org	Non-profit organizations	1985	No
aero	Air transport	2001	Yes
biz	Businesses	2001	No
coop	Cooperatives	2001	Yes
info	Informational	2002	No
museum	Museums	2002	Yes
name	People	2002	No
pro	Professionals	2002	Yes
cat	Catalan	2005	Yes
jobs	Employment	2005	Yes
mobi	Mobile devices	2005	Yes
tel	Contact details	2005	Yes
travel	Travel industry	2005	Yes
xxx	Sex industry	2010	No

Figure 7-2. Generic top-level domains.

for example. It is for qualified professionals. But who is a professional? Doctors and lawyers clearly are professionals. But what about freelance photographers, piano teachers, magicians, plumbers, barbers, exterminators, tattoo artists, mercenaries, and prostitutes? Are these occupations eligible? According to whom?

There is also money in names. Tuvalu (the country) sold a lease on its *tv* domain for $50 million, all because the country code is well-suited to advertising television sites. Virtually every common (English) word has been taken in the *com* domain, along with the most common misspellings. Try household articles, animals, plants, body parts, etc. The practice of registering a domain only to turn around and sell it off to an interested party at a much higher price even has a name. It is called **cybersquatting**. Many companies that were slow off the mark when the Internet era began found their obvious domain names already taken when they tried to acquire them. In general, as long as no trademarks are being violated and no fraud is involved, it is first-come, first-served with names. Nevertheless, policies to resolve naming disputes are still being refined.

Each domain is named by the path upward from it to the (unnamed) root. The components are separated by periods (pronounced "dot"). Thus, the engineering department at Cisco might be *eng.cisco.com.*, rather than a UNIX-style name such as */com/cisco/eng*. Notice that this hierarchical naming means that *eng.cisco.com.* does not conflict with a potential use of *eng* in *eng.washington.edu.*, which might be used by the English department at the University of Washington.

Domain names can be either absolute or relative. An absolute domain name always ends with a period (e.g., *eng.cisco.com.*), whereas a relative one does not. Relative names have to be interpreted in some context to uniquely determine their true meaning. In both cases, a named domain refers to a specific node in the tree and all the nodes under it.

Domain names are case-insensitive, so *edu*, *Edu*, and *EDU* mean the same thing. Component names can be up to 63 characters long, and full path names must not exceed 255 characters.

In principle, domains can be inserted into the tree in either generic or country domains. For example, *cs.washington.edu* could equally well be listed under the *us* country domain as *cs.washington.wa.us*. In practice, however, most organizations in the United States are under generic domains, and most outside the United States are under the domain of their country. There is no rule against registering under multiple top-level domains. Large companies often do so (e.g., *sony.com*, *sony.net*, and *sony.nl*).

Each domain controls how it allocates the domains under it. For example, Japan has domains *ac.jp* and *co.jp* that mirror *edu* and *com*. The Netherlands does not make this distinction and puts all organizations directly under *nl*. Thus, all three of the following are university computer science departments:

1. *cs.washington.edu* (University of Washington, in the U.S.).

2. *cs.vu.nl* (Vrije Universiteit, in The Netherlands).

3. *cs.keio.ac.jp* (Keio University, in Japan).

To create a new domain, permission is required of the domain in which it will be included. For example, if a VLSI group is started at the University of Washington and wants to be known as *vlsi.cs.washington.edu*, it has to get permission from whoever manages *cs.washington.edu*. Similarly, if a new university is chartered, say, the University of Northern South Dakota, it must ask the manager of the *edu* domain to assign it *unsd.edu* (if that is still available). In this way, name conflicts are avoided and each domain can keep track of all its subdomains. Once a new domain has been created and registered, it can create subdomains, such as *cs.unsd.edu*, without getting permission from anybody higher up the tree.

Naming follows organizational boundaries, not physical networks. For example, if the computer science and electrical engineering departments are located in the same building and share the same LAN, they can nevertheless have distinct domains. Similarly, even if computer science is split over Babbage Hall and Turing Hall, the hosts in both buildings will normally belong to the same domain.

7.1.2 Domain Resource Records

Every domain, whether it is a single host or a top-level domain, can have a set of **resource records** associated with it. These records are the DNS database. For a single host, the most common resource record is just its IP address, but many other kinds of resource records also exist. When a resolver gives a domain name to DNS, what it gets back are the resource records associated with that name. Thus, the primary function of DNS is to map domain names onto resource records.

A resource record is a five-tuple. Although they are encoded in binary for efficiency, in most expositions resource records are presented as ASCII text, one line per resource record. The format we will use is as follows:

```
Domain_name   Time_to_live   Class   Type   Value
```

The *Domain_name* tells the domain to which this record applies. Normally, many records exist for each domain and each copy of the database holds information about multiple domains. This field is thus the primary search key used to satisfy queries. The order of the records in the database is not significant.

The *Time_to_live* field gives an indication of how stable the record is. Information that is highly stable is assigned a large value, such as 86400 (the number of seconds in 1 day). Information that is highly volatile is assigned a small value, such as 60 (1 minute). We will come back to this point later when we have discussed caching.

The third field of every resource record is the *Class*. For Internet information, it is always *IN*. For non-Internet information, other codes can be used, but in practice these are rarely seen.

The *Type* field tells what kind of record this is. There are many kinds of DNS records. The important types are listed in Fig. 7-3.

An *SOA* record provides the name of the primary source of information about the name server's zone (described below), the email address of its administrator, a unique serial number, and various flags and timeouts.

The most important record type is the *A* (Address) record. It holds a 32-bit IPv4 address of an interface for some host. The corresponding *AAAA*, or "quad A," record holds a 128-bit IPv6 address. Every Internet host must have at least one IP address so that other machines can communicate with it. Some hosts have two or more network interfaces, in which case they will have two or more type *A* or *AAAA* resource records. Consequently, DNS can return multiple addresses for a single name.

A common record type is the *MX* record. It specifies the name of the host prepared to accept email for the specified domain. It is used because not every

Type	Meaning	Value
SOA	Start of authority	Parameters for this zone
A	IPv4 address of a host	32-Bit integer
AAAA	IPv6 address of a host	128-Bit integer
MX	Mail exchange	Priority, domain willing to accept email
NS	Name server	Name of a server for this domain
CNAME	Canonical name	Domain name
PTR	Pointer	Alias for an IP address
SPF	Sender policy framework	Text encoding of mail sending policy
SRV	Service	Host that provides it
TXT	Text	Descriptive ASCII text

Figure 7-3. The principal DNS resource record types.

machine is prepared to accept email. If someone wants to send email to, for example, *bill@microsoft.com*, the sending host needs to find some mail server located at *microsoft.com* that is willing to accept email. The *MX* record can provide this information.

Another important record type is the *NS* record. It specifies a name server for the domain or subdomain. This is a host that has a copy of the database for a domain. It is used as part of the process to look up names, which we will describe shortly.

CNAME records allow aliases to be created. For example, a person familiar with Internet naming in general and wanting to send a message to user *paul* in the computer science department at M.I.T. might guess that *paul@cs.mit.edu* will work. Actually, this address will not work, because the domain for M.I.T.'s computer science department is *csail.mit.edu*. However, as a service to people who do not know this, M.I.T. could create a *CNAME* entry to point people and programs in the right direction. An entry like this one might do the job:

```
cs.mit.edu   86400   IN   CNAME   csail.mit.edu
```

Like *CNAME*, *PTR* points to another name. However, unlike *CNAME*, which is really just a macro definition (i.e., a mechanism to replace one string by another), *PTR* is a regular DNS data type whose interpretation depends on the context in which it is found. In practice, it is nearly always used to associate a name with an IP address to allow lookups of the IP address and return the name of the corresponding machine. These are called **reverse lookups**.

SRV is a newer type of record that allows a host to be identified for a given service in a domain. For example, the Web server for *cs.washington.edu* could be identified as *cockatoo.cs.washington.edu*. This record generalizes the *MX* record that performs the same task but it is just for mail servers.

SPF is also a newer type of record. It lets a domain encode information about what machines in the domain will send mail to the rest of the Internet. This helps receiving machines check that mail is valid. If mail is being received from a machine that calls itself *dodgy* but the domain records say that mail will only be sent out of the domain by a machine called *smtp*, chances are that the mail is forged junk mail.

Last on the list, *TXT* records were originally provided to allow domains to identify themselves in arbitrary ways. Nowadays, they usually encode machine-readable information, typically the *SPF* information.

Finally, we have the *Value* field. This field can be a number, a domain name, or an ASCII string. The semantics depend on the record type. A short description of the *Value* fields for each of the principal record types is given in Fig. 7-3.

For an example of the kind of information one might find in the DNS database of a domain, see Fig. 7-4. This figure depicts part of a (hypothetical) database for the *cs.vu.nl* domain shown in Fig. 7-1. The database contains seven types of resource records.

```
; Authoritative data for cs.vu.nl
cs.vu.nl.        86400  IN  SOA    star boss (9527,7200,7200,241920,86400)
cs.vu.nl.        86400  IN  MX     1 zephyr
cs.vu.nl.        86400  IN  MX     2 top
cs.vu.nl.        86400  IN  NS     star

star             86400  IN  A      130.37.56.205
zephyr           86400  IN  A      130.37.20.10
top              86400  IN  A      130.37.20.11
www              86400  IN  CNAME  star.cs.vu.nl
ftp              86400  IN  CNAME  zephyr.cs.vu.nl

flits            86400  IN  A      130.37.16.112
flits            86400  IN  A      192.31.231.165
flits            86400  IN  MX     1 flits
flits            86400  IN  MX     2 zephyr
flits            86400  IN  MX     3 top

rowboat                 IN  A      130.37.56.201
                        IN  MX     1 rowboat
                        IN  MX     2 zephyr

little-sister           IN  A      130.37.62.23

laserjet                IN  A      192.31.231.216
```

Figure 7-4. A portion of a possible DNS database for *cs.vu.nl*.

The first noncomment line of Fig. 7-4 gives some basic information about the domain, which will not concern us further. Then come two entries giving the first and second places to try to deliver email sent to *person@cs.vu.nl*. The *zephyr* (a specific machine) should be tried first. If that fails, the *top* should be tried as the next choice. The next line identifies the name server for the domain as *star*.

After the blank line (added for readability) come lines giving the IP addresses for the *star*, *zephyr*, and *top*. These are followed by an alias, *www.cs.vu.nl*, so that this address can be used without designating a specific machine. Creating this alias allows *cs.vu.nl* to change its World Wide Web server without invalidating the address people use to get to it. A similar argument holds for *ftp.cs.vu.nl*.

The section for the machine *flits* lists two IP addresses and three choices are given for handling email sent to *flits.cs.vu.nl*. First choice is naturally the *flits* itself, but if it is down, the *zephyr* and *top* are the second and third choices.

The next three lines contain a typical entry for a computer, in this case, *rowboat.cs.vu.nl*. The information provided contains the IP address and the primary and secondary mail drops. Then comes an entry for a computer that is not capable of receiving mail itself, followed by an entry that is likely for a printer that is connected to the Internet.

7.1.3 Name Servers

In theory at least, a single name server could contain the entire DNS database and respond to all queries about it. In practice, this server would be so overloaded as to be useless. Furthermore, if it ever went down, the entire Internet would be crippled.

To avoid the problems associated with having only a single source of information, the DNS name space is divided into nonoverlapping **zones**. One possible way to divide the name space of Fig. 7-1 is shown in Fig. 7-5. Each circled zone contains some part of the tree.

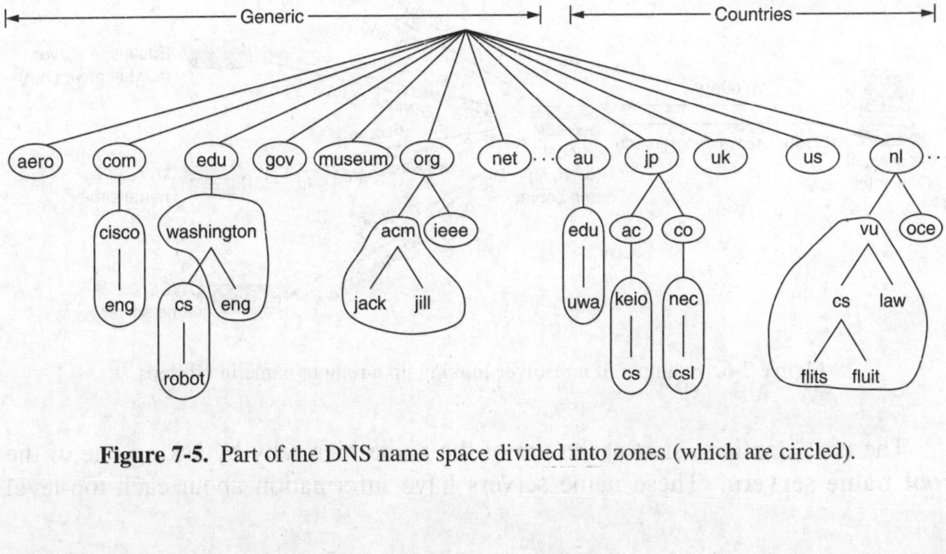

Figure 7-5. Part of the DNS name space divided into zones (which are circled).

Where the zone boundaries are placed within a zone is up to that zone's administrator. This decision is made in large part based on how many name servers are desired, and where. For example, in Fig. 7-5, the University of Washington has a zone for *washington.edu* that handles *eng.washington.edu* but does not handle *cs.washington.edu*. That is a separate zone with its own name servers. Such a decision might be made when a department such as English does not wish to run its own name server, but a department such as Computer Science does.

Each zone is also associated with one or more name servers. These are hosts that hold the database for the zone. Normally, a zone will have one primary name server, which gets its information from a file on its disk, and one or more secondary name servers, which get their information from the primary name server. To improve reliability, some of the name servers can be located outside the zone.

The process of looking up a name and finding an address is called **name resolution**. When a resolver has a query about a domain name, it passes the query to a local name server. If the domain being sought falls under the jurisdiction of the name server, such as *top.cs.vu.nl* falling under *cs.vu.nl*, it returns the authoritative resource records. An **authoritative record** is one that comes from the authority that manages the record and is thus always correct. Authoritative records are in contrast to **cached records**, which may be out of date.

What happens when the domain is remote, such as when *flits.cs.vu.nl* wants to find the IP address of *robot.cs.washington.edu* at UW (University of Washington)? In this case, and if there is no cached information about the domain available locally, the name server begins a remote query. This query follows the process shown in Fig. 7-6. Step 1 shows the query that is sent to the local name server. The query contains the domain name sought, the type (*A*), and the class(*IN*).

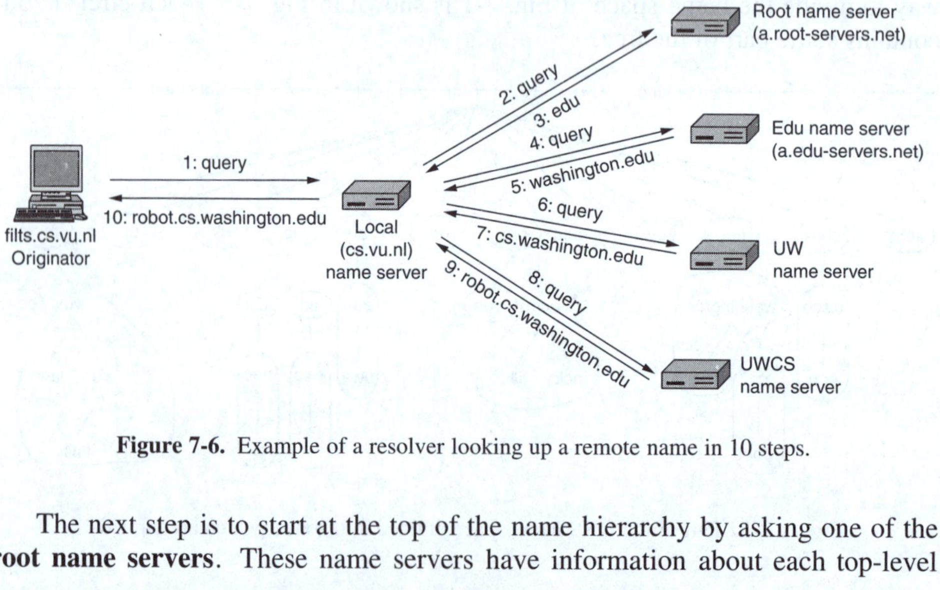

Figure 7-6. Example of a resolver looking up a remote name in 10 steps.

The next step is to start at the top of the name hierarchy by asking one of the **root name servers**. These name servers have information about each top-level domain. This is shown as step 2 in Fig. 7-6. To contact a root server, each name server must have information about one or more root name servers. This information is normally present in a system configuration file that is loaded into the DNS cache when the DNS server is started. It is simply a list of *NS* records for the root and the corresponding *A* records.

There are 13 root DNS servers, unimaginatively called *a-root-servers.net* through *m.root-servers.net*. Each root server could logically be a single computer. However, since the entire Internet depends on the root servers, they are powerful and heavily replicated computers. Most of the servers are present in multiple geographical locations and reached using anycast routing, in which a packet is delivered to the nearest instance of a destination address; we described anycast in Chap. 5 The replication improves reliability and performance.

The root name server is unlikely to know the address of a machine at UW, and probably does not know the name server for UW either. But it must know the name server for the *edu* domain, in which *cs.washington.edu* is located. It returns the name and IP address for that part of the answer in step 3.

The local name server then continues its quest. It sends the entire query to the *edu* name server (*a.edu-servers.net*). That name server returns the name server for UW. This is shown in steps 4 and 5. Closer now, the local name server sends the query to the UW name server (step 6). If the domain name being sought was in the English department, the answer would be found, as the UW zone includes the English department. But the Computer Science department has chosen to run its own name server. The query returns the name and IP address of the UW Computer Science name server (step 7).

Finally, the local name server queries the UW Computer Science name server (step 8). This server is authoritative for the domain *cs.washington.edu*, so it must have the answer. It returns the final answer (step 9), which the local name server forwards as a response to *flits.cs.vu.nl* (step 10). The name has been resolved.

You can explore this process using standard tools such as the *dig* program that is installed on most UNIX systems. For example, typing

```
dig@a.edu-servers.net robot.cs.washington.edu
```

will send a query for *robot.cs.washington.edu* to the *a.edu-servers.net* name server and print out the result. This will show you the information obtained in step 4 in the example above, and you will learn the name and IP address of the UW name servers.

There are three technical points to discuss about this long scenario. First, two different query mechanisms are at work in Fig. 7-6. When the host *flits.cs.vu.nl* sends its query to the local name server, that name server handles the resolution on behalf of *flits* until it has the desired answer to return. It does *not* return partial answers. They might be helpful, but they are not what the query was seeking. This mechanism is called a **recursive query**.

On the other hand, the root name server (and each subsequent name server) does not recursively continue the query for the local name server. It just returns a partial answer and moves on to the next query. The local name server is responsible for continuing the resolution by issuing further queries. This mechanism is called an **iterative query**.

One name resolution can involve both mechanisms, as this example showed. A recursive query may always seem preferable, but many name servers (especially the root) will not handle them. They are too busy. Iterative queries put the burden on the originator. The rationale for the local name server supporting a recursive query is that it is providing a service to hosts in its domain. Those hosts do not have to be configured to run a full name server, just to reach the local one.

The second point is caching. All of the answers, including all the partial answers returned, are cached. In this way, if another *cs.vu.nl* host queries for *robot.cs.washington.edu* the answer will already be known. Even better, if a host queries for a different host in the same domain, say *galah.cs.washington.edu*, the query can be sent directly to the authoritative name server. Similarly, queries for other domains in *washington.edu* can start directly from the *washington.edu* name server. Using cached answers greatly reduces the steps in a query and improves performance. The original scenario we sketched is in fact the worst case that occurs when no useful information is cached.

However, cached answers are not authoritative, since changes made at *cs.washington.edu* will not be propagated to all the caches in the world that may know about it. For this reason, cache entries should not live too long. This is the reason that the *Time_to_live* field is included in each resource record. It tells remote name servers how long to cache records. If a certain machine has had the same IP address for years, it may be safe to cache that information for 1 day. For more volatile information, it might be safer to purge the records after a few seconds or a minute.

The third issue is the transport protocol that is used for the queries and responses. It is UDP. DNS messages are sent in UDP packets with a simple format for queries, answers, and name servers that can be used to continue the resolution. We will not go into the details of this format. If no response arrives within a short time, the DNS client repeats the query, trying another server for the domain after a small number of retries. This process is designed to handle the case of the server being down as well as the query or response packet getting lost. A 16-bit identifier is included in each query and copied to the response so that a name server can match answers to the corresponding query, even if multiple queries are outstanding at the same time.

Even though its purpose is simple, it should be clear that DNS is a large and complex distributed system that is comprised of millions of name servers that work together. It forms a key link between human-readable domain names and the IP addresses of machines. It includes replication and caching for performance and reliability and is designed to be highly robust.

We have not covered security, but as you might imagine, the ability to change the name-to-address mapping can have devastating consequences if done maliciously. For that reason, security extensions called DNSSEC have been developed for DNS. We will describe them in Chap. 8.

There is also application demand to use names in more flexible ways, for example, by naming content and resolving to the IP address of a nearby host that has the content. This fits the model of searching for and downloading a movie. It is the movie that matters, not the computer that has a copy of it, so all that is wanted is the IP address of any nearby computer that has a copy of the movie. Content distribution networks are one way to accomplish this mapping. We will describe how they build on the DNS later in this chapter, in Sec. 7.5.

7.2 ELECTRONIC MAIL

Electronic mail, or more commonly **email**, has been around for over three decades. Faster and cheaper than paper mail, email has been a popular application since the early days of the Internet. Before 1990, it was mostly used in academia. During the 1990s, it became known to the public at large and grew exponentially, to the point where the number of emails sent per day now is vastly more than the number of **snail mail** (i.e., paper) letters. Other forms of network communication, such as instant messaging and voice-over-IP calls have expanded greatly in use over the past decade, but email remains the workhorse of Internet communication. It is widely used within industry for intracompany communication, for example, to allow far-flung employees all over the world to cooperate on complex projects. Unfortunately, like paper mail, the majority of email—some 9 out of 10 messages—is junk mail or **spam** (McAfee, 2010).

Email, like most other forms of communication, has developed its own conventions and styles. It is very informal and has a low threshold of use. People who would never dream of calling up or even writing a letter to a Very Important Person do not hesitate for a second to send a sloppily written email to him or her. By eliminating most cues associated with rank, age, and gender, email debates often focus on content, not status. With email, a brilliant idea from a summer student can have more impact than a dumb one from an executive vice president.

Email is full of jargon such as BTW (By The Way), ROTFL (Rolling On The Floor Laughing), and IMHO (In My Humble Opinion). Many people also use little ASCII symbols called **smileys**, starting with the ubiquitous ":-)". Rotate the book 90 degrees clockwise if this symbol is unfamiliar. This symbol and other **emoticons** help to convey the tone of the message. They have spread to other terse forms of communication, such as instant messaging.

The email protocols have evolved during the period of their use, too. The first email systems simply consisted of file transfer protocols, with the convention that the first line of each message (i.e., file) contained the recipient's address. As time went on, email diverged from file transfer and many features were added, such as the ability to send one message to a list of recipients. Multimedia capabilities became important in the 1990s to send messages with images and other non-text material. Programs for reading email became much more sophisticated too, shifting from text-based to graphical user interfaces and adding the ability for users to access their mail from their laptops wherever they happen to be. Finally, with the prevalence of spam, mail readers and the mail transfer protocols must now pay attention to finding and removing unwanted email.

In our description of email, we will focus on the way that mail messages are moved between users, rather than the look and feel of mail reader programs. Nevertheless, after describing the overall architecture, we will begin with the user-facing part of the email system, as it is familiar to most readers.

7.2.1 Architecture and Services

In this section, we will provide an overview of how email systems are organized and what they can do. The architecture of the email system is shown in Fig. 7-7. It consists of two kinds of subsystems: the **user agents**, which allow people to read and send email, and the **message transfer agents**, which move the messages from the source to the destination. We will also refer to message transfer agents informally as **mail servers**.

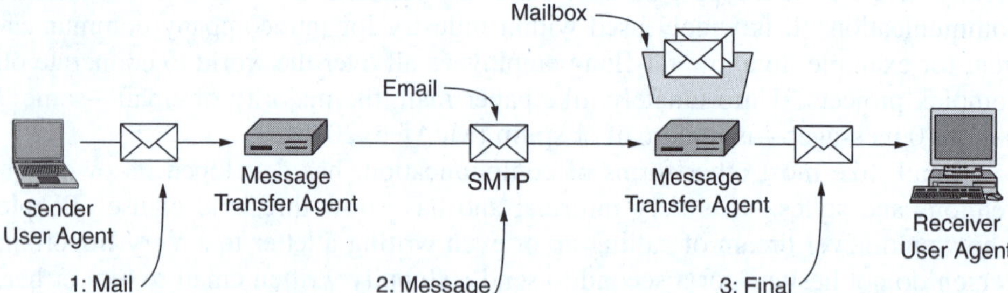

Figure 7-7. Architecture of the email system.

The user agent is a program that provides a graphical interface, or sometimes a text- and command-based interface that lets users interact with the email system. It includes a means to compose messages and replies to messages, display incoming messages, and organize messages by filing, searching, and discarding them. The act of sending new messages into the mail system for delivery is called **mail submission**.

Some of the user agent processing may be done automatically, anticipating what the user wants. For example, incoming mail may be filtered to extract or deprioritize messages that are likely spam. Some user agents include advanced features, such as arranging for automatic email responses ("I'm having a wonderful vacation and it will be a while before I get back to you"). A user agent runs on the same computer on which a user reads her mail. It is just another program and may be run only some of the time.

The message transfer agents are typically system processes. They run in the background on mail server machines and are intended to be always available. Their job is to automatically move email through the system from the originator to the recipient with **SMTP (Simple Mail Transfer Protocol)**. This is the message transfer step.

SMTP was originally specified as RFC 821 and revised to become the current RFC 5321. It sends mail over connections and reports back the delivery status and any errors. Numerous applications exist in which confirmation of delivery is important and may even have legal significance ("Well, Your Honor, my email system is just not very reliable, so I guess the electronic subpoena just got lost somewhere").

Message transfer agents also implement **mailing lists**, in which an identical copy of a message is delivered to everyone on a list of email addresses. Other advanced features are carbon copies, blind carbon copies, high-priority email, secret (i.e., encrypted) email, alternative recipients if the primary one is not currently available, and the ability for assistants to read and answer their bosses' email.

Linking user agents and message transfer agents are the concepts of mailboxes and a standard format for email messages. **Mailboxes** store the email that is received for a user. They are maintained by mail servers. User agents simply present users with a view of the contents of their mailboxes. To do this, the user agents send the mail servers commands to manipulate the mailboxes, inspecting their contents, deleting messages, and so on. The retrieval of mail is the final delivery (step 3) in Fig. 7-7. With this architecture, one user may use different user agents on multiple computers to access one mailbox.

Mail is sent between message transfer agents in a standard format. The original format, RFC 822, has been revised to the current RFC 5322 and extended with support for multimedia content and international text. This scheme is called MIME and will be discussed later. People still refer to Internet email as RFC 822, though.

A key idea in the message format is the distinction between the **envelope** and its contents. The envelope encapsulates the message. It contains all the information needed for transporting the message, such as the destination address, priority, and security level, all of which are distinct from the message itself. The message transport agents use the envelope for routing, just as the post office does.

The message inside the envelope consists of two separate parts: the **header** and the **body**. The header contains control information for the user agents. The body is entirely for the human recipient. None of the agents care much about it. Envelopes and messages are illustrated in Fig. 7-8.

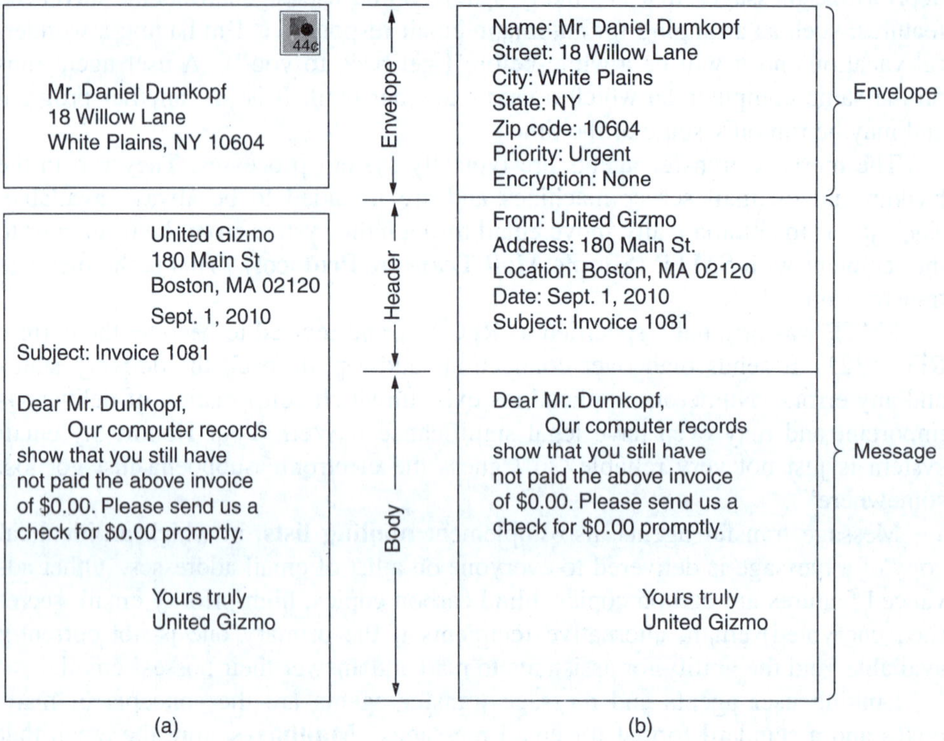

Figure 7-8. Envelopes and messages. (a) Paper mail. (b) Electronic mail.

We will examine the pieces of this architecture in more detail by looking at the steps that are involved in sending email from one user to another. This journey starts with the user agent.

7.2.2 The User Agent

A user agent is a program (sometimes called an **email reader**) that accepts a variety of commands for composing, receiving, and replying to messages, as well as for manipulating mailboxes. There are many popular user agents, including Google gmail, Microsoft Outlook, Mozilla Thunderbird, and Apple Mail. They can vary greatly in their appearance. Most user agents have a menu- or icon-driven graphical interface that requires a mouse, or a touch interface on smaller mobile devices. Older user agents, such as Elm, mh, and Pine, provide text-based interfaces and expect one-character commands from the keyboard. Functionally, these are the same, at least for text messages.

The typical elements of a user agent interface are shown in Fig. 7-9. Your mail reader is likely to be much flashier, but probably has equivalent functions.

When a user agent is started, it will usually present a summary of the messages in the user's mailbox. Often, the summary will have one line for each message in some sorted order. It highlights key fields of the message that are extracted from the message envelope or header.

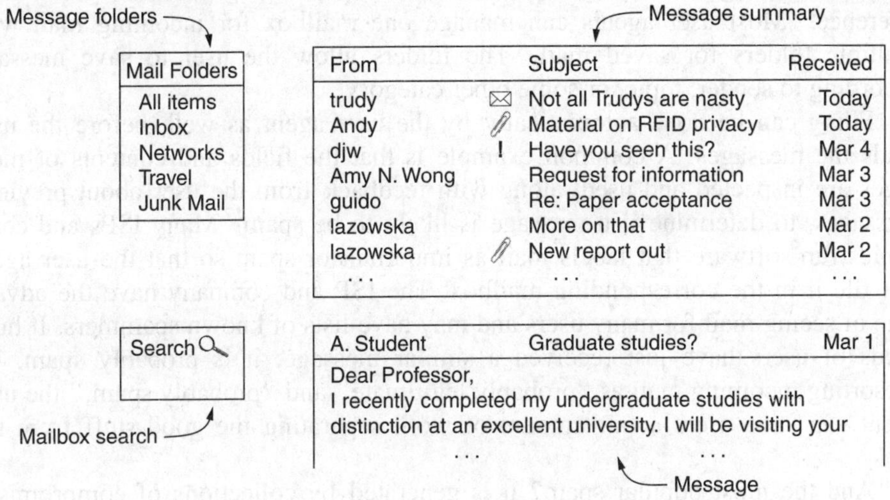

Figure 7-9. Typical elements of the user agent interface.

Seven summary lines are shown in the example of Fig. 7-9. The lines use the *From*, *Subject*, and *Received* fields, in that order, to display who sent the message, what it is about, and when it was received. All the information is formatted in a user-friendly way rather than displaying the literal contents of the message fields, but it is based on the message fields. Thus, people who fail to include a *Subject* field often discover that responses to their emails tend not to get the highest priority.

Many other fields or indications are possible. The icons next to the message subjects in Fig. 7-9 might indicate, for example, unread mail (the envelope), attached material (the paperclip), and important mail, at least as judged by the sender (the exclamation point).

Many sorting orders are also possible. The most common is to order messages based on the time that they were received, most recent first, with some indication as to whether the message is new or has already been read by the user. The fields in the summary and the sort order can be customized by the user according to her preferences.

User agents must also be able to display incoming messages as needed so that people can read their email. Often a short preview of a message is provided, as in Fig. 7-9, to help users decide when to read further. Previews may use small icons or images to describe the contents of the message. Other presentation processing includes reformatting messages to fit the display, and translating or converting contents to more convenient formats (e.g., digitized speech to recognized text).

After a message has been read, the user can decide what to do with it. This is called **message disposition**. Options include deleting the message, sending a reply, forwarding the message to another user, and keeping the message for later reference. Most user agents can manage one mailbox for incoming mail with multiple folders for saved mail. The folders allow the user to save message according to sender, topic, or some other category.

Filing can be done automatically by the user agent as well, before the user reads the messages. A common example is that the fields and contents of messages are inspected and used, along with feedback from the user about previous messages, to determine if a message is likely to be spam. Many ISPs and companies run software that labels mail as important or spam so that the user agent can file it in the corresponding mailbox. The ISP and company have the advantage of seeing mail for many users and may have lists of known spammers. If hundreds of users have just received a similar message, it is probably spam. By presorting incoming mail as "probably legitimate" and "probably spam," the user agent can save users a fair amount of work separating the good stuff from the junk.

And the most popular spam? It is generated by collections of compromised computers called **botnets** and its content depends on where you live. Fake diplomas are topical in Asia, and cheap drugs and other dubious product offers are topical in the U.S. Unclaimed Nigerian bank accounts still abound. Pills for enlarging various body parts are common everywhere.

Other filing rules can be constructed by users. Each rule specifies a condition and an action. For example, a rule could say that any message received from the boss goes to one folder for immediate reading and any message from a particular mailing list goes to another folder for later reading. Several folders are shown in Fig. 7-9. The most important folders are the Inbox, for incoming mail not filed elsewhere, and Junk Mail, for messages that are thought to be spam.

As well as explicit constructs like folders, user agents now provide rich capabilities to search the mailbox. This feature is also shown in Fig. 7-9. Search capabilities let users find messages quickly, such as the message about "where to buy Vegemite" that someone sent in the last month.

Email has come a long way from the days when it was just file transfer. Providers now routinely support mailboxes with up to 1 GB of stored mail that details a user's interactions over a long period of time. The sophisticated mail handling of user agents with search and automatic forms of processing is what makes it possible to manage these large volumes of email. For people who send and receive thousands of messages a year, these tools are invaluable.

Another useful feature is the ability to automatically respond to messages in some way. One response is to forward incoming email to a different address, for example, a computer operated by a commercial paging service that pages the user by using radio or satellite and displays the *Subject:* line on his pager. These **autoresponders** must run in the mail server because the user agent may not run all the time and may only occasionally retrieve email. Because of these factors, the user agent cannot provide a true automatic response. However, the interface for automatic responses is usually presented by the user agent.

A different example of an automatic response is a **vacation agent**. This is a program that examines each incoming message and sends the sender an insipid reply such as: "Hi. I'm on vacation. I'll be back on the 24th of August. Talk to you then." Such replies can also specify how to handle urgent matters in the interim, other people to contact for specific problems, etc. Most vacation agents keep track of whom they have sent canned replies to and refrain from sending the same person a second reply. There are pitfalls with these agents, however. For example, it is not advisable to send a canned reply to a large mailing list.

Let us now turn to the scenario of one user sending a message to another user. One of the basic features user agents support that we have not yet discussed is mail composition. It involves creating messages and answers to messages and sending these messages into the rest of the mail system for delivery. Although any text editor can be used to create the body of the message, editors are usually integrated with the user agent so that it can provide assistance with addressing and the numerous header fields attached to each message. For example, when answering a message, the email system can extract the originator's address from the incoming email and automatically insert it into the proper place in the reply. Other common features are appending a **signature block** to the bottom of a message, correcting spelling, and computing digital signatures that show the message is valid.

Messages that are sent into the mail system have a standard format that must be created from the information supplied to the user agent. The most important part of the message for transfer is the envelope, and the most important part of the envelope is the destination address. This address must be in a format that the message transfer agents can deal with.

The expected form of an address is *user@dns-address*. Since we studied DNS earlier in this chapter, we will not repeat that material here. However, it is worth noting that other forms of addressing exist. In particular, **X.400** addresses look radically different from DNS addresses.

X.400 is an ISO standard for message-handling systems that was at one time a competitor to SMTP. SMTP won out handily, though X.400 systems are still used, mostly outside of the U.S. X.400 addresses are composed of *attribute=value* pairs separated by slashes, for example,

/C=US/ST=MASSACHUSETTS/L=CAMBRIDGE/PA=360 MEMORIAL DR./CN=KEN SMITH/

This address specifies a country, state, locality, personal address, and common name (Ken Smith). Many other attributes are possible, so you can send email to someone whose exact email address you do not know, provided you know enough other attributes (e.g., company and job title).

Although X.400 names are considerably less convenient than DNS names, the issue is moot for user agents because they have user-friendly aliases (sometimes called nicknames) that allow users to enter or select a person's name and get the correct email address. Consequently, it is usually not necessary to actually type in these strange strings.

A final point we will touch on for sending mail is mailing lists, which let users send the same message to a list of people with a single command. There are two choices for how the mailing list is maintained. It might be maintained locally, by the user agent. In this case, the user agent can just send a separate message to each intended recipient.

Alternatively, the list may be maintained remotely at a message transfer agent. Messages will then be expanded in the message transfer system, which has the effect of allowing multiple users to send to the list. For example, if a group of bird watchers has a mailing list called *birders* installed on the transfer agent *meadowlark.arizona.edu*, any message sent to *birders@meadowlark.arizona.edu* will be routed to the University of Arizona and expanded into individual messages to all the mailing list members, wherever in the world they may be. Users of this mailing list cannot tell that it is a mailing list. It could just as well be the personal mailbox of Prof. Gabriel O. Birders.

7.2.3 Message Formats

Now we turn from the user interface to the format of the email messages themselves. Messages sent by the user agent must be placed in a standard format to be handled by the message transfer agents. First we will look at basic ASCII email using RFC 5322, which is the latest revision of the original Internet message format as described in RFC 822. After that, we will look at multimedia extensions to the basic format.

RFC 5322—The Internet Message Format

Messages consist of a primitive envelope (described as part of SMTP in RFC 5321), some number of header fields, a blank line, and then the message body. Each header field (logically) consists of a single line of ASCII text containing the field name, a colon, and, for most fields, a value. The original RFC 822 was designed decades ago and did not clearly distinguish the envelope fields from the header fields. Although it has been revised to RFC 5322, completely redoing it was not possible due to its widespread usage. In normal usage, the user agent builds a message and passes it to the message transfer agent, which then uses some of the header fields to construct the actual envelope, a somewhat old-fashioned mixing of message and envelope.

The principal header fields related to message transport are listed in Fig. 7-10. The *To:* field gives the DNS address of the primary recipient. Having multiple recipients is also allowed. The *Cc:* field gives the addresses of any secondary recipients. In terms of delivery, there is no distinction between the primary and secondary recipients. It is entirely a psychological difference that may be important to the people involved but is not important to the mail system. The term *Cc:* (Carbon copy) is a bit dated, since computers do not use carbon paper, but it is well established. The *Bcc:* (Blind carbon copy) field is like the *Cc:* field, except that this line is deleted from all the copies sent to the primary and secondary recipients. This feature allows people to send copies to third parties without the primary and secondary recipients knowing this.

Header	Meaning
To:	Email address(es) of primary recipient(s)
Cc:	Email address(es) of secondary recipient(s)
Bcc:	Email address(es) for blind carbon copies
From:	Person or people who created the message
Sender:	Email address of the actual sender
Received:	Line added by each transfer agent along the route
Return-Path:	Can be used to identify a path back to the sender

Figure 7-10. RFC 5322 header fields related to message transport.

The next two fields, *From:* and *Sender:*, tell who wrote and sent the message, respectively. These need not be the same. For example, a business executive may write a message, but her assistant may be the one who actually transmits it. In this case, the executive would be listed in the *From:* field and the assistant in the *Sender:* field. The *From:* field is required, but the *Sender:* field may be omitted if it is the same as the *From:* field. These fields are needed in case the message is undeliverable and must be returned to the sender.

A line containing *Received:* is added by each message transfer agent along the way. The line contains the agent's identity, the date and time the message was received, and other information that can be used for debugging the routing system.

The *Return-Path:* field is added by the final message transfer agent and was intended to tell how to get back to the sender. In theory, this information can be gathered from all the *Received:* headers (except for the name of the sender's mailbox), but it is rarely filled in as such and typically just contains the sender's address.

In addition to the fields of Fig. 7-10, RFC 5322 messages may also contain a variety of header fields used by the user agents or human recipients. The most common ones are listed in Fig. 7-11. Most of these are self-explanatory, so we will not go into all of them in much detail.

Header	Meaning
Date:	The date and time the message was sent
Reply-To:	Email address to which replies should be sent
Message-Id:	Unique number for referencing this message later
In-Reply-To:	Message-Id of the message to which this is a reply
References:	Other relevant Message-Ids
Keywords:	User-chosen keywords
Subject:	Short summary of the message for the one-line display

Figure 7-11. Some fields used in the RFC 5322 message header.

The *Reply-To:* field is sometimes used when neither the person composing the message nor the person sending the message wants to see the reply. For example, a marketing manager may write an email message telling customers about a new product. The message is sent by an assistant, but the *Reply-To:* field lists the head of the sales department, who can answer questions and take orders. This field is also useful when the sender has two email accounts and wants the reply to go to the other one.

The *Message-Id:* is an automatically generated number that is used to link messages together (e.g., when used in the *In-Reply-To:* field) and to prevent duplicate delivery.

The RFC 5322 document explicitly says that users are allowed to invent optional headers for their own private use. By convention since RFC 822, these headers start with the string *X-*. It is guaranteed that no future headers will use names starting with *X-*, to avoid conflicts between official and private headers. Sometimes wiseguy undergraduates make up fields like *X-Fruit-of-the-Day:* or *X-Disease-of-the-Week:*, which are legal, although not always illuminating.

After the headers comes the message body. Users can put whatever they want here. Some people terminate their messages with elaborate signatures, including quotations from greater and lesser authorities, political statements, and disclaimers of all kinds (e.g., The XYZ Corporation is not responsible for my opinions; in fact, it cannot even comprehend them).

MIME—The Multipurpose Internet Mail Extensions

In the early days of the ARPANET, email consisted exclusively of text messages written in English and expressed in ASCII. For this environment, the early RFC 822 format did the job completely: it specified the headers but left the content entirely up to the users. In the 1990s, the worldwide use of the Internet and demand to send richer content through the mail system meant that this approach was no longer adequate. The problems included sending and receiving messages in languages with accents (e.g., French and German), non-Latin alphabets (e.g., Hebrew and Russian), or no alphabets (e.g., Chinese and Japanese), as well as sending messages not containing text at all (e.g., audio, images, or binary documents and programs).

The solution was the development of **MIME (Multipurpose Internet Mail Extensions)**. It is widely used for mail messages that are sent across the Internet, as well as to describe content for other applications such as Web browsing. MIME is described in RFCs 2045–2047, 4288, 4289, and 2049.

The basic idea of MIME is to continue to use the RFC 822 format (the precursor to RFC 5322 the time MIME was proposed) but to add structure to the message body and define encoding rules for the transfer of non-ASCII messages. Not deviating from RFC 822 allowed MIME messages to be sent using the existing mail transfer agents and protocols (based on RFC 821 then, and RFC 5321 now). All that had to be changed were the sending and receiving programs, which users could do for themselves.

MIME defines five new message headers, as shown in Fig. 7-12. The first of these simply tells the user agent receiving the message that it is dealing with a MIME message, and which version of MIME it uses. Any message not containing a *MIME-Version:* header is assumed to be an English plaintext message (or at least one using only ASCII characters) and is processed as such.

Header	Meaning
MIME-Version:	Identifies the MIME version
Content-Description:	Human-readable string telling what is in the message
Content-Id:	Unique identifier
Content-Transfer-Encoding:	How the body is wrapped for transmission
Content-Type:	Type and format of the content

Figure 7-12. Message headers added by MIME.

The *Content-Description:* header is an ASCII string telling what is in the message. This header is needed so the recipient will know whether it is worth decoding and reading the message. If the string says "Photo of Barbara's hamster" and the person getting the message is not a big hamster fan, the message will probably be discarded rather than decoded into a high-resolution color photograph.

The *Content-Id:* header identifies the content. It uses the same format as the standard *Message-Id:* header.

The *Content-Transfer-Encoding:* tells how the body is wrapped for transmission through the network. A key problem at the time MIME was developed was that the mail transfer (SMTP) protocols expected ASCII messages in which no line exceeded 1000 characters. ASCII characters use 7 bits out of each 8-bit byte. Binary data such as executable programs and images use all 8 bits of each byte, as do extended character sets. There was no guarantee this data would be transferred safely. Hence, some method of carrying binary data that made it look like a regular ASCII mail message was needed. Extensions to SMTP since the development of MIME do allow 8-bit binary data to be transferred, though even today binary data may not always go through the mail system correctly if unencoded.

MIME provides five transfer encoding schemes, plus an escape to new schemes—just in case. The simplest scheme is just ASCII text messages. ASCII characters use 7 bits and can be carried directly by the email protocol, provided that no line exceeds 1000 characters.

The next simplest scheme is the same thing, but using 8-bit characters, that is, all values from 0 up to and including 255 are allowed. Messages using the 8-bit encoding must still adhere to the standard maximum line length.

Then there are messages that use a true binary encoding. These are arbitrary binary files that not only use all 8 bits but also do not adhere to the 1000-character line limit. Executable programs fall into this category. Nowadays, mail servers can negotiate to send data in binary (or 8-bit) encoding, falling back to ASCII if both ends do not support the extension.

The ASCII encoding of binary data is called **base64 encoding**. In this scheme, groups of 24 bits are broken up into four 6-bit units, with each unit being sent as a legal ASCII character. The coding is "A" for 0, "B" for 1, and so on, followed by the 26 lowercase letters, the 10 digits, and finally + and / for 62 and 63, respectively. The == and = sequences indicate that the last group contained only 8 or 16 bits, respectively. Carriage returns and line feeds are ignored, so they can be inserted at will in the encoded character stream to keep the lines short enough. Arbitrary binary text can be sent safely using this scheme, albeit inefficiently. This encoding was very popular before binary-capable mail servers were widely deployed. It is still commonly seen.

For messages that are almost entirely ASCII but with a few non-ASCII characters, base64 encoding is somewhat inefficient. Instead, an encoding known as **quoted-printable encoding** is used. This is just 7-bit ASCII, with all the characters above 127 encoded as an equals sign followed by the character's value as two hexadecimal digits. Control characters, some punctuation marks and math symbols, as well as trailing spaces are also so encoded.

Finally, when there are valid reasons not to use one of these schemes, it is possible to specify a user-defined encoding in the *Content-Transfer-Encoding:* header.

The last header shown in Fig. 7-12 is really the most interesting one. It specifies the nature of the message body and has had an impact well beyond email. For instance, content downloaded from the Web is labeled with MIME types so that the browser knows how to present it. So is content sent over streaming media and real-time transports such as voice over IP.

Initially, seven MIME types were defined in RFC 1521. Each type has one or more available subtypes. The type and subtype are separated by a slash, as in

"Content-Type: video/mpeg". Since then, hundreds of subtypes have been added, along with another type. Additional entries are being added all the time as new types of content are developed. The list of assigned types and subtypes is maintained online by IANA at *www.iana.org/assignments/media-types*.

The types, along with examples of commonly used subtypes, are given in Fig. 7-13. Let us briefly go through them, starting with *text*. The *text/plain* combination is for ordinary messages that can be displayed as received, with no encoding and no further processing. This option allows ordinary messages to be transported in MIME with only a few extra headers. The *text/html* subtype was added when the Web became popular (in RFC 2854) to allow Web pages to be sent in RFC 822 email. A subtype for the eXtensible Markup Language, *text/xml*, is defined in RFC 3023. XML documents have proliferated with the development of the Web. We will study HTML and XML in Sec. 7.3.

Type	Example subtypes	Description
text	plain, html, xml, css	Text in various formats
image	gif, jpeg, tiff	Pictures
audio	basic, mpeg, mp4	Sounds
video	mpeg, mp4, quicktime	Movies
model	vrml	3D model
application	octet-stream, pdf, javascript, zip	Data produced by applications
message	http, rfc822	Encapsulated message
multipart	mixed, alternative, parallel, digest	Combination of multiple types

Figure 7-13. MIME content types and example subtypes.

The next MIME type is *image*, which is used to transmit still pictures. Many formats are widely used for storing and transmitting images nowadays, both with and without compression. Several of these, including GIF, JPEG, and TIFF, are built into nearly all browsers. Many other formats and corresponding subtypes exist as well.

The *audio* and *video* types are for sound and moving pictures, respectively. Please note that *video* may include only the visual information, not the sound. If a movie with sound is to be transmitted, the video and audio portions may have to be transmitted separately, depending on the encoding system used. The first video format defined was the one devised by the modestly named Moving Picture Experts Group (MPEG), but others have been added since. In addition to *audio/basic*, a new audio type, *audio/mpeg*, was added in RFC 3003 to allow people to email MP3 audio files. The *video/mp4* and *audio/mp4* types signal video and audio data that are stored in the newer MPEG 4 format.

The *model* type was added after the other content types. It is intended for describing 3D model data. However, it has not been widely used to date.

The *application* type is a catchall for formats that are not covered by one of the other types and that require an application to interpret the data. We have listed the subtypes *pdf*, *javascript*, and *zip* as examples for PDF documents, JavaScript programs, and Zip archives, respectively. User agents that receive this content use a third-party library or external program to display the content; the display may or may not appear to be integrated with the user agent.

By using MIME types, user agents gain the extensibility to handle new types of application content as it is developed. This is a significant benefit. On the other hand, many of the new forms of content are executed or interpreted by applications, which presents some dangers. Obviously, running an arbitrary executable program that has arrived via the mail system from "friends" poses a security hazard. The program may do all sorts of nasty damage to the parts of the computer to which it has access, especially if it can read and write files and use the network. Less obviously, document formats can pose the same hazards. This is because formats such as PDF are full-blown programming languages in disguise. While they are interpreted and restricted in scope, bugs in the interpreter often allow devious documents to escape the restrictions.

Besides these examples, there are many more application subtypes because there are many more applications. As a fallback to be used when no other subtype is known to be more fitting, the *octet-stream* subtype denotes a sequence of uninterpreted bytes. Upon receiving such a stream, it is likely that a user agent will display it by suggesting to the user that it be copied to a file. Subsequent processing is then up to the user, who presumably knows what kind of content it is.

The last two types are useful for composing and manipulating messages themselves. The *message* type allows one message to be fully encapsulated inside another. This scheme is useful for forwarding email, for example. When a complete RFC 822 message is encapsulated inside an outer message, the *rfc822* subtype should be used. Similarly, it is common for HTML documents to be encapsulated. And the *partial* subtype makes it possible to break an encapsulated message into pieces and send them separately (for example, if the encapsulated message is too long). Parameters make it possible to reassemble all the parts at the destination in the correct order.

Finally, the *multipart* type allows a message to contain more than one part, with the beginning and end of each part being clearly delimited. The *mixed* subtype allows each part to be a different type, with no additional structure imposed. Many email programs allow the user to provide one or more attachments to a text message. These attachments are sent using the *multipart* type.

In contrast to *mixed*, the *alternative* subtype allows the same message to be included multiple times but expressed in two or more different media. For example, a message could be sent in plain ASCII, in HMTL, and in PDF. A properly designed user agent getting such a message would display it according to user preferences. Likely PDF would be the first choice, if that is possible. The second choice would be HTML. If neither of these were possible, then the flat ASCII text would be displayed. The parts should be ordered from simplest to most complex to help recipients with pre-MIME user agents make some sense of the message (e.g., even a pre-MIME user can read flat ASCII text).

The *alternative* subtype can also be used for multiple languages. In this context, the Rosetta Stone can be thought of as an early *multipart/alternative* message.

Of the other two example subtypes, the *parallel* subtype is used when all parts must be "viewed" simultaneously. For example, movies often have an audio channel and a video channel. Movies are more effective if these two channels are played back in parallel, instead of consecutively. The *digest* subtype is used when multiple messages are packed together into a composite message. For example, some discussion groups on the Internet collect messages from subscribers and then send them out to the group periodically as a single *multipart/digest* message.

As an example of how MIME types may be used for email messages, a multimedia message is shown in Fig. 7-14. Here, a birthday greeting is transmitted in alternative forms as HTML and as an audio file. Assuming the receiver has audio capability, the user agent there will play the sound file. In this example, the sound is carried by reference as a *message/external-body* subtype, so first the user agent must fetch the sound file *birthday.snd* using FTP. If the user agent has no audio capability, the lyrics are displayed on the screen in stony silence. The two parts are delimited by two hyphens followed by a (software-generated) string specified in the *boundary* parameter.

Note that the *Content-Type* header occurs in three positions within this example. At the top level, it indicates that the message has multiple parts. Within each part, it gives the type and subtype of that part. Finally, within the body of the second part, it is required to tell the user agent what kind of external file it is to fetch. To indicate this slight difference in usage, we have used lowercase letters here, although all headers are case insensitive. The *Content-Transfer-Encoding* is similarly required for any external body that is not encoded as 7-bit ASCII.

7.2.4 Message Transfer

Now that we have described user agents and mail messages, we are ready to look at how the message transfer agents relay messages from the originator to the recipient. The mail transfer is done with the SMTP protocol.

The simplest way to move messages is to establish a transport connection from the source machine to the destination machine and then just transfer the message. This is how SMTP originally worked. Over the years, however, two different uses of SMTP have been differentiated. The first use is **mail submission**, step 1 in the email architecture of Fig. 7-7. This is the means by which user agents send messages into the mail system for delivery. The second use is to transfer messages between message transfer agents (step 2 in Fig. 7-7). This

```
From: alice@cs.washington.edu
To: bob@ee.uwa.edu.au
MIME-Version: 1.0
Message-Id: <0704760941.AA00747@cs.washington.edu>
Content-Type: multipart/alternative; boundary=qwertyuiopasdfghjklzxcvbnm
Subject: Earth orbits sun integral number of times

This is the preamble. The user agent ignores it. Have a nice day.

--qwertyuiopasdfghjklzxcvbnm
Content-Type: text/html

<p>Happy birthday to you<br>
Happy birthday to you<br>
Happy birthday dear <b> Bob </b><br>
Happy birthday to you</p>

--qwertyuiopasdfghjklzxcvbnm
Content-Type: message/external-body;
      access-type="anon-ftp";
      site="bicycle.cs.washington.edu";
      directory="pub";
      name="birthday.snd"

content-type: audio/basic
content-transfer-encoding: base64
--qwertyuiopasdfghjklzxcvbnm--
```

Figure 7-14. A multipart message containing HTML and audio alternatives.

sequence delivers mail all the way from the sending to the receiving message transfer agent in one hop. Final delivery is accomplished with different protocols that we will describe in the next section.

In this section, we will describe the basics of the SMTP protocol and its extension mechanism. Then we will discuss how it is used differently for mail submission and message transfer.

SMTP (Simple Mail Transfer Protocol) and Extensions

Within the Internet, email is delivered by having the sending computer establish a TCP connection to port 25 of the receiving computer. Listening to this port is a mail server that speaks **SMTP (Simple Mail Transfer Protocol)**. This server accepts incoming connections, subject to some security checks, and accepts messages for delivery. If a message cannot be delivered, an error report containing the first part of the undeliverable message is returned to the sender.

SMTP is a simple ASCII protocol. This is not a weakness but a feature. Using ASCII text makes protocols easy to develop, test, and debug. They can be tested by sending commands manually, and records of the messages are easy to read. Most application-level Internet protocols now work this way (e.g., HTTP).

We will walk through a simple message transfer between mail servers that delivers a message. After establishing the TCP connection to port 25, the sending machine, operating as the client, waits for the receiving machine, operating as the server, to talk first. The server starts by sending a line of text giving its identity and telling whether it is prepared to receive mail. If it is not, the client releases the connection and tries again later.

If the server is willing to accept email, the client announces whom the email is coming from and whom it is going to. If such a recipient exists at the destination, the server gives the client the go-ahead to send the message. Then the client sends the message and the server acknowledges it. No checksums are needed because TCP provides a reliable byte stream. If there is more email, that is now sent. When all the email has been exchanged in both directions, the connection is released. A sample dialog for sending the message of Fig. 7-14, including the numerical codes used by SMTP, is shown in Fig. 7-15. The lines sent by the client (i.e., the sender) are marked *C:*. Those sent by the server (i.e., the receiver) are marked *S:*.

The first command from the client is indeed meant to be *HELO*. Of the various four-character abbreviations for *HELLO*, this one has numerous advantages over its biggest competitor. Why all the commands had to be four characters has been lost in the mists of time.

In Fig. 7-15, the message is sent to only one recipient, so only one *RCPT* command is used. Such commands are allowed to send a single message to multiple receivers. Each one is individually acknowledged or rejected. Even if some recipients are rejected (because they do not exist at the destination), the message can be sent to the other ones.

Finally, although the syntax of the four-character commands from the client is rigidly specified, the syntax of the replies is less rigid. Only the numerical code really counts. Each implementation can put whatever string it wants after the code.

The basic SMTP works well, but it is limited in several respects. It does not include authentication. This means that the *FROM* command in the example could give any sender address that it pleases. This is quite useful for sending spam. Another limitation is that SMTP transfers ASCII messages, not binary data. This is why the base64 MIME content transfer encoding was needed. However, with that encoding the mail transmission uses bandwidth inefficiently, which is an issue for large messages. A third limitation is that SMTP sends messages in the clear. It has no encryption to provide a measure of privacy against prying eyes.

To allow these and many other problems related to message processing to be addressed, SMTP was revised to have an extension mechanism. This mechanism is a mandatory part of the RFC 5321 standard. The use of SMTP with extensions is called **ESMTP (Extended SMTP)**.

```
                        S: 220 ee.uwa.edu.au SMTP service ready
C: HELO abcd.com
                        S: 250 cs.washington.edu says hello to ee.uwa.edu.au
C: MAIL FROM: <alice@cs.washington.edu>
                        S: 250 sender ok
C: RCPT TO: <bob@ee.uwa.edu.au>
                        S: 250 recipient ok
C: DATA
                        S: 354 Send mail; end with "." on a line by itself
C: From: alice@cs.washington.edu
C: To: bob@ee.uwa.edu.au
C: MIME-Version: 1.0
C: Message-Id: <0704760941.AA00747@ee.uwa.edu.au>
C: Content-Type: multipart/alternative; boundary=qwertyuiopasdfghjklzxcvbnm
C: Subject: Earth orbits sun integral number of times
C:
C: This is the preamble. The user agent ignores it. Have a nice day.
C:
C: --qwertyuiopasdfghjklzxcvbnm
C: Content-Type: text/html
C:
C: <p>Happy birthday to you
C: Happy birthday to you
C: Happy birthday dear <bold> Bob </bold>
C: Happy birthday to you
C:
C: --qwertyuiopasdfghjklzxcvbnm
C: Content-Type: message/external-body;
C:       access-type="anon-ftp";
C:       site="bicycle.cs.washington.edu";
C:       directory="pub";
C:       name="birthday.snd"
C:
C: content-type: audio/basic
C: content-transfer-encoding: base64
C: --qwertyuiopasdfghjklzxcvbnm
C: .
                        S: 250 message accepted
C: QUIT
                        S: 221 ee.uwa.edu.au closing connection
```

Figure 7-15. Sending a message from *alice@cs.washington.edu* to *bob@ee.uwa.edu.au*.

Clients wanting to use an extension send an *EHLO* message instead of *HELO* initially. If this is rejected, the server is a regular SMTP server, and the client should proceed in the usual way. If the *EHLO* is accepted, the server replies with the extensions that it supports. The client may then use any of these extensions. Several common extensions are shown in Fig. 7-16. The figure gives the keyword as used in the extension mechanism, along with a description of the new functionality. We will not go into extensions in further detail.

Keyword	Description
AUTH	Client authentication
BINARYMIME	Server accepts binary messages
CHUNKING	Server accepts large messages in chunks
SIZE	Check message size before trying to send
STARTTLS	Switch to secure transport (TLS; see Chap. 8)
UTF8SMTP	Internationalized addresses

Figure 7-16. Some SMTP extensions.

To get a better feel for how SMTP and some of the other protocols described in this chapter work, try them out. In all cases, first go to a machine connected to the Internet. On a UNIX (or Linux) system, in a shell, type

```
telnet mail.isp.com 25
```

substituting the DNS name of your ISP's mail server for *mail.isp.com*. On a Windows XP system, click on Start, then Run, and type the command in the dialog box. On a Vista or Windows 7 machine, you may have to first install the telnet program (or equivalent) and then start it yourself. This command will establish a telnet (i.e., TCP) connection to port 25 on that machine. Port 25 is the SMTP port; see Fig. 6-34 for the ports for other common protocols. You will probably get a response something like this:

```
Trying 192.30.200.66...
Connected to mail.isp.com
Escape character is '^]'.
220 mail.isp.com Smail #74 ready at Thu, 25 Sept 2002 13:26 +0200
```

The first three lines are from telnet, telling you what it is doing. The last line is from the SMTP server on the remote machine, announcing its willingness to talk to you and accept email. To find out what commands it accepts, type

```
HELP
```

From this point on, a command sequence such as the one in Fig. 7-16 is possible if the server is willing to accept mail from you.

Mail Submission

Originally, user agents ran on the same computer as the sending message transfer agent. In this setting, all that is required to send a message is for the user agent to talk to the local mail server, using the dialog that we have just described. However, this setting is no longer the usual case.

User agents often run on laptops, home PCs, and mobile phones. They are not always connected to the Internet. Mail transfer agents run on ISP and company servers. They are always connected to the Internet. This difference means that a user agent in Boston may need to contact its regular mail server in Seattle to send a mail message because the user is traveling.

By itself, this remote communication poses no problem. It is exactly what the TCP/IP protocols are designed to support. However, an ISP or company usually does not want any remote user to be able to submit messages to its mail server to be delivered elsewhere. The ISP or company is not running the server as a public service. In addition, this kind of **open mail relay** attracts spammers. This is because it provides a way to launder the original sender and thus make the message more difficult to identify as spam.

Given these considerations, SMTP is normally used for mail submission with the *AUTH* extension. This extension lets the server check the credentials (username and password) of the client to confirm that the server should be providing mail service.

There are several other differences in the way SMTP is used for mail submission. For example, port 587 is used in preference to port 25 and the SMTP server can check and correct the format of the messages sent by the user agent. For more information about the restricted use of SMTP for mail submission, please see RFC 4409.

Message Transfer

Once the sending mail transfer agent receives a message from the user agent, it will deliver it to the receiving mail transfer agent using SMTP. To do this, the sender uses the destination address. Consider the message in Fig. 7-15, addressed to *bob@ee.uwa.edu.au*. To what mail server should the message be delivered?

To determine the correct mail server to contact, DNS is consulted. In the previous section, we described how DNS contains multiple types of records, including the *MX*, or mail exchanger, record. In this case, a DNS query is made for the *MX* records of the domain *ee.uwa.edu.au*. This query returns an ordered list of the names and IP addresses of one or more mail servers.

The sending mail transfer agent then makes a TCP connection on port 25 to the IP address of the mail server to reach the receiving mail transfer agent, and uses SMTP to relay the message. The receiving mail transfer agent will then place mail for the user *bob* in the correct mailbox for Bob to read it at a later time. This local delivery step may involve moving the message among computers if there is a large mail infrastructure.

With this delivery process, mail travels from the initial to the final mail transfer agent in a single hop. There are no intermediate servers in the message transfer stage. It is possible, however, for this delivery process to occur multiple times. One example that we have described already is when a message transfer agent implements a mailing list. In this case, a message is received for the list. It is then expanded as a message to each member of the list that is sent to the individual member addresses.

As another example of relaying, Bob may have graduated from M.I.T. and also be reachable via the address *bob@alum.mit.edu*. Rather than reading mail on multiple accounts, Bob can arrange for mail sent to this address to be forwarded to *bob@ee.uwa.edu*. In this case, mail sent to *bob@alum.mit.edu* will undergo two deliveries. First, it will be sent to the mail server for *alum.mit.edu*. Then, it will be sent to the mail server for *ee.uwa.edu.au*. Each of these legs is a complete and separate delivery as far as the mail transfer agents are concerned.

Another consideration nowadays is spam. Nine out of ten messages sent today are spam (McAfee, 2010). Few people want more spam, but it is hard to avoid because it masquerades as regular mail. Before accepting a message, additional checks may be made to reduce the opportunities for spam. The message for Bob was sent from *alice@cs.washington.edu*. The receiving mail transfer agent can look up the sending mail transfer agent in DNS. This lets it check that the IP address of the other end of the TCP connection matches the DNS name. More generally, the receiving agent may look up the sending domain in DNS to see if it has a mail sending policy. This information is often given in the *TXT* and *SPF* records. It may indicate that other checks can be made. For example, mail sent from *cs.washington.edu* may always be sent from the host *june.cs.washington.edu*. If the sending mail transfer agent is not *june*, there is a problem.

If any of these checks fail, the mail is probably being forged with a fake sending address. In this case, it is discarded. However, passing these checks does not imply that mail is not spam. The checks merely ensure that the mail seems to be coming from the region of the network that it purports to come from. The idea is that spammers should be forced to use the correct sending address when they send mail. This makes spam easier to recognize and delete when it is unwanted.

7.2.5 Final Delivery

Our mail message is almost delivered. It has arrived at Bob's mailbox. All that remains is to transfer a copy of the message to Bob's user agent for display. This is step 3 in the architecture of Fig. 7-7. This task was straightforward in the early Internet, when the user agent and mail transfer agent ran on the same machine as different processes. The mail transfer agent simply wrote new messages to the end of the mailbox file, and the user agent simply checked the mailbox file for new mail.

Nowadays, the user agent on a PC, laptop, or mobile, is likely to be on a different machine than the ISP or company mail server. Users want to be able to access their mail remotely, from wherever they are. They want to access email from work, from their home PCs, from their laptops when on business trips, and from cybercafes when on so-called vacation. They also want to be able to work offline, then reconnect to receive incoming mail and send outgoing mail. Moreover, each user may run several user agents depending on what computer it is convenient to use at the moment. Several user agents may even be running at the same time.

In this setting, the job of the user agent is to present a view of the contents of the mailbox, and to allow the mailbox to be remotely manipulated. Several different protocols can be used for this purpose, but SMTP is not one of them. SMTP is a push-based protocol. It takes a message and connects to a remote server to transfer the message. Final delivery cannot be achieved in this manner both because the mailbox must continue to be stored on the mail transfer agent and because the user agent may not be connected to the Internet at the moment that SMTP attempts to relay messages.

IMAP—The Internet Message Access Protocol

One of the main protocols that is used for final delivery is **IMAP** (**Internet Message Access Protocol**). Version 4 of the protocol is defined in RFC 3501. To use IMAP, the mail server runs an IMAP server that listens to port 143. The user agent runs an IMAP client. The client connects to the server and begins to issue commands from those listed in Fig. 7-17.

First, the client will start a secure transport if one is to be used (in order to keep the messages and commands confidential), and then log in or otherwise authenticate itself to the server. Once logged in, there are many commands to list folders and messages, fetch messages or even parts of messages, mark messages with flags for later deletion, and organize messages into folders. To avoid confusion, please note that we use the term "folder" here to be consistent with the rest of the material in this section, in which a user has a single mailbox made up of multiple folders. However, in the IMAP specification, the term *mailbox* is used instead. One user thus has many IMAP mailboxes, each of which is typically presented to the user as a folder.

IMAP has many other features, too. It has the ability to address mail not by message number, but by using attributes (e.g., give me the first message from Alice). Searches can be performed on the server to find the messages that satisfy certain criteria so that only those messages are fetched by the client.

IMAP is an improvement over an earlier final delivery protocol, **POP3** (**Post Office Protocol, version 3**), which is specified in RFC 1939. POP3 is a simpler protocol but supports fewer features and is less secure in typical usage. Mail is usually downloaded to the user agent computer, instead of remaining on the mail server. This makes life easier on the server, but harder on the user. It is not easy to read mail on multiple computers, plus if the user agent computer breaks, all email may be lost permanently. Nonetheless, you will still find POP3 in use.

Proprietary protocols can also be used because the protocol runs between a mail server and user agent that can be supplied by the same company. Microsoft Exchange is a mail system with a proprietary protocol.

Command	Description
CAPABILITY	List server capabilities
STARTTLS	Start secure transport (TLS; see Chap. 8)
LOGIN	Log on to server
AUTHENTICATE	Log on with other method
SELECT	Select a folder
EXAMINE	Select a read-only folder
CREATE	Create a folder
DELETE	Delete a folder
RENAME	Rename a folder
SUBSCRIBE	Add folder to active set
UNSUBSCRIBE	Remove folder from active set
LIST	List the available folders
LSUB	List the active folders
STATUS	Get the status of a folder
APPEND	Add a message to a folder
CHECK	Get a checkpoint of a folder
FETCH	Get messages from a folder
SEARCH	Find messages in a folder
STORE	Alter message flags
COPY	Make a copy of a message in a folder
EXPUNGE	Remove messages flagged for deletion
UID	Issue commands using unique identifiers
NOOP	Do nothing
CLOSE	Remove flagged messages and close folder
LOGOUT	Log out and close connection

Figure 7-17. IMAP (version 4) commands.

Webmail

An increasingly popular alternative to IMAP and SMTP for providing email service is to use the Web as an interface for sending and receiving mail. Widely used **Webmail** systems include Google Gmail, Microsoft Hotmail and Yahoo! Mail. Webmail is one example of software (in this case, a mail user agent) that is provided as a service using the Web.

In this architecture, the provider runs mail servers as usual to accept messages for users with SMTP on port 25. However, the user agent is different. Instead of being a standalone program, it is a user interface that is provided via Web pages. This means that users can use any browser they like to access their mail and send new messages.

We have not yet studied the Web, but a brief description that you might come back to is as follows. When the user goes to the email Web page of the provider, a form is presented in which the user is asked for a login name and password. The login name and password are sent to the server, which then validates them. If the login is successful, the server finds the user's mailbox and builds a Web page listing the contents of the mailbox on the fly. The Web page is then sent to the browser for display.

Many of the items on the page showing the mailbox are clickable, so messages can be read, deleted, and so on. To make the interface responsive, the Web pages will often include JavaScript programs. These programs are run locally on the client in response to local events (e.g., mouse clicks) and can also download and upload messages in the background, to prepare the next message for display or a new message for submission. In this model, mail submission happens using the normal Web protocols by posting data to a URL. The Web server takes care of injecting messages into the traditional mail delivery system that we have described. For security, the standard Web protocols can be used as well. These protocols concern themselves with encrypting Web pages, not whether the content of the Web page is a mail message.

7.3 THE WORLD WIDE WEB

The Web, as the World Wide Web is popularly known, is an architectural framework for accessing linked content spread out over millions of machines all over the Internet. In 10 years it went from being a way to coordinate the design of high-energy physics experiments in Switzerland to the application that millions of people think of as being "The Internet." Its enormous popularity stems from the fact that it is easy for beginners to use and provides access with a rich graphical interface to an enormous wealth of information on almost every conceivable subject, from aardvarks to Zulus.

The Web began in 1989 at CERN, the European Center for Nuclear Research. The initial idea was to help large teams, often with members in half a dozen or more countries and time zones, collaborate using a constantly changing collection of reports, blueprints, drawings, photos, and other documents produced by experiments in particle physics. The proposal for a web of linked documents came from CERN physicist Tim Berners-Lee. The first (text-based) prototype was operational 18 months later. A public demonstration given at the Hypertext '91 conference caught the attention of other researchers, which led Marc Andreessen at the University of Illinois to develop the first graphical browser. It was called Mosaic and released in February 1993.

The rest, as they say, is now history. Mosaic was so popular that a year later Andreessen left to form a company, Netscape Communications Corp., whose goal was to develop Web software. For the next three years, Netscape Navigator and Microsoft's Internet Explorer engaged in a "browser war," each one trying to capture a larger share of the new market by frantically adding more features (and thus more bugs) than the other one.

Through the 1990s and 2000s, Web sites and Web pages, as Web content is called, grew exponentially until there were millions of sites and billions of pages. A small number of these sites became tremendously popular. Those sites and the companies behind them largely define the Web as people experience it today. Examples include: a bookstore (Amazon, started in 1994, market capitalization $50 billion), a flea market (eBay, 1995, $30B), search (Google, 1998, $150B), and social networking (Facebook, 2004, private company valued at more than $15B). The period through 2000, when many Web companies became worth hundreds of millions of dollars overnight, only to go bust practically the next day when they turned out to be hype, even has a name. It is called the **dot com era**. New ideas are still striking it rich on the Web. Many of them come from students. For example, Mark Zuckerberg was a Harvard student when he started Facebook, and Sergey Brin and Larry Page were students at Stanford when they started Google. Perhaps you will come up with the next big thing.

In 1994, CERN and M.I.T. signed an agreement setting up the **W3C** (**World Wide Web Consortium**), an organization devoted to further developing the Web, standardizing protocols, and encouraging interoperability between sites. Berners-Lee became the director. Since then, several hundred universities and companies have joined the consortium. Although there are now more books about the Web than you can shake a stick at, the best place to get up-to-date information about the Web is (naturally) on the Web itself. The consortium's home page is at *www.w3.org*. Interested readers are referred there for links to pages covering all of the consortium's numerous documents and activities.

7.3.1 Architectural Overview

From the users' point of view, the Web consists of a vast, worldwide collection of content in the form of **Web pages**, often just called **pages** for short. Each page may contain links to other pages anywhere in the world. Users can follow a link by clicking on it, which then takes them to the page pointed to. This process can be repeated indefinitely. The idea of having one page point to another, now called **hypertext**, was invented by a visionary M.I.T. professor of electrical engineering, Vannevar Bush, in 1945 (Bush, 1945). This was long before the Internet was invented. In fact, it was before commercial computers existed although several universities had produced crude prototypes that filled large rooms and had less power than a modern pocket calculator.

Pages are generally viewed with a program called a **browser**. Firefox, Internet Explorer, and Chrome are examples of popular browsers. The browser fetches the page requested, interprets the content, and displays the page, properly formatted, on the screen. The content itself may be a mix of text, images, and formatting commands, in the manner of a traditional document, or other forms of content such as video or programs that produce a graphical interface with which users can interact.

A picture of a page is shown on the top-left side of Fig. 7-18. It is the page for the Computer Science & Engineering department at the University of Washington. This page shows text and graphical elements (that are mostly too small to read). Some parts of the page are associated with links to other pages. A piece of text, icon, image, and so on associated with another page is called a **hyperlink**. To follow a link, the user places the mouse cursor on the linked portion of the page area (which causes the cursor to change shape) and clicks. Following a link is simply a way of telling the browser to fetch another page. In the early days of the Web, links were highlighted with underlining and colored text so that they would stand out. Nowadays, the creators of Web pages have ways to control the look of linked regions, so a link might appear as an icon or change its appearance when the mouse passes over it. It is up to the creators of the page to make the links visually distinct, to provide a usable interface.

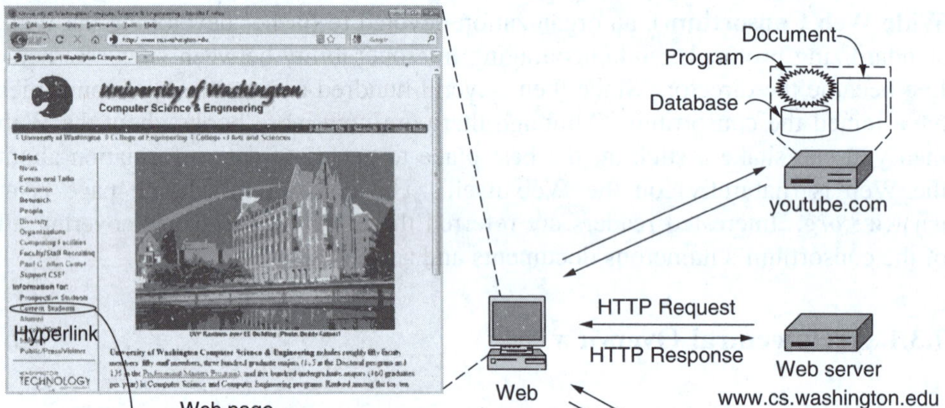

Figure 7-18. Architecture of the Web.

Students in the department can learn more by following a link to a page with information especially for them. This link is accessed by clicking in the circled area. The browser then fetches the new page and displays it, as partially shown in the bottom left of Fig. 7-18. Dozens of other pages are linked off the first page besides this example. Every other page can be comprised of content on the same machine(s) as the first page, or on machines halfway around the globe. The user cannot tell. Page fetching is done by the browser, without any help from the user. Thus, moving between machines while viewing content is seamless.

The basic model behind the display of pages is also shown in Fig. 7-18. The browser is displaying a Web page on the client machine. Each page is fetched by sending a request to one or more servers, which respond with the contents of the page. The request-response protocol for fetching pages is a simple text-based protocol that runs over TCP, just as was the case for SMTP. It is called **HTTP** (**HyperText Transfer Protocol**). The content may simply be a document that is read off a disk, or the result of a database query and program execution. The page is a **static page** if it is a document that is the same every time it is displayed. In contrast, if it was generated on demand by a program or contains a program it is a **dynamic page**.

A dynamic page may present itself differently each time it is displayed. For example, the front page for an electronic store may be different for each visitor. If a bookstore customer has bought mystery novels in the past, upon visiting the store's main page, the customer is likely to see new thrillers prominently displayed, whereas a more culinary-minded customer might be greeted with new cookbooks. How the Web site keeps track of who likes what is a story to be told shortly. But briefly, the answer involves cookies (even for culinarily challenged visitors).

In the figure, the browser contacts three servers to fetch the two pages, *cs.washington.edu*, *youtube.com*, and *google-analytics.com*. The content from these different servers is integrated for display by the browser. Display entails a range of processing that depends on the kind of content. Besides rendering text and graphics, it may involve playing a video or running a script that presents its own user interface as part of the page. In this case, the *cs.washington.edu* server supplies the main page, the *youtube.com* server supplies an embedded video, and the *google-analytics.com* server supplies nothing that the user can see but tracks visitors to the site. We will have more to say about trackers later.

The Client Side

Let us now examine the Web browser side in Fig. 7-18 in more detail. In essence, a browser is a program that can display a Web page and catch mouse clicks to items on the displayed page. When an item is selected, the browser follows the hyperlink and fetches the page selected.

When the Web was first created, it was immediately apparent that having one page point to another Web page required mechanisms for naming and locating pages. In particular, three questions had to be answered before a selected page could be displayed:

1. What is the page called?
2. Where is the page located?
3. How can the page be accessed?

If every page were somehow assigned a unique name, there would not be any ambiguity in identifying pages. Nevertheless, the problem would not be solved. Consider a parallel between people and pages. In the United States, almost everyone has a social security number, which is a unique identifier, as no two people are supposed to have the same one. Nevertheless, if you are armed only with a social security number, there is no way to find the owner's address, and certainly no way to tell whether you should write to the person in English, Spanish, or Chinese. The Web has basically the same problems.

The solution chosen identifies pages in a way that solves all three problems at once. Each page is assigned a **URL** (**Uniform Resource Locator**) that effectively serves as the page's worldwide name. URLs have three parts: the protocol (also known as the **scheme**), the DNS name of the machine on which the page is located, and the path uniquely indicating the specific page (a file to read or program to run on the machine). In the general case, the path has a hierarchical name that models a file directory structure. However, the interpretation of the path is up to the server; it may or may not reflect the actual directory structure.

As an example, the URL of the page shown in Fig. 7-18 is

http://www.cs.washington.edu/index.html

This URL consists of three parts: the protocol (*http*), the DNS name of the host (*www.cs.washington.edu*), and the path name (*index.html*).

When a user clicks on a hyperlink, the browser carries out a series of steps in order to fetch the page pointed to. Let us trace the steps that occur when our example link is selected:

1. The browser determines the URL (by seeing what was selected).
2. The browser asks DNS for the IP address of the server *www.cs.washington.edu*.
3. DNS replies with 128.208.3.88.
4. The browser makes a TCP connection to 128.208.3.88 on port 80, the well-known port for the HTTP protocol.
5. It sends over an HTTP request asking for the page */index.html*.

6. The *www.cs.washington.edu* server sends the page as an HTTP response, for example, by sending the file */index.html*.
7. If the page includes URLs that are needed for display, the browser fetches the other URLs using the same process. In this case, the URLs include multiple embedded images also fetched from *www.cs.washington.edu*, an embedded video from *youtube.com*, and a script from *google-analytics.com*.
8. The browser displays the page */index.html* as it appears in Fig. 7-18.
9. The TCP connections are released if there are no other requests to the same servers for a short period.

Many browsers display which step they are currently executing in a status line at the bottom of the screen. In this way, when the performance is poor, the user can see if it is due to DNS not responding, a server not responding, or simply page transmission over a slow or congested network.

The URL design is open-ended in the sense that it is straightforward to have browsers use multiple protocols to get at different kinds of resources. In fact, URLs for various other protocols have been defined. Slightly simplified forms of the common ones are listed in Fig. 7-19.

Name	Used for	Example
http	Hypertext (HTML)	http://www.ee.uwa.edu/~rob/
https	Hypertext with security	https://www.bank.com/accounts/
ftp	FTP	ftp://ftp.cs.vu.nl/pub/minix/README
file	Local file	file:///usr/suzanne/prog.c
mailto	Sending email	mailto:JohnUser@acm.org
rtsp	Streaming media	rtsp://youtube.com/montypython.mpg
sip	Multimedia calls	sip:eve@adversary.com
about	Browser information	about:plugins

Figure 7-19. Some common URL schemes.

Let us briefly go over the list. The *http* protocol is the Web's native language, the one spoken by Web servers. **HTTP** stands for **HyperText Transfer Protocol**. We will examine it in more detail later in this section.

The *ftp* protocol is used to access files by FTP, the Internet's file transfer protocol. FTP predates the Web and has been in use for more than three decades. The Web makes it easy to obtain files placed on numerous FTP servers throughout the world by providing a simple, clickable interface instead of a command-line interface. This improved access to information is one reason for the spectacular growth of the Web.

It is possible to access a local file as a Web page by using the *file* protocol, or more simply, by just naming it. This approach does not require having a server. Of course, it works only for local files, not remote ones.

The *mailto* protocol does not really have the flavor of fetching Web pages, but is useful anyway. It allows users to send email from a Web browser. Most browsers will respond when a *mailto* link is followed by starting the user's mail agent to compose a message with the address field already filled in.

The *rtsp* and *sip* protocols are for establishing streaming media sessions and audio and video calls.

Finally, the *about* protocol is a convention that provides information about the browser. For example, following the *about:plugins* link will cause most browsers to show a page that lists the MIME types that they handle with browser extensions called plug-ins.

In short, the URLs have been designed not only to allow users to navigate the Web, but to run older protocols such as FTP and email as well as newer protocols for audio and video, and to provide convenient access to local files and browser information. This approach makes all the specialized user interface programs for those other services unnecessary and integrates nearly all Internet access into a single program: the Web browser. If it were not for the fact that this idea was thought of by a British physicist working a research lab in Switzerland, it could easily pass for a plan dreamed up by some software company's advertising department.

Despite all these nice properties, the growing use of the Web has turned up an inherent weakness in the URL scheme. A URL points to one specific host, but sometimes it is useful to reference a page without simultaneously telling where it is. For example, for pages that are heavily referenced, it is desirable to have multiple copies far apart, to reduce the network traffic. There is no way to say: "I want page *xyz*, but I do not care where you get it."

To solve this kind of problem, URLs have been generalized into **URIs** (**Uniform Resource Identifiers**). Some URIs tell how to locate a resource. These are the URLs. Other URIs tell the name of a resource but not where to find it. These URIs are called **URNs** (**Uniform Resource Names**). The rules for writing URIs are given in RFC 3986, while the different URI schemes in use are tracked by IANA. There are many different kinds of URIs besides the schemes listed in Fig. 7-19, but those schemes dominate the Web as it is used today.

MIME Types

To be able to display the new page (or any page), the browser has to understand its format. To allow all browsers to understand all Web pages, Web pages are written in a standardized language called HTML. It is the lingua franca of the Web (for now). We will discuss it in detail later in this chapter.

Although a browser is basically an HTML interpreter, most browsers have numerous buttons and features to make it easier to navigate the Web. Most have a button for going back to the previous page, a button for going forward to the next page (only operative after the user has gone back from it), and a button for going straight to the user's preferred start page. Most browsers have a button or menu item to set a bookmark on a given page and another one to display the list of bookmarks, making it possible to revisit any of them with only a few mouse clicks.

As our example shows, HTML pages can contain rich content elements and not simply text and hypertext. For added generality, not all pages need contain HTML. A page may consist of a video in MPEG format, a document in PDF format, a photograph in JPEG format, a song in MP3 format, or any one of hundreds of other file types. Since standard HTML pages may link to any of these, the browser has a problem when it hits a page it does not know how to interpret.

Rather than making the browsers larger and larger by building in interpreters for a rapidly growing collection of file types, most browsers have chosen a more general solution. When a server returns a page, it also returns some additional information about the page. This information includes the MIME type of the page (see Fig. 7-13). Pages of type *text/html* are just displayed directly, as are pages in a few other built-in types. If the MIME type is not one of the built-in ones, the browser consults its table of MIME types to determine how to display the page. This table associates MIME types with viewers.

There are two possibilities: plug-ins and helper applications. A **plug-in** is a third-party code module that is installed as an extension to the browser, as illustrated in Fig. 7-20(a). Common examples are plug-ins for PDF, Flash, and Quicktime to render documents and play audio and video. Because plug-ins run inside the browser, they have access to the current page and can modify its appearance.

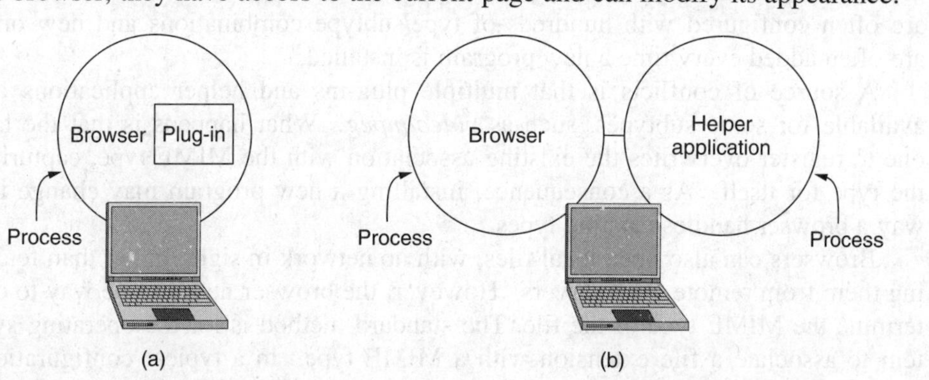

Figure 7-20. (a) A browser plug-in. (b) A helper application.

Each browser has a set of procedures that all plug-ins must implement so the browser can call the plug-ins. For example, there is typically a procedure the browser's base code calls to supply the plug-in with data to display. This set of procedures is the plug-in's interface and is browser specific.

In addition, the browser makes a set of its own procedures available to the plug-in, to provide services to plug-ins. Typical procedures in the browser interface are for allocating and freeing memory, displaying a message on the browser's status line, and querying the browser about parameters.

Before a plug-in can be used, it must be installed. The usual installation procedure is for the user to go to the plug-in's Web site and download an installation file. Executing the installation file unpacks the plug-in and makes the appropriate calls to register the plug-in's MIME type with the browser and associate the plug-in with it. Browsers usually come preloaded with popular plug-ins.

The other way to extend a browser is make use of a **helper application**. This is a complete program, running as a separate process. It is illustrated in Fig. 7-20(b). Since the helper is a separate program, the interface is at arm's length from the browser. It usually just accepts the name of a scratch file where the content file has been stored, opens the file, and displays the contents. Typically, helpers are large programs that exist independently of the browser, for example, Microsoft Word or PowerPoint.

Many helper applications use the MIME type *application*. As a consequence, a considerable number of subtypes have been defined for them to use, for example, *application/vnd.ms-powerpoint* for PowerPoint files. *vnd* denotes vendor-specific formats. In this way, a URL can point directly to a PowerPoint file, and when the user clicks on it, PowerPoint is automatically started and handed the content to be displayed. Helper applications are not restricted to using the *application* MIME type.. Adobe Photoshop uses *image/x-photoshop*, for example.

Consequently, browsers can be configured to handle a virtually unlimited number of document types with no changes to themselves. Modern Web servers are often configured with hundreds of type/subtype combinations and new ones are often added every time a new program is installed.

A source of conflicts is that multiple plug-ins and helper applications are available for some subtypes, such as *video/mpeg*. What happens is that the last one to register overwrites the existing association with the MIME type, capturing the type for itself. As a consequence, installing a new program may change the way a browser handles existing types.

Browsers can also open local files, with no network in sight, rather than fetching them from remote Web servers. However, the browser needs some way to determine the MIME type of the file. The standard method is for the operating system to associate a file extension with a MIME type. In a typical configuration, opening *foo.pdf* will open it in the browser using an *application/pdf* plug-in and opening *bar.doc* will open it in Word as the *application/msword* helper.

Here, too, conflicts can arise, since many programs are willing—no, make that eager—to handle, say, mpg. During installation, programs intended for sophisticated users often display checkboxes for the MIME types and extensions they are prepared to handle to allow the user to select the appropriate ones and thus not overwrite existing associations by accident. Programs aimed at the consumer market assume that the user does not have a clue what a MIME type is and simply grab everything they can without regard to what previously installed programs have done.

The ability to extend the browser with a large number of new types is convenient but can also lead to trouble. When a browser on a Windows PC fetches a file with the extension *exe*, it realizes that this file is an executable program and therefore has no helper. The obvious action is to run the program. However, this could be an enormous security hole. All a malicious Web site has to do is produce a Web page with pictures of, say, movie stars or sports heroes, all of which are linked to a virus. A single click on a picture then causes an unknown and potentially hostile executable program to be fetched and run on the user's machine. To prevent unwanted guests like this, Firefox and other browsers come configured to be cautious about running unknown programs automatically, but not all users understand what choices are safe rather than convenient.

The Server Side

So much for the client side. Now let us take a look at the server side. As we saw above, when the user types in a URL or clicks on a line of hypertext, the browser parses the URL and interprets the part between *http://* and the next slash as a DNS name to look up. Armed with the IP address of the server, the browser establishes a TCP connection to port 80 on that server. Then it sends over a command containing the rest of the URL, which is the path to the page on that server. The server then returns the page for the browser to display.

To a first approximation, a simple Web server is similar to the server of Fig. 6-6. That server is given the name of a file to look up and return via the network. In both cases, the steps that the server performs in its main loop are:

1. Accept a TCP connection from a client (a browser).
2. Get the path to the page, which is the name of the file requested.
3. Get the file (from disk).
4. Send the contents of the file to the client.
5. Release the TCP connection.

Modern Web servers have more features, but in essence, this is what a Web server does for the simple case of content that is contained in a file. For dynamic content, the third step may be replaced by the execution of a program (determined from the path) that returns the contents.

However, Web servers are implemented with a different design to serve many requests per second. One problem with the simple design is that accessing files is often the bottleneck. Disk reads are very slow compared to program execution, and the same files may be read repeatedly from disk using operating system calls. Another problem is that only one request is processed at a time. The file may be large, and other requests will be blocked while it is transferred.

One obvious improvement (used by all Web servers) is to maintain a cache in memory of the *n* most recently read files or a certain number of gigabytes of content. Before going to disk to get a file, the server checks the cache. If the file is there, it can be served directly from memory, thus eliminating the disk access. Although effective caching requires a large amount of main memory and some extra processing time to check the cache and manage its contents, the savings in time are nearly always worth the overhead and expense.

To tackle the problem of serving a single request at a time, one strategy is to make the server **multithreaded**. In one design, the server consists of a front-end module that accepts all incoming requests and *k* processing modules, as shown in Fig. 7-21. The $k + 1$ threads all belong to the same process, so the processing modules all have access to the cache within the process' address space. When a request comes in, the front end accepts it and builds a short record describing it. It then hands the record to one of the processing modules.

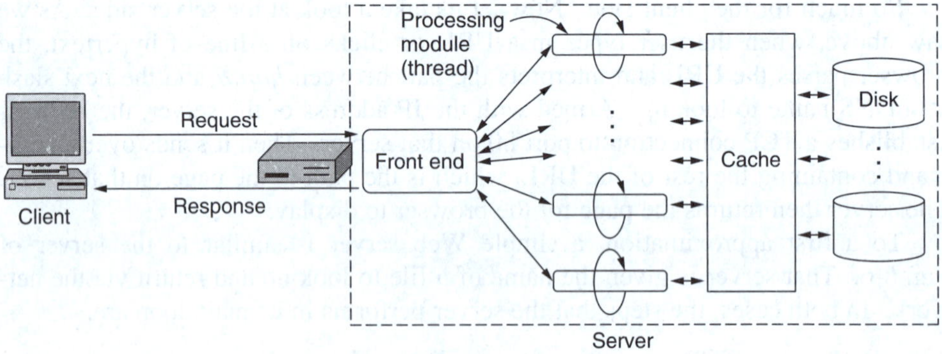

Figure 7-21. A multithreaded Web server with a front end and processing modules.

The processing module first checks the cache to see if the file needed is there. If so, it updates the record to include a pointer to the file in the record. If it is not there, the processing module starts a disk operation to read it into the cache (possibly discarding some other cached file(s) to make room for it). When the file comes in from the disk, it is put in the cache and also sent back to the client.

The advantage of this scheme is that while one or more processing modules are blocked waiting for a disk or network operation to complete (and thus consuming no CPU time), other modules can be actively working on other requests. With *k* processing modules, the throughput can be as much as *k* times higher than with a single-threaded server. Of course, when the disk or network is the limiting factor, it is necessary to have multiple disks or a faster network to get any real improvement over the single-threaded model.

Modern Web servers do more than just accept path names and return files. In fact, the actual processing of each request can get quite complicated. For this reason, in many servers each processing module performs a series of steps. The front end passes each incoming request to the first available module, which then carries it out using some subset of the following steps, depending on which ones are needed for that particular request. These steps occur after the TCP connection and any secure transport mechanism (such as SSL/TLS, which will be described in Chap. 8) have been established.

1. Resolve the name of the Web page requested.
2. Perform access control on the Web page.
3. Check the cache.
4. Fetch the requested page from disk or run a program to build it.
5. Determine the rest of the response (e.g., the MIME type to send).
6. Return the response to the client.
7. Make an entry in the server log.

Step 1 is needed because the incoming request may not contain the actual name of a file or program as a literal string. It may contain built-in shortcuts that need to be translated. As a simple example, the URL *http://www.cs.vu.nl/* has an empty file name. It has to be expanded to some default file name that is usually *index.html*. Another common rule is to map *~user/* onto *user*'s Web directory. These rules can be used together. Thus, the home page of one of the authors (AST) can be reached at

http://www.cs.vu.nl/~ast/

even though the actual file name is *index.html* in a certain default directory.

Also, modern browsers can specify configuration information such as the browser software and the user's default language (e.g., Italian or English). This makes it possible for the server to select a Web page with small pictures for a mobile device and in the preferred language, if available. In general, name expansion is not quite so trivial as it might at first appear, due to a variety of conventions about how to map paths to the file directory and programs.

Step 2 checks to see if any access restrictions associated with the page are met. Not all pages are available to the general public. Determining whether a client can fetch a page may depend on the identity of the client (e.g., as given by usernames and passwords) or the location of the client in the DNS or IP space. For example, a page may be restricted to users inside a company. How this is accomplished depends on the design of the server. For the popular Apache server, for instance, the convention is to place a file called *.htaccess* that lists the access restrictions in the directory where the restricted page is located.

Steps 3 and 4 involve getting the page. Whether it can be taken from the cache depends on processing rules. For example, pages that are created by running programs cannot always be cached because they might produce a different result each time they are run. Even files should occasionally be checked to see if their contents have changed so that the old contents can be removed from the cache. If the page requires a program to be run, there is also the issue of setting the program parameters or input. These data come from the path or other parts of the request.

Step 5 is about determining other parts of the response that accompany the contents of the page. The MIME type is one example. It may come from the file extension, the first few words of the file or program output, a configuration file, and possibly other sources.

Step 6 is returning the page across the network. To increase performance, a single TCP connection may be used by a client and server for multiple page fetches. This reuse means that some logic is needed to map a request to a shared connection and to return each response so that it is associated with the correct request.

Step 7 makes an entry in the system log for administrative purposes, along with keeping any other important statistics. Such logs can later be mined for valuable information about user behavior, for example, the order in which people access the pages.

Cookies

Navigating the Web as we have described it so far involves a series of independent page fetches. There is no concept of a login session. The browser sends a request to a server and gets back a file. Then the server forgets that it has ever seen that particular client.

This model is perfectly adequate for retrieving publicly available documents, and it worked well when the Web was first created. However, it is not suited for returning different pages to different users depending on what they have already done with the server. This behavior is needed for many ongoing interactions with Web sites. For example, some Web sites (e.g., newspapers) require clients to register (and possibly pay money) to use them. This raises the question of how servers can distinguish between requests from users who have previously registered and everyone else. A second example is from e-commerce. If a user wanders around an electronic store, tossing items into her virtual shopping cart from time to time, how does the server keep track of the contents of the cart? A third example is customized Web portals such as Yahoo!. Users can set up a personalized detailed initial page with only the information they want (e.g., their stocks and their favorite sports teams), but how can the server display the correct page if it does not know who the user is?

At first glance, one might think that servers could track users by observing their IP addresses. However, this idea does not work. Many users share computers, especially at home, and the IP address merely identifies the computer, not the user. Even worse, many companies use NAT, so that outgoing packets bear the same IP address for all users. That is, all of the computers behind the NAT box look the same to the server. And many ISPs assign IP addresses to customers with DHCP. The IP addresses change over time, so to a server you might suddenly look like your neighbor. For all of these reasons, the server cannot use IP addresses to track users.

This problem is solved with an oft-critized mechanism called **cookies**. The name derives from ancient programmer slang in which a program calls a procedure and gets something back that it may need to present later to get some work done. In this sense, a UNIX file descriptor or a Windows object handle can be considered to be a cookie. Cookies were first implemented in the Netscape browser in 1994 and are now specified in RFC 2109.

When a client requests a Web page, the server can supply additional information in the form of a cookie along with the requested page. The cookie is a rather small, named string (of at most 4 KB) that the server can associate with a browser. This association is not the same thing as a user, but it is much closer and more useful than an IP address. Browsers store the offered cookies for an interval, usually in a cookie directory on the client's disk so that the cookies persist across browser invocations, unless the user has disabled cookies. Cookies are just strings, not executable programs. In principle, a cookie could contain a virus, but since cookies are treated as data, there is no official way for the virus to actually run and do damage. However, it is always possible for some hacker to exploit a browser bug to cause activation.

A cookie may contain up to five fields, as shown in Fig. 7-22. The *Domain* tells where the cookie came from. Browsers are supposed to check that servers are not lying about their domain. Each domain should store no more than 20 cookies per client. The *Path* is a path in the server's directory structure that identifies which parts of the server's file tree may use the cookie. It is often /, which means the whole tree.

The *Content* field takes the form *name* = *value*. Both *name* and *value* can be anything the server wants. This field is where the cookie's content is stored.

The *Expires* field specifies when the cookie expires. If this field is absent, the browser discards the cookie when it exits. Such a cookie is called a **nonpersistent cookie**. If a time and date are supplied, the cookie is said to be a **persistent cookie** and is kept until it expires. Expiration times are given in Greenwich Mean Time. To remove a cookie from a client's hard disk, a server just sends it again, but with an expiration time in the past.

Domain	Path	Content	Expires	Secure
toms-casino.com	/	CustomerID=297793521	15-10-10 17:00	Yes
jills-store.com	/	Cart=1-00501;1-07031;2-13721	11-1-11 14:22	No
aportal.com	/	Prefs=Stk:CSCO+ORCL;Spt:Jets	31-12-20 23:59	No
sneaky.com	/	UserID=4627239101	31-12-19 23:59	No

Figure 7-22. Some examples of cookies.

Finally, the *Secure* field can be set to indicate that the browser may only return the cookie to a server using a secure transport, namely SSL/TLS (which we will describe in Chap. 8). This feature is used for e-commerce, banking, and other secure applications.

We have now seen how cookies are acquired, but how are they used? Just before a browser sends a request for a page to some Web site, it checks its cookie directory to see if any cookies there were placed by the domain the request is going to. If so, all the cookies placed by that domain, and only that domain, are included in the request message. When the server gets them, it can interpret them any way it wants to.

Let us examine some possible uses for cookies. In Fig. 7-22, the first cookie was set by *toms-casino.com* and is used to identify the customer. When the client returns next week to throw away some more money, the browser sends over the cookie so the server knows who it is. Armed with the customer ID, the server can look up the customer's record in a database and use this information to build an appropriate Web page to display. Depending on the customer's known gambling habits, this page might consist of a poker hand, a listing of today's horse races, or a slot machine.

The second cookie came from *jills-store.com*. The scenario here is that the client is wandering around the store, looking for good things to buy. When she finds a bargain and clicks on it, the server adds it to her shopping cart (maintained on the server) and also builds a cookie containing the product code of the item and sends the cookie back to the client. As the client continues to wander around the store by clicking on new pages, the cookie is returned to the server on every new page request. As more purchases accumulate, the server adds them to the cookie. Finally, when the client clicks on PROCEED TO CHECKOUT, the cookie, now containing the full list of purchases, is sent along with the request. In this way, the server knows exactly what the customer wants to buy.

The third cookie is for a Web portal. When the customer clicks on a link to the portal, the browser sends over the cookie. This tells the portal to build a page containing the stock prices for Cisco and Oracle, and the New York Jets' football results. Since a cookie can be up to 4 KB, there is plenty of room for more detailed preferences concerning newspaper headlines, local weather, special offers, etc.

A more controversial use of cookies is to track the online behavior of users. This lets Web site operators understand how users navigate their sites, and advertisers build up profiles of the ads or sites a particular user has viewed. The controversy is that users are typically unaware that their activity is being tracked, even with detailed profiles and across seemingly unrelated Web sites. Nonetheless, **Web tracking** is big business. DoubleClick, which provides and tracks ads, is ranked among the 100 busiest Web sites in the world by the Web monitoring company Alexa. Google Analytics, which tracks site usage for operators, is used by more than half of the busiest 100,000 sites on the Web.

It is easy for a server to track user activity with cookies. Suppose a server wants to keep track of how many unique visitors it has had and how many pages each visitor looked at before leaving the site. When the first request comes in, there will be no accompanying cookie, so the server sends back a cookie containing *Counter = 1*. Subsequent page views on that site will send the cookie back to the server. Each time the counter is incremented and sent back to the client. By keeping track of the counters, the server can see how many people give up after seeing the first page, how many look at two pages, and so on.

Tracking the browsing behavior of users across sites is only slightly more complicated. It works like this. An advertising agency, say, Sneaky Ads, contacts major Web sites and places ads for its clients' products on their pages, for which it pays the site owners a fee. Instead, of giving the sites the ad as a GIF file to place on each page, it gives them a URL to add to each page. Each URL it hands out contains a unique number in the path, such as

```
http://www.sneaky.com/382674902342.gif
```

When a user first visits a page, *P*, containing such an ad, the browser fetches the HTML file. Then the browser inspects the HTML file and sees the link to the image file at *www.sneaky.com*, so it sends a request there for the image. A GIF file containing an ad is returned, along with a cookie containing a unique user ID, 4627239101 in Fig. 7-22. Sneaky records the fact that the user with this ID visited page *P*. This is easy to do since the path requested (*382674902342.gif*) is referenced only on page *P*. Of course, the actual ad may appear on thousands of pages, but each time with a different name. Sneaky probably collects a fraction of a penny from the product manufacturer each time it ships out the ad.

Later, when the user visits another Web page containing any of Sneaky's ads, the browser first fetches the HTML file from the server. Then it sees the link to, say, *http://www.sneaky.com/193654919923.gif* on the page and requests that file. Since it already has a cookie from the domain *sneaky.com*, the browser includes Sneaky's cookie containing the user's ID. Sneaky now knows a second page the user has visited.

In due course, Sneaky can build up a detailed profile of the user's browsing habits, even though the user has never clicked on any of the ads. Of course, it does not yet have the user's name (although it does have his IP address, which may be enough to deduce the name from other databases). However, if the user ever supplies his name to any site cooperating with Sneaky, a complete profile along with a name will be available for sale to anyone who wants to buy it. The sale of this information may be profitable enough for Sneaky to place more ads on more Web sites and thus collect more information.

And if Sneaky wants to be supersneaky, the ad need not be a classical banner ad. An "ad" consisting of a single pixel in the background color (and thus invisible) has exactly the same effect as a banner ad: it requires the browser to go fetch the 1×1-pixel GIF image and send it all cookies originating at the pixel's domain.

Cookies have become a focal point for the debate over online privacy because of tracking behavior like the above. The most insidious part of the whole business is that many users are completely unaware of this information collection and may even think they are safe because they do not click on any of the ads. For this reason, cookies that track users across sites are considered by many to be **spyware**. Have a look at the cookies that are already stored by your browser. Most browsers will display this information along with the current privacy preferences. You might be surprised to find names, email addresses, or passwords as well as opaque identifiers. Hopefully, you will not find credit card numbers, but the potential for abuse is clear.

To maintain a semblance of privacy, some users configure their browsers to reject all cookies. However, this can cause problems because many Web sites will not work properly without cookies. Alternatively, most browsers let users block **third-party cookies**. A third-party cookie is one from a different site than the main page that is being fetched, for example, the *sneaky.com* cookie that is used when interacting with page *P* on a completely different Web site. Blocking these cookies helps to prevent tracking across Web sites. Browser extensions can also be installed to provide fine-grained control over how cookies are used (or, rather, not used). As the debate continues, many companies are developing privacy policies that limit how they will share information to prevent abuse. Of course, the policies are simply how the companies say they will handle information. For example: "We may use the information collected from you in the conduct of our business"—which might be selling the information.

7.3.2 Static Web Pages

The basis of the Web is transferring Web pages from server to client. In the simplest form, Web pages are static. That is, they are just files sitting on some server that present themselves in the same way each time they are fetched and viewed. Just because they are static does not mean that the pages are inert at the browser, however. A page containing a video can be a static Web page.

As mentioned earlier, the lingua franca of the Web, in which most pages are written, is HTML. The home pages of teachers are usually static HTML pages.

The home pages of companies are usually dynamic pages put together by a Web design company. In this section, we will take a brief look at static HTML pages as a foundation for later material. Readers already familiar with HTML can skip ahead to the next section, where we describe dynamic content and Web services.

HTML—The HyperText Markup Language

HTML (**HyperText Markup Language**) was introduced with the Web. It allows users to produce Web pages that include text, graphics, video, pointers to other Web pages, and more. HTML is a markup language, or language for describing how documents are to be formatted. The term "markup" comes from the old days when copyeditors actually marked up documents to tell the printer—in those days, a human being—which fonts to use, and so on. Markup languages thus contain explicit commands for formatting. For example, in HTML, <b> **means start boldface mode, and** </b> means leave boldface mode. LaTeX and TeX are other examples of markup languages that are well known to most academic authors.

The key advantage of a markup language over one with no explicit markup is that it separates content from how it should be presented. Writing a browser is then straightforward: the browser simply has to understand the markup commands and apply them to the content. Embedding all the markup commands within each HTML file and standardizing them makes it possible for any Web browser to read and reformat any Web page. That is crucial because a page may have been produced in a 1600×1200 window with 24-bit color on a high-end computer but may have to be displayed in a 640×320 window on a mobile phone.

While it is certainly possible to write documents like this with any plain text editor, and many people do, it is also possible to use word processors or special HTML editors that do most of the work (but correspondingly give the user less direct control over the details of the final result).

A simple Web page written in HTML and its presentation in a browser are given in Fig. 7-23. A Web page consists of a head and a body, each enclosed by <html> and </html> **tags** (formatting commands), although most browsers do not complain if these tags are missing. As can be seen in Fig. 7-23(a), the head is bracketed by the <head> and </head> tags and the body is bracketed by the <body> and </body> tags. The strings inside the tags are called **directives**. Most, but not all, HTML tags have this format. That is, they use <something> to mark the beginning of something and </something> to mark its end.

Tags can be in either lowercase or uppercase. Thus, <head> and <HEAD> mean the same thing, but lower case is best for compatibility. Actual layout of the HTML document is irrelevant. HTML parsers ignore extra spaces and carriage returns since they have to reformat the text to make it fit the current display area. Consequently, white space can be added at will to make HTML documents more readable, something most of them are badly in need of. As another consequence, blank lines cannot be used to separate paragraphs, as they are simply ignored. An explicit tag is required.

Some tags have (named) parameters, called **attributes**. For example, the <img> tag in Fig. 7-23 is used for including an image inline with the text. It has two attributes, src and alt. The first attribute gives the URL for the image. The HTML standard does not specify which image formats are permitted. In practice, all browsers support GIF and JPEG files. Browsers are free to support other formats, but this extension is a two-edged sword. If a user is accustomed to a browser that supports, say, TIFF files, he may include these in his Web pages and later be surprised when other browsers just ignore all of his wonderful art.

The second attribute gives alternate text to use if the image cannot be displayed. For each tag, the HTML standard gives a list of what the permitted parameters, if any, are, and what they mean. Because each parameter is named, the order in which the parameters are given is not significant.

Technically, HTML documents are written in the ISO 8859-1 Latin-1 character set, but for users whose keyboards support only ASCII, escape sequences are present for the special characters, such as è. The list of special characters is given in the standard. All of them begin with an ampersand and end with a semicolon. For example,   produces a space, è produces è and é produces é. Since <, >, and & have special meanings, they can be expressed only with their escape sequences, <, >, and &, respectively.

The main item in the head is the title, delimited by <title> and </title>. Certain kinds of metainformation may also be present, though none are present in our example. The title itself is not displayed on the page. Some browsers use it to label the page's window.

Several headings are used in Fig. 7-23. Each heading is generated by an <h*n*> tag, where *n* is a digit in the range 1 to 6. Thus, <h1> is the most important heading; <h6> is the least important one. It is up to the browser to render these appropriately on the screen. Typically, the lower-numbered headings will be displayed in a larger and heavier font. The browser may also choose to use different colors for each level of heading. Usually, <h1> headings are large and boldface with at least one blank line above and below. In contrast, <h2> headings are in a smaller font with less space above and below.

The tags <b> and <i> are used to enter boldface and italics mode, respectively. The <hr> tag forces a break and draws a horizontal line across the display.

The <p> tag starts a paragraph. The browser might display this by inserting a blank line and some indentation, for example. Interestingly, the </p> tag that exists to mark the end of a paragraph is often omitted by lazy HTML programmers.

HTML provides various mechanisms for making lists, including nested lists. Unordered lists, like the ones in Fig. 7-23 are started with <ul>, with <li> used to mark the start of items. There is also an <ol> tag to starts an ordered list. The

```
<html>
<head> <title> AMALGAMATED WIDGET, INC. </title> </head>
<body> <h1> Welcome to AWI's Home Page </h1>
<img src="http://www.widget.com/images/logo.gif" ALT="AWI Logo"> <br>
We are so happy that you have chosen to visit <b> Amalgamated Widget's</b>
home page. We hope <i> you </i> will find all the information you need here.
<p>Below we have links to information about our many fine products.
You can order electronically (by WWW), by telephone, or by email. </p>
<hr>
<h2> Product information </h2>
<ul>
  <li> <a href="http://widget.com/products/big"> Big widgets </a> </li>
  <li> <a href="http://widget.com/products/little"> Little widgets </a> </li>
</ul>
<h2> Contact information </h2>
<ul>
  <li> By telephone: 1-800-WIDGETS </li>
  <li> By email: info@amalgamated-widget.com </li>
</ul>
</body>
</html>
```

(a)

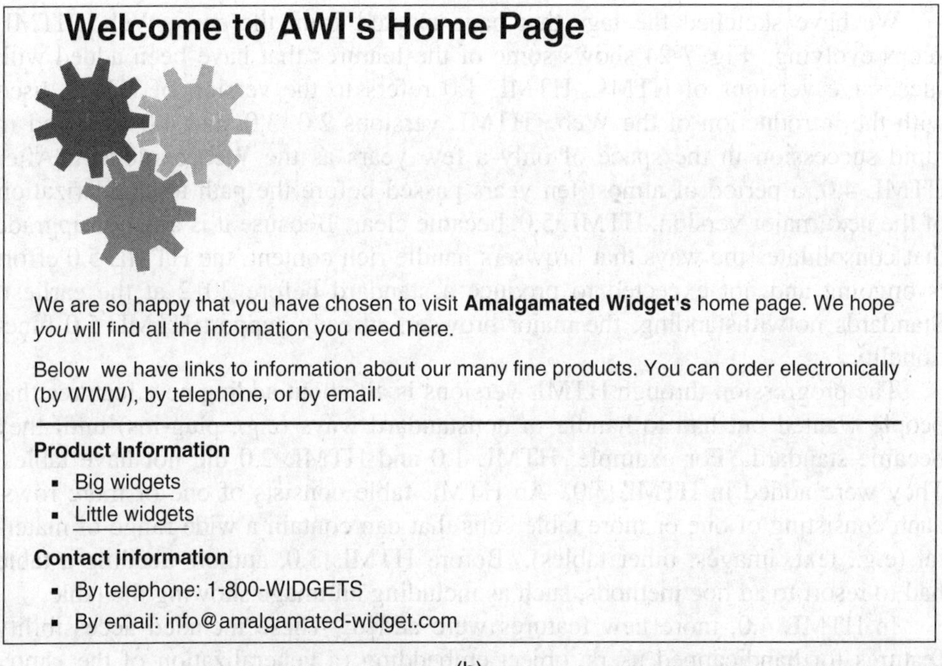

(b)

Figure 7-23. (a) The HTML for a sample Web page. (b) The formatted page.

individual items in unordered lists often appear with bullets (•) in front of them. Items in ordered lists are numbered by the browser.

Finally, we come to hyperlinks. Examples of these are seen in Fig. 7-23 using the <a> (anchor) and </a> tags. The <a> tag has various parameters, the most important of which is *href* the linked URL. The text between the <a> and </a> is displayed. If it is selected, the hyperlink is followed to a new page. It is also permitted to link other elements. For example, an image can be given between the <a> and </a> tags using <img>. In this case, the image is displayed and clicking on it activates the hyperlink.

There are many other HTML tags and attributes that we have not seen in this simple example. For instance, the <a> tag can take a parameter *name* to plant a hyperlink, allowing a hyperlink to point to the middle of a page. This is useful, for example, for Web pages that start out with a clickable table of contents. By clicking on an item in the table of contents, the user jumps to the corresponding section of the same page. An example of a different tag is <br>. It forces the browser to break and start a new line.

Probably the best way to understand tags is to look at them in action. To do this, you can pick a Web page and look at the HTML in your browser to see how the page was put together. Most browsers have a VIEW SOURCE menu item (or something similar). Selecting this item displays the current page's HTML source, instead of its formatted output.

We have sketched the tags that have existed from the early Web. HTML keeps evolving. Fig. 7-24 shows some of the features that have been added with successive versions of HTML. HTML 1.0 refers to the version of HTML used with the introduction of the Web. HTML versions 2.0, 3.0, and 4.0 appeared in rapid succession in the space of only a few years as the Web exploded. After HTML 4.0, a period of almost ten years passed before the path to standarization of the next major version, HTML 5.0, became clear. Because it is a major upgrade that consolidates the ways that browsers handle rich content, the HTML 5.0 effort is ongoing and not expected to produce a standard before 2012 at the earliest. Standards notwithstanding, the major browsers already support HTML 5.0 functionality.

The progression through HTML versions is all about adding new features that people wanted but had to handle in nonstandard ways (e.g., plug-ins) until they became standard. For example, HTML 1.0 and HTML 2.0 did not have tables. They were added in HTML 3.0. An HTML table consists of one or more rows, each consisting of one or more table cells that can contain a wide range of material (e.g., text, images, other tables). Before HTML 3.0, authors needing a table had to resort to ad hoc methods, such as including an image showing the table.

In HTML 4.0, more new features were added. These included accessibility features for handicapped users, object embedding (a generalization of the <img> tag so other objects can also be embedded in pages), support for scripting languages (to allow dynamic content), and more.

Item	HTML 1.0	HTML 2.0	HTML 3.0	HTML 4.0	HTML 5.0
Hyperlinks	x	x	x	x	x
Images	x	x	x	x	x
Lists	x	x	x	x	x
Active maps & images		x	x	x	x
Forms		x	x	x	x
Equations			x	x	x
Toolbars			x	x	x
Tables			x	x	x
Accessibility features				x	x
Object embedding				x	x
Style sheets				x	x
Scripting				x	x
Video and audio					x
Inline vector graphics					x
XML representation					x
Background threads					x
Browser storage					x
Drawing canvas					x

Figure 7-24. Some differences between HTML versions.

HTML 5.0 includes many features to handle the rich media that are now routinely used on the Web. Video and audio can be included in pages and played by the browser without requiring the user to install plug-ins. Drawings can be built up in the browser as vector graphics, rather than using bitmap image formats (like JPEG and GIF) There is also more support for running scripts in browsers, such as background threads of computation and access to storage. All of these features help to support Web pages that are more like traditional applications with a user interface than documents. This is the direction the Web is heading.

Input and Forms

There is one important capability that we have not discussed yet: input. HTML 1.0 was basically one-way. Users could fetch pages from information providers, but it was difficult to send information back the other way. It quickly became apparent that there was a need for two-way traffic to allow orders for products to be placed via Web pages, registration cards to be filled out online, search terms to be entered, and much, much more.

Sending input from the user to the server (via the browser) requires two kinds of support. First, it requires that HTTP be able to carry data in that direction. We describe how this is done in a later section; it uses the *POST* method. The second requirement is to be able to present user interface elements that gather and package up the input. **Forms** were included with this functionality in HTML 2.0.

Forms contain boxes or buttons that allow users to fill in information or make choices and then send the information back to the page's owner. Forms are written just like other parts of HTML, as seen in the example of Fig. 7-25. Note that forms are still static content. They exhibit the same behavior regardless of who is using them. Dynamic content, which we will cover later, provides more sophisticated ways to gather input by sending a program whose behavior may depend on the browser environment.

Like all forms, this one is enclosed between the <form> and </form> tags. The attributes of this tag tell what to do with the data that are input, in this case using the *POST* method to send the data to the specified URL. Text not enclosed in a tag is just displayed. All the usual tags (e.g., <b>) are allowed in a form to let the author of the page control the look of the form on the screen.

Three kinds of input boxes are used in this form, each of which uses the <input> tag. It has a variety of parameters for determining the size, nature, and usage of the box displayed. The most common forms are blank fields for accepting user text, boxes that can be checked, and *submit* buttons that cause the data to be returned to the server.

The first kind of input box is a *text* box that follows the text "Name". The box is 46 characters wide and expects the user to type in a string, which is then stored in the variable *customer*.

The next line of the form asks for the user's street address, 40 characters wide. Then comes a line asking for the city, state, and country. Since no <p> tags are used between these fields, the browser displays them all on one line (instead of as separate paragraphs) if they will fit. As far as the browser is concerned, the one paragraph contains just six items: three strings alternating with three boxes. The next line asks for the credit card number and expiration date. Transmitting credit card numbers over the Internet should only be done when adequate security measures have been taken. We will discuss some of these in Chap. 8.

Following the expiration date, we encounter a new feature: radio buttons. These are used when a choice must be made among two or more alternatives. The intellectual model here is a car radio with half a dozen buttons for choosing stations. Clicking on one button turns off all the other ones in the same group. The visual presentation is up to the browser. Widget size also uses two radio buttons. The two groups are distinguished by their *name* parameter, not by static scoping using something like <radiobutton> ... </radiobutton>.

The *value* parameters are used to indicate which radio button was pushed. For example, depending on which credit card options the user has chosen, the variable *cc* will be set to either the string "mastercard" or the string "visacard".

```
<html>
<head> <title> AWI CUSTOMER ORDERING FORM </title> </head>
<body>
<h1> Widget Order Form </h1>
<form ACTION="http://widget.com/cgi-bin/order.cgi" method=POST>
<p> Name <input name="customer" size=46> </p>
<p> Street address <input name="address" size=40> </p>
<p> City <input name="city" size=20> State <input name="state" size =4>
Country <input name="country" size=10> </p>
<p> Credit card # <input name="cardno" size=10>
Expires <input name="expires" size=4>
M/C <input name="cc" type=radio value="mastercard">
VISA <input name="cc" type=radio value="visacard"> </p>
<p> Widget size Big <input name="product" type=radio value="expensive">
Little <input name="product" type=radio value="cheap">
Ship by express courier <input name="express" type=checkbox> </p>
<p><input type=submit value="Submit order"> </p>
Thank you for ordering an AWI widget, the best widget money can buy!
</form>
</body>
</html>
```

(a)

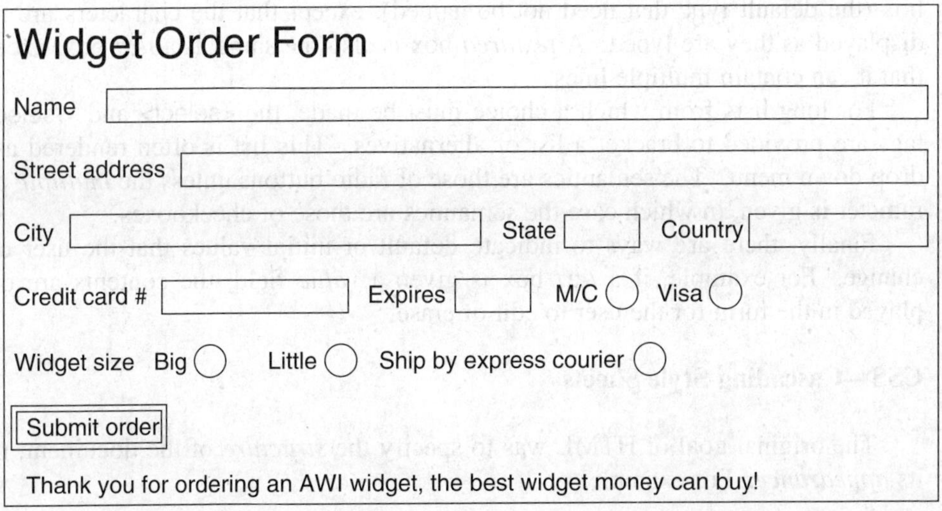

(b)

Figure 7-25. (a) The HTML for an order form. (b) The formatted page.

After the two sets of radio buttons, we come to the shipping option, represented by a box of type *checkbox*. It can be either on or off. Unlike radio buttons, where exactly one out of the set must be chosen, each box of type *checkbox* can be on or off, independently of all the others.

Finally, we come to the *submit* button. The *value* string is the label on the button and is displayed. When the user clicks the *submit* button, the browser packages the collected information into a single long line and sends it back to the server to the URL provided as part of the <form> tag. A simple encoding is used. The & is used to separate fields and + is used to represent space. For our example form, the line might look like the contents of Fig. 7-26.

```
customer=John+Doe&address=100+Main+St.&city=White+Plains&
state=NY&country=USA&cardno=1234567890&expires=6/14&cc=mastercard&
product=cheap&express=on
```

Figure 7-26. A possible response from the browser to the server with information filled in by the user.

The string is sent back to the server as one line. (It is broken into three lines here because the page is not wide enough.) It is up to the server to make sense of this string, most likely by passing the information to a program that will process it. We will discuss how this can be done in the next section.

There are also other types of input that are not shown in this simple example. Two other types are *password* and *textarea*. A *password* box is the same as a *text* box (the default type that need not be named), except that the characters are not displayed as they are typed. A *textarea* box is also the same as a *text* box, except that it can contain multiple lines.

For long lists from which a choice must be made, the <select> and </select> tags are provided to bracket a list of alternatives. This list is often rendered as a drop-down menu. The semantics are those of radio buttons unless the *multiple* parameter is given, in which case the semantics are those of checkboxes.

Finally, there are ways to indicate default or initial values that the user can change. For example, if a *text* box is given a *value* field, the contents are displayed in the form for the user to edit or erase.

CSS—Cascading Style Sheets

The original goal of HTML was to specify the *structure* of the document, not its *appearance*. For example,

```
<h1> Deborah's Photos </h1>
```

instructs the browser to emphasize the heading, but does not say anything about the typeface, point size, or color. That is left up to the browser, which knows the properties of the display (e.g., how many pixels it has). However, many Web page designers wanted absolute control over how their pages appeared, so new tags were added to HTML to control appearance, such as

```
<font face="helvetica" size="24" color="red"> Deborah's Photos </font>
```

Also, ways were added to control positioning on the screen accurately. The trouble with this approach is that it is tedious and produces bloated HTML that is not portable. Although a page may render perfectly in the browser it is developed on, it may be a complete mess in another browser or another release of the same browser or at a different screen resolution.

A better alternative is the use of style sheets. Style sheets in text editors allow authors to associate text with a logical style instead of a physical style, for example, "initial paragraph" instead of "italic text." The appearance of each style is defined separately. In this way, if the author decides to change the initial paragraphs from 14-point italics in blue to 18-point boldface in shocking pink, all it requires is changing one definition to convert the entire document.

CSS (**Cascading Style Sheets**) introduced style sheets to the Web with HTML 4.0, though widespread use and browser support did not take off until 2000. CSS defines a simple language for describing rules that control the appearance of tagged content. Let us look at an example. Suppose that AWI wants snazzy Web pages with navy text in the Arial font on an off-white background, and level headings that are an extra 100% and 50% larger than the text for each level, respectively. The CSS definition in Fig. 7-27 gives these rules.

```
body {background-color:linen; color:navy; font-family:Arial;}
h1 {font-size:200%;}
h2 {font-size:150%;}
```

Figure 7-27. CSS example.

As can be seen, the style definitions can be compact. Each line selects an element to which it applies and gives the values of properties. The properties of an element apply as defaults to all other HTML elements that it contains. Thus, the style for body sets the style for paragraphs of text in the body. There are also convenient shorthands for color names (e.g., red). Any style parameters that are not defined are filled with defaults by the browser. This behavior makes style sheet definitions optional; some reasonable presentation will occur without them.

Style sheets can be placed in an HTML file (e.g., using the <style> tag), but it is more common to place them in a separate file and reference them. For example, the <head> tag of the AWI page can be modified to refer to a style sheet in the file *awistyle.css* as shown in Fig. 7-28. The example also shows the MIME type of CSS files to be *text/css*.

```
<head>
<title> AMALGAMATED WIDGET, INC. </title>
<link rel="stylesheet" type="text/css" href="awistyle.css" />
</head>
```

Figure 7-28. Including a CSS style sheet.

This strategy has two advantages. First, it lets one set of styles be applied to many pages on a Web site. This organization lends a consistent appearance to pages even if they were developed by different authors at different times, and allows the look of the entire site to be changed by editing one CSS file and not the HTML. This method can be compared to an #include file in a C program: changing one macro definition there changes it in all the program files that include the header. The second advantage is that the HTML files that are downloaded are kept small. This is because the browser can download one copy of the CSS file for all pages that reference it. It does not need to download a new copy of the definitions along with each Web page.

7.3.3 Dynamic Web Pages and Web Applications

The static page model we have used so far treats pages as multimedia documents that are conveniently linked together. It was a fitting model in the early days of the Web, as vast amounts of information were put online. Nowadays, much of the excitement around the Web is using it for applications and services. Examples include buying products on e-commerce sites, searching library catalogs, exploring maps, reading and sending email, and collaborating on documents.

These new uses are like traditional application software (e.g., mail readers and word processors). The twist is that these applications run inside the browser, with user data stored on servers in Internet data centers. They use Web protocols to access information via the Internet, and the browser to display a user interface. The advantage of this approach is that users do not need to install separate application programs, and user data can be accessed from different computers and backed up by the service operator. It is proving so successful that it is rivaling traditional application software. Of course, the fact that these applications are offered for free by large providers helps. This model is the prevalent form of **cloud computing**, in which computing moves off individual desktop computers and into shared clusters of servers in the Internet.

To act as applications, Web pages can no longer be static. Dynamic content is needed. For example, a page of the library catalog should reflect which books are currently available and which books are checked out and are thus not available. Similarly, a useful stock market page would allow the user to interact with the page to see stock prices over different periods of time and compute profits and losses. As these examples suggest, dynamic content can be generated by programs running on the server or in the browser (or in both places).

In this section, we will examine each of these two cases in turn. The general situation is as shown in Fig. 7-29. For example, consider a map service that lets the user enter a street address and presents a corresponding map of the location. Given a request for a location, the Web server must use a program to create a page that shows the map for the location from a database of streets and other geographic information. This action is shown as steps 1 through 3. The request (step

1) causes a program to run on the server. The program consults a database to generate the appropriate page (step 2) and returns it to the browser (step 3).

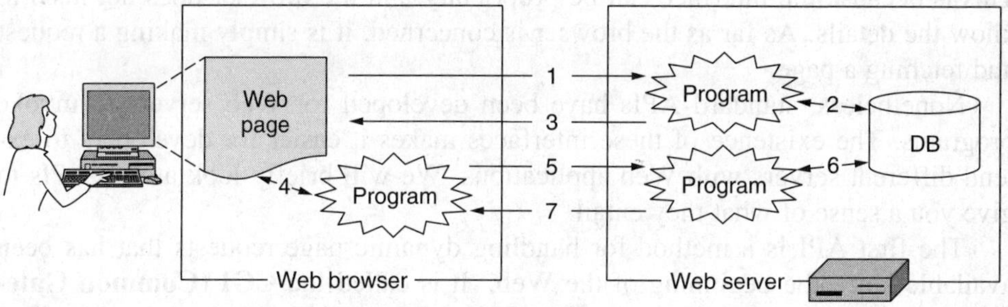

Figure 7-29. Dynamic pages.

There is more to dynamic content, however. The page that is returned may itself contain programs that run in the browser. In our map example, the program would let the user find routes and explore nearby areas at different levels of detail. It would update the page, zooming in or out as directed by the user (step 4). To handle some interactions, the program may need more data from the server. In this case, the program will send a request to the server (step 5) that will retrieve more information from the database (step 6) and return a response (step 7). The program will then continue updating the page (step 4). The requests and responses happen in the background; the user may not even be aware of them because the page URL and title typically do not change. By including client-side programs, the page can present a more responsive interface than with server-side programs alone.

Server-Side Dynamic Web Page Generation

Let us look at the case of server-side content generation in more detail. A simple situation in which server-side processing is necessary is the use of forms. Consider the user filling out the AWI order form of Fig. 7-25(b) and clicking the *Submit order* button. When the user clicks, a request is sent to the server at the URL specified with the form (a *POST* to *http://widget.com/cgi-bin/order.cgi* in this case) along with the contents of the form as filled in by the user. These data must be given to a program or script to process. Thus, the URL identifies the program to run; the data are provided to the program as input. In this case, processing would involve entering the order in AWI's internal system, updating customer records, and charging the credit card. The page returned by this request will depend on what happens during the processing. It is not fixed like a static page. If the order succeeds, the page returned might give the expected shipping date. If it is unsuccessful, the returned page might say that widgets requested are out of stock or the credit card was not valid for some reason.

Exactly how the server runs a program instead of retrieving a file depends on the design of the Web server. It is not specified by the Web protocols themselves. This is because the interface can be proprietary and the browser does not need to know the details. As far as the browser is concerned, it is simply making a request and fetching a page.

Nonetheless, standard APIs have been developed for Web servers to invoke programs. The existence of these interfaces makes it easier for developers to extend different servers with Web applications. We will briefly look at two APIs to give you a sense of what they entail.

The first API is a method for handling dynamic page requests that has been available since the beginning of the Web. It is called the **CGI** (**Common Gateway Interface**) and is defined in RFC 3875. CGI provides an interface to allow Web servers to talk to back-end programs and scripts that can accept input (e.g., from forms) and generate HTML pages in response. These programs may be written in whatever language is convenient for the developer, usually a scripting language for ease of development. Pick Python, Ruby, Perl or your favorite language.

By convention, programs invoked via CGI live in a directory called *cgi-bin*, which is visible in the URL. The server maps a request to this directory to a program name and executes that program as a separate process. It provides any data sent with the request as input to the program. The output of the program gives a Web page that is returned to the browser.

In our example, the program *order.cgi* is invoked with input from the form encoded as shown in Fig. 7-26. It will parse the parameters and process the order. A useful convention is that the program will return the HTML for the order form if no form input is provided. In this way, the program will be sure to know the representation of the form.

The second API we will look at is quite different. The approach here is to embed little scripts inside HTML pages and have them be executed by the server itself to generate the page. A popular language for writing these scripts is **PHP** (**PHP: Hypertext Preprocessor**). To use it, the server has to understand PHP, just as a browser has to understand CSS to interpret Web pages with style sheets. Usually, servers identify Web pages containing PHP from the file extension *php* rather than *html* or *htm*.

PHP is simpler to use than CGI. As an example of how it works with forms, see the example in Fig. 7-30(a). The top part of this figure contains a normal HTML page with a simple form in it. This time, the <form> tag specifies that *action.php* is to be invoked to handle the parameters when the user submits the form. The page displays two text boxes, one with a request for a name and one with a request for an age. After the two boxes have been filled in and the form submitted, the server parses the Fig. 7-26-type string sent back, putting the name in the *name* variable and the age in the *age* variable. It then starts to process the *action.php* file, shown in Fig. 7-30(b), as a reply. During the processing of this file, the PHP commands are executed. If the user filled in "Barbara" and "24" in the boxes, the HTML file sent back will be the one given in Fig. 7-30(c). Thus, handling forms becomes extremely simple using PHP.

```
<html>
<body>
<form action="action.php" method="post">
<p> Please enter your name: <input type="text" name="name"> </p>
<p> Please enter your age: <input type="text" name="age"> </p>
<input type="submit">
</form>
</body>
</html>
```

(a)

```
<html>
<body>
<h1> Reply: </h1>
Hello <?php echo $name; ?>.
Prediction: next year you will be <?php echo $age + 1; ?>
</body>
</html>
```

(b)

```
<html>
<body>
<h1> Reply: </h1>
Hello Barbara.
Prediction: next year you will be 33
</body>
</html>
```

(c)

Figure 7-30. (a) A Web page containing a form. (b) A PHP script for handling the output of the form. (c) Output from the PHP script when the inputs are "Barbara" and "32", respectively.

Although PHP is easy to use, it is actually a powerful programming language for interfacing the Web and a server database. It has variables, strings, arrays, and most of the control structures found in C, but much more powerful I/O than just *printf*. PHP is open source code, freely available, and widely used. It was designed specifically to work well with Apache, which is also open source and is the world's most widely used Web server. For more information about PHP, see Valade (2009).

We have now seen two different ways to generate dynamic HTML pages: CGI scripts and embedded PHP. There are several others to choose from. **JSP** (**JavaServer Pages**) is similar to PHP, except that the dynamic part is written in the Java programming language instead of in PHP. Pages using this technique have the file extension *.jsp*. **ASP.NET** (**Active Server Pages .NET**) is Microsoft's version of PHP and JavaServer Pages. It uses programs written in Microsoft's proprietary .NET networked application framework for generating the dynamic content. Pages using this technique have the extension *.aspx*. The choice among these three techniques usually has more to do with politics (open source vs. Microsoft) than with technology, since the three languages are roughly comparable.

Client-Side Dynamic Web Page Generation

PHP and CGI scripts solve the problem of handling input and interactions with databases on the server. They can all accept incoming information from forms, look up information in one or more databases, and generate HTML pages with the results. What none of them can do is respond to mouse movements or interact with users directly. For this purpose, it is necessary to have scripts embedded in HTML pages that are executed on the client machine rather than the server machine. Starting with HTML 4.0, such scripts are permitted using the tag <script>. The technologies used to produce these interactive Web pages are broadly referred to as **dynamic HTML**

The most popular scripting language for the client side is **JavaScript**, so we will now take a quick look at it. Despite the similarity in names, JavaScript has almost nothing to do with the Java programming language. Like other scripting languages, it is a very high-level language. For example, in a single line of JavaScript it is possible to pop up a dialog box, wait for text input, and store the resulting string in a variable. High-level features like this make JavaScript ideal for designing interactive Web pages. On the other hand, the fact that it is mutating faster than a fruit fly trapped in an X-ray machine makes it extremely difficult to write JavaScript programs that work on all platforms, but maybe some day it will stabilize.

As an example of a program in JavaScript, consider that of Fig. 7-31. Like that of Fig. 7-30, it displays a form asking for a name and age, and then predicts how old the person will be next year. The body is almost the same as the PHP example, the main difference being the declaration of the *Submit* button and the assignment statement in it. This assignment statement tells the browser to invoke the *response* script on a button click and pass it the form as a parameter.

What is completely new here is the declaration of the JavaScript function *response* in the head of the HTML file, an area normally reserved for titles, background colors, and so on. This function extracts the value of the *name* field from the form and stores it in the variable *person* as a string. It also extracts the value of the *age* field, converts it to an integer by using the *eval* function, adds 1 to it, and stores the result in *years*. Then it opens a document for output, does four

```
<html>
<head>
<script language="javascript" type="text/javascript">
function response(test_form) {
  var person = test_form.name.value;
  var years = eval(test_form.age.value) + 1;
  document.open();
  document.writeln("<html> <body>");
  document.writeln("Hello " + person + ".<br>");
  document.writeln("Prediction: next year you will be " + years + ".");
  document.writeln("</body> </html>");
  document.close();
}
</script>
</head>
<body>
<form>
Please enter your name: <input type="text" name="name">
<p>
Please enter your age: <input type="text" name="age">
<p>
<input type="button" value="submit" onclick="response(this.form)">
</form>
</body>
</html>
```

Figure 7-31. Use of JavaScript for processing a form.

writes to it using the *writeln* method, and closes the document. The document is an HTML file, as can be seen from the various HTML tags in it. The browser then displays the document on the screen.

It is very important to understand that while PHP and JavaScript look similar in that they both embed code in HTML files, they are processed totally differently. In the PHP example of Fig. 7-30, after the user has clicked on the *submit* button, the browser collects the information into a long string and sends it off to the server as a request for a PHP page. The server loads the PHP file and executes the PHP script that is embedded in to produce a new HTML page. That page is sent back to the browser for display. The browser cannot even be sure that it was produced by a program. This processing is shown as steps 1 to 4 in Fig. 7-32(a).

In the JavaScript example of Fig. 7-31, when the *submit* button is clicked the browser interprets a JavaScript function contained on the page. All the work is done locally, inside the browser. There is no contact with the server. This processing is shown as steps 1 and 2 in Fig. 7-32(b). As a consequence, the result is displayed virtually instantaneously, whereas with PHP there can be a delay of several seconds before the resulting HTML arrives at the client.

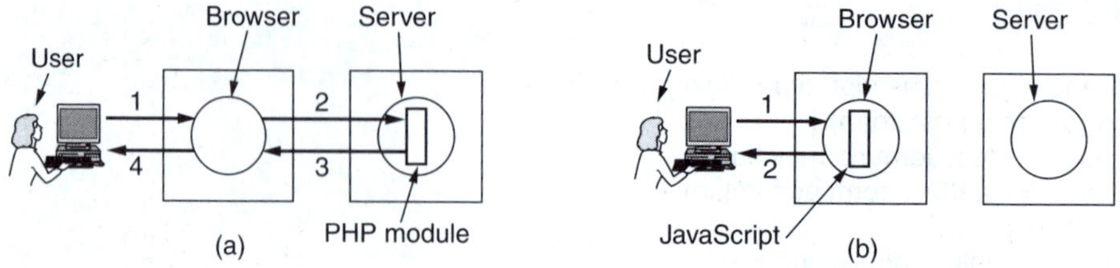

Figure 7-32. (a) Server-side scripting with PHP. (b) Client-side scripting with JavaScript.

This difference does not mean that JavaScript is better than PHP. Their uses are completely different. PHP (and, by implication, JSP and ASP) is used when interaction with a database on the server is needed. JavaScript (and other client-side languages we will mention, such as VBScript) is used when the interaction is with the user at the client computer. It is certainly possible to combine them, as we will see shortly.

JavaScript is not the only way to make Web pages highly interactive. An alternative on Windows platforms is **VBScript**, which is based on Visual Basic. Another popular method across platforms is the use of **applets**. These are small Java programs that have been compiled into machine instructions for a virtual computer called the **JVM** (**Java Virtual Machine**). Applets can be embedded in HTML pages (between <applet> and </applet>) and interpreted by JVM-capable browsers. Because Java applets are interpreted rather than directly executed, the Java interpreter can prevent them from doing Bad Things. At least in theory. In practice, applet writers have found a nearly endless stream of bugs in the Java I/O libraries to exploit.

Microsoft's answer to Sun's Java applets was allowing Web pages to hold **ActiveX controls**, which are programs compiled to x86 machine language and executed on the bare hardware. This feature makes them vastly faster and more flexible than interpreted Java applets because they can do anything a program can do. When Internet Explorer sees an ActiveX control in a Web page, it downloads it, verifies its identity, and executes it. However, downloading and running foreign programs raises enormous security issues, which we will discuss in Chap. 8.

Since nearly all browsers can interpret both Java programs and JavaScript, a designer who wants to make a highly interactive Web page has a choice of at least two techniques, and if portability to multiple platforms is not an issue, ActiveX in addition. As a general rule, JavaScript programs are easier to write, Java applets execute faster, and ActiveX controls run fastest of all. Also, since all browsers implement exactly the same JVM but no two browsers implement the same version of JavaScript, Java applets are more portable than JavaScript programs. For more information about JavaScript, there are many books, each with many (often with more than 1000) pages. See, for example, Flanagan (2010).

AJAX—Asynchronous JavaScript and XML

Compelling Web applications need responsive user interfaces and seamless access to data stored on remote Web servers. Scripting on the client (e.g., with JavaScript) and the server (e.g., with PHP) are basic technologies that provide pieces of the solution. These technologies are commonly used with several other key technologies in a combination called **AJAX (Asynchronous JAvascript and Xml)**. Many full-featured Web applications, such as Google's Gmail, Maps, and Docs, are written with AJAX.

AJAX is somewhat confusing because it is not a language. It is a set of technologies that work together to enable Web applications that are every bit as responsive and powerful as traditional desktop applications. The technologies are:

1. HTML and CSS to present information as pages.
2. DOM (Document Object Model) to change parts of pages while they are viewed.
3. XML (eXtensible Markup Language) to let programs exchange application data with the server.
4. An asynchronous way for programs to send and retrieve XML data.
5. JavaScript as a language to bind all this functionality together.

As this is quite a collection, we will go through each piece to see what it contributes. We have already seen HTML and CSS. They are standards for describing content and how it should be displayed. Any program that can produce HTML and CSS can use a Web browser as a display engine.

DOM (Document Object Model) is a representation of an HTML page that is accessible to programs. This representation is structured as a tree that reflects the structure of the HTML elements. For instance, the DOM tree of the HTML in Fig. 7-30(a) is given in Fig. 7-33. At the root is an *html* element that represents the entire HTML block. This element is the parent of the *body* element, which is in turn parent to a *form* element. The form has two attributes that are drawn to the right-hand side, one for the form method (a *POST*) and one for the form action (the URL to request). This element has three children, reflecting the two paragraph tags and one input tag that are contained within the form. At the bottom of the tree are leaves that contain either elements or literals, such as text strings.

The significance of the DOM model is that it provides programs with a straightforward way to change parts of the page. There is no need to rewrite the entire page. Only the node that contains the change needs to be replaced. When this change is made, the browser will correspondingly update the display. For example, if an image on part of the page is changed in DOM, the browser will update that image without changing the other parts of the page. We have already seen DOM in action when the JavaScript example of Fig. 7-31 added lines to the

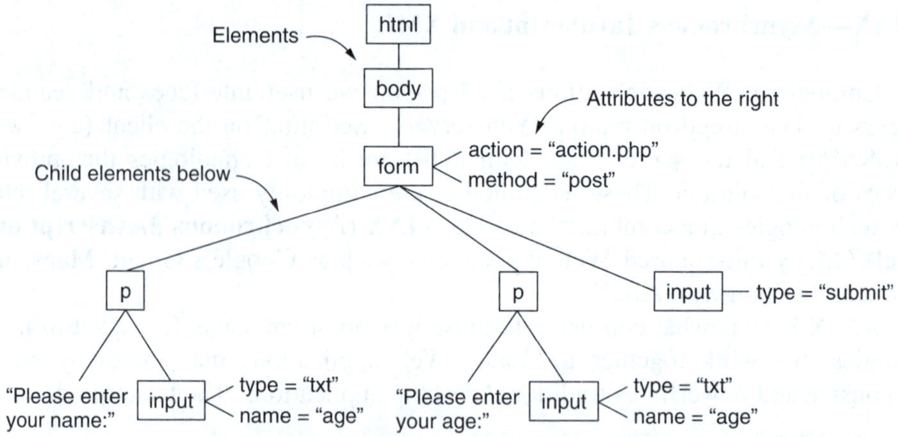

Figure 7-33. The DOM tree for the HTML in Fig. 7-30(a).

document element to cause new lines of text to appear at the bottom of the browser window. The DOM is a powerful method for producing pages that can evolve.

The third technology, **XML (eXtensible Markup Language)**, is a language for specifying structured content. HTML mixes content with formatting because it is concerned with the presentation of information. However, as Web applications become more common, there is an increasing need to separate structured content from its presentation. For example, consider a program that searches the Web for the best price for some book. It needs to analyze many Web pages looking for the item's title and price. With Web pages in HTML, it is very difficult for a program to figure out where the title is and where the price is.

For this reason, the W3C developed XML (Bray et al., 2006) to allow Web content to be structured for automated processing. Unlike HTML, there are no defined tags for XML. Each user can define her own tags. A simple example of an XML document is given in Fig. 7-34. It defines a structure called book_list, which is a list of books. Each book has three fields, the title, author, and year of publication. These structures are extremely simple. It is permitted to have structures with repeated fields (e.g., multiple authors), optional fields (e.g., URL of the audio book), and alternative fields (e.g., URL of a bookstore if it is in print or URL of an auction site if it is out of print).

In this example, each of the three fields is an indivisible entity, but it is also permitted to further subdivide the fields. For example, the author field could have been done as follows to give finer-grained control over searching and formatting:

```
<author>
    <first_name> George </first_name>
    <last_name> Zipf </last_name>
</author>
```

Each field can be subdivided into subfields and subsubfields, arbitrarily deeply.

```
<?xml version="1.0" ?>
<book_list>
<book>
  <title> Human Behavior and the Principle of Least Effort </title>
  <author> George Zipf </author>
  <year> 1949 </year>
</book>
<book>
  <title> The Mathematical Theory of Communication </title>
  <author> Claude E. Shannon </author>
  <author> Warren Weaver </author>
  <year> 1949 </year>
</book>
<book>
  <title> Nineteen Eighty-Four </title>
  <author> George Orwell </author>
  <year> 1949 </year>
</book>
</book_list>
```

Figure 7-34. A simple XML document.

All the file of Fig. 7-34 does is define a book list containing three books. It is well suited for transporting information between programs running in browsers and servers, but it says nothing about how to display the document as a Web page. To do that, a program that consumes the information and judges 1949 to be a fine year for books might output HTML in which the titles are marked up as italic text. Alternatively, a language called **XSLT (eXtensible Stylesheet Language Transformations**), can be used to define how XML should be transformed into HTML. XSLT is like CSS, but much more powerful. We will spare you the details.

The other advantage of expressing data in XML, instead of HTML, is that it is easier for programs to analyze. HTML was originally written manually (and often is still) so a lot of it is a bit sloppy. Sometimes the closing tags, like </p>, are left out. Other tags do not have a matching closing tag, like <br>. Still other tags may be nested improperly, and the case of tag and attribute names can vary. Most browsers do their best to work out what was probably intended. XML is stricter and cleaner in its definition. Tag names and attributes are always lowercase, tags must always be closed in the reverse of the order that they were opened (or indicate clearly if they are an empty tag with no corresponding close), and attribute values must be enclosed in quotation marks. This precision makes parsing easier and unambiguous.

HTML is even being defined in terms of XML. This approach is called **XHTML (eXtended HyperText Markup Language**). Basically, it is a Very

Picky version of HTML. XHTML pages must strictly conform to the XML rules, otherwise they are not accepted by the browser. No more shoddy Web pages and inconsistencies across browsers. As with XML, the intent is to produce pages that are better for programs (in this case Web applications) to process. While XHTML has been around since 1998, it has been slow to catch on. People who produce HTML do not see why they need XHTML, and browser support has lagged. Now HTML 5.0 is being defined so that a page can be represented as either HTML or XHTML to aid the transition. Eventually, XHTML should replace HTML, but it will be a long time before this transition is complete.

XML has also proved popular as a language for communication between programs. When this communication is carried by the HTTP protocol (described in the next section) it is called a Web service. In particular, **SOAP** (**Simple Object Access Protocol**) is a way of implementing Web services that performs RPC between programs in a language- and system-independent way. The client just constructs the request as an XML message and sends it to the server, using the HTTP protocol. The server sends back a reply as an XML-formatted message. In this way, applications on heterogeneous platforms can communicate.

Getting back to AJAX, our point is simply that XML is a useful format to exchange data between programs running in the browser and the server. However, to provide a responsive interface in the browser while sending or receiving data, it must be possible for scripts to perform **asynchronous I/O** that does not block the display while awaiting the response to a request. For example, consider a map that can be scrolled in the browser. When it is notified of the scroll action, the script on the map page may request more map data from the server if the view of the map is near the edge of the data. The interface should not freeze while those data are fetched. Such an interface would win no user awards. Instead, the scrolling should continue smoothly. When the data arrive, the script is notified so that it can use the data. If all goes well, new map data will be fetched before it is needed. Modern browsers have support for this model of communication.

The final piece of the puzzle is a scripting language that holds AJAX together by providing access to the above list of technologies. In most cases, this language is JavaScript, but there are alternatives such as VBScript. We presented a simple example of JavaScript earlier. Do not be fooled by this simplicity. JavaScript has many quirks, but it is a full-blown programming language, with all the power of C or Java. It has variables, strings, arrays, objects, functions, and all the usual control structures. It also has interfaces specific to the browser and Web pages. JavaScript can track mouse motion over objects on the screen, which makes it easy to make a menu suddenly appear and leads to lively Web pages. It can use DOM to access pages, manipulate HTML and XML, and perform asynchronous HTTP communication.

Before leaving the subject of dynamic pages, let us briefly summarize the technologies we have covered so far by relating them on a single figure. Complete Web pages can be generated on the fly by various scripts on the server machine. The scripts can be written in server extension languages like PHP, JSP, or ASP.NET, or run as separate CGI processes and thus be written in any language. These options are shown in Fig. 7-35.

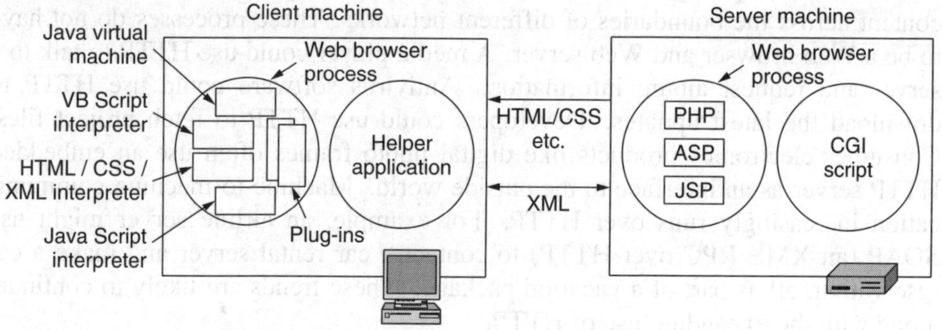

Figure 7-35. Various technologies used to generate dynamic pages.

Once these Web pages are received by the browser, they are treated as normal pages in HTML, CSS and other MIME types and just displayed. Plug-ins that run in the browser and helper applications that run outside of the browser can be installed to extend the MIME types that are supported by the browser.

Dynamic content generation is also possible on the client side. The programs that are embedded in Web pages can be written in JavaScript, VBScript, Java, and other languages. These programs can perform arbitrary computations and update the display. With AJAX, programs in Web pages can asynchronously exchange XML and other kinds of data with the server. This model supports rich Web applications that look just like traditional applications, except that they run inside the browser and access information that is stored at servers on the Internet.

7.3.4 HTTP—The HyperText Transfer Protocol

Now that we have an understanding of Web content and applications, it is time to look at the protocol that is used to transport all this information between Web servers and clients. It is **HTTP (HyperText Transfer Protocol)**, as specified in RFC 2616.

HTTP is a simple request-response protocol that normally runs over TCP. It specifies what messages clients may send to servers and what responses they get back in return. The request and response headers are given in ASCII, just like in SMTP. The contents are given in a MIME-like format, also like in SMTP. This simple model was partly responsible for the early success of the Web because it made development and deployment straightforward.

In this section, we will look at the more important properties of HTTP as it is used nowadays. However, before getting into the details we will note that the way it is used in the Internet is evolving. HTTP is an application layer protocol because it runs on top of TCP and is closely associated with the Web. That is why we are covering it in this chapter. However, in another sense HTTP is becoming more like a transport protocol that provides a way for processes to communicate content across the boundaries of different networks. These processes do not have to be a Web browser and Web server. A media player could use HTTP to talk to a server and request album information. Antivirus software could use HTTP to download the latest updates. Developers could use HTTP to fetch project files. Consumer electronics products like digital photo frames often use an embedded HTTP server as an interface to the outside world. Machine-to-machine communication increasingly runs over HTTP. For example, an airline server might use SOAP (an XML RPC over HTTP) to contact a car rental server and make a car reservation, all as part of a vacation package. These trends are likely to continue, along with the expanding use of HTTP.

Connections

The usual way for a browser to contact a server is to establish a TCP connection to port 80 on the server's machine, although this procedure is not formally required. The value of using TCP is that neither browsers nor servers have to worry about how to handle long messages, reliability, or congestion control. All of these matters are handled by the TCP implementation.

Early in the Web, with HTTP 1.0, after the connection was established a single request was sent over and a single response was sent back. Then the TCP connection was released. In a world in which the typical Web page consisted entirely of HTML text, this method was adequate. Quickly, the average Web page grew to contain large numbers of embedded links for content such as icons and other eye candy. Establishing a separate TCP connection to transport each single icon became a very expensive way to operate.

This observation led to HTTP 1.1, which supports **persistent connections**. With them, it is possible to establish a TCP connection, send a request and get a response, and then send additional requests and get additional responses. This strategy is also called **connection reuse**. By amortizing the TCP setup, startup, and release costs over multiple requests, the relative overhead due to TCP is reduced per request. It is also possible to pipeline requests, that is, send request 2 before the response to request 1 has arrived.

The performance difference between these three cases is shown in Fig. 7-36. Part (a) shows three requests, one after the other and each in a separate connection. Let us suppose that this represents a Web page with two embedded images on the same server. The URLs of the images are determined as the main page is fetched, so they are fetched after the main page. Nowadays, a typical page has around 40 other objects that must be fetched to present it, but that would make our figure far too big so we will use only two embedded objects.

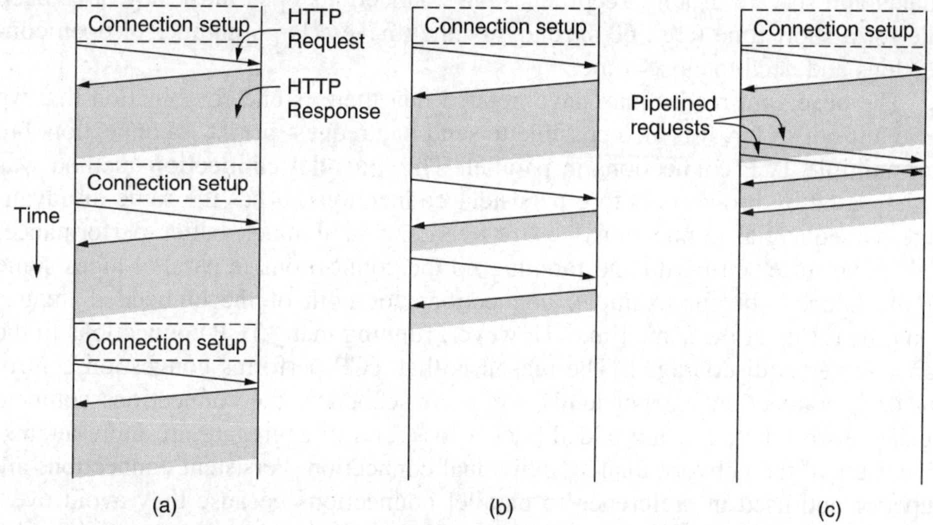

Figure 7-36. HTTP with (a) multiple connections and sequential requests. (b) A persistent connection and sequential requests. (c) A persistent connection and pipelined requests.

In Fig. 7-36(b), the page is fetched with a persistent connection. That is, the TCP connection is opened at the beginning, then the same three requests are sent, one after the other as before, and only then is the connection closed. Observe that the fetch completes more quickly. There are two reasons for the speedup. First, time is not wasted setting up additional connections. Each TCP connection requires at least one round-trip time to establish. Second, the transfer of the same images proceeds more quickly. Why is this? It is because of TCP congestion control. At the start of a connection, TCP uses the slow-start procedure to increase the throughput until it learns the behavior of the network path. The consequence of this warmup period is that multiple short TCP connections take disproportionately longer to transfer information than one longer TCP connection.

Finally, in Fig. 7-36(c), there is one persistent connection and the requests are pipelined. Specifically, the second and third requests are sent in rapid succession as soon as enough of the main page has been retrieved to identify that the images must be fetched. The responses for these requests follow eventually. This method cuts down the time that the server is idle, so it further improves performance.

Persistent connections do not come for free, however. A new issue that they raise is when to close the connection. A connection to a server should stay open while the page loads. What then? There is a good chance that the user will click on a link that requests another page from the server. If the connection remains open, the next request can be sent immediately. However, there is no guarantee that the client will make another request of the server any time soon. In practice, clients and servers usually keep persistent connections open until they have been idle for a short time (e.g., 60 seconds) or they have a large number of open connections and need to close some.

The observant reader may have noticed that there is one combination that we have left out so far. It is also possible to send one request per TCP connection, but run multiple TCP connections in parallel. This **parallel connection** method was widely used by browsers before persistent connections. It has the same disadvantage as sequential connections—extra overhead—but much better performance. This is because setting up and ramping up the connections in parallel hides some of the latency. In our example, connections for both of the embedded images could be set up at the same time. However, running many TCP connections to the same server is discouraged. The reason is that TCP performs congestion control for each connection independently. As a consequence, the connections compete against each other, causing added packet loss, and in aggregate are more aggressive users of the network than an individual connection. Persistent connections are superior and used in preference to parallel connections because they avoid overhead and do not suffer from congestion problems.

Methods

Although HTTP was designed for use in the Web, it was intentionally made more general than necessary with an eye to future object-oriented uses. For this reason, operations, called **methods**, other than just requesting a Web page are supported. This generality is what permitted SOAP to come into existence.

Each request consists of one or more lines of ASCII text, with the first word on the first line being the name of the method requested. The built-in methods are listed in Fig. 7-37. The names are case sensitive, so *GET* is allowed but not *get*.

Method	Description
GET	Read a Web page
HEAD	Read a Web page's header
POST	Append to a Web page
PUT	Store a Web page
DELETE	Remove the Web page
TRACE	Echo the incoming request
CONNECT	Connect through a proxy
OPTIONS	Query options for a page

Figure 7-37. The built-in HTTP request methods.

The *GET* method requests the server to send the page. (When we say "page" we mean "object" in the most general case, but thinking of a page as the contents of a file is sufficient to understand the concepts.) The page is suitably encoded in MIME. The vast majority of requests to Web servers are *GET*s. The usual form of *GET* is

```
GET filename HTTP/1.1
```

where *filename* names the page to be fetched and 1.1 is the protocol version.

The *HEAD* method just asks for the message header, without the actual page. This method can be used to collect information for indexing purposes, or just to test a URL for validity.

The *POST* method is used when forms are submitted. Both it and *GET* are also used for SOAP Web services. Like *GET*, it bears a URL, but instead of simply retrieving a page it uploads data to the server (i.e., the contents of the form or RPC parameters). The server then does something with the data that depends on the URL, conceptually appending the data to the object. The effect might be to purchase an item, for example, or to call a procedure. Finally, the method returns a page indicating the result.

The remaining methods are not used much for browsing the Web. The *PUT* method is the reverse of *GET*: instead of reading the page, it writes the page. This method makes it possible to build a collection of Web pages on a remote server. The body of the request contains the page. It may be encoded using MIME, in which case the lines following the *PUT* might include authentication headers, to prove that the caller indeed has permission to perform the requested operation.

DELETE does what you might expect: it removes the page, or at least it indicates that the Web server has agreed to remove the page. As with *PUT*, authentication and permission play a major role here.

The *TRACE* method is for debugging. It instructs the server to send back the request. This method is useful when requests are not being processed correctly and the client wants to know what request the server actually got.

The *CONNECT* method lets a user make a connection to a Web server through an intermediate device, such as a Web cache.

The *OPTIONS* method provides a way for the client to query the server for a page and obtain the methods and headers that can be used with that page.

Every request gets a response consisting of a status line, and possibly additional information (e.g., all or part of a Web page). The status line contains a three-digit status code telling whether the request was satisfied and, if not, why not. The first digit is used to divide the responses into five major groups, as shown in Fig. 7-38. The 1xx codes are rarely used in practice. The 2xx codes mean that the request was handled successfully and the content (if any) is being returned. The 3xx codes tell the client to look elsewhere, either using a different URL or in its own cache (discussed later). The 4xx codes mean the request failed due to a client error such an invalid request or a nonexistent page. Finally, the 5xx errors mean the server itself has an internal problem, either due to an error in its code or to a temporary overload.

Code	Meaning	Examples
1xx	Information	100 = server agrees to handle client's request
2xx	Success	200 = request succeeded; 204 = no content present
3xx	Redirection	301 = page moved; 304 = cached page still valid
4xx	Client error	403 = forbidden page; 404 = page not found
5xx	Server error	500 = internal server error; 503 = try again later

Figure 7-38. The status code response groups.

Message Headers

The request line (e.g., the line with the *GET* method) may be followed by additional lines with more information. They are called **request headers**. This information can be compared to the parameters of a procedure call. Responses may also have **response headers**. Some headers can be used in either direction. A selection of the more important ones is given in Fig. 7-39. This list is not short, so as you might imagine there is often a variety of headers on each request and response.

The *User-Agent* header allows the client to inform the server about its browser implementation (e.g., *Mozilla/5.0* and *Chrome/5.0.375.125*). This information is useful to let servers tailor their responses to the browser, since different browsers can have widely varying capabilities and behaviors.

The four *Accept* headers tell the server what the client is willing to accept in the event that it has a limited repertoire of what is acceptable. The first header specifies the MIME types that are welcome (e.g., *text/html*). The second gives the character set (e.g., *ISO-8859-5* or *Unicode-1-1*). The third deals with compression methods (e.g., *gzip*). The fourth indicates a natural language (e.g., Spanish). If the server has a choice of pages, it can use this information to supply the one the client is looking for. If it is unable to satisfy the request, an error code is returned and the request fails.

The *If-Modified-Since* and *If-None-Match* headers are used with caching. They let the client ask for a page to be sent only if the cached copy is no longer valid. We will describe caching shortly.

The *Host* header names the server. It is taken from the URL. This header is mandatory. It is used because some IP addresses may serve multiple DNS names and the server needs some way to tell which host to hand the request to.

The *Authorization* header is needed for pages that are protected. In this case, the client may have to prove it has a right to see the page requested. This header is used for that case.

The client uses the misspelled *Referer* header to give the URL that referred to the URL that is now requested. Most often this is the URL of the previous page.

Header	Type	Contents
User-Agent	Request	Information about the browser and its platform
Accept	Request	The type of pages the client can handle
Accept-Charset	Request	The character sets that are acceptable to the client
Accept-Encoding	Request	The page encodings the client can handle
Accept-Language	Request	The natural languages the client can handle
If-Modified-Since	Request	Time and date to check freshness
If-None-Match	Request	Previously sent tags to check freshness
Host	Request	The server's DNS name
Authorization	Request	A list of the client's credentials
Referer	Request	The previous URL from which the request came
Cookie	Request	Previously set cookie sent back to the server
Set-Cookie	Response	Cookie for the client to store
Server	Response	Information about the server
Content-Encoding	Response	How the content is encoded (e.g., *gzip*)
Content-Language	Response	The natural language used in the page
Content-Length	Response	The page's length in bytes
Content-Type	Response	The page's MIME type
Content-Range	Response	Identifies a portion of the page's content
Last-Modified	Response	Time and date the page was last changed
Expires	Response	Time and date when the page stops being valid
Location	Response	Tells the client where to send its request
Accept-Ranges	Response	Indicates the server will accept byte range requests
Date	Both	Date and time the message was sent
Range	Both	Identifies a portion of a page
Cache-Control	Both	Directives for how to treat caches
ETag	Both	Tag for the contents of the page
Upgrade	Both	The protocol the sender wants to switch to

Figure 7-39. Some HTTP message headers.

This header is particularly useful for tracking Web browsing, as it tells servers how a client arrived at the page.

Although cookies are dealt with in RFC 2109 rather than RFC 2616, they also have headers. The *Set-Cookie* header is how servers send cookies to clients. The client is expected to save the cookie and return it on subsequent requests to the server by using the *Cookie* header. (Note that there is a more recent specification for cookies with newer headers, RFC 2965, but this has largely been rejected by industry and is not widely implemented.)

Many other headers are used in responses. The *Server* header allows the server to identify its software build if it wishes. The next five headers, all starting with *Content-*, allow the server to describe properties of the page it is sending.

The *Last-Modified* header tells when the page was last modified, and the *Expires* header tells for how long the page will remain valid. Both of these headers play an important role in page caching.

The *Location* header is used by the server to inform the client that it should try a different URL. This can be used if the page has moved or to allow multiple URLs to refer to the same page (possibly on different servers). It is also used for companies that have a main Web page in the *com* domain but redirect clients to a national or regional page based on their IP addresses or preferred language.

If a page is very large, a small client may not want it all at once. Some servers will accept requests for byte ranges, so the page can be fetched in multiple small units. The *Accept-Ranges* header announces the server's willingness to handle this type of partial page request.

Now we come to headers that can be used in both directions. The *Date* header can be used in both directions and contains the time and date the message was sent, while the *Range* header tells the byte range of the page that is provided by the response.

The *ETag* header gives a short tag that serves as a name for the content of the page. It is used for caching. The *Cache-Control* header gives other explicit instructions about how to cache (or, more usually, how not to cache) pages.

Finally, the *Upgrade* header is used for switching to a new communication protocol, such as a future HTTP protocol or a secure transport. It allows the client to announce what it can support and the server to assert what it is using.

Caching

People often return to Web pages that they have viewed before, and related Web pages often have the same embedded resources. Some examples are the images that are used for navigation across the site, as well as common style sheets and scripts. It would be very wasteful to fetch all of these resources for these pages each time they are displayed because the browser already has a copy.

Squirreling away pages that are fetched for subsequent use is called **caching**. The advantage is that when a cached page can be reused, it is not necessary to repeat the transfer. HTTP has built-in support to help clients identify when they can safely reuse pages. This support improves performance by reducing both network traffic and latency. The trade-off is that the browser must now store pages, but this is nearly always a worthwhile trade-off because local storage is inexpensive. The pages are usually kept on disk so that they can be used when the browser is run at a later date.

The difficult issue with HTTP caching is how to determine that a previously cached copy of a page is the same as the page would be if it was fetched again.

This determination cannot be made solely from the URL. For example, the URL may give a page that displays the latest news item. The contents of this page will be updated frequently even though the URL stays the same. Alternatively, the contents of the page may be a list of the gods from Greek and Roman mythology. This page should change somewhat less rapidly.

HTTP uses two strategies to tackle this problem. They are shown in Fig. 7-40 as forms of processing between the request (step 1) and the response (step 5). The first strategy is page validation (step 2). The cache is consulted, and if it has a copy of a page for the requested URL that is known to be fresh (i.e., still valid), there is no need to fetch it anew from the server. Instead, the cached page can be returned directly. The *Expires* header returned when the cached page was originally fetched and the current date and time can be used to make this determination.

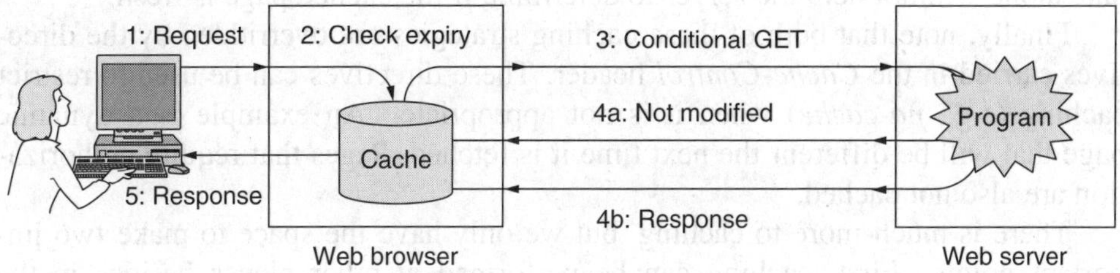

Figure 7-40. HTTP caching.

However, not all pages come with a convenient *Expires* header that tells when the page must be fetched again. After all, making predictions is hard—especially about the future. In this case, the browser may use heuristics. For example, if the page has not been modified in the past year (as told by the *Last-Modified* header) it is a fairly safe bet that it will not change in the next hour. There is no guarantee, however, and this may be a bad bet. For example, the stock market might have closed for the day so that the page will not change for hours, but it will change rapidly once the next trading session starts. Thus, the cacheability of a page may vary wildly over time. For this reason, heuristics should be used with care, though they often work well in practice.

Finding pages that have not expired is the most beneficial use of caching because it means that the server does not need to be contacted at all. Unfortunately, it does not always work. Servers must use the *Expires* header conservatively, since they may be unsure when a page will be updated. Thus, the cached copies may still be fresh, but the client does not know.

The second strategy is used in this case. It is to ask the server if the cached copy is still valid. This request is a **conditional GET**, and it is shown in Fig. 7-40 as step 3. If the server knows that the cached copy is still valid, it can send a short reply to say so (step 4a). Otherwise, it must send the full response (step 4b).

More header fields are used to let the server check whether a cached copy is still valid. The client has the time a cached page was last updated from the *Last-Modified* header. It can send this time to the server using the *If-Modified-Since* header to ask for the page only if it has been changed in the meantime.

Alternatively, the server may return an *ETag* header with a page. This header gives a tag that is a short name for the content of the page, like a checksum but better. (It can be a cryptographic hash, which we will describe in Chap. 8.) The client can validate cached copies by sending the server an *If-None-Match* header listing the tags of the cached copies. If any of the tags match the content that the server would respond with, the corresponding cached copy may be used. This method can be used when it is not convenient or useful to determine freshness. For example, a server may return different content for the same URL depending on what languages and MIME types are preferred. In this case, the modification date alone will not help the server to determine if the cached page is fresh.

Finally, note that both of these caching strategies are overridden by the directives carried in the *Cache-Control* header. These directives can be used to restrict caching (e.g., *no-cache*) when it is not appropriate. An example is a dynamic page that will be different the next time it is fetched. Pages that require authorization are also not cached.

There is much more to caching, but we only have the space to make two important points. First, caching can be performed at other places besides in the browser. In the general case, HTTP requests can be routed through a series of caches. The use of a cache external to the browser is called **proxy caching**. Each added level of caching can help to reduce requests further up the chain. It is common for organizations such as ISPs and companies to run proxy caches to gain the benefits of caching pages across different users. We will discuss proxy caching with the broader topic of content distribution in Sec. 7.5 at the end of this chapter.

Second, caches provide an important boost to performance, but not as much as one might hope. The reason is that, while there are certainly popular documents on the Web, there are also a great many unpopular documents that people fetch, many of which are also very long (e.g., videos). The "long tail" of unpopular documents take up space in caches, and the number of requests that can be handled from the cache grows only slowly with the size of the cache. Web caches are always likely to be able to handle less than half of the requests. See Breslau et al. (1999) for more information.

Experimenting with HTTP

Because HTTP is an ASCII protocol, it is quite easy for a person at a terminal (as opposed to a browser) to directly talk to Web servers. All that is needed is a TCP connection to port 80 on the server. Readers are encouraged to experiment with the following command sequence. It will work in most UNIX shells and the command window on Windows (once the telnet program is enabled).

```
telnet www.ietf.org 80
GET /rfc.html HTTP/1.1
Host: www.ietf.org
```

This sequence of commands starts up a telnet (i.e., TCP) connection to port 80 on IETF's Web server, *www.ietf.org*. Then comes the *GET* command naming the path of the URL and the protocol. Try servers and URLs of your choosing. The next line is the mandatory *Host* header. A blank line following the last header is mandatory. It tells the server that there are no more request headers. The server will then send the response. Depending on the server and the URL, many different kinds of headers and pages can be observed.

7.3.5 The Mobile Web

The Web is used from most every type of computer, and that includes mobile phones. Browsing the Web over a wireless network while mobile can be very useful. It also presents technical problems because much Web content was designed for flashy presentations on desktop computers with broadband connectivity. In this section we will describe how Web access from mobile devices, or the **mobile Web**, is being developed.

Compared to desktop computers at work or at home, mobile phones present several difficulties for Web browsing:

1. Relatively small screens preclude large pages and large images.
2. Limited input capabilities make it tedious to enter URLs or other lengthy input.
3. Network bandwidth is limited over wireless links, particularly on cellular (3G) networks, where it is often expensive too.
4. Connectivity may be intermittent.
5. Computing power is limited, for reasons of battery life, size, heat dissipation, and cost.

These difficulties mean that simply using desktop content for the mobile Web is likely to deliver a frustrating user experience.

Early approaches to the mobile Web devised a new protocol stack tailored to wireless devices with limited capabilities. **WAP (Wireless Application Protocol)** is the most well-known example of this strategy. The WAP effort was started in 1997 by major mobile phone vendors that included Nokia, Ericsson, and Motorola. However, something unexpected happened along the way. Over the next decade, network bandwidth and device capabilities grew tremendously with the deployment of 3G data services and mobile phones with larger color displays, faster processors, and 802.11 wireless capabilities. All of a sudden, it was possible for mobiles to run simple Web browsers. There is still a gap between these mobiles and desktops that will never close, but many of the technology problems that gave impetus to a separate protocol stack have faded.

The approach that is increasingly used is to run the same Web protocols for mobiles and desktops, and to have Web sites deliver mobile-friendly content when the user happens to be on a mobile device. Web servers are able to detect whether to return desktop or mobile versions of Web pages by looking at the request headers. The *User-Agent* header is especially useful in this regard because it identifies the browser software. Thus, when a Web server receives a request, it may look at the headers and return a page with small images, less text, and simpler navigation to an iPhone and a full-featured page to a user on a laptop.

W3C is encouraging this approach in several ways. One way is to standardize best practices for mobile Web content. A list of 60 such best practices is provided in the first specification (Rabin and McCathieNevile, 2008). Most of these practices take sensible steps to reduce the size of pages, including by the use of compression, since the costs of communication are higher than those of computation, and by maximizing the effectiveness of caching. This approach encourages sites, especially large sites, to create mobile Web versions of their content because that is all that is required to capture mobile Web users. To help those users along, there is also a logo to indicate pages that can be viewed (well) on the mobile Web.

Another useful tool is a stripped-down version of HTML called **XHTML Basic**. This language is a subset of XHTML that is intended for use by mobile phones, televisions, PDAs, vending machines, pagers, cars, game machines, and even watches. For this reason, it does not support style sheets, scripts, or frames, but most of the standard tags are there. They are grouped into 11 modules. Some are required; some are optional. All are defined in XML. The modules and some example tags are listed in Fig. 7-41.

However, not all pages will be designed to work well on the mobile Web. Thus, a complementary approach is the use of **content transformation** or **transcoding**. In this approach, a computer that sits between the mobile and the server takes requests from the mobile, fetches content from the server, and transforms it to mobile Web content. A simple transformation is to reduce the size of large images by reformatting them at a lower resolution. Many other small but useful transformations are possible. Transcoding has been used with some success since the early days of the mobile Web. See, for example, Fox et al. (1996). However, when both approaches are used there is a tension between the mobile content decisions that are made by the server and by the transcoder. For instance, a Web site may select a particular combination of image and text for a mobile Web user, only to have a transcoder change the format of the image.

Our discussion so far has been about content, not protocols, as it is the content that is the biggest problem in realizing the mobile Web. However, we will briefly mention the issue of protocols. The HTTP, TCP, and IP protocols used by the

Module	Req.?	Function	Example tags
Structure	Yes	Doc. structure	body, head, html, title
Text	Yes	Information	br, code, dfn, em, h*n*, kbd, p, strong
Hypertext	Yes	Hyperlinks	a
List	Yes	Itemized lists	dl, dt, dd, ol, ul, li
Forms	No	Fill-in forms	form, input, label, option, textarea
Tables	No	Rectangular tables	caption, table, td, th, tr
Image	No	Pictures	img
Object	No	Applets, maps, etc.	object, param
Meta-information	No	Extra info	meta
Link	No	Similar to <a>	link
Base	No	URL starting point	base

Figure 7-41. The XHTML Basic modules and tags.

Web may consume a significant amount of bandwidth on protocol overheads such as headers. To tackle this problem, WAP and other solutions defined special-purpose protocols. This turns out to be largely unecessary. Header compression technologies, such as ROHC (RObust Header Compression) described in Chap. 6, can reduce the overheads of these protocols. In this way, it is possible to have one set of protocols (HTTP, TCP, IP) and use them over either high- or low- bandwidth links. Use over the low-bandwidth links simply requires that header compression be turned on.

7.3.6 Web Search

To finish our description of the Web, we will discuss what is arguably the most successful Web application: search. In 1998, Sergey Brin and Larry Page, then graduate students at Stanford, formed a startup called Google to build a better Web search engine. They were armed with the then-radical idea that a search algorithm that counted how many times each page was pointed to by other pages was a better measure of its importance than how many times it contained the key words being sought. For instance, many pages link to the main Cisco page, which makes this page more important to a user searching for "Cisco" than a page outside of the company that happens to use the word "Cisco" many times.

They were right. It did prove possible to build a better search engine, and people flocked to it. Backed by venture capital, Google grew tremendously. It became a public company in 2004, with a market capitalization of $23 billion. By 2010, it was estimated to run more than one million servers in data centers throughout the world.

In one sense, search is simply another Web application, albeit one of the most mature Web applications because it has been under development since the early days of the Web. However, Web search has proved indispensible in everyday usage. Over one billion Web searches are estimated to be done each day. People looking for all manner of information use search as a starting point. For example, to find out where to buy Vegemite in Seattle, there is no obvious Web site to use as a starting point. But chances are that a search engine knows of a page with the desired information and can quickly direct you to the answer.

To perform a Web search in the traditional manner, the user directs her browser to the URL of a Web search site. The major search sites include Google, Yahoo!, and Bing. Next, the user submits search terms using a form. This act causes the search engine to perform a query on its database for relevant pages or images, or whatever kind of resource is being searched for, and return the result as a dynamic page. The user can then follow links to the pages that have been found.

Web search is an interesting topic for discussion because it has implications for the design and use of networks. First, there is the question of how Web search finds pages. The Web search engine must have a database of pages to run a query. Each HTML page may contain links to other pages, and everything interesting (or at least searchable) is linked somewhere. This means that it is theoretically possible to start with a handful of pages and find all other pages on the Web by doing a traversal of all pages and links. This process is called **Web crawling**. All Web search engines use Web crawlers.

One issue with crawling is the kind of pages that it can find. Fetching static documents and following links is easy. However, many Web pages contain programs that display different pages depending on user interaction. An example is an online catalog for a store. The catalog may contain dynamic pages created from a product database and queries for different products. This kind of content is different from static pages that are easy to traverse. How do Web crawlers find these dynamic pages? The answer is that, for the most part, they do not. This kind of hidden content is called the **deep Web**. How to search the deep Web is an open problem that researchers are now tackling. See, for example, madhavan et al. (2008). There are also conventions by which sites make a page (known as *robots.txt*) to tell crawlers what parts of the sites should or should not be visited.

A second consideration is how to process all of the crawled data. To let indexing algorithms be run over the mass of data, the pages must be stored. Estimates vary, but the main search engines are thought to have an index of tens of billions of pages taken from the visible part of the Web. The average page size is estimated at 320 KB. These figures mean that a crawled copy of the Web takes on the order of 20 petabytes or 2×10^{16} bytes to store. While this is a truly huge number, it is also an amount of data that can comfortably be stored and processed in Internet data centers (Chang et al., 2006). For example, if disk storage costs \$20/TB, then 2×10^4 TB costs \$400,000, which is not exactly a huge amount for companies the size of Google, Microsoft, and Yahoo!. And while the Web is expanding, disk costs are dropping dramatically, so storing the entire Web may continue to be feasible for large companies for the foreseeable future.

Making sense of this data is another matter. You can appreciate how XML can help programs extract the structure of the data easily, while ad hoc formats will lead to much guesswork. There is also the issue of conversion between formats, and even translation between languages. But even knowing the structure of data is only part of the problem. The hard bit is to understand what it means. This is where much value can be unlocked, starting with more relevant result pages for search queries. The ultimate goal is to be able to answer questions, for example, where to buy a cheap but decent toaster oven in your city.

A third aspect of Web search is that it has come to provide a higher level of naming. There is no need to remember a long URL if it is just as reliable (or perhaps more) to search for a Web page by a person's name, assuming that you are better at remembering names than URLs. This strategy is increasingly successful. In the same way that DNS names relegated IP addresses to computers, Web search is relegating URLs to computers. Also in favor of search is that it corrects spelling and typing errors, whereas if you type in a URL wrong, you get the wrong page.

Finally, Web search shows us something that has little to do with network design but much to do with the growth of some Internet services: there is much money in advertising. Advertising is the economic engine that has driven the growth of Web search. The main change from print advertising is the ability to target advertisements depending on what people are searching for, to increase the relevance of the advertisements. Variations on an auction mechanism are used to match the search query to the most valuable advertisement (Edelman et al., 2007). This new model has given rise to new problems, of course, such as **click fraud**, in which programs imitate users and click on advertisements to cause payments that have not been fairly earned.

7.4 STREAMING AUDIO AND VIDEO

Web applications and the mobile Web are not the only exciting developments in the use of networks. For many people, audio and video are the holy grail of networking. When the word "multimedia" is mentioned, both the propellerheads and the suits begin salivating as if on cue. The former see immense technical challenges in providing voice over IP and video-on-demand to every computer. The latter see equally immense profits in it.

While the idea of sending audio and video over the Internet has been around since the 1970s at least, it is only since roughly 2000 that **real-time audio** and **real-time video** traffic has grown with a vengeance. Real-time traffic is different from Web traffic in that it must be played out at some predetermined rate to be useful. After all, watching a video in slow motion with fits and starts is not most people's idea of fun. In contrast, the Web can have short interruptions, and page loads can take more or less time, within limits, without it being a major problem.

Two things happened to enable this growth. First, computers have became much more powerful and are equipped with microphones and cameras so that they can input, process, and output audio and video data with ease. Second, a flood of Internet bandwidth has come to be available. Long-haul links in the core of the Internet run at many gigabits/sec, and broadband and 802.11 wireless reaches users at the edge of the Internet. These developments allow ISPs to carry tremendous levels of traffic across their backbones and mean that ordinary users can connect to the Internet 100–1000 times faster than with a 56-kbps telephone modem.

The flood of bandwidth caused audio and video traffic to grow, but for different reasons. Telephone calls take up relatively little bandwidth (in principle 64 kbps but less when compressed) yet telephone service has traditionally been expensive. Companies saw an opportunity to carry voice traffic over the Internet using existing bandwidth to cut down on their telephone bills. Startups such as Skype saw a way to let customers make free telephone calls using their Internet connections. Upstart telephone companies saw a cheap way to carry traditional voice calls using IP networking equipment. The result was an explosion of voice data carried over Internet networks that is called **voice over IP** or **Internet telephony**.

Unlike audio, video takes up a large amount of bandwidth. Reasonable quality Internet video is encoded with compression at rates of around 1 Mbps, and a typical DVD movie is 2 GB of data. Before broadband Internet access, sending movies over the network was prohibitive. Not so any more. With the spread of broadband, it became possible for the first time for users to watch decent, streamed video at home. People love to do it. Around a quarter of the Internet users on any given day are estimated to visit YouTube, the popular video sharing site. The movie rental business has shifted to online downloads. And the sheer size of videos has changed the overall makeup of Internet traffic. The majority of Internet traffic is already video, and it is estimated that 90% of Internet traffic will be video within a few years (Cisco, 2010).

Given that there is enough bandwidth to carry audio and video, the key issue for designing streaming and conferencing applications is network delay. Audio and video need real-time presentation, meaning that they must be played out at a predetermined rate to be useful. Long delays mean that calls that should be interactive no longer are. This problem is clear if you have ever talked on a satellite phone, where the delay of up to half a second is quite distracting. For playing music and movies over the network, the absolute delay does not matter, because it only affects when the media starts to play. But the variation in delay, called **jitter**, still matters. It must be masked by the player or the audio will sound unintelligible and the video will look jerky.

In this section, we will discuss some strategies to handle the delay problem, as well as protocols for setting up audio and video sessions. After an introduction to digital audio and video, our presentation is broken into three cases for which different designs are used. The first and easiest case to handle is streaming stored media, like watching a video on YouTube. The next case in terms of difficulty is streaming live media. Two examples are Internet radio and IPTV, in which radio and television stations broadcast to many users live on the Internet. The last and most difficult case is a call as might be made with Skype, or more generally an interactive audio and video conference.

As an aside, the term **multimedia** is often used in the context of the Internet to mean video and audio. Literally, multimedia is just two or more media. That definition makes this book a multimedia presentation, as it contains text and graphics (the figures). However, that is probably not what you had in mind, so we use the term "multimedia" to imply two or more **continuous media**, that is, media that have to be played during some well-defined time interval. The two media are normally video with audio, that is, moving pictures with sound. Many people also refer to pure audio, such as Internet telephony or Internet radio, as multimedia as well, which it is clearly not. Actually, a better term for all these cases is **streaming media**. Nonetheless, we will follow the herd and consider real-time audio to be multimedia as well.

7.4.1 Digital Audio

An audio (sound) wave is a one-dimensional acoustic (pressure) wave. When an acoustic wave enters the ear, the eardrum vibrates, causing the tiny bones of the inner ear to vibrate along with it, sending nerve pulses to the brain. These pulses are perceived as sound by the listener. In a similar way, when an acoustic wave strikes a microphone, the microphone generates an electrical signal, representing the sound amplitude as a function of time.

The frequency range of the human ear runs from 20 Hz to 20,000 Hz. Some animals, notably dogs, can hear higher frequencies. The ear hears loudness logarithmically, so the ratio of two sounds with power A and B is conventionally expressed in **dB (decibels)** as the quantity $10 \log_{10}(A/B)$. If we define the lower limit of audibility (a sound pressure of about 20 μPascals) for a 1-kHz sine wave as 0 dB, an ordinary conversation is about 50 dB and the pain threshold is about 120 dB. The dynamic range is a factor of more than 1 million.

The ear is surprisingly sensitive to sound variations lasting only a few milliseconds. The eye, in contrast, does not notice changes in light level that last only a few milliseconds. The result of this observation is that jitter of only a few milliseconds during the playout of multimedia affects the perceived sound quality much more than it affects the perceived image quality.

Digital audio is a digital representation of an audio wave that can be used to recreate it. Audio waves can be converted to digital form by an **ADC (Analog-to-Digital Converter)**. An ADC takes an electrical voltage as input and generates a binary number as output. In Fig. 7-42(a) we see an example of a sine wave.

To represent this signal digitally, we can sample it every ΔT seconds, as shown by the bar heights in Fig. 7-42(b). If a sound wave is not a pure sine wave but a linear superposition of sine waves where the highest frequency component present is f, the Nyquist theorem (see Chap. 2) states that it is sufficient to make samples at a frequency $2f$. Sampling more often is of no value since the higher frequencies that such sampling could detect are not present.

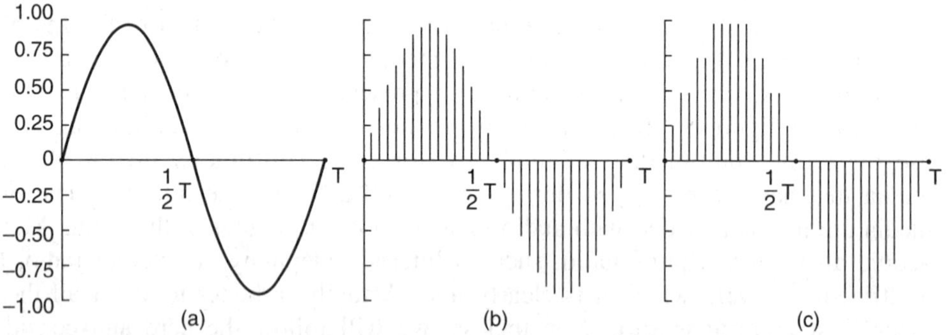

Figure 7-42. (a) A sine wave. (b) Sampling the sine wave. (c) Quantizing the samples to 4 bits.

The reverse process takes digital values and produces an analog electrical voltage. It is done by a **DAC** (**Digital-to-Analog Converter**). A loudspeaker can then convert the analog voltage to acoustic waves so that people can hear sounds.

Digital samples are never exact. The samples of Fig. 7-42(c) allow only nine values, from −1.00 to +1.00 in steps of 0.25. An 8-bit sample would allow 256 distinct values. A 16-bit sample would allow 65,536 distinct values. The error introduced by the finite number of bits per sample is called the **quantization noise**. If it is too large, the ear detects it.

Two well-known examples where sampled sound is used are the telephone and audio compact discs. Pulse code modulation, as used within the telephone system, uses 8-bit samples made 8000 times per second. The scale is nonlinear to minimize perceived distortion, and with only 8000 samples/sec, frequencies above 4 kHz are lost. In North America and Japan, the **μ-law** encoding is used. In Europe and internationally, the **A-law** encoding is used. Each encoding gives a data rate of 64,000 bps.

Audio CDs are digital with a sampling rate of 44,100 samples/sec, enough to capture frequencies up to 22,050 Hz, which is good enough for people but bad for canine music lovers. The samples are 16 bits each and are linear over the range of amplitudes. Note that 16-bit samples allow only 65,536 distinct values, even though the dynamic range of the ear is more than 1 million. Thus, even though CD-quality audio is much better than telephone-quality audio, using only 16 bits per sample introduces noticeable quantization noise (although the full dynamic range is not covered—CDs are not supposed to hurt). Some fanatic audiophiles still prefer 33-RPM LP records to CDs because records do not have a Nyquist frequency cutoff at 22 kHz and have no quantization noise. (But they do have scratches unless handled very carefully) With 44,100 samples/sec of 16 bits each, uncompressed CD-quality audio needs a bandwidth of 705.6 kbps for monaural and 1.411 Mbps for stereo.

Audio Compression

Audio is often compressed to reduce bandwidth needs and transfer times, even though audio data rates are much lower than video data rates. All compression systems require two algorithms: one for compressing the data at the source, and another for decompressing it at the destination. In the literature, these algorithms are referred to as the **encoding** and **decoding** algorithms, respectively. We will use this terminology too.

Compression algorithms exhibit certain asymmetries that are important to understand. Even though we are considering audio first, these asymmetries hold for video as well. For many applications, a multimedia document will only be encoded once (when it is stored on the multimedia server) but will be decoded thousands of times (when it is played back by customers). This asymmetry means that it is acceptable for the encoding algorithm to be slow and require expensive hardware provided that the decoding algorithm is fast and does not require expensive hardware. The operator of a popular audio (or video) server might be quite willing to buy a cluster of computers to encode its entire library, but requiring customers to do the same to listen to music or watch movies is not likely to be a big success. Many practical compression systems go to great lengths to make decoding fast and simple, even at the price of making encoding slow and complicated.

On the other hand, for live audio and video, such as a voice-over-IP calls, slow encoding is unacceptable. Encoding must happen on the fly, in real time. Consequently, real-time multimedia uses different algorithms or parameters than stored audio or videos on disk, often with appreciably less compression.

A second asymmetry is that the encode/decode process need not be invertible. That is, when compressing a data file, transmitting it, and then decompressing it, the user expects to get the original back, accurate down to the last bit. With multimedia, this requirement does not exist. It is usually acceptable to have the audio (or video) signal after encoding and then decoding be slightly different from the original as long as it sounds (or looks) the same. When the decoded output is not exactly equal to the original input, the system is said to be **lossy**. If the input and output are identical, the system is **lossless**. Lossy systems are important because accepting a small amount of information loss normally means a huge payoff in terms of the compression ratio possible.

Historically, long-haul bandwidth in the telephone network was very expensive, so there is a substantial body of work on **vocoders** (short for "voice coders") that compress audio for the special case of speech. Human speech tends to be in the 600-Hz to 6000-Hz range and is produced by a mechanical process that depends on the speaker's vocal tract, tongue, and jaw. Some vocoders make use of models of the vocal system to reduce speech to a few parameters (e.g., the sizes and shapes of various cavities) and a data rate of as little as 2.4 kbps. How these vocoders work is beyond the scope of this book, however.

We will concentrate on audio as sent over the Internet, which is typically closer to CD-quality. It is also desirable to reduce the data rates for this kind of audio. At 1.411 Mbps, stereo audio would tie up many broadband links, leaving less room for video and other Web traffic. Its data rate with compression can be reduced by an order of magnitude with little to no perceived loss of quality.

Compression and decompression require signal processing. Fortunately, digitized sound and movies can be easily processed by computers in software. In fact, dozens of programs exist to let users record, display, edit, mix, and store media from multiple sources. This has led to large amounts of music and movies being available on the Internet—not all of it legal—which has resulted in numerous lawsuits from the artists and copyright owners.

Many audio compression algorithms have been developed. Probably the most popular formats are **MP3 (MPEG audio layer 3)** and **AAC (Advanced Audio Coding)** as carried in **MP4 (MPEG-4)** files. To avoid confusion, note that MPEG provides audio and video compression. MP3 refers to the audio compression portion (part 3) of the MPEG-1 standard, not the third version of MPEG. In fact, no third version of MPEG was released, only MPEG-1, MPEG-2, and MPEG-4. AAC is the successor to MP3 and the default audio encoding used in MPEG-4. MPEG-2 allows both MP3 and AAC audio. Is that clear now? The nice thing about standards is that there are so many to choose from. And if you do not like any of them, just wait a year or two.

Audio compression can be done in two ways. In **waveform coding**, the signal is transformed mathematically by a Fourier transform into its frequency components. In Chap. 2, we showed an example function of time and its Fourier amplitudes in Fig. 2-1(a). The amplitude of each component is then encoded in a minimal way. The goal is to reproduce the waveform fairly accurately at the other end in as few bits as possible.

The other way, **perceptual coding**, exploits certain flaws in the human auditory system to encode a signal in such a way that it sounds the same to a human listener, even if it looks quite different on an oscilloscope. Perceptual coding is based on the science of **psychoacoustics**—how people perceive sound. Both MP3 and AAC are based on perceptual coding.

The key property of perceptual coding is that some sounds can **mask** other sounds. Imagine you are broadcasting a live flute concert on a warm summer day. Then all of a sudden, out of the blue, a crew of workmen nearby turn on their jackhammers and start tearing up the street. No one can hear the flute any more. Its sounds have been masked by the jackhammers. For transmission purposes, it is now sufficient to encode just the frequency band used by the jackhammers because the listeners cannot hear the flute anyway. This is called **frequency masking**—the ability of a loud sound in one frequency band to hide a softer sound in another frequency band that would have been audible in the absence of the loud sound. In fact, even after the jackhammers stop, the flute will be inaudible for a short period of time because the ear turns down its gain when they start and it takes a finite time to turn it up again. This effect is called **temporal masking**.

To make these effects more quantitative, imagine experiment 1. A person in a quiet room puts on headphones connected to a computer's sound card. The computer generates a pure sine wave at 100 Hz at low, but gradually increasing, power. The subject is instructed to strike a key when she hears the tone. The computer records the current power level and then repeats the experiment at 200 Hz, 300 Hz, and all the other frequencies up to the limit of human hearing. When averaged over many people, a log-log graph of how much power it takes for a tone to be audible looks like that of Fig. 7-43(a). A direct consequence of this curve is that it is never necessary to encode any frequencies whose power falls below the threshold of audibility. For example, if the power at 100 Hz were 20 dB in Fig. 7-43(a), it could be omitted from the output with no perceptible loss of quality because 20 dB at 100 Hz falls below the level of audibility.

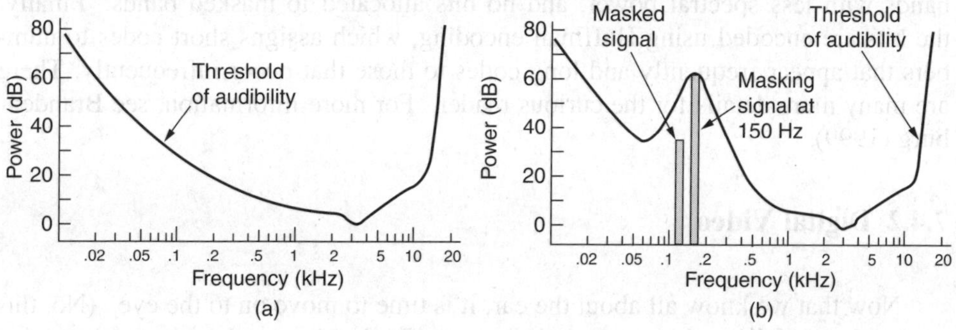

Figure 7-43. (a) The threshold of audibility as a function of frequency. (b) The masking effect.

Now consider experiment 2. The computer runs experiment 1 again, but this time with a constant-amplitude sine wave at, say, 150 Hz superimposed on the test frequency. What we discover is that the threshold of audibility for frequencies near 150 Hz is raised, as shown in Fig. 7-43(b).

The consequence of this new observation is that by keeping track of which signals are being masked by more powerful signals in nearby frequency bands, we can omit more and more frequencies in the encoded signal, saving bits. In Fig. 7-43, the 125-Hz signal can be completely omitted from the output and no one will be able to hear the difference. Even after a powerful signal stops in some frequency band, knowledge of its temporal masking properties allows us to continue to omit the masked frequencies for some time interval as the ear recovers. The essence of MP3 and AAC is to Fourier-transform the sound to get the power at each frequency and then transmit only the unmasked frequencies, encoding these in as few bits as possible.

With this information as background, we can now see how the encoding is done. The audio compression is done by sampling the waveform at a rate from 8 to 96 kHz for AAC, often at 44.1 kHz, to mimic CD sound. Sampling can be done on one (mono) or two (stereo) channels. Next, the output bit rate is chosen. MP3 can compress a stereo rock 'n roll CD down to 96 kbps with little perceptible loss in quality, even for rock 'n roll fans with no hearing loss. For a piano concert, AAC with at least 128 kbps is needed. The difference is because the signal-to-noise ratio for rock 'n roll is much higher than for a piano concert (in an engineering sense, anyway). It is also possible to choose lower output rates and accept some loss in quality.

The samples are processed in small batches. Each batch is passed through a bank of digital filters to get frequency bands. The frequency information is fed into a psychoacoustic model to determine the masked frequencies. Then the available bit budget is divided among the bands, with more bits allocated to the bands with the most unmasked spectral power, fewer bits allocated to unmasked bands with less spectral power, and no bits allocated to masked bands. Finally, the bits are encoded using Huffman encoding, which assigns short codes to numbers that appear frequently and long codes to those that occur infrequently. There are many more details for the curious reader. For more information, see Brandenburg (1999).

7.4.2 Digital Video

Now that we know all about the ear, it is time to move on to the eye. (No, this section is not followed by one on the nose.) The human eye has the property that when an image appears on the retina, the image is retained for some number of milliseconds before decaying. If a sequence of images is drawn at 50 images/sec, the eye does not notice that it is looking at discrete images. All video systems exploit this principle to produce moving pictures.

The simplest digital representation of video is a sequence of frames, each consisting of a rectangular grid of picture elements, or **pixels**. Each pixel can be a single bit, to represent either black or white. However, the quality of such a system is awful. Try using your favorite image editor to convert the pixels of a color image to black and white (and *not* shades of gray).

The next step up is to use 8 bits per pixel to represent 256 gray levels. This scheme gives high-quality "black-and-white" video. For color video, many systems use 8 bits for each of the red, green and blue (RGB) primary color components. This representation is possible because any color can be constructed from a linear superposition of red, green, and blue with the appropriate intensities. With

24 bits per pixel, there are about 16 million colors, which is more than the human eye can distinguish.

On color LCD computer monitors and televisions, each discrete pixel is made up of closely spaced red, green and blue subpixels. Frames are displayed by setting the intensity of the subpixels, and the eye blends the color components.

Common frame rates are 24 frames/sec (inherited from 35mm motion-picture film), 30 frames/sec (inherited from NTSC U.S. televisions), and 30 frames/sec (inherited from the PAL television system used in nearly all the rest of the world). (For the truly picky, NTSC color television runs at 29.97 frames/sec. The original black-and-white system ran at 30 frames/sec, but when color was introduced, the engineers needed a bit of extra bandwidth for signaling so they reduced the frame rate to 29.97. NTSC videos intended for computers really use 30.) PAL was invented after NTSC and really uses 25.000 frames/sec. To make this story complete, a third system, SECAM, is used in France, Francophone Africa, and Eastern Europe. It was first introduced into Eastern Europe by then Communist East Germany so the East German people could not watch West German (PAL) television lest they get Bad Ideas. But many of these countries are switching to PAL. Technology and politics at their best.

Actually, for broadcast television, 25 frames/sec is not quite good enough for smooth motion so the images are split into two **fields**, one with the odd-numbered scan lines and one with the even-numbered scan lines. The two (half-resolution) fields are broadcast sequentially, giving almost 60 (NTSC) or exactly 50 (PAL) fields/sec, a system known as **interlacing**. Videos intended for viewing on a computer are **progressive**, that is, do not use interlacing because computer monitors have buffers on their graphics cards, making it possible for the CPU to put a new image in the buffer 30 times/sec but have the graphics card redraw the screen 50 or even 100 times/sec to eliminate flicker. Analog television sets do not have a frame buffer the way computers do. When an interlaced video with rapid movement is displayed on a computer, short horizontal lines will be visible near sharp edges, an effect known as **combing**.

The frame sizes used for video sent over the Internet vary widely for the simple reason that larger frames require more bandwidth, which may not always be available. Low-resolution video might be 320 by 240 pixels, and "full-screen" video is 640 by 480 pixels. These dimensions approximate those of early computer monitors and NTSC television, respectively. The **aspect ratio**, or width to height ratio, of 4:3, is the same as a standard television. **HDTV (High-Definition TeleVision)** videos can be downloaded with 1280 by 720 pixels. These "widescreen" images have an aspect ratio of 16:9 to more closely match the 3:2 aspect ratio of film. For comparison, standard DVD video is usually 720 by 480 pixels, and video on Blu-ray discs is usually HDTV at 1080 by 720 pixels.

On the Internet, the number of pixels is only part of the story, as media players can present the same image at different sizes. Video is just another window on a computer screen that can be blown up or shrunk down. The role of more pixels is to increase the quality of the image, so that it does not look blurry when it is expanded. However, many monitors can show images (and hence videos) with even more pixels than even HDTV.

Video Compression

It should be obvious from our discussion of digital video that compression is critical for sending video over the Internet. Even a standard-quality video with 640 by 480 pixel frames, 24 bits of color information per pixel, and 30 frames/sec takes over 200 Mbps. This far exceeds the bandwidth by which most company offices are connected to the Internet, let alone home users, and this is for a single video stream. Since transmitting uncompressed video is completely out of the question, at least over wide area networks, the only hope is that massive compression is possible. Fortunately, a large body of research over the past few decades has led to many compression techniques and algorithms that make video transmission feasible.

Many formats are used for video that is sent over the Internet, some proprietary and some standard. The most popular encoding is MPEG in its various forms. It is an open standard found in files with mpg and mp4 extensions, as well as in other container formats. In this section, we will look at MPEG to study how video compression is accomplished. To begin, we will look at the compression of still images with JPEG. A video is just a sequence of images (plus sound). One way to compress video is to encode each image in succession. To a first approximation, MPEG is just the JPEG encoding of each frame, plus some extra features for removing the redundancy across frames.

The JPEG Standard

The **JPEG** (**Joint Photographic Experts Group**) standard for compressing continuous-tone still pictures (e.g., photographs) was developed by photographic experts working under the joint auspices of ITU, ISO, and IEC, another standards body. It is widely used (look for files with the extension jpg) and often provides compression ratios of 10:1 or better for natural images.

JPEG is defined in International Standard 10918. Really, it is more like a shopping list than a single algorithm, but of the four modes that are defined only the lossy sequential mode is relevant to our discussion. Furthermore, we will concentrate on the way JPEG is normally used to encode 24-bit RGB video images and will leave out some of the options and details for the sake of simplicity.

The algorithm is illustrated in Fig. 7-44. Step 1 is block preparation. For the sake of specificity, let us assume that the JPEG input is a 640×480 RGB image with 24 bits/pixel, as shown in Fig. 7-44(a). RGB is not the best color model to use for compression. The eye is much more sensitive to the **luminance**, or brightness, of video signals than the **chrominance**, or color, of video signals. Thus, we first compute the luminance, *Y*, and the two chrominances, *Cb* and *Cr*, from the *R*, *G*, and *B* components. The following formulas are used for 8-bit values that range from 0 to 255:

$$\begin{aligned} Y &= 16 + 0.26R + 0.50G + 0.09B \\ Cb &= 128 + 0.15R - 0.29G - 0.44B \\ Cr &= 128 + 0.44R - 0.37G + 0.07B \end{aligned}$$

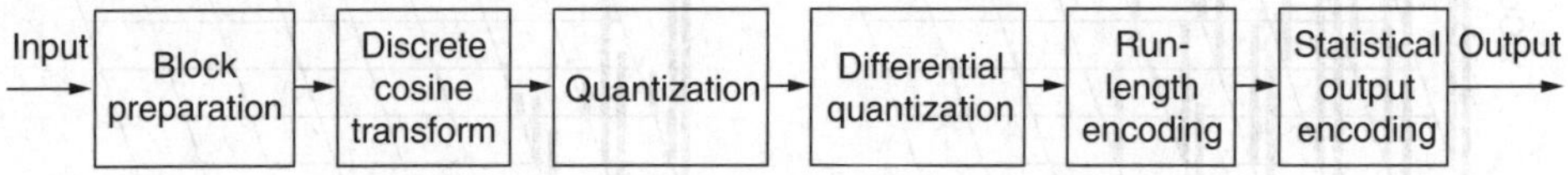

Figure 7-44. Steps in JPEG lossy sequential encoding.

Separate matrices are constructed for *Y*, *Cb*, and *Cr*. Next, square blocks of four pixels are averaged in the *Cb* and *Cr* matrices to reduce them to 320 × 240. This reduction is lossy, but the eye barely notices it since the eye responds to luminance more than to chrominance. Nevertheless, it compresses the total amount of data by a factor of two. Now 128 is subtracted from each element of all three matrices to put 0 in the middle of the range. Finally, each matrix is divided up into 8 × 8 blocks. The *Y* matrix has 4800 blocks; the other two have 1200 blocks each, as shown in Fig. 7-45(b).

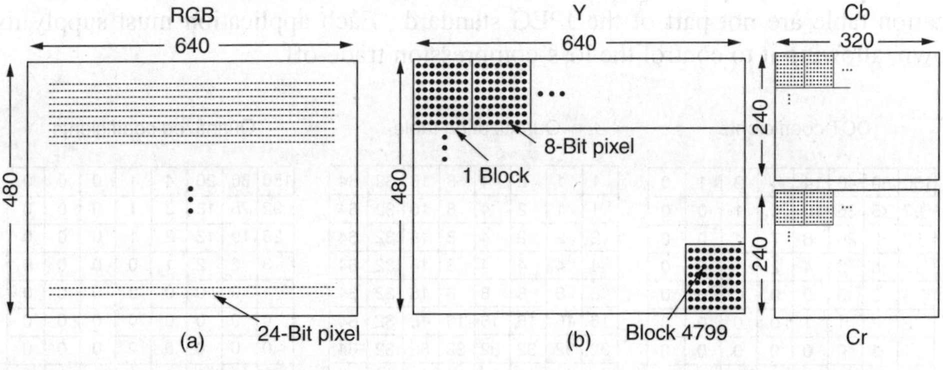

Figure 7-45. (a) RGB input data. (b) After block preparation.

Step 2 of JPEG encoding is to apply a **DCT** (**Discrete Cosine Transformation**) to each of the 7200 blocks separately. The output of each DCT is an 8 × 8 matrix of DCT coefficients. DCT element (0, 0) is the average value of the block. The other elements tell how much spectral power is present at each spatial frequency. Normally, these elements decay rapidly with distance from the origin, (0, 0), as suggested by Fig. 7-46.

Once the DCT is complete, JPEG encoding moves on to step 3, called **quantization**, in which the less important DCT coefficients are wiped out. This (lossy)

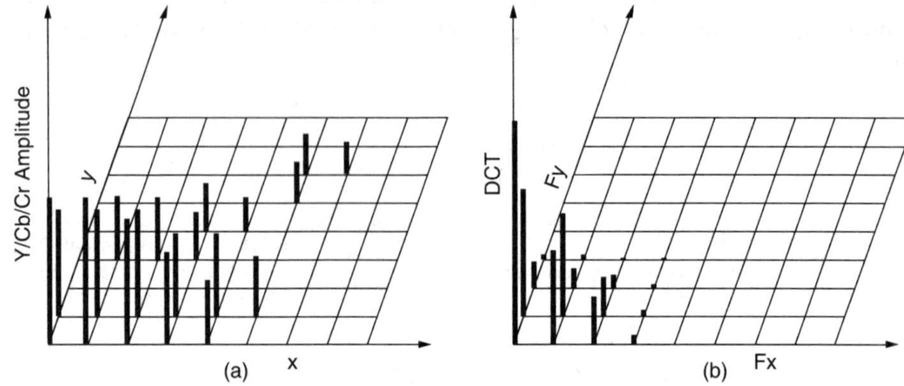

Figure 7-46. (a) One block of the Y matrix. (b) The DCT coefficients.

transformation is done by dividing each of the coefficients in the 8×8 DCT matrix by a weight taken from a table. If all the weights are 1, the transformation does nothing. However, if the weights increase sharply from the origin, higher spatial frequencies are dropped quickly.

An example of this step is given in Fig. 7-47. Here we see the initial DCT matrix, the quantization table, and the result obtained by dividing each DCT element by the corresponding quantization table element. The values in the quantization table are not part of the JPEG standard. Each application must supply its own, allowing it to control the loss-compression trade-off.

DCT coefficients

150	80	40	14	4	2	1	0
92	75	36	10	6	1	0	0
52	38	26	8	7	4	0	0
12	8	6	4	2	1	0	0
4	3	2	0	0	0	0	0
2	2	1	1	0	0	0	0
1	1	0	0	0	0	0	0
0	0	0	0	0	0	0	0

Quantization table

1	1	2	4	8	16	32	64
1	1	2	4	8	16	32	64
2	2	2	4	8	16	32	64
4	4	4	4	8	16	32	64
8	8	8	8	8	16	32	64
16	16	16	16	16	16	32	64
32	32	32	32	32	32	32	64
64	64	64	64	64	64	64	64

Quantized coefficients

150	80	20	4	1	0	0	0
92	75	18	3	1	0	0	0
26	19	13	2	1	0	0	0
3	2	2	1	0	0	0	0
1	0	0	0	0	0	0	0
0	0	0	0	0	0	0	0
0	0	0	0	0	0	0	0
0	0	0	0	0	0	0	0

Figure 7-47. Computation of the quantized DCT coefficients.

Step 4 reduces the (0, 0) value of each block (the one in the upper-left corner) by replacing it with the amount it differs from the corresponding element in the previous block. Since these elements are the averages of their respective blocks, they should change slowly, so taking the differential values should reduce most of them to small values. No differentials are computed from the other values.

Step 5 linearizes the 64 elements and applies run-length encoding to the list. Scanning the block from left to right and then top to bottom will not concentrate the zeros together, so a zigzag scanning pattern is used, as shown in Fig. 7-48. In this example, the zigzag pattern produces 38 consecutive 0s at the end of the matrix. This string can be reduced to a single count saying there are 38 zeros, a technique known as **run-length encoding**.

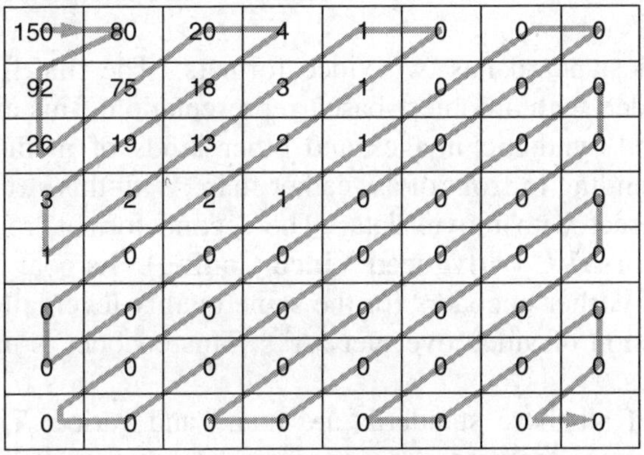

Figure 7-48. The order in which the quantized values are transmitted.

Now we have a list of numbers that represent the image (in transform space). Step 6 Huffman-encodes the numbers for storage or transmission, assigning common numbers shorter codes than uncommon ones.

JPEG may seem complicated, but that is because it *is* complicated. Still, the benefits of up to 20:1 compression are worth it. Decoding a JPEG image requires running the algorithm backward. JPEG is roughly symmetric: decoding takes as long as encoding. This property is not true of all compression algorithms, as we shall now see.

The MPEG Standard

Finally, we come to the heart of the matter: the **MPEG** (**Motion Picture Experts Group**) standards. Though there are many proprietary algorithms, these standards define the main algorithms used to compress videos. They have been international standards since 1993. Because movies contain both images and sound, MPEG can compress both audio and video. We have already examined audio compression and still image compression, so let us now examine video compression.

The MPEG-1 standard (which includes MP3 audio) was first published in 1993 and is still widely used. Its goal was to produce video-recorder-quality output that was compressed 40:1 to rates of around 1 Mbps. This video is suitable for broad Internet use on Web sites. Do not worry if you do not remember video recorders—MPEG-1 was also used for storing movies on CDs when they existed. If you do not know what CDs are, we will have to move on to MPEG-2.

The MPEG-2 standard, released in 1996, was designed for compressing broadcast-quality video. It is very common now, as it is used as the basis for video encoded on DVDs (which inevitably finds its way onto the Internet) and for digital broadcast television (as DVB). DVD quality video is typically encoded at rates of 4–8 Mbps.

The MPEG-4 standard has two video formats. The first format, released in 1999, encodes video with an object-based representation. This allows for the mixing of natural and synthetic images and other kinds of media, for example, a weatherperson standing in front of a weather map. With this structure, it is easy to let programs interact with movie data. The second format, released in 2003, is known as **H.264** or **AVC** (**Advanced Video Coding**). Its goal is to encode video at half the rate of earlier encoders for the same quality level, all the better to support the transmission of video over networks. This encoder is used for HDTV on most Blu-ray discs.

The details of all these standards are many and varied. The later standards also have many more features and encoding options than the earlier standards. However, we will not go into the details. For the most part, the gains in video compression over time have come from numerous small improvements, rather than fundamental shifts in how video is compressed. Thus, we will sketch the overall concepts.

MPEG compresses both audio and video. Since the audio and video encoders work independently, there is an issue of how the two streams get synchronized at the receiver. The solution is to have a single clock that outputs timestamps of the current time to both encoders. These timestamps are included in the encoded output and propagated all the way to the receiver, which can use them to synchronize the audio and video streams.

MPEG video compression takes advantage of two kinds of redundancies that exist in movies: spatial and temporal. Spatial redundancy can be utilized by simply coding each frame separately with JPEG. This approach is occasionally used, especially when random access to each frame is needed, as in editing video productions. In this mode, JPEG levels of compression are achieved.

Additional compression can be achieved by taking advantage of the fact that consecutive frames are often almost identical. This effect is smaller than it might first appear since many movie directors cut between scenes every 3 or 4 seconds (time a movie fragment and count the scenes). Nevertheless, runs of 75 or more highly similar frames offer the potential of a major reduction over simply encoding each frame separately with JPEG.

For scenes in which the camera and background are stationary and one or two actors are moving around slowly, nearly all the pixels will be identical from frame to frame. Here, just subtracting each frame from the previous one and running

JPEG on the difference would do fine. However, for scenes where the camera is panning or zooming, this technique fails badly. What is needed is some way to compensate for this motion. This is precisely what MPEG does; it is the main difference between MPEG and JPEG.

MPEG output consists of three kinds of frames:

1. I- (Intracoded) frames: self-contained compressed still pictures.

2. P- (Predictive) frames: block-by-block difference with the previous frames.

3. B- (Bidirectional) frames: block-by-block differences between previous and future frames.

I-frames are just still pictures. They can be coded with JPEG or something similar. It is valuable to have I-frames appear in the output stream periodically (e.g., once or twice per second) for three reasons. First, MPEG can be used for a multicast transmission, with viewers tuning in at will. If all frames depended on their predecessors going back to the first frame, anybody who missed the first frame could never decode any subsequent frames. Second, if any frame were received in error, no further decoding would be possible: everything from then on would be unintelligble junk. Third, without I-frames, while doing a fast forward or rewind the decoder would have to calculate every frame passed over so it would know the full value of the one it stopped on.

P-frames, in contrast, code interframe differences. They are based on the idea of **macroblocks**, which cover, for example, 16×16 pixels in luminance space and 8×8 pixels in chrominance space. A macroblock is encoded by searching the previous frame for it or something only slightly different from it.

An example of where P-frames would be useful is given in Fig. 7-49. Here we see three consecutive frames that have the same background, but differ in the position of one person. The macroblocks containing the background scene will match exactly, but the macroblocks containing the person will be offset in position by some unknown amount and will have to be tracked down.

Figure 7-49. Three consecutive frames.

The MPEG standards do not specify how to search, how far to search, or how good a match has to be in order to count. This is up to each implementation. For example, an implementation might search for a macroblock at the current position in the previous frame, and all other positions offset $\pm \Delta x$ in the x direction and $\pm \Delta y$ in the y direction. For each position, the number of matches in the luminance matrix could be computed. The position with the highest score would be declared the winner, provided it was above some predefined threshold. Otherwise, the macroblock would be said to be missing. Much more sophisticated algorithms are also possible, of course.

If a macroblock is found, it is encoded by taking the difference between its current value and the one in the previous frame (for luminance and both chrominances). These difference matrices are then subjected to the discrete cosine transformation, quantization, run-length encoding, and Huffman encoding, as usual. The value for the macroblock in the output stream is then the motion vector (how far the macroblock moved from its previous position in each direction), followed by the encoding of its difference. If the macroblock is not located in the previous frame, the current value is encoded, just as in an I-frame.

Clearly, this algorithm is highly asymmetric. An implementation is free to try every plausible position in the previous frame if it wants to, in a desperate attempt to locate every last macroblock, no matter where it has moved to. This approach will minimize the encoded MPEG stream at the expense of very slow encoding. This approach might be fine for a one-time encoding of a film library but would be terrible for real-time videoconferencing.

Similarly, each implementation is free to decide what constitutes a "found" macroblock. This freedom allows implementers to compete on the quality and speed of their algorithms, but always produce compliant MPEG output.

So far, decoding MPEG is straightforward. Decoding I-frames is similar to decoding JPEG images. Decoding P-frames requires the decoder to buffer the previous frames so it can build up the new one in a separate buffer based on fully encoded macroblocks and macroblocks containing differences from the previous frames. The new frame is assembled macroblock by macroblock.

B-frames are similar to P-frames, except that they allow the reference macroblock to be in either previous frames or succeeding frames. This additional freedom allows for improved motion compensation. It is useful, for example, when objects pass in front of, or behind, other objects. To do B-frame encoding, the encoder needs to hold a sequence of frames in memory at once: past frames, the current frame being encoded, and future frames. Decoding is similarly more complicated and adds some delay. This is because a given B-frame cannot be decoded until the successive frames on which it depends are decoded. Thus, although B-frames give the best compression, they are not always used due to their greater complexity and buffering requirements.

The MPEG standards contain many enhancements to these techniques to achieve excellent levels of compression. AVC can be used to compress video at ratios in excess of 50:1, which reduces network bandwidth requirements by the same factor. For more information on AVC, see Sullivan and Wiegand (2005).

7.4.3 Streaming Stored Media

Let us now move on to network applications. Our first case is streaming media that is already stored in files. The most common example of this is watching videos over the Internet. This is one form of **VoD** (**Video on Demand**). Other forms of video on demand use a provider network that is separate from the Internet to deliver the movies (e.g., the cable network).

In the next section, we will look at streaming live media, for example, broadcast IPTV and Internet radio. Then we will look at the third case of real-time conferencing. An example is a voice-over-IP call or video conference with Skype. These three cases place increasingly stringent requirements on how we can deliver the audio and video over the network because we must pay increasing attention to delay and jitter.

The Internet is full of music and video sites that stream stored media files. Actually, the easiest way to handle stored media is *not* to stream it. Imagine you want to create an online movie rental site to compete with Apple's iTunes. A regular Web site will let users download and then watch videos (after they pay, of course). The sequence of steps is shown in Fig. 7-50. We will spell them out to contrast them with the next example.

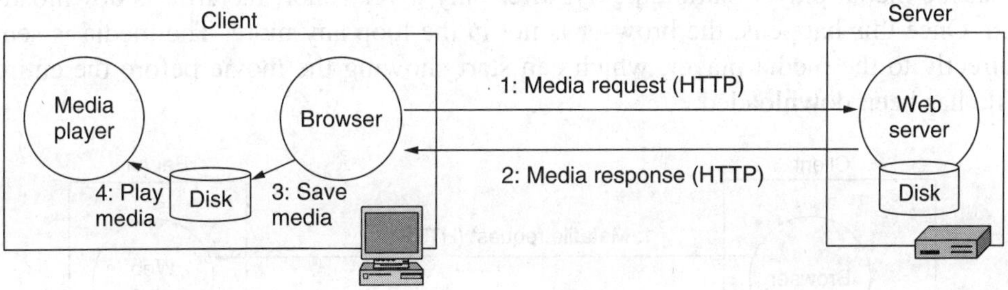

Figure 7-50. Playing media over the Web via simple downloads.

The browser goes into action when the user clicks on a movie. In step 1, it sends an HTTP request for the movie to the Web server to which the movie is linked. In step 2, the server fetches the movie (which is just a file in MP4 or some other format) and sends it back to the browser. Using the MIME type, for example, *video/mp4*, the browser looks up how it is supposed to display the file. In this case, it is with a media player that is shown as a helper application, though it could also be a plug-in. The browser saves the entire movie to a scratch file on disk in step 3. It then starts the media player, passing it the name of the scratch file. Finally, in step 4 the media player starts reading the file and playing the movie.

In principle, this approach is completely correct. It will play the movie. There is no real-time network issue to address either because the download is simply a file download. The only trouble is that the entire video must be transmitted over the network before the movie starts. Most customers do not want to wait an hour for their "video on demand." This model can be problematic even for audio. Imagine previewing a song before purchasing an album. If the song is 4 MB, which is a typical size for an MP3 song, and the broadband connectivity is 1 Mbps, the user will be greeted by half a minute of silence before the preview starts. This model is unlikely to sell many albums.

To get around this problem without changing how the browser works, sites can use the design shown in Fig. 7-51. The page linked to the movie is not the actual movie file. Instead, it is what is called a **metafile**, a very short file just naming the movie (and possibly having other key descriptors). A simple metafile might be only one line of ASCII text and look like this:

```
rtsp://joes-movie-server/movie-0025.mp4
```

The browser gets the page as usual, now a one-line file, in steps 1 and 2. Then it starts the media player and hands it the one-line file in step 3, all as usual. The media player reads the metafile and sees the URL of where to get the movie. It contacts *joes-video-server* and asks for the movie in step 4. The movie is then streamed back to the media player in step 5. The advantage of this arrangement is that the media player starts quickly, after only a very short metafile is downloaded. Once this happens, the browser is not in the loop any more. The media is sent directly to the media player, which can start showing the movie before the entire file has been downloaded.

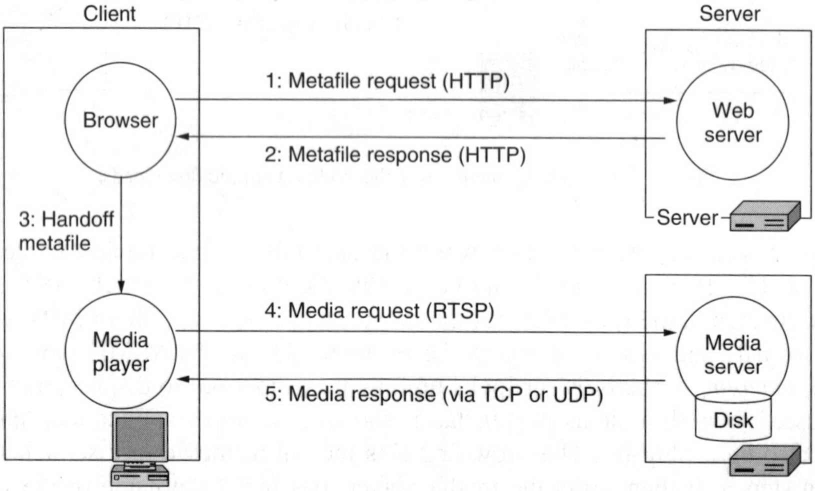

Figure 7-51. Streaming media using the Web and a media server.

We have shown two servers in Fig. 7-51 because the server named in the metafile is often not the same as the Web server. In fact, it is generally not even an HTTP server, but a specialized media server. In this example, the media server uses **RTSP (Real Time Streaming Protocol)**, as indicated by the scheme name *rtsp*.

The media player has four major jobs to do:

1. Manage the user interface.
2. Handle transmission errors.
3. Decompress the content.
4. Eliminate jitter.

Most media players nowadays have a glitzy user interface, sometimes simulating a stereo unit, with buttons, knobs, sliders, and visual displays. Often there are interchangeable front panels, called **skins**, that the user can drop onto the player. The media player has to manage all this and interact with the user.

The other jobs are related and depend on the network protocols. We will go through each one in turn, starting with handling transmission errors. Dealing with errors depends on whether a TCP-based transport like HTTP is used to transport the media, or a UDP-based transport like RTP is used. Both are used in practice. If a TCP-based transport is being used then there are no errors for the media player to correct because TCP already provides reliability by using retransmissions. This is an easy way to handle errors, at least for the media player, but it does complicate the removal of jitter in a later step.

Alternatively, a UDP-based transport like RTP can be used to move the data. We studied it in Chap. 6. With these protocols, there are no retransmissions. Thus, packet loss due to congestion or transmission errors will mean that some of the media does not arrive. It is up to the media player to deal with this problem.

Let us understand the difficulty we are up against. The loss is a problem because customers do not like large gaps in their songs or movies. However, it is not as much of a problem as loss in a regular file transfer because the loss of a small amount of media need not degrade the presentation for the user. For video, the user is unlikely to notice if there are occasionally 24 new frames in some second instead of 25 new frames. For audio, short gaps in the playout can be masked with sounds close in time. The user is unlikely to detect this substitution unless they are paying *very* close attention.

The key to the above reasoning, however, is that the gaps are very short. Network congestion or a transmission error will generally cause an entire packet to be lost, and packets are often lost in small bursts. Two strategies can be used to reduce the impact of packet loss on the media that is lost: FEC and interleaving. We will describe each in turn.

FEC (Forward Error Correction) is simply the error-correcting coding that we studied in Chap. 3 applied at the application level. Parity across packets provides an example (Shacham and McKenny, 1990). For every four data packets that are sent, a fifth **parity packet** can be constructed and sent. This is shown in Fig. 7-52 with packets *A*, *B*, *C*, and *D*. The parity packet, *P*, contains redundant bits that are the parity or exclusive-OR sums of the bits in each of the four data packets. Hopefully, all of the packets will arrive for most groups of five packets. When this happens, the parity packet is simply discarded at the receiver. Or, if only the parity packet is lost, no harm is done.

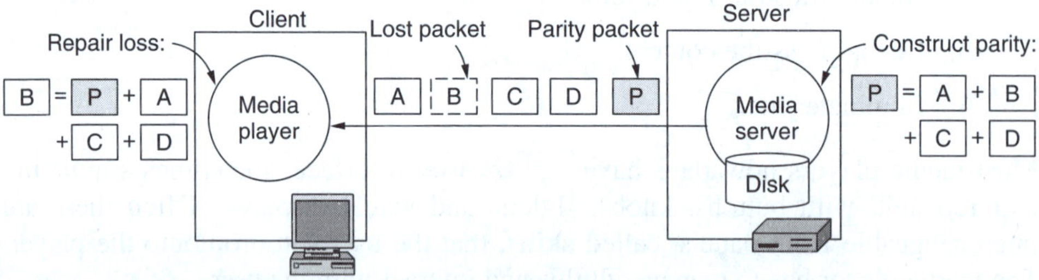

Figure 7-52. Using a parity packet to repair loss.

Occasionally, however, a data packet may be lost during transmission, as *B* is in Fig. 7-52. The media player receives only three data packets, *A*, *C*, and *D*, plus the parity packet, *P*. By design, the bits in the missing data packet can be reconstructed from the parity bits. To be specific, using "+" to represent exclusive-OR or modulo 2 addition, *B* can be reconstructed as $B = P + A + C + D$ by the properties of exclusive-OR (i.e., $X + Y + Y = X$).

FEC can reduce the level of loss seen by the media player by repairing some of the packet losses, but it only works up to a certain level. If two packets in a group of five are lost, there is nothing we can do to recover the data. The other property to note about FEC is the cost that we have paid to gain this protection. Every four packets have become five packets, so the bandwidth requirements for the media are 25% larger. The latency of decoding has increased too, as we may need to wait until the parity packet has arrived before we can reconstruct a data packet that came before it.

There is also one clever trick in the technique above. In Chap. 3, we described parity as providing error detection. Here we are providing error-correction. How can it do both? The answer is that in this case it is known which packet was lost. The lost data is called an **erasure**. In Chap. 3, when we considered a frame that was received with some bits in error, we did not know which bit was errored. This case is harder to deal with than erasures. Thus, with erasures parity can provide error correction, and without erasures parity can only provide error detection. We will see another unexpected benefit of parity soon, when we get to multicast scenarios.

The second strategy is called **interleaving**. This approach is based on mixing up or interleaving the order of the media before transmission and unmixing or deinterleaving it on reception. That way, if a packet (or burst of packets) is lost, the loss will be spread out over time by the unmixing. It will not result in a single, large gap when the media is played out. For example, a packet might contain 220 stereo samples, each containing a pair of 16-bit numbers, normally good for 5 msec of music. If the samples were sent in order, a lost packet would represent a 5 msec gap in the music. Instead, the samples are transmitted as shown in Fig. 7-53. All the even samples for a 10-msec interval are sent in one packet, followed by all the odd samples in the next one. The loss of packet 3 now does not represent a 5-msec gap in the music, but the loss of every other sample for 10 msec. This loss can be handled easily by having the media player interpolate using the previous and succeeding samples. The result is lower temporal resolution for 10 msec, but not a noticeable time gap in the media.

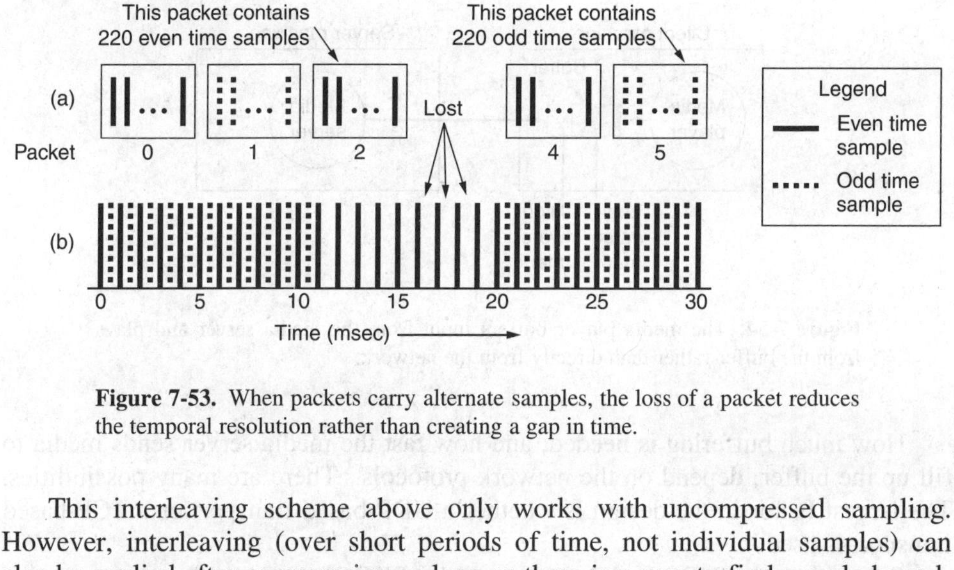

Figure 7-53. When packets carry alternate samples, the loss of a packet reduces the temporal resolution rather than creating a gap in time.

This interleaving scheme above only works with uncompressed sampling. However, interleaving (over short periods of time, not individual samples) can also be applied after compression as long as there is a way to find sample boundaries in the compressed stream. RFC 3119 gives a scheme that works with compressed audio.

Interleaving is an attractive technique when it can be used because it needs no additional bandwidth, unlike FEC. However, interleaving adds to the latency, just like FEC, because of the need to wait for a group of packets to arrive (so they can be de-interleaved).

The media player's third job is decompressing the content. Although this task is computationally intensive, it is fairly straightforward. The thorny issue is how to decode media if the network protocol does not correct transmission errors. In many compression schemes, later data cannot be decompressed until the earlier data has been decompressed, because the later data is encoded relative to the earlier data. For a UDP-based transport, there can be packet loss. Thus, the encoding process must be designed to permit decoding despite packet loss. This requirement is why MPEG uses I-, P- and B-frames. Each I-frame can be decoded independently of the other frames to recover from the loss of any earlier frames.

The fourth job is to eliminate jitter, the bane of all real-time systems. The general solution that we described in Sec. 6.4.3 is to use a playout buffer. All streaming systems start by buffering 5–10 sec worth of media before starting to play, as shown in Fig. 7-54. Playing drains media regularly from the buffer so that the audio is clear and the video is smooth. The startup delay gives the buffer a chance to fill to the **low-water mark**. The idea is that data should now arrive regularly enough that the buffer is never completely emptied. If that were to happen, the media playout would stall. The value of buffering is that if the data are sometimes slow to arrive due to congestion, the buffered media will allow the playout to continue normally until new media arrive and the buffer is replenished.

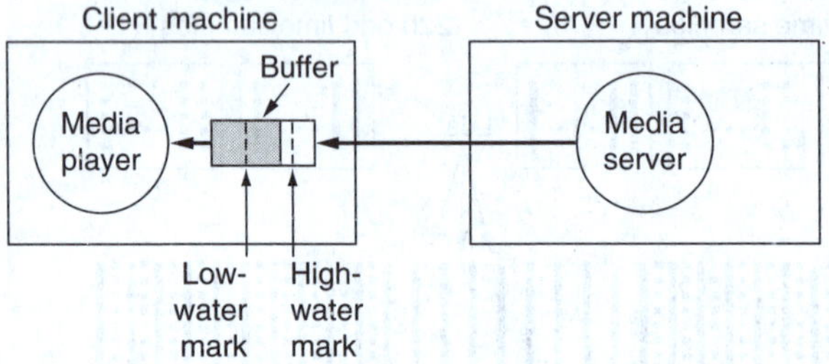

Figure 7-54. The media player buffers input from the media server and plays from the buffer rather than directly from the network.

How much buffering is needed, and how fast the media server sends media to fill up the buffer, depend on the network protocols. There are many possibilities. The largest factor in the design is whether a UDP-based transport or a TCP-based transport is used.

Suppose that a UDP-based transport like RTP is used. Further suppose that there is ample bandwidth to send packets from the media server to the media player with little loss, and little other traffic in the network. In this case, packets can be sent at the exact rate that the media is being played. Each packet will transit the network and, after a propagation delay, arrive at about the right time for the media player to present the media. Very little buffering is needed, as there is no variability in delay. If interleaving or FEC is used, more buffering is needed for at least the group of packets over which the interleaving or FEC is performed. However, this adds only a small amount of buffering.

Unfortunately, this scenario is unrealistic in two respects. First, bandwidth varies over network paths, so it is usually not clear to the media server whether there will be sufficient bandwidth before it tries to stream the media. A simple solution is to encode media at multiple resolutions and let each user choose a resolution that is supported by his Internet connectivity. Often there are just two levels: high quality, say, encoded at 1.5 Mbps or better, and low quality, say encoded at 512 kbps or less.

Second, there will be some jitter, or variation in how long it takes media samples to cross the network. This jitter comes from two sources. There is often an appreciable amount of competing traffic in the network—some of which can come from multitasking users themselves browsing the Web while ostensibly watching a streamed movie). This traffic will cause fluctuations in when the media arrives. Moreover, we care about the arrival of video frames and audio samples, not packets. With compression, video frames in particular may be larger or smaller depending on their content. An action sequence will typically take more bits to encode than a placid landscape. If the network bandwidth is constant, the rate of media delivery versus time will vary. The more jitter, or variation in delay, from these sources, the larger the low-water mark of the buffer needs to be to avoid underrun.

Now suppose that a TCP-based transport like HTTP is used to send the media. By performing retransmissions and waiting to deliver packets until they are in order, TCP will increase the jitter that is observed by the media player, perhaps significantly. The result is that a larger buffer and higher low-water mark are needed. However, there is an advantage. TCP will send data as fast as the network will carry it. Sometimes media may be delayed if loss must be repaired. But much of the time, the network will be able to deliver media faster than the player consumes it. In these periods, the buffer will fill and prevent future underruns. If the network is significantly faster than the average media rate, as is often the case, the buffer will fill rapidly after startup such that emptying it will soon cease to be a concern.

With TCP, or with UDP and a transmission rate that exceeds the playout rate, a question is how far ahead of the playout point the media player and media server are willing to proceed. Often they are willing to download the entire file.

However, proceeding far ahead of the playout point performs work that is not yet needed, may require significant storage, and is not necessary to avoid buffer underruns. When it is not wanted, the solution is for the media player to define a **high-water mark** in the buffer. Basically, the server just pumps out data until the buffer is filled to the high-water mark. Then the media player tells it to pause. Since data will continue to pour in until the server has gotten the pause request, the distance between the high-water mark and the end of the buffer has to be greater than the bandwidth-delay product of the network. After the server has stopped, the buffer will begin to empty. When it hits the low-water mark, the media player tells the media server to start again. To avoid underrun, the low-water mark must also take the bandwidth-delay product of the network into account when asking the media server to resume sending the media.

To start and stop the flow of media, the media player needs a remote control for it. This is what RTSP provides. It is defined in RFC 2326 and provides the mechanism for the player to control the server. As well as starting and stopping the stream, it can seek back or forward to a position, play specified intervals, and play at fast or slow speeds. It does not provide for the data stream, though, which is usually RTP over UDP or RTP over HTTP over TCP.

The main commands provided by RTSP are listed in Fig. 7-55. They have a simple text format, like HTTP messages, and are usually carried over TCP. RTSP can run over UDP too, since each command is acknowledged (and so can be resent if it is not acknowledged).

Command	Server action
DESCRIBE	List media parameters
SETUP	Establish a logical channel between the player and the server
PLAY	Start sending data to the client
RECORD	Start accepting data from the client
PAUSE	Temporarily stop sending data
TEARDOWN	Release the logical channel

Figure 7-55. RTSP commands from the player to the server.

Even though TCP would seem a poor fit to real-time traffic, it is often used in practice. The main reason is that it is able to pass through firewalls more easily than UDP, especially when run over the HTTP port. Most administrators configure firewalls to protect their networks from unwelcome visitors. They almost always allow TCP connections from remote port 80 to pass through for HTTP and Web traffic. Blocking that port quickly leads to unhappy campers. However, most other ports are blocked, including for RSTP and RTP, which use ports 554 and 5004, amongst others. Thus, the easiest way to get streaming media through the firewall is for the Web site to pretend it is an HTTP server sending a regular HTTP response, at least to the firewall.

There are some other advantages of TCP, too. Because it provides reliability, TCP gives the client a complete copy of the media. This makes it easy for a user to rewind to a previously viewed playout point without concern for lost data. Finally, TCP will buffer as much of the media as possible as quickly as possible. When buffer space is cheap (which it is when the disk is used for storage), the media player can download the media while the user watches. Once the download is complete, the user can watch uninterrupted, even if he loses connectivity. This property is helpful for mobiles because connectivity can change rapidly with motion.

The disadvantage of TCP is the added startup latency (because of TCP startup) and also a higher low-water mark. However, this is rarely much of a penalty as long as the network bandwidth exceeds the media rate by a large factor.

7.4.4 Streaming Live Media

It is not only recorded videos that are tremendously popular on the Web. Live media streaming is very popular too. Once it became possible to stream audio and video over the Internet, commercial radio and TV stations got the idea of broadcasting their content over the Internet as well as over the air. Not so long after that, college stations started putting their signals out over the Internet. Then college *students* started their own Internet broadcasts.

Today, people and companies of all sizes stream live audio and video. The area is a hotbed of innovation as the technologies and standards evolve. Live streaming is used for an online presence by major television stations. This is called **IPTV** (**IP TeleVision**). It is also used to broadcast radio stations like the BBC. This is called **Internet radio**. Both IPTV and Internet radio reach audiences worldwide for events ranging from fashion shows to World Cup soccer and test matches live from the Melbourne Cricket Ground. Live streaming over IP is used as a technology by cable providers to build their own broadcast systems. And it is widely used by low-budget operations from adult sites to zoos. With current technology, virtually anyone can start live streaming quickly and with little expense.

One approach to live streaming is to record programs to disk. Viewers can connect to the server's archives, pull up any program, and download it for listening. A **podcast** is an episode retrieved in this manner. For scheduled events, it is also possible to store content just after it is broadcast live, so the archive is only running, say, half an hour or less behind the live feed.

In fact, this approach is exactly the same as that used for the streaming media we just discussed. It is easy to do, all the techniques we have discussed work for it, and viewers can pick and choose among all the programs in the archive.

A different approach is to broadcast live over the Internet. Viewers tune in to an ongoing media stream, just like turning on the television. However, media players provide the added features of letting the user pause or rewind the playout. The live media will continue to be streamed and will be buffered by the player until the user is ready for it. From the browser's point of view, it looks exactly like the case of streaming stored media. It does not matter to the player whether the content comes from a file or is being sent live, and usually the player will not be able to tell (except that it is not possible to skip forward with a live stream). Given the similarity of mechanism, much of our previous discussion applies, but there are also some key differences.

Importantly, there is still the need for buffering at the client side to smooth out jitter. In fact, a larger amount of buffering is often needed for live streaming (independent of the consideration that the user may pause playback). When streaming from a file, the media can be pushed out at a rate that is greater than the playback rate. This will build up a buffer quickly to compensate for network jitter (and the player will stop the stream if it does not want to buffer more data). In contrast, live media streaming is always transmitted at precisely the rate it is generated, which is the same as the rate at which it is played back. It cannot be sent faster than this. As a consequence, the buffer must be large enough to handle the full range of network jitter. In practice, a 10–15 second startup delay is usually adequate, so this is not a large problem.

The other important difference is that live streaming events usually have hundreds or thousands of simultaneous viewers of the same content. Under these circumstances, the natural solution for live streaming is to use multicasting. This is not the case for streaming stored media because the users typically stream different content at any given time. Streaming to many users then consists of many individual streaming sessions that happen to occur at the same time.

A multicast streaming scheme works as follows. The server sends each media packet once using IP multicast to a group address. The network delivers a copy of the packet to each member of the group. All of the clients who want to receive the stream have joined the group. The clients do this using IGMP, rather than sending an RTSP message to the media server. This is because the media server is already sending the live stream (except before the first user joins). What is needed is to arrange for the stream to be received locally.

Since multicast is a one-to-many delivery service, the media is carried in RTP packets over a UDP transport. TCP only operates between a single sender and a single receiver. Since UDP does not provide reliability, some packets may be lost. To reduce the level of media loss to an acceptable level, we can use FEC and interleaving, as before.

In the case of FEC, there is a beneficial interaction with multicast that is shown in the parity example of Fig. 7-56. When the packets are multicast, different clients may lose different packets. For example, client 1 has lost packet *B*, client 2 lost the parity packet *P*, client 3 lost *D*, and client 4 did not lose any packets. However, even though three different packets are lost across the clients, each client can recover all of the data packets in this example. All that is required is that each client lose no more than one packet, whichever one it may be, so that the missing packet can be recovered by a parity computation. Nonnenmacher et al. (1997) describe how this idea can be used to boost reliability.

For a server with a large number of clients, multicast of media in RTP and UDP packets is clearly the most efficient way to operate. Otherwise, the server must transmit *N* streams when it has *N* clients, which will require a very large amount of network bandwidth at the server for large streaming events.

It may surprise you to learn that the Internet does not work like this in practice. What usually happens is that each user establishes a separate TCP connection to the server, and the media is streamed over that connection. To the client, this is the same as streaming stored media. And as with streaming stored media, there are several reasons for this seemingly poor choice.

The first reason is that IP multicast is not broadly available on the Internet. Some ISPs and networks support it internally, but it is usually not available across network boundaries as is needed for wide-area streaming. The other reasons are

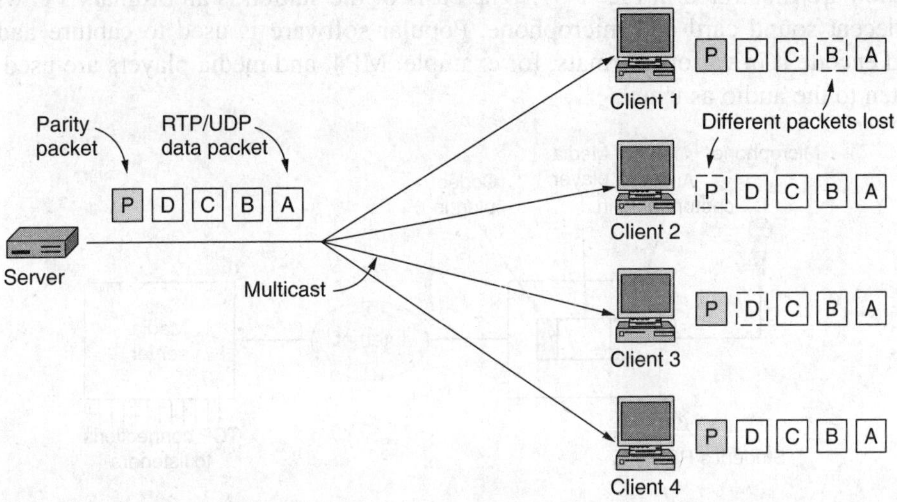

Figure 7-56. Multicast streaming media with a parity packet.

the same advantages of TCP over UDP as discussed earlier. Streaming with TCP will reach nearly all clients on the Internet, particularly when disguised as HTTP to pass through firewalls, and reliable media delivery allows users to rewind easily.

There is one important case in which UDP and multicast can be used for streaming, however: within a provider network. For example, a cable company might decide to broadcast TV channels to customer set-top boxes using IP technology instead of traditional video broadcasts. The use of IP to distribute broadcast video is broadly called IPTV, as discussed above. Since the cable company has complete control of its own network, it can engineer it to support IP multicast and have sufficient bandwidth for UDP-based distribution. All of this is invisible to the customer, as the IP technology exists within the **walled garden** of the provider. It looks just like cable TV in terms of service, but it is IP underneath, with the set-top box being a computer running UDP and the TV set being simply a monitor attached to the computer.

Back to the Internet case, the disadvantage of live streaming over TCP is that the server must send a separate copy of the media for each client. This is feasible for a moderate number of clients, especially for audio. The trick is to place the server at a location with good Internet connectivity so that there is sufficient bandwidth. Usually this means renting a server in a data center from a hosting provider, not using a server at home with only broadband Internet connectivity. There is a very competitive hosting market, so this need not be expensive.

In fact, it is easy for anybody, even a student, to set up and operate a streaming media server such as an Internet radio station. The main components of this station are illustrated in Fig. 7-57. The basis of the station is an ordinary PC with a decent sound card and microphone. Popular software is used to capture audio and encode it in various formats, for example, MP4, and media players are used to listen to the audio as usual.

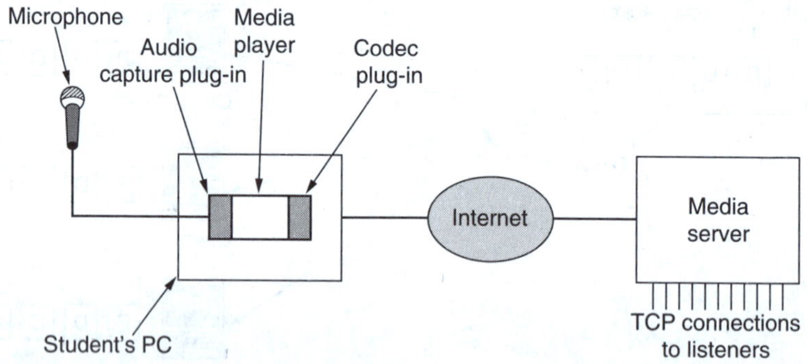

Figure 7-57. A student radio station.

The audio stream captured on the PC is then fed over the Internet to a media server with good network connectivity, either as podcasts for stored file streaming or for live streaming. The server handles the task of distributing the media via large numbers of TCP connections. It also presents a front-end Web site with pages about the station and links to the content that is available for streaming. There are commercial software packages for managing all the pieces, as well as open source packages such as icecast.

However, for a very large number of clients, it becomes infeasible to use TCP to send media to each client from a single server. There is simply not enough bandwidth to the one server. For large streaming sites, the streaming is done using a set of servers that are geographically spread out, so that a client can connect to the nearest server. This is a content distribution network that we will study at the end of the chapter.

7.4.5 Real-Time Conferencing

Once upon a time, voice calls were carried over the public switched telephone network, and network traffic was primarily voice traffic, with a little bit of data traffic here and there. Then came the Internet, and the Web. The data traffic grew and grew, until by 1999 there was as much data traffic as voice traffic (since voice is now digitized, both can be measured in bits). By 2002, the volume of data traffic was an order of magnitude more than the volume of voice traffic and still growing exponentially, with voice traffic staying almost flat.

The consequence of this growth has been to flip the telephone network on its head. Voice traffic is now carried using Internet technologies, and represents only a tiny fraction of the network bandwidth. This disruptive technology is known as **voice over IP**, and also as **Internet telephony**.

Voice-over-IP is used in several forms that are driven by strong economic factors. (English translation: it saves money so people use it.) One form is to have what look like regular (old-fashioned?) telephones that plug into the Ethernet and send calls over the network. Pehr Anderson was an undergraduate student at M.I.T. when he and his friends prototyped this design for a class project. They got a "B" grade. Not content, he started a company called NBX in 1996, pioneered this kind of voice over IP, and sold it to 3Com for $90 million three years later. Companies love this approach because it lets them do away with separate telephone lines and make do with the networks that they have already.

Another approach is to use IP technology to build a long-distance telephone network. In countries such as the U.S., this network can be accessed for competitive long-distance service by dialing a special prefix. Voice samples are put into packets that are injected into the network and pulled out of the packets when they leave it. Since IP equipment is much cheaper than telecommunications equipment this leads to cheaper services.

As an aside, the difference in price is not entirely technical. For many decades, telephone service was a regulated monopoly that guaranteed the phone companies a fixed percentage profit over their costs. Not surprisingly, this led them to run up costs, for example, by having lots and lots of redundant hardware, justified in the name of better reliability (the telephone system was only allowed to be down for a total of 2 hours every 40 years, or 3 min/year on average). This effect was often referred to as the "gold-plated telephone pole syndrome." Since deregulation, the effect has decreased, of course, but legacy equipment still exists. The IT industry never had any history operating like this, so it has always been lean and mean.

However, we will concentrate on the form of voice over IP that is likely the most visible to users: using one computer to call another computer. This form became commonplace as PCs began shipping with microphones, speakers, cameras, and CPUs fast enough to process media, and people started connecting to the Internet from home at broadband rates. A well-known example is the Skype software that was released starting in 2003. Skype and other companies also provide gateways to make it easy to call regular telephone numbers as well as computers with IP addresses.

As network bandwidth increased, video calls joined voice calls. Initially, video calls were in the domain of companies. Videoconferencing systems were designed to exchange video between two or more locations enabling executives at different locations to see each other while they held their meetings. However, with good broadband Internet connectivity and video compression software, home users can also videoconference. Tools such as Skype that started as audio-only now routinely include video with the calls so that friends and family across the world can see as well as hear each other.

From our point of view, Internet voice or video calls are also a media streaming problem, but one that is much more constrained than streaming a stored file or a live event. The added constraint is the low latency that is needed for a two-way conversation. The telephone network allows a one-way latency of up to 150 msec for acceptable usage, after which delay begins to be perceived as annoying by the participants. (International calls may have a latency of up to 400 msec, by which point they are far from a positive user experience.)

This low latency is difficult to achieve. Certainly, buffering 5–10 seconds of media is not going to work (as it would for broadcasting a live sports event). Instead, video and voice-over-IP systems must be engineered with a variety of techniques to minimize latency. This goal means starting with UDP as the clear choice rather than TCP, because TCP retransmissions introduce at least one round-trip worth of delay. Some forms of latency cannot be reduced, however, even with UDP. For example, the distance between Seattle and Amsterdam is close to 8,000 km. The speed-of-light propagation delay for this distance in optical fiber is 40 msec. Good luck beating that. In practice, the propagation delay through the network will be longer because it will cover a larger distance (the bits do not follow a great circle route) and have transmission delays as each IP router stores and forwards a packet. This fixed delay eats into the acceptable delay budget.

Another source of latency is related to packet size. Normally, large packets are the best way to use network bandwidth because they are more efficient. However, at an audio sampling rate of 64 kbps, a 1-KB packet would take 125 msec to fill (and even longer if the samples are compressed). This delay would consume most of the overall delay budget. In addition, if the 1-KB packet is sent over a broadband access link that runs at just 1 Mbps, it will take 8 msec to transmit. Then add another 8 msec for the packet to go over the broadband link at the other end. Clearly, large packets will not work.

Instead, voice-over-IP systems use short packets to reduce latency at the cost of bandwidth efficiency. They batch audio samples in smaller units, commonly 20 msec. At 64 kbps, this is 160 bytes of data, less with compression. However, by definition the delay from this packetization will be 20 msec. The transmission delay will be smaller as well because the packet is shorter. In our example, it would reduce to around 1 msec. By using short packets, the minimum one-way delay for a Seattle-to-Amsterdam packet has been reduced from an unacceptable 181 msec (40 + 125 + 16) to an acceptable 62 msec (40 + 20 + 2).

We have not even talked about the software overhead, but it, too, will eat up some of the delay budget. This is especially true for video, since compression is usually needed to fit video into the available bandwidth. Unlike streaming from a stored file, there is no time to have a computationally intensive encoder for high levels of compression. The encoder and the decoder must both run quickly.

Buffering is still needed to play out the media samples on time (to avoid unintelligible audio or jerky video), but the amount of buffering must be kept very small since the time remaining in our delay budget is measured in milliseconds.

When a packet takes too long to arrive, the player will skip over the missing samples, perhaps playing ambient noise or repeating a frame to mask the loss to the user. There is a trade-off between the size of the buffer used to handle jitter and the amount of media that is lost. A smaller buffer reduces latency but results in more loss due to jitter. Eventually, as the size of the buffer shrinks, the loss will become noticeable to the user.

Observant readers may have noticed that we have said nothing about the network layer protocols so far in this section. The network can reduce latency, or at least jitter, by using quality of service mechanisms. The reason that this issue has not come up before is that streaming is able to operate with substantial latency, even in the live streaming case. If latency is not a major concern, a buffer at the end host is sufficient to handle the problem of jitter. However, for real-time conferencing, it is usually important to have the network reduce delay and jitter to help meet the delay budget. The only time that it is not important is when there is so much network bandwidth that everyone gets good service.

In Chap. 5, we described two quality of service mechanisms that help with this goal. One mechanism is DS (Differentiated Services), in which packets are marked as belonging to different classes that receive different handling within the network. The appropriate marking for voice-over-IP packets is low delay. In practice, systems set the DS codepoint to the well-known value for the *Expedited Forwarding* class with *Low Delay* type of service. This is especially useful over broadband access links, as these links tend to be congested when Web traffic or other traffic competes for use of the link. Given a stable network path, delay and jitter are increased by congestion. Every 1-KB packet takes 8 msec to send over a 1-Mbps link, and a voice-over-IP packet will incur these delays if it is sitting in a queue behind Web traffic. However, with a low delay marking the voice-over-IP packets will jump to the head of the queue, bypassing the Web packets and lowering their delay.

The second mechanism that can reduce delay is to make sure that there is sufficient bandwidth. If the available bandwidth varies or the transmission rate fluctuates (as with compressed video) and there is sometimes not sufficient bandwidth, queues will build up and add to the delay. This will occur even with DS. To ensure sufficient bandwidth, a reservation can be made with the network. This capability is provided by integrated services. Unfortunately, it is not widely deployed. Instead, networks are engineered for an expected traffic level or network customers are provided with service-level agreements for a given traffic level. Applications must operate below this level to avoid causing congestion and introducing unnecessary delays. For casual videoconferencing at home, the user may choose a video quality as a proxy for bandwidth needs, or the software may test the network path and select an appropriate quality automatically.

Any of the above factors can cause the latency to become unacceptable, so real-time conferencing requires that attention be paid to all of them. For an overview of voice over IP and analysis of these factors, see Goode (2002).

Now that we have discussed the problem of latency in the media streaming path, we will move on to the other main problem that conferencing systems must address. This problem is how to set up and tear down calls. We will look at two protocols that are widely used for this purpose, H.323 and SIP. Skype is another important system, but its inner workings are proprietary.

H.323

One thing that was clear to everyone before voice and video calls were made over the Internet was that if each vendor designed its own protocol stack, the system would never work. To avoid this problem, a number of interested parties got together under ITU auspices to work out standards. In 1996, ITU issued recommendation **H.323**, entitled "Visual Telephone Systems and Equipment for Local Area Networks Which Provide a Non-Guaranteed Quality of Service." Only the telephone industry would think of such a name. It was quickly changed to "Packet-based Multimedia Communications Systems" in the 1998 revision. H.323 was the basis for the first widespread Internet conferencing systems. It remains the most widely deployed solution, in its seventh version as of 2009.

H.323 is more of an architectural overview of Internet telephony than a specific protocol. It references a large number of specific protocols for speech coding, call setup, signaling, data transport, and other areas rather than specifying these things itself. The general model is depicted in Fig. 7-58. At the center is a **gateway** that connects the Internet to the telephone network. It speaks the H.323 protocols on the Internet side and the PSTN protocols on the telephone side. The communicating devices are called **terminals**. A LAN may have a **gatekeeper**, which controls the end points under its jurisdiction, called a **zone**.

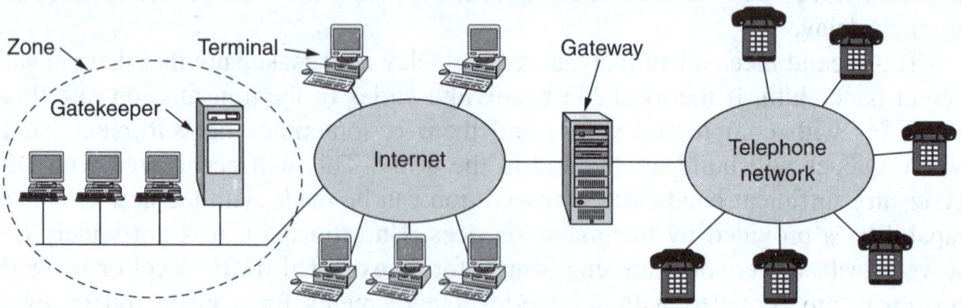

Figure 7-58. The H.323 architectural model for Internet telephony.

A telephone network needs a number of protocols. To start with, there is a protocol for encoding and decoding audio and video. Standard telephony representations of a single voice channel as 64 kbps of digital audio (8000 samples of 8 bits per second) are defined in ITU recommendation **G.711**. All H.323 systems must support G.711. Other encodings that compress speech are permitted, but not required. They use different compression algorithms and make different trade-offs between quality and bandwidth. For video, the MPEG forms of video compression that we described above are supported, including H.264.

Since multiple compression algorithms are permitted, a protocol is needed to allow the terminals to negotiate which one they are going to use. This protocol is called **H.245**. It also negotiates other aspects of the connection such as the bit rate. RTCP is need for the control of the RTP channels. Also required is a protocol for establishing and releasing connections, providing dial tones, making ringing sounds, and the rest of the standard telephony. ITU **Q.931** is used here. The terminals need a protocol for talking to the gatekeeper (if present) as well. For this purpose, **H.225** is used. The PC-to-gatekeeper channel it manages is called the **RAS** (**Registration/Admission/Status**) channel. This channel allows terminals to join and leave the zone, request and return bandwidth, and provide status updates, among other things. Finally, a protocol is needed for the actual data transmission. RTP over UDP is used for this purpose. It is managed by RTCP, as usual. The positioning of all these protocols is shown in Fig. 7-59.

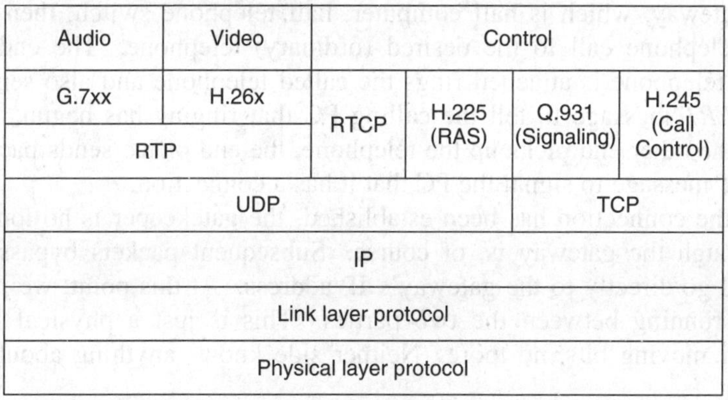

Figure 7-59. The H.323 protocol stack.

To see how these protocols fit together, consider the case of a PC terminal on a LAN (with a gatekeeper) calling a remote telephone. The PC first has to discover the gatekeeper, so it broadcasts a UDP gatekeeper discovery packet to port 1718. When the gatekeeper responds, the PC learns the gatekeeper's IP address. Now the PC registers with the gatekeeper by sending it a RAS message in a UDP packet. After it has been accepted, the PC sends the gatekeeper a RAS admission message requesting bandwidth. Only after bandwidth has been granted may call setup begin. The idea of requesting bandwidth in advance is to allow the gatekeeper to limit the number of calls. It can then avoid oversubscribing the outgoing line in order to help provide the necessary quality of service.

As an aside, the telephone system does the same thing. When you pick up the receiver, a signal is sent to the local end office. If the office has enough spare capacity for another call, it generates a dial tone. If not, you hear nothing. Nowadays, the system is so overdimensioned that the dial tone is nearly always instantaneous, but in the early days of telephony, it often took a few seconds. So if your grandchildren ever ask you "Why are there dial tones?" now you know. Except by then, probably telephones will no longer exist.

The PC now establishes a TCP connection to the gatekeeper to begin call setup. Call setup uses existing telephone network protocols, which are connection oriented, so TCP is needed. In contrast, the telephone system has nothing like RAS to allow telephones to announce their presence, so the H.323 designers were free to use either UDP or TCP for RAS, and they chose the lower-overhead UDP.

Now that it has bandwidth allocated, the PC can send a Q.931 *SETUP* message over the TCP connection. This message specifies the number of the telephone being called (or the IP address and port, if a computer is being called). The gatekeeper responds with a Q.931 *CALL PROCEEDING* message to acknowledge correct receipt of the request. The gatekeeper then forwards the *SETUP* message to the gateway.

The gateway, which is half computer, half telephone switch, then makes an ordinary telephone call to the desired (ordinary) telephone. The end office to which the telephone is attached rings the called telephone and also sends back a Q.931 *ALERT* message to tell the calling PC that ringing has begun. When the person at the other end picks up the telephone, the end office sends back a Q.931 *CONNECT* message to signal the PC that it has a connection.

Once the connection has been established, the gatekeeper is no longer in the loop, although the gateway is, of course. Subsequent packets bypass the gatekeeper and go directly to the gateway's IP address. At this point, we just have a bare tube running between the two parties. This is just a physical layer connection for moving bits, no more. Neither side knows anything about the other one.

The H.245 protocol is now used to negotiate the parameters of the call. It uses the H.245 control channel, which is always open. Each side starts out by announcing its capabilities, for example, whether it can handle video (H.323 can handle video) or conference calls, which codecs it supports, etc. Once each side knows what the other one can handle, two unidirectional data channels are set up and a codec and other parameters are assigned to each one. Since each side may have different equipment, it is entirely possible that the codecs on the forward and reverse channels are different. After all negotiations are complete, data flow can begin using RTP. It is managed using RTCP, which plays a role in congestion control. If video is present, RTCP handles the audio/video synchronization. The various channels are shown in Fig. 7-60. When either party hangs up, the Q.931 call signaling channel is used to tear down the connection after the call has been completed in order to free up resources no longer needed.

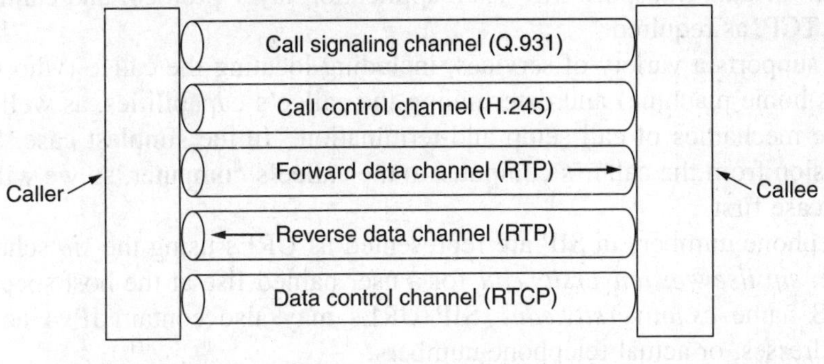

Figure 7-60. Logical channels between the caller and callee during a call.

When the call is terminated, the calling PC contacts the gatekeeper again with a RAS message to release the bandwidth it has been assigned. Alternatively, it can make another call.

We have not said anything about quality of service as part of H.323, even though we have said it is an important part of making real-time conferencing a success. The reason is that QoS falls outside the scope of H.323. If the underlying network is capable of producing a stable, jitter-free connection from the calling PC to the gateway, the QoS on the call will be good; otherwise, it will not be. However, any portion of the call on the telephone side will be jitter-free, because that is how the telephone network is designed.

SIP—The Session Initiation Protocol

H.323 was designed by ITU. Many people in the Internet community saw it as a typical telco product: large, complex, and inflexible. Consequently, IETF set up a committee to design a simpler and more modular way to do voice over IP. The major result to date is **SIP (Session Initiation Protocol)**. The latest version is described in RFC 3261, which was written in 2002. This protocol describes how to set up Internet telephone calls, video conferences, and other multimedia connections. Unlike H.323, which is a complete protocol suite, SIP is a single module, but it has been designed to interwork well with existing Internet applications. For example, it defines telephone numbers as URLs, so that Web pages can contain them, allowing a click on a link to initiate a telephone call (the same way the *mailto* scheme allows a click on a link to bring up a program to send an email message).

SIP can establish two-party sessions (ordinary telephone calls), multiparty sessions (where everyone can hear and speak), and multicast sessions (one sender, many receivers). The sessions may contain audio, video, or data, the latter being useful for multiplayer real-time games, for example. SIP just handles setup, management, and termination of sessions. Other protocols, such as RTP/RTCP, are also used for data transport. SIP is an application-layer protocol and can run over UDP or TCP, as required.

SIP supports a variety of services, including locating the callee (who may not be at his home machine) and determining the callee's capabilities, as well as handling the mechanics of call setup and termination. In the simplest case, SIP sets up a session from the caller's computer to the callee's computer, so we will examine that case first.

Telephone numbers in SIP are represented as URLs using the *sip* scheme, for example, *sip:ilse@cs.university.edu* for a user named Ilse at the host specified by the DNS name *cs.university.edu*. SIP URLs may also contain IPv4 addresses, IPv6 addresses, or actual telephone numbers.

The SIP protocol is a text-based protocol modeled on HTTP. One party sends a message in ASCII text consisting of a method name on the first line, followed by additional lines containing headers for passing parameters. Many of the headers are taken from MIME to allow SIP to interwork with existing Internet applications. The six methods defined by the core specification are listed in Fig. 7-61.

Method	Description
INVITE	Request initiation of a session
ACK	Confirm that a session has been initiated
BYE	Request termination of a session
OPTIONS	Query a host about its capabilities
CANCEL	Cancel a pending request
REGISTER	Inform a redirection server about the user's current location

Figure 7-61. SIP methods.

To establish a session, the caller either creates a TCP connection with the callee and sends an *INVITE* message over it or sends the *INVITE* message in a UDP packet. In both cases, the headers on the second and subsequent lines describe the structure of the message body, which contains the caller's capabilities, media types, and formats. If the callee accepts the call, it responds with an HTTP-type reply code (a three-digit number using the groups of Fig. 7-38, 200 for acceptance). Following the reply-code line, the callee also may supply information about its capabilities, media types, and formats.

Connection is done using a three-way handshake, so the caller responds with an *ACK* message to finish the protocol and confirm receipt of the 200 message.

Either party may request termination of a session by sending a message with the *BYE* method. When the other side acknowledges it, the session is terminated.

The *OPTIONS* method is used to query a machine about its own capabilities. It is typically used before a session is initiated to find out if that machine is even capable of voice over IP or whatever type of session is being contemplated.

The *REGISTER* method relates to SIP's ability to track down and connect to a user who is away from home. This message is sent to a SIP location server that keeps track of who is where. That server can later be queried to find the user's current location. The operation of redirection is illustrated in Fig. 7-62. Here, the caller sends the *INVITE* message to a proxy server to hide the possible redirection. The proxy then looks up where the user is and sends the *INVITE* message there. It then acts as a relay for the subsequent messages in the three-way handshake. The *LOOKUP* and *REPLY* messages are not part of SIP; any convenient protocol can be used, depending on what kind of location server is used.

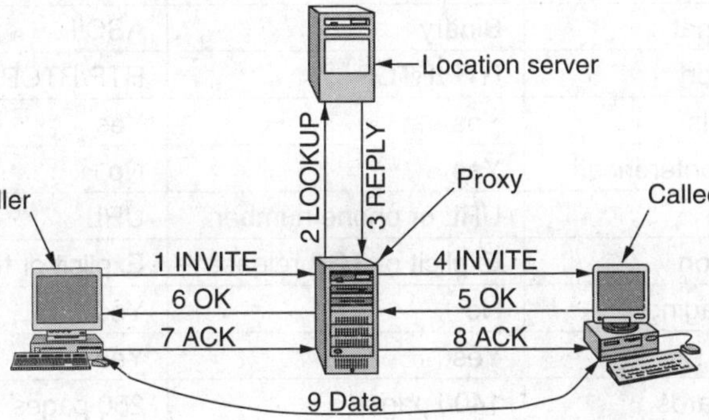

Figure 7-62. Use of a proxy server and redirection with SIP.

SIP has a variety of other features that we will not describe here, including call waiting, call screening, encryption, and authentication. It also has the ability to place calls from a computer to an ordinary telephone, if a suitable gateway between the Internet and telephone system is available.

Comparison of H.323 and SIP

Both H.323 and SIP allow two-party and multiparty calls using both computers and telephones as end points. Both support parameter negotiation, encryption, and the RTP/RTCP protocols. A summary of their similarities and differences is given in Fig. 7-63.

Although the feature sets are similar, the two protocols differ widely in philosophy. H.323 is a typical, heavyweight, telephone-industry standard, specifying the complete protocol stack and defining precisely what is allowed and what is forbidden. This approach leads to very well defined protocols in each layer, easing the task of interoperability. The price paid is a large, complex, and rigid standard that is difficult to adapt to future applications.

In contrast, SIP is a typical Internet protocol that works by exchanging short lines of ASCII text. It is a lightweight module that interworks well with other Internet protocols but less well with existing telephone system signaling protocols.

Item	H.323	SIP
Designed by	ITU	IETF
Compatibility with PSTN	Yes	Largely
Compatibility with Internet	Yes, over time	Yes
Architecture	Monolithic	Modular
Completeness	Full protocol stack	SIP just handles setup
Parameter negotiation	Yes	Yes
Call signaling	Q.931 over TCP	SIP over TCP or UDP
Message format	Binary	ASCII
Media transport	RTP/RTCP	RTP/RTCP
Multiparty calls	Yes	Yes
Multimedia conferences	Yes	No
Addressing	URL or phone number	URL
Call termination	Explicit or TCP release	Explicit or timeout
Instant messaging	No	Yes
Encryption	Yes	Yes
Size of standards	1400 pages	250 pages
Implementation	Large and complex	Moderate, but issues
Status	Widespread, esp. video	Alternative, esp. voice

Figure 7-63. Comparison of H.323 and SIP.

Because the IETF model of voice over IP is highly modular, it is flexible and can be adapted to new applications easily. The downside is that is has suffered from ongoing interoperability problems as people try to interpret what the standard means.

7.5 CONTENT DELIVERY

The Internet used to be all about communication, like the telephone network. Early on, academics would communicate with remote machines, logging in over the network to perform tasks. People have used email to communicate with each other for a long time, and now use video and voice over IP as well. Since the Web grew up, however, the Internet has become more about content than communication. Many people use the Web to find information, and there is a tremendous amount of peer-to-peer file sharing that is driven by access to movies, music, and programs. The switch to content has been so pronounced that the majority of Internet bandwidth is now used to deliver stored videos.

Because the task of distributing content is different from that of communication, it places different requirements on the network. For example, if Sally wants to talk to Jitu, she may make a voice-over-IP call to his mobile. The communication must be with a particular computer; it will do no good to call Paul's computer. But if Jitu wants to watch his team's latest cricket match, he is happy to stream video from whichever computer can provide the service. He does not mind whether the computer is Sally's or Paul's, or, more likely, an unknown server in the Internet. That is, location does not matter for content, except as it affects performance (and legality).

The other difference is that some Web sites that provide content have become tremendously popular. YouTube is a prime example. It allows users to share videos of their own creation on every conceivable topic. Many people want to do this. The rest of us want to watch. With all of these bandwidth-hungry videos, it is estimated that YouTube accounts for up to 10% of Internet traffic today.

No single server is powerful or reliable enough to handle such a startling level of demand. Instead, YouTube and other large content providers build their own content distribution networks. These networks use data centers spread around the world to serve content to an extremely large number of clients with good performance and availability.

The techniques that are used for content distribution have been developed over time. Early in the growth of the Web, its popularity was almost its undoing. More demands for content led to servers and networks that were frequently overloaded. Many people began to call the WWW the World Wide Wait.

In response to consumer demand, very large amounts of bandwidth were provisioned in the core of the Internet, and faster broadband connectivity was rolled out at the edge of the network. This bandwidth was key to improving performance, but it is only part of the solution. To reduce the endless delays, researchers also developed different architectures to use the bandwidth for distributing content.

One architecture is a **CDN (Content Distribution Network)**. In it, a provider sets up a distributed collection of machines at locations inside the Internet and uses them to serve content to clients. This is the choice of the big players. An alternative architecture is a **P2P (Peer-to-Peer)** network. In it, a collection of computers pool their resources to serve content to each other, without separately provisioned servers or any central point of control. This idea has captured people's imagination because, by acting together, many little players can pack an enormous punch.

In this section, we will look at the problem of distributing content on the Internet and some of the solutions that are used in practice. After briefly discussing content popularity and Internet traffic, we will describe how to build powerful Web servers and use caching to improve performance for Web clients. Then we will come to the two main architectures for distributing content: CDNs and P2P networks. There design and properties are quite different, as we will see.

7.5.1 Content and Internet Traffic

To design and engineer networks that work well, we need an understanding of the traffic that they must carry. With the shift to content, for example, servers have migrated from company offices to Internet data centers that provide large numbers of machines with excellent network connectivity. To run even a small server nowadays, it is easier and cheaper to rent a virtual server hosted in an Internet data center than to operate a real machine in a home or office with broadband connectivity to the Internet.

Fortunately, there are only two facts about Internet traffic that is it essential to know. The first fact is that it changes quickly, not only in the details but in the overall makeup. Before 1994, most traffic was traditional FTP file transfer (for moving programs and data sets between computers) and email. Then the Web arrived and grew exponentially. Web traffic left FTP and email traffic in the dust long before the dot com bubble of 2000. Starting around 2000, P2P file sharing for music and then movies took off. By 2003, most Internet traffic was P2P traffic, leaving the Web in the dust. Sometime in the late 2000s, video streamed using content distribution methods by sites like YouTube began to exceed P2P traffic. By 2014, Cisco predicts that 90% of all Internet traffic will be video in one form or another (Cisco, 2010).

It is not always traffic volume that matters. For instance, while voice-over-IP traffic boomed even before Skype started in 2003, it will always be a minor blip on the chart because the bandwidth requirements of audio are two orders of magnitude lower than for video. However, voice-over-IP traffic stresses the network in other ways because it is sensitive to latency. As another example, online social networks have grown furiously since Facebook started in 2004. In 2010, for the first time, Facebook reached more users on the Web per day than Google. Even putting the traffic aside (and there is an awful lot of traffic), online social networks are important because they are changing the way that people interact via the Internet.

The point we are making is that seismic shifts in Internet traffic happen quickly, and with some regularity. What will come next? Please check back in the 6th edition of this book and we will let you know.

The second essential fact about Internet traffic is that it is highly skewed. Many properties with which we are familiar are clustered around an average. For instance, most adults are close to the average height. There are some tall people and some short people, but few very tall or very short people. For these kinds of properties, it is possible to design for a range that is not very large but nonetheless captures the majority of the population.

Internet traffic is not like this. For a long time, it has been known that there are a small number of Web sites with massive traffic and a vast number of Web site with much smaller traffic. This feature has become part of the language of networking. Early papers talked about traffic in terms of **packet trains**, the idea being that express trains with a large number of packets would suddenly travel down a link (Jain and Routhier, 1986). This was formalized as the notion of **self-similarity**, which for our purposes can be thought of as network traffic that exhibits many short and many long gaps even when viewed at different time scales (Leland et al., 1994). Later work spoke of long traffic flows as **elephants** and short traffic flows as **mice**. The idea is that there are only a few elephants and many mice, but the elephants matter because they are so big.

Returning to Web content, the same sort of skew is evident. Experience with video rental stores, public libraries, and other such organizations shows that not all items are equally popular. Experimentally, when N movies are available, the fraction of all requests for the kth most popular one is approximately C/k. Here, C is computed to normalize the sum to 1, namely,

$$C = 1/(1 + 1/2 + 1/3 + 1/4 + 1/5 + \cdots + 1/N)$$

Thus, the most popular movie is seven times as popular as the number seven movie. This result is known as **Zipf's law** (Zipf, 1949). It is named after George Zipf, a professor of linguistics at Harvard University who noted that the frequency of a word's usage in a large body of text is inversely proportional to its rank. For example, the 40th most common word is used twice as much as the 80th most common word and three times as much as the 120th most common word.

A Zipf distribution is shown in Fig. 7-64(a). It captures the notion that there are a small number of popular items and a great many unpopular items. To recognize distributions of this form, it is convenient to plot the data on a log scale on both axes, as shown in Fig. 7-64(b). The result should be a straight line.

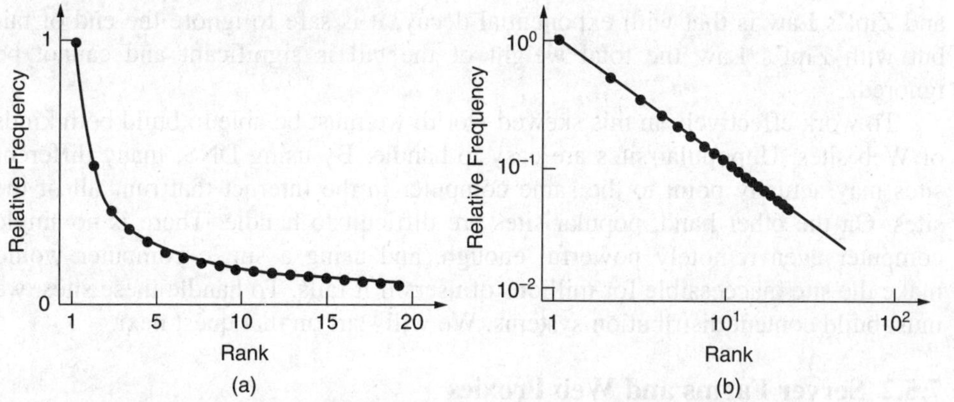

Figure 7-64. Zipf distribution (a) On a linear scale. (b) On a log-log scale.

When people looked at the popularity of Web pages, it also turned out to roughly follow Zipf's law (Breslau et al., 1999). A Zipf distribution is one example in a family of distributions known as **power laws**. Power laws are evident in many human phenomena, such as the distribution of city populations and of wealth. They have the same propensity to describe a few large players and a great many smaller players, and they too appear as a straight line on a log-log plot. It was soon discovered that the topology of the Internet could be roughly described with power laws (Faloutsos et al., 1999). Next, researchers began plotting every imaginable property of the Internet on a log scale, observing a straight line, and shouting: "Power law!"

However, what matters more than a straight line on a log-log plot is what these distributions mean for the design and use of networks. Given the many forms of content that have Zipf or power law distributions, it seems fundamental that Web sites on the Internet are Zipf-like in popularity. This in turn means that an average site is not a useful representation. Sites are better described as either popular or unpopular. Both kinds of sites matter. The popular sites obviously matter, since a few popular sites may be responsible for most of the traffic on the Internet. Perhaps surprisingly, the unpopular sites can matter too. This is because the total amount of traffic directed to the unpopular sites can add up to a large fraction of the overall traffic. The reason is that there are so many unpopular sites. The notion that, collectively, many unpopular choices can matter has been popularized by books such as *The Long Tail* (Anderson, 2008a).

Curves showing decay like that of Fig. 7-64(a) are common, but they are not all the same. In particular, situations in which the rate of decay is proportional to how much material is left (such as with unstable radioactive atoms) exhibit **exponential decay**, which drops off much faster than Zipf's Law. The number of items, say atoms, left after time t is usually expressed as $e^{-t/\alpha}$, where the constant α determines how fast the decay is. The difference between exponential decay and Zipf's Law is that with exponential decay, it is safe to ignore the end of tail but with Zipf's Law the total weight of the tail is significant and cannot be ignored.

To work effectively in this skewed world, we must be able to build both kinds of Web sites. Unpopular sites are easy to handle. By using DNS, many different sites may actually point to the same computer in the Internet that runs all of the sites. On the other hand, popular sites are difficult to handle. There is no single computer even remotely powerful enough, and using a single computer would make the site inaccessible for millions of users if it fails. To handle these sites, we must build content distribution systems. We will start on that quest next.

7.5.2 Server Farms and Web Proxies

The Web designs that we have seen so far have a single server machine talking to multiple client machines. To build large Web sites that perform well, we can speed up processing on either the server side or the client side. On the server side, more powerful Web servers can be built with a server farm, in which a cluster of computers acts as a single server. On the client side, better performance can be achieved with better caching techniques. In particular, proxy caches provide a large shared cache for a group of clients.

We will describe each of these techniques in turn. However, note that neither technique is sufficient to build the largest Web sites. Those popular sites require the content distribution methods that we describe in the following sections, which combine computers at many different locations.

Server Farms

No matter how much bandwidth one machine has, it can only serve so many Web requests before the load is too great. The solution in this case is to use more than one computer to make a Web server. This leads to the **server farm** model of Fig. 7-65.

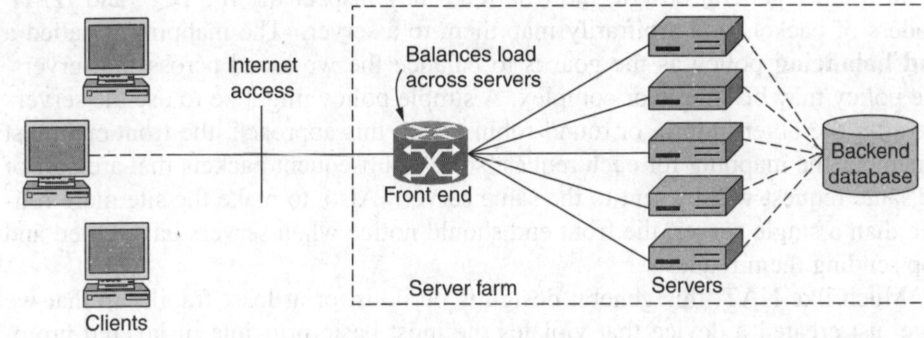

Figure 7-65. A server farm.

The difficulty with this seemingly simple model is that the set of computers that make up the server farm must look like a single logical Web site to clients. If they do not, we have just set up different Web sites that run in parallel.

There are several possible solutions to make the set of servers appear to be one Web site. All of the solutions assume that any of the servers can handle a request from any client. To do this, each server must have a copy of the Web site. The servers are shown as connected to a common back-end database by a dashed line for this purpose.

One solution is to use DNS to spread the requests across the servers in the server farm. When a DNS request is made for the Web URL, the DNS server returns a rotating list of the IP addresses of the servers. Each client tries one IP address, typically the first on the list. The effect is that different clients contact different servers to access the same Web site, just as intended. The DNS method is at the heart of CDNs, and we will revisit it later in this section.

The other solutions are based on a **front end** that sprays incoming requests over the pool of servers in the server farm. This happens even when the client contacts the server farm using a single destination IP address. The front end is usually a link-layer switch or an IP router, that is, a device that handles frames or packets. All of the solutions are based on it (or the servers) peeking at the network, transport, or application layer headers and using them in nonstandard ways. A Web request and response are carried as a TCP connection. To work correctly, the front end must distribute all of the packets for a request to the same server.

A simple design is for the front end to broadcast all of the incoming requests to all of the servers. Each server answers only a fraction of the requests by prior agreement. For example, 16 servers might look at the source IP address and reply to the request only if the last 4 bits of the source IP address match their configured selectors. Other packets are discarded. While this is wasteful of incoming bandwidth, often the responses are much longer than the request, so it is not nearly as inefficient as it sounds.

In a more general design, the front end may inspect the IP, TCP, and HTTP headers of packets and arbitrarily map them to a server. The mapping is called a **load balancing** policy as the goal is to balance the workload across the servers. The policy may be simple or complex. A simple policy might be to use the servers one after the other in turn, or round-robin. With this approach, the front end must remember the mapping for each request so that subsequent packets that are part of the same request will be sent to the same server. Also, to make the site more reliable than a single server, the front end should notice when servers have failed and stop sending them requests.

Much like NAT, this general design is perilous, or at least fragile, in that we have just created a device that violates the most basic principle of layered protocols: each layer must use its own header for control purposes and may not inspect and use information from the payload for any purpose. But people design such systems anyway and when they break in the future due to changes in higher layers, they tend to be surprised. The front end in this case is a switch or router, but it may take action based on transport layer information or higher. Such a box is called a **middlebox** because it interposes itself in the middle of a network path in which it has no business, according to the protocol stack. In this case, the front end is best considered an internal part of a server farm that terminates all layers up to the application layer (and hence can use all of the header information for those layers).

Nonetheless, as with NAT, this design is useful in practice. The reason for looking at TCP headers is that it is possible to do a better job of load balancing than with IP information alone. For example, one IP address may represent an entire company and make many requests. It is only by looking at TCP or higher-layer information that these requests can be mapped to different servers.

The reason for looking at the HTTP headers is somewhat different. Many Web interactions access and update databases, such as when a customer looks up her most recent purchase. The server that fields this request will have to query the back-end database. It is useful to direct subsequent requests from the same user to the same server, because that server has already cached information about the user. The simplest way to cause this to happen is to use Web cookies (or other information to distinguish the user) and to inspect the HTTP headers to find the cookies.

As a final note, although we have described this design for Web sites, a server farm can be built for other kinds of servers as well. An example is servers streaming media over UDP. The only change that is required is for the front end to be able to load balance these requests (which will have different protocol header fields than Web requests).

Web Proxies

Web requests and responses are sent using HTTP. In Sec. 7.3, we described how browsers can cache responses and reuse them to answer future requests. Various header fields and rules are used by the browser to determine if a cached copy of a Web page is still fresh. We will not repeat that material here.

Caching improves performance by shortening the response time and reducing the network load. If the browser can determine that a cached page is fresh by itself, the page can be fetched from the cache immediately, with no network traffic at all. However, even if the browser must ask the server for confirmation that the page is still fresh, the response time is shortened and the network load is reduced, especially for large pages, since only a small message needs to be sent.

However, the best the browser can do is to cache all of the Web pages that the user has previously visited. From our discussion of popularity, you may recall that as well as a few popular pages that many people visit repeatedly, there are many, many unpopular pages. In practice, this limits the effectiveness of browser caching because there are a large number of pages that are visited just once by a given user. These pages always have to be fetched from the server.

One strategy to make caches more effective is to share the cache among multiple users. That way, a page already fetched for one user can be returned to another user when that user makes the same request. Without browser caching, both users would need to fetch the page from the server. Of course, this sharing cannot be done for encrypted traffic, pages that require authentication, and uncacheable pages (e.g., current stock prices) that are returned by programs. Dynamic pages created by programs, especially, are a growing case for which caching is not effective. Nonetheless, there are plenty of Web pages that are visible to many users and look the same no matter which user makes the request (e.g., images).

A **Web proxy** is used to share a cache among users. A proxy is an agent that acts on behalf of someone else, such as the user. There are many kinds of proxies. For instance, an ARP proxy replies to ARP requests on behalf of a user who is elsewhere (and cannot reply for himself). A Web proxy fetches Web requests on behalf of its users. It normally provides caching of the Web responses, and since it is shared across users it has a substantially larger cache than a browser.

When a proxy is used, the typical setup is for an organization to operate one Web proxy for all of its users. The organization might be a company or an ISP. Both stand to benefit by speeding up Web requests for its users and reducing its bandwidth needs. While flat pricing, independent of usage, is common for end users, most companies and ISPs are charged according to the bandwidth that they use.

This setup is shown in Fig. 7-66. To use the proxy, each browser is configured to make page requests to the proxy instead of to the page's real server. If the proxy has the page, it returns the page immediately. If not, it fetches the page from the server, adds it to the cache for future use, and returns it to the client that requested it.

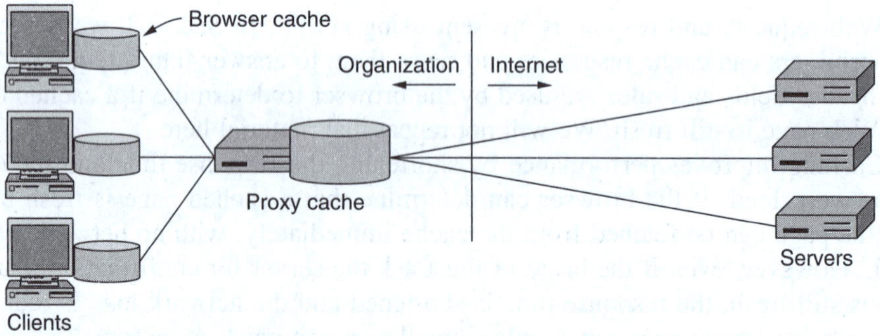

Figure 7-66. A proxy cache between Web browsers and Web servers.

As well as sending Web requests to the proxy instead of the real server, clients perform their own caching using its browser cache. The proxy is only consulted after the browser has tried to satisfy the request from its own cache. That is, the proxy provides a second level of caching.

Further proxies may be added to provide additional levels of caching. Each proxy (or browser) makes requests via its **upstream proxy**. Each upstream proxy caches for the **downstream proxies** (or browsers). Thus, it is possible for browsers in a company to use a company proxy, which uses an ISP proxy, which contacts Web servers directly. However, the single level of proxy caching we have shown in Fig. 7-66 is often sufficient to gain most of the potential benefits, in practice. The problem again is the long tail of popularity. Studies of Web traffic have shown that shared caching is especially beneficial until the number of users reaches about the size of a small company (say, 100 people). As the number of people grows larger, the benefits of sharing a cache become marginal because of the unpopular requests that cannot be cached due to lack of storage space (Wolman et al., 1999).

Web proxies provide additional benefits that are often a factor in the decision to deploy them. One benefit is to filter content. The administrator may configure the proxy to blacklist sites or otherwise filter the requests that it makes. For example, many administrators frown on employees watching YouTube videos (or worse yet, pornography) on company time and set their filters accordingly. Another benefit of having proxies is privacy or anonymity, when the proxy shields the identity of the user from the server.

7.5.3 Content Delivery Networks

Server farms and Web proxies help to build large sites and to improve Web performance, but they are not sufficient for truly popular Web sites that must serve content on a global scale. For these sites, a different approach is needed.

CDNs (**Content Delivery Networks**) turn the idea of traditional Web caching on its head. Instead, of having clients look for a copy of the requested page in a nearby cache, it is the provider who places a copy of the page in a set of nodes at different locations and directs the client to use a nearby node as the server.

An example of the path that data follows when it is distributed by a CDN is shown in Fig. 7-67. It is a tree. The origin server in the CDN distributes a copy of the content to other nodes in the CDN, in Sydney, Boston, and Amsterdam, in this example. This is shown with dashed lines. Clients then fetch pages from the nearest node in the CDN. This is shown with solid lines. In this way, the clients in Sydney both fetch the page copy that is stored in Sydney; they do not both fetch the page from the origin server, which may be in Europe.

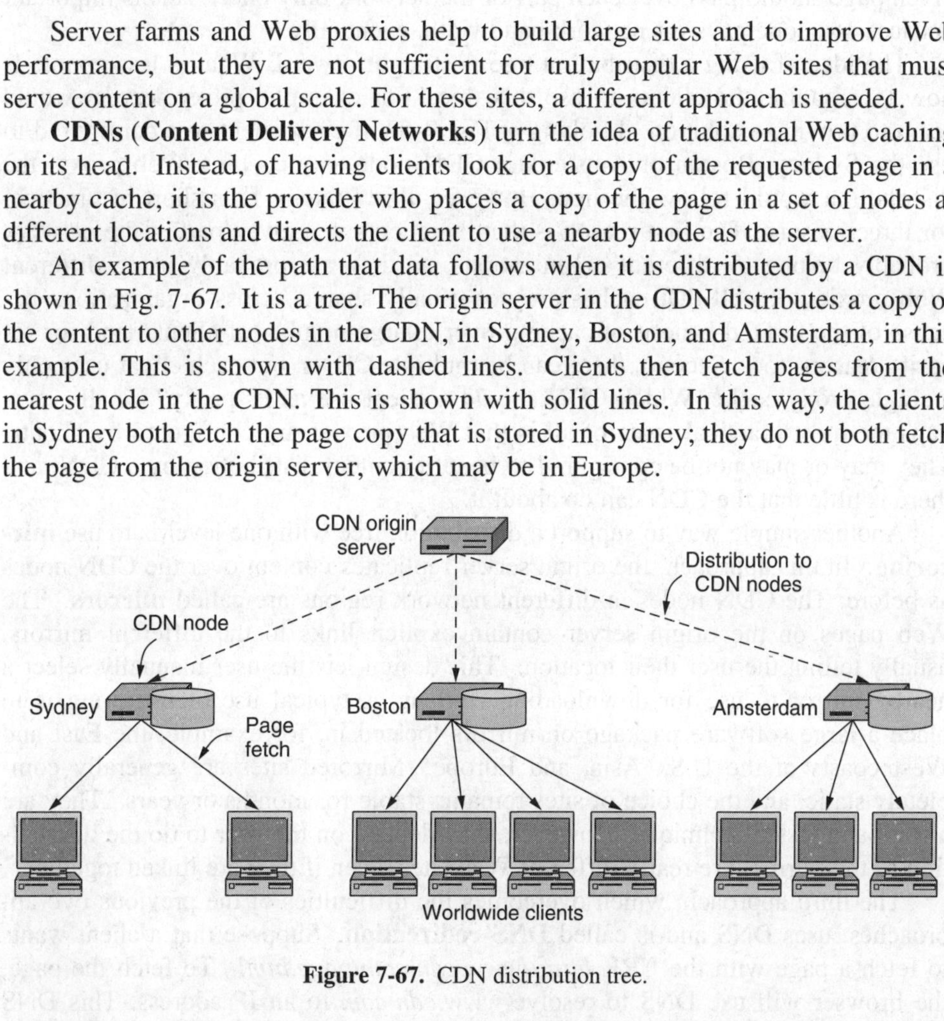

Figure 7-67. CDN distribution tree.

Using a tree structure has three virtues. First, the content distribution can be scaled up to as many clients as needed by using more nodes in the CDN, and more levels in the tree when the distribution among CDN nodes becomes the bottleneck. No matter how many clients there are, the tree structure is efficient. The origin server is not overloaded because it talks to the many clients via the tree of CDN nodes; it does not have to answer each request for a page by itself. Second, each client gets good performance by fetching pages from a nearby server instead of a distant server. This is because the round-trip time for setting up a connection is shorter, TCP slow-start ramps up more quickly because of the shorter round-trip time, and the shorter network path is less likely to pass through regions of congestion in the Internet. Finally, the total load that is placed on the network is also kept at a minimum. If the CDN nodes are well placed, the traffic for a given page should pass over each part of the network only once. This is important because someone pays for network bandwidth, eventually.

The idea of using a distribution tree is straightforward. What is less simple is how to organize the clients to use this tree. For example, proxy servers would seem to provide a solution. Looking at Fig. 7-67, if each client was configured to use the Sydney, Boston or Amsterdam CDN node as a caching Web proxy, the distribution would follow the tree. However, this strategy falls short in practice, for three reasons. The first reason is that the clients in a given part of the network probably belong to different organizations, so they are probably using different Web proxies. Recall that caches are not usually shared across organizations because of the limited benefit of caching over a large number of clients, and for security reasons too. Second, there can be multiple CDNs, but each client uses only a single proxy cache. Which CDN should a client use as its proxy? Finally, perhaps the most practical issue of all is that Web proxies are configured by clients. They may or may not be configured to benefit content distribution by a CDN, and there is little that the CDN can do about it.

Another simple way to support a distribution tree with one level is to use **mirroring**. In this approach, the origin server replicates content over the CDN nodes as before. The CDN nodes in different network regions are called **mirrors**. The Web pages on the origin server contain explicit links to the different mirrors, usually telling the user their location. This design lets the user manually select a nearby mirror to use for downloading content. A typical use of mirroring is to place a large software package on mirrors located in, for example, the East and West coasts of the U.S., Asia, and Europe. Mirrored sites are generally completely static, and the choice of sites remains stable for months or years. They are a tried and tested technique. However, they depend on the user to do the distribution as the mirrors are really different Web sites, even if they are linked together.

The third approach, which overcomes the difficulties of the previous two approaches, uses DNS and is called **DNS redirection**. Suppose that a client wants to fetch a page with the URL *http://www.cdn.com/page.html*. To fetch the page, the browser will use DNS to resolve *www.cdn.com* to an IP address. This DNS lookup proceeds in the usual manner. By using the DNS protocol, the browser learns the IP address of the name server for *cdn.com*, then contacts the name server to ask it to resolve *www.cdn.com*. Now comes the really clever bit. The name server is run by the CDN. Instead, of returning the same IP address for each request, it will look at the IP address of the client making the request and return different answers. The answer will be the IP address of the CDN node that is nearest the client. That is, if a client in Sydney asks the CDN name server to resolve *www.cdn.com*, the name server will return the IP address of the Sydney CDN node, but if a client in Amsterdam makes the same request, the name server will return the IP address of the Amsterdam CDN node instead.

This strategy is perfectly legal according to the semantics of DNS. We have previously seen that name servers may return changing lists of IP addresses. After the name resolution, the Sydney client will fetch the page directly from the Sydney CDN node. Further pages on the same "server" will be fetched directly from the Sydney CDN node as well because of DNS caching. The overall sequence of steps is shown in Fig. 7-68.

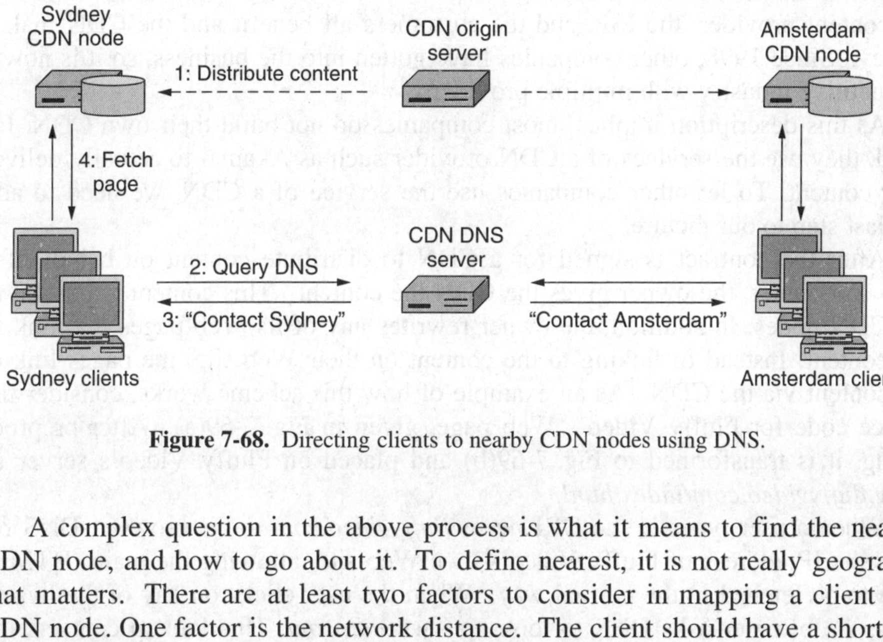

Figure 7-68. Directing clients to nearby CDN nodes using DNS.

A complex question in the above process is what it means to find the nearest CDN node, and how to go about it. To define nearest, it is not really geography that matters. There are at least two factors to consider in mapping a client to a CDN node. One factor is the network distance. The client should have a short and high-capacity network path to the CDN node. This situation will produce quick downloads. CDNs use a map they have previously computed to translate between the IP address of a client and its network location. The CDN node that is selected might be the one at the shortest distance as the crow flies, or it might not. What matters is some combination of the length of the network path and any capacity limits along it. The second factor is the load that is already being carried by the CDN node. If the CDN nodes are overloaded, they will deliver slow responses, just like the overloaded Web server that we sought to avoid in the first place. Thus, it may be necessary to balance the load across the CDN nodes, mapping some clients to nodes that are slightly further away but more lightly loaded.

The techniques for using DNS for content distribution were pioneered by Akamai starting in 1998, when the Web was groaning under the load of its early growth. Akamai was the first major CDN and became the industry leader. Probably even more clever than the idea of using DNS to connect clients to nearby nodes was the incentive structure of their business. Companies pay Akamai to deliver their content to clients, so that they have responsive Web sites that customers like to use. The CDN nodes must be placed at network locations with good connectivity, which initially meant inside ISP networks. For the ISPs, there is a benefit to having a CDN node in their networks, namely that the CDN node cuts down the amount of upstream network bandwidth that they need (and must pay for), just as with proxy caches. In addition, the CDN node improves responsiveness for the ISP's customers, which makes the ISP look good in their eyes, giving them a competitive advantage over ISPs that do not have a CDN node. These benefits (at no cost to the ISP) makes installing a CDN node a no brainer for the ISP. Thus, the content provider, the ISP, and the customers all benefit and the CDN makes money. Since 1998, other companies have gotten into the business, so it is now a competitive industry with multiple providers.

As this description implies, most companies do not build their own CDN. Instead, they use the services of a CDN provider such as Akamai to actually deliver their content. To let other companies use the service of a CDN, we need to add one last step to our picture.

After the contract is signed for a CDN to distribute content on behalf of a Web site owner, the owner gives the CDN the content. This content is pushed to the CDN nodes. In addition, the owner rewrites any of its Web pages that link to the content. Instead of linking to the content on their Web site, the pages link to the content via the CDN. As an example of how this scheme works, consider the source code for Fluffy Video's Web page, given in Fig. 7-69(a). After preprocessing, it is transformed to Fig. 7-69(b) and placed on Fluffy Video's server as *www.fluffyvideo.com/index.html*.

When a user types in the URL *www.fluffyvideo.com* to his browser, DNS returns the IP address of Fluffy Video's own Web site, allowing the main (HTML) page to be fetched in the normal way. When the user clicks on any of the hyperlinks, the browser asks DNS to look up *www.cdn.com*. This lookup contacts the CDN's DNS server, which returns the IP address of the nearby CDN node. The browser then sends a regular HTTP request to the CDN node, for example, for */fluffyvideo/koalas.mpg*. The URL identifies the page to return, starting the path with *fluffyvideo* so that the CDN node can separate requests for the different companies that it serves. Finally, the video is returned and the user sees cute fluffy animals.

The strategy behind this split of content hosted by the CDN and entry pages hosted by the content owner is that it gives the content owner control while letting the CDN move the bulk of the data. Most entry pages are tiny, being just HTML text. These pages often link to large files, such as videos and images. It is precisely these large files that are served by the CDN, even though the use of a CDN is completely transparent to users. The site looks the same, but performs faster.

```
<html>
<head> <title> Fluffy Video </title> </head>
<body>
<h1> Fluffy Video's Product List </h1>
<p> Click below for free samples. </p>
<a href="koalas.mpg"> Koalas Today </a> <br>
<a href="kangaroos.mpg"> Funny Kangaroos </a> <br>
<a href="wombats.mpg"> Nice Wombats </a> <br>
</body>
</html>
```

(a)

```
<html>
<head> <title> Fluffy Video </title> </head>
<body>
<h1> Fluffy Video's Product List </h1>
<p> Click below for free samples. </p>
<a href="http://www.cdn.com/fluffyvideo/koalas.mpg"> Koalas Today </a> <br>
<a href="http://www.cdn.com/fluffyvideo/kangaroos.mpg"> Funny Kangaroos </a> <br>
<a href="http://www.cdn.com/fluffyvideo/wombats.mpg"> Nice Wombats </a> <br>
</body>
</html>
```

(b)

Figure 7-69. (a) Original Web page. (b) Same page after linking to the CDN.

There is another advantage for sites using a shared CDN. The future demand for a Web site can be difficult to predict. Frequently, there are surges in demand known as **flash crowds**. Such a surge may happen when the latest product is released, there is a fashion show or other event, or the company is otherwise in the news. Even a Web site that was a previously unknown, unvisited backwater can suddenly become the focus of the Internet if it is newsworthy and linked from popular sites. Since most sites are not prepared to handle massive increases in traffic, the result is that many of them crash when traffic surges.

Case in point. Normally the Florida Secretary of State's Web site is not a busy place, although you can look up information about Florida corporations, notaries, and cultural affairs, as well as information about voting and elections there. For some odd reason, on Nov. 7, 2000 (the date of the U.S. presidential election with Bush vs. Gore), a whole lot of people were suddenly interested in the election results page of this site. The site suddenly became one of the busiest Web sites in the world and naturally crashed as a result. If it had been using a CDN, it would probably have survived.

By using a CDN, a site has access to a very large content-serving capacity. The largest CDNs have tens of thousands of servers deployed in countries all over the world. Since only a small number of sites will be experiencing a flash crowd at any one time (by definition), those sites may use the CDN's capacity to handle the load until the storm passes. That is, the CDN can quickly scale up a site's serving capacity.

The preceding discussion above is a simplified description of how Akamai works. There are many more details that matter in practice. The CDN nodes pictured in our example are normally clusters of machines. DNS redirection is done with two levels: one to map clients to the approximate network location, and another to spread the load over nodes in that location. Both reliability and performance are concerns. To be able to shift a client from one machine in a cluster to another, DNS replies at the second level are given with short TTLs so that the client will repeat the resolution after a short while. Finally, while we have concentrated on distributing static objects like images and videos, CDNs can also support dynamic page creation, streaming media, and more. For more information about CDNs, see Dilley et al. (2002).

7.5.4 Peer-to-Peer Networks

Not everyone can set up a 1000-node CDN at locations around the world to distribute their content. (Actually, it is not hard to rent 1000 virtual machines around the globe because of the well-developed and competitive hosting industry. However, setting up a CDN only starts with getting the nodes.) Luckily, there is an alternative for the rest of us that is simple to use and can distribute a tremendous amount of content. It is a P2P (Peer-to-Peer) network.

P2P networks burst onto the scene starting in 1999. The first widespread application was for mass crime: 50 million Napster users were exchanging copyrighted songs without the copyright owners' permission until Napster was shut down by the courts amid great controversy. Nevertheless, peer-to-peer technology has many interesting and legal uses. Other systems continued development, with such great interest from users that P2P traffic quickly eclipsed Web traffic. Today, BitTorrent is the most popular P2P protocol. It is used so widely to share (licensed and public domain) videos, as well as other content, that it accounts for a large fraction of all Internet traffic. We will look at it in this section.

The basic idea of a **P2P (Peer-to-Peer)** file-sharing network is that many computers come together and pool their resources to form a content distribution system. The computers are often simply home computers. They do not need to be machines in Internet data centers. The computers are called peers because each one can alternately act as a client to another peer, fetching its content, and as a server, providing content to other peers. What makes peer-to-peer systems interesting is that there is no dedicated infrastructure, unlike in a CDN. Everyone participates in the task of distributing content, and there is often no central point of control.

Many people are excited about P2P technology because it is seen as empowering the little guy. The reason is not only that it takes a large company to run a

CDN, while anyone with a computer can join a P2P network. It is that P2P networks have a formidable capacity to distribute content that can match the largest of Web sites.

Consider a P2P network made up of *N* average users, each with broadband connectivity at 1 Mbps. The aggregate upload capacity of the P2P network, or rate at which the users can send traffic into the Internet, is *N* Mbps. The download capacity, or rate at which the users can receive traffic, is also *N* Mbps. Each user can upload and download at the same time, too, because they have a 1-Mbps link in each direction.

It is not obvious that this should be true, but it turns out that all of the capacity can be used productively to distribute content, even for the case of sharing a single copy of a file with all the other users. To see how this can be so, imagine that the users are organized into a binary tree, with each non-leaf user sending to two other users. The tree will carry the single copy of the file to all the other users. To use the upload bandwidth of as many users as possible at all times (and hence distribute the large file with low latency), we need to pipeline the network activity of the users. Imagine that the file is divided into 1000 pieces. Each user can receive a new piece from somewhere up the tree and send the previously received piece down the tree at the same time. This way, once the pipeline is started, after a small number of pieces (equal to the depth of the tree) are sent, all non-leaf users will be busy uploading the file to other users. Since there are approximately *N*/2 non-leaf users, the upload bandwidth of this tree is *N*/2 Mbps. We can repeat this trick and create another tree that uses the other *N*/2 Mbps of upload bandwidth by swapping the roles of leaf and non-leaf nodes. Together, this construction uses all of the capacity.

This argument means that P2P networks are self-scaling. Their usable upload capacity grows in tandem with the download demands that can be made by their users. They are always "large enough" in some sense, without the need for any dedicated infrastructure. In contrast, the capacity of even a large Web site is fixed and will either be too large or too small. Consider a site with only 100 clusters, each capable of 10 Gbps. This enormous capacity does not help when there are a small number of users. The site cannot get information to *N* users at a rate faster than *N* Mbps because the limit is at the users and not the Web site. And when there are more than one million 1-Mbps users, the Web site cannot pump out data fast enough to keep all the users busy downloading. That may seem like a large number of users, but large BitTorrent networks (e.g., Pirate Bay) claim to have more than 10,000,000 users. That is more like 10 terabits/sec in terms of our example!

You should take these back-of-the-envelope numbers with a grain (or better yet, a metric ton) of salt because they oversimplify the situation. A significant challenge for P2P networks is to use bandwidth well when users can come in all shapes and sizes, and have different download and upload capacities. Nevertheless, these numbers do indicate the enormous potential of P2P.

There is another reason that P2P networks are important. CDNs and other centrally run services put the providers in a position of having a trove of personal information about many users, from browsing preferences and where people shop online, to people's locations and email addresses. This information can be used to provide better, more personalized service, or it can be used to intrude on people's privacy. The latter may happen either intentionally—say as part of a new product—or through an accidental disclosure or compromise. With P2P systems, there can be no single provider that is capable of monitoring the entire system. This does not mean that P2P systems will necessarily provide privacy, as users are trusting each other to some extent. It only means that they can provide a different form of privacy than centrally managed systems. P2P systems are now being explored for services beyond file sharing (e.g., storage, streaming), and time will tell whether this advantage is significant.

P2P technology has followed two related paths as it has been developed. On the more practical side, there are the systems that are used every day. The most well known of these systems are based on the BitTorrent protocol. On the more academic side, there has been intense interest in DHT (Distributed Hash Table) algorithms that let P2P systems perform well as a whole, yet rely on no centralized components at all. We will look at both of these technologies.

BitTorrent

The BitTorrent protocol was developed by Brahm Cohen in 2001 to let a set of peers share files quickly and easily. There are dozens of freely available clients that speak this protocol, just as there are many browsers that speak the HTTP protocol to Web servers. The protocol is available as an open standard at *www.bittorrent.org*.

In a typical peer-to-peer system, like that formed with BitTorrent, the users each have some information that may be of interest to other users. This information may be free software, music, videos, photographs, and so on. There are three problems that need to be solved to share content in this setting:

1. How does a peer find other peers that have the content it wants to download?
2. How is content replicated by peers to provide high-speed downloads for everyone?
3. How do peers encourage each other to upload content to others as well as download content for themselves?

The first problem exists because not all peers will have all of the content, at least initially. The approach taken in BitTorrent is for every content provider to create a content description called a **torrent**. The torrent is much smaller than the content, and is used by a peer to verify the integrity of the data that it downloads from other peers. Other users who want to download the content must first obtain the torrent, say, by finding it on a Web page advertising the content.

The torrent is just a file in a specified format that contains two key kinds of information. One kind is the name of a **tracker**, which is a server that leads peers to the content of the torrent. The other kind of information is a list of equal-sized pieces, or **chunks**, that make up the content. Different chunk sizes can be used for different torrents, typically 64 KB to 512 KB. The torrent file contains the name of each chunk, given as a 160-bit SHA-1 hash of the chunk. We will cover cryptographic hashes such as SHA-1 in Chap. 8. For now, you can think of a hash as a longer and more secure checksum. Given the size of chunks and hashes, the torrent file is at least three orders of magnitude smaller than the content, so it can be transferred quickly.

To download the content described in a torrent, a peer first contacts the tracker for the torrent. The **tracker** is a server that maintains a list of all the other peers that are actively downloading and uploading the content. This set of peers is called a **swarm**. The members of the swarm contact the tracker regularly to report that they are still active, as well as when they leave the swarm. When a new peer contacts the tracker to join the swarm, the tracker tells it about other peers in the swarm. Getting the torrent and contacting the tracker are the first two steps for downloading content, as shown in Fig. 7-70.

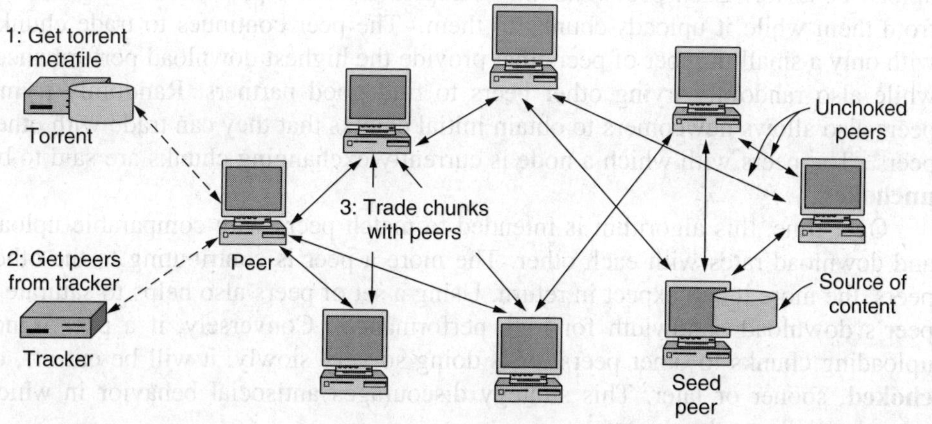

Figure 7-70. BitTorrent.

The second problem is how to share content in a way that gives rapid downloads. When a swarm is first formed, some peers must have all of the chunks that make up the content. These peers are called **seeders**. Other peers that join the swarm will have no chunks; they are the peers that are downloading the content.

While a peer participates in a swarm, it simultaneously downloads chunks that it is missing from other peers, and uploads chunks that it has to other peers who need them. This trading is shown as the last step of content distribution in Fig. 7-70. Over time, the peer gathers more chunks until it has downloaded all of the content. The peer can leave the swarm (and return) at any time. Normally a peer will stay for a short period after finishes its own download. With peers coming and going, the rate of churn in a swarm can be quite high.

For the above method to work well, each chunk should be available at many peers. If everyone were to get the chunks in the same order, it is likely that many peers would depend on the seeders for the next chunk. This would create a bottleneck. Instead, peers exchange lists of the chunks they have with each other. Then they select rare chunks that are hard to find to download. The idea is that downloading a rare chunk will make a copy of it, which will make the chunk easier for other peers to find and download. If all peers do this, after a short while all chunks will be widely available.

The third problem is perhaps the most interesting. CDN nodes are set up exclusively to provide content to users. P2P nodes are not. They are users' computers, and the users may be more interested in getting a movie than helping other users with their downloads. Nodes that take resources from a system without contributing in kind are called **free-riders** or **leechers**. If there are too many of them, the system will not function well. Earlier P2P systems were known to host them (Saroiu et al., 2003) so BitTorrent sought to minimize them.

The approach taken in BitTorrent clients is to reward peers who show good upload behavior. Each peer randomly samples the other peers, retrieving chunks from them while it uploads chunks to them. The peer continues to trade chunks with only a small number of peers that provide the highest download performance, while also randomly trying other peers to find good partners. Randomly trying peers also allows newcomers to obtain initial chunks that they can trade with other peers. The peers with which a node is currently exchanging chunks are said to be **unchoked**.

Over time, this algorithm is intended to match peers with comparable upload and download rates with each other. The more a peer is contributing to the other peers, the more it can expect in return. Using a set of peers also helps to saturate a peer's download bandwidth for high performance. Conversely, if a peer is not uploading chunks to other peers, or is doing so very slowly, it will be cut off, or **choked**, sooner or later. This strategy discourages antisocial behavior in which peers free-ride on the swarm.

The choking algorithm is sometimes described as implementing the **tit-for-tat** strategy that encourages cooperation in repeated interactions. However, it does not prevent clients from gaming the system in any strong sense (Piatek et al., 2007). Nonetheless, attention to the issue and mechanisms that make it more difficult for casual users to free-ride have likely contributed to the success of BitTorrent.

As you can see from our discussion, BitTorrent comes with a rich vocabulary. There are torrents, swarms, leechers, seeders, and trackers, as well as snubbing, choking, lurking, and more. For more information see the short paper on BitTorrent (Cohen, 2003) and look on the Web starting with *www.bittorrent.org*.

DHTs—Distributed Hash Tables

The emergence of P2P file sharing networks around 2000 sparked much interest in the research community. The essence of P2P systems is that they avoid the centrally managed structures of CDNs and other systems. This can be a significant advantage. Centrally managed components become a bottleneck as the system grows very large and are a single point of failure. Central components can also be used as a point of control (e.g., to shut off the P2P network). However, the early P2P systems were only partly decentralized, or, if they were fully decentralized, they were inefficient.

The traditional form of BitTorrent that we just described uses peer-to-peer transfers and a centralized tracker for each swarm. It is the tracker that turns out to be the hard part to decentralize in a peer-to-peer system. The key problem is how to find out which peers have specific content that is being sought. For example, each user might have one or more data items such as songs, photographs, programs, files, and so on that other users might want to read. How do the other users find them? Making one index of who has what is simple, but it is centralized. Having every peer keep its own index does not help. True, it is distributed. However, it requires so much work to keep the indexes of all peers up to date (as content is moved about the system) that it is not worth the effort.

The question tackled by the research community was whether it was possible to build P2P indexes that were entirely distributed but performed well. By perform well, we mean three things. First, each node keeps only a small amount of information about other nodes. This property means that it will not be expensive to keep the index up to date. Second, each node can look up entries in the index quickly. Otherwise, it is not a very useful index. Third, each node can use the index at the same time, even as other nodes come and go. This property means the performance of the index grows with the number of nodes.

The answer is to the question was: "Yes." Four different solutions were invented in 2001. They are Chord (Stoica et al., 2001), CAN (Ratnasamy et al., 2001), Pastry (Rowstron and Druschel, 2001), and Tapestry (Zhao et al., 2004). Other solutions were invented soon afterwards, including Kademlia, which is used in practice (Maymounkov and Mazieres, 2002). The solutions are known as **DHTs** (**Distributed Hash Tables**) because the basic functionality of an index is to map a key to a value. This is like a hash table, and the solutions are distributed versions, of course.

DHTs do their work by imposing a regular structure on the communication between the nodes, as we will see. This behavior is quite different than that of traditional P2P networks that use whatever connections peers happen to make.

For this reason, DHTs are called **structured P2P networks**. Traditional P2P protocols build **unstructured P2P networks**.

The DHT solution that we will describe is Chord. As a scenario, consider how to replace the centralized tracker traditionally used in BitTorrent with a fully-distributed tracker. Chord can be used to solve this problem. In this scenario, the overall index is a listing of all of the swarms that a computer may join to download content. The key used to look up the index is the torrent description of the content. It uniquely identifies a swarm from which content can be downloaded as the hashes of all the content chunks. The value stored in the index for each key is the list of peers that comprise the swarm. These peers are the computers to contact to download the content. A person wanting to download content such as a movie has only the torrent description. The question the DHT must answer is how, lacking a central database, does a person find out which peers (out of the millions of BitTorrent nodes) to download the movie from?

A Chord DHT consists of n participating nodes. They are nodes running BitTorrent in our scenario. Each node has an IP address by which it may be contacted. The overall index is spread across the nodes. This implies that each node stores bits and pieces of the index for use by other nodes. The key part of Chord is that it navigates the index using identifiers in a virtual space, not the IP addresses of nodes or the names of content like movies. Conceptually, the identifiers are simply m-bit numbers that can be arranged in ascending order into a ring.

To turn a node address into an identifier, it is mapped to an m-bit number using a hash function, *hash*. Chord uses SHA-1 for *hash*. This is the same hash that we mentioned when describing BitTorrent. We will look at it when we discuss cryptography in Chap. 8. For now, suffice it to say that it is just a function that takes a variable-length byte string as an argument and produces a highly random 160-bit number. Thus, we can use it to convert any IP address to a 160-bit number called the **node identifier**.

In Fig. 7-71(a), we show the node identifier circle for $m = 5$. (Just ignore the arcs in the middle for the moment.) Some of the identifiers correspond to nodes, but most do not. In this example, the nodes with identifiers 1, 4, 7, 12, 15, 20, and 27 correspond to actual nodes and are shaded in the figure; the rest do not exist.

Let us now define the function $successor(k)$ as the node identifier of the first actual node following k around the circle, clockwise. For example, $successor(6) = 7$, $successor(8) = 12$, and $successor(22) = 27$.

A **key** is also produced by hashing a content name with *hash* (i.e., SHA-1) to generate a 160-bit number. In our scenario, the content name is the torrent. Thus, in order to convert *torrent* (the torrent description file) to its key, we compute $key = hash(torrent)$. This computation is just a local procedure call to *hash*.

To start a new a swarm, a node needs to insert a new key-value pair consisting of (*torrent*, *my-IP-address*) into the index. To accomplish this, the node asks *successor*(*hash*(*torrent*)) to store *my-IP-address*. In this way, the index is distributed over the nodes at random. For fault tolerance, p different hash functions

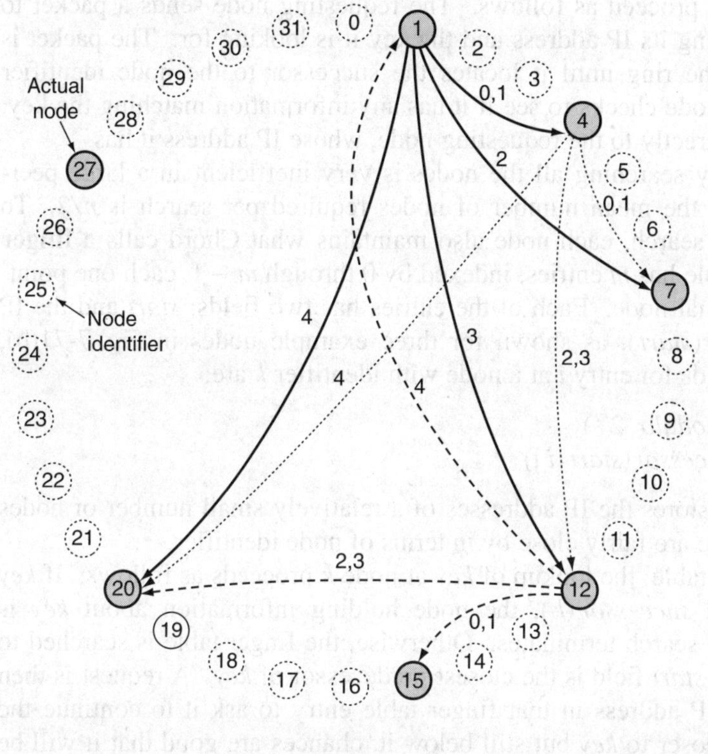

(a)

Start	IP addr of successor
2	4
3	4
5	7
9	12
17	20

Node 1's finger table

Start	IP addr of successor
5	7
6	7
8	12
12	12
20	20

Node 4's finger table

Start	IP addr of successor
13	15
14	15
16	20
20	20
28	1

Node 12's finger table

(b)

Figure 7-71. (a) A set of 32 node identifiers arranged in a circle. The shaded ones correspond to actual machines. The arcs show the fingers from nodes 1, 4, and 12. The labels on the arcs are the table indices. (b) Examples of the finger tables.

could be used to store the data at *p* nodes, but we will not consider the subject of fault tolerance further here.

Some time after the DHT is constructed, another node wants to find a torrent so that it can join the swarm and download content. A node looks up *torrent* by first hashing it to get *key*, and second using *successor* (*key*) to find the IP address of the node storing the corresponding value. The value is the list of peers in the swarm; the node can add its IP address to the list and contact the other peers to download content with the BitTorrent protocol.

The first step is easy; the second one is not easy. To make it possible to find the IP address of the node corresponding to a certain key, each node is required to maintain certain administrative data structures. One of these is the IP address of its successor node along the node identifier circle. For example, in Fig. 7-71, node 4's successor is 7 and node 7's successor is 12.

Lookup can now proceed as follows. The requesting node sends a packet to its successor containing its IP address and the key it is looking for. The packet is propagated around the ring until it locates the successor to the node identifier being sought. That node checks to see if it has any information matching the key, and if so, returns it directly to the requesting node, whose IP address it has.

However, linearly searching all the nodes is very inefficient in a large peer-to-peer system since the mean number of nodes required per search is $n/2$. To greatly speed up the search, each node also maintains what Chord calls a **finger table**. The finger table has m entries, indexed by 0 through $m - 1$, each one pointing to a different actual node. Each of the entries has two fields: *start* and the IP address of $successor(start)$, as shown for three example nodes in Fig. 7-71(b). The values of the fields for entry i at a node with identifier k are:

$$start = k + 2^i \ (modulo \ \ 2^m)$$
$$\text{IP address of } successor(start\,[i\,])$$

Note that each node stores the IP addresses of a relatively small number of nodes and that most of these are fairly close by in terms of node identifier.

Using the finger table, the lookup of *key* at node k proceeds as follows. If *key* falls between k and $successor(k)$, the node holding information about *key* is $successor(k)$ and the search terminates. Otherwise, the finger table is searched to find the entry whose *start* field is the closest predecessor of *key*. A request is then sent directly to the IP address in that finger table entry to ask it to continue the search. Since it is closer to *key* but still below it, chances are good that it will be able to return the answer with only a small number of additional queries. In fact, since every lookup halves the remaining distance to the target, it can be shown that the average number of lookups is $\log_2 n$.

As a first example, consider looking up $key = 3$ at node 1. Since node 1 knows that 3 lies between it and its successor, 4, the desired node is 4 and the search terminates, returning node 4's IP address.

As a second example, consider looking up $key = 16$ at node 1. Since 16 does not lie between 1 and 4, the finger table is consulted. The closest predecessor to 16 is 9, so the request is forwarded to the IP address of 9's entry, namely, that of node 12. Node 12 also does not know the answer itself, so it looks for the node most closely preceding 16 and finds 14, which yields the IP address of node 15. A query is then sent there. Node 15 observes that 16 lies between it and its successor (20), so it returns the IP address of 20 to the caller, which works its way back to node 1.

Since nodes join and leave all the time, Chord needs a way to handle these operations. We assume that when the system began operation it was small enough that the nodes could just exchange information directly to build the first circle and finger tables. After that, an automated procedure is needed. When a new node, *r*, wants to join, it must contact some existing node and ask it to look up the IP address of *successor*(*r*) for it. Next, the new node then asks *successor*(*r*) for its predecessor. The new node then asks both of these to insert *r* in between them in the circle. For example, if 24 in Fig. 7-71 wants to join, it asks any node to look up *successor*(24), which is 27. Then it asks 27 for its predecessor (20). After it tells both of those about its existence, 20 uses 24 as its successor and 27 uses 24 as its predecessor. In addition, node 27 hands over those keys in the range 21–24, which now belong to 24. At this point, 24 is fully inserted.

However, many finger tables are now wrong. To correct them, every node runs a background process that periodically recomputes each finger by calling *successor*. When one of these queries hits a new node, the corresponding finger entry is updated.

When a node leaves gracefully, it hands its keys over to its successor and informs its predecessor of its departure so the predecessor can link to the departing node's successor. When a node crashes, a problem arises because its predecessor no longer has a valid successor. To alleviate this problem, each node keeps track not only of its direct successor but also its *s* direct successors, to allow it to skip over up to $s - 1$ consecutive failed nodes and reconnect the circle if disaster strikes.

There has been a tremendous amount of research on DHTs since they were invented. To give you an idea of just how much research, let us pose a question: what is the most-cited networking paper of all time? You will find it difficult to come up with a paper that is cited more than the seminal Chord paper (Stoica et al., 2001). Despite this veritable mountain of research, applications of DHTs are only slowly beginning to emerge. Some BitTorrent clients use DHTs to provide a fully distributed tracker of the kind that we described. Large commercial cloud services such as Amazon's Dynamo also incorporate DHT techniques (DeCandia et al., 2007).

7.6 SUMMARY

Naming in the ARPANET started out in a very simple way: an ASCII text file listed the names of all the hosts and their corresponding IP addresses. Every night all the machines downloaded this file. But when the ARPANET morphed into the Internet and exploded in size, a far more sophisticated and dynamic naming scheme was required. The one used now is a hierarchical scheme called the Domain Name System. It organizes all the machines on the Internet into a set of trees. At the top level are the well-known generic domains, including *com* and *edu*, as well as about 200 country domains. DNS is implemented as a distributed database with servers all over the world. By querying a DNS server, a process can map an Internet domain name onto the IP address used to communicate with a computer for that domain.

Email is the original killer app of the Internet. It is still widely used by everyone from small children to grandparents. Most email systems in the world use the mail system now defined in RFCs 5321 and 5322. Messages have simple ASCII headers, and many kinds of content can be sent using MIME. Mail is submitted to message transfer agents for delivery and retrieved from them for presentation by a variety of user agents, including Web applications. Submitted mail is delivered using SMTP, which works by making a TCP connection from the sending message transfer agent to the receiving one.

The Web is the application that most people think of as being the Internet. Originally, it was a system for seamlessly linking hypertext pages (written in HTML) across machines. The pages are downloaded by making a TCP connection from the browser to a server and using HTTP. Nowadays, much of the content on the Web is produced dynamically, either at the server (e.g., with PHP) or in the browser (e.g., with JavaScript). When combined with back-end databases, dynamic server pages allow Web applications such as e-commerce and search. Dynamic browser pages are evolving into full-featured applications, such as email, that run inside the browser and use the Web protocols to communicate with remote servers.

Caching and persistent connections are widely used to enhance Web performance. Using the Web on mobile devices can be challenging, despite the growth in the bandwidth and processing power of mobiles. Web sites often send tailored versions of pages with smaller images and less complex navigation to devices with small displays.

The Web protocols are increasingly being used for machine-to-machine communication. XML is preferred to HTML as a description of content that is easy for machines to process. SOAP is an RPC mechanism that sends XML messages using HTTP.

Digital audio and video have been key drivers for the Internet since 2000. The majority of Internet traffic today is video. Much of it is streamed from Web sites over a mix of protocols (including RTP/UDP and RTP/HTTP/TCP). Live media is streamed to many consumers. It includes Internet radio and TV stations that broadcast all manner of events. Audio and video are also used for real-time conferencing. Many calls use voice over IP, rather than the traditional telephone network, and include videoconferencing.

There are a small number of tremendously popular Web sites, as well as a very large number of less popular ones. To serve the popular sites, content distribution networks have been deployed. CDNs use DNS to direct clients to a nearby server; the servers are placed in data centers all around the world. Alternatively, P2P networks let a collection of machines share content such as movies among themselves. They provide a content distribution capacity that scales with the number of machines in the P2P network and which can rival the largest of sites.

PROBLEMS

1. Many business computers have three distinct and worldwide unique identifiers. What are they?

2. In Fig. 7-4, there is no period after *laserjet*. Why not?

3. Consider a situation in which a cyberterrorist makes all the DNS servers in the world crash simultaneously. How does this change one's ability to use the Internet?

4. DNS uses UDP instead of TCP. If a DNS packet is lost, there is no automatic recovery. Does this cause a problem, and if so, how is it solved?

5. John wants to have an original domain name and uses a randomized program to generate a secondary domain name for him. He wants to register this domain name in the *com* generic domain. The domain name that was generated is 253 characters long. Will the *com* registrar allow this domain name to be registered?

6. Can a machine with a single DNS name have multiple IP addresses? How could this occur?

7. The number of companies with a Web site has grown explosively in recent years. As a result, thousands of companies are registered in the *com* domain, causing a heavy load on the top-level server for this domain. Suggest a way to alleviate this problem without changing the naming scheme (i.e., without introducing new top-level domain names). It is permitted that your solution requires changes to the client code.

8. Some email systems support a *Content Return:* header field. It specifies whether the body of a message is to be returned in the event of nondelivery. Does this field belong to the envelope or to the header?

9. Electronic mail systems need directories so people's email addresses can be looked up. To build such directories, names should be broken up into standard components (e.g., first name, last name) to make searching possible. Discuss some problems that must be solved for a worldwide standard to be acceptable.

10. A large law firm, which has many employees, provides a single email address for each employee. Each employee's email address is *<login>@lawfirm.com*. However, the firm did not explicitly define the format of the login. Thus, some employees use their first names as their login names, some use their last names, some use their initials, etc. The firm now wishes to make a fixed format, for example:

    firstname.lastname@lawfirm.com,

    that can be used for the email addresses of all its employees. How can this be done without rocking the boat too much?

11. A binary file is 4560 bytes long. How long will it be if encoded using base64 encoding, with a CR+LF pair inserted after every 110 bytes sent and at the end?

12. Name five MIME types not listed in this book. You can check your browser or the Internet for information.

13. Suppose that you want to send an MP3 file to a friend, but your friend's ISP limits the size of each incoming message to 1 MB and the MP3 file is 4 MB. Is there a way to handle this situation by using RFC 5322 and MIME?

14. Suppose that John just set up an auto-forwarding mechanism on his work email address, which receives all of his business-related emails, to forward them to his personal email address, which he shares with his wife. John's wife was unaware of this, and activated a vacation agent on their personal account. Because John forwarded his email, he did not set up a vacation daemon on his work machine. What happens when an email is received at John's work email address?

15. In any standard, such as RFC 5322, a precise grammar of what is allowed is needed so that different implementations can interwork. Even simple items have to be defined carefully. The SMTP headers allow white space between the tokens. Give *two* plausible alternative definitions of white space between tokens.

16. Is the vacation agent part of the user agent or the message transfer agent? Of course, it is set up using the user agent, but does the user agent actually send the replies? Explain your answer.

17. In a simple version of the Chord algorithm for peer-to-peer lookup, searches do not use the finger table. Instead, they are linear around the circle, in either direction. Can a node accurately predict which direction it should search in? Discuss your answer.

18. IMAP allows users to fetch and download email from a remote mailbox. Does this mean that the internal format of mailboxes has to be standardized so any IMAP program on the client side can read the mailbox on any mail server? Discuss your answer.

19. Consider the Chord circle of Fig. 7-71. Suppose that node 18 suddenly goes online. Which of the finger tables shown in the figure are affected? how?

20. Does Webmail use POP3, IMAP, or neither? If one of these, why was that one chosen? If neither, which one is it closer to in spirit?

21. When Web pages are sent out, they are prefixed by MIME headers. Why?

22. Is it possible that when a user clicks on a link with Firefox, a particular helper is started, but clicking on the same link in Internet Explorer causes a completely different helper to be started, even though the MIME type returned in both cases is identical? Explain your answer.

23. Although it was not mentioned in the text, an alternative form for a URL is to use the IP address instead of its DNS name. Use this information to explain why a DNS name cannot end with a digit.

24. Imagine that someone in the math department at Stanford has just written a new document including a proof that he wants to distribute by FTP for his colleagues to review. He puts the program in the FTP directory *ftp/pub/forReview/newProof.pdf*. What is the URL for this program likely to be?

25. In Fig. 7-22, *www.aportal.com* keeps track of user preferences in a cookie. A disadvantage of this scheme is that cookies are limited to 4 KB, so if the preferences are

extensive, for example, many stocks, sports teams, types of news stories, weather for multiple cities, specials in numerous product categories, and more, the 4-KB limit may be reached. Design an alternative way to keep track of preferences that does not have this problem.

26. Sloth Bank wants to make online banking easy for its lazy customers, so after a customer signs up and is authenticated by a password, the bank returns a cookie containing a customer ID number. In this way, the customer does not have to identify himself or type a password on future visits to the online bank. What do you think of this idea? Will it work? Is it a good idea?

27. (a) Consider the following HTML tag:

```
<h1 title="this is the header"> HEADER 1 </h1>
```

Under what conditions does the browser use the *TITLE* attribute, and how?
(b) How does the *TITLE* attribute differ from the *ALT* attribute?

28. How do you make an image clickable in HTML? Give an example.

29. Write an HTML page that includes a link to the email address *username@DomainName.com*. What happens when a user clicks this link?

30. Write an XML page for a university registrar listing multiple students, each having a name, an address, and a GPA.

31. For each of the following applications, tell whether it would be (1) possible and (2) better to use a PHP script or JavaScript, and why:
(a) Displaying a calendar for any requested month since September 1752.
(b) Displaying the schedule of flights from Amsterdam to New York.
(c) Graphing a polynomial from user-supplied coefficients.

32. Write a program in JavaScript that accepts an integer greater than 2 and tells whether it is a prime number. Note that JavaScript has if and while statements with the same syntax as C and Java. The modulo operator is %. If you need the square root of x, use *Math.sqrt* (x).

33. An HTML page is as follows:

```
<html> <body>
<a href="www.info-source.com/welcome.html"> Click here for info </a>
</body> </html>
```

If the user clicks on the hyperlink, a TCP connection is opened and a series of lines is sent to the server. List all the lines sent.

34. The *If-Modified-Since* header can be used to check whether a cached page is still valid. Requests can be made for pages containing images, sound, video, and so on, as well as HTML. Do you think the effectiveness of this technique is better or worse for JPEG images as compared to HTML? Think carefully about what "effectiveness" means and explain your answer.

35. On the day of a major sporting event, such as the championship game in some popular sport, many people go to the official Web site. Is this a flash crowd in the same sense as the 2000 Florida presidential election? Why or why not?

36. Does it make sense for a single ISP to function as a CDN? If so, how would that work? If not, what is wrong with the idea?

37. Assume that compression is not used for audio CDs. How many MB of data must the compact disc contain in order to be able to play two hours of music?

38. In Fig. 7-42(c), quantization noise occurs due to the use of 4-bit samples to represent nine signal values. The first sample, at 0, is exact, but the next few are not. What is the percent error for the samples at 1/32, 2/32, and 3/32 of the period?

39. Could a psychoacoustic model be used to reduce the bandwidth needed for Internet telephony? If so, what conditions, if any, would have to be met to make it work? If not, why not?

40. An audio streaming server has a one-way "distance" of 100 msec to a media player. It outputs at 1 Mbps. If the media player has a 2-MB buffer, what can you say about the position of the low-water mark and the high-water mark?

41. Does voice over IP have the same problems with firewalls that streaming audio does? Discuss your answer.

42. What is the bit rate for transmitting uncompressed 1200×800 pixel color frames with 16 bits/pixel at 50 frames/sec?

43. Can a 1-bit error in an MPEG frame affect more than the frame in which the error occurs? Explain your answer.

44. Consider a 50,000-customer video server, where each customer watches three movies per month. Two-thirds of the movies are served at 9 P.M. How many movies does the server have to transmit at once during this time period? If each movie requires 6 Mbps, how many OC-12 connections does the server need to the network?

45. Suppose that Zipf's law holds for accesses to a 10,000-movie video server. If the server holds the most popular 1000 movies in memory and the remaining 9000 on disk, give an expression for the fraction of all references that will be to memory. Write a little program to evaluate this expression numerically.

46. Some cybersquatters have registered domain names that are misspellings of common corporate sites, for example, *www.microsfot.com*. Make a list of at least five such domains.

47. Numerous people have registered DNS names that consist of *www.word.com*, where *word* is a common word. For each of the following categories, list five such Web sites and briefly summarize what it is (e.g., *www.stomach.com* belongs to a gastroenterologist on Long Island). Here is the list of categories: animals, foods, household objects, and body parts. For the last category, please stick to body parts above the waist.

48. Rewrite the server of Fig. 6-6 as a true Web server using the *GET* command for HTTP 1.1. It should also accept the *Host* message. The server should maintain a cache of files recently fetched from the disk and serve requests from the cache when possible.

8

NETWORK SECURITY

For the first few decades of their existence, computer networks were primarily used by university researchers for sending email and by corporate employees for sharing printers. Under these conditions, security did not get a lot of attention. But now, as millions of ordinary citizens are using networks for banking, shopping, and filing their tax returns, and weakness after weakness has been found, network security has become a problem of massive proportions. In this chapter, we will study network security from several angles, point out numerous pitfalls, and discuss many algorithms and protocols for making networks more secure.

Security is a broad topic and covers a multitude of sins. In its simplest form, it is concerned with making sure that nosy people cannot read, or worse yet, secretly modify messages intended for other recipients. It is concerned with people trying to access remote services that they are not authorized to use. It also deals with ways to tell whether that message purportedly from the IRS "Pay by Friday, or else" is really from the IRS and not from the Mafia. Security also deals with the problems of legitimate messages being captured and replayed, and with people later trying to deny that they sent certain messages.

Most security problems are intentionally caused by malicious people trying to gain some benefit, get attention, or harm someone. A few of the most common perpetrators are listed in Fig. 8-1. It should be clear from this list that making a network secure involves a lot more than just keeping it free of programming errors. It involves outsmarting often intelligent, dedicated, and sometimes well-funded adversaries. It should also be clear that measures that will thwart casual attackers will have little impact on the serious ones. Police records show that the most damaging attacks are not perpetrated by outsiders tapping a phone line but by insiders bearing a grudge. Security systems should be designed accordingly.

Adversary	Goal
Student	To have fun snooping on people's email
Cracker	To test out someone's security system; steal data
Sales rep	To claim to represent all of Europe, not just Andorra
Corporation	To discover a competitor's strategic marketing plan
Ex-employee	To get revenge for being fired
Accountant	To embezzle money from a company
Stockbroker	To deny a promise made to a customer by email
Identity thief	To steal credit card numbers for sale
Government	To learn an enemy's military or industrial secrets
Terrorist	To steal biological warfare secrets

Figure 8-1. Some people who may cause security problems, and why.

Network security problems can be divided roughly into four closely intertwined areas: secrecy, authentication, nonrepudiation, and integrity control. Secrecy, also called confidentiality, has to do with keeping information out of the grubby little hands of unauthorized users. This is what usually comes to mind when people think about network security. Authentication deals with determining whom you are talking to before revealing sensitive information or entering into a business deal. Nonrepudiation deals with signatures: how do you prove that your customer really placed an electronic order for ten million left-handed doohickeys at 89 cents each when he later claims the price was 69 cents? Or maybe he claims he never placed any order. Finally, integrity control has to do with how you can be sure that a message you received was really the one sent and not something that a malicious adversary modified in transit or concocted.

All these issues (secrecy, authentication, nonrepudiation, and integrity control) occur in traditional systems, too, but with some significant differences. Integrity and secrecy are achieved by using registered mail and locking documents up. Robbing the mail train is harder now than it was in Jesse James' day.

Also, people can usually tell the difference between an original paper document and a photocopy, and it often matters to them. As a test, make a photocopy of a valid check. Try cashing the original check at your bank on Monday. Now try cashing the photocopy of the check on Tuesday. Observe the difference in the bank's behavior. With electronic checks, the original and the copy are indistinguishable. It may take a while for banks to learn how to handle this.

People authenticate other people by various means, including recognizing their faces, voices, and handwriting. Proof of signing is handled by signatures on letterhead paper, raised seals, and so on. Tampering can usually be detected by handwriting, ink, and paper experts. None of these options are available electronically. Clearly, other solutions are needed.

Before getting into the solutions themselves, it is worth spending a few moments considering where in the protocol stack network security belongs. There is probably no one single place. Every layer has something to contribute. In the physical layer, wiretapping can be foiled by enclosing transmission lines (or better yet, optical fibers) in sealed tubes containing an inert gas at high pressure. Any attempt to drill into a tube will release some gas, reducing the pressure and triggering an alarm. Some military systems use this technique.

In the data link layer, packets on a point-to-point line can be encrypted as they leave one machine and decrypted as they enter another. All the details can be handled in the data link layer, with higher layers oblivious to what is going on. This solution breaks down when packets have to traverse multiple routers, however, because packets have to be decrypted at each router, leaving them vulnerable to attacks from within the router. Also, it does not allow some sessions to be protected (e.g., those involving online purchases by credit card) and others not. Nevertheless, **link encryption**, as this method is called, can be added to any network easily and is often useful.

In the network layer, firewalls can be installed to keep good packets and bad packets out. IP security also functions in this layer.

In the transport layer, entire connections can be encrypted end to end, that is, process to process. For maximum security, end-to-end security is required.

Finally, issues such as user authentication and nonrepudiation can only be handled in the application layer.

Since security does not fit neatly into any layer, it does not fit into any chapter of this book. For this reason, it rates its own chapter.

While this chapter is long, technical, and essential, it is also quasi-irrelevant for the moment. It is well documented that most security failures at banks, for example, are due to lax security procedures and incompetent employees, numerous implementation bugs that enable remote break-ins by unauthorized users, and so-called social engineering attacks, where customers are tricked into revealing their account details. All of these security problems are more prevalent than clever criminals tapping phone lines and then decoding encrypted messages. If a person can walk into a random branch of a bank with an ATM slip he found on the street claiming to have forgotten his PIN and get a new one on the spot (in the name of good customer relations), all the cryptography in the world will not prevent abuse. In this respect, Ross Anderson's (2008a) book is a real eye-opener, as it documents hundreds of examples of security failures in numerous industries, nearly all of them due to what might politely be called sloppy business practices or inattention to security. Nevertheless, the technical foundation on which e-commerce is built when all of these other factors are done well is cryptography.

Except for physical layer security, nearly all network security is based on cryptographic principles. For this reason, we will begin our study of security by examining cryptography in some detail. In Sec. 8.1, we will look at some of the basic principles. In Sec. 8-2 through Sec. 8-5, we will examine some of the fundamental algorithms and data structures used in cryptography. Then we will examine in detail how these concepts can be used to achieve security in networks. We will conclude with some brief thoughts about technology and society.

Before starting, one last thought is in order: what is not covered. We have tried to focus on networking issues, rather than operating system and application issues, although the line is often hard to draw. For example, there is nothing here about user authentication using biometrics, password security, buffer overflow attacks, Trojan horses, login spoofing, code injection such as cross-site scripting, viruses, worms, and the like. All of these topics are covered at length in Chap. 9 of *Modern Operating Systems* (Tanenbaum, 2007). The interested reader is referred to that book for the systems aspects of security. Now let us begin our journey.

8.1 CRYPTOGRAPHY

Cryptography comes from the Greek words for "secret writing." It has a long and colorful history going back thousands of years. In this section, we will just sketch some of the highlights, as background information for what follows. For a complete history of cryptography, Kahn's (1995) book is recommended reading. For a comprehensive treatment of modern security and cryptographic algorithms, protocols, and applications, and related material, see Kaufman et al. (2002). For a more mathematical approach, see Stinson (2002). For a less mathematical approach, see Burnett and Paine (2001).

Professionals make a distinction between ciphers and codes. A **cipher** is a character-for-character or bit-for-bit transformation, without regard to the linguistic structure of the message. In contrast, a **code** replaces one word with another word or symbol. Codes are not used any more, although they have a glorious history. The most successful code ever devised was used by the U.S. armed forces during World War II in the Pacific. They simply had Navajo Indians talking to each other using specific Navajo words for military terms, for example *chay-da-gahi-nail-tsaidi* (literally: tortoise killer) for antitank weapon. The Navajo language is highly tonal, exceedingly complex, and has no written form. And not a single person in Japan knew anything about it.

In September 1945, the *San Diego Union* described the code by saying "For three years, wherever the Marines landed, the Japanese got an earful of strange gurgling noises interspersed with other sounds resembling the call of a Tibetan monk and the sound of a hot water bottle being emptied." The Japanese never broke the code and many Navajo code talkers were awarded high military honors for extraordinary service and bravery. The fact that the U.S. broke the Japanese code but the Japanese never broke the Navajo code played a crucial role in the American victories in the Pacific.

8.1.1 Introduction to Cryptography

Historically, four groups of people have used and contributed to the art of cryptography: the military, the diplomatic corps, diarists, and lovers. Of these, the military has had the most important role and has shaped the field over the centuries. Within military organizations, the messages to be encrypted have traditionally been given to poorly paid, low-level code clerks for encryption and transmission. The sheer volume of messages prevented this work from being done by a few elite specialists.

Until the advent of computers, one of the main constraints on cryptography had been the ability of the code clerk to perform the necessary transformations, often on a battlefield with little equipment. An additional constraint has been the difficulty in switching over quickly from one cryptographic method to another one, since this entails retraining a large number of people. However, the danger of a code clerk being captured by the enemy has made it essential to be able to change the cryptographic method instantly if need be. These conflicting requirements have given rise to the model of Fig. 8-2.

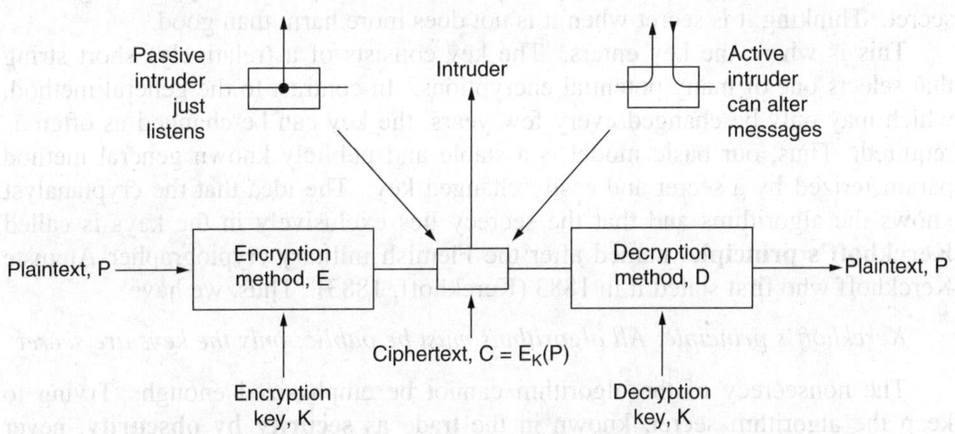

Figure 8-2. The encryption model (for a symmetric-key cipher).

The messages to be encrypted, known as the **plaintext**, are transformed by a function that is parameterized by a **key**. The output of the encryption process, known as the **ciphertext**, is then transmitted, often by messenger or radio. We assume that the enemy, or **intruder**, hears and accurately copies down the complete ciphertext. However, unlike the intended recipient, he does not know what the decryption key is and so cannot decrypt the ciphertext easily. Sometimes the intruder can not only listen to the communication channel (passive intruder) but can also record messages and play them back later, inject his own messages, or modify legitimate messages before they get to the receiver (active intruder). The art of breaking ciphers, known as **cryptanalysis**, and the art of devising them (cryptography) are collectively known as **cryptology**.

It will often be useful to have a notation for relating plaintext, ciphertext, and keys. We will use $C = E_K(P)$ to mean that the encryption of the plaintext P using key K gives the ciphertext C. Similarly, $P = D_K(C)$ represents the decryption of C to get the plaintext again. It then follows that

$$D_K(E_K(P)) = P$$

This notation suggests that E and D are just mathematical functions, which they are. The only tricky part is that both are functions of two parameters, and we have written one of the parameters (the key) as a subscript, rather than as an argument, to distinguish it from the message.

A fundamental rule of cryptography is that one must assume that the cryptanalyst knows the methods used for encryption and decryption. In other words, the cryptanalyst knows how the encryption method, E, and decryption, D, of Fig. 8-2 work in detail. The amount of effort necessary to invent, test, and install a new algorithm every time the old method is compromised (or thought to be compromised) has always made it impractical to keep the encryption algorithm secret. Thinking it is secret when it is not does more harm than good.

This is where the key enters. The key consists of a (relatively) short string that selects one of many potential encryptions. In contrast to the general method, which may only be changed every few years, the key can be changed as often as required. Thus, our basic model is a stable and publicly known general method parameterized by a secret and easily changed key. The idea that the cryptanalyst knows the algorithms and that the secrecy lies exclusively in the keys is called **Kerckhoff's principle**, named after the Flemish military cryptographer Auguste Kerckhoff who first stated it in 1883 (Kerckhoff, 1883). Thus, we have

Kerckhoff's principle: All algorithms must be public; only the keys are secret

The nonsecrecy of the algorithm cannot be emphasized enough. Trying to keep the algorithm secret, known in the trade as **security by obscurity**, never works. Also, by publicizing the algorithm, the cryptographer gets free consulting from a large number of academic cryptologists eager to break the system so they can publish papers demonstrating how smart they are. If many experts have tried to break the algorithm for a long time after its publication and no one has succeeded, it is probably pretty solid.

Since the real secrecy is in the key, its length is a major design issue. Consider a simple combination lock. The general principle is that you enter digits in sequence. Everyone knows this, but the key is secret. A key length of two digits means that there are 100 possibilities. A key length of three digits means 1000 possibilities, and a key length of six digits means a million. The longer the key, the higher the **work factor** the cryptanalyst has to deal with. The work factor for breaking the system by exhaustive search of the key space is exponential in the key length. Secrecy comes from having a strong (but public) algorithm and a long key. To prevent your kid brother from reading your email, 64-bit keys will do. For routine commercial use, at least 128 bits should be used. To keep major governments at bay, keys of at least 256 bits, preferably more, are needed.

From the cryptanalyst's point of view, the cryptanalysis problem has three principal variations. When he has a quantity of ciphertext and no plaintext, he is confronted with the **ciphertext-only** problem. The cryptograms that appear in the puzzle section of newspapers pose this kind of problem. When the cryptanalyst has some matched ciphertext and plaintext, the problem is called the **known plaintext** problem. Finally, when the cryptanalyst has the ability to encrypt pieces of plaintext of his own choosing, we have the **chosen plaintext** problem. Newspaper cryptograms could be broken trivially if the cryptanalyst were allowed to ask such questions as "What is the encryption of ABCDEFGHIJKL?"

Novices in the cryptography business often assume that if a cipher can withstand a ciphertext-only attack, it is secure. This assumption is very naive. In many cases, the cryptanalyst can make a good guess at parts of the plaintext. For example, the first thing many computers say when you call them up is "login:". Equipped with some matched plaintext-ciphertext pairs, the cryptanalyst's job becomes much easier. To achieve security, the cryptographer should be conservative and make sure that the system is unbreakable even if his opponent can encrypt arbitrary amounts of chosen plaintext.

Encryption methods have historically been divided into two categories: substitution ciphers and transposition ciphers. We will now deal with each of these briefly as background information for modern cryptography.

8.1.2 Substitution Ciphers

In a **substitution cipher**, each letter or group of letters is replaced by another letter or group of letters to disguise it. One of the oldest known ciphers is the **Caesar cipher**, attributed to Julius Caesar. With this method, *a* becomes *D*, *b* becomes *E*, *c* becomes *F*, . . . , and *z* becomes *C*. For example, *attack* becomes *DWWDFN*. In our examples, plaintext will be given in lowercase letters, and ciphertext in uppercase letters.

A slight generalization of the Caesar cipher allows the ciphertext alphabet to be shifted by *k* letters, instead of always three. In this case, *k* becomes a key to the general method of circularly shifted alphabets. The Caesar cipher may have fooled Pompey, but it has not fooled anyone since.

The next improvement is to have each of the symbols in the plaintext, say, the 26 letters for simplicity, map onto some other letter. For example,

```
plaintext:   a b c d e f g h i j k l m n o p q r s t u v w x y z
ciphertext:  Q W E R T Y U I O P A S D F G H J K L Z X C V B N M
```

The general system of symbol-for-symbol substitution is called a **monoalphabetic substitution cipher**, with the key being the 26-letter string corresponding to the full alphabet. For the key just given, the plaintext *attack* would be transformed into the ciphertext *QZZQEA*.

At first glance this might appear to be a safe system because although the cryptanalyst knows the general system (letter-for-letter substitution), he does not know which of the $26! \approx 4 \times 10^{26}$ possible keys is in use. In contrast with the Caesar cipher, trying all of them is not a promising approach. Even at 1 nsec per solution, a million computer chips working in parallel would take 10,000 years to try all the keys.

Nevertheless, given a surprisingly small amount of ciphertext, the cipher can be broken easily. The basic attack takes advantage of the statistical properties of natural languages. In English, for example, *e* is the most common letter, followed by *t*, *o*, *a*, *n*, *i*, etc. The most common two-letter combinations, or **digrams**, are *th*, *in*, *er*, *re*, and *an*. The most common three-letter combinations, or **trigrams**, are *the*, *ing*, *and*, and *ion*.

A cryptanalyst trying to break a monoalphabetic cipher would start out by counting the relative frequencies of all letters in the ciphertext. Then he might tentatively assign the most common one to *e* and the next most common one to *t*. He would then look at trigrams to find a common one of the form *tXe*, which strongly suggests that *X* is *h*. Similarly, if the pattern *thYt* occurs frequently, the *Y* probably stands for *a*. With this information, he can look for a frequently occurring trigram of the form *aZW*, which is most likely *and*. By making guesses at common letters, digrams, and trigrams and knowing about likely patterns of vowels and consonants, the cryptanalyst builds up a tentative plaintext, letter by letter.

Another approach is to guess a probable word or phrase. For example, consider the following ciphertext from an accounting firm (blocked into groups of five characters):

```
CTBMN BYCTC BTJDS QXBNS GSTJC BTSWX CTQTZ CQVUJ
QJSGS TJQZZ MNQJS VLNSX VSZJU JDSTS JQUUS JUBXJ
DSKSU JSNTK BGAQJ ZBGYQ TLCTZ BNYBN QJSW
```

A likely word in a message from an accounting firm is *financial*. Using our knowledge that *financial* has a repeated letter (*i*), with four other letters between their occurrences, we look for repeated letters in the ciphertext at this spacing. We find 12 hits, at positions 6, 15, 27, 31, 42, 48, 56, 66, 70, 71, 76, and 82. However, only two of these, 31 and 42, have the next letter (corresponding to *n* in the plaintext) repeated in the proper place. Of these two, only 31 also has the *a* correctly positioned, so we know that *financial* begins at position 30. From this point on, deducing the key is easy by using the frequency statistics for English text and looking for nearly complete words to finish off.

8.1.3 Transposition Ciphers

Substitution ciphers preserve the order of the plaintext symbols but disguise them. **Transposition ciphers**, in contrast, reorder the letters but do not disguise them. Figure 8-3 depicts a common transposition cipher, the columnar transposition. The cipher is keyed by a word or phrase not containing any repeated letters. In this example, MEGABUCK is the key. The purpose of the key is to order the columns, with column 1 being under the key letter closest to the start of the alphabet, and so on. The plaintext is written horizontally, in rows, padded to fill the matrix if need be. The ciphertext is read out by columns, starting with the column whose key letter is the lowest.

M	E	G	A	B	U	C	K
7	4	5	1	2	8	3	6
p	l	e	a	s	e	t	r
a	n	s	f	e	r	o	n
e	m	i	l	l	i	o	n
d	o	l	l	a	r	s	t
o	m	y	s	w	i	s	s
b	a	n	k	a	c	c	o
u	n	t	s	i	x	t	w
o	t	w	o	a	b	c	d

Plaintext

pleasetransferonemilliondollarsto
myswissbankaccountsixtwotwo

Ciphertext

AFLLSKSOSELAWAIATOOSSCTCLNMOMANT
ESILYNTWRNNTSOWDPAEDOBUOERIRICXB

Figure 8-3. A transposition cipher.

To break a transposition cipher, the cryptanalyst must first be aware that he is dealing with a transposition cipher. By looking at the frequency of *E*, *T*, *A*, *O*, *I*, *N*, etc., it is easy to see if they fit the normal pattern for plaintext. If so, the cipher is clearly a transposition cipher, because in such a cipher every letter represents itself, keeping the frequency distribution intact.

The next step is to make a guess at the number of columns. In many cases, a probable word or phrase may be guessed at from the context. For example, suppose that our cryptanalyst suspects that the plaintext phrase *milliondollars* occurs somewhere in the message. Observe that digrams *MO*, *IL*, *LL*, *LA*, *IR*, and *OS* occur in the ciphertext as a result of this phrase wrapping around. The ciphertext letter *O* follows the ciphertext letter *M* (i.e., they are vertically adjacent in column 4) because they are separated in the probable phrase by a distance equal to the key length. If a key of length seven had been used, the digrams *MD*, *IO*, *LL*, *LL*, *IA*, *OR*, and *NS* would have occurred instead. In fact, for each key length, a different set of digrams is produced in the ciphertext. By hunting for the various possibilities, the cryptanalyst can often easily determine the key length.

The remaining step is to order the columns. When the number of columns, k, is small, each of the $k(k-1)$ column pairs can be examined in turn to see if its digram frequencies match those for English plaintext. The pair with the best match is assumed to be correctly positioned. Now each of the remaining columns is tentatively tried as the successor to this pair. The column whose digram and trigram frequencies give the best match is tentatively assumed to be correct. The next column is found in the same way. The entire process is continued until a potential ordering is found. Chances are that the plaintext will be recognizable at this point (e.g., if *milloin* occurs, it is clear what the error is).

Some transposition ciphers accept a fixed-length block of input and produce a fixed-length block of output. These ciphers can be completely described by giving a list telling the order in which the characters are to be output. For example, the cipher of Fig. 8-3 can be seen as a 64 character block cipher. Its output is 4, 12, 20, 28, 36, 44, 52, 60, 5, 13, . . . , 62. In other words, the fourth input character, *a*, is the first to be output, followed by the twelfth, *f*, and so on.

8.1.4 One-Time Pads

Constructing an unbreakable cipher is actually quite easy; the technique has been known for decades. First choose a random bit string as the key. Then convert the plaintext into a bit string, for example, by using its ASCII representation. Finally, compute the XOR (eXclusive OR) of these two strings, bit by bit. The resulting ciphertext cannot be broken because in a sufficiently large sample of ciphertext, each letter will occur equally often, as will every digram, every trigram, and so on. This method, known as the **one-time pad**, is immune to all present and future attacks, no matter how much computational power the intruder has. The reason derives from information theory: there is simply no information in the message because all possible plaintexts of the given length are equally likely.

An example of how one-time pads are used is given in Fig. 8-4. First, message 1, "I love you." is converted to 7-bit ASCII. Then a one-time pad, pad 1, is chosen and XORed with the message to get the ciphertext. A cryptanalyst could try all possible one-time pads to see what plaintext came out for each one. For example, the one-time pad listed as pad 2 in the figure could be tried, resulting in plaintext 2, "Elvis lives", which may or may not be plausible (a subject beyond the scope of this book). In fact, for every 11-character ASCII plaintext, there is a one-time pad that generates it. That is what we mean by saying there is no information in the ciphertext: you can get any message of the correct length out of it.

One-time pads are great in theory but have a number of disadvantages in practice. To start with, the key cannot be memorized, so both sender and receiver must carry a written copy with them. If either one is subject to capture, written keys are clearly undesirable. Additionally, the total amount of data that can be transmitted is limited by the amount of key available. If the spy strikes it rich and discovers a wealth of data, he may find himself unable to transmit them back to

```
Message 1:    1001001 0100000 1101100 1101111 1110110 1100101 0100000 1111001 1101111 1110101 0101110
Pad 1:        1010010 1001011 1110010 1010101 1010010 1100011 0001011 0101010 1010111 1100110 0101011
Ciphertext:   0011011 1101011 0011110 0111010 0100100 0000110 0101011 1010011 0111000 0010011 0000101

Pad 2:        1011110 0000111 1101000 1010011 1010111 0100110 1000111 0111010 1001110 1110110 1110110
Plaintext 2:  1000101 1101100 1110110 1101001 1110011 0100000 1101100 1101001 1110110 1100101 1110011
```

Figure 8-4. The use of a one-time pad for encryption and the possibility of getting any possible plaintext from the ciphertext by the use of some other pad.

headquarters because the key has been used up. Another problem is the sensitivity of the method to lost or inserted characters. If the sender and receiver get out of synchronization, all data from then on will appear garbled.

With the advent of computers, the one-time pad might potentially become practical for some applications. The source of the key could be a special DVD that contains several gigabytes of information and, if transported in a DVD movie box and prefixed by a few minutes of video, would not even be suspicious. Of course, at gigabit network speeds, having to insert a new DVD every 30 sec could become tedious. And the DVDs must be personally carried from the sender to the receiver before any messages can be sent, which greatly reduces their practical utility.

Quantum Cryptography

Interestingly, there may be a solution to the problem of how to transmit the one-time pad over the network, and it comes from a very unlikely source: quantum mechanics. This area is still experimental, but initial tests are promising. If it can be perfected and be made efficient, virtually all cryptography will eventually be done using one-time pads since they are provably secure. Below we will briefly explain how this method, **quantum cryptography**, works. In particular, we will describe a protocol called **BB84** after its authors and publication year (Bennet and Brassard, 1984).

Suppose that a user, Alice, wants to establish a one-time pad with a second user, Bob. Alice and Bob are called **principals**, the main characters in our story. For example, Bob is a banker with whom Alice would like to do business. The names "Alice" and "Bob" have been used for the principals in virtually every paper and book on cryptography since Ron Rivest introduced them many years ago (Rivest et al., 1978). Cryptographers love tradition. If we were to use "Andy" and "Barbara" as the principals, no one would believe anything in this chapter. So be it.

If Alice and Bob could establish a one-time pad, they could use it to communicate securely. The question is: how can they establish it without previously exchanging DVDs? We can assume that Alice and Bob are at the opposite ends of an optical fiber over which they can send and receive light pulses. However, an intrepid intruder, Trudy, can cut the fiber to splice in an active tap. Trudy can read all the bits sent in both directions. She can also send false messages in both directions. The situation might seem hopeless for Alice and Bob, but quantum cryptography can shed some new light on the subject.

Quantum cryptography is based on the fact that light comes in little packets called **photons**, which have some peculiar properties. Furthermore, light can be polarized by being passed through a polarizing filter, a fact well known to both sunglasses wearers and photographers. If a beam of light (i.e., a stream of photons) is passed through a polarizing filter, all the photons emerging from it will be polarized in the direction of the filter's axis (e.g., vertically). If the beam is now passed through a second polarizing filter, the intensity of the light emerging from the second filter is proportional to the square of the cosine of the angle between the axes. If the two axes are perpendicular, no photons get through. The absolute orientation of the two filters does not matter; only the angle between their axes counts.

To generate a one-time pad, Alice needs two sets of polarizing filters. Set one consists of a vertical filter and a horizontal filter. This choice is called a **rectilinear basis**. A basis (plural: bases) is just a coordinate system. The second set of filters is the same, except rotated 45 degrees, so one filter runs from the lower left to the upper right and the other filter runs from the upper left to the lower right. This choice is called a **diagonal basis**. Thus, Alice has two bases, which she can rapidly insert into her beam at will. In reality, Alice does not have four separate filters, but a crystal whose polarization can be switched electrically to any of the four allowed directions at great speed. Bob has the same equipment as Alice. The fact that Alice and Bob each have two bases available is essential to quantum cryptography.

For each basis, Alice now assigns one direction as 0 and the other as 1. In the example presented below, we assume she chooses vertical to be 0 and horizontal to be 1. Independently, she also chooses lower left to upper right as 0 and upper left to lower right as 1. She sends these choices to Bob as plaintext.

Now Alice picks a one-time pad, for example based on a random number generator (a complex subject all by itself). She transfers it bit by bit to Bob, choosing one of her two bases at random for each bit. To send a bit, her photon gun emits one photon polarized appropriately for the basis she is using for that bit. For example, she might choose bases of diagonal, rectilinear, rectilinear, diagonal, rectilinear, etc. To send her one-time pad of 1001110010100110 with these bases, she would send the photons shown in Fig. 8-5(a). Given the one-time pad and the sequence of bases, the polarization to use for each bit is uniquely determined. Bits sent one photon at a time are called **qubits**.

Bob does not know which bases to use, so he picks one at random for each arriving photon and just uses it, as shown in Fig. 8-5(b). If he picks the correct basis, he gets the correct bit. If he picks the incorrect basis, he gets a random bit

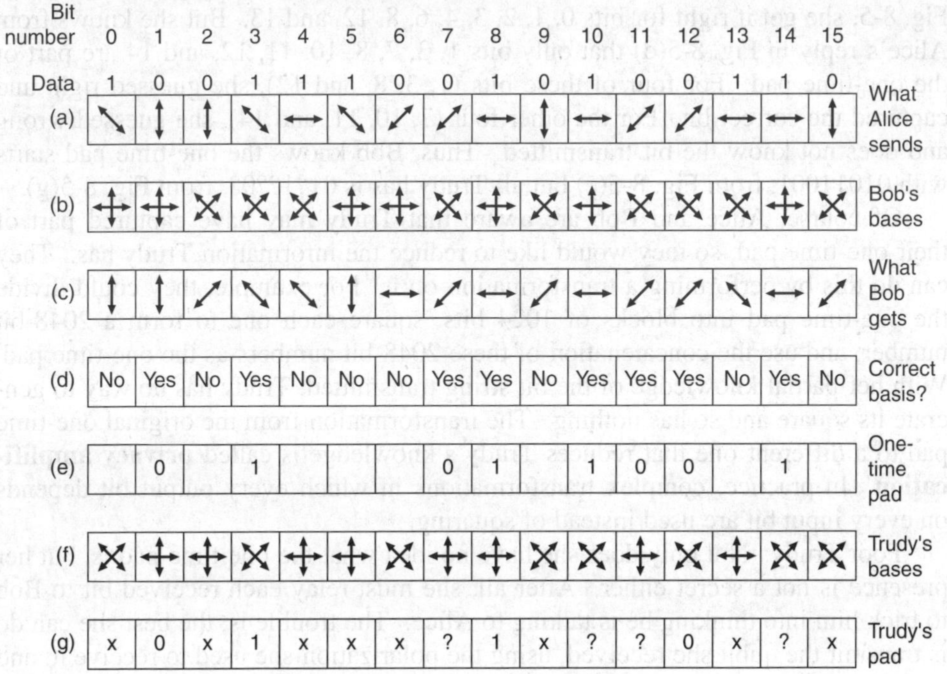

Figure 8-5. An example of quantum cryptography.

because if a photon hits a filter polarized at 45 degrees to its own polarization, it randomly jumps to the polarization of the filter or to a polarization perpendicular to the filter, with equal probability. This property of photons is fundamental to quantum mechanics. Thus, some of the bits are correct and some are random, but Bob does not know which are which. Bob's results are depicted in Fig. 8-5(c).

How does Bob find out which bases he got right and which he got wrong? He simply tells Alice which basis he used for each bit in plaintext and she tells him which are right and which are wrong in plaintext, as shown in Fig. 8-5(d). From this information, both of them can build a bit string from the correct guesses, as shown in Fig. 8-5(e). On the average, this bit string will be half the length of the original bit string, but since both parties know it, they can use it as a one-time pad. All Alice has to do is transmit a bit string slightly more than twice the desired length, and she and Bob will have a one-time pad of the desired length. Done.

But wait a minute. We forgot Trudy. Suppose that she is curious about what Alice has to say and cuts the fiber, inserting her own detector and transmitter. Unfortunately for her, she does not know which basis to use for each photon either. The best she can do is pick one at random for each photon, just as Bob does. An example of her choices is shown in Fig. 8-5(f). When Bob later reports (in plaintext) which bases he used and Alice tells him (in plaintext) which ones are correct, Trudy now knows when she got it right and when she got it wrong. In Fig. 8-5, she got it right for bits 0, 1, 2, 3, 4, 6, 8, 12, and 13. But she knows from Alice's reply in Fig. 8-5(d) that only bits 1, 3, 7, 8, 10, 11, 12, and 14 are part of the one-time pad. For four of these bits (1, 3, 8, and 12), she guessed right and captured the correct bit. For the other four (7, 10, 11, and 14), she guessed wrong and does not know the bit transmitted. Thus, Bob knows the one-time pad starts with 01011001, from Fig. 8-5(e) but all Trudy has is 01?1??0?, from Fig. 8-5(g).

Of course, Alice and Bob are aware that Trudy may have captured part of their one-time pad, so they would like to reduce the information Trudy has. They can do this by performing a transformation on it. For example, they could divide the one-time pad into blocks of 1024 bits, square each one to form a 2048-bit number, and use the concatenation of these 2048-bit numbers as the one-time pad. With her partial knowledge of the bit string transmitted, Trudy has no way to generate its square and so has nothing. The transformation from the original one-time pad to a different one that reduces Trudy's knowledge is called **privacy amplification**. In practice, complex transformations in which every output bit depends on every input bit are used instead of squaring.

Poor Trudy. Not only does she have no idea what the one-time pad is, but her presence is not a secret either. After all, she must relay each received bit to Bob to trick him into thinking he is talking to Alice. The trouble is, the best she can do is transmit the qubit she received, using the polarization she used to receive it, and about half the time she will be wrong, causing many errors in Bob's one-time pad.

When Alice finally starts sending data, she encodes it using a heavy forward-error-correcting code. From Bob's point of view, a 1-bit error in the one-time pad is the same as a 1-bit transmission error. Either way, he gets the wrong bit. If there is enough forward error correction, he can recover the original message despite all the errors, but he can easily count how many errors were corrected. If this number is far more than the expected error rate of the equipment, he knows that Trudy has tapped the line and can act accordingly (e.g., tell Alice to switch to a radio channel, call the police, etc.). If Trudy had a way to clone a photon so she had one photon to inspect and an identical photon to send to Bob, she could avoid detection, but at present no way to clone a photon perfectly is known. And even if Trudy could clone photons, the value of quantum cryptography to establish one-time pads would not be reduced.

Although quantum cryptography has been shown to operate over distances of 60 km of fiber, the equipment is complex and expensive. Still, the idea has promise. For more information about quantum cryptography, see Mullins (2002).

8.1.5 Two Fundamental Cryptographic Principles

Although we will study many different cryptographic systems in the pages ahead, two principles underlying all of them are important to understand. Pay attention. You violate them at your peril.

Redundancy

The first principle is that all encrypted messages must contain some redundancy, that is, information not needed to understand the message. An example may make it clear why this is needed. Consider a mail-order company, The Couch Potato (TCP), with 60,000 products. Thinking they are being very efficient, TCP's programmers decide that ordering messages should consist of a 16-byte customer name followed by a 3-byte data field (1 byte for the quantity and 2 bytes for the product number). The last 3 bytes are to be encrypted using a very long key known only by the customer and TCP.

At first, this might seem secure, and in a sense it is because passive intruders cannot decrypt the messages. Unfortunately, it also has a fatal flaw that renders it useless. Suppose that a recently fired employee wants to punish TCP for firing her. Just before leaving, she takes the customer list with her. She works through the night writing a program to generate fictitious orders using real customer names. Since she does not have the list of keys, she just puts random numbers in the last 3 bytes, and sends hundreds of orders off to TCP.

When these messages arrive, TCP's computer uses the customers' name to locate the key and decrypt the message. Unfortunately for TCP, almost every 3-byte message is valid, so the computer begins printing out shipping instructions. While it might seem odd for a customer to order 837 sets of children's swings or 540 sandboxes, for all the computer knows, the customer might be planning to open a chain of franchised playgrounds. In this way, an active intruder (the ex-employee) can cause a massive amount of trouble, even though she cannot understand the messages her computer is generating.

This problem can be solved by the addition of redundancy to all messages. For example, if order messages are extended to 12 bytes, the first 9 of which must be zeros, this attack no longer works because the ex-employee can no longer generate a large stream of valid messages. The moral of the story is that all messages must contain considerable redundancy so that active intruders cannot send random junk and have it be interpreted as a valid message.

However, adding redundancy makes it easier for cryptanalysts to break messages. Suppose that the mail-order business is highly competitive, and The Couch Potato's main competitor, The Sofa Tuber, would dearly love to know how many sandboxes TCP is selling so it taps TCP's phone line. In the original scheme with 3-byte messages, cryptanalysis was nearly impossible because after guessing a key, the cryptanalyst had no way of telling whether it was right because almost every message was technically legal. With the new 12-byte scheme, it is easy for the cryptanalyst to tell a valid message from an invalid one. Thus, we have

Cryptographic principle 1: Messages must contain some redundancy

In other words, upon decrypting a message, the recipient must be able to tell whether it is valid by simply inspecting the message and perhaps performing a simple computation. This redundancy is needed to prevent active intruders from sending garbage and tricking the receiver into decrypting the garbage and acting on the "plaintext." However, this same redundancy makes it much easier for passive intruders to break the system, so there is some tension here. Furthermore, the redundancy should never be in the form of *n* 0s at the start or end of a message, since running such messages through some cryptographic algorithms gives more predictable results, making the cryptanalysts' job easier. A CRC polynomial is much better than a run of 0s since the receiver can easily verify it, but it generates more work for the cryptanalyst. Even better is to use a cryptographic hash, a concept we will explore later. For the moment, think of it as a better CRC.

Getting back to quantum cryptography for a moment, we can also see how redundancy plays a role there. Due to Trudy's interception of the photons, some bits in Bob's one-time pad will be wrong. Bob needs some redundancy in the incoming messages to determine that errors are present. One very crude form of redundancy is repeating the message two times. If the two copies are not identical, Bob knows that either the fiber is very noisy or someone is tampering with the transmission. Of course, sending everything twice is overkill; a Hamming or Reed-Solomon code is a more efficient way to do error detection and correction. But it should be clear that some redundancy is needed to distinguish a valid message from an invalid message, especially in the face of an active intruder.

Freshness

The second cryptographic principle is that measures must be taken to ensure that each message received can be verified as being fresh, that is, sent very recently. This measure is needed to prevent active intruders from playing back old messages. If no such measures were taken, our ex-employee could tap TCP's phone line and just keep repeating previously sent valid messages. Thus,

Cryptographic principle 2: Some method is needed to foil replay attacks

One such measure is including in every message a timestamp valid only for, say, 10 seconds. The receiver can then just keep messages around for 10 seconds and compare newly arrived messages to previous ones to filter out duplicates. Messages older than 10 seconds can be thrown out, since any replays sent more than 10 seconds later will be rejected as too old. Measures other than timestamps will be discussed later.

8.2 SYMMETRIC-KEY ALGORITHMS

Modern cryptography uses the same basic ideas as traditional cryptography (transposition and substitution), but its emphasis is different. Traditionally, cryptographers have used simple algorithms. Nowadays, the reverse is true: the object is to make the encryption algorithm so complex and involuted that even if the cryptanalyst acquires vast mounds of enciphered text of his own choosing, he will not be able to make any sense of it at all without the key.

The first class of encryption algorithms we will study in this chapter are called **symmetric-key algorithms** because they use the same key for encryption and decryption. Fig. 8-2 illustrates the use of a symmetric-key algorithm. In particular, we will focus on **block ciphers**, which take an *n*-bit block of plaintext as input and transform it using the key into an *n*-bit block of ciphertext.

Cryptographic algorithms can be implemented in either hardware (for speed) or software (for flexibility). Although most of our treatment concerns the algorithms and protocols, which are independent of the actual implementation, a few words about building cryptographic hardware may be of interest. Transpositions and substitutions can be implemented with simple electrical circuits. Figure 8-6(a) shows a device, known as a **P-box** (P stands for permutation), used to effect a transposition on an 8-bit input. If the 8 bits are designated from top to bottom as 01234567, the output of this particular P-box is 36071245. By appropriate internal wiring, a P-box can be made to perform any transposition and do it at practically the speed of light since no computation is involved, just signal propagation. This design follows Kerckhoff's principle: the attacker knows that the general method is permuting the bits. What he does not know is which bit goes where.

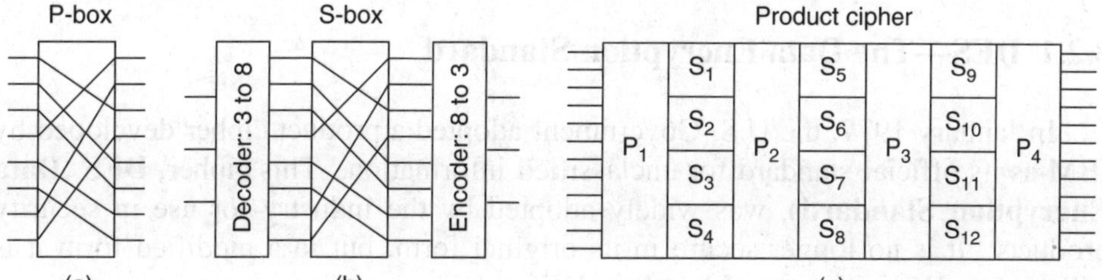

Figure 8-6. Basic elements of product ciphers. (a) P-box. (b) S-box. (c) Product.

Substitutions are performed by **S-boxes**, as shown in Fig. 8-6(b). In this example, a 3-bit plaintext is entered and a 3-bit ciphertext is output. The 3-bit input selects one of the eight lines exiting from the first stage and sets it to 1; all the other lines are 0. The second stage is a P-box. The third stage encodes the selected input line in binary again. With the wiring shown, if the eight octal numbers 01234567 were input one after another, the output sequence would be 24506713. In other words, 0 has been replaced by 2, 1 has been replaced by 4, etc. Again, by appropriate wiring of the P-box inside the S-box, any substitution can be accomplished. Furthermore, such a device can be built in hardware to achieve great speed, since encoders and decoders have only one or two (subnanosecond) gate delays and the propagation time across the P-box may well be less than 1 picosec.

The real power of these basic elements only becomes apparent when we cascade a whole series of boxes to form a **product cipher**, as shown in Fig. 8-6(c). In this example, 12 input lines are transposed (i.e., permuted) by the first stage (P_1). In the second stage, the input is broken up into four groups of 3 bits, each of which is substituted independently of the others (S_1 to S_4). This arrangement shows a method of approximating a larger S-box from multiple, smaller S-boxes. It is useful because small S-boxes are practical for a hardware implementation (e.g., an 8-bit S-box can be realized as a 256-entry lookup table), but large S-boxes become unwieldy to build (e.g., a 12-bit S-box would at a minimum need $2^{12} = 4096$ crossed wires in its middle stage). Although this method is less general, it is still powerful. By inclusion of a sufficiently large number of stages in the product cipher, the output can be made to be an exceedingly complicated function of the input.

Product ciphers that operate on *k*-bit inputs to produce *k*-bit outputs are very common. Typically, *k* is 64 to 256. A hardware implementation usually has at least 10 physical stages, instead of just 7 as in Fig. 8-6(c). A software implementation is programmed as a loop with at least eight iterations, each one performing S-box-type substitutions on subblocks of the 64- to 256-bit data block, followed by a permutation that mixes the outputs of the S-boxes. Often there is a special initial permutation and one at the end as well. In the literature, the iterations are called **rounds**.

8.2.1 DES—The Data Encryption Standard

In January 1977, the U.S. Government adopted a product cipher developed by IBM as its official standard for unclassified information. This cipher, **DES (Data Encryption Standard)**, was widely adopted by the industry for use in security products. It is no longer secure in its original form, but in a modified form it is still useful. We will now explain how DES works.

An outline of DES is shown in Fig. 8-7(a). Plaintext is encrypted in blocks of 64 bits, yielding 64 bits of ciphertext. The algorithm, which is parameterized by a 56-bit key, has 19 distinct stages. The first stage is a key-independent transposition on the 64-bit plaintext. The last stage is the exact inverse of this transposition. The stage prior to the last one exchanges the leftmost 32 bits with the rightmost 32 bits. The remaining 16 stages are functionally identical but are parameterized by different functions of the key. The algorithm has been designed to allow decryption to be done with the same key as encryption, a property needed in any symmetric-key algorithm. The steps are just run in the reverse order.

The operation of one of these intermediate stages is illustrated in Fig. 8-7(b). Each stage takes two 32-bit inputs and produces two 32-bit outputs. The left output is simply a copy of the right input. The right output is the bitwise XOR of the left input and a function of the right input and the key for this stage, K_i. Pretty much all the complexity of the algorithm lies in this function.

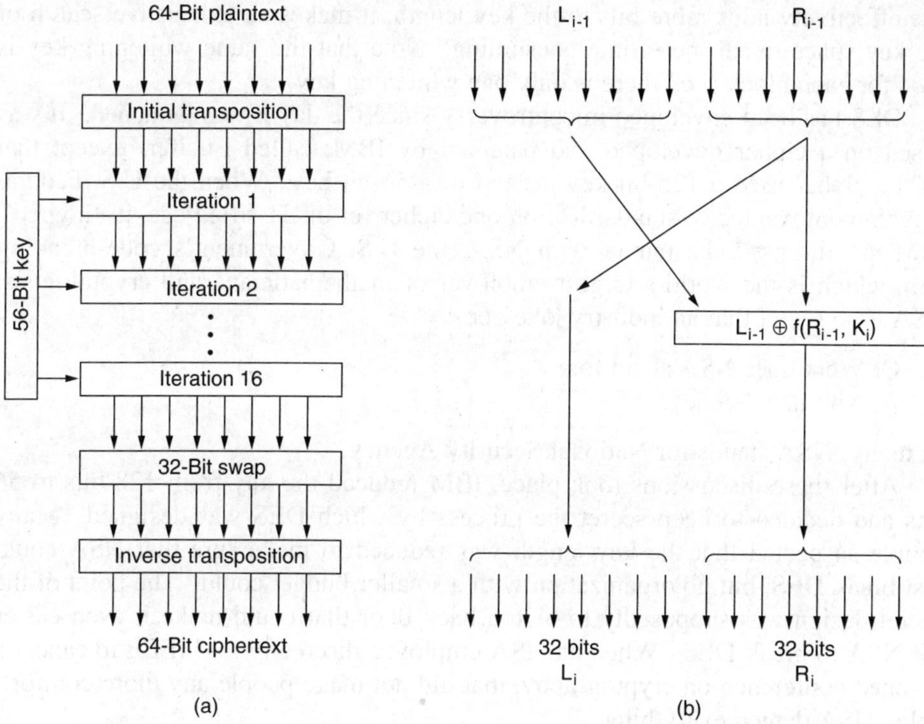

Figure 8-7. The Data Encryption Standard. (a) General outline. (b) Detail of one iteration. The circled + means exclusive OR.

The function consists of four steps, carried out in sequence. First, a 48-bit number, E, is constructed by expanding the 32-bit R_{i-1} according to a fixed transposition and duplication rule. Second, E and K_i are XORed together. This output is then partitioned into eight groups of 6 bits each, each of which is fed into a different S-box. Each of the 64 possible inputs to an S-box is mapped onto a 4-bit output. Finally, these 8×4 bits are passed through a P-box.

In each of the 16 iterations, a different key is used. Before the algorithm starts, a 56-bit transposition is applied to the key. Just before each iteration, the key is partitioned into two 28-bit units, each of which is rotated left by a number of bits dependent on the iteration number. K_i is derived from this rotated key by applying yet another 56-bit transposition to it. A different 48-bit subset of the 56 bits is extracted and permuted on each round.

A technique that is sometimes used to make DES stronger is called **whitening**. It consists of XORing a random 64-bit key with each plaintext block before feeding it into DES and then XORing a second 64-bit key with the resulting ciphertext before transmitting it. Whitening can easily be removed by running the reverse operations (if the receiver has the two whitening keys). Since this technique effectively adds more bits to the key length, it makes an exhaustive search of the key space much more time consuming. Note that the same whitening key is used for each block (i.e., there is only one whitening key).

DES has been enveloped in controversy since the day it was launched. It was based on a cipher developed and patented by IBM, called Lucifer, except that IBM's cipher used a 128-bit key instead of a 56-bit key. When the U.S. Federal Government wanted to standardize on one cipher for unclassified use, it "invited" IBM to "discuss" the matter with NSA, the U.S. Government's code-breaking arm, which is the world's largest employer of mathematicians and cryptologists. NSA is so secret that an industry joke goes:

Q: What does NSA stand for?
A: No Such Agency.

Actually, NSA stands for National Security Agency.

After these discussions took place, IBM reduced the key from 128 bits to 56 bits and decided to keep secret the process by which DES was designed. Many people suspected that the key length was reduced to make sure that NSA could just break DES, but no organization with a smaller budget could. The point of the secret design was supposedly to hide a back door that could make it even easier for NSA to break DES. When an NSA employee discreetly told IEEE to cancel a planned conference on cryptography, that did not make people any more comfortable. NSA denied everything.

In 1977, two Stanford cryptography researchers, Diffie and Hellman (1977), designed a machine to break DES and estimated that it could be built for 20 million dollars. Given a small piece of plaintext and matched ciphertext, this machine could find the key by exhaustive search of the 2^{56}-entry key space in under 1 day. Nowadays, the game is up. Such a machine exists, is for sale, and costs less than \$10,000 to make (Kumar et al., 2006).

Triple DES

As early as 1979, IBM realized that the DES key length was too short and devised a way to effectively increase it, using triple encryption (Tuchman, 1979). The method chosen, which has since been incorporated in International Standard 8732, is illustrated in Fig. 8-8. Here, two keys and three stages are used. In the first stage, the plaintext is encrypted using DES in the usual way with K_1. In the second stage, DES is run in decryption mode, using K_2 as the key. Finally, another DES encryption is done with K_1.

This design immediately gives rise to two questions. First, why are only two keys used, instead of three? Second, why is **EDE (Encrypt Decrypt Encrypt)** used, instead of **EEE (Encrypt Encrypt Encrypt)**? The reason that two keys are used is that even the most paranoid of cryptographers believe that 112 bits is

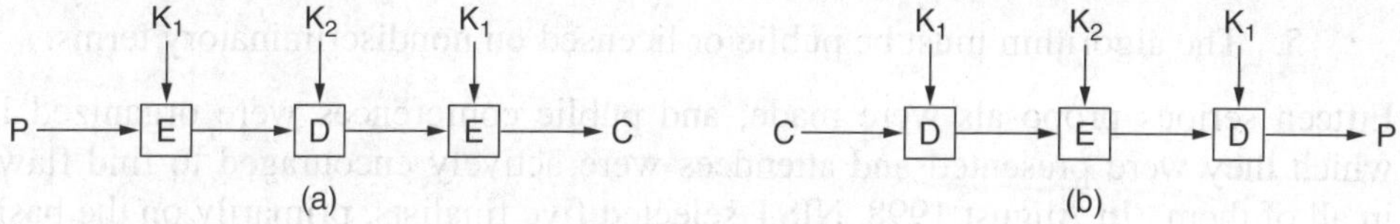

Figure 8-8. (a) Triple encryption using DES. (b) Decryption.

adequate for routine commercial applications for the time being. (And among cryptographers, paranoia is considered a feature, not a bug.) Going to 168 bits would just add the unnecessary overhead of managing and transporting another key for little real gain.

The reason for encrypting, decrypting, and then encrypting again is backward compatibility with existing single-key DES systems. Both the encryption and decryption functions are mappings between sets of 64-bit numbers. From a cryptographic point of view, the two mappings are equally strong. By using EDE, however, instead of EEE, a computer using triple encryption can speak to one using single encryption by just setting $K_1 = K_2$. This property allows triple encryption to be phased in gradually, something of no concern to academic cryptographers but of considerable importance to IBM and its customers.

8.2.2 AES—The Advanced Encryption Standard

As DES began approaching the end of its useful life, even with triple DES, **NIST** (**National Institute of Standards and Technology**), the agency of the U.S. Dept. of Commerce charged with approving standards for the U.S. Federal Government, decided that the government needed a new cryptographic standard for unclassified use. NIST was keenly aware of all the controversy surrounding DES and well knew that if it just announced a new standard, everyone knowing anything about cryptography would automatically assume that NSA had built a back door into it so NSA could read everything encrypted with it. Under these conditions, probably no one would use the standard and it would have died quietly.

So, NIST took a surprisingly different approach for a government bureaucracy: it sponsored a cryptographic bake-off (contest). In January 1997, researchers from all over the world were invited to submit proposals for a new standard, to be called **AES** (**Advanced Encryption Standard**). The bake-off rules were:

1. The algorithm must be a symmetric block cipher.
2. The full design must be public.
3. Key lengths of 128, 192, and 256 bits must be supported.

4. Both software and hardware implementations must be possible.
5. The algorithm must be public or licensed on nondiscriminatory terms.

Fifteen serious proposals were made, and public conferences were organized in which they were presented and attendees were actively encouraged to find flaws in all of them. In August 1998, NIST selected five finalists, primarily on the basis of their security, efficiency, simplicity, flexibility, and memory requirements (important for embedded systems). More conferences were held and more potshots taken.

In October 2000, NIST announced that it had selected Rijndael, by Joan Daemen and Vincent Rijmen. The name Rijndael, pronounced Rhine-doll (more or less), is derived from the last names of the authors: Rijmen + Daemen. In November 2001, Rijndael became the AES U.S. Government standard, published as FIPS (Federal Information Processing Standard) 197. Due to the extraordinary openness of the competition, the technical properties of Rijndael, and the fact that the winning team consisted of two young Belgian cryptographers (who were unlikely to have built in a back door just to please NSA), Rijndael has become the world's dominant cryptographic cipher. AES encryption and decryption is now part of the instruction set for some microprocessors (e.g., Intel).

Rijndael supports key lengths and block sizes from 128 bits to 256 bits in steps of 32 bits. The key length and block length may be chosen independently. However, AES specifies that the block size must be 128 bits and the key length must be 128, 192, or 256 bits. It is doubtful that anyone will ever use 192-bit keys, so de facto, AES has two variants: a 128-bit block with a 128-bit key and a 128-bit block with a 256-bit key.

In our treatment of the algorithm, we will examine only the 128/128 case because this is likely to become the commercial norm. A 128-bit key gives a key space of $2^{128} \approx 3 \times 10^{38}$ keys. Even if NSA manages to build a machine with 1 billion parallel processors, each being able to evaluate one key per picosecond, it would take such a machine about 10^{10} years to search the key space. By then the sun will have burned out, so the folks then present will have to read the results by candlelight.

Rijndael

From a mathematical perspective, Rijndael is based on Galois field theory, which gives it some provable security properties. However, it can also be viewed as C code, without getting into the mathematics.

Like DES, Rijndael uses substitution and permutations, and it also uses multiple rounds. The number of rounds depends on the key size and block size, being 10 for 128-bit keys with 128-bit blocks and moving up to 14 for the largest key or the largest block. However, unlike DES, all operations involve entire bytes, to allow for efficient implementations in both hardware and software. An outline of the code is given in Fig. 8-9. Note that this code is for the purpose of illustration. Good implementations of security code will follow additional practices, such as zeroing out sensitive memory after it has been used. See, for example, Ferguson et al. (2010).

```
#define LENGTH 16                                  /* # bytes in data block or key */
#define NROWS 4                                    /* number of rows in state */
#define NCOLS 4                                    /* number of columns in state */
#define ROUNDS 10                                  /* number of iterations */
typedef unsigned char byte;                        /* unsigned 8-bit integer */

rijndael(byte plaintext[LENGTH], byte ciphertext[LENGTH], byte key[LENGTH])
{
  int r;                                           /* loop index */
  byte state[NROWS][NCOLS];                        /* current state */
  struct {byte k[NROWS][NCOLS];} rk[ROUNDS + 1];  /* round keys */

  expand_key(key, rk);                             /* construct the round keys */
  copy_plaintext_to_state(state, plaintext);       /* init current state */
  xor_roundkey_into_state(state, rk[0]);           /* XOR key into state */
  for (r = 1; r <= ROUNDS; r++) {
       substitute(state);                          /* apply S-box to each byte */
       rotate_rows(state);                         /* rotate row i by i bytes */
       if (r < ROUNDS) mix_columns(state);         /* mix function */
       xor_roundkey_into_state(state, rk[r]);      /* XOR key into state */
  }
  copy_state_to_ciphertext(ciphertext, state);     /* return result */
}
```

Figure 8-9. An outline of Rijndael in C.

The function *rijndael* has three parameters. They are: *plaintext*, an array of 16 bytes containing the input data; *ciphertext*, an array of 16 bytes where the enciphered output will be returned; and *key*, the 16-byte key. During the calculation, the current state of the data is maintained in a byte array, *state*, whose size is $NROWS \times NCOLS$. For 128-bit blocks, this array is 4×4 bytes. With 16 bytes, the full 128-bit data block can be stored.

The *state* array is initialized to the plaintext and modified by every step in the computation. In some steps, byte-for-byte substitution is performed. In others, the bytes are permuted within the array. Other transformations are also used. At the end, the contents of the *state* are returned as the ciphertext.

The code starts out by expanding the key into 11 arrays of the same size as the state. They are stored in *rk*, which is an array of structs, each containing a state array. One of these will be used at the start of the calculation and the other 10 will be used during the 10 rounds, one per round. The calculation of the round keys from the encryption key is too complicated for us to get into here. Suffice it to say that the round keys are produced by repeated rotation and XORing of various groups of key bits. For all the details, see Daemen and Rijmen (2002).

The next step is to copy the plaintext into the *state* array so it can be processed during the rounds. It is copied in column order, with the first 4 bytes going into column 0, the next 4 bytes going into column 1, and so on. Both the columns and the rows are numbered starting at 0, although the rounds are numbered starting at 1. This initial setup of the 12 byte arrays of size 4×4 is illustrated in Fig. 8-10.

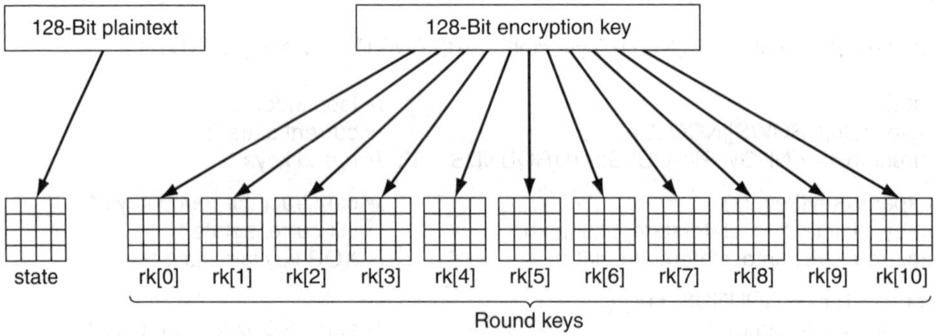

Figure 8-10. Creating the *state* and *rk* arrays.

There is one more step before the main computation begins: $rk[0]$ is XORed into *state*, byte for byte. In other words, each of the 16 bytes in *state* is replaced by the XOR of itself and the corresponding byte in $rk[0]$.

Now it is time for the main attraction. The loop executes 10 iterations, one per round, transforming *state* on each iteration. The contents of each round is produced in four steps. Step 1 does a byte-for-byte substitution on *state*. Each byte in turn is used as an index into an S-box to replace its value by the contents of that S-box entry. This step is a straight monoalphabetic substitution cipher. Unlike DES, which has multiple S-boxes, Rijndael has only one S-box.

Step 2 rotates each of the four rows to the left. Row 0 is rotated 0 bytes (i.e., not changed), row 1 is rotated 1 byte, row 2 is rotated 2 bytes, and row 3 is rotated 3 bytes. This step diffuses the contents of the current data around the block, analogous to the permutations of Fig. 8-6.

Step 3 mixes up each column independently of the other ones. The mixing is done using matrix multiplication in which the new column is the product of the old column and a constant matrix, with the multiplication done using the finite Galois field, $GF(2^8)$. Although this may sound complicated, an algorithm exists that allows each element of the new column to be computed using two table lookups and three XORs (Daemen and Rijmen, 2002, Appendix E).

Finally, step 4 XORs the key for this round into the *state* array for use in the next round.

Since every step is reversible, decryption can be done just by running the algorithm backward. However, there is also a trick available in which decryption can be done by running the encryption algorithm using different tables.

The algorithm has been designed not only for great security, but also for great speed. A good software implementation on a 2-GHz machine should be able to achieve an encryption rate of 700 Mbps, which is fast enough to encrypt over 100 MPEG-2 videos in real time. Hardware implementations are faster still.

8.2.3 Cipher Modes

Despite all this complexity, AES (or DES, or any block cipher for that matter) is basically a monoalphabetic substitution cipher using big characters (128-bit characters for AES and 64-bit characters for DES). Whenever the same plaintext block goes in the front end, the same ciphertext block comes out the back end. If you encrypt the plaintext *abcdefgh* 100 times with the same DES key, you get the same ciphertext 100 times. An intruder can exploit this property to help subvert the cipher.

Electronic Code Book Mode

To see how this monoalphabetic substitution cipher property can be used to partially defeat the cipher, we will use (triple) DES because it is easier to depict 64-bit blocks than 128-bit blocks, but AES has exactly the same problem. The straightforward way to use DES to encrypt a long piece of plaintext is to break it up into consecutive 8-byte (64-bit) blocks and encrypt them one after another with the same key. The last piece of plaintext is padded out to 64 bits, if need be. This technique is known as **ECB mode** (**Electronic Code Book mode**) in analogy with old-fashioned code books where each plaintext word was listed, followed by its ciphertext (usually a five-digit decimal number).

In Fig. 8-11, we have the start of a computer file listing the annual bonuses a company has decided to award to its employees. This file consists of consecutive 32-byte records, one per employee, in the format shown: 16 bytes for the name, 8 bytes for the position, and 8 bytes for the bonus. Each of the sixteen 8-byte blocks (numbered from 0 to 15) is encrypted by (triple) DES.

Leslie just had a fight with the boss and is not expecting much of a bonus. Kim, in contrast, is the boss' favorite, and everyone knows this. Leslie can get access to the file after it is encrypted but before it is sent to the bank. Can Leslie rectify this unfair situation, given only the encrypted file?

No problem at all. All Leslie has to do is make a copy of the 12th ciphertext block (which contains Kim's bonus) and use it to replace the fourth ciphertext block (which contains Leslie's bonus). Even without knowing what the 12th

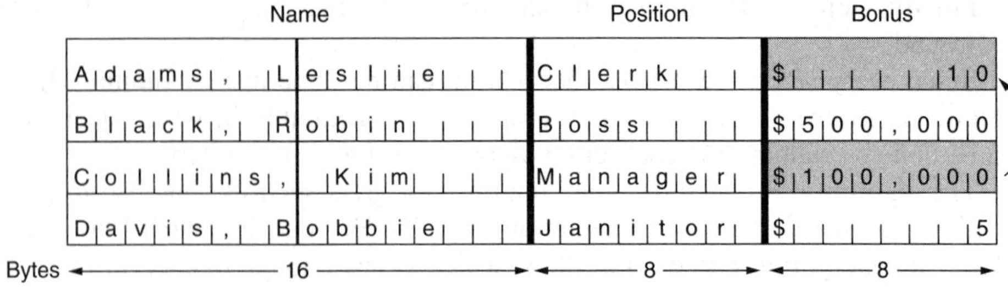

Figure 8-11. The plaintext of a file encrypted as 16 DES blocks.

block says, Leslie can expect to have a much merrier Christmas this year. (Copying the eighth ciphertext block is also a possibility, but is more likely to be detected; besides, Leslie is not a greedy person.)

Cipher Block Chaining Mode

To thwart this type of attack, all block ciphers can be chained in various ways so that replacing a block the way Leslie did will cause the plaintext decrypted starting at the replaced block to be garbage. One way of chaining is **cipher block chaining**. In this method, shown in Fig. 8-12, each plaintext block is XORed with the previous ciphertext block before being encrypted. Consequently, the same plaintext block no longer maps onto the same ciphertext block, and the encryption is no longer a big monoalphabetic substitution cipher. The first block is XORed with a randomly chosen **IV (Initialization Vector)**, which is transmitted (in plaintext) along with the ciphertext.

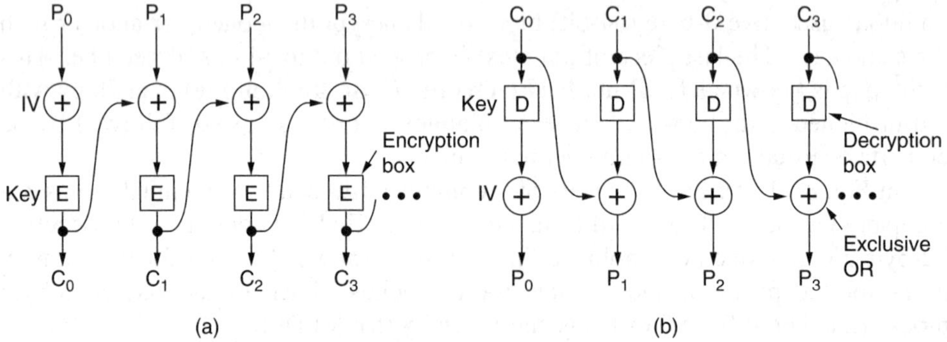

Figure 8-12. Cipher block chaining. (a) Encryption. (b) Decryption.

We can see how cipher block chaining mode works by examining the example of Fig. 8-12. We start out by computing $C_0 = E(P_0 \text{ XOR } IV)$. Then we compute $C_1 = E(P_1 \text{ XOR } C_0)$, and so on. Decryption also uses XOR to reverse the process, with $P_0 = IV \text{ XOR } D(C_0)$, and so on. Note that the encryption of block i is a function of all the plaintext in blocks 0 through $i - 1$, so the same plaintext generates different ciphertext depending on where it occurs. A transformation of the type Leslie made will result in nonsense for two blocks starting at Leslie's bonus field. To an astute security officer, this peculiarity might suggest where to start the ensuing investigation.

Cipher block chaining also has the advantage that the same plaintext block will not result in the same ciphertext block, making cryptanalysis more difficult. In fact, this is the main reason it is used.

Cipher Feedback Mode

However, cipher block chaining has the disadvantage of requiring an entire 64-bit block to arrive before decryption can begin. For byte-by-byte encryption, **cipher feedback mode** using (triple) DES is used, as shown in Fig. 8-13. For AES, the idea is exactly the same, only a 128-bit shift register is used. In this figure, the state of the encryption machine is shown after bytes 0 through 9 have been encrypted and sent. When plaintext byte 10 arrives, as illustrated in Fig. 8-13(a), the DES algorithm operates on the 64-bit shift register to generate a 64-bit ciphertext. The leftmost byte of that ciphertext is extracted and XORed with P_{10}. That byte is transmitted on the transmission line. In addition, the shift register is shifted left 8 bits, causing C_2 to fall off the left end, and C_{10} is inserted in the position just vacated at the right end by C_9.

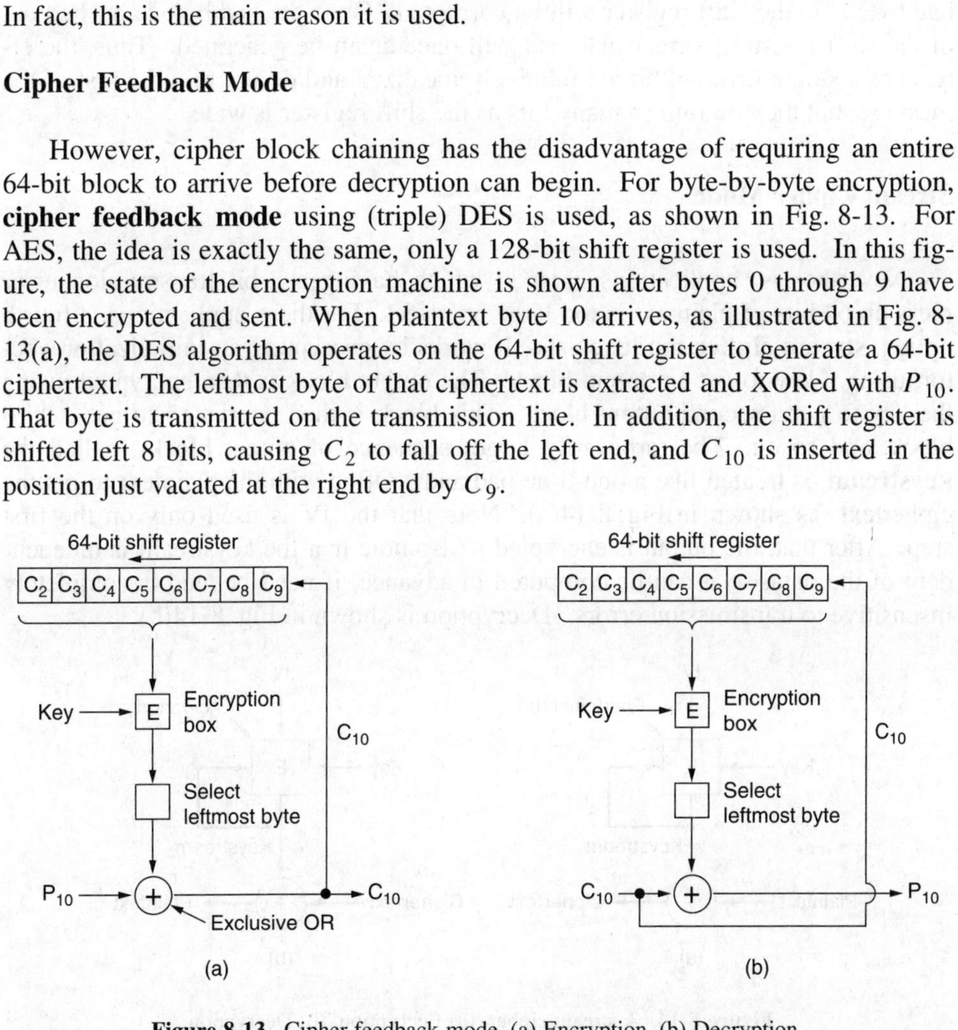

Figure 8-13. Cipher feedback mode. (a) Encryption. (b) Decryption.

Note that the contents of the shift register depend on the entire previous history of the plaintext, so a pattern that repeats multiple times in the plaintext will be encrypted differently each time in the ciphertext. As with cipher block chaining, an initialization vector is needed to start the ball rolling.

Decryption with cipher feedback mode works the same way as encryption. In particular, the content of the shift register is *encrypted*, not *decrypted*, so the selected byte that is XORed with C_{10} to get P_{10} is the same one that was XORed with P_{10} to generate C_{10} in the first place. As long as the two shift registers remain identical, decryption works correctly. This is illustrated in Fig. 8-13(b).

A problem with cipher feedback mode is that if one bit of the ciphertext is accidentally inverted during transmission, the 8 bytes that are decrypted while the bad byte is in the shift register will be corrupted. Once the bad byte is pushed out of the shift register, correct plaintext will once again be generated. Thus, the effects of a single inverted bit are relatively localized and do not ruin the rest of the message, but they do ruin as many bits as the shift register is wide.

Stream Cipher Mode

Nevertheless, applications exist in which having a 1-bit transmission error mess up 64 bits of plaintext is too large an effect. For these applications, a fourth option, **stream cipher mode**, exists. It works by encrypting an initialization vector, using a key to get an output block. The output block is then encrypted, using the key to get a second output block. This block is then encrypted to get a third block, and so on. The (arbitrarily large) sequence of output blocks, called the **keystream**, is treated like a one-time pad and XORed with the plaintext to get the ciphertext, as shown in Fig. 8-14(a). Note that the IV is used only on the first step. After that, the output is encrypted. Also note that the keystream is independent of the data, so it can be computed in advance, if need be, and is completely insensitive to transmission errors. Decryption is shown in Fig. 8-14(b).

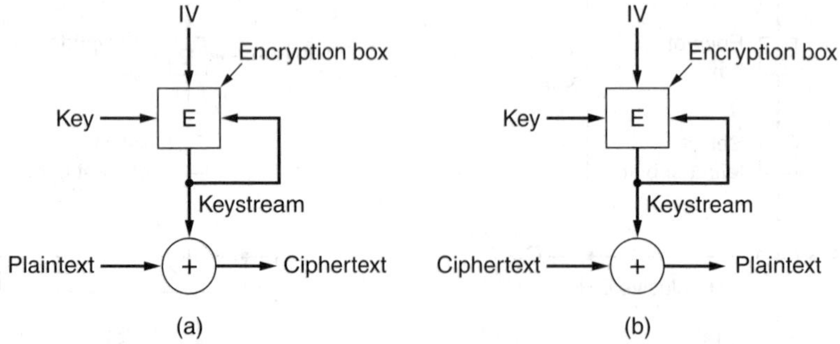

Figure 8-14. A stream cipher. (a) Encryption. (b) Decryption.

Decryption occurs by generating the same keystream at the receiving side. Since the keystream depends only on the IV and the key, it is not affected by transmission errors in the ciphertext. Thus, a 1-bit error in the transmitted ciphertext generates only a 1-bit error in the decrypted plaintext.

It is essential never to use the same (key, IV) pair twice with a stream cipher because doing so will generate the same keystream each time. Using the same keystream twice exposes the ciphertext to a **keystream reuse attack**. Imagine that the plaintext block, P_0, is encrypted with the keystream to get P_0 XOR K_0. Later, a second plaintext block, Q_0, is encrypted with the same keystream to get Q_0 XOR K_0. An intruder who captures both of these ciphertext blocks can simply XOR them together to get P_0 XOR Q_0, which eliminates the key. The intruder now has the XOR of the two plaintext blocks. If one of them is known or can be guessed, the other can also be found. In any event, the XOR of two plaintext streams can be attacked by using statistical properties of the message. For example, for English text, the most common character in the stream will probably be the XOR of two spaces, followed by the XOR of space and the letter "e", etc. In short, equipped with the XOR of two plaintexts, the cryptanalyst has an excellent chance of deducing both of them.

Counter Mode

One problem that all the modes except electronic code book mode have is that random access to encrypted data is impossible. For example, suppose a file is transmitted over a network and then stored on disk in encrypted form. This might be a reasonable way to operate if the receiving computer is a notebook computer that might be stolen. Storing all critical files in encrypted form greatly reduces the damage due to secret information leaking out in the event that the computer falls into the wrong hands.

However, disk files are often accessed in nonsequential order, especially files in databases. With a file encrypted using cipher block chaining, accessing a random block requires first decrypting all the blocks ahead of it, an expensive proposition. For this reason, yet another mode has been invented: **counter mode**, as illustrated in Fig. 8-15. Here, the plaintext is not encrypted directly. Instead, the initialization vector plus a constant is encrypted, and the resulting ciphertext is XORed with the plaintext. By stepping the initialization vector by 1 for each new block, it is easy to decrypt a block anywhere in the file without first having to decrypt all of its predecessors.

Although counter mode is useful, it has a weakness that is worth pointing out. Suppose that the same key, K, is used again in the future (with a different plaintext but the same IV) and an attacker acquires all the ciphertext from both runs. The keystreams are the same in both cases, exposing the cipher to a keystream reuse attack of the same kind we saw with stream ciphers. All the cryptanalyst has to do is XOR the two ciphertexts together to eliminate all the cryptographic protection and just get the XOR of the plaintexts. This weakness does not mean counter mode is a bad idea. It just means that both keys and initialization vectors should be chosen independently and at random. Even if the same key is accidentally used twice, if the IV is different each time, the plaintext is safe.

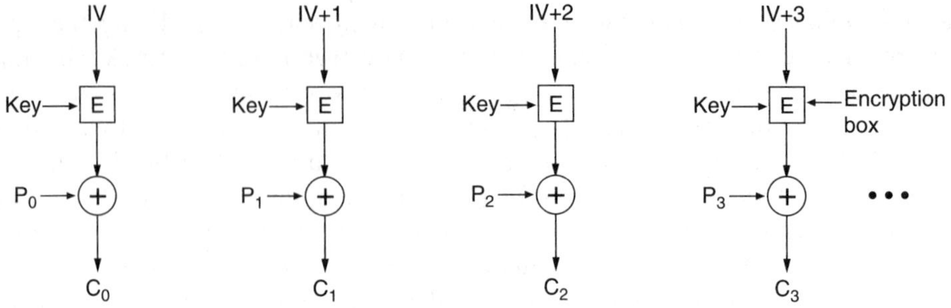

Figure 8-15. Encryption using counter mode.

8.2.4 Other Ciphers

AES (Rijndael) and DES are the best-known symmetric-key cryptographic algorithms, and the standard industry choices, if only for liability reasons. (No one will blame you if you use AES in your product and AES is cracked, but they will certainly blame you if you use a nonstandard cipher and it is later broken.) However, it is worth mentioning that numerous other symmetric-key ciphers have been devised. Some of these are embedded inside various products. A few of the more common ones are listed in Fig. 8-16. It is possible to use combinations of these ciphers, for example, AES over Twofish, so that both ciphers need to be broken to recover the data.

Cipher	Author	Key length	Comments
DES	IBM	56 bits	Too weak to use now
RC4	Ronald Rivest	1–2048 bits	Caution: some keys are weak
RC5	Ronald Rivest	128–256 bits	Good, but patented
AES (Rijndael)	Daemen and Rijmen	128–256 bits	Best choice
Serpent	Anderson, Biham, Knudsen	128–256 bits	Very strong
Triple DES	IBM	168 bits	Good, but getting old
Twofish	Bruce Schneier	128–256 bits	Very strong; widely used

Figure 8-16. Some common symmetric-key cryptographic algorithms.

8.2.5 Cryptanalysis

Before leaving the subject of symmetric-key cryptography, it is worth at least mentioning four developments in cryptanalysis. The first development is **differential cryptanalysis** (Biham and Shamir, 1997). This technique can be used to attack any block cipher. It works by beginning with a pair of plaintext blocks differing in only a small number of bits and watching carefully what happens on each internal iteration as the encryption proceeds. In many cases, some bit patterns are more common than others, which can lead to probabilistic attacks.

The second development worth noting is **linear cryptanalysis** (Matsui, 1994). It can break DES with only 2^{43} known plaintexts. It works by XORing certain bits in the plaintext and ciphertext together and examining the result. When done repeatedly, half the bits should be 0s and half should be 1s. Often, however, ciphers introduce a bias in one direction or the other, and this bias, however small, can be exploited to reduce the work factor. For the details, see Matsui's paper.

The third development is using analysis of electrical power consumption to find secret keys. Computers typically use around 3 volts to represent a 1 bit and 0 volts to represent a 0 bit. Thus, processing a 1 takes more electrical energy than processing a 0. If a cryptographic algorithm consists of a loop in which the key bits are processed in order, an attacker who replaces the main *n*-GHz clock with a slow (e.g., 100-Hz) clock and puts alligator clips on the CPU's power and ground pins can precisely monitor the power consumed by each machine instruction. From this data, deducing the key is surprisingly easy. This kind of cryptanalysis can be defeated only by carefully coding the algorithm in assembly language to make sure power consumption is independent of the key and also independent of all the individual round keys.

The fourth development is timing analysis. Cryptographic algorithms are full of `if` statements that test bits in the round keys. If the `then` and `else` parts take different amounts of time, by slowing down the clock and seeing how long various steps take, it may also be possible to deduce the round keys. Once all the round keys are known, the original key can usually be computed. Power and timing analysis can also be employed simultaneously to make the job easier. While power and timing analysis may seem exotic, in reality they are powerful techniques that can break any cipher not specifically designed to resist them.

8.3 PUBLIC-KEY ALGORITHMS

Historically, distributing the keys has always been the weakest link in most cryptosystems. No matter how strong a cryptosystem was, if an intruder could steal the key, the system was worthless. Cryptologists always took for granted that the encryption key and decryption key were the same (or easily derived from one another). But the key had to be distributed to all users of the system. Thus, it seemed as if there was an inherent problem. Keys had to be protected from theft, but they also had to be distributed, so they could not be locked in a bank vault.

In 1976, two researchers at Stanford University, Diffie and Hellman (1976), proposed a radically new kind of cryptosystem, one in which the encryption and decryption keys were so different that the decryption key could not feasibly be derived from the encryption key. In their proposal, the (keyed) encryption algorithm, E, and the (keyed) decryption algorithm, D, had to meet three requirements. These requirements can be stated simply as follows:

1. $D(E(P)) = P$.
2. It is exceedingly difficult to deduce D from E.
3. E cannot be broken by a chosen plaintext attack.

The first requirement says that if we apply D to an encrypted message, $E(P)$, we get the original plaintext message, P, back. Without this property, the legitimate receiver could not decrypt the ciphertext. The second requirement speaks for itself. The third requirement is needed because, as we shall see in a moment, intruders may experiment with the algorithm to their hearts' content. Under these conditions, there is no reason that the encryption key cannot be made public.

The method works like this. A person, say, Alice, who wants to receive secret messages, first devises two algorithms meeting the above requirements. The encryption algorithm and Alice's key are then made public, hence the name **public-key cryptography**. Alice might put her public key on her home page on the Web, for example. We will use the notation E_A to mean the encryption algorithm parameterized by Alice's public key. Similarly, the (secret) decryption algorithm parameterized by Alice's private key is D_A. Bob does the same thing, publicizing E_B but keeping D_B secret.

Now let us see if we can solve the problem of establishing a secure channel between Alice and Bob, who have never had any previous contact. Both Alice's encryption key, E_A, and Bob's encryption key, E_B, are assumed to be in publicly readable files. Now Alice takes her first message, P, computes $E_B(P)$, and sends it to Bob. Bob then decrypts it by applying his secret key D_B [i.e., he computes $D_B(E_B(P)) = P$]. No one else can read the encrypted message, $E_B(P)$, because the encryption system is assumed to be strong and because it is too difficult to derive D_B from the publicly known E_B. To send a reply, R, Bob transmits $E_A(R)$. Alice and Bob can now communicate securely.

A note on terminology is perhaps useful here. Public-key cryptography requires each user to have two keys: a public key, used by the entire world for encrypting messages to be sent to that user, and a private key, which the user needs for decrypting messages. We will consistently refer to these keys as the *public* and *private* keys, respectively, and distinguish them from the *secret* keys used for conventional symmetric-key cryptography.

8.3.1 RSA

The only catch is that we need to find algorithms that indeed satisfy all three requirements. Due to the potential advantages of public-key cryptography, many researchers are hard at work, and some algorithms have already been published.

One good method was discovered by a group at M.I.T. (Rivest et al., 1978). It is known by the initials of the three discoverers (Rivest, Shamir, Adleman): **RSA**. It has survived all attempts to break it for more than 30 years and is considered very strong. Much practical security is based on it. For this reason, Rivest, Shamir, and Adleman were given the 2002 ACM Turing Award. Its major disadvantage is that it requires keys of at least 1024 bits for good security (versus 128 bits for symmetric-key algorithms), which makes it quite slow.

The RSA method is based on some principles from number theory. We will now summarize how to use the method; for details, consult the paper.

1. Choose two large primes, p and q (typically 1024 bits).
2. Compute $n = p \times q$ and $z = (p - 1) \times (q - 1)$.
3. Choose a number relatively prime to z and call it d.
4. Find e such that $e \times d = 1 \; mod \; z$.

With these parameters computed in advance, we are ready to begin encryption. Divide the plaintext (regarded as a bit string) into blocks, so that each plaintext message, P, falls in the interval $0 \le P < n$. Do that by grouping the plaintext into blocks of k bits, where k is the largest integer for which $2^k < n$ is true.

To encrypt a message, P, compute $C = P^e \pmod{n}$. To decrypt C, compute $P = C^d \pmod{n}$. It can be proven that for all P in the specified range, the encryption and decryption functions are inverses. To perform the encryption, you need e and n. To perform the decryption, you need d and n. Therefore, the public key consists of the pair (e, n) and the private key consists of (d, n).

The security of the method is based on the difficulty of factoring large numbers. If the cryptanalyst could factor the (publicly known) n, he could then find p and q, and from these z. Equipped with knowledge of z and e, d can be found using Euclid's algorithm. Fortunately, mathematicians have been trying to factor large numbers for at least 300 years, and the accumulated evidence suggests that it is an exceedingly difficult problem.

According to Rivest and colleagues, factoring a 500-digit number would require 10^{25} years using brute force. In both cases, they assumed the best known algorithm and a computer with a 1-μsec instruction time. With a million chips running in parallel, each with an instruction time of 1 nsec, it would still take 10^{16} years. Even if computers continue to get faster by an order of magnitude per decade, it will be many years before factoring a 500-digit number becomes feasible, at which time our descendants can simply choose p and q still larger.

A trivial pedagogical example of how the RSA algorithm works is given in Fig. 8-17. For this example, we have chosen $p = 3$ and $q = 11$, giving $n = 33$ and $z = 20$. A suitable value for d is $d = 7$, since 7 and 20 have no common factors. With these choices, e can be found by solving the equation $7e = 1 \pmod{20}$, which yields $e = 3$. The ciphertext, C, corresponding to a plaintext message, P, is given by $C = P^3 \pmod{33}$. The ciphertext is decrypted by the receiver by making use of the rule $P = C^7 \pmod{33}$. The figure shows the encryption of the plaintext "SUZANNE" as an example.

Plaintext (P)			Ciphertext (C)		After decryption	
Symbolic	Numeric	P^3	P^3 (mod 33)	C^7	C^7 (mod 33)	Symbolic
S	19	6859	28	13492928512	19	S
U	21	9261	21	1801088541	21	U
Z	26	17576	20	1280000000	26	Z
A	01	1	1	1	01	A
N	14	2744	5	78125	14	N
N	14	2744	5	78125	14	N
E	05	125	26	8031810176	05	E
Sender's computation				Receiver's computation		

Figure 8-17. An example of the RSA algorithm.

Because the primes chosen for this example are so small, P must be less than 33, so each plaintext block can contain only a single character. The result is a monoalphabetic substitution cipher, not very impressive. If instead we had chosen p and $q \approx 2^{512}$, we would have $n \approx 2^{1024}$, so each block could be up to 1024 bits or 128 eight-bit characters, versus 8 characters for DES and 16 characters for AES.

It should be pointed out that using RSA as we have described is similar to using a symmetric algorithm in ECB mode—the same input block gives the same output block. Therefore, some form of chaining is needed for data encryption. However, in practice, most RSA-based systems use public-key cryptography primarily for distributing one-time session keys for use with some symmetric-key algorithm such as AES or triple DES. RSA is too slow for actually encrypting large volumes of data but is widely used for key distribution.

8.3.2 Other Public-Key Algorithms

Although RSA is widely used, it is by no means the only public-key algorithm known. The first public-key algorithm was the knapsack algorithm (Merkle and Hellman, 1978). The idea here is that someone owns a large number of objects, each with a different weight. The owner encodes the message by secretly selecting a subset of the objects and placing them in the knapsack. The total weight of the objects in the knapsack is made public, as is the list of all possible objects and their corresponding weights. The list of objects in the knapsack is kept secret. With certain additional restrictions, the problem of figuring out a possible list of objects with the given weight was thought to be computationally infeasible and formed the basis of the public-key algorithm.

The algorithm's inventor, Ralph Merkle, was quite sure that this algorithm could not be broken, so he offered a $100 reward to anyone who could break it. Adi Shamir (the "S" in RSA) promptly broke it and collected the reward. Undeterred, Merkle strengthened the algorithm and offered a $1000 reward to anyone who could break the new one. Ronald Rivest (the "R" in RSA) promptly broke the new one and collected the reward. Merkle did not dare offer $10,000 for the next version, so "A" (Leonard Adleman) was out of luck. Nevertheless, the knapsack algorithm is not considered secure and is not used in practice any more.

Other public-key schemes are based on the difficulty of computing discrete logarithms. Algorithms that use this principle have been invented by El Gamal (1985) and Schnorr (1991).

A few other schemes exist, such as those based on elliptic curves (Menezes and Vanstone, 1993), but the two major categories are those based on the difficulty of factoring large numbers and computing discrete logarithms modulo a large prime. These problems are thought to be genuinely difficult to solve—mathematicians have been working on them for many years without any great breakthroughs.

8.4 DIGITAL SIGNATURES

The authenticity of many legal, financial, and other documents is determined by the presence or absence of an authorized handwritten signature. And photocopies do not count. For computerized message systems to replace the physical transport of paper-and-ink documents, a method must be found to allow documents to be signed in an unforgeable way.

The problem of devising a replacement for handwritten signatures is a difficult one. Basically, what is needed is a system by which one party can send a signed message to another party in such a way that the following conditions hold:

1. The receiver can verify the claimed identity of the sender.
2. The sender cannot later repudiate the contents of the message.
3. The receiver cannot possibly have concocted the message himself.

The first requirement is needed, for example, in financial systems. When a customer's computer orders a bank's computer to buy a ton of gold, the bank's computer needs to be able to make sure that the computer giving the order really belongs to the customer whose account is to be debited. In other words, the bank has to authenticate the customer (and the customer has to authenticate the bank).

The second requirement is needed to protect the bank against fraud. Suppose that the bank buys the ton of gold, and immediately thereafter the price of gold drops sharply. A dishonest customer might then proceed to sue the bank, claiming that he never issued any order to buy gold. When the bank produces the message in court, the customer may deny having sent it. The property that no party to a contract can later deny having signed it is called **nonrepudiation**. The digital signature schemes that we will now study help provide it.

The third requirement is needed to protect the customer in the event that the price of gold shoots up and the bank tries to construct a signed message in which the customer asked for one bar of gold instead of one ton. In this fraud scenario, the bank just keeps the rest of the gold for itself.

8.4.1 Symmetric-Key Signatures

One approach to digital signatures is to have a central authority that knows everything and whom everyone trusts, say, Big Brother (*BB*). Each user then chooses a secret key and carries it by hand to *BB*'s office. Thus, only Alice and *BB* know Alice's secret key, K_A, and so on.

When Alice wants to send a signed plaintext message, *P*, to her banker, Bob, she generates $K_A(B, R_A, t, P)$, where *B* is Bob's identity, R_A is a random number chosen by Alice, *t* is a timestamp to ensure freshness, and $K_A(B, R_A, t, P)$ is the message encrypted with her key, K_A. Then she sends it as depicted in Fig. 8-18. *BB* sees that the message is from Alice, decrypts it, and sends a message to Bob as shown. The message to Bob contains the plaintext of Alice's message and also the signed message $K_{BB}(A, t, P)$. Bob now carries out Alice's request.

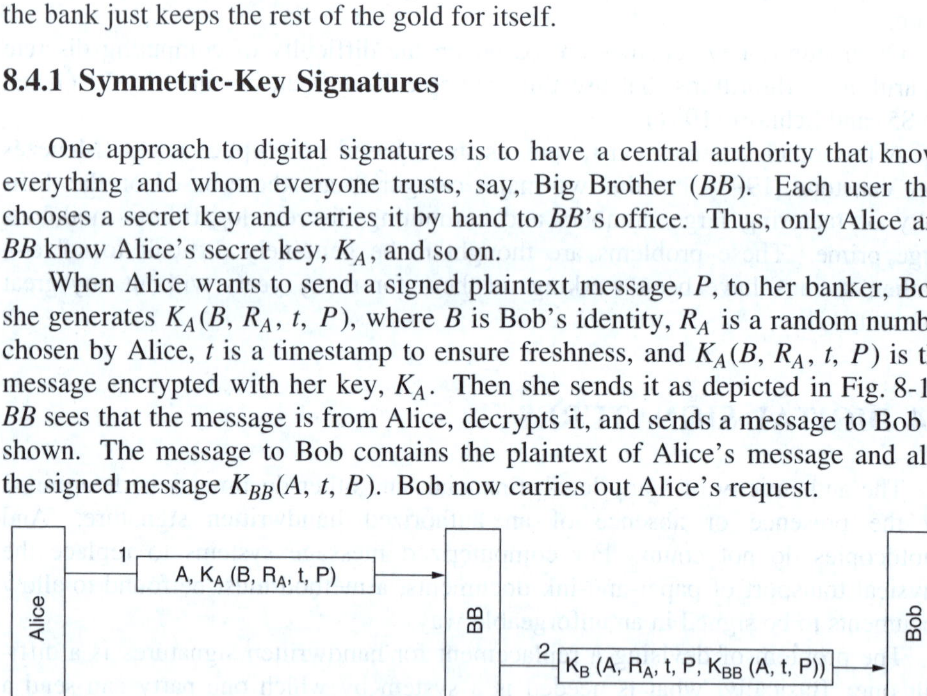

Figure 8-18. Digital signatures with Big Brother.

What happens if Alice later denies sending the message? Step 1 is that everyone sues everyone (at least, in the United States). Finally, when the case comes to court and Alice vigorously denies sending Bob the disputed message, the judge will ask Bob how he can be sure that the disputed message came from Alice and not from Trudy. Bob first points out that *BB* will not accept a message from Alice unless it is encrypted with K_A, so there is no possibility of Trudy sending *BB* a false message from Alice without BB detecting it immediately.

Bob then dramatically produces Exhibit A: $K_{BB}(A, t, P)$. Bob says that this is a message signed by *BB* that proves Alice sent *P* to Bob. The judge then asks *BB* (whom everyone trusts) to decrypt Exhibit A. When *BB* testifies that Bob is telling the truth, the judge decides in favor of Bob. Case dismissed.

One potential problem with the signature protocol of Fig. 8-18 is Trudy replaying either message. To minimize this problem, timestamps are used throughout. Furthermore, Bob can check all recent messages to see if R_A was used in any of them. If so, the message is discarded as a replay. Note that based on the timestamp, Bob will reject very old messages. To guard against instant replay attacks, Bob just checks the R_A of every incoming message to see if such a message has been received from Alice in the past hour. If not, Bob can safely assume this is a new request.

8.4.2 Public-Key Signatures

A structural problem with using symmetric-key cryptography for digital signatures is that everyone has to agree to trust Big Brother. Furthermore, Big Brother gets to read all signed messages. The most logical candidates for running the Big Brother server are the government, the banks, the accountants, and the lawyers. Unfortunately, none of these inspire total confidence in all citizens. Hence, it would be nice if signing documents did not require a trusted authority.

Fortunately, public-key cryptography can make an important contribution in this area. Let us assume that the public-key encryption and decryption algorithms have the property that $E(D(P)) = P$, in addition, of course, to the usual property that $D(E(P)) = P$. (RSA has this property, so the assumption is not unreasonable.) Assuming that this is the case, Alice can send a signed plaintext message, P, to Bob by transmitting $E_B(D_A(P))$. Note carefully that Alice knows her own (private) key, D_A, as well as Bob's public key, E_B, so constructing this message is something Alice can do.

When Bob receives the message, he transforms it using his private key, as usual, yielding $D_A(P)$, as shown in Fig. 8-19. He stores this text in a safe place and then applies E_A to get the original plaintext.

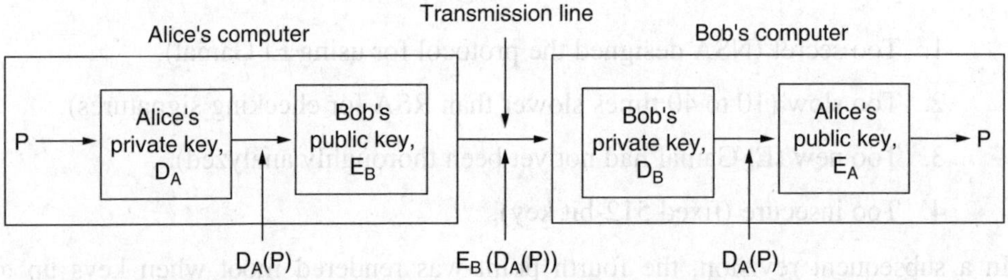

Figure 8-19. Digital signatures using public-key cryptography.

To see how the signature property works, suppose that Alice subsequently denies having sent the message P to Bob. When the case comes up in court, Bob can produce both P and $D_A(P)$. The judge can easily verify that Bob indeed has a valid message encrypted by D_A by simply applying E_A to it. Since Bob does not know what Alice's private key is, the only way Bob could have acquired a message encrypted by it is if Alice did indeed send it. While in jail for perjury and fraud, Alice will have much time to devise interesting new public-key algorithms.

Although using public-key cryptography for digital signatures is an elegant scheme, there are problems that are related to the environment in which they operate rather than to the basic algorithm. For one thing, Bob can prove that a message was sent by Alice only as long as D_A remains secret. If Alice discloses her secret key, the argument no longer holds, because anyone could have sent the message, including Bob himself.

The problem might arise, for example, if Bob is Alice's stockbroker. Suppose that Alice tells Bob to buy a certain stock or bond. Immediately thereafter, the price drops sharply. To repudiate her message to Bob, Alice runs to the police claiming that her home was burglarized and the PC holding her key was stolen. Depending on the laws in her state or country, she may or may not be legally liable, especially if she claims not to have discovered the break-in until getting home from work, several hours after it allegedly happened.

Another problem with the signature scheme is what happens if Alice decides to change her key. Doing so is clearly legal, and it is probably a good idea to do so periodically. If a court case later arises, as described above, the judge will apply the *current* E_A to $D_A(P)$ and discover that it does not produce P. Bob will look pretty stupid at this point.

In principle, any public-key algorithm can be used for digital signatures. The de facto industry standard is the RSA algorithm. Many security products use it. However, in 1991, NIST proposed using a variant of the El Gamal public-key algorithm for its new **Digital Signature Standard (DSS)**. El Gamal gets its security from the difficulty of computing discrete logarithms, rather than from the difficulty of factoring large numbers.

As usual when the government tries to dictate cryptographic standards, there was an uproar. DSS was criticized for being

1. Too secret (NSA designed the protocol for using El Gamal).
2. Too slow (10 to 40 times slower than RSA for checking signatures).
3. Too new (El Gamal had not yet been thoroughly analyzed).
4. Too insecure (fixed 512-bit key).

In a subsequent revision, the fourth point was rendered moot when keys up to 1024 bits were allowed. Nevertheless, the first two points remain valid.

8.4.3 Message Digests

One criticism of signature methods is that they often couple two distinct functions: authentication and secrecy. Often, authentication is needed but secrecy is not always needed. Also, getting an export license is often easier if the system in question provides only authentication but not secrecy. Below we will describe an authentication scheme that does not require encrypting the entire message.

This scheme is based on the idea of a one-way hash function that takes an arbitrarily long piece of plaintext and from it computes a fixed-length bit string. This hash function, *MD*, often called a **message digest**, has four important properties:

1. Given P, it is easy to compute $MD(P)$.
2. Given $MD(P)$, it is effectively impossible to find P.
3. Given P, no one can find P' such that $MD(P') = MD(P)$.
4. A change to the input of even 1 bit produces a very different output.

To meet criterion 3, the hash should be at least 128 bits long, preferably more. To meet criterion 4, the hash must mangle the bits very thoroughly, not unlike the symmetric-key encryption algorithms we have seen.

Computing a message digest from a piece of plaintext is much faster than encrypting that plaintext with a public-key algorithm, so message digests can be used to speed up digital signature algorithms. To see how this works, consider the signature protocol of Fig. 8-18 again. Instead, of signing P with $K_{BB}(A, t, P)$, *BB* now computes the message digest by applying *MD* to P, yielding $MD(P)$. *BB* then encloses $K_{BB}(A, t, MD(P))$ as the fifth item in the list encrypted with K_B that is sent to Bob, instead of $K_{BB}(A, t, P)$.

If a dispute arises, Bob can produce both P and $K_{BB}(A, t, MD(P))$. After Big Brother has decrypted it for the judge, Bob has $MD(P)$, which is guaranteed to be genuine, and the alleged P. However, since it is effectively impossible for Bob to find any other message that gives this hash, the judge will easily be convinced that Bob is telling the truth. Using message digests in this way saves both encryption time and message transport costs.

Message digests work in public-key cryptosystems, too, as shown in Fig. 8-20. Here, Alice first computes the message digest of her plaintext. She then signs the message digest and sends both the signed digest and the plaintext to Bob. If Trudy replaces P along the way, Bob will see this when he computes $MD(P)$.

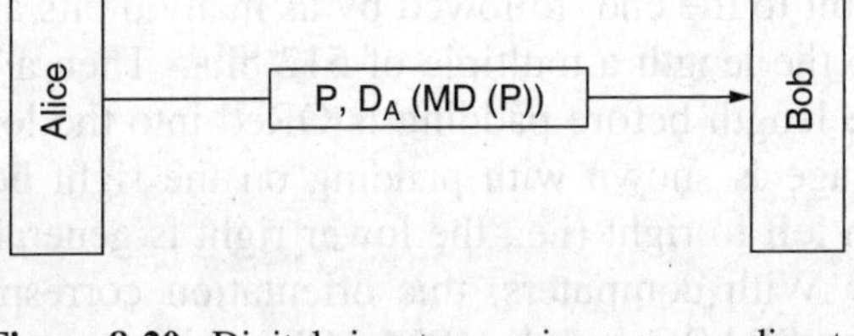

Figure 8-20. Digital signatures using message digests.

SHA-1 and SHA-2

A variety of message digest functions have been proposed. One of the most widely used functions is **SHA-1 (Secure Hash Algorithm 1)** (NIST, 1993). Like all message digests, it operates by mangling bits in a sufficiently complicated way that every output bit is affected by every input bit. SHA-1 was developed by NSA and blessed by NIST in FIPS 180-1. It processes input data in 512-bit blocks, and it generates a 160-bit message digest. A typical way for Alice to send a nonsecret but signed message to Bob is illustrated in Fig. 8-21. Here, her plaintext message is fed into the SHA-1 algorithm to get a 160-bit SHA-1 hash. Alice then signs the hash with her RSA private key and sends both the plaintext message and the signed hash to Bob.

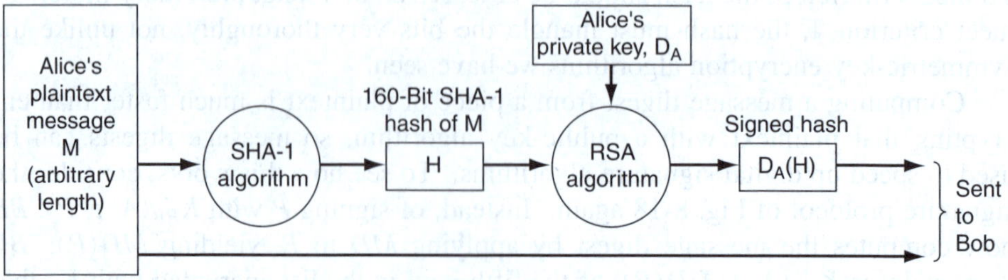

Figure 8-21. Use of SHA-1 and RSA for signing nonsecret messages.

After receiving the message, Bob computes the SHA-1 hash himself and also applies Alice's public key to the signed hash to get the original hash, H. If the two agree, the message is considered valid. Since there is no way for Trudy to modify the (plaintext) message while it is in transit and produce a new one that hashes to H, Bob can easily detect any changes Trudy has made to the message. For messages whose integrity is important but whose contents are not secret, the scheme of Fig. 8-21 is widely used. For a relatively small cost in computation, it guarantees that any modifications made to the plaintext message in transit can be detected with very high probability.

Now let us briefly see how SHA-1 works. It starts out by padding the message by adding a 1 bit to the end, followed by as many 0 bits as are necessary, but at least 64, to make the length a multiple of 512 bits. Then a 64-bit number containing the message length before padding is ORed into the low-order 64 bits. In Fig. 8-22, the message is shown with padding on the right because English text and figures go from left to right (i.e., the lower right is generally perceived as the end of the figure). With computers, this orientation corresponds to big-endian machines such as the SPARC and the IBM 360 and its successors, but SHA-1 always pads the end of the message, no matter which endian machine is used.

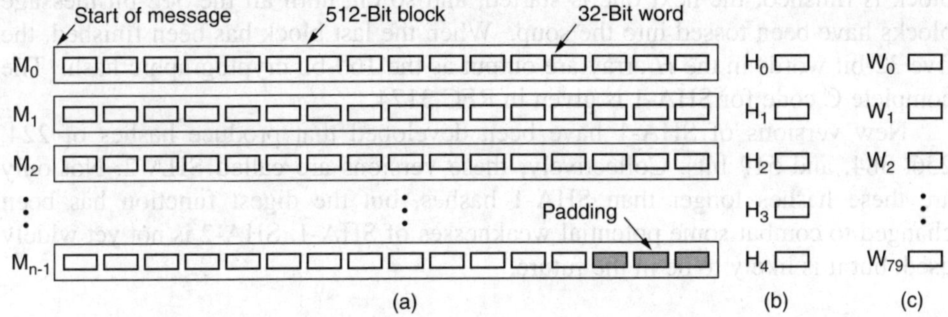

Figure 8-22. (a) A message padded out to a multiple of 512 bits. (b) The output variables. (c) The word array.

During the computation, SHA-1 maintains five 32-bit variables, H_0 through H_4, where the hash accumulates. These are shown in Fig. 8-22(b). They are initialized to constants specified in the standard.

Each of the blocks M_0 through M_{n-1} is now processed in turn. For the current block, the 16 words are first copied into the start of an auxiliary 80-word array, W, as shown in Fig. 8-22(c). Then the other 64 words in W are filled in using the formula

$$W_i = S^1(W_{i-3} \text{ XOR } W_{i-8} \text{ XOR } W_{i-14} \text{ XOR } W_{i-16}) \quad (16 \le i \le 79)$$

where $S^b(W)$ represents the left circular rotation of the 32-bit word, W, by b bits. Now five scratch variables, A through E, are initialized from H_0 through H_4, respectively.

The actual calculation can be expressed in pseudo-C as

```
for (i = 0; i< 80; i++) {
    temp = S^5(A) + f_i (B, C, D) + E + W_i + K_i;
    E = D;  D = C;  C = S^30(B);  B = A;  A = temp;
}
```

where the K_i constants are defined in the standard. The mixing functions f_i are defined as

$$f_i(B,C,D) = (B \text{ AND } C) \text{ OR } (\text{NOT } B \text{ AND } D) \quad (0 \le i \le 19)$$
$$f_i(B,C,D) = B \text{ XOR } C \text{ XOR } D \quad (20 \le i \le 39)$$
$$f_i(B,C,D) = (B \text{ AND } C) \text{ OR } (B \text{ AND } D) \text{ OR } (C \text{ AND } D) \quad (40 \le i \le 59)$$
$$f_i(B,C,D) = B \text{ XOR } C \text{ XOR } D \quad (60 \le i \le 79)$$

When all 80 iterations of the loop are completed, A through E are added to H_0 through H_4, respectively.

Now that the first 512-bit block has been processed, the next one is started. The W array is reinitialized from the new block, but H is left as it was. When this block is finished, the next one is started, and so on, until all the 512-bit message blocks have been tossed into the soup. When the last block has been finished, the five 32-bit words in the *H* array are output as the 160-bit cryptographic hash. The complete C code for SHA-1 is given in RFC 3174.

New versions of SHA-1 have been developed that produce hashes of 224, 256, 384, and 512 bits. Collectively, these versions are called SHA-2. Not only are these hashes longer than SHA-1 hashes, but the digest function has been changed to combat some potential weaknesses of SHA-1. SHA-2 is not yet widely used, but it is likely to be in the future.

MD5

For completeness, we will mention another digest that is popular. **MD5** (Rivest, 1992) is the fifth in a series of message digests designed by Ronald Rivest. Very briefly, the message is padded to a length of 448 bits (modulo 512). Then the original length of the message is appended as a 64-bit integer to give a total input whose length is a multiple of 512 bits. Each round of the computation takes a 512-bit block of input and mixes it thoroughly with a running 128-bit buffer. For good measure, the mixing uses a table constructed from the sine function. The point of using a known function is to avoid any suspicion that the designer built in a clever back door through which only he can enter. This process continues until all the input blocks have been consumed. The contents of the 128-bit buffer form the message digest.

After more than a decade of solid use and study, weaknesses in MD5 have led to the ability to find collisions, or different messages with the same hash (Sotirov, et al., 2008). This is the death knell for a digest function because it means that the digest cannot safely be used to represent a message. Thus, the security community considers MD5 to be broken; it should be replaced where possible and no new systems should use it as part of their design. Nevertheless, you may still see MD5 used in existing systems.

8.4.4 The Birthday Attack

In the world of crypto, nothing is ever what it seems to be. One might think that it would take on the order of 2^m operations to subvert an m-bit message digest. In fact, $2^{m/2}$ operations will often do using the **birthday attack,** an approach published by Yuval (1979) in his now-classic paper "How to Swindle Rabin."

The idea for this attack comes from a technique that math professors often use in their probability courses. The question is: how many students do you need in a class before the probability of having two people with the same birthday exceeds 1/2? Most students expect the answer to be way over 100. In fact, probability theory says it is just 23. Without giving a rigorous analysis, intuitively, with 23 people, we can form $(23 \times 22)/2 = 253$ different pairs, each of which has a probability of 1/365 of being a hit. In this light, it is not really so surprising any more.

More generally, if there is some mapping between inputs and outputs with n inputs (people, messages, etc.) and k possible outputs (birthdays, message digests, etc.), there are $n(n-1)/2$ input pairs. If $n(n-1)/2 > k$, the chance of having at least one match is pretty good. Thus, approximately, a match is likely for $n > \sqrt{k}$. This result means that a 64-bit message digest can probably be broken by generating about 2^{32} messages and looking for two with the same message digest.

Let us look at a practical example. The Department of Computer Science at State University has one position for a tenured faculty member and two candidates, Tom and Dick. Tom was hired two years before Dick, so he goes up for review first. If he gets it, Dick is out of luck. Tom knows that the department chairperson, Marilyn, thinks highly of his work, so he asks her to write him a letter of recommendation to the Dean, who will decide on Tom's case. Once sent, all letters become confidential.

Marilyn tells her secretary, Ellen, to write the Dean a letter, outlining what she wants in it. When it is ready, Marilyn will review it, compute and sign the 64-bit digest, and send it to the Dean. Ellen can send the letter later by email.

Unfortunately for Tom, Ellen is romantically involved with Dick and would like to do Tom in, so she writes the following letter with the 32 bracketed options:

Dear Dean Smith,

This [*letter* | *message*] is to give my [*honest* | *frank*] opinion of Prof. Tom Wilson, who is [*a candidate* | *up*] for tenure [*now* | *this year*]. I have [*known* | *worked with*] Prof. Wilson for [*about* | *almost*] six years. He is an [*outstanding* | *excellent*] researcher of great [*talent* | *ability*] known [*worldwide* | *internationally*] for his [*brilliant* | *creative*] insights into [*many* | *a wide variety of*] [*difficult* | *challenging*] problems.

He is also a [*highly* | *greatly*] [*respected* | *admired*] [*teacher* | *educator*]. His students give his [*classes* | *courses*] [*rave* | *spectacular*] reviews. He is [*our* | *the Department's*] [*most popular* | *best-loved*] [*teacher* | *instructor*].

[*In addition* | *Additionally*] Prof. Wilson is a [*gifted* | *effective*] fund raiser. His [*grants* | *contracts*] have brought a [*large* | *substantial*] amount of money into [*the* | *our*] Department. [*This money has* | *These funds have*] [*enabled* | *permitted*] us to [*pursue* | *carry out*] many [*special* | *important*] programs, [*such as* | *for example*] your State 2000 program. Without these funds we would [*be unable* | *not be able*] to continue this program, which is so [*important* | *essential*] to both of us. I strongly urge you to grant him tenure.

Unfortunately for Tom, as soon as Ellen finishes composing and typing in this letter, she also writes a second one:

Dear Dean Smith,

This [*letter* | *message*] is to give my [*honest* | *frank*] opinion of Prof. Tom Wilson, who is [*a candidate* | *up*] for tenure [*now* | *this year*]. I have [*known* | *worked with*] Tom for [*about* | *almost*] six years. He is a [*poor* | *weak*] researcher not well known in his [*field* | *area*]. His research [*hardly ever* | *rarely*] shows [*insight in* | *understanding of*] the [*key* | *major*] problems of [*the* | *our*] day.

Furthermore, he is not a [*respected* | *admired*] [*teacher* | *educator*]. His students give his [*classes* | *courses*] [*poor* | *bad*] reviews. He is [*our* | *the Department's*] least popular [*teacher* | *instructor*], known [*mostly* | *primarily*] within [*the* | *our*] Department for his [*tendency* | *propensity*] to [*ridicule* | *embarrass*] students [*foolish* | *imprudent*] enough to ask questions in his classes.

[*In addition* | *Additionally*] Tom is a [*poor* | *marginal*] fund raiser. His [*grants* | *contracts*] have brought only a [*meager* | *insignificant*] amount of money into [*the* | *our*] Department. Unless new [*money is* | *funds are*] quickly located, we may have to cancel some essential programs, such as your State 2000 program. Unfortunately, under these [*conditions* | *circumstances*] I cannot in good [*conscience* | *faith*] recommend him to you for [*tenure* | *a permanent position*].

Now Ellen programs her computer to compute the 2^{32} message digests of each letter overnight. Chances are, one digest of the first letter will match one digest of the second. If not, she can add a few more options and try again tonight. Suppose that she finds a match. Call the "good" letter *A* and the "bad" one *B*.

Ellen now emails letter *A* to Marilyn for approval. Letter *B* she keeps secret, showing it to no one. Marilyn, of course, approves it, computes her 64-bit message digest, signs the digest, and emails the signed digest off to Dean Smith. Independently, Ellen emails letter *B* to the Dean (not letter *A*, as she is supposed to).

After getting the letter and signed message digest, the Dean runs the message digest algorithm on letter *B*, sees that it agrees with what Marilyn sent him, and fires Tom. The Dean does not realize that Ellen managed to generate two letters with the same message digest and sent her a different one than the one Marilyn saw and approved. (Optional ending: Ellen tells Dick what she did. Dick is appalled and breaks off the affair. Ellen is furious and confesses to Marilyn. Marilyn calls the Dean. Tom gets tenure after all.) With SHA-1, the birthday attack is difficult because even at the ridiculous speed of 1 trillion digests per second, it would take over 32,000 years to compute all 2^{80} digests of two letters with 80 variants each, and even then a match is not guaranteed. With a cloud of 1,000,000 chips working in parallel, 32,000 years becomes 2 weeks.

8.5 MANAGEMENT OF PUBLIC KEYS

Public-key cryptography makes it possible for people who do not share a common key in advance to nevertheless communicate securely. It also makes signing messages possible without the presence of a trusted third party. Finally, signed message digests make it possible for the recipient to verify the integrity of received messages easily and securely.

However, there is one problem that we have glossed over a bit too quickly: if Alice and Bob do not know each other, how do they get each other's public keys to start the communication process? The obvious solution—put your public key on your Web site—does not work, for the following reason. Suppose that Alice wants to look up Bob's public key on his Web site. How does she do it? She starts by typing in Bob's URL. Her browser then looks up the DNS address of Bob's home page and sends it a *GET* request, as shown in Fig. 8-23. Unfortunately, Trudy intercepts the request and replies with a fake home page, probably a copy of Bob's home page except for the replacement of Bob's public key with Trudy's public key. When Alice now encrypts her first message with E_T, Trudy decrypts it, reads it, re-encrypts it with Bob's public key, and sends it to Bob, who is none the wiser that Trudy is reading his incoming messages. Worse yet, Trudy could modify the messages before reencrypting them for Bob. Clearly, some mechanism is needed to make sure that public keys can be exchanged securely.

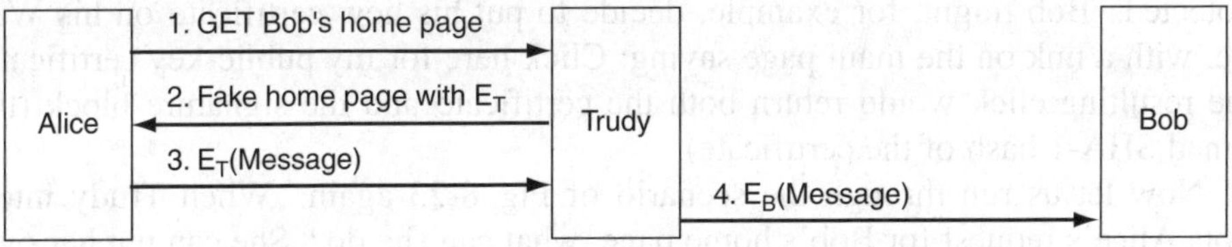

Figure 8-23. A way for Trudy to subvert public-key encryption.

8.5.1 Certificates

As a first attempt at distributing public keys securely, we could imagine a **KDC key distribution center** available online 24 hours a day to provide public keys on demand. One of the many problems with this solution is that it is not scalable, and the key distribution center would rapidly become a bottleneck. Also, if it ever went down, Internet security would suddenly grind to a halt.

For these reasons, people have developed a different solution, one that does not require the key distribution center to be online all the time. In fact, it does not have to be online at all. Instead, what it does is certify the public keys belonging to people, companies, and other organizations. An organization that certifies public keys is now called a **CA** (**Certification Authority**).

As an example, suppose that Bob wants to allow Alice and other people he does not know to communicate with him securely. He can go to the CA with his public key along with his passport or driver's license and ask to be certified. The CA then issues a certificate similar to the one in Fig. 8-24 and signs its SHA-1 hash with the CA's private key. Bob then pays the CA's fee and gets a CD-ROM containing the certificate and its signed hash.

I hereby certify that the public key
    19836A8B03030CF83737E3837837FC3s87092827262643FFA82710382828282A
belongs to
    Robert John Smith
    12345 University Avenue
    Berkeley, CA 94702
    Birthday: July 4, 1958
    Email: bob@superdupernet.com

SHA-1 hash of the above certificate signed with the CA's private key

Figure 8-24. A possible certificate and its signed hash.

The fundamental job of a certificate is to bind a public key to the name of a principal (individual, company, etc.). Certificates themselves are not secret or protected. Bob might, for example, decide to put his new certificate on his Web site, with a link on the main page saying: Click here for my public-key certificate. The resulting click would return both the certificate and the signature block (the signed SHA-1 hash of the certificate).

Now let us run through the scenario of Fig. 8-23 again. When Trudy intercepts Alice's request for Bob's home page, what can she do? She can put her own certificate and signature block on the fake page, but when Alice reads the contents of the certificate she will immediately see that she is not talking to Bob because Bob's name is not in it. Trudy can modify Bob's home page on the fly, replacing Bob's public key with her own. However, when Alice runs the SHA-1 algorithm on the certificate, she will get a hash that does not agree with the one she gets when she applies the CA's well-known public key to the signature block. Since Trudy does not have the CA's private key, she has no way of generating a signature block that contains the hash of the modified Web page with her public key on it. In this way, Alice can be sure she has Bob's public key and not Trudy's or someone else's. And as we promised, this scheme does not require the CA to be online for verification, thus eliminating a potential bottleneck.

While the standard function of a certificate is to bind a public key to a principal, a certificate can also be used to bind a public key to an **attribute**. For example, a certificate could say: "This public key belongs to someone over 18." It could be used to prove that the owner of the private key was not a minor and thus allowed to access material not suitable for children, and so on, but without disclosing the owner's identity. Typically, the person holding the certificate would send it to the Web site, principal, or process that cared about age. That site, principal, or process would then generate a random number and encrypt it with the public key in the certificate. If the owner were able to decrypt it and send it back, that would be proof that the owner indeed had the attribute stated in the certificate. Alternatively, the random number could be used to generate a session key for the ensuing conversation.

Another example of where a certificate might contain an attribute is in an object-oriented distributed system. Each object normally has multiple methods. The owner of the object could provide each customer with a certificate giving a bit map of which methods the customer is allowed to invoke and binding the bit map to a public key using a signed certificate. Again, if the certificate holder can prove possession of the corresponding private key, he will be allowed to perform the methods in the bit map. This approach has the property that the owner's identity need not be known, a property useful in situations where privacy is important.

8.5.2 X.509

If everybody who wanted something signed went to the CA with a different kind of certificate, managing all the different formats would soon become a problem. To solve this problem, a standard for certificates has been devised and approved by ITU. The standard is called **X.509** and is in widespread use on the Internet. It has gone through three versions since the initial standardization in 1988. We will discuss V3.

X.509 has been heavily influenced by the OSI world, borrowing some of its worst features (e.g., naming and encoding). Surprisingly, IETF went along with X.509, even though in nearly every other area, from machine addresses to transport protocols to email formats, IETF generally ignored OSI and tried to do it right. The IETF version of X.509 is described in RFC 5280.

At its core, X.509 is a way to describe certificates. The primary fields in a certificate are listed in Fig. 8-25. The descriptions given there should provide a general idea of what the fields do. For additional information, please consult the standard itself or RFC 2459.

For example, if Bob works in the loan department of the Money Bank, his X.500 address might be

```
/C=US/O=MoneyBank/OU=Loan/CN=Bob/
```

where *C* is for country, *O* is for organization, *OU* is for organizational unit, and *CN* is for common name. CAs and other entities are named in a similar way. A substantial problem with X.500 names is that if Alice is trying to contact *bob@moneybank.com* and is given a certificate with an X.500 name, it may not be obvious to her that the certificate refers to the Bob she wants. Fortunately, starting with version 3, DNS names are now permitted instead of X.500 names, so this problem may eventually vanish.

Certificates are encoded using OSI **ASN.1 (Abstract Syntax Notation 1)**, which is sort of like a struct in C, except with a extremely peculiar and verbose notation. More information about X.509 is given by Ford and Baum (2000).

Field	Meaning
Version	Which version of X.509
Serial number	This number plus the CA's name uniquely identifies the certificate
Signature algorithm	The algorithm used to sign the certificate
Issuer	X.500 name of the CA
Validity period	The starting and ending times of the validity period
Subject name	The entity whose key is being certified
Public key	The subject's public key and the ID of the algorithm using it
Issuer ID	An optional ID uniquely identifying the certificate's issuer
Subject ID	An optional ID uniquely identifying the certificate's subject
Extensions	Many extensions have been defined
Signature	The certificate's signature (signed by the CA's private key)

Figure 8-25. The basic fields of an X.509 certificate.

8.5.3 Public Key Infrastructures

Having a single CA to issue all the world's certificates obviously would not work. It would collapse under the load and be a central point of failure as well. A possible solution might be to have multiple CAs, all run by the same organization and all using the same private key to sign certificates. While this would solve the load and failure problems, it introduces a new problem: key leakage. If there were dozens of servers spread around the world, all holding the CA's private key, the chance of the private key being stolen or otherwise leaking out would be greatly increased. Since the compromise of this key would ruin the world's electronic security infrastructure, having a single central CA is very risky.

In addition, which organization would operate the CA? It is hard to imagine any authority that would be accepted worldwide as legitimate and trustworthy. In some countries, people would insist that it be a government, while in other countries they would insist that it not be a government.

For these reasons, a different way for certifying public keys has evolved. It goes under the general name of **PKI** (**Public Key Infrastructure**). In this section, we will summarize how it works in general, although there have been many proposals, so the details will probably evolve in time.

A PKI has multiple components, including users, CAs, certificates, and directories. What the PKI does is provide a way of structuring these components and define standards for the various documents and protocols. A particularly simple form of PKI is a hierarchy of CAs, as depicted in Fig. 8-26. In this example we have shown three levels, but in practice there might be fewer or more. The top-level CA, the root, certifies second-level CAs, which we here call **RA**s (**Regional**

Authorities) because they might cover some geographic region, such as a country or continent. This term is not standard, though; in fact, no term is really standard for the different levels of the tree. These in turn certify the real CAs, which issue the X.509 certificates to organizations and individuals. When the root authorizes a new RA, it generates an X.509 certificate stating that it has approved the RA, includes the new RA's public key in it, signs it, and hands it to the RA. Similarly, when an RA approves a new CA, it produces and signs a certificate stating its approval and containing the CA's public key.

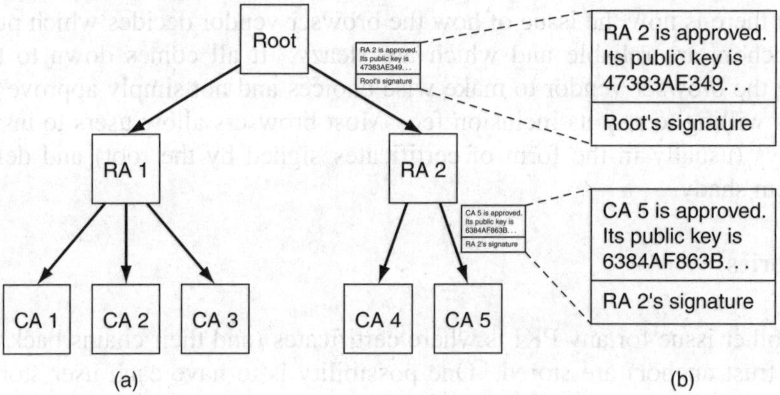

Figure 8-26. (a) A hierarchical PKI. (b) A chain of certificates.

Our PKI works like this. Suppose that Alice needs Bob's public key in order to communicate with him, so she looks for and finds a certificate containing it, signed by CA 5. But Alice has never heard of CA 5. For all she knows, CA 5 might be Bob's 10-year-old daughter. She could go to CA 5 and say: "Prove your legitimacy." CA 5 will respond with the certificate it got from RA 2, which contains CA 5's public key. Now armed with CA 5's public key, she can verify that Bob's certificate was indeed signed by CA 5 and is thus legal.

Unless RA 2 is Bob's 12-year-old son. So, the next step is for her to ask RA 2 to prove it is legitimate. The response to her query is a certificate signed by the root and containing RA 2's public key. Now Alice is sure she has Bob's public key.

But how does Alice find the root's public key? Magic. It is assumed that everyone knows the root's public key. For example, her browser might have been shipped with the root's public key built in.

Bob is a friendly sort of guy and does not want to cause Alice a lot of work. He knows that she is going to have to check out CA 5 and RA 2, so to save her some trouble, he collects the two needed certificates and gives her the two certificates along with his. Now she can use her own knowledge of the root's public key to verify the top-level certificate and the public key contained therein to verify the second one. Alice does not need to contact anyone to do the verification.

Because the certificates are all signed, she can easily detect any attempts to tamper with their contents. A chain of certificates going back to the root like this is sometimes called a **chain of trust** or a **certification path**. The technique is widely used in practice.

Of course, we still have the problem of who is going to run the root. The solution is not to have a single root, but to have many roots, each with its own RAs and CAs. In fact, modern browsers come preloaded with the public keys for over 100 roots, sometimes referred to as **trust anchors**. In this way, having a single worldwide trusted authority can be avoided.

But there is now the issue of how the browser vendor decides which purported trust anchors are reliable and which are sleazy. It all comes down to the user trusting the browser vendor to make wise choices and not simply approve all trust anchors willing to pay its inclusion fee. Most browsers allow users to inspect the root keys (usually in the form of certificates signed by the root) and delete any that seem shady.

Directories

Another issue for any PKI is where certificates (and their chains back to some known trust anchor) are stored. One possibility is to have each user store his or her own certificates. While doing this is safe (i.e., there is no way for users to tamper with signed certificates without detection), it is also inconvenient. One alternative that has been proposed is to use DNS as a certificate directory. Before contacting Bob, Alice probably has to look up his IP address using DNS, so why not have DNS return Bob's entire certificate chain along with his IP address?

Some people think this is the way to go, but others would prefer dedicated directory servers whose only job is managing X.509 certificates. Such directories could provide lookup services by using properties of the X.500 names. For example, in theory such a directory service could answer a query such as: "Give me a list of all people named Alice who work in sales departments anywhere in the U.S. or Canada."

Revocation

The real world is full of certificates, too, such as passports and drivers' licenses. Sometimes these certificates can be revoked, for example, drivers' licenses can be revoked for drunken driving and other driving offenses. The same problem occurs in the digital world: the grantor of a certificate may decide to revoke it because the person or organization holding it has abused it in some way. It can also be revoked if the subject's private key has been exposed or, worse yet, the CA's private key has been compromised. Thus, a PKI needs to deal with the issue of revocation. The possibility of revocation complicates matters.

A first step in this direction is to have each CA periodically issue a **CRL** (**Certificate Revocation List**) giving the serial numbers of all certificates that it has revoked. Since certificates contain expiry times, the CRL need only contain the serial numbers of certificates that have not yet expired. Once its expiry time has passed, a certificate is automatically invalid, so no distinction is needed between those that just timed out and those that were actually revoked. In both cases, they cannot be used any more.

Unfortunately, introducing CRLs means that a user who is about to use a certificate must now acquire the CRL to see if the certificate has been revoked. If it has been, it should not be used. However, even if the certificate is not on the list, it might have been revoked just after the list was published. Thus, the only way to really be sure is to ask the CA. And on the next use of the same certificate, the CA has to be asked again, since the certificate might have been revoked a few seconds ago.

Another complication is that a revoked certificate could conceivably be reinstated, for example, if it was revoked for nonpayment of some fee that has since been paid. Having to deal with revocation (and possibly reinstatement) eliminates one of the best properties of certificates, namely, that they can be used without having to contact a CA.

Where should CRLs be stored? A good place would be the same place the certificates themselves are stored. One strategy is for the CA to actively push out CRLs periodically and have the directories process them by simply removing the revoked certificates. If directories are not used for storing certificates, the CRLs can be cached at various places around the network. Since a CRL is itself a signed document, if it is tampered with, that tampering can be easily detected.

If certificates have long lifetimes, the CRLs will be long, too. For example, if credit cards are valid for 5 years, the number of revocations outstanding will be much longer than if new cards are issued every 3 months. A standard way to deal with long CRLs is to issue a master list infrequently, but issue updates to it more often. Doing this reduces the bandwidth needed for distributing the CRLs.

8.6 COMMUNICATION SECURITY

We have now finished our study of the tools of the trade. Most of the important techniques and protocols have been covered. The rest of the chapter is about how these techniques are applied in practice to provide network security, plus some thoughts about the social aspects of security at the end of the chapter.

In the following four sections, we will look at communication security, that is, how to get the bits secretly and without modification from source to destination and how to keep unwanted bits outside the door. These are by no means the only security issues in networking, but they are certainly among the most important ones, making this a good place to start our study.

8.6.1 IPsec

IETF has known for years that security was lacking in the Internet. Adding it was not easy because a war broke out about where to put it. Most security experts believe that to be really secure, encryption and integrity checks have to be end to end (i.e., in the application layer). That is, the source process encrypts and/or integrity protects the data and sends them to the destination process where they are decrypted and/or verified. Any tampering done in between these two processes, including within either operating system, can then be detected. The trouble with this approach is that it requires changing all the applications to make them security aware. In this view, the next best approach is putting encryption in the transport layer or in a new layer between the application layer and the transport layer, making it still end to end but not requiring applications to be changed.

The opposite view is that users do not understand security and will not be capable of using it correctly and nobody wants to modify existing programs in any way, so the network layer should authenticate and/or encrypt packets without the users being involved. After years of pitched battles, this view won enough support that a network layer security standard was defined. In part, the argument was that having network layer encryption does not prevent security-aware users from doing it right and it does help security-unaware users to some extent.

The result of this war was a design called **IPsec (IP security)**, which is described in RFCs 2401, 2402, and 2406, among others. Not all users want encryption (because it is computationally expensive). Rather than make it optional, it was decided to require encryption all the time but permit the use of a null algorithm. The null algorithm is described and praised for its simplicity, ease of implementation, and great speed in RFC 2410.

The complete IPsec design is a framework for multiple services, algorithms, and granularities. The reason for multiple services is that not everyone wants to pay the price for having all the services all the time, so the services are available a la carte. The major services are secrecy, data integrity, and protection from replay attacks (where the intruder replays a conversation). All of these are based on symmetric-key cryptography because high performance is crucial.

The reason for having multiple algorithms is that an algorithm that is now thought to be secure may be broken in the future. By making IPsec algorithm-independent, the framework can survive even if some particular algorithm is later broken.

The reason for having multiple granularities is to make it possible to protect a single TCP connection, all traffic between a pair of hosts, or all traffic between a pair of secure routers, among other possibilities.

One slightly surprising aspect of IPsec is that even though it is in the IP layer, it is connection oriented. Actually, that is not so surprising because to have any security, a key must be established and used for some period of time—in essence, a kind of connection by a different name. Also, connections amortize the setup costs over many packets. A "connection" in the context of IPsec is called an **SA** (**Security Association**). An SA is a simplex connection between two endpoints and has a security identifier associated with it. If secure traffic is needed in both directions, two security associations are required. Security identifiers are carried in packets traveling on these secure connections and are used to look up keys and other relevant information when a secure packet arrives.

Technically, IPsec has two principal parts. The first part describes two new headers that can be added to packets to carry the security identifier, integrity control data, and other information. The other part, **ISAKMP** (**Internet Security Association and Key Management Protocol**), deals with establishing keys. ISAKMP is a framework. The main protocol for carrying out the work is **IKE** (**Internet Key Exchange**). Version 2 of IKE as described in RFC 4306 should be used, as the earlier version was deeply flawed, as pointed out by Perlman and Kaufman (2000).

IPsec can be used in either of two modes. In **transport mode**, the IPsec header is inserted just after the IP header. The *Protocol* field in the IP header is changed to indicate that an IPsec header follows the normal IP header (before the TCP header). The IPsec header contains security information, primarily the SA identifier, a new sequence number, and possibly an integrity check of the payload.

In **tunnel mode**, the entire IP packet, header and all, is encapsulated in the body of a new IP packet with a completely new IP header. Tunnel mode is useful when the tunnel ends at a location other than the final destination. In some cases, the end of the tunnel is a security gateway machine, for example, a company firewall. This is commonly the case for a VPN (Virtual Private Network). In this mode, the security gateway encapsulates and decapsulates packets as they pass through it. By terminating the tunnel at this secure machine, the machines on the company LAN do not have to be aware of IPsec. Only the security gateway has to know about it.

Tunnel mode is also useful when a bundle of TCP connections is aggregated and handled as one encrypted stream because it prevents an intruder from seeing who is sending how many packets to whom. Sometimes just knowing how much traffic is going where is valuable information. For example, if during a military crisis, the amount of traffic flowing between the Pentagon and the White House were to drop sharply, but the amount of traffic between the Pentagon and some military installation deep in the Colorado Rocky Mountains were to increase by the same amount, an intruder might be able to deduce some useful information from these data. Studying the flow patterns of packets, even if they are encrypted, is called **traffic analysis**. Tunnel mode provides a way to foil it to some extent. The disadvantage of tunnel mode is that it adds an extra IP header, thus increasing packet size substantially. In contrast, transport mode does not affect packet size as much.

The first new header is **AH** (**Authentication Header**). It provides integrity checking and antireplay security, but not secrecy (i.e., no data encryption). The use of AH in transport mode is illustrated in Fig. 8-27. In IPv4, it is interposed between the IP header (including any options) and the TCP header. In IPv6, it is just another extension header and is treated as such. In fact, the format is close to that of a standard IPv6 extension header. The payload may have to be padded out to some particular length for the authentication algorithm, as shown.

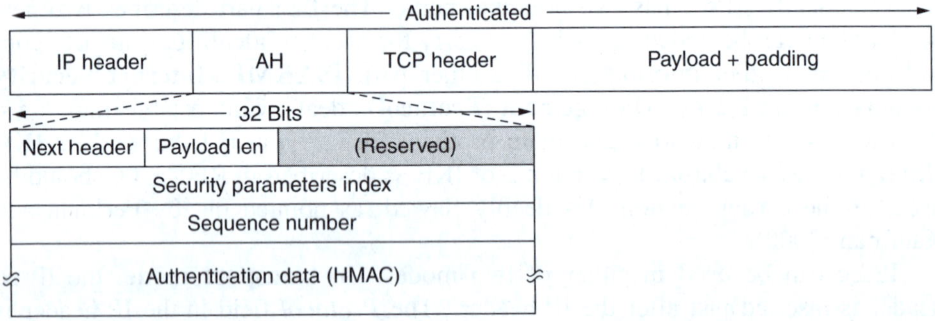

Figure 8-27. The IPsec authentication header in transport mode for IPv4.

Let us now examine the AH header. The *Next header* field is used to store the value that the IP *Protocol* field had before it was replaced with 51 to indicate that an AH header follows. In most cases, the code for TCP (6) will go here. The *Payload length* is the number of 32-bit words in the AH header minus 2.

The *Security parameters index* is the connection identifier. It is inserted by the sender to indicate a particular record in the receiver's database. This record contains the shared key used on this connection and other information about the connection. If this protocol had been invented by ITU rather than IETF, this field would have been called *Virtual circuit number*.

The *Sequence number* field is used to number all the packets sent on an SA. Every packet gets a unique number, even retransmissions. In other words, the retransmission of a packet gets a different number here than the original (even though its TCP sequence number is the same). The purpose of this field is to detect replay attacks. These sequence numbers may not wrap around. If all 2^{32} are exhausted, a new SA must be established to continue communication.

Finally, we come to *Authentication data*, which is a variable-length field that contains the payload's digital signature. When the SA is established, the two sides negotiate which signature algorithm they are going to use. Normally, public-key cryptography is not used here because packets must be processed extremely rapidly and all known public-key algorithms are too slow. Since IPsec is based on symmetric-key cryptography and the sender and receiver negotiate a shared key before setting up an SA, the shared key is used in the signature computation. One simple way is to compute the hash over the packet plus the shared key. The shared key is not transmitted, of course. A scheme like this is called an **HMAC**

(**Hashed Message Authentication Code**). It is much faster to compute than first running SHA-1 and then running RSA on the result.

The AH header does not allow encryption of the data, so it is mostly useful when integrity checking is needed but secrecy is not needed. One noteworthy feature of AH is that the integrity check covers some of the fields in the IP header, namely, those that do not change as the packet moves from router to router. The *Time to live* field changes on each hop, for example, so it cannot be included in the integrity check. However, the IP source address is included in the check, making it impossible for an intruder to falsify the origin of a packet.

The alternative IPsec header is **ESP** (**Encapsulating Security Payload**). Its use for both transport mode and tunnel mode is shown in Fig. 8-28.

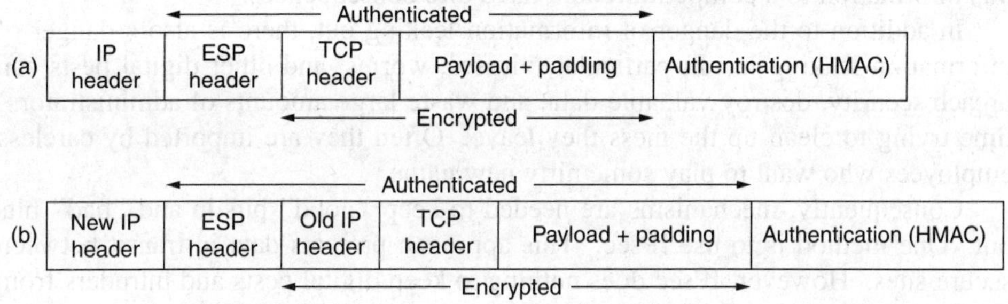

Figure 8-28. (a) ESP in transport mode. (b) ESP in tunnel mode.

The ESP header consists of two 32-bit words. They are the *Security parameters index* and *Sequence number* fields that we saw in AH. A third word that generally follows them (but is technically not part of the header) is the *Initialization vector* used for the data encryption, unless null encryption is used, in which case it is omitted.

ESP also provides for HMAC integrity checks, as does AH, but rather than being included in the header, they come after the payload, as shown in Fig. 8-28. Putting the HMAC at the end has an advantage in a hardware implementation: the HMAC can be calculated as the bits are going out over the network interface and appended to the end. This is why Ethernet and other LANs have their CRCs in a trailer, rather than in a header. With AH, the packet has to be buffered and the signature computed before the packet can be sent, potentially reducing the number of packets/sec that can be sent.

Given that ESP can do everything AH can do and more and is more efficient to boot, the question arises: why bother having AH at all? The answer is mostly historical. Originally, AH handled only integrity and ESP handled only secrecy. Later, integrity was added to ESP, but the people who designed AH did not want to let it die after all that work. Their only real argument is that AH checks part of the IP header, which ESP does not, but other than that it is really a weak argument. Another weak argument is that a product supporting AH but not ESP might have less trouble getting an export license because it cannot do encryption. AH is likely to be phased out in the future.

8.6.2 Firewalls

The ability to connect any computer, anywhere, to any other computer, anywhere, is a mixed blessing. For individuals at home, wandering around the Internet is lots of fun. For corporate security managers, it is a nightmare. Most companies have large amounts of confidential information online—trade secrets, product development plans, marketing strategies, financial analyses, etc. Disclosure of this information to a competitor could have dire consequences.

In addition to the danger of information leaking out, there is also a danger of information leaking in. In particular, viruses, worms, and other digital pests can breach security, destroy valuable data, and waste large amounts of administrators' time trying to clean up the mess they leave. Often they are imported by careless employees who want to play some nifty new game.

Consequently, mechanisms are needed to keep "good" bits in and "bad" bits out. One method is to use IPsec. This approach protects data in transit between secure sites. However, IPsec does nothing to keep digital pests and intruders from getting onto the company LAN. To see how to accomplish this goal, we need to look at firewalls.

Firewalls are just a modern adaptation of that old medieval security standby: digging a deep moat around your castle. This design forced everyone entering or leaving the castle to pass over a single drawbridge, where they could be inspected by the I/O police. With networks, the same trick is possible: a company can have many LANs connected in arbitrary ways, but all traffic to or from the company is forced through an electronic drawbridge (firewall), as shown in Fig. 8-29. No other route exists.

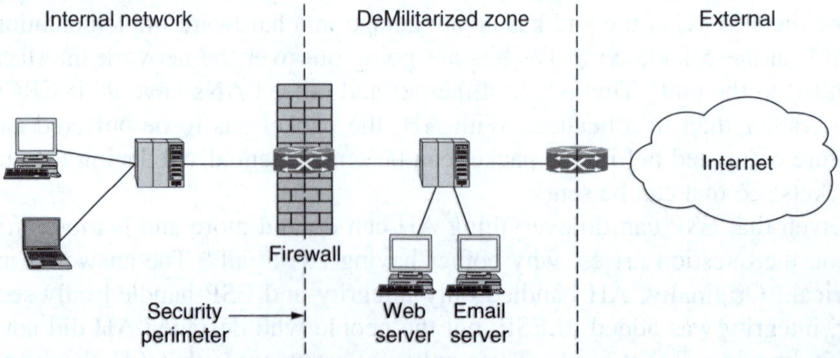

Figure 8-29. A firewall protecting an internal network.

The firewall acts as a **packet filter**. It inspects each and every incoming and outgoing packet. Packets meeting some criterion described in rules formulated by the network administrator are forwarded normally. Those that fail the test are uncermoniously dropped.

The filtering criterion is typically given as rules or tables that list sources and destinations that are acceptable, sources and destinations that are blocked, and default rules about what to do with packets coming from or going to other machines. In the common case of a TCP/IP setting, a source or destination might consist of an IP address and a port. Ports indicate which service is desired. For example, TCP port 25 is for mail, and TCP port 80 is for HTTP. Some ports can simply be blocked. For example, a company could block incoming packets for all IP addresses combined with TCP port 79. It was once popular for the Finger service to look up people's email addresses but is little used today.

Other ports are not so easily blocked. The difficulty is that network administrators want security but cannot cut off communication with the outside world. That arrangement would be much simpler and better for security, but there would be no end to user complaints about it. This is where arrangements such as the **DMZ (DeMilitarized Zone)** shown in Fig. 8-29 come in handy. The DMZ is the part of the company network that lies outside of the security perimeter. Anything goes here. By placing a machine such as a Web server in the DMZ, computers on the Internet can contact it to browse the company Web site. Now the firewall can be configured to block incoming TCP traffic to port 80 so that computers on the Internet cannot use this port to attack computers on the internal network. To allow the Web server to be managed, the firewall can have a rule to permit connections between internal machines and the Web server.

Firewalls have become much more sophisticated over time in an arms race with attackers. Originally, firewalls applied a rule set independently for each packet, but it proved difficult to write rules that allowed useful functionality but blocked all unwanted traffic. **Stateful firewalls** map packets to connections and use TCP/IP header fields to keep track of connections. This allows for rules that, for example, allow an external Web server to send packets to an internal host, but only if the internal host first establishes a connection with the external Web server. Such a rule is not possible with stateless designs that must either pass or drop all packets from the external Web server.

Another level of sophistication up from stateful processing is for the firewall to implement **application-level gateways**. This processing involves the firewall looking inside packets, beyond even the TCP header, to see what the application is doing. With this capability, it is possible to distinguish HTTP traffic used for Web browsing from HTTP traffic used for peer-to-peer file sharing. Administrators can write rules to spare the company from peer-to-peer file sharing but allow Web browsing that is vital for business. For all of these methods, outgoing traffic can be inspected as well as incoming traffic, for example, to prevent sensitive documents from being emailed outside of the company.

As the above discussion should make clear, firewalls violate the standard layering of protocols. They are network layer devices, but they peek at the transport and applications layers to do their filtering. This makes them fragile. For instance, firewalls tend to rely on standard port numbering conventions to determine what kind of traffic is carried in a packet. Standard ports are often used, but not by all computers, and not by all applications either. Some peer-to-peer applications select ports dynamically to avoid being easily spotted (and blocked). Encryption with IPSEC or other schemes hides higher-layer information from the firewall. Finally, a firewall cannot readily talk to the computers that communicate through it to tell them what policies are being applied and why their connection is being dropped. It must simply pretend to be a broken wire. For all these reasons, networking purists consider firewalls to be a blemish on the architecture of the Internet. However, the Internet can be a dangerous place if you are a computer. Firewalls help with that problem, so they are likely to stay.

Even if the firewall is perfectly configured, plenty of security problems still exist. For example, if a firewall is configured to allow in packets from only specific networks (e.g., the company's other plants), an intruder outside the firewall can put in false source addresses to bypass this check. If an insider wants to ship out secret documents, he can encrypt them or even photograph them and ship the photos as JPEG files, which bypasses any email filters. And we have not even discussed the fact that, although three-quarters of all attacks come from outside the firewall, the attacks that come from inside the firewall, for example, from disgruntled employees, are typically the most damaging (Verizon, 2009).

A different problem with firewalls is that they provide a single perimeter of defense. If that defense is breached, all bets are off. For this reason, firewalls are often used in a layered defense. For example, a firewall may guard the entrance to the internal network and each computer may also run its own firewall. Readers who think that one security checkpoint is enough clearly have not made an international flight on a scheduled airline recently.

In addition, there is a whole other class of attacks that firewalls cannot deal with. The basic idea of a firewall is to prevent intruders from getting in and secret data from getting out. Unfortunately, there are people who have nothing better to do than try to bring certain sites down. They do this by sending legitimate packets at the target in great numbers until it collapses under the load. For example, to cripple a Web site, an intruder can send a TCP *SYN* packet to establish a connection. The site will then allocate a table slot for the connection and send a *SYN* + *ACK* packet in reply. If the intruder does not respond, the table slot will be tied up for a few seconds until it times out. If the intruder sends thousands of connection requests, all the table slots will fill up and no legitimate connections will be able to get through. Attacks in which the intruder's goal is to shut down the target rather than steal data are called **DoS** (**Denial of Service**) attacks. Usually, the request packets have false source addresses so the intruder cannot be traced easily. DoS attacks against major Web sites are common on the Internet.

An even worse variant is one in which the intruder has already broken into hundreds of computers elsewhere in the world, and then commands all of them to attack the same target at the same time. Not only does this approach increase the intruder's firepower, but it also reduces his chances of detection since the packets are coming from a large number of machines belonging to unsuspecting users. Such an attack is called a **DDoS** (**Distributed Denial of Service**) attack. This attack is difficult to defend against. Even if the attacked machine can quickly recognize a bogus request, it does take some time to process and discard the request, and if enough requests per second arrive, the CPU will spend all its time dealing with them.

8.6.3 Virtual Private Networks

Many companies have offices and plants scattered over many cities, sometimes over multiple countries. In the olden days, before public data networks, it was common for such companies to lease lines from the telephone company between some or all pairs of locations. Some companies still do this. A network built up from company computers and leased telephone lines is called a **private network**.

Private networks work fine and are very secure. If the only lines available are the leased lines, no traffic can leak out of company locations and intruders have to physically wiretap the lines to break in, which is not easy to do. The problem with private networks is that leasing a dedicated T1 line between two points costs thousands of dollars a month, and T3 lines are many times more expensive. When public data networks and later the Internet appeared, many companies wanted to move their data (and possibly voice) traffic to the public network, but without giving up the security of the private network.

This demand soon led to the invention of **VPNs** (**Virtual Private Networks**), which are overlay networks on top of public networks but with most of the properties of private networks. They are called "virtual" because they are merely an illusion, just as virtual circuits are not real circuits and virtual memory is not real memory.

One popular approach is to build VPNs directly over the Internet. A common design is to equip each office with a firewall and create tunnels through the Internet between all pairs of offices, as illustrated in Fig. 8-30(a). A further advantage of using the Internet for connectivity is that the tunnels can be set up on demand to include, for example, the computer of an employee who is at home or traveling as long as the person has an Internet connection. This flexibility is much greater then is provided with leased lines, yet from the perspective of the computers on the VPN, the topology looks just like the private network case, as shown in Fig. 8-30(b). When the system is brought up, each pair of firewalls has to negotiate the parameters of its SA, including the services, modes, algorithms, and keys. If IPsec is used for the tunneling, it is possible to aggregate all traffic between any

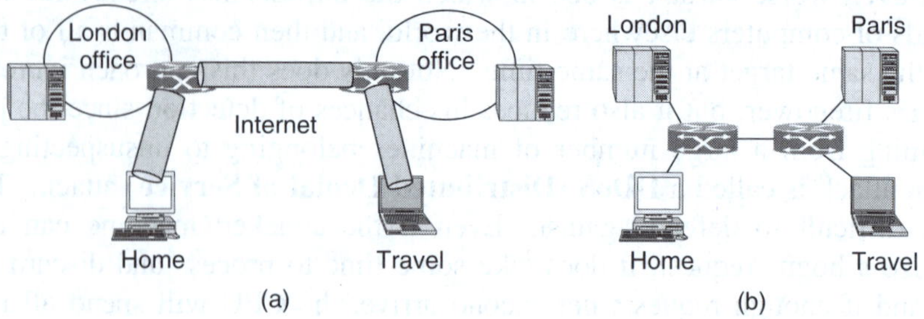

Figure 8-30. (a) A virtual private network. (b) Topology as seen from the inside.

two pairs of offices onto a single authenticated, encrypted SA, thus providing integrity control, secrecy, and even considerable immunity to traffic analysis. Many firewalls have VPN capabilities built in. Some ordinary routers can do this as well, but since firewalls are primarily in the security business, it is natural to have the tunnels begin and end at the firewalls, providing a clear separation between the company and the Internet. Thus, firewalls, VPNs, and IPsec with ESP in tunnel mode are a natural combination and widely used in practice.

Once the SAs have been established, traffic can begin flowing. To a router within the Internet, a packet traveling along a VPN tunnel is just an ordinary packet. The only thing unusual about it is the presence of the IPsec header after the IP header, but since these extra headers have no effect on the forwarding process, the routers do not care about this extra header.

Another approach that is gaining popularity is to have the ISP set up the VPN. Using MPLS (as discussed in Chap. 5), paths for the VPN traffic can be set up across the ISP network between the company offices. These paths keep the VPN traffic separate from other Internet traffic and can be guaranteed a certain amount of bandwidth or other quality of service.

A key advantage of a VPN is that it is completely transparent to all user software. The firewalls set up and manage the SAs. The only person who is even aware of this setup is the system administrator who has to configure and manage the security gateways, or the ISP administrator who has to configure the MPLS paths. To everyone else, it is like having a leased-line private network again. For more about VPNs, see Lewis (2006).

8.6.4 Wireless Security

It is surprisingly easy to design a system using VPNs and firewalls that is logically completely secure but that, in practice, leaks like a sieve. This situation can occur if some of the machines are wireless and use radio communication, which passes right over the firewall in both directions. The range of 802.11 networks is often a few hundred meters, so anyone who wants to spy on a company can simply drive into the employee parking lot in the morning, leave an 802.11-enabled notebook computer in the car to record everything it hears, and take off for the day. By late afternoon, the hard disk will be full of valuable goodies. Theoretically, this leakage is not supposed to happen. Theoretically, people are not supposed to rob banks, either.

Much of the security problem can be traced to the manufacturers of wireless base stations (access points) trying to make their products user friendly. Usually, if the user takes the device out of the box and plugs it into the electrical power socket, it begins operating immediately—nearly always with no security at all, blurting secrets to everyone within radio range. If it is then plugged into an Ethernet, all the Ethernet traffic suddenly appears in the parking lot as well. Wireless is a snooper's dream come true: free data without having to do any work. It therefore goes without saying that security is even more important for wireless systems than for wired ones. In this section, we will look at some ways wireless networks handle security. Some additional information is given by Nichols and Lekkas (2002).

802.11 Security

Part of the 802.11 standard, originally called **802.11i**, prescribes a data link-level security protocol for preventing a wireless node from reading or interfering with messages sent between another pair of wireless nodes. It also goes by the trade name **WPA2 (WiFi Protected Access 2)**. Plain WPA is an interim scheme that implements a subset of 802.11i. It should be avoided in favor of WPA2.

We will describe 802.11i shortly, but will first note that it is a replacement for **WEP (Wired Equivalent Privacy)**, the first generation of 802.11 security protocols. WEP was designed by a networking standards committee, which is a completely different process than, for example, the way NIST selected the design of AES. The results were devastating. What was wrong with it? Pretty much everything from a security perspective as it turns out. For example, WEP encrypted data for confidentiality by XORing it with the output of a stream cipher. Unfortunately, weak keying arrangements meant that the output was often reused. This led to trivial ways to defeat it. As another example, the integrity check was based on a 32-bit CRC. That is an efficient code for detecting transmission errors, but it is not a cryptographically strong mechanism for defeating attackers.

These and other design flaws made WEP very easy to compromise. The first practical demonstration that WEP was broken came when Adam Stubblefield was an intern at AT&T (Stubblefield et al., 2002). He was able to code up and test an attack outlined by Fluhrer et al. (2001) in one week, of which most of the time was spent convincing management to buy him a WiFi card to use in his experiments. Software to crack WEP passwords within a minute is now freely available and the use of WEP is very strongly discouraged. While it does prevent casual access it does not provide any real form of security. The 802.11i group was put together in a hurry when it was clear that WEP was seriously broken. It produced a formal standard by June 2004.

Now we will describe 802.11i, which does provide real security if it is set up and used properly. There are two common scenarios in which WPA2 is used. The first is a corporate setting, in which a company has a separate authentication server that has a username and password database that can be used to determine if a wireless client is allowed to access the network. In this setting, clients use standard protocols to authenticate themselves to the network. The main standards are **802.1X**, with which the access point lets the client carry on a dialogue with the authentication server and observes the result, and **EAP** (**Extensible Authentication Protocol**) (RFC 3748), which tells how the client and the authentication server interact. Actually, EAP is a framework and other standards define the protocol messages. However, we will not delve into the many details of this exchange because they do not much matter for an overview.

The second scenario is in a home setting in which there is no authentication server. Instead, there is a single shared password that is used by clients to access the wireless network. This setup is less complex than having an authentication server, which is why it is used at home and in small businesses, but it is less secure as well. The main difference is that with an authentication server each client gets a key for encrypting traffic that is not known by the other clients. With a single shared password, different keys are derived for each client, but all clients have the same password and can derive each others' keys if they want to.

The keys that are used to encrypt traffic are computed as part of an authentication handshake. The handshake happens right after the client associates with a wireless network and authenticates with an authentication server, if there is one. At the start of the handshake, the client has either the shared network password or its password for the authentication server. This password is used to derive a master key. However, the master key is not used directly to encrypt packets. It is standard cryptographic practice to derive a session key for each period of usage, to change the key for different sessions, and to expose the master key to observation as little as possible. It is this session key that is computed in the handshake.

The session key is computed with the four-packet handshake shown in Fig. 8-31. First, the AP (access point) sends a random number for identification. Random numbers used just once in security protocols like this one are called **nonces**, which is more-or-less a contraction of "number used once." The client also picks its own nonce. It uses the nonces, its MAC address and that of the AP, and the master key to compute a session key, K_S. The session key is split into portions, each of which is used for different purposes, but we have omitted this detail. Now the client has session keys, but the AP does not. So the client sends its nonce to the AP, and the AP performs the same computation to derive the same session keys. The nonces can be sent in the clear because the keys cannot be derived from them without extra, secret information. The message from the client is protected with an integrity check called a **MIC (Message Integrity Check)** based on the session key. The AP can check that the MIC is correct, and so the message indeed must have come from the client, after it computes the session keys. A MIC is just another name for a message authentication code, as in an HMAC. The term MIC is often used instead for networking protocols because of the potential for confusion with MAC (Medium Access Control) addresses.

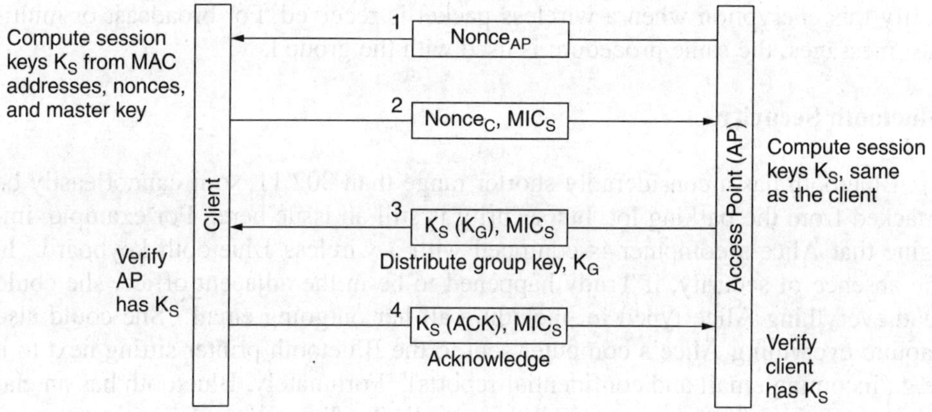

Figure 8-31. The 802.11i key setup handshake.

In the last two messages, the AP distributes a group key, K_G, to the client, and the client acknowledges the message. Receipt of these messages lets the client verify that the AP has the correct session keys, and vice versa. The group key is used for broadcast and multicast traffic on the 802.11 LAN. Because the result of the handshake is that every client has its own encryption keys, none of these keys can be used by the AP to broadcast packets to all of the wireless clients; a separate copy would need to be sent to each client using its key. Instead, a shared key is distributed so that broadcast traffic can be sent only once and received by all the clients. It must be updated as clients leave and join the network.

Finally, we get to the part where the keys are actually used to provide security. Two protocols can be used in 802.11i to provide message confidentiality, integrity, and authentication. Like WPA, one of the protocols, called **TKIP (Temporary Key Integrity Protocol)**, was an interim solution. It was designed to improve security on old and slow 802.11 cards, so that at least some security that is better than WEP can be rolled out as a firmware upgrade. However, it, too, has now been broken so you are better off with the other, recommended protocol, **CCMP**. What does CCMP stand for? It is short for the somewhat spectacular name Counter mode with Cipher block chaining Message authentication code Protocol. We will just call it CCMP. You can call it anything you want.

CCMP works in a fairly straightforward way. It uses AES encryption with a 128-bit key and block size. The key comes from the session key. To provide confidentiality, messages are encrypted with AES in counter mode. Recall that we discussed cipher modes in Sec. 8.2.3. These modes are what prevent the same message from being encrypted to the same set of bits each time. Counter mode mixes a counter into the encryption. To provide integrity, the message, including header fields, is encrypted with cipher block chaining mode and the last 128-bit block is kept as the MIC. Then both the message (encrypted with counter mode) and the MIC are sent. The client and the AP can each perform this encryption, or verify this encryption when a wireless packet is received. For broadcast or multicast messages, the same procedure is used with the group key.

Bluetooth Security

Bluetooth has a considerably shorter range than 802.11, so it cannot easily be attacked from the parking lot, but security is still an issue here. For example, imagine that Alice's computer is equipped with a wireless Bluetooth keyboard. In the absence of security, if Trudy happened to be in the adjacent office, she could read everything Alice typed in, including all her outgoing email. She could also capture everything Alice's computer sent to the Bluetooth printer sitting next to it (e.g., incoming email and confidential reports). Fortunately, Bluetooth has an elaborate security scheme to try to foil the world's Trudies. We will now summarize the main features of it.

Bluetooth version 2.1 and later has four security modes, ranging from nothing at all to full data encryption and integrity control. As with 802.11, if security is disabled (the default for older devices), there is no security. Most users have security turned off until a serious breach has occurred; then they turn it on. In the agricultural world, this approach is known as locking the barn door after the horse has escaped.

Bluetooth provides security in multiple layers. In the physical layer, frequency hopping provides a tiny little bit of security, but since any Bluetooth device that moves into a piconet has to be told the frequency hopping sequence, this sequence is obviously not a secret. The real security starts when the newly arrived slave asks for a channel with the master. Before Bluetooth 2.1, two devices were assumed to share a secret key set up in advance. In some cases, both are hardwired by the manufacturer (e.g., for a headset and mobile phone sold as a unit). In other cases, one device (e.g., the headset) has a hardwired key and the user has to enter that key into the other device (e.g., the mobile phone) as a decimal number. These shared keys are called **passkeys**. Unfortunately, the passkeys are often hardcoded to "1234" or another predictable value, and in any case are four decimal digits, allowing only 10^4 choices. With simple secure pairing in Bluetooth 2.1, devices pick a code from a six-digit range, which makes the passkey much less predictable but still far from secure.

To establish a channel, the slave and master each check to see if the other one knows the passkey. If so, they negotiate whether that channel will be encrypted, integrity controlled, or both. Then they select a random 128-bit session key, some of whose bits may be public. The point of allowing this key weakening is to comply with government restrictions in various countries designed to prevent the export or use of keys longer than the government can break.

Encryption uses a stream cipher called $\mathbf{E_0}$; integrity control uses **SAFER+**. Both are traditional symmetric-key block ciphers. SAFER+ was submitted to the AES bake-off but was eliminated in the first round because it was slower than the other candidates. Bluetooth was finalized before the AES cipher was chosen; otherwise, it would most likely have used Rijndael.

The actual encryption using the stream cipher is shown in Fig. 8-14, with the plaintext XORed with the keystream to generate the ciphertext. Unfortunately, E_0 itself (like RC4) may have fatal weaknesses (Jakobsson and Wetzel, 2001). While it was not broken at the time of this writing, its similarities to the A5/1 cipher, whose spectacular failure compromises all GSM telephone traffic, are cause for concern (Biryukov et al., 2000). It sometimes amazes people (including the authors of this book), that in the perennial cat-and-mouse game between the cryptographers and the cryptanalysts, the cryptanalysts are so often on the winning side.

Another security issue is that Bluetooth authenticates only devices, not users, so theft of a Bluetooth device may give the thief access to the user's financial and other accounts. However, Bluetooth also implements security in the upper layers, so even in the event of a breach of link-level security, some security may remain, especially for applications that require a PIN code to be entered manually from some kind of keyboard to complete the transaction.

8.7 AUTHENTICATION PROTOCOLS

Authentication is the technique by which a process verifies that its communication partner is who it is supposed to be and not an imposter. Verifying the identity of a remote process in the face of a malicious, active intruder is surprisingly difficult and requires complex protocols based on cryptography. In this section, we will study some of the many authentication protocols that are used on insecure computer networks.

As an aside, some people confuse authorization with authentication. Authentication deals with the question of whether you are actually communicating with a specific process. Authorization is concerned with what that process is permitted to do. For example, say a client process contacts a file server and says: "I am Scott's process and I want to delete the file *cookbook.old*." From the file server's point of view, two questions must be answered:

1. Is this actually Scott's process (authentication)?
2. Is Scott allowed to delete *cookbook.old* (authorization)?

Only after both of these questions have been unambiguously answered in the affirmative can the requested action take place. The former question is really the key one. Once the file server knows to whom it is talking, checking authorization is just a matter of looking up entries in local tables or databases. For this reason, we will concentrate on authentication in this section.

The general model that essentially all authentication protocols use is this. Alice starts out by sending a message either to Bob or to a trusted **KDC (Key Distribution Center)**, which is expected to be honest. Several other message exchanges follow in various directions. As these messages are being sent, Trudy may intercept, modify, or replay them in order to trick Alice and Bob or just to gum up the works.

Nevertheless, when the protocol has been completed, Alice is sure she is talking to Bob and Bob is sure he is talking to Alice. Furthermore, in most of the protocols, the two of them will also have established a secret **session key** for use in the upcoming conversation. In practice, for performance reasons, all data traffic is encrypted using symmetric-key cryptography (typically AES or triple DES), although public-key cryptography is widely used for the authentication protocols themselves and for establishing the session key.

The point of using a new, randomly chosen session key for each new connection is to minimize the amount of traffic that gets sent with the users' secret keys or public keys, to reduce the amount of ciphertext an intruder can obtain, and to minimize the damage done if a process crashes and its core dump falls into the wrong hands. Hopefully, the only key present then will be the session key. All the permanent keys should have been carefully zeroed out after the session was established.

8.7.1 Authentication Based on a Shared Secret Key

For our first authentication protocol, we will assume that Alice and Bob already share a secret key, K_{AB}. This shared key might have been agreed upon on the telephone or in person, but, in any event, not on the (insecure) network.

This protocol is based on a principle found in many authentication protocols: one party sends a random number to the other, who then transforms it in a special way and returns the result. Such protocols are called **challenge-response** protocols. In this and subsequent authentication protocols, the following notation will be used:

A, B are the identities of Alice and Bob.
R_i's are the challenges, where i identifies the challenger.
K_i's are keys, where i indicates the owner.
K_S is the session key.

The message sequence for our first shared-key authentication protocol is illustrated in Fig. 8-32. In message 1, Alice sends her identity, A, to Bob in a way that Bob understands. Bob, of course, has no way of knowing whether this message came from Alice or from Trudy, so he chooses a challenge, a large random number, R_B, and sends it back to "Alice" as message 2, in plaintext. Alice then encrypts the message with the key she shares with Bob and sends the ciphertext, $K_{AB}(R_B)$, back in message 3. When Bob sees this message, he immediately knows that it came from Alice because Trudy does not know K_{AB} and thus could not have generated it. Furthermore, since R_B was chosen randomly from a large space (say, 128-bit random numbers), it is very unlikely that Trudy would have seen R_B and its response in an earlier session. It is equally unlikely that she could guess the correct response to any challenge.

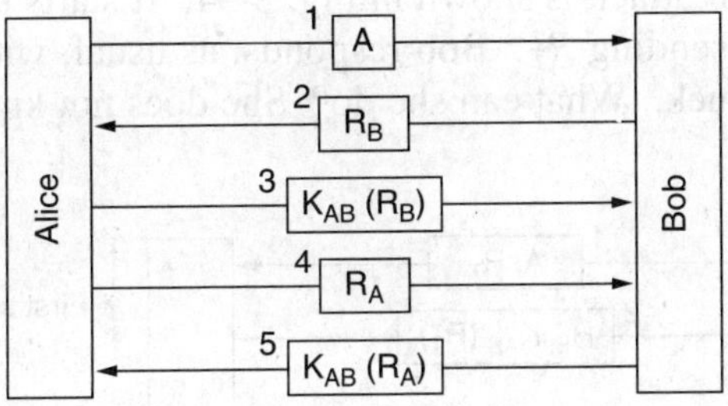

Figure 8-32. Two-way authentication using a challenge-response protocol.

At this point, Bob is sure he is talking to Alice, but Alice is not sure of anything. For all Alice knows, Trudy might have intercepted message 1 and sent back R_B in response. Maybe Bob died last night. To find out to whom she is talking, Alice picks a random number, R_A, and sends it to Bob as plaintext, in message 4. When Bob responds with $K_{AB}(R_A)$, Alice knows she is talking to Bob. If they wish to establish a session key now, Alice can pick one, K_S, and send it to Bob encrypted with K_{AB}.

The protocol of Fig. 8-32 contains five messages. Let us see if we can be clever and eliminate some of them. One approach is illustrated in Fig. 8-33. Here Alice initiates the challenge-response protocol instead of waiting for Bob to do it. Similarly, while he is responding to Alice's challenge, Bob sends his own. The entire protocol can be reduced to three messages instead of five.

Is this new protocol an improvement over the original one? In one sense it is: it is shorter. Unfortunately, it is also wrong. Under certain circumstances, Trudy can defeat this protocol by using what is known as a **reflection attack**. In particular, Trudy can break it if it is possible to open multiple sessions with Bob at once. This situation would be true, for example, if Bob is a bank and is prepared to accept many simultaneous connections from teller machines at once.

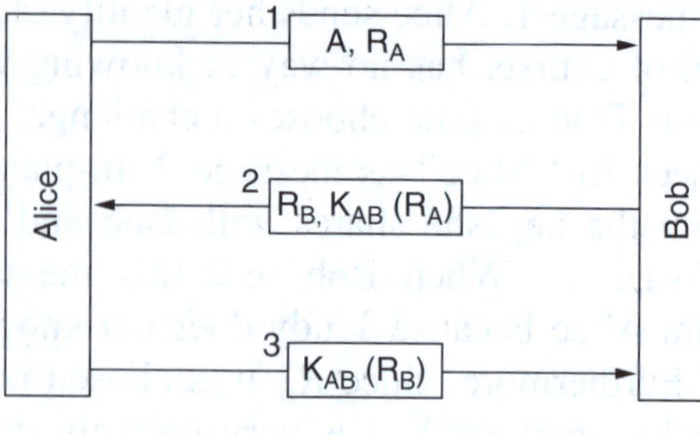

Figure 8-33. A shortened two-way authentication protocol.

Trudy's reflection attack is shown in Fig. 8-34. It starts out with Trudy claiming she is Alice and sending R_T. Bob responds, as usual, with his own challenge, R_B. Now Trudy is stuck. What can she do? She does not know $K_{AB}(R_B)$.

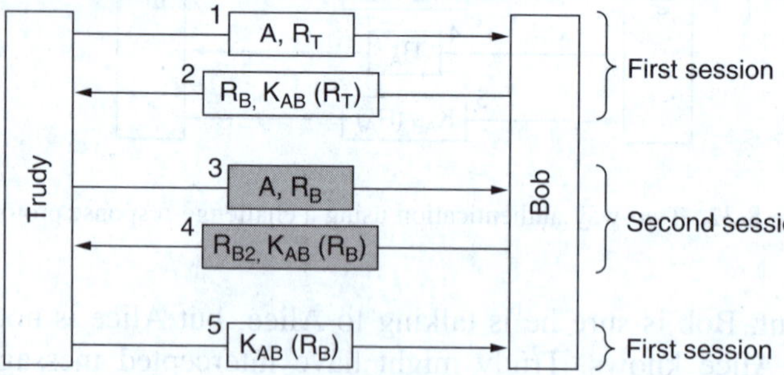

Figure 8-34. The reflection attack.

She can open a second session with message 3, supplying the R_B taken from message 2 as her challenge. Bob calmly encrypts it and sends back $K_{AB}(R_B)$ in message 4. We have shaded the messages on the second session to make them stand out. Now Trudy has the missing information, so she can complete the first session and abort the second one. Bob is now convinced that Trudy is Alice, so when she asks for her bank account balance, he gives it to her without question. Then when she asks him to transfer it all to a secret bank account in Switzerland, he does so without a moment's hesitation.

The moral of this story is:

Designing a correct authentication protocol is much harder than it looks.

The following four general rules often help the designer avoid common pitfalls:

1. Have the initiator prove who she is before the responder has to. This avoids Bob giving away valuable information before Trudy has to give any evidence of who she is.

2. Have the initiator and responder use different keys for proof, even if this means having two shared keys, K_{AB} and K'_{AB}.

3. Have the initiator and responder draw their challenges from different sets. For example, the initiator must use even numbers and the responder must use odd numbers.

4. Make the protocol resistant to attacks involving a second parallel session in which information obtained in one session is used in a different one.

If even one of these rules is violated, the protocol can frequently be broken. Here, all four rules were violated, with disastrous consequences.

Now let us go take a closer look at Fig. 8-32. Surely that protocol is not subject to a reflection attack? Maybe. It is quite subtle. Trudy was able to defeat our protocol by using a reflection attack because it was possible to open a second session with Bob and trick him into answering his own questions. What would happen if Alice were a general-purpose computer that also accepted multiple sessions, rather than a person at a computer? Let us take a look what Trudy can do.

To see how Trudy's attack works, see Fig. 8-35. Alice starts out by announcing her identity in message 1. Trudy intercepts this message and begins her own session with message 2, claiming to be Bob. Again we have shaded the session 2 messages. Alice responds to message 2 by saying in message 3: "You claim to be Bob? Prove it." At this point, Trudy is stuck because she cannot prove she is Bob.

What does Trudy do now? She goes back to the first session, where it is her turn to send a challenge, and sends the R_A she got in message 3. Alice kindly responds to it in message 5, thus supplying Trudy with the information she needs to send in message 6 in session 2. At this point, Trudy is basically home free because she has successfully responded to Alice's challenge in session 2. She can now cancel session 1, send over any old number for the rest of session 2, and she will have an authenticated session with Alice in session 2.

But Trudy is nasty, and she really wants to rub it in. Instead, of sending any old number over to complete session 2, she waits until Alice sends message 7, Alice's challenge for session 1. Of course, Trudy does not know how to respond, so she uses the reflection attack again, sending back R_{A2} as message 8. Alice conveniently encrypts R_{A2} in message 9. Trudy now switches back to session 1 and sends Alice the number she wants in message 10, conveniently copied from what Alice sent in message 9. At this point Trudy has two fully authenticated sessions with Alice.

This attack has a somewhat different result than the attack on the three-message protocol that we saw in Fig. 8-34. This time, Trudy has two authenticated

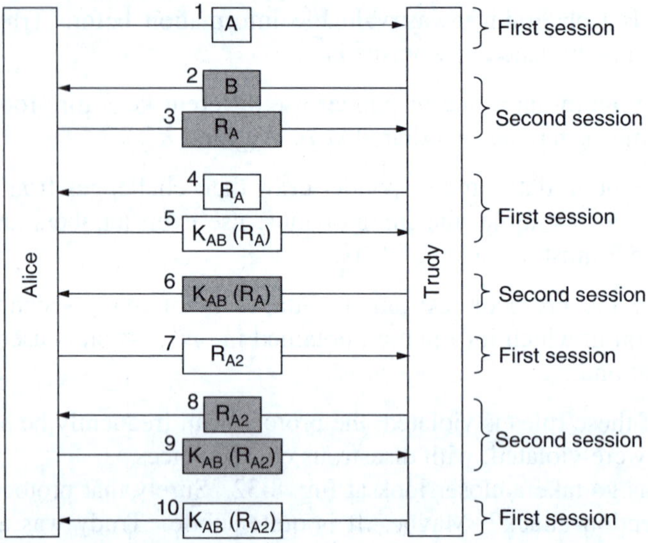

Figure 8-35. A reflection attack on the protocol of Fig. 8-32.

connections with Alice. In the previous example, she had one authenticated connection with Bob. Again here, if we had applied all the general authentication protocol rules discussed earlier, this attack could have been stopped. For a detailed discussion of these kinds of attacks and how to thwart them, see Bird et al. (1993). They also show how it is possible to systematically construct protocols that are provably correct. The simplest such protocol is nevertheless a bit complicated, so we will now show a different class of protocol that also works.

The new authentication protocol is shown in Fig. 8-36 (Bird et al., 1993). It uses an HMAC of the type we saw when studying IPsec. Alice starts out by sending Bob a nonce, R_A, as message 1. Bob responds by selecting his own nonce, R_B, and sending it back along with an HMAC. The HMAC is formed by building a data structure consisting of Alice's nonce, Bob's nonce, their identities, and the shared secret key, K_{AB}. This data structure is then hashed into the HMAC, for example, using SHA-1. When Alice receives message 2, she now has R_A (which she picked herself), R_B, which arrives as plaintext, the two identities, and the secret key, K_{AB}, which she has known all along, so she can compute the HMAC herself. If it agrees with the HMAC in the message, she knows she is talking to Bob because Trudy does not know K_{AB} and thus cannot figure out which HMAC to send. Alice responds to Bob with an HMAC containing just the two nonces.

Can Trudy somehow subvert this protocol? No, because she cannot force either party to encrypt or hash a value of her choice, as happened in Fig. 8-34 and Fig. 8-35. Both HMACs include values chosen by the sending party, something that Trudy cannot control.

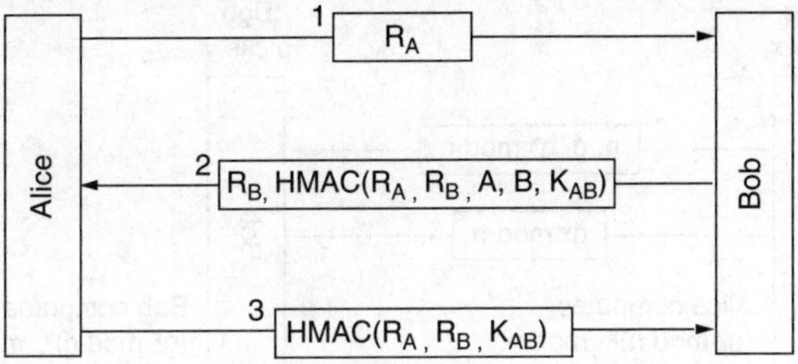

Figure 8-36. Authentication using HMACs.

Using HMACs is not the only way to use this idea. An alternative scheme that is often used instead of computing the HMAC over a series of items is to encrypt the items sequentially using cipher block chaining.

8.7.2 Establishing a Shared Key: The Diffie-Hellman Key Exchange

So far, we have assumed that Alice and Bob share a secret key. Suppose that they do not (because so far there is no universally accepted PKI for signing and distributing certificates). How can they establish one? One way would be for Alice to call Bob and give him her key on the phone, but he would probably start out by saying: "How do I know you are Alice and not Trudy?" They could try to arrange a meeting, with each one bringing a passport, a driver's license, and three major credit cards, but being busy people, they might not be able to find a mutually acceptable date for months. Fortunately, incredible as it may sound, there is a way for total strangers to establish a shared secret key in broad daylight, even with Trudy carefully recording every message.

The protocol that allows strangers to establish a shared secret key is called the **Diffie-Hellman key exchange** (Diffie and Hellman, 1976) and works as follows. Alice and Bob have to agree on two large numbers, n and g, where n is a prime, $(n-1)/2$ is also a prime, and certain conditions apply to g. These numbers may be public, so either one of them can just pick n and g and tell the other openly. Now Alice picks a large (say, 1024-bit) number, x, and keeps it secret. Similarly, Bob picks a large secret number, y.

Alice initiates the key exchange protocol by sending Bob a message containing $(n, g, g^x \bmod n)$, as shown in Fig. 8-37. Bob responds by sending Alice a message containing $g^y \bmod n$. Now Alice raises the number Bob sent her to the xth power modulo n to get $(g^y \bmod n)^x$ *mod n*. Bob performs a similar operation to get $(g^x \bmod n)^y$ *mod n*. By the laws of modular arithmetic, both calculations yield $g^{xy} \bmod n$. Lo and behold, as if by magic, Alice and Bob suddenly share a secret key, $g^{xy} \bmod n$.

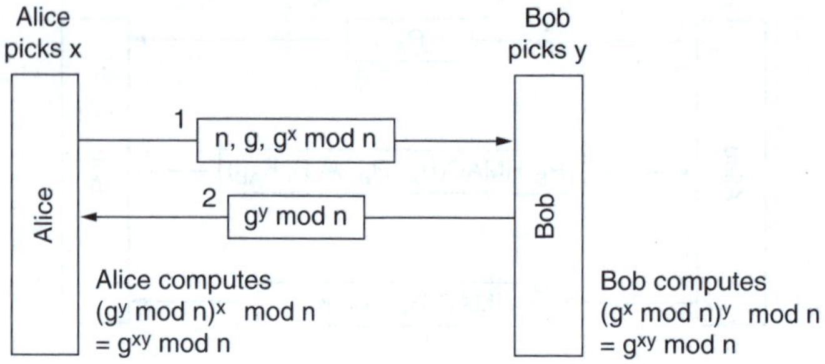

Figure 8-37. The Diffie-Hellman key exchange.

Trudy, of course, has seen both messages. She knows g and n from message 1. If she could compute x and y, she could figure out the secret key. The trouble is, given only $g^x \bmod n$, she cannot find x. No practical algorithm for computing discrete logarithms modulo a very large prime number is known.

To make this example more concrete, we will use the (completely unrealistic) values of $n = 47$ and $g = 3$. Alice picks $x = 8$ and Bob picks $y = 10$. Both of these are kept secret. Alice's message to Bob is (47, 3, 28) because $3^8 \bmod 47$ is 28. Bob's message to Alice is (17). Alice computes $17^8 \bmod 47$, which is 4. Bob computes $28^{10} \bmod 47$, which is 4. Alice and Bob have now independently determined that the secret key is now 4. To find the key, Trudy now has to solve the equation $3^x \bmod 47 = 28$, which can be done by exhaustive search for small numbers like this, but not when all the numbers are hundreds of bits long. All currently known algorithms simply take far too long, even on massively parallel, lightning fast supercomputers.

Despite the elegance of the Diffie-Hellman algorithm, there is a problem: when Bob gets the triple (47, 3, 28), how does he know it is from Alice and not from Trudy? There is no way he can know. Unfortunately, Trudy can exploit this fact to deceive both Alice and Bob, as illustrated in Fig. 8-38. Here, while Alice and Bob are choosing x and y, respectively, Trudy picks her own random number, z. Alice sends message 1, intended for Bob. Trudy intercepts it and sends message 2 to Bob, using the correct g and n (which are public anyway) but with her own z instead of x. She also sends message 3 back to Alice. Later Bob sends message 4 to Alice, which Trudy again intercepts and keeps.

Now everybody does the modular arithmetic. Alice computes the secret key as $g^{xz} \bmod n$, and so does Trudy (for messages to Alice). Bob computes $g^{yz} \bmod n$ and so does Trudy (for messages to Bob). Alice thinks she is talking to Bob, so she establishes a session key (with Trudy). So does Bob. Every message that Alice sends on the encrypted session is captured by Trudy, stored, modified if desired, and then (optionally) passed on to Bob. Similarly, in the other direction, Trudy sees everything and can modify all messages at will, while both Alice and Bob are under the illusion that they have a secure channel to one another. For this

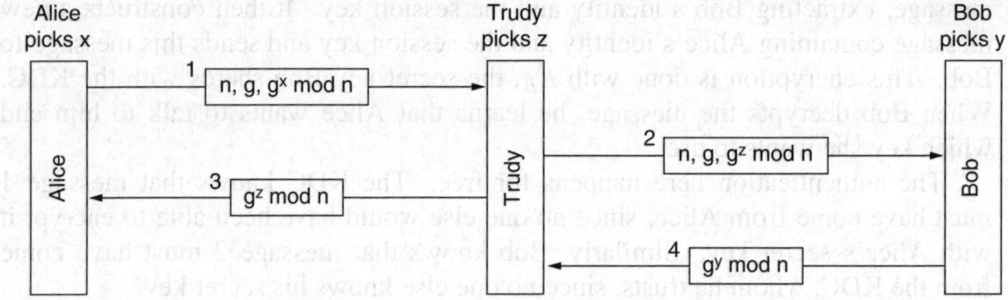

Figure 8-38. The man-in-the-middle attack.

reason, the attack is known as the **man-in-the-middle attack**. It is also called the **bucket brigade attack**, because it vaguely resembles an old-time volunteer fire department passing buckets along the line from the fire truck to the fire.

8.7.3 Authentication Using a Key Distribution Center

Setting up a shared secret with a stranger almost worked, but not quite. On the other hand, it probably was not worth doing in the first place (sour grapes attack). To talk to *n* people this way, you would need *n* keys. For popular people, key management would become a real burden, especially if each key had to be stored on a separate plastic chip card.

A different approach is to introduce a trusted key distribution center. In this model, each user has a single key shared with the KDC. Authentication and session key management now go through the KDC. The simplest known KDC authentication protocol involving two parties and a trusted KDC is depicted in Fig. 8-39.

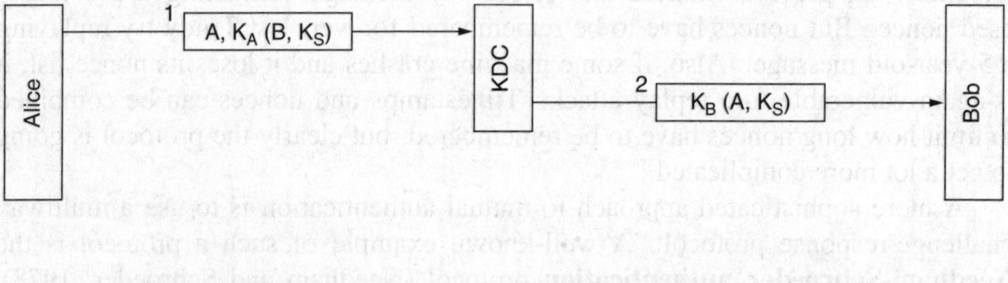

Figure 8-39. A first attempt at an authentication protocol using a KDC.

The idea behind this protocol is simple: Alice picks a session key, K_S, and tells the KDC that she wants to talk to Bob using K_S. This message is encrypted with the secret key Alice shares (only) with the KDC, K_A. The KDC decrypts this message, extracting Bob's identity and the session key. It then constructs a new message containing Alice's identity and the session key and sends this message to Bob. This encryption is done with K_B, the secret key Bob shares with the KDC. When Bob decrypts the message, he learns that Alice wants to talk to him and which key she wants to use.

The authentication here happens for free. The KDC knows that message 1 must have come from Alice, since no one else would have been able to encrypt it with Alice's secret key. Similarly, Bob knows that message 2 must have come from the KDC, whom he trusts, since no one else knows his secret key.

Unfortunately, this protocol has a serious flaw. Trudy needs some money, so she figures out some legitimate service she can perform for Alice, makes an attractive offer, and gets the job. After doing the work, Trudy then politely requests Alice to pay by bank transfer. Alice then establishes a session key with her banker, Bob. Then she sends Bob a message requesting money to be transferred to Trudy's account.

Meanwhile, Trudy is back to her old ways, snooping on the network. She copies both message 2 in Fig. 8-39 and the money-transfer request that follows it. Later, she replays both of them to Bob who thinks: "Alice must have hired Trudy again. She clearly does good work." Bob then transfers an equal amount of money from Alice's account to Trudy's. Some time after the 50th message pair, Bob runs out of the office to find Trudy to offer her a big loan so she can expand her obviously successful business. This problem is called the **replay attack**.

Several solutions to the replay attack are possible. The first one is to include a timestamp in each message. Then, if anyone receives an obsolete message, it can be discarded. The trouble with this approach is that clocks are never exactly synchronized over a network, so there has to be some interval during which a timestamp is valid. Trudy can replay the message during this interval and get away with it.

The second solution is to put a nonce in each message. Each party then has to remember all previous nonces and reject any message containing a previously used nonce. But nonces have to be remembered forever, lest Trudy try replaying a 5-year-old message. Also, if some machine crashes and it loses its nonce list, it is again vulnerable to a replay attack. Timestamps and nonces can be combined to limit how long nonces have to be remembered, but clearly the protocol is going to get a lot more complicated.

A more sophisticated approach to mutual authentication is to use a multiway challenge-response protocol. A well-known example of such a protocol is the **Needham-Schroeder authentication** protocol (Needham and Schroeder, 1978), one variant of which is shown in Fig. 8-40.

The protocol begins with Alice telling the KDC that she wants to talk to Bob. This message contains a large random number, R_A, as a nonce. The KDC sends back message 2 containing Alice's random number, a session key, and a ticket

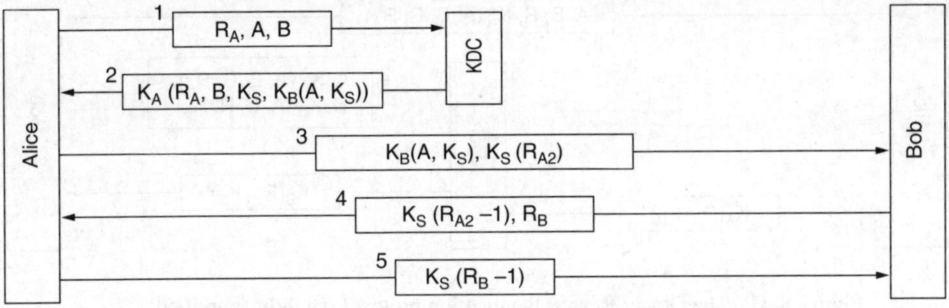

Figure 8-40. The Needham-Schroeder authentication protocol.

that she can send to Bob. The point of the random number, R_A, is to assure Alice that message 2 is fresh, and not a replay. Bob's identity is also enclosed in case Trudy gets any funny ideas about replacing B in message 1 with her own identity so the KDC will encrypt the ticket at the end of message 2 with K_T instead of K_B. The ticket encrypted with K_B is included inside the encrypted message to prevent Trudy from replacing it with something else on the way back to Alice.

Alice now sends the ticket to Bob, along with a new random number, R_{A2}, encrypted with the session key, K_S. In message 4, Bob sends back $K_S(R_{A2} - 1)$ to prove to Alice that she is talking to the real Bob. Sending back $K_S(R_{A2})$ would not have worked, since Trudy could just have stolen it from message 3.

After receiving message 4, Alice is now convinced that she is talking to Bob and that no replays could have been used so far. After all, she just generated R_{A2} a few milliseconds ago. The purpose of message 5 is to convince Bob that it is indeed Alice he is talking to, and no replays are being used here either. By having each party both generate a challenge and respond to one, the possibility of any kind of replay attack is eliminated.

Although this protocol seems pretty solid, it does have a slight weakness. If Trudy ever manages to obtain an old session key in plaintext, she can initiate a new session with Bob by replaying the message 3 that corresponds to the compromised key and convince him that she is Alice (Denning and Sacco, 1981). This time she can plunder Alice's bank account without having to perform the legitimate service even once.

Needham and Schroeder (1987) later published a protocol that corrects this problem. In the same issue of the same journal, Otway and Rees (1987) also published a protocol that solves the problem in a shorter way. Figure 8-41 shows a slightly modified Otway-Rees protocol.

In the Otway-Rees protocol, Alice starts out by generating a pair of random numbers: R, which will be used as a common identifier, and R_A, which Alice will use to challenge Bob. When Bob gets this message, he constructs a new message from the encrypted part of Alice's message and an analogous one of his own.

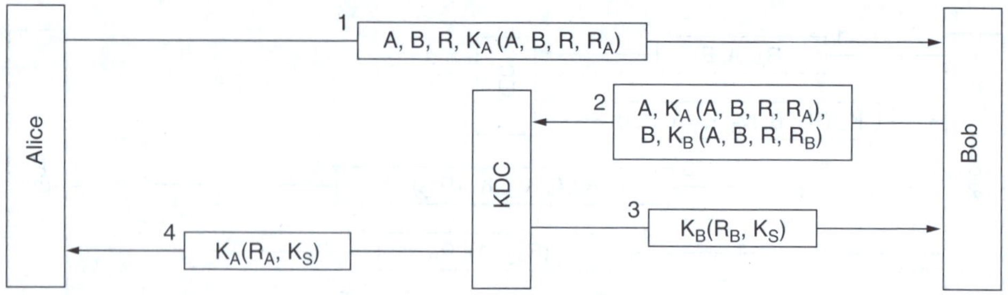

Figure 8-41. The Otway-Rees authentication protocol (slightly simplified).

Both the parts encrypted with K_A and K_B identify Alice and Bob, contain the common identifier, and contain a challenge.

The KDC checks to see if the *R* in both parts is the same. It might not be if Trudy has tampered with *R* in message 1 or replaced part of message 2. If the two *R*s match, the KDC believes that the request message from Bob is valid. It then generates a session key and encrypts it twice, once for Alice and once for Bob. Each message contains the receiver's random number, as proof that the KDC, and not Trudy, generated the message. At this point, both Alice and Bob are in possession of the same session key and can start communicating. The first time they exchange data messages, each one can see that the other one has an identical copy of K_S, so the authentication is then complete.

8.7.4 Authentication Using Kerberos

An authentication protocol used in many real systems (including Windows 2000 and later versions) is **Kerberos**, which is based on a variant of Needham-Schroeder. It is named for a multiheaded dog in Greek mythology that used to guard the entrance to Hades (presumably to keep undesirables out). Kerberos was designed at M.I.T. to allow workstation users to access network resources in a secure way. Its biggest difference from Needham-Schroeder is its assumption that all clocks are fairly well synchronized. The protocol has gone through several iterations. V5 is the one that is widely used in industry and defined in RFC 4120. The earlier version, V4, was finally retired after serious flaws were found (Yu et al., 2004). V5 improves on V4 with many small changes to the protocol and some improved features, such as the fact that it no longer relies on the now-dated DES. For more information, see Neuman and Ts'o (1994).

Kerberos involves three servers in addition to Alice (a client workstation):

1. Authentication Server (AS): Verifies users during login.
2. Ticket-Granting Server (TGS): Issues "proof of identity tickets."
3. Bob the server: Actually does the work Alice wants performed.

AS is similar to a KDC in that it shares a secret password with every user. The TGS's job is to issue tickets that can convince the real servers that the bearer of a TGS ticket really is who he or she claims to be.

To start a session, Alice sits down at an arbitrary public workstation and types her name. The workstation sends her name and the name of the TGS to the AS in plaintext, as shown in message 1 of Fig. 8-42. What comes back is a session key and a ticket, $K_{TGS}(A, K_S, t)$, intended for the TGS. The session key is encrypted using Alice's secret key, so that only Alice can decrypt it. Only when message 2 arrives does the workstation ask for Alice's password—not before then. The password is then used to generate K_A in order to decrypt message 2 and obtain the session key.

At this point, the workstation overwrites Alice's password to make sure that it is only inside the workstation for a few milliseconds at most. If Trudy tries logging in as Alice, the password she types will be wrong and the workstation will detect this because the standard part of message 2 will be incorrect.

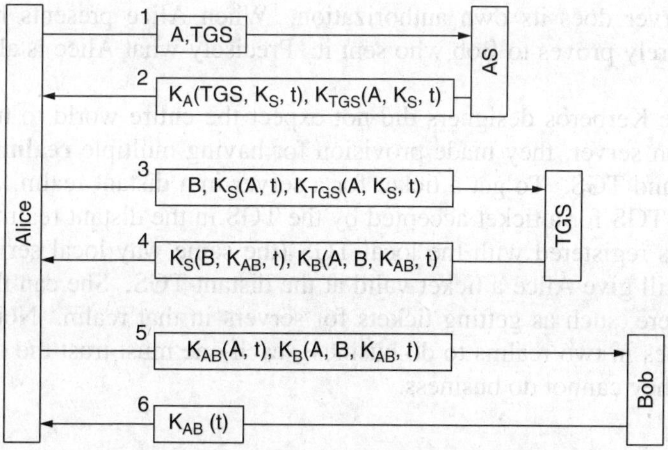

Figure 8-42. The operation of Kerberos V5.

After she logs in, Alice may tell the workstation that she wants to contact Bob the file server. The workstation then sends message 3 to the TGS asking for a ticket to use with Bob. The key element in this request is the ticket $K_{TGS}(A, K_S, t)$, which is encrypted with the TGS's secret key and used as proof that the sender really is Alice. The TGS responds in message 4 by creating a session key, K_{AB}, for Alice to use with Bob. Two versions of it are sent back. The first is encrypted with only K_S, so Alice can read it. The second is another ticket, encrypted with Bob's key, K_B, so Bob can read it.

Trudy can copy message 3 and try to use it again, but she will be foiled by the encrypted timestamp, *t*, sent along with it. Trudy cannot replace the timestamp with a more recent one, because she does not know K_S, the session key Alice uses to talk to the TGS. Even if Trudy replays message 3 quickly, all she will get is another copy of message 4, which she could not decrypt the first time and will not be able to decrypt the second time either.

Now Alice can send K_{AB} to Bob via the new ticket to establish a session with him (message 5). This exchange is also timestamped. The optional response (message 6) is proof to Alice that she is actually talking to Bob, not to Trudy.

After this series of exchanges, Alice can communicate with Bob under cover of K_{AB}. If she later decides she needs to talk to another server, Carol, she just repeats message 3 to the TGS, only now specifying C instead of B. The TGS will promptly respond with a ticket encrypted with K_C that Alice can send to Carol and that Carol will accept as proof that it came from Alice.

The point of all this work is that now Alice can access servers all over the network in a secure way and her password never has to go over the network. In fact, it only had to be in her own workstation for a few milliseconds. However, note that each server does its own authorization. When Alice presents her ticket to Bob, this merely proves to Bob who sent it. Precisely what Alice is allowed to do is up to Bob.

Since the Kerberos designers did not expect the entire world to trust a single authentication server, they made provision for having multiple **realms**, each with its own AS and TGS. To get a ticket for a server in a distant realm, Alice would ask her own TGS for a ticket accepted by the TGS in the distant realm. If the distant TGS has registered with the local TGS (the same way local servers do), the local TGS will give Alice a ticket valid at the distant TGS. She can then do business over there, such as getting tickets for servers in that realm. Note, however, that for parties in two realms to do business, each one must trust the other's TGS. Otherwise, they cannot do business.

8.7.5 Authentication Using Public-Key Cryptography

Mutual authentication can also be done using public-key cryptography. To start with, Alice needs to get Bob's public key. If a PKI exists with a directory server that hands out certificates for public keys, Alice can ask for Bob's, as shown in Fig. 8-43 as message 1. The reply, in message 2, is an X.509 certificate containing Bob's public key. When Alice verifies that the signature is correct, she sends Bob a message containing her identity and a nonce.

When Bob receives this message, he has no idea whether it came from Alice or from Trudy, but he plays along and asks the directory server for Alice's public key (message 4), which he soon gets (message 5). He then sends Alice message 6, containing Alice's R_A, his own nonce, R_B, and a proposed session key, K_S.

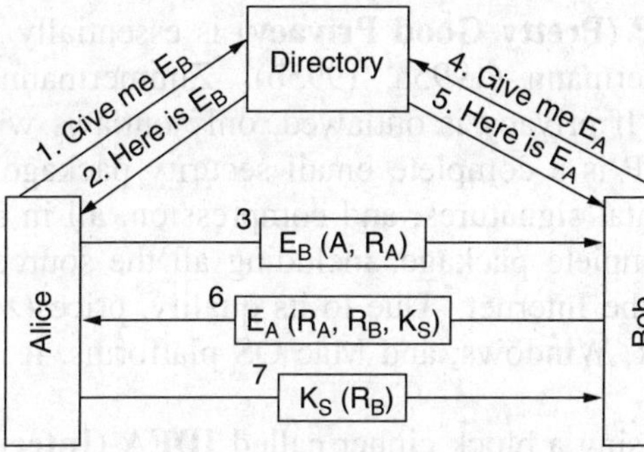

Figure 8-43. Mutual authentication using public-key cryptography.

When Alice gets message 6, she decrypts it using her private key. She sees R_A in it, which gives her a warm feeling inside. The message must have come from Bob, since Trudy has no way of determining R_A. Furthermore, it must be fresh and not a replay, since she just sent Bob R_A. Alice agrees to the session by sending back message 7. When Bob sees R_B encrypted with the session key he just generated, he knows Alice got message 6 and verified R_A. Bob is now a happy camper.

What can Trudy do to try to subvert this protocol? She can fabricate message 3 and trick Bob into probing Alice, but Alice will see an R_A that she did not send and will not proceed further. Trudy cannot forge message 7 back to Bob because she does not know R_B or K_S and cannot determine them without Alice's private key. She is out of luck.

8.8 EMAIL SECURITY

When an email message is sent between two distant sites, it will generally transit dozens of machines on the way. Any of these can read and record the message for future use. In practice, privacy is nonexistent, despite what many people think. Nevertheless, many people would like to be able to send email that can be read by the intended recipient and no one else: not their boss and not even their government. This desire has stimulated several people and groups to apply the cryptographic principles we studied earlier to email to produce secure email. In the following sections we will study a widely used secure email system, PGP, and then briefly mention one other, S/MIME. For additional information about secure email, see Kaufman et al. (2002) and Schneier (1995).

8.8.1 PGP—Pretty Good Privacy

Our first example, **PGP** (**Pretty Good Privacy**) is essentially the brainchild of one person, Phil Zimmermann (1995a, 1995b). Zimmermann is a privacy advocate whose motto is: "If privacy is outlawed, only outlaws will have privacy." Released in 1991, PGP is a complete email security package that provides privacy, authentication, digital signatures, and compression, all in an easy-to-use form. Furthermore, the complete package, including all the source code, is distributed free of charge via the Internet. Due to its quality, price (zero), and easy availability on UNIX, Linux, Windows, and Mac OS platforms, it is widely used today.

PGP encrypts data by using a block cipher called **IDEA** (**International Data Encryption Algorithm**), which uses 128-bit keys. It was devised in Switzerland at a time when DES was seen as tainted and AES had not yet been invented. Conceptually, IDEA is similar to DES and AES: it mixes up the bits in a series of rounds, but the details of the mixing functions are different from DES and AES. Key management uses RSA and data integrity uses MD5, topics that we have already discussed.

PGP has also been embroiled in controversy since day 1 (Levy, 1993). Because Zimmermann did nothing to stop other people from placing PGP on the Internet, where people all over the world could get it, the U.S. Government claimed that Zimmermann had violated U.S. laws prohibiting the export of munitions. The U.S. Government's investigation of Zimmermann went on for 5 years but was eventually dropped, probably for two reasons. First, Zimmermann did not place PGP on the Internet himself, so his lawyer claimed that *he* never exported anything (and then there is the little matter of whether creating a Web site constitutes export at all). Second, the government eventually came to realize that winning a trial meant convincing a jury that a Web site containing a downloadable privacy program was covered by the arms-trafficking law prohibiting the export of war materiel such as tanks, submarines, military aircraft, and nuclear weapons. Years of negative publicity probably did not help much, either.

As an aside, the export rules are bizarre, to put it mildly. The government considered putting code on a Web site to be an illegal export and harassed Zimmermann about it for 5 years. On the other hand, when someone published the complete PGP source code, in C, as a book (in a large font with a checksum on each page to make scanning it in easy) and then exported the book, that was fine with the government because books are not classified as munitions. The sword is mightier than the pen, at least for Uncle Sam.

Another problem PGP ran into involved patent infringement. The company holding the RSA patent, RSA Security, Inc., alleged that PGP's use of the RSA algorithm infringed on its patent, but that problem was settled with releases starting at 2.6. Furthermore, PGP uses another patented encryption algorithm, IDEA, whose use caused some problems at first.

Since PGP is open source, various people and groups have modified it and produced a number of versions. Some of these were designed to get around the munitions laws, others were focused on avoiding the use of patented algorithms, and still others wanted to turn it into a closed-source commercial product. Although the munitions laws have now been slightly liberalized (otherwise, products using AES would not have been exportable from the U.S.), and the RSA patent expired in September 2000, the legacy of all these problems is that several incompatible versions of PGP are in circulation, under various names. The discussion below focuses on classic PGP, which is the oldest and simplest version. Another popular version, Open PGP, is described in RFC 2440. Yet another is the GNU Privacy Guard.

PGP intentionally uses existing cryptographic algorithms rather than inventing new ones. It is largely based on algorithms that have withstood extensive peer review and were not designed or influenced by any government agency trying to weaken them. For people who distrust government, this property is a big plus.

PGP supports text compression, secrecy, and digital signatures and also provides extensive key management facilities, but, oddly enough, not email facilities. It is like a preprocessor that takes plaintext as input and produces signed ciphertext in base64 as output. This output can then be emailed, of course. Some PGP implementations call a user agent as the final step to actually send the message.

To see how PGP works, let us consider the example of Fig. 8-44. Here, Alice wants to send a signed plaintext message, P, to Bob in a secure way. Both Alice and Bob have private (D_X) and public (E_X) RSA keys. Let us assume that each one knows the other's public key; we will cover PGP key management shortly.

Alice starts out by invoking the PGP program on her computer. PGP first hashes her message, P, using MD5, and then encrypts the resulting hash using her private RSA key, D_A. When Bob eventually gets the message, he can decrypt the hash with Alice's public key and verify that the hash is correct. Even if someone else (e.g., Trudy) could acquire the hash at this stage and decrypt it with Alice's known public key, the strength of MD5 guarantees that it would be computationally infeasible to produce another message with the same MD5 hash.

The encrypted hash and the original message are now concatenated into a single message, *P1*, and compressed using the ZIP program, which uses the Ziv-Lempel algorithm (Ziv and Lempel, 1977). Call the output of this step *P1.Z*.

Next, PGP prompts Alice for some random input. Both the content and the typing speed are used to generate a 128-bit IDEA message key, K_M (called a session key in the PGP literature, but this is really a misnomer since there is no session). K_M is now used to encrypt *P1.Z* with IDEA in cipher feedback mode. In addition, K_M is encrypted with Bob's public key, E_B. These two components are then concatenated and converted to base64, as we discussed in the section on MIME in Chap. 7. The resulting message contains only letters, digits, and the symbols +, /, and =, which means it can be put into an RFC 822 body and be expected to arrive unmodified.

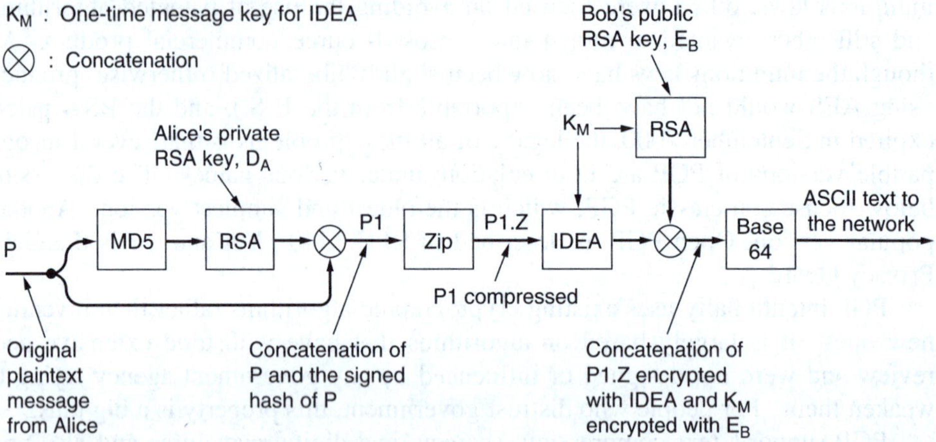

Figure 8-44. PGP in operation for sending a message.

When Bob gets the message, he reverses the base64 encoding and decrypts the IDEA key using his private RSA key. Using this key, he decrypts the message to get *P1.Z*. After decompressing it, Bob separates the plaintext from the encrypted hash and decrypts the hash using Alice's public key. If the plaintext hash agrees with his own MD5 computation, he knows that *P* is the correct message and that it came from Alice.

It is worth noting that RSA is only used in two places here: to encrypt the 128-bit MD5 hash and to encrypt the 128-bit IDEA key. Although RSA is slow, it has to encrypt only 256 bits, not a large volume of data. Furthermore, all 256 plaintext bits are exceedingly random, so a considerable amount of work will be required on Trudy's part just to determine if a guessed key is correct. The heavy-duty encryption is done by IDEA, which is orders of magnitude faster than RSA. Thus, PGP provides security, compression, and a digital signature and does so in a much more efficient way than the scheme illustrated in Fig. 8-19.

PGP supports four RSA key lengths. It is up to the user to select the one that is most appropriate. The lengths are:

1. Casual (384 bits): Can be broken easily today.
2. Commercial (512 bits): Breakable by three-letter organizations.
3. Military (1024 bits): Not breakable by anyone on earth.
4. Alien (2048 bits): Not breakable by anyone on other planets, either.

Since RSA is only used for two small computations, everyone should use alien-strength keys all the time.

The format of a classic PGP message is shown in Fig. 8-45. Numerous other formats are also in use. The message has three parts, containing the IDEA key, the signature, and the message, respectively. The key part contains not only the key, but also a key identifier, since users are permitted to have multiple public keys.

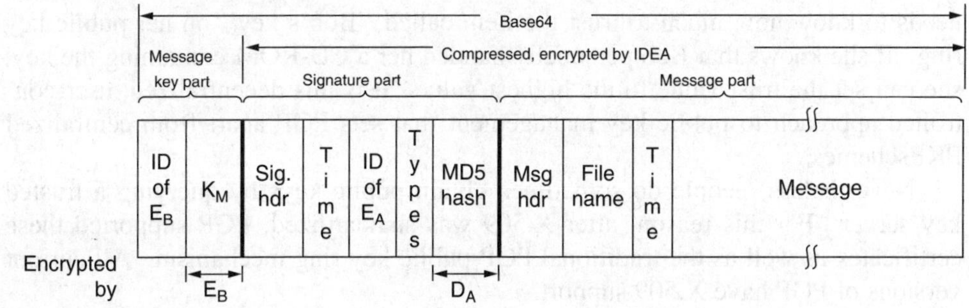

Figure 8-45. A PGP message.

The signature part contains a header, which will not concern us here. The header is followed by a timestamp, the identifier for the sender's public key that can be used to decrypt the signature hash, some type information that identifies the algorithms used (to allow MD6 and RSA2 to be used when they are invented), and the encrypted hash itself.

The message part also contains a header, the default name of the file to be used if the receiver writes the file to the disk, a message creation timestamp, and, finally, the message itself.

Key management has received a large amount of attention in PGP as it is the Achilles' heel of all security systems. Key management works as follows. Each user maintains two data structures locally: a private key ring and a public key ring. The **private key ring** contains one or more personal private/public key pairs. The reason for supporting multiple pairs per user is to permit users to change their public keys periodically or when one is thought to have been compromised, without invalidating messages currently in preparation or in transit. Each pair has an identifier associated with it so that a message sender can tell the recipient which public key was used to encrypt it. Message identifiers consist of the low-order 64 bits of the public key. Users are themselves responsible for avoiding conflicts in their public-key identifiers. The private keys on disk are encrypted using a special (arbitrarily long) password to protect them against sneak attacks.

The **public key ring** contains public keys of the user's correspondents. These are needed to encrypt the message keys associated with each message. Each entry on the public key ring contains not only the public key, but also its 64-bit identifier and an indication of how strongly the user trusts the key.

The problem being tackled here is the following. Suppose that public keys are maintained on bulletin boards. One way for Trudy to read Bob's secret email is to attack the bulletin board and replace Bob's public key with one of her choice. When Alice later fetches the key allegedly belonging to Bob, Trudy can mount a bucket brigade attack on Bob.

To prevent such attacks, or at least minimize the consequences of them, Alice needs to know how much to trust the item called "Bob's key" on her public key ring. If she knows that Bob personally handed her a CD-ROM containing the key, she can set the trust value to the highest value. It is this decentralized, user-controlled approach to public-key management that sets PGP apart from centralized PKI schemes.

Nevertheless, people do sometimes obtain public keys by querying a trusted key server. For this reason, after X.509 was standardized, PGP supported these certificates as well as the traditional PGP public key ring mechanism. All current versions of PGP have X.509 support.

8.8.2 S/MIME

IETF's venture into email security, called **S/MIME** (**Secure/MIME**), is described in RFCs 2632 through 2643. It provides authentication, data integrity, secrecy, and nonrepudiation. It also is quite flexible, supporting a variety of cryptographic algorithms. Not surprisingly, given the name, S/MIME integrates well with MIME, allowing all kinds of messages to be protected. A variety of new MIME headers are defined, for example, for holding digital signatures.

S/MIME does not have a rigid certificate hierarchy beginning at a single root, which had been one of the political problems that doomed an earlier system called PEM (Privacy Enhanced Mail). Instead, users can have multiple trust anchors. As long as a certificate can be traced back to some trust anchor the user believes in, it is considered valid. S/MIME uses the standard algorithms and protocols we have been examining so far, so we will not discuss it any further here. For the details, please consult the RFCs.

8.9 WEB SECURITY

We have just studied two important areas where security is needed: communications and email. You can think of these as the soup and appetizer. Now it is time for the main course: Web security. The Web is where most of the Trudies hang out nowadays and do their dirty work. In the following sections, we will look at some of the problems and issues relating to Web security.

Web security can be roughly divided into three parts. First, how are objects and resources named securely? Second, how can secure, authenticated connections be established? Third, what happens when a Web site sends a client a piece of executable code? After looking at some threats, we will examine all these issues.

8.9.1 Threats

One reads about Web site security problems in the newspaper almost weekly. The situation is really pretty grim. Let us look at a few examples of what has already happened. First, the home pages of numerous organizations have been attacked and replaced by new home pages of the crackers' choosing. (The popular press calls people who break into computers "hackers," but many programmers reserve that term for great programmers. We prefer to call these people "crackers.") Sites that have been cracked include those belonging to Yahoo!, the U.S. Army, the CIA, NASA, and the *New York Times*. In most cases, the crackers just put up some funny text and the sites were repaired within a few hours.

Now let us look at some much more serious cases. Numerous sites have been brought down by denial-of-service attacks, in which the cracker floods the site with traffic, rendering it unable to respond to legitimate queries. Often, the attack is mounted from a large number of machines that the cracker has already broken into (DDoS attacks). These attacks are so common that they do not even make the news any more, but they can cost the attacked sites thousands of dollars in lost business.

In 1999, a Swedish cracker broke into Microsoft's Hotmail Web site and created a mirror site that allowed anyone to type in the name of a Hotmail user and then read all of the person's current and archived email.

In another case, a 19-year-old Russian cracker named Maxim broke into an e-commerce Web site and stole 300,000 credit card numbers. Then he approached the site owners and told them that if they did not pay him $100,000, he would post all the credit card numbers to the Internet. They did not give in to his blackmail, and he indeed posted the credit card numbers, inflicting great damage on many innocent victims.

In a different vein, a 23-year-old California student emailed a press release to a news agency falsely stating that the Emulex Corporation was going to post a large quarterly loss and that the C.E.O. was resigning immediately. Within hours, the company's stock dropped by 60%, causing stockholders to lose over $2 billion. The perpetrator made a quarter of a million dollars by selling the stock short just before sending the announcement. While this event was not a Web site break-in, it is clear that putting such an announcement on the home page of any big corporation would have a similar effect.

We could (unfortunately) go on like this for many more pages. But it is now time to examine some of the technical issues related to Web security. For more information about security problems of all kinds, see Anderson (2008a); Stuttard and Pinto (2007); and Schneier (2004). Searching the Internet will also turn up vast numbers of specific cases.

8.9.2 Secure Naming

Let us start with something very basic: Alice wants to visit Bob's Web site. She types Bob's URL into her browser and a few seconds later, a Web page appears. But is it Bob's? Maybe yes and maybe no. Trudy might be up to her old tricks again. For example, she might be intercepting all of Alice's outgoing packets and examining them. When she captures an HTTP *GET* request headed to Bob's Web site, she could go to Bob's Web site herself to get the page, modify it as she wishes, and return the fake page to Alice. Alice would be none the wiser. Worse yet, Trudy could slash the prices at Bob's e-store to make his goods look very attractive, thereby tricking Alice into sending her credit card number to "Bob" to buy some merchandise.

One disadvantage of this classic man-in-the-middle attack is that Trudy has to be in a position to intercept Alice's outgoing traffic and forge her incoming traffic. In practice, she has to tap either Alice's phone line or Bob's, since tapping the fiber backbone is fairly difficult. While active wiretapping is certainly possible, it is a fair amount of work, and while Trudy is clever, she is also lazy. Besides, there are easier ways to trick Alice.

DNS Spoofing

One way would be for Trudy to crack the DNS system or maybe just the DNS cache at Alice's ISP, and replace Bob's IP address (say, 36.1.2.3) with her (Trudy's) IP address (say, 42.9.9.9). That leads to the following attack. The way it is supposed to work is illustrated in Fig. 8-46(a). Here, Alice (1) asks DNS for Bob's IP address, (2) gets it, (3) asks Bob for his home page, and (4) gets that, too. After Trudy has modified Bob's DNS record to contain her own IP address instead of Bob's, we get the situation in Fig. 8-46(b). Here, when Alice looks up Bob's IP address, she gets Trudy's, so all her traffic intended for Bob goes to Trudy. Trudy can now mount a man-in-the-middle attack without having to go to the trouble of tapping any phone lines. Instead, she has to break into a DNS server and change one record, a much easier proposition.

How might Trudy fool DNS? It turns out to be relatively easy. Briefly summarized, Trudy can trick the DNS server at Alice's ISP into sending out a query to look up Bob's address. Unfortunately, since DNS uses UDP, the DNS server has no real way of checking who supplied the answer. Trudy can exploit this property by forging the expected reply and thus injecting a false IP address into the DNS server's cache. For simplicity, we will assume that Alice's ISP does not initially have an entry for Bob's Web site, *bob.com*. If it does, Trudy can wait until it times out and try later (or use other tricks).

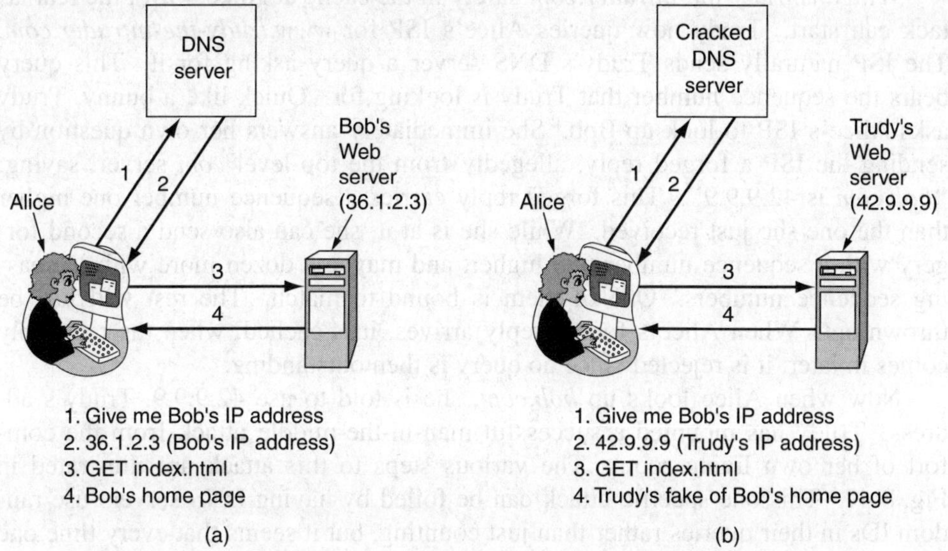

Figure 8-46. (a) Normal situation. (b) An attack based on breaking into a DNS server and modifying Bob's record.

Trudy starts the attack by sending a lookup request to Alice's ISP asking for the IP address of *bob.com*. Since there is no entry for this DNS name, the cache server queries the top-level server for the *com* domain to get one. However, Trudy beats the *com* server to the punch and sends back a false reply saying: "*bob.com* is 42.9.9.9," where that IP address is hers. If her false reply gets back to Alice's ISP first, that one will be cached and the real reply will be rejected as an unsolicited reply to a query no longer outstanding. Tricking a DNS server into installing a false IP address is called **DNS spoofing**. A cache that holds an intentionally false IP address like this is called a **poisoned cache**.

Actually, things are not quite that simple. First, Alice's ISP checks to see that the reply bears the correct IP source address of the top-level server. But since Trudy can put anything she wants in that IP field, she can defeat that test easily since the IP addresses of the top-level servers have to be public.

Second, to allow DNS servers to tell which reply goes with which request, all requests carry a sequence number. To spoof Alice's ISP, Trudy has to know its current sequence number. The easiest way to learn the current sequence number is for Trudy to register a domain herself, say, *trudy-the-intruder.com*. Let us assume its IP address is also 42.9.9.9. She also creates a DNS server for her newly hatched domain, *dns.trudy-the-intruder.com*. It, too, uses Trudy's 42.9.9.9 IP address, since Trudy has only one computer. Now she has to make Alice's ISP aware of her DNS server. That is easy to do. All she has to do is ask Alice's ISP for *foobar.trudy-the-intruder.com*, which will cause Alice's ISP to find out who serves Trudy's new domain by asking the top-level *com* server.

With *dns.trudy-the-intruder.com* safely in the cache at Alice's ISP, the real attack can start. Trudy now queries Alice's ISP for *www.trudy-the-intruder.com*. The ISP naturally sends Trudy's DNS server a query asking for it. This query bears the sequence number that Trudy is looking for. Quick like a bunny, Trudy asks Alice's ISP to look up Bob. She immediately answers her own question by sending the ISP a forged reply, allegedly from the top-level *com* server, saying: "*bob.com* is 42.9.9.9". This forged reply carries a sequence number one higher than the one she just received. While she is at it, she can also send a second forgery with a sequence number two higher, and maybe a dozen more with increasing sequence numbers. One of them is bound to match. The rest will just be thrown out. When Alice's forged reply arrives, it is cached; when the real reply comes in later, it is rejected since no query is then outstanding.

Now when Alice looks up *bob.com*, she is told to use 42.9.9.9, Trudy's address. Trudy has mounted a successful man-in-the-middle attack from the comfort of her own living room. The various steps to this attack are illustrated in Fig. 8-47. This one specific attack can be foiled by having DNS servers use random IDs in their queries rather than just counting, but it seems that every time one hole is plugged, another one turns up. In particular, the IDs are only 16 bits, so working through all of them is easy when it is a computer that is doing the guessing.

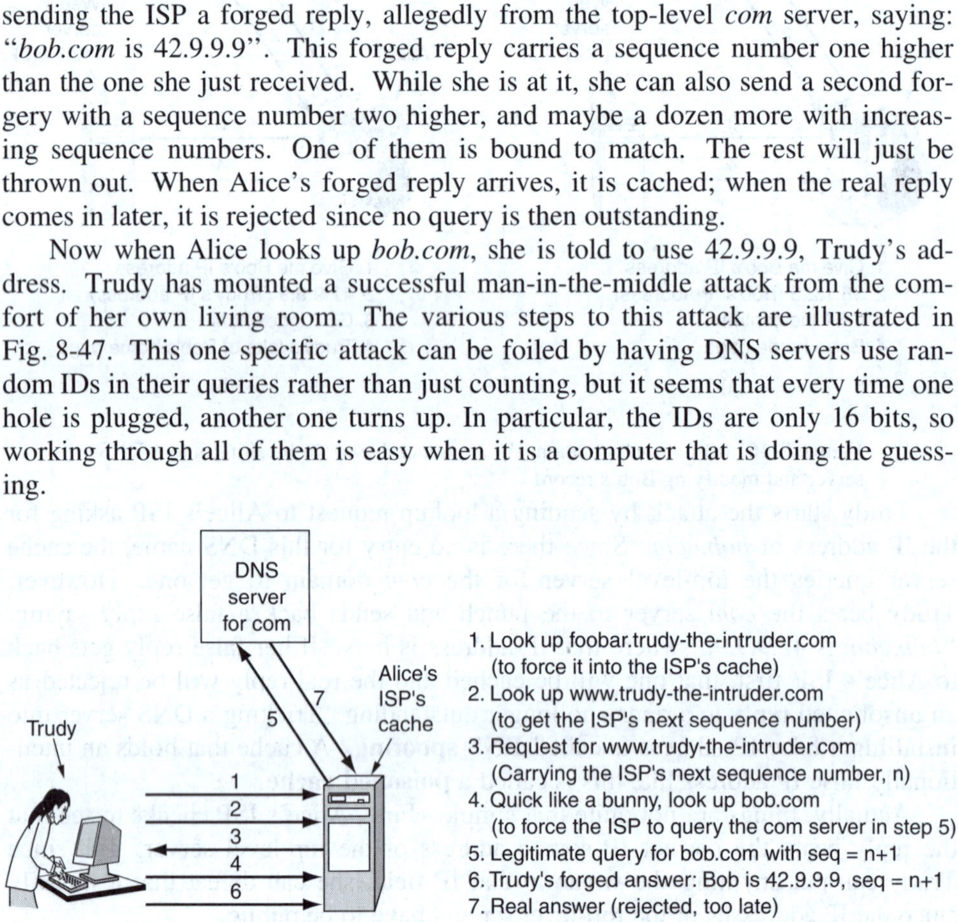

Figure 8-47. How Trudy spoofs Alice's ISP.

Secure DNS

The real problem is that DNS was designed at a time when the Internet was a research facility for a few hundred universities, and neither Alice, nor Bob, nor Trudy was invited to the party. Security was not an issue then; making the Internet work at all was the issue. The environment has changed radically over the years, so in 1994 IETF set up a working group to make DNS fundamentally secure. This (ongoing) project is known as **DNSsec** (**DNS security**); its first output was presented in RFC 2535. Unfortunately, DNSsec has not been fully deployed yet, so numerous DNS servers are still vulnerable to spoofing attacks.

DNSsec is conceptually extremely simple. It is based on public-key cryptography. Every DNS zone (in the sense of Fig. 7-5) has a public/private key pair. All information sent by a DNS server is signed with the originating zone's private key, so the receiver can verify its authenticity.

DNSsec offers three fundamental services:

1. Proof of where the data originated.
2. Public key distribution.
3. Transaction and request authentication.

The main service is the first one, which verifies that the data being returned has been approved by the zone's owner. The second one is useful for storing and retrieving public keys securely. The third one is needed to guard against playback and spoofing attacks. Note that secrecy is not an offered service since all the information in DNS is considered public. Since phasing in DNSsec is expected to take several years, the ability for security-aware servers to interwork with security-ignorant servers is essential, which implies that the protocol cannot be changed. Let us now look at some of the details.

DNS records are grouped into sets called **RRSets** (**Resource Record Sets**), with all the records having the same name, class, and type being lumped together in a set. An RRSet may contain multiple *A* records, for example, if a DNS name resolves to a primary IP address and a secondary IP address. The RRSets are extended with several new record types (discussed below). Each RRSet is cryptographically hashed (e.g., using SHA-1). The hash is signed by the zone's private key (e.g., using RSA). The unit of transmission to clients is the signed RRSet. Upon receipt of a signed RRSet, the client can verify whether it was signed by the private key of the originating zone. If the signature agrees, the data are accepted. Since each RRSet contains its own signature, RRSets can be cached anywhere, even at untrustworthy servers, without endangering the security.

DNSsec introduces several new record types. The first of these is the *KEY* record. This records holds the public key of a zone, user, host, or other principal, the cryptographic algorithm used for signing, the protocol used for transmission, and a few other bits. The public key is stored naked. X.509 certificates are not used due to their bulk. The algorithm field holds a 1 for MD5/RSA signatures (the preferred choice), and other values for other combinations. The protocol field can indicate the use of IPsec or other security protocols, if any.

The second new record type is the *SIG* record. It holds the signed hash according to the algorithm specified in the *KEY* record. The signature applies to all the records in the RRSet, including any *KEY* records present, but excluding itself. It also holds the times when the signature begins its period of validity and when it expires, as well as the signer's name and a few other items.

The DNSsec design is such that a zone's private key can be kept offline. Once or twice a day, the contents of a zone's database can be manually transported (e.g., on CD-ROM) to a disconnected machine on which the private key is located. All the RRSets can be signed there and the *SIG* records thus produced can be conveyed back to the zone's primary server on CD-ROM. In this way, the private key can be stored on a CD-ROM locked in a safe except when it is inserted into the disconnected machine for signing the day's new RRSets. After signing is completed, all copies of the key are erased from memory and the disk and the CD-ROM are returned to the safe. This procedure reduces electronic security to physical security, something people understand how to deal with.

This method of presigning RRSets greatly speeds up the process of answering queries since no cryptography has to be done on the fly. The trade-off is that a large amount of disk space is needed to store all the keys and signatures in the DNS databases. Some records will increase tenfold in size due to the signature.

When a client process gets a signed RRSet, it must apply the originating zone's public key to decrypt the hash, compute the hash itself, and compare the two values. If they agree, the data are considered valid. However, this procedure begs the question of how the client gets the zone's public key. One way is to acquire it from a trusted server, using a secure connection (e.g., using IPsec).

However, in practice, it is expected that clients will be preconfigured with the public keys of all the top-level domains. If Alice now wants to visit Bob's Web site, she can ask DNS for the RRSet of *bob.com*, which will contain his IP address and a *KEY* record containing Bob's public key. This RRSet will be signed by the top-level *com* domain, so Alice can easily verify its validity. An example of what this RRSet might contain is shown in Fig. 8-48.

Domain name	Time to live	Class	Type	Value
bob.com.	86400	IN	A	36.1.2.3
bob.com.	86400	IN	KEY	3682793A7B73F731029CE2737D...
bob.com.	86400	IN	SIG	86947503A8B848F5272E53930C...

Figure 8-48. An example RRSet for *bob.com*. The *KEY* record is Bob's public key. The *SIG* record is the top-level *com* server's signed hash of the *A* and *KEY* records to verify their authenticity.

Now armed with a verified copy of Bob's public key, Alice can ask Bob's DNS server (run by Bob) for the IP address of *www.bob.com*. This RRSet will be signed by Bob's private key, so Alice can verify the signature on the RRSet Bob returns. If Trudy somehow manages to inject a false RRSet into any of the caches, Alice can easily detect its lack of authenticity because the *SIG* record contained in it will be incorrect.

However, DNSsec also provides a cryptographic mechanism to bind a response to a specific query, to prevent the kind of spoof Trudy managed to pull off in Fig. 8-47. This (optional) antispoofing measure adds to the response a hash of the query message signed with the respondent's private key. Since Trudy does not know the private key of the top-level *com* server, she cannot forge a response to a query Alice's ISP sent there. She can certainly get her response back first, but it will be rejected due to its invalid signature over the hashed query.

DNSsec also supports a few other record types. For example, the *CERT* record can be used for storing (e.g., X.509) certificates. This record has been provided because some people want to turn DNS into a PKI. Whether this will actually happen remains to be seen. We will stop our discussion of DNSsec here. For more details, please consult RFC 2535.

8.9.3 SSL—The Secure Sockets Layer

Secure naming is a good start, but there is much more to Web security. The next step is secure connections. We will now look at how secure connections can be achieved. Nothing involving security is simple and this is not either.

When the Web burst into public view, it was initially used for just distributing static pages. However, before long, some companies got the idea of using it for financial transactions, such as purchasing merchandise by credit card, online banking, and electronic stock trading. These applications created a demand for secure connections. In 1995, Netscape Communications Corp., the then-dominant browser vendor, responded by introducing a security package called **SSL** (**Secure Sockets Layer**) to meet this demand. This software and its protocol are now widely used, for example, by Firefox, Safari, and Internet Explorer, so it is worth examining in some detail.

SSL builds a secure connection between two sockets, including

1. Parameter negotiation between client and server.
2. Authentication of the server by the client.
3. Secret communication.
4. Data integrity protection.

We have seen these items before, so there is no need to elaborate on them.

The positioning of SSL in the usual protocol stack is illustrated in Fig. 8-49. Effectively, it is a new layer interposed between the application layer and the transport layer, accepting requests from the browser and sending them down to TCP for transmission to the server. Once the secure connection has been established, SSL's main job is handling compression and encryption. When HTTP is used over SSL, it is called **HTTPS** (**Secure HTTP**), even though it is the standard HTTP protocol. Sometimes it is available at a new port (443) instead of port 80.

As an aside, SSL is not restricted to Web browsers, but that is its most common application. It can also provide mutual authentication.

Application (HTTP)
Security (SSL)
Transport (TCP)
Network (IP)
Data link (PPP)
Physical (modem, ADSL, cable TV)

Figure 8-49. Layers (and protocols) for a home user browsing with SSL.

The SSL protocol has gone through several versions. Below we will discuss only version 3, which is the most widely used version. SSL supports a variety of different options. These options include the presence or absence of compression, the cryptographic algorithms to be used, and some matters relating to export restrictions on cryptography. The last is mainly intended to make sure that serious cryptography is used only when both ends of the connection are in the United States. In other cases, keys are limited to 40 bits, which cryptographers regard as something of a joke. Netscape was forced to put in this restriction in order to get an export license from the U.S. Government.

SSL consists of two subprotocols, one for establishing a secure connection and one for using it. Let us start out by seeing how secure connections are established. The connection establishment subprotocol is shown in Fig. 8-50. It starts out with message 1 when Alice sends a request to Bob to establish a connection. The request specifies the SSL version Alice has and her preferences with respect to compression and cryptographic algorithms. It also contains a nonce, R_A, to be used later.

Now it is Bob's turn. In message 2, Bob makes a choice among the various algorithms that Alice can support and sends his own nonce, R_B. Then, in message 3, he sends a certificate containing his public key. If this certificate is not signed by some well-known authority, he also sends a chain of certificates that can be followed back to one. All browsers, including Alice's, come preloaded with about 100 public keys, so if Bob can establish a chain anchored to one of these, Alice will be able to verify Bob's public key. At this point, Bob may send some other messages (such as a request for Alice's public-key certificate). When Bob is done, he sends message 4 to tell Alice it is her turn.

Alice responds by choosing a random 384-bit **premaster key** and sending it to Bob encrypted with his public key (message 5). The actual session key used for encrypting data is derived from the premaster key combined with both nonces in a complex way. After message 5 has been received, both Alice and Bob are able to compute the session key. For this reason, Alice tells Bob to switch to the

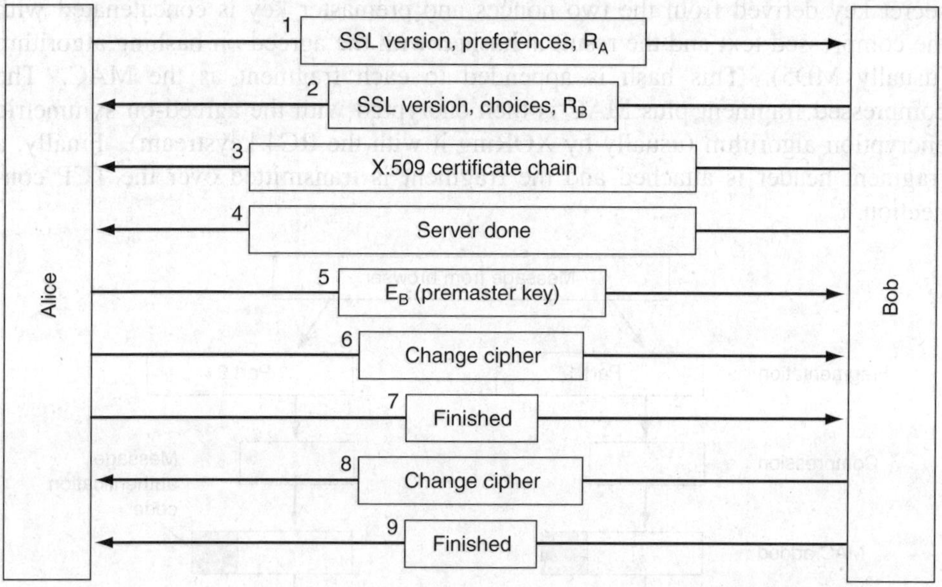

Figure 8-50. A simplified version of the SSL connection establishment subprotocol.

new cipher (message 6) and also that she is finished with the establishment subprotocol (message 7). Bob then acknowledges her (messages 8 and 9).

However, although Alice knows who Bob is, Bob does not know who Alice is (unless Alice has a public key and a corresponding certificate for it, an unlikely situation for an individual). Therefore, Bob's first message may well be a request for Alice to log in using a previously established login name and password. The login protocol, however, is outside the scope of SSL. Once it has been accomplished, by whatever means, data transport can begin.

As mentioned above, SSL supports multiple cryptographic algorithms. The strongest one uses triple DES with three separate keys for encryption and SHA-1 for message integrity. This combination is relatively slow, so it is mostly used for banking and other applications in which the highest security is required. For ordinary e-commerce applications, RC4 is used with a 128-bit key for encryption and MD5 is used for message authentication. RC4 takes the 128-bit key as a seed and expands it to a much larger number for internal use. Then it uses this internal number to generate a keystream. The keystream is XORed with the plaintext to provide a classical stream cipher, as we saw in Fig. 8-14. The export versions also use RC4 with 128-bit keys, but 88 of the bits are made public to make the cipher easy to break.

For actual transport, a second subprotocol is used, as shown in Fig. 8-51. Messages from the browser are first broken into units of up to 16 KB. If data compression is enabled, each unit is then separately compressed. After that, a secret key derived from the two nonces and premaster key is concatenated with the compressed text and the result is hashed with the agreed-on hashing algorithm (usually MD5). This hash is appended to each fragment as the MAC. The compressed fragment plus MAC is then encrypted with the agreed-on symmetric encryption algorithm (usually by XORing it with the RC4 keystream). Finally, a fragment header is attached and the fragment is transmitted over the TCP connection.

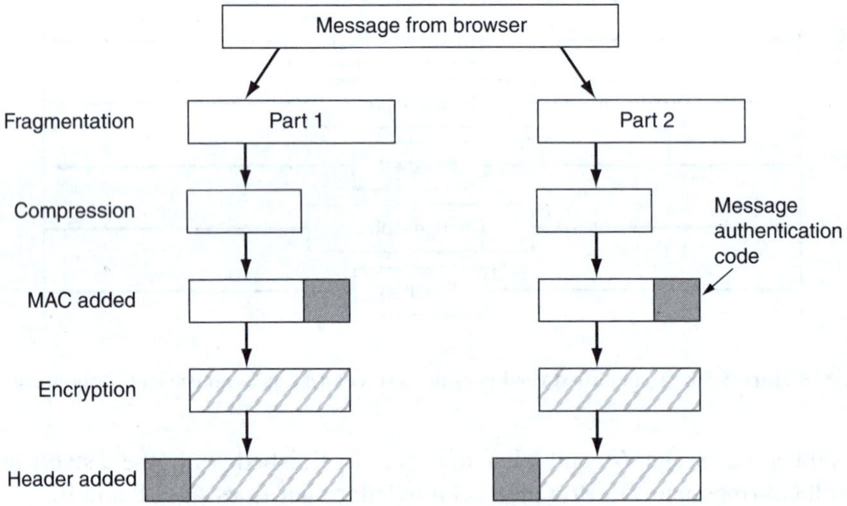

Figure 8-51. Data transmission using SSL.

A word of caution is in order, however. Since it has been shown that RC4 has some weak keys that can be easily cryptanalyzed, the security of SSL using RC4 is on shaky ground (Fluhrer et al., 2001). Browsers that allow the user to choose the cipher suite should be configured to use triple DES with 168-bit keys and SHA-1 all the time, even though this combination is slower than RC4 and MD5. Or, better yet, users should upgrade to browsers that support the successor to SSL that we describe shortly.

A problem with SSL is that the principals may not have certificates, and even if they do, they do not always verify that the keys being used match them.

In 1996, Netscape Communications Corp. turned SSL over to IETF for standardization. The result was **TLS (Transport Layer Security)**. It is described in RFC 5246.

TLS was built on SSL version 3. The changes made to SSL were relatively small, but just enough that SSL version 3 and TLS cannot interoperate. For example, the way the session key is derived from the premaster key and nonces was changed to make the key stronger (i.e., harder to cryptanalyze). Because of this incompatibility, most browsers implement both protocols, with TLS falling back to SSL during negotiation if necessary. This is referred to as SSL/TLS. The first TLS implementation appeared in 1999 with version 1.2 defined in August 2008. It includes support for stronger cipher suites (notably AES). SSL has remained strong in the marketplace although TLS will probably gradually replace it.

8.9.4 Mobile Code Security

Naming and connections are two areas of concern related to Web security. But there are more. In the early days, when Web pages were just static HTML files, they did not contain executable code. Now they often contain small programs, including Java applets, ActiveX controls, and JavaScripts. Downloading and executing such **mobile code** is obviously a massive security risk, so various methods have been devised to minimize it. We will now take a quick peek at some of the issues raised by mobile code and some approaches to dealing with it.

Java Applet Security

Java applets are small Java programs compiled to a stack-oriented machine language called **JVM** (**Java Virtual Machine**). They can be placed on a Web page for downloading along with the page. After the page is loaded, the applets are inserted into a JVM interpreter inside the browser, as illustrated in Fig. 8-52.

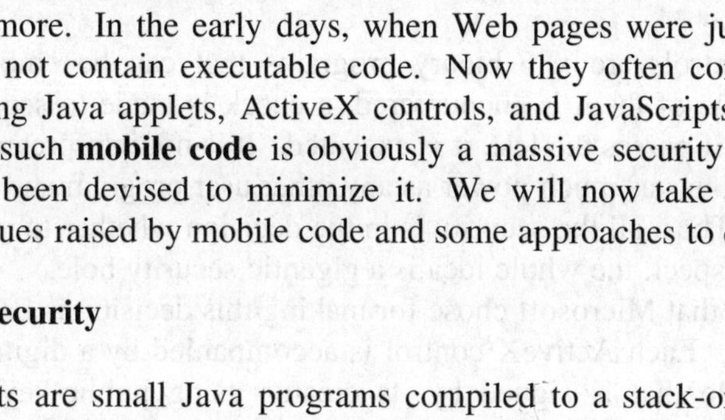

Figure 8-52. Applets can be interpreted by a Web browser.

The advantage of running interpreted code over compiled code is that every instruction is examined by the interpreter before being executed. This gives the interpreter the opportunity to check whether the instruction's address is valid. In addition, system calls are also caught and interpreted. How these calls are handled is a matter of the security policy. For example, if an applet is trusted (e.g., it came from the local disk), its system calls could be carried out without question. However, if an applet is not trusted (e.g., it came in over the Internet), it could be encapsulated in what is called a **sandbox** to restrict its behavior and trap its attempts to use system resources.

When an applet tries to use a system resource, its call is passed to a security monitor for approval. The monitor examines the call in light of the local security policy and then makes a decision to allow or reject it. In this way, it is possible to give applets access to some resources but not all. Unfortunately, the reality is that the security model works badly and that bugs in it crop up all the time.

ActiveX

ActiveX controls are x86 binary programs that can be embedded in Web pages. When one of them is encountered, a check is made to see if it should be executed, and it if passes the test, it is executed. It is not interpreted or sandboxed in any way, so it has as much power as any other user program and can potentially do great harm. Thus, all the security is in the decision whether to run the ActiveX control. In retrospect, the whole idea is a gigantic security hole.

The method that Microsoft chose for making this decision is based on the idea of **code signing**. Each ActiveX control is accompanied by a digital signature—a hash of the code that is signed by its creator using public-key cryptography. When an ActiveX control shows up, the browser first verifies the signature to make sure it has not been tampered with in transit. If the signature is correct, the browser then checks its internal tables to see if the program's creator is trusted or there is a chain of trust back to a trusted creator. If the creator is trusted, the program is executed; otherwise, it is not. The Microsoft system for verifying ActiveX controls is called **Authenticode**.

It is useful to contrast the Java and ActiveX approaches. With the Java approach, no attempt is made to determine who wrote the applet. Instead, a run-time interpreter makes sure it does not do things the machine owner has said applets may not do. In contrast, with code signing, there is no attempt to monitor the mobile code's run-time behavior. If it came from a trusted source and has not been modified in transit, it just runs. No attempt is made to see whether the code is malicious or not. If the original programmer *intended* the code to format the hard disk and then erase the flash ROM so the computer can never again be booted, and if the programmer has been certified as trusted, the code will be run and destroy the computer (unless ActiveX controls have been disabled in the browser).

Many people feel that trusting an unknown software company is scary. To demonstrate the problem, a programmer in Seattle formed a software company and got it certified as trustworthy, which is easy to do. He then wrote an ActiveX control that did a clean shutdown of the machine and distributed his ActiveX control widely. It shut down many machines, but they could just be rebooted, so no harm was done. He was just trying to expose the problem to the world. The official response was to revoke the certificate for this specific ActiveX control, which ended a short episode of acute embarrassment, but the underlying problem is still there for an evil programmer to exploit (Garfinkel with Spafford, 2002). Since there is no way to police the thousands of software companies that might write mobile code, the technique of code signing is a disaster waiting to happen.

JavaScript

JavaScript does not have any formal security model, but it does have a long history of leaky implementations. Each vendor handles security in a different way. For example, Netscape Navigator version 2 used something akin to the Java model, but by version 4 that had been abandoned for a code-signing model.

The fundamental problem is that letting foreign code run on your machine is asking for trouble. From a security standpoint, it is like inviting a burglar into your house and then trying to watch him carefully so he cannot escape from the kitchen into the living room. If something unexpected happens and you are distracted for a moment, bad things can happen. The tension here is that mobile code allows flashy graphics and fast interaction, and many Web site designers think that this is much more important than security, especially when it is somebody else's machine at risk.

Browser Extensions

As well as extending Web pages with code, there is a booming marketplace in **browser extensions**, **add-ons**, and **plug-ins**. They are computer programs that extend the functionality of Web browsers. Plug-ins often provide the capability to interpret or display a certain type of content, such as PDFs or Flash animations. Extensions and add-ons provide new browser features, such as better password management, or ways to interact with pages by, for example, marking them up or enabling easy shopping for related items.

Installing an extension, add-on, or plug-in is as simple as coming across something you want when browsing and following the link to install the program. This action will cause code to be downloaded across the Internet and installed into the browser. All of these programs are written to frameworks that differ depending on the browser that is being enhanced. However, to a first approximation, they become part of the trusted computing base of the browser. That is, if the code that is installed is buggy, the entire browser can be compromised.

There are two other obvious failure modes as well. The first is that the program may behave maliciously, for example, by gathering personal information and sending it to a remote server. For all the browser knows, the user installed the extension for precisely this purpose. The second problem is that plug-ins give the browser the ability to interpret new types of content. Often this content is a full blown programming language itself. PDF and Flash are good examples. When users view pages with PDF and Flash content, the plug-ins in their browser are executing the PDF and Flash code. That code had better be safe; often there are vulnerabilities that it can exploit. For all of these reasons, add-ons and plug-ins should only be installed as needed and only from trusted vendors.

Viruses

Viruses are another form of mobile code. Only, unlike the examples above, viruses are not invited in at all. The difference between a virus and ordinary mobile code is that viruses are written to reproduce themselves. When a virus arrives, either via a Web page, an email attachment, or some other way, it usually starts out by infecting executable programs on the disk. When one of these programs is run, control is transferred to the virus, which usually tries to spread itself to other machines, for example, by emailing copies of itself to everyone in the victim's email address book. Some viruses infect the boot sector of the hard disk, so when the machine is booted, the virus gets to run. Viruses have become a huge problem on the Internet and have caused billions of dollars' worth of damage. There is no obvious solution. Perhaps a whole new generation of operating systems based on secure microkernels and tight compartmentalization of users, processes, and resources might help.

8.10 SOCIAL ISSUES

The Internet and its security technology is an area where social issues, public policy, and technology meet head on, often with huge consequences. Below we will just briefly examine three areas: privacy, freedom of speech, and copyright. Needless to say, we can only scratch the surface. For additional reading, see Anderson (2008a), Garfinkel with Spafford (2002), and Schneier (2004). The Internet is also full of material. Just type words such as "privacy," "censorship," and "copyright" into any search engine. Also, see this book's Web site for some links. It is at *http://www.pearsonhighered.com/tanenbaum*.

8.10.1 Privacy

Do people have a right to privacy? Good question. The Fourth Amendment to the U.S. Constitution prohibits the government from searching people's houses, papers, and effects without good reason, and goes on to restrict the circumstances under which search warrants shall be issued. Thus, privacy has been on the public agenda for over 200 years, at least in the U.S.

What has changed in the past decade is both the ease with which governments can spy on their citizens and the ease with which the citizens can prevent such spying. In the 18th century, for the government to search a citizen's papers, it had to send out a policeman on a horse to go to the citizen's farm demanding to see certain documents. It was a cumbersome procedure. Nowadays, telephone companies and Internet providers readily provide wiretaps when presented with search warrants. It makes life much easier for the policeman and there is no danger of falling off a horse.

Cryptography changes all that. Anybody who goes to the trouble of downloading and installing PGP and who uses a well-guarded alien-strength key can be fairly sure that nobody in the known universe can read his email, search warrant or no search warrant. Governments well understand this and do not like it. Real privacy means it is much harder for them to spy on criminals of all stripes, but it is also much harder to spy on journalists and political opponents. Consequently, some governments restrict or forbid the use or export of cryptography. In France, for example, prior to 1999, all cryptography was banned unless the government was given the keys.

France was not alone. In April 1993, the U.S. Government announced its intention to make a hardware cryptoprocessor, the **clipper chip**, the standard for all networked communication. It was said that this would guarantee citizens' privacy. It also mentioned that the chip provided the government with the ability to decrypt all traffic via a scheme called **key escrow**, which allowed the government access to all the keys. However, the government promised only to snoop when it had a valid search warrant. Needless to say, a huge furor ensued, with privacy advocates denouncing the whole plan and law enforcement officials praising it. Eventually, the government backed down and dropped the idea.

A large amount of information about electronic privacy is available at the Electronic Frontier Foundation's Web site, *www.eff.org*.

Anonymous Remailers

PGP, SSL, and other technologies make it possible for two parties to establish secure, authenticated communication, free from third-party surveillance and interference. However, sometimes privacy is best served by *not* having authentication, in fact, by making communication anonymous. The anonymity may be desired for point-to-point messages, newsgroups, or both.

Let us consider some examples. First, political dissidents living under authoritarian regimes often wish to communicate anonymously to escape being jailed or killed. Second, wrongdoing in many corporate, educational, governmental, and other organizations has often been exposed by whistleblowers, who frequently prefer to remain anonymous to avoid retribution. Third, people with unpopular social, political, or religious views may wish to communicate with each other via email or newsgroups without exposing themselves. Fourth, people may wish to discuss alcoholism, mental illness, sexual harassment, child abuse, or being a member of a persecuted minority in a newsgroup without having to go public. Numerous other examples exist, of course.

Let us consider a specific example. In the 1990s, some critics of a nontraditional religious group posted their views to a USENET newsgroup via an **anonymous remailer**. This server allowed users to create pseudonyms and send email to the server, which then remailed or re-posted them using the pseudonyms, so no one could tell where the messages really came from. Some postings revealed what the religious group claimed were trade secrets and copyrighted documents. The religious group responded by telling local authorities that its trade secrets had been disclosed and its copyright infringed, both of which were crimes where the server was located. A court case followed and the server operator was compelled to turn over the mapping information that revealed the true identities of the persons who had made the postings. (Incidentally, this was not the first time that a religious group was unhappy when someone leaked its trade secrets: William Tyndale was burned at the stake in 1536 for translating the Bible into English).

A substantial segment of the Internet community was completely outraged by this breach of confidentiality. The conclusion that everyone drew is that an anonymous remailer that stores a mapping between real email addresses and pseudonyms (now called a type 1 remailer) is not worth much. This case stimulated various people into designing anonymous remailers that could withstand subpoena attacks.

These new remailers, often called **cypherpunk remailers**, work as follows. The user produces an email message, complete with RFC 822 headers (except *From:*, of course), encrypts it with the remailer's public key, and sends it to the remailer. There the outer RFC 822 headers are stripped off, the content is decrypted and the message is remailed. The remailer has no accounts and maintains no logs, so even if the server is later confiscated, it retains no trace of messages that have passed through it.

Many users who wish anonymity chain their requests through multiple anonymous remailers, as shown in Fig. 8-53. Here, Alice wants to send Bob a really, really, really anonymous Valentine's Day card, so she uses three remailers. She composes the message, M, and puts a header on it containing Bob's email address. Then she encrypts the whole thing with remailer 3's public key, E_3 (indicated by horizontal hatching). To this she prepends a header with remailer 3's email address in plaintext. This is the message shown between remailers 2 and 3 in the figure.

Then she encrypts this message with remailer 2's public key, E_2 (indicated by vertical hatching) and prepends a plaintext header containing remailer 2's email address. This message is shown between 1 and 2 in Fig. 8-53. Finally, she encrypts the entire message with remailer 1's public key, E_1, and prepends a plaintext header with remailer 1's email address. This is the message shown to the right of Alice in the figure and this is the message she actually transmits.

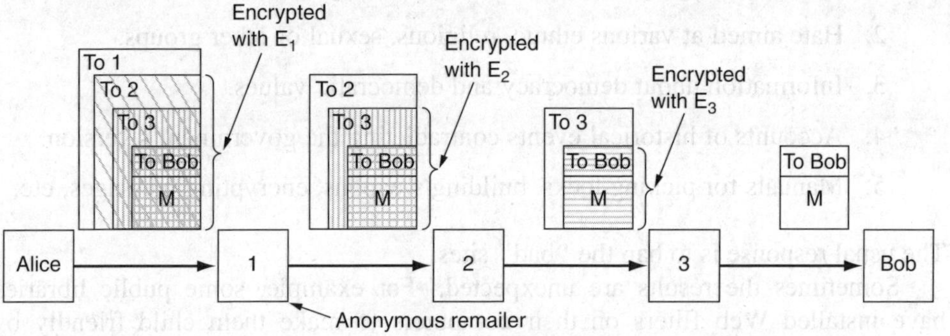

Figure 8-53. How Alice uses three remailers to send Bob a message.

When the message hits remailer 1, the outer header is stripped off. The body is decrypted and then emailed to remailer 2. Similar steps occur at the other two remailers.

Although it is extremely difficult for anyone to trace the final message back to Alice, many remailers take additional safety precautions. For example, they may hold messages for a random time, add or remove junk at the end of a message, and reorder messages, all to make it harder for anyone to tell which message output by a remailer corresponds to which input, in order to thwart traffic analysis. For a description of this kind of remailer, see Mazières and Kaashoek (1998).

Anonymity is not restricted to email. Services also exist that allow anonymous Web surfing using the same form of layered path in which one node only knows the next node in the chain. This method is called **onion routing** because each node peels off another layer of the onion to determine where to forward the packet next. The user configures his browser to use the anonymizer service as a proxy. Tor is a well-known example of such a system (Dingledine et al., 2004). Henceforth, all HTTP requests go through the anonymizer network, which requests the page and sends it back. The Web site sees an exit node of the anonymizer network as the source of the request, not the user. As long as the anonymizer network refrains from keeping a log, after the fact no one can determine who requested which page.

8.10.2 Freedom of Speech

Privacy relates to individuals wanting to restrict what other people can see about them. A second key social issue is freedom of speech, and its opposite, censorship, which is about governments wanting to restrict what individuals can read and publish. With the Web containing millions and millions of pages, it has become a censor's paradise. Depending on the nature and ideology of the regime, banned material may include Web sites containing any of the following:

1. Material inappropriate for children or teenagers.
2. Hate aimed at various ethnic, religious, sexual or other groups.
3. Information about democracy and democratic values.
4. Accounts of historical events contradicting the government's version.
5. Manuals for picking locks, building weapons, encrypting messages, etc.

The usual response is to ban the "bad" sites.

Sometimes the results are unexpected. For example, some public libraries have installed Web filters on their computers to make them child friendly by blocking pornography sites. The filters veto sites on their blacklists but also check pages for dirty words before displaying them. In one case in Loudoun County, Virginia, the filter blocked a patron's search for information on breast cancer because the filter saw the word "breast." The library patron sued Loudoun County. However, in Livermore, California, a parent sued the public library for *not* installing a filter after her 12-year-old son was caught viewing pornography there. What's a library to do?

It has escaped many people that the World Wide Web is a worldwide Web. It covers the whole world. Not all countries agree on what should be allowed on the Web. For example, in November 2000, a French court ordered Yahoo!, a California Corporation, to block French users from viewing auctions of Nazi memorabilia on Yahoo!'s Web site because owning such material violates French law. Yahoo! appealed to a U.S. court, which sided with it, but the issue of whose laws apply where is far from settled.

Just imagine. What would happen if some court in Utah instructed France to block Web sites dealing with wine because they do not comply with Utah's much stricter laws about alcohol? Suppose that China demanded that all Web sites dealing with democracy be banned as not in the interest of the State. Do Iranian laws on religion apply to more liberal Sweden? Can Saudi Arabia block Web sites dealing with women's rights? The whole issue is a veritable Pandora's box.

A relevant comment from John Gilmore is: "The net interprets censorship as damage and routes around it." For a concrete implementation, consider the **eternity service** (Anderson, 1996). Its goal is to make sure published information cannot be depublished or rewritten, as was common in the Soviet Union during Josef Stalin's reign. To use the eternity service, the user specifies how long the material is to be preserved, pays a fee proportional to its duration and size, and uploads it. Thereafter, no one can remove or edit it, not even the uploader.

How could such a service be implemented? The simplest model is to use a peer-to-peer system in which stored documents would be placed on dozens of participating servers, each of which gets a fraction of the fee, and thus an incentive to join the system. The servers should be spread over many legal jurisdictions for maximum resilience. Lists of 10 randomly selected servers would be stored securely in multiple places, so that if some were compromised, others would still exist. An authority bent on destroying the document could never be sure it had found all copies. The system could also be made self-repairing in the sense that if it became known that some copies had been destroyed, the remaining sites would attempt to find new repositories to replace them.

The eternity service was the first proposal for a censorship-resistant system. Since then, others have been proposed and, in some cases, implemented. Various new features have been added, such as encryption, anonymity, and fault tolerance. Often the files to be stored are broken up into multiple fragments, with each fragment stored on many servers. Some of these systems are Freenet (Clarke et al., 2002), PASIS (Wylie et al., 2000), and Publius (Waldman et al., 2000). Other work is reported by Serjantov (2002).

Increasingly, many countries are trying to regulate the export of intangibles, which often include Web sites, software, scientific papers, email, telephone helpdesks, and more. Even the U.K., which has a centuries-long tradition of freedom of speech, is now seriously considering highly restrictive laws, that would, for example, define technical discussions between a British professor and his foreign Ph.D. student, both located at the University of Cambridge, as regulated export needing a government license (Anderson, 2002). Needless to say, many people consider such a policy to be outrageous.

Steganography

In countries where censorship abounds, dissidents often try to use technology to evade it. Cryptography allows secret messages to be sent (although possibly not lawfully), but if the government thinks that Alice is a Bad Person, the mere fact that she is communicating with Bob may get him put in this category, too, as repressive governments understand the concept of transitive closure, even if they are short on mathematicians. Anonymous remailers can help, but if they are banned domestically and messages to foreign ones require a government export license, they cannot help much. But the Web can.

People who want to communicate secretly often try to hide the fact that any communication at all is taking place. The science of hiding messages is called **steganography**, from the Greek words for "covered writing." In fact, the ancient Greeks used it themselves. Herodotus wrote of a general who shaved the head of a messenger, tattooed a message on his scalp, and let the hair grow back before sending him off. Modern techniques are conceptually the same, only they have a higher bandwidth, lower latency, and do not require the services of a barber.

As a case in point, consider Fig. 8-54(a). This photograph, taken by one of the authors (AST) in Kenya, contains three zebras contemplating an acacia tree. Fig. 8-54(b) appears to be the same three zebras and acacia tree, but it has an extra added attraction. It contains the complete, unabridged text of five of

Shakespeare's plays embedded in it: *Hamlet*, *King Lear*, *Macbeth*, *The Merchant of Venice*, and *Julius Caesar*. Together, these plays total over 700 KB of text.

(a) (b)

Figure 8-54. (a) Three zebras and a tree. (b) Three zebras, a tree, and the complete text of five plays by William Shakespeare.

How does this steganographic channel work? The original color image is 1024×768 pixels. Each pixel consists of three 8-bit numbers, one each for the red, green, and blue intensity of that pixel. The pixel's color is formed by the linear superposition of the three colors. The steganographic encoding method uses the low-order bit of each RGB color value as a covert channel. Thus, each pixel has room for 3 bits of secret information, 1 in the red value, 1 in the green value, and 1 in the blue value. With an image of this size, up to $1024 \times 768 \times 3$ bits or 294,912 bytes of secret information can be stored in it.

The full text of the five plays and a short notice add up to 734,891 bytes. This text was first compressed to about 274 KB using a standard compression algorithm. The compressed output was then encrypted using IDEA and inserted into the low-order bits of each color value. As can be seen (or actually, cannot be seen), the existence of the information is completely invisible. It is equally invisible in the large, full-color version of the photo. The eye cannot easily distinguish 21-bit color from 24-bit color.

Viewing the two images in black and white with low resolution does not do justice to how powerful the technique is. To get a better feel for how steganography works, we have prepared a demonstration, including the full-color high-resolution image of Fig. 8-54(b) with the five plays embedded in it. The demonstration, including tools for inserting and extracting text into images, can be found at the book's Web site.

To use steganography for undetected communication, dissidents could create a Web site bursting with politically correct pictures, such as photographs of the Great Leader, local sports, movie, and television stars, etc. Of course, the pictures would be riddled with steganographic messages. If the messages were first compressed and then encrypted, even someone who suspected their presence would have immense difficulty in distinguishing the messages from white noise. Of course, the images should be fresh scans; copying a picture from the Internet and changing some of the bits is a dead giveaway.

Images are by no means the only carrier for steganographic messages. Audio files also work fine. Hidden information can be carried in a voice-over-IP call by manipulating the packet delays, distorting the audio, or even in the header fields of packets (Lubacz et al., 2010). Even the layout and ordering of tags in an HTML file can carry information.

Although we have examined steganography in the context of free speech, it has numerous other uses. One common use is for the owners of images to encode secret messages in them stating their ownership rights. If such an image is stolen and placed on a Web site, the lawful owner can reveal the steganographic message in court to prove whose image it is. This technique is called **watermarking**. It is discussed in Piva et al. (2002).

For more on steganography, see Wayner (2008).

8.10.3 Copyright

Privacy and censorship are just two areas where technology meets public policy. A third one is the copyright law. **Copyright** is granting to the creators of **IP** (**Intellectual Property**), including writers, poets, artists, composers, musicians, photographers, cinematographers, choreographers, and others, the exclusive right to exploit their IP for some period of time, typically the life of the author plus 50 years or 75 years in the case of corporate ownership. After the copyright of a work expires, it passes into the public domain and anyone can use or sell it as they wish. The Gutenberg Project (*www.promo.net/pg*), for example, has placed thousands of public-domain works (e.g., by Shakespeare, Twain, and Dickens) on the Web. In 1998, the U.S. Congress extended copyright in the U.S. by another 20 years at the request of Hollywood, which claimed that without an extension nobody would create anything any more. By way of contrast, patents last for only 20 years and people still invent things.

Copyright came to the forefront when Napster, a music-swapping service, had 50 million members. Although Napster did not actually copy any music, the courts held that its holding a central database of who had which song was contributory infringement, that is, it was helping other people infringe. While nobody seriously claims copyright is a bad idea (although many claim that the term is far too long, favoring big corporations over the public), the next generation of music sharing is already raising major ethical issues.

For example, consider a peer-to-peer network in which people share legal files (public-domain music, home videos, religious tracts that are not trade secrets, etc.) and perhaps a few that are copyrighted. Assume that everyone is online all the time via ADSL or cable. Each machine has an index of what is on the hard disk, plus a list of other members. Someone looking for a specific item can pick a random member and see if he has it. If not, he can check out all the members in that person's list, and all the members in their lists, and so on. Computers are very good at this kind of work. Having found the item, the requester just copies it.

If the work is copyrighted, chances are the requester is infringing (although for international transfers, the question of whose law applies matters because in some countries uploading is illegal but downloading is not). But what about the supplier? Is it a crime to keep music you have paid for and legally downloaded on your hard disk where others might find it? If you have an unlocked cabin in the country and an IP thief sneaks in carrying a notebook computer and scanner, scans a copyrighted book to the notebook's hard disk, and sneaks out, are *you* guilty of the crime of failing to protect someone else's copyright?

But there is more trouble brewing on the copyright front. There is a huge battle going on now between Hollywood and the computer industry. The former wants stringent protection of all intellectual property but the latter does not want to be Hollywood's policeman. In October 1998, Congress passed the **DMCA** (**Digital Millennium Copyright Act**), which makes it a crime to circumvent any protection mechanism present in a copyrighted work or to tell others how to circumvent it. Similar legislation has been enacted in the European Union. While virtually no one thinks that pirates in the Far East should be allowed to duplicate copyrighted works, many people think that the DMCA completely shifts the balance between the copyright owner's interest and the public interest.

A case in point: in September 2000, a music industry consortium charged with building an unbreakable system for selling music online sponsored a contest inviting people to try to break the system (which is precisely the right thing to do with any new security system). A team of security researchers from several universities, led by Prof. Edward Felten of Princeton, took up the challenge and broke the system. They then wrote a paper about their findings and submitted it to a USENIX security conference, where it underwent peer review and was accepted. Before the paper was to be presented, Felten received a letter from the Recording Industry Association of America that threatened to sue the authors under the DMCA if they published the paper.

Their response was to file a lawsuit asking a federal court to rule on whether publishing scientific papers on security research was still legal. Fearing a definitive court ruling against it, the industry withdrew its threat and the court dismissed Felten's suit. No doubt the industry was motivated by the weakness of its case: it had invited people to try to break its system and then threatened to sue some of them for accepting its own challenge. With the threat withdrawn, the paper was published (Craver et al., 2001). A new confrontation is virtually certain.

Meanwhile, pirated music and movies have fueled the massive growth of peer-to-peer networks. This has not pleased the copyright holders, who have used the DMCA to take action. There are now automated systems that search peer-to-peer networks and then fire off warnings to network operators and users who are suspected of infringing copyright. In the United States, these warnings are known as **DMCA takedown notices**. This search is an arms' race because it is hard to reliably catch copyright infringers. Even your printer might be mistaken for a culprit (Piatek et al., 2008).

A related issue is the extent of the **fair use doctrine**, which has been established by court rulings in various countries. This doctrine says that purchasers of a copyrighted work have certain limited rights to copy the work, including the right to quote parts of it for scientific purposes, use it as teaching material in schools or colleges, and in some cases make backup copies for personal use in case the original medium fails. The tests for what constitutes fair use include (1) whether the use is commercial, (2) what percentage of the whole is being copied, and (3) the effect of the copying on sales of the work. Since the DMCA and similar laws within the European Union prohibit circumvention of copy protection schemes, these laws also prohibit legal fair use. In effect, the DMCA takes away historical rights from users to give content sellers more power. A major showdown is inevitable.

Another development in the works that dwarfs even the DMCA in its shifting of the balance between copyright owners and users is **trusted computing** as advocated by industry bodies such as the **TCG** (**Trusted Computing Group**), led by companies like Intel and Microsoft. The idea is to provide support for carefully monitoring user behavior in various ways (e.g., playing pirated music) at a level below the operating system in order to prohibit unwanted behavior. This is accomplished with a small chip, called a **TPM** (**Trusted Platform Module**), which it is difficult to tamper with. Most PCs sold nowadays come equipped with a TPM. The system allows software written by content owners to manipulate PCs in ways that users cannot change. This raises the question of who is trusted in trusted computing. Certainly, it is not the user. Needless to say, the social consequences of this scheme are immense. It is nice that the industry is finally paying attention to security, but it is lamentable that the driver is enforcing copyright law rather than dealing with viruses, crackers, intruders, and other security issues that most people are concerned about.

In short, the lawmakers and lawyers will be busy balancing the economic interests of copyright owners with the public interest for years to come. Cyberspace is no different from meatspace: it constantly pits one group against another, resulting in power struggles, litigation, and (hopefully) eventually some kind of resolution, at least until some new disruptive technology comes along.

8.11 SUMMARY

Cryptography is a tool that can be used to keep information confidential and to ensure its integrity and authenticity. All modern cryptographic systems are based on Kerckhoff's principle of having a publicly known algorithm and a secret key. Many cryptographic algorithms use complex transformations involving substitutions and permutations to transform the plaintext into the ciphertext. However, if quantum cryptography can be made practical, the use of one-time pads may provide truly unbreakable cryptosystems.

Cryptographic algorithms can be divided into symmetric-key algorithms and public-key algorithms. Symmetric-key algorithms mangle the bits in a series of rounds parameterized by the key to turn the plaintext into the ciphertext. AES (Rijndael) and triple DES are the most popular symmetric-key algorithms at present. These algorithms can be used in electronic code book mode, cipher block chaining mode, stream cipher mode, counter mode, and others.

Public-key algorithms have the property that different keys are used for encryption and decryption and that the decryption key cannot be derived from the encryption key. These properties make it possible to publish the public key. The main public-key algorithm is RSA, which derives its strength from the fact that it is very difficult to factor large numbers.

Legal, commercial, and other documents need to be signed. Accordingly, various schemes have been devised for digital signatures, using both symmetric-key and public-key algorithms. Commonly, messages to be signed are hashed using algorithms such as SHA-1, and then the hashes are signed rather than the original messages.

Public-key management can be done using certificates, which are documents that bind a principal to a public key. Certificates are signed by a trusted authority or by someone (recursively) approved by a trusted authority. The root of the chain has to be obtained in advance, but browsers generally have many root certificates built into them.

These cryptographic tools can be used to secure network traffic. IPsec operates in the network layer, encrypting packet flows from host to host. Firewalls can screen traffic going into or out of an organization, often based on the protocol and port used. Virtual private networks can simulate an old leased-line network to provide certain desirable security properties. Finally, wireless networks need good security lest everyone read all the messages, and protocols like 802.11i provide it.

When two parties establish a session, they have to authenticate each other and, if need be, establish a shared session key. Various authentication protocols exist, including some that use a trusted third party, Diffie-Hellman, Kerberos, and public-key cryptography.

Email security can be achieved by a combination of the techniques we have studied in this chapter. PGP, for example, compresses messages, then encrypts them with a secret key and sends the secret key encrypted with the receiver's public key. In addition, it also hashes the message and sends the signed hash to verify message integrity.

Web security is also an important topic, starting with secure naming. DNSsec provides a way to prevent DNS spoofing. Most e-commerce Web sites use

SSL/TLS to establish secure, authenticated sessions between the client and server. Various techniques are used to deal with mobile code, especially sandboxing and code signing.

The Internet raises many issues in which technology interacts strongly with public policy. Some of the areas include privacy, freedom of speech, and copyright.

PROBLEMS

1. Break the following monoalphabetic substitution cipher. The plaintext, consisting of letters only, is an excerpt from a poem by Lewis Carroll.

mvyy bek mnyx n yvjjyr snijrh invq n muvjvdt je n idnvy
jurhri n fehfevir pyeir oruvdq ki ndq uri jhrnqvdt ed zb jnvy
Irr uem rntrhyb jur yeoijrhi ndq jur jkhjyri nyy nqlndpr
Jurb nhr mnvjvdt ed jur iuvdtyr mvyy bek pezr ndq wevd jur qndpr
mvyy bek, medj bek, mvyy bek, medj bek, mvyy bek wevd jur qndpr
mvyy bek, medj bek, mvyy bek, medj bek wevd jur qndpr

2. An affine cipher is a version of a monoalphabetic substitution cipher, in which the letters of an alphabet of size *m* are first map to the integers in the range 0 to *m*-1. Subsequently, the integer representing each plaintext letter is transformed to an integer representing the corresponding cipher text letter. The encryption function for a single letter is $E(x) = (ax + b) \bmod m$, where *m* is the size of the alphabet and *a* and *b* are the key of the cipher, and are co-prime. Trudy finds out that Bob generated a ciphertext using an affine cipher. She gets a copy of the ciphertext, and finds out that the most frequent letter of the ciphertext is 'R', and the second most frequent letter of the ciphertext is 'K'. Show how Trudy can break the code and retrieve the plaintext.

3. Break the following columnar transposition cipher. The plaintext is taken from a popular computer textbook, so "computer" is a probable word. The plaintext consists entirely of letters (no spaces). The ciphertext is broken up into blocks of five characters for readability.

aauan cvlre rurnn dltme aeepb ytust iceat npmey iicgo gorch srsoc
nntii imiha oofpa gsivt tpsit lbolr otoex

4. Alice used a transposition cipher to encrypt her messages to Bob. For added security, she encrypted the transposition cipher key using a substitution cipher, and kept the encrypted cipher in her computer. Trudy managed to get hold of the encrypted transposition cipher key. Can Trudy decipher Alice's messages to Bob? Why or why not?

5. Find a 77-bit one-time pad that generates the text "Hello World" from the ciphertext of Fig. 8-4.

6. You are a spy, and, conveniently, have a library with an infinite number of books at your disposal. Your operator also has such a library at his disposal. You have agreed to use *Lord of the Rings* as a one-time pad. Explain how you could use these assets to generate an infinitely long one-time pad.

7. Quantum cryptography requires having a photon gun that can, on demand, fire a single photon carrying 1 bit. In this problem, calculate how many photons a bit carries on a 250-Gbps fiber link. Assume that the length of a photon is equal to its wavelength, which for purposes of this problem, is 1 micron. The speed of light in fiber is 20 cm/nsec.

8. If Trudy captures and regenerates photons when quantum cryptography is in use, she will get some of them wrong and cause errors to appear in Bob's one-time pad. What fraction of Bob's one-time pad bits will be in error, on average?

9. A fundamental cryptographic principle states that all messages must have redundancy. But we also know that redundancy helps an intruder tell if a guessed key is correct. Consider two forms of redundancy. First, the initial n bits of the plaintext contain a known pattern. Second, the final n bits of the message contain a hash over the message. From a security point of view, are these two equivalent? Discuss your answer.

10. In Fig. 8-6, the P-boxes and S-boxes alternate. Although this arrangement is esthetically pleasing, is it any more secure than first having all the P-boxes and then all the S-boxes? Discuss your answer.

11. Design an attack on DES based on the knowledge that the plaintext consists exclusively of uppercase ASCII letters, plus space, comma, period, semicolon, carriage return, and line feed. Nothing is known about the plaintext parity bits.

12. In the text, we computed that a cipher-breaking machine with a million processors that could analyze a key in 1 nanosecond would take 10^{16} years to break the 128-bit version of AES. Let us compute how long it will take for this time to get down to 1 year, still along time, of course. To achieve this goal, we need computers to be 10^{16} times faster. If Moore's Law (computing power doubles every 18 months) continues to hold, how many years will it take before a parallel computer can get the cipher-breaking time down to a year?

13. AES supports a 256-bit key. How many keys does AES-256 have? See if you can find some number in physics, chemistry, or astronomy of about the same size. Use the Internet to help search for big numbers. Draw a conclusion from your research.

14. Suppose that a message has been encrypted using DES in counter mode. One bit of ciphertext in block C_i is accidentally transformed from a 0 to a 1 during transmission. How much plaintext will be garbled as a result?

15. Now consider ciphertext block chaining again. Instead of a single 0 bit being transformed into a 1 bit, an extra 0 bit is inserted into the ciphertext stream after block C_i. How much plaintext will be garbled as a result?

16. Compare cipher block chaining with cipher feedback mode in terms of the number of encryption operations needed to transmit a large file. Which one is more efficient and by how much?

17. Using the RSA public key cryptosystem, with $a = 1$, $b = 2 \cdots y = 25$, $z = 26$.
(a) If $p = 5$ and $q = 13$, list five legal values for d.

(b) If $p = 5$, $q = 31$, and $d = 37$, find e.
(c) Using $p = 3$, $q = 11$, and $d = 9$, find e and encrypt "hello".

18. Alice and Bob use RSA public key encryption in order to communicate between them. Trudy finds out that Alice and Bob shared one of the primes used to determine the number n of their public key pairs. In other words, Trudy found out that $n_a = p_a \times q$ and $n_b = p_b \times q$. How can Trudy use this information to break Alice's code?

19. Consider the use of counter mode, as shown in Fig. 8-15, but with $IV = 0$. Does the use of 0 threaten the security of the cipher in general?

20. In Fig. 8-20, we see how Alice can send Bob a signed message. If Trudy replaces P, Bob can detect it. But what happens if Trudy replaces both P and the signature?

21. Digital signatures have a potential weakness due to lazy users. In e-commerce transactions, a contract might be drawn up and the user asked to sign its SHA-1 hash. If the user does not actually verify that the contract and hash correspond, the user may inadvertently sign a different contract. Suppose that the Mafia try to exploit this weakness to make some money. They set up a pay Web site (e.g., pornography, gambling, etc.) and ask new customers for a credit card number. Then they send over a contract saying that the customer wishes to use their service and pay by credit card and ask the customer to sign it, knowing that most of them will just sign without verifying that the contract and hash agree. Show how the Mafia can buy diamonds from a legitimate Internet jeweler and charge them to unsuspecting customers.

22. A math class has 25 students. Assuming that all of the students were born in the first half of the year—between January 1st and June 30th— what is the probability that at least two students have the same birthday? Assume that nobody was born on leap day, so there are 181 possible birthdays.

23. After Ellen confessed to Marilyn about tricking her in the matter of Tom's tenure, Marilyn resolved to avoid this problem by dictating the contents of future messages into a dictating machine and having her new secretary just type them in. Marilyn then planned to examine the messages on her terminal after they had been typed in to make sure they contained her exact words. Can the new secretary still use the birthday attack to falsify a message, and if so, how? *Hint*: She can.

24. Consider the failed attempt of Alice to get Bob's public key in Fig. 8-23. Suppose that Bob and Alice already share a secret key, but Alice still wants Bob's public key. Is there now a way to get it securely? If so, how?

25. Alice wants to communicate with Bob, using public-key cryptography. She establishes a connection to someone she hopes is Bob. She asks him for his public key and he sends it to her in plaintext along with an X.509 certificate signed by the root CA. Alice already has the public key of the root CA. What steps does Alice carry out to verify that she is talking to Bob? Assume that Bob does not care who he is talking to (e.g., Bob is some kind of public service).

26. Suppose that a system uses PKI based on a tree-structured hierarchy of CAs. Alice wants to communicate with Bob, and receives a certificate from Bob signed by a CA X after establishing a communication channel with Bob. Suppose Alice has never heard of X. What steps does Alice take to verify that she is talking to Bob?

27. Can IPsec using AH be used in transport mode if one of the machines is behind a NAT box? Explain your answer.

28. Alice wants to send a message to Bob using SHA-1 hashes. She consults with you regarding the appropriate signature algorithm to be used. What would you suggest?

29. Give one reason why a firewall might be configured to inspect incoming traffic. Give one reason why it might be configured to inspect outgoing traffic. Do you think the inspections are likely to be successful?

30. Suppose an organization uses VPN to securely connect its sites over the Internet. Jim, a user in the organization, uses the VPN to communicate with his boss, Mary. Describe one type of communication between Jim and Mary which would not require use of encryption or other security mechanism, and another type of communication which would require encryption or other security mechanisms. Explain your answer.

31. Change one message in the protocol of Fig. 8-34 in a minor way to make it resistant to the reflection attack. Explain why your change works.

32. The Diffie-Hellman key exchange is being used to establish a secret key between Alice and Bob. Alice sends Bob (227, 5, 82). Bob responds with (125). Alice's secret number, x, is 12, and Bob's secret number, y, is 3. Show how Alice and Bob compute the secret key.

33. Two users can establish a shared secret key using the Diffie-Hellman algorithm, even if they have never met, share no secrets, and have no certificates
(a) Explain how this algorithm is susceptible to a man-in-the-middle attack.
(b) How would this susceptibility change if n or g were secret?

34. In the protocol of Fig. 8-39, why is A sent in plaintext along with the encrypted session key?

35. In the Needham-Schroeder protocol, Alice generates two challenges, R_A and R_{A2}. This seems like overkill. Would one not have done the job?

36. Suppose an organization uses Kerberos for authentication. In terms of security and service availability, what is the effect if AS or TGS goes down?

37. Alice is using the public-key authentication protocol of Fig. 8-43 to authenticate communication with Bob. However, when sending message 7, Alice forgot to encrypt R_B. Trudy now knows the value of R_B. Do Alice and Bob need to repeat the authentication procedure with new parameters in order to ensure secure communication? Explain your answer.

38. In the public-key authentication protocol of Fig. 8-43, in message 7, R_B is encrypted with K_S. Is this encryption necessary, or would it have been adequate to send it back in plaintext? Explain your answer.

39. Point-of-sale terminals that use magnetic-stripe cards and PIN codes have a fatal flaw: a malicious merchant can modify his card reader to log all the information on the card and the PIN code in order to post additional (fake) transactions in the future. Next generation terminals will use cards with a complete CPU, keyboard, and tiny display on the card. Devise a protocol for this system that malicious merchants cannot break.

40. Is it possible to multicast a PGP message? What restrictions would apply?

41. Assuming that everyone on the Internet used PGP, could a PGP message be sent to an arbitrary Internet address and be decoded correctly by all concerned? Discuss your answer.

42. The attack shown in Fig. 8-47 leaves out one step. The step is not needed for the spoof to work, but including it might reduce potential suspicion after the fact. What is the missing step?

43. The SSL data transport protocol involves two nonces as well as a premaster key. What value, if any, does using the nonces have?

44. Consider an image of 2048×512 pixels. You want to encrypt a file sized 2.5 MB. What fraction of the file can you encrypt in this image? What fraction would you be able to encrypt if you compressed the file to a quarter of its original size? Show your calculations.

45. The image of Fig. 8-54(b) contains the ASCII text of five plays by Shakespeare. Would it be possible to hide music among the zebras instead of text? If so, how would it work and how much could you hide in this picture? If not, why not?

46. You are given a text file of size 60 MB, which is to be encrypted using steganography in the low-order bits of each color in an image file. What size image would be required in order to encrypt the entire file? What size would be needed if the file were first compressed to a third of its original size? Give your answer in pixels, and show your calculations. Assume that the images have an aspect ratio of 3:2, for example, 3000×2000 pixels.

47. Alice was a heavy user of a type 1 anonymous remailer. She would post many messages to her favorite newsgroup, *alt.fanclub.alice*, and everyone would know they all came from Alice because they all bore the same pseudonym. Assuming that the remailer worked correctly, Trudy could not impersonate Alice. After type 1 remailers were all shut down, Alice switched to a cypherpunk remailer and started a new thread in her newsgroup. Devise a way for her to prevent Trudy from posting new messages to the newsgroup, impersonating Alice.

48. Search the Internet for an interesting case involving privacy and write a one-page report on it.

49. Search the Internet for some court case involving copyright versus fair use and write a 1-page report summarizing your findings.

50. Write a program that encrypts its input by XORing it with a keystream. Find or write as good a random number generator as you can to generate the keystream. The program should act as a filter, taking plaintext on standard input and producing ciphertext on standard output (and vice versa). The program should take one parameter, the key that seeds the random number generator.

51. Write a procedure that computes the SHA-1 hash of a block of data. The procedure should have two parameters: a pointer to the input buffer and a pointer to a 20-byte output buffer. To see the exact specification of SHA-1, search the Internet for FIPS 180-1, which is the full specification.

52. Write a function that accepts a stream of ASCII characters and encrypts this input using a substitution cipher with the Cipher Block Chaining mode. The block size should be 8 bytes. The program should take plaintext from the standard input and print the ciphertext on the standard output. For this problem, you are allowed to select any reasonable system to determine that the end of the input is reached, and/or when padding should be applied to complete the block. You may select any output format, as long as it is unambiguous. The program should receive two parameters:

    1. A pointer to the initializing vector; and
    2. A number, k, representing the substitution cipher shift, such that each ASCII character would be encrypted by the kth character ahead of it in the alphabet.

    For example, if $x = 3$, then A is encoded by D, B is encoded by E etc. Make reasonable assumptions with respect to reaching the last character in the ASCII set. Make sure to document clearly in your code any assumptions you make about the input and encryption algorithm.

53. The purpose of this problem is to give you a better understanding as to the mechanisms of RSA. Write a function that receives as its parameters primes p and q, calculates public and private RSA keys using these parameters, and outputs n, z, d and e as printouts to the standard output. The function should also accept a stream of ASCII characters and encrypt this input using the calculated RSA keys. The program should take plaintext from the standard input and print the ciphertext to the standard output. The encryption should be carried out character-wise, that is, take each character in the input and encrypt it independently of other characters in the input. For this problem, you are allowed to select any reasonable system to determine that the end of the input is reached. You may select any output format, as long as it is unambiguous. Make sure to document clearly in your code any assumptions you make about the input and encryption algorithm.

9

READING LIST AND BIBLIOGRAPHY

We have now finished our study of computer networks, but this is only the beginning. Many interesting topics have not been treated in as much detail as they deserve, and others have been omitted altogether for lack of space. In this chapter, we provide some suggestions for further reading and a bibliography, for the benefit of readers who wish to continue their study of computer networks.

9.1 SUGGESTIONS FOR FURTHER READING

There is an extensive literature on all aspects of computer networks. Two journals that publish papers in this area are *IEEE/ACM Transactions on Networking* and *IEEE Journal on Selected Areas in Communications*.

The periodicals of the ACM Special Interest Groups on Data Communications (SIGCOMM) and Mobility of Systems, Users, Data, and Computing (SIGMOBILE) publish many papers of interest, especially on emerging topics. They are *Computer Communication Review* and *Mobile Computing and Communications Review*.

IEEE also publishes three magazines—*IEEE Internet Computing*, *IEEE Network Magazine*, and *IEEE Communications Magazine*—that contain surveys, tutorials, and case studies on networking. The first two emphasize architecture, standards, and software, and the last tends toward communications technology (fiber optics, satellites, and so on).

There are a number of annual or biannual conferences that attract numerous papers on networks. In particular, look for the *SIGCOMM* conference, *NSDI* (Symposium on Networked Systems Design and Implementation), *MobiSys* (Conference on Mobile Systems, Applications, and Services), *SOSP* (Symposium on Operating Systems Principles) and *OSDI* (Symposium on Operating Systems Design and Implementation).

Below we list some suggestions for supplementary reading, keyed to the chapters of this book. Many of the suggestions are books of chapters in books, with some tutorials and surveys. Full references are in Sec. 9.2.

9.1.1 Introduction and General Works

Comer, *The Internet Book*, 4th ed.

Anyone looking for an easygoing introduction to the Internet should look here. Comer describes the history, growth, technology, protocols, and services of the Internet in terms that novices can understand, but so much material is covered that the book is also of interest to more technical readers.

Computer Communication Review, 25th Anniversary Issue, Jan. 1995

For a firsthand look at how the Internet developed, this special issue collects important papers up to 1995. Included are papers that show the development of TCP, multicast, the DNS, Ethernet, and the overall architecture.

Crovella and Krishnamurthy, *Internet Measurement*

How do we know how well the Internet works anyway? This question is not trivial to answer because no one is in charge of the Internet. This book describes the techniques that have been developed to measure the operation of the Internet, from network infrastructure to applications.

IEEE Internet Computing, Jan.–Feb. 2000

The first issue of *IEEE Internet Computing* in the new millennium did exactly what you would expect: it asked the people who helped create the Internet in the previous millennium to speculate on where it is going in the next one. The experts are Paul Baran, Lawrence Roberts, Leonard Kleinrock, Stephen Crocker, Danny Cohen, Bob Metcalfe, Bill Gates, Bill Joy, and others. See how well their predictions have fared over a decade later.

Kipnis, "Beating the System: Abuses of the Standards Adoption Process"

Standards committees try to be fair and vendor neutral in their work, but unfortunately there are companies that try to abuse the system. For example, it has happened repeatedly that a company helps develop a standard and then after it is approved, announces that the standard is based on a patent it owns and which it will license to companies that it likes and not to companies that it does not like, at prices that it alone determines. For a look at the dark side of standardization, this article is an excellent start.

Hafner and Lyon, *Where Wizards Stay Up Late*
Naughton, *A Brief History of the Future*

Who invented the Internet, anyway? Many people have claimed credit. And rightly so, since many people had a hand in it, in different ways. There was Paul Baran, who wrote a report describing packet switching, there were the people at various universities who designed the ARPANET architecture, there were the people at BBN who programmed the first IMPs, there were Bob Kahn and Vint Cerf who invented TCP/IP, and so on. These books tell the story of the Internet, at least up to 2000, replete with many anecdotes.

9.1.2 The Physical Layer

Bellamy, *Digital Telephony*, 3rd ed.

For a look back at that other important network, the telephone network, this authoritative book contains everything you ever wanted to know and more. Particularly interesting are the chapters on transmission and multiplexing, digital switching, fiber optics, mobile telephony, and DSL.

Hu and Li, "Satellite-Based Internet: A Tutorial"

Internet access via satellite is different from using terrestrial lines. Not only is there the issue of delay, but routing and switching are also different. In this paper, the authors examine the issues related to using satellites for Internet access.

Joel, "Telecommunications and the IEEE Communications Society"

For a compact but surprisingly comprehensive history of telecommunications, starting with the telegraph and ending with 802.11, this article is the place to look. It also covers radio, telephones, analog and digital switching, submarine cables, digital transmission, television broadcasting, satellites, cable TV, optical communications, mobile phones, packet switching, the ARPANET, and the Internet.

Palais, *Fiber Optic Communication*, 5th ed.

Books on fiber optic technology tend to be aimed at the specialist, but this one is more accessible than most. It covers waveguides, light sources, light detectors, couplers, modulation, noise, and many other topics.

Su, *The UMTS Air Interface in RF Engineering*

This book provides a detailed overview of one of the main 3G cellular systems. It is focused on the air interface, or wireless protocols that are used between mobiles and the network infrastructure.

Want, *RFID Explained*

Want's book is an easy-to-read primer on how the unusual technology of the RFID physical layer works. It covers all aspects of RFID, including its potential applications. Some real-world examples of RFID deployments and the experience gained from them is also convered.

9.1.3 The Data Link Layer

Kasim, *Delivering Carrier Ethernet*

Nowadays, Ethernet is not only a local-area technology. The new fashion is to use Ethernet as a long-distance link for carrier-grade Ethernet. This book brings together essays to cover the topic in depth.

Lin and Costello, *Error Control Coding*, 2nd ed.

Codes to detect and correct errors are central to reliable computer networks. This popular textbook explains some of the most important codes, from simple linear Hamming codes to more complex low-density parity check codes. It tries to do so with the minimum algebra necessary, but that is still a lot.

Stallings, *Data and Computer Communications*, 9th ed.

Part two covers digital data transmission and a variety of links, including error detection, error control with retransmissions, and flow control.

9.1.4 The Medium Access Control Sublayer

Andrews et al., *Fundamentals of WiMAX*

This comprehensive book gives a definitive treatment of WiMAX technology, from the idea of broadband wireless, to the wireless techniques using OFDM and multiple antennas, through the multi-access system. Its tutorial style gives about the most accessible treatment you will find for this heavy material.

Gast, *802.11 Wireless Networks*, 2nd ed.

For a readable introduction to the technology and protocols of 802.11, this is a good place to start. It begins with the MAC sublayer, then introduces material on the different physical layers and also security. However, the second edition is not new enough to have much to say about 802.11n.

Perlman, *Interconnections*, 2nd ed.

For an authoritative but entertaining treatment of bridges, routers, and routing in general, Perlman's book is the place to look. The author designed the algorithms used in the IEEE 802 spanning tree bridge and she is one of the world's leading authorities on various aspects of networking.

9.1.5 The Network Layer

Comer, *Internetworking with TCP/IP*, Vol. 1, 5th ed.

Comer has written the definitive work on the TCP/IP protocol suite, now in its fifth edition. Most of the first half deals with IP and related protocols in the network layer. The other chapters deal primarily with the higher layers and are also worth reading.

Grayson et al., *IP Design for Mobile Networks*

Traditional telephone networks and the Internet are on a collision course, with mobile phone networks being implemented with IP on the inside. This book tells how to design a network using the IP protocols that supports mobile telephone service.

Huitema, *Routing in the Internet*, 2nd ed.

If you want to gain a deep understanding of routing protocols, this is a very good book. Both pronounceable algorithms (e.g., RIP, and CIDR) and unpronounceable algorithms (e.g., OSPF, IGRP, and BGP) are treated in great detail. Newer developments are not covered since this is an older book, but what is covered is explained very well.

Koodli and Perkins, *Mobile Inter-networking with IPv6*

Two important network layer developments are presented in one volume: IPv6 and Mobile IP. Both topics are covered well, and Perkins was one of the driving forces behind Mobile IP.

Nucci and Papagiannaki, *Design, Measurement and Management of Large-Scale IP Networks*

We talked a great deal about how networks work, but not how you would design, deploy and manage one if you were an ISP. This book fills that gap, looking at modern methods for traffic engineering and how ISPs provide services using networks.

Perlman, *Interconnections*, 2nd ed.

In Chaps. 12 through 15, Perlman describes many of the issues involved in unicast and multicast routing algorithm design, both for wide area networks and networks of LANs. But by far, the best part of the book is Chap. 18, in which the author distills her many years of experience with network protocols into an informative and fun chapter. It is required reading for protocol designers.

Stevens, *TCP/IP Illustrated*, Vol. 1

Chapters 3–10 provide a comprehensive treatment of IP and related protocols (ARP, RARP, and ICMP), illustrated by examples.

Varghese, *Network Algorithmics*

We have spent much time talking about how routers and other network elements interact with each other. This book is different: it is about how routers are actually designed to forward packets at prodigious speeds. For the inside scoop on that and related questions, this is the book to read. The author is an authority on clever algorithms that are used in practice to implement high-speed network elements in software and hardware.

9.1.6 The Transport Layer

Comer, *Internetworking with TCP/IP*, Vol. 1, 5th ed.

As mentioned above, Comer has written the definitive work on the TCP/IP protocol suite. The second half of the book is about UDP and TCP.

Farrell and Cahill, *Delay- and Disruption-Tolerant Networking*

This short book is the one to read for a deeper look at the architecture, protocols, and applications of "challenged networks" that must operate under harsh conditions of connectivity. The authors have participated in the development of DTNs in the IETF DTN Research Group.

Stevens, *TCP/IP Illustrated*, Vol. 1

Chapters 17–24 provide a comprehensive treatment of TCP illustrated by examples.

9.1.7 The Application Layer

Berners-Lee et al., "The World Wide Web"

Take a trip back in time for a perspective on the Web and where it is going by the person who invented it and some of his colleagues at CERN. The article focuses on the Web architecture, URLs, HTTP, and HTML, as well as future directions, and compares it to other distributed information systems.

Held, *A Practical Guide to Content Delivery Networks*, 2nd ed.

This book gives a down-to-earth exposition of how CDNs work, emphasizing the practical considerations in designing and operating a CDN that performs well.

Hunter et al., *Beginning XML*, 4th ed.

There are many, many books on HTML, XML and Web services. This 1000-page book covers most of what you are likely to want to know. It explains not only how to write XML and XHTML, but also how to develop Web services that produce and manipulate XML using Ajax, SOAP, and other techniques that are commonly used in practice.

Krishnamurthy and Rexford, *Web Protocols and Practice*

It would be hard to find a more comprehensive book about all aspects of the Web than this one. It covers clients, servers, proxies, and caching, as you might expect. But there are also chapters on Web traffic and measurements as well as chapters on current research and improving the Web.

Simpson, *Video Over IP*, 2nd ed.

The author takes a broad look at how IP technology can be used to move video across networks, both on the Internet and in private networks designed to carry video. Interestingly, this book is oriented for the video professional learning about networking, rather than the other way around.

Wittenburg, *Understanding Voice Over IP Technology*

This book covers how voice over IP works, from carrying audio data with the IP protocols and quality-of-service issues, through to the SIP and H.323 suite of protocols. It is necessarily detailed given the material, but accessible and broken up into digestible units.

9.1.8 Network Security

Anderson, *Security Engineering*, 2nd. ed.

This book presents a wonderful mix of security techniques couched in an understanding of how people use (and misuse) them. It is more technical than *Secrets and Lies*, but less technical than *Network Security* (see below). After an introduction to the basic security techniques, entire chapters are devoted to various applications, including banking, nuclear command and control, security printing, biometrics, physical security, electronic warfare, telecom security, e-commerce, and copyright protection.

Ferguson et al., *Cryptography Engineering*

Many books tell you how the popular cryptographic algorithms work. This book tells you how to use cryptography—why cryptographic protocols are designed the way they are and how to put them together into a system that will meet your security goals. It is a fairly compact book that is essential reading for anyone designing systems that depend on cryptography.

Fridrich, *Steganography in Digital Media*

Steganography goes back to ancient Greece, where the wax was melted off blank tablets so secret messages could be applied to the underlying wood before the wax was reapplied. Nowadays, videos, audio, and other content on the Internet provide different carriers for secret messages. Various modern techniques for hiding and finding information in images are discussed here.

Kaufman et al., *Network Security*, 2nd ed.

This authoritative and witty book is the first place to look for more technical information on network security algorithms and protocols. Secret and public key algorithms and protocols, message hashes, authentication, Kerberos, PKI, IPsec, SSL/TLS, and email security are all explained carefully and at considerable length, with many examples. Chapter 26, on security folklore, is a real gem. In security, the devil is in the details. Anyone planning to design a security system that will actually be used will learn a lot from the real-world advice in this chapter.

Schneier, *Secrets and Lies*

If you read *Cryptography Engineering* from cover to cover, you will know everything there is to know about cryptographic algorithms. If you then read *Secrets and Lies* cover to cover (which can be done in a lot less time), you will learn that cryptographic algorithms are not the whole story. Most security weaknesses are not due to faulty algorithms or even keys that are too short, but to flaws in the security environment. For a nontechnical and fascinating discussion of computer security in the broadest sense, this book is a very good read.

Skoudis and Liston, *Counter Hack Reloaded*, 2nd ed.

The best way to stop a hacker is to think like a hacker. This book shows how hackers see a network, and argues that security should be a function of the entire network's design, not an afterthought based on one specific technology. It covers almost all common attacks, including the "social engineering" types that take advantage of users who are not always familiar with computer security measures.

9.2 ALPHABETICAL BIBLIOGRAPHY

ABRAMSON, N.: "Internet Access Using VSATs," *IEEE Commun. Magazine*, vol. 38, pp. 60–68, July 2000.

AHMADI, S.: "An Overview of Next-Generation Mobile WiMAX Technology," *IEEE Commun. Magazine*, vol. 47, pp. 84–88, June 2009.

ALLMAN, M., and PAXSON, V.: "On Estimating End-to-End Network Path Properties," *Proc. SIGCOMM '99 Conf.*, ACM, pp. 263–274, 1999.

ANDERSON, C.: *The Long Tail: Why the Future of Business is Selling Less of More*, rev. upd. ed., New York: Hyperion, 2008a.

ANDERSON, R.J.: *Security Engineering: A Guide to Building Dependable Distributed Systems*, 2nd ed., New York: John Wiley & Sons, 2008b.

ANDERSON, R.J.: "Free Speech Online and Offline," *IEEE Computer*, vol. 25, pp. 28–30, June 2002.

ANDERSON, R.J.: "The Eternity Service," *Proc. Pragocrypt Conf.*, CTU Publishing House, pp. 242–252, 1996.

ANDREWS, J., GHOSH, A., and MUHAMED, R.: *Fundamentals of WiMAX: Understanding Broadband Wireless Networking*, Upper Saddle River, NJ: Pearson Education, 2007.

ASTELY, D., DAHLMAN, E., FURUSKAR, A., JADING, Y., LINDSTROM, M., and PARKVALL, S.: "LTE: The Evolution of Mobile Broadband," *IEEE Commun. Magazine*, vol. 47, pp. 44–51, Apr. 2009.

BALLARDIE, T., FRANCIS, P., and CROWCROFT, J.: "Core Based Trees (CBT)," *Proc. SIGCOMM '93 Conf.*, ACM, pp. 85–95, 1993.

BARAN, P.: "On Distributed Communications: I. Introduction to Distributed Communication Networks," *Memorandum RM-420-PR*, Rand Corporation, Aug. 1964.

BELLAMY, J.: *Digital Telephony*, 3rd ed., New York: John Wiley & Sons, 2000.

BELLMAN, R.E.: *Dynamic Programming*, Princeton, NJ: Princeton University Press, 1957.

BELLOVIN, S.: "The Security Flag in the IPv4 Header," RFC 3514, Apr. 2003.

BELSNES, D.: "Flow Control in the Packet Switching Networks," *Communications Networks*, Uxbridge, England: Online, pp. 349–361, 1975.

BENNET, C.H., and BRASSARD, G.: "Quantum Cryptography: Public Key Distribution and Coin Tossing," *Int'l Conf. on Computer Systems and Signal Processing*, pp. 175–179, 1984.

BERESFORD, A., and STAJANO, F.: "Location Privacy in Pervasive Computing," *IEEE Pervasive Computing*, vol. 2, pp. 46–55, Jan. 2003.

BERGHEL, H.L.: "Cyber Privacy in the New Millennium," *IEEE Computer*, vol. 34, pp. 132–134, Jan. 2001.

BERNERS-LEE, T., CAILLIAU, A., LOUTONEN, A., NIELSEN, H.F., and SECRET, A.: "The World Wide Web," *Commun. of the ACM*, vol. 37, pp. 76–82, Aug. 1994.

BERTSEKAS, D., and GALLAGER, R.: *Data Networks*, 2nd ed., Englewood Cliffs, NJ: Prentice Hall, 1992.

BHATTI, S.N., and CROWCROFT, J.: "QoS Sensitive Flows: Issues in IP Packet Handling," *IEEE Internet Computing*, vol. 4, pp. 48–57, July–Aug. 2000.

BIHAM, E., and SHAMIR, A.: "Differential Fault Analysis of Secret Key Cryptosystems," *Proc. 17th Ann. Int'l Cryptology Conf.*, Berlin: Springer-Verlag LNCS 1294, pp. 513–525, 1997.

BIRD, R., GOPAL, I., HERZBERG, A., JANSON, P.A., KUTTEN, S., MOLVA, R., and YUNG, M.: "Systematic Design of a Family of Attack-Resistant Authentication Protocols," *IEEE J. on Selected Areas in Commun.*, vol. 11, pp. 679–693, June 1993.

BIRRELL, A.D., and NELSON, B.J.: "Implementing Remote Procedure Calls," *ACM Trans. on Computer Systems*, vol. 2, pp. 39–59, Feb. 1984.

BIRYUKOV, A., SHAMIR, A., and WAGNER, D.: "Real Time Cryptanalysis of A5/1 on a PC," *Proc. Seventh Int'l Workshop on Fast Software Encryption*, Berlin: Springer-Verlag LNCS 1978, pp. 1–8, 2000.

BLAZE, M., and BELLOVIN, S.: "Tapping on My Network Door," *Commun. of the ACM*, vol. 43, p. 136, Oct. 2000.

BOGGS, D., MOGUL, J., and KENT, C.: "Measured Capacity of an Ethernet: Myths and Reality," *Proc. SIGCOMM '88 Conf.*, ACM, pp. 222–234, 1988.

BORISOV, N., GOLDBERG, I., and WAGNER, D.: "Intercepting Mobile Communications: The Insecurity of 802.11," *Seventh Int'l Conf. on Mobile Computing and Networking*, ACM, pp. 180–188, 2001.

BRADEN, R.: "Requirements for Internet Hosts—Communication Layers," RFC 1122, Oct. 1989.

BRADEN, R., BORMAN, D., and PARTRIDGE, C.: "Computing the Internet Checksum," RFC 1071, Sept. 1988.

BRANDENBURG, K.: "MP3 and AAC Explained," *Proc. 17th Intl. Conf.: High-Quality Audio Coding*, Audio Engineering Society, pp. 99–110, Aug. 1999.

BRAY, T., PAOLI, J., SPERBERG-MCQUEEN, C., MALER, E., YERGEAU, F., and COWAN, J.: "Extensible Markup Language (XML) 1.1 (Second Edition)," W3C Recommendation, Sept. 2006.

BRESLAU, L., CAO, P., FAN, L., PHILLIPS, G., and SHENKER, S.: "Web Caching and Zipf-like Distributions: Evidence and Implications," *Proc. INFOCOM Conf.*, IEEE, pp. 126–134, 1999.

BURLEIGH, S., HOOKE, A., TORGERSON, L., FALL, K., CERF, V., DURST, B., SCOTT, K., and WEISS, H.: "Delay-Tolerant Networking: An Approach to Interplanetary Internet," *IEEE Commun. Magazine*, vol. 41, pp. 128–136, June 2003.

BURNETT, S., and PAINE, S.: *RSA Security's Official Guide to Cryptography*, Berkeley, CA: Osborne/McGraw-Hill, 2001.

BUSH, V.: "As We May Think," *Atlantic Monthly*, vol. 176, pp. 101–108, July 1945.

CAPETANAKIS, J.I.: "Tree Algorithms for Packet Broadcast Channels," *IEEE Trans. on Information Theory*, vol. IT–5, pp. 505–515, Sept. 1979.

CASTAGNOLI, G., BRAUER, S., and HERRMANN, M.: "Optimization of Cyclic Redundancy-Check Codes with 24 and 32 Parity Bits," *IEEE Trans. on Commun.*, vol. 41, pp. 883–892, June 1993.

CERF, V., and KAHN, R.: "A Protocol for Packet Network Interconnection," *IEEE Trans. on Commun.*, vol. COM–2, pp. 637–648, May 1974.

CHANG, F., DEAN, J., GHEMAWAT, S., HSIEH, W., WALLACH, D., BURROWS, M., CHANDRA, T., FIKES, A., and GRUBER, R.: "Bigtable: A Distributed Storage System for Structured Data," *Proc. OSDI 2006 Symp.*, USENIX, pp. 15–29, 2006.

CHASE, J.S., GALLATIN, A.J., and YOCUM, K.G.: "End System Optimizations for High-Speed TCP," *IEEE Commun. Magazine*, vol. 39, pp. 68–75, Apr. 2001.

CHEN, S., and NAHRSTEDT, K.: "An Overview of QoS Routing for Next-Generation Networks," *IEEE Network Magazine*, vol. 12, pp. 64–69, Nov./Dec. 1998.

CHIU, D., and JAIN, R.: "Analysis of the Increase and Decrease Algorithms for Congestion Avoidance in Computer Networks," *Comput. Netw. ISDN Syst.*, vol. 17, pp. 1–4, June 1989.

CISCO: "Cisco Visual Networking Index: Forecast and Methodology, 2009–2014," Cisco Systems Inc., June 2010.

CLARK, D.D.: "The Design Philosophy of the DARPA Internet Protocols," *Proc. SIGCOMM '88 Conf.*, ACM, pp. 106–114, 1988.

CLARK, D.D.: "Window and Acknowledgement Strategy in TCP," RFC 813, July 1982.

CLARK, D.D., JACOBSON, V., ROMKEY, J., and SALWEN, H.: "An Analysis of TCP Processing Overhead," *IEEE Commun. Magazine*, vol. 27, pp. 23–29, June 1989.

CLARK, D.D., SHENKER, S., and ZHANG, L.: "Supporting Real-Time Applications in an Integrated Services Packet Network," *Proc. SIGCOMM '92 Conf.*, ACM, pp. 14–26, 1992.

CLARKE, A.C.: "Extra-Terrestrial Relays," *Wireless World*, 1945.

CLARKE, I., MILLER, S.G., HONG, T.W., SANDBERG, O., and WILEY, B.: "Protecting Free Expression Online with Freenet," *IEEE Internet Computing*, vol. 6, pp. 40–49, Jan.–Feb. 2002.

COHEN, B.: "Incentives Build Robustness in BitTorrent," *Proc. First Workshop on Economics of Peer-to-Peer Systems*, June 2003.

COMER, D.E.: *The Internet Book*, 4th ed., Englewood Cliffs, NJ: Prentice Hall, 2007.

COMER, D.E.: *Internetworking with TCP/IP*, vol. 1, 5th ed., Englewood Cliffs, NJ: Prentice Hall, 2005.

CRAVER, S.A., WU, M., LIU, B., STUBBLEFIELD, A., SWARTZLANDER, B., WALLACH, D.W., DEAN, D., and FELTEN, E.W.: "Reading Between the Lines: Lessons from the SDMI Challenge," *Proc. 10th USENIX Security Symp.*, USENIX, 2001.

CROVELLA, M., and KRISHNAMURTHY, B.: *Internet Measurement*, New York: John Wiley & Sons, 2006.

DAEMEN, J., and RIJMEN, V.: *The Design of Rijndael*, Berlin: Springer-Verlag, 2002.

DALAL, Y., and METCLFE, R.: "Reverse Path Forwarding of Broadcast Packets," *Commun. of the ACM*, vol. 21, pp. 1040–1048, Dec. 1978.

DAVIE, B., and FARREL, A.: *MPLS: Next Steps*, San Francisco: Morgan Kaufmann, 2008.

DAVIE, B., and REKHTER, Y.: *MPLS Technology and Applications*, San Francisco: Morgan Kaufmann, 2000.

DAVIES, J.: *Understanding IPv6*, 2nd ed., Redmond, WA: Microsoft Press, 2008.

DAY, J.D.: "The (Un)Revised OSI Reference Model," *Computer Commun. Rev.*, vol. 25, pp. 39–55, Oct. 1995.

DAY, J.D., and ZIMMERMANN, H.: "The OSI Reference Model," *Proc. of the IEEE*, vol. 71, pp. 1334–1340, Dec. 1983.

DECANDIA, G., HASTORIN, D., JAMPANI, M., KAKULAPATI, G., LAKSHMAN, A., PILCHIN, A., SIVASUBRAMANIAN, S., VOSSHALL, P., and VOGELS, W.: "Dynamo: Amazon's Highly Available Key-value Store," *Proc. 19th Symp. on Operating Systems Prin.*, ACM, pp. 205–220, Dec. 2007.

DEERING, S.E.: "SIP: Simple Internet Protocol," *IEEE Network Magazine*, vol. 7, pp. 16–28, May/June 1993.

DEERING, S., and CHERITON, D.: "Multicast Routing in Datagram Networks and Extended LANs," *ACM Trans. on Computer Systems*, vol. 8, pp. 85–110, May 1990.

DEMERS, A., KESHAV, S., and SHENKER, S.: "Analysis and Simulation of a Fair Queueing Algorithm," *Internetwork: Research and Experience*, vol. 1, pp. 3–26, Sept. 1990.

DENNING, D.E., and SACCO, G.M.: "Timestamps in Key Distribution Protocols," *Commun. of the ACM*, vol. 24, pp. 533–536, Aug. 1981.

DEVARAPALLI, V., WAKIKAWA, R., PETRESCU, A., and THUBERT, P.: "Network Mobility (NEMO) Basic Support Protocol," RFC 3963, Jan. 2005.

DIFFIE, W., and HELLMAN, M.E.: "Exhaustive Cryptanalysis of the NBS Data Encryption Standard," *IEEE Computer*, vol. 10, pp. 74–84, June 1977.

DIFFIE, W., and HELLMAN, M.E.: "New Directions in Cryptography," *IEEE Trans. on Information Theory*, vol. IT–2, pp. 644–654, Nov. 1976.

DIJKSTRA, E.W.: "A Note on Two Problems in Connexion with Graphs," *Numer. Math.*, vol. 1, pp. 269–271, Oct. 1959.

DILLEY, J., MAGGS, B., PARIKH, J., PROKOP, H., SITARAMAN, R., and WHEIL, B.: "Globally Distributed Content Delivery," *IEEE Internet Computing*, vol. 6, pp. 50–58, 2002.

DINGLEDINE, R., MATHEWSON, N., SYVERSON, P.: "Tor: The Second-Generation Onion Router," *Proc. 13th USENIX Security Symp.*, USENIX, pp. 303–320, Aug. 2004.

DONAHOO, M., and CALVERT, K.: *TCP/IP Sockets in C*, 2nd ed., San Francisco: Morgan Kaufmann, 2009.

DONAHOO, M., and CALVERT, K.: *TCP/IP Sockets in Java*, 2nd ed., San Francisco: Morgan Kaufmann, 2008.

DONALDSON, G., and JONES, D.: "Cable Television Broadband Network Architectures," *IEEE Commun. Magazine*, vol. 39, pp. 122–126, June 2001.

DORFMAN, R.: "Detection of Defective Members of a Large Population," *Annals Math. Statistics*, vol. 14, pp. 436–440, 1943.

DUTCHER, B.: *The NAT Handbook*, New York: John Wiley & Sons, 2001.

DUTTA-ROY, A.: "An Overview of Cable Modem Technology and Market Perspectives," *IEEE Commun. Magazine*, vol. 39, pp. 81–88, June 2001.

EDELMAN, B., OSTROVSKY, M., and SCHWARZ, M.: "Internet Advertising and the Generalized Second-Price Auction: Selling Billions of Dollars Worth of Keywords," *American Economic Review*, vol. 97, pp. 242–259, Mar. 2007.

EL GAMAL, T.: "A Public-Key Cryptosystem and a Signature Scheme Based on Discrete Logarithms," *IEEE Trans. on Information Theory*, vol. IT–1, pp. 469–472, July 1985.

EPCGLOBAL: *EPC Radio-Frequency Identity Protocols Class– Generation– UHF RFID Protocol for Communication at 860-MHz to 960-MHz Version 1.2.0*, Brussels: EPCglobal Inc., Oct. 2008.

FALL, K.: "A Delay-Tolerant Network Architecture for Challenged Internets," *Proc. SIGCOMM 2003 Conf.*, ACM, pp. 27–34, Aug. 2003.

FALOUTSOS, M., FALOUTSOS, P., and FALOUTSOS, C.: "On Power-Law Relationships of the Internet Topology," *Proc. SIGCOMM '99 Conf.*, ACM, pp. 251–262, 1999.

FARRELL, S., and CAHILL, V.: *Delay- and Disruption-Tolerant Networking*, London: Artech House, 2007.

FELLOWS, D., and JONES, D.: "DOCSIS Cable Modem Technology," *IEEE Commun. Magazine*, vol. 39, pp. 202–209, Mar. 2001.

FENNER, B., HANDLEY, M., HOLBROOK, H., and KOUVELAS, I.: "Protocol Independent Multicast-Sparse Mode (PIM-SM)," RFC 4601, Aug. 2006.

FERGUSON, N., SCHNEIER, B., and KOHNO, T.: *Cryptography Engineering: Design Principles and Practical Applications*, New York: John Wiley & Sons, 2010.

FLANAGAN, D.: *JavaScript: The Definitive Guide*, 6th ed., Sebastopol, CA: O'Reilly, 2010.

FLETCHER, J.: "An Arithmetic Checksum for Serial Transmissions," *IEEE Trans. on Commun.*, vol. COM–0, pp. 247–252, Jan. 1982.

FLOYD, S., HANDLEY, M., PADHYE, J., and WIDMER, J.: "Equation-Based Congestion Control for Unicast Applications," *Proc. SIGCOMM 2000 Conf.*, ACM, pp. 43–56, Aug. 2000.

FLOYD, S., and JACOBSON, V.: "Random Early Detection for Congestion Avoidance," *IEEE/ACM Trans. on Networking*, vol. 1, pp. 397–413, Aug. 1993.

FLUHRER, S., MANTIN, I., and SHAMIR, A.: "Weakness in the Key Scheduling Algorithm of RC4," *Proc. Eighth Ann. Workshop on Selected Areas in Cryptography*, Berlin: Springer-Verlag LNCS 2259, pp. 1–24, 2001.

FORD, B.: "Structured Streams: A New Transport Abstraction," *Proc. SIGCOMM 2007 Conf.*, ACM, pp. 361–372, 2007.

FORD, L.R., Jr., and FULKERSON, D.R.: *Flows in Networks*, Princeton, NJ: Princeton University Press, 1962.

FORD, W., and BAUM, M.S.: *Secure Electronic Commerce*, Upper Saddle River, NJ: Prentice Hall, 2000.

FORNEY, G.D.: "The Viterbi Algorithm," *Proc. of the IEEE*, vol. 61, pp. 268–278, Mar. 1973.

FOULI, K., and MALER, M.: "The Road to Carrier-Grade Ethernet," *IEEE Commun. Magazine*, vol. 47, pp. S30–S38, Mar. 2009.

FOX, A., GRIBBLE, S., BREWER, E., and AMIR, E.: "Adapting to Network and Client Variability via On-Demand Dynamic Distillation," *SIGOPS Oper. Syst. Rev.*, vol. 30, pp. 160–170, Dec. 1996.

FRANCIS, P.: "A Near-Term Architecture for Deploying Pip," *IEEE Network Magazine*, vol. 7, pp. 30–37, May/June 1993.

FRASER, A.G.: "Towards a Universal Data Transport System," *IEEE J. on Selected Areas in Commun.*, vol. 5, pp. 803–816, Nov. 1983.

FRIDRICH, J.: *Steganography in Digital Media: Principles, Algorithms, and Applications*, Cambridge: Cambridge University Press, 2009.

FULLER, V., and LI, T.: "Classless Inter-domain Routing (CIDR): The Internet Address Assignment and Aggregation Plan," RFC 4632, Aug. 2006.

GALLAGHER, R.G.: "A Minimum Delay Routing Algorithm Using Distributed Computation," *IEEE Trans. on Commun.*, vol. COM–5, pp. 73–85, Jan. 1977.

GALLAGHER, R.G.: "Low-Density Parity Check Codes," *IRE Trans. on Information Theory*, vol. 8, pp. 21–28, Jan. 1962.

GARFINKEL, S., with SPAFFORD, G.: *Web Security, Privacy, and Commerce*, Sebastopol, CA: O'Reilly, 2002.

GAST, M.: *802.11 Wireless Networks: The Definitive Guide*, 2nd ed., Sebastopol, CA: O'Reilly, 2005.

GERSHENFELD, N., and KRIKORIAN, R., and COHEN, D.: "The Internet of Things," *Scientific American*, vol. 291, pp. 76–81, Oct. 2004.

GILDER, G.: "Metcalfe's Law and Legacy," *Forbes ASAP*, Sepy. 13, 1993.

GOODE, B.: "Voice over Internet Protocol," *Proc. of the IEEE*, vol. 90, pp. 1495–1517, Sept. 2002.

GORALSKI, W.J.: *SONET*, 2nd ed., New York: McGraw-Hill, 2002.

GRAYSON, M., SHATZKAMER, K., and WAINNER, S.: *IP Design for Mobile Networks*, Indianapolis, IN: Cisco Press, 2009.

GROBE, K., and ELBERS, J.: "PON in Adolescence: From TDMA to WDM-PON," *IEEE Commun. Magazine*, vol. 46, pp. 26–34, Jan. 2008.

GROSS, G., KAYCEE, M., LIN, A., MALIS, A., and STEPHENS, J.: "The PPP Over AAL5," RFC 2364, July 1998.

HA, S., RHEE, I., and LISONG, X.: "CUBIC: A New TCP-Friendly High-Speed TCP Variant," *SIGOPS Oper. Syst. Rev.*, vol. 42, pp. 64–74, June 2008.

HAFNER, K., and LYON, M.: *Where Wizards Stay Up Late*, New York: Simon & Schuster, 1998.

HALPERIN, D., HEYDT-BENJAMIN, T., RANSFORD, B., CLARK, S., DEFEND, B., MORGAN, W., FU, K., KOHNO, T., and MAISEL, W.: "Pacemakers and Implantable Cardiac Defibrillators: Software Radio Attacks and Zero-Power Defenses," *IEEE Symp. on Security and Privacy*, pp. 129–142, May 2008.

HALPERIN, D., HU, W., SHETH, A., and WETHERALL, D.: "802.11 with Multiple Antennas for Dummies," *Computer Commun. Rev.*, vol. 40, pp. 19–25, Jan. 2010.

HAMMING, R.W.: "Error Detecting and Error Correcting Codes," *Bell System Tech. J.*, vol. 29, pp. 147–160, Apr. 1950.

HARTE, L., KELLOGG, S., DREHER, R., and SCHAFFNIT, T.: *The Comprehensive Guide to Wireless Technology*, Fuquay-Varina, NC: APDG Publishing, 2000.

HAWLEY, G.T.: "Historical Perspectives on the U.S. Telephone Loop," *IEEE Commun. Magazine*, vol. 29, pp. 24–28, Mar. 1991.

HECHT, J.: *Understanding Fiber Optics*, Upper Saddle River, NJ: Prentice Hall, 2005.

HELD, G.: *A Practical Guide to Content Delivery Networks*, 2nd ed., Boca Raton, FL: CRC Press, 2010.

HEUSSE, M., ROUSSEAU, F., BERGER-SABBATEL, G., DUDA, A.: "Performance Anomaly of 802.11b," *Proc. INFOCOM Conf.*, IEEE, pp. 836–843, 2003.

HIERTZ, G., DENTENEER, D., STIBOR, L., ZANG, Y., COSTA, X., and WALKE, B.: "The IEEE 802.11 Universe," *IEEE Commun. Magazine*, vol. 48, pp. 62–70, Jan. 2010.

HOE, J.: "Improving the Start-up Behavior of a Congestion Control Scheme for TCP," *Proc. SIGCOMM '96 Conf.*, ACM, pp. 270–280, 1996.

HU, Y., and LI, V.O.K.: "Satellite-Based Internet: A Tutorial," *IEEE Commun. Magazine*, vol. 30, pp. 154–162, Mar. 2001.

HUITEMA, C.: *Routing in the Internet*, 2nd ed., Englewood Cliffs, NJ: Prentice Hall, 1999.

HULL, B., BYCHKOVSKY, V., CHEN, K., GORACZKO, M., MIU, A., SHIH, E., ZHANG, Y., BALAKRISHNAN, H., and MADDEN, S.: "CarTel: A Distributed Mobile Sensor Computing System," *Proc. Sensys 2006 Conf.*, ACM, pp. 125–138, Nov. 2006.

HUNTER, D., RAFTER, J., FAWCETT, J., VAN DER LIST, E., AYERS, D., DUCKETT, J., WATT, A., and MCKINNON, L.: *Beginning XML*, 4th ed., New Jersey: Wrox, 2007.

IRMER, T.: "Shaping Future Telecommunications: The Challenge of Global Standardization," *IEEE Commun. Magazine*, vol. 32, pp. 20–28, Jan. 1994.

ITU (INTERNATIONAL TELECOMMUNICATION UNION): *ITU Internet Reports 2005: The Internet of Things*, Geneva: ITU, Nov. 2005.

ITU (INTERNATIONAL TELECOMMUNICATION UNION): *Measuring the Information Society: The ICT Development Index*, Geneva: ITU, Mar. 2009.

JACOBSON, V.: "Compressing TCP/IP Headers for Low-Speed Serial Links," RFC 1144, Feb. 1990.

JACOBSON, V.: "Congestion Avoidance and Control," *Proc. SIGCOMM '88 Conf.*, ACM, pp. 314–329, 1988.

JAIN, R., and ROUTHIER, S.: "Packet Trains—Measurements and a New Model for Computer Network Traffic," *IEEE J. on Selected Areas in Commun.*, vol. 6, pp. 986–995, Sept. 1986.

JAKOBSSON, M., and WETZEL, S.: "Security Weaknesses in Bluetooth," *Topics in Cryptology: CT-RSA 2001*, Berlin: Springer-Verlag LNCS 2020, pp. 176–191, 2001.

JOEL, A.: "Telecommunications and the IEEE Communications Society," *IEEE Commun. Magazine*, 50th Anniversary Issue, pp. 6–14 and 162–167, May 2002.

JOHNSON, D., PERKINS, C., and ARKKO, J.: "Mobility Support in IPv6," RFC 3775, June 2004.

JOHNSON, D.B., MALTZ, D., and BROCH, J.: "DSR: The Dynamic Source Routing Protocol for Multi-Hop Wireless Ad Hoc Networks," *Ad Hoc Networking*, Boston: Addison-Wesley, pp. 139–172, 2001.

JUANG, P., OKI, H., WANG, Y., MARTONOSI, M., PEH, L., and RUBENSTEIN, D.: "Energy-Efficient Computing for Wildlife Tracking: Design Tradeoffs and Early Experiences with ZebraNet," *SIGOPS Oper. Syst. Rev.*, vol. 36, pp. 96–107, Oct. 2002.

KAHN, D.: *The Codebreakers*, 2nd ed., New York: Macmillan, 1995.

KAMOUN, F., and KLEINROCK, L.: "Stochastic Performance Evaluation of Hierarchical Routing for Large Networks," *Computer Networks*, vol. 3, pp. 337–353, Nov. 1979.

KARN, P.: "MACA—A New Channel Access Protocol for Packet Radio," *ARRL/CRRL Amateur Radio Ninth Computer Networking Conf.*, pp. 134–140, 1990.

KARN, P., and PARTRIDGE, C.: "Improving Round-Trip Estimates in Reliable Transport Protocols," *Proc. SIGCOMM '87 Conf.*, ACM, pp. 2–7, 1987.

KARP, B., and KUNG, H.T.: "GPSR: Greedy Perimeter Stateless Routing for Wireless Networks," *Proc. MOBICOM 2000 Conf.*, ACM, pp. 243–254, 2000.

KASIM, A.: *Delivering Carrier Ethernet*, New York: McGraw-Hill, 2007.

KATABI, D., HANDLEY, M., and ROHRS, C.: "Internet Congestion Control for Future High Bandwidth-Delay Product Environments," *Proc. SIGCOMM 2002 Conf.*, ACM, pp. 89–102, 2002.

KATZ, D., and FORD, P.S.: "TUBA: Replacing IP with CLNP," *IEEE Network Magazine*, vol. 7, pp. 38–47, May/June 1993.

KAUFMAN, C., PERLMAN, R., and SPECINER, M.: *Network Security*, 2nd ed., Englewood Cliffs, NJ: Prentice Hall, 2002.

KENT, C., and MOGUL, J.: "Fragmentation Considered Harmful," *Proc. SIGCOMM '87 Conf.*, ACM, pp. 390–401, 1987.

KERCKHOFF, A.: "La Cryptographie Militaire," *J. des Sciences Militaires*, vol. 9, pp. 5–38, Jan. 1883 and pp. 161–191, Feb. 1883.

KHANNA, A., and ZINKY, J.: "The Revised ARPANET Routing Metric," *Proc. SIGCOMM '89 Conf.*, ACM, pp. 45–56, 1989.

KIPNIS, J.: "Beating the System: Abuses of the Standards Adoption Process," *IEEE Commun. Magazine*, vol. 38, pp. 102–105, July 2000.

KLEINROCK, L.: "Power and Other Deterministic Rules of Thumb for Probabilistic Problems in Computer Communications," *Proc. Intl. Conf. on Commun.*, pp. 43.1.1–43.1.10, June 1979.

KLEINROCK, L., and TOBAGI, F.: "Random Access Techniques for Data Transmission over Packet-Switched Radio Channels," *Proc. Nat. Computer Conf.*, pp. 187–201, 1975.

KOHLER, E., HANDLEY, H., and FLOYD, S.: "Designing DCCP: Congestion Control without Reliability," *Proc. SIGCOMM 2006 Conf.*, ACM, pp. 27–38, 2006.

KOODLI, R., and PERKINS, C.E.: *Mobile Inter-networking with IPv6*, New York: John Wiley & Sons, 2007.

KOOPMAN, P.: "32-Bit Cyclic Redundancy Codes for Internet Applications," *Proc. Intl. Conf. on Dependable Systems and Networks.*, IEEE, pp. 459–472, 2002.

KRISHNAMURTHY, B., and REXFORD, J.: *Web Protocols and Practice*, Boston: Addison-Wesley, 2001.

KUMAR, S., PAAR, C., PELZL, J., PFEIFFER, G., and SCHIMMLER, M.: "Breaking Ciphers with COPACOBANA: A Cost-Optimized Parallel Code Breaker," *Proc. 8th Cryptographic Hardware and Embedded Systems Wksp.*, IACR, pp. 101–118, Oct. 2006.

LABOVITZ, C., AHUJA, A., BOSE, A., and JAHANIAN, F.: "Delayed Internet Routing Convergence," *IEEE/ACM Trans. on Networking*, vol. 9, pp. 293–306, June 2001.

LAM, C.K.M., and TAN, B.C.Y.: "The Internet Is Changing the Music Industry," *Commun. of the ACM*, vol. 44, pp. 62–66, Aug. 2001.

LAOUTARIS, N., SMARAGDAKIS, G., RODRIGUEZ, P., and SUNDARAM, R.: "Delay Tolerant Bulk Data Transfers on the Internet," *Proc. SIGMETRICS 2009 Conf.*, ACM, pp. 229–238, June 2009.

LARMO, A., LINDSTROM, M., MEYER, M., PELLETIER, G., TORSNER, J., and WIEMANN, H.: "The LTE Link-Layer Design," *IEEE Commun. Magazine*, vol. 47, pp. 52–59, Apr. 2009.

LEE, J.S., and MILLER, L.E.: *CDMA Systems Engineering Handbook*, London: Artech House, 1998.

LELAND, W., TAQQU, M., WILLINGER, W., and WILSON, D.: "On the Self-Similar Nature of Ethernet Traffic," *IEEE/ACM Trans. on Networking*, vol. 2, pp. 1–15, Feb. 1994.

LEMON, J.: "Resisting SYN Flood DOS Attacks with a SYN Cache," *Proc. BSDCon Conf.*, USENIX, pp. 88–98, 2002.

LEVY, S.: "Crypto Rebels," *Wired*, pp. 54–61, May/June 1993.

LEWIS, M.: *Comparing, Designing, and Deploying VPNs*, Indianapolis, IN: Cisco Press, 2006.

LI, M., AGRAWAL, D., GANESAN, D., and VENKATARAMANI, A.: "Block-Switched Networks: A New Paradigm for Wireless Transport," *Proc. NSDI 2009 Conf.*, USENIX, pp. 423–436, 2009.

LIN, S., and COSTELLO, D.: *Error Control Coding*, 2nd ed., Upper Saddle River, NJ: Pearson Education, 2004.

LUBACZ, J., MAZURCZYK, W., and SZCZYPIORSKI, K.: "Vice over IP," *IEEE Spectrum*, pp. 42–47, Feb. 2010.

MACEDONIA, M.R.: "Distributed File Sharing," *IEEE Computer*, vol. 33, pp. 99–101, 2000.

MADHAVAN, J., KO, D., LOT, L., GANGPATHY, V., RASMUSSEN, A., and HALEVY, A.: "Google's Deep Web Crawl," *Proc. VLDB 2008 Conf.*, VLDB Endowment, pp. 1241–1252, 2008.

MAHAJAN, R., RODRIG, M., WETHERALL, D., and ZAHORJAN, J.: "Analyzing the MAC-Level Behavior of Wireless Networks in the Wild," *Proc. SIGCOMM 2006 Conf.*, ACM, pp. 75–86, 2006.

MALIS, A., and SIMPSON, W.: "PPP over SONET/SDH," RFC 2615, June 1999.

MASSEY, J.L.: "Shift-Register Synthesis and BCH Decoding," *IEEE Trans. on Information Theory*, vol. IT–5, pp. 122–127, Jan. 1969.

MATSUI, M.: "Linear Cryptanalysis Method for DES Cipher," *Advances in Cryptology—Eurocrypt 1993 Proceedings*, Berlin: Springer-Verlag LNCS 765, pp. 386–397, 1994.

MAUFER, T.A.: *IP Fundamentals*, Upper Saddle River, NJ: Prentice Hall, 1999.

MAYMOUNKOV, P., and MAZIERES, D.: "Kademlia: A Peer-to-Peer Information System Based on the XOR Metric," *Proc. First Intl. Wksp. on Peer-to-Peer Systems*, Berlin: Springer-Verlag LNCS 2429, pp. 53–65, 2002.

MAZIERES, D., and KAASHOEK, M.F.: "The Design, Implementation, and Operation of an Email Pseudonym Server," *Proc. Fifth Conf. on Computer and Commun. Security*, ACM, pp. 27–36, 1998.

MCAFEE LABS: *McAfee Threat Reports: First Quarter 2010*, McAfee Inc., 2010.

MENEZES, A.J., and VANSTONE, S.A.: "Elliptic Curve Cryptosystems and Their Implementation," *Journal of Cryptology*, vol. 6, pp. 209–224, 1993.

MERKLE, R.C., and HELLMAN, M.: "Hiding and Signatures in Trapdoor Knapsacks," *IEEE Trans. on Information Theory*, vol. IT–4, pp. 525–530, Sept. 1978.

METCALFE, R.M.: "Computer/Network Interface Design: Lessons from Arpanet and Ethernet," *IEEE J. on Selected Areas in Commun.*, vol. 11, pp. 173–179, Feb. 1993.

METCALFE, R.M., and BOGGS, D.R.: "Ethernet: Distributed Packet Switching for Local Computer Networks," *Commun. of the ACM*, vol. 19, pp. 395–404, July 1976.

METZ, C: "Interconnecting ISP Networks," *IEEE Internet Computing*, vol. 5, pp. 74–80, Mar.–Apr. 2001.

MISHRA, P.P., KANAKIA, H., and TRIPATHI, S.: "On Hop by Hop Rate-Based Congestion Control," *IEEE/ACM Trans. on Networking*, vol. 4, pp. 224–239, Apr. 1996.

MOGUL, J.C.: "IP Network Performance," in *Internet System Handbook*, D.C. Lynch and M.Y. Rose (eds.), Boston: Addison-Wesley, pp. 575–575, 1993.

MOGUL, J., and DEERING, S.: "Path MTU Discovery," RFC 1191, Nov. 1990.

MOGUL, J., and MINSHALL, G.: "Rethinking the Nagle Algorithm," *Comput. Commun. Rev.*, vol. 31, pp. 6–20, Jan. 2001.

MOY, J.: "Multicast Routing Extensions for OSPF," *Commun. of the ACM*, vol. 37, pp. 61–66, Aug. 1994.

MULLINS, J.: "Making Unbreakable Code," *IEEE Spectrum*, pp. 40–45, May 2002.

NAGLE, J.: "On Packet Switches with Infinite Storage," *IEEE Trans. on Commun.*, vol. COM–5, pp. 435–438, Apr. 1987.

NAGLE, J.: "Congestion Control in TCP/IP Internetworks," *Computer Commun. Rev.*, vol. 14, pp. 11–17, Oct. 1984.

NAUGHTON, J.: *A Brief History of the Future*, Woodstock, NY: Overlook Press, 2000.

NEEDHAM, R.M., and SCHROEDER, M.D.: "Using Encryption for Authentication in Large Networks of Computers," *Commun. of the ACM*, vol. 21, pp. 993–999, Dec. 1978.

NEEDHAM, R.M., and SCHROEDER, M.D.: "Authentication Revisited," *Operating Systems Rev.*, vol. 21, p. 7, Jan. 1987.

NELAKUDITI, S., and ZHANG, Z.-L.: "A Localized Adaptive Proportioning Approach to QoS Routing," *IEEE Commun. Magazine* vol. 40, pp. 66–71, June 2002.

NEUMAN, C., and TS'O, T.: "Kerberos: An Authentication Service for Computer Networks," *IEEE Commun. Mag.*, vol. 32, pp. 33–38, Sept. 1994.

NICHOLS, R.K., and LEKKAS, P.C.: *Wireless Security*, New York: McGraw-Hill, 2002.

NIST: "Secure Hash Algorithm," U.S. Government Federal Information Processing Standard 180, 1993.

NONNENMACHER, J., BIERSACK, E., and TOWSLEY, D.: "Parity-Based Loss Recovery for Reliable Multicast Transmission," *Proc. SIGCOMM '97 Conf.*, ACM, pp. 289–300, 1997.

NUCCI, A., and PAPAGIANNAKI, D.: *Design, Measurement and Management of Large-Scale IP Networks*, Cambridge: Cambridge University Press, 2008.

NUGENT, R., MUNAKANA, R., CHIN, A., COELHO, R., and PUIG-SUARI, J.: "The CubeSat: The PicoSatellite Standard for Research and Education," *Proc. SPACE 2008 Conf.*, AIAA, 2008.

ORAN, D.: "OSI IS-IS Intra-domain Routing Protocol," RFC 1142, Feb. 1990.

OTWAY, D., and REES, O.: "Efficient and Timely Mutual Authentication," *Operating Systems Rev.*, pp. 8–10, Jan. 1987.

PADHYE, J., FIROIU, V., TOWSLEY, D., and KUROSE, J.: "Modeling TCP Throughput: A Simple Model and Its Empirical Validation," *Proc. SIGCOMM '98 Conf.*, ACM, pp. 303–314, 1998.

PALAIS, J.C.: *Fiber Optic Commun.*, 5th ed., Englewood Cliffs, NJ: Prentice Hall, 2004.

PARAMESWARAN, M., SUSARLA, A., and WHINSTON, A.B.: "P2P Networking: An Information-Sharing Alternative," *IEEE Computer*, vol. 34, pp. 31–38, July 2001.

PAREKH, A., and GALLAGHER, R.: "A Generalized Processor Sharing Approach to Flow Control in Integrated Services Networks: The Multiple-Node Case," *IEEE/ACM Trans. on Networking*, vol. 2, pp. 137–150, Apr. 1994.

PAREKH, A., and GALLAGHER, R.: "A Generalized Processor Sharing Approach to Flow Control in Integrated Services Networks: The Single-Node Case," *IEEE/ACM Trans. on Networking*, vol. 1, pp. 344–357, June 1993.

PARTRIDGE, C., HUGHES, J., and STONE, J.: "Performance of Checksums and CRCs over Real Data," *Proc. SIGCOMM '95 Conf.*, ACM, pp. 68–76, 1995.

PARTRIDGE, C., MENDEZ, T., and MILLIKEN, W.: "Host Anycasting Service," RFC 1546, Nov. 1993.

PAXSON, V., and FLOYD, S.: "Wide-Area Traffic: The Failure of Poisson Modeling," *IEEE/ACM Trans. on Networking*, vol. 3, pp. 226–244, June 1995.

PERKINS, C.: "IP Mobility Support for IPv4," RFC 3344, Aug. 2002.

PERKINS, C.E.: *RTP: Audio and Video for the Internet*, Boston: Addison-Wesley, 2003.

PERKINS, C.E. (ed.): *Ad Hoc Networking*, Boston: Addison-Wesley, 2001.

PERKINS, C.E.: *Mobile IP Design Principles and Practices*, Upper Saddle River, NJ: Prentice Hall, 1998.

PERKINS, C.E., and ROYER, E.: "The Ad Hoc On-Demand Distance-Vector Protocol," in *Ad Hoc Networking*, edited by C. Perkins, Boston: Addison-Wesley, 2001.

PERLMAN, R.: *Interconnections*, 2nd ed., Boston: Addison-Wesley, 2000.

PERLMAN, R.: *Network Layer Protocols with Byzantine Robustness*, Ph.D. thesis, M.I.T., 1988.

PERLMAN, R.: "An Algorithm for the Distributed Computation of a Spanning Tree in an Extended LAN," *Proc. SIGCOMM '85 Conf.*, ACM, pp. 44–53, 1985.

PERLMAN, R., and KAUFMAN, C.: "Key Exchange in IPsec," *IEEE Internet Computing*, vol. 4, pp. 50–56, Nov.–Dec. 2000.

PETERSON, W.W., and BROWN, D.T.: "Cyclic Codes for Error Detection," *Proc. IRE*, vol. 49, pp. 228–235, Jan. 1961.

PIATEK, M., KOHNO, T., and KRISHNAMURTHY, A.: "Challenges and Directions for Monitoring P2P File Sharing Networks—or Why My Printer Received a DMCA Takedown Notice," *3rd Workshop on Hot Topics in Security*, USENIX, July 2008.

PIATEK, M., ISDAL, T., ANDERSON, T., KRISHNAMURTHY, A., and VENKATARAMANI, V.: "Do Incentives Build Robustness in BitTorrent?," *Proc. NSDI 2007 Conf.*, USENIX, pp. 1–14, 2007.

PISCITELLO, D.M., and CHAPIN, A.L.: *Open Systems Networking: TCP/IP and OSI*, Boston: Addison-Wesley, 1993.

PIVA, A., BARTOLINI, F., and BARNI, M.: "Managing Copyrights in Open Networks," *IEEE Internet Computing*, vol. 6, pp. 18–26, May– 2002.

POSTEL, J.: "Internet Control Message Protocols," RFC 792, Sept. 1981.

RABIN, J., and McCATHIENEVILE, C.: "Mobile Web Best Practices 1.0," W3C Recommendation, July 2008.

RAMAKRISHNAM, K.K., FLOYD, S., and BLACK, D.: "The Addition of Explicit Congestion Notification (ECN) to IP," RFC 3168, Sept. 2001.

RAMAKRISHNAN, K.K., and JAIN, R.: "A Binary Feedback Scheme for Congestion Avoidance in Computer Networks with a Connectionless Network Layer," *Proc. SIGCOMM '88 Conf.*, ACM, pp. 303–313, 1988.

RAMASWAMI, R., KUMAR, S., and SASAKI, G.: *Optical Networks: A Practical Perspective*, 3rd ed., San Francisco: Morgan Kaufmann, 2009.

RATNASAMY, S., FRANCIS, P., HANDLEY, M., KARP, R., and SHENKER, S.: "A Scalable Content-Addressable Network," *Proc. SIGCOMM 2001 Conf.*, ACM, pp. 161–172, 2001.

RIEBACK, M., CRISPO, B., and TANENBAUM, A.: "Is Your Cat Infected with a Computer Virus?," *Proc. IEEE Percom*, pp. 169–179, Mar. 2006.

RIVEST, R.L.: "The MD5 Message-Digest Algorithm," RFC 1320, Apr. 1992.

RIVEST, R.L., SHAMIR, A., and ADLEMAN, L.: "On a Method for Obtaining Digital Signatures and Public Key Cryptosystems," *Commun. of the ACM*, vol. 21, pp. 120–126, Feb. 1978.

ROBERTS, L.G.: "Extensions of Packet Communication Technology to a Hand Held Personal Terminal," *Proc. Spring Joint Computer Conf.*, AFIPS, pp. 295–298, 1972.

ROBERTS, L.G.: "Multiple Computer Networks and Intercomputer Communication," *Proc. First Symp. on Operating Systems Prin.*, ACM, pp. 3.1–3.6, 1967.

ROSE, M.T.: *The Simple Book*, Englewood Cliffs, NJ: Prentice Hall, 1994.

ROSE, M.T.: *The Internet Message*, Englewood Cliffs, NJ: Prentice Hall, 1993.

ROWSTRON, A., and DRUSCHEL, P.: "Pastry: Scalable, Distributed Object Location and Routing for Large-Scale Peer-to-Peer Storage Utility," *Proc. 18th Int'l Conf. on Distributed Systems Platforms*, London: Springer-Verlag LNCS 2218, pp. 329–350, 2001.

RUIZ-SANCHEZ, M.A., BIERSACK, E.W., and DABBOUS, W.: "Survey and Taxonomy of IP Address Lookup Algorithms," *IEEE Network Magazine*, vol. 15, pp. 8–23, Mar.–Apr. 2001.

SALTZER, J.H., REED, D.P., and CLARK, D.D.: "End-to-End Arguments in System Design," *ACM Trans. on Computer Systems*, vol. 2, pp. 277–288, Nov. 1984.

SAMPLE, A., YEAGER, D., POWLEDGE, P., MAMISHEV, A., and SMITH, J.: "Design of an RFID-Based Battery-Free Programmable Sensing Platform," *IEEE Trans. on Instrumentation and Measurement*, vol. 57, pp. 2608–2615, Nov. 2008.

SAROIU, S., GUMMADI, K., and GRIBBLE, S.: "Measuring and Analyzing the Characteristics of Napster & Gnutella Hosts," *Multim. Syst.*, vol. 9,, pp. 170–184, Aug. 2003.

SCHALLER, R.: "Moore's Law: Past, Present and Future," *IEEE Spectrum*, vol. 34, pp. 52–59, June 1997.

SCHNEIER, B.: *Secrets and Lies*, New York: John Wiley & Sons, 2004.

SCHNEIER, B.: *E-Mail Security*, New York: John Wiley & Sons, 1995.

SCHNORR, C.P.: "Efficient Signature Generation for Smart Cards," *Journal of Cryptology*, vol. 4, pp. 161–174, 1991.

SCHOLTZ, R.A.: "The Origins of Spread-Spectrum Communications," *IEEE Trans. on Commun.*, vol. COM–0, pp. 822–854, May 1982.

SCHWARTZ, M., and ABRAMSON, N.: "The AlohaNet: Surfing for Wireless Data," *IEEE Commun. Magazine*, vol. 47, pp. 21–25, Dec. 2009.

SEIFERT, R., and EDWARDS, J.: *The All-New Switch Book*, NY: John Wiley, 2008.

SENN, J.A.: "The Emergence of M-Commerce," *IEEE Computer*, vol. 33, pp. 148–150, Dec. 2000.

SERJANTOV, A.: "Anonymizing Censorship Resistant Systems," *Proc. First Int'l Workshop on Peer-to-Peer Systems*, London: Springer-Verlag LNCS 2429, pp. 111–120, 2002.

SHACHAM, N., and MCKENNY, P.: "Packet Recovery in High-Speed Networks Using Coding and Buffer Management," *Proc. INFOCOM Conf.*, IEEE, pp. 124–131, June 1990.

SHAIKH, A., REXFORD, J., and SHIN, K.: "Load-Sensitive Routing of Long-Lived IP Flows," *Proc. SIGCOMM '99 Conf.*, ACM, pp. 215–226, Sept. 1999.

SHALUNOV, S., and CARLSON, R.: "Detecting Duplex Mismatch on Ethernet," *Passive and Active Network Measurement*, Berlin: Springer-Verlag LNCS 3431, pp. 3135–3148, 2005.

SHANNON, C.: "A Mathematical Theory of Communication," *Bell System Tech. J.*, vol. 27, pp. 379–423, July 1948; and pp. 623–656, Oct. 1948.

SHEPARD, S.: *SONET/SDH Demystified*, New York: McGraw-Hill, 2001.

SHREEDHAR, M., and VARGHESE, G.: "Efficient Fair Queueing Using Deficit Round Robin," *Proc. SIGCOMM '95 Conf.*, ACM, pp. 231–243, 1995.

SIMPSON, W.: *Video Over IP*, 2nd ed., Burlington, MA: Focal Press, 2008.

SIMPSON, W.: "PPP in HDLC-like Framing," RFC 1662, July 1994b.

SIMPSON, W.: "The Point-to-Point Protocol (PPP)," RFC 1661, July 1994a.

SIU, K., and JAIN, R.: "A Brief Overview of ATM: Protocol Layers, LAN Emulation, and Traffic," *ACM Computer Communications Review*, vol. 25, pp. 6–20, Apr. 1995.

SKOUDIS, E., and LISTON, T.: *Counter Hack Reloaded*, 2nd ed., Upper Saddle River, NJ: Prentice Hall, 2006.

SMITH, D.K., and ALEXANDER, R.C.: *Fumbling the Future*, New York: William Morrow, 1988.

SNOEREN, A.C., and BALAKRISHNAN, H.: "An End-to-End Approach to Host Mobility," *Int'l Conf. on Mobile Computing and Networking* , ACM, pp. 155–166, 2000.

SOBEL, D.L.: "Will Carnivore Devour Online Privacy," *IEEE Computer*, vol. 34, pp. 87–88, May 2001.

SOTIROV, A., STEVENS, M., APPELBAUM, J., LENSTRA, A., MOLNAR, D., OSVIK, D., and DE WEGER, B.: "MD5 Considered Harmful Today," *Proc. 25th Chaos Communication Congress*, Verlag Art d'Ameublement, 2008.

SOUTHEY, R.: *The Doctors*, London: Longman, Brown, Green and Longmans, 1848.

SPURGEON, C.E.: *Ethernet: The Definitive Guide*, Sebastopol, CA: O'Reilly, 2000.

STALLINGS, W.: *Data and Computer Communications*, 9th ed., Upper Saddle River, NJ: Pearson Education, 2010.

STARR, T., SORBARA, M., COIFFI, J., and SILVERMAN, P.: "DSL Advances," Upper Saddle River, NJ: Prentice Hall, 2003.

STEVENS, W.R.: *TCP/IP Illustrated: The Protocols*, Boston: Addison Wesley, 1994.

STINSON, D.R.: *Cryptography Theory and Practice*, 2nd ed., Boca Raton, FL: CRC Press, 2002.

STOICA, I., MORRIS, R., KARGER, D., KAASHOEK, M.F., and BALAKRISHNAN, H.: "Chord: A Scalable Peer-to-Peer Lookup Service for Internet Applications," *Proc. SIGCOMM 2001 Conf.*, ACM, pp. 149–160, 2001.

STUBBLEFIELD, A., IOANNIDIS, J., and RUBIN, A.D.: "Using the Fluhrer, Mantin, and Shamir Attack to Break WEP," *Proc. Network and Distributed Systems Security Symp.*, ISOC, pp. 1–11, 2002.

STUTTARD, D., and PINTO, M.: *The Web Application Hacker's Handbook*, New York: John Wiley & Sons, 2007.

SU, S.: *The UMTS Air Interface in RF Engineering*, New York: McGraw-Hill, 2007.

SULLIVAN, G., and WIEGAND, T.: "Tree Algorithms for Packet Broadcast Channels," *Proc. of the IEEE*, vol. 93, pp. 18–31, Jan. 2005.

SUNSHINE, C.A., and DALAL, Y.K.: "Connection Management in Transport Protocols," *Computer Networks*, vol. 2, pp. 454–473, 1978.

TAN, K., SONG, J., ZHANG, Q., and SRIDHARN, M.: "A Compound TCP Approach for High-Speed and Long Distance Networks," *Proc. INFOCOM Conf.*, IEEE, pp. 1–12, 2006.

TANENBAUM, A.S.: *Modern Operating Systems*, 3rd ed., Upper Saddle River, NJ: Prentice Hall, 2007.

TANENBAUM, A.S., and VAN STEEN, M.: *Distributed Systems: Principles and Paradigms*, Upper Saddle River, NJ: Prentice Hall, 2007.

TOMLINSON, R.S.: "Selecting Sequence Numbers," *Proc. SIGCOMM/SIGOPS Interprocess Commun. Workshop*, ACM, pp. 11–23, 1975.

TUCHMAN, W.: "Hellman Presents No Shortcut Solutions to DES," *IEEE Spectrum*, vol. 16, pp. 40–41, July 1979.

TURNER, J.S.: "New Directions in Communications (or Which Way to the Information Age)," *IEEE Commun. Magazine*, vol. 24, pp. 8–15, Oct. 1986.

UNGERBOECK, G.: "Trellis-Coded Modulation with Redundant Signal Sets Part I: Introduction," *IEEE Commun. Magazine*, vol. 25, pp. 5–11, Feb. 1987.

VALADE, J.: *PHP & MySQL for Dummies*, 5th ed., New York: John Wiley & Sons, 2009.

VARGHESE, G.: *Network Algorithmics*, San Francisco: Morgan Kaufmann, 2004.

VARGHESE, G., and LAUCK, T.: "Hashed and Hierarchical Timing Wheels: Data Structures for the Efficient Implementation of a Timer Facility," *Proc. 11th Symp. on Operating Systems Prin.*, ACM, pp. 25–38, 1987.

VERIZON BUSINESS: *2009 Data Breach Investigations Report*, Verizon, 2009.

VITERBI, A.: *CDMA: Principles of Spread Spectrum Communication*, Englewood Cliffs, NJ: Prentice Hall, 1995.

VON AHN, L., BLUM, B., and LANGFORD, J.: "Telling Humans and Computers Apart Automatically," *Commun. of the ACM*, vol. 47, pp. 56–60, Feb. 2004.

WAITZMAN, D., PARTRIDGE, C., and DEERING, S.: "Distance Vector Multicast Routing Protocol," RFC 1075, Nov. 1988.

WALDMAN, M., RUBIN, A.D., and CRANOR, L.F.: "Publius: A Robust, Tamper-Evident, Censorship-Resistant Web Publishing System," *Proc. Ninth USENIX Security Symp.*, USENIX, pp. 59–72, 2000.

WANG, Z., and CROWCROFT, J.: "SEAL Detects Cell Misordering," *IEEE Network Magazine*, vol. 6, pp. 8–9, July 1992.

WANT, R.: *RFID Explained*, San Rafael, CA: Morgan Claypool, 2006.

WARNEKE, B., LAST, M., LIEBOWITZ, B., and PISTER, K.S.J.: "Smart Dust: Communicating with a Cubic Millimeter Computer," *IEEE Computer*, vol. 34, pp. 44–51, Jan. 2001.

WAYNER, P.: *Disappearing Cryptography: Information Hiding, Steganography, and Watermarking*, 3rd ed., San Francisco: Morgan Kaufmann, 2008.

WEI, D., CHENG, J., LOW, S., and HEGDE, S.: "FAST TCP: Motivation, Architecture, Algorithms, Performance," *IEEE/ACM Trans. on Networking*, vol. 14, pp. 1246–1259, Dec. 2006.

WEISER, M.: "The Computer for the Twenty-First Century," *Scientific American*, vol. 265, pp. 94–104, Sept. 1991.

WELBOURNE, E., BATTLE, L., COLE, G., GOULD, K., RECTOR, K., RAYMER, S., BALAZINSKA, M., and BORRIELLO, G.: "Building the Internet of Things Using RFID," *IEEE Internet Computing*, vol. 13, pp. 48–55, May 2009.

WITTENBURG, N.: *Understanding Voice Over IP Technology*, Clifton Park, NY: Delmar Cengage Learning, 2009.

WOLMAN, A., VOELKER, G., SHARMA, N., CARDWELL, N., KARLIN, A., and LEVY, H.: "On the Scale and Performance of Cooperative Web Proxy Caching," *Proc. 17th Symp. on Operating Systems Prin.*, ACM, pp. 16–31, 1999.

WOOD, L., IVANCIC, W., EDDY, W., STEWART, D., NORTHAM, J., JACKSON, C., and DA SILVA CURIEL, A.: "Use of the Delay-Tolerant Networking Bundle Protocol from Space," *Proc. 59th Int'l Astronautical Congress*, Int'l Astronautical Federation, pp. 3123–3133, 2008.

WU, T.: "Network Neutrality, Broadband Discrimination," *Journal on Telecom. and High-Tech. Law*, vol. 2, pp. 141–179, 2003.

WYLIE, J., BIGRIGG, M.W., STRUNK, J.D., GANGER, G.R., KILICCOTE, H., and KHOSLA, P.K.: "Survivable Information Storage Systems," *IEEE Computer*, vol. 33, pp. 61–68, Aug. 2000.

YU, T., HARTMAN, S., and RAEBURN, K.: "The Perils of Unauthenticated Encryption: Kerberos Version 4," *Proc. NDSS Symposium*, Internet Society, Feb. 2004.

YUVAL, G.: "How to Swindle Rabin," *Cryptologia*, vol. 3, pp. 187–190, July 1979.

ZACKS, M.: "Antiterrorist Legislation Expands Electronic Snooping," *IEEE Internet Computing*, vol. 5, pp. 8–9, Nov.–Dec. 2001.

ZHANG, Y., BRESLAU, L., PAXSON, V., and SHENKER, S.: "On the Characteristics and Origins of Internet Flow Rates," *Proc. SIGCOMM 2002 Conf.*, ACM, pp. 309–322, 2002.

ZHAO, B., LING, H., STRIBLING, J., RHEA, S., JOSEPH, A., and KUBIATOWICZ, J.: "Tapestry: A Resilient Global-Scale Overlay for Service Deployment," *IEEE J. on Selected Areas in Commun.*, vol. 22, pp. 41–53, Jan. 2004.

ZIMMERMANN, P.R.: *The Official PGP User's Guide*, Cambridge, MA: M.I.T. Press, 1995a.

ZIMMERMANN, P.R.: *PGP: Source Code and Internals*, Cambridge, MA: M.I.T. Press, 1995b.

ZIPF, G.K.: *Human Behavior and the Principle of Least Effort: An Introduction to Human Ecology*, Boston: Addison-Wesley, 1949.

ZIV, J., and LEMPEL, Z.: "A Universal Algorithm for Sequential Data Compression," *IEEE Trans. on Information Theory*, vol. IT–3, pp. 337–343, May 1977.

INDEX

INDEX

Numbers

A

B

D

E

G

H

I

N

O

P

S

T

U

V

W

X

Z

Also by Andrew S. Tanenbaum

Modern Operating Systems, 3rd ed.

This worldwide best-seller incorporates the latest developments in operating systems. The book starts with chapters on the principles, including processes, memory management, file systems, I/O, and so on. Then it goes into three chapter-long case studies: Linux, Windows, and Symbian. Tanenbaum's experience as the designer of three operating systems (Amoeba, Globe, and MINIX) gives him a background few other authors can match, so the final chapter distills his long experience into advice for operating system designers.

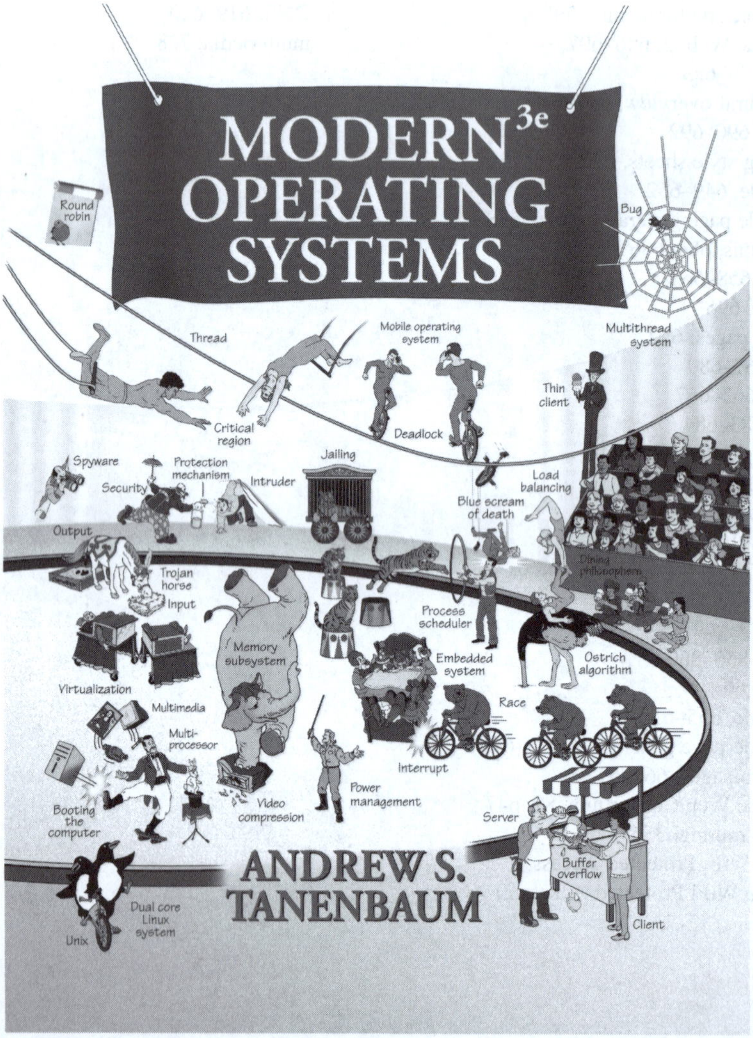

Also by Andrew S. Tanenbaum and Albert S. Woodhull

Operating Systems: Design and Implementation, 3rd ed.

All other textbooks on operating systems are long on theory and short on practice. This one is different. In addition to the usual material on processes, memory management, file systems, I/O, and so on, it contains a CD-ROM with the source code (in C) of a small, but complete, POSIX-conformant operating system called MINIX 3 (see *www.minix3.org*). All the principles are illustrated by showing how they apply to MINIX 3. The reader can also compile, test, and experiment with MINIX 3, leading to in-depth knowledge of how an operating system really works.

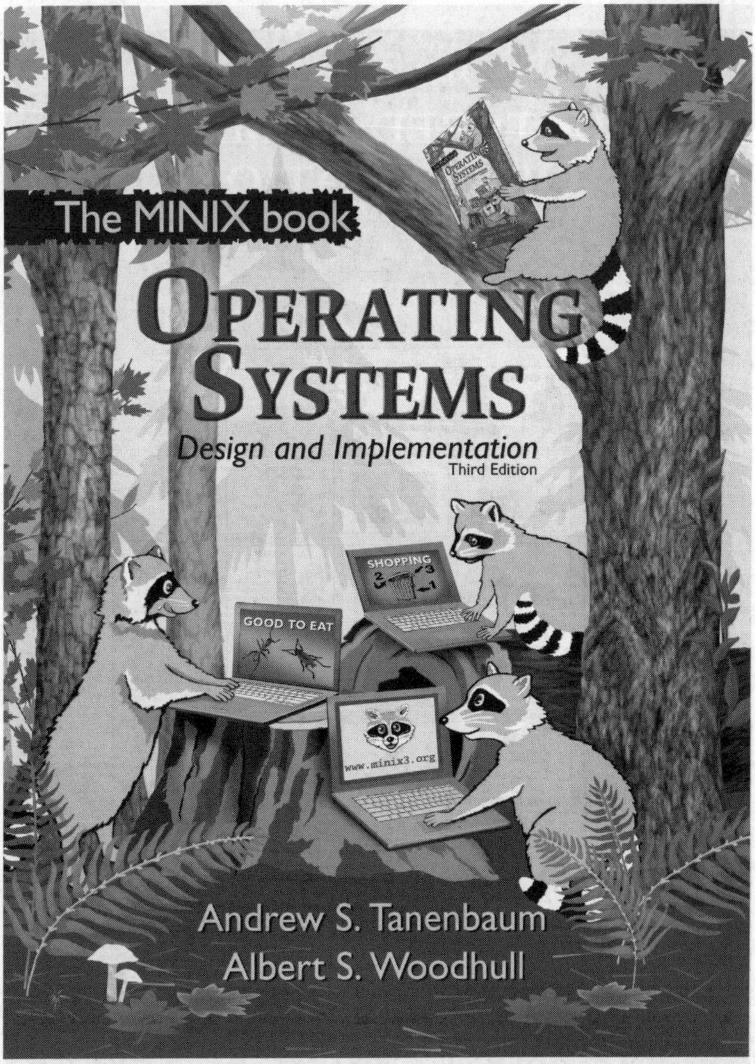

Also by Andrew S. Tanenbaum

Structured Computer Organization, 5th ed.

A computer can be structured as a hierarchy of levels, from the hardware up through the operating system. This book treats all of them, starting with how a transistor works and ending with operating system design. No previous experience with either hardware or software is needed to follow this book, however, as all the topics are self contained and explained in simple terms starting right at the beginning. The running examples used throughout the book range from the high-end UltraSPARC III, through the ever-popular x86 (Pentium) to the tiny Intel 8051 used in small embedded systems.

Also by Andrew S. Tanenbaum and Maarten van Steen

Distributed Systems: Principles and Paradigms, 2nd ed.

Distributed systems are becoming ever-more important in the world and this book explains their principles and illustrates them with numerous examples. Among the topics covered are architectures, processes, communication, naming, synchronization, consistency, fault tolerance, and security. Examples are taken from distributed object-based, file, Web-based, and coordination-based systems.

ABOUT THE AUTHORS

Andrew S. Tanenbaum has an S.B. degree from M.I.T. and a Ph.D. from the University of California at Berkeley. He is currently a Professor of Computer Science at the Vrije Universiteit where he has taught operating systems, networks, and related topics for over 30 years. His current research is on highly reliable operating systems although he has worked on compilers, distributed systems, security, and other topics over the years. These research projects have led to over 150 refereed papers in journals and conferences.

Prof. Tanenbaum has also (co)authored five books which have now appeared in 19 editions. The books have been translated into 21 languages, ranging from Basque to Thai and are used at universities all over the world. In all, there are 159 versions (language/edition combinations), which are listed at *www.cs.vu.nl/~ast/publications.*

Prof. Tanenbaum has also produced a considerable volume of software, including the Amsterdam Compiler Kit (a retargetable portable compiler), Amoeba (an early distributed system used on LANs), and Globe (a wide-area distributed system).

He is also the author of MINIX, a small UNIX clone initially intended for use in student programming labs. It was the direct inspiration for Linux and the platform on which Linux was initially developed. The current version of MINIX, called MINIX 3, is now focused on being an extremely reliable and secure operating system. Prof. Tanenbaum will consider his work done when no computer is equipped with a reset button and no living person has ever experienced a system crash. MINIX 3 is an on-going open-source project to which you are invited to contribute. Go to *www.minix3.org* to download a free copy and find out what is happening.

Tanenbaum is a Fellow of the ACM, a Fellow of the the IEEE, and a member of the Royal Netherlands Academy of Arts and Sciences. He has also won numerous scientific prizes, including:

- 2010 TAA McGuffey Award for Computer Science and Engineering books
- 2007 IEEE James H. Mulligan, Jr. Education Medal
- 2002 TAA Texty Award for Computer Science and Engineering books
- 1997 ACM/SIGCSE Award for Outstanding Contributions to Computer Science Education
- 1994 ACM Karl V. Karlstrom Outstanding Educator Award

His home page on the World Wide Web can be found at *http://www.cs.vu.nl/~ast/.*

David J. Wetherall is an Associate Professor of Computer Science and Engineering at the University of Washington in Seattle, and advisor to Intel Labs in Seattle. He hails from Australia, where he received his B.E. in electrical enginering from the University of Western Australia and his Ph.D. in computer science from M.I.T.

Prof. Wetherall has worked in the area of networking for the past two decades. His research is focused on network systems, especially wireless networks and mobile computing, the design of Internet protocols, and network measurement.

He received the ACM SIGCOMM Test-of-Time award for research that pioneered active networks, an architecture for rapidly introducing new network services. He received the IEEE William Bennett Prize for breakthroughs in Internet mapping. His research was recognized with an NSF CAREER award in 2002, and he became a Sloan Fellow in 2004.

As well as teaching networking, Prof. Wetherall participates in the networking research community. He has co-chaired the program committees of SIGCOMM, NSDI and MobiSys, and co-founded the ACM HotNets workshops. He has served on numerous program committees for networking conferences, and is an editor for ACM Computer Communication Review.

His home page on the World Wide Web can be found at *http://djw.cs.washington.edu*.